T0134689

Lecture Notes in Computer Science 12113

More information about this series at http://www.springer.com/series/7409

Yunmook Nah · Bin Cui ·
Sang-Won Lee · Jeffrey Xu Yu ·
Yang-Sae Moon · Steven Euijong Whang (Eds.)

Database Systems
for Advanced Applications

25th International Conference, DASFAA 2020
Jeju, South Korea, September 24–27, 2020
Proceedings, Part II

 Springer

Editors
Yunmook Nah
Dankook University
Yongin, Korea (Republic of)

Sang-Won Lee
Sungkyunkwan University
Suwon, Korea (Republic of)

Yang-Sae Moon (iD)
Kangwon National University
Chunchon, Korea (Republic of)

Bin Cui
Peking University
Haidian, China

Jeffrey Xu Yu
Department of System Engineering
and Engineering Management
The Chinese University of Hong Kong
Hong Kong, Hong Kong

Steven Euijong Whang (iD)
Korea Advanced Institute of Science
and Technology
Daejeon, Korea (Republic of)

ISSN 0302-9743   ISSN 1611-3349 (electronic)
Lecture Notes in Computer Science
ISBN 978-3-030-59415-2   ISBN 978-3-030-59416-9 (eBook)
https://doi.org/10.1007/978-3-030-59416-9

LNCS Sublibrary: SL3 – Information Systems and Applications, incl. Internet/Web, and HCI

This Springer imprint is published by the registered company Springer Nature Switzerland AG
The registered company address is: Gewerbestrasse 11, 6330 Cham, Switzerland

Preface

It is our great pleasure to introduce the proceedings of the 25th International Conference on Database Systems for Advanced Applications (DASFAA 2020), held during September 24–27, 2020, in Jeju, Korea. The conference was originally scheduled for May 21–24, 2020, but inevitably postponed due to the outbreak of COVID-19 and its continual spreading all over the world. DASFAA provides a leading international forum for discussing the latest research on database systems and advanced applications. The conference's long history has established the event as the premier research conference in the database area.

To rigorously review the 487 research paper submissions, we conducted a double-blind review following the tradition of DASFAA and constructed the large committee consisting of 16 Senior Program Committee (SPC) members and 212 Program Committee (PC) members. Each valid submission was reviewed by three PC members and meta-reviewed by one SPC member who also led the discussion with the PC members. We, the PC co-chairs, considered the recommendations from the SPC members and looked into each submission as well as its reviews to make the final decisions. As a result, 119 full papers (acceptance ratio of 24.4%) and 23 short papers were accepted. The review process was supported by the EasyChair system. During the three main conference days, these 142 papers were presented in 27 research sessions. The dominant keywords for the accepted papers included neural network, knowledge graph, time series, social networks, and attention mechanism. In addition, we included 4 industrial papers, 15 demo papers, and 3 tutorials in the program. Last but not least, to shed the light on the direction where the database field is headed to, the conference program included four invited keynote presentations by Amr El Abbadi (University of California, Santa Barbara, USA), Kian-Lee Tan (National University of Singapore, Singapore), Wolfgang Lehner (TU Dresden, Germany), and Sang Kyun Cha (Seoul National University, South Korea).

Five workshops were selected by the workshop co-chairs to be held in conjunction with DASFAA 2020: the 7th Big Data Management and Service (BDMS 2020); the 6th International Symposium on Semantic Computing and Personalization (SeCoP 2020); the 5th Big Data Quality Management (BDQM 2020); the 4th International Workshop on Graph Data Management and Analysis (GDMA 2020); and the First International Workshop on Artificial Intelligence for Data Engineering (AIDE 2020). The workshop papers are included in a separate volume of the proceedings also published by Springer in its *Lecture Notes in Computer Science* series.

We would like to thank all SPC members, PC members, and external reviewers for their hard work to provide us with thoughtful and comprehensive reviews and recommendations. Many thanks to the authors who submitted their papers to the conference. In addition, we are grateful to all the members of the Organizing Committee, and many volunteers, for their great support in the conference organization. Also, we would like to express our sincere thanks to Yang-Sae Moon for compiling all accepted papers and for working with the Springer team to produce the proceedings. Lastly, we acknowledge the generous financial support from IITP[1], Dankook University SW Centric University Project Office, DKU RICT, OKESTRO, SUNJESOFT, KISTI, LG CNS, INZENT, Begas, SK Broadband, MTDATA, WAVUS, SELIMTSG, and Springer.

We hope that the readers of the proceedings find the content interesting, rewarding, and beneficial to their research.

September 2020

Bin Cui
Sang-Won Lee
Jeffrey Xu Yu

---

[1] Institute of Information & communications Technology Planning & Evaluation (IITP) grant funded by the Korea government (MSIT) (No. 2020-0-01356, 25th International Conference on Database Systems for Advanced Applications (DASFAA)).

Organization

Organizing Committee

General Chair

Yunmook Nah   Dankook University, South Korea

Program Co-chairs

Bin Cui   Peking University, China
Sang-Won Lee   Sungkyunkwan University, South Korea
Jeffrey Xu Yu   The Chinese University of Hong Kong, Hong Kong

Industry Program Co-chairs

Jinyang Gao   Alibaba Group, China
Sangjun Lee   Soongsil University, South Korea
Eenjun Hwang   Korea University, South Korea

Demo Co-chairs

Makoto P. Kato   Kyoto University, Japan
Hwanjo Yu   POSTECH, South Korea

Tutorial Chair

U. Kang   Seoul National University, South Korea

Workshop Co-chairs

Chulyun Kim   Sookmyung Women's University, South Korea
Seon Ho Kim   USC, USA

Panel Chair

Wook-Shin Han   POSTECH, South Korea

Organizing Committee Chair

Jinseok Chae   Incheon National University, South Korea

Local Arrangement Co-chairs

Jun-Ki Min   Koreatec, South Korea
Haejin Chung   Dankook University, South Korea

Registration Chair

Min-Soo Kim   DGIST, South Korea

Publication Co-chairs

Yang-Sae Moon   Kangwon National University, South Korea
Steven Euijong Whang   KAIST, South Korea

Publicity Co-chairs

Yingxia Shao   Beijing University of Posts and Telecommunications,
                             China
Taehyung Wang   California State University Northridge, USA
Jonghoon Chun   Myongji University, South Korea

Web Chair

Ha-Joo Song   Pukyong National University, South Korea

Finance Chair

Dongseop Kwon   Myongji University, South Korea

Sponsor Chair

Junho Choi   Sunjesoft Inc., South Korea

DASFAA Steering Committee Liaison

Kyuseok Shim   Seoul National University, South Korea

Program Committee

Senior Program Committee Members

K. Selcuk Candan   Arizona State University, USA
Lei Chen   The Hong Kong University of Science
                             and Technology, Hong Kong
Wook-Shin Han   POSTECH, South Korea
Christian S. Jensen   Aalborg University, Denmark
Feifei Li   University of Utah, USA
Chengfei Liu   Swinburne University of Technology, Australia
Werner Nutt   Free University of Bozen-Bolzano, Italy
Makoto Onizuka   Osaka University, Japan
Kyuseok Shim   Seoul National University, South Korea
Yongxin Tong   Beihang University, China
Xiaokui Xiao   National University of Singapore, Singapore
Junjie Yao   East China Normal University, China
Hongzhi Yin   The University of Queensland, Australia
Ce Zhang   ETH Zurich, Switzerland

| Qiang Zhu | University of Michigan, USA |
| Eenjun Hwang | Korea University, South Korea |

Program Committee Members

Alberto Abello	Universitat Politècnica de Catalunya, Spain
Marco Aldinucci	University of Turin, Italy
Akhil Arora	Ecole Polytechnique Fédérale de Lausanne, Switzerland
Jie Bao	JD Finance, China
Zhifeng Bao	RMIT University, Australia
Ladjel Bellatreche	LIAS, ENSMA, France
Andrea Calì	University of London, Birkbeck College, UK
Xin Cao	The University of New South Wales, Australia
Yang Cao	Kyoto University, Japan
Yang Cao	The University of Edinburgh, UK
Barbara Catania	DIBRIS, University of Genoa, Italy
Chengliang Chai	Tsinghua University, China
Lijun Chang	The University of Sydney, Australia
Chen Chen	Arizona State University, USA
Cindy Chen	University of Massachusetts Lowell, USA
Huiyuan Chen	Case Western Reserve University, USA
Shimin Chen	ICT CAS, China
Wei Chen	Soochow University, China
Yang Chen	Fudan University, China
Peng Cheng	East China Normal University, China
Reynold Cheng	The University of Hong Kong, Hong Kong
Theodoros Chondrogiannis	University of Konstanz, Germany
Jaegul Choo	Korea University, South Korea
Lingyang Chu	Simon Fraser University, Canada
Gao Cong	Nanyang Technological University, Singapore
Antonio Corral	University of Almeria, Spain
Lizhen Cui	Shandong University, China
Lars Dannecker	SAP SE, Germany
Ernesto Damiani	University of Milan, Italy
Sabrina De Capitani	University of Milan, Italy
Dong Den	Rutgers University, USA
Anton Dignös	Free University of Bozen-Bolzano, Italy
Lei Duan	Sichuan University, China
Amr Ebaid	Google, USA
Ju Fan Renmin	University of China, China
Yanjie Fu	University of Central Florida, USA
Hong Gao	Harbin Institute of Technology, China
Xiaofeng Gao	Shanghai Jiao Tong University, China
Yunjun Gao	Zhejiang University, China
Tingjian Ge	University of Massachusetts Lowell, USA

Boris Glavic	Illinois Institute of Technology, USA
Neil Gong	Iowa State University, USA
Zhiguo Gong	University of Macau, Macau
Yu Gu	Northeastern University, China
Lei Guo	Shandong Normal University, China
Long Guo	Alibaba Group, China
Yuxing Han	Alibaba Group, China
Peng Hao	Beihang University, China
Huiqi Hu	East China Normal University, China
Juhua Hu	University of Washington Tacoma, USA
Zhiting Hu	Carnegie Mellon University, USA
Wen Hua	The University of Queensland, Australia
Chao Huang	University of Notre Dame, USA
Zi Huang	The University of Queensland, Australia
Seung-Won Hwang	Yonsei University, South Korea
Matteo Interlandi	Microsoft, USA
Md. Saiful Islam	Griffith University, Australia
Di Jiang	WeBank, China
Jiawei Jiang	ETH Zurich, Switzerland
Lilong Jiang	Twitter, USA
Cheqing Jin	East China Normal University, China
Peiquan Jin	University of Science and Technology of China, China
Woon-Hak Kang	e-Bay Inc., USA
Jongik Kim	JeonBuk National University, South Korea
Min-Soo Kim	KAIST, South Korea
Sang-Wook Kim	Hanyang University, South Korea
Younghoon Kim	Hanyang University, South Korea
Peer Kröger	Ludwig Maximilian University of Munich, Germany
Anne Laurent	University of Montpellier, France
Julien Leblay	National Institute of Advanced Industrial Science and Technology (AIST), Japan
Dong-Ho Lee	Hanyang University, South Korea
Jae-Gil Lee	KAIST, South Korea
Jongwuk Lee	Sungkyunkwan University, South Korea
Young-Koo Lee	Kyung Hee University, South Korea
Bohan Li	Nanjing University of Aeronautics and Astronautics, China
Cuiping Li	Renmin University of China, China
Guoliang Li	Tsinghua University, China
Jianxin Li	Deakin University, Australia
Yawen Li	Beijing University of Posts and Telecommunications, China
Zhixu Li	Soochow University, China
Xiang Lian	Kent State University, USA
Qing Liao	Harbin Institute of Technology, China

Zheng Liu	Nanjing University of Posts and Telecommunications, China
Chunbin Lin	Amazon Web Services, USA
Guanfeng Liu	Macquarie University, Australia
Hailong Liu	Northwestern Polytechnical University, China
Qing Liu	CSIRO, Australia
Qingyun Liu	Facebook, USA
Eric Lo	The Chinese University of Hong Kong, Hong Kong
Cheng Long	Nanyang Technological University, Singapore
Guodong Long	University of Technology Sydney, Australia
Hua Lu	Aalborg University, Denmark
Wei Lu	Renmin University of China, China
Shuai Ma	Beihang University, China
Yannis Manolopoulos	Open University of Cyprus, Cyprus
Jun-Ki Min	Korea University of Technology and Education, South Korea
Yang-Sae Moon	Kangwon National University, South Korea
Mikolaj Morzy	Poznan University of Technology, Poland
Parth Nagarkar	New Mexico State University, USA
Liqiang Nie	Shandong University, China
Baoning Niu	Taiyuan University of Technology, China
Kjetil Nørvåg	Norwegian University of Science and Technology, Norway
Vincent Oria	New Jersey Institute of Technology, USA
Noseong Park	George Mason University, USA
Dhaval Patel	IBM, USA
Wen-Chih Peng	National Chiao Tung University, Taiwan
Ruggero G. Pensa	University of Turin, Italy
Dieter Pfoser	George Mason University, USA
Silvestro R. Poccia	Polytechnic of Turin, Italy
Shaojie Qiao	Chengdu University of Information Technology, China
Lu Qin	University of Technology Sydney, Australia
Weixiong Rao	Tongji University, China
Oscar Romero	Universitat Politènica de Catalunya, Spain
Olivier Ruas	Peking University, China
Babak Salimi	University of Washington, USA
Maria Luisa Sapino	University of Turin, Italy
Claudio Schifanella	University of Turin, Italy
Shuo Shang	Inception Institute of Artificial Intelligence, UAE
Xuequn Shang	Northwestern Polytechnical University, China
Zechao Shang	The University of Chicago, USA
Jie Shao	University of Electronic Science and Technology of China, China
Yingxia Shao	Beijing University of Posts and Telecommunications, China
Wei Shen	Nankai University, China

Yanyan Shen	Shanghai Jiao Tong University, China
Xiaogang Shi	Tencent, China
Kijung Shin	KAIST, South Korea
Alkis Simitsis	HP Labs, USA
Chunyao Song	Nankai University, China
Guojie Song	Peking University, China
Shaoxu Song	Tsinghua University, China
Fei Sun	Huawei, USA
Hailong Sun	Beihang University, China
Han Sun	University of Electronic Science and Technology of China, China
Weiwei Sun	Fudan University, China
Yahui Sun	Nanyang Technological University, Singapore
Jing Tang	National University of Singapore, Singapore
Nan Tang	Hamad Bin Khalifa University, Qatar
Ismail Toroslu	Middle East Technical University, Turkey
Vincent Tseng	National Chiao Tung University, Taiwan
Leong Hou	University of Macau, Macau
Bin Wang	Northeastern University, China
Chang-Dong Wang	Sun Yat-sen University, China
Chaokun Wang	Tsinghua University, China
Chenguang Wang	IBM, USA
Hongzhi Wang	Harbin Institute of Technology, China
Jianmin Wang	Tsinghua University, China
Jin Wang	University of California, Los Angeles, USA
Ning Wang	Beijing Jiaotong University, China
Pinghui Wang	Xi'an Jiaotong University, China
Senzhang Wang	Nanjing University of Aeronautics and Astronautics, China
Sibo Wang	The Chinese University of Hong Kong, Hong Kong
Wei Wang	National University of Singapore, Singapore
Wei Wang	The University of New South Wales, Australia
Weiqing Wang	Monash University, Australia
Xiaoling Wang	East China Normal University, China
Xin Wang	Tianjin University, China
Zeke Wang	ETH Zurich, Switzerland
Joyce Whang	Sungkyunkwan University, South Korea
Steven Whang	KAIST, South Korea
Kesheng Wu	Lawrence Berkeley Laboratory, USA
Sai Wu	Zhejiang University, China
Yingjie Wu	Fuzhou University, China
Mingjun Xiao	University of Science and Technology of China, China
Xike Xie	University of Science and Technology of China, China
Guandong Xu	University of Technology Sydney, Australia
Jianliang Xu	Hong Kong Baptist University, Hong Kong

Jianqiu Xu	Nanjing University of Aeronautics and Astronautics, China
Quanqing Xu	A*STAR, Singapore
Tong Yang	Peking University, China
Yu Yang	City University of Hong Kong, Hong Kong
Zhi Yang	Peking University, China
Bin Yao	Shanghai Jiao Tong University, China
Lina Yao	The University of New South Wales, Australia
Man Lung Yiu	The Hong Kong Polytechnic University, Hong Kong
Ge Yu	Northeastern University, China
Lele Yu	Tencent, China
Minghe Yu	Northeastern University, China
Ye Yuan	Northeastern University, China
Dongxiang Zhang	Zhejiang University, China
Jilian Zhang	Jinan University, China
Rui Zhang	The University of Melbourne, Australia
Tieying Zhang	Alibaba Group, USA
Wei Zhang	East China Normal University, China
Xiaofei Zhang	The University of Memphis, USA
Xiaowang Zhang	Tianjin University, China
Ying Zhang	University of Technology Sydney, Australia
Yong Zhang	Tsinghua University, China
Zhenjie Zhang	Yitu Technology, Singapore
Zhipeng Zhang	Peking University, China
Jun Zhao	Nanyang Technological University, Singapore
Kangfei Zhao	The Chinese University of Hong Kong, Hong Kong
Pengpeng Zhao	Soochow University, China
Xiang Zhao	National University of Defense Technology, China
Bolong Zheng	Huazhong University of Science and Technology, China
Kai Zheng	University of Electronic Science and Technology of China, China
Weiguo Zheng	Fudan University, China
Yudian Zheng	Twitter, USA
Chang Zhou	Alibaba Group, China
Rui Zhou	Swinburne University of Technology, Australia
Xiangmin Zhou	RMIT University, Australia
Xuan Zhou	East China Normal University, China
Yongluan Zhou	University of Copenhagen, Denmark
Zimu Zhou	Singapore Management University, Singapore
Yuanyuan Zhu	Wuhan University, China
Lei Zou	Peking University, China
Zhaonian Zou	Harbin Institute of Technology, China
Andreas Züfle	George Mason University, USA

External Reviewers

Ahmed Al-Baghdadi
Alberto R. Martinelli
Anastasios Gounaris
Antonio Corral
Antonio Jesus
Baozhu Liu
Barbara Cantalupo
Bayu Distiawan
Besim Bilalli
Bing Tian
Caihua Shan
Chen Li
Chengkun He
Chenhao Ma
Chris Liu
Chuanwen Feng
Conghui Tan
Davide Colla
Deyu Kong
Dimitrios Rafailidis
Dingyuan Shi
Dominique Laurent
Dong Wen
Eleftherios Tiakas
Elena Battaglia
Feng Yuan
Francisco Garcia-Garcia
Fuxiang Zhang
Gang Qian
Gianluca Mittone
Hans Behrens
Hanyuan Zhang
Huajun He
Huan Li
Huaqiang Xu
Huasha Zhao
Iacopo Colonnelli
Jiaojiao Jiang
Jiejie Zhao
Jiliang Tang
Jing Nathan Yan
Jinglin Peng
Jithin Vachery

Joon-Seok Kim
Junhua Zhang
Kostas Tsichlas
Liang Li
Lin Sun
Livio Bioglio
Lu Liu
Luigi Di Caro
Mahmoud Mohammadi
Massimo Torquati
Mengmeng Yang
Michael Vassilakopoulos
Moditha Hewasinghage
Mushfiq Islam
Nhi N.Y. Vo
Niccolo Meneghetti
Niranjan Rai
Panayiotis Bozanis
Peilun Yang
Pengfei Li
Petar Jovanovic
Pietro Galliani
Qian Li
Qian Tao
Qiang Fu
Qianhao Cong
Qianren Mao
Qinyong Wang
Qize Jiang
Ran Gao
Rongzhong Lian
Rosni Lumbantoruan
Ruixuan Liu
Ruiyuan Li
Saket Gurukar
San Kim
Seokki Lee
Sergi Nadal
Shaowu Liu
Shiquan Yang
Shuyuan Li
Sicong Dong
Sicong Liu

Sijie Ruan
Sizhuo Li
Tao Shen
Teng Wang
Tianfu He
Tiantian Liu
Tianyu Zhao
Tong Chen
Waqar Ali
Weilong Ren
Weiwei Zhao
Weixue Chen
Wentao Li
Wenya Sun
Xia Hu
Xiang Li
Xiang Yu
Xiang Zhang
Xiangguo Sun
Xianzhe Wu
Xiao He
Xiaocong Chen
Xiaocui Li
Xiaodong Li
Xiaojie Wang
Xiaolin Han
Xiaoqi Li
Xiaoshuang Chen
Xing Niu
Xinting Huang
Xinyi Zhang
Xinyu Zhang
Yang He
Yang Zhao
Yao Wan
Yaohua Tang
Yash Garg
Yasir Arfat
Yijian Liu
Yilun Huang
Yingjun Wu
Yixin Su
Yu Yang

Yuan Liang
Yuanfeng Song
Yuanhang Yu
Yukun Cao
Yuming Huang
Yuwei Wang

Yuxing Han
Yuxuan Qiu
Yuyu Luo
Zelei Cheng
Zhangqing Shan
Zhuo Ma

Zicun Cong
Zili Zhou
Zisheng Yu
Zizhe Wang
Zonghan Wu

Financial Sponsors

 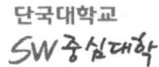  

Academic Sponsors

Contents – Part II

Graph Data

Spatial Data

Data Mining

EPARS: Early Prediction of At-Risk Students with Online and Offline Learning Behaviors

Yu Yang[1]([✉]), Zhiyuan Wen[1], Jiannong Cao[1], Jiaxing Shen[1], Hongzhi Yin[2], and Xiaofang Zhou[2]

[1] Department of Computing, The Hong Kong Polytechnic University, Hong Kong SAR, China
{csyyang,cszwen,csjshen}@comp.polyu.edu.hk
jiannong.cao@polyu.edu.hk
[2] School of ITEE, The University of Queensland, Brisbane, Australia
h.yin1@uq.edu.au, zxf@itee.uq.edu.au

Abstract. Early prediction of students at risk (STAR) is an effective and significant means to provide timely intervention for dropout and suicide. Existing works mostly rely on either online or offline learning behaviors which are not comprehensive enough to capture the whole learning processes and lead to unsatisfying prediction performance. We propose a novel algorithm (EPARS) that could early predict STAR in a semester by modeling online and offline learning behaviors. The online behaviors come from the log of activities when students use the online learning management system. The offline behaviors derive from the check-in records of the library. Our main observations are two folds. Significantly different from good students, STAR barely have regular and clear study routines. We devised a multi-scale bag-of-regularity method to extract the regularity of learning behaviors that is robust to sparse data. Second, friends of STAR are more likely to be at risk. We constructed a co-occurrence network to approximate the underlying social network and encode the social homophily as features through network embedding. To validate the proposed algorithm, extensive experiments have been conducted among an Asian university with $15,503$ undergraduate students. The results indicate EPARS outperforms baselines by 14.62%–38.22% in predicting STAR.

Keywords: Learning analytics · At-risk student prediction · Learning behavior · Regularity patterns · Social homophily

1 Introduction

Predicting students at risk (STAR) plays a crucial and significant role in education as STAR keep raising public concern of dropout and suicide among

Y. Yang and Z. Wen—These authors have contributed equally to this work.

© Springer Nature Switzerland AG 2020
Y. Nah et al. (Eds.): DASFAA 2020, LNCS 12113, pp. 3–19, 2020.
https://doi.org/10.1007/978-3-030-59416-9_1

adolescents [16, 22]. STAR refer to students requiring temporary or ongoing intervention to succeed academically [18]. Students may be at risk for several reasons like family problems and personal issues including poor academic performance. Those students will gradually fail to sustain their studies and then drop out which is also a waste of educational resources [1]. Early prediction of STAR offer educators the opportunity to intervene in a timely manner.

Traditionally, many universities identify STAR by their academic performance which sometimes is too late to intervene. Existing works are largely based on either online behaviors or offline behaviors of students [8, 12, 14]. For example, STAR are predicted in a particular course from in-class feedback such as the grade of homework, quiz, and mid-term examination [14]. However, due to the complex nature of STAR [5], either online and offline behaviors only capture part of the learning processes. For example, some students prefer learning with printed documents so they become inactive in online learning platforms after downloading learning materials. This process is difficult to capture through their online learning behaviors. Therefore, existing work can hardly capture the whole learning processes in a comprehensive way and thus leads to poor performance in the early prediction of STAR.

In this work, we aim to predict STAR before the end of a semester using both online and offline learning behaviors. STAR are defined as students with an average GPA below 2.0 in a semester. Online behaviors are extracted from click-stream traces on a learning management system (LMS). These traces reveal how students use various functionalities of LMS. While the offline behaviors derive from library check-in records. To achieve the goal, we encounter the following three major challenges: (1) **Lable imbalance**. The number of STAR is significantly smaller than that of normal students, which makes it an extreme label-imbalance classification problem. The classifier will be easily dominated by the majority class (normal students). (2) **Data density imbalance**. The library check-in records are much sparser than click-stream traces on the online learning platform so that it is challenging to fuse them fairly well for classifying STAR. (3) **Data insufficiency**. Students, especially STAR, are usually inactive at the early stage of a semester. As a result, the behavior traces are far from enough for accurate early prediction of STAR.

In light of these challenges, we propose a novel algorithm (EPARS) for early prediction of at-risk students. EPARS captures students' regularity patterns of learning processes in a robust manner. Besides, it also models social homophily among students to perform highly accurate early STAR prediction. The intuitions behind EPARS are two-fold. First, good students usually follow their study routines periodically and show clear regularities of learning patterns [24]. However, the study routines of STAR are disorganized leading to irregular learning patterns, which is different from good students. Second, students tend to have social tie with others who are similar to them according to the theory of social homophily [15] and existing studies found that at-risk students had more dropout friends [5].

Based on both intuitions, we first propose a multi-scale bag-of-regularity method to extract discriminative features from the regularity patterns of students' learning behaviors. Unlike the traditional approaches using entropy for measuring the regularities, which cannot work well on sparse data, we ignore the inactive behavior subsequence and capture the regularity patterns in a multi-scale manner. Our approach can capture the regularity patterns fairly well even though the data are very sparse. Therefore, it overcomes the challenge of data density imbalance and extracts discriminative features from regularity patterns for classifying STAR. In order to model the social homophily, we construct a co-occurrence network from the library check-in records to approximate social relationships among students. Co-occurrence networks have been widely used in modeling social relationship and achieved great success in many application scenarios [20, 21] After that, we embed the co-occurrence networks and learn a representation vector for every student with the assumption that students' representation vectors are close when they have similar social connections. Modeling the social homophily provides extra information to supplement the lack of behavior trace for STAR at the beginning of a semester, which solves the data insufficiency problems and makes EPARS capable of early predicting STAR. Moreover, we oversample the training samples of STAR by random interpolating using SMOTE [2], which overcomes the label imbalance problem while training the classifiers.

We conducted extensive experiments on a large scale dataset covering all 15, 503 undergraduate students from freshmen to senior students in the whole university. The experimental results show that the proposed EPARS achieves 0.7237 accuracy in predicting STAR before the end of a semester and 0.6184 prediction accuracy after the first week of the semester, which outperforms the baseline by 34.14% and 38.22% respectively. Comparative experiments found that our proposed multi-scale bag-of-regularity method and modeling students' social homophily by the co-occurrence network improve the performance of STAR early prediction 26.82% and 14.62% respectively. From the data analysis, we also found that STAR engaged less than normal students in learning in the early semester. Besides, the results confirm that the friends of STAR are more likely to be at risk if they have similar regularity patterns of learning behaviors, which in line with the conclusion drawn by an existing experimental study [5].

The our contributions are summarized as follows.

- We propose a multi-scale bag-of-regularity approach to extract regularity patterns of learning behaviors, which is robust for sparse data. This approach is also generic for extracting repeated patterns from any given sequence.
- We model the social homophily among students by embedding a co-occurrence network constructed from their library check-in records, which reliefs the data insufficiency issues.
- Extensive experiments on a university-scale dataset show that our proposed EPARS is effective on STAR early prediction in terms of 14.62%–38.22% accuracy improvement to the baselines.

The remainder of this paper is organized as follows. We review the relative works in the next section and formally formulate the STAR early prediction problem in Sect. 3. The data description are reported in Sect. 4. In Sect. 5, we present the proposed EPARS in detail and evaluate its effectiveness in Sect. 6 before we conclude the paper in the last section.

2 Related Works

There are various reasons for students being at-risk, including school factors, community factors, and family factors. Most of the existing works focus on school factors due to the convenience of data collection. The classification models used include Logistic Regression, Decision Trees, and Support Vector Machines. The main difference of these works relies on the input features, which could be generally classified into offline and online.

The offline learning behaviors contain check-ins of classes or libraries, quiz and homework grades, and records of other activities conduct in the offline environment. These kinds of works are quite straight forward to monitor the student learning activities for identification. Early researchers design the Personal Response system and utilize the order of students' device registration to help identify STAR [6]. Besides, questionnaires and personal interviews are also applied to collect student information for identification [3]. These methods show accurate results in an early stage of a semester. Moreover, Marbouti et al. also proposed to identify STAR at three time-points (week 2, 4, and 9) in a semester using in-term performance consists of homework and quiz grades and mid-term exam scores [14]. These methods rely heavily on domain knowledge, and collecting these offline learning data is very high labor cost and time-consuming, such that they are not practical for large scale STAR prediction.

With the popularization of online learning, researchers have turned their attention to analyzing student behavioral data on online learning platforms such as MOOCs and Open edX. The online learning behaviors are collected from the trace that students left in the online learning system such as click-stream logs in functional modules of the systems, forum posts, assignment submission, etc. Kondo et al. early detect STAR from the system login and assignment submission logs on the LMS [11], but their results may be partial since most students are not actively engaged with LMS. Shelton et al. designed a multi-tasks model to predict outstanding students and STAR [19], which purely uses the frequency of module access as features. [9] proposed a personalized model for predicting STAR enrolling in different courses, but it is hardly generalized to various courses, especially the totally new one. Instead of purely using statistic features, we further extract students' regularity patterns and social homophily for early predicting STAR.

3   Problem Formulation

This section gives the formal problem definition of STAR early prediction which is essentially a binary classification problem. We will introduce the exact definition of STAR, the input data, and the meaning of early prediction.

According to the student handbook of the university, when a student has a Grade Point Average (GPA) lower than 2.0, he/she will be put on academic probation in the following semester. If a student is able to pull his/her GPA up to 2.0 or above at the end of the semester, the status of academic probation will be lifted. Otherwise, he/she will be dropped out. Therefore, we define STAR as students whose average GPA is below 2.0 in a semester.

The input data are two folds. One is the records of students' online activities in the Blackboard, a learning management system. The Blackboard has several modules including course participation, communication and collaboration, assessment and assignments. Students could browse and download course-related materials including lecture keynotes, assignments, quizzes, lab documents etc. They can also take online quizzes and upload their answers for assessment. Besides, students could communicate over the different posts and collaborate on their group assignments. Students' click operations in the Blackboard will be recorded (online traces). The other is the check-in records of the library. Students have to tap their student cards before entering the library (offline records).

Early prediction means the input data are collected before the end of a semester. Given online traces and offline records accumulated within t ($t < t_{end}$) where t_{end} is the end time of a semester, our objective is to identify STAR as accurate as possible.

4   Data Description

We collect students' online and offline learning traces and their average GPA in an Asian University in 2016 to 2017 academic year. The online learning traces come from how students use the Blackboard, a learning management system, to learn. There are many functions in the Blackboard but some of them are rare to be used by students. Thus, we collect the click-stream data with timestamps from some of the most popular modules in the Blackboard including log-in, log-out, course materials access, assignment, grade center, discussion board, announcement board, group activity, personal information pages, etc. Offline learning traces come from students' library check-in records which indicating when they go to library. Since students do not need to tap their student cards when they leave the library, the check-out records will not be marked down and we exclude it in this study.

All 15,503 undergraduate students in the whole university involved in this study. Every student has a unique but encrypted ID for linking their LMS click-stream data, library check-in records, and GPA. The overview of collected data are showed in Table 1. There are 225 and 319 STAR in semester one and two respectively, which are 1.45% and 2.06% of all students. This makes our STAR

Table 1. Data overview.

	Semester 1		Semester 2	
	STAR	Other Std	STAR	Other Std
Population	391	15,112	225	15,278
# click-stream logs in LMS	2,225,605	95,949,014	1,019,134	70,874,428
Avg. # click-stream logs	5,692.0844	6,349.1936	4,529.4844	4,638.9860
Avg. # click-stream logs in first 2 weeks	301.4041	399.9502	243.0400	284.4368
Avg. # click-stream logs in last 2 weeks	526.6522	545.4346	336.9133	304.7331
# library check-in	14,045	636,353	6,245	517,557
Avg. # library check-in	35.9207	42.1091	27.7556	33.8760
Avg. # library check-in in first 2 weeks	1.7877	2.3303	1.3889	1.8424
Avg. # library check-in in last 2 weeks	2.9834	3.3760	2.3444	2.4547

early prediction as an extremely label imbalance classification problem, which is our first challenge. In addition, students left over 170 million click-stream logs but only 1.7 million library check-in records in the whole academic year such that the data density between online and offline learning trace are also imbalance. Compared to the last two weeks of the semester, all students are less active in the first two weeks and STAR are even less active than normal students which cause data inefficiency problems for early predict STAR at the beginning of the semester.

5 Methodologies

In this section, we will elaborate on the proposed EPARS including multi-scale bag-of-regularity, social homophily, and data augmentation.

5.1 Multi-scale Bag-of-Regularity

In order to extract the regularity patterns from students' learning traces, we propose multi-scale bag-of-regularity here, which is robust for sparse data.

Based on Hugh Drummond's definition, behavior regularity is repeatedly occurring of a certain behavior in descriptions of patterns [4]. Students usually have their own repeated patterns for using LMS and going to the library. For instance, some students prefer to go to the library every Monday and Thursday. It is possible for us to illustrate their repeated patterns on multiple scales such as they will not go to library after the day they go there; they go to the library two and three days apart alternately. If we purely extract the regularity patterns on a single scale, it hardly captures the complete picture and leads to information loss. This motivates us to extract the regularity patterns in multi-scales. In addition, traditional approaches, such as entropy, measure the regularities in a global perspective. When students' library check-in data are sparse, those approaches will regard their library check-in as outliers and consider their general regularity patterns as never go to the library, which are incorrect. Therefore, we focus on the every behavior trace students leave during learning for extracting their learning regularity patterns.

First of all, we construct a binary sequence from students' behavior traces. When they have certain behaviors, such as check-in to the library, we mark it as 1 in the sequence. The time granularity for constructing the binary sequence depends on the application and the time granularity we used in this study is a day. Next, We sample subsequences of length ℓ centered on every nonzero element in the sequence. The length of subsequences $\ell = 2 + (s - 1) \times z$ where $s \in \{1, 2, \cdots, S\}$ is scale and z is the step-size between scales. This sampling approach guarantees that no all-zeros sequence will be sampled for the following regularity measurement which gives our method the ability to overcome data sparsity issues. Every subsequence actually is a behavior pattern that is viewed on different scales.

After sampling the behavior patterns, we explore the repeated patterns from them to obtain the regularities. Since the regularity is repeatedly occurring of behavior patterns, we ignore the subsequences that the times of occurrences are less than a threshold n. For the subsequence of length ℓ in scale s, it contains $2^\ell - 1$ different behavior pattern excluding all-zeros one. We regard them as a bag and count the number of occurrences of every behavior pattern. Finally, a $(2^\ell - 1) \times 1$ vector r_s is obtained, which carries the behavior regularities on scale s. Lastly, we concatenate the regularity vectors r_s in every scale as the representation of regularity on multi-scales. Our bag-of-regularity approach explores the regularity patterns of behaviors in multi-scales such that it can extract richer information from the sparse input sequence. The regularity features extracted from dense LMS data and sparse library check-in records by our multi-scale bag-of-regularity are on the same scale-space so that we can simply concatenate them together as the final regularity features for STAR prediction and the performance is fairly well. In addition, the proposed multi-scale bag-of-regularity is generic for extracting repeated patterns from any given sequence since it will transform the input sequence into a binary sequence before extracting regularities.

5.2   Social Homophily

We construct a co-occurrence network to model the social relationship among students. If students are friends, they are more likely to learn together because of the social homophily [15]. They have a higher probability to go to the library together comparing to strangers. Thus, we assume that two students are friends if they go to library together. If the time difference of the library check-in between two students is less than a threshold δ, we treat this as the co-occurrence of two students in the library. In other words, they go to the library together. Based on this, we construct a co-occurrence network $G(V, E, W)$ where nodes V are students and there is an edge $e \in E$ linking two nodes if students go to the library together. Each edge is accompanied by a weight value $w \in W$ showing how many times they co-occurrence in the library. We constrain $w \geq \sigma$ which is a threshold to filter out the "familiar strangers". We do not construct the co-occurrence network from the LMS log-in traces because the LMS log-in frequency is too high and it will involve too many "familiar strangers" in the network. This will introduce significant biases for learning the social homophily later.

Next step is to learn students' social homophily from the co-occurrence network. Network embedding has been widely applied in encoding the connectivities among nodes as representation and well preserves the graph properties [13, 23]. Here, we embed the co-occurrence network by Node2Vec [7] and learn a representation vector for every node which preserves the connectivities among students. In addition, we constrain that the learned representation of nodes should be close when they have similar connections. Specifically, we first exploring diverse neighborhoods for every node by a biased random walk. Let us denote c_i as the ith node in the walk. We sample node sequences with transition probability

$$p(c_i = u | c_{i-1} = v) = \begin{cases} \frac{\alpha_{pq} w_{uv}}{Z} & \text{if } (u, v) \in E \\ 0 & \text{Otherwise} \end{cases} \tag{1}$$

where Z is a constant for normalization and α_{pq} in Eq. (2) is the sampling bias.

$$\alpha_{pq} = \begin{cases} 1/p & \text{if } d_{uv} = 0 \\ 1 & \text{if } d_{uv} = 1 \\ 1/q & \text{if } d_{uv} = 2 \\ 0 & \text{Otherwise} \end{cases} \tag{2}$$

d_{uv} denotes the shortest path distance between nodes u and v. Parameters p and q make the trade-offs between depth-first and breadth-first neighborhood sampling.

To learning the final representation of every node, we train a Skip-gram model [17] by maximizing the log-probability of its network neighborhood conditioned on its feature representation as showed in Eq. (3) where $f(\cdot)$ is a mapping function from node to feature representations and $N_s(u)$ is u's neighborhood sampling by the above random walk.

$$\max_f \sum_{u \in V} \log \left(\prod_{v_i \in N_s(u)} \frac{\exp \left(f(u) \cdot f(v_i) \right)}{\sum_{v \in V} \exp \left(f(u) \cdot f(v) \right)} \right) \tag{3}$$

We adopt the stochastic gradient ascent to optimize the above objective function over the model parameters and obtain the representation of every node which carrying its social homophily. Learning students' social homophily provides extra information for dealing with the data insufficiency issues such that it makes our EPARS have the ability to early predict STAR.

5.3 Data Augmentation

To deal with the extremely label imbalance issues, we oversample the STAR by a synthetic minority over-sampling technique (SMOTE) [2] while constructing the training set. For each STAR training sample, denoted as x, we first search its k-nearest neighbors from all STAR samples in training set by the Euclidean distance in the feature space, and the k is set to 10 in our experiment. Next, we randomly select a sample x' from the k nearest neighbors and synthesize a new STAR example by Eq. (4) where ω is a random number between 0 and 1.

$$x_{new} = x + (x' - x) \times \omega \qquad (4)$$

After the data augmentation, STAR have the same amount as the normal students in the training set; this allows the classifier to avoid being dominated by the majority of the normal students during training. SMOTE synthesizes new examples between any of the two existing minority samples by a linear interpolation approach. Compared with a widely used under-sampling technique EasyEnsemble, SMOTE introduces random perturbation into the training set while generating the synthetic examples, which provide the trained classifier better generalization.

6 Experiments

We conduct experiments to showcase the effectiveness of proposed EPARS. In particular, we aim to answer the following research questions (RQ) via experiments:

- RQ1: How effective is the EPARS in predicting STAR?
- RQ2: How early does the EPARS well predict STAR?
- RQ3: How effective is SMOTE for data augmentation in EPARS?
- RQ4: Is the EPARS sensitive to hyper-parameters?

6.1 Experiment Protocol

Experiment Setting. In our dataset, each student has an independent label of either STAR or the normal student in each semester. Thus, we treat students in different semesters as a whole in our experiments. When predicting STAR at any time t before the end of the semester t_{end}, we extract features from their online and offline learning traces from the beginning of a semester to the current time t. After feature extraction, we synthesize new STAR examples to augment the training set. We conduct experiments under the 5-fold cross-validation setting and repeat 10 times. The average results will be reported in the next subsection. Several classifiers are tested, including the Logistic Regression, Support Vector Machine (SVM), Decision Tree, Random Forest, and the Gradient Boosting Decision Tree (GBDT). GBDT outperforms all other classifiers in our experiments, so we only report the results of GBDT due to the space limit.

Parameter Setting. We set the maximum scale of regularity $S = 4$, the co-occurrence threshold δ to be 30 s, the linking threshold $\sigma = 2$, and the dimension of embedding to be 64 for EPARS. We select $k = 10$ neighborhood for SMOTE to augment the training set. The classifier GBDT is trained with parameters that the number of estimators is 100, maximum depth of the decision tree is 10, and the learning rate is 0.1.

Evaluation Metrics. We evaluate the performance of EPARS from two aspects. Since the STAR prediction is a binary classification problem, we adopt Area Under the receiver operating characteristics Curve (AUC) to measure the classification performance. The AUC indicates how capable the model is to distinguish between STAR and the normal students. Moreover, since our focus is to find out the STAR as accurate as possible, we measure the accuracy of our model in predicting STAR by the number of true positive predictions divided by the total number of STAR in the test set. We denote it as ACC-STAR, which indicates how many percentages of STAR are correctly predicted.

Baseline Approaches. As mentioned in the introduction, our major contribution is to achieve better STAR early prediction performance, in terms of higher AUC and ACC-STAR, with features extracted from students' learning regularity and social homophily. To verify the effectiveness of EPARS, we set four baseline models, including SF, DA, DA-Reg, and DA-SoH. SF uses only the statistically significant behavior features as input to predict STAR without data augmentation. The process of discovering significant statistical features will be presented in the next paragraph. DA uses the same features as SF and augments the training set using SMOTE. Comparing SF and DA, we can verify whether SMOTE can solve the label imbalance challenge well and results in better classification performance. DA-Reg and DA-SoH integrate the regularity features and the social homophily to the DA, respectively. They are to verify the effectiveness of our proposed multi-scale bag-of-regularity and the social homophily modeling approach in STAR prediction.

To discover the significant statistical features, we perform an ANOVA (analysis of variance) test to figure out what behaviors are statistically significant for distinguishing between STAR and the normal students. We have 13 kinds of clickstream behaviors on the LMS and 28 kinds of library check-in behaviors at different times of the day and different periods in the semester. Due to the space limited, we report the statistically significant features and some of the insignificant features discovered from the ANOVA in Table 2. It is interesting to note that STAR use the LMS less than the normal students, but they will check the announcement and lectures' information more. There is no significant difference in accessing the course materials and checking assignment results. Besides, STAR go to the library less than the normal students at the beginning of a semester. Still, they prefer more to be there after business hours. Lastly, we select the statistically significant features as the SF baseline to benchmark our proposed EPARS.

Table 2. Results of the ANOVA test.

Features	P-value	F-value	Mean STAR	Mean others
# LMS Login	0.0020	9.5112	127.4987	144.8043
# LMS Logout	0.0000	34.5301	8.9318	20.1348
# Check announcement	0.0158	5.8311	41.4436	36.8361
# Course access	0.7328	0.1165	4.2677	4.5667
# Grade center access	0.7694	0.0859	10.5486	10.2108
# Discussion board access	0.0020	9.5951	11.7979	19.2444
# Group access	0.0209	5.3385	13.2782	20.1268
# Check personal info	0.0000	16.7953	0.2283	1.6585
# Check lecturer info	0.0000	106.1638	9.7297	5.5440
# Journal page access	0.0199	5.4191	0.2283	1.6585
# Lib check-in	0.0700	3.2829	42.8163	47.3589
# Lib check-in in the morning	0.0001	14.7133	7.0367	9.4206
# Lib check-in in the afternoon	0.0023	9.3196	27.0604	31.9419
# Lib check-in after midnight	0.0000	43.9327	4.0105	1.6927
# Lib check-in before exam months	0.0123	6.2740	33.9265	39.0143
# Lib check-in at the first month	0.0004	12.5447	8.4724	10.6052

Table 3. Results of predicting STAR using the whole semester learning behavior data.

Metric	SF	DA	DA-Reg	DA-SoH	EPARS
AUC	0.8423	0.8442	0.8611	0.8623	**0.8684**
ACC-STAR	0.5395	0.6079	0.6842	0.6184	**0.7237**

6.2   Experimental Results

RQ1: To verify the effectiveness of our proposed EPARS in predicting STAR, we extract features from the whole semester data to train the GBDT and benchmark EPARS with four baselines. This experiment evaluates the performance of EPARS when students' all learning behaviors in a whole semester is known. The results are presented in Table 3.

Comparing the experimental results between SF and DA, it is confirmed that our data augmentation approach overcomes the data imbalance challenges to some extent and achieves improvement in both AUC and ACC-STAR. In addition, the regularity features extracted by our multi-scale bag-of-regularity method can improve the accuracy of predicting STAR a lot, which indicates that the regularity of learning is a distinguished feature between STAR and the normal students, and the multi-scale bag-of-regularity can well extract their regularity patterns efficiently. Compared with DA-Reg, DA-SoH achieves a higher AUC score and has better overall classification performance. However, its ACC-STAR is much lower than DA-Reg's, suggesting that it cannot identify STAR as accurate as DA-Reg. In other words, social homophily helps identify the normal students a lot rather than recognizing STAR. This shows that our approach is capable of well modeling the social homophily among students. Nevertheless, STAR may have similar linkage patterns with "familiar strangers" in the co-occurrence network since STAR are very handful. Combining the regularity patterns of learning and social homophily, which is our proposed EPARS, achieves the best performance in predicting STA in terms of 19.05%, 5.77% and 17.03% ACC-STAR improvement to DA, DA-Reg and DA-SoH, respectively. This indicates that friends of STAR are more likely to be at-risk if their regularity patterns of learning behaviors are also similar. Therefore, the regularity features can help eliminate the "familiar strangers" and result in better STAR prediction performance.

RQ2: To demonstrate the effectiveness of our methods in early predicting STAR, we conduct experiments in every week's data of the semester. For each week, we extract features of students' learning traces from the beginning of the semester to the end of that week. We repeat the experiment for 10 times, and the average ACC-STAR of early predicting STAR is presented in Fig. (1) in which the solid lines are the average ACC-STAR, and the shadows represent the error spans.

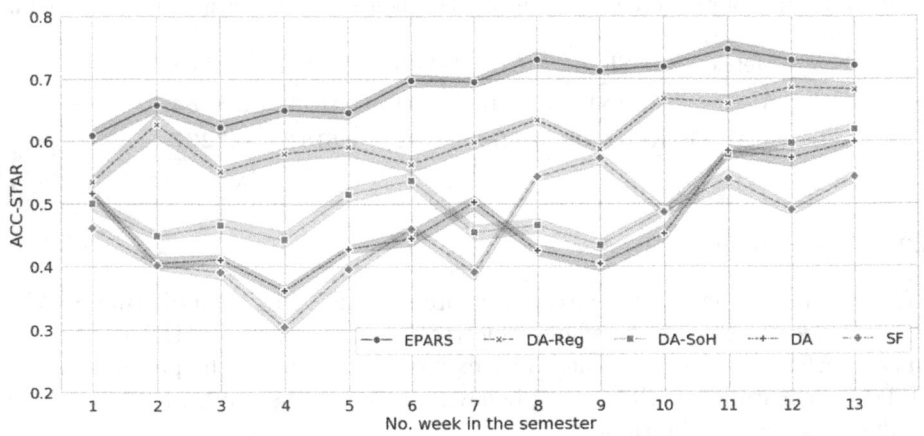

Fig. 1. Results of STAR early prediction.

Our EPARS outperforms all other baselines from the first week to the end of the semester. It is worth mention that our EPARS can correctly predict 61.84% STAR only based on the online and offline learning traces of the students in the first week, which outperforms SF, DA, DA-Reg, and DA-SoH 38.22%, 17.50%, 14.62%, and 22.38%, respectively. In the first four weeks, the prediction performance of SF keeps on decreasing. One possible reason is that some normal students are not active in the beginning of the semester, so that they may have similar behavior patterns with STAR and cause misclassification. Students' social homophily and regularity patterns of learning behaviors are much more discriminable especially in the early stage of a semester. The performance of EPARS is almost converged in the middle of a semester while other baselines are still gradually increasing or concussion. It shows that our EPARS can leverage less information but achieves better performance in early predicting STAR.

RQ3: To verify the effectiveness of using SMOTE for dealing with the label imbalance issues, we conduct a comparative experiment among random undersampling (RU), random oversampling (RO) and SMOTE. RU and RO are widely adopted in existing work for STAR prediction [8,10]. RU randomly deletes examples with the majority labels until the labels of training samples are balanced while RO randomly resamples the minority examples until the numbers of the minority are the same as the majority one. We regard SF as baseline and launch above data augmentation approach for predicting STAR before the end of a semester. We repeat the experiment 10 times and report the average AUC and ACC-STAR in Table 4.

The first two columns show the number of examples in the training set after data augmentation in each fold of the experiment. Experimental results show that RO slightly outperforms the baselines but the performance of RU is worse than the baselines. In the case of extremely label imbalance, undersampling technique drops most of negative training samples and constructs a very small training set, which cannot provide enough information to well train a classifier. Although RO augments the minority examples by oversampling, most synthesis examples are the same so that the classifier is very easy to overfit and results in poor testing accuracy. SMOTE synthesizes the minority examples by linear interpolation which not only increases the number of minority samples but also enriches the diversity of the training set. Thus, it achieves the best STAR prediction accuracy in such an extremely label imbalance classification task.

Table 4. Evaluation of data augmentation.

	# STAR after DA	# Normal Std after DA	AUC	ACC-STAR
SF	305	11295	0.8342	0.5526
RU	305	305	0.8211	0.5316
RO	11295	11295	0.8458	0.5645
SMOTE	11295	11295	**0.8684**	**0.7237**

RQ4: We test how sensitive EPARS is to the hyper-parameters and discuss how to select hyper-parameters for EPARS. We focus on three hyper-parameters of EPARS. One is the maximum scale S of multi-scale bag-of-regularity. The other two are co-occurrence threshold δ and linking threshold σ between pairs

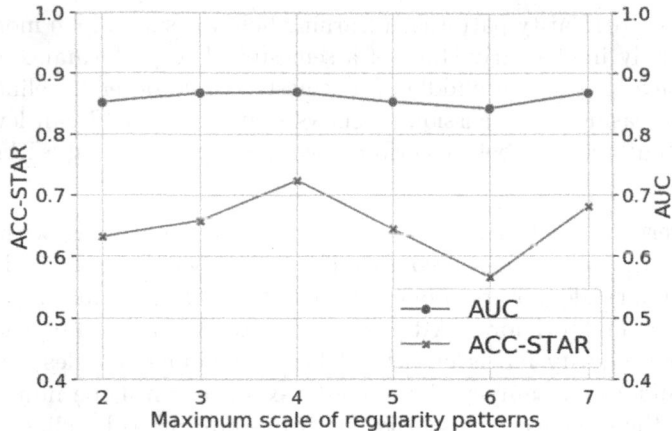

Fig. 2. Results of testing the maximum scale S of multi-scale bag-of-regularity.

of students when constructing co-occurrence networks for further modeling the social homophily.

While we are testing the maximum scale S, we fix all other parameters and vary S from 2 to 7 because the minimum time length of the repeated pattern is two days, and the course schedule is a 7-day cycle. The prediction results are shown in Fig. (2). We found that the overall classification performance measured by AUC is not sensitive to the maximum scale S, but it affects a lot on the correctness of identifying STAR. EPARS achieves the best performance when $S = 4$. The reason may be in two folds. One reason is that the regularity patterns of the scale 5 to 7 can be synthesized by the scale of 2 to 4. Thus it has already captured almost all regularity when setting the maximum scale $S = 4$. The other reason is that the output feature vector of multi-scale bag-of-regularity is short and dense when $S = 4$. It will dramatically become sparse when $S \geq 4$ in our cases, which makes the performance worse.

Table 5. Results of testing co-occurrence threshold δ.

δ	Ave #edge per week	AUC	ACC-STAR
10 s	14263	**0.8699**	0.5921
30 s	39386	0.8684	**0.7237**
60 s	77318	0.8576	0.6316

We further test how co-occurrence threshold δ and linking threshold σ affect the modeling of social homophily and present the results in Table 5 and 6. $\delta = 30$ is the best since smaller δ will make the co-occurrence network unable to capture enough social relationship for learning the social homophily and larger

Table 6. Results of testing linking threshold σ.

σ	AUC	ACC-STAR
2 times	**0.8684**	**0.7237**
3 times	0.8615	0.6184
4 times	0.8554	0.5658
5 times	0.8122	0.5395

δ will introduce a large number of "familiar strangers" which also damages the prediction performance. Similar results are found in the result of testing linking threshold σ. When increase σ, both AUC and ACC-STAR are dropping. The reason is that STAR and some ordinary students go to the library less often than outstanding students so that higher σ may filter out their social interaction and results in worse prediction performance.

7   Conclusion

In this paper, we propose EPARS, a novel algorithm to extract students' regularity patterns of learning and social homophily from online and offline learning behaviors for early predicting STAR. One of our major contributions is to devise a multi-scale bag-of-regularity method to extract regularity features from sequential learning behaviors, which is robust for sparse data. In addition, we model students' social relationships by constructing a co-occurrence network from library check-in records and embed their social homophily as feature vectors. Before training a classifier, we oversample the minority examples to overcome the label imbalance issues. Extensive experiments are conducted on a large scale dataset covering all undergraduate students in the whole university. Experimental results indicate that our EPARS improves the accuracy of baselines by $14.62\% \sim 38.22\%$ and $5.77\% \sim 34.14\%$ in predicting STAR in the first week and the last week of a semester, respectively.

Acknowledgement. This research has been supported by the PolyU Teaching Development (Grant No. 1.61.xx.9A5V) and ARC Discovery Project (Grant No. DP190101985, DP170103954 and DP170101172).

References

1. Berens, J., Schneider, K., Görtz, S., Oster, S., Burghoff, J.: Early detection of students at risk-predicting student dropouts using administrative student data and machine learning methods. CESifo Working Paper Series (2018)
2. Chawla, N.V., Bowyer, K.W., Hall, L.O., Kegelmeyer, W.P.: SMOTE: synthetic minority over-sampling technique. J. Artif. Intell. Res. **16**, 321–357 (2002)
3. Choi, S.P., Lam, S.S., Li, K.C., Wong, B.T.: Learning analytics at low cost: at-risk student prediction with clicker data and systematic proactive interventions. J. Educ. Technol. Soc. **21**(2), 273–290 (2018)

4. Drummond, H.: The nature and description of behavior patterns. In: Bateson, P.P.G., Klopfer, P.H. (eds.) Perspectives in Ethology, pp. 1–33. Springer, Boston (1981). https://doi.org/10.1007/978-1-4615-7575-7_1

5. Ellenbogen, S., Chamberland, C.: The peer relations of dropouts: a comparative study of at-risk and not at-risk youths. J. Adolesc. **20**(4), 355–367 (1997)

6. Griff, E.R., Matter, S.F.: Early identification of at-risk students using a personal response system. Br. J. Educ. Technol. **39**(6), 1124–1130 (2008)

7. Grover, A., Leskovec, J.: node2vec: scalable feature learning for networks. In: Proceedings of the 22nd ACM SIGKDD International Conference on Knowledge Discovery and Data Mining, pp. 855–864. ACM (2016)

8. He, J., Bailey, J., Rubinstein, B.I., Zhang, R.: Identifying at-risk students in massive open online courses. In: Twenty-Ninth AAAI Conference on Artificial Intelligence (2015)

9. Ho, L.C., Shim, K.J.: Data mining approach to the identification of at-risk students. In: 2018 IEEE International Conference on Big Data (Big Data), pp. 5333–5335. IEEE (2018)

10. Jayaprakash, S.M., Moody, E.W., Lauría, E.J., Regan, J.R., Baron, J.D.: Early alert of academically at-risk students: an open source analytics initiative. J. Learn. Anal. **1**(1), 6–47 (2014)

11. Kondo, N., Okubo, M., Hatanaka, T.: Early detection of at-risk students using machine learning based on LMS log data. In: 2017 6th IIAI International Congress on Advanced Applied Informatics (IIAI-AAI), pp. 198–201. IEEE (2017)

12. Koprinska, I., Stretton, J., Yacef, K.: Students at risk: detection and remediation. In: Proceedings of the 8th International Conference on Educational Data Mining, pp. 512–515 (2015)

13. Li, C., et al.: PPNE: property preserving network embedding. In: Candan, S., Chen, L., Pedersen, T.B., Chang, L., Hua, W. (eds.) DASFAA 2017. LNCS, vol. 10177, pp. 163–179. Springer, Cham (2017). https://doi.org/10.1007/978-3-319-55753-3_11

14. Marbouti, F., Diefes-Dux, H.A., Madhavan, K.: Models for early prediction of at-risk students in a course using standards-based grading. Comput. Educ. **103**, 1–15 (2016)

15. Marsden, P.V.: Homogeneity in confiding relations. Soc. Netw. **10**(1), 57–76 (1988)

16. Orozco, R., et al.: Association between attempted suicide and academic performance indicators among middle and high school students in Mexico: results from a national survey. Child Adolesc. Psychiatry Mental Health **12**(1), 9 (2018)

17. Perozzi, B., Al-Rfou, R., Skiena, S.: Deepwalk: online learning of social representations. In: Proceedings of the 20th ACM SIGKDD International Conference on Knowledge Discovery and Data Mining, pp. 701–710. ACM (2014)

18. Richardson, V.: At-risk student intervention implementation guide. The Education and Economic Development Coordinating Council At-Risk Student Committee, p. 18 (2005)

19. Shelton, B.E., Yang, J., Hung, J.-L., Du, X.: Two-stage predictive modeling for identifying at-risk students. In: Wu, T.-T., Huang, Y.-M., Shadieva, R., Lin, L., Starčič, A.I. (eds.) ICITL 2018. LNCS, vol. 11003, pp. 578–583. Springer, Cham (2018). https://doi.org/10.1007/978-3-319-99737-7_61

20. Shen, J., Cao, J., Liu, X.: BaG: behavior-aware group detection in crowded urban spaces using WiFi probes. In: The World Wide Web Conference, pp. 1669–1678. ACM (2019)

21. Shen, J., Cao, J., Liu, X., Tang, S.: Snow: detecting shopping groups using WiFi. IEEE Internet Things J. **5**(5), 3908–3917 (2018)

22. Stinebrickner, R., Stinebrickner, T.: Academic performance and college dropout: using longitudinal expectations data to estimate a learning model. J. Lab. Econ. **32**(3), 601–644 (2014)
23. Yang, D., Wang, S., Li, C., Zhang, X., Li, Z.: From properties to links: deep network embedding on incomplete graphs. In: Proceedings of the 2017 ACM on Conference on Information and Knowledge Management, pp. 367–376 (2017)
24. Yao, H., Lian, D., Cao, Y., Wu, Y., Zhou, T.: Predicting academic performance for college students: a campus behavior perspective. ACM Trans. Intell. Syst. Technol. (TIST) **10**(3), 24 (2019)

MRMRP: Multi-source Review-Based Model for Rating Prediction

Xiaochen Wang[1], Tingsong Xiao[1], Jie Tan[2], Deqiang Ouyang[1(⊠)], and Jie Shao[1,3]

[1] University of Electronic Science and Technology of China, Chengdu 611731, China
{wangxiaochen,xiaotingsong,ouyangdeqiang}@std.uestc.edu.cn
shaojie@uestc.edu.cn
[2] Zhejiang University, Hangzhou 310027, China
tanjie95@zju.edu.cn
[3] Sichuan Artificial Intelligence Research Institute, Yibin 644000, China

Abstract. Reviews written by users often contain rich semantic information which can reflect users' preferences for different attributes of items. For the past few years, many studies in recommender systems take user reviews into consideration and achieve promising performance. However, in daily life, most consumers are used to leaving no comments for products purchased and most reviews written by consumers are short, which leads to the performance degradation of most existing review-based methods. In order to alleviate the data sparsity problem of user reviews, in this paper, we propose a novel review-based model MRMRP, which stands for Multi-source Review-based Model for Rating Prediction. In this model, to build multi-source user reviews, we collect supplementary reviews from similar users for each user, where similar users refer to users who have similar consuming behaviors and historical rating records. MRMRP is capable of extracting useful features from supplementary reviews to further improve recommendation performance by applying a deep learning based method. Moreover, the supplementary reviews can be incorporated into different neural models to boost rating prediction accuracy. Experiments are conducted on four real-world datasets and the results demonstrate that MRMRP achieves better rating prediction accuracy than the state-of-the-art methods.

Keywords: Recommender systems · Rating prediction · Deep learning

1 Introduction

With an increasing number of choices available online, recommender system becomes more and more important in our daily life. Recommender systems help customers by presenting products or services based on their demographic information and past buying behaviors, which can improve user experience. In activities including online shopping, reading articles, and watching movies, most purchasers are used to considering suggestions from recommendation systems.

Y. Nah et al. (Eds.): DASFAA 2020, LNCS 12113, pp. 20–35, 2020.
https://doi.org/10.1007/978-3-030-59416-9_2

Besides, recommender systems are widely used in applications and websites such as Taobao and Netflix to drive sales.

A large number of approaches employed in recommender systems are based on Collaborative Filtering (CF) algorithm [4,7,11,18,21,25,26,32], whose core philosophy is "birds of a feather flock together". CF obtains user preferences and item attributes by exploiting historical user consuming records. Despite its great performance, the CF-based recommender system cannot provide nice personalized recommendation services for users who have few consuming records. In this sense, CF methods have the cold start and data sparsity problems. In many applications, users are allowed to leave reviews to express their views on their consumed products. The information contained in reviews can be exploited to uncover the preferences of consumers and the features of items as well, thereby alleviating the data sparsity problem.

To tackle the sparsity of data, review-based recommender systems consider not only user-item interactions but also user preferences and item attributes extracted from user reviews for making recommendations. Many of them such as CARP [12] and CARL [28] achieve better performance than approaches without using user reviews. Although the utilization of user reviews can improve the performance of these recommender systems, their performance is hindered by the sparsity problem of user reviews. This is because only a few users are willing to write detailed comments to share their experiences about consumed items.

To address the sparsity problem of user reviews, in this paper, we propose an algorithm to supplement profiles of users, which appends reviews written by similar users. Here, similar users refer to the users who give close ratings to the same item and have the highest similarity score. For instance, Fig. 1 compares the reviews given by two audiences with the nicknames "SomeDisneyGuy" and "namob" who give the rating of 9 points and 10 points respectively to the film named "Frozen II". For the user SomeDisneyGuy, our algorithm selects namob as the only similar user on this film. Our goal is to use namob's review on this film to supplement SomeDisneyGuy's review. We believe that some information which are not fully expressed in SomeDisneyGuy's review can be contained in reviews written by its similar users such as namob. From the sentences circled by green boxes in both reviews, we can see that SomeDisneyGuy and namob have the common movie experience of expecting more content in this film. On the other hand, they have different interests presented in their reviews. We can infer that SomeDisneyGuy is possibly interested in magical things and is likely to give a high score to magical films from the review written by namob. Besides, we speculate that namob may be a fan of 80's Kristoff's songs according to SomeDisneyGuy's review. For each item SomeDisneyGuy has consumed, we collect reviews from its similar users and integrate these reviews to the document called the user supplementary review document.

Frozen II (2019)
User Reviews
⊕ Review this title

★ 9/10

It's all about change. If you think the teasers are somewhat dark, Frozen 2 will deliver that,. And a good sequel I would say.
SomeDisneyGuy   20 November 2019

(This has a post-credit scene in case you're wondering)

Anna, Elsa, Kristoff, Olaf and Sven leave Arendelle to travel to an ancient, autumn-bound forest of an enchanted land. They set out to find the origin of Elsa's powers in order to save their kingdom.

The songs are great. Especially Kristoff's song, an 80's jam as Jonathan Groff would say it. Even the animation looks like an 80's music video which I find funny. Olaf's comedic skits are even funnier. For Into the Unknown, not as catchy as Let it Go but time will tell. The animation, the best. Elsa got even beautifuller. If you saw the water animation you would see "much" more of that. The story is bigger, questions are answered, but there are some points that look silly. The plot is predictable but personally I enjoyed it.

★ 10/10

Lovely beautiful movie and better than the first
namob-43673   22 November 2019

Seeing this in a theatre filled with families and kids was an almost magical experience. It is like seeing kids meeting Santa for the first time. Consequently I have no doubt this sequel will make all the billions and be just as, if not more loved than the first.

This movie does a few things better than the first movie. I think the story is more, which is not necessarily better for the kids since it need a bit more thinking and understanding, but as an adult this sequel has a lot more to offer. I also think this is funnier, and oh God it is beautiful to watch. The cinematic experience of seeing this beauty on screen is magical .. and yes, magical is the word of the day. Elsa also goes fully magical and has several really cool superpower moments. And did I mention how beautiful this movie is to watch?

Fig. 1. Examples of reviews written by two audiences for the film "Frozen II" on IMDB. Two users rate 9 and 10 to Frozen II respectively. Both similar and different interests are presented by their reviews.

In this paper, we develop a Multi-source Review-based Model for Rating Prediction called MRMRP to effectively exploit informative features from supplementary reviews and thus improve rating prediction accuracy. The user supplementary review document can be regarded as a supplementary information source for the user and it is expected that this additional information can improve recommendation performance. Inspired by [31], MRMRP extracts information from user review document (aggregation of reviews written by a user), item review document (aggregation of reviews written for an item) and user supplementary review documents with three parallel neural networks. It then extracts useful information in supplementary reviews by using the latent representation of the user review document to filter the latent representation of the user supplementary review document. Finally, the obtained features can be incorporated into neural network models to improve recommendation performance. In our model, we use a Multi-Layer Perceptron (MLP) for final rating prediction. The contributions of our work can be summarized as follows:

- To address the data sparsity problem of review, for each user, we collect reviews from their similar users and add these reviews to the user's supplementary review document. Note that, we design a new similarity estimation method to compute the similarity between different users.
- We develop a deep leaning-based model to extract useful features from the user supplementary review document and implement a filtering layer to obtain

informative features from user supplementary reviews. Besides, we consider mean value of all ratings in training data to alleviate rating variation.
– The experiments conducted on four real-world datasets demonstrate that our MRMRP model achieves better rating prediction performance than the existing methods.

The rest of this paper is organized as follows: Sect. 2 states related work; Sect. 3 formulates our approach; Sect. 4 presents our experiments; Sect. 5 concludes our work.

2 Related Work

CF-based recommender systems which only utilize user-item interaction records to give recommendations to users are prevalent in the past decades. However, the performance of most existing CF-based methods is hindered by the data sparsity and cold-start problems. For example, Probabilistic Matrix Factorization (PMF) [20], which is a conventional latent model, has a poor performance when the dataset is very sparse. User preferences and item attributes extracted from user reviews can overcome the serious data sparsity to some extent, so many works exploit textual information from review text and integrate them with ratings to improve rating prediction accuracy. Prior models such as RBLT [23] use topic modeling techniques to derive latent features from user reviews and achieve better rating prediction accuracy. These models outperform most interaction-based models that only use user-item interactions for making recommendations. Although these approaches have made some progress, they employ the bag-of-words (BOW) techniques to generate review representations and thus ignore the word order information, which could impede their performance.

To tackle this limitation, Collaborative Multi-Level Embedding (CMLE) [30] utilizes a word embedding model with a standard matrix factorization model to extract semantic context information in the review documents. Recent years have witnessed the successful use of Deep Neural Networks (DNN) in the field of natural language processing [5,24]. Inspired by these studies, many neural network based recommender systems [1,3,8,12,22,27] propose to generate better latent semantic representations from reviews with neural networks. Deep Cooperative Neural Networks (DeepCoNN) [31] utilizes two parallel neural networks to learn latent representations for users and items from the user review document and the item review document respectively. Then, the two latent representations are coupled by Factorization Machines (FM) [17] for the final rating prediction. Neural Factorization Machines (NFM) [8] applies MLP to abstract the high-level features of both users and items by modeling user-item interactions in a non-linear way, and then it puts the high-level features into FM. FM is a popular solution to utilize second-order feature interactions and many extensions of it have been developed and achieve comparable performance [6,8,9,16,29]. Since FM is incapable of learning complex user-item rating behaviors through high-order feature interactions, Deep&Crossing [22] and Wide&Deep [2] not only model features in a linear way but also import MLP to learn high-order feature interactions, which is proved to be effective in enhancing the click-through rate prediction model capability greatly.

However, in the real world, few users are likely to comment on purchased products and most reviews written by users are short. As a result, the review text is extremely sparse. PARL [27] extracts extra user features from user auxiliary reviews from like-minded users to tackle this problem. This model picks auxiliary review by randomly selecting the review written by another user who gives the same rating score as the specified user. We think the approach PARL generates the user auxiliary reviews ignores much information implied in the user historical ratings and does not consider the different user scoring habits.

In this paper, we introduce a more reasonable algorithm to supplement profiles of users, which collects reviews written by similar users. Here, similar users refer to the users who give close ratings to the same item and have the highest similarity with the specified user. Besides, we extract useful features from these supplementary reviews with a neural network architecture. Our proposed model can alleviate the data sparsity problem of user reviews and thus improve the recommendation performance of review-based recommendation systems.

3   MRMRP

In this section, we describe the details of the proposed MRMRP model. We first introduce how our model constructs the user supplementary review document. Note that, we consider the scoring habits and user historical rating records as well in our algorithm. After that, we elaborate the process of extracting features from reviews including supplementary reviews in MRMRP. Then, we describe how these features are fused and applied to make rating prediction. Finally, we discuss the optimization objective of our model.

3.1   Construction of User Supplementary Review Document

Our goal is to alleviate the sparsity of user reviews by extracting extra information from the user supplementary review document. Given a specified user u, we show the details of the construction process of the supplementary review document in Algorithm 1.

The user supplementary review document contains reviews written by other users with the highest similarity score with the user u and give the close rating value as user u. These users have consumed at least one same item with user u. We design a formula to compute the similarity score between users, which is an extension of the Pearson correlation coefficient. Equation 1 gives the definition of our similarity formula:

$$r_{xy} = \sqrt{|I_x \cap I_y|} \frac{\sum_{i \in I_x \cap I_y}(x_i - \bar{x})(y_i - \bar{y})}{\sqrt{\sum_{i \in I_x}(x_i - \bar{x})^2}\sqrt{\sum_{i \in I_y}(y_i - \bar{y})^2}} \tag{1}$$

where x and y are two different users, I_x and I_y denote the collection of items that user x and user y have consumed respectively, and $I_x \cap I_y$ means the collection

---

Algorithm 1: User supplementary review document construction.

Input: identification of user u

Output: supplementary review document of user u

    // get user $u's$ consumption record in training data

1 *record = get_record(u)* ;

2 *supplementary_doc = None*;

3 **for** *item i in record* **do**

      // get user $u's$ rating of item i

4   *rate = get_rate(u, i)* ;

      // get identifications of users who score item i between $[rate-1, rate+1]$

5   *user_set = seek_user(i, rate)*;

      // compute similarity score of users in user_set with user u

6   *users_similarity = compute_user_similarity(u, user_set)*;

      // get the identification of the user who is most similar with user u

7   *u_selected = max(users_similarity)*;

8   **if** *u_selected ≠ Null* **then**

9         $\lfloor$ *review = review_{u_selected,i}*;

10   **else**

11        $\lfloor$ *review = None*;

12    $\lfloor$ *supplementary_doc+ = review*;

13 *return supplementary_doc*;

---

of items that both user x and user y have consumed. x_i, y_i are the rating scores of user x, y on item i respectively, $\bar{x}, \bar{y}$ are the average value of all ratings of user x, y respectively, and $|I_x \cap I_y|$ are the number of items that user x and user y have both consumed. Besides, user rating records are extremely sparse and it indicates that two users are very likely to have common habits if they have consumed many same items, so we add the $\sqrt{|I_x \cap I_y|}$ to make such two users get a larger similarity score.

For each item i consumed by user u, we will first select all the instances containing item i in the training data. In reality, some users tend to give high ratings and some tend to give low ratings. Hence, all instances whose scores on item i differ from the score given by user u by no more than 1 are selected as instances of similar users. Then, the similarity score between each candidate user and user u is calculated according to the consumption records of the corresponding users. At last, we select the review written by the user who has the highest similarity score with user u and add it into the supplementary review document.

MRMRP takes rating tendencies and historical purchased records into considerations when deciding supplementary reviews written by similar users. Therefore, it is not surprising that similar users will present similar comments on the same item. On the other hand, they will also show different interests in their reviews which can enrich the profiles of users and therefore improve recommendation performance. This is because supplementary reviews of user u are collected from various users who may have many similar interests with this spec-

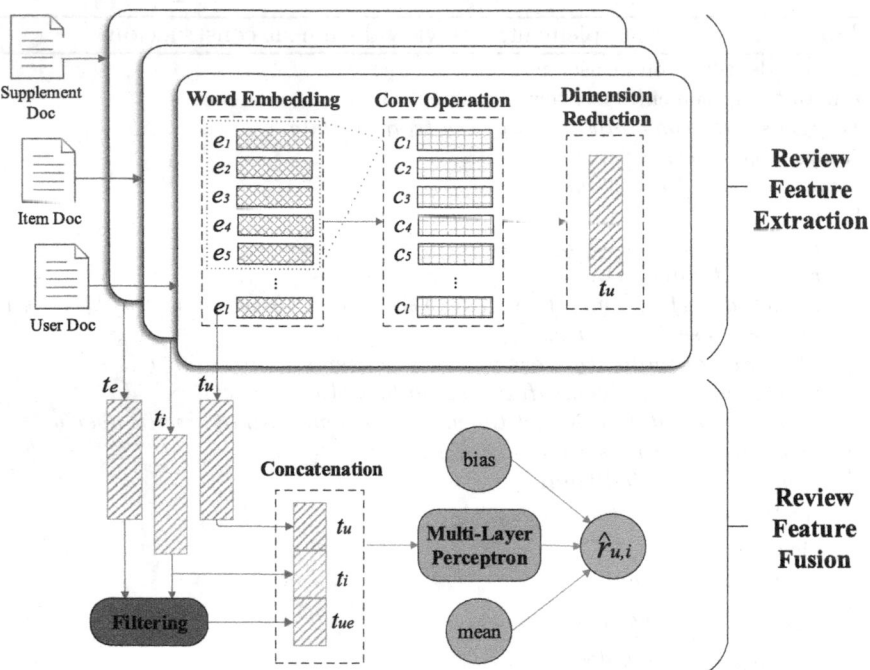

Fig. 2. Architecture of the MRMRP model.

ified user. It is expected that we can capture extra interests that may not be fully expressed in the user review document from supplementary reviews and thus improve rating prediction accuracy.

3.2 Review Feature Extraction

The task of review-based feature extraction is to learn the latent feature vectors of three kinds of documents. Since the reviews written by users can reflect their personal preferences, we collect all the reviews written by the same user to make the user review document. For the same reason, we take all the reviews that an item received from all users to form the item review document. In the last section, we create the user supplementary review document for each user as a supplementary review source.

As shown in Fig. 2, MRMRP exploits three neural networks to capture useful features from the user review document, the user supplementary review document and the item review document. It aims to model user preferences, user additional preferences, and item attributes from these three review documents. Specifically, the convolution operation is used to extract different aspects covered by the review documents and a dimension reduction operation is employed to merge information included in different channels. Finally, we obtain latent representations of these three review documents.

Word Embedding: Given a review document $D = (w_1, w_2, ..., w_l)$, we first employ an embedding layer to project each word to its corresponding embedding vector $e_i \in \mathbb{R}^n$. Then, we concatenate these embedding vectors according to the order their corresponding words appear in the review document. Finally, we obtain a review document matrix $D \in \mathbb{R}^{n \times l}$:

$$D = [e_1, e_2, ..., e_l] \tag{2}$$

where l is the length of the review document, n is the embedding dimension of each word and e_i represents the word embedding vector of the $i - th$ word in the review document D.

Convolution Operation: Given a review document matrix D, the convolution layer is exploited for semantic information extraction. To obtain various features, we use multiple convolution filters with different convolution weights to capture the context features for the review document matrix D. To be specific, the $j - th$ convolution filter on a window of words with size ω is used to extract the local contextual feature c^j. Finally, the feature extracted from the window centered at position h can be defined as follows:

$$c_h^j = f(W^j * D_{h:h+\omega-1, 0:n}) \tag{3}$$

where $*$ is the convolution operator, f is a nonlinear activation function, and W^j is the convolution weight represents the convolution weight vector for the $j - th$ convolution filter. $D_{h:h+\omega-1, 0:n}$ consists of context words that appear from $h - position$ within a window of size ω in the review document matrix D.

After the convolution operation, we can represent the feature extracted from the review document D by concatenating these convolutional results as follows:

$$C = [c_1, c_2, ..., c_m]^T \tag{4}$$

where $C \in \mathbb{R}^{m \times l}$, m is the number of filters, and c_i denotes the contextual feature extracted by the $i - th$ convolution filter.

Dimension Reduction: The contextual matrix C is first passed to a max-pooling layer. This operation can better compress the information contained in different channels. After the max-pooling operation, we get a contextual vector t_m as follows:

$$t_m = [t_1, t_2, ..., t_m] \tag{5}$$

$$t = [t_1, t_2, ..., t_k] \tag{6}$$

After the max-pooling operation, we utilize a fully connected layer to integrate the semantic features. Finally, we get the latent representation vector t of the review document D.

3.3   Review Feature Fusion

Filtering Layer: After adopting the above operation steps on the user review document, the item review document and the user supplementary review document, we can get three vectors t_u, t_i and t_s. These extracted vectors are the latent representations of their corresponding review documents. The user supplementary review document serves as a supplementary document to the user review document that contains very sparse review data. Reviews in the user supplementary documents are extra information which may help in rating prediction. Because supplementary reviews are written by different users, we need to extract informative features related to the specified user when these additional reviews are used to make recommendations. We define a filtering layer to filter out t_s as follows:

$$g = sigmoid(\boldsymbol{W_g} * \boldsymbol{t_u} + b_g) \tag{7}$$

$$\boldsymbol{t_{us}} = \boldsymbol{g} \odot \boldsymbol{t_s} \tag{8}$$

where $\boldsymbol{W_g}$ is the weight vector, b_g is the bias, $\boldsymbol{g}$ is the filtering gate that controls the flow of information and $\odot$ denotes the element-wise product operation.

Fusion Layer: After obtaining three vectors $\boldsymbol{t_u}$, $\boldsymbol{t_i}$ and $\boldsymbol{t_{us}}$, we concatenate them as $\boldsymbol{a^0}$ and feed it into the Multi-Layer Perceptron (MLP) to predict the rating of user u upon item i as follows:

$$\boldsymbol{a^0} = [\boldsymbol{t_u}, \boldsymbol{t_i}, \boldsymbol{t_{us}}] \tag{9}$$

$$\boldsymbol{a^{l+1}} = f(\boldsymbol{W_l} * \boldsymbol{a^l} + b_l) \tag{10}$$

where $\boldsymbol{a^0}$ is the concatenation vector of $\boldsymbol{t_u}$, $\boldsymbol{t_i}$ and $\boldsymbol{t_{ue}}$, and l is the hidden layer number in MLP. $\boldsymbol{a^l}$, $\boldsymbol{W_l}$ and b_l are the output, weight vector and bias at l-th hidden layer. After that, a scalar is generated, which is fed into the addition for the final rating prediction. MLP is effective in processing low-dimensional dense embedding vectors. Compared with FM, which achieves great performance in modelling low-order interactions between features in a linear way, MLP can learn high-order feature interactions at the bit-wise level.

In particular, rating behaviors contain multiple inherent tendencies, which is known as bias. According to our analysis for some rating samples, many ratings are related only to users or items but have nothing to do with the interaction between user and item. In other words, some users tend to rate a high score for all items and some items are likely to receive higher ratings from all users. Incorporating user biases and item biases have been proven to alleviate rating variations and thus yield better rating prediction performance [19]. We encapsulate factors that are irrelevant to user-item interactions into the final prediction as follows:

$$\widehat{r}_{u,i} = \widehat{b}_{u,i} + \mu + b_u + b_i \tag{11}$$

where μ is the mean value of all ratings in training data, and b_u and b_i are the biases for user u and item i.

3.4 Optimization Objective

We take the square loss as the objective function for parameter optimization:

$$L = \frac{1}{M} \sum_{i=1}^{M} (r_{u,i} - \widehat{r}_{u,i})^2 \tag{12}$$

Table 1. Statistics of four evaluated datasets.

Datasets	#users	#items	#ratings	#w_u	#w_i	#w_s	density
Musical instruments	1429	900	10261	141.32	200.12	182.33	0.798%
Office products	405	2420	53227	197.93	229.52	239.81	0.448%
Tools improvement	16638	10217	134321	162.52	212.48	177.25	0.079%
Beer	7725	21976	66625	34.06	103.20	78.01	0.039%

where M is the number of instances in the training data, $\widehat{r}_{u,i}$ denotes the prediction rating value and $r_{u,i}$ is the true rating value.

4   Experiments

In this section, we first introduce experimental settings including datasets and evaluation metric, baselines and parameter settings. Subsequently, we make comparison of different models and validate the effectiveness of our model. Then, we perform ablation experiments to prove that different components contribute positively to the overall performance of MRMRP. Finally, we present how different parameter settings influence the performance of MRMRP.

4.1   Datasets and Evaluation Metric

The experiments are on four publicly accessible datasets that provide user reviews. The four datasets includes Amazon-5cores datasets[1] (Musical Instruments, Office Products and Tools Improvement) and a dataset called Beer collected from the RateBeer website [14]. 5-core means that each user and each item in the dataset have no less than 5 reviews. Note that, we also conduct 5-core operation on the Beer dataset. These four datasets consist of users' explicit ratings on items ranging from 1 to 5 and contain review texts.

We use similar preprocessing steps mentioned in [10] to preprocess review documents for all datasets. Initially, we remove stop words and words that have the document frequency higher than 0.5. Second, we calculate tf-idf score for each word and select the top 20,000 distinct words as vocabulary. Then, we remove all words out of the vocabulary from raw documents and amputate (pad) the long (short) review documents to the same length of 300 words. Finally, we filter out the rating records which contain empty review after preprocessing.

Table 1 summarizes the statistics of the four datasets after four preprocessing steps. To save space, we write some phrases in a simplified form as follows: w_u means words per user review document, w_i represents words per item review document, and w_s means words per user supplementary document. For each dataset, we randomly choose 72% of each dataset as the training data, 8% of each dataset as the validation data and the remaining 20% of each dataset as the

---

[1] http://jmcauley.ucsd.edu/data/amazon/.

testing data. Moreover, each user and each item have at least one rating in the training data. The training data is selected such that at least one interaction for each user-item pair should be contained. Following the work in [1], the reviews in the validation data and testing data are excluded because they are unavailable during rating prediction. Similar with prior work [12,27], the performance of our proposed algorithm is judged by Mean Squared Error (MSE) metric:

$$MSE = \frac{1}{N} \sum_{i=1}^{N} (r_{u,i} - \widehat{r}_{u,i})^2 \tag{13}$$

where $\widehat{r}_{u,i}$ denotes the prediction rating value, $r_{u,i}$ is the true rating value and N is the number of instances in the testing data.

4.2   Baselines

PMF: Probabilistic Matrix Factorization (PMF) is a classical Matrix Factorization (MF) method that can greatly predict rating while data volume is large and user data is sparse [20].

RBLT: Rating-Boosted Latent Topics (RBLT) models user preferences and item attributes in a shared topic space and then feeds them into an MF model for the final rating prediction [23].

CMLE: Collaborative Multi-Level Embedding (CMLE) combines a word embedding model with an MF model to extract user preferences and item attributes from both reviews and user-item interactions [30].

DeepCoNN: Deep Cooperative Neural Networks (DeepCoNN) utilizes two parallel neural networks to learn the latent representations of user and item and subsequently introduce them into FM for the final prediction [31].

TransNets: TransNets is an extension of the DeepCoNN model [1]. It adds an neural layer to model the target user-item review.

TARMF: TARMF co-learns user preferences and item attributes from both user reviews and user-item interactions by optimizing the MF algorithm and an attention-based recurrent neural network [13].

ANR: ANR imports the attention mechanism to perform aspect-based representation learning for users and items [3]. Aspect means from which perspective the user writes reviews or from which perspective the item is introduced, such as price, performance and service.

PARL: PARL exploits extra user preferences from auxiliary reviews written by users who give the same scores to address the sparsity problem of user reviews and produce extra information of users [27].

CARP: CARP learns the informative logic units from the reviews written by users and infer their corresponding sentiments [12]. It can also discover the interpretable reasons at a fine level of granularity.

4.3 Parameter Settings

We exploit the grid search to tune the parameters for our model and all baselines mentioned above. For the purpose of fair comparisons, we train all deep learning models by employing RMSprop optimization [15] to minimize the MSE loss (Eq. 13) and tune their learning rate from {0.0015, 0.003, 0.005, 0.01}. The word embedding matrix is randomly initialized at first and we go through the dimension of each word embedding in the set {25, 50, 100, 200}. The number of convolution filters in the convolution layer is optimized from {64, 128, 256, 512}. In addition, we tune the keep probability of dropout from {0.6, 0.7, 0.8}.

Besides, the window size of all convolution layers is set to 5. The batch size for Musical Instruments is set to 64. For the other three datasets containing more instances, the batch size is set to 256. Once the result on the training data becomes worse, we stop training the model. We only save the model which achieves the best result on the validation data for the final rating prediction on testing data.

Table 2. Performance comparison of MSE on four real-world datasets. Our results are highlighted in boldface, and the best results of baselines are highlighted in underline. △% denotes the relative improvement of MRMRP over the review-based baselines. † means that the variation in achieving the best result is statistically significant at the 0.05 level.

Datasets	Musical instruments	Office Products	Tools improvement	Beer
PMF [20]	1.398†	1.092†	1.566†	1.641†
RBLT [23]	0.815†	0.759†	0.983†	0.576†
CMLE [30]	0.817†	0.759†	1.020†	0.605†
DeepCoNN [31]	0.814†	0.860†	1.061†	0.618†
TransNets [1]	0.798†	0.759†	1.003†	0.581†
TARMF [13]	0.943†	0.789†	1.160†	0.912†
ANR [3]	0.795†	0.742†	0.975†	0.590†
PARL [27]	0.782	0.731	<u>0.955</u>	0.561
CARP [12]	<u>0.773</u>	<u>0.719</u>	0.960	<u>0.556</u>
MRMRP	**0.715**	**0.711**	**0.941**	**0.546**
△%	7.5–24.2	1.1–17.3	1.5–19.5	1.8–40.0

4.4 Model Comparison

Table 2 compares the performance of our method and baselines on the three Amazon-5cores datasets and the Beer dataset. The line below the performance of MRMRP also presents the percentage of improvements achieved by MRMRP compared with our review-based baselines. The best results are highlighted in bold and the second best results are underlined.

It is clear that our proposed model MRMRP achieves the best performance across four benchmark datasets. Our method obtains 7.5% improvement on the

Table 3. Effect of different components in MRMRP.

Methods	Musical instruments	Office products	Tools improvement	Beer
DeepCoNN	0.814	0.860	1.063	0.617
+bias	0.756	0.783	0.995	0.589
+supplementary	0.745	0.729	0.956	0.559
+mean	0.717	0.714	0.948	0.553
FM→MLP	0.715	0.711	0.941	0.546

dataset of Musical Instruments compared with the best baseline on this dataset. By contrast, the figure for the Beer dataset is 1.8%. Intuitively, this is because reviews in the Beer dataset is very sparse and the performance of our model is closely related to data sparsity of dataset. We ascribe the success of our model to the user supplementary document created by our algorithm and the effective way we fuse the latent representations of review documents. In the following experiments, we further analyze how the specific designs of MRMRP boost its performance.

Besides, we can observe that the review-based method outperforms the rating-based method. All the models using reviews outperform PMF on all datasets. This demonstrates that information implied in reviews can boost recommendation performance. In general, deep learning based methods outperform shallow methods such as PMF and CMLE. This is because neural modes are capable of learning powerful representations of data.

4.5   Ablation Study

In this paper, we develop a review-based model for rating prediction. It collects the user supplementary reviews as a complementary information source. Moreover, it uses an architecture consists of a filtering layer and an MLP to fuse review features for final rating prediction. Note that, our model considers global mean value and bias as well. In this section, we conduct ablation experiments to validate the effect of different components in our proposed MRMRP. These components are sequentially stacked on top of the DeepCoNN model each time to explain their effectiveness. The experimental results are shown in Table 3.

DeepCoNN utilizes two parallel neural networks to separately learn latent representation from user review document and item review document, and then incorporates them into the FM for final rating prediction. DeepCoNN + bias can be regarded as DeepCoNN plus the user and item bias values. +supplementary utilizes three parallel neural networks to obtain latent representation from user review document, item review document and user supplementary review document respectively. +mean additionally considers the mean value of all ratings in the training data. FM→MLP replaces the FM in DeepCoNN with MLP to fuse latent representations extracted from three review documents.

From the results in Table 3, we can see the contributions of different components in our proposed model. The +bias component is designed for alleviating

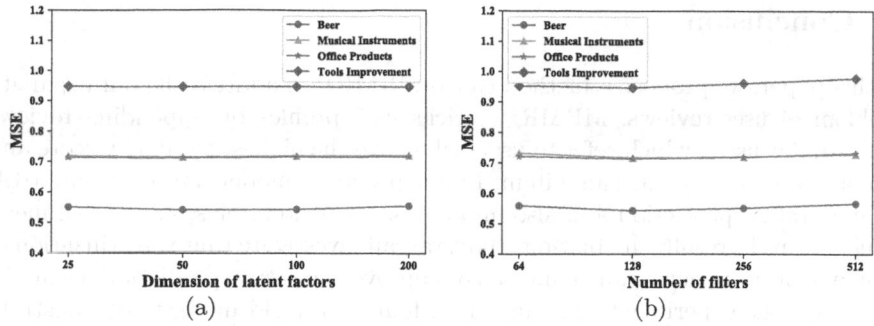

Fig. 3. Effects of the dimension of latent factors and the number of convolution filters on the performance of MRMRP.

rating variation and this experiment confirms its effectiveness. The results of the +supplementary experiment demonstrate that our constructed user supplementary review document can significantly improve recommendation performance. Besides, MRMRP introduces the mean value of all ratings in the training data to alleviate rating variation and the +mean experiment validates the effectiveness of this design. Finally, FM→MLP demonstrates that MLP is more effective in modeling high-order feature interactions.

4.6 Parameter Sensitivity Analysis

Finally, we empirically study the impact of the dimension of latent factors and the number of filters in the convolutional neural layer.

Effect of the Dimension of Latent Factors: Figure 3(a) depicts the performance of MRMRP by varying the dimension of latent factors in {25, 50, 100, 200} on the four datasets. Our model achieves the optimal rating prediction accuracy at the latent factor dimension of 50, after which its performance will experience a slight decline. We can conclude that the dimension of latent factors has little effect on experimental performance and high dimension of the latent factor may cause over-fitting. Therefore, the dimension of the latent factor is set to 50.

Effect of the Number of Convolution Filters: Figure 3(b) shows the performance of MRMRP by varying the number of filters in {64, 128, 256, 512} on the four datasets. We can see that with the change of the filter number, the performance of our model changes variously. Our model reaches the best performance at the convolution filter number of 128. Besides, it is observed that too many filters or too few filters can cause the performance degradation of our model. When we set the number of filters to a large value, it may cause an over-fitting phenomenon and thus result in poor performance. When we set the number of filters to a small value, the convolution layer cannot capture the context features adequately. Hence, the number of filters in the convolutional neural layer is set to 128.

5 Conclusion

In this paper, we propose a method called MRMRP to address the data sparsity problem of user reviews. MRMRP enrichs user profiles by appending reviews from similar users, which refer to users who have the highest similarity score and give a close score on the same item. In our proposed model, we utilize an MLP for final rating prediction and also import user bias, item bias, and global mean value. From the results in ablation study, we can investigate that the utilization of supplementary reviews can significantly improve the rating prediction accuracy. Moreover, the experiments conducted on four real-world datasets demonstrate that our MRMRP model outperforms all baseline recommendation systems.

Acknowledgments. This work is supported by the National Nature Science Foundation of China (No. 61672133 and No. 61832001) and Sichuan Science and Technology Program (No. 2019YFG0535).

References

1. Catherine, R., Cohen, W.W.: TransNets: learning to transform for recommendation. In: RecSys, pp. 288–296 (2017)
2. Cheng, H., et al.: Wide & deep learning for recommender systems. In: DLRS@RecSys, pp. 7–10 (2016)
3. Chin, J.Y., Zhao, K., Joty, S.R., Cong, G.: ANR: aspect-based neural recommender. In: CIKM, pp. 147–156 (2018)
4. Deshpande, M., Karypis, G.: Item-based top-N recommendation algorithms. ACM Trans. Inf. Syst. **22**(1), 143–177 (2004)
5. Devlin, J., Chang, M., Lee, K., Toutanova, K.: BERT: pre-training of deep bidirectional transformers for language understanding. In: NAACL-HLT, no. 1, pp. 4171–4186 (2019)
6. Guo, H., Tang, R., Ye, Y., Li, Z., He, X.: DeepFM: a factorization-machine based neural network for CTR prediction. In: IJCAI, pp. 1725–1731 (2017)
7. Guo, L., Shao, J., Tan, K., Yang, Y.: WhereToGo: personalized travel recommendation for individuals and groups. In: MDM, vol. 1, pp. 49–58 (2014)
8. He, X., Chua, T.: Neural factorization machines for sparse predictive analytics. In: SIGIR, pp. 355–364 (2017)
9. Hong, L., Doumith, A.S., Davison, B.D.: Co-factorization machines: modeling user interests and predicting individual decisions in Twitter. In: WSDM (2013)
10. Kim, D.H., Park, C., Oh, J., Lee, S., Yu, H.: Convolutional matrix factorization for document context-aware recommendation. In: RecSys, pp. 233–240 (2016)
11. Koren, Y., Bell, R.M., Volinsky, C.: Matrix factorization techniques for recommender systems. IEEE Comput. **42**(8), 30–37 (2009)
12. Li, C., Quan, C., Peng, L., Qi, Y., Deng, Y., Wu, L.: A capsule network for recommendation and explaining what you like and dislike. In: SIGIR, pp. 275–284 (2019)
13. Lu, Y., Dong, R., Smyth, B.: Coevolutionary recommendation model: mutual learning between ratings and reviews. In: WWW, pp. 773–782 (2018)
14. McAuley, J.J., Leskovec, J., Jurafsky, D.: Learning attitudes and attributes from multi-aspect reviews. In: ICDM, pp. 1020–1025 (2012)

15. Mukkamala, M.C., Hein, M.: Variants of RMSProp and adagrad with logarithmic regret bounds. In: ICML, pp. 2545–2553 (2017)
16. Oentaryo, R.J., Lim, E., Low, J., Lo, D., Finegold, M.: Predicting response in mobile advertising with hierarchical importance-aware factorization machine. In: WSDM, pp. 123–132 (2014)
17. Rendle, S.: Factorization machines. In: ICDM, pp. 995–1000 (2010)
18. Rendle, S., Gantner, Z., Freudenthaler, C., Schmidt-Thieme, L.: Fast context-aware recommendations with factorization machines. In: SIGIR, pp. 635–644 (2011)
19. Burke, R., O'Mahony, M.P., Hurley, N.J.: Robust collaborative recommendation. In: Ricci, F., Rokach, L., Shapira, B., Kantor, P.B. (eds.) Recommender Systems Handbook, pp. 805–835. Springer, Boston (2011). https://doi.org/10.1007/978-0-387-85820-3_25
20. Salakhutdinov, R., Mnih, A.: Probabilistic matrix factorization. In: NIPS, pp. 1257–1264 (2007)
21. Salakhutdinov, R., Mnih, A., Hinton, G.E.: Restricted Boltzmann machines for collaborative filtering. In: ICML, pp. 791–798 (2007)
22. Shan, Y., Hoens, T.R., Jiao, J., Wang, H., Yu, D., Mao, J.C.: Deep crossing: web-scale modeling without manually crafted combinatorial features. In: KDD, pp. 255–262 (2016)
23. Tan, Y., Zhang, M., Liu, Y., Ma, S.: Rating-boosted latent topics: understanding users and items with ratings and reviews. In: IJCAI, pp. 2640–2646 (2016)
24. Vaswani, A., et al.: Attention is all you need. In: NIPS, pp. 5998–6008 (2017)
25. Wang, X., Hu, G., Lin, H., Sun, J.: A novel ensemble approach for click-through rate prediction based on factorization machines and gradient boosting decision trees. In: Shao, J., Yiu, M.L., Toyoda, M., Zhang, D., Wang, W., Cui, B. (eds.) APWeb-WAIM 2019. LNCS, vol. 11642, pp. 152–162. Springer, Cham (2019). https://doi.org/10.1007/978-3-030-26075-0_12
26. Wu, H., Shao, J., Yin, H., Shen, H.T., Zhou, X.: Geographical constraint and temporal similarity modeling for point-of-interest recommendation. In: Wang, J., et al. (eds.) WISE 2015. LNCS, vol. 9419, pp. 426–441. Springer, Cham (2015). https://doi.org/10.1007/978-3-319-26187-4_40
27. Wu, L., Quan, C., Li, C., Ji, D.: PARL: let strangers speak out what you like. In: CIKM, pp. 677–686 (2018)
28. Wu, L., Quan, C., Li, C., Wang, Q., Zheng, B., Luo, X.: A context-aware user-item representation learning for item recommendation. ACM Trans. Inf. Syst. **37**(2), 22:1–22:29 (2019)
29. Xiao, J., Ye, H., He, X., Zhang, H., Wu, F., Chua, T.: Attentional factorization machines: learning the weight of feature interactions via attention networks. In: IJCAI, pp. 3119–3125 (2017)
30. Zhang, W., Yuan, Q., Han, J., Wang, J.: Collaborative multi-level embedding learning from reviews for rating prediction. In: IJCAI, pp. 2986–2992 (2016)
31. Zheng, L., Noroozi, V., Yu, P.S.: Joint deep modeling of users and items using reviews for recommendation. In: WSDM, pp. 425–434 (2017)
32. Zhou, G., et al.: Deep interest evolution network for click-through rate prediction. In: AAAI, pp. 5941–5948 (2019)

Discovering Real-Time Reachable Area
Using Trajectory Connections

Ruiyuan Li[1,2], Jie Bao[2], Huajun He[2,3], Sijie Ruan[1,2], Tianfu He[2,4], Liang Hong[5], Zhongyuan Jiang[1], and Yu Zheng[1,2(✉)]

[1] Xidian University, Xi'an, China
`liruiyuan@whu.edu.cn, sjruan94@gmail.com, zyjiang@xidian.edu.cn`
[2] JD Intelligent City Research, Beijing, China
`baojie@jd.com, msyuzheng@outlook.com`
[3] Southwest Jiaotong University, Chengdu, China
`hehuajun@my.swjtu.edu.cn`
[4] Harbin Institute of Technology, Harbin, China
`Tianfu.D.He@outlook.com`
[5] Wuhan University, Wuhan, China
`hong@whu.edu.cn`

Abstract. Discovering real-time reachable areas of a specified location is of importance for many location-based applications. The real-time reachable area of given location changes with different environments. Existing methods fail to capture real-time traffic conditions instantly. This paper provides the first attempt to discover real-time reachable areas with real-time trajectories. To address the data sparsity issue raised by the limited real-time trajectories, we propose a trajectory connection technique, which connects sub-trajectories passing the same location. Specifically, we propose a framework that combines indexing and machine learning techniques: 1) we propose a set of indexing and query processing techniques to efficiently find reachable areas with an arbitrary number of trajectory connections; 2) we propose to predict the best number of connections in any location and at any time based on multiple datasets. Extensive experiments and one case study demonstrate the effectiveness and efficiency of our methods.

1 Introduction

Real-time reachable area discovery aims to find the reachable area from a specified location within a given time period in real-time conditions. It is very useful in many urban applications: 1) Location-based recommendation. As depicted in Fig. 1(a), a user wants to find the restaurants that can be reached from her current location within 5 min; and 2) Vehicle dispatching. As illustrated in Fig. 1(b), a user calls for a taxi to pick her up in 10 min. Taxi companies would use this function to find the candidate drivers. Traditional methods are based on the static spatial range query over either Euclidean distance [1] or road network distance [2,3], which find the same reachable areas without considering the highly skewed traffic conditions at different time (e.g., late night

Y. Nah et al. (Eds.): DASFAA 2020, LNCS 12113, pp. 36–53, 2020.
https://doi.org/10.1007/978-3-030-59416-9_3

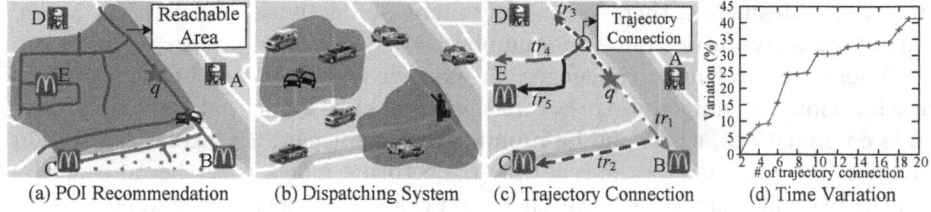

(a) POI Recommendation   (b) Dispatching System   (c) Trajectory Connection   (d) Time Variation

Fig. 1. Application scenarios and trajectory connections.

vs. rush hours). Optional methods first estimate the travel time of each road segment [4–7], then find reachable areas using road network expansion techniques [2,8]. However, these methods ignore the delays of intersections. Besides, they are designed to model the regular traffic conditions, but can hardly capture abnormal events, such as accidents. With the availability of massive trajectories, [9] takes advantage of historical trajectories that passed the query location during the request hour to find the reachable area. However, this approach cannot be applied directly in a real-time scenario, as it does not consider real-time contexts, such as weather, traffic conditions, accidents and other events in a city.

An intuitive idea is to use only real-time trajectories (e.g., generated within the most recent one hour). However, we cannot apply directly the techniques in [9] to real-time trajectories, due to the **data sparsity** issue (i.e., the number of trajectories passing the query location in a short time window is very limited). To solve this issue, we propose a **trajectory connection** technique. As illustrated in Fig. 1(c), if we consider only the trajectories that exactly pass the query location q, i.e., tr_1 and tr_3, only B can be reached. Suppose the trajectories can be connected if they share the same locations, e.g., tr_1 and tr_2, C is also in the reachable area. Further, if the trajectories can be connected twice, E can be reached as well by connecting tr_5 to tr_4, which significantly improves the coverage of the reachable area. However, the reliability of discovered reachable areas may be affected by trajectory connections, as the connected trajectories are generated by different moving objects, where the time cost of connections (e.g., waiting time in crossroads) is ignored. To study the effects of trajectory connections on reliability, we compare the estimated travel time of a path using different numbers of trajectory connections with the real travel time, as shown in Fig. 1(d). It shows that, with more connections, the accuracy of estimation becomes lower. But if we limit the number less than five, the estimation variation is less than 10%, which guarantees a reasonable reachable area. However, a small trajectory connection number may cause a coverage problem. As a result, the number of trajectory connections is a trade-off between reliability and coverage.

An appropriate connection number is determined by the real-time trajectories. If there are fewer real-time trajectories, a bigger connection number should be assigned to achieve a good coverage. However, it is hard to determine a good connection number, as the spatio-temporal distribution of trajectories is skewed severely. For example, downtown areas contain more taxi activities than suburb areas. Meanwhile, there are usually more taxi activities during rush hours. Therefore, a **dynamic** connection number is needed when a query arrives.

There are three main challenges. 1) As each trajectory can be connected at any location with numerous trajectories, it results in exponential numbers of possible combinations, which can be prohibitively inefficient. 2) A good connection number is determined by the real-time trajectories, which is further affected by multiple complex factors, e.g. weather conditions, road networks, and land usage around the request location [10]. 3) there is even no ground truth of reachable areas in our datasets, which leads to lack of the labels of connection numbers for model learning. The main contributions of this paper are summarized as follows:

(1) We provide the first attempt to discover real-time reachable areas with dynamic trajectory connections, and design a framework that combines indexing with machine learning techniques to solve this problem (Sect. 3).
(2) We design a set of indexing and query processing techniques to prune redundant trajectory connections, which can efficiently answer real-time reachable area discovery requests with arbitrary connection numbers (Sect. 4).
(3) We propose a method to generate the labels of connection numbers using historical trajectories, and identify spatio-temporal features to predict a good connection number in any location and at any time (Sect. 5).
(4) Extensive experiments are conducted using multiple real datasets, verifying the effectiveness and efficiency of our solutions. Readers can experience our demo system in http://r-area.urban-computing.com/ (Sect. 6).

2   Preliminary

Definition 1 (Road Network). *A road network RN is a directed graph $G = (V, E)$, where $V = \{v_1, v_2, ..., v_m\}$ is a set of vertices representing the intersections, and $E = \{e_1, e_2, ..., e_n\}$ is a set of road segments (edges) with directions. $e.v_{start}$ and $e.v_{end}$ represent the start vertex and end vertex of edge e respectively.*

Definition 2 (Map-Matched Trajectory). *A map-matched trajectory $tr =< (e_1, t_1) \rightarrow (e_2, t_2) \rightarrow ... \rightarrow (e_n, t_n) >$ is generated by mapping raw GPS points onto the corresponding road segments, where t_i is the time when the trajectory enters edge e_i. The time cost to traverse e_i is $Cost(tr.e_i) = t_{i+1} - t_i$.*

For simplicity, in this paper, we represent a map-matched trajectory without detailed temporal information, i.e., $tr =< e_1 \rightarrow e_2 \rightarrow ... \rightarrow e_n >$. $tr[i...j]$ denotes the sub-trajectory of tr that starts from i-th edge to j-th edge in tr.

Definition 3 (Connected Trajectory). *A connected trajectory $ctr =< tr_1[i_1...j_1] \rightarrow tr_2[i_2...j_2] \rightarrow ... \rightarrow tr_n[i_n...j_n] >$ consists of a sequence of sub-trajectories, where the last edge of the previous sub-trajectory shares the same intersection with the first edge of the next sub-trajectory, i.e., $tr_m[j_m].v_{end} = tr_{m+1}[i_{m+1}].v_{start}$.*

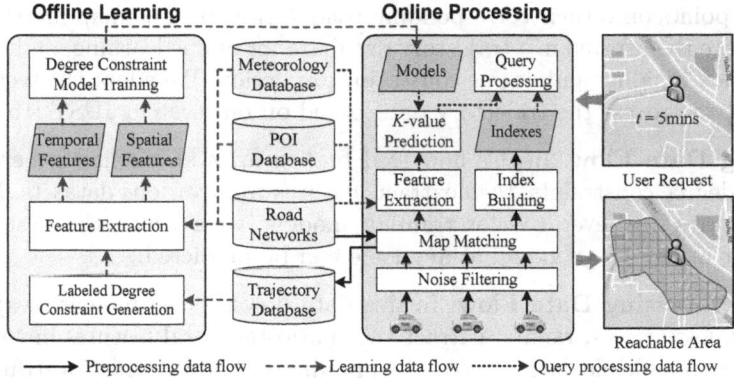

Fig. 2. System framework.

The number of sub-trajectories in a connected trajectory ctr is its ***degree***, denoted by $D(ctr)$. Specifically, there is $D(ctr) - 1$ connections in ctr.

Problem Definition. Given a real-time trajectory database $\mathcal{T}$ generated in the most recent time δ, a query location q, a time budget t, and external environmental data around q (e.g. POIs, road networks, and meteorological data), we first predict a reasonable degree constraint $k \geq 1$ of q, and then find a set of road segments as the reachable area $RA(\mathcal{T}, q, t, k)$, such that for any $e_i \in RA$, there exists at least one connected trajectory $ctr = < q \rightarrow ... \rightarrow e_i >$ that connects e_i from q, satisfying the following two constraints:

(1) **Time Constraint.** The time cost of ctr is not greater than t:

$$Cost(ctr) = \sum_{m=1}^{D(ctr)} Cost(tr_m[i_m, j_m]) \leq t \qquad (1)$$

(2) **Degree Constraint.** The degree of ctr is not greater than k:

$$D(ctr) \leq k \qquad (2)$$

The degree constraint k defines the maximum number of sub-trajectories in a connected trajectory, which provides a trade-off between the coverage and reliability of reachable areas. To guarantee a high reliability, we set $1 \leq k \leq 5$ according to Fig. 1(d). Besides, we focus on reachable area discovery in a very short time ahead, e.g., $t \leq 30$ min, as it can satisfy most dispatching or emergency scenarios. We also have $\delta \times k \geq t$, to make the connection feasible.

3 Framework

Figure 2 gives the framework with two major parts, offline learning and online processing, which generates three data flows:

Preprocessing Data Flow. This data flow (black solid arrows) takes real-time GPS updates as input, removes the trajectories with abnormal speed, and maps the GPS points onto their corresponding road segments. The map-matched trajectories are then stored in a trajectory database for offline learning, and used for online index building and degree constraint prediction. We adopt the techniques in [11–14] to process the trajectory data based on our system JUST [15,16].

Learning Data Flow. In this flow (red broken arrows), we first generate the labels of degree constraints, then extract features from various datasets. Finally, these features are leveraged for training models, with which the best degree constraint in any location and at any time can be predicted.

Query Processing Data Flow. In this data flow (dotted blue arrows), when a user request arrives, we first extract the spatio-temporal features in the given location from multiple data sources, then predict the best degree constraint with the models trained offline. Finally, the real-time reachable area is calculated by means of the built indexes and predicted degree constraint.

As we will apply the indexing techniques to degree constraint model learning, we first introduce the index building and query processing techniques in Sect. 4, and then detail degree constraint model training and prediction in Sect. 5.

4   Index Building and Query Processing

In this section, we assume the degree constraint k is already predicted. If we apply the traditional network expansion based algorithm [2,8] directly, in each expansion step, each candidate road segment is associated with a status of two different dimensions, i.e., time cost t_c and degree cost k_c, which makes it impossible to select the "best" candidate. Therefore, it is required to build an effective index and an efficient pruning strategy to discover real-time reachable areas.

4.1   Traj-Index

Data Structure. *Traj-index* builds links between edges and trajectories. Figure 3(a) gives an example with two parts: 1) *Trajectory-Edge (TE) hash* uses trajectory IDs as hash keys, and each value is a list of edge IDs passed by the trajectory within the most recent δ minutes; 2) *Edge-Trajectory (ET) hash* is an inverted index where the keys are edge IDs, and each value is a list of trajectory IDs passing the edge ordered by arriving time within the most recent δ minutes. To efficiently expand the search via sub-trajectories, a pointer is maintained to link the same trajectory-edge combination between the two hash tables.

Construction. *Traj-index* is updated in a streaming way, where each update is processed incrementally. The complexity is $\mathcal{O}(m \times n)$, where m is the number of new trajectories, and n is the average size of each trajectory. As a result, it is efficient to handle large-scale trajectory updates in a real-time manner.

Query Processing. With *Traj-index*, we propose a query processing method *trajectory expansion* based on an intuitive idea: 1) traversing all trajectories passing q, and finding covered road segments; 2) for each qualified road segment,

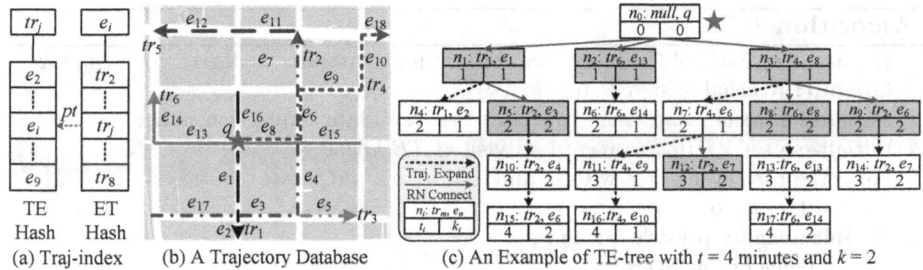

(a) Traj-index   (b) A Trajectory Database   (c) An Example of TE-tree with $t = 4$ minutes and $k = 2$

Fig. 3. Example of Traj-index and TE-tree.

identifying all possible trajectory connections, and updating new qualified road segments; and 3) repeating the previous step, until the budget t or k is used up.

To realize the discovery of reachable areas with *Traj-index*, a *TE-tree* is created during the search process. For example, given a trajectory database as Fig. 3(b), we get a *TE-tree* shown as Fig. 3(c), where the query location q forms the root. The *TE-tree* consists of one type of nodes and two types of links: 1) **TE-node.** Each node contains five properties: an identifier n, a trajectory tr, an edge e, a time cost t_c, and a degree cost k_c. A *TE-node* indicates the current search status (i.e., trajectory tr at edge e), where the time cost t_c and degree cost k_c are the corresponding costs traveling from the root. 2) **Expansion Link.** This link (denoted as the dotted black arrows) is generated by accessing the *TE hash* in *Traj-index*. The nodes, e.g., $n_i \& n_j$, along a link belong to the same trajectory, with an increasing time cost t_c and the same degree cost k_c, i.e., $n_j.tr = n_i.tr$, $n_j.t_c = n_i.t_c + Cost(n_j.e)$, $n_j.k_c = n_i.k_c$. 3) **Connection Link.** This link (denoted as the blue solid arrows) is generated by the connection of different two sub-trajectories, which can be built efficiently with road networks and the *ET hash*. The nodes, e.g., $n_i \& n_j$, connected by this type of link have an increasing time cost t_c and an increasing degree cost k_c, i.e. $n_j.tr \neq n_i.tr$, $n_j.t_c = n_i.t_c + Cost(n_j.e)$, $n_j.k_c = n_i.k_c + 1$.

Note that *TE-tree* is constructed during the search process, which cannot be pre-computed. As we enumerate all possibly connected trajectories for each candidate edge via the nodes in *TE-tree*, finding a reachable area of a position can be reduced to traversing its corresponding *TE-tree*. An intuitive idea uses a depth-first approach, until the budget t or k are used up (denoted as **TE**). However, there will be many edges being visited redundantly. For example in Fig. 3(c), n_2 and n_{13} are traversed with the same trajectory tr_6 and edge e_{13}. As shown in Fig. 3(b), there is an illogical path combination: the user first goes right with tr_4 on e_8, and then makes a U-turn and goes back to e_{13}. A more reasonable route should go directly to e_{13}, which is represented as n_2 in *TE-tree*.

To avoid redundant computation, we design a pruning strategy based on the observation that, illogical routes always start by a *TE-node* with the same trajectory and edge of some visited nodes, but with higher time and degree costs than them, e.g., n_{13} and n_2 in Fig. 3(c). We call this as *node domination*.

Algorithm 1: TE+

    Input: *Traj-index* of $\mathcal{T}$, query location q, time constraint t, degree constraint k.
    Output: Reachable area $RA(\mathcal{T}, q, t, k)$.

1 Initialize a queue *ConQueue* to record the candidate connection node;
2 Initialize a set *Visited* to record all visited *TE-nodes*;
3 Form the root of *TE-tree* with q, and add it to *ConQueue*;
4 for $i = 1$ *to* k **do**
5   Init a empty priority queue *pq*;
         // Connection Step
6   Pop all nodes in *ConQueue*, create new nodes based on the road network
         adjacency and *Edge-Trajectory Hash*, and add the new nodes to *pq*;
         // Expansion Step
7   **while** *pq is not empty* **do**
8   Pop a node n_{min} from *pq*, and add it to *Visited* and *ConQueue*;
9   Create a new node n along the same trajectory in n_{min};
10   **if** $n.t_c \geq t$ *and not* $(\exists n' \in Visited$ *that* $n' \succeq n)$ **then**
11   Add n to *pq*;

12 return the edges in *Visited* as *RA*;

Definition 4 (Node Domination in TE-tree). *Given two nodes n_i and n_j in TE-tree, if $n_i.tr = n_j.tr$, $n_i.e = n_j.e$, $n_i.t_c \leq n_j.t_c$, and $n_i.k_c \leq n_j.k_c$, then n_i dominates n_j, denoted as $n_i \succeq n_j$.*

Theorem 1. *If $n_i \succeq n_j$, n_j and all the children of n_j can be pruned.*

Proof. As $n_i \succeq n_j$, both nodes have the same trajectory and edge, all possible connected trajectories from n_j (which generate the children nodes of n_j in *TE-tree*) can also be attached to n_i. As a result, all edges covered in n_j's children are also covered in n_i's children. Thus, we can safely prune n_j and all of its children.

To maximize the pruning ability, it is important to apply a good order to traverse *TE-tree*. For example, in Fig. 3(c), n_{13} and its children can be pruned only if n_2 is visited before n_{13}. As a result, the nodes with smaller t_c and k_c should be searched as early as possible. We propose two heuristics: 1) *H1:* Nodes with the same trajectory are searched in priority, as it guarantees not to increase the degree cost; 2) *H2:* For multiple sub-trajectories connecting to the same node, we search the trajectory with the lowest time cost first.

The proposed method **TE+** (Algorithm 1) with the two heuristics starts from the root of *TE-tree*, and performs a k-iteration process, where each iteration has two steps: 1) *Connection*, which connects the existing *TE-nodes* with possible road segments based on the road network adjacency. Each connection consumes one degree budget. 2) *Expansion*, which generates new *TE-nodes* by expanding trajectories from the newly added road segments. To ensure *H2*, we resort to a priority queue to store all candidate *TE-nodes* based on their time costs. We also record all visited *TE-nodes* with a set. If there exists a visited node dominating the newly generated node n, we prune n according to Theorem 1.

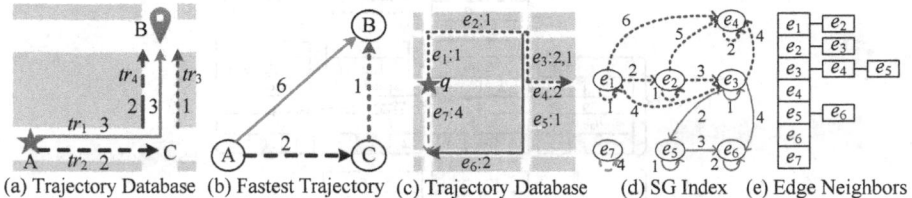

(a) Trajectory Database (b) Fastest Trajectory (c) Trajectory Database   (d) SG Index   (e) Edge Neighbors

Fig. 4. Inspiration for *SG-index*. (Color figure online)

4.2 Skip Graph Index

Observation. In essence, TE and TE+ enumerate all possible trajectory connections. However, it is not necessary to keep all trajectories and explore every possible trajectory connection. For example, as shown in Fig. 4(a), we have four trajectories in different colors and time costs. We do not need to explore any trajectory connection with tr_4, as any trajectory connection containing tr_4 can be replaced by tr_3 with a better time cost. Keeping tr_4 here only increases the computation cost. Furthermore, for each pair of origin and destination (OD), we only need to keep track of the fastest sub-trajectory. Figure 4(b) gives all of the fastest trajectories extracted from Fig. 4(a) based on different OD pairs.

Theorem 2 *For any edge e_i in the real-time reachable area, it can be reached from the query location by connecting no more than k sub-trajectories, where each sub-trajectory is the fastest one between its origin and destination.*

Proof. Each qualified edge is reachable from q via at least one qualified ctr, which can be segmented into no more than k sub-trajectories. By connecting the OD of each sub-trajectory with the fastest sub-trajectory between them, we can create a new connected trajectory ctr', where $Cost(ctr') \leq Cost(ctr)$ and $D(ctr') \leq D(ctr)$. If $D(ctr') < D(ctr)$, there at least exists two neighbor sub-trajectories in ctr' belonging to the same trajectory.

Data Structure. With the insight above, we propose Skip Graph index (*SG-index*), which preserves the fastest sub-trajectories connecting every OD pair. Indeed, *SG-index* is a weighted directed graph, in which a node (*SG-node*) is a road segment on road networks, an edge (*SG-link*) connecting two *SG-nodes* e_i and e_j represents there is at least one sub-trajectory traveling from $e_i.v_{start}$ to $e_j.v_{end}$, and the weight of an *SG-link* is the minimum time cost on it. Figure 4(d) is the *SG-index* of the trajectory database demonstrated in Fig. 4(c).

Construction. *SG-index* is constructed by scanning trajectories. For each trajectory, all of its sub-trajectories are examined to create *SG-links*. The weight of an *SG-link* is assigned as the time cost of the fastest sub-trajectory traversing it. The time complexity of *SG-index* construction is $\mathcal{O}(m \times n^2)$, where m is the number of trajectories in $\mathcal{T}$, and n is the average length of each trajectory. *SG-index* stores the minimum time cost of sub-trajectories in a time period, e.g.,

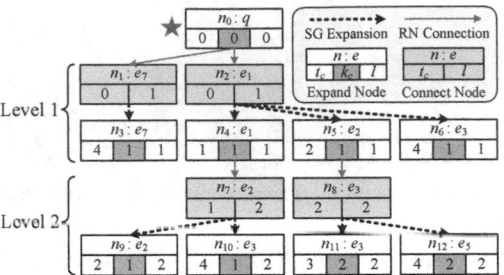

Fig. 5. An Example of *SGE-tree* with $t = 4$ min and $k = 2$.

the most recent 30 min, so it cannot be updated incrementally with new trajectory updates. Instead, it needs to be rebuilt periodically, e.g., every one minute. We can also deploy a distributed streaming framework, like Flink of Storm, to reduce the construction time.

Query Processing. We propose *SGE-tree* (Skip Graph Expansion tree) to find all k-hop neighbours of q based on *SG-index* and road networks, where *SG-index* provides the minimum time cost information between two edges, and road networks give the hints of trajectory connections. Figure 5 is the *SGE-tree* based on Fig. 4(c), which is organized into k levels with the query location as root. *SGE-tree* consists of two types of nodes and two types of links: 1) **Connect Node.** This node (marked in grey) is generated based on the neighbour of road segments, with four properties: an identifier n, an edge e, a time cost t_c, and a level number l. 2) **Expand Node.** This node (marked in white) is generated based on the expansion of *SG-index*. It contains five properties: an identifier n, an edge e, a time cost t_c, a degree cost k_c, and a level number l. 3) **Road Network Connection.** RN connection (blue solid arrow) connects an *expand node* to a *connect node*, based on the neighbours of road segments. Along this type of link, the nodes ($n_i \& n_j$) have the same time cost $n_j.t_c = n_i.t_c$, but an increasing level number $n_j.l = n_i.l + 1$. 4) **SG Expansion.** This link (black dotted arrow) connects a *connect node* to an *expand node*, based on the neighbours of *SG-nodes* in *SG-index*. Along this type of link, the nodes ($n_i \& n_j$) have an increasing time cost $n_j.t_c = n_i.t_c + Cost(n_i.e \rightarrow n_j.e)$, and the same level number $n_j.l = n_i.l$, where $Cost(n_i.e \rightarrow n_j.e)$ is the weight from $n_i.e$ to $n_j.e$ in *SG-index*.

Note that the level number l on an *expand node* is not equivalent to its degree cost k_c. l means the i-th hop neighbours of the root, but multiple hops in *SGE-tree* may belong to the same trajectory. For example in Fig. 5, $n_9.l = 2$, as it is a two hop neighbour from q. However, both of the hops are the sub-trajectories of the red dotted trajectory in Fig. 4(c), i.e., $tr_{red}[e_1...e_1] \rightarrow tr_{red}[e_2...e_2]$, which makes the degree cost only one. As a result, we know that in *SGE-tree*, $l \geq k_c$.

Theorem 3. *An SGE-tree with the level number of k covers all qualified edges e_i in reachable area $RA(\mathcal{T}, q, t, k)$.*

Proof. Suppose edge e is in the reachable area RA, but does not appear in *SGE-tree* with a level of k. As e does not appear in *SGE-tree* with a level of k, it means that e cannot be reached from q by connecting any k fastest sub-trajectories. In other words, to reach e, more than k fastest sub-trajectories should be connected. Thus, it disqualifies e to be reachable, which is contradictory to our assumption.

Therefore, finding a reachable area with k trajectory connections is equivalent to finding the k-hop neighbors of q in *SG-index*. A basic idea is to search the *SGE-tree* level by level using a breath-first search, as this order guarantees the trajectory connections with a smaller degree cost is searched first (denoted as **SGE**). However, we can observe that there are still redundant computations. For example in Fig. 5, n_9 should not be searched when n_5 exists, as they have the same time cost and edge. We can avoid this situation based on *node domination*.

Definition 5 (Node Domination in SGE-tree). *Given two expand nodes n_i and n_j, if $n_i.e = n_j.e$, $n_i.t_c \leq n_j.t_c$, and $n_i.l \leq n_j.l$, then n_i dominates n_j, denoted as $n_i \succeq n_j$.*

Lemma 1. *If an expand node n_j in an SGE-tree has $n_j.l > n_j.k_c$, there must exist an expand node n_i in level $n_j.k_c$, with $n_i.k_c = n_i.l = n_j.k_c$ and $n_i.t_c = n_j.t_c$.*

Although l is not equivalent to k_c, we can still use the domination relation to prune the disqualified nodes, when applying the breath-first search.

Theorem 4. *If there exist two expand nodes n_i and n_j such that $n_i \succeq n_j$, then n_j and all its children can be pruned, when using the breath-first search.*

Proof. Suppose $n_i \succeq n_j$, then $n_i.e = n_j.e$, $n_i.t_c \leq n_j.t_c$ and $n_i.l \leq n_j.l$. There are two possible cases between $n_i.k_c$ and $n_j.k_c$: 1) $n_i.k_c \leq n_j.k_c$, in this case, n_j can be pruned, as all the children of n_j can be attached to n_i; or 2) $n_i.k_c > n_j.k_c$, in this case, $n_j.k_c \neq n_j.l$. Otherwise, if $n_j.k_c = n_j.l$, we will have $n_i.l \geq n_i.k_c > n_j.k_c = n_j.l$, which contradicts to the domination relation $n_i.l \leq n_j.l$. Thus, $n_j.k_c < n_j.l$. According to Lemma 1, there must exist a node in level $n_j.k_c$ that covers the same trajectory connection. As a result, we can safely remove n_j and all its children from further expansion.

According to Theorem 4, we propose **SGE+** (Algorithm 2) to prune all disqualified *expand nodes* based on SGE. SGE+ performs a k-iteration process, where each iteration executes two functions: 1) *RNConnection*, which creates *connect nodes* based on the road network neighbours of *expand nodes* in the previous level; and 2) *SGExpansion*, which identifies qualified *expand nodes* in this level based on the links in *SG-index* and the *connect nodes* in the previous step. We discard the disqualified *expand node* if either it has a time cost more than t or its edge has been searched before with a smaller time cost.

It is worth noting that we only leverage the time costs t_c and the level numbers l of *expand nodes* to perform the pruning process. As a result, in implementation, it is unnecessary to store the degree costs k_c in *expand nodes*.

Algorithm 2: SGE+

Input: *SG-index* of $\mathcal{T}$, query location q, time constraint t, degree constraint k.
Output: Reachable area $RA(\mathcal{T}, q, t, k)$.

1 Init a key-value store *Edge2MinT* to track the min time cost of edges from q;
2 Init two sets *Exp* and *Con* to store *expand nodes* and *connect nodes* in a level;
3 Form the root of *SGE-tree* with q, and add it to *Exp*;
4 **for** $i = 1$ *to* k **do**
    // RNConnect Step
5   Pop all *expand nodes* in *Exp*, create new *connect nodes* based on the road network neighbours, and add them to *Con*;
    // SGExpansion Step
6   **while** *Con is not empty* **do**
7   Pop a node n_c from *Con*;
8   Create a new *expand node* n_e based on n_c and *SG-index*;
9   **if** $n_e.t_c \leq t$ *and* $Edge2MinT[n_e.e] > n_e.t_c$ **then**
10   Add n_e to *Exp*; $Edge2MinT[n_e.e] = n_e.t_c$;

11 **return** the edges in *Edge2MinT* as *RA*;

---

5 Model Learning and Prediction

The degree constraint k is intangible for users. We cannot assign a fixed k at all places and all times, as k is affected by various external factors. To this end, we propose to dynamically predict the k value in any location and at any time.

5.1 Label Generation

One of the challenges to predict k is that there is no label of reachable areas in our dataset. As k is a trade-off between coverage and reliability, a bigger k achieves a higher coverage, but results in a lower reliability. The intuition is to get a reasonable coverage with the k as small as possible. As a result, we generate the labels of k using historical trajectories. More specifically, we regard the reachable area without any trajectory connection based on "future" trajectories as partial ground truth, and find reachable areas with different k values using "recent" trajectories. The minimum k that satisfies a coverage threshold is set as the label. To get labels for a time budget t_b using the trajectories in most recent time δ, three tasks are performed: 1) **Trajectory Partition.** The historical trajectories are partitioned by a sliding window of size $\delta + t_b$. The trajectories in a time window are further divided into two sets, $\mathcal{T}_1$ and $\mathcal{T}_2$, as shown in Fig. 6(a). 2) **Reachable Area Discovery.** In each time window, we take each edge e at the time t as a start location. For each $k \in \{1, 2, ..., 5\}$, a reachable area $E_k = RA(\mathcal{T}_1, e, t_b, k)$ with trajectory connections is discovered, using the techniques introduced in Sect. 4. Besides, we find the reachable area E_{GT} starting from e without any trajectory connection as the partial ground truth of the real reachable area, using the technique in [9]. 3) k-**Selection.** As shown in Fig. 6(b),

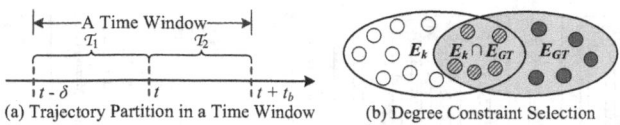

(a) Trajectory Partition in a Time Window   (b) Degree Constraint Selection

Fig. 6. Illustration of label generation.

for each $k \in \{1, 2, ..., 5\}$, we calculate the ratio between $|E_k \cap E_{GT}|$ and $|E_{GT}|$, where $|*|$ is the cardinality of a set. We then select the minimum k as the label k_l that makes the ratio greater than η, $0 \leq \eta \leq 1$, formally defined as Eq. (3). It means that E_k covers the most edges in E_{GT}, but k is as small as possible. To achieve a high reliability, we set $\eta = 0.9$ in implementation.

$$k_l = \min k, \quad s.t. \ |E_k \cap E_t| / |E_t| \geq \eta \text{ and } k \in \{1, 2, ..., 5\} \tag{3}$$

5.2 Feature Extraction

We identify five types of features from multiple data sources: 1) **Traffic Features.** For each road segment, we extract two traffic features, i.e., traffic flow and average speed, from the nearby real-time trajectories. 2) **Time Features.** The time of day, day of the week, and holidays are extracted, to capture the periodicity of traffic conditions. 3) **Meteorological Features.** We extract the meteorological features of each query location, such as rainfall, temperature and weather conditions (e.g., cloudy, sunny and rainy). 4) **POI Features.** We calculate the POI distribution within 1 km of each query location. The POIs are categorized into food, shopping, company and etc. 5) **Road Network Features.** The structure of road networks affects traffic conditions. For each road segment, we extract the features from nearby road networks, including intersection number and the length of each road level (e.g., highway, main road, side road and so on).

5.3 Model Training

The extracted features are first standardized, and then fed into the-state-of-art model ST-ResNet [10], as it can capture the spatial dependencies, temporal dependencies, and external factors of the traffic conditions. Although k is discrete, we regard this problem as a regression instead of a classification, because the penalties should be different for different predicted k values. For example, if the label is 2, it is better to predict k as 3 than 5. For each discrete $t \in [1, 20]$, we train a model individually. The model that is closest to the given continuous time budget is used when predicting.

6 Evaluation

6.1 Datasets and Settings

Datasets. We adopt four real datasets in our experiments: 1) **Road Networks.** The road networks of Shanghai, China are extracted from OpenStreetMap with

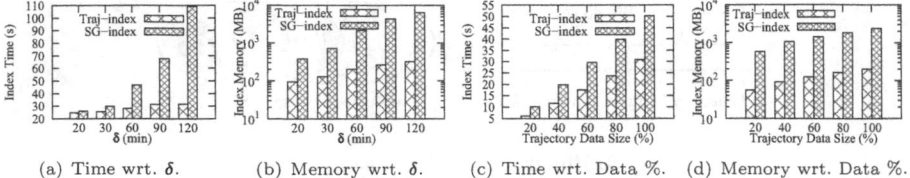

| (a) Time wrt. δ. | (b) Memory wrt. δ. | (c) Time wrt. Data %. | (d) Memory wrt. Data %. |

Fig. 7. Indexing performance.

333,766 vertices and 440,922 road segments. 2) **POIs.** We extract the POIs of Shanghai from OpenStreetMap, which contains 1,111,188 records. 3) **Meteorology.** We collect the meteorological data in Shanghai ranging from Dec. 23rd to Dec. 30th, 2016. The data is updated every hour. 4) **Trajectories.** We extract the taxi trajectories from Dec. 23rd to Dec. 30th, 2016 in Shanghai. It contains 303,673,097 GPS points of 5,669 taxis, whose average sampling rate is 10 seconds. The trajectories generated in most recent δ minutes to the query time is used to simulate the real-time trajectory updates.

Comparing Methods. We compare our proposed method (i.e. SGE+) with its variants (i.e., TE, TE+ and SGE) and two advanced methods: 1) **SQMB** [9], which finds reachable areas using historical trajectories; and 2) **TTE**, which first estimates the travel time of each road segment [4], then discovers reachable areas based on network expansion method [2]. We also verify the effectiveness of ST-ResNet for our problem, comparing with multiple models including GBDT, RF, SVR and XGBoost.

Experimental Settings. We focus on the efficiency of indexing and query processing (implemented in C#), and the effectiveness of k value prediction (implemented in Python). We randomly select 100 edges as query locations and calculate the average query processing time. 70% of trajectory and meteorology data are used for k value model training, and the left are used for validation. All experiments are performed on a 64-bit Windows Server 2012 with octa-core 2.2GHz CPU and 56 GB RAM. If not specified, we set the default real-time window $\delta = 60$ minutes, time budget $t = 15$ minutes, and degree constraint $k = 3$. Besides, we use 100% available real-time taxi trajectory data by default.

6.2   Indexing Performance

Different Real-Time Windows. Figure 7(a) depicts the indexing time of *Traj-index* and *SG-index* with different real-time windows δ. There are two observations: 1) with a bigger δ, both *Traj-index* and *SG-index* need more time to build, as we need to process more trajectories; 2) compared with *Traj-index*, the indexing time of *SG-index* increases more significantly with a larger δ, as more sub-trajectories are examined to update *SG-index*. Figure 7(b) shows the memory usage of *Traj-index* and *SG-index* with the increasing real-time window δ. It is clear that more spaces are used for both indexes. Moreover, the space

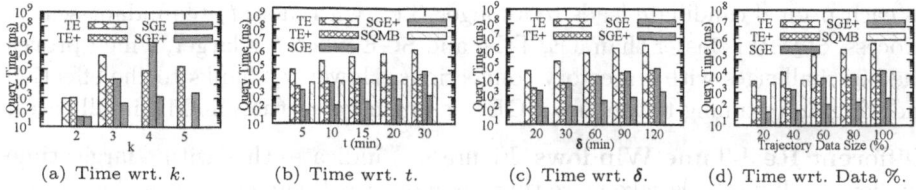

(a) Time wrt. k. (b) Time wrt. t. (c) Time wrt. δ. (d) Time wrt. Data %.

Fig. 8. Query processing performance.

consumed by *SG-index* grows exponentially with a larger δ, as longer trajectories are generated, which creates exponentially more sub-trajectory candidates to create the links in *SG-index*.

Different Trajectory Data Sizes. Figure 7(c) presents the construction time for two indexes, where the dataset contains different numbers of trajectories randomly sampled from 20% to 100%. It is observed that the indexing time of both indexes grows linearly with an increasing sample ratio, because for both indexes, they need to scan the dataset for one time. Moreover, *SG-index* consumes much more time, as it needs to check all sub-trajectories to create the links. Figure 7(d) indicates that the memory usage of both indexes increases with more trajectories. It is interesting to see that the memory growth of *SG-index* is slower comparing to different δ, because more trajectories introduce a limited number of sub-trajectories with distinct OD pairs as the links in *SG-index*.

We do not compare the indexing performance with SQMB and TTE here, as SQMB scans all historical trajectories when building indexes (which is time-consuming), and TTE does not build indexes. Besides, in the next subsection, we do not compare the query efficiency of TTE, because it is unfair for TTE if we consider its prediction time, which is costly.

6.3   Query Processing Performance

Different Degree Constraints. Figure 8(a) shows the query processing time with different k, from 2 to 5 ($k = 1$ is not tested, as it does not involve any trajectory connection). With an increasing k, the query processing time of all methods increases. Moreover, TE+ (or SGE+) is more efficient than TE (or SGE), as redundant computations are avoided. Furthermore, SGE takes more time than TE+ when k is large. Because with more combinations of sub-trajectories, pruning the disqualified nodes in *TE-tree* or *SGE-tree* is more effective. In fact, TE is not able to compute the results when $k \geq 4$. Similarly, SGE also fails when $k \geq 5$. SQMB is not tested here as it does not involve trajectory connections.

Different Time Constraints. As depicted in Fig. 8(b), with the growth of t, the query processing time of all methods increases. It is clear that with a larger t, more candidate road segments are tested. We can also notice that TE+ (or SGE+) is much better than TE (or SGE), and SGE+ is the most efficient. It is interesting to see that the performance of TE+ exceeds SGE when t is large, as each pruned candidate leads to a longer (i.e., with more t) redundant search process. SQMB is faster than TE, TE+ and SGE when t is larger, which proves the big challenges with trajectory connections. However, thanks to the effective indexing and pruning techniques, SGE+ is much faster than SQMB in all cases.

Different Real-Time Windows. Figure 8(c) indicates that with a larger time window δ, all methods take more time, as more road segments are included in a trajectory, leading to a larger *TE-tree* or *SGE-tree*. Here we do not test SQMB as it uses all historical trajectories, which is not affected by the real-time window.

Different Trajectory Data Sizes. Figure 8(d) shows that the query processing time increases with more trajectories, as more trajectory connection candidates are tested. TE+ is comparable to SGE, because the pruning techniques based on node domination play a major factor in improving the querying efficiency.

6.4 Effectiveness of k Prediction

Figure 9 shows the average RMSE (Root Mean Square Error) and MAE (Mean Absolute Error) of different models, which indicates that ST-ResNet is the best model for our problem, in terms of both RMSE and MAE. Because ST-ResNet not only captures the temporal closeness, period, and trend properties of traffic conditions, but also model the spatial dependency among different locations.

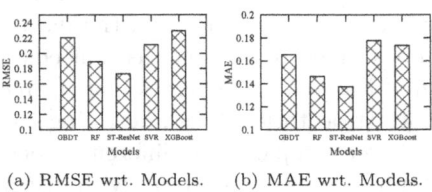

(a) RMSE wrt. Models.   (b) MAE wrt. Models.

Fig. 9. Effectiveness of k prediction.

6.5 Case Study

Figure 10 shows the reachable areas in the Mercedes-Benz Arena, Shanghai at the same time on two different days using different methods. Although both days are Friday, the reachable area in Fig. 10(b) is much smaller than that in Fig. 10(a), because there is a concert in the arena at 19:30, Dec. 30th, 2016[1].

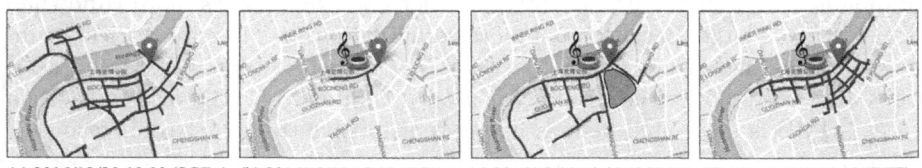

(a) 2016/12/23 19:00 (SGE+) (b) 2016/12/30 19:00 (SGE+) (c) 2016/12/30 19:00 (SQMB) (d) 2016/12/30 19:00 (TTE)

Fig. 10. A case of concert ($t = 5$ min, $\delta = 30$ min). (Color figure online)

---

[1] http://bit.ly/2y6f3BF.

More than 10,000 fans gathered here, causing a heavy traffic jam. As a result, our solutions reflect the traffic jam, where the reachable area only covers the nearby road segments. Comparing to SGE+, SQMB gives the same reachable area in all days as shown in Fig. 10(c), and TTE gives a reachable area as shown in Fig. 10(d), thus they can hardly capture the real-time traffic conditions such as events. Besides, SQMB could miss some reachable road segments if there is no trajectory that exactly traverses from the query location to them (i.e., the orange area). However, the trajectory connection techniques proposed by this paper can mitigate this situation.

7 Related Works

Reachability Query. The conventional reachability query is one of the fundamental graph operations, asking if two nodes are connected in a directed graph [17–23]. These works can be categorized into two main categories: 1) reachability query on static graphs, e.g., [17] introduces a graph reduction method, while other works [20,23] propose different labeling methods to reduce the index size; and 2) reachability query on dynamic graphs, whose edges and vertexes change over time. For example, [22] proposes different indexes to efficiently handle vertex insertions and deletions. The conventional reachability query problem is very different from our real-time reachable area discovery task, as their reachability only considers the graph structure. The closest work is [9], which finds reachable areas based on massive historical trajectories that passed the query location during the request hour. By analyzing the daily statistics of the qualified trajectories, the reachable area with a certain probability can be identified. However, this method cannot capture weather, traffic conditions and events, which is not suitable for real-time reachable area discovery.

Travel Time Estimation. Travel time estimation calculates the time cost on a given path. [4–7] leverage the readings of loop detectors or trajectories to infer the time cost on each road segment. Then, the time cost of a path is estimated by summing up all costs of the road segments along the given path. These works ignore the dependencies between road segments. To capture the delays of road intersections/traffic lights and improve the estimation accuracy, [24–26] estimate the travel time of a path by considering the trajectories passed the entire path, and [27] proposes an end-to-end deep learning framework to estimate the travel time. The techniques of travel time estimation cannot be applied directly to the discovery of real-time reachable areas, as they require the predefinition of a path, including the origin and destination locations. In the scenario of reachable area discovery, the destinations and the paths from the query location are not predefined. As a consequence, directly applying travel time estimation methods requires to examine all possible destinations and possible paths to them, which is inefficient and infeasible in a real-time scenario.

8   Conclusion

This paper provides the first attempt to discover real-time reachable areas with dynamic trajectory connections. A framework that combines indexing techniques with machine learning is proposed. Our proposed indexing and query processing methods can efficiently find real-time reachable areas with an arbitrary number of trajectory connections. We also propose to predict the best connection number that achieves a good coverage while guarantees reliability. Extensive experiments and one case study on four real datasets confirm the effectiveness and efficiency of our proposed methods for the real-time scenarios.

Acknowledgement. This work was supported by NSFC (No. 61976168, No. 61672399, No. U1609217) and the Science Foundation of Hubei Province (No. 2019CFA025). We would like to thank Yuxuan Liang to discuss the label generation methods of connection number.

References

1. Beckmann, N., Kriegel, H.-P., Schneider, R., Seeger, B.: The r*-tree: an efficient and robust access method for points and rectangles. In: SIGMOD, vol. 19, no. 2, pp. 322–331. ACM (1990)
2. Papadias, D., Zhang, J., Mamoulis, N., Tao, Y.: Query processing in spatial network databases. In: VLDB, pp. 802–813 (2003)
3. Bauer, V., Gamper, J., Loperfido, R., Profanter, S., Putzer, S., Timko, I.: Computing isochrones in multi-modal, schedule-based transport networks. In: ACM SIGSPATIAL, pp. 1–2 (2008)
4. Wang, J., Gu, Q., Wu, J., Liu, G., Xiong, Z.: Traffic speed prediction and congestion source exploration: a deep learning method. In: ICDM, pp. 499–508. IEEE (2016)
5. Wang, D., Cao, W., Xu, M., Li, J.: ETCPS: an effective and scalable traffic condition prediction system. In: Navathe, S.B., Wu, W., Shekhar, S., Du, X., Wang, X.S., Xiong, H. (eds.) DASFAA 2016. LNCS, vol. 9643, pp. 419–436. Springer, Cham (2016). https://doi.org/10.1007/978-3-319-32049-6_26
6. Lin, X., Wang, Y., Xiao, X., Li, Z., Bhowmick, S.S.: Path travel time estimation using attribute-related hybrid trajectories network. In: CIKM, pp. 1973–1982. ACM (2019)
7. Xie, Q., Guo, T., Chen, Y., Xiao, Y., Wang, X., Zhao, B.Y.: How do urban incidents affect traffic speed? A deep graph convolutional network for incident-driven traffic speed prediction, arXiv preprint arXiv:1912.01242 (2019)
8. Skiena, S.: Dijkstra's algorithm. In: Implementing Discrete Mathematics: Combinatorics and Graph Theory with Mathematica, pp. 225–227. Addison-Wesley, Reading (1990)
9. Wu, G., Ding, Y., Li, Y., Bao, J., Zheng, Y.: Mining spatio-temporal reachable regions over massive trajectory data. In: ICDE, pp. 1283–1294. IEEE (2017)
10. Zhang, J., Zheng, Y., Qi, D., Li, R., Yi, X., Li, T.: Predicting citywide crowd flows using deep spatio-temporal residual networks. Artif. Intell. **259**, 147–166 (2018)
11. Ruan, S., Li, R., Bao, J., He, T., Zheng, Y.: CloudTP: a cloud-based flexible trajectory preprocessing framework. In: ICDE. IEEE (2018)
12. Bao, J., Li, R., Yi, X., Zheng, Y.: Managing massive trajectories on the cloud. In: SIGSPATIAL, p. 41. ACM (2016)

13. Li, R., Ruan, S., Bao, J., Zheng, Y.: A cloud-based trajectory data management system. In: ACM SIGSPATIAL, pp. 1–4 (2017)
14. Li, R., et al.: Efficient path query processing over massive trajectories on the cloud. IEEE Trans. Big Data (2018)
15. Li, R., et al.: Just: JD urban spatio-temporal data engine. In: ICDE. IEEE (2020)
16. Li, R., et al.: TrajMesa: a distributed NoSQL storage engine for big trajectory data. In: ICDE. IEEE (2020)
17. Zhou, J., Zhou, S., Yu, J.X., Wei, H., Chen, Z., Tang, X.: Dag reduction: fast answering reachability queries. In: SIGMOD, pp. 375–390. ACM (2017)
18. Valstar, L.D., Fletcher, G.H., Yoshida, Y.: Landmark indexing for evaluation of label-constrained reachability queries. In: SIGMOD, pp. 345–358. ACM (2017)
19. Anirban, S., Wang, J., Saiful Islam, M.: Multi-level graph compression for fast reachability detection. In: Li, G., Yang, J., Gama, J., Natwichai, J., Tong, Y. (eds.) DASFAA 2019. LNCS, vol. 11447, pp. 229–246. Springer, Cham (2019). https://doi.org/10.1007/978-3-030-18579-4_14
20. Su, J., Zhu, Q., Wei, H., Yu, J.X.: Reachability querying: can it be even faster? TKDE **29**(3), 683–697 (2017)
21. Sarwat, M., Sun, Y.: Answering location-aware graph reachability queries on geosocial data. In: ICDE, pp. 207–210. IEEE (2017)
22. Wu, H., Huang, Y., Cheng, J., Li, J., Ke, Y.: Reachability and time-based path queries in temporal graphs. In: ICDE, pp. 145–156. IEEE (2016)
23. Wei, H., Yu, J.X., Lu, C., Jin, R.: Reachability querying: an independent permutation labeling approach. VLDB J. **27**(1), 1–26 (2017). https://doi.org/10.1007/s00778-017-0468-3
24. Wang, Y., Zheng, Y., Xue, Y.: Travel time estimation of a path using sparse trajectories. In: SIGKDD, pp. 25–34. ACM (2014)
25. Dai, J., Yang, B., Guo, C., Jensen, C.S., Hu, J.: Path cost distribution estimation using trajectory data. VLDB **10**(3), 85–96 (2016)
26. Xu, J., Zhang, Y., Chao, L., Xing, C.: STDR: a deep learning method for travel time estimation. In: Li, G., Yang, J., Gama, J., Natwichai, J., Tong, Y. (eds.) DASFAA 2019. LNCS, vol. 11447, pp. 156–172. Springer, Cham (2019). https://doi.org/10.1007/978-3-030-18579-4_10
27. Wang, D., Zhang, J., Cao, W., Li, J., Yu, Z.: When will you arrive? Estimating travel time based on deep neural networks. In: AAAI (2018)

Few-Shot Human Activity Recognition on Noisy Wearable Sensor Data

Shizhuo Deng[1]([✉]), Wen Hua[2], Botao Wang[1], Guoren Wang[3],
and Xiaofang Zhou[2]

[1] School of Computer Science and Engineering,
Northeastern University, Shenyang, China
dengshizhuo@gmail.com, wangbotao@cse.neu.edu.cn
[2] School of ITEE, The University of Queensland, Brisbane, Australia
[3] School of Computer Science and Technology,
Beijing Institute of Technology, Beijing, China

Abstract. Most existing wearable sensor-based human activity recognition (HAR) models are trained on substantial labeled data. It is difficult for HAR to learn new-class activities unseen during training from a few samples. Very few researches of few-shot learning (FSL) have been done in HAR to address the above problem, though FSL has been widely used in computer vision tasks. Besides, it is impractical to annotate sensor data with accurate activity labels in real-life applications. The noisy labels have great negative effects on FSL due to the limited samples. The weakly supervised few-shot learning in HAR is challenging, significant but rarely researched in existing literature. In this paper, we propose an end-to-end **W**eakly supervised **P**rototypical **N**etworks (WPN) to learn more latent information from noisy data with multiple instance learning (MIL). In MIL, the noisy instances (subsequences of segmentation) have different labels from the bag's (segmentation's) label. The prototype is the center of the instances in WPN rather than less discriminative bags, which determines the bag-level classification accuracy. To get the most representative instance-level prototype, we propose two strategies to refine the prototype by selecting high-probability instances same as their bag's label iteratively based on the distance-metric. The model is trained by minimizing the instance-level loss function and infers the final bag-level labels from instance-level labels. In the experiments, our proposals outperform existing approaches and achieve higher average ranks.

Keywords: Few-shot learning · Weakly supervised models · Wearable sensors · Human activity recognition

1 Introduction

Human activity recognition (HAR) based on wearable sensors (accelerometer, gyroscope, etc.) plays a key role in research areas and real-world applications,

© Springer Nature Switzerland AG 2020
Y. Nah et al. (Eds.): DASFAA 2020, LNCS 12113, pp. 54–72, 2020.
https://doi.org/10.1007/978-3-030-59416-9_4

for example, health care [1] and sports monitoring [12]. Most existing supervised models are usually trained on substantial well-labeled data. However, the noisy data is ubiquitous in real-world applications because labeling datasets correctly is a time-consuming task [19]. In addition, the existing HAR models learn new-class activities from a few training samples by re-training, which leads to overfitting and imbalance problems.

People can learn new concepts given just a few samples. Thus Artificial Intelligence should have the similar ability to recognize new activities from a few samples. In addition, the quality of the activity labels has a great impact on the effectiveness due to the limited samples. For example, in Fig. 1, new activity *Run* has a few samples (segmentations from raw data) including noisy activities *Walk* (W) which are subsequences in one segmentation. The weakly-labeled segmentation leads to less discriminative features. Our goal is to recognize *Run* based on a few samples with noisy labels from the knowledge in the existing models without retraining.

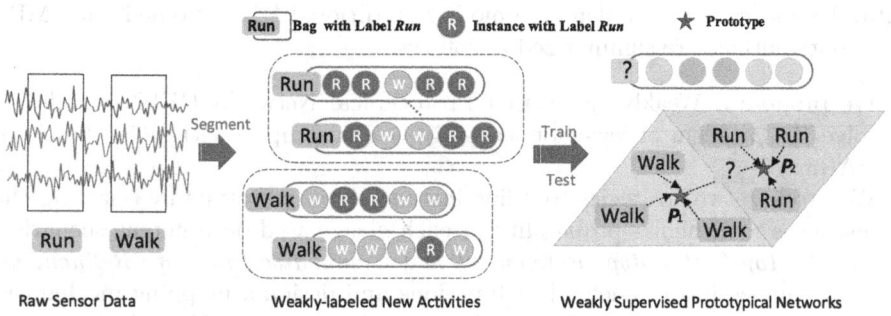

Fig. 1. An example of weakly supervised Prototypical Networks for HAR

Although few-shot learning (FSL) [7] and multiple instance learning (MIL) [6] could solve the problems caused by new-class learning on few samples and weakly-labeled learning respectively, they are studied separately in most existing researches. On one hand, most significant researches on FSL have achieved satisfying performance on vision tasks, such as metric learning and meta learning [13,18]. Among these networks, *Prototypical Networks* (PN) [23] and semi-supervised models based on PN [2,22] are effective to avoid overfitting. However, there are few works concentrating on HAR with wearable sensor data [8,16,20]. On the other hand, these models assume to be trained on well-labeled data which requires a time-consuming work in real-life applications. MIL has better performance in weakly supervised HAR with less annotation effort [3,10,24]. One segmentation (bag) of time series data with a bag-level label consists of several subsequences (instances) with unknown instance-level labels which may be different from their bag's label (*Run* example illustrated in Fig. 1). MIL can recognize the bag-level label from the noisy data if the bag contains the objective activity.

A natural improvement would be to combine the power of both few-shot learning and weakly supervised learning. In this line, weakly supervised PN based on attention mechanism has been used in image classification [14] and natural language processing (NLP) [9]. However, they cannot be used on HAR task directly for the different kinds of noisy data. Therefore, we aim to build an end-to-end model to recognize new activities leveraging the advantages of PN and MIL. To the best of our knowledge, we are the first to leverage the weakly-labeled information in few-shot learning on time series data in HAR. However, there is still one great challenge as below:

How to Obtain the Accurate Prototype Feature from Noisy Instances? PN extracts prototype features for each class and classifies samples based on the distance metric to each prototype as shown in Fig. 1. The prototype in our model is calculated on instance-level features rather than less discriminative bag-level features. However, the noisy instances may result in the bias of the instance-level prototypes. Hence, refining the prototype by selecting the most representative instances in each class is the key to guarantee the effectiveness of PN on noisy data. To address this problem, we modify traditional PN combined with MIL. Our contributions are summarized as follows:

1) We propose a Weakly supervised Prototypical Networks (WPN) model to solve the problem of few-shot learning on few samples with noisy labels in HAR.
2) We propose two strategies to refine instance-level prototype by selecting the instances with higher probability in each class based on different scenarios, namely *Top-K Prototype Refinement* and *Cumulative Prototype Refinement*.
3) We minimize instance-level loss functions and design a mapping mechanism from instance label to bag label to improve the accuracy of bag classification.
4) In the experiments, WPN with two refinement strategies outperforms the existing approaches on three benchmark datasets, which demonstrates the effectiveness of our model.

The rest of the paper is organized as follows. Section 2 reviews related work. Section 3 gives the preliminary and problem definition. We propose an end-to-end weakly supervised model with two refinement strategies in Sect. 4 and evaluate the performance of our proposals in Sect. 5. Finally, we conclude our work in Sect. 6.

2 Related Work

Weakly supervised human activity recognition aims to solve the inaccurate label annotation problem. As the development of hardware and software technologies [21], people have growing interest to HAR. Therefore, the accuracy of recognition is more important especially on weakly-labeled data. Multiple instance learning (MIL), one of the weakly supervised methods, is robust to noisy data and reduce the laborious labeling effort with good performance. In MIL for

HAR, one bag (segmentation of sequence with fixed window size) with known label consists of multiple instances (subsequences in the window) without labels. MIL on wearable sensors is firstly used in research [24] which proposes new annotation strategies to reduce the frequency of annotation. A generative graphical model for MIL is presented on time series data based on auto-regressive hidden Markov model which can annotate both bag and instance labels [10]. However, they can not learn the new-class activities from a few bag-level training samples.

Few-Shot learning (FSL) is a task learning process in which the classifier generalizes well even on very few samples of new classes not seen in the training dataset without re-training the model [15]. Metric-based few-shot learning approaches aim to learn an end-to-end model where the parameters can be transferred to new-classes classification leveraging nearest neighbor based on the given distance metric. The nearest neighbor classifier in *Matching Networks* [25] is implemented with an attention mechanism over the embedding labeled samples (the support set) to predict the unlabeled samples (the query set) both during training and testing. The embedding features in *Siamese Networks* [13] are extracted from pair samples and classified by the pair-wise distance. *Prototypical Networks* [23] solve the overfitting problem in metric-based few-shot learning. To leverage the unlabeled data, semi-supervised FSL models [2,22] are proposed.

Few-shot Learning for HAR. Although FSL is widely used in HAR based on image and video [17,28], there are few studies on few-shot learning based on wearable sensor data. Recently, FSHAR (few-shot human activity recognition) [8] is proposed to recognize new activities by transferring the model parameters from source domain to target domain. In the literature [16] it only compares the performance of *Siamese Networks*, *Triplet Networks* [11] and *Matching Network* in wearable sensor-based HAR. The importance of attributes for zero-shot pose-classification is discussed in [20]. However, all of them are supposed to be trained on high-quality well-labeled data in supervised models. In real-life applications, it is common that the labels are inaccurate and ambiguous, which is also challenging in FSL.

Recently, weakly supervised PN is proposed for noisy few-shot relation classification (RC) with hybrid-attention in natural language processing (NLP) [9]. The weights of the final prototype are calculated by the distance between the support set and query set through the linear layer. However, it does not fit for time series data in HAR because samples in both support set and query set have weakly-labeled data which leads to the bias of the weights. Considering the character of time series data and the problem of few-shot learning on weakly-labeled data, we provide a different view of refining final prototype which is suitable for noisy data in HAR.

3   Preliminary and Problem Formulation

In this section, we review the notations of multiple instance learning and Prototype Networks and give the problem formulation.

3.1 Multiple Instance Learning

Given a set of N samples $D = \{(X_1, y_1), \ldots, (X_N, y_N)\}$ where $X_i = [x_{i1}, x_{i2}, \ldots, x_{iT}]$ is the set of time series data points where $x_{it} \in \mathbb{R}^d$ is d-dimensional sensor data and $y_i \in [0, 1, 2, \ldots, C]$ is the corresponding label for each X_i. It means that x_{it} is the t-th time step data point of the i-th sample and $y_i = 0$ denotes the null class.

For multiple instance learning in HAR, the bag B_i corresponding to the sample X_i is $B_i = [I_{i,1}, \ldots, I_{i,(T-l+1)}]$ where $I_{i,j} = [x_{i,j}, \ldots, x_{i,(j+l-1)}]$ denotes the j-th instance in B_i with the instance sliding window size 1. Usually, the ground-truth label of bag y_i is annotated by human and the label of instance $y_{i,j}$ is unknown. Some instances' labels in each bag are the same as the bag's label. However, some labels are different from the bag's label, which are known as noisy labeled data as illustrated in Fig. 1. To get the bag-level label, one strategy is to infer the instance-level label and then get the bag-level label. The other strategy is to learn bag representation without inferring the instance probabilities of each class.

3.2 Prototype Networks

In Prototype Networks (PN), the model samples mini-batches (episodes) from support set S and query set Q to mimic the few-shot task in test sets including new categories. PN first extracts feature from S through an embedding function f_ϕ to get the prototype representation. Then it classifies the samples in Q by minimizing the loss. D_c is the subset of D, denoting the set of class c. In each episode of supervised PN, we select subset C' of C classes (C'-way) and n samples (n-shot) for each class. Let $S = \{D_1, \ldots, D_{C'}\}$ be the support set where D_c contains $|D_c|$ time series X_i of class c and $Q = \{D_1^*, \ldots, D_{C'}^*\}$ be the query set where D_c^* contains $|D_c^*|$ time series X_i^*. The prototype of class c is the average of feaures from embedded samples

$$\mathbf{p}_c = \frac{1}{|D_c|} \sum_{(X_i, y_i) \in D_c} f_\phi(X_i) \tag{1}$$

The classification for query X_i^* is the probability over classes produced based on softmax with the pre-defined distances function d [23] as follows

$$P(c \mid (X_i^*, \mathbf{p}_c)) = \frac{exp(-d(f_\phi(X_i^*), \mathbf{p}_c))}{\sum_{c'=1}^{C'} exp(-d(f_\phi(X_i^*), \mathbf{p}_{c'}))} \tag{2}$$

For all the query samples in Q, the loss function in each training episode is the average negative log-probability for the objective class:

$$\mathcal{J} = -\frac{1}{|Q|} \sum log P(y_i^* \mid (X_i^*, \mathbf{p}_c)) \tag{3}$$

3.3   Problem Formulation

We aim to train an end-to-end model to recognize the previously unseen activities in the circumstance of a few low-quality samples for each new class based on Prototypical Networks. Given the set of few weakly-labeled bags $D_c = \{B_1^c, \ldots, B_n^c\}$ sampled from known class c in each episode, the model is trained to learn the function f_ϕ with parameters ϕ to improve the classification accuracy. Since the number of labeled bags is not large and the labels are ambiguous, it would result in heavy bias in prototype on B_i and affect the effectiveness of PN. In weakly supervised models, each bag has a certain signature in the sequential data [5], which may be one instance or several instances. It is necessary to get the most representative instance-level prototype to avoid the negative effect of bag-level prototype. There are two goals in our model:

1) Efficient strategies to get the most representative instance-level prototype $\mathbf{p}_c$ by selecting instances $I_{i,j}$ with high probabilities from all bags B_i in D_c.
2) Efficient loss function and mapping mechanism in classification to infer the bag-level label y_i from instance-level label $y_{i,j}$.

4   Weakly Supervised Prototypical Networks for HAR

To address the problem of human new-class activities classification on few weakly-labeled samples, we propose an end-to-end model, Weakly supervised Prototypical Networks (WPN). In our model two strategies are used to get the most representative instance-level prototype. The bag-level label is inferred from the instance-level label recognized by the model.

4.1   Overview of WPN Model

To solve the problems defined and achieve the goals set in Sect. 3.3, we propose an end-to-end model Weakly supervised Prototypical Networks (WPN) leveraging PN and MIL. We train and test on instances instead of bags and infer the bag-level labels from the instance-level labels. To make it easier to understand the model, we take one-shot learning for example as shown in Fig. 2. It shows the architecture of the training phase for WPN. In the support set (bag-level) and query set (bag-level), different classes are shown as different coloured shapes. There is more than one instance in one bag shown as smaller size shapes. Obviously, not all the instances'labels correspond with their bag's label. Even there is *null-class* instance in the bag. For example, it is supposed that the bag with label *Class 1* in support bag set has six instances (three *Class 1*, two *Class 2* and one *null class*). The model selects the embedded instances with high probabilities of *Class 1* after refining operation. The selected instances in *Class 1* are used to update the instance-level prototype of *Class 1*.

Similar refinement could be an optional operation for query set and the model computes the instance-level loss between selected embedded instances and the prototype. There are three modules in our model:

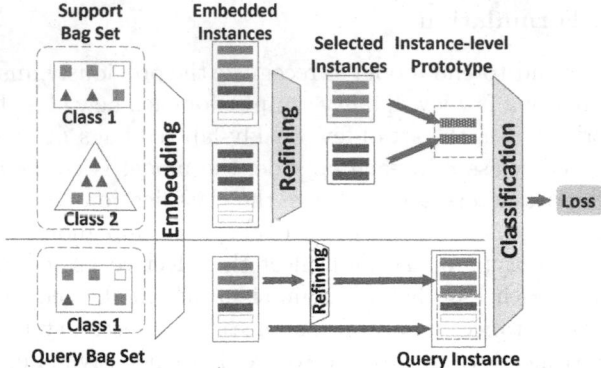

Fig. 2. One-shot learning in WPN HAR model

- **Embedding Module**
  To extract instance-level feature vector, all the instances in the bags with the same bag label are embedded by embedding function.
- **Refinement Module**
  To refine the instance-level prototype, an important role in PN, this module selects instances with high probability from all the instances mixed with noisy labels for each class and two refinement strategies are proposed under different scenarios.
- **Classification Module**
  To optimize the parameters, the model classifies the instances based on the distances between the instances in Q and the prototypes for all classes, minimizes instance-level loss functions and infers the bag label from its instance labels.

During testing, we utilize the trained model to annotate bag-level time series data for new class. Few bag samples or one sample are treated as support set to refine the prototype by selecting the embedded instances like what it does during training. After labeling the instances, this module adopts majority vote to infer the final bag-level label.

4.2 Embedding Module

This module extracts feature from input raw data through an embedding function f_ϕ with the learnable parameters ϕ. Our weakly supervised model uses f_ϕ to embed the instances ($I_{i,j} \in \mathbb{R}^{l \times d}$) for each class. Convolutional neural network (CNN) provides better representation in times series and spatio-temporal data [4,26]. The embedding module consists of two steps:

Step One: Feature Extraction. Multiple sets of CNN layers with 2-dimension kernels and max pooling layers are used to extract temporal and spacial information for each instance.

Step Two: Dimension Transformation. The output of the pooling layer is reshaped as 1-dimension feature space which is adaptive to the Prototype Networks.

4.3   Refinement Module

In MIL, only the label of bag is annotated and the labels of its instances are not given exactly. Actually, the labels of some instances are the same as their bag label and the other instances are treated as noisy data. Therefore, we give two assumptions considering the number of noisy instances: (i) the instances include a large quantity of noisy data; (ii) the instances include a small quantity of noisy data. Based on these two assumptions, we propose two strategies to refine the instance-level prototype by selecting the instances with high probability for the same class.

4.3.1   *Top-K* Prototype Refinement

Actually, it is difficult to know the ground-truth labels of the instances in the bags. It is supposed that there are large quantity of instances with different labels from the bag's label in the first assumption. The intuitional solution is to select the high-probability instances and abandon low-probability instances. Therefore, we propose *Top-K Prototype Refinement* strategy to select the K nearest instances based on the distance between the instances and the initial prototype for the same class. The selected instances are used to calculate the new prototype. There are three steps in this strategy.

Step One: Initializing Prototype. Different from the traditional PN, we focus on the instance-level prototype in our model. We assume that all the instances have the same label as their bag's label, that is $y_{i,j} = c$ if $y_i = c$. Since we do not consider the noisy instances, the initial instance-level prototype $\mathbf{p}_c$ is the average vector of all the embedded instances in the support set labeled class c. For each class c, there are n bags and m instances in each bag, denoted as $D_c = \{B_1^c, \ldots, B_n^c\}$ and $B_i^c = \{I_{i,j}^c, \ldots, I_{i,m}^c\}$. We modify Eq. (1) as Eq. (4), where $I_{i,j}^c \in \mathcal{D}_c$, $i \in [1, n]$, $j \in [1, m]$, $\mathcal{D}_c$ denotes set of $n \times m$ instances in D_c set and all $\omega_{i,j} = 1$ here indicate that all the instances $I_{i,j}^c$ are selected during initialization.

$$\mathbf{p}_c = \frac{\sum\sum \omega_{i,j} f_\phi(I_{i,j}^c)}{\sum\sum \omega_{i,j}} \tag{4}$$

Step Two: Selecting Instances. For all the instances in $\mathcal{D}_c$, the model calculates the distance between them and $\mathbf{p}_c$ and select the K instances nearest to the initial prototype denoted as $\mathcal{D}_c^K$. It is supposed these instances in $\mathcal{D}_c^K$ have high probability corresponding with the bag label. Therefore, the weight $\omega_{i,j}$ is updated by

$$\omega_{i,j} = \begin{cases} 1, if\ I_{i,j}^c \in \mathcal{D}_c^K \\ 0, if\ I_{i,j}^c \notin \mathcal{D}_c^K \end{cases} \tag{5}$$

Step Three: Updating Prototype. The model updates $\mathbf{p}_c$ based on Eq. (4) after updating all the weights. It aims to get the more representative prototype from the noisy labeled instances by iteratively selecting the instances and updating the average vector. When the number of iterations is more than τ or the variance of the selected instances to prototype increases which is calculated in Eq. (6), we would get the final prototype and selected instances. $\omega'_{i,j}$ and $\mathbf{p}'_c$ are updated on the previous iterative step.

$$\Delta = \frac{\sum \left| \omega_{i,j} I^c_{i,j} - \mathbf{p}_c \right|^2}{\sum \omega_{i,j}} - \frac{\sum \left| \omega'_{i,j} I^c_{i,j} - \mathbf{p}'_c \right|^2}{\sum \omega'_{i,j}} \tag{6}$$

The Algorithm 1 describes the pseudo code of *Top-K Prototype Refinement*. According to the length of the instance, it splits the bags into the instances for each class in line 1. Since the number of selected instances is becoming smaller in each iteration, K is calculated by the ratio of the size of instances set on each iterative step. It is not practical to iterate too many times, which results in much bias when there are very few instances. Lines 5 to 9 describe step two and step three in detail.

During training, the Algorithm 1 also fits on the query set since the query set has the noisy labeling problem. The difference is that the $\mathcal{D}^K_c$ set is the final output used to calculate the distance between the query set and prototype.

4.3.2   Cumulative Prototype Refinement

Considering the second assumption that there is a small number of noisy instances in support set, *Top-K Prototype Refinement* strategy ignores the contributions of the unselected instances. They may have a latent relationship with the selected instances. In MIL, the label of the instance is uncertain because there is no ground truth for the label of instance. Although we suppose that the K instances have the high probabilities corresponding with the bag label, it can not judge the unselected instances as noisy data definitely. The useful information is significant, especially in few-shot learning. Hence we utilize the information of the unselected instances and the prototypes are given with gradually increasing weights as the number of iterations increases.

The basic idea is that the new prototype in each iteration is the average of the previous prototype and the current prototype produced by *Top-K Prototype Refinement* strategy. It preserves the information of unselected instances in the current iteration. However, they have low contributions to the new prototype because the selected instances are the subset of the previous set. The new prototype, the previous prototype and the current prototype in k-*th* iteration step with class c are denoted as $\mathbf{p}^k_c$, $\mathbf{p}^{k-1}_c$ and $\mathbf{p}'^k_c$ respectively. The $\mathbf{p}^k_c$ is updated by

---

Algorithm 1. Top-K Prototype Refinement

Input:
 D_c: The set of bag samples for class c; l: The length of each instance;
 τ: The iterative times; γ: Ratio used in *Top-K* ;
Output:
 $\mathbf{p}_c$: The prototype vector for class c;
1: Split all the bags in D_c to get the instances set $\mathcal{D}_c$ with the parameters l;
2: Initialize $\omega_{i,j} = 1$, $k = 1$, $\Delta = -1$;
3: Initialize the $\mathbf{p}_c$ based on $\mathcal{D}_c$ with Equation (4);
4: **While($\Delta < 0$ and $k \leq \tau$);**
5: Calculate K with γ and the size of $\mathcal{D}_c$;
6: Select *Top-K* nearest instances $\mathcal{D}_c^K$ from $\mathcal{D}_c$;
7: Update $\omega_{i,j}$ with Equation (5);
8: Update $\mathbf{p}_c$ with Equation (4);
9: Compute Δ, $k = k + 1$, $\mathcal{D}_c = \mathcal{D}_c^K$;
10. return $\mathbf{p}_c$;

$$\begin{aligned}
\mathbf{p}_c^k &= \frac{1}{2}(\mathbf{p}_c^{k-1} + \mathbf{p'}_c^k) \\
&= \frac{1}{2}(\frac{1}{2}(\mathbf{p}_c^{k-2} + \mathbf{p'}_c^{k-1}) + \mathbf{p'}_c^k) \\
&= \frac{1}{2^2}\mathbf{p}_c^{k-2} + \frac{1}{2^2}\mathbf{p'}_c^{k-1} + \frac{1}{2}\mathbf{p'}_c^k \\
&= \frac{1}{2^k}\mathbf{p}_c^0 + \frac{1}{2^k}\mathbf{p'}_c^1 + \frac{1}{2^{k-1}}\mathbf{p'}_c^2 + \cdots + \frac{1}{2^1}\mathbf{p'}_c^k
\end{aligned} \tag{7}$$

According to the Eq. (7) the final prototype is cumulated by the prototypes generated in all the iteration steps with different weights. However, they have gradually decreasing weights to the final prototype which means the initial prototypes calculated by noisy data have the least influence. The prototypes produced by selected instances have more contributions to the final prototype. In addition, the number of iterations has little influence on classification performance in *Cumulative Prototype Refinement* strategy because the prototype in current iteration includes all the historic information of the instances with different weights. It avoids the problem encountered by *Top-K Prototype Refinement* strategy for multiple iterations. The *Cumulative Prototype Refinement* is different from the existing semi-prototype work [22] in which the weight of the unlabeled sample is the distance to the original prototype. *Top-K Prototype Refinement* strategy is the basic of *Cumulative Prototype Refinement* strategy, therefore, we modify step 3 in Algorithm 1 with *Initialize* $\mathbf{p}_c^0$, the step 8 with *Compute* $\mathbf{p'}_c^k$ *with Eq. (4)*, and add *Update* $\mathbf{p}_c^k$ *with Eq. (7)* between step 8 and step 9.

4.4 Classification Module

Although the final classification task is the bag annotation, the individual instance labels also contribute to the bag labels in the real world. The final bag label is determined by the instance labels in the bag. Therefore the objective is to classify instances individually and then infer the bag label. Different from the traditional Prototypical Networks, we modify the Eq. (2) to fit in our model as follows

$$P_I(c \mid (I_{i,j}^*, \mathbf{P}_c)) = \frac{exp(-\omega_{i,j} \cdot d(f_\phi(I_{i,j}^*), \mathbf{P}_c))}{\sum_{c'-1}^{C'} exp(-\omega_{i,j} \cdot d(f_\phi(I_{i,j}^*), \mathbf{P}_{c'}))} \qquad (8)$$

where $I_{i,j}^*$ is the j-th instances in query B_i^*. $\omega_{i,j}$ in Q is updated after selecting instances with high probability during training by using step 7 in Algorithm 1.

For all the selected query instances, Eq. (3) is modified to fit in our model for each given training episode:

$$\mathcal{J}_I = -\frac{1}{\sum \omega_{i,j}} \sum log P_I(y_{i,j}^* \mid (I_{i,j}^*, \mathbf{P}_c)) \qquad (9)$$

Training in each episode minimizes the average loss for all the selected instances. Therefore, the gradient descent updating depends on refinement prototypes and selected query instances to improve the accuracy of instance classification.

During testing, the support set is composed of the few bag-level samples. We refine the instance-level prototype based on two strategies. The predicted label of the query instance $I_{i,j}^*$ during testing is the mostly likely class $\hat{y_{i,j}} = argmax_c P_I(c \mid (I_{i,j}^*, \mathbf{P}_c))$. Considering the witness rate in most situations, we set a majority vote mapping mechanism in which the label of instance with highest frequency in one bag is the final label of bag, $\hat{y_i} = argmax_c Count(c \mid (\hat{y_{i,j}}, \mathbf{P}_c))$.

5 Evaluation

5.1 Experimental Setup

5.1.1 Datasets

PAMAP2[1] consists of 12 activities from 9 different subjects following a protocol with a sampling frequency 100 Hz. We use the sensor data with 36 attributes generated by accelerations and gyroscope from 3 inertial measurement units. It is split into 80% for training and 20% for testing. The last 6 activities are selected as the new classes during testing shown in Table 1 according to the activity ids order. We just choose one of the split methods. Other split strategies are optional.

Skoda[2] describes 10 manipulative gestures performed in a car maintenance scenario with the original sample rates 98 Hz. There are 20 acceleration sensors on both arms. Model is trained on 10 sensors from right arms with 80% of the dataset. We split the classes randomly into train set and test set, shown as Table 1.

---

[1] https://archive.ics.uci.edu/ml/datasets/PAMAP2+Physical+Activity+Monitoring.
[2] http://har-dataset.org/doku.php?id=wiki:dataset.

UCI-HAR[3] records 6 activities from 30 subjects using a waist-mounted smart phone with built-in embedded accelerometer and gyroscope. The sample rate is 50 Hz and the public data has been sampled in fix-width sliding windows of 2.56 seconds (128 steps per window). The ground truth is labeled according to the video-recording manually. 70% of the dataset is selected for training and the remaining is test data. Some repetitive classes are used during testing in Table 1 because of very few classes.

Table 1. Classes split for datasets

Dataset	Train classes	Test classes
PAMAP2	Lying, sitting, standing, walking, running, cycling	Nordic walking, ascending stairs, ironing, rope jumping
Skoda	Write on notepad, open hood close hood, check gaps (front door) open left front door	Close left front door, close both left door check trunk gaps,open and close trunk check steering wheel
UCI-HAR	Walk, walk-upstairs, walk-downstairs, sit	Walk, walk-upstairs, Walk-downstairs, sit, stand, lay

5.1.2   Parameters Settings

Two sets of CNN layers and max pooling layers are used to extract features with all parameters of Prototypical Networks. On Skoda and PAMAP2 the CNN kernel size is 5*3 with strides 2*1. On UCI-HAR the kernel size is 3*3 with the strides 1*1. The number of filters is 64 and the max pooling size is 2*2 on all datasets. Time window is used here [24,27] and the window size of bag for all datasets is set as 128. The size of the sliding window in Skoda and PAMAP2 is 100 to avoid the overlap of instances in set S and Q. To verify the performance of MIL with different number of instances in each bag, we set the number of instances as 4, 5, 6, 7 corresponding to the size of instances 80, 64, 48, 32 (default size) with 50% overlap respectively. We evaluate 1-shot and 5-shot cases frequently used in FSL following [2,8,22]. We follow the episodes [23,25], effective training paradigm in meta learning. The number of iterations are set as 1 (default value), 2, and 3. The ratio in *Top-K* is 0.8 in S. If the ratio is too small, there would be very few selected instances resulting in the similar problem of bag-level classification. The ratio is 1 for refinement in Q to select all the instances in this setup.

---

[3] https://archive.ics.uci.edu/ml/datasets/human+activity+recognition+using+smart phones.

5.1.3   Baselines

We compare the accuracy of our model with existing approaches (supervised models and weakly supervised models) in the experiment.

Supervised FSL Baselines. PN and FSHAR [8] are trained on bag-level data.

Weakly Supervised Baselines. WPN-I and Proto-IATT [9] are trained on instance-level data. WPN-I is the WPN without prototype refinement. Proto-IATT [9] is similar to our motivation but it is first proposed in NLP. We only choose Proto-IATT since there is no problem of feature sparsity in HAR and modify Proto-IATT to fit in HAR.

Our Weakly Supervised Models. WPN-T and WPN-C are WPN models with our two refinement strategies, *Top-K Prototype Refinement* and *Cumulative Prototype Refinement* respectively.

5.2   Evaluation Result

5.2.1   Accuracy

Table 2 shows the test accuracy of different models on benchmark datasets. **ACC-I** and **ACC-B** indicate the accuracy of instance and the bag respectively. In FSHAR, S/H means soft/hard normalization and Cos/SR means cosine similarly and sparse reconstruction respectively. As shown in Table 2, the performance in 5-shot learning is much better than that in 1-shot learning because more samples can generate more general feature comparing with one sample. We mainly describe the performance and analyze the reasons as the following two aspects.

Table 2. Accuracy of different models on different datasets

Datasets		PN	WPN-I	WPN-T	WPN-C	Proto-IATT	FSHAR			
							S-Cos	S-SR	H-Cos	H-SR
PAMAP2	Acc-I	–	57.11	58.11	**60.45**	57.99	–	–	–	–
5-shot	Acc-B	58.36	61.6	62.38	**65.53**	63.34	35.74	42.78	40.19	41.29
PAMAP2	Acc-I	–	44.68	43.4	**46.4**	40.1	–	–	–	–
1-shot	Acc-B	42.66	47.61	45.87	**49.4**	42.34	35.37	42.04	37.04	35
UCI-HAR	Acc-I	–	89.12	**89.89**	88.72	88.13	–	–	–	- -
5-shot	Acc-B	85.59	90.76	**91.3**	90.13	90.25	83.75	78.33	77.39	79.17
UCI-HAR	Acc-I	–	78.48	**79.71**	78.96	77.35	–	–	–	–
1-shot	Acc-B	70.77	80.64	**81.56**	80.83	79.54	76.25	74.08	73.64	65.63
Skoda	Acc-I	-	73.01	71.66	**76.17**	72.17	–	–	–	–
5-shot	Acc-B	73.59	77.67	75.98	**80.17**	76.1	67.2	62.4	65.6	62.1
Skoda	Acc-I	–	59.63	**62.88**	61.12	59.87	–	–	–	–
1-shot	Acc-B	58.75	62.38	**65.88**	63.78	63.09	56.8	50.8	54.4	56.4

The Effectiveness of MIL in Few-shot Learning. All the four weakly supervised models significantly outperform supervised models. It demonstrates the effectiveness of the weakly supervised method for few-shot learning. The reason is that the bag with large window size contains more noisy data than the instances. The feature of the bag may be extracted inaccurately. On the contrary, instances have better signatures although their labels are not given exactly. Besides, the number of instances is much larger than that of bags, which provides more trainable samples with inaccurate labels. That is why it is necessary to select more representative prototypes from the instances with high probability corresponding with ground-truth classes. Our weakly supervised models learn more hidden information from the noisy-labeling instances to improve the annotation accuracy dramatically.

The Effectiveness of Refinement Strategies. On the benchmarks, at least one of WPN-T and WPN-C has better performance than native WPN-I and Proto-IATT in the default experiment setup, demonstrating that our proposed refinement strategies have the ability to refine the prototype from the instances including noisy labels. The different performance of the proposals in three datasets may be caused by the different distribution of noisy instances. In most cases, the accuracy of WPN-C is higher than that of WPN-I because WPN-C preserves the useful information as well as reduces the negative effect of the noisy data. However, WPN-T abandons some useful information in the selecting phase which results in lower accuracy comparing with WPN-I in some cases. Proto-IATT has less ability to refine the prototypes than our models because the noisy labels exist both in S set and Q set in HAR and the weights in Proto-IATT are determined by the distance between supports and queries. Our proposals avoid the negative influence of the noisy instances in the query set. We refine the prototypes only in S set during training. The slight improvement may be caused by the original annotation techniques for the current benchmark datasets. The current datasets usually record repetition activity for a long time which is suitable for the supervised models. In addition, activities last for the longer time than the window size and the number of bags with noisy label is reduced. Therefore the improvement is slight but significant in FSL.

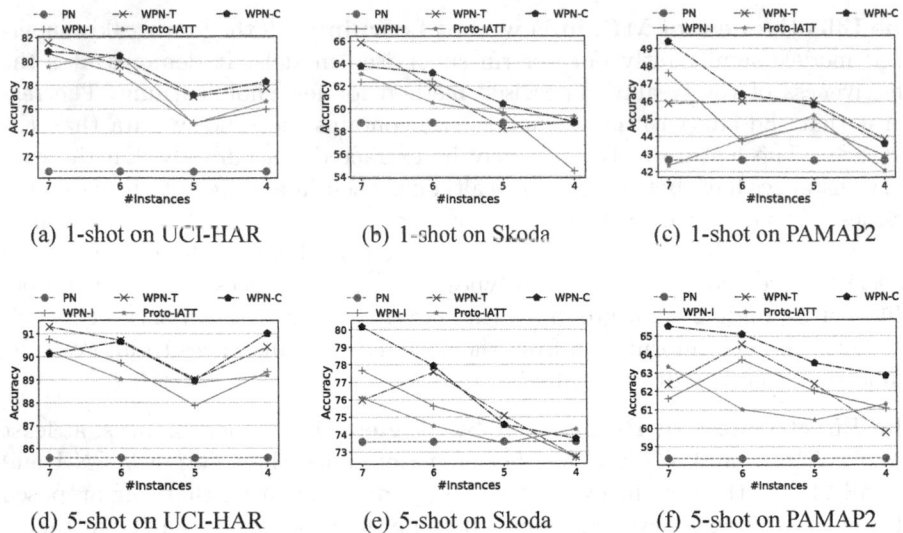

Fig. 3. The accuracy of the different number of instances

5.2.2   The Influence of the Number of Instances

In this part, we evaluate the performance of all the models above when the number of instances is different in each bag. The accuracy of all the experiments of PN displays the same value because there is only bag-level classification. The accuracy values of FSHAR are not displayed since PN performs better than FSHAR in default parameters setting except the accuracy of 1-shot learning on UCI-HAR. Performance of MIL has a relationship with the number of instances, especially in time-series data. As shown in Fig. 3, the accuracy of most of the models decreases with the fluctuation when the number of instances decreases on all datasets. When the window size of the instance is nearly close to the window size of the bag, it would lead to the same problems as bag classification with noisy labeled data.

In addition, more instances in one bag will have a positive effect on the bag-level classification according to the majority vote mapping mechanism in the classification module. When one bag contains 4 instances WPN-I and WPN-T have poorer performance in 5-shot learning on Skoda. One reason is that WPN-T may abandon some information from the few instances and obtain prototype with bias which leads to the low accuracy of the classification of the instances. The other reason is that there are not enough instances to vote the most possible bag label from the noisy instances. On UCI-HAR our models have the poorest performance of 5 instances in each bag comparing with themselves. The reason is that the feature of instance is not representative with unsuitable instance window size and the number of instances is too small as well.

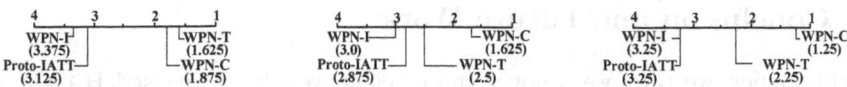

(a) Average ranks on UCI-HAR   (b) Average ranks on Skoda   (c) Average ranks on PAMAP2

Fig. 4. The average ranks of different models

The accuracy of our methods in weakly supervised models is higher than that of the baselines on three datasets in most cases. It also demonstrates the effectiveness of our refinement methods in weakly Prototype Networks. The average ranks of all the models in all the cases on each dataset are illustrated in Fig. 4. WPN-C ranks first on both PAMAP2 and Skoda and ranks second in UCI-HAR. WPN-T ranks first on Skoda with a little gap between WPN-T and WPN-C. When the bag consists of many instances with noisy labels, the WPN-T is much better due to the abandonment of the noisy instances. However, the instances in one bag have some relationships with each other, WPN-C can preserve partial original information and has perfect generalization on different datasets.

5.2.3 The Influence of the Number of Iterations

Table 3 lists the accuracy of WPN-T and WPN-C with the different number of iterations. The number of iterations has a great influence on WPN-T and a little influence on WPN-C. WPN-C outperforms WPN-T as the number of iterations increases because too many iterations will abandon too much useful information and lead to the problems similar to one-shot learning. WPN-C reserves all the information with different weights of the prototype in each iteration. Based on the experiment, we conclude that 1 is the best choice of iterations in few-shot learning for weakly supervised HAR.

Table 3. Accuracy on different number of iterations

Datasets	Models	5-shot			1-shot		
		$\tau = 1$	$\tau = 2$	$\tau = 3$	$\tau = 1$	$\tau = 2$	$\tau = 3$
PAMAP2	WPN-T	**62.38**	59.01	55.82	**45.87**	45.81	45.69
	WPN-C	**65.53**	63.86	65.05	**49.4**	46.67	47.56
UCI-HAR	WPN-T	**91.3**	91.26	91.28	**81.56**	80.41	79.3
	WPN-C	90.13	90.54	**91.58**	80.83	80.18	**80.9**
Skoda	WPN-T	**75.98**	74.6	72.72	**65.88**	64.07	65.76
	WPN-C	**80.17**	77.63	77.89	63.78	63.83	**66.09**

6   Conclusion and Future Work

In this paper, we propose a novel and efficient weakly supervised HAR model WPN to solve the problem of new-class activities recognition from a few noisy train data after reviewing related work. We propose two strategies, *Top-K Prototype Refinement* and *Cumulative Prototype Refinement*, both of which refine the prototype from the embedding instances to improve the accuracy of instance classification. The model minimizes the instance-level loss functions to optimize the network parameters and get the bag-level labels during classification. We compare our proposals with several existing approaches including supervised models and weakly supervised models on three benchmark datasets. The performance is evaluated in three aspects, which are accuracy, the influence of the number of instances, and the influence of the number of iterations. It demonstrates that our proposals perform better than existing models in accuracy. We further observe that more instances and smaller number of iterations have a positive influence on the accuracy of the bag-level classification.

The future work will be focused on the bag-level loss function based on the relationship between the bag and its instances. The bag-level labels are predicted directly without inferring the instance-level label. A framework will be proposed to adaptively determine when should use which prototype refinement strategies

Acknowledgements. This work is partially supported by the National Natural Science Foundation of China (Grant No. 61732003 61729201, 61932004 and N181605012), the Australian Queensland Government (Grant No. AQRF12516), and the Australian Research Council (DP170101172).

References

1. Arifoglu, D., Bouchachia, A.: Activity recognition and abnormal behaviour detection with recurrent neural networks. Proc. Comput. Sci. **110**, 86–93 (2017)
2. Boney, R., Ilin, A.: Semi-supervised few-shot learning with prototypical networks. CoRR (2017)
3. Cao, J., Li, W., Ma, C., Tao, Z.: Optimizing multi-sensor deployment via ensemble pruning for wearable activity recognition. Inf. Fusion **41**, 68–79 (2018)
4. Deng, S., Wang, B., Yang, C., Wang, G.: Convolutional neural networks for human activity recognition using multi-location wearable sensors. Ruan Jian Xue Bao/J. Softw. **30**(3), 718–737 (2019)
5. Dennis, D., Pabbaraju, C., Simhadri, H.V., Jain, P.: Multiple instance learning for efficient sequential data classification on resource-constrained devices. In: Advances in Neural Information Processing Systems (Nips), vol. 31, pp. 10976–10987 (2018)
6. Dietterich, T.G., Lathrop, R.H., Lozano-Pérez, T.: Solving the multiple instance problem with axis-parallel rectangles. Artif. Intell. **89**(1–2), 31–71 (1997)
7. Fe-Fei, L., et al.: A bayesian approach to unsupervised one-shot learning of object categories. In: Proceedings Ninth IEEE International Conference on Computer Vision, pp. 1134–1141. IEEE (2003)

8. Feng, S., Duarte, M.F.: Few-shot learning-based human activity recognition. arXiv preprint arXiv:1903.10416 (2019)
9. Gao, T., Han, X., Liu, Z., Sun, M.: Hybrid attention-based prototypical networks for noisy few-shot relation classification. In: Proceedings of the Thirty-Second AAAI Conference on Artificial Intelligence, (AAAI-19), New York, USA (2019)
10. Guan, X., Raich, R., Wong, W.K.: Efficient multi-instance learning for activity recognition from time series data using an auto-regressive hidden markov model. In: International Conference on Machine Learning, pp. 2330–2339 (2016)
11. Hoffer, E., Ailon, N.: Deep metric learning using triplet network. In: Feragen, A., Pelillo, M., Loog, M. (eds.) SIMBAD 2015. LNCS, vol. 9370, pp. 84–92. Springer, Cham (2015). https://doi.org/10.1007/978-3-319-24261-3_7
12. Kautz, T., Groh, B.H., Hannink, J., Jensen, U., Strubberg, H., Eskofier, B.M.: Activity recognition in beach volleyball using a deep convolutional neural network. Data Mining Knowl. Disc. **31**(6), 1678–1705 (2017)
13. Koch, G., Zemel, R., Salakhutdinov, R.: Siamese neural networks for one-shot image recognition. In: ICML deep learning workshop, vol. 2 (2015)
14. Liu, L., Zhou, T., Long, G., Jiang, J., Yao, L., Zhang, C.: Prototype propagation networks (ppn) for weakly-supervised few-shot learning on category graph. arXiv preprint arXiv:1905.04042 (2019)
15. Liu, Y., et al.: Learning to propagate labels: transductive propagation network for few-shot learning. arXiv preprint arXiv:1805.10002 (2018)
16. Martin, K., Wijekoon, A., Wiratunga, N.: Human activity recognition with deep metric learners. In: CEUR Workshop Proceedings (2019)
17. Mishra, A., Verma, V.K., Reddy, M.S.K., Arulkumar, S., Rai, P., Mittal, A.: A generative approach to zero-shot and few-shot action recognition. In: 2018 IEEE Winter Conference on Applications of Computer Vision (WACV), pp. 372–380. IEEE (2018)
18. Munkhdalai, T., Yu, H.: Meta networks. In: Proceedings of the 34th International Conference on Machine Learning-Volume 70, pp. 2554–2563. JMLR. org (2017)
19. Nguyen-Dinh, L.V., Calatroni, A., Tröster, G.: Supporting one-time point annotations for gesture recognition. IEEE Trans. Pattern Anal. Mach. Intell. **39**(11), 2270–2283 (2016)
20. Ohashi, H., Al-Naser, M., Ahmed, S., Nakamura, K., Sato, T., Dengel, A.: Attributes' importance for zero-shot pose-classification based on wearable sensors. Sensors **18**(8), 2485 (2018)
21. Pan, W., Li, Z., Zhang, Y., Weng, C.: The new hardware development trend and the challenges in data management and analysis. Data Sci. Eng. **3**(3), 263–276 (2018). https://doi.org/10.1007/s41019-018-0072-6
22. Ren, M., et al.: Meta-learning for semi-supervised few-shot classification. arXiv preprint arXiv:1803.00676 (2018)
23. Snell, J., Swersky, K., Zemel, R.: Prototypical networks for few-shot learning. In: Advances in Neural Information Processing Systems, pp. 4077–4087 (2017)
24. Stikic, M., Larlus, D., Ebert, S., Schiele, B.: Weakly supervised recognition of daily life activities with wearable sensors. IEEE Trans. Pattern Anal. Mach. Intell. **33**(12), 2521–2537 (2011)
25. Vinyals, O., Blundell, C., Lillicrap, T., Wierstra, D., et al.: Matching networks for one shot learning. In: Advances in Neural Information Processing Systems, pp. 3630–3638 (2016)
26. Wang, S., Cao, J., Yu, P.S.: Deep learning for spatio-temporal data mining: A survey. arXiv preprint arXiv:1906.04928 (2019)

27. Wang, Y., Yuan, Y., Ma, Y., Wang, G.: Time-dependent graphs: definitions, applications, and algorithms. Data Sci. Eng. **4**(4), 352–366 (2019)
28. Xu, B., Ye, H., Zheng, Y., Wang, H., Luwang, T., Jiang, Y.G.: Dense dilated network for few shot action recognition. In: Proceedings of the 2018 ACM on International Conference on Multimedia Retrieval, pp. 379–387. ACM (2018)

Adversarial Generation of Target Review for Rating Prediction

Huilin Yu[1], Tieyun Qian[1(✉)], Yile Liang[1], and Bing Liu[2]

[1] School of Computer Science, Wuhan University, Hubei, China
{huilin_yu,qty,liangyile}@whu.edu.cn
[2] Department of Computer Science,
University of Illinois at Chicago, Chicago, IL, USA
liub@uic.edu

Abstract. Recent years have witnessed a growing trend of utilizing reviews to improve the performance and interpretability of recommender systems. Almost all existing methods learn the latent representations from the user's and the item's historical reviews, and then combine these two representations for rating prediction. The fatal limitation in these methods is that they are unable to utilize the most predictive review of the target user for the target item since such a review is not available at test time.

In this paper, we propose a novel recommendation model, called GTR, which can *generate the unseen target review with adversarial training for rating prediction*. To this end, we develop a unified framework to combine *the rating tailored generative adversarial nets* (RTGAN) for synthetic review generation and *the neural latent factor module* (NLFM) using the generated target review along with historical reviews for rating prediction. Extensive experiments on four real-world datasets demonstrate that our model achieves the state-of-the-art performance in both rating prediction and review generation tasks.

Keywords: Recommender systems · Review aware recommendation · Generative adversarial network

1 Introduction

A user's rating indicates his/her attitude towards an purchased item. Rating prediction aims to predict the user's ratings on unrated items which may reflect his/her potential interests on these items. Collaborative filtering (CF) approaches, which mainly depend on historical ratings, have aroused great research interests and become the dominant method in recommender systems. As a typical CF technique, matrix factorization (MF) learns the latent features of users and items by decomposing the user-item rating matrix, and then uses these two feature vectors to predict the rating that the user would assign to the item.

© Springer Nature Switzerland AG 2020
Y. Nah et al. (Eds.): DASFAA 2020, LNCS 12113, pp. 73–89, 2020.
https://doi.org/10.1007/978-3-030-59416-9_5

MF is the most widely used technique for rating prediction. However, MF based methods suffer from the data sparsity problem and the predicted rating lacks the interpretability on why the user gives high or low scores. To tackle these issues, textual reviews have become a key complementary data source to enhance the performance and interpretation of the rating prediction task [1, 8,20,32]. In particular, due to the power of non-linear combination of different types of information, impressive progress has been made by applying deep neural networks to this problem [3,4,6,18,26,33].

The pioneering work by Zheng et al. [33] proposed a DeepCoNN model to represent both users and items in a joint manner using all the reviews of users and items. As proven in [3], *the target review*, which is written by the target user for the target item, provides much of the predictive value for rating prediction. The performance of the DeepCoNN model [33] drops severely when the target reviews are omitted. Indeed, the target review usually contains the target user's preference on the target item's attributes or properties and is closely related to the rating score. However, the target review will not be available at test time in real-world recommendation settings. The hereafter studies along this line do not access the target reviews in the validation and test set at any time to simulate a real world scenario. Clearly, the inherent limitation in these methods is that they are unable to utilize the most predictive target review.

In light of this, we propose a novel framework, namely GTR, to generate the target review for rating prediction. Our model has two distinguishing characteristics. Firstly, we *generate the target review with rating tailored generative adversarial nets (RTGAN)* which incorporates the rating into its objective function in addition to the user's and the item's historical reviews. Secondly, we *develop a neural latent factor module (NLFM) to accurately predict the rating score* by learning from the generated target review which encodes the user's specific preference on the item. In such a way, the target review naturally provides guidance for the rating prediction task beyond the above mentioned review-aware deep recommendation approaches [3,4,6,18,26]. Meanwhile, the rating drives the RTGAN module to produce a target review conveying consistent sentiment with the rating score.

We are aware of a few existing studies for generating reviews [5,19,28] or abstractive tips [15]. However, our GTR model is fundamentally different from the NRT [15], MT [19], and CAML [5] models, in the sense that all these approaches do not directly utilize the target review for rating prediction. Although the neural memory (NM) model proposed by Wang and Zhang [28] also integrates the target review in their prediction step, we distinguish our model with NM in both the review generation and rating prediction modules. We present a conditional GAN architecture for review generation, whereas NM [28] uses the sequence-to-sequence (seq2seq) [24] generative model. More importantly, we design a novel neural latent factor model to stress the target review to make good use of its predictive ability, while NM simply feeds the target review as the input of rating prediction in the last layer.

We have realized the proposed GTR model in both the rating prediction and review generation tasks. Empirical evaluation on four real world datasets proves that our proposed GTR model ahieves the state-of-the-art performance on both tasks.

2   Related Work

We summarize the research progress in review-aware rating prediction, categorized by the traditional methods and deep learning based methods. We omit the classic CF based methods which do not use text reviews.

2.1   Traditional Methods

When integrating review texts, the traditional methods can be roughly classified into three categories. The first one is to extract useful textual information such as topics or aspects from review texts and learn latent factors from ratings, and then link the textual information and latent factors together using linear [2,20,25,31] or Bayesian combination [17,29]. The second one is by extending the latent factor model [7,11,21,22,32] to encode the textual influence. The third one is to modify graphic models to include latent factors from ratings [1,8,27].

2.2   Deep Learning Based Methods

The first type of deep learning based methods only uses historical reviews without generating the target review. These approaches differ mainly in how they combine reviews with ratings. For example, NARRE [4] jointly learns hidden latent features for users and items using two parallel neural networks with the attention mechanism [4]. TARMF [18] adopts a neural network for mutual learning between reviews and ratings, where the features from reviews are optimized by an attention-based GRU network. A^3NCF [6] extracts features from reviews using topic models and fuses them with the embeddings from ratings, and it then captures a user's attention on the item with an attention network. MPCN [26] presents a pointer-based co-attention mechanism which can extracts multiple interactions between user and item reviews.

The second type of deep learning based methods generates the target review, but not all of them exploits the predictive ability of the target review. As we have illustrated this issue in the introduction section, here we discuss these methods on how they generate target reviews. NRT [15] is mainly for the purpose of enhancing explainability by generating tips based on a standard generative model with the GRU architecture. NM [28] adopts the seq2seq modeling [24] technique for review generation. Meanwhile, MT [19] uses an adversarial training process which helps overcome the problem of exposure bias in seq2seq models.

Our proposed GTR model falls into the second type of deep learning based methods. Similar to MT [19] in this type, our model also employs GAN for review generation. However, our model incorporates rating as one of the conditions in both the generator and discriminator, whereas MT relies purely on reviews. More importantly, MT adopts a traditional MF method for rating prediction, which does not take the target review into consideration. In contrast, our GTR can fully utilize the target review with a carefully designed neural latent factor model.

3   Problem Definition

This section presents the problem definition and notations. Let $\mathcal{U}$ be a user set and $\mathcal{I}$ be an item set, and $\mathcal{D}$ be a review set on the items in $\mathcal{I}$ written by a set of users in $\mathcal{U}$. Each review d_{ui} written by user u on item i has an accompanying rating r_{ui} indicating u's overall satisfaction towards i. We refer to all historical reviews written by the user, i.e., except that on item i, as the *user's historical review document d_u*. Similarly, the set of historical reviews on item i, except the one written by u, is referred to as the *item's historical review document d_i*. Each training instance is denoted as a sextuple $(u, i, d_{ui}, r_{ui}, d_u, d_i)$. The goal is to predict a rating $\hat{r}_{ui}$ and learn a synthetic target review s_{ui} for each item i that u does not interact with.

For ease of presentation, we summarize the notations in Table 1.

Table 1. Notations used in this paper

Variable	Interpretation
$\mathcal{U}$	User set
$\mathcal{I}$	Item set
$\mathcal{R}$	Rating set
$\mathcal{D}$	Review set
$u \in \mathcal{U}$	A user $u \in \mathcal{U}$
$i \in \mathcal{I}$	An item $i \in \mathcal{I}$
$r_{ui} \in \mathcal{R}$	User u's rating on item i
$d_{ui} \in \mathcal{D}$	User u's review on item i
$d_u \subset \mathcal{D}$	User u's all reviews except d_{ui}
$d_i \subset \mathcal{D}$	Item i's all reviews except d_{ui}
$\hat{r}_{ui}$	User u's predicted rating on item i
s_{ui}	User u's generated review on item i

4   Our Proposed Model

In this section, we introduce our proposed model. We begin with the overall architecture and then go to the details of two modules.

4.1   Model Overview

Our model consists of two modules. One is the rating tailored GAN (RTGAN), which takes the rating as an important condition in the generator and the discriminator of GAN for review generation. The other is the neural latent factor module (NLFM) that leverages the generated target review along with the historical reviews for ration prediction using a neural network. The overall architecture of our model is shown in Fig. 1.

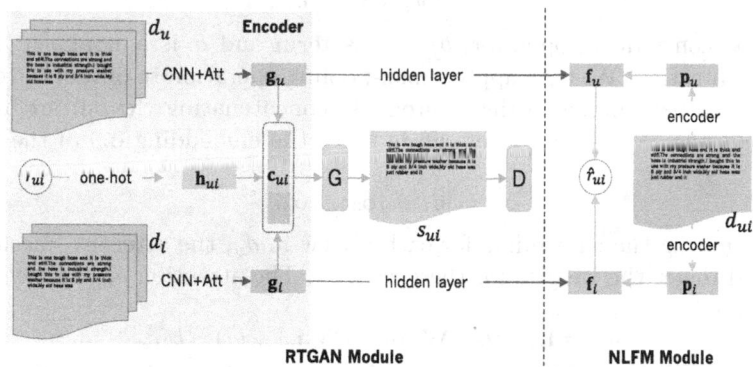

Fig. 1. The architecture of our GTR model

4.2   Rating Tailored GAN (RTGAN) Module

We have two basic assumptions for generating the synthetic target review s_{ui}. Firstly, s_{ui} should reflect the user u's preferences and the item i's features. Secondly, the sentiment expressed in s_{ui} should be consistent with the rating score r_{ui}. Following these assumptions, we design our rating tailored GAN (RTGAN) module conditioned on three types of information: 1) the user's historical review document d_u to capture u's preferences, 2) the item's historical review document d_i to represent i's features, and 3) the rating r_{ui} of the user u to the item i to serve as a constraint. During training, we learn a generator G using three types of condition information to produce a synthetic review, and a discriminator D to distinguish it with the real one.

4.2.1   Condition Information Encoder

We first introduce the condition information encoder (the left grey part in Fig. 1). It maps three types of condition information into user's general preference embedding $\mathbf{g}_u$, item's feature embedding $\mathbf{g}_i$, and the rating embedding $\mathbf{h}_{ui}$.

We take the process of mapping user's review document d_u to his/her preference embedding $\mathbf{g}_u$ as an example. Each word in d_u is randomly initialized as a d dimensional vector, and each review in d_u is transformed into a matrix with the fixed length T (padded with 0 if necessary). Since the text processing is not the focus of this study, we take the same TextCNN [4] approach to encode each review in d_u. Essentially, TextCNN can be summarized as a CNN structure followed by an attention mechanism. The convolution layer consists of m neurons. Each neuron is associated with a filter $\mathbf{K} \in \mathbb{R}^{t \times d}$ which produces features by applying convolution operator on word vectors. Let $\mathbf{V}_{ul}$ be the embedding matrix corresponding to the lth review in d_u, the jth neuron in CNN produces its feature as:

$$\mathbf{z}_j = \sigma(\mathbf{V}_{ul} * \mathbf{K}_j + b_j), \tag{1}$$

where $*$ is convolution operator, b_j is bias term and σ is a nonlinear RELU activation function. We then apply a max-pooling operation to obtain the output feature $\mathbf{o}_j$ corresponding to this neuron. By concatenating the output from all m neurons, the convolution layer can produce the embedding $\mathbf{o}_{ul}$ of the review d_{ul} as:

$$\mathbf{o}_{ul} = [\mathbf{o}_1, \mathbf{o}_2, \mathbf{o}_3, ..., \mathbf{o}_m], \tag{2}$$

After getting the embedding for each review in d_u, the attention mechanism is adopted to get the weights for these reviews. The attention a_{ul} for review d_{ul} is defined as:

$$a_{ul}^* = \mathbf{h}_a^T ReLU(\mathbf{W}_O \mathbf{o}_{ul} + \mathbf{W}_i \mathbf{i}_{ul} + b_1) + b_2, \tag{3}$$

where $\mathbf{h}_a \in \mathbb{R}^t$, $\mathbf{W}_O \in \mathbb{R}^{t \times k_1}$, $\mathbf{W}_i \in \mathbb{R}^{t \times k_2}$, $b_1 \in \mathbb{R}^t$, $b_2 \in \mathbb{R}^1$ are model parameters, $\mathbf{i}_{ul} \in \mathbb{R}^K$ is the embedding of the item which the user write this review for.

A softmax function is used to normalize the above a_{ul}^* to get the final attention a_{ul}. The user's u general preference embedding $\mathbf{g}_u$ is then calculated as the attention weighted sum of all reviews $d_{ul} \in d_u$, i.e.,

$$\mathbf{g}_u = \sum\nolimits_{l=1,...|d_u|} a_{ul} \mathbf{o}_{ul} \tag{4}$$

The process of mapping item's review document d_i to its feature embedding $\mathbf{g}_i$ is all the same. Hence we have:

$$\mathbf{g}_i = \sum\nolimits_{l=1,...|d_i|} a_{il} \mathbf{o}_{il} \tag{5}$$

The mapping from the original rating r_{ui} to an one-hot embedding h_{ui} is straight-forward. We simply discretize the rating r_{ui} into a m-dimension vector ($m = 5$ in our case). If the value falls into an interval, the corresponding dimension is set to 1 and other dimensions are set to 0. For example, a rating $r_{ui} = 3.78$ will be mapped into a $\mathbf{h}_{ui}$ as $(0,0,0,1,0)^T$. Note that the rating r_{ui} is known only in training. During validation or test, we will use a basic rating from NLFM module instead. The detail will be given later.

4.2.2   RTGAN for Target Review Generation

A good number of generative methods have been proposed for text generation in recent years, such as seq2seq [24] based models, SeqGAN [30], and

RankGAN [16]. Since the reviews are usually long (with average length > 40), we adopt the state-of-the-art LeakGAN [9] model to generate reviews in this paper, and extend it by incorporating three types of condition information into both the generator and the discriminator.

Conditional Generator. Starting from the random state, LeakGAN generates texts via the adversarial generation of synthetic texts against real texts. This implies that, if simply adopting LeakGAN in our model, the generated reviews are only ensured to be written in a human-like style. However, we need to generate the target review that is written by a specific user for a specific item.

In order to provide additional information for guiding the target review generation, we incorporate LeakGAN with the conditional GAN by taking three types of information as the condition of the generator in LeakGAN. We call the combination of these three types of information as a condition vector c_{ui}, and define it as:

$$c_{ui} = g_u \oplus g_i \oplus (W_r * h_{ui}), \tag{6}$$

where W_r is a mapping matrix to transform the sparse h_{ui} to a dense vector.

Similar to many text generation methods [9,19], we employ a decoder GRU to iteratively generate a review word by word. Different from these methods, the decoder layer in our RTGAN module is conditioned on c_{ui}, which is the combination of three types of information. By doing so, our generator produces a synthetic target review that reflects not only the user u's preferences but also the item i's features. Moreover, the sentiment contained in the synthetic review is also forced to match the rating score.

To ensure that the condition information is maintained during the generation process, the condition vector c_{ui} is concatenated with the word vector before it is fed into the decoder GRU at each time step. Suppose x_t is the embedding for the current word being processed at time step t, the concatenated vector $x_t' = c_{ui} \oplus x_t$ is input into the decoder GRU to get the hidden state h_t. And then, the hidden state h_t is multiplied by an output projection matrix and passed through a softmax over all the words in the vocabulary to obtain the probability of each word in the current context. Finally, the output word y_t at time t is sampled from the multi-nominal distribution through a softmax layer.

The difference between the generator in our RTGAN module and that in LeakGAN is that, our generator is conditioned on the additional information as discussed above. For learning, we follow the generator training method in LeakGAN [9] by adopting a hierarchical architecture to effectively generate long texts.

Briefly, the hierarchical generator G consists of a high-level MANAGER module and a low-level WORKER module. At each step, the MANAGER receives a leaked feature vector f_t (which is the last layer in discriminator D), and uses f_t to form the guiding goal vector g_t for the WORKER module. Compared to the scalar classification probability of D, the leaked feature vector f_t is a much more informative guiding signal for G, since it tells what the position of currently-generated word is in the extracted feature space.

The loss for the MANAGER module is defined as:

$$L_{G_M} = -\sum_{t=1}^{T} Q(\mathbf{f}_t, \mathbf{g}_t) * d_{cos}(\mathbf{f}_{t+c} - \mathbf{f}_t, \mathbf{g}_t), \tag{7}$$

where $Q(\mathbf{f}_t, \mathbf{g}_t)$ is the expected reward (the classification probability output by D) under the current policy, and d_{cos} represents the cosine similarity between the change of leaked feature representation of discriminator after c-step transition (from $\mathbf{f}_t$ to $\mathbf{f}_{t+c}$) and the goal vector $\mathbf{g}_t$, and T is the maximum sequence length we set for review. The loss function aims to force the goal vector to match the transition in the feature space while achieving high reward. Meanwhile, the loss for the WORKER module is defined as:

$$L_{G_W} = -\sum_{t=1}^{T} r_t^I \cdot p(y_t|s_{t-1}, \mathbf{c}_{ui}), \tag{8}$$

where $p(y_t|s_{t-1}, \mathbf{c}_{ui})$ denotes the conditional generative probability of the next token y_t given a sequence $s_{t-1} = [y_0, y_1, ..., y_{t-1}]$ and the condition vector $\mathbf{c}_{ui}$ in WORKER module. r_t^I is the intrinsic reward defined as:

$$r_t^I = \frac{1}{c} \sum_{i=1}^{T} d_{cos}(\mathbf{f}_t - \mathbf{f}_{t-i}, \mathbf{g}_{t-i}) \tag{9}$$

The objective in G is to minimize L_{G_M} and L_{G_W} in two modules, which are alternatively trained while fixing the other.

Conditional Discriminator. The discriminator learns to distinguish the ground-truth review d_{ui} from the synthetic one s_{ui}. We adopt the same CNN structure in the generator to process review texts, and we can get the embedding $\mathbf{d}_{ui}$ for d_{ui} and $\mathbf{s}_{ui}$ for s_{ui}, respectively. Different from the discriminator that only distinguishes between the real and the synthetic one, our discriminator needs to determine whether the review is related to the user and the item, and whether the review is written by the user for this item. Therefore, we take the condition information $\mathbf{c}_{ui}$ into account in the discrimination as well. The loss for the discriminator D is defined as:

$$L_D = -(log(D(\mathbf{d}_{ui}|\mathbf{c}_{ui})) + log(1 - D(\mathbf{s}_{ui}|\mathbf{c}_{ui}))), \tag{10}$$

where $D()$ is the probability function computed by applying a softmax layer to the concatenation of $\mathbf{d}_{ui}/\mathbf{s}_{ui}$ and $\mathbf{c}_{ui}$. The objective in D is to maximize the probability of classifying the ground-truth review as positive, and to minimize the probability of classifying the synthetic one as authentic.

The training of G and D in RTGAN module is an adversarial process. The goal of generator is to produce the most indistinguishable synthetic reviews to fool the discriminator, while the discriminator aims to distinguish synthetic and ground-truth reviews as much as possible. Hence we iteratively train G and D to reach an equilibrium.

4.3   Neural Latent Factor Model (NLFM) Module

Inspired by the neural latent factor models in [4,10], we propose our NLFM module by extending these neural models in the following ways. Firstly, we represent *general latent factors* of user and item merely based on historical reviews without ratings. Secondly, we extend to exploit the *special latent factors* which encode the user's preference on the item in the target review.

Specifically, the embeddings of user preferences and item features, i.e., $\mathbf{g_u}$ and $\mathbf{g_i}$, are passed from the RTGAN module, and then we map them with a hidden layer to get the general latent factors of user and item. To obtain the special latent factors, we transform the target review d_{ui} (s_{ui} when testing) through a CNN structure and a hidden layer as follows:

$$\mathbf{p}_u = tanh(\mathbf{W}_{su} * CNN(d_{ui}) + b_{su}), \tag{11}$$

$$\mathbf{p}_i = tanh(\mathbf{W}_{si} * CNN(d_{ui}) + b_{si}), \tag{12}$$

where $CNN()$ is a convolutional neural network that maps the target review d_{ui} into a feature vector, and $\mathbf{W}_{su}$, $\mathbf{W}_{si}$ are the projection matrices and b_{su}, b_{si} are biases.

Combining the general and special latent factors together, we can obtain the user's and item's overall representations:

$$\mathbf{f}_u = tanh(\mathbf{W}_{gu} * \mathbf{g}_u) + tanh(\mathbf{W}_{pu} * \mathbf{p}_u), \tag{13}$$

$$\mathbf{f}_i = tanh(\mathbf{W}_{gi} * \mathbf{g}_i) + tanh(\mathbf{W}_{pi} * \mathbf{p}_i), \tag{14}$$

where $\mathbf{W}_{gu}$, $\mathbf{W}_{pu}$, $\mathbf{W}_{gi}$, $\mathbf{W}_{pi}$ are weight matrices.

We then pass these two overall representations $\mathbf{f}_u$ and $\mathbf{f}_i$ to a prediction layer to get a real-valued rating $\hat{r}_{ui}$:

$$\hat{r}_{ui} = \mathbf{f}_u^T \mathbf{f}_i + b_u + b_i + b, \tag{15}$$

where b_u, b_i, and b denotes the user bias, item bias and global bias, respectively. Clearly, our predicted rating $\hat{r}_{ui}$ encodes the general user interests and item features as well as the user's specific interest on this item.

Since rating prediction is actually a regression problem, a commonly used squared loss is adopted as the objective function for our NLFM module:

$$L_r = \sum_{u,i \in \mathcal{U},\mathcal{I}} (\hat{r}_{ui} - r_{ui})^2, \tag{16}$$

where U, I denotes the user and item set respectively, and r_{ui} is the ground-truth rating assigned by u on i.

4.4   Training and Prediction

We iteratively train the RTGAN and NLFM modules. Since these two modules share the parameters in the historical reviews encoder layer, the parameters will be iteratively updated.

At the time of validation and testing, we first get a basic rating using the user's and item's embeddings saved in NLFM after training. We then input this basic rating as a condition to RTGAN to generate the synthetic target review. Finally, the generated review is fed into NLFM to get the final rating score. Note that though we add the RTGAN module in order to generate and utilize the synthetic review, the rating prediction task in our GTR model can be performed offline like MF methods.

5 Experiments

5.1 Experimental Setup

Datasets We conduct experiments on two publicly accessible data sources: Amazon product review[1] and Yelp 2017[2]. We use three of product categories in Amazon: *Patio, Lawn and Garden, Automotive,* and *Grocery and Gourmet Food.* We take the 5-core version for experiments following the previous studies [4,6,26]. In this version, each user or item has at least 5 interactions. For all datasets, we extract the textual reviews as well as the numerical ratings to conduct experiments. The basic statistics of the datasets are shown in Table 2.

Table 2. Statistics of the datasets

Datasets	Users	Items	Ratings	Sparsity
Garden	1686	962	13272	0.9918
Automotive	2928	1834	20473	0.9962
Grocery	14679	8711	151254	0.9988
Yelp2017	29406	39643	1239518	0.9990

Evaluation Metrics. For rating prediction, we employ MAE [15] and MSE [19,26, 28] as evaluation metrics. For review generation, we report the results in terms of negative log-likelyhood (NLL) [9,30] and ROUGE-1 [15,28]. All these metrics are widely used in text generation and recommendation systems.

Compared Methods. We compare our GTR model with the following state-of-the-art methods.

SentiRec [12] first encodes each review into a fixed-size vector using CNN and then generates recommendations using vector-encoded reviews.

MPCN [26] exploits review-level co-attention mechanism to determine the most informative reviews and gets the representations of users and items.

A³NCF [6] designs a new topic model to extract user preferences and item characteristics from review texts and then feeds them into a neural network for rating prediction.

---

[1] https://jmcauley.ucsd.edu/data/amazon/html.
[2] www.yelp.com/datasetchallenge/.

ALFM [7] develops an aspect-aware latent factor model where a new topic model in integrated to model user preferences and item features from different aspects.

NARRE [4] processes each review using CNN and adopts attention mechanism to build the recommendation model and select useful reviews simultaneously.

TARMF [18] adopts attention-based RNN to extract textual features and maximizes the similarity between latent factors and textual features.

MT [19] jointly learns to perform rating prediction and recommendation explanation by combining MF for rating prediction and SeqGan [30] for review generation.

NRT [15] uses MF and generation networks to combine ratings, reviews, and tips for rating prediction and abstractive tips generation.

NM [28] uses a single neural network to model users and products, and generates customized product representations using a deep memory network, from which customized ratings and reviews are constructed jointly.

CAML [5] uses an encoder-selector-decoder architecture to model the cross knowledge transferred for both the recommendation task and the explanation task using a multi-task framework.

In addition to the above baselines, we propose two variants for MT and our GTR models. Specifically, **MT-lg** replaces SeqGan [30] in the review generation module of MT [19] with LeakGan [9] in our model to exclude the potential influence caused by using different generation models. **GTR-r** removes the rating condition from the generation module in our GTR model to investigate the effects of our rating tailored GAN.

We do not compare our model with other methods like DeepCoNN [33] and TransNet [3] using reviews for rating prediction, neither with the traditional methods like NMF [14], FM [23], and NeuMF [10] which do not use reviews. These methods have been shown to be weaker than the baselines [7,18,26] used in our experiments, thus we only show improvements over the baselines.

Parameter Settings. Each dataset is divided into 80%/10%/10% splits for training, validation, and testing, respectively. We train the model on the training set and tune the hyper-parameters on the validation set. The ground-truth reviews in the training set are used for training the model. Note that those in validation or testing sets are never accessed. Instead, only the generated target reviews are used for validation or testing.

The parameters of all baselines are the same as those in the corresponding original papers. For our GTR model, we set dimensionality to 32 for all embeddings of users, items, and word latent factors. In review generation, the maximum review length T is set to 40 words, and other parameters such as the kernel size of CNN are the same as those in LeakGAN. We use Adam [13] for optimization. We set learning rate $= 0.002$, minibatch size $= 64$, and dropout ratio $= 0.5$ for all the datasets.

Table 3. Rating prediction performance in terms of MAE and MSE. The best results are in bold and the second best ones (except those in our GTR-r variant) are underlined. - and * denote significant difference according to paired t-test between our model and each baseline for $p < 0.05$ and $p < 0.01$, respectively.

	Garden		Automotive		Grocery		Yelp	
	MAE	MSE	MAE	MSE	MAE	MSE	MAE	MSE
SentiRec	0.833*	1.067*	0.637*	0.824*	0.742*	1.014*	0.926*	1.371*
MPCN	0.852*	1.166*	0.576*	0.815*	0.821*	1.904*	0.902*	1.286*
A³NCF	0.793*	1.035*	0.696*	0.823*	0.777*	1.020*	0.846*	1.137*
ALFM	0.749*	0.984*	0.631*	0.772*	0.746*	1.001*	0.828*	1.096*
NARRE	0.772*	0.990*	0.621*	0.781*	0.743*	0.997*	0.819*	1.105*
TARMF	0.832*	1.103*	0.730*	0.868*	0.775*	1.073*	0.849*	1.196*
MT	0.848*	1.112*	0.747*	0.879*	0.769*	1.015*	0.852*	1.191*
MT-lg	0.799*	1.074*	0.701*	0.851*	0.762*	1.005*	0.855*	1.148*
NM	0.810⁻	1.181⁻	0.602⁻	0.829⁻	0.724*	1.020*	0.819*	1.116*
NRT	0.874*	1.109*	0.769*	0.814*	0.868*	1.174*	0.912*	1.127*
CAML	0.742	1.023*	0.625*	0.775*	**0.704**	**0.979**	0.815⁻	1.089*
GTR-r	0.750	0.972	0.602	0.767	0.737	0.994	0.821	1.091
GTR	**0.743**	**0.955**	**0.566**	**0.754**	0.706	0.981	**0.808**	**1.073**

5.2 Rating Prediction

The results of all methods for rating prediction are presented in Table 3. (1) The upper six rows from SentiRec to TARMF are *the first type* of review-aware rating prediction methods which do not generate target reviews. (2) The middle five rows from MT to CAML are *the second type* which generates target reviews/tips. (3) The last two rows are our GTR model and its variant. From Table 3, we have the following important observations.

Firstly, our GTR model statistically significantly outperforms all baselines in terms of MAE and MSE metrics on three of the four datasets. The baselines' performances fluctuate among different datasets. MPCN, ALFM, and CAML once becomes the second best in some cases. This shows that it is hard to get the consistently better performance for one method due to the characteristics of the different datasets. In contrast, our model achieves the best performance on Garden, Automotive, and Yelp datasets. CAML is the best on Grocery. However, the difference between our model and CAML on this dataset is not significant. All these results clearly demonstrate the effectiveness of our model.

Secondly, among six methods in the first type, ALFM and NARRE are generally better than other methods. Both these methods differentiate the importance of each review or each aspect. This infers that a fine-grained analysis on the reviews has great impacts on the related rating prediction task. Among five methods in the second type, CAML benefits a lot from the joint training of two tasks under the multi-task framework. Moreover, NM performs better than

MT and NRT which only generate but do not integrate target reviews for rating prediction. Both these clearly show the predictive ability of target reviews. Our GTR model's superior performance over NM can be due to our carefully designed NLFM module, which makes the best use of the target review. The other reason is that the quality of our generated reviews is higher than that of NM with the help of rating tailored adversarial learning.

Thirdly, MT-lg is better than the original MT, suggesting the importance of generative model. On the other hand, GRT-r performs worse than GTR, showing that rating condition plays a critical role in generating reviews consistent with rating scores. However, the enhanced MT-lg is still worse than our simplified version GRT-r. This indicates that our NLFM module performs much better the matrix factorization model in MT. NRT is designed for abstractive tips generation, which results in its inferior performance.

5.3 Review Generation

This section evaluates the performance of our GTR model on review generation by comparing it with the second-type baselines. The results are presented in Table 4. NLL measures the negative log likelihood of the test data under the generated language model, and ROUGE-1 counts the number of overlapping unigrams between each pair of the generated review and the ground truth one. For NLL, the smaller the better, whereas the larger the better for ROUGE-1. The best results are in bold and the second best ones (except those in our GTR-r variant) are underlined.

Table 4. Review generation performance in terms of NLL and ROUGE-1 (R-1)

	Garden		Auto.		Grocery		Yelp	
	NLL	R-1	NLL	R-1	NLL	R-1	NLL	R-1
MT	5.74	3.22	4.01	2.95	4.28	5.20	5.19	5.22
MT-lg	5.61	3.25	3.96	2.94	4.30	5.01	5.14	5.31
NM	5.63	3.33	4.06	2.98	4.81	4.40	5.84	6.25
NRT	6.24	0.52	4.34	1.72	4.57	7.51	5.43	6.21
CAML	**5.45**	**4.96**	**3.28**	**3.33**	_3.51_	_7.57_	**4.84**	**7.38**
GTR-r	5.68	3.42	3.99	2.74	4.34	4.54	5.08	5.74
GTR	_5.51_	_3.49_	_3.86_	_3.01_	**3.25**	**7.73**	_4.99_	_6.43_

From Table 4, it is clear that our GTR model can generate the best or second best reviews in terms of NLL and ROUGE-1 metrics on all datasets. Moreover, GTR-r's results are not as good as GTR. This, once again, demonstrates that our strategy of taking rating as the condition in GAN helps generate high-quality reviews. Among the baselines, CAML can generate good reviews with the help of supervision from the rating subtask under the multi-task learning framework.

We also find that both NRT and NM perform relatively poorly. The reason might be that they only adopt the maximum likelihood estimation to generate reviews without exploiting the adversarial network. On the other hand, MT-lg is better than MT, indicating that LeakGAN performs better than SeqGAN.

5.4　Case Study

In order to capture more details, we provide several examples in Table 5 to analyze the relevance between the generated synthetic reviews/ratings and the real ones.

Table 5. Examples of the predicted ratings and the generated reviews (Ref. denotes the ground-truth review and rating)

	Rating	Review
Ref	5.0	last very long time stainless steel very good quality i not buy another sure use alot
MT	4.25	good want use like another days earth hubby metal very activity...
MT-lg	4.47	think nice product use buy but still want again skin cool cold rarely does like...
NRT	4.17	shaped nice seldom introduced so sneak transplanting still momentum ...
NM	4.33	activity absolutely very well down won cool quality skin sheath ...
CAML	4.84	bought happy grill test propane ignition roast mind what built ...
GTR-r	4.68	good product use still some lot not very operate only so middle ...
GTR	4.85	worked very well very easy use still from some quality rain not sure good value few days ...

As can be seen, our GTR model gets the highest rating score, i.e., 4.85, which is very close to the real score. Furthermore, our generated review is suitable to express the strong positive sentiment reflected by the full credit, and it is most similar to the real review. We also need to point out that, the words in the latter half of our generated review are not very accurate. This also happens to other generated reviews. The reason is that some unrelated words are padded into the short reviews when training the model to reach the fixed length. Consequently, the network is unable to generate accurate words for the latter part of the sentence.

5.5   Parameter Analysis

In this subsection, we investigate the effects of two parameters, i.e., the number of latent factors and the max length of reviews. We first examine the effect of the latent factor size in Fig. 2(a) and 2(b). We can see that, with the increase number of latent factors, the performance could be enhanced since more latent factors bring better representation capability. However, too many latent factors may cause over-fitting and result in the decrease of performance.

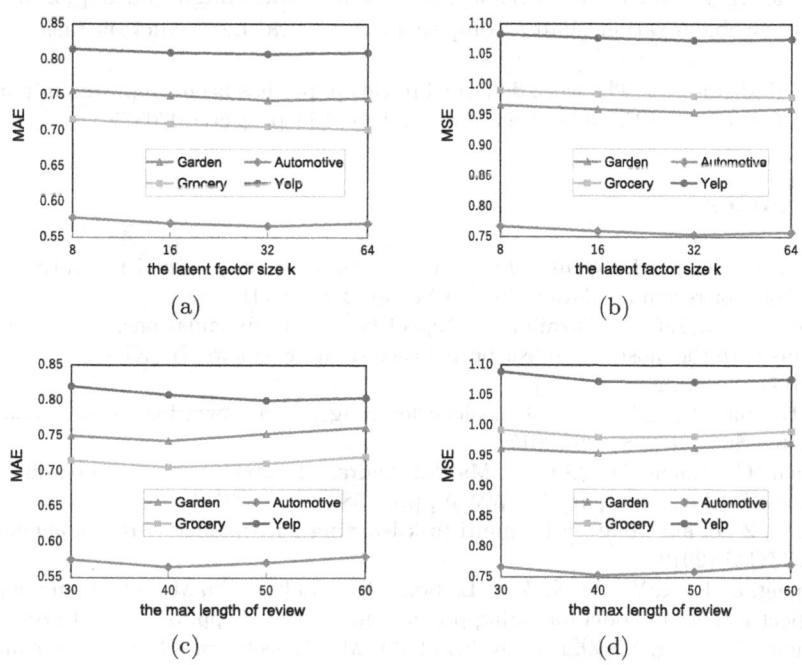

(a)   (b)

(c)   (d)

Fig. 2. Performance of different size of latent factor and max length of review.

We then study the effects of the max length of reviews in Fig. 2(c) and 2(d). When the review length is small, the part of texts that exceeds the specified length need to be truncated when preprocessing, which will result in a information loss. In this case, the smaller the specified length, the more information is missing, and thus the performance will decrease. When the review length increases, the reviews which is shorter than the threshold need to be padded. The irrelevant words padded would bring noises to the model, which will harm the performance of the model.

6   Conclusion

In this paper, we presented a novel GTR model to leverage the predictive ability of target reviews. We developed a unified framework to generate target reviews using a rating tailored GAN and to do rating prediction with a neural latent factor model which well exploits the generated target review besides historical reviews. We conducted extensive experiments on four real world datasets. Results demonstrate our model achieves the state-of-the-art performance in both rating prediction and review generation tasks.

As for future work, one possible direction is to generate target reviews with variable length. The second is to enhance the interaction between two modules under the multi-task framework. The third is to develop new approach instead of extending LeakGAN for review generation, which might be explored as a separate problem rather than a component in our rating prediction task.

Acknowledgments. The work described in this paper has been supported in part by the NSFC projects (61572376, 91646206), and the 111 project(B07037).

References

1. Bao, Y., Fang, H., Zhang, J.: Topicmf: simultaneously exploiting ratings and reviews for recommendation. In: AAAI, pp. 2–8 (2014)
2. Bauman, K., Liu, B., Tuzhilin, A.: Aspect based recommendations: recommending items with the most valuable aspects based on user reviews. In: KDD, pp. 717–725 (2017)
3. Catherine, R., Cohen, W.: Transnets: learning to transform for recommendation. In: RecSys, pp. 288–296 (2017)
4. Chen, C., Zhang, M., Liu, Y., Ma, S.: Neural attentional rating regression with review-level explanations. In: WWW, pp. 1583–1592 (2018)
5. Chen, Z., et al.: Co-attentive multi-task learning for explainable recommendation. In: IJCAI (2019)
6. Cheng, Z., Ding, Y., He, X., Zhu, L., Song, X., Kankanhalli, M.: A^3ncf: an adaptive aspect attention model for rating prediction. In: IJCAI, pp. 3748–3754 (2018)
7. Cheng, Z., Ding, Y., Zhu, L., Kankanhalli, M.: Aspect-aware latent factor model: rating prediction with ratings and reviews. In: WWW, pp. 639–648 (2018)
8. Diao, Q., Qiu, M., Wu, C.Y., Smola, A.J., Jiang, J., Wang, C.: Jointly modeling aspects, ratings and sentiments for movie recommendation (jmars). In: KDD, pp. 193–202 (2014)
9. Guo, J., Lu, S., Cai, H., Zhang, W., Yu, Y., Wang, J.: Long text generation via adversarial training with leaked information. In: AAAI (2018)
10. He, X., Liao, L., Zhang, H., Nie, L., Hu, X., Chua, T.S.: Neural collaborative filtering. In: WWW, pp. 173–182 (2017)
11. Hu, L., Sun, A., Liu, Y.: Your neighbors affect your ratings: on geographical neighborhood influence to rating prediction. In: SIGIR, pp. 345–354 (2014)
12. Hyun, D., Park, C., Yang, M.C., , J.T., Yu, HSong, I., Lee.: Review sentiment-guided scalable deep recommender system. In: SIGIR, pp. 965–968 (2018)
13. Kingma, D., Ba, J.: Adam: a method for stochastic optimization. In: Computer Science (2014)
14. Lee, D.D., Seung, H.S.: Algorithms for non-negative matrix factorization. In: NIPS, pp. 556-562 (2001)
15. Li, P., Wang, Z., Ren, Z., Bing, L., Lam, W.: Neural rating regression with abstractive tips generation for recommendation. In: SIGIR, pp. 345–354 (2017)

16. Lin, K., Li, D., He, X., Zhang, Z. and Sun, M.T.: Adversarial ranking for language generation. In: NIPS (2017)
17. Ling, G., Lyu, M.R., King, I.: Ratings meet reviews, a combined approach to recommend. In: RecSys, pp. 105–112 (2014)
18. Lu, Y., Dong, R., Smyth, B.: Coevolutionary recommendation model: mutual learning between ratings and reviews. In: WWW, pp. 773–782 (2018)
19. Lu, Y., Dong, R., Smyth, B.: Why i like it: multi-task learning for recommendation and explanation. In: RecSys, pp. 4–12 (2018)
20. McAuley, J., Leskovec, J.: Hidden factors and hidden topics: understanding rating dimensions with review text. In: RecSys, pp. 165–172 (2013)
21. Pappas, N., Popescu-Belis, A.: Sentiment analysis of user comments for one-class collaborative filtering over ted talks. In: SIGIR, pp. 773–776 (2013)
22. Š. Pero, Horáth, T.: Opinion-driven matrix factorization for rating prediction. In: UMAP, pp. 1–13 (2013)
23. Rendle, S.: Factorization machines. In: ICDM, pp. 995–1000 (2010)
24. Sutskever, I., Vinynls, O., Le, Q.V.: Sequence to sequence learning with neural networks. In: NIPS, pp. 3104–3112 (2014)
25. Tan, Y., Zhang, M., Liu, Y., Ma, S.: Rating-boosted latent topics: understanding users and items with ratings and reviews. In: IJCAI, pp. 2640–2646 (2016)
26. Tay, Y., Luu, A.T., Hui, S.C.: Multi-pointer co-attention networks for recommendation. In: KDD, pp. 2309–2318 (2018)
27. Wang, C., Blei, D.M.: Collaborative topic modeling for recommending scientific articles. In: KDD, pp. 448–456 (2011)
28. Wang, Z., Zhang, Y.: Opinion recommendation using a neural model. In: EMNLP, pp. 1626–1637 (2017)
29. Xu, Y., Lam, W., Lin, T.: Collaborative filtering incorporating review text and co-clusters of hidden user communities and item groups. In: CIKM, pp. 1661–1670 (2014)
30. Yu, L.T., Zhang, W.N., Wang, J., Yu, Y.: Seqgan: sequence generative adversarial nets with policy gradient. In: AAAI (2016)
31. Zhang, W., Wang, J.: Integrating topic and latent factors for scalable personalized review-based rating prediction. TKDE **28**(11), 3013–3027 (2016)
32. Zhang, Y., Lai, G., Zhang, M., Zhang, Y., Liu, Y., Ma, S.: Explicit factor models for explainable recommendation based on phrase-level sentiment analysis. In: SIGIR, pp. 83–92 (2014)
33. Zheng, L., Noroozi, V., Yu, P.S.: Joint deep modeling of users and items using reviews for recommendation. In: WSDM, pp. 425–434 (2017)

Hybrid Attention Based Neural Architecture for Text Semantics Similarity Measurement

Kaixin Liu, Yong Zhang$^{(\boxtimes)}$, and Chunxiao Xing

BNRist, Department of Computer Science and Technology, RIIT,
Institute of Internet Industry, Tsinghua University, Beijing, China
lkx17@mails.tsinghua.edu.cn, {zhangyong05,xingcx}@tsinghua.edu.cn

Abstract. Text semantics similarity measurement is a crucial problem in many real world applications, such as text mining, information retrieval and natural language processing. It is a complicated task due to the ambiguity and variability of linguistic expression. Previous studies focus on modeling the representation of a sentence in multiple granularities and then measure the similarity based on the representations. However, above methods cannot make full use of the diverse importance of different parts in a sentence. To address this problem, in this paper we propose a neural architecture with hybrid attention mechanism to highlight the important signals in different granularities within a text. We first utilize a Bi-directional Long Short Term Memory (BiLSTM) network to encode each sentence. Then we apply the hybrid attention mechanism on top of BiLSTM network. To detect the important parts of a sentence, we adopt a self-attention component to generate sentence level representations and then measure their relevance with a neural tensor network. To better utilize the interaction information, we devise an inter-attention component to further consider the influence of one sentence on another when modeling finer granularity interactions. We evaluate our proposed method on the task of paraphrase identification using two real world datasets. Experimental results demonstrate the superiority of this framework.

Keywords: Sentene modeling · Semantic similarity · Deep neural network · Attention · Bi-directional long short term memory

1 Introduction

Text semantic similarity modeling is a fundamental problem in the field of natural language processing. It is widely applied in many real world scenarios, such as paraphrase identification [7], information retrieval [25], question answering [8] and textual entailment [23]. For instance, in the problem of paraphrase identification, given a pair of sentences, the task is to first compute their similarity in term of a score and then determine whether they are paraphrases or not by comparing to a threshold [4].

© Springer Nature Switzerland AG 2020
Y. Nah et al. (Eds.): DASFAA 2020, LNCS 12113, pp. 90–106, 2020.
https://doi.org/10.1007/978-3-030-59416-9_6

The problem of measuring text similarity is challenging due to the semantic ambiguity and variability of linguistic expression. Traditional approaches use hand-crafted features i.e. lexicon [36], syntax parsing [6] and machine translation [17] to map similar sentences together. However, such methods suffered from the problems of data sparsity, inherent errors in external NLP tools and limited amount of annotated training data. Recently deep learning based techniques have been applied in natural language processing [16,30,34,40]. There are also many studies in the problem of evaluating text semantic similarity and achieved some major successes. Compared with traditional ML approaches, deep neural networks can automatically learn patterns from implicit representations with low-dimensional vectors. Without generality, in this work we will focus on the case of sentence pair modeling, which is a typical application scenario of text semantic similarity evaluation. Existing deep learning based methods mainly follow two paradigms: sentence representation learning and local feature matching.

Table 1. An example of sentences

Label	Sentence
X	She struck a deal with Warner to publish a new album this week
Y_1	She canceled the deal with Warner to publish a new album this week
Y_2	She canceled the deal with Warner to publish a new album last week and postpone the date by one week

The first category of studies directly works on sentence representation. They first learn the representation of two sentences separately and then compute the similarity score between them based on some distance functions, such as cosine, Euclidean distance and element-wise difference. Examples include MPCNN [7],Tree-LSTM [29] and Ma-LSTM [20]. However, due to the lack of interactions, such approaches cannot capture well enough local information within a sentence. For example, given a pair of sentences X and Y_1 in Table 1, we can see that the keywords such as *canceled the deal, this week* are crucial in deciding the relatedness of two sentences. However, by directly representing a complicated sentence with a single vector, it is difficult to capture such local information [1].

Another category of studies focuses on local feature matching between sentences. They build the interaction between sentences at finer granularity, such as SIN [14], DF-LSTM [15] and PWIM [8]. Compared with the first category, these methods can achieve better results by taking different granularities of interactions between two sentences into consideration. But they just treat all words in the two sentences with equal importance. In real scenarios, different words or phrases could play different roles in deciding the semantics of a sentence. Therefore, they would fail to recognize the varied contributions different parts make to the composition of sentence. Let us look at sentence Y_2 in Table 1. Obviously, Y_2 should be a paraphrase of X and not one of Y_1. In order to distinguish the semantic between Y_1 and Y_2, the parts *last week, postpone, one week* in Y_2 should be highlighted. However, if we treat every word equally, it is very likely to ignore such important signals and identify these two sentences as paraphrase since they have many common words e.g. *canceled, deal, Warner, publish* etc.

In this paper, we propose a new deep neural network based framework which employ **Bi**directional **L**ong **T**erm **S**hort **M**emory (BiLSTM) network with **H**ybrid **A**ttention (HA-BLSTM) for sentence similarity modeling. The attention model can be described as mapping a query and a set of key-value pairs to an output, where the query, keys, values, and output are all vectors [31]. With the help of it, we can compute a representation of the sentence by assigning different weights to different positions of it to denote the varied importance. Our framework integrates two attention components upon the sentence representation and adopts effective similarity measurement techniques to evaluate the semantic similarity.

Firstly, for a single sentence, we adopt a BiLSTM network to generate its positional representation so as to capture rich contextual information. Next we propose a hybrid attention mechanism: on one hand, we incorporate a self-attention component on top of the positional representation of each sentence to distinguish the importance of different parts so as to enhance the sentence level representation. Correspondingly, the representation of a single sentence would be the output of self-attention component. On the other hand, as we need to measure the similarity between a pair of sentences, the importance of each part is decided not only by the sentence itself, but also by its partner. Thus we also devise an inter-attention component which assign a weight to each part in a sentence considering the influence from its partner. In this way, we can detect the key information from the interactions in finer granularity. After applying both attention mechanisms to model the sentence, we apply different similarity measurement methods on the representation vectors of sentences and use a vector as the output for both components. Finally, we combine the output of both self-attention and inter-attention components into a fully connected layer and obtain the similarity score between two sentences.

We argue that by taking the output of both self-attention and inter-attention components, we can capture not only the features from different granularities, but also detect the important parts within each sentence. To justify it, we conduct an extensive set of experiments on two real world datasets. Experimental results demonstrate the effectiveness of our proposed method.

The rest of this paper is organized as follows. We summarize the related work in Sect. 2. We introduce our HA-BLSTM framework in Sect. 3. We report the experimental results in Sect. 4. Finally we conclude in Sect. 5.

2   Related Work

Paraphrase Identification. Paraphrase Identification is a typical task of sentence similarity modeling. There is a large body of studies regarding text similarity in database and information retrieval [32,33,37,41,42] It has also attracted much attention from the nature language processing community. Ji et al. [11] used matrix factorization to obtain the representation of sentences and fed them into a classifier for similarity predication. Kenter et al. [12] devised a feature interaction based approach to evaluate the short text similarity. Recently many deep learning based approaches have been proposed to further improve the performance. Socher et al. [27] proposed recursive auto-encoders to model the representation of the sentence, phrase and words in a hierarchical manner. Hu et al. [10] proposed two kinds of architectures to learn the text relevance in different granularity. He et al. [7] and Yin et al. [38] designed two CNN-based models which can extract and match features in different granularities from sentences. Yin et al. [39] combined CNN and attention model to capture the informative contents within a sentence.

Attention Based Models. Attention based models have become an effective mechanism to obtain superior results in a variety of applications. Mnih et al. [19] integrated attention into RNN model for image classification. Chorowski et al. [3] applied attention in speech recognition. Attention has also been applied in many NLP applications. Hermann et al. [9] utilized attention model in the problem of question answering which help provide richer signals for the matching process. Rush et al. [24] focused the problem of text reconstruction with the help of attention weight. Parikh addressed the problem of natural language inference by assigning an attention layer for text encoding [21]. Recently Vaswani et al. [31] adopted attention models in the task of machine translation and achieved a very significant improvement.

LSTM in Sentence Similarity Modeling. The LSTM model has been widely applied in sentence modeling as it is very effective to model word sequences and learn contextual information. Tai et al. [29] and Zhou et al. [43] proposed tree-based LSTM neural network for sentence modeling. Liu et al. [15] devised a Sentence Interaction Network on the basis of LSTM and applied it in the task of question answering. Liu et al. [15] proposed DF-LSTM framework to model the strong interactions of two texts. Chen et al. [2] encoded parsing information with LSTM model for sentence modeling. Wang et al. [35] adopted two levels of BiLSTM layers to learn matching steps from multiple perspectives. Such methods mainly focused on improving the interaction mechanism between sentences and ignored detecting the important parts within a sentence. Muller et al. [20] proposed MaLSTM, a Siamese architecture for sentence pair modeling.

There exists a recent study [23] which integrated the attention model into LSTM to improve the performance of textual entailment task. As this method used one LSTM network to jointly learn the premise and hypothesis and assigned attention weight among them, it might lose the sentence level information as it does not generate a representation for each sentence.

3   Methodology

In this section, we introduce our proposed HA-BLSTM framework. The overall architecture is shown in Fig. 1. It consists of three layers: representation layer, attention layer and output layer. The representation layer takes the word embeddings as input and learns the context-aware representation with a BiLSTM network. The attention layer includes both self-attention and inter-attention components to assign weights to words within a sentence from different perspectives. For each components, it first uses BiLSTM network and attention mechanism to encode the sentence and then adopts a similarity measurement method (e.g. Neural Tensor Layer/Element-wise operations) to model the interaction of two sentences. The output layer combined the representative vectors from both components in attention layer into a fully connected layer and output the similarity score.

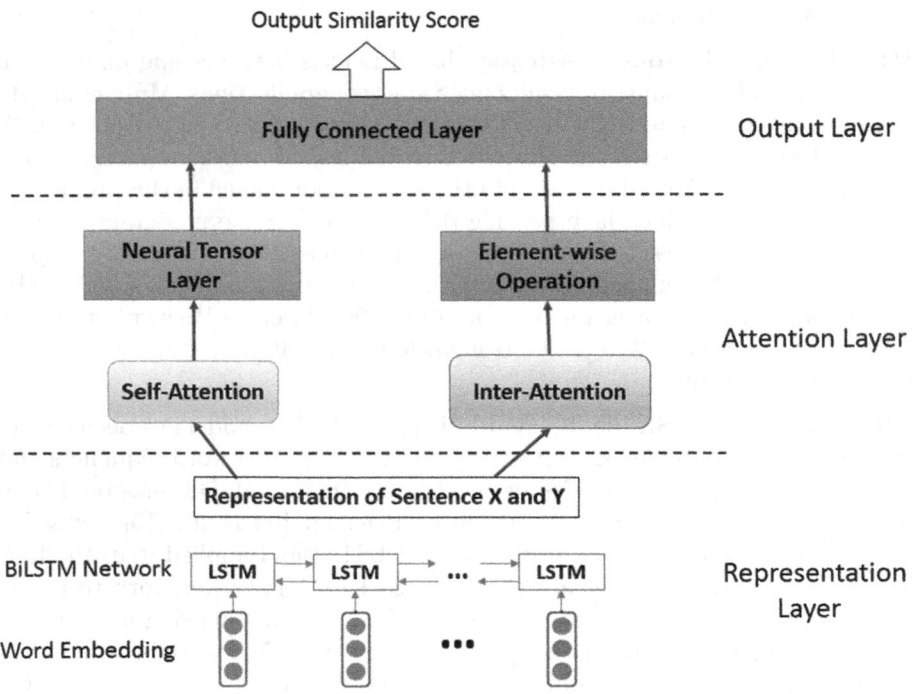

Fig. 1. The overall architecture of HA-BLSTM

3.1   Representation Layer

Given two sentences X and Y, we first obtain the embedding matrices of them with pre-trained word embedding. To reach the goal, we first apply an embedding layer that transforms the sentence into matrix representation. Specifically, we transform the sentence X into a matrix representation, denoted as $X_e \in R^{L \times m}$ as the input of the network, where L and m are the number of words in a sentence and dimension of word embedding, respectively. We obtain X_e by concatenating the embedding of words together. The way to construct X_e is rather straightforward: suppose the text consists of L words, and $\mathbf{x}_i \in R^m$ is an m-dimensional vector of the ith word in the sentence. We can get X_e by simply concatenating them:

$$X_e = \mathbf{x}_1 \oplus \mathbf{x}_2 \oplus ... \oplus \mathbf{x}_L \tag{1}$$

where for the whole dataset, L is decided by the longest sentence. We use zero padding for other shorter sentences to make the length equal.

Then we utilize the Long Term Short Memory (LSTM) network to learn the sentence representation for each sentence. It has been proved to be very powerful to learn on data with long range temporal dependencies. Given an input sequence $V = \{v_1, v_2, ...v_L\}$, LSTM computes an output vector sequence with a series of hidden states. At each time step t, an LSTM layer takes the input vector v_t, the hidden state vector h_{t-1} and a memory cell vector c_{t-1} and produces the next hidden state h_t and memory cell vector c_t. At $t = 1$, the parameters h_0 and c_0 will be initialized to zero vectors. This process is controlled by a set of gates, i.e. the input gate i_t, the forget gate f_t and the output gate o_t, as the transition function. With the help of forget gate, the model can decide the portion of information in old memory cells to be discarded. The details are shown in Eq. 2.

$$
\begin{aligned}
i_t &= \sigma(W_i h_{t-1} + V_i x_t + b_i) \\
f_t &= \sigma(W_f h_{t-1} + V_f x_t + b_f) \\
o_t &= \sigma(W_o h_{t-1} + V_o x_t + b_o) \\
g_t &= \phi(W_g h_{t-1} + V_g x_t + b_g) \\
c_t &= f_t \odot c_{t-1} + i_t \odot g_t \\
h_t &= o_t \odot \phi(c_t)
\end{aligned}
\tag{2}
$$

where all the W_j, V_j and b_j ($j \in i, f, o, g$) are the parameters to be learned during training. σ and ϕ denote the *sigmoid* and *tanh* function, respectively. And $\odot$ is the element-wise multiplication of two vectors.

We adopt Bidirectional LSTM (Bi-LSTM) for sentence modeling in this work. Compared with the single directional LSTM, Bi-LSTM utilizes both previous and future context with two LSTM networks that run on parallel in opposite direction: one forward and another backward. At the time step t, we obtain two vectors denoted as $\overrightarrow{h_t}$ and $\overleftarrow{h_t}$, respectively. Since $\overrightarrow{h_t}$ and $\overleftarrow{h_t}$ reflect the meaning of the whole sentence from two directions, we define the hidden vector at time step t denoted as $v_t \in R^{2 \times r}$ by concatenating them:

$$v_t = [\overrightarrow{h_t} \parallel \overleftarrow{h_t}] \tag{3}$$

In our framework, we feed X_e and Y_e separately into a parameter shared BiLSTM network. The outputs of BiLSTM at time step t for X_e and Y_e are v_t^X and v_t^Y respectively.

3.2 Attention Layer

Although the BiLSTM network provides rich contextual information in text representation, it cannot detect the diverse contributions that different parts make to the overall composition of the sentence. To address this issue, we adopt

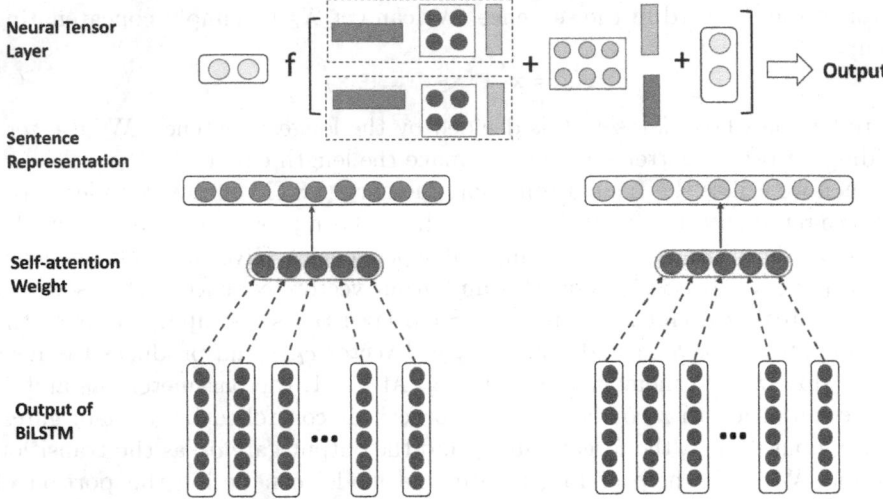

Fig. 2. The attention layer in HA-BLSTM: self-attention

an attention layer on top of representation layer to enable our model to focus on certain parts of the sentence. The attention layer consists of two components: the *self-attention* component helps find important parts within a sentence; while the *inter-attention* component focuses on representing the interactions between two sentences so as to find the relatedness between them. The input of each component is the output of BiLSTM network of the two sentences. By combining these two components, we can learn richer information for sentence interaction.

Self-attention Component. As is shown in Fig. 2, the self-attention mechanism is applied on the representation of X and Y separately. As X and Y share the parameter of attention layer, we just introduce the case of X here. Let $H_X \in R^{2L \times r}$ be a matrix of hidden vectors $[v_1^X, v_2^X, \cdots v_L^X]$ produced by the BiLSTM network. The self-attention mechanism is implemented with a feed forward neural layer and outputs a hidden representation r_X. We obtain a weighted vector α which represent the importance of each word from a non-linear transformation on the projection of positional representation H_X itself.

Details are shown in Eq. 4:

$$N = tanh(W_1 H_X)$$
$$\alpha = softmax(W_2 N) \qquad (4)$$
$$r_X = H_X \alpha^T$$

where W_1 and W_2 are projection parameters to be learned. The final sentence representation of self-attention $T_{self}^X \in R^r$ is obtained by a non-linear layer:

$$T_{self}^X = tanh(W_3 r_X) \qquad (5)$$

where W_3 is a parameter to be learned.

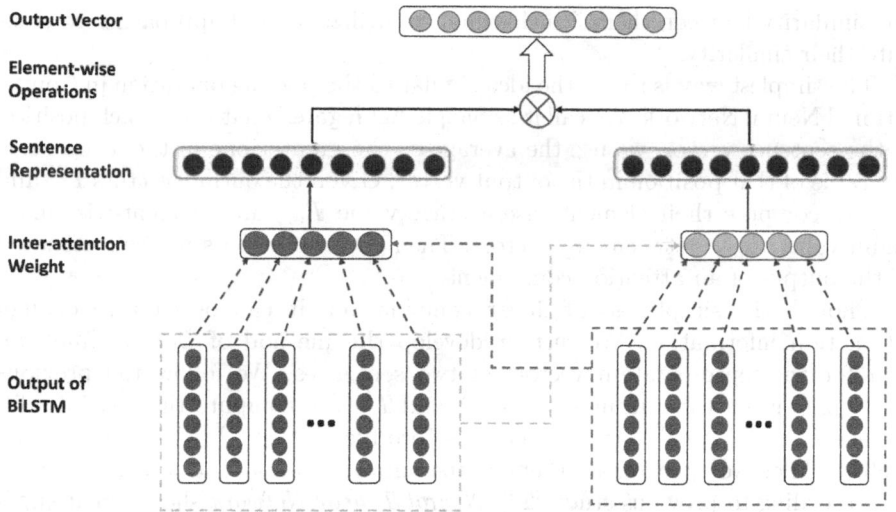

Fig. 3. The attention layer in HA-BLSTM: inter-attention

Inter-Attention Component. Though the effectiveness of self-attention mechanism, it can only detect the importance of different parts within a sentence. As we need to evaluate the degree of matching between two sentences, the importance of each part in one sentence should also be influenced by the other sentence. Inspired by this idea, we propose the inter-attention component. As is shown in Fig. 3, it assigns attention weights to each part of one sentence by considering the interaction with the other sentence. Similarly, parameters in the inter-attention component is shared by X and Y. So we only introduce the case of X as is shown in Eq. 6.

$$\hat{N} = tanh(W_4 H_Y)$$
$$\hat{\alpha} = softmax(W_5 \hat{N}) \tag{6}$$
$$\hat{r_X} = H_X \hat{\alpha}^T$$

where W_4 and W_5 are projection parameters to be learned and $\hat{r_X}$ is the hidden representation of inter-attention. Different from self-attention, the weight vector $\hat{\alpha}$ here models the interaction of H_Y on H_X. This is done by computing $\hat{\alpha}$ using H_Y instead of H_X in Eq. 8. The final text representation of inter-attention $T^X_{inter} \in R^r$ is:

$$T^X_{inter} = tanh(W_6 \hat{r_X}) \tag{7}$$

where W_6 is a parameter to be learned.

3.3 Similarity Measurement Layer

After we obtain the sentence level representation T^X_{self} and T^Y_{self} (T^X_{inter} and T^Y_{inter}) from the self-attention(inter-attention) component, we further measure the similarity between them. To this end, we utilize several approaches to compute their similarity.

The simplest way is to use the idea similar to the pooling operation in Convolutional Neural Network. We call it as Simple Aggregate. That is, for each position in the sentence vector, we use the average or the greater one of them to decide the value of that position in the output vector. Given the output vectors T^X and T^Y, we compute their element-wise average value T_{avg} and element-wise maximum value T_{max} between two vectors. Then the two vectors are concatenated as the output of an attention component.

Though the simpleness of linear combination, it cannot capture enough interaction information. We further develop the method of *Linear Combination* for the representation vectors of two sentences. We follow the previous study [29]: given the output vectors T^X and T^Y, we compute the absolute difference $T^+ = |T^X - T^Y|$ and element-wise product $T^\times = T^X \odot T^Y$ between two vectors. Then we concatenate them as the output of an attention component.

According to previous study [26], *Neural Tensor Network* shows great superiority in modeling complicated interactions between two vectors compared with traditional ways, e.g. cosine and Euclidean distance. Therefore, we put a neural tensor layer on top of the self-attention component to model the matching degree of two sentences.

The tensor layer takes the vectors $x = T_X$ and $y = T_Y$ as input and outputs a vector to represent their similarity as shown in Eq. 8:

$$v(x,y) = f(x^T M^i y + W_{xy}\begin{bmatrix} x \\ y \end{bmatrix} + b) \tag{8}$$

where $M^i, i \in [1, c]$ is one slice of tensor parameter. W_{xy} and b are parameters to be learned. f is a non-linear function. Here we use ReLU as the function because it can always speed up convergence.

In this work, we empirically design our models as following. For the self-attention component, we adopt Neural Tensor Network to measure the similarity. For the inter-attention component, we do not apply the neural tensor layer to model the interaction. Instead, we just use linear combination of the two feature vectors. The reason is that T_{inter}^X (T_{inter}^Y) has already contains interactive information from its partner. Therefore the simple element-wise operations are good enough to capture the interaction information. Details of evaluating the similarity measurement methods are shown in Sect. 4.4 later.

3.4 Output Layer

Finally, we combine the results of attention layer as a vector S and feed it into the fully connected layer:

$$S = [v(T_{self}^X, T_{self}^Y), T_{inter}^+, T_{inter}^\times] \tag{9}$$

On top of the fully connected layer, we further apply Dropout [28] to avoid overfitting. As is shown in many previous studies, the sentence pair similarity computation can be treated as a classification task. Thus we calculate a probability distribution with a hidden layer and a softmax layer:

$$\hat{p} = softmax(W_s ReLU(S) + b_s) \tag{10}$$

where W_s and b_s are parameters in the softmax layer.

4 Evaluation

4.1 Experiment Setup

To evaluate the proposed methods, we conduct experiments on the task of paraphrase identification using two datasets: PAN and SICK.

The PAN corpus[1] is collected from the PAN 2010 plagiarism detection competition. This dataset consists of text documents from Project Gutenberg with some cases of plagiarism inserted. Each sentence pair is annotated with a binary label indicating whether they are paraphrase. We use its original split: the sizes of training and test sets are 10000 and 3000, respectively. The evaluation metric used on this dataset is accuracy and F_1.

The Sentence Involving Compositional Knowledge (SICK) dataset is from SemEval 2014 competition [18]. It consists of 9927 sentence pairs with 4500 as training set, 500 as development set and 4927 as test set. Each sentence pair is annotated with a relatedness score $y \in [1,5]$. A higher score means closer relatedness of the two sentences. Following many previous studies, the evaluation metrics used for this dataset are Pearson's r, Spearman's ρ and Mean Squared Error (MSE).

In the experiments on both datasets, we use pre-trained word embedding from GloVe [22]. For out-of-box words, we will randomly initialize its embedding vector within the range of $[-0.01, 0.01]$. The hyper-parameters are as following: The dimension of word embedding is 300. The output dimension of LSTM is 64. The size of hidden layers is 50. The dropout rate is 0.5.

4.2 Training

Next we talk about the settings of training process. Here θ is the parameters to be learned. m_1 and m_2 are the cardinality of two training sets, respectively. And λ is the regularization parameter.

For experiments on PAN, it can be regarded as a binary classification problem. Then the objective is to minimize the negative log-likelihood:

$$J(\theta) = -\frac{1}{m_1} \sum_{i=1}^{m_1} \log p_\theta^{(i)}(y^{(i)} \mid x^{(i)}) + \frac{\lambda}{2} \| \theta \|_2^2 \tag{11}$$

where $x^{(i)}$ is a pair of texts and $y^{(i)}$ is the predicted label about whether the pair of texts are similar.

---

[1] http://bit.ly/mt-para.

For the SICK dataset, we use the same techniques as [29] to transform the score of relatedness into a sparse target distribution. For the learned parameters θ, the predicted distribution with model weight vector θ would be $\hat{p}_\theta$. Then the objective is to minimize the regularized KL-divergence between $\hat{p}_\theta$ and the ground truth p.

$$J(\theta) = \frac{1}{m_2} \sum_{i=1}^{m_2} KL(p^i \parallel \hat{p}_\theta{}^i) + \frac{\lambda}{2} \parallel \theta \parallel_2^2 \tag{12}$$

For both datasets, we perform optimization using Adagrad [5] algorithm with the learning rate 0.01. All the parameters are initialized from a uniform distribution.

4.3   Results and Discussion

We first compare our method with several state-of-the-art methods: one feature based method i.e. OoB, four CNN-based methods i.e. ARC-I, ARC-II, MPCNN, ABCNN, one Recursive Neural Network method i.e. RAE and two RNN-based methods i.e. MaLSTM and BiMPM. The results are shown in Table 2. For the compared methods, we obtain the source code from the authors and run them by ourselves. We can see that our HA-BLSTM achieved the best results. The OoB method is designed to measure the similarity between short texts. Although it works well for short text, it fails to capture the inherited structure within a sentence. The CNN methods encode the sentence by aggregating the neighborhood information with convolution operations. However, their performances are suboptimal compared with HA-BLSTM since we adopt attention based mechanism to recognize important parts that decide the semantic of sentence. Although ABCNN [39] also integrated attention mechanism, it did not include enough contextual and dependency information when generating the representation of sentences. BiMPM [35] is a up-to-date model that integrates self-attention into LSTM network. Compared with our method, it fails to consider the sentence

Table 2. Results on PAN dataset: accuracy and F_1

Model	Accuracy	F_1
OoB [4]	84.4	82.3
ARC-I [10]	61.4	60.3
ARC-II [10]	64.9	63.5
MPCNN [7]	91.5	91.3
ABCNN [39]	90.3	89.8
RAE [27]	89.2	88.8
MaLSTM [20]	93.6	93.5
BiMPM [35]	94.0	93.9
HA-BLSTM	**94.4**	**94.2**

level representation of each sentence. Therefore, it does not perform as well as our method.

Table 3 shows the results on SICK dataset. For the results of state-of-the-art methods, we include the methods with best results reported by [20] and [8]. We can see that our method outperforms all other deep learning based methods when measured by Pearson's r. While other LSTM-based methods in Table 3 rely on the dependency parser, our method directly learns the features from the sentences. PWIM [8] is another method that does not rely on external tools e.g POS tagging, dependency parsing. It is superior than previous deep learning based methods because it takes the word level interaction into consideration. Our HA-BLSTM beats PWIM on all metrics because we adopted inter-attention to assign weight to different parts when incorporating interactions. The recent proposed DRCN [13] does not perform well on this task. The reason might be due to overfitting. Therefore, HA-BLSTM can better capture the key information in the interactions.

Table 3. Results on SICK dataset: r, ρ and MSE

Model	r	ρ	MSE
LSTM [29]	0.8477	0.7921	0.2949
BiLSTM [29]	0.8522	0.7952	0.2850
Tree-LSTM [29]	0.8676	0.8083	0.2532
MPCNN [7]	0.8686	0.8047	0.2606
AttTree-LSTM [43]	0.8730	0.8117	0.2426
PWIM [8]	0.8784	0.8199	0.2329
MaLSTM [20]	0.8822	0.8345	0.2286
DRCN [13]	0.8796	0.8251	0.2367
HA-BLSTM	**0.8825**	0.8304	**0.2257**

4.4   Effectiveness of Proposed Techniques

In this section, we further conducted more experiments to evaluate the proposed techniques in this paper.

Table 4. Ablation test on two datasets

Ablation settings	PAN (Accuracy)	SICK (Pearson's r)
Full model	94.4	0.8825
Remove attention layer	91.6	0.8641
Remove inter-attention mechanism	92.3	0.8715
Remove self-attention mechanism	92.9	0.8749
Replace similarity measuring with direct concatenation	90.8	0.8701
Replace BiLSTM with LSTM	94.2	0.8742

We first evaluate the contribution of each component of HA-BLSTM with the ablation test on the two datasets. We identify 5 major components of our method and remove one at a time. The results of accuracy (PAN) and Pearson's r (SICK) are reported in Table 4. We can see that there is a large drop in the performance when removing the attention layer. This demonstrates the importance of our proposed hybrid attention component. By removing only self-attention or inter-attention component, there is also degradation in different degrees. We further investigate the similarity measurements for sentence representations. We did this by replacing the neural tensor layer in the self-attention component and the element-wise operations in inter-attention component with direct concatenation of two vectors. Then on both two datasets, the performance drops obviously. It shows the necessity of applying proper mechanisms for both components.

We then evaluate the different similarity measurement methods for both intra-attention and inter-attention component. Here we focus on 3 mechanisms discussion in Sect. 3.2: LC is the simplest way using element-wise average and max to construct the output vector; LC is the Linear Concatenation method that combines the result of absolute difference and element-wise product; NTN is the Neural Tensor Network model [26]. In this experiment, we apply the combination of above methods on both self and inter attention components and evaluate the results of accuracy/mean squared error, respectively. The results are shown in Table 5. From these results, we have the following observations: Firstly, we can see that applying NTN can improve the performance of interaction in most cases. This demonstrates the effectiveness of NTN as is consistence of previous studies. However, applying NTN will also significantly increase the number of parameters of the whole model. Thus here we need a trade-off when designing the model. Secondly, we can observe that generally BiI performs better than LC. And the performance gain is more obvious for self-attention than that of inter-attention. This phenomenon is reasonable since the inter-attention mechanism has enabled interaction between two sentences in a finer granularity. We can see from the results on both datasets that when we apply NTN on the self-attention component, applying BiI and NTN on the inter-attention component will not lead to better performance. Meanwhile, it will increase the complexity of model. Therefore, we construct the model by using NTN and LC as the similarity measurement for self-attention and inter-attention components, respectively.

Table 5. Effect of different interaction methods

(a) **PAN**(Accuracy)

Self \ Inter	SA	LC	NTN
SA	92.5	92.6	93.0
LC	93.2	93.2	93.1
NTN	94.2	**94.4**	**94.4**

(b) **SICK** (Pearson's r)

Self \ Inter	SA	LC	NTN
SA	0.8749	0.8773	0.8802
LC	0.8814	0.8816	0.8816
NTN	0.8824	**0.8825**	0.8824

4.5 Case Study

Next we take a pair of sentence from SICK dataset to visualize the assigned weights of the attention layer. The results of self-attention and inter-attention are shown in Fig. 4. We can see that with only self-attention, the words with top-3 attention in sentence X and Y are $\{man, cutting, paper\}$ and $\{person, not, paper\}$, respectively. Then it seems that they are not relevant due to the large attention value on "not". However, with the help of inter-attention, the weight of "not" is alleviated and the weight of "tearing" increases. Therefore, this is a more accurate representation of the sentence. The ground truth of this pair of sentence is 3.1. With only self-attention mechanism, the result of prediction is 2.545. But by adding the inter-attention mechanism, the result of prediction becomes 2.920. This is because inter-attention mechanism successfully recognizes that the word "not" itself does not make a large contribution in deciding the relatedness.

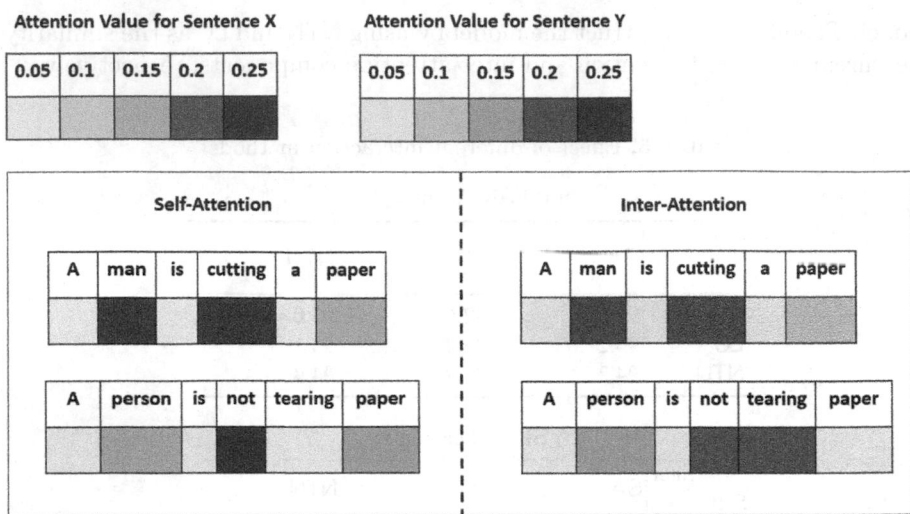

Fig. 4. Visualization of self-attention and inter-attention mechanisms

5 Conclusion

In this paper, we propose a novel LSTM based framework with hybrid attention mechanism for sentence similarity modeling. Our method utilizes a self-attention component to find the key part of a sentence so as to generate better sentence representation. Moreover, we devise an inter-attention layer to further distinguish the importance of different parts in a sentence by leveraging the information from its partner. Experimental results on the paraphrase identification task show that our proposed method outperforms state-of-the-art methods on two popular datasets. For future work, we will generalize our framework to more tasks, such as question answering, sentence completion and textual entailment. We also consider extending our framework to measure the similarity between a short query and sub-parts from documents in information retrieval related tasks.

Acknowledgments. This work was supported by NSFC(91646202), National Key R&D Program of China(2018YFB1404401,2018YFB1402701).

References

1. Bahdanau, D., Cho, K., Bengio, Y.: Neural machine translation by jointly learning to align and translate. CoRR abs/1409.0473 (2014)
2. Chen, Q., Zhu, X., Ling, Z., Wei, S., Jiang, H., Inkpen, D.: Enhanced LSTM for natural language inference. In: ACL, pp. 1657–1668 (2017)
3. Chorowski, J., Bahdanau, D., Serdyuk, D., Cho, K., Bengio, Y.: Attention-based models for speech recognition. In: NIPS, pp. 577–585 (2015)
4. Dolan, B., Quirk, C., Brockett, C.: Unsupervised construction of large paraphrase corpora: exploiting massively parallel news sources. In: COLING (2004)

5. Duchi, J.C., Hazan, E., Singer, Y.: Adaptive subgradient methods for online learning and stochastic optimization. JMLR **12**, 2121–2159 (2011)
6. Filice, S., Martino, G.D.S., Moschitti, A.: Structural representations for learning relations between pairs of texts. In: ACL, pp. 1003–1013 (2015)
7. He, H., Gimpel, K., Lin, J.J.: Multi-perspective sentence similarity modeling with convolutional neural networks. In: EMNLP, pp. 1576–1586 (2015)
8. He, H., Lin, J.J.: Pairwise word interaction modeling with deep neural networks for semantic similarity measurement. In: NAACL-HLT, pp. 937–948 (2016)
9. Hermann, K.M., et al.: Teaching machines to read and comprehend. In: NIPS, pp. 1693–1701 (2015)
10. Hu, B., Lu, Z., Li, H., Chen, Q.: Convolutional neural network architectures for matching natural language sentences. In: NIPS, pp. 2042–2050 (2014)
11. Ji, Y., Eisenstein, J.: Discriminative improvements to distributional sentence similarity. In: EMNLP, pp. 891–896 (2013)
12. Kenter, T., de Rijke, M.: Short text similarity with word embeddings. In: CIKM, pp. 1411–1420 (2015)
13. Kim, S., Kang, I., Kwak, N.: Semantic sentence matching with densely-connected recurrent and co-attentive information. In: AAAI, pp. 6586–6593 (2019)
14. Liu, B., Huang, M.: A sentence interaction network for modeling dependence between sentences. In: ACL (2016)
15. Liu, P., Qiu, X., Chen, J., Huang, X.: Deep fusion LSTMs for text semantic matching. In: ACL (2016)
16. Luo, L., et al.: Beyond polarity: interpretable financial sentiment analysis with hierarchical query-driven attention. In: IJCAI, pp. 4244–4250 (2018)
17. Madnani, N., Tetreault, J.R., Chodorow, M.: Re-examining machine translation metrics for paraphrase identification. In: NAACL, pp. 182–190 (2012)
18. Marelli, M., Bentivogli, L., Baroni, M., Bernardi, R., Menini, S., Zamparelli, R.: Semeval-2014 task 1: evaluation of compositional distributional semantic models on full sentences through semantic relatedness and textual entailment. In: SemEval@COLING, pp. 1–8 (2014)
19. Mnih, V., Heess, N., Graves, A., Kavukcuoglu, K.: Recurrent models of visual attention. In: NIPS, pp. 2204–2212 (2014)
20. Mueller, J., Thyagarajan, A.: Siamese recurrent architectures for learning sentence similarity. In: AAAI, pp. 2786–2792 (2016)
21. Parikh, A.P., Täckström, O., Das, D., Uszkoreit, J.: A decomposable attention model for natural language inference. In: EMNLP, pp. 2249–2255 (2016)
22. Pennington, J., Socher, R., Manning, C.D.: Glove: global vectors for word representation. In: EMNLP, pp. 1532–1543 (2014)
23. Rocktäschel, T., Grefenstette, E., Hermann, K.M., Kociský, T., Blunsom, P.: Reasoning about entailment with neural attention. ICLR (2016)
24. Rush, A.M., Chopra, S., Weston, J.: A neural attention model for abstractive sentence summarization. In: EMNLP, pp. 379–389 (2015)
25. Severyn, A., Moschitti, A.: Learning to rank short text pairs with convolutional deep neural networks. In: SIGIR, pp. 373–382 (2015)
26. Socher, R., Chen, D., Manning, C.D., Ng, A.Y.: Reasoning with neural tensor networks for knowledge base completion. In: NIPS, pp. 926–934 (2013)
27. Socher, R., Huang, E.H., Pennington, J., Ng, A.Y., Manning, C.D.: Dynamic pooling and unfolding recursive autoencoders for paraphrase detection. In: NIPS, pp. 801–809 (2011)

28. Srivastava, N., Hinton, G.E., Krizhevsky, A., Sutskever, I., Salakhutdinov, R.: Dropout: a simple way to prevent neural networks from overfitting. JMLR **15**(1), 1929–1958 (2014)
29. Tai, K.S., Socher, R., Manning, C.D.: Improved semantic representations from tree-structured long short-term memory networks. In: ACL, pp. 1556–1566 (2015)
30. Tian, B., Zhang, Y., Wang, J., Xing, C.: Hierarchical inter-attention network for document classification with multi-task learning. In: IJCAI, pp. 3569–3575 (2019)
31. Vaswani, A., et al.: Attention is all you need. In: NIPS, pp. 6000–6010 (2017)
32. Wang, J., Lin, C., Li, M., Zaniolo, C.: An efficient sliding window approach for approximate entity extraction with synonyms. In: EDBT, pp. 109–120 (2019)
33. Wang, J., Lin, C., Zaniolo, C.: Mf-join: Efficient fuzzy string similarity join with multi-level filtering. In: ICDE, pp. 386–397 (2019)
34. Wang, W., Zhang, W., Wang, J., Yan, J., Zha, H.: Learning sequential correlation for user generated textual content popularity prediction. In: IJCAI, pp. 1625–1631 (2018)
35. Wang, Z., Hamza, W., Florian, R.: Bilateral multi-perspective matching for natural language sentences. In: IJCAI, pp. 4144–4150 (2017)
36. Wang, Z., Mi, H., Ittycheriah, A.: Sentence similarity learning by lexical decomposition and composition. In: COLING, pp. 1340–1349 (2016)
37. Yang, J., Zhang, Y., Zhou, X., Wang, J., Hu, H., Xing, C.: A hierarchical framework for top-k location-aware error-tolerant keyword search. In: ICDE, pp. 986–997 (2019)
38. Yin, W., Schütze, H.: MultiGranCNN: an architecture for general matching of text chunks on multiple levels of granularity. In: ACL, pp. 63–73 (2015)
39. Yin, W., Schütze, H., Xiang, B., Zhou, B.: ABCNN: attention-based convolutional neural network for modeling sentence pairs. TACL **4**, 259–272 (2016)
40. Zhang, W., Yuan, Q., Han, J., Wang, J.: Collaborative multi-level embedding learning from reviews for rating prediction. In: IJCAI, pp. 2986–2992 (2016)
41. Zhang, Y., Li, X., Wang, J., Zhang, Y., Xing, C., Yuan, X.: An efficient framework for exact set similarity search using tree structure indexes. In: ICDE, pp. 759–770 (2017)
42. Zhang, Y., Wu, J., Wang, J., Xing, C.: A transformation-based framework for KNN set similarity search. IEEE Trans. Knowl. Data Eng. **32**(3), 409–423 (2020)
43. Zhou, Y., Liu, C., Pan, Y.: Modelling sentence pairs with tree-structured attentive encoder. In: COLING, pp. 2912–2922 (2016)

Instance Explainable Multi-instance Learning for ROI of Various Data

Xu Zhao, Zihao Wang, Yong Zhang$^{(\boxtimes)}$, and Chunxiao Xing

BNRist, Department of Computer Science and Technology, RIIT,
Institute of Internet Industry, Tsinghua University, Beijing 100084, China
{zhaoxu18,wzh17}@mails.tsinghua.edu.cn,
{zhangyong05,xingcx}@tsinghua.edu.cn

Abstract. Estimating the Region of Interest (ROI) for images is a classic problem in the field of computer vision. In a broader sense, the object of ROI estimation can be generalized to the bag containing multiple data instances, i.e., identify the instances that probably arouse our interest. Under the circumstance without instance labels, generalized ROI estimation problem can be addressed in the framework of Multi-Instance Learning (MIL). MIL is a variation of supervised learning where a bag containing multiple instances is assigned a single class label. Though the success in bag-level classification, when bags contain a large number of instances, existing works ignore instance-level interpretation which is the key to ROI estimation. In this paper we propose an instance explainable MIL method to solve the problem. We devise a generalized permutation-invariant operator with the idea of utility and show that the interpretation issues can be addressed by including a family of utility functions in the space of instance embedding. Following this route, we propose a novel Permutation-Invariant Operator to improve the instance-level interpretability of MIL as well as the overall performance. We also point out that existing approaches can be regarded as a special case of our framework and qualitatively analyze the superiority of our work. Furthermore we give a criterion to measure the linear separability in the instance embedding space. We conduct extensive evaluations on both classic MIL benchmarks and a real-life histopathology dataset. Experimental results show that our method achieves a significant improvement in the performance of both instance-level ROI estimation and bag-level classification compared to state-of-the-art methods.

Keywords: Region of interest · Multi-instance learning · Instance level interpretability

---

X. Zhao and Z. Wang—Contributed equally to this paper.
This work was supported by NSFC(91646202), National Key R&D Program of China(2018YFB1404401,2018YFB1402701).

1   Introduction

Estimating the Region of Interest(ROI) [2,3] for images is a classic problem in the field of computer vision. In a broader sense, the object of ROI estimation can be generalized to the bag containing any objects that can be embedded, i.e., identify the instances that probably arouse our interest, but not only for images. For example, tissue images consisting of patches of cells for cancer diagnosis can be considered as bags to be classified. The annotated malignant cells by pathologists are essential evidence for the diagnose results. In this case, an ROI algorithm is expected to show whether each cell, i.e., each instance, is malignant or not. Another example is online shopping. Given a large scale collection of commodities, users need an algorithm to preliminary screen out the products that probably arouse their interest. In order to identify the instances we are interested in, it's crucial to find a supportive explanation at the instance level, which has both legal[1] and practical significance.

Concretely given a bag containing multiple data instances, the goal is to identify the instances we are probably interested in, i.e., each instance will be given a label indicating whether we are interested in it. Except for the instance-level label, a bag-level label will also be used to indicate whether any positive instances(instances we are interested in) belong to the bag. The bag-level classifying task is known as Multi-Instance learning (MIL) [5], a variation of supervised learning where a single class label is assigned to a bag of instances. It is good at dealing with weakly annotated data where only the ground-truth for bag is given while the instance label is not accessible. Since there is no assumption about the order of instances, the bag classifiers are required to be *permutation-invariant* to the instances in MIL.

The main goal of MIL is to learn a model to predict the labels for bags. Traditional studies addressed the task of bag-level classification with feature based methods, such as Support Vector Machine [1,8] and similarity estimation [4]. Recently, deep neural networks have shown superior performance in many areas such as document classification [17,20], information extraction [26], because they can automatically extract features and support end-to-end training. Deep learning can also bring improvement to MIL [14]. The neural network-based MIL framework consists of three components [9,21]: Instance Encoder, Permutation-Invariant Operator (PIO) and Bag Classifier. Details are shown in Fig. 1.

Apparently, instance-level interpretation is crucial to ROI estimation. However previous MIL approaches are rather lacking in instance interpretability. As Recently the Attention-based (ATT) PIO [9] approach steps further towards instance-level explanation by parameterizing the PIO using neural network and attention mechanism. Specifically, it constructs the bag representation with weighted averaging of instance representations learned from attention mechanism. Intuitively, the attention weights also provide evidence to explain the instance-level results. However, ATT ignores explanation at the instance-level.

---

[1] According to the European Union General Data Protection Regulation (since 2018), a user should have the right to obtain an explanation of the decision reached.

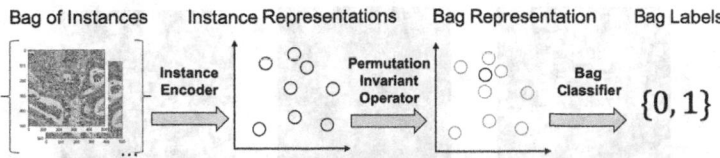

Fig. 1. Bird-view of MIL and deep neural network, from left to right: (1) Instance Encoder: It is designed task-specifically and can extract the features of each instance to generate instance representation. (2) Permutation-Invariant Operator (PIO): It aggregates the instance features (gray circle) to generate the bag representation (black circle); (3) Bag Classifier: It predicts bag label with bag representation

We observe that ATT generates highly skewed importance scores and only regards very few instances as positive. The performance deteriorates seriously when the bag contains a large number of instances. Figure 2(b) displays the example in a real-world colon cancer image task [16]. We can see that the attention-based approach ATT [9] misses many positive instances in the ground truth shown in Fig. 2(a). To get enough instance-level interpretation of MIL, we face the following three challenges:

- How to quantify the representation of instance-level interpretation?
- How to capture the nonlinear factor int instance embedding space?
- How to analyze the effectiveness of a method in the excavation of instance-level interpretation?

In this paper, we try to gain more understanding in the instance level of MIL by applying *utility functions*. Following this route, we propose the Multi-Utility (MU) Permutation-Invariant Operator that ensembles multiple utility functions as a solution for more reliable instance explanation as well as bag classification. Moreover, the previous approach ATT can be regarded as a special case that employs single utility function which is linear to instance representations. Compared with previous approaches, our approach is able to capture the implicit non-linearity of dataset and thus can produce high-quality importance weights that identify more positive instances.

To answer why previous attention-based methods don't provide good instance explanation, we employ an auxiliary linear discriminator on instance embedding space to give a criterion of linear separability in instance embedding space. We have shown that the linear separability of positive and negative instances are closely related to the instance explanation performance of previous attention-based methods. Based on this point of view, our proposed MU captures the non-linearity in the instance embedding space and generate high-quality representations for bags.

To sum up, our contributions are concluded as follows:

- We enhance MIL with instance interpretability to solve the ROI estimation problem of various data.

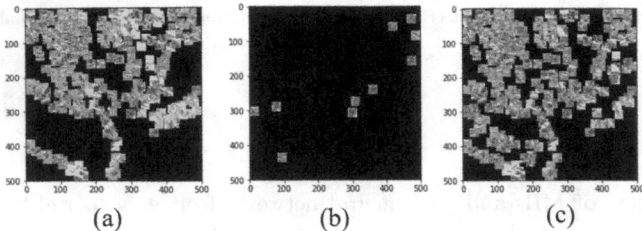

(a)   (b)   (c)

Fig. 2. Attention-based MIL [9] with correct bag-level prediction cannot offer reliable instance-level explanation with acceptable recall. *(a)*: the ground truth of the positive instances. *(b)*: instance-level prediction by attention-based MIL ($p = 0.80$, $r = 0.03$, $f = 0.06$). *(c)*: instance-level prediction by our multi-utility MIL ($p = 0.81$, $r = 0.84$, $f = 0.83$)

- We propose a brand new method MU PIO to capture the nonlinear factor in instance embedding space by multiple utility functions.
- We propose an auxiliary linear discriminator as a criterion of the linear separability for the instance embedding space.

The remaining of this paper is structured as follows. Section 2 lists the related works of this paper. Section 3 introduces the preliminary knowledge of the MIL. Section 4 describes our proposed methodology. Section 5 presents the experiment results. Section 6 gives analysis based on the experiment results. Section 7 concludes the paper.

2   Related Work

In this section we list related work of two fields. Firstly we introduce some traditional Permutation-Invariant Operators for MIL. Secondly we discuss the applications of attention in the field of MIL.

Permutation-Invariant Operators for Multi-instance Learning. Previous work have always employed the parameter-free `mean` pooling, `max` pooling or `log-sum-exp` pooling as the permutation-invariant operator [6,21]. While it is guaranteed that PIOs like `mean` pooling [24] and `max` pooling [13] are universally approximated, they fail to explain the MIL instances sufficiently. [11] introduces `Noisy-AND` with two global parameters. Those operators have little flexibility to adjust to the complexity of data.

Attention and Multi-instance Learning. The *attention* [18] mechanism is widely used in different fields for its great interpretability and flexibility. It has been adapted to PIO in many MIL applications: relation extraction [22], pixel/fine-grained object labeling [12] and image classification [13]. According to the scores assigned to each instance, it seems much easier to give some instance-level interpretation. However the score distribution generated by attention always gets into the trouble of skewness, and attention-based PIO does not always guarantee better performance than traditional PIOs such as MAX pooling [13].

3 Preliminary

In this section we introduce some preliminary knowledge, which is the basis of the paper. Firstly the formal definition of Multi-Instance (MIL) Learning is presented as follows.

Definition 1. *Let $\mathcal{X}$ denotes the instance space and $\Omega = \{0,1\}$ denotes the binary label set. Given a dataset $\bigcup_{i=1}^{m}\{(X_i, Y_i)\}$, where $X_i = \bigcup_{j=1}^{n_i}\{x_{ij}\} \subseteq \mathcal{X}(i = 1,\dots,m)$ is a set of instances called a bag and $Y_i \in \Omega$ is the bag class label, here $x_{ij} \in \mathcal{X}(j \in \{1,\dots,n_i\})$ is an instance and n_i denotes the number of instances in X_i, the goal is to learn a function $S : \mathbb{N}^{\mathcal{X}} \mapsto \Omega$ to predict the label for an unseen bag, where $\mathbb{N}^{\mathcal{X}}$ is the collection of all multiple discrete subsets of $\mathcal{X}$ [7]. We call this task **Multi-Instance Learning**.*

As an extension to Definition 1, we present the definition of instance-level hidden label which could be regarded as instance-level interpretation hidden in MIL framework.

Definition 2. *As defined in Definition 1, $x_{ij} \in \mathcal{X}(j \in \{1,\dots,n_i\})$ denotes an instance. For every instance x_{ij}, we define $y_{ij} \in \{0,1\}$ as the **hidden label** to indicate whether it triggers the positive bag label Y_i, i.e., the bag label Y_i is positive if and only if there exists at least one positive instance label: $Y_i = \max_{j=1,\dots,n_i} y_{ij}$.*

Moreover, MIL assumes that there is no dependency or order among the instances. Thus the target function $S : \mathbb{N}^{\mathcal{X}} \to \Omega$ described in Definition 1 need to possess the permutation invariant property whose definition is as follows.

Property 1. A function $f : \mathbb{N}^{\mathcal{X}} \mapsto \Omega$ acting on sets must be **permutation invariant** to the order of objects in the set, i.e., for any permutation π: $f(\{x_1,\dots,x_I\}) = f(\{x_{\pi(1)},\dots,x_{\pi(I)}\})$

MIL models the bag label Y as a Bernoulli distribution with parameter $S(X)$ of the bag X. For convenience, in the remaining of the paper, we use i as the iterator for instances in X. It has been proved in the previous work [24] that any permutation-invariant function has the following decomposition:

$$S(X) = g\left(\sum_i f(x_i)\right) \tag{1}$$

for suitable transformations f and g. It is shown in another previous work [13] that the decomposition in Inequation (2) holds for arbitrary $\epsilon > 0$ and suitable transformations f and g.

$$\|S(X) - g(\max_i f(x_i))\| < \epsilon \tag{2}$$

Such conclusions about the universal approximation suggest that any permutation-invariant function can be constructed with three consecutive components: (a) instance-level function f, (b) permutation-invariant operator (PIO), eg the sum operator in Eq. (1) and the max operator in Inequation (2), (c) bag-level function g. The neural network-based MIL is designed following this idea [9] and its three components are detailed as follows:

(a) An instance encoding network $f : \mathcal{X} \mapsto \mathbb{R}^n$ to obtain the instance embedding $z_i = f(x_i)$.
(b) The PIO T between f and g to link the bag and its instances, which are differentiable to enable gradient descent. The input of PIO T is a bag of instance representation $\{z_i, ..., z_I\}$ (I is the instance number) and the output is the bag representation $\bar{z}$.
(c) A bag classification network: $g : \mathbb{R}^n \mapsto \{0, 1\}$ to make prediction of bag label $\hat{Y}$.
In this framework, PIO is the only part that provides instance-level explanation. It connects the bag and instance representations by $\bar{z} = T(z_1, ..., z_I)$.

We only focus on the form of PIO, (a) and (c) are not in our scope. We are interested in the form of weighted average $\bar{z} = \sum_i^I \alpha_i z_i$ where the weights α_i are interpreted as the importance of instances. The key issue here is how to calculates the importance weights $\{\alpha_i, i = 1, ..., I\}$. Next we will provide the details of our interpretable PIO.

4   Methodology

In this section, we describe the ATT as of *Single Utility PIO* and then introduce our proposed MU as *Multiple Utility PIO*. Then we optimize the training process by randomly dropout of utility functions. Finally, we introduce the linear discriminator loss as a useful metric to detect when the single utility PIO fails to capture the non-linearity in the data.

4.1   Attention-Based PIO as Single-Utility PIO

In this section, we describe the proposed PIOs by introducing a generalized framework. We argue that previous attention-based MIL approaches [9,12] can be expressed with a particular *utility function*. The utility function $\mathcal{U}$ is defined by inner-product in the instance embedding space $\mathcal{H}$:

$$\mathcal{U}(\xi_i) = \mathbf{w}^T \xi, \tag{3}$$

where $\xi = \phi(z_i) \in \mathcal{H}$ is the instance embedding and ϕ is a transform. ϕ takes all the non-linear parts from z_i to $u_i = \mathcal{U}(\phi(z_i))$ and $\mathcal{U}$ parameterized by $\mathbf{w}$ is a linear function defined on $\mathcal{H}$. The vector $\mathbf{w}$ provides a preferred "direction" in the instance space. Specifically, instances in that direction get higher utility values and are more important when predicting the bag label. For example,

ATT [9] applied a neural network ϕ that transforms the instance representation z_i to the instance embedding ξ_i in Eq. (4).

$$\xi_i = \phi(z_i) = \tanh(\mathbf{V}^T z_i) \in \mathcal{H}. \tag{4}$$

Given utility u_i for the i-th instance, the importance score α_i can be calculated by softmax in Eq. (5):

$$\alpha_i = \texttt{softmax}(u_i) = \exp(u_i)/Z \tag{5}$$

where $Z = \sum_{j=1}^{I} \exp(u_j)$ is the partition function.

We can see that the importance scores α_i by ATT are generated based on one utility function $\mathcal{U}$, which selects *only one* preferred direction in $\mathcal{H}$. Therefore, the attention mechanism ATT can be abstracted as single utility function imposed on the bag of instances. When applied to MIL, the attention weights could be further interpreted as the importance scores $\alpha_i > 0$ of corresponding instances ($\sum_i \alpha_i = 1$). Such an interpretation of MIL requires that the attention weight for each instance is a scalar. More complicated attention models such as multi-head attention [18] cannot be directly applied to MIL since their output for each instance is a vector. What is worse, since the utility function is linear, the performance of such single-utility approaches will be deteriorated when the data distribution is nonlinear.

4.2 Multi-utility PIO

To capture the non-linearity in $\mathcal{H}$, we further need to fuse multiple utility functions together. To this end, we step from single-utility PIO (i.e. ATT) to *multi-utility PIO*. Given K different utility functions $\mathcal{U}_k, k \in \{1, ..., K\}$, we obtain K utilities $u_i^{(k)} = \mathcal{U}_k(\phi(z_i))$ for i-th instance. Our goal is to properly generate the importance weights α_i from $u_i^{(k)}$. Since softmax operation is not applied to set of vectors, we need to provide a generalized format for the multiple utility framework.

One straightforward solution to reach this goal is to directly average multi-head attention weights [18]. In this approach, the importance weights are calculated by Eq. (6).

$$\alpha_i = \sum_{k=1}^{K} \beta_i^{(k)}/K \tag{6}$$

This baseline is named as MHATT.

Another alternative method is named by DATT, which replaces one-layer representation PIO with two-layer one by the following equation:

$$\alpha_i = \texttt{softmax}(\sum_{k}^{K} x_k \beta_i^{(k)}). \tag{7}$$

DATT employs an additional fully-connected layer along with softmax to merge re-scaled scores from multiple utility functions.

Next we introduce our generalized framework MU for this problem. Considering the multiple utility functions independently, we have independent importance scores $\beta_i^{(k)} = \mathtt{softmax}(u_i^{(k)})$ given the value of k. We define the importance score α_i based on multiple utility functions as the solution of following linear equation system:

$$\sum_{i=1}^{I} \alpha_i \mathbf{u}_i = \mathbf{t}, \quad s.t. \sum_{i-1}^{I} \alpha_i = 1, \quad \alpha_i \geq 0, i = 1, ..., I \tag{8}$$

where the *utility vector* $\mathbf{u}_i = [u_i^{(1)}, ..., u_i^{(K)}]$ contains K utilities for i-th instance. And the *target vector* $\mathbf{t} = [\sum_i u_i^{(1)} \beta_i^{(1)}, ..., \sum_i u_i^{(K)} \beta_i^{(K)}]$ combines all results of different utility functions together[2]. Each dimension of $\mathbf{t}$ is the weighted average of the utility values based on the corresponding importance score $\beta_i^{(k)}$. It is observed that when $K = 1$, $\alpha_i = \beta_i^{(1)}$, $\mathtt{softmax}$ in Eq. (5) is the unique solution of Eq. (8) for all $I \in \mathbb{N}$.

However, when $K > 1$, there might be no solution when $\mathbf{t}$ locates out of the convex hull of $\{\mathbf{u}_i\}_{i=1}^{I}$. To relax the problem, we use the inner product of the target vector and normalized utility vector to approximate the importance score. Similar idea could be found in dynamic routing mechanism of the capsule network [15]. Hence, given the utilities of i-th instance $\mathbf{u}_i = [u_i^{(1)}, ..., u_i^{(K)}]$, the importance scores are calculated by Eq. (9).

$$\alpha_i = \mathtt{softmax}\left(\langle \mathbf{t}, \frac{\mathbf{u}_i}{\|\mathbf{u}_i\|}\rangle\right). \tag{9}$$

In the experimental part, we will compare MHATT and DATT with our approach MU in benchmark datasets and a real-life dataset. MHATT and MU are different because merge calculation mechanism is either average or $\mathtt{softmax}$.

Utility Dropout. To optimize the training process of MU PIO, we enforce every utility function taking effect by randomly dropout at the utility function level. We assign K i.i.d Bernoulli random variables $\{\eta_k\}_{k=1}^{K}$ of probability p (in our case 0.5) for K different utility functions $\{\mathcal{U}_k\}_{k=1}^{K}$ respectively. We define the utility dropout random matrix as Eq. (10)

$$D = \mathtt{diag}(\eta_1, ..., \eta_K). \tag{10}$$

This matrix D takes $\{\eta_k\}_{k=1}^{K}$ as the diagonal. To apply the dropout, we need to apply this matrix to target vector $\mathbf{t}$. And the importance scores in the training process are finally computed by applying $\mathtt{softmax}$ on $\langle D\mathbf{t}, \frac{\mathbf{u}_i}{\|\mathbf{u}_i\|}\rangle$. The backpropagation will only update the utility whose value of η_k is 1, thus force every utility function taking effect independently.

---

[2] Actually Eq. 6 is a special case when $\mathbf{t}$ is an all-one vector.

Algorithm 1. Training Process of MIL with MU **PIO**

Input: training set $\mathcal{D} = \bigcup_i^m \{(X_i(I \times d), Y_i(bool))\}$
Parameters: $V(d \times n), T(n \times K), \mathbf{v}(n \times 1)$

1: Initialize $V, T, \mathbf{v}$
2: **for** each $e \in [1, \ldots, E]$ **do**
3:    Draw $\mathcal{D}_b$ with size b from $\mathcal{D}$
4:    $G_V, G_T, G_\mathbf{w} = 0, 0, 0$
5:    **for** each $(X_i, Y_i) \in \mathcal{D}_b$ **do**
6:       $Z = \tanh(X_i V)$
7:       $U = ZT$
8:       $B_{ij} = \exp(U_{ij}) / \sum_p \exp(U_{ip})$
9:       $\mathbf{t} = (B \odot U)^T \mathbb{1}_I$
10:       Normalize U by row and obtain U'
11:       Generate Bernoulli random variables $\{\eta_k\}_{k=1}^K$
12:       $D = \texttt{diag}(\eta_1, \ldots, \eta_K)$
13:       $\mathbf{a} = \texttt{softmax}(U'D\mathbf{t})$
14:       Re-scale $\mathbf{a}$ to $[0, 1]$
15:       $\bar{\mathbf{z}} = Z^T \mathbf{a}$
16:       $\bar{Y}_i = \texttt{logistic}(\mathbf{v}^T \bar{\mathbf{z}})$
17:       $\mathcal{L} = -Y_i \log \bar{Y}_i - (1 - Y_i) \log (1 - \bar{Y}_i)$
18:       $G_V = G_V + \nabla_V \mathcal{L}$
19:       $G_T = G_T + \nabla_T \mathcal{L}$
20:       $G_\mathbf{v} = G_\mathbf{v} + \nabla_\mathbf{v} \mathcal{L}$
21:    **end for**
22:    Update $V, T, \mathbf{v}$ by AdamGrad
23: **end for**

Output: $V, T, \mathbf{v}$

The training process of MIL with MU **PIO** is summarized in Algorithm 1. Given a training date set, the goal is to optimize three parameters: two matrices $V(d \times n), T(n \times K)$ and one vector $\mathbf{v}(n \times 1)$. We use Adam Gradient Descent(AdamGrad) as optimization method. Thus Lines 3–4 describe the sampling process in each epoch. Lines 6–16 are the forward procedure. In line 6, instance representations are mapped to instance embedding space $\mathbb{R}^n$. Lines 7–8 generate multi-head attention weights $B(I \times K)$ by multiple utilities stored in T. In lines 9–13, we compute the approximate solution of Eq. (8) and apply the utility dropout mechanism. The vector $\mathbf{a} = \{\alpha_1, \ldots, \alpha_I\}^T$ stores the instance important weights and is the key for instance interpretability. In lines 14–15, we compute the bag representation $\bar{\mathbf{z}}$ and use the logistic function to estimate the probability that bag X_i contains positive instances. Lines 16-21 describe the formulation of loss function and the procedure of AdamGrad.

4.3 Discriminator over Instance Embedding Space

Finally we make a qualitative analysis of the superiority of our approach. We argue that the limited linear separability in $\mathcal{H}$ leads to inadequate instance explanation in single utility PIO (ATT). To demonstrate this, we provide an approach to measure the linear separability experimentally for ATT. In the instance embedding space $\mathcal{H}$, positive instances are expected to have higher utilities. For single utility PIO (ATT), higher utility means that the instance embedding should have a large projection on some certain direction (see Eq. (3)). To evaluate the linear separability in the instance embedding space $\mathcal{H}$, we train a logistic discriminator $\mathcal{D}$ with cross-entropy loss which is generally used as the metric between distributions:

$$L = -\frac{1}{I} \sum_i \left[y_i \log(\mathcal{D}(\xi_i)) + (1 - y_i) \log(1 - \mathcal{D}(\xi_i)) \right]. \tag{11}$$

Note that the instance label is used only in Eq. (11) and the weights in the discriminator are different from **w** in the utility function in Eq. (3). This discriminator quantifies the non-linearity of the data distribution, i.e., how well the instances could be linearly separated, in instance embedding space $\mathcal{H}$. It is easy to see that theoretically, the smaller loss would lead to better instance explanation performance. It is shown that when this loss is large, ATT generates poorly instance explanation and our MU model has significant advantage. To sum up, our approach works exactly when the data has strong implicit non-linearity and cannot be well linearly separated.

5   Experiments

In this section, we systematically evaluate the performance in both bag-level and instance-level. Firstly, we look at bag-level performance. We demonstrate how MU outperforms other classic and deep MIL methods on five benchmark datasets: MUSK1, MUSK2, Fox, Tiger, Elephant, which are first used in [1]. Secondly, we investigate what happens when employing more utility functions. Since the only difference between ATT and MU is the number of utility functions, we compare ATT with MU at both bag level and instance level on the MNIST-bags dataset. MNIST-bags is a controllable artificial MIL dataset generated from MNIST with balanced positive/negative instances [9]. We change the condition of the MNIST-bags dataset to discuss the effectiveness of multiple utility functions. Finally, we further show the advantage of MU on Colon Cancer dataset, which is a human-annotated histopathology dataset [16] in a real-world scenario. We open the source code on github[3].

5.1   Experiment Setup

For all experiments, we follow the original split of training and test sets and perform 5-fold cross-validation. All reported results are averaged from 5 evaluations. Some standard deviation is not reported due to the limited space and the bold value indicates the most significant model. The evaluation metrics are **P**recision, **R**ecall, **A**ccuracy, AUC and F_1 score.

We want to make further clarification about why not report the instance-level AUC for the following reasons. For the five MIL benchmark datasets, the state-of-the-art methods do not support reporting AUC. For the MINST-bags and Colon Cancer datasets, the reasons are explained as following. Note that the importance weights α_i are re-scaled into $\bar{\alpha}_i \in [0, 1]$ as follows:

$$\bar{\alpha}_i = \frac{\alpha_i - \min_k \alpha_k}{\max_k \alpha_k - \min_k \alpha_k} \tag{12}$$

When the bag label is positive, the instance with higher re-scaled importance score $\bar{\alpha}_i$ should be assigned an instance label $y_i = 1$. In practice, the classification

---

[3] https://github.com/thu-west/MU-MIL.

Table 1. Accuracy results on classic MIL datasets. ±: a standard error of a mean. Bold values indicate the best performance, and the underlined values indicate the best performance over previous approaches

Model	MUSK1	MUSK2	Fox	Tiger	Elephant
mi-SVM	0.874	0.836	0.582	0.784	0.822
MI-SVM	0.779	0.843	0.578	0.840	0.843
MI-Kernel	0.880 ± 0.031	0.893 ± 0.015	0.603 ± 0.028	0.842 ± 0.010	0.843 ± 0.016
EM-DD	0.849 ± 0.044	0.869 ± 0.048	0.609 ± 0.730	0.730 ± 0.043	0.771 ± 0.016
mi-Graph	0.889 ± 0.033	$\underline{0.903 \pm 0.039}$	0.620 ± 0.044	$\underline{0.860 \pm 0.037}$	$\underline{0.869 \pm 0.035}$
miVLAD	0.871 ± 0.043	0.872 ± 0.042	0.620 ± 0.044	0.811 ± 0.039	0.850 ± 0.036
miFV	$\underline{0.909 \pm 0.040}$	0.884 ± 0.042	0.621 ± 0.049	0.813 ± 0.037	0.852 ± 0.036
mi-Net	0.889 ± 0.039	0.858 ± 0.049	0.613 ± 0.035	0.824 ± 0.034	0.858 ± 0.037
MI-Net	0.887 ± 0.041	0.858 ± 0.049	0.622 ± 0.038	0.830 ± 0.032	0.862 ± 0.034
MI-Net+DS	0.894 ± 0.042	0.874 ± 0.043	$\underline{0.630 \pm 0.037}$	0.845 ± 0.039	0.872 ± 0.032
MI-Net+RC	0.898 ± 0.043	0.873 ± 0.044	0.619 ± 0.047	0.836 ± 0.037	0.857 ± 0.040
ATT	0.892 ± 0.040	0.858 ± 0.048	0.615 ± 0.043	0.839 ± 0.022	0.868 ± 0.022
GATT	0.900 ± 0.050	0.863 ± 0.042	0.603 ± 0.029	0.845 ± 0.018	0.857 ± 0.027
MHATT	0.889 ± 0.022	0.900 ± 0.043	0.627 ± 0.015	0.831 ± 0.021	0.830 ± 0.050
DATT	0.926 ± 0.011	0.883 ± 0.024	0.627 ± 0.061	0.834 ± 0.042	0.775 ± 0.027
MU w.o. utility dropout	0.889 ± 0.064	0.844 ± 0.120	0.559 ± 0.044	0.847 ± 0.017	0.813 ± 0.076
MU	$\mathbf{0.941 \pm 0.055}$	$\mathbf{0.913 \pm 0.065}$	$\mathbf{0.646 \pm 0.025}$	$\mathbf{0.867 \pm 0.025}$	$\mathbf{0.879 \pm 0.036}$

is based on a tunable threshold thr. If $\bar{\alpha}_i > thr$, then $y_i = 1$; Otherwise $y_i = 0$. Since we cannot access the instance label, the threshold in our study is set as 0.5 without prior distribution knowledge of $\bar{\alpha}_i$. In this case, AUC score has little practical significance.

Hyper-Parameter Setting. For all experiments, we adopt the Adam optimizer [10] in the training process with parameters $\beta_1 = 0.9, \beta_2 = 0.999$. The weight decay is 0.0005. We conduct grid search to select the best hyperparameters as following: The learning rate is selected from $[0.01, \mathbf{0.001}, 0.0001]$ and the number of utility functions is selected from $[2, \mathbf{5}, 10, 15]$, where the bold values are the ones that are applied in most experiments. We train each model for 100 epoches and take the early-stop criteria as the lowest validation error and loss.

5.2 Results on Classic MIL Benchmarks

The detailed description of the 5 classic MIL benchmarks is as following. Musk1 and Musk2 are traditional drug-activity datasets. A molecule holds the desired effect iff it contains a targeted conformation bind. As for the MIL, the bag is a molecule to be classified. Each instance is a conformation bind described by the pre-computed features. Fox, Tiger, and Elephant are three image classification datasets. The positive image is labeled iff it contains the targeted animal (fox, tiger or elephant). For MIL formulation, each bag is an image containing a set of image segments of animals. Moreover, pre-computed features are extracted for each instance (image segments). We focus on the accuracy of bag classification task.

Table 2. Bag classification and instance explanation performance on MNIST-bags. Since we focus on the differences of single utility function and multiple utility functions under varying dataset conditions, we restrict our comparison within ATT and MU.

size	# train	model	dloss	Skewness	Bag Classification					Instance Explanation		
					AUC	P	R	F1	A	P	R	F1
10	10	ATT	0.461	0.863	0.625	0.582	**0.734**	**0.645**	0.595	0.091	0.318	0.141
		MU	0.332	0.245	**0.701**	**0.651**	0.646	0.642	**0.651**	**0.192**	**0.850**	**0.310**
	50	ATT	0.267		0.831	0.757	**0.790**	0.773	0.768	**0.616**	0.617	0.615
		MU	0.222		**0.845**	**0.808**	0.751	**0.777**	**0.785**	0.477	**0.878**	**0.595**
	100	ATT	0.239		0.917	0.862	0.846	0.853	0.854	**0.814**	0.700	0.752
		MU	0.153		**0.937**	**0.893**	**0.860**	**0.875**	**0.877**	0.672	**0.914**	**0.767**
50	10	ATT	0.474		0.710	0.699	0.536	0.596	0.645	0.132	0.492	0.207
		MU	0.273		**0.772**	**0.710**	**0.675**	**0.690**	**0.694**	**0.173**	**0.832**	**0.286**
	50	ATT	0.188		0.957	0.890	0.901	0.893	0.894	**0.884**	0.237	0.373
		MU	0.152		**0.972**	**0.962**	**0.919**	**0.940**	**0.941**	0.776	**0.750**	**0.759**
	100	ATT	0.147		0.989	0.984	0.953	0.968	0.969	**0.986**	0.262	0.413
		MU	0.073		**0.993**	**0.997**	**0.973**	**0.985**	**0.985**	0.920	**0.801**	**0.850**
100	10	ATT	0.494		0.763	0.737	0.549	0.627	0.678	0.119	0.234	0.149
		MU	0.244		**0.880**	**0.789**	**0.815**	**0.797**	**0.796**	**0.226**	**0.769**	**0.333**
	50	ATT	0.182		0.998	0.990	0.983	0.986	0.986	**0.990**	0.155	0.269
		MU	0.089		**0.999**	**0.998**	**0.995**	**0.996**	**0.996**	0.934	**0.784**	**0.852**
	100	ATT	0.180		0.998	0.997	0.985	0.991	0.991	**0.995**	0.160	0.276
		MU	0.082		**0.999**	**0.999**	**0.998**	**0.999**	**0.999**	0.979	**0.807**	**0.885**

We compared our method with many successful classic MIL methods: mi-SVM and MI-SVM [1], MI-Kernel [8], EM-DD [25], mi-Graph [27], miVLAD and miFV [23]. We also include multi-instance neural network models mi-Net, MI-Net, MI-Net+DS, and MI-Net+RC [21] as well as the latest attention-based approach ATT and GATT (ATT with gates) [9] as well as another method MHATT with multi-head attention [18] introduced before. Besides, we include two straightforward baselines MHATT and ATT introduced before, as well as MU without utility dropout. We use the default settings of the baseline methods. Experiment results are displayed in Table 1.

5.3 Results on MNIST-bags Dataset: Single or Multiple Utility Functions Under Varying Conditions

For the instance-level task, we focus on the reliability of the interpretation with the threshold 0.5. The number of test samples is 500. For each case, we evaluate the trained model at both bag level and instance level. For bag-level task, we focus on the complete performance of the classifier. We report the precision, recall, F1, accuracy (with threshold 0.5) and ROC-AUC scores. For the baseline methods, we use the default settings of [9].

We report the AUC, Precision, Recall and F1 scores of the interpreted positive instances. For each case, we record the discriminator loss in column "dloss". In practice, we choose label '9' as a targeted class. The training and test sets are

Table 3. Bag classification instance explanation for colon cancer. Skewness of a distribution is $|\mathbb{E}(x-\mu)^3|/\sigma^{3/2}$, where μ and σ are the mean and variance. Larger skewness indicates more skewed distribution.

Method	AUC	P (bag)	R (bag)	F_1 (bag)	Acc (bag)	P (ins)	R (ins)	F_1 (ins)	Skewness	dloss
Max	0.918	0.884	0.753	0.813	0.824	–	–	–	–	–
Mean	0.940	0.911	0.804	0.853	0.860	–	–	–	–	–
ATT	0.968	0.953	0.855	0.901	0.904	**0.663**	0.036	0.064	4.039	0.602
GATT	0.968	0.944	0.851	0.893	0.898	0.633	0.124	0.206	2.571	0.570
MHATT	0.959	0.936	0.906	0.920	0.917	0.659	0.120	0.204	2.560	0.615
DATT	**0.982**	**0.989**	0.896	0.939	0.938	0.000	0.000	0.000	0.000	0.676
MU	0.979	0.984	**0.938**	**0.960**	**0.958**	0.644	**0.225**	**0.333**	0.370	**0.557**

sampled from the original MNIST training/test split respectively. The sampling process is parametrized to generate MIL data of varying conditions. First, The bag size is controlled by a Gaussian random variable with adjustable mean and variance. In this way, we adjust the complexity of the bag. Secondly, we control the size of the training set. The number of training samples also affects the training process of MIL classifiers. Thirdly, the number of test samples is set to be much larger than the number of training samples to keep a fair evaluation. Also, we keep the ratio of positive to negative samples to be 1 in both training and test sets. Table 2 shows the evaluation results on MNIST-bags dataset.

5.4 Results on Colon Cancer Dataset

This dataset contains 100 tissue images stained by hematoxylin and eosin (H&E) [16]. There are 22,444 nuclei with human-annotated labels, including epithelial, inflammatory, fibroblast and miscellaneous. Tagging epithelial cells is an essential biomedical task since the epithelial cells are highly relevant to the early stage of colon cancer. The MIL bag is an H&E image. It contains the segmentation where coarse-grained recognized cells are centered in a sub-image of size 27x27 pixels. The bag is labeled positive if it contains at least one epithelial cell instance. Also, the instance is labeled positive if it is epithelial. In this experiment, we aimed at evaluating different pooling operations, i.e., mean, max, ATT, GATT, MHATT, and DATT that serve as PIO. Data preprocessing and the neural network structure of baselines keep the same with [9,16]. Table 3 presents the results of bag classification and instance explanation.

6 Dicussion

In this section, we give analysis based on the experiment results from four aspects.In Sect. 6.1 and Sect. 6.2, we compare MU with other methods in the bag level and instance level respectively. Section 6.3 presents analysis about dloss and the skewness score. Section 6.4 discusses the reason of DATT's collapse on colon cancer dataset.

6.1   Bag-Level Analysis

From the results in Table 1, we could see that MU significantly outperforms state-of-the-art methods, including the attention-based ones on all datasets. The reason is that it can take advantage of incorporating multiple utility functions, which shows the advantage of our model at bag level. We can also see that MU obviously beats that of MHATT and DATT. It demonstrates that simply averaging the multi-head vectors of instances or adding fully connected layer is' not as good as our generalized method, even though DATT has more parameters to fit. Also, utility dropout is necessary for MU to work efficiently.

According to the results in Table 2, it is observed that our multi-utility app-roach MU performs the best under most settings. In the case of small mean bag size (10) and small number of training samples (10, 50), we could see that the recall of MU is worse than single-utility PIO while the precision is better. The reason is that due to its larger number of parameters, overfitting occurs on the extremely limited training data for MU. As a consequence, MU remembers some certain modes and makes more precise prediction on them while ignores other possibilities. On the contrary, when training data is sufficient, the multi-utility model(MU) could fit more complex data distribution and perform clearly better, which is proven by results in Table 3.

As shown in Table 3, MU has best overall performance with the highest F_1 score. DATT has better AUC and precision score but significantly worse recall score. Given more number of parameters to learn in DATT model, we conclude DATT does not outperform MU, especially for cancer detection where *recall is more important than precision.*

6.2   Instance-Level Analysis

From the results in Table 2, we could observe that under all settings MU has the best results in F_1 score. The precision and recall scores of two approaches behave differently. We conclude such behaviors from three aspects: (1) For ATT approach, the precision score increases along with both mean size of bag and the number of training samples. However, given the cardinality of training set, the recall score decreases with the increasing mean size of bag. Those two contradict-ing trends make the F_1 score improve slowly; (2) For MU approach, all precision, recall and F1 scores increase along with the mean size of bag and the number of training samples; (3) When the cardinality of training set is small (e.g., 10), MU achieves the best precision, recall and F1 scores. As the cardinality increases, the precision score of MU is slightly lower than ATT while the recall score is significantly higher. Thus, the overall performance of MU is notably better.

For the Colon Cancer Dataset evaluation, our MU significantly improves the recall score (about $0.1 \sim 0.2$) and at the cost of no more than 0.02 lower in precision score compared to the highest one, which is shown in Table 3.

6.3   dloss and Skewness Analysis

From the results in Table 2, we see that under *every dataset condition*, MU always has higher instance recall with lower dloss than ATT. We believe ATT-like single utility PIO has its **intrinsic deficiency of the worse linear-separability** compared to its multi-utility generalization, especially in high-dimension. Here is our analysis:

   We explain the skewness of importance score α_i from single-utility (attention-based) approach by a positive feedback process. The principle is that the importance score α_i acts like a gradient update filter [19] during back-propagation. Once an instance embedding $z_i^{(l)}$ is assigned by highest importance score $\alpha_i^{(l)}$ in iteration l, its learning rate must be higher than other instances. If the update in next iteration $l + 1$ further reduces the loss (this actually happens when one positive instance is selected correctly in a positive bag), then its importance score $\alpha_i^{(l+1)}$ gets even higher. By softmax, small step of ξ_i towards direction of $\mathbf{w} \in \mathcal{H}$ $(\mathbf{w}^T(\xi_i^{(l+1)} - \xi_i^{(l)}) > 0)$ will be exponentially amplified in the importance weights as well as reduce the weight of other instances. Eventually, this process will further limit the update on other instances. And the model is only trained on few instances with very high importance scores. Insufficient training of most instances in single utility function model is responsible for the higher dloss, which results in the low recall.

   Empirical results support this explanation. Firstly, the instance-level recall largely drops with the increase of mean bag size. This means that the importance score is highly skewed. Secondly, given dataset condition, the discriminator loss of MU is much less than ATT. This loss shows that the instance encoder network is not fully trained on all instances with single-utility PIO. So the data distribution in the instance embedding space $\mathcal{H}$ gets more disordered. On the contrary, MU mildly filters the back-propagated gradient by the redundancy of utility functions.

   In Table 3, the dloss as well as skewness score reveals the superiority of MU again. We could see that MU has lowest skewness despite of the collapsed DATT model. This explains why MU has highest recall score. Also, MU has the lowest dloss than all other attention based PIOs. Compared to single utility ATT and GATT PIOs, MU makes the instances more linearly separable with more utility functions. Compared to other multiple-utility baselines MHATT and DATT, only our approach reduces dloss. We see MHATT and DATT increased dloss.

6.4 DATT Collapse Analysis

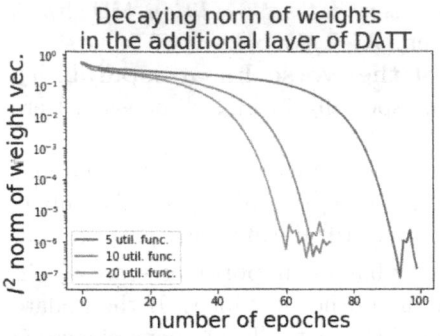

Fig. 3. The weights of DATT decayed with training ($\sum_k x_k^2$ in Eq. (7))

Interestingly, from the results in Table 3 we observe that **DATT** collapses in experiments. We can see that the instance-level precision, recall and F_1 scores of DATT are all zeros. We find the norm of weights in the additional layer converges to zero during training (see Fig. 3), thus leading to the observed almost same importance scores (like MEAN PIO, which is totally not interpretable, resulting in the collapsed results in Table 3).

This is because the training dynamics of DATT is totally different compared to MU. Intuitively, the additional layer in DATT gives utility functions that recognize more pos/nag samples more weights and vise versa. In high-dimensional instance embedding space, finding some certain direction is extremely hard in probability due to the high complexity of sampling. So at each update step, most of the random initiated utility functions are penalized with fewer weights. In the figure above, we see the l^2-norm of weights with larger number of utility functions decays faster and earlier.

As a result, simply stacking more layers like DATT does not improve instance explanation. We argue that our MU approach is a novel and effective attempt to handle this problem. Though seems similar to a PIO with more "operations", MU's unique advantage can not be achieved by either adding non-parametric average MHATT or parametric neural network layer DATT.

7 Conclusion

In this paper, we extend the object of Region of Interest estimation to a wider range of any objects that can be embedded. We regard it as a problem of Multi-Instance Learning and introduce a new Permutation-Invariant Operator MU for MIL. With the help of utility functions imposed on instance space, our approach naturally generalizes the previous attention-based MIL methods. Our approach is capable of fitting more complex multi-instance data by leveraging multiple utility functions, which is more effective than simple adding-layer approaches MHATT and DATT. We provide a discriminator loss to explain why the previous attention-based approaches generates skewed importance scores and indicates the superiority of MU. Empirical results on multiple benchmark datasets show that our method achieves state-of-the-art performance in both bag-level and instance-level tasks. Notably, our approach also provides obviously more reliable instance-level interpretation in real-life weakly labeled tasks, which also indicates some possible directions for automatic labeling.

References

1. Andrews, S., Tsochantaridis, I., Hofmann, T.: Support vector machines for multiple-instance learning. In: NIPS, pp. 561–568 (2002)
2. Askelöf, J., Carlander, M.L., Christopoulos, C.: Region of interest coding in JPEG 2000. Sig. Process.: Image Commun. **17**(1), 105–111 (2002)
3. Brett, M., Anton, J.L., Valabregue, R., Poline, J.B., et al.: Region of interest analysis using an SPM toolbox. In: 8th International Conference on Functional Mapping of the Human Brain, vol. 16, p. 497. Sendai, Japan (2002)
4. Cheplygina, V., Tax, D.M.J., Loog, M.: Multiple instance learning with bag dissimilarities. Pattern Recogn. **48**(1), 264–275 (2015)
5. Dietterich, T.G., Lathrop, R.H., Lozano-Pérez, T.: Solving the multiple instance problem with axis-parallel rectangles. Artif. Intell. **89**(1–2), 31–71 (1997)
6. Feng, J., Zhou, Z.: Deep MIML network. In: AAAI, pp. 1884–1890 (2017)
7. Foulds, J., Frank, E.: A review of multi-instance learning assumptions. Knowl. Eng. Rev. **25**(1), 1–25 (2010)
8. Gärtner, T., Flach, P.A., Kowalczyk, A., Smola, A.J.: Multi-instance kernels. In: ICML, pp. 179–186 (2002)
9. Ilse, M., Tomczak, J.M., Welling, M.: Attention-based deep multiple instance learning. In: ICML, pp. 2132–2141 (2018)
10. Kingma, D.P., Ba, J.: Adam: a method for stochastic optimization. In: Bengio, Y., LeCun, Y. (eds.) ICLR (2015). http://arxiv.org/abs/1412.6980
11. Kraus, O.Z., Ba, L.J., Frey, B.J.: Classifying and segmenting microscopy images with deep multiple instance learning. Bioinformatics **32**(12), 52–59 (2016)
12. Pinheiro, P.H.O., Collobert, R.: From image-level to pixel-level labeling with convolutional networks. In: CVPR, pp. 1713–1721 (2015)
13. Qi, C.R., Su, H., Mo, K., Guibas, L.J.: Pointnet: deep learning on point sets for 3D classification and segmentation. In: CVPR, pp. 77–85 (2017)
14. Ramon, J., Raedt, L.D.: Multi-instance neural networks (2000)
15. Sabour, S., Frosst, N., Hinton, G.E.: Dynamic routing between capsules. In: NIPS, pp. 3859–3869 (2017)
16. Sirinukunwattana, K., e Ahmed Raza, S., Tsang, Y., Snead, D.R.J., Cree, I.A., Rajpoot, N.M.: Locality sensitive deep learning for detection and classification of nuclei in routine colon cancer histology images. IEEE Trans. Med. Imaging **35**(5), 1196–1206 (2016)
17. Tian, B., Zhang, Y., Wang, J., Xing, C.: Hierarchical inter-attention network for document classification with multi-task learning. In: Proceedings of the Twenty-Eighth International Joint Conference on Artificial Intelligence, IJCAI 2019, Macao, China, 10–16 August 2019, pp. 3569–3575 (2019). https://doi.org/10.24963/ijcai.2019/495
18. Vaswani, A., et al.: Attention is all you need. In: NIPS, pp. 6000–6010 (2017)
19. Wang, F., et al.: Residual attention network for image classification. In: CVPR, pp. 6450–6458 (2017)
20. Wang, J., Wang, Z., Zhang, D., Yan, J.: Combining knowledge with deep convolutional neural networks for short text classification. In: Proceedings of the Twenty-Sixth International Joint Conference on Artificial Intelligence, IJCAI 2017, Melbourne, Australia, 19–25 August 2017, pp. 2915–2921 (2017). https://doi.org/10.24963/ijcai.2017/406
21. Wang, X., Yan, Y., Tang, P., Bai, X., Liu, W.: Revisiting multiple instance neural networks. Pattern Recogn. **74**, 15–24 (2018)

22. Wang, Z., Zhang, Y., Xing, C.: Reducing wrong labels for distant supervision relation extraction with selective capsule network. In: Shao, J., Yiu, M.L., Toyoda, M., Zhang, D., Wang, W., Cui, B. (eds.) APWeb-WAIM 2019. LNCS, vol. 11641, pp. 77–92. Springer, Cham (2019). https://doi.org/10.1007/978-3-030-26072-9_6
23. Wei, X., Wu, J., Zhou, Z.: Scalable algorithms for multi-instance learning. IEEE Trans. Neural Netw. Learn. Syst. **28**(4), 975–987 (2017)
24. Zaheer, M., Kottur, S., Ravanbakhsh, S., Póczos, B., Salakhutdinov, R.R., Smola, A.J.: Deep sets. In: NIPS, pp. 3394–3404 (2017)
25. Zhang, Q., Goldman, S.A.: EM-DD: an improved multiple-instance learning technique. In: NIPS, pp. 1073–1080 (2001)
26. Zhao, K., et al.: Modeling patient visit using electronic medical records for cost profile estimation. In: Database Systems for Advanced Applications - 23rd International Conference, DASFAA 2018, Gold Coast, QLD, Australia, 21–24 May 2018, Proceedings, Part II, pp. 20–36 (2018). https://doi.org/10.1007/978-3-319-91458-9_2
27. Zhou, Z., Sun, Y., Li, Y.: Multi-instance learning by treating instances as non-I.I.D. samples. In: ICML, pp. 1249–1256 (2009)

Anomaly Detection in High-Dimensional Data Based on Autoregressive Flow

Yanwei Yu[1(✉)], Peng Lv[2], Xiangrong Tong[2], and Junyu Dong[1]

[1] Department of Computer Science and Technology, Ocean University of China, Qingdao, China
{yuyanwei,dongjunyu}@ouc.edu.cn
[2] School of Computer and Control Engineering, Yantai University, Yantai, China
lvpeng4869@outlook.com, txr@ytu.edu.cn

Abstract. Anomaly detection of high-dimensional data is an important but yet challenging problem in research and application domains. Unsupervised techniques typically rely on the density distribution of the data to detect anomalies, where objects with low density are considered to be abnormal. The state-of-the-art methods solve this problem by first applying dimension reduction techniques to the data and then detecting anomalies in the low dimensional space. However, these methods suffer from inappropriate density estimation modeling and decoupled models with inconsistent objectives. In this work, we propose an effective Anomaly Detection model based on Autoregressive Flow (ADAF). The key idea is to unify the distribution mapping capability of flow-based models with the neural density estimation power of autoregressive models. We design an autoregressive flow-based model to infer the latent variables of input data by minimizing the combination of latent error and neural density. The neural density of input data can be estimated naturally by ADAF, along with the latent variable inference, rather than through an additional stitched density estimation network. Unlike stitching decoupled models, ADAF optimizes the same network parameters simultaneously by balancing latent error and neural density estimation in a unified training fashion to effectively separate the anomalies out. Experimental results on six public benchmark datasets show that, ADAF achieves better performance than state-of-the-art anomaly detection techniques by up to 20% improvement on the standard F_1 score.

Keywords: Anomaly detection · Flow-based model · Neural density estimation · Deep learning

1 Introduction

Anomaly detection is a fundamental and hence well-studied problem in many areas, such as cyber-security [26], manufacturing [19], system management [16], and medicine [7]. Anomaly detection, also known as outlier detection, is to identify the objects that significantly differ from the majority of objects in the data

© Springer Nature Switzerland AG 2020
Y. Nah et al. (Eds.): DASFAA 2020, LNCS 12113, pp. 125–140, 2020.
https://doi.org/10.1007/978-3-030-59416-9_8

space. In general, normal data is large and consistent with certain distribution, while abnormal data is small and discrete; therefore anomalies are residing in low density areas.

Although great progress has been made in anomaly detection in the past few decades, anomaly detection for high-dimensional data is still a huge challenge. Due to the dimensional disaster, it is increasingly difficult for traditional density estimation models to implement density estimation in the original data space. But unfortunately for a real-world problem, the dimensionality of data could be very large. To address this challenge, a two-step framework is usually applied into high-dimensional data [5,12]. It first performs dimensionality reduction on high-dimensional data and then detect anomalies in the low-dimensional space. In recent years, deep learning has achieved great success in anomaly detection [6]. Generative adversarial networks (GANs) [13] and autoencoder [30] and their variants have been widely used for anomaly detection, such as variational autoencoder (VAE) [1], and adversarial autoencoder (AAE) [21]. The core idea of these methods is to encode input data into a low dimensional representation, and then decode the low dimensional representation into the original data space by minimizing the reconstruction error. In this process, the essential features of the original data are extracted in latent data space through training autoencoder, without noise and unnecessary features. Several recent studies have applied this structure into practical problems. For example, DAGMM [31] combines deep autoencoder and Gaussian mixture model (GMM) in anomaly detection. However, the real-world data may not only have high dimensions, but also lack a clear predefined distribution (e.g., GMM). Manual parameter adjustment is also required in GMM when modeling the density distribution of input data, which has a serious impact on detection performance. Additionally, all these methods based on two steps have two main limitations: (1) the loss of information in original data is caused by the irreversible dimensionality reduction. (2) the decoupled models of dimensionality reduction and density estimation are easily trapped in local optima during training.

Recently, several flow-based models are proposed to generate data and have proved to be successful in many fields, such as Parallel WaveNet [20] for speech synthesis, and Glow [17] and NICE [9] for image generation. Flow-based models map original data to a latent space so as to make the transformed data conform to a factorized distribution, i.e., resulting in independent latent variables. This is a revertible non-dimensional reduction process, meaning that there is no loss of information. Compared with GANs and VAEs, which have shown great success in the field of high-dimensional data anomaly detection, flow-based models have not received much attention. Nevertheless, flow-based models possess the following advantages: First, flow-based models perform exact latent variable inference and log-likelihood evaluation. VAEs can only infer the approximate value of the latent variable corresponding to the input data point after encoding. GANs have no encoder at all to infer the latent variable. In reversible generative models like Glow [17], exact inference of latent variables can be achieved without approximation, and the exact log-likelihood of the data also can be optimized, instead of a lower bound of it. Second, flow-based models are efficient to parallelize for both inference and synthesis, such as Glow [17] and RealNVP [10]. Third, there is significant potential for memory savings. Computing gradients in reversible neural networks requires a certain amount of memory, instead of linear in their depth. The fourth is natural neural density estimation. Autoregressive models and normalizing flows are the main members of the family of neural density estimation. The neural density of input data can be estimated while inferring latent variable.

In this paper, we propose an effective Anomaly Detection method based on Autoregressive Flow-based generative model, called ADAF, which is a deep learning framework that addresses the aforementioned challenges in anomaly detection from high-dimensional datasets. ADAF is a *neural density estimation* model, which unifies the distribution mapping capacity of flow-based model with the density estimation power of autoregressive model to provide a neural density estimation of high dimensional data for effectively identifying anomalies. First, we design an autoregressive flow-based model to infer the latent variables of input data by minimizing the combination of latent error and sample neural density. Second, neural density of input data can be estimated naturally by ADAF, which is totally different from traditional surrounding point-based density estimation. The neural density of a data point is calculated directly along with the latent variable inference and log-likelihood evaluation, rather than through an additional stitched density estimation network. Finally, ADAF is an absolute end-to-end model that optimizes both latent error and neural density estimation simultaneously for the same network parameters, which avoids getting into local optima.

We conduct comprehensive experiments on six public benchmark datasets to valuate the effectiveness of our proposed model. ADAF is significantly better than state-of-the-art methods by up to 20% improvement in standard F_1 score for anomaly detection. It is worth noting that ADAF achieves better results with fewer training samples compared to existing methods based on deep learning.

To summarize, we make the following contributions:

- We propose a deep anomaly detection model based on autoregressive flow for anomaly detection from high-dimensional datasets.
- We propose to combine the latent error and neural density together to optimize latent variable inference and log-likelihood estimation simultaneously in autoregressive flow model for effectively identifying anomalies.
- We conduct extensive evaluations on six benchmark datasets. Experimental results demonstrate that our method significantly outperforms state-of-the-art methods.

2   Related Work

In recent years, varieties of studies focus on anomaly detection in data mining and machine learning [11]. Distance-based model [18] detects anomalies through global density criterion. Density-based methods [4,27] uses local relative density as anomaly criterion to detect anomalies. Several studies [15,25] apply KDE into density-based local outlier detection to improve the detection accuracy. However, such methods rely on an appropriate distance metric, which are only feasible for handling low-dimensional data, but not for anomaly detection of high dimensional data. One-class classification approaches trained by normal data are widely used for anomaly detection, such as one-class SVMs [8] and SVDD [22]. The core of these methods is to find a decision boundary that separates abnormal data from normal data. Another category of anomaly detection framework is mainly based on reconstruction errors to determine whether a sample is anomalous, such as conventional Principal Component Analysis (PCA), kernel PAC, and Robust PCA (RPCA) [5,14].

Recently, varieties of anomaly detection methods based on deep neural networks are proposed to detect anomalies [6]. GANs, Autoencoder and their variants have been widely used in anomaly detection, especially for high-dimensional data anomaly detection. The variational autoencoder is used directly for anomaly detection by using reconstruction error in [1]. Inspired by RPCA [5], Zhou et al. [30] propose a Robust Deep Autoencoder (RDA), and use the reconstruction error to detect anomalies for high-dimensional data. AnoGAN [3] uses a Generative Adversarial Network [13] to detect anomalies in the context of medical images by reconstruction error. In a follow-up work, f-AnoGAN [23] introduces Wasserstein GAN [2] to improve AnoGAN to be adaptable to real-time anomaly detection applications. However, these methods only consider reconstruction errors as anomaly criterion, thus the performance of these methods is limited in detecting anomalies.

Deep structured energy based model (DSEBM) [29] directly simulates the data distribution through the deep architectures to detect data anomalies. DSEBM integrates Energy-Based Models (EBMs) with various types of datasets, including spatial data, static data, and sequential data. DSEBM has two anomaly criteria to identify anomalies: the energy score (DSEBM-e) and the reconstruction error (DSEBM-r). Deep Autoencoding Gaussian Mixture Model (DAGMM) [31] consists of a compression network and an estimation network. The compression network reduces the dimensionality of input samples through a deep autoencoder, prepares their low-dimensional representations from the reduced space and reconstruction error features, and provides the representations to the subsequent estimation network. Estimation networks take feeds and predict their likelihood/energy in the framework of a Gaussian Mixture Model (GMM). These models first reduce the dimensionality of the data, and then detect anomalies in the low-dimensional space through the energy model or GMM. As GANs are able to model the complex high-dimensional distributions of real-world data, and Adversarially Learned Anomaly Detection (ALAD) is a GAN based methods [28], which considers both data distribution and reconstruction error. ALAD derives adversarially learned features for the anomaly detection task based on bi-directional GANs, and then uses reconstruction errors based on these adversarially learned features to separate out anomalies.

Our proposed method is most related to DAGMM. However, unlike DAGMM, ADAF uses an autoregressive flow-based model to accurately extract independent latent variables. And ADAF directly obtain the neural density estimation of the original data with latent variable mapping, rather than a predefined GMM distribution. Most importantly, ADAF can independently estimate the neural density of a data point without having to rely on other constraints, such as distance or density from other data points, and show a powerful ability of anomaly detection with few training samples.

3 Autoregressive Flow-Based Anomaly Detection Model

3.1 Normalizing Flows

Flow refers to the data "flowing" through a series of bijections (revertible mapping), and finally maps to a suitable representation space. Normalizing means that the variable integral of the representation space is 1, which meets the definition of probability distribution function.

Given an observed data $x \in X$, an explicit invertible non-linear transformation $f : \mathbb{R}^d \to \mathbb{R}^d$ of a simple tractable distribution $p_Z(z)$ (e.g., an isotropic Gaussian distribution) on a latent variable $z \in Z$, $X = f(Z)$ and $Z = f^{-1}(X)$, the change of variable formula defines a model distribution on X by:

$$p_X(x) = p_Z(f^{-1}(x))|det(\frac{\partial f^{-1}(x)}{\partial x})|, \tag{1}$$

where $\frac{\partial f^{-1}(x)}{\partial x}$ is the Jacobian of f at x. The transformation f is typically chosen so that it is invertible and its Jacobian determinant is easy to compute.

Therefore, the probability density function of the model given a data can be calculated from a log probability:

$$\log(p_X(x)) = \log(p_Z(f^{-1}(x))) + \log(|det(\frac{\partial f^{-1}(x)}{\partial x})|). \tag{2}$$

3.2 Autoregressive Density Estimation

Autoregressive density estimation uses the chain rule of probability to learn the joint probability density by decomposing it into the product of one-dimensional conditional probability density. Given an observation x which contains d attributes, its joint probability density is calculated as follows:

$$p(x) = \prod_{i=1}^{d} p(x_i|x_{1:i-1}), \tag{3}$$

Formally, the generation of the variable x_i in the i-th dimension depends only on the previously generated variable $x_{1:i-1}$, that is:

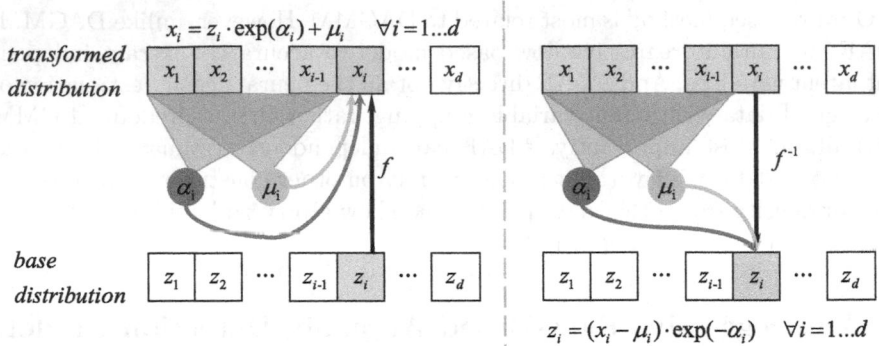

Fig. 1. Specific process of single model. The gray cells are the cells that are currently being calculated, and the blue cells represent the cells on which they depend. (Color figure online)

$$p(x_i|x_{1:i-1}) = \mathcal{N}(x_i|\mu_i, (\exp(\alpha_i))^2), \ \mu_i = g_{\mu_i}(x_{1:i-1}), \ \alpha_i = g_{\alpha_i}(x_{1:i-1}), \quad (4)$$

where g_{μ_i} and g_{α_i} are functions that compute the mean and log standard deviation of the i-th attribute given all previous variables. Autoregressive probability density has two parameters: mean μ_i and log standard deviation α_i.

We use the recursive operation of the above Eq. (3) and Eq. (4) to generate data:

$$x_i = z_i \exp(\alpha_i) + \mu_i, \ z_i \sim \mathcal{N}(0, 1), \quad (5)$$

where $z = (z_1, z_2, ..., z_d)$ is the vector of random numbers the model uses internally to generate data.

3.3 Anomaly Detection Based on Autoregressive Flow (ADAF)

Single Module. From Eq. (5), we can see that the autoregressive model provides an alternative characterization as a transformation f from the space of random numbers Z to the space of data X. We express this model as $X = f(Z)$. Given data point x which contains d dimensions, we can get z by the following reverse operation:

$$z_i = (x_i - \mu_i) \exp(-\alpha_i), \mu_i = g_{\mu_i}(x_{1:i-1}), \alpha_i = g_{\alpha_i}(x_{1:i-1}), \quad (6)$$

The specific process of a single module is shown in Fig. 1. The figure on the left is the generation process f of x. For any distribution x_i, it is calculated from α_i, μ_i and z_i, which means that x_i depends on all previous variables (i.e., $x_1, \ldots, x_{i-1}$) and corresponding z_i. The figure on the right is the inverse generation process f^{-1} of z. For any distribution z_i, it is obtained from α_i, μ_i and

x_i, which means that z_i also only depends on all previously generated variables (i.e., $x_1, \ldots, x_{i-1}$).

Because of autoregressive structure, the Jacobian of f^{-1} is triangular by design. We can calculate its absolute determinant as follows:

$$|det(\frac{\partial f^{-1}(x)}{\partial x})| = \exp(-\sum_{i=1}^{d} \alpha_i), \ \alpha_i = g_{\alpha_i}(x_{1:i-1}). \tag{7}$$

Therefore, the autoregressive model can be equivalently regarded as a normalizing flow, which can calculate density $p(x)$ by substituting Eq. (6) and (7) into Eq. (2):

$$\log(p_X(x)) = \log(p_Z(f^{-1}(x))) + \log(\exp(-\sum_{i=1}^{d} \alpha_i)). \tag{8}$$

Multiple Modules. We improve the model fit by stacking multiple instances of the single model into a deeper flow:

$$x = f_K \circ \ldots \circ f_2 \circ f_1(z), \tag{9}$$

$$z = f_1^{-1} \circ \ldots \circ f_{K-1}^{-1} \circ f_K^{-1}(x), \tag{10}$$

where x is the input data for d dimensions, K is the number of single module, f_i represents an autoregressive module, z is the latent variable.

Combining Eq. (7), (8), and Eq. (10), then sample neural density can be further inferred by:

$$D(x) = -\log(p_X(x))$$
$$= -[\log(p_Z(\prod_{k=1}^{K} f_i^{-1}(x))) + \sum_{k=1}^{K}[\log(\exp(-\sum_{i=1}^{d} \alpha_{ki}))]], \tag{11}$$

where p_Z is a simple tractable distribution (e.g., an isotropic Gaussian distribution).

Objective Function. Given a dataset of N instances, which contain d attributes. The objective function guides ADAF training is constructed as follows:

$$\mathcal{J}(\mu, \alpha) = \frac{1}{N} \sum_{j=1}^{N} L(x^j, z^j) + \frac{\lambda}{N} \sum_{j=1}^{N} D(x^j). \tag{12}$$

This objective function includes two components.

- $L(x^j, z^j)$ is the latent error, which is the error between input data x^j and its latent data z^j. Latent data is the key information of the input data, so we expect the value of latent error is as low as possible. In practice, we use L_2-norm for this purpose, as $L(x^j, z^j) = \|x^j - z^j\|_2^2$.
- $D(x^j)$ is the sample neural density of input data. By minimizing negative log-likelihood density estimations, we can better fit the observed data to high-density space. We optimize the combination of neural density and latent error until the two reach a equilibrium, which makes our objective function better serve the objective of anomaly detection.
- λ is the coefficient parameter in ADAF, which controls the objective to be biased towards latent error or neural density.
- $\mathcal{J}(\mu, \alpha)$, μ and α represent all related parameters μ_i and α_i in the model.

Although our objective function consists of two components, it is totally different from DAGMM. In our objective function, the latent error and the neural density together optimize the same network parameters, which is a thorough end-to-end model. DAGMM is also an end-to-end training model, but the two parts of its objective function optimize different network parts, respectively. Therefore, our model is an absolute end-to-end framework that jointly optimizes latent error and neural density estimation simultaneously. More specifically, we use stochastic gradient descent to optimize the objective during training. Finally, the latent error and the sample neural density are used as anomaly criteria to detect anomalies. That is, a data sample has a higher latent error and sample neural density value, it is more likely to be an anomaly.

4   Experiments

In this section, we use six public benchmark datasets to evaluate the effectiveness and robustness of ADAF in anomaly detection. The code of the baseline methods is available at GitHub[1] released by ALAD. The code of our ADAF can be available at GitHub[2].

Table 1. Statistics of the public benchmark datasets

Dataset	#Dimensions	#Instances	Anomaly ratio (ρ)
Thyroid	36	3,772	0.025
KDDCUP	118	494,021	0.2
SpamBase	58	3485	0.2
Arrhythmia	274	432	0.15
KDDCUP-Rev	118	121,597	0.2
Cardiotocography	22	2068	0.2

---

[1] https://github.com/houssamzenati/Adversarially-Learned-Anomaly-Detection.
[2] https://github.com/1246170471/ADAF.

4.1   Datasets

We conduct experiments on six public datasets in the field of anomaly detection: KDDCUP, Thyroid, Arrhythmia, KDDCUP-Rev, SpamBase, and Cardiotocography. The details of the datasets are shown in Table 1.

- **Thyroid:** Thyroid is from UCI Machine Learning Repository[3] thyroid disease classification dataset, which contains samples of 36 dimensions. There are 3 classes in original dataset. As hyperfunction is a minority class, we treat hyperfunction as anomaly class in our experiment.
- **KDDCUP:** The KDDCUP 10% dataset from UCI Machine Learning Repository is a network intrusion dataset, which originally contains 41 dimensions. 34 of them are continuous data, and another 7 represent categories. We use one-hot representation to encoder them, and eventually obtain a 118-dimensional dataset. As 20% of them are marked as "normal" and meanwhile others are marked as "attack", and "normal" samples constitute a small portion, therefore, we treat "normal" samples as anomalies in our experiment.
- **SpamBase:** SpamBase is from UCI Machine Learning Repository, which collects spam emails filed by postmaster and individuals and non-spam emails from filed work and personal emails. We treat the spam emails as outliers, and the anomaly ratio is 0.2.
- **Arrhythmia:** Arrhythmia dataset is also obtained from the UCI Machine Learning Repository. This dataset contains 274 attributes, 206 of them are linear valued and the rest are nominal. The smallest classes, including 3, 4, 5, 7, 8, 9, 14 and 15, are combined to form the anomaly class, and the rest of the classes are combined to form the normal class.
- **KDDCUP-Rev:** This dataset is an abbreviated version extracted from KDDCUP. We retain all "normal" data in this dataset, and randomly draw "attack" samples to keep the anomaly ratio as 0.2. As "attack" data is in minority part, we treat "attack" data as anomalies.
- **Cardiotocography:** Cardiotocography is also from UCI Machine Learning Repository which related to heart diseases. This dataset contains 22 attributes, and the instances in the dataset are classified by three expert obstetricians into 3 classes: normal, suspect, or pathological. Normal instances are treated as inliers and the remaining as outliers.

4.2   Baseline Methods

We compare our method with the following traditional and state-of-the-art deep learning methods:

- **OC-SVM** [8]: One Class Support Vector Machines (OC-SVM) is a classic kernel method for novelty detection that only use normal data to learn a decision boundary. We adopt the widely used radial basis function (RBF) kernel. In our experiments, we assume that the abnormal proportion is known.

---

[3] https://archive.ics.uci.edu/ml/.

We set the parameter ν to the anomaly proportion, and set γ to $1/m$, where m is the number of input features.

- **DSEBM** [29]: Deep Structured Energy Based Models(DSEBM) is a deep learning method for anomaly detection. They tackle the anomaly detection problem by directly modeling the data distribution with deep architectures. DSEBM contains two decision criteria for performing anomaly detection: the energy score (**DSEBM-e**) and the reconstruction error (**DSEBM-r**).
- **DAGMM** [31]: Deep Autoencoding Gaussian Mixture Model (DAGMM) is a state-of-the-art method for anomaly detection, which consists of two major components: a compression network and an estimation network. The compression network performs dimensionality reduction for input samples by a deep autoencoder, and feeds the low-dimensional representations with the reconstruction error to the subsequent estimation network. The estimation network takes the feed, and predicts their likelihood/energy in the framework of GMM.
- **AnoGAN** [24]: AnoGAN is a GAN-based method for anomaly detection. AnoGAN is trained with normal data, and using it to recover a latent representation for each input test data. AnoGAN uses both reconstruction error and discrimination components as the anomaly criterion. Reconstruction error ensures how well the GAN is able to reconstruct the data via the generator, while the discrimination component considers a score based on the discriminator. There are two approaches for the anomaly score in the original paper and we choose the best variant in our tasks.
- **ALAD** [28]: Adversarially Learned Anomaly Detection (ALAD) is also a state-of-the-art method based on bi-directional GANs, which derives adversarially learned features for the anomaly detection task. ALAD uses reconstruction error based on these adversarially learned features to determine if a data sample is anomalous.

4.3   Experiment Configuration

The configurations of baselines used in experiments follows their original configurations. We follow the setting in [29,31] with completely clean training data: in each run, we take $\tau\%$ of data by randomly sampling for training with the rest $(1-\tau\%)$ reserved for testing, and only data samples from the normal data are used for training models. Specifically, for our ADAF and all baselines, we set $\tau = 50$ in KDDCUP and KDDCUP-Rev, $\tau = 80$ in other datasets. Without special statement, we set λ to 1 by default.

We set different K values (i.e., the number of distribution mappings) on different datasets in our network structure. K is set to 4 in KDDCUP and KDDCUP-Rev, $K = 8$ in Cardiotocography, $K = 16$ in Arrhythmia, $K = 16$ in SpamBase, and $K=10$ in Thyroid. See our code for more detailed network structure settings.

4.4 Evaluation Metrics

We consider average precision, recall, and F_1 score to quantify the results. We choose a threshold based on the anomaly ratio in the test set. For example, if the anomaly ratio in the test set is ρ, the top ρ data of the objective function value is marked as anomalies.

The precision and recall are defined as follows: $Precision = \frac{|G \cap R|}{|R|}$ and $Recall = \frac{|G \cap R|}{|G|}$, where G denotes the set of ground truth anomalies in the dataset, and R denotes the set of anomalies reported by the methods. F_1 score is defined as follows: $F_1 = \frac{2*Precision*Recall}{Precision+Recall}$.

Table 2. Average precision, recall, and F_1 from ADAF and all baselines. For each metric, the best result is shown in bold.

Method	KDDCUP			Thyroid		
	Precision	Recall	F_1	Precision	Recall	F_1
OC-SVM	0.7457	0.8523	0.7954	0.3639	0.4239	0.3887
DSEBM-r	0.8744	0.8414	0.8575	0.0400	0.0403	0.0403
DSEBM-e	0.2151	0.2180	0.2170	0.1319	0.1319	0.1319
DAGMM	0.9297	0.9442	0.9369	0.4766	0.4834	0.4782
AnoGAN	0.8786	0.8297	0.8865	0.0412	0.0430	0.0421
ALAD	0.9427	0.9577	0.9501	0.3196	0.3333	0.3263
ADAF	**0.9877**	**0.9926**	**0.9901**	**0.5102**	**0.5321**	**0.5209**
Method	Arrhythmia			KDDCUP-Rev		
	Precision	Recall	F_1	Precision	Recall	F_1
OC-SVM	0.5397	0.4082	0.4581	0.7148	0.9940	0.8316
DSEBM-r	0.4286	0.5000	0.4615	0.2036	0.2036	0.2036
DSEBM-e	0.4643	0.4645	0.4643	0.2212	0.2213	0.2213
DAGMM	0.4909	0.5078	0.4983	0.9370	0.9390	0.9380
AnoGAN	0.4118	0.4375	0.4242	0.8422	0.8305	0.8363
ALAD	0.5000	0.5313	0.5152	0.9547	0.9678	0.9612
ADAF	**0.7172**	**0.7171**	**0.7171**	**0.9895**	**0.9941**	**0.9918**
Method	SpamBase			Cardiotocography		
	Precision	Recall	F_1	Precision	Recall	F_1
OC-SVM	0.7440	0.7972	0.7694	0.7366	0.6848	0.7051
DSEBM-r	0.4296	0.3085	0.3574	0.5584	0.5467	0.5365
DSEBM-e	0.4356	0.3185	0.3679	0.5564	0.5367	0.5515
DAGMM	0.9435	0.7233	0.7970	0.5024	0.4905	0.4964
AnoGAN	0.4963	0.5313	0.5132	0.4446	0.4360	0.4412
ALAD	0.5344	0.5206	0.5274	0.5983	0.5841	0.5911
ADAF	**0.8381**	**0.8393**	**0.8387**	**0.7435**	**0.7432**	**0.7433**

4.5 Effectiveness Evaluation

First, we valuate the overall effectiveness of our proposed model compared with all baseline methods on six benchmark datasets. We repeat 20 runs for all methods on each dataset and the average precision, recall, and F_1 score are shown in Table 2.

From Table 2, we can see that ADAF is significantly better than all baselines in terms of average precision, recall, and F_1 score on six datasets. On the KDD-CUP and KDDCUP-Rev, ADAF achieves 4% and 2.4% improvement in standard F_1 score compared to state-of-the-art ALAD, reaching over 98% in all terms of precision, recall and F_1 score. On Thyroid and Arrhythmia, ADAF significantly performs better than state-of-the-art DAGMM and ALAD by over 4.2% and 20.1% improvement in standard F_1 score. On SpamBase and Cardiotocography, ADAF is 4.1% and 3.7% better than DAGMM and OC-SVM methods, respectively. The reasons why ADAF is better than DAGMM may be attributed as: (1) ADAF obtains latent variables based on a reversible flow model. There is no loss of dimensional information in the reversible process, and exact latent variables can be obtained. DAGMM uses an autoencoder to obtain the latent variables, which is an irreversible dimensionality reduction operation and will inevitably lose the information of the original input data; (2) ADAF uses a neural density estimator for density estimation instead of Gaussian mixture model. Deep neural density estimation is superior to Gaussian mixture model, because GMM is a parameter estimation that refers to the process of using sample data to estimate the parameters of the selected distribution, while neural density estimator compute the probability density jointly combining with the generation of latent variables. Additionally, GMM also needs to manually select the number of mixed Gaussian models, which is very tricky in the absence of domain knowledge.

For AnoGAN, it adopts adversarial autoencoder to recover a latent representation for each input data, and uses both reconstruction error and discrimination components as the anomaly criterion, but AnoGAN does not make full use of the low-dimensional representation. Although ALAD can simulate the distribution of data well when the experimental data is large enough, it also ignores the consideration of latent representation. Another potential reason why our method is better than all baselines is that we use an autoregressive flow model to obtain the latent variables and neural density of input data at the same time without dimensionality reduction, avoiding the loss of information.

4.6 Performance w.r.t. Training Set

Second, we investigate the impact of different training data on ADAF and all baselines. We use $\tau\%$ of the normal dataset as the training set for all methods. We repeat the experiments on Arrhythmia and KDDCUP datasets 20 times and report the average results in Table 3 and Table 4.

As we can see, only when the training data is 30%, our results are slightly lower than DSEBM-e on Arrhythmia. In all other cases, our ADAF significantly outperforms than all baselines in terms of precision, recall and F_1 score on both

Table 3. Performance comparison w.r.t. training ratio on Arrhythmia

Ratio	ADAF			ALAD			DAGMM		
$\tau\%$	Precision	Recall	F_1	Precision	Recall	F_1	Precision	Recall	F_1
30%	0.4607	0.4747	0.4676	0.4641	0.5250	0.4926	0.3750	0.4500	0.4091
40%	0.5024	0.5252	0.5135	0.4634	0.5278	0.4935	0.3902	0.4444	0.4156
50%	0.5539	0.5707	0.5621	0.5000	0.5312	0.5152	0.3824	0.4062	0.3939
60%	0.5808	0.5808	0.5808	0.4643	0.4643	0.4643	0.4643	0.4643	0.4643
70%	0.6286	0.6363	0.6315	0.3810	0.4000	0.3902	0.4286	0.4500	0.4390
80%	0.7172	0.7171	0.7171	0.3571	0.4167	0.3846	0.3571	0.4167	0.3846

Ratio	DSEBM-e			DSEBM-r			AnoGAN		
$\tau\%$	Precision	Recall	F_1	Precision	Recall	F_1	Precision	Recall	F_1
30%	0.4583	0.5500	0.5000	0.3542	0.4250	0.3864	0.2917	0.3500	0.3182
40%	0.4634	0.5278	0.4935	0.3902	0.4444	0.4156	0.3415	0.3889	0.3636
50%	0.5000	0.5312	0.5152	0.4118	0.4375	0.4242	0.3529	0.3750	0.3636
60%	0.4643	0.4643	0.4643	0.4286	0.4286	0.4286	0.4286	0.4286	0.4286
70%	0.4286	0.4500	0.4390	0.3810	0.4000	0.3902	0.4286	0.4500	0.4390
80%	0.4286	0.5000	0.4615	0.4286	0.5000	0.4615	0.3571	0.4167	0.3846

Table 4. Performance comparison w.r.t. training ratio on KDDCUP

Ratio	ADAF			ALAD			DAGMM		
$\tau\%$	Precision	Recall	F_1	Precision	Recall	F_1	Precision	Recall	F_1
10%	0.9873	0.9938	0.9906	0.9576	0.9727	0.9651	0.9234	0.9382	0.9308
20%	0.9896	0.9942	0.9919	0.9554	0.9691	0.9622	0.9041	0.9171	0.9106
30%	0.9863	0.9889	0.9876	0.9513	0.9513	0.9513	0.9290	0.9437	0.9363
40%	0.9888	0.9895	0.9892	0.9466	0.9625	0.9545	0.9469	0.9628	0.9548
50%	0.9833	0.9941	0.9887	0.9513	0.9664	0.9588	0.9315	0.9464	0.9389
60%	0.9890	0.9959	0.9925	0.9502	0.9624	0.9563	0.9448	0.9570	0.9509

Ratio	DSEBM-e			DSEBM-r			AnoGAN		
$\tau\%$	Precision	Recall	F_1	Precision	Recall	F_1	Precision	Recall	F_1
10%	0.1121	0.1142	0.1131	0.8535	0.8233	0.8381	0.9166	0.8362	0.8667
20%	0.1322	0.1333	0.1332	0.8472	0.8166	0.8316	0.8590	0.8590	0.8590
30%	0.0830	0.0840	0.0830	0.8732	0.8403	0.8564	0.8344	0.8476	0.8409
40%	0.1311	0.1332	0.1321	0.8745	0.8422	0.8576	0.8343	0.8344	0.8344
50%	0.2151	0.2180	0.2170	0.8744	0.8414	0.8575	0.9472	0.8163	0.8630
60%	0.0401	0.0411	0.0410	0.8756	0.8399	0.8573	0.8496	0.8605	0.8550

Arrhythmia and KDDCUP. As the ratio of training data increases, the performance of our model is getting better and better on both datasets, especially on Arrhythmia ADAF achieves a significant improvement. The performance of ALAD and AnoGAN on KDDCUP dataset is relatively stable, and has some fluctuations on Arrhythmia. From Table 4, DSEBM-e that uses energy score as detection criterion is not suitable for KDDCUP. This is because the data distribution of KDDCUP is more complicated than that of the energy model. The experimental results of ALAD, DSEBM-r and AnoGAN are similar because they all use the reconstruction error as the criterion for anomaly detection. Although the results of DAGMM also increases with the increase of training data, our ADAF is far superior to DAGMM, even using less training data.

In summary, this experiment confirms that our ADAF can achieve better results with fewer training samples compared to state-of-the-art baselines.

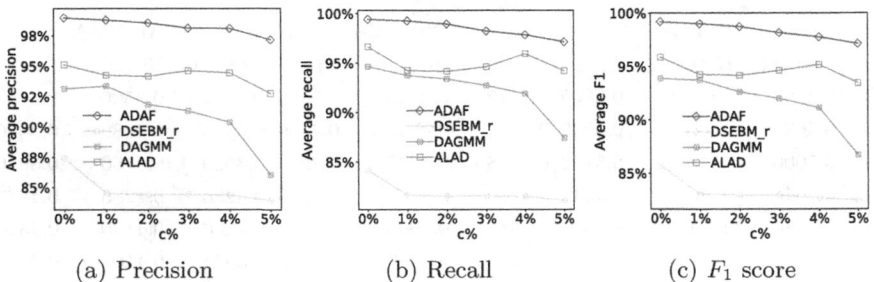

| (a) Precision | (b) Recall | (c) F_1 score |

Fig. 2. Anomaly detection results on contaminated training data on KDDCUP

4.7 Robustness Evaluation

Finally, we evaluate the robustness of our ADAF compared to the baselines on KDDCUP. We only use 10% of the normal data as the training set for our ADAF, and meanwhile we mix $c\%$ of samples from the anomalous data into the training set. In term of ALAD, DSEBM and DAGMM, we select 50% of the normal data as the training set, while mixing $c\%$ of samples from anomaly data into their training set.

Figure 2 shows the average precision, recall, and F_1 score results of ADAF, DSEBM-e, DAGMM and ALAD with different contaminated training data. When the contamination ratio c increases from 1% to 5%, the average precision, recall, and F_1 score of all methods decrease. However, we also observe that our model is only affected slightly and maintains an extremely robust performance. As $c\%$ increases, the performance of DAGMM declines sharply, but the impact on DSEBM-r and ALAD is not very significant. This may be because the GMM model in DAGMM is more sensitive to noise compared to the reconstruction error used in DSEBM-r and ALAD. Nevertheless, our ADAF is still significantly better than all baseline methods.

5 Conclusion

In this paper, we propose an Anomaly Detection model based on Autoregressive Flow (ADAF) for detecting anomalies in high-dimensional data. ADAF uses an autoregressive flow to obtain the latent variable, which holds the key information of the original input data. Because of the reversibility of flow model, the latent variables completely inherit the essential information of the original input data. Unlike the traditional two-step methods, ADAF is an absolute end-to-end framework that jointly optimizes the latent error and probability density estimation simultaneously. Finally, both latent error and neural density are used as decision criteria in anomaly detection. Our experimental results on public benchmark datasets show that ADAF is significantly better than state-of-the-art methods by up to 20% improvement on the standard F_1 score.

Acknowledgments. This work is partially supported by the National Natural Science Foundation of China under grant Nos. 61773331, U1706218 and 61572418, and the Natural Science Foundation of Shandong Province under grant No. ZR2018ZB0852.

References

1. An, J., Cho, S.: Variational autoencoder based anomaly detection using reconstruction probability. Spec. Lect. IE **2**, 1–18 (2015)
2. Arjovsky, M., Chintala, S., Bottou, L.: Wasserstein generative adversarial networks. In: ICML, pp. 214–223 (2017)
3. Baur, C., Wiestler, B., Albarqouni, S., Navab, N.: Deep autoencoding models for unsupervised anomaly segmentation in brain MR images. In: Crimi, A., Bakas, S., Kuijf, H., Keyvan, F., Reyes, M., van Walsum, T. (eds.) BrainLes 2018. LNCS, vol. 11383, pp. 161–169. Springer, Cham (2019). https://doi.org/10.1007/978-3-030-11723-8_16
4. Breunig, M.M., Kriegel, H.P., Ng, R.T., Sander, J.: LOF: identifying density-based local outliers. In: ACM Sigmod Record, vol. 29, pp. 93–104. ACM (2000)
5. Candès, E.J., Li, X., Ma, Y., Wright, J.: Robust principal component analysis? J. ACM (JACM) **58**(3), 11 (2011)
6. Chalapathy, R., Chawla, S.: Deep learning for anomaly detection: A survey. arXiv:1901.03407 (2019)
7. Chandola, V., Banerjee, A., Kumar, V.: Anomaly detection: a survey. ACM Comput. Surv. (CSUR) **41**(3), 15 (2009)
8. Chen, Y., Zhou, X.S., Huang, T.S.: One-class SVM for learning in image retrieval. In: ICIP, pp. 34–37. Citeseer (2001)
9. Dinh, L., Krueger, D., Bengio, Y.: Nice: Non-linear independent components estimation. arXiv preprint arXiv:1410.8516 (2014)
10. Dinh, L., Sohl-Dickstein, J., Bengio, S.: Density estimation using real NVP. arXiv preprint arXiv:1605.08803 (2016)
11. Domingues, R., Filippone, M., Michiardi, P., Zouaoui, J.: A comparative evaluation of outlier detection algorithms: experiments and analyses. Pattern Recogn. **74**, 406–421 (2018)
12. Erfani, S.M., Rajasegarar, S., Karunasekera, S., Leckie, C.: High-dimensional and large-scale anomaly detection using a linear one-class SVM with deep learning. Pattern Recogn. **58**, 121–134 (2016)
13. Goodfellow, I., et al.: Generative adversarial nets. In: NeurIPS, pp. 2672–2680 (2014)
14. Günter, S., Schraudolph, N.N., Vishwanathan, S.: Fast iterative kernel principal component analysis. J. Mach. Learn. Res. 8(Aug), 1893–1918 (2007)

15. Hu, W., Gao, J., Li, B., Wu, O., Du, J., Maybank, S.J.: Anomaly detection using local kernel density estimation and context-based regression. IEEE Trans. Knowl. Data Eng. (2018)
16. Keller, F., Muller, E., Bohm, K.: HiCS: high contrast subspaces for density-based outlier ranking. In: ICDE, pp. 1037–1048. IEEE (2012)
17. Kingma, D.P., Dhariwal, P.: Glow: generative flow with invertible 1x1 convolutions. In: NeurIPS, pp. 10215–10224 (2018)
18. Knorr, E M., Ng, R.T., Tucakov, V.: Distance-based outliers: algorithms and applications. VLDB J. **8**(3–4), 237–253 (2000)
19. Liu, F.T., Ting, K.M., Zhou, Z.H.: Isolation forest. In: ICDM, pp. 413–422. IEEE (2008)
20. van den Oord, A., et al.: Parallel wavenet: Fast high-fidelity speech synthesis. arXiv preprint arXiv:1711.10433 (2017)
21. Ravanbakhsh, M., Nabi, M., Mousavi, H., Sangineto, E., Sebe, N.: Plug-and-play CNN for crowd motion analysis: an application in abnormal event detection. In: WACV, pp. 1689–1698. IEEE (2018)
22. Ruff, L., et al.: Deep one-class classification. In: ICML, pp. 4393–4402 (2018)
23. Schlegl, T., Seeböck, P., Waldstein, S.M., Langs, G., Schmidt-Erfurth, U.: f-AnoGAN: fast unsupervised anomaly detection with generative adversarial networks. Med. Image Anal. **54**, 30–44 (2019)
24. Schlegl, T., Seeböck, P., Waldstein, S.M., Schmidt-Erfurth, U., Langs, G.: Unsupervised anomaly detection with generative adversarial networks to guide marker discovery. In: Niethammer, M., Styner, M., Aylward, S., Zhu, H., Oguz, I., Yap, P.-T., Shen, D. (eds.) IPMI 2017. LNCS, vol. 10265, pp. 146–157. Springer, Cham (2017). https://doi.org/10.1007/978-3-319-59050-9_12
25. Schubert, E., Zimek, A., Kriegel, H.P.: Generalized outlier detection with flexible kernel density estimates. In: SDM, pp. 542–550. SIAM (2014)
26. Tan, S.C., Ting, K.M., Liu, T.F.: Fast anomaly detection for streaming data. In: IJCAI (2011)
27. Yan, Y., Cao, L., Rundensteiner, E.A.: Scalable top-n local outlier detection. In: KDD, pp. 1235–1244. ACM (2017)
28. Zenati, H., Romain, M., Foo, C.S., Lecouat, B., Chandrasekhar, V.: Adversarially learned anomaly detection. In: ICDM, pp. 727–736. IEEE (2018)
29. Zhai, S., Cheng, Y., Lu, W., Zhang, Z.: Deep structured energy based models for anomaly detection. ICML **48** (2016)
30. Zhou, C., Paffenroth, R.C.: Anomaly detection with robust deep autoencoders. In: KDD, pp. 665–674. ACM (2017)
31. Zong, B., et al.: Deep autoencoding Gaussian mixture model for unsupervised anomaly detection. ICLR (2018)

Fine-Grained Entity Typing
for Relation-Sparsity Entities

Lei Niu[1], Binbin Gu[2], Zhixu Li[1(✉)], Wei Chen[1], Ying He[3], Zhaoyin Zhang[3],
and Zhigang Chen[4]

[1] Institute of Artificial Intelligence, School of Computer Science and Technology,
Soochow University, Suzhou, China
lniu@stu.suda.edu.cn, {zhixuli,robertchen}@suda.edu.cn
[2] University of California, Santa Cruz, USA
gu.binbin@hotmail.com
[3] IFLYTEK Research, Suzhou, China
{yinghe,zyzhang27}@iflytek.com
[4] State Key Laboratory of Cognitive Intelligence, iFLYTEK, Hefei, China
zgchen27@iflytek.com

Abstract. This paper works on fine-grained entity typing without using external knowledge for Knowledge Graphs (KGs). Aiming at identifying the semantic type of an entity, this task has been studied predominantly in KGs. Provided with dense enough relations among entities, the existing mainstream KG embedding based approaches could achieve great performance on the task. However, many entities are sparse in their relations with other entities in KGs, which fails the existing KG embedding models in fine-grained entity typing. In this paper, we propose a novel KG embedding model for relation-sparsity entities in KGs. In our model, we map all attributes and types into the same vector sapce, where attributes could be granted with different weights according to an employed attention mechanism, while attribute values could be trained as bias vectors from attribute vectors pointing to type vectors. Based on this KG embedding model, we perform entity typing from coarse-grained level to more fine-grained level hierarchically. Besides, we also propose ways to utilize zero-shot attribute values that never appear in the training set. Our experiments performed on real-world KGs show that our approach is superior to the most advanced models in most cases.

Keywords: Fine-grained entity typing · Knowledge graph embedding · Knowledge graph

1 Introduction

Type information of entities is very important in Knowledge Graphs (KGs). Unfortunately, many entities' type information is usually missing for many entities even in some well-known KGs such as Yago [20] and DBPedia [1]. To complete the missing type information in KGs, the task of **entity typing** [15] is

© Springer Nature Switzerland AG 2020
Y. Nah et al. (Eds.): DASFAA 2020, LNCS 12113, pp. 141–157, 2020.
https://doi.org/10.1007/978-3-030-59416-9_9

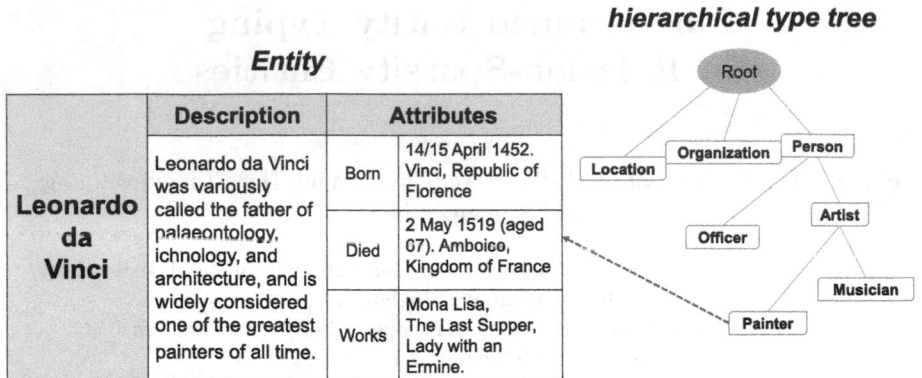

Fig. 1. An example of fine-grained entity typing in KG

proposed, aiming at identifying the semantic type (e.g., Artist) of an entity (e.g., Leonardo da Vinci) in KGs.

While traditional entity typing approaches only focus on assigning entities with a small set of coarse-grained types including Person, Organization, Location and Others [19], **fine-grained entity typing** assigns more specific types to entities, which could form a type-path in the type hierarchy in KGs [18]. As the example shown in Fig. 1, "Leonardo da Vinci" is associated with a type-path *"thing/person/artist/painter"*. Apparently, fine-grained types (e.g., *Painter* and *Artist*) make more sense in data mining than coarse-grained types (e.g., *Person*) since they provide us with more specific semantic information [22]. Therefore, the more fine-grained the types are, the more instrumental they would be in many of the KG-based tasks, such as knowledge base completion [5], entity linking [12], relation extraction [13], and question answering [25].

Plenty of work has been done on fine-grained entity typing. While traditional information extraction based approaches focus on extracting type information for entities from external text resource [3,14,26], in recent years, more and more work tend to infer missing entity types for entities based on KGs' internal information. The existing work on KG-based fine-grained entity typing mainly relies on KG embedding for entity typing, i.e., the entities are first embedded based on information in KGs including relations, continuous attribute values and descriptions etc., and then classified into different semantic types according to their embedded results. However, although the TransE [2] and its variants [10,11,21] are widely applied to many KG-relevant applications, they are helpless to those entities having sparse relations with other entities. Some work also infers missing types for entities according to the embedding results of entities based on their text descriptions [16]. But text descriptions are not always in high-quality. Recent work inputs the relations of entities and continuous attributes into a multi-layer perceptron to train the representation of entities for entity typing and achieves state-of-the-art results [8]. However, without dense enough relations among entities for embedding learning, they are difficult to achieve

Table 1. Percentage of Entities having Sparse Relations (1, 2, or 3) with Other Entities, and the Average Number of Triples with them on DBpedia, CN-DBpedia and Yago3

	0 Relation		1 Relation		2 Relation		3 Relation	
DBpedia	5%	3.5	2%	3.9	7%	5.1	12%	6.3
CN-DBpedia	11%	4.3	6%	4.7	5%	5.3	9%	6.1
Yogo3	7%	3.8	3%	4.4	6%	5.6	10%	6.4

desirable results. In practice, there are a large proportion of entities having very sparse relations with other entities in KGs. As listed in Table 1, there are more than 20% entities having no more than 3 relational triples with other entities on DBpedia, CN-DBpedia, and Yogo3. On the other hand, the average number of triples for such entities are not that small, which can also be observed in Table 1. While some of these triples are just attribute triples describing an attribute and corresponding attribute value of an entity, other triples are "unlinked" relational triples, which have their tail entity mentions unlinked to their corresponding KG entities.

To address fine-grained entity typing for relation-sparsity entities in KGs, this paper proposes a novel KG embedding model based on attributes and attribute values of entities. Particularly, this KG embedding model maps all the attributes and types into the same vector space in a TransE-like way, where "unlinked" relational triples are also taken as attribute triples. In this model, attributes are granted with different weights according to a selective attention mechanism [7], while attribute values could be trained as bias vectors from attribute vectors to type vectors. Based on this KG embedding model, we perform entity typing from coarse-grained level to more fine-grained level hierarchically. Besides, it is common to meet zero-shot attribute values that never appear in the training set in the entity typing process. To handle these special cases, we also design a similarity measurement to find a set of closest attribute values to denote the zero-shot one, such that the robustness of our model could be further improved.

We summarize our contributions as follows:

- We propose a new KG embedding model based on attributes and attribute values, which is particularly designed for fine-grained entity typing to relation-sparsity entities in KGs.
- Based on this embedding model, we then propose to perform entity typing from coarse-grained level to more fine-grained level hierarchically.
- We design an algorithm to handle the entities with untrained (zero-shot) triple tails to ensure the robustness of our model.

We use two datasets from real-world KGs for experimental study. Our experiments performed on these two KGs show that our approach is superior to the most advanced models in most cases.

Roadmap. The rest of the paper is organized as follows: We cover the related work in Sect. 2, and then formulate the problem in Sect. 3. After present our approach in Sect. 4, we report our empirical study in Sect. 5. We finally conclude in Sect. 6.

2   Related Work

Entity typing is a long-standing problem in the Knowledge Graph (KG) construction research field. In this section, we first introduce the traditional solutions using external textual semantic information, and then cover the mainstream methods on entity typing within KGs.

2.1   Entity Typing with Texts

The goal of entity typing is to give entities more specific types after they have been recognized from text. As the number of types and the complexity of the problem increases, researchers try many ways to organize hierarchical information of types [26]. In recent work, Choi et al. [3] constructs an ultra-fine-grained dataset with 10,201 types at the most fine granularity. Based on the same dataset, Federico et al. [14] map all types onto a sphere space and train a transpose matrix to obtain the types of entities. This work achieve the state-of-art results in entity typing with texts. However, the information used for entity typing is usually about the sentences themselves, so the performance of entity typing in fine granularity is still unsatisfactory.

2.2   Entity Typing in KGs

The classification of entities KG becomes a classical problem that refers to KG completion. In KG completion, KG embedding is often used to solve such problems. For example, TransE [2], which is the basic of all KG embedding methods, trains vector expressions of entities and relationships based on relations between entities. In TransE, relations are trained as transitions from head entities to tail entities, which can be expressed as $\mathbf{h} + \mathbf{r} = \mathbf{t}$. Since then, various KG embedding methods focus on how to obtain a better representation of KG based on the relations between entities, such as TransR [11], PTrans [10], TransH [21] and so on.

Another kind of methods is to obtain the low-dimensional vector representations of entities semantics and then use the vectors to classify the entities. These methods are based on various kinds information in KGs rather than just relational triples. For example, Neelakantan and Chang [16] generate feature vectors from the description of entities in KG. Xu et al. [22] adopt a multi-labelled hierarchical classification method to assign Chinese entities of DBpedia types according to attributes and category information. In recent work, Jin et al. [8] comprehensively consider the relationship between entities and continuous attribute values, and combine them with a multi-layer perceptron to obtain the semantic vectors of entities.

The above methods consider entity typing in a complete KG. Nevertheless, there are many relation-sparsity entities in KGs during the actual construction process. These relation-sparsity entities tend to have many triples with unsplit and unlinked tails, so that the above methods may fail to address such triples. Our approach is designed to solve the problem of entity typing in this case. We take full use of discontinuous attribute values which mostly come from unsplit and unlinked tails to ensure that the relation information in such tails is not lost.

3   Problem Formulation

A typical KG consists of a number of facts, usually in the form of *triples* denoted by *(head, predicate, tail)*, where *head* is the *subject entity* and *tail* is either the *object entity* or an *attribute value* of the subject entity. We call a triple as a *relational triple* if the *object* of the triple is an entity and the *predicate* denotes the relation between the two entities. And we call a triple as an *attribute triple* if the *predicate* denotes an attribute of the entity [6].

Given a KG with a hierachical type tree such as the one shown in Fig. 1, the task of fine-grained entity typing aims at finding fine-grained semantic types for entities with missing type information in the KG, w.r.t. the given hierachical type tree. The hierachical type tree reflects the hypernym-hyponym relations between types, for example, "person" is the hypernym of "artist". More formally, we give the relevant definitions with fine-grained entity typing task as follows.

Definition 1 (Knowledge Graph). *Knowledge graph $KG = \{E, RT, AT\}$ is defined as a set of entities E, their relation triples RT and their attribute triples AT.*

Definition 2 (Hierarchical Type Tree). *Hierarchical type tree organizes types in the form of a tree which provides hypernym-hyponym relations between types. Formally, Hierarchical type tree $Ttr = \{TS, TR\}$ contains the set of types TS and the relations between types TR.*

Definition 3 (Fine-grained Entity Typing). *Given a knowledge graph $KG = \{E, RT, AT\}$ and a hierarchical type tree $Ttr = \{TS, TR\}$, **Fine-grained Entity Typing** aims to find a path $\{t_1, t_2...t_n\}$ in Ttr for each entity in E, where t_i is the hypernym of t_{i-1}.*

Example 1. As shown in Fig. 1, **hierarchical type tree** is a tree which reflects hypernym-hyponym relations between types, while **knowledge graph** is a collection which contains entities like "Leonardo da Vinci" and their attributes and relations between each other. The task of **fine-grained entity typing** is to find a type path in **hierarchical type tree** for each entity in **knowledge graph**, such as *"thing/person/artist/painter"* for *"Leonardo da Vinci"*.

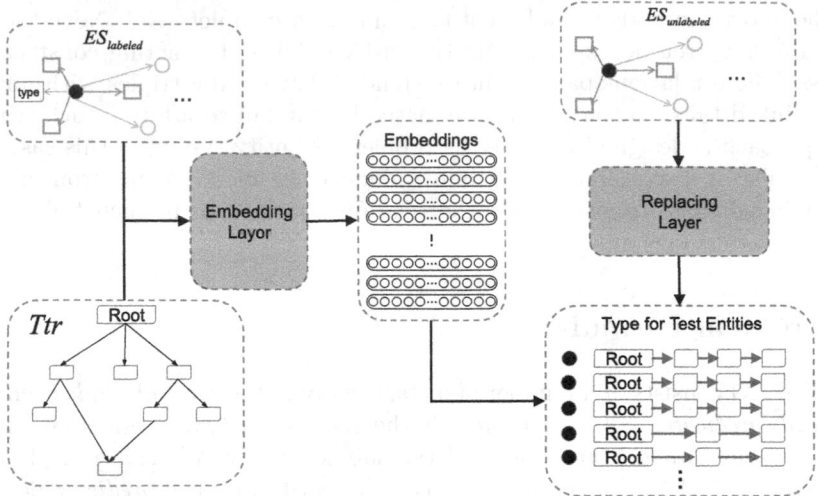

Fig. 2. Architecture of our approach

4 Our Approach

The architecture of our approach is given in Fig. 2. Our model mainly consists of two modules: embedding layer and replacing layer. We obtain vector representations of triples at the embedding layer which needs labeled entities and a hierarchical type tree Ttr as input. The role of the replacing layer is to classify the unlabeled entities based on the embedded results and handle the entities with untrained (zero-shot) triple tails. In the following, we briefly introduce how to build a proper hierarchical type tree and then present the embedding layer and replacing layer respectively.

- **Hierarchical Type Tree:** Types are naturally hierarchical, we start with the coarse-grained typing of entities, and then we gradually get more fine-grained types. To this end, we construct a tree that can reflect the hypernym-hyponym relationship of types at the semantic level which can be used to carry out hierarchical classification.

  Given a set of types denoted as TS, for each pair of type combination $<t_1, t_2>$ in TS, we calculate the possibility that t_1, t_2 have hypernym-hyponym relationship according to the entity set of types t_1 and t_2:

$$P_{hyp}(t_1, t_2) = \sqrt{\frac{|ES(t_1) \cap ES(t_2)|}{|ES(t_1)|} \times (1 - \frac{|ES(t_1) \cap ES(t_2)|}{|ES(t_2)|})} \quad (1)$$

  where $ES(t)$ is the set of entities of type t. This formula is proposed by Lenci et al. [9], which calculates confidence based on the coincidence between the sets of entities. If $P_{hyp}(t_1, t_2) > \theta$, we consider that t_1 is the hypernym of

t_2, where θ is threshold value. The set of hypernym-hyponym relationships between types is denoted as TR which is formulated as follows:

$$TR = \{< t_1, t_2 > |t_1, t_2 \in Ts \ \& \ P_{hyp}(t_1, t_2) > \theta\} \tag{2}$$

To ensure the accuracy of TR, we perform a manual filtering where each hypernym-hyponym relationship in TR is checked by three people and only those confirmed correct by at least two people would be kept. After that, we also need to remove some redundant relationships to ensure that the children of each node are at the same layer of the tree. For example, if $<$"person", "artist"$>$, $<$"artist", "painter"$>$ and $<$"person", "painter"$>$ $\in TR$, we remove $<$"person", "painter"$>$ from TR so that the children of node "person" in Ttr are at the same layer, which means they are of the similar granularity.

- **Embedding Layer:** The main task of the embedding layer is to construct classifiers and train the vector representation of elements in triples and types. To obtain the type path of the entity, we build several classifiers to identify types of different granularities. Also, we propose to fully use discontinuous attribute values, which are trained as bias vector in this layer. We give more details in Sect. 4.1.

- **Replacing Layer:** The replacing layer will be triggered when unlabeled entities are classified by embedding results. This is because we often encounter entities with untrained (zero-shot) triples which have no corresponding vector representation. So we use replacing layer to handle such entities to ensure the robustness of our model. More details could be found in Sect. 4.2.

4.1 Embedding Layer

The architecture of the embedded layer is shown in Fig. 3. There are two main inputs to the embedded layer, one is the set of labeled entities ($ES_{labeled}$), and the other is the hierarchical type tree Ttr. In Ttr, the coarser the type granularity is, the closer it is to the root node. There are three coarse-grained types: "person" ("Per"), "organization" ("Org"), and "location" ("Loc"). We start by training a classifier to classify these three types, and we denote it as $classifier_1$. Then three classifiers are trained to classify the sub-types of "Per", "Org" and "Loc" respectively. For example, if "Per" has five sub-types including artist, officials..., we train a classifier to classify entities which has been classified by $classifier_1$ as "Per" into five more fine-grained types.

In each classifier, we first learn the low-dimensional vector representation of each triple's predicate and tail in embedding layer. After that, the representation of each entity is calculated by the representation of its triples and should be as close to the representation of entity's type as possible. The validity of the method of obtaining types by triples' information has been proved by multiple experiments [8]. But all of these approaches only consider predicate information in triples, and they can only work when the tails of triples are entities which have been linked. However, relation-sparsity entities have a small number of such triple tails.

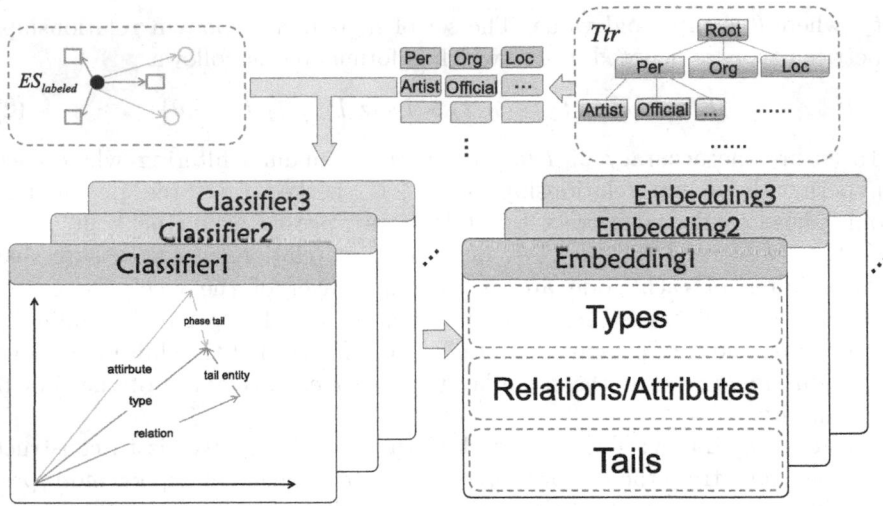

Fig. 3. Architecture of embedding layer

As shown in Table 1, most relation-sparsity entities also have rich triples that contain many undiscovered relations. These relations are mainly derived from the tails of unsplit and unlinked triples, or from phrase tails that have not yet been refined, and they will be treated as discontinuous attribute values. For example, ("Leonardo da Vinci", "born", "14/15 April 1452.Republic of Florence") can be spilt into an attribute triple ("Leonardo da Vinci", "birthday", "14/15 April 1452") and a relation triple ("Leonardo da Vinci", "birthplace", "Republic of Florence"). The goal of our model is to make full use of discontinuous attribute values in fine-grained entity typing.

1) Embedding with Predicates in Triples. In triples, predicates are usually relation names or attribute names. These predicates themselves can reflect the type information of the corresponding head entity. For example, "Leonardo da Vinci" has an attribute: "bron", which obviously tends to be the attribute of entities whose type is "Per". In previous work, SDType [17] proposed a method to calculate the type probability distribution of entities based on their triples' predicates, which indicates that the predicates of entities can indeed reflect the type information of entities. In our approach, we map entities' attribute/relation name and type into the same vector space. Vector representations of entities can be obtained by weighted summation of their attribute/relation vectors and should be as close as possible to the entity's type vector. For an entity in training set, the embedded target can be represented as follows when considering only the average weights:

$$\frac{\sum_{i=0}^{|PS|} \overrightarrow{p_i}}{|PS|} = \overrightarrow{type} \tag{3}$$

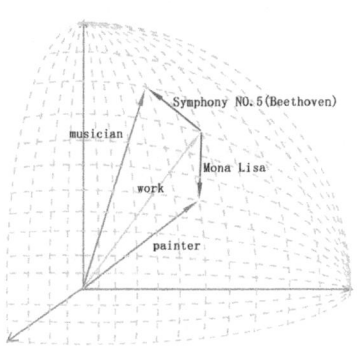

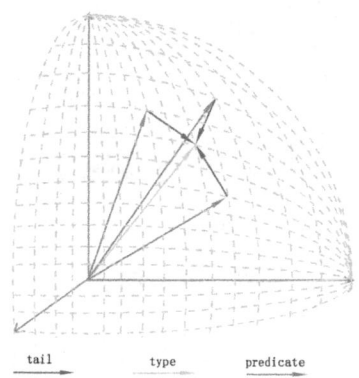

tail   type   predicate

Fig. 4. Example of bias vector   **Fig. 5.** Training target

where PS means the set of predicates in entity's triples and $p_i \in PS$, $type$ means entity's type. In the vector space that satisfies the above formula, the more a predicate P is monopolized by a type T, the closer the $\overrightarrow{P}$ is to the $\overrightarrow{T}$. A predicate P being monopolized by a type T means if an entity's triples have predicate P, the entity's type is mostly likely to T. As shown in Fig. 6, predicate "born" exists in triples of entities whose type is "Per" in most cases, so $\overrightarrow{born}$ is close to $\overrightarrow{Per}$ but far from $\overrightarrow{Loc}$ and $\overrightarrow{Org}$.

2) Embedding with Triple Tails. If we just use predicates of triples to train the entity representation, it does work well at coarse granularity. However, as the granularity increases, it becomes difficult to identify the more accurate type of an entity due to insufficient information. For example, "Leonardo da Vinci" has a predicate "work", which can help us know he is a "Per". However, both entities of type "musician" and entities of type "painter" have predicate "work". We could hardly know whether "Leonardo da Vinci" is a "painter" or a "musician" simply by the predicate "work", while the object of predicate "work" can help us identify him as a "painter".

So we consider training the tails of triples as bias vectors pointing to more specific types, as shown in Fig. 4, the vector of predicate "work" is close both to the vector of type "musician" and the vector of type "painter". Apparently, when the object of "work" is a painting like "Mona Lisa," the entity is more likely to be a "painter", and when the object of "work" is a music like "Symphony No. 5 (Beethoven)" the entity is more likely to be a "musician". So we train the tails like "Mona Lisa" and "Symphony No. 5 (Beethoven)" to be bias vectors pointing to more specific types. When considering the tails of triples, we can obtain the type vector of each entity from its predicate vector plus the vector of the corresponding triple tail. The training target and the example are shown in Fig. 5 and Fig. 4 respectively. The formal expression is as follows:

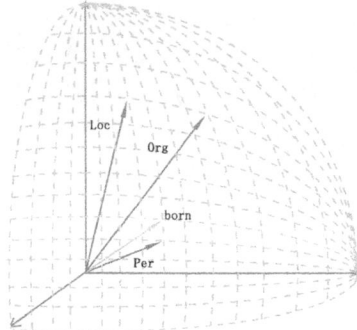

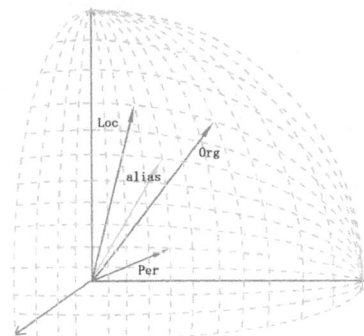

Fig. 6. "born"   **Fig. 7.** "alias"

$$\frac{\sum\limits_{i=0}^{|PS|} (\overrightarrow{p_i} + \overrightarrow{t_i})}{|PS|} = type \tag{4}$$

where t_i is the corresponding triple tail of predicate p_i. For continuous attribute values, we train them after discretizing them by clustering.

3) Getting Weights for Predicates. Each predicate is supposed to have a different weight when judging the type. For example, "born" is a common predicate that "Per", "Org", and "Loc" can have, whereas "alias" is usually only reserved for "Per". This is reflected in low-dimensional vector space where $\overrightarrow{born}$ is very close to $\overrightarrow{Per}$ and $\overrightarrow{alias}$ is not particularly close to the vector of any type. Figure 6 and Fig. 7 illustrate this phenomenon. Clearly "born" is more significant and should have a higher weight. Based on this idea, we use a selective attention mechanism to obtain the weight of the predicate, and the training objective is defined as follows:

$$\frac{\sum\limits_{i=0}^{|PS|} e^{Weight(p_i)} (\overrightarrow{p_i} + \overrightarrow{t_i})}{\sum\limits_{i=0}^{|PS|} e^{Weight(p_i)}} = \overrightarrow{type} \tag{5}$$

The weights of predicates, denoted by $Weight(p_i, TS)$, defines the variance of the distances between $\overrightarrow{p_i}$ and the vectors of each class.

$$Weight(p_i, TS) = \frac{\sum\limits_{j=0}^{|TS|} \left(\left\| \overrightarrow{p_i} - \overrightarrow{type_j} \right\|_2 - Avg_{dis}(p_i, TS) \right)^2}{|TS|} \tag{6}$$

where TS means the set of types that the current classifier needs to distinguish and $type_j \in TS$. $Avg_{dis}(p_i, TS)$ is the average distance between $\overrightarrow{p_i}$ and the vector of each type in TS:

$$Avg_{dis}(p_i, TS) = \frac{\sum_{j=0}^{|TS|} \left\| \overrightarrow{p_i} - \overrightarrow{type_j} \right\|_2}{|TS|} \quad (7)$$

During the process of training, negative samples are obtained by replacing the types of positive samples. For example, the negative sample of ("Leonardo da Vinci", "painter") can be ("Leonardo da Vinci", "musician"). The loss function for each positive sample is defined as follows:

$$l_{(e,type)} = \left\| \frac{\sum_{i=0}^{|PS|} e^{Weight(p_i,TS)} (\overrightarrow{p_i} + \overrightarrow{t_i})}{\sum_{i=0}^{|PS|} e^{Weight(p_i,TS)}} - \overrightarrow{type} \right\|_2 \quad (8)$$

For each positive sample $(e, type)$ and the corresponding negative sample $(e, type')$, where $type'$ is the error label after replacing. We use hinge loss to get the loss of each sample. The hinge loss is defined as:

$$l_{hinge} = max(0, l_{(e,type)} - l_{(e,type')} + \xi) \quad (9)$$

where ξ is the fixed margin. Finally, our loss function is defined as:

$$L = \sum_{e \in ES} max(0, l_{(e,type)} - l_{(e,type')} + \xi) \quad (10)$$

where ES is the entity set in training.

4.2 Replacing Layer

In the real world, there are an infinite number of possible objects corresponding to predicates in triples, and even the triple tails with the same semantic meaning may have different but similar expressions. The training set cannot contain all possible triple tails. In fact, we often encounter untrained tails during testing, so we design a replacing layer to replace such tails with the closest trained tails. We mainly adopt three kinds of similarity: gensim[1] (Bag of Words), longest common sub-sequence (LCS) and BERT-wwm [4]. The gensim similarity is defined as follows:

$$Sim_{gensim}(s_1, s_2) = \frac{|Bow(s_1) \cap Bow(s_2)|^2}{|Bow(s_1)| \times |Bow(s_2)|} \quad (11)$$

where $Bow(s)$ means the "Bag of Words" of s. s_1, s_2 are two phrases used to judge similarity. And the longest common sub-sequence (LCS) similarity is as follows:

$$Sim_{LCS}(s_1, s_2) = \frac{len(LCS(s_1, s_2))^2}{len(s_1) \times len(s_2)} \quad (12)$$

---

[1] https://pypi.org/project/gensim/.

Table 2. Statistics of the datasets

	Entities	Types	Predicates	Rel.triples	Attr.triples	
					Continuous	Discontinuous
CN-DBpedia	198,546	175	2185	178,554	515,862	1,270,694
DBpeadia	300,000	214	1426	5,243,230	849,387	0

where $LCS(s_1, s_2)$ means the longest common sub-sequence of s_1 and s_2 and $len(\ldots)$ means the number of characters in the phrase.

Here we use BERT-wwm [4] to get the vector presentations of phrases and then calculate the similarity by cosine function.

Based on the above three similarities, we define the final similarity as follows:

$$Sim = Sim_{gensim} + \lambda_1 \cdot Sim_{LCS} + \lambda_2 \cdot Sim_{BERT-wwm} \tag{13}$$

λ_1 and λ_2 are weight parameters. The above formula expresses the semantic similarity between phrases, triple tails with similar semantics should have similar representation in the vector space in our model. So we use formula 13 to replace untrained triple tails with tails that are already trained.

5   Experiments and Analysis

In this section, we first introduce our datasets and the metrics we use for evaluation in Sect. 5.1 and then explain methods we compare with in Sect. 5.2. Finally, we present the experimental results and analysis in Sect. 5.3.

5.1   Datasets and Experimental Setup

Datasets: We collect our data from CN-DBpedia[2] and DBpedia[3]. The data in CN-DBpedia is mainly collected from the inforbox if BaiduBaike which contains many unsplit and unlinked relation triples. So, a large number of relation-sparsity entities exist in this dataset, which is specifically used to test the performance of our method on relation-sparsity entities. The DBpedia dataset is proposed by Jin et al. [8], which is extracted from DBpedia. In this dataset, each entity has rich relationships and continuous attribute values. As we can see in Table 2, both datasets have about 200 fine-grained types, and the second dataset has a much larger proportion of relational triples than the first one.

Metris: As for the evaluation metrics, we use Micro-averaged F1 (Mi-F1) and Macro-averaged F1 (Ma-F1), which have been used in many fine-grained typing systems [18,23,24].

---

[2] http://kw.fudan.edu.cn/cndbpedia/intro/.
[3] https://wiki.dbpedia.org.

Parameter Settings: In our experiments, all predicate vectors are normalized: $\|\overrightarrow{p_i}\|_2 = 1$, and the length of bias vector is positioned to $1/6$ of the length of predicate vector: $\left\|\overrightarrow{t_i}\right\|_2 = 1/6$. A batch of 500 samples is used to update the model parameter per step with learning rate set as 0.002, training time is limited to at most 200 epochs over the training set. And we set fixed margin in loss function $\xi = 1$. In replacing layer, both λ_1 and λ_2 are chosen among$\{0.2, 0.4, 0.6, 0.8\}$, we found $\lambda_1 = 0.4$ and $\lambda_2 = 0.8$ achieve best performance.

5.2 Approaches for Comparison

In this section, we briefly introduce five comparative methods including *TransE* [2], *SDType* [17] *APE* [8], our proposed *Baseline Model* and *Final Model*.

- The *TransE* method aims to learn representations of all entities and relations in KGs. In *TransE*, the relation r in each relation triple: (h,r,t) can be considered as a translating from the head entity to the tail entity. By constantly adjusting the vector representation of h, r and t, we wish (h+r) is equal to t as much as possible, that is, $h + r = t$. This method is mainly used for prediction of tail entities, but vector representation of entities can also be used for entity typing. So, we input the entity representation obtained by *TransE* into a linear classifier for entity typing. For CN-DBpedia, due to the lack of relations, we link some tail entities to ensure that *TransE* could train normally.
- The *SDType* method is a heuristic model which counts on the distribution of head entities' types and tail entities' types for each predicate, respectively. For unlabeled entity, SDType calculates the probability that it is of each type based on these distribution.
- The *APE* method inputs the one-hot encoding of the entity's owned predicates and the vector of the continuous attribute values into a multi-layer perceptron. After that it uses a softmax layer to get the entity's type at the last layer of the network.
- The *Baseline1* considers only the predicates themself without the triple tails information, and each predicate has an average weight when the weighted sum is taken.
- The *Baseline2* does not replace untrained (zero-shot) triple tails by the replacing layer. It assigns vectors of untrained tails to the average of vectors of trained tails which are owned by untrained tails corresponding predicates.
- The *Final Model (TransCate)* adds the triple tails information to the loss function and uses the selective attention mechanism to obtain the predicates' weight. Besides, replacing layer is introduced to handle the untrained triple tails.

Table 3. The overall of the comparsion results

Approaches	CN-DBpedia		DBpeadia	
	Mi-F1	Ma-F1	Mi-F1	Ma-F1
TransE	0.375	0.261	0.519	0.512
SDType	0.558	0.447	0.577	0.569
APE	0.732	0.597	0.657	0.649
Baseline1	0.638	0.493	0.628	0.621
Baseline2	0.723	0.517	0.654	0.646
TransCate	**0.761**	**0.563**	**0.662**	**0.651**

5.3   Experimental Results

1) Overall Comparsion Results. We assign 40% of the entities in each dataset to test the performance of the entity typing. Each dataset is subjected to multiple experiments to get the average result except SDType as it relies on probability distribution and the effect of multiple experiments remained unchanged. As can be seen from Table 3, our method has obtained the desired performance, with a 3% improvement over the best methods of the past in CN-DBpedia since CN-DBpedia contains a large number of relation-sparsity entities. For DBpedia, our method only has tiny improvement. It is worth mentioning that TransE's performance is poor on both datasets. We notice that its performance is close to SDType, but much lower than other methods in most cases. The main reason for this is that TransE is designed for tail entity prediction rather than entity typing.

Analysis: In CN-DBpedia, the performance of TransE is much lower than that of other methods due to the sparse relations, and the performance of the baseline1 is lower than that of APE because it only uses predicate information of triples, while APE also use the information of continuous attribute values in triples. When our method uses triple tails information, the results are the best among all the comparison methods. In DBpedia, as the relations become denser, the performance of other methods approaches that of ours. The use of the replacing layer improves performance in CN-DBpedia more than it does in DBpedia because the test set of CN-DBpedia has more untrained triple tails.

2) The Effectiveness of Tails and Attention. We also evaluate the results for different granularity types when our approach use predicates information in triples, tails information and attention mechanisms. Table 4 shows the experimental results on CN-DBpedia. We observe that even simple typing with predicates can achieve good results when judging only three types: person, organization and location. However, the improvement brought by triple tails and attention mechanism becomes larger and larger as the granularity increases.

Table 4. The effectiveness of tails and attention

	3 types		23 types		149 types	
	Mi-F1	Ma-F1	Mi-F1	Ma-F1	Mi-F1	Ma-F1
Predicates	0.982	0.961	0.829	0.737	0.638	0.493
P+Tails	0.986	0.970	0.887	0.804	0.744	0.545
P+T+Attentions	0.991	0.983	0.904	0.826	0.761	0.563

6   Conclusions and Future Work

In this paper, we propose a new KG embedding model based on attributes and attribute values, which is particularly designed for fine-grained entity typing to relation-sparsity entities in KGs. Based on this KG embedding model, we perform entity typing from coarse-grained level to more fine-grained level hierarchically. We also design an algorithm to handle the entities with untrained (zero-shot) triple tails to ensure the robustness of our model. Our experiments performed on two real-world KGs show that our approach is superior to the most advanced models in most cases.

Future work looks forward to finding a better replacing algorithm for the untrained triple tails. In addition, we would like to consider the description text of the entity as an important information for better entity typing performance to triple-sparsity entities.

Acknowledgments. This research is partially supported by Natural Science Foundation of Jiangsu Province (No. BK20191420), National Natural Science Foundation of China (Grant No. 61632016, 61572336, 61572335, 61772356), Natural Science Research Project of Jiangsu Higher Education Institution (No. 17KJA520003, 18KJA520010), and the Open Program of Neusoft Corporation (No. SKLSAOP1801).

References

1. Auer, S., Bizer, C., Kobilarov, G., Lehmann, J., Cyganiak, R., Ives, Z.: DBpedia: a nucleus for a web of open data. In: Aberer, K., et al. (eds.) ASWC/ISWC -2007. LNCS, vol. 4825, pp. 722–735. Springer, Heidelberg (2007). https://doi.org/10.1007/978-3-540-76298-0_52
2. Bordes, A., Usunier, N., Garcia-Duran, A., Weston, J., Yakhnenko, O.: Translating embeddings for modeling multi-relational data. In: Advances in Neural Information Processing Systems, pp. 2787–2795 (2013)
3. Choi, E., Levy, O., Choi, Y., Zettlemoyer, L.: Ultra-fine entity typing. arXiv preprint arXiv:1807.04905 (2018)
4. Cui, Y., et al.: Pre-training with whole word masking for Chinese bert. arXiv preprint arXiv:1906.08101 (2019)
5. Dong, X., et al.: Knowledge vault: a web-scale approach to probabilistic knowledge fusion. In: Proceedings of the 20th ACM SIGKDD International Conference on Knowledge Discovery and Data Mining, pp. 601–610. ACM (2014)

6. He, F., et al.: Unsupervised entity alignment using attribute triples and relation triples. In: Li, G., Yang, J., Gama, J., Natwichai, J., Tong, Y. (eds.) DASFAA 2019. LNCS, vol. 11446, pp. 367–382. Springer, Cham (2019). https://doi.org/10.1007/978-3-030-18576-3_22

7. Jiang, T., Liu, M., Qin, B., Liu, T.: Attribute acquisition in ontology based on representation learning of hierarchical classes and attributes. arXiv preprint arXiv:1903.03282 (2019)

8. Jin, H., Hou, L., Li, J., Dong, T.: Attributed and predictive entity embedding for fine-grained entity typing in knowledge bases. In: Proceedings of the 27th International Conference on Computational Linguistics, pp. 282–292 (2018)

9. Lenci, A., Benotto, G.: Identifying hypernyms in distributional semantic spaces. In: * SEM 2012: The First Joint Conference on Lexical and Computational Semantics-Volume 1: Proceedings of the Main Conference and the Shared Task, and Volume 2: Proceedings of the Sixth International Workshop on Semantic Evaluation (SemEval 2012), pp. 75–79 (2012)

10. Lin, Y., Liu, Z., Luan, H., Sun, M., Rao, S., Liu, S.: Modeling relation paths for representation learning of knowledge bases. arXiv preprint arXiv:1506.00379 (2015)

11. Lin, Y., Liu, Z., Sun, M., Liu, Y., Zhu, X.: Learning entity and relation embeddings for knowledge graph completion. In: AAAI, vol. 15, pp. 2181–2187 (2015)

12. Ling, X., Singh, S., Weld, D.S.: Design challenges for entity linking. Trans. Assoc. Comput. Linguist. **3**, 315–328 (2015)

13. Liu, Y., Liu, K., Xu, L., Zhao, J., et al.: Exploring fine-grained entity type constraints for distantly supervised relation extraction (2014)

14. López, F., Heinzerling, B., Strube, M.: Fine-grained entity typing in hyperbolic space. arXiv preprint arXiv:1906.02505 (2019)

15. Nadeau, D., Sekine, S.: A survey of named entity recognition and classification. Lingvisticae Investigationes **30**(1), 3–26 (2007)

16. Neelakantan, A., Chang, M.W.: Inferring missing entity type instances for knowledge base completion: New dataset and methods. arXiv preprint arXiv:1504.06658 (2015)

17. Paulheim, H., Bizer, C.: Type inference on noisy RDF data. In: Alani, H., et al. (eds.) ISWC 2013. LNCS, vol. 8218, pp. 510–525. Springer, Heidelberg (2013). https://doi.org/10.1007/978-3-642-41335-3_32

18. Ren, X., He, W., Qu, M., Huang, L., Ji, H., Han, J.: AFET: automatic fine-grained entity typing by hierarchical partial-label embedding. In: Proceedings of the 2016 Conference on Empirical Methods in Natural Language Processing, pp. 1369–1378 (2016)

19. Sang, E.F., De Meulder, F.: Introduction to the conll-2003 shared task: Language-independent named entity recognition. arXiv preprint cs/0306050 (2003)

20. Suchanek, F.M., Kasneci, G., Weikum, G.: Yago: a core of semantic knowledge. In: Proceedings of the 16th International Conference on World Wide Web, pp. 697–706. ACM (2007)

21. Wang, Z., Zhang, J., Feng, J., Chen, Z.: Knowledge graph embedding by translating on hyperplanes. In: AAAI, vol. 14, pp. 1112–1119 (2014)

22. Xu, B., Zhang, Y., Liang, J., Xiao, Y., Hwang, S., Wang, W.: Cross-lingual type inference. In: Navathe, S.B., Wu, W., Shekhar, S., Du, X., Wang, X.S., Xiong, H. (eds.) DASFAA 2016. LNCS, vol. 9642, pp. 447–462. Springer, Cham (2016). https://doi.org/10.1007/978-3-319-32025-0_28

23. Yaghoobzadeh, Y., Schütze, H.: Multi-level representations for fine-grained typing of knowledge base entities. arXiv preprint arXiv:1701.02025 (2017)

24. Yaghoobzadeh, Y., Tze, H.S.: Corpus-level fine-grained entity typing using contextual information. arXiv preprint arXiv:1606.07901 (2016)
25. Yahya, M., Berberich, K., Elbassuoni, S., Weikum, G.: Robust question answering over the web of linked data. In: Proceedings of the 22nd ACM International Conference on Conference on Information & Knowledge Management, pp. 1107–1116. ACM (2013)
26. Yavuz, S., Gur, I., Su, Y., Srivatsa, M., Yan, X.: Improving semantic parsing via answer type inference. In: Proceedings of the 2016 Conference on Empirical Methods in Natural Language Processing, pp. 149–159 (2016)

Progressive Term Frequency Analysis on Large Text Collections

Yazhong Zhang[1,3], Hanbing Zhang[2,3], Zhenying He[2,3](✉), Yinan Jing[2,3](✉),
Kai Zhang[2,3], and X. Sean Wang[1,2,3,4](✉)

[1] School of Software, Fudan University, Shanghai, China
[2] School of Computer Science, Fudan University, Shanghai, China
{zhangyz17,hbzhang17,zhenying,jingyn,zhangk,xywangcs}@fudan.edu.cn
[3] Shanghai Key Laboratory of Data Science, Shanghai, China
[4] Shanghai Insititute of Intelligent Electronics and Systems, Shanghai, China

Abstract. The size of textual data continues to grow along with the need for timely and cost-effective analysis, while the growth of computation power cannot keep up with the growth of data. The delays when processing huge textual data can negatively impact user activity and insight. This calls for a paradigm shift from blocking fashion to progressive processing. In this paper, we propose a sample-based progressive processing model that focuses on term frequency calculation on text. The model is based on an incremental execution engine and will calculate a series of approximate results for a single query in a progressive way to provide a smooth trade-off between accuracy and latency. As a part, we proposed a new variant of the bootstrap technique to quantify result error progressively. We implemented this method in our system called Parrot on top of Apache Spark and used real-world data to test its performance. Experiments demonstrate that our method is 2.4x–19.7x faster to get a result within 1% error while the confidence interval always covers the accurate results very well.

1 Introduction

A huge amount of textual data is increasingly produced on the Internet. In twitter, for example, more than 500 million tweets were published per day in 2017[1]. These data are of great analytic values across many fields including hot topic analysis, social public sentiment, etc. Compared to structured data, textual data contains more semantic information such as term frequency and tf-idf whereas existing SQL aggregation functions focused mainly on numerical values, and, thus, are not suitable. And due to the non-correlated relationship between documents, people have much less priori about the distribution of words, especially on a subset. Analyzing textual data through a collection of fixed workload becomes unrealistic. Therefore, the way of interactive exploration becomes popular. The interactive exploration tool gives the user opportunities to continuously

---

[1] http://www.internetlivestats.com/twitter-statistics/.

© Springer Nature Switzerland AG 2020
Y. Nah et al. (Eds.): DASFAA 2020, LNCS 12113, pp. 158–174, 2020.
https://doi.org/10.1007/978-3-030-59416-9_10

approach the final goal by iteratively executing queries using varying predicates [6]. A key requirement of these tools is the ability to provide query results at "human speed". Previous literature [20] has demonstrated that a great delay can negatively impact user activity and insight discovery. However, the term frequency calculation on a 100 GB text collection costs more than 10 min in our experiment.

For analyzing structured data, lots of previous works attempt to speed up query execution through Data Cube or AQP (Approximate Query Processing) techniques. For data cube [8] and its successors, e.g., imMens [13] and NanoCubes [12], they either suffer from the curse of dimensionality or restrict the number of attributes that can be filtered at the same time. When limited by response time and computing resources, AQP systems (e.g., AQUA [2], IDEA [7], VerdictDB [14]) only return a single approximate result regardless of how long the user waits. However, there is an increasing need for interactive human-driven exploratory analysis, whose desired accuracy or the time-criticality cannot be known a priori and change dynamically based on unquantifiable human factors [18]. Besides, due to the difference in data structure, these technologies cannot be migrated to apply to text data easily. For semi-structured and unstructured data, state-of-the-art solutions are based on the content management system or cube structures, such as ElasticSearch [1] and Text Cube [11]. ElasticSearch supports simple queries with key-value based filtering as well as full-text searching for fuzzy matching over the entire dataset. However, it doesn't have good support for ad-hoc queries on subset and cannot return an accurate total term frequency through the *termvectors* API. Text Cube uses techniques to pre-aggregate data and gives the user the possibility to make a semantic navigation in data dimensions [4]. Text Cube can significantly reduce query latency, but it requires extensive preprocessing and suffer from the curse of dimensionality.

The universality and the demand for performance motivate us to utilize sampling techniques to return approximate answers to shorten response latency. However, approximate answers are most useful when accompanied by accuracy guarantees. Most commonly, the accuracy is guaranteed by *error estimation*, which comes in the form of the confidence interval (a.k.a., "error bound") [10]. The error estimation can be reported directly to users, who can factor the uncertainty of the query results in their analysis and decisions. Many methods have been proposed for producing reliable error bounds - the earliest is closed-form estimates based on either the central limit theorem (CLT) [15] or large deviation inequalities such as Hoeffding bounds [9]. Unfortunately, these techniques either compute an error bound much wider than the real which lost guidance to users or require data to follow the normal distribution while the distribution of terms frequency often obeys the Zipf law [5]. This has motivated the use of resampling methods like bootstrap [19], which requires no such normal distribution and can be applied to arbitrary queries. However, traditional bootstrap and its variant, variational subsampling technique proposed by VerdictDB [14] remain high complexity in our progressive execution model due to lots of duplicate computation.

In this paper, we first present a new query formulation by extending SQL grammar with UDF (user-defined function) for term frequency analysis on text data. Then, we propose a sample-based progressive process model to continuously refine the approximate result in the user-think period. Longer the waiting time becomes, the more accurate the result will be. As a part of our progressive execution model, we present a new error estimation method, progressive bootstrap. Moreover, to achieve a good performance over rare words, we present a new low-overhead sampling method, *Tail Sampling*. In summary, this paper claims to make the following contributions:

- We propose a new query formulation that extends SQL grammar with UDF to support term frequency calculation on text data.
- We apply AQP techniques to get the approximate result to shorten the response latency on large text datasets.
- We present a sample-based progressive execution model and a progressive bootstrap method to continuously refine the approximate result.
- We integrate these methods into the system called Parrot. Experiments show that Parrot can provide smooth trade-off between accuracy and latency while the quantified error bound covers the accurate result well.

Paper Outline: Sect. 2 introduces an overview of Parrot. Section 3 describes Parrot's sample-based progressive processing. Section 4 explains how our progressive error estimation works. Section 5 presents our experiments. Finally, we review the related work in Sect. 6 and conclude this paper in Sect. 7.

2   Overview

2.1   System Architecture

Parrot is placed between the user and an off-the-shelf database. The user submits queries through any application that issues SQL queries to Parrot and obtains the result directly from Parrot without interacting with the underlying database. Parrot communicates with the underlying text collection for accessing and processing data when sampling. Figure 1 shows the workflow and internal components of Parrot, which contains two stages, *online* and *offline*. In the offline phase, the sample preparation module first normalizes data into a unified format which is JSON-based with a "text" attribute to store text, a "desc" object to store other attributes, and a "words" array to store words that appeared in the text. In Parrot, we use Stanford NLP[2] and Jieba[3] to do word segmentation. Then samplers build different types of *sample set* which is a logical concept and composed of multiple *sample blocks*. Each diagonal filled box in Fig. 1 represents a sample block that stores a part of the original data. The data stored in each block of one sample set are distinct. At runtime, the query parser and

---

[2] https://stanfordnlp.github.io/CoreNLP/.
[3] https://github.com/fxsjy/jieba.

analyzer analyze the issued SQL and generate a progressive execution plan. The execution plan contains two parts - a reference to the best sample set which is chosen according to our sample planner and an error estimation instance. Then the execution engine fetches blocks from the best sample set and calculates the result in the progressive mode which means that the user will receive an approximate result within a short time and the approximate result will be continuously refined until the whole sample set has been processed or Parrot is stopped by manual. Meanwhile, Parrot uses progressive bootstrap to estimate the error by the confidence interval according to a given confidence level. Generally, the width of the confidence interval can reflect the accuracy of the current result.

In the remainder of this paper, we use T to represent the underlying text collection, T_s to represent a sample set, $|T|$ to represent the cardinality of T and b_i to represent the i-th block. Actually, a sample set T_s is built by a sampler with a group of specified parameters applied on the underlying text data T.

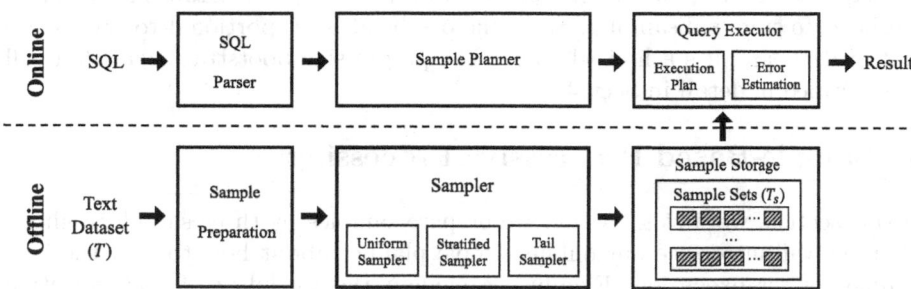

Fig. 1. System overview of Parrot

2.2 Query Formulation

We extend the standard SQL grammar with UDF (user-defined function) to support analysis for text collections. Here is an example of inquiring the frequency of word *bank* in the date range between Jan. 1, 2018 and Jan. 31, 2018:

```
SELECT FREQ('bank')
FROM news
WHERE date BETWEEN '2018-01-01' AND '2018-01-31'
```

Note that, FREQ function is similar to a standard *count* aggregation after *group-by*. We support selecting multiple terms frequencies or using other select clauses in a mixture of FREQ in one single SQL. In addition to the FREQ function, we also support the TF_IDF which is a numerical statistic widely used in information retrieval and TOP_K to find the k most frequent words. Since the core of these functions is about term frequency, we will focus on FREQ function in the following sections.

2.3 Quantifying Result Error

Our error estimation is in the form of confidence interval with a given confidence level associated with the continuously updated result. For example, the confidence interval [3.5, 5.5] with the confidence level 95% means that we have 95% confidence to ensure that the accurate result will fall into the interval [3.5, 5.5]. As discussed before, the Zipf law of natural languages motivates us to use bootstrap techniques. However, traditional bootstrap and variational subsampling bootstrap proposed by VerdictDB, need to generate many resamples (usually a large number, e.g., 100 or 1000) of the entire proceeded data when proceeding a new sample block, which will lead to lots of duplicate computations in our progressive execution model. Inspired by Verdict, we propose the progressive bootstrap which has a lower time complexity by maintaining subsamples throughout the execution process to avoid redundant re-generating subsamples. Actually, the time complexity is only related to the size of the new block. At the expense of that, the progressive bootstrap requires an additional memory overhead to store subsamples. Since the overhead is proportional to the square root of data size, it's a limited value. The progressive bootstrap algorithm will be described in detail in Sect. 4.

3 Sample-Based Progressive Processing

In this section, we first show how we prepare samples by three samplers offline. Then we will introduce our online sample planner about how to pick the best sample set for execution. Finally, we explain the workflow of our execution engine, which utilizes delta computation to minimize re-computation.

3.1 Offline Sample Preparation

Uniform Sampler. Given the text dataset T and the number of blocks B, uniform sampler generates a random integer i in $[1, B]$ for each document which represents the block number to output. Then the sampler clusters documents by i and output into the i-th block. Both every single block and any combinations of these blocks could be seen as an independent uniform sample.

Stratified Sampler. Stratified sampler optimizes queries over rare subpopulations by applying a biased sampling on different groups [3]. Given a column set C and a number k, stratified sampling ensures that at least k documents pass through for every distinct value of the columns in C[4]. To satisfy smooth convergence of results, the stratified sampler needs to ensure that each sample block has almost the same and enough number of documents. Therefore, for generating a stratified sample block each time, we need to dynamically adjust k to an appropriate value. Suppose there are m groups and the requested cardinality of each block is $|b|$. We first collect the cardinality of each group ($|c_i|$ for the i-th group) on C. Then we minimize the value of *diff* in Formula 1 by binary

---

[4] Precisely, at least min(k, number of documents for that distinct value).

searching an appropriate value $k = \hat{k}$ in the range of $[1, |b|]$. Since we get the $\hat{k}$, we apply a stratified sampling and output the chosen documents to a new block. Then remove them from the dataset and update the left cardinalities for each group. The above process will be repeated until there is no left document.

$$diff = |\sum_{i=1}^{m} min(|c_i|, k) - |b|| \qquad (1)$$

Besides, to maximize the number of documents selected by the query within the same time, the stratified sampler records the *disappearance block* (abbr. *d-block*) for each group. The *d-block* of a group refers to the block number that after outputting to that block, the remaining cardinality of this group reduces to 0. Thus the cardinality of a group Ω in the i-th block (i.e., b_i) is no more than that in the j-th block (i.e., b_j) if (1) $i \leq j$, and (2) $j < d - block_\Omega$. In the execution phase, for a specified group Ω and its $d-block_\Omega$, traversing from $d-block_\Omega$ down to 1 (in reversed order) will maximum the query selecting ratio. For queries over multiple groups, we first retrieve the maximum *d-block* ($d-block_{max}$) among all groups in the query and then read blocks from $d-block_{max}$ down to 1.

Tail Sampler. Queries over rare words occur frequently in the interactive data exploration but often lead to large errors due to its much small selectivity. Tail sampler, a low-overhead partial sampler, collects these rare words and documents. Tail sampler firstly determines whether a given document is rare and then constructs the sample set on the subset of all rare documents. It works as Algorithm 1 shown. The input contains text collection T and two parameters - tail threshold τ and sample overhead λ. We define γ_{word} as the ratio of appearance times of the word to $|T|$ and γ_{doc} as the minimum γ_{word} of words appeared in the document. Tail threshold τ refers to the maximum γ_{word} allowed to be included in the tail sample. Sample overhead λ refers to the maximum ratio of the size of the tail sample set to the original dataset. With these inputs, tail sampler firstly builds the inverted index for each word in T. Then for each word, we calculate γ_{word} (line 3–5). Next, we scan words in the ascending order of γ. For each word, if $\gamma \leq \tau$, and the size ratio not exceeds λ, then add the word into the set of rare words and add documents in which the word appears into the sample document set, D_s, without duplicates (line 7–12). Finally, the tail sampler builds the tail sample set T_s based on the D_s by the uniform sampler.

3.2   Online Sample Planning

A *sample plan* is composed of a reference to a sample set with some extra information (e.g., traversal order of the chosen sample set). Parrot's sample planner aims to find the *best* sample set for the query, i.e., the sample plan that results in the lowest approximation errors within the same latency. Our strategy is based on the *selectivity* which is defined as the ratio (i) the number of documents selected by the query, to (ii) the number of documents read by the query. At runtime, the response time increases with more number of documents being

---

Algorithm 1: Tail Sampling

Input: text collection T, tail threshold τ, sample overhead λ
Output: tail sample set T_s, rare words set W

1 initialize $T_s = \{\}$, $W = \{\}$ $D_s = \{\}$;
2 build *inverted index* for each word in T;
3 **foreach** *word* $\in$ *inverted index* **do**
4 $\quad$ $n =$ number of documents which this word appears in;
5 $\quad$ $\gamma_{word} = n/|T|$;

6 sort words by γ in ascending order;
7 **foreach** *word* in ascending order of γ **do**
8 $\quad$ **if** $\gamma_{word} <= \tau$ **then**
9 $\quad\quad$ $D_w =$ documents which this word appears in;
10 $\quad\quad$ **if** $|D_s$ union $D_w|/|T| \leq \lambda$ **then**
11 $\quad\quad\quad$ $D_s = D_s + D_w$;
12 $\quad\quad\quad$ $W = W + word$;

13 build T_s based on D_s by uniform sampler;
14 return T_s and W

---

read and the error decreases with more number of documents WHERE/GROUP BY clause selects. For this, Parrot generates many possible sample plans (called *candidate plans*) and selects the *best*.

Candidate Plans. Candidate plans contain all sample sets that can be used to answer the issued query. For a uniform sample, it's always a candidate plan. For a stratified sample, if SCS $\supseteq$ QCS, then it's a candidate plan. The SCS (sample column set) is the column set that stratified sampler builds on. The QCS (query column set) is the set of all columns that appears in the WHERE/GROUP BY clauses. For a tail sample set, if the issued word of the query belongs to the rare words, then it is a candidate plan.

Selecting a Plan. We first take the sampling strategy into account. Tail sample is the best as it only includes documents that have rare words and can reduce the total size of the sample set. Stratified sampler gives different groups different traversal orders (from $d - block_\Omega$ down to 1). For a rare subpopulation, it has a small $d - block_{rare}$ value (only appear in the first few blocks) to reduce the total sample size. For a popular subpopulation, the reversed traversal order makes a higher selectivity. Therefore, the stratified sample can provide a higher selectivity than the uniform. Then among all stratified samples, we choose the sample set with the lowest $d - block$ for the query. For tail samples, we choose the sample set of the lowest overhead λ as it has the highest selectivity.

3.3 Query Execution Model

Our execution engine computes an approximate result $\hat{\theta}^T_{word}$ on a sample to estimate the accurate result θ^T_{word}. Here the *word* refers to the issued word in the FREQ function. Then, by *maximum likelihood estimation* (MLE)[16], we can get an approximation $\hat{\theta}^{\mathrm{MLE}}_{\mathrm{word}} = \theta^{S}_{\mathrm{word}}/|S|$ of the accurate result θ_{word}, where the S refers to the sample, $|S|$ refers to the cardinality of S, and $\theta^{S}_{\mathrm{word}}$ refers to the result on S. Intuitively, this approximation $\hat{\theta}^{\mathrm{MLE}}_{\mathrm{word}}$ represents the estimated frequency of the word in each document of the dataset. Multiplying a frequency estimate $\hat{\theta}^{\mathrm{MLE}}_{\mathrm{word}}$ by the total number $|T|$ of documents will (i.e., $\hat{\theta}^{T}_{\mathrm{word}} = \hat{\theta}^{\mathrm{MLE}}_{\mathrm{word}} \cdot |T|$)therefore yield an approximate frequency of the word.

Our execution engine works in the progressive fashion. The process contains many *rounds*, where each round means a new block data is being proceeded and a refined result will be returned after proceeding. The guiding design principle behind Parrot is to take full advantage of delta computation to minimize re-computation. In other words, before the i-th round, suppose we have finished processing data S_{i-1} (i.e., $S_{i-1} = b_1 \cup b_2 \cup ... \cup b_{i-1}$) and get result $\theta^{S_{i-1}}_{\mathrm{word}}$. Then, instead of computing query on S_i directly, we compute $\theta^{b_i}_{word}$ and merge it into previous result $\theta^{S_{i-1}}_{\mathrm{word}}$ since $S_i = S_{i-1} + b_i$ and $\theta^{S_i}_{\mathrm{word}}$ can be calculated from the previous result $\theta^{S_{i-1}}_{\mathrm{word}}$ by a delta query $\theta^{b_i}_{\mathrm{word}}$ (shown as Formula 2).

$$\hat{\theta}^{T}_{\mathrm{word}} = \left(\frac{\theta^{S_{i-1}}_{\mathrm{word}} + \theta^{b_i}_{\mathrm{word}}}{|S_{i-1}| + |b_i|}\right) \cdot |T| \tag{2}$$

4   Error Estimation

In this section, we describe our new bootstrap method for progressive query execution. We will start with traditional bootstrap and variational subsampling bootstrap (Sect. 4.1). Then we introduce our method, progressive bootstrap in detail (Sect. 4.2).

4.1   Traditional Bootstrap and Variational Subsampling Bootstrap

Bootstrap is the state-of-the-art error estimation mechanism used by previous AQP engines. Let θ be the accurate result of an aggregate function on N real values and $\hat{\theta}$ be an estimator of θ on a random sample with size n. To measure the quality of the estimate, bootstrap recomputes the aggregate on many resamples of the sample. In traditional bootstrap, each resample is constructed with replacement and has the same size n_s as the sample itself (i.e., $n_s = n$) while in variational subsampling bootstrap it's without replacement and of size n_s where $n_s \ll n$ (a.k.a. subsample). Bootstrap will construct m such resamples. Let $\hat{\theta}_j$ be the value of the estimator computed on the j-th resample. Then bootstrap uses $\hat{\theta}_1, ..., \hat{\theta}_m$ to construct an empirical distribution of the original sample. Let $\hat{\theta}_0$ be the estimator's value on the sample itself, and t_α be the α-quantile of $\hat{\theta}_0 - \hat{\theta}_j$. Then, the $1 - \alpha$ confidence interval can be computed as:

$$[\hat{\theta}_0 - t_{1-\alpha/2} \cdot \sqrt{n_s/n}, \quad \hat{\theta}_0 - t_{\alpha/2} \cdot \sqrt{n_s/n}] \tag{3}$$

4.2 Progressive Bootstrap

Both two bootstrap methods introduced before, they need to perform bootstrap over the entire proceeded data and lead to lots of duplicate computations. Suppose the cardinality of the sample set is n, the number of resamples is m, and there are p rounds in total, traditional bootstrap and variational subsampling bootstrap have unaffordable time complexity $O(n \cdot m \cdot p)$ and $O(n \cdot p)$ respectively. Inspired by Verdict, we propose the progressive bootstrap by maintaining all needed sub-samples through the progressive process to avoid duplicate resampling from past blocks. VerdictDB has proved that the bootstrap has the lowest error when the cardinality of each subsample equals to $\sqrt{n}$. Thus, in the best case, the subsampling ratio is $r = m \cdot \sqrt{n}/n = m/\sqrt{n}$. As n grows (more and more data has proceeded), the ratio will drop. Therefore, if we have preserved all subsamples s (composed of s_1, s_2, ..., s_m) and when new block b_i is being proceeded, we can directly update subsamples based on s with b_i instead of re-subsampling overall past data. For documents in b_i, we apply a Bernoulli sampling with ratio $r_i = m/\sqrt{n}$. For maintained subsamples, let E_i refers to the event of a document being picked into subsamples at i-th round and we can also apply a Bernoulli sampling with ratio Δr calculated by conditional probability as shown in Formular 4.

$$\Delta r = P(E_i|E_{i-1}) = \frac{P(E_i \cap E_{i-1})}{P(E_{i-1})} = \frac{r_i}{r_{i-1}} \tag{4}$$

Algorithm 2 gives a detailed illustration. The input includes the issued word set $words$ in FREQ functions, the cardinality of underlying dataset N, proceeded data S_{i-1} (i.e., $b_1 \cup b_2 \cup ... \cup b_{i-1}$), new block b_i, past sub-samples s (composed of s_1, s_2, ..., s_m), past counters c ($c[word]$ for $word$ and composed of $c[word]_1$, $c[word]_2$, ..., $c[word]_m$), confidence level α (e.g., 0.95), and the approximate result $\hat{\theta}$. Our algorithm first filters out documents which should be excluded from the past subsamples (line 3–7) and update counters of each word for each subsample (line 8–10). Then it picks out documents which should be included into sub-samples from the new block (line 11–15) and update counters (line 16–18). Then for each word, we sort m counters in ascending order and collect the error bound σ_{word} according to the subsamples distribution (line 19–21). Finally, return the updated subsamples, counters and error bound (line 22). Progressive bootstrap has a lower time complexity $O(\sqrt{n} \cdot m \cdot p)$.

5 Experiment

5.1 Experiment Setup

We implemented the methods in our system - Parrot, and the baseline - blocking, on top of Spark 2.4.3. The baseline implements the same SQL parser and UDF as Parrot but reads documents from the underlying collection directly and processes in a blocking fashion. All the following experiments are performed on a 10-node cluster (each with Intel Xeon E5-2620, 64 GB RAM, and 1.77 TB HDD) under

---

Algorithm 2: Progressive Bootstrap

Input: issued word set $words$, dataset cardinality N, proceeded data S_{i-1}, new block b_i, past subsamples s, past counters c, confidence level α, approximate result $\hat{\theta}$

Output: updated subsamples s', updated counters c', error bound σ

1 $n' = |S_{i-1}| + |b_i|$;

2 $n'_s = \sqrt{n'}$;

3 **foreach** document $doc \in s$ **do**

4   suppose the document is in the ε-th subsample s_ε;

5       $r = $ a random number in $[0, n')$;

6   **if** $r < |b_i|$ **then**

7           $s_\varepsilon = s_\varepsilon - doc$;

8   **foreach** word $\in words$ **do**

9               $f = word$ frequency in doc;

10              $c[word]_\varepsilon = c[word]_\varepsilon - f$;

11 **foreach** document $doc \in b_i$ **do**

12      $r = $ a random number in $[0, n')$;

13      $\varepsilon = r/n'_s + 1$;

14   **if** $\varepsilon < m$ **then**

15          $s_\varepsilon = s_\varepsilon + doc$;

16   **foreach** word $\in words$ **do**

17              $f = word$ frequency in doc;

18              $c[word]_\varepsilon = c[word]_\varepsilon + f$;

19 **foreach** $word \in words$ **do**

20   sort $c[word]$ in ascending order;

21      $\sigma_{word} = [\hat{\theta} - c[word]_{\alpha/2} \cdot \sqrt{n'_s/n'} \cdot N/n'_s, \ \hat{\theta} - c[word]_{1-\alpha/2} \cdot \sqrt{n'_s/n'} \cdot N/n'_s]$;

22 **return** updated subsamples $s' = s$, updated counters $c' = c$ and error bound σ;

Apache Spark 2.4.3 and Ubuntu Linux 14.04 LTS. Our data is stored in Hadoop distributed file system and organized in JSON format.

Performance Metrics: Two metrics are used: (1) the relative error of the approximate result in each round; (2) the response latency for the first acceptable result. The relative error (RE) is calculated by $RE = |\hat{\theta} - \theta|/\theta$ where θ is the accurate result and $\hat{\theta}$ is the approximate result based on the sample. The relative confidence interval (RCI) is calculated by $RCI = (|\sigma_x - \sigma_y|/2)/\hat{\theta}$, where the $[\sigma_x, \sigma_y]$ represents the error bound. When the RCI of an approximate result is less than the given (1% as default in our experiment), we say it is an acceptable result. The confidence level is set to 95% as default.

Synthetic Dataset: We use the mix of Reuters news dataset[5] and Webhose English articles[6] as our dataset. After data cleaning and word segmentation,

---

[5] https://trec.nist.gov/data/reuters/reuters.html.

[6] https://webhose.io/free-datasets/english-news-articles/.

this dataset is about 10.9 GB and contains about 3 million documents. Then we scale up the data to 100 GB in proportion to ensure that the distribution and skewness are similar to the original. We built a uniform sample, a stratified sample on the *date* column, and a tail sample with $\tau = 0.01$ and $\lambda = 0.5$. We fix the block size of samples to 128 MB. To evaluate the performance, we use the following 6 queries:

Q_1: **SELECT FREQ**('bank') **FROM** news;
Q_2: **SELECT FREQ**('bank') **FROM** news **WHERE** location= 'LONDON';
Q_3: **SELECT FREQ**('government') **FROM** news
WHERE date **BETWEEN** '2015-10-01' **AND** '2015-10-31';
Q_4: **SELECT FREQ**('president') **FROM** news
WHERE date **BETWEEN** '2008-01-01' **AND** '2008-01-31';
Q_5: **SELECT FREQ**('top-asia') **FROM** news;
Q_6: **SELECT FREQ**('chronology-bird') **FROM** news
WHERE location <> 'PARIS';

Among them, Q_1, Q_2 run on the uniform sample, Q_3, Q_4 run on the stratified sample as their *where* clauses are on *date* column and Q_5, Q_6 run on the tail sample as words "*top-asia*" and "*chronology-bird*" are very rare words. Selectivity of Q_1–Q_6 is shown in Table 1. The lower the selectivity, the larger the error and oscillation of the approximate result may occur. As Q_2–Q_6 are on very rare sub-populations, these queries can test the performance of all three kinds of samples comprehensively.

Real-World Dataset: The second dataset is a real-world Chinese dataset, which comprises about 60 million articles from the Sina website with size 64 GB. We built a uniform sample, a stratified sample on the *channel* column and a tail sample with $\tau = 0.01$ and $\lambda = 0.5$. We fix the block size of samples to 128 MB. Then we use three queries, Q_7–Q_9[7], to evaluate the performance. Selectivity of Q_7–Q_9 is shown in Table 1. In this experiment, Q_7, Q_8, Q_9 run on the uniform sample, stratified sample and tail sample respectively.

Q_7: **SELECT FREQ**('Netizen') **FROM** article **WHERE LEN**(text) < 1000;
Q_8: **SELECT FREQ**('Female') **FROM** article **WHERE** channel= 'Health';
Q_9: **SELECT FREQ**('Guangxu') **FROM** article;

5.2 Experiment Results

Performance on Synthetic Dataset. In this experiment, we compare the performance between Parrot and baseline on the 100 GB synthetic dataset by Q_1–Q_6. As shown in Fig. 2(a), the time cost to get the first acceptable result of Parrot

---

[7] For convenience, we use English words with the same meaning in the paper.

Table 1. Selectivity of Q_1–Q_9.

	Q_1	Q_2	Q_3	Q_4	Q_5	Q_6	Q_7	Q_8	Q_9
Selectivity	17.5%	0.42%	0.98%	0.48%	0.16%	0.038%	6.58%	2.95%	0.53%

is much shorter than the baseline since Parrot uses a sample-based progressive execution model. Taking Q_1 as an example, Parrot costs about 23 s whereas blocking takes more than 450 s. However, Parrot brings different improvements for different queries. As we can see, Q_1, Q_3, Q_4 have more improvement than the other three. It's mainly due to two reasons: (1) for queries running on the same sample set, queries with higher selectivity may faster converge to 1% RCI as more documents can be selected within the same time; and (2) for queries of very low selectivity, RCI by bootstrap is much harder to converge to 1% as too few documents may cause unstable distribution of subsamples. Low selectivity may also cause fluctuations of RCI through the progressive process. Figure 3 (a) - (f) show how RE and RCI converge during the execution process. The horizontal dotted line marks the 1% RCI. We can see that the *RE* and the *RCI* converge smoothly and fast except for some fluctuations when executing queries of very low selectivity (e.g. Q_6). Besides, Parrot can return the first result in about 15 seconds for all of the six queries. The length of this period mainly depends on block size and we will evaluate it in later experiments.

In summary, on the synthetic dataset, the first acceptable result of Parrot is 2.4x–19.7x faster compared with the blocking fashion. Besides, Parrot can provide a smooth trade-off between accuracy and latency. Only queries with very small selectivity may lead to some fluctuations.

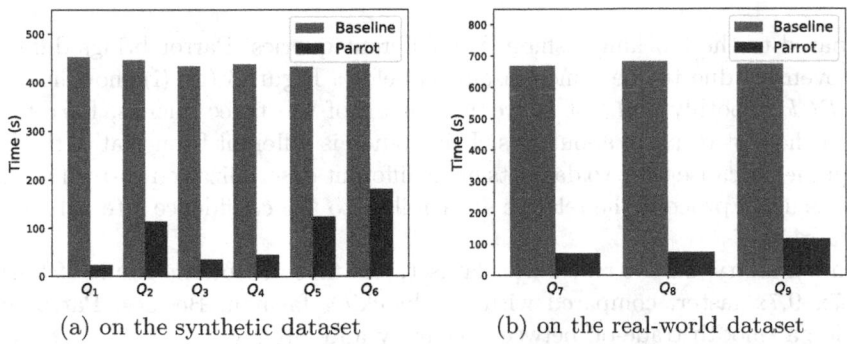

(a) on the synthetic dataset   (b) on the real-world dataset

Fig. 2. Time to get the first acceptable result.

Performance on Real-World Dataset. In this experiment, we compare the performance between Parrot and baseline on the 64 GB real-word dataset by Q_7–Q_9. As shown in Fig. 2(b), Parrot can achieve 1% RCI at a very fast speed

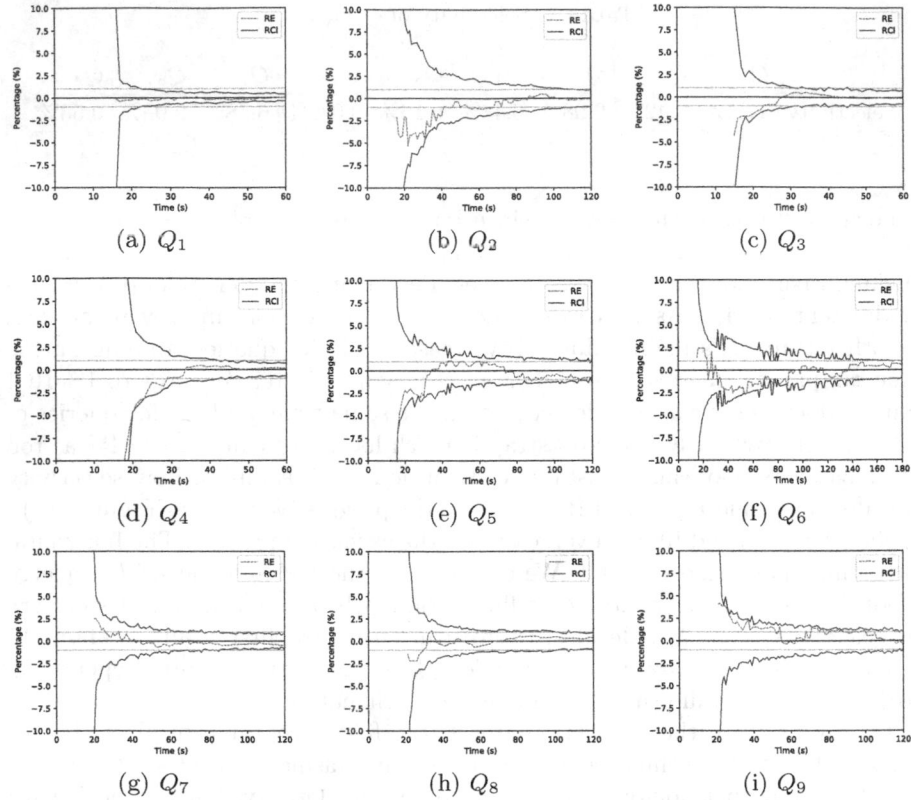

Fig. 3. The convergence of RE and RCI for Q_1–Q_9.

compared to the blocking fashion. For different queries, Parrot brings different improvement due to the same reasons as before. Figure 3 (g)–(i) show how *RE* and *RCI* smoothly and fast converge. For all of the three queries, Parrot can return the first result in about 20 s. The latency is different from that of the first six queries because the two datasets have different deserialization costs. Through the execution process, the relative error falls into the confidence interval almost all the time.

In summary, on the real-world dataset, the first acceptable result of Parrot is 5.7x–9.7x faster, compared with the blocking fashion. Besides, Parrot can provide a smooth trade-off between accuracy and latency.

Performance of Bootstrap. In this experiment, we compare the performance of three different bootstrap methods - traditional bootstrap, variational subsampling bootstrap, and progressive bootstrap. We run Q_1 on the 100 GB synthetic dataset and record the time cost of the error estimation phase in each round from the beginning until the first acceptable result returned. The average time cost is shown in Fig. 4. We can see that traditional bootstrap costs more than 128 s

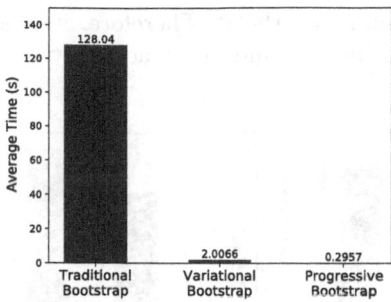
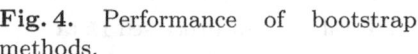
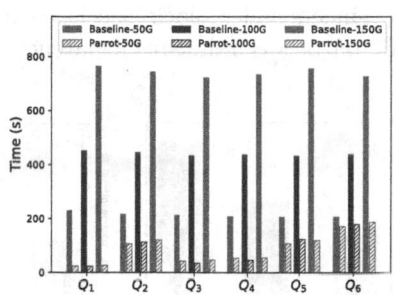

Fig. 4. Performance of bootstrap methods.

Fig. 5. Performance on different data sizes.

on average while it's unacceptable in our interactive exploration scenario. The variational subsampling bootstrap costs from 0.307 to 4.14 s with an average of 2.0066 s. It's fast in the first few rounds and then becomes slower and slower with more and more data being processed as its time complexity is proportional to the amount of data that has been proceeded. Our progressive bootstrap gets the best performance with an average cost of 0.2957 s and can perform bootstrap within almost a fixed time cost. The cost mainly depends on the block size.

Effect of Data Size. In this experiment, we evaluate the effect of text data size. We use three text collections scaled from the synthetic dataset with size 50 GB, 100 GB, and 150 GB. We generate samples of these three collections with the same parameters and the fixed block size (i.e., 128 MB). Then we run Q_1 - Q_6, both through Parrot and baseline. As shown in Fig. 5, the time cost for baseline increases with the data size increases (e.g., 100 GB 452s vs. 150 GB 766s for Q_1) since it needs to calculate on the entire dataset. We also find that the data size has a limited effect on the time cost of the first acceptable result by Parrot (e.g., 100 GB 23s vs. 150 GB 26s for Q_1), because Parrot mainly relies on a sufficient number of documents in the sample to be processed. Therefore, Parrot can provide a good and stable performance on large text collections.

Effect of Block Size. In this experiment, we evaluate the effect of different block sizes on the 100 GB synthetic dataset. We construct three groups of samples under the same parameters except for the block size - 64 MB, 128 MB, and 256 MB, respectively. We run Q_1 by Parrot on the three groups of samples and record the time cost of the first estimate result, the average updating interval of result, and the processed data within 100 seconds. We use b_{64}, b_{128}, b_{256} to represent the block sizes with 64 MB, 128 MB, and 256 MB respectively. Figure 6 (a) shows that smaller the block size, the shorter the latency of the first estimate result will be (e.g., b_{64} 11.7s vs. b_{128} 15.4s). Figure 6 (b) shows that the increment of block size cause longer result updating interval (e.g., b_{64} 0.558s vs. b_{128} 0.759s). That's because smaller block size has less I/O and CPU cost for processing each single block. Figure 6 (c) shows that smaller block size results in less data being processed within the same time (e.g., b_{64} 9.3 GB vs. b_{128} 13.1

GB) since smaller block size leads to more shuffle overhead. Therefore, it is a trade-off between first-result latency, updating interval and query accuracy.

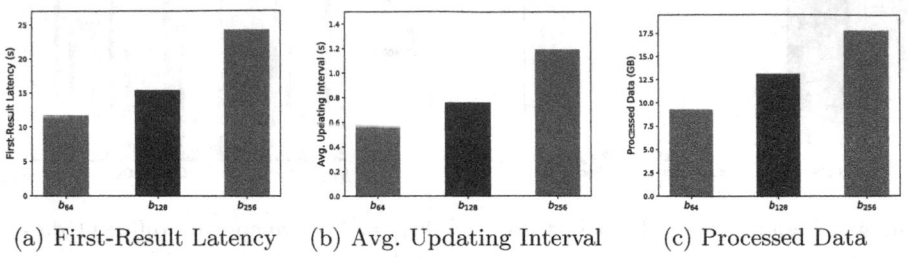

(a) First-Result Latency   (b) Avg. Updating Interval   (c) Processed Data

Fig. 6. Performance on different block sizes.

6   Related Work

Interactive Exploration on Text. For structured data, lots of previous works attempt to speed up query execution through AQP (Approximate Query Processing) technique (e.g., AQUA [2], IDEA [7], VerdictDB [14]), which aims to find an approximate answer by samples [17] as close as to the exact answer efficiently. While limited by response time and computing resources, the before-mentioned AQP systems only return a single approximate result. However, there is an increasing need for interactive human-driven exploratory analysis, whose desired accuracy cannot be known a priori and change dynamically based on unquantifiable factors [18]. For semi-structured and unstructured data, the state-of-the-art solutions are base on the content management system or the cube structure, such as ElasticSearch [1] and Text Cube [11]. ElasticSearch supports simple queries with key-value based filtering as well as full-text searching for fuzzy matching over the entire dataset. But it doesn't have good support for ad-hoc queries of term frequency on a subset. Text Cube uses techniques to pre-aggregate data and gives the user the possibility to make semantic navigation in the data dimension but requires extensive preprocessing and suffers from the curse of dimensionality.

Error Estimation. To make approximate answers useful, lots of error estimation techniques have been proposed - the earliest being closed-form estimates based on either the central limit theorem (CLT) [15] or large deviation inequalities such as Hoeffding bounds [9]. These techniques either compute an error bound much wider than the real which lost guidance to users or require data to follow the normal distribution while it's not suitable for natural languages. Another estimation technique, bootstrap [14,19], can be applied to arbitrary queries. However, before bootstrap techniques have poor performance to apply in our progressive execution model due to lots of duplicate computation.

7   Conclusion

In this paper, we propose a new query formulation by extending SQL grammar with UDF for term frequency calculation on text data. We apply AQP techniques to return an approximate result within a short time. We present a sample-based progressive processing model and progressive bootstrap to continuously refine the approximate result. We implement these methods in the system called Parrot. Experiment results show that Parrot is about 2.4x–19.7x faster than the blocking fashion for the first acceptable result and can provide a smooth trade-off between accuracy and latency. Meanwhile, the quantified error bound covers the accurate result well.

Acknowledgements. This work is supported by the National Key R&D Program of China (No. 2018YFB1004404 and No. 2018YFB1402600), the NSFC (No. 61732004 and No. 61802066) and the Shanghai Sailing Program (No. 18YF1401300).

References

1. https://www.elastic.co/, ElasticSearch 7.4.2
2. Acharya, S., Gibbons, P.B., Poosala, V., Ramaswamy, S.: The aqua approximate query answering system. In: SIGMOD 1999 (1999)
3. Agarwal, S., Mozafari, B., Panda, A., Milner, H., Madden, S., Stoica, I.: BlinkDB: queries with bounded errors and bounded response times on very large data. In: EuroSys 2013 (2013)
4. Bouakkaz, M., Ouinten, Y., Loudcher, S., Strekalova, Y.: Textual aggregation approaches in OLAP context: a survey. Int J. Inf. Manag. **37**(6), 684–692 (2017)
5. Corral, A., Boleda, G., Ferrer-i-Cancho, R.: Zipf's law for word frequencies: word forms versus lemmas in long texts. CoRR abs/1407.8322 (2014)
6. Dimitriadou, K., Papaemmanouil, O., Diao, Y.: Interactive data exploration based on user relevance feedback. In: ICDE 2014 (2014)
7. Galakatos, A., Crotty, A., Zgraggen, E., Binnig, C., Kraska, T.: Revisiting reuse for approximate query processing. PVLDB **10**(10), 1142–1153 (2017)
8. Gray J., et al.: Data cube: a relational aggregation operator generalizing group-by, cross-tab, and sub-totals. CoRR abs/cs/0701155 (2007)
9. Haas, P.J.: Hoeffding inequalities for join-selectivity estimation and online aggregation. IBM (1996)
10. Li, K., Li, G.: Approximate query processing: what is new and where to go? - A survey on approximate query processing. Data Sci. Eng. **3**(4), 379–397 (2018)
11. Lin, C.X., Ding, B., Han, J., Zhu, F., Zhao, B.: Text cube: computing IR measures for multidimensional text database analysis. In: ICDM 2008 (2008)
12. Lins, L.D., Klosowski, J.T., Scheidegger, C.E.: Nanocubes for real-time exploration of spatiotemporal datasets. IEEE Trans. Vis. Comput. Graph. **19**(12), 2456–2465 (2013)
13. Liu, Z., Jiang, B., Heer, J.: imMens: real-time visual querying of big data. Comput. Graph. Forum **32**(3), 421–430 (2013)
14. Park, Y., Mozafari, B., Sorenson, J., Wang, J.: VerdictDB: universalizing approximate query processing. In: SIGMOD 2018 (2018)
15. Rice, J.A.: Mathematical statistics and data analysis. Cengage Learning (2006)

16. Rossi, R.J.: Mathematical Statistics An Introduction to Likelihood Based Inference. Wiley, Hoboken (2018)
17. Wu, Z., Jing, Y., He, Z., Guo, C., Wang, X.S.: Polytope: a flexible sampling system for answering exploratory queries. In: World Wide Web, pp. 1–22 (2019)
18. Zeng, K., Agarwal, S., Stoica, I.: iOLAP: managing uncertainty for efficient incremental OLAP. In: SIGMOD 2016 (2016)
19. Zeng, K., Gao, S., Mozafari, B., Zaniolo, C.: The analytical bootstrap: a new method for fast error estimation in approximate query processing. In: SIGMOD 2014 (2014)
20. Zgraggen, E., Galakatos, A., Crotty, A., Fekete, J., Kraska, T.: How progressive visualizations affect exploratory analysis. IEEE Trans. Vis. Comput. Graph. **23**(8), 1977–1987 (2017)

Learning a Cost-Effective Strategy on Incomplete Medical Data

Mengxiao Zhu[1,2] and Haogang Zhu[1,2(✉)]

[1] State Key Laboratory of Software Development Environment Lab,
Beihang University, Beijing, China
[2] Beijing Advanced Innovation Center for Biomedical Engineering, Beijing, China
{zhumx,haogangzhu}@buaa.edu.cn

Abstract. Deep learning techniques have shown remarkable success in classification tasks. However, the prerequisite for high accuracy is that data is easily accessible, which is unrealistic since most features come at a cost. Under a medical scenario, each feature is associated with a medical test that costs a certain amount of money. And doctors would ask patients to do consecutive tests until they are confident enough to make a final diagnosis, whereas the overall cost incurred during the process is often ignored. In this paper, we propose to learn a cost-effective strategy which at the same time hastens the decision process. As is often the case where both medical records and initial feature values of a new patient are incomplete, we design a framework consisting of two components, the oracle classifier and the feature selector, to tackle the challenges. The classifier incorporates a sequence encoder that can handle any set of feature values in various sizes. And the selector efficiently learns the cost-effective strategy based on the state-of-art reinforcement learning techniques. Experimental results have shown that under the same classification accuracy, our strategy is superior to other related approaches in terms of the overall cost.

Keywords: Medical data · Feature acquisition · Cost-effective strategy · Reinforcement learning

1 Introduction

Classification tasks have been equipped with mature machine learning techniques in recent years. Given sufficient features about a disease, a well-trained classifier can rival many medical practitioners in the accuracy of detecting the disease. The underlying assumption is that comprehensive feature values for both the new instance and training data are readily available. Yet in real scenarios, such an assumption does not hold since most features are acquired at a cost. Consider the process of medical inquiry. A doctor, starting the diagnosis with few symptoms initially stated by a patient, would require her to conduct some medical tests which cost a certain amount of money to measure some feature values.

© Springer Nature Switzerland AG 2020
Y. Nah et al. (Eds.): DASFAA 2020, LNCS 12113, pp. 175–191, 2020.
https://doi.org/10.1007/978-3-030-59416-9_11

Gestational weeks	Biparietal diameter	Left pulmonary artery	Right ventricular diameter	...	Tetralogy of Fallot (TOF)
21	-	1.1	8.0	...	1
22	56	-	7.8	...	0

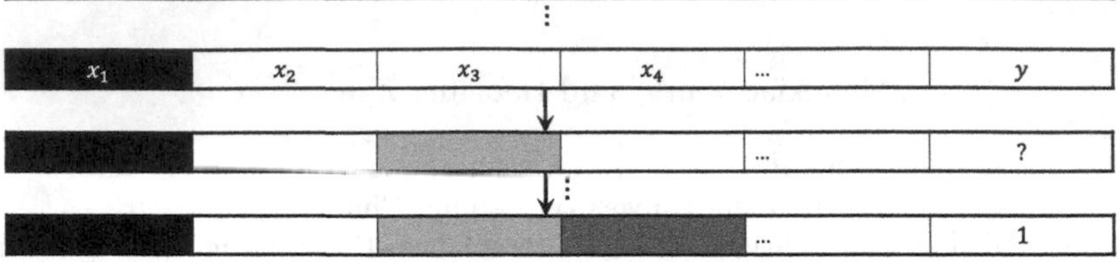

$\vdots$

x_1	x_2	x_3	x_4	...	y
				...	?

$\vdots$

| | | | | ... | 1 |

Fig. 1. Illustrated example of the TOF. The training data on top has missing terms in these two instances. The process below shows that we sequentially acquire the feature values of each new patient until the final classification.

Furthermore, since the examination results can either increase or decrease the confidence of the doctor's conjecture about potential diseases, the patient is instructed to do consecutive tests until the doctor's preliminary diagnosis takes shape. According to personalized experience of doctors, their choices of tests depend primarily on how quickly they can gain enough confidence in the final judgment instead of the overall cost incurred during the process. Therefore, it is significant to learn a strategy that quickly forms a diagnosis and minimizes the cost at the same time.

We illustrate two main challenges by the example of Tetralogy of Fallot (TOF), which is a type of heart defect present at birth. Pregnant women are often required to do medical tests with different amounts of money, such as the blood test and ultrasound examination, to measure some feature values as shown in the top part of Fig. 1. For one thing, some feature values in the training data are missing. That may be because some patients do not conduct some tests due to a limited budget, or the doctors are incapable of measuring some values for the abnormal locations of the fetus. For another, we need to learn a cost-effective strategy personalized to each new patient; after seeing one feature value, we should test the next feature based on the trade-off between lowering the overall cost and converging to the final judgment as soon as possible.

Previous work partially considers the above issues [4, 8, 17]. First, they assume that training data is complete, which is unrealistic in our medical case. Second, they often make the trade-off by using a linear combination of the classification accuracy and the overall cost balanced by a hyperparameter λ. However, it is often hard to find a real sense of λ and set an appropriate value in practice.

In this paper, we first formulate the real setting as a constrained optimization problem, which captures both the confidence and the feature cost in the sequential process, and propose a framework to solve it. In particular, we first view the sequential process as a Markov Decision Process (MDP), where we simulate the environment exactly as the interactions between doctors and patients, then design two components: the oracle classifier and the feature selector. The former one is mainly made up of a sequence encoder, which addresses the first issue where the training data is incomplete. The idea is based on the techniques of document classification in natural language processing, which record the information of each feature value in the sequence. And the feature selector tackles the second issue by adopting the state-of-art reinforcement learning techniques with the elaborate design of the behavioral policy.

Our contributions in this work are listed below:

- We identify the problem of learning a cost-effective strategy that accurately characterizes the real scenario of medical inquiry.
- We design a general framework consisting of the feature selector and the oracle classifier to tackle the problem.
- We verify the effectiveness of the proposed solution through extensive experiments on real medical data.

2 Problem Statement

Let (x, y) be a sample drawn from the data distribution $\mathcal{D}$ on $\mathcal{X} \times \mathcal{Y}$. Vector $x \in \mathcal{X} \subseteq \mathbf{R}^n$ is described by a set of n features $\mathcal{F} = \{f_1, \ldots, f_n\}$, where x_i is the value of feature f_i, and $y \in \{0, 1\}$ is the class. Each feature f is associated with a cost c_f when it is acquired. Let $g_{\mathcal{I}}(x) = \{x_i | \forall f_i \in \mathcal{I}\}$ be the set of feature values for any $\mathcal{I} \subseteq \mathcal{F}$.

Suppose there is an oracle classifier h_ϑ (parameterized by ϑ) which bears a similar ability of diagnosis as the doctor. Given any set of feature values $g_{\mathcal{I}}(x)$, the oracle classifier outputs the probability of class 1, i.e., $h_\vartheta(g_{\mathcal{I}}(x)) = P(y = 1|g_{\mathcal{I}}(x))$.

We now state the process of feature acquisition. At time step $t = 0$, we start with an empty acquired feature set $\mathcal{I}_0 = \emptyset$. At each time step t, we could select one feature $f \in \mathcal{F} \backslash \mathcal{I}_{t-1}$ to obtain its value with a cost c_f. With acquired feature values $g_{\mathcal{I}_t}(x)$, we could ask the oracle classifier about the probability of class 1, i.e., $h_\vartheta(g_{\mathcal{I}_t}(x))$. And we would use the log-odds function $\delta(p) = |\log \frac{p}{1-p}|$ to represent the confidence of the classification. If we are confident enough, where the confidence is higher than a threshold α:

$$\delta(h_\vartheta(g_{\mathcal{I}_t}(x))) = |\log \frac{h_\vartheta(g_{\mathcal{I}_t}(x))}{1 - h_\vartheta(g_{\mathcal{I}_t}(x))}| \geq \alpha, \tag{1}$$

we would stop the feature acquisition. The problem is to find a strategy π_θ (parameterized by θ) to select an appropriate feature at each step so as to minimize the overall cost.

Note that the threshold α can be easily set by an experienced doctor. The threshold α corresponds to some probability p; that is, $\delta(x) \geq \alpha$ is equivalent to $x \geq p$ or $x \leq 1 - p$ for some $p \in (0, 1)$.

We also assume that the threshold α is set so that Eq. (1) can be met when all the feature values are acquired (i.e., $g_{\mathcal{F}}(x)$). This accords with the real scenario where the doctor can finally make a decisive diagnosis for each patient, sometimes even a false judgment. Those uncertain cases are beyond the scope of the paper, since they only take up a tiny fraction, which is demonstrated in Fig. 2.

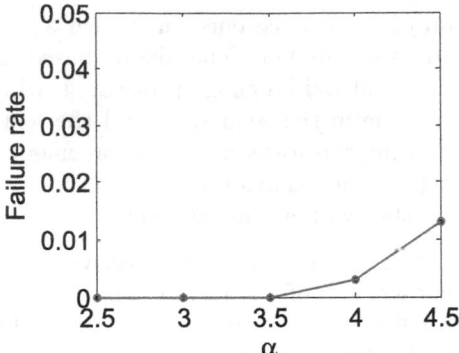

Fig. 2. The failure rate w.r.t. α on the TOF data. The failure rate represents the percentage of the instances whose confidence cannot meet the threshold. As the confidence level increases, there are still few uncertain instances.

3   Methodology

3.1   Overview

The problem is first formulated as the Markov decision process (MDP) and the proposed model is based on the framework of reinforcement learning (RL). It consists of two components: the *feature selector* π_θ and the *oracle classifier* h_ϑ, as showed in Fig. 3. The feature selector is realized by a Q-network which would select one remaining feature according to the current state in the MDP. Learning the network requires that an agent repeatedly explores the environment to receive rewards to update the parameters. The oracle classifier, which is a part of the environment, would output the confidence and decide if it satisfies Eq. 1. If the new state is a terminal state, the agent cannot make a transition and would be reset. For the oracle classifier, it can be realized by any mature solutions from the literature of binary classification. However, each state represents a set of feature values, which requires to be encoded so that it can fit into the Q-network. Therefore, we adopt the Gate Recurrent Units (GRU) [3], and design a bidirectional GRU-based sequence encoder shared by both the feature selector and the oracle classifier. We further use the attention mechanism, as the name suggests, to identify the significance of individual features. The encoder would be trained during learning the classifier and the feature selector.

3.2   MDP Construction

MDP includes a set of states $\mathcal{S}$, a set of actions $\mathcal{A}$ per state, and the environment which an agent interacts with. In state $s_t \in \mathcal{S}$, the agent selects an action a_t according to its policy $\pi_\theta(a|s)$. The environment returns the agent a reward r_t and let the agent enter a new state s_{t+1}. The goal is to maximize the accumulative rewards till the terminal state.

State. The state $s_t = (g_{\mathcal{I}_t}(x), \mathcal{I}_t)$ consists of the current set of acquired features $\mathcal{I}_t \subseteq \mathcal{F}$ and the corresponding values $g_{\mathcal{I}_t}(x)$. As the states are actually set variables, we use a sequence encoder (detailed below) to transform them into vectors of fixed length so that they can be fed into the model.

Action. The set of actions per state depends on the set of remaining features $\mathcal{F}\backslash\mathcal{I}_t$. We assume that the agent can only select one feature at each state for clarity. The approach can be easily extended to the case of multiple features at a time. Note that some actions would be invalid if the corresponding features can not be acquired for the personal reasons or limits of medical conditions.

Rewards. It is straightforward to define each step's reward as the negative feature cost c_f if the agent selects the feature f, since minimizing the overall cost is equivalent to maximizing the overall reward.

Environment. Given an action a_t, the state transition in the environment is deterministic from $(g_{\mathcal{I}_t}(x), \mathcal{I}_t)$ to $(g_{\mathcal{I}_{t+1}}(x), \mathcal{I}_{t+1})$. But if the oracle classifier claims that its confidence holds the Eq. (1), the agent would be in the terminal state, and the final judgment is also given by the model.

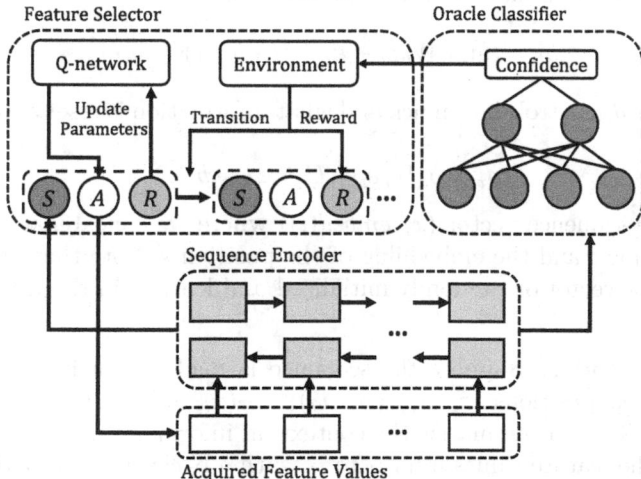

Fig. 3. The overall framework. The sequence encoder shared by both two components handles various sizes of sets of feature values. The oracle classifier produces the confidence given any set of feature values. The feature selector interacts with the classifier to find a currently appropriate feature.

3.3   Oracle Classifier

The oracle classifier is composed of two parts: a sequence encoder for feature encoding and fully-connected layers for classification. The encoder adopts the bidirectional GRU-based architecture (which is a kind of recurrent neural network) with the attention mechanism [1]. The reason why we use a sequence encoder is that the contextual information is useful in selecting the next action, since we will use the same encoder in the feature selector. For example, the doctor would ask you to do another medical test according to the previous results of the test. The current set of feature values would guide the next action.

GRU. The GRU [3] tracks the states of sequences based on a gating system. Two kinds of gates, including the reset gate d_t and the update gate z_t, are used to control how the information is updated. The new state is computed as

$$h_t = (1 - z_t) \odot h_{t-1} + z_t \odot \tilde{h}_t, \tag{2}$$

where $\odot$ is the element-wise multiplication. The update gate z_t allow each unit to maintain its previous information and we update it by

$$z_t = \sigma(W_z e_t + U_z h_{t-1} + b_z). \tag{3}$$

And $\tilde{h}_t$ is the newly updated state, computed as

$$\tilde{h}_t = \tanh(W_h e_t + d_t \odot (U_h h_{t-1}) + b_h). \tag{4}$$

The reset gate d_t controls how much and what information is reset and is updated as

$$d_t = \sigma(W_r e_t + U_r h_{t-1} + b_r), \tag{5}$$

And e_t is the sequence vector $(x_i, embed(i))$ where we concatenate the feature value x_i at time t and the embedding of the position i. Note that $embed(i)$ can be the one-hot vector or randomly initialized and learned in the training phase.

Sequence Encoder. Suppose the sequence is made up of individual feature values and their positions $(x_{i_1}, i_1), (x_{i_2}, i_2), \ldots, (x_{i_t}, i_t), \ldots, (x_{i_T}, i_T)$. We use a bidirectional GRU to summarize the contextual information. The forward GRU $\overrightarrow{GRU}$ reads the feature values from i_1 to i_t, with a backward one $\overleftarrow{GRU}$ from i_t to i_1. With the position further embedded into the vector e_t, we obtain the hidden vector by concatenating both two directions, i.e., $h_t = [\overrightarrow{GRU}(e_t), \overleftarrow{GRU}(e_t)]$.

Note that not all feature values are informative in the representation of the sequence. We adopt the attention mechanism [1] to distinguish the feature values that are important to the meaning of the sequence. Specifically, the hidden vector h_t is first fed into a one-layer MLP to get u_t as a hidden representation of h_t:

$$u_t = \tanh(W_w h_t + b_w). \tag{6}$$

The importance of the feature values is then measured by a context vector W_u and normalized by the softmax function:

$$\beta_t = \frac{\exp(u_t^\top W_u)}{\sum_t \exp(u_t^\top W_u)}. \tag{7}$$

Note that the context vector W_u is randomly initialized and jointly learned during the process of training. The final representation of the sequence is

$$v = \sum_t \beta_t h_t. \tag{8}$$

Classifier. The representation v would then be fed into two fully connected layers to make the classification. Because of the biased data where few samples are abnormal, we use the weighted cross-entropy loss as the objective function:

$$L = -\beta \sum_{g_{\mathcal{I}_t}(x) \in D^+} \log h_\vartheta(g_{\mathcal{I}_t}(x)) - (1 - \beta) \sum_{g_{\mathcal{I}_t}(x) \in D^-} \log(1 - h_\vartheta(g_{\mathcal{I}_t}(x))), \tag{9}$$

where $\beta = |D^-|/(|D^+| + |D^-|)$, and D^+/D^- represents the positive/negative sample set.

Before learning the feature selector, the oracle classifier has been pre-trained and would output the confidence to decide if the condition (Eq. 1) holds.

3.4 Feature Selector

The feature selector uses the value-based techniques in RL which learn a score function for state-action pairs and adopts the strategy which selects the action with the highest score. We realize the score function by the state-of-art dueling network [20] and follow a traditional Q-learning way [12]. However, as the exploration of the environment during the training can be more efficient, we do not stick to the greedy policy in Q-learning but design a new policy. In the following, we will first introduce the background of deep Q-learning that we used and then present the details of our model.

Deep Q-Learning. Q-learning mainly learns the state-action function $Q^*(s,a)$, representing the expected future reward when the agent on state s selects action a. Such function is modeled by a neural network (called Q-network and parameterized by θ) with inputs corresponding to states and outputs to Q-function values of different actions a. Using the Bellman equation, the Q-function can be calculated by

$$Q^*(s,a) = r(s,a) + \gamma \max_{a'} Q^*(s',a'), \tag{10}$$

where $r(s,a)$ is the reward by taking action a and $\gamma \leq 1$ is a discount factor.

Since both sides of Eq. (10) has the $Q^*(s,a)$, it is impossible to converge if we use the same network to realize them. We usually regard the left side as a target which would be fixed for a period of time, and optimize the network of the right side to approach the target [12]. Besides, we adopt the technique of double Q-learning [6] to alleviate the overestimate of action values. That is, the action is selected based on the right network, and its value is taken from the target network. The left one has the parameters θ^- which follow the right one θ with a delay. It is then optimized by minimize the mean squared error empirically experienced by an agent following a greedy policy that selects the action with the currently highest Q-value. Formally, if the agent travels through the trajectory τ, we minimize the loss w.r.t. θ

$$\mathcal{L}_\theta(\tau) = \frac{1}{|\tau|} \sum_{(s_t, a_t) \in \tau} (r_t + \gamma Q^{\theta^-}(s_{t+1}, \max_a Q^\theta(s_{t+1}, a)) - Q^\theta(s_t, a_t))^2. \quad (11)$$

Note that we do not have to use such a greedy policy to get the trajectory, since the action may be locally optimal w.r.t. the current Q-function.

Network Architecture. As the input of the Q-network requires the vector representation of the state, we would use the sequence encoder to transform it. As the states in the trajectory naturally form a sequence, we encode the states in the same way in the oracle classifier; that is, each new state $(x_i, embed(i))$ is incorporated by the bidirectional GRU with the attention mechanism. The output of the sequence encoder is then fed into the Q-network, which is basically an MLP by convention.

We adopt the technique in [20] to decompose the $Q^*(s, a)$ into two functions: the expected future rewards at state s $V(s)$ and the advantage of taking action a versus all other possible actions $A(s, a)$. The output network is accordingly divided into such two estimates, which are then aggregated to the final output

$$Q^\theta(s, a) = V^\theta(s) + A^\theta(s, a) - \frac{1}{|\mathcal{A}|} \sum_{a'} A^\theta(s, a'). \quad (12)$$

This technique is proved useful in accelerating and stabilizing the training.

Behavioral Policy. As stated above, the agent would follow a behavioral policy to experience the environment. The traditional ways, such as the ϵ-greedy policy, all tend to select a better action according to the current Q-function values. However, when the training starts, since they do not converge to their true expected values, the Q-function is inaccurate and may guide us in the wrong way. Therefore, we design a new behavioral policy to ameliorate such a cold start problem in training.

We still use the framework of ϵ-greedy, where we select a random feature with some small probability ϵ and the feature which achieves the most "bang for the buck" with probability $1 - \epsilon$.

$$\underset{f \in \mathcal{F} \backslash \mathcal{I}_t}{\arg\max} \frac{\delta(h_\vartheta(g_{\mathcal{I}_t \cup \{f\}}(x))) - \delta(h_\vartheta(g_{\mathcal{I}_t}(x)))}{c_f}. \quad (13)$$

Algorithm 1: Training Procedure

---

1 Initialize the parameters ϑ for oracle classifier and θ for feature selector randomly
2 Pretrain the classifier which incorporates the sequence encoder by using the cross-entropy loss
3 Initialize a target network with parameters $\theta^- = \theta$
4 $t = 0$
5 **for** $l = 1, 2 \ldots$ **do**
6   //Run N agents in parallel
7   Initialize an experienced buffer $\mathcal{B}$
8   Get state $s_t = (g_{\mathcal{I}_t}(x), \mathcal{I}_t)$
9   **for** $i = 1, 2 \ldots$ **do**
10   Take action a_t according to the behavioral policy
11   Receive reward $r_t = -c_{a_t}$
12   Update state $s_{t+1} = (g_{\mathcal{I}_{t+1}}(x), \mathcal{I}_{t+1})$
13   **if** $\delta(h_{\vartheta}(g_{\mathcal{I}_{t+1}}(x))) \geq \alpha$ **then**
14   Reset s_{t+1} with a new sample from the environment
15   Add trajectory (s_t, a_t, r_t, s_{t+1}) into buffer $\mathcal{B}$
16          $t = t + 1$
17   **for** $(s_i, a_i, r_i, s_{i+1}) \in \mathcal{B}$ **do**
18   Compute target q_i according to Eq. 10
19   Compute the loss w.r.t. θ according to Eq. 11
20   Update θ with gradient descent
21   **if** $t \bmod freq_{clf}$ *is equal to 0* **then**
22   Compute the loss w.r.t. ϑ according to Eq. 9
23   Update ϑ with gradient descent
24   **if** $t \bmod freq_{target}$ *is equal to 0* **then**
25          $\theta^- = \theta$

That is, such a feature would bring about the most increase in confidence over the cost. Such a choice has been proved a good approximation of the optimal solution when the objective function is submodular.

Besides, as the number of remaining features is lower than some small number N, we could easily try all the $N!$ permutations and obtain the optimal policy which satisfies Eq. (1) and achieves the smallest cost. The last few steps will be directly recorded into the trajectory and used in optimization.

3.5 Model Training

The whole training process is described in Algorithm 1. We first train the oracle classifier on incomplete medical records before learning the feature selector. To enlarge the training samples, we randomly discard some features values for each instance to make new instances, as used in [17]. Note that the classifier could still be improved when we train the feature selector.

To optimize the Q-network, we run multiple agents in parallel and each agent would interact with the environment for a fixed number of steps to produce the trajectories, which are then recorded in an experienced buffer. At each step, a valid action is selected by the behavioral policy based on the current state. The corresponding reward is presented for this action and the state is accordingly updated. Then the new state is fed into the classifier to estimate the confidence. If it is greater than the threshold α, the state is reset with a new sample from the environment.

We next compute the target Q-value for each trajectory, The network parameters θ are updated by the gradient descent method to minimize the empirical loss in Eq. 11. Since we delay the update of the target Q-network, the parameters are only updated for every $freq_{target}$ steps. Besides, we also update the parameters of the classifier for every $freq_{clf}$ steps to improve its capability on incomplete data. Note that the sequence encoder can be further learned both by the Q-network and the oracle classifier.

Table 1. Details of real datasets.

Datasets	#Instances	#Features	#Class 0: #Class 1
TOF	11115	45	27.4:1
PAA	10896	45	62.3:1
TR	12181	45	7.4:1

4 Experiments

4.1 Experiment Setup

Datasets. To evaluate our strategy, we use three medical datasets from a major hospital in Beijing. They all include medical records of pregnant women and fetuses, such as the gestational weeks, the diameters of ventricles, and the status of arteries and veins. These tests are used for diagnosing whether fetuses have congenital heart diseases, such as the Tetralogy of Tallot (TOF). The first dataset is to diagnose whether fetuses suffer from the TOF, the second one is for Pulmonary Artery Atresia (PAA), and the third one is for Tricuspid Regurgitation (TR). The costs of features are first shared equally within each medical test and then normalized into $[0, 1]$. For all datasets, we split the data randomly into the training/validation/test sets by the 0.6/0.2/0.2 ratio. Details about the datasets are listed in Table 1.

Compared Strategies. We compare two state-of-art strategies with our cost-effective feature selector (CFS). Note that they all directly minimize a loss function on training data which is essentially a linear combination between the classification accuracy and the feature cost, balanced by the hyperparameter λ. To minimize the function, they all adopt the reinforcement learning techniques.

(1) JLAFA [17] uses an LSTM model to encode the state. Its reward for each step involves both the classification loss and the negative feature cost.

(2) RLCwCF [8] uses all the feature values as each state. If some values have not been acquired, it simply assigns them 0. And the classifier is SVM.

We set the λ as 0.01, 0.001, 0.0001, respectively, which refers to their papers. Then three versions of strategies for each one are obtained.

Parameter Setting. For the parameters of the oracle classifier, we set the dimension of the hidden vector of each direction in sequence encoder as 16, and the learning rate as 0.01. The $freq_{clf}$ is set to 50, indicating that the oracle classifier is updated for every 50 iterations.

For the parameters of feature selector, we set the number of agents as 128 and the number of steps as 4, meaning that 128 agents run in parallel for 4 steps per iteration. The feature selector consists of the MLP with two hidden layers of each 32 units. For the behavioral policy, ϵ linearly decreases from 1 to 0.1 with the speed 0.02 for each iteration. Besides, the discount factor γ is set to 1, the learning rate is set to 0.001 and the target network is updated for every 100 iterations. We set the batch size as 128 and apply the Adam optimizer.

Metrics and Implementation. The goal of our strategy is to find a strategy to minimize the overall cost while satisfying the confidence threshold. So we choose the average cost and the failure rate as the metrics to evaluate the overall performance for different confidence thresholds α. The failure rate represents the ratio of the instances that do not satisfy α.

Note that we only consider the instances that satisfy α with all feature values given, as stated in the problem statement. However, since the compared strategies with inappropriate λ may choose only a small number of features and be unable to fulfill the confidence threshold. To ensure fairness, we remove those instances for which the compared strategies cannot satisfy the threshold.

We directly use their public source codes of the compared algorithms. All algorithms are implemented by Python 3.6.6 and PyTorch. All tests are repeated over 5 times and we report the average values.

4.2   Experimental Results

Overall Performance. To test the performance of our strategy, we compare 6 different versions of related strategies. Note that the costs of these strategies are tested under the problem setting which adopts the same oracle classifier.

We vary the confidence threshold α from 2.5 to 4.5 while fixing the other parameters to their default values. The results of the average cost and the failure rate on two datasets are presented in Fig. 4.

On the TOF dataset, due to a high failure rate when the parameter λ of RLCwCF is set to 0.01 and 0.001, we just report the result of the RLCwCF-0.0001 version. For the average cost, it can be seen that most strategies incur a higher cost as we increase the confidence threshold. However, the costs of

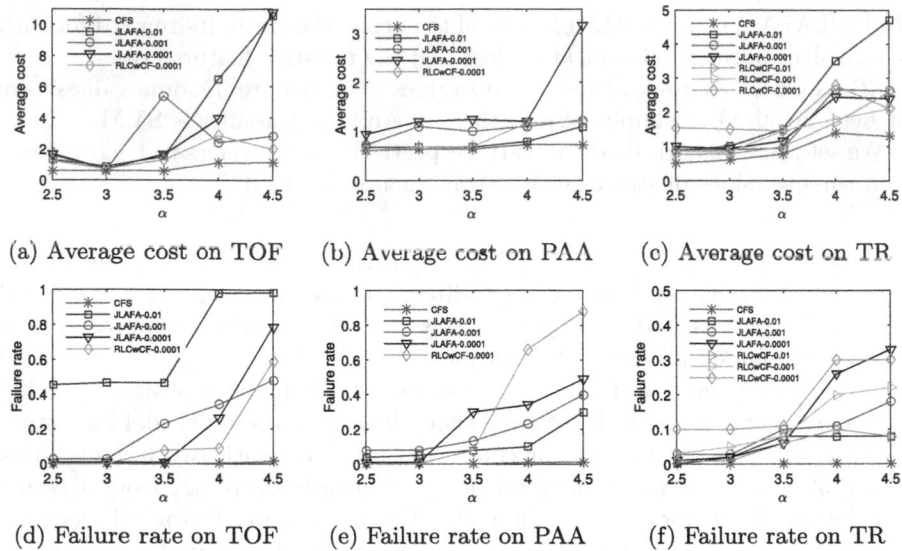

(a) Average cost on TOF   (b) Average cost on PAA   (c) Average cost on TR

(d) Failure rate on TOF   (e) Failure rate on PAA   (f) Failure rate on TR

Fig. 4. Effectiveness on TOF, PAA, and TR

JLAFA-0.0001 and RLCwCF-0.0001 decrease when α is 4 and 4.5, which may be because too many instances cannot meet the threshold (which coincides with Fig. 4d) and the successful ones are easy to be classified with few features. Among all the strategies, our CFS always achieves the smallest cost. For the failure rate, all the compared strategies tend to increase with larger thresholds, since they would stop the process of feature selection when the instances can be classified and hence do not acquire more features to enhance the confidence. But CFS is trained to meet the predetermined threshold. It can be observed that CFS always achieves a high success rate.

On the PAA and TR datasets, the results are similar to that on TOF dataset. It can be seen that the average cost of CFS is lower than all compared strategies across different confidence thresholds, and the failure rate of CFS is almost zero for different thresholds. In conclusion, CFS performs the best on three datasets among all the strategies and is effective.

Classification Accuracy. Apart from the average cost and failure rate, the accuracy of the diagnoses is also important. Due to the imbalance of the data, we use the area under the receiving operating curve (AUC score) as the metric to measure the classification accuracy. In this experiment, we directly use all the compared strategies to choose the features and calculate the predicted probabilities. For the compared strategies, we would view CFS trained with different thresholds as different versions of our strategy. And for the RLCwCF-0.01 and RLCwCF-0.001, since they often fail to select features on the TOF and PAA datasets (which is because larger λ indicates a very small total feature cost) and

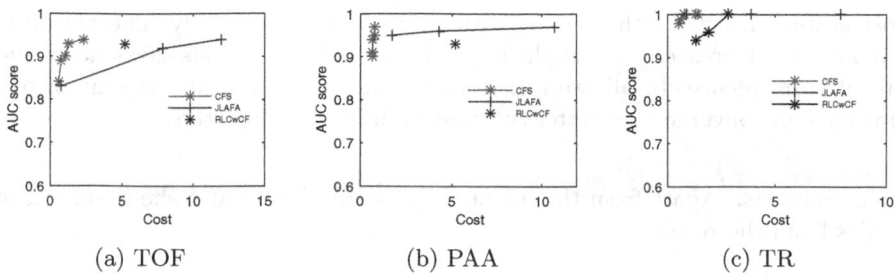

(a) TOF   (b) PAA   (c) TR

Fig. 5. AUC scores of different costs on TOF, PAA and TR

directly make the prediction, we just show the results of the RLCwCF-0.0001 version on TOF and PAA dataset. The results are reported in Fig. 5.

From the results on three datasets, we can observe that the AUC scores of these strategies increase as the cost is larger, which is consistent with the fact that the prediction would be more accurate with more features acquired. It can be seen that the points of our CFS method concentrate on the top left part of the figures, which implies that we only take a small cost to obtain a high classification accuracy. Besides, under the same cost, the AUC score of our strategy is larger than that of JLAFA and RLCwCF. Superiority can also be seen when we fix the AUC score. Therefore, we can conclude that our strategy performs better than JLAFA and RLCwCF.

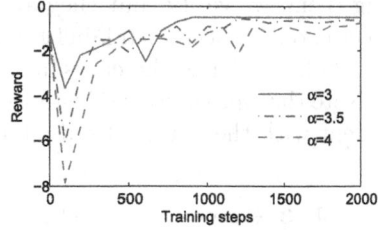

Fig. 6. Average rewards during training

Convergence Analysis. We analyze the convergence of our strategy by considering the average rewards during training. Take the TOF as an example, we investigate different versions of our strategy w.r.t. the confidence threshold α. The results are reported in Fig. 6.

It can be observed that the performance of all versions has a similar trend. The average rewards of all versions fluctuate at first, then tend to be stable in the later phase. However, another fact is that there are differences in the convergence speeds of different versions. The version with $\alpha = 3$ converges fastest and is the most stable one, while the version with $\alpha = 4$ converges slowly. The reason is that larger α increases the complexity of feature selection, thus slows down the rate of convergence. In all, we can draw a conclusion that all versions of our strategy can converge to a better solution in finite training steps.

Case Studies. Apart from the quantitative analysis, we also show some case studies from the results.

Table 2. Case studies on TOF.

	Instance 1	Instance 2
Features selected	Gestational weeks	Gestational weeks
	Annulus diameter of pulmonary valve	Diameter of the aortic ends of ductus arteriosus
	Width of descending aorta	Annulus diameter of pulmonary valve
	Diameter of left ventricle	–
Label	1	0

(1) For the TOF, we select two instances with different labels, and the features selected of CFS are showed in Table 2. For Instance 1, CFS selects four features and makes a correct judgment. And for Instance 2, only three features are acquired. By analyzing them, we verify that they are related to the TOF.

(2) For the TR, we select two instances with label 1, and the features selected of CFS are presented in Table 3. Similar to the cases in TOF, only a few features are selected for diagnosis. Note that for these two instances, CFS selects different features, which are coincident with the personalized instances.

Table 3. Case studies on TR.

	Instance 1	Instance 2
Features selected	Gestational weeks	Gestational weeks
	Diameter of right ventricle	Diastolic peak of the aortic arch
	Systolic peak of pulmonary venous flow	Peak A of the tricuspid valve
	–	Peak E of the tricuspid valve
Label	1	1

5   Related Work

The studied problem of learning a cost-effective strategy on incomplete medical data is related to the traditional problem of active feature acquisition. However, ours is unique in that we capture the core characteristics of the medical inquiry where consecutive tests are conducted until the doctors gain enough confidence. So the related approaches may not be easily applied to our problem. We just review them below.

Some existing work deals with the problem in a Bayesian setting [5,9,10, 18]. They assume that the probability distribution of the data is given and can be estimated from the data. Their approaches minimize the feature acquisition cost by inferring the feature dependencies. Note that their approaches are only applicable in low-dimensional data so that the probability models can be reliably learned.

Another type of method constructs the decision trees on the training data to guide the feature selection [2,11,13–15,21]. The tree is learned by minimizing the elaborate empirical loss, which combines the cost of used features and classification accuracy. The construction follows some purity metrics such as the entropy. Note that they still focus on the training data and use some hyperparameters which balance the two goals but are hard to set in practice.

Other heuristics include using a crowdsourcing-based approach to generate high-quality rules to largely reduce the cost while preserving quality [22], solving an lp to select the model with the best accuracy and the lowest cost from those pre-trained candidates which utilize different sets of features [19], or adopting imitation learning to follow the reference policy provided by an oracle of feature selection [7]. However, their approaches are not specific to the problem of medical inquiry and fail to capture the real characteristics of that.

Recently, reinforcement learning (RL) has shown remarkable success in various domains. Some works formulate the feature acquisition problem as a Markov Decision Process (MDP) or a partial observable MDP (POMDP) and adopt the mature solutions in RL to learn the best feature acquisition strategy that gives maximum returns [4,8,16,17]. As stated in the introduction, the main problem is that it is hard to find the real sense of the hyperparameter which balances the loss of classification and the feature cost and overlooks the real characteristics of the medical inquiry.

6   Conclusion

The problem of learning a cost-effective strategy on incomplete medical data generalizes the traditional problem of sequential feature acquisition but uniquely characterizes the process of medical inquiry. The proposed formulation, based on the success of modern classification techniques, captures the practical issues of quickly converging into a diagnosis but incurring a smaller cost. The proposed framework of of learning the strategy follows the traditional reinforcement learning where each element in the MDP is defined and the environment is accordingly modeled by an oracle classifier. To tackle the challenge of coding the variable sets, we adopt the bidirectional GRU-based architecture with the attention mechanism as the encoder. Sharing this encoder with the classifier can further improve its accuracy of classification. Extensive experiments demonstrate that the simulation indeed coincides with our expectation of the real process of medical inquiry and our strategy outperforms the other state-of-the-art baseline strategies in many respects.

Acknowledgments. This research was supported by the National Natural Science Foundation under Grant 61702027, the Beijing Science and Technology Plan Project under Grant Z171100000117022, the Beijing Municipal Science & Technology Commission under Grant Z181100001918008.

References

1. Bahdanau, D., Cho, K., Bengio, Y.: Neural machine translation by jointly learning to align and translate. In: ICLR 2015 (2015)
2. Bilgic, M., Getoor, L.: VOILA: efficient feature-value acquisition for classification. In: AAAI 2007, pp. 1225–1230 (2007)
3. Cho, K., et al.: Learning phrase representations using RNN encoder-decoder for statistical machine translation. In: EMNLP 2014, pp. 1724–1734 (2014)
4. Dulac-Arnold, G., Denoyer, L., Preux, P., Gallinari, P.: Datum-wise classification: a sequential approach to sparsity. In: Gunopulos, D., Hofmann, T., Malerba, D., Vazirgiannis, M. (eds.) ECML PKDD 2011. LNCS (LNAI), vol. 6911, pp. 375–390. Springer, Heidelberg (2011). https://doi.org/10.1007/978-3-642-23780-5_34
5. Gao, T., Koller, D.: Active classification based on value of classifier. In: NeurIPS 2011, pp. 1062–1070 (2011)
6. van Hasselt, H., Guez, A., Silver, D.: Deep reinforcement learning with double q-learning. In: AAAI 2016, pp. 2094–2100 (2016)
7. He, H., III, H.D., Eisner, J.: Imitation learning by coaching. In: NeurIPS 2012, pp. 3158–3166 (2012)
8. Janisch, J., Pevný, T., Lisý, V.: Classification with costly features using deep reinforcement learning. In: AAAI 2019, pp. 3959–3966 (2019)
9. Ji, S., Carin, L.: Cost-sensitive feature acquisition and classification. Pattern Recogn. **40**(5), 1474–1485 (2007)
10. Kapoor, A., Horvitz, E.: Breaking boundaries between induction time and diagnosis time active information acquisition. In: NeurIPS 2009, pp. 898–906 (2009)
11. Maliah, S., Shani, G.: MDP-based cost sensitive classification using decision trees. In: AAAI 2018, pp. 3746–3753 (2018)
12. Mnih, V., et al.: Human-level control through deep reinforcement learning. Nature **518**(7540), 529–533 (2015)
13. Nan, F., Saligrama, V.: Adaptive classification for prediction under a budget. In: NeurIPS 2017, pp. 4727–4737 (2017)
14. Nan, F., Wang, J., Saligrama, V.: Feature-budgeted random forest. In: ICML 2015, pp. 1983–1991 (2015)
15. Nan, F., Wang, J., Saligrama, V.: Pruning random forests for prediction on a budget. In: NeurIPS 2016, pp. 2334–2342 (2016)

16. Rückstieß, T., Osendorfer, C., van der Smagt, P.: Sequential feature selection for classification. In: Wang, D., Reynolds, M. (eds.) AI 2011. LNCS (LNAI), vol. 7106, pp. 132–141. Springer, Heidelberg (2011). https://doi.org/10.1007/978-3-642-25832-9_14

17. Shim, H., Hwang, S.J., Yang, E.: Joint active feature acquisition and classification with variable-size set encoding. In: NeurIPS 2018, pp. 1375–1385 (2018)

18. Trapeznikov, K., Saligrama, V.: Supervised sequential classification under budget constraints. In: AISTATS 2013, pp. 581–589 (2013)

19. Wang, J., Trapeznikov, K., Saligrama, V.: An LP for sequential learning under budgets. In: AISTATS 2014, pp. 987–995 (2014)

20. Wang, Z., Schaul, T., Hessel, M., van Hasselt, H., Lanctot, M., de Freitas, N.: Dueling network architectures for deep reinforcement learning. In: ICML 2016, pp. 1995–2003 (2016)

21. Xu, Z.E., Kusner, M.J., Weinberger, K.Q., Chen, M.: Cost-sensitive tree of classifiers. In: ICML 2013, pp. 133–141 (2013)

22. Yang, J., Fan, J., Wei, Z., Li, G., Liu, T., Du, X.: Cost-effective data annotation using game-based crowdsourcing. PVLDB **12**(1), 57–70 (2018)

Bus Frequency Optimization: When Waiting Time Matters in User Satisfaction

Songsong Mo[1], Zhifeng Bao[2], Baihua Zheng[3], and Zhiyong Peng[1(✉)]

[1] School of Computer Science, Wuhan University, Hubei, China
{songsong945,peng}@whu.edu.cn
[2] RMIT University, Melbourne, Australia
zhifeng.bao@rmit.edu.au
[3] Singapore Management University, Singapore, Singapore
bhzheng@smu.edu.sg

Abstract. Reorganizing bus frequency to cater for the actual travel demand can save the cost of the public transport system significantly. Many, if not all, existing studies formulate this as a bus frequency optimization problem which tries to minimize passengers' average waiting time. However, many investigations have confirmed that the user satisfaction drops faster as the waiting time increases. Consequently, this paper studies the bus frequency optimization problem considering the user satisfaction. Specifically, for the first time to our best knowledge, we study how to schedule the buses such that the total number of passengers who could receive their bus services within the waiting time threshold is maximized. We prove that this problem is NP-hard, and present an index-based algorithm with $(1-1/e)$ approximation ratio. By exploiting the locality property of routes in a bus network, we propose a partition-based greedy method which achieves a $(1-\rho)(1-1/e)$ approximation ratio. Then we propose a progressive partition-based greedy method to further improve the efficiency while achieving a $(1 - \rho)(1 - 1/e - \varepsilon)$ approximation ratio. Experiments on a real city-wide bus dataset in Singapore verify the efficiency, effectiveness, and scalability of our methods.

Keywords: Bus frequency scheduling optimization · User waiting time minimization · Approximate algorithm

1 Introduction

Public transport and the services delivered by buses are essential to our daily life. Bus services provide us with the capability to move around, which shapes where we can work and live, where we shop and how we spend our leisure time. In this paper, we focus on bus frequency design which plays a very important role in urban public transport systems, as reorganizing bus frequencies to meet the actual travel demands is expected to achieve significant savings in cost. Taking

New York City as an example, the cost of each bus is around $550,000 and the operating cost of transit agencies reaches $215 per hour[1]. If we re-organize the bus frequencies based on real travel demands and save 10% bus departures, we can save $20 operating costs per hour and $55,000 per vehicle.

In the literature, there are many studies focusing on the problem of bus frequency optimization. Most of them share a common objective, which is to minimize the *average* travel cost (in terms of waiting time) of passengers [3,5,9, 10,13]. Moreover, their solutions are usually heuristic rather than approximate (with theoretical guarantees). However, most, if not all, existing works ignore an important aspect, the *user satisfaction*. Many studies have confirmed that the user satisfaction drops faster as the waiting time increases [1,8]. Motivated by this finding, we aim to schedule the buses in a way to serve more passengers within a given waiting time threshold θ but not to minimize the average waiting time. In addition, our algorithms are adaptive to cater for different settings of θ.

We call this novel problem as SatisFAction-BooST Bus Scheduling (FAST). Given a bus database $\mathcal{B}$, a bus route database $\mathcal{R}$, a passenger database $\mathcal{P}$, and a vector $\mathcal{N}$ $\langle n_1, n_2, \cdots, n_i, \cdots, n_{|\mathcal{R}|} \rangle$ that specifies the expected number of bus departures for each bus route, it chooses n_i buses for each route $r_i \in \mathcal{R}$ such that the whole bus system is able to satisfy the most passengers. The analysis shows that the objective function of FAST is submodular and FAST is NP-hard.

To resolve the FAST problem, we develop a range of approximate algorithms with non-trivial theoretical guarantees. First, we propose an index-based greedy method (Greedy), which can provide $(1 - 1/e)$ approximation factor for FAST as the baseline, and two enhanced versions, namely PartGreedy and ProPart-Greedy. PartGreedy is inspired from [18] and by the fact that a bus network is designed to cover different parts of the city and it tries to avoid unnecessary overlapping among routes [4,16]. It adopts a partitioning algorithm to divide the bus network into several disjoint partitions. Accordingly, it invokes local greedy search within each partition, which effectively reduces the computation cost of the original greedy algorithm. On the other hand, ProPartGreedy adopts a different strategy to address the efficiency issue. Instead of finding one bus that contributes the most to the objective function in each iteration of the local greedy search, it fetches multiple buses in each iteration of the local greedy search to cut down the total number of iterations required. Meanwhile, ProPartGreedy has a tunable parameter that could determine roughly how many buses could be fetched in each iteration and hence provide a trade-off between efficiency and effectiveness.

In summary, we make the following contributions.

- We propose and study the FAST problem. To the best of our knowledge, this is the first study on bus frequency optimization that considers user satisfaction. We prove that the objective function of FAST is monotone and submodular, and FAST is NP-hard.
- We propose an index-based greedy method (Greedy), a partition-based greedy method (PartGreedy) and a progressive partition-based greedy method

---

[1] https://www.liveabout.com/bus-cost-to-purchase-and-operate-2798845.

(ProPartGreedy) to solve the FAST problem efficiently. They can achieve an approximation ratio of $(1 - \frac{1}{e})$, $(1 - \rho)(1 - \frac{1}{e})$, and $(1 - \rho)(1 - \frac{1}{e} - \varepsilon)$ respectively, where ρ and ε are the user-defined parameters.
- We conduct extensive experiments on real-world bus route and bus touch-on/touch-off records in Singapore (396 routes, 28 million trip records of one week) to demonstrate the effectiveness, efficiency and scalability of our methods.

2   Related Work

In this section, we will review existing related work and report the difference between this work and existing ones.

We divide the literature into two categories based on the overall optimization objective. One is called the travel time driven bus frequency optimization problem (Travel-BFO), which aims to minimize the average/total travel time of passengers for either one bus route or a bus route network, based on passenger demands. It treats each ride as a new trip. Another is called the transfer time driven bus frequency optimization problem (Transfer-BFO), which aims to minimize the total transfer time of the transfer passengers.

Travel-BFO. Here, the passenger demands are usually abstracted as origin-destination (OD) pairs. The model proposed in [13] treats the travel time of passengers as an aggregation of the walking time, the waiting time, and the on-board travel time. The problem is usually formulated as a nonconvex objective function with linear or convex constraints. In [3], it is modeled as a nonlinear bilevel problem: the upper level represents the planner who wants to ensure minimal total travel time under fleet size constraints; the lower level represents the users who act by minimizing the travel time. In [5], a multi-objective model is proposed, seeking to minimize the overall travel time of the users and the operational cost of the operators (assumed to be linearly proportional to the frequencies). Martínez et al. [10] study the transit frequency optimization problem to determine the time interval between subsequent buses for a set of bus lines. They propose a mixed-integer linear programming (MILP) formulation for an existing bilevel model [3], and present a metaheuristic method. A new model considering user behavior is proposed in [9]. It assigns a user's trip to three stages (pre-trip, on-board and end-trip) and aims to minimize users' total travel costs of the objective bus line.

Differences. Although different bus frequency optimization models have been proposed, they share a very similar optimization objective, i.e., minimizing the average/total travel cost of passengers. Different from the above literature, we aim to improve the *overall passenger satisfaction* by scheduling the buses such that they can serve more passengers within the given waiting time threshold. Our work is mainly motivated by the following two findings. *First*, waiting time has a direct impact on the user satisfaction, as evident by many studies [1,8]. *Second*, the waiting time threshold is tunable, hence the bus company can adjust thresholds to cater to various concerns on budget, government needs, passengers' tolerance of waiting, etc.

Transfer-BFO. Transfer time driven bus frequency optimization problem is an extension of single bus route timetabling. It determines the departure time of each trip of all lines in the bus network with the consideration of passenger transfer activities at transfer stations [6].

This problem is modeled by mixed integer programming models to maximize the number of synchronized bus arrivals at transfer nodes [2]. Ibarra-Rojas et al. [7] extend the work of Ceder et al. [2] to address a flexible Transfer-BFO problem with almost evenly spaced departures and preventing bus bunching. The model proposed in [14] tries to minimize the total transfer time experienced by passengers. Parbo et al. [12] studied a bi-level bus timetabling problem to minimize the weighted transfer waiting time of passengers, and a Tabu Search algorithm was applied to solve the bilevel model. Recently a nonlinear mixed integer-programming model is proposed to maximize the number of total transferring passengers with small excess transfer time [17].

Differences. The above studies on the Transfer-BFO problem mainly focus on minimizing the total transfer cost for passengers on transfer, which can only improve the satisfaction of the transfer passengers. In contrast, our problem aims to improve overall passenger satisfaction by serving them within a given time threshold.

For all the above work in both categories, despite the difference, all existing approaches only propose heuristic methods without theoretical guarantees, while we propose algorithms with non-trivial theoretical guarantees.

3   Problem Formulation

In a bus route database $\mathcal{R}$, a route r is a sequence of bus stations $(s_1, s_2, \cdots, s_i, \cdots, s_m)$, where s_i is a bus station represented by (latitude, longitude). In a passenger database $\mathcal{P}$, a passenger $p \in \mathcal{P}$ is in form of a tuple $\{s_b, s_e, t\}$, where s_b denotes the boarding station, s_e denotes the alighting station, and t denotes the time when p reaches s_b. A bus b_{ij} is in form of a tuple $\{r_i, dt_j\}$, where r_i and dt_j denote the bus service route and the departure time from $r_i.s_1$ respectively.

Definition 1. *We define that a bus b_{ij} can serve a passenger p, if r_i contains $p.s_b$ and $p.s_e$ in order, and $0 \le dt_j + T(r_i.s_1, p.s_b) - t \le \theta$, where $T(r_i.s_1, p.s_b)$ denotes the travel time required by bus b_{ij} from $r_i.s_1$ to $p.s_b$ via the bus route r_i, and θ is a given waiting time threshold.*

There are multiple ways available to approximate $T(r_i.s_1, p.s_b)$. In this paper, we utilize the historical average travel time from $r_i.s_1$ to $p.s_b$ via the route r_i to compute $T(s_1, s_b)$. Based on Definition 1, we formally introduce $\mathcal{S}(b_{ij}, p_k)$ to denote the service of b_{ij} to p_k, as presented in Eq. (1).

$$\mathcal{S}(b_{ij}, p_k) = \begin{cases} 1 \text{ if } b_{ij} \text{ can serve } p_k \\ 0 \text{ otherwise} \end{cases} \tag{1}$$

Next, we introduce the concept of bus service frequency in Definition 2. Let the bus service frequency $\mathcal{F}$ for $\mathcal{R}$ be a set, with each element $f_i \in \mathcal{F}$ corresponding to a bus route $r_i \in \mathcal{R}$, i.e., $\mathcal{F} = \{\cup_{\forall r_i \in \mathcal{R}} f_i\}$. Then, the service of $\mathcal{F}$ to a passenger p_k can be computed by Eq. (2). Note $\mathcal{S}(\mathcal{F}, p_k) = 1$ as long as any $b_{ij} \in \mathcal{F}$ can serve p_k; otherwise, $\mathcal{S}(\mathcal{F}, p_k) = 0$.

$$\mathcal{S}(\mathcal{F}, p_k) = 1 - \prod_{b_{ij} \in \mathcal{F}} (1 - \mathcal{S}(b_{ij}, p_k)) \tag{2}$$

Definition 2. *A bus service frequency (f_i) for r_i refers to a set of buses $(b_{i1}, b_{i2}, \cdots, b_{in_i})$ that serve the route r_i, where n_i $(n_i \geq 1)$ denotes the total number of bus departures corresponding to the route r_i within a day.*

Next, we formulate our problem in Definition 3 and show its NP-hardness. Note that we ignore the passenger capacity of the bus in our problem definition.

Definition 3 (SatisFAction-BooST Bus Scheduling (FAST)). *Given a bus route database $\mathcal{R}$, a passenger database $\mathcal{P}$, a waiting time threshold θ, and a vector $\mathcal{N}\langle n_1, n_2, \cdots, n_i, \cdots, n_{|\mathcal{R}|}\rangle$ where n_i (≥ 1) denotes the total number of bus departures of bus route $r_i \in \mathcal{R}$, we output a bus service frequency $\mathcal{F}$ which can maximize $\mathcal{G}(\mathcal{F}) = \sum_{p_k \in \mathcal{P}} \mathcal{S}(\mathcal{F}, p_k)$, where $\mathcal{G}(\mathcal{F})$ denotes the total number of passengers served by $\mathcal{F}$.*

Theorem 1. *The objective function $\mathcal{G}$ of FAST is monotone and submodular.*

Proof. We skip the proof of the monotonicity of $\mathcal{G}$ as it is straightforward. In the following, we prove that $\mathcal{G}$ is submodular. Let $V \subseteq T \subset \mathcal{B}$, where $\mathcal{B}$ denotes the universe of buses, and b refers to a bus in $\mathcal{B} \backslash T$. According to [11], $\mathcal{G}(V)$ is submodular if it satisfies: $\mathcal{G}(V \cup b) - \mathcal{G}(V) \geq \mathcal{G}(T \cup b) - \mathcal{G}(T)$. To facilitate the proof, we define $V_b = V \cup b$ and $\mathcal{G}_b(V) = \mathcal{G}(V \cup b) - \mathcal{G}(V)$. Then, we have:

$$\mathcal{G}_b(V) - \mathcal{G}_b(T) = \left(\sum_{p_k \in \mathcal{P}} \mathcal{S}(V_b, p_k) - \sum_{p_k \in \mathcal{P}} \mathcal{S}(V, p_k)\right)$$
$$-\left(\sum_{p_k \in \mathcal{P}} \mathcal{S}(T_b, p_k) - \sum_{p_k \in \mathcal{P}} \mathcal{S}(T, p_k)\right) \tag{3}$$
$$= \sum_{p_k \in \mathcal{P}} (\mathcal{S}(V_b, p_k) - \mathcal{S}(V, p_k) - \mathcal{S}(T_b, p_k) + \mathcal{S}(T, p_k)).$$

To show the submodularity of $\mathcal{G}$, we first prove Inequality (4).

$$\mathcal{S}(V_b, p_k) - \mathcal{S}(V, p_k) - \mathcal{S}(T_b, p_k) + \mathcal{S}(T, p_k) \geq 0 \tag{4}$$

According to whether p_k can be served by buses in V or buses in $T \backslash V$ or bus b, there are in total four cases corresponding to Inequality (4). Case 1: p_k can be served by a bus $b_0 \in V$. Then we have $\mathcal{S}(V, p_k) = \mathcal{S}(V_b, p_k) = \mathcal{S}(T, p_k) = \mathcal{S}(T_b, p_k) = 1$, because $V \subset V_b$ and $V \subseteq T \subset T_b$. Thus, $\mathcal{S}(V_b, p_k) - \mathcal{S}(V, p_k) - \mathcal{S}(T_b, p_k) + \mathcal{S}(T, p_k) = 0$. Case 2: p_k cannot be served by any bus $b_0 \in V$ but it can be served by a bus $b_1 \in T \backslash V$. Then we have $\mathcal{S}(V, p_k) = 0$, $\mathcal{S}(V_b, p_k) \geq 0$ and $\mathcal{S}(T, p_k) = \mathcal{S}(T_b, p_k) = 1$. Thus, $\mathcal{S}(V_b, p_k) - \mathcal{S}(V, p_k) - \mathcal{S}(T_b, p_k) + \mathcal{S}(T, p_k) \geq 0$.

Algorithm 1: Greedy $(\mathcal{B}, \mathcal{R}, \mathcal{P}, \mathcal{N})$

1.1 Input: a bus database $\mathcal{B}$, a bus route database $\mathcal{R}$, a passenger database $\mathcal{P}$, and a vector $\mathcal{N} \langle n_1, n_2, \cdots, n_{|\mathcal{R}|} \rangle$

1.2 Output: a bus service frequency $\mathcal{F}$

1.3 Initialize $\mathcal{F} \leftarrow \phi,\ n \leftarrow \sum_{i=1}^{|\mathcal{N}|} n_i$

1.4 Initialize a $|\mathcal{N}|$-dimension vector $\langle k_1, k_2, \cdots, k_{|\mathcal{N}|} \rangle$ with zero

1.5 for $i \leftarrow 1$ *to* n **do**

1.6   Select a bus $b_{jl} \leftarrow \arg\max_{b \in \mathcal{B} \setminus \mathcal{F}}(\mathcal{G}(\mathcal{F} \cup b) - \mathcal{G}(\mathcal{F}))$

1.7 $k_j ++$

1.8   **if** $k_j \leq n_j$ **then**

1.9 | $\mathcal{F} \leftarrow \mathcal{F} \cup b_{jl}$

1.10   **if** $k_j \geq n_j$ **then**

1.11 | remove all the buses serving the route j from $\mathcal{B}$

1.12 return $\mathcal{F}$

<u>Case 3</u>: p_k cannot be served by any bus $b_0 \in T$ and can be served by the bus b. Then we have $\mathcal{S}(V, p_k) = \mathcal{S}(T, p_k) = 0$ and $\mathcal{S}(V_b, p_k) = \mathcal{S}(T_b, p_k) = 1$. Thus, $\mathcal{S}(V_b, p_k) - \mathcal{S}(V, p_k) - \mathcal{S}(T_b, p_k) + \mathcal{S}(T, p_k) = 0$. <u>Case 4</u>: p_k cannot be served by any bus $b_0 \in T$ or the bus b. Then we have $\mathcal{S}(V, p_k) = \mathcal{S}(V_b, p_k) = \mathcal{S}(T, p_k) = \mathcal{S}(T_b, p_k) = 0$. Thus, $\mathcal{S}(V_b, p_k) - \mathcal{S}(V, p_k) - \mathcal{S}(T_b, p_k) + \mathcal{S}(T, p_k) = 0$. The above shows the correctness of Inequality (4). Based on Eq. (3) and Inequality (4), we have $\mathcal{G}_b(V) - \mathcal{G}_b(T) \geq 0$ and hence $\mathcal{G}$ is a submodular function. ∎

Theorem 2. *The FAST problem is NP-hard.*

Proof. It is worth noting that the minimum unit of time is second in daily life. Therefore, $\mathcal{B}$ is a finite set. Based on this, we prove it by reducing the Set Cover problem to the FAST problem. In the Set Cover problem, given a collection of subsets $S_1, \cdots, S_i, \cdots, S_j$ of a universe of elements U, we wish to know whether there exist k of the subsets whose union is equal to U. We map each element in U in the Set Cover problem to each passenger in $\mathcal{P}$, and map each subset S_i to the set of passengers server by a bus $b \in \mathcal{B}$. Consequently, if all passengers in U are served by S, the total number of passengers served by S is $|U|$. Subsequently, $n = \sum_{i=1}^{|\mathcal{R}|} n_i$ is set to k (selecting k buses). The Set Cover problem is equivalent to deciding if there is a k-bus set with the maximum served passenger number U in FAST. As the Set Cover problem is NP-complete, the decision problem of FAST is NP-complete, and the optimization problem is NP-hard. ∎

4   Basic Greedy Method

To address FAST, we first present a baseline which extends the basic greedy method for the problem of submodular function maximization. To accelerate the marginal gain computation, we propose a mapping structure to index the bus and passenger database. The basic greedy method is guaranteed to achieve $(1 - 1/e)$-approximation, as proved by Nemhauser et al. [11].

Bus List	$N_{ToBeServed}$	L_P
b_1	3	$p_1, p_3, p_{|\mathcal{P}|}$
b_2	2	p_1, p_2
b_3	1	p_3
...	...	...
$b_{|\mathcal{B}|}$	1	p_2

Passenger List	$IsServed$	Optional Buses
p_1	$false$	b_1, b_2
p_2	$false$	$b_2, b_{|\mathcal{B}|}$
p_3	$false$	b_1, b_3
...	...	...
$p_{|\mathcal{P}|}$	$false$	b_1

Fig. 1. Forward list

Fig. 2. Inverted list

4.1   A Basic Greedy Method

The pseudo-code of the greedy method is listed in Algorithm 1. In each iteration, it selects a bus $b_{jl} \in \mathcal{B} \backslash \mathcal{F}$ with the largest marginal gain, such that $b_{jl} = \arg\max_{b \in \mathcal{B} \backslash \mathcal{F}}(\mathcal{G}(\mathcal{F} \cup b) - \mathcal{G}(\mathcal{F}))$, and inserts it to the current service frequency $\mathcal{F}$. In lines 1.8-1.11, it checks whether the number of bus departures of route j, which b_{jl} serves, has reached the total number of bus departures required by this route. If so, it removes all buses serving the route j from $\mathcal{B}$. Such an iteration is repeated n times, with n being the total number of bus departures required by all the bus routes. Finally, it returns $\mathcal{F}$ as the solution.

Time Complexity. In each iteration, Algorithm 1 needs to scan all the buses in $\mathcal{B} \backslash \mathcal{F}$ and computes their marginal gain to the chosen set. Each marginal gain computation needs to traverse $\mathcal{P}$ once in the worst case. Thus, adding one bus into $\mathcal{F}$ takes $O(|\mathcal{P}| \cdot |\mathcal{B}|)$ time, and the total complexity is $O(n \cdot |\mathcal{P}| \cdot |\mathcal{B}|)$.

4.2   Index for Efficient Marginal Gain Computation

To accelerate the marginal gain computation, which is the main bottleneck of Algorithm 1, we propose two mapping indexes, *forward list* and *inverted list* as shown in Fig. 1 and Fig. 2 respectively. The former is for buses $b_i \in \mathcal{B}$, maintaining a list of passengers L_P that could be served by bus b_i. Note that a passenger could be served by multiple buses. To avoid counting the same passenger multiple times when we calculate the marginal gain, we maintain another parameter $N_{ToBeServed}$ to capture the number of passengers in L_P that are still waiting for services. The initial value of $N_{ToBeServed}$ is set to be the cardinality of L_P, and its value will be reduced every time when a passenger in L_P is served by another bus. The latter is for passengers $p \in \mathcal{P}$, maintaining a list of buses that could serve the passenger p. The boolean $IsServed$ is to indicate whether any of the optional buses has been scheduled with an initial value being $false$. For example, if bus b_1 is selected, it could serve three passengers based on $N_{ToBeServed}$'s value associated with b_1 in forward list. Meanwhile, $IsServed$'s value of passengers in L_P of b_1 (i.e., $p_1, p_3, p_{|\mathcal{P}|}$) will be changed to $true$, all the buses that could serve p_1 or p_3 or $p_{|\mathcal{P}|}$ have to update $N_{ToBeServed}$'s value to reflect the fact that some of their potential passengers have already been served.

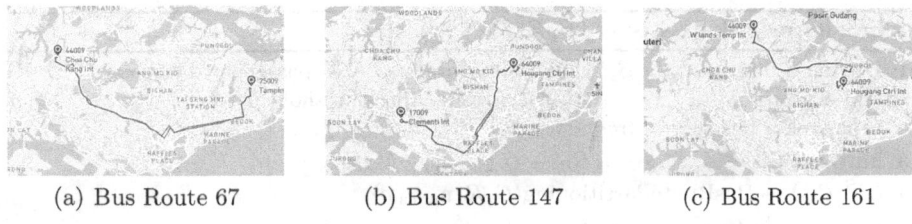

(a) Bus Route 67   (b) Bus Route 147   (c) Bus Route 161

Fig. 3. Visualization of three popular bus routes in Singapore

5 Partition-Based Greedy Method

In practice, a bus network is designed to cover different parts of a city to meet residents' various travel demands. By design, it tries to avoid unnecessary overlapping among routes [4, 16]. For example, Fig. 3 plots three popular bus routes in Singapore. A passenger whose travel demand could be served by route 67 will not consider route 161 or route 147 as these routes have *zero* overlap. This observation suggests that it might be unnecessary to scan the entire bus network when calculating the marginal gains of certain buses. This motivates us to design a partition-based greedy method. In the following, we first introduce a novel concept namely *service overlap ratio* to guide the partitioning process, and then present the algorithm.

Our main idea is to partition the bus routes (and buses) into disjoint clusters, and then use a divide-and-conquer strategy to find local optimal frequencies for routes in each partition. This approach is expected to reduce the time complexity of the basic greedy by a factor of m^2 with m being the number of partitions. The speedup is contributed by the fact that it invokes the greedy algorithm for each cluster and hence it only needs to scan the buses and passengers corresponding to the routes in a cluster during the greedy search. Meanwhile, in term of accuracy, we introduce a novel concept called *service overlap ratio* to achieve an approximation ratio with non-trivial theoretical guarantee, as shown later.

Definition 4 (Partition). *A partition of a set S is denoted as a cluster set $\mathcal{C}=\{\mathcal{C}_1, \mathcal{C}_2, \cdots, \mathcal{C}_m\}$, where m denotes the total number of clusters, such that $S = \cup_{i=1}^{m}\mathcal{C}_i$, $\forall\mathcal{C}_i \in \mathcal{C}$, $\mathcal{C}_i \neq \phi$, and $\forall\mathcal{C}_i, \mathcal{C}_j \in \mathcal{C}$ with $i \neq j$, $\mathcal{C}_i \cap \mathcal{C}_j = \phi$.*

To better illustrate the service overlap ratio, we define a function $\mathsf{Serve}(P,R)$ that takes a passenger set P and a route set R as inputs and returns the passengers in P that could be served by any route in R without considering the temporal factor. To be more specific, a passenger p will be returned by $\mathsf{Serve}(P,R)$ if there is a route $r_i \in R$ such that r_i contains $p.s_b$ and $p.s_e$ in order, which is different from the "bus serves passengers" defined in Definition 1. We name the set of passengers returned by $\mathsf{Serve}(P,R)$ as the passenger pool w.r.t. bus routes R.

As stated in Definition 5, the service overlap ratio ρ_i of a bus route cluster $\mathcal{C}_i^R$ tries to measure the number of passengers in the passenger pool w.r.t. $\mathcal{C}_i^R$ that actually also belong to the passenger pools w.r.t. other clusters. Let $|A|$ denote

---

Algorithm 2: PartGreedy $(\mathcal{B}, \mathcal{R}, \mathcal{P}, \mathcal{N}, \rho)$

2.1 Input: a bus database $\mathcal{B}$, a bus route database $\mathcal{R}$, a passenger database $\mathcal{P}$,
and a vector $\mathcal{N}$ $\langle n_1, n_2, \cdots, n_{|\mathcal{R}|} \rangle$, a controlling threshold ρ
2.2 Output: a bus service frequency $\mathcal{F}$
2.3 initialize $\mathcal{C}^R \leftarrow \phi$, $\mathcal{C}^B \leftarrow \phi$, $S_P \leftarrow \phi$, $n_{min} \leftarrow Min_{1 \le i \le |\mathcal{R}|} n_i$, $\mathcal{F} \leftarrow \phi$
2.4 $(\mathcal{C}^B, \mathcal{C}^R) \leftarrow$ BusRoutePartitioning$(\mathcal{B}, \mathcal{R}, n_{min}, \rho)$
2.5 for *each cluster* $\mathcal{C}_i^R \in \mathcal{C}^R$ **do**
2.6 $S_P \leftarrow$ Serve$(\mathcal{P}, Cluster_i^R)$, $\mathcal{F} \leftarrow \mathcal{F} \sqcup$ Greedy$(\mathcal{C}_i^B, \mathcal{C}_i^R, S_P, \mathcal{N})$
2.7 return $\mathcal{F}$

---

the cardinality of the set A, and $\overline{\mathcal{F}}_i$ denote a bus service frequency returned by Greedy$(\mathcal{C}_i^B, \mathcal{C}_i^R, \mathcal{C}_i^P, N_{min})$. $\mathcal{C}_i^B$, $\mathcal{C}_i^R$, and $\mathcal{C}_i^P$ refer to a cluster of buses, a cluster of routes and a cluster of passengers respectively, and N_{min} refers to a $|\mathcal{C}_i^R|$-dimensional vector in the form of $\langle n_{min}, n_{min}, \cdots, n_{min} \rangle$. The parameter n_{min} is set to the minimum number of buses required by any route. Although there are different ways to quantify the overlaps between bus routes, we define ρ_i in such a way that a partition-based greedy guided by ρ_i can achieve a theoretical bound, as to be detailed next.

Definition 5 (Service overlap ratio). *Given a partition $\mathcal{C}^R$ of the original bus route database $\mathcal{R}$, for a cluster $\mathcal{C}_i^R$, the ratio ρ_i of the service overlap between*

$\mathcal{C}_i^R$ *and the rest clusters is* $\dfrac{\left| \bigcup_{\mathcal{C}_j^R \in \mathcal{C}^R \setminus \mathcal{C}_i^R} \text{Serve}(\mathcal{P}, \mathcal{C}_i^R) \cap \text{Serve}(\mathcal{P}, \mathcal{C}_j^R) \right|}{\mathcal{G}(\overline{\mathcal{F}}_i)}$.

Partitioning of Bus Routes and Buses. Algorithm 3 lists the pseudo-code of a bus route partitioning method guided by service overlap ratio. It first partitions the routes using the finest granularity by forming a cluster for each bus route. Thereafter, it checks the service overlap ratio ρ_i for each cluster $\mathcal{C}_i^R$ and picks the one with the largest ρ_i, denoted as $\mathcal{C}_k^R$, for expansion (Line 3.9). It selects the cluster $\mathcal{C}_j^R$ that shares the largest common passenger pool with $\mathcal{C}_k^R$ (Line 3.11) and merges $\mathcal{C}_j^R$ with $\mathcal{C}_k^R$ (Lines 3.12 - 3.14). Note that when cluster $\mathcal{C}_k^R$ is expanded, let $\overline{\mathcal{F}}_k$ denote the new frequency returned by Greedy$(\mathcal{C}_k^B, \mathcal{C}_k^R, \mathcal{P}, N_{min})$. $\mathcal{G}(\overline{\mathcal{F}}_k)$ is actually required when calculating ρ_k for this expanded cluster, by Definition 5. However, to reduce the computation cost and the complexity, we use $\mathcal{L} = max\{\mathcal{G}(\overline{\mathcal{F}}_k) + \mathcal{G}(\overline{\mathcal{F}}_j) - |S_k \cap S_j|, \mathcal{G}(\overline{\mathcal{F}}_k), \mathcal{G}(\overline{\mathcal{F}}_j)\}$ as an approximation of $\mathcal{G}(\overline{\mathcal{F}}_k)$. According to our merger rules, $\mathcal{L}$ is a lower bound of $\mathcal{G}(\overline{\mathcal{F}}_k)$ and it does not affect the accuracy of our partition algorithm. This merge-and-expansion process continues until the ρ_is associated with all the clusters $\mathcal{C}_i^R$ fall below the input threshold ρ.

When the bus routes and buses are partitioned, it invokes the basic greedy method (Sect. 4) to find the frequency for each cluster, and merges the local frequencies for $|\mathcal{C}^R|$ clusters as the final answer. We name this approach as PartGreedy. Its pseudo-code is shown in Algorithm 2 and its approximation ratio is analyzed in Lemma 1.

Algorithm 3: BusRoutePartitioning $(\mathcal{B}, \mathcal{R}, n_{min}, \rho)$

3.1 **Input:** a bus database $\mathcal{B}$, a bus route database $\mathcal{R}$, an integer n_{min}, and a controlling threshold ρ

3.2 **Output:** a partition $\mathcal{C}^B$ of $\mathcal{B}$ and a partition $\mathcal{C}^R$ of $\mathcal{R}$

3.3 **for** *each bus route* $r_i \in$ *Route* **do**

3.4 $\quad$ initialize $\mathcal{C}_i^R \leftarrow \{r_i\}$, $\mathcal{C}_i^B \leftarrow \{b_{ab} \in \mathcal{B}|a=i\}$, $S_i \leftarrow \mathsf{Serve}(\mathcal{P}, Cluster_i^R)$

3.5 $\quad$ $\overline{\mathcal{F}}_i \leftarrow \mathsf{Greedy}(\mathcal{C}_i^B, \mathcal{C}_i^R, \mathcal{P}, \mathrm{N_{min}})$

3.6 initialize $\mathcal{C}^R \leftarrow \cup_{r_i \in \mathcal{R}} \mathcal{C}_i^R$

3.7 **for** $\mathcal{C}_i^R \in \mathcal{C}^R$ **do**

3.8 $\quad$ $\rho_i \leftarrow \left|\bigcup_{\mathcal{C}_j^R \in \mathcal{C}^R \setminus \mathcal{C}_i^R} S_i \cap S_j\right| / \mathcal{G}(\overline{\mathcal{F}}_i)$

3.9 $k \leftarrow \mathrm{argmax}_{\mathcal{C}_k^R \in \mathcal{C}^R} \rho_k$, $Max \leftarrow \rho_k$

3.10 **while** $Max > \rho$ **do**

3.11 $\quad$ $j \leftarrow \mathrm{argmax}_{\mathcal{C}_j^R \in \mathcal{C}^R \setminus \mathcal{C}_k^R} |(S_j \cap S_k)|$

3.12 $\quad$ $\mathcal{C}_k^R \leftarrow \mathcal{C}_k^R \cup \mathcal{C}_j^R$, $\mathcal{C}^R \leftarrow \mathcal{C}^R - \mathcal{C}_j^R$, $\mathcal{C}_k^B \leftarrow \mathcal{C}_k^B \cup \mathcal{C}_j^B$, $\mathcal{C}^B \leftarrow \mathcal{C}^B - \mathcal{C}_j^B$

3.13 $\quad$ $\mathcal{G}(\overline{\mathcal{F}}_k) \leftarrow max\{\mathcal{G}(\overline{\mathcal{F}}_k) + \mathcal{G}(\overline{\mathcal{F}}_j) - |S_k \cap S_j|, \mathcal{G}(\overline{\mathcal{F}}_k), \mathcal{G}(\overline{\mathcal{F}}_j)\}$, $S_k \leftarrow S_k \cup S_j$

3.14 $\quad$ $\rho_k \leftarrow \dfrac{\left|\bigcup_{\mathcal{C}_i^R \in \mathcal{C}^R \setminus \mathcal{C}_k^R} S_i \cap S_k\right|}{\mathcal{G}(\overline{\mathcal{F}}_k)}$

3.15 $\quad$ $k \leftarrow \mathrm{argmax}_{\mathcal{C}_k^R \in \mathcal{C}^R} \rho_k$, $Max \leftarrow \rho_k$

3.16 **return** $\mathcal{C}^B, \mathcal{C}^R$

Lemma 1. *Given a partition* $\mathcal{C}^R = \{\mathcal{C}_1^R, \mathcal{C}_2^R, \cdots, \mathcal{C}_i^R, \cdots, \mathcal{C}_m^R\}$ *of the bus route database* $\mathcal{R}$ *and the maximum service overlap ratio* ρ, *PartGreedy achieves a* $(1 - \rho)(1 - 1/e)$ *approximation ratio to solve the FAST problem.*

Proof. Let $\mathcal{F}_i$ denote the solution obtained by Greedy for cluster $\mathcal{C}_i^R$, $\mathcal{F}^*$ denote the solution obtained by PartGreedy, $\mathcal{O}_i$ denote the optimal solution for cluster $\mathcal{C}_i^R$, and $\mathcal{O}$ denote the global optimal solution. In Algorithm 3, it uses the lower bound of the $\mathcal{G}(\overline{\mathcal{F}}_k)$ to compute the upper bound of ρ_k and terminates when the upper bound of ρ_i for every cluster $\mathcal{C}_i^R \in \mathcal{C}^R$ is no greater than the given threshold ρ. Then we have $\rho \geq \rho_i$ for any $\mathcal{C}_i^R \in \mathcal{C}^R$. Recall Sect. 3, the basic greedy method is proved to achieve $(1-1/e)$-approximation. Therefore, we have $\mathcal{G}(\mathcal{F}_i) \geq (1-1/e)\mathcal{G}(\mathcal{O}_i)$. Because of the submodularity and monotonicity of $\mathcal{G}$, we have $\sum_{i=1}^m \mathcal{G}(\mathcal{O}_i) \geq \mathcal{G}(\mathcal{O})$ and $\mathcal{G}(\mathcal{F}_i) \geq \mathcal{G}(\overline{\mathcal{F}}_i)$. Then, by Definition 5 we have:

$$\left|\bigcup_{\mathcal{C}_j^R \in \mathcal{C}^R \setminus \mathcal{C}_i^R} \mathsf{Serve}(\mathcal{P}, \mathcal{C}_i^R) \cap \mathsf{Serve}(\mathcal{P}, \mathcal{C}_j^R)\right| = \rho_i \mathcal{G}(\overline{\mathcal{F}}_i) \leq \rho\mathcal{G}(\mathcal{F}_i). \quad (5)$$

In addition, Inequality (6) holds according to Definition 3.

$$\left|\bigcup_{\mathcal{C}_j^R \in \mathcal{C}^R \setminus \mathcal{C}_i^R} \mathsf{Serve}(\mathcal{P}, \mathcal{C}_i^R) \cap \mathsf{Serve}(\mathcal{P}, \mathcal{C}_j^R)\right| \geq \mathcal{G}(\mathcal{F}_i) - (\mathcal{G}(\mathcal{F}^*) - \mathcal{G}(\mathcal{F}^* \setminus \mathcal{F}_i)) \quad (6)$$

Based on Inequality (5) and Inequality (6), we have $\mathcal{G}(\mathcal{F}^*) - \mathcal{G}(\mathcal{F}^* \setminus \mathcal{F}_i) \geq (1 - \rho)\mathcal{G}(\mathcal{F}_i)$. Using the principle of inclusion-exclusion, we have $\mathcal{G}(\mathcal{F}^*) = \mathcal{G}(\mathcal{F}_1 \cup$

Function 1: ProGreedy $(\mathcal{B}, \mathcal{R}, \mathcal{N}, \varepsilon)$

1.1 **Input:** a bus database $\mathcal{B}$, a bus route database $\mathcal{R}$, a vector $\mathcal{N}$, and a parameter ε

1.2 **Output:** a bus service frequency $\mathcal{F}$

1.3 Initialize $\mathcal{F} \leftarrow \phi,\, n \leftarrow \sum_{i=1}^{|\mathcal{N}|} n_i$

1.4 Initialize a $|\mathcal{N}|$-dimension vector $\langle k_1, k_2, \cdots, k_{|\mathcal{N}|} \rangle$ with zero

1.5 Sort $b \in \mathcal{B}$ based on descending order of $\mathcal{G}(b)$

1.6 Initialize $h \leftarrow \max_{b \in \mathcal{B}}(\mathcal{G}(b))$

1.7 **while** $|\mathcal{F}| \leq n$ **do**

1.8   **for** *each* $b_{jl} \in \mathcal{B}$ **do**

1.9   **if** $|\mathcal{F}| \leq n$ **then**

1.10 $\mathcal{G}_{b_{jl}}(\mathcal{F}) \leftarrow \mathcal{G}(\mathcal{F} \cup b_{jl}) - \mathcal{G}(\mathcal{F})$

1.11   **if** $\mathcal{G}_{b_{jl}}(\mathcal{F}) \geq h$ **then**

1.12 $\mathcal{F} \leftarrow \mathcal{F} \cup b_{jl},\, \mathcal{B} \leftarrow \mathcal{B} \backslash b_{jl}$

1.13 $k_j + +$

1.14   **if** $k_j \geq n_j$ **then**

1.15   remove all bus serve the route r_j from $\mathcal{B}$

1.16   **if** $\mathcal{G}(b_{jl}) < h$ **then**

1.17   break

1.18   **else**

1.19   break

1.20 $h \leftarrow \frac{h}{1+\epsilon}$

1.21 **return** $\mathcal{F}$

$\mathcal{F}_2 \cup \ldots \cup \mathcal{F}_m) \geq \sum_{i=1}^{m}(\mathcal{G}(\mathcal{F}^*) - \mathcal{G}(\mathcal{F}^* \backslash \mathcal{F}_i)) \geq (1 - \rho) \sum_{i=1}^{m} \mathcal{G}(\mathcal{F}_i) \geq (1 - \rho)(1 - 1/e) \sum_{i=1}^{m} \mathcal{G}(\mathcal{O}_i) \geq (1 - \rho)(1 - 1/e)\mathcal{G}(\mathcal{O})$.

Thus, this lemma is proved. ∎

6 Progressive Partition-Based Greedy Method

Although PartGreedy improves the efficiency of basic greedy by conducting the search within each partition (though not the original route/bus database), it still suffers from a high computational cost. To be more specific, in each iteration of the greedy search (either a global search or a local search by Greedy), in order to find the one with the maximum gain, it has to recalculate the marginal gain $\mathcal{G}(\mathcal{F} \cup b) - \mathcal{G}(\mathcal{F})$ for all the buses not yet scheduled.

Motivated by this observation, we propose a progressive partition-based greedy method (ProPartGreedy). It selects multiple, but not only one, buses in each local greedy search iteration to cut down the total number of iterations required and hence the computation cost. The pseudo-code of ProPartGreedy is the same as Algorithm 2 except that the call of Greedy is replaced with Function 1 (ProGreedy) in line 2.6 of Algorithm 2. Meanwhile, we will prove that it can achieve an approximation ratio of $(1 - \rho)(1 - 1/e - \varepsilon)$, where ρ and ε are tunable parameters that provide a trade-off between efficiency and accuracy.

As presented in Function 1, ProGreedy first sorts $b \in \mathcal{B}$ by $\mathcal{G}(b)$ and initializes the threshold h to the value of $\max_{b \in \mathcal{B}}(\mathcal{G}(b))$. Then, it iteratively fetches all the buses with their marginal gains not smaller than h into $\mathcal{F}$ and meanwhile lowers the threshold h by a factor of $(1 + \varepsilon)$ for next iteration (Lines 1.8–1.20). The iteration continues until there are n buses in $\mathcal{F}$. Unlike the basic greedy method that has to check all the potential buses in $\mathcal{B}$ or a cluster of $\mathcal{B}$ in each iteration, it is not necessary for ProGreedy as it implements an early termination (Lines 1.16–1.17). Since buses are sorted by $\mathcal{G}(b)$ values, if $\mathcal{G}(b_{jl})$ of the current bus is smaller than h, all the buses b pending for evaluation will have their $\mathcal{G}(b)$ values smaller than h and hence could be skipped from evaluation. In the following, we first analyze the approximation ratio of Function 1 by Lemma 2. Based on Lemma 2, we show the approximation ratio of ProPartGreedy by Lemma 3.

Lemma 2. *ProGreedy achieves a* $(1 - 1/e - \varepsilon)$ *approximation ratio.*

Proof. Let b_i be the bus selected at a given threshold h and $\mathcal{O}$ denote the optimal local solution to the problem of selecting n buses that can maximize $\mathcal{G}$. Because of the submodularity of $\mathcal{G}$, we have:

$$\mathcal{G}_b(\mathcal{F}) = \begin{cases} \geq h & \text{if } b = b_i \\ \leq h \cdot (1 + \varepsilon) & \text{if } b \in \mathcal{O}\backslash(\mathcal{F} \cup b_i), \end{cases} \tag{7}$$

where $\mathcal{F}$ is the current partial solution. Equation (7) implies that $\mathcal{G}_{b_i}(\mathcal{F}) \geq \mathcal{G}_b(\mathcal{F})/(1 + \varepsilon)$ for any $b \in \mathcal{O}\backslash\mathcal{F}$. Thus, we have $\mathcal{G}_{b_i}(\mathcal{F}) \geq \frac{1}{(1+\varepsilon)|\mathcal{O}\backslash\mathcal{F}|} \sum_{b \in \mathcal{O}\backslash\mathcal{F}} \mathcal{G}_b(\mathcal{F}) \geq \frac{1}{(1+\varepsilon)n} \sum_{b \in \mathcal{O}\backslash\mathcal{F}} \mathcal{G}_b(\mathcal{F})$. Let $\mathcal{F}_i$ denote the partial solution that b_i has been included and b_{i+1} be the bus selected at the $(i + 1)$th step. Then we have $\mathcal{G}(\mathcal{F}_{i+1}) - \mathcal{G}(\mathcal{F}_i) = \mathcal{G}_{b_{i+1}}(\mathcal{F}_i) \geq \frac{1}{(1+\varepsilon)n} \sum_{b \in \mathcal{O}\backslash\mathcal{F}_i} \mathcal{G}_b(\mathcal{F}_i) \geq \frac{1}{(1+\varepsilon)n}(\mathcal{G}(\mathcal{O} \cup \mathcal{F}_i) - \mathcal{G}(\mathcal{F}_i)) \geq \frac{1}{(1+\varepsilon)n}(\mathcal{G}(\mathcal{O}) - \mathcal{G}(\mathcal{F}_i))$.

The solution $\mathcal{F}^*$ obtained by Function 1 with $|\mathcal{F}^*| = n$. Using the geometric series formula, we have $\mathcal{G}(\mathcal{F}^*) \geq \left(1 - \left(1 - \frac{1}{(1+\varepsilon)n}\right)^n\right) \mathcal{G}(\mathcal{O}) \geq \left(1 - e^{\frac{-n}{(1+\varepsilon)n}}\right) \mathcal{G}(\mathcal{O}) = \left(1 - e^{\frac{-1}{(1+\varepsilon)}}\right) \mathcal{G}(\mathcal{O}) \geq ((1 - 1/e - \varepsilon)) \mathcal{G}(\mathcal{O})$.

Hence, the lemma is proved. ∎

Lemma 3. *Given a partition* $\mathcal{C}^R = \{\mathcal{C}_1^R, \mathcal{C}_2^R, \cdots, \mathcal{C}_i^R, \cdots, \mathcal{C}_m^R\}$ *of the bus route database* $\mathcal{R}$ *and the maximum service overlap ratio* ρ, *ProPartGreedy achieves a* $(1 - \rho)(1 - 1/e - \varepsilon)$ *approximation ratio to solve the FAST problem.*

Proof. Based on Lemma 2, this proof is similar to the proof of Lemma 1, so we omit it due to space limit. ∎

Table 1. Statistics of datasets

Database	Amount	AvgDistance	AvgTravelTime
$\mathcal{B}$	451k	N.A	N.A.
$\mathcal{R}$	396	19.91 km	5159 s
$\mathcal{P}$	28 m	4.2 km	1342 s

7   Experiment

In this section, we first explain the experimental setup; we then conduct sensitivity tests to tune the parameters to their reasonable settings, as our algorithms have several tunable parameters; we finally report the performance, in terms of effectiveness, efficiency, and scalability, of all the algorithms.

Datasets. We crawl the real bus routes ($\mathcal{R}$) from transitlink[2] in Singapore. Each route is represented by the sequence of bus stop IDs it passes sequentially, together with the distance between two consecutive bus stops. The travel time from a stop to another stop via a route r_i is estimated by the ratio of the distance between those two stops along the route to the average bus speed of the route. We use bus touch-on record data (shown later) to find the average travel speed of a particular bus line. For the passenger database ($\mathcal{P}$), due to the exhibit regular travel patterns of passengers [15], we use the real bus touch-on record data in a week of April 2016 in Singapore, which is obtained from the authors of [15] and contains 28 million trip records. Each trip record includes the IDs/timestamps of the boarding and alighting bus stops, the bus route, and the trip distance. We assume passengers spend x minutes waiting for their buses, with x following a random distribution between 1 and 5 min. Then, we generate the bus candidate set ($\mathcal{B}$) based on the route and service time range. For each route, we use buses that depart every minute between 5am and 12am as the superset of candidate buses. The statistics of those datasets are shown in Table 1.

Parameters. Table 2 lists the parameter settings, with values in bold being default. In all experiments, we vary one parameter and set the rest to their defaults. We assume all bus routes require the same number of bus departures in our study. Notation $\langle 20 \rangle$ represents the vector $\langle 20, \cdots, 20 \rangle$ for brevity.

Algorithm. To the best of our knowledge, this is the first work to study the FAST problem, and thus no previous work is available for direct comparison. In particular, we compare the following five methods. FixInterval that fixes the time interval between two bus departures as $\lfloor$(service time range) / (bus number)$\rfloor$ for each line and chooses the bus that departures at 5am as the first bus; Top-k that picks top-k buses, which could serve the most number of passengers ($k = n_i$); Greedy, PartGreedy, and ProPartGreedy, i.e., Algorithm 1, Algorithm 2, and the progressive partition-based method proposed in this paper.

---

[2] https://www.transitlink.com.sg/eservice/eguide/service_idx.php.

Table 2. Parameter settings

Parameter	Values
Number of bus departures $\mathcal{N} = \langle n_1, n_2, \cdots \rangle$	$\langle 10 \rangle$, $\langle 20 \rangle$, $\langle \mathbf{30} \rangle$, $\langle 40 \rangle$, $\langle 50 \rangle$
Total passenger number $|\mathcal{P}|$	100k, 200k, **300k**, 400k, 500k
Waiting time threshold θ	1 min, 2 min, **3 min**, 4 min, 5 min
Tunable parameter used by ProPartGreedy ε	10^{-4}, 10^{-3}, $\mathbf{10^{-2}}$, 10^{-1}
Controlling threshold used by PartGreedy ρ	0.1, **0.2**, 0.3, 0.4

Performance Measurement. We adopt the *total running time* of each algorithm and the *total served passenger number (SPN)* of the scheduled buses as the main performance metrics. We randomly choose 5 million passengers from a week of data and pre-process the passenger dataset to build the index, which takes 5,690 s and occupies 585 MB disk space. Each experiment is repeated ten times, and the average result is reported.

Setup. All codes are implemented in C++. Experiments are conducted on a server with 24 Intel X5690 CPU and 140 GB memory running CentOS release 6.10. We will release the code publicly once the paper is published.

Parameter Sensitivity Test - θ. The impact of waiting time threshold θ on the running time and SPN are reported in Fig. 4(a) and (d), respectively. Parameter θ has an almost-zero impact on the running time. On the other hand, it affects SPN. As θ increases, all the algorithms are able to serve more passengers, which is consistent with our expectations. We set $\theta = 3$, the mean value.

Parameter Sensitivity Test - ρ. The impact of parameter ρ on the running time and SPN are reported in Fig. 4(b) and (e), respectively. It has a positive impact on the running time performance but a negative impact on SPN. As ρ increases its value, PartGreedy and ProPartGreedy both incur shorter running time but serve less number of passengers. We choose $\rho = 0.2$ as the default setting.

Parameter Sensitivity Test - ε. Parameter ε only affects ProPartGreedy. It controls the trade-off between efficiency and accuracy. As ε increases its value, ProPartGreedy incurs shorter running time and serves less number of passengers, as reported in Fig. 4(b) and (f), respectively. We choose $\varepsilon = 0.01$ as the default setting.

Effectiveness Study. We report the effectiveness of different algorithms in Fig. 5. We observe that (1) FixInterval is most *ineffective*; (2) the three algorithms proposed in this work perform much better than the other two, e.g., ProPartGreedy doubles (or even triples in some cases) the SPN of FixInterval; and (3) Greedy performs the best while PartGreedy and ProPartGreedy achieve comparable performance (only up to 9.4% below that of Greedy).

Efficiency Study. Figure 6 shows the running time of each method w.r.t. varying $\mathcal{N}$ and $|\mathcal{P}|$. We have two main observations. (1) The time gap among Greedy,

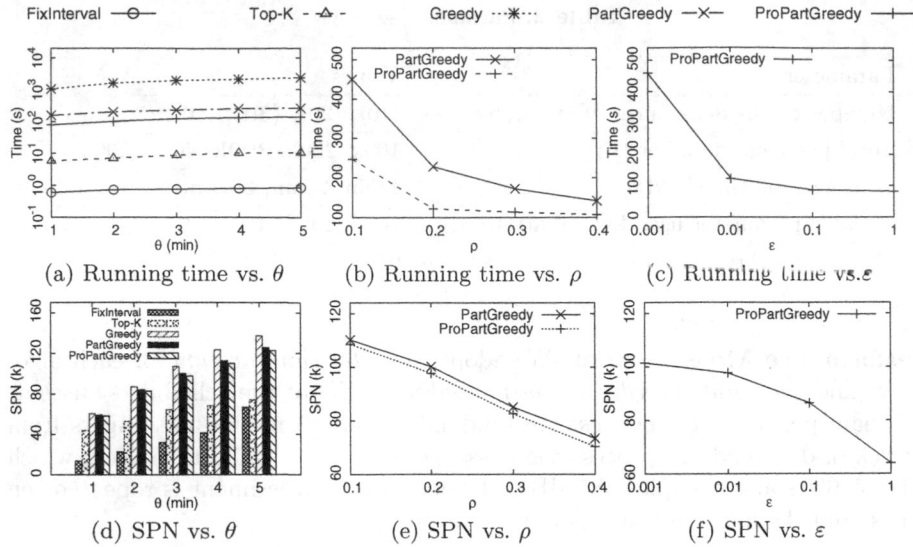

(a) Running time vs. θ (b) Running time vs. ρ (c) Running time vs. ε

(d) SPN vs. θ (e) SPN vs. ρ (f) SPN vs. ε

Fig. 4. Effect of parameters

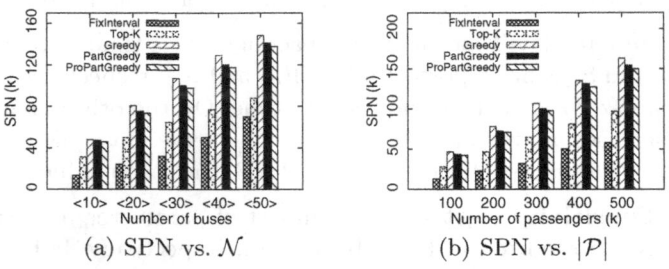

(a) SPN vs. $\mathcal{N}$ (b) SPN vs. $|\mathcal{P}|$

Fig. 5. Effectiveness study: SPN vs. $\mathcal{N}$ or $|\mathcal{P}|$

PartGreedy and ProPartGreedy becomes more significant with the increase of $\mathcal{N}$. This could be the increase of $\mathcal{N}$ causes an increase in the number of clusters and n_{min}. On the other hand, PartGreedy and ProPartGreedy only need to scan one cluster when selecting buses. (2) The improvement of PartGreedy and ProPartGreedy over Greedy decreases with the increase of $|\mathcal{P}|$. This is because the overlap between clusters increases with the increase of $|\mathcal{P}|$, which leads to a reduction in the number of clusters and an increase in partition time.

Scalability Study. To evaluate the scalability of our methods, we vary $\mathcal{N}$ from $\langle 100 \rangle$ to $\langle 500 \rangle$, and $|\mathcal{P}|$ from 1 million to 5 million. From Fig. 7(a), we find that the efficiency of Greedy is more sensitive to $\mathcal{N}$, as compared to PartGreedy and ProPartGreedy. It's worth noting that the results are omitted for Greedy when it cannot terminate within 10^4 s. As shown in Fig. 7(b), PartGreedy and ProPartGreedy are about ten times faster than Greedy when $|\mathcal{P}|$ is varying.

(a) Running time vs. $\mathcal{N}$ (b) Running time vs. $|\mathcal{P}|$

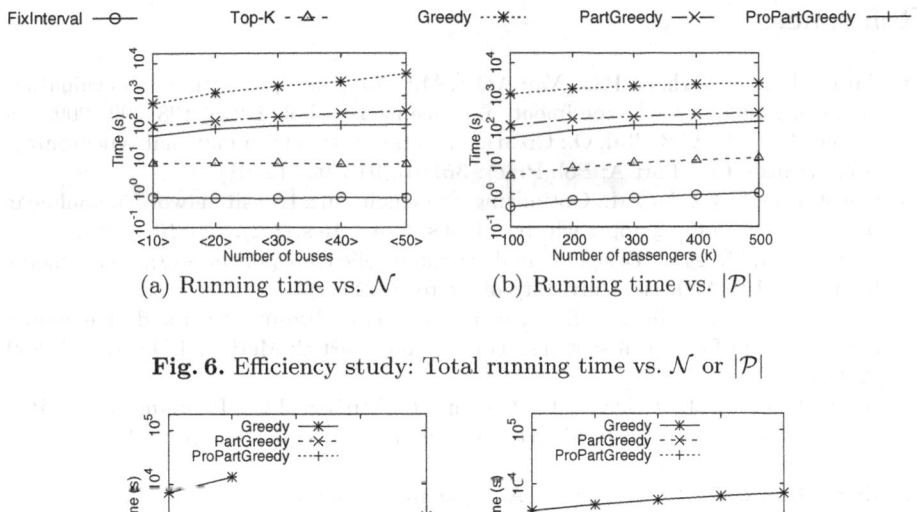

Fig. 6. Efficiency study: Total running time vs. $\mathcal{N}$ or $|\mathcal{P}|$

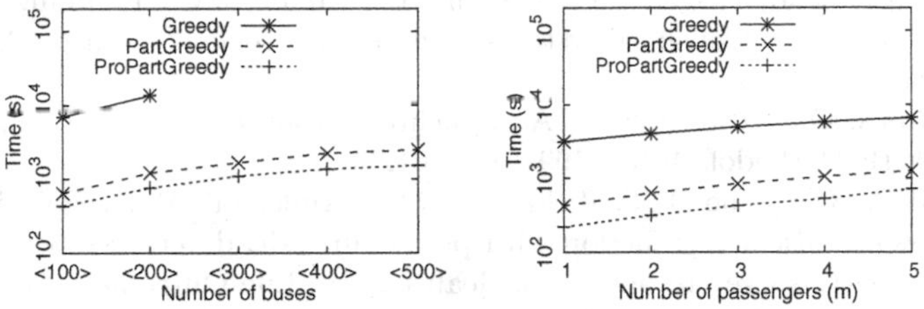

(a) Running time vs. $\mathcal{N}$ (b) Running time vs. $|\mathcal{P}|$

Fig. 7. Scalability study

8 Conclusion

In this paper we studied the bus frequency optimization problem considering user satisfaction for the first time. Our target is to schedule the buses in such a way that the total number of passengers who could receive their bus services within the waiting time threshold is maximized. We showed that this problem is NP-hard, and proposed three approximation algorithms with non-trivial theoretical guarantees. Lastly, we conducted experiments on real-world datasets to verify the efficiency, effectiveness, and scalability of our methods.

Acknowledgements. Zhiyong Peng is supported in part by the National Key Research and Development Program of China (Project Number: 2018YFB1003400), Key Project of the National Natural Science Foundation of China (Project Number: U1811263) and the Research Fund from Alibaba Group. Zhifeng Bao is supported in part by ARC DP200102611, DP180102050, NSFC 91646204, and a Google Faculty Award. Baihua Zheng is supported in part by Prime Minister's Office, Singapore under its International Research Centres in Singapore Funding Initiative.

References

1. Antonides, G., Verhoef, P.C., Van Aalst, M.: Consumer perception and evaluation of waiting time: a field experiment. J. Consum. Psychol. **12**(3), 193–202 (2002)
2. Ceder, A., Golany, B., Tal, O.: Creating bus timetables with maximal synchronization. Transp. Res. Part A: Pol. Pract. **35**(10), 913–928 (2001)
3. Constantin, I., Florian, M.: Optimizing frequencies in a transit network: a nonlinear bi-level programming approach. Int. Trans. Oper. Res. **2**(2), 149–164 (1995)
4. Fletterman, M., et al.: Designing multimodal public transport networks using meta-heuristics. Ph.D. thesis, University of Pretoria (2009)
5. Gao, Z., Sun, H., Shan, L.L.: A continuous equilibrium network design model and algorithm for transit systems. Transp. Res. Part B: Methodol. **38**(3), 235–250 (2004)
6. Ibarra-Rojas, O.J., Delgado, F., Giesen, R., Muñoz, J.C.: Planning, operation, and control of bus transport systems: a literature review. Transp. Res. Part B: Methodol. **77**, 38–75 (2015)
7. Ibarra-Rojas, O.J., Rios-Solis, Y.A.: Synchronization of bus timetabling. Transp. Res. Part B: Methodol. **46**(5), 599–614 (2012)
8. Kong, M.C., Camacho, F.T., Feldman, S.R., Anderson, R.T., Balkrishnan, R.: Correlates of patient satisfaction with physician visit: differences between elderly and non-elderly survey respondents. Health Qual. Life Outcomes **5**(1), 62 (2007). https://doi.org/10.1186/1477-7525-5-62
9. Lin, N., Ma, W., Chen, X.: Bus frequency optimisation considering user behaviour based on mobile bus applications. IET Intel. Transp. Syst. **13**(4), 596–604 (2019)
10. Martínez, H., Mauttone, A., Urquhart, M.E.: Frequency optimization in public transportation systems: formulation and metaheuristic approach. Eur. J. Oper. Res. **236**(1), 27–36 (2014)
11. Nemhauser, G.L., Wolsey, L.A., Fisher, M.L.: An analysis of approximations for maximizing submodular set functions - I. Math. Program. **14**(1), 265–294 (1978). https://doi.org/10.1007/BF01588971
12. Parbo, J., Nielsen, O.A., Prato, C.G.: User perspectives in public transport timetable optimisation. Transp. Res. Part C: Emerg. Technol. **48**, 269–284 (2014)
13. Schéele, S.: A supply model for public transit services. Transp. Res. Part B: Methodol. **14**(1–2), 133–146 (1980)
14. Shafahi, Y., Khani, A.: A practical model for transfer optimization in a transit network: Model formulations and solutions. Transportation Research Part A: Policy and Practice **44**(6), 377–389 (2010)
15. Tian, X., Zheng, B.: Using smart card data to model commuters' responses upon unexpected train delays. In: Big Data, pp. 831–840. IEEE (2018)
16. Wang, S., Bao, Z., Culpepper, J.S., Sellis, T., Cong, G.: Reverse k nearest neighbor search over trajectories. IEEE Trans. Knowl. Data Eng. **30**(4), 757–771 (2018)
17. Wu, Y.: Combining local search into genetic algorithm for bus schedule coordination through small timetable modifications. Int. J. Intell. Transp. Syst. Res. **17**(2), 102–113 (2019). https://doi.org/10.1007/s13177-018-0165-7
18. Zhang, P., Bao, Z., Li, Y., Li, G., Zhang, Y., Peng, Z.: Trajectory-driven influential billboard placement. In: SIGKDD, pp. 2748–2757. ACM (2018)

Incorporating Boundary and Category Feature for Nested Named Entity Recognition

Jin Cao[1], Guohua Wang[1], Canguang Li[1], Haopeng Ren[1], Yi Cai[1(✉)],
Raymond Chi-Wing Wong[2], and Qing Li[3]

[1] School of Software Engineering, South China University of Technology,
GuangZhou, China
{sejincao,secanguangli,se_renhp}@mail.scut.edu.cn,
{ghwang,ycai}@scut.edu.cn
[2] Department of Computer Science and Engineering,
The Hong Kong University of Science and Technology, Hong Kong, China
raywong@cse.ust.hk
[3] Department of Computing, The Hong Kong Polytechnic University,
Hung Hom, Kowloon, Hong Kong
csqli@comp.polyu.edu.hk

Abstract. In the natural language processing (NLP) field, it is fairly common that an entity is nested in another entity. Most existing named entity recognition (NER) models focus on flat entities but ignore nested entities. In this paper, we propose a neural model for nested named entity recognition. Our model employs a multi-label boundary detection module to detect entity boundaries, avoiding boundary detection conflict existing in the boundary-aware model. Besides, our model with a boundary detection module and a category detection module detects entity boundaries and entity categories simultaneously, avoiding the error propagation problem existing in current pipeline models. Furthermore, we introduce multitask learning to train the boundary detection module and the category detection module to capture the underlying association between entity boundary information and entity category information. In this way, our model achieves better performance of entity extraction. In evaluations on two nested NER datasets and a flat NER dataset, we show that our model outperforms previous state-of-the-art models on nested and flat NER.

Keywords: Natural language processing · Nested named entity recognition · Multitask learning

1 Introduction

Named entity recognition is a task of identifying named entities in texts and classifying them into pre-defined categories such as *person*, *location*, *DNA* and

© Springer Nature Switzerland AG 2020
Y. Nah et al. (Eds.): DASFAA 2020, LNCS 12113, pp. 209–226, 2020.
https://doi.org/10.1007/978-3-030-59416-9_13

so on. NER is generally treated as a sequential labeling task, where each word is tagged with one label. The label is composed of an entity boundary label and a category label. One example is showed in Fig. 1. Considering the entity "terminally differentiated cells", the word "terminally" is tagged with a boundary label "B" and a category label "Cell-Line", where "B" indicates the boundary of an entity and "Cell-Line" indicates the corresponding entity category. In natural language, many entities are included in other entities. They are known as nested entities [6]. A word included in several entities may have multiple boundary labels and category labels. As shown in Fig. 1, an entity of *Cell-Type* ("DC") is included in an entity of *Cell-Line* ("monocyte - derived DC"). In this case, word "DC" should be tagged with two category labels ("Cell-Line" and "Cell-Type") instead of one. However, most of the existing works [12,15,20] for NER focus on non-nested entities (flat entities) but ignore nested entities.

words:	the	monocyte	-	derived	DC	were	not	terminally	differentiated	cells
boundary:	O	B	I	I	S E	O	O	B	I	E
category 1:	O	O	O	O	Cell-Type	O	O	O	O	O
category 2:	O	Cell-Line	Cell-Line	Cell-Line	Cell-Line	O	O	Cell-Line	Cell-Line	Cell-Line

Fig. 1. An example of flat entity and nested entities from the GENIA dataset [9]: "DC" is an single-token entity of *Cell-Type* and "monocyte - derived DC" is an entity of *Cell-Line*, the former entity is included in the latter. "terminally differentiated cells" is a flat entity of *Cell-Line*. "B", "I" and "E" denote the beginning, inside and end of an entity. They indicate the boundary labels of entities. "S" denotes the boundary label of single-token entity. "O" denotes outside of any entities. *Cell-Type* and *Cell-Line* denote categories of entities.

To identify the nested entities, several models [3,5,18,23,25] are proposed based on feature-engineering. These models heavily rely on hand-crafted features which are time-consuming to construct. Recently, neural networks are proved to be efficient in NER without relying on hand-crafted features. Therefore, several models [6,19,24] based on neural networks for nested NER have been proposed. Most of them handle nested NER in a pipelined manner, such as the layered model [6] and the boundary-aware model [24]. They divide the nested NER task into two phases. The error caused by the first phase will affect the performance of the second phase, which leads to the error propagation problem. What's more, the boundary-aware model achieves better performance by explicitly utilizing boundary information. However, when a word in nested entities is simultaneously the beginning of an entity and the end of another entity, the boundary-aware model only tags it with one kind of boundary label, which leads to boundary detection conflict. According to our statistics, there are 8.1% of such nested entities in GENIA dataset. Considering the example in Fig. 1, word "DC" is both the beginning of the entity "DC" and the end of the entity "monocyte -

derived DC". If the boundary-aware model tags "DC" with the boundary label "E", the single-token entity "DC" will be ignored and vice versa. We call this problem as boundary detection conflict.

In order to overcome the problem of error propagation and boundary detection conflict, we propose a neural model in this paper. Our model is composed of a multi-label boundary detection module and a multi-label category detection module. On the one hand, to tackle the boundary detection conflict problem, we propose a multi-label boundary detection module which tags each word with multiple kinds of boundary labels. Considering the example in Fig. 1, the word "DC" is tagged with two kinds of boundary labels ("S" and "E") by our multi-label boundary detection module, where "S" denotes the boundary label of single-token entity. With the multi-label boundary detection module, our model does not suffer from boundary detection conflict. On the other hand, to avoid error propagation problem, we propose our model with the boundary detection module and the category detection module. These two modules detect entity boundaries and entity categories simultaneously. In this way, the entity category detection does not depend on the boundary detection, which avoids error propagation.

Furthermore, we train our model in a multitask learning way to capture the underlying association between the entity boundary information and the entity category information. They are complementary to each other. On the one hand, the boundary information is beneficial to detect entity categories. Considering an example in GENIA dataset, "cat reporter gene" is an entity of *DNA* but "the cat reporter gene" is not an entity. The boundary detection module focuses on detecting entity boundaries. It is more likely to identify that "cat" and "gene" are entity boundaries and "the" is not. And this information can be shared by the category detection module through multitask learning. With the information that "the" is not entity boundary, the category detection model tends to identify that the category of "the" is non-entity. On the other hand, the category information is also beneficial to detect entity boundaries. The word "gene" in GENIA dataset is often the inside word of entities of *protein* and the end word of entities of *DNA*. The category detection module focuses on detecting entity categories. It is more likely to identify that "gene" in the example mentioned above is a part of the entity of *DNA* ("cat reporter gene"). And this information can be shared by the boundary detection module through multitask learning. With the information that "gene" is a part of an entity of *DNA*, the boundary detection module tends to identify that "gene" is the end word of the entity "cat reporter gene".

The main contributions of this paper are summarized as follows:

1. We propose a multi-label boundary detection module to overcome the boundary detection conflict existing in the boundary-aware model [24].
2. We propose our model with the boundary detection module and the category detection model to overcome the error propagation problem which exists in current pipeline models.

3. We introduce multitask learning to capture the underlying association between the entity boundary information and the entity category information. Entity boundary information and entity category information are complementary to each other. By capturing their underlying association, we improve the performance of our model.
4. Experiments are conducted on three datasets to illustrate that our model outperforms previous state-of-the-art models.

2   Related Work

NER is a foundational task in natural language processing field and has been studied for decades. The development of NER can boost many downstream tasks, such as question answering [8,21], entity linking [22], relation extraction [13] and so on. Many methods [11,12,15,20] have been proposed for flat NER, but few of them address nested NER.

Early works for nested NER mainly rely on hand-crafted features. Some methods [18,23,25] employ a Hidden Markov Model to extract inner entities and then detect outer entities through rule-based methods. Gu [5] identifies inner entities and outmost entities separately based on SVM. Finkel and Manning [3] propose a constituency parser based on conditional random filed (CRF) for nested named entities such that each named entity is a constituent in the parse tree. However, their method is not scalable to larger corpus with a cubic time complexity. Later on, Lu and Roth [14] propose a hypergraph-based model for nested NER. One issue of their model is the spurious structure of hypergraphs. Mius and Lu [16] incorporate mention separators to overcome the spurious structure and achieve better performance. These methods all depend on hand-crafted features which are time-consuming to construct.

In recent years, neural networks are proved to be efficient in many NLP tasks because of their powerful ability of auto-feature extraction. Therefore, neural network-based models are not only proposed for flat NER but also proposed for nested NER. Ma and Hovy [15] and Lample et al. [12] propose their neural models based on bidirectional long short-term memory network (LSTM) for flat NER and significantly improve the performance. Ju et al. [6], Sohrab and Miwa [19] and Zheng et al. [24] apply LSTM on nested NER and also achieve performance improvement. Ju et al. [6] identify nested entities by dynamically stacking flat NER layer. Each flat NER layer is composed of a Bi-LSTM layer and a cascaded CRF layer. However, their model suffers from error propagation from layer to layer. An inner entity can not be identified when an outer entity is identified first. Sohrab and Miwa [19] enumerate all possible regions in a sentence as candidate entities and classify them into pre-defined entity categories. Their model ignores explicit boundary information of the entity. Non-entity regions may be classifies into entities incorrectly. Zheng et al. [24] combine the methods of Ju et al. [6] and Sohrab and Miwa [19], and propose a boundary-aware model which explicitly utilizes boundary information to predict entity categories. However, their model has two issues. One issue of their model is the boundary detection conflict. In nested NER, words included in several entities may have multiple kinds of boundary labels but their single-label sequence labeling model can only tag each word with one kind of boundary label. In our method, we propose a multi-label sequence labeling module to detect entity boundaries, avoiding the boundary detection conflict. Another issue is that their model also suffers from error propagation caused by its pipeline structure. In our method, we identify entity boundaries and entity categories simultaneously, avoiding the error propagation problem.

3   Method

Our proposed model for extracting nested entities is composed of a boundary detection module and a category detection module. The architecture of our model is shown in Fig. 2.

There are three layers in our model. The first layer is the word representation layer which converts words in input sentences to their word representation. The second layer is the feature extraction layer. We employ a multi-layer bidirectional LSTM as the shared feature extractor to extract the shared context feature for modules in the next layer. The third layer includes two modules: the boundary detection module and the category detection module. These two modules are used to predict entity boundaries and entity categories, respectively.

We train the boundary detection module and category detection module by multitask learning to capture the underlying association between the entity boundary information and the entity category information. These two information are complementary to each other. In this way, we can improve the performance of our model.

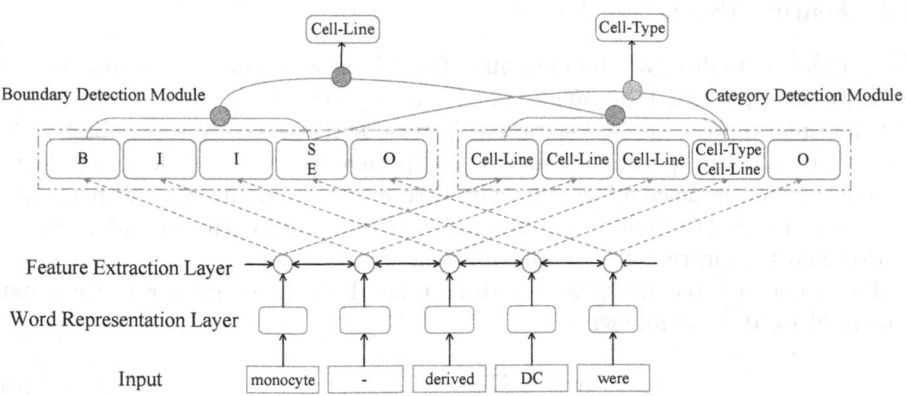

Fig. 2. Architecture of our model. Our model employs a boundary detection module and a category detection module to detect entity boundaries and entity categories simultaneously. Then we can obtain the entities according to the detected entity boundaries and entity categories.

3.1 Word Representation Layer

Following the success of Ma and Hovy [15] and Lample et al. [12] that represent each word by concatenating its word embedding and its character-level representation for the flat NER task, we represent each word in the same way. For the word embedding, pre-trained word embedding is used to initialize it. For the character-level representation, a character-level bidirectional LSTM is applied to character sequence of the word to capture the orthographic and morphological features and obtain the character-level representation.

For a given sentence consisting of n words $\{w_1, w_2, ..., w_n\}$, the word embedding of i-th word w_i is represented as: $\mathbf{e}^w(w_i)$, where $\mathbf{e}^w$ denotes the word embedding lookup table which is initialized by pre-trained word embedding.

For the character sequence $\{c_1, c_2, ..., c_m\}$ of the i-th word w_i, each character c_k is represented as $\mathbf{e}^c(c_k)$, where $\mathbf{e}^c$ denotes the character embedding lookup table which is initialized randomly.

Then a bidirectional LSTM is applied to sequence $\{\mathbf{e}^c(c_1), \mathbf{e}^c(c_2), ..., \mathbf{e}^c(c_m)\}$ to obtain a left-to-right sequence of hidden states $\{\overrightarrow{\mathbf{h}_1^c}, \overrightarrow{\mathbf{h}_2^c}, ..., \overrightarrow{\mathbf{h}_m^c}\}$ and a right-to-left sequence of hidden states $\{\overleftarrow{\mathbf{h}_1^c}, \overleftarrow{\mathbf{h}_2^c}, ..., \overleftarrow{\mathbf{h}_m^c}\}$ for the characters $\{c_1, c_2, ..., c_m\}$, respectively. The final character-level representation of word w_i is:

$$\mathbf{x}_i^c = [\overrightarrow{\mathbf{h}_m^c}, \overleftarrow{\mathbf{h}_1^c}] \tag{1}$$

where $[,]$ denotes concatenation.

The final word representation is the concatenation of $\mathbf{e}^w(w_i)$ and $\mathbf{x}_i^c$:

$$\mathbf{x}_i^w = [\mathbf{e}^w(w_i), \mathbf{x}_i^c] \tag{2}$$

3.2 Feature Extraction Layer

We employ a multi-layer bidirectional LSTM as a feature extractor, for its strength in capturing long-range dependencies between words, a useful property for information extraction tasks [7]. The multi-layer bidirectional LSTM also severs as a hard parameter sharing component for multitask learning. Hard parameter sharing mechanism is beneficial to avoid overfitting [1] and helps our model to capture the underlying association between the entity boundary information and the entity category information.

By employing the multi-layer bidirectional LSTM, we gather the context feature of word w_i as follow:

$$\overrightarrow{\mathbf{h}_i} = \overrightarrow{\mathrm{LSTM}}(\mathbf{x}_i^w, \overrightarrow{\mathbf{h}}_{i-1}) \tag{3}$$

$$\overleftarrow{\mathbf{h}_i} = \overleftarrow{\mathrm{LSTM}}(\mathbf{x}_i^w, \overleftarrow{\mathbf{h}}_{i+1}) \tag{4}$$

$$\mathbf{h}_i = [\overrightarrow{\mathbf{h}_i}, \overleftarrow{\mathbf{h}_i}] \tag{5}$$

where $\mathbf{h}_i$ denotes the context feature representation of word w_i, $\overrightarrow{\mathbf{h}_i}$ and $\overleftarrow{\mathbf{h}_i}$ denote the hidden states in the forward direction and backward direction, respectively.

3.3   Boundary Detection and Category Detection

In the flat NER (non-nested NER) task, each word has only one kind of boundary label and one kind of category label. However, in nested NER, an individual word included in several nested entities has multiple kinds of boundary labels and category labels. Thus, we employ two multi-label modules to tag words. In our model, words included in several nested entities are tagged with multiple kinds of boundary labels and category labels.

There are two modules in our model: the boundary detection module and the category detection module. The first module is designed for detecting entity boundaries and the second is designed for detecting entity categories. We will describe these two modules in detail.

Boundary Detection Module. We use $E(p, q)$ to denote an entity, whose region starts from position p and ends at position q of the sentence. Given an input sentence $S = \{w_1, w_2, ..., w_n\}$ and two nested entities in this sentence: entity $E(i, j)$ of *DNA* and entity $E(i, k)$ of *protein*, where $j < k$. Specially, w_i is the common beginning word of two entities, so our model tags this word with the boundary label "B". w_j is the inside word of entity $E(i, k)$ and the end word of entity $E(i, j)$, so this word is tagged with two kinds of boundary labels ("I" and "E"). w_k is the end word of entity $E(i, k)$, so our model tags this word with "E". Words inside entities that are neither beginning words nor end words are tagged with "I". Words that are outside of any entities are tagged with "O".

In the boundary detection module, for each word w_i in the sentence, we feed its feature representation $\mathbf{h}_i$ obtained from the shared feature extractor to a fully connected layer. Finally, the output of the fully connected layer is fed to a sigmoid activation function to predict the boundary labels:

$$\mathbf{o}_i^b = \mathbf{W}\mathbf{h}_i + \mathbf{b} \tag{6}$$

$$\mathbf{e}_i^b = \text{sigmoid}(\mathbf{o}_i^b) \tag{7}$$

where $\mathbf{W}$ and $\mathbf{b}$ are trainable parameters and $\mathbf{e}_i^b$ is the output of the sigmoid function. As described above, words included in nested entities may have multiple boundary labels, so we use binary cross entropy loss function to optimize this module:

$$L_b = \sum_{t=1}^{u} \mathbf{y}_{i,t}^b \cdot \log(\mathbf{e}_{i,t}^b) + (1 - \mathbf{y}_{i,t}^b) \cdot \log(1 - \mathbf{e}_{i,t}^b) \tag{8}$$

where u denotes the number of all kinds of boundary labels, $\mathbf{y}_{i,t}^b$ denotes the true label of t-th boundary label and $\mathbf{e}_{i,t}^b$ denotes the corresponding probability predicted by the boundary detection module.

Category Detection Module. Considering the example mentioned above, input sentence $S = \{w_1, w_2, ..., w_n\}$ contains two entities: entity $E(i, j)$ of *DNA* and entity $E(i, k)$ of *protein*, where $j < k$. Words $\{w_i, w_{i+1}, ..., w_j\}$ are included in two different kinds of categories of entities, so they are tagged with two kinds of category labels ("DNA" and "protein") by the category detection module. Words $\{w_{j+1}, ..., w_k\}$ are only included in entity of *protein*, so the category detection module tags them with category label "protein". Words that are outside of any entities are tagged with "O".

For each word w_i in the input sentence, the category detection module predicts its category labels by feeding its feature representation $\mathbf{h}_i$ to a fully connected layer and a sigmoid activation function:

$$\mathbf{o}_i^c = \widehat{\mathbf{W}}\mathbf{h}_i + \hat{\mathbf{b}} \tag{9}$$

$$\mathbf{e}_i^c = \text{sigmoid}(\mathbf{o}_i^c) \tag{10}$$

where $\widehat{\mathbf{W}}$ and $\hat{\mathbf{b}}$ are trainable parameters and $\mathbf{e}_i^c$ is the output of sigmoid function. Just like the boundary labels, words included in several nested entities may also have multiple kinds of category labels. We also use binary cross entropy loss function to optimize this module:

$$L_c = \sum_{t=1}^{v} \mathbf{y}_{i,t}^c \cdot \log(\mathbf{e}_{i,t}^c) + (1 - \mathbf{y}_{i,t}^c) \cdot \log(1 - \mathbf{e}_{i,t}^c) \tag{11}$$

where v denotes the number of all kinds of category labels, $\mathbf{y}_{i,t}^c$ denotes the true label of t-th category label and $\mathbf{e}_{i,t}^c$ denotes the corresponding probability predicted by the category detection module.

3.4   Entity Output

We obtain entities according to the detected entity boundaries and the detected entity categories. For nested entities, we obtain the outer entities first and then obtain the inner entities. Considering the example in Fig. 2, there is an inner entity "DC" nested in an outer entity "monocyte - derived DC". We first obtain the outer entity "monocyte - derived DC" whose region determined by continuous boundary labels "B I I E" exactly matches the region determined by continuous category labels "Cell-Line Cell-Line Cell-Line Cell-Line". Then we obtain the inner entity "DC" whose region determined by boundary label "S" exactly matches the region determined by category label "Cell-Type". In this way, we can obtain these two nested entities ("DC" and "monocyte - derived DC").

3.5   Multitask Learning

In our method, the nested NER task can be regarded as a combination of two subtasks: detecting entity boundaries and detecting entity categories. We employ a boundary detection module and a category detection module to detect entity boundaries and entity categories, respectively. Considering the entity boundary information and the entity category information are complementary to each other, we train the boundary detection module and the category detection module by multitask learning to capture the underlying association between the boundary information and the category information.

The final objective function of our model is the sum of the boundary detection loss and category detection loss as follows:

$$L = L_b + L_c \tag{12}$$

where L_b and L_c denote the boundary detection loss and category detection loss.

4   Evaluation Settings

4.1   Dataset and Evaluation Metrics

To demonstrate the effectiveness of our model on detecting nested and flat entities, we evaluate our model on three datasets: GENIA [9], JNLPBA [10] and GermEval 2014 [2].

GENIA dataset is constructed on the GENIA v3.0.2 corpus. We follow the dataset settings of Zheng et al. [24]. The dataset is split into 8.1:0.9:1 for training, development and testing. Table 1 shows the statistics of GENIA dataset.

JNLPBA dataset is originally from GENIA corpus. It is a flat NER dataset which only contains flat and topmost entities. Following the settings of GENIA dataset, the subcategories are collapsed into 5 categories.

GermEval 2014 dataset is a German NER dataset from KONVENS 2014 shared task. It contains German nested named entities. The dataset consists of a total of 31, 300 sentences corresponding respectively 591, 006 tokens.

We use a strict evaluation metrics similar to Zheng et al. [24]. The extracted entities are considered correct if both the entity boundary labels and the entity category labels are exactly correct. We employ precision (P), recall (R) and F-score (F) to evaluate the performance.

Table 1. Statistics of GENIA dataset.

Dataset	DNA	RNA	Protein	Cell-Line	Cell-Type	Overall
Train	7650	692	28728	3027	5832	45929
Development	1026	132	2303	325	551	4337
Test	1257	109	3066	438	604	5474
Overall	9933	933	34097	3790	6987	55740
Nested	1744	407	1902	347	389	4789

4.2 Baselines and Previous Models

We compare our model with several previous state-of-the-art models. These models can be summarized into three types as follows:

(1) The CRF-based constituency parser model in [3] which is denoted as CRF-constituency.
(2) Graph-based models: Mention hypergraph model (MH) [14], Multigraph model (MG) [16].
(3) Neural network models: Layered sequence labeling model (LSLM) [6], Exhaustive region classification model (ERCM) [19], Boundary-aware model (BM) [24].

4.3 Parameters Settings and Tagging Schemes

We use Adam optimizer for training our model. We use the same 200-dimension pre-trained word embedding [6,24] to initialize our word embedding. The character embedding is initialized randomly and set to 50-dimension. We regularize our model using dropout, with the dropout rate set to 0.5. The hidden state size of LSTM is set to 200. Our model is implemented using the PyTorch framework and all of our experiments are conducted on the NVIDIA RTX2080Ti GPU.

We use the BIOES tagging schemes for tagging entity boundary labels. The meaning of BIOES is: B (the beginning of an entity), I (the inside of an entity), O (outside of any entities), E (the end of an entity), S (the single-token entity).

5 Results and Analysis

5.1 Nested NER and Flat NER

Table 2 presents the comparison of our model with several previous state-of-the-art models on GENIA dataset for nested NER. The results show our model outperforms the state-of-the-art models in terms of precision, recall, and F-score. Besides, we observe that BM [24] and our model achieve 73.6% and 74.6% respectively in terms of recall, which is much better than other models. We analysis that both of BM and our model explicitly utilize entity boundary information to extract entities while other models does not. Comparing with BM, our model does not suffer from boundary detection conflict and error propagation, which helps our model achieve better performance. Furthermore, we introduce multi-task learning to train our boundary detection module and category detection module to capture the underlying association between entity boundary information and entity category information. In this way, our model can locate entities more precisely and achieves the best performance on GENIA dataset compared to other models. We conduct an experiment in the next subsection to further illustrate that our model can locate entities more precisely by capturing the underlying association between entity boundary information and category information.

Table 2. Performance comparison of our model with other state-of-the-art models on GENIA test set.

Model	P(%)	R(%)	F(%)
CRF-constituency [3][a]	75.4	65.9	70.3
MH [14][a]	72.5	65.2	68.7
MG [16][a]	75.4	66.8	70.8
ERCM [19][a]	73.3	68.3	70.7
LSLM [6][a]	76.1	66.8	71.1
BM [24][a]	75.9	73.6	74.7
Our model	**76.4**	**74.6**	**75.5**

[a]The results are taken from [24].

Table 3. Statistics of five entity categories on GENIA test set and our results compared to ERCM [19], LSLM [6] and BM [24].

Category	Statistics	P(%)	R(%)	F(%)	ERCM.F(%)[a]	LSLM.F(%)[a]	BM.F(%)[a]
DNA	1257	72.3	69.8	**71.0**	67.8	70.1	70.6
RNA	109	80.1	77.9	79.0	75.9	80.8	**81.5**
Protein	3066	77.8	78.2	**78.0**	72.9	72.7	76.4
Cell-Line	438	79.8	65.2	**71.8**	63.6	66.9	71.3
Cell-Type	604	74.2	72.0	**73.1**	69.8	71.3	72.5
Overall	5474	76.4	74.6	**75.5**	70.7	71.1	74.7

[a]The results are taken from [24].

Table 3 shows the comparison of our model with three previous state-of-the-art models on five entity categories on GENIA test set. Without error propagation and boundary detection conflict, our model outperforms LSLM [6] and BM [24] on almost all entity categories. By capturing underlying association between entity boundary information and category information, our model can locate entities more precisely and outperforms ERCM [19] on all entity categories.

Table 4. Performance comparison on GermEval 2014 test set.

Model	P(%)	R(%)	F(%)
ECRM [19][b]	75.0	60.8	67.2
LSLM [6][b]	72.9	61.5	66.7
BM [24][b]	74.5	**69.1**	71.7
Our model	**78.5**	67.6	**72.7**

[b]The results are taken from [24].

Table 4 shows the comparison of our model with three previous state-of-the-art models on GermEval 2014 dataset. Previous works on this dataset either ignore nested entities or extract inner entities and outer entities through two independent models [24]. Different from them, our model can extract both flat entities and nested entities in a unified model. Compared to LSLM [6] and BM [24], our model does not suffer from error propagation and boundary detection conflict and achieves better performance. Moreover, by capturing the underlying association between entity boundary information and category information, our model outperforms all three models. Besides, we observe that our model outperforms other models especially in terms of precision. This is likely because we introduce multitask learning to train our model to capture the underlying association between entity boundary information and category information. In this way, our model tends to extract entities more likely to be true entities.

To illustrate that our model can handle not only nested NER but also flat NER, we evaluate our model on JNLPBA dataset. JNLPBA dataset is a flat NER dataset. Our model achieves 74.6% in terms of F-score, outperforming BM [24] which is also designed for nested NER and achieves 73.6% in terms of F-score. Besides, our model is competitive to the state-of-the-art model [4] which is especially designed for flat NER.

Table 5. Performance comparison of Boundary Detection on GENIA test set and GermEval 2014 test set.

Model	GENIA			GermEval 2014		
	P(%)	R(%)	F(%)	P(%)	R(%)	F(%)
ECRM [19]	76.6	69.2	72.7	**83.5**	66.0	73.8
LSLM [6]	**79.9**	67.08	73.4	83.2	65.1	73.0
BM [24]	79.7	76.9	78.3	81.4	75.1	78.1
Our model	78.4	**80.0**	**79.2**	82.9	**79.9**	**81.4**

5.2 Performance of Boundary Detection

To illustrate that our model can identify entity boundaries more precisely by capturing the underlying association between entity boundary information and category information, we conduct several experiments.

Table 5[1] shows the comparison of our model with three previous state-of-the-art models on boundary detection. The performance of boundary detection evaluates the model's ability of identifying entity regions. Compared with other models, our model achieves best performance in terms of F-score. Compared with BM [24] which only utilizes entity boundary information, we introduce multitask

---

[1] The results on GENIA test set are taken from [24], and the results on GermEval 2014 test set are obtained by running the codes shared by [24].

Table 6. Performance comparison of Boundary Label Prediction on GENIA test set.

Boundary label	P(%)	R(%)	F(%)
O(non-entity)	97.6	96.0	96.8
B(beginning)	83.6	87.2	85.3
I(inner-entity)	85.7	93.0	89.2
E(end)	84.7	90.1	87.3
S(single)	79.4	71.6	75.3

Table 7. Performance comparison of non-multitask learning model and multitask learning model on GENIA dataset and GermEval 2014 dataset.

Model	GENIA			GermEval 2014		
	P(%)	R(%)	F(%)	P(%)	R(%)	F(%)
Non-multitask learning	70.7	73.1	74.9	79.1	66.2	72.1
Multitask learning	76.4	74.6	**75.5**	78.5	67.6	**72.7**

learning to capture the underlying association between entity boundary information and category information and achieve better performance on boundary detection. It illustrates that our model can locate entities more precisely by capturing the underlying association between entity boundary information and category information.

Table 6 shows the performance of boundary label prediction of our model. The performance of boundary label prediction evaluates the model's ability of predicting the boundary label of each word in sentences. With the help of multitask learning, our model can capture the underlying association between entity boundary information and category information. It helps our model achieve relatively high performance on boundary label prediction. This gives a reason why our model can achieve good performance on boundary detection. The performance of our model to predict the boundary label "S" is not so good as other boundary labels. This is likely because the amount of the boundary label "S" is much less than other labels.

5.3   Performance of Multitask Learning

To prove that we can improve the performance of our model through multitask learning, we conduct experiments on the GENIA and GermEval 2014 datasets. Table 7 shows that our multitask learning model outperforms our non-multitask learning model. The architecture of our non-multitask learning model is shown is Fig. 3. In non-multitask learning model, we train two individual multi-label sequence labeling modules for entity boundary prediction and entity category prediction without sharing any components. Therefore, entity boundary prediction and entity category prediction are separate and do not share any information. In multitask learning model, we jointly train two modules through a

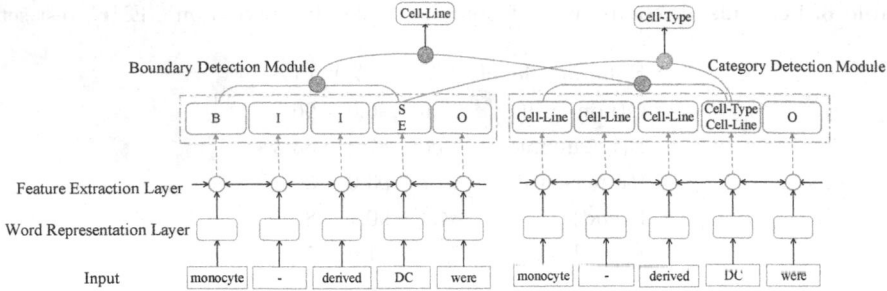

Fig. 3. Architecture of our non-multitask learning model. The model is composed by two individual multi-label sequence labeling modules without sharing any components.

shared multi-layer Bi-LSTM which serves as the shared component. In this way, the boundary detection module and category detection module can share information with each other through the shared component. Multitask learning helps our model focus attention on features that actually matter [17]. With multitask learning, our model can capture the underlying association between entity boundary information and category information. It means that our model can capture features that not only matter to entity boundary detection but also matter to entity category detection. Therefore, our model can locate entities more precisely. The results in Table 7 illustrate that multitask learning improves the performance of our model.

Table 8. Results of Ablation Tests on GENIA test set and GermEval 2014 test set ("w/o" means "without").

Setting	GENIA			GermEval 2014		
	P(%)	R(%)	F(%)	P(%)	R(%)	F(%)
Our model	**76.4**	**74.6**	**75.5**	**78.5**	**67.6**	**72.7**
w/o Dropout	74.2	71.1	72.6	70.9	63.7	67.1
w/o Character representation	76.0	73.0	74.5	74.7	58.4	65.6
w/o Pre-trained Word Embedding	73.7	73.9	73.8	76.3	66.7	71.2

5.4   Ablation Tests

Our model has several components that we could tweak to understand their impact on the overall performance. We explore the impact that the dropout layer, the character-level LSTM and the pre-trained word embedding have on our model. Table 8 shows the results of the ablation experiments on GENIA test set and GermEval 2014 test set. From the results, we observe that all components contribute to the overall performance to varying degrees.

6   Case Study

To specifically illustrate that our model does not suffer from boundary detection conflict which BM [24] suffers from, we show case 1 in Table 9. There are three entities in this case, including "mAb", "NFATc" and "T cell NFATc". The word "NFATc" is simultaneously the beginning of entity "NFATc" and the end of entity "T cell NFATc". In this case, BM [24] only identifies the entity "NFATc" but ignores the entity "T cell NFATc" because it only tags each word with one kind of boundary label, which leads to boundary detection conflict. Different from BM, our model tags each word with multiple kinds of boundary labels, thus our model does not suffer from boundary detection conflict and successfully identifies both "NFATc" and "T cell NFATc".

Table 9. Two cases of predicted results in GENIA test dataset.

Case 1	However, supershift assays using the available mAb recognizing the T cell NFATc
Ground truth	protein:{mAb; NFATc; T cell NFATc}
BM [24]	protein: {NFATc}
Our multitask model	protein: {mAb; NFATc; T cell NFATc}
Case 2	human FKBP cDNA were detected
Ground truth	protein: {FKBP} DNA: {human FKBP cDNA}
LSLM [6]	DNA: {human FKBP cDNA}
ERCM [19]	protein: {human FKBP} DNA: {human FKBP cDNA}
BM [24]	DNA: {human FKBP cDNA}
Our non-multitask model	DNA: {human FKBP cDNA}
Our multitask model	protein: {FKBP} DNA: {human FKBP cDNA}

To specifically illustrate that the performance of our multitask model outperforms previous models and our non-multitask model, we show case 2 in Table 9. There are two entities in this case, including "FKBP" and "human FKBP cDNA". LSLM [6] only extracts the outer entity "human FKBP cDNA" but ignores the inner entity "FKBP" because it suffers from error propagation caused by its pipeline structure. The exhaustive model incorrectly extracts the non-entity "human FKBP" because it does not explicitly utilize boundary information. BM [24] explicitly utilizes the boundary information so that it does not extract the non-entity, but it ignores some entities, as same as our non-multitask model. As for our multitask model, it successfully identifies all entities. This is likely because our multitask model captures the underlying association between entity boundary information and entity category information through multitask learning, thus it locates entities more precisely and achieves better performance.

7 Conclusion

This paper presents a neural model with a multi-label boundary detection module and a multi-label category detection module to extract nested entities. Our model detects entity boundaries and entity categories simultaneously, which avoids boundary detection conflict and error propagation problem. Furthermore, our model captures the underlying association between the boundary information and the category information through multitask learning. In this way, our model extracts entities more precisely and achieves better performance. Experiments conducted on two nested NER dataset and a flat NER dataset show that our model outperforms existing models both on nested NER and flat NER.

In future work, it would be interesting to model the explicit association between the boundary and category information. It may help to better detect entity boundaries and entity categories.

Acknowledgements. This work was supported by the Fundamental Research Funds for the Central Universities, SCUT (No. 2017ZD048, D2182480), the Science and Technology Planning Project of Guangdong Province (No.2017B050506004), the Science and Technology Programs of Guangzhou (No.201704030076, 201802010027, 201902010046), the Hong Kong Research Grants Council (project no. PolyU 1121417), and an internal research grant from the Hong Kong Polytechnic University (project 1.9B0V).

References

1. Baxter, J.: A Bayesian/information theoretic model of learning to learn via multiple task sampling. Mach. Learn. **28**(1), 7–39 (1997). https://doi.org/10.1023/A:1007327622663
2. Benikova, D., Biemann, C., Reznicek, M.: NoSta-d named entity annotation for German: guidelines and dataset. In: Proceedings of the Ninth International Conference on Language Resources and Evaluation (LREC 2014), pp. 2524–2531 (2014)
3. Finkel, J.R., Manning, C.D.: Nested named entity recognition. In: Proceedings of the 2009 Conference on Empirical Methods in Natural Language Processing, vol. 1-vol. 1, pp. 141–150. Association for Computational Linguistics (2009)
4. Gridach, M.: Character-level neural network for biomedical named entity recognition. J. Biomed. Inform. **70**, 85–91 (2017)
5. Gu, B.: Recognizing nested named entities in GENIA corpus. In: Proceedings of the HLT-NAACL BioNLP Workshop on Linking Natural Language and Biology, pp. 112–113 (2006)
6. Ju, M., Miwa, M., Ananiadou, S.: A neural layered model for nested named entity recognition. In: Proceedings of the 2018 Conference of the North American Chapter of the Association for Computational Linguistics: Human Language Technologies, pp. 1446–1459 (2018). https://doi.org/10.18653/v1/N18-1131
7. Katiyar, A., Cardie, C.: Nested named entity recognition revisited. In: Proceedings of the 2018 Conference of the North American Chapter of the Association for Computational Linguistics: Human Language Technologies, vol. 1 (Long Papers), pp. 861–871. Association for Computational Linguistics (2018)

8. Khot, T., Balasubramanian, N., Gribkoff, E., Sabharwal, A., Clark, P., Etzioni, O.: Exploring Markov logic networks for question answering. In: Proceedings of the 2015 Conference on Empirical Methods in Natural Language Processing, pp. 685–694 (2015). https://doi.org/10.18653/v1/D15-1080

9. Kim, J.D., Ohta, T., Tateisi, Y., Tsujii, J.: Genia corpus–a semantically annotated corpus for bio-textmining. Bioinformatics, 19(suppl_1), i180–i182 (2003)

10. Kim, J.D., Ohta, T., Tsuruoka, Y., Tateisi, Y., Collier, N.: Introduction to the bio-entity recognition task at JNLPBA. In: Proceedings of the International Joint Workshop on Natural Language Processing in Biomedicine and its Applications, pp. 70–75. Citeseer (2004)

11. Lafferty, J., McCallum, A., Pereira, F.C.: Conditional random fields: probabilistic models for segmenting and labeling sequence data (2001)

12. Lample, G., Ballesteros, M., Subramanian, S., Kawakami, K., Dyer, C.: Neural architectures for named entity recognition. In: Proceedings of the 2016 Conference of the North American Chapter of the Association for Computational Linguistics: Human Language Technologies, pp. 260–270 (2016)

13. Lin, B., Cao, H., Qi, G., Duan, S., Wu, T., Wang, M.: Adversarial discriminative denoising for distant supervision relation extraction. In: Li, G., Yang, J., Gama, J., Natwichai, J., Tong, Y. (eds.) DASFAA 2019. LNCS, vol. 11448, pp. 282–286. Springer, Cham (2019). https://doi.org/10.1007/978-3-030-18590-9_29

14. Lu, W., Roth, D.: Joint mention extraction and classification with mention hypergraphs. In: Proceedings of the 2015 Conference on Empirical Methods in Natural Language Processing, pp. 857–867 (2015). https://doi.org/10.18653/v1/D15-1102

15. Ma, X., Hovy, E.: End-to-end sequence labeling via bi-directional LSTM-CNNs-CRF. In: Proceedings of the 54th Annual Meeting of the Association for Computational Linguistics (Volume 1: Long Papers), pp. 1064–1074 (2016)

16. Muis, A.O., Lu, W.: Labeling gaps between words: recognizing overlapping mentions with mention separators. In: Proceedings of the 2017 Conference on Empirical Methods in Natural Language Processing, pp. 2608–2618 (2017)

17. Ruder, S.: An overview of multi-task learning in deep neural networks. arXiv preprint arXiv:1706.05098 (2017)

18. Shen, D., Zhang, J., Zhou, G., Su, J., Tan, C.L.: Effective adaptation of hidden Markov model-based named entity recognizer for biomedical domain. In: Proceedings of the ACL 2003 Workshop on Natural Language Processing in Biomedicine, pp. 49–56 (2003). https://doi.org/10.3115/1118958.1118965

19. Sohrab, M.G., Miwa, M.: Deep exhaustive model for nested named entity recognition. In: Proceedings of the 2018 Conference on Empirical Methods in Natural Language Processing, pp. 2843–2849 (2018). https://doi.org/10.18653/v1/D18-1309

20. Sun, Y., Li, L., Xie, Z., Xie, Q., Li, X., Xu, G.: Co-training an improved recurrent neural network with probability statistic models for named entity recognition. In: Candan, S., Chen, L., Pedersen, T.B., Chang, L., Hua, W. (eds.) DASFAA 2017. LNCS, vol. 10178, pp. 545–555. Springer, Cham (2017). https://doi.org/10.1007/978-3-319-55699-4_33

21. Tong, P., Zhang, Q., Yao, J.: Leveraging domain context for question answering over knowledge graph. Data Sci. Eng. 4(4), 323–335 (2019). https://doi.org/10.1007/s41019-019-00109-w

22. Zhang, J., Li, J., Li, X.-L., Shi, Y., Li, J., Wang, Z.: Domain-specific entity linking via fake named entity detection. In: Navathe, S.B., Wu, W., Shekhar, S., Du, X., Wang, X.S., Xiong, H. (eds.) DASFAA 2016. LNCS, vol. 9642, pp. 101–116. Springer, Cham (2016). https://doi.org/10.1007/978-3-319-32025-0_7

23. Zhang, J., Shen, D., Zhou, G., Su, J., Tan, C.L.: Enhancing HMM-based biomedical named entity recognition by studying special phenomena. J. Biomed. Inform. **37**(6), 411–422 (2004)
24. Zheng, C., Cai, Y., Xu, J., Leung, H.F., Xu, G.: A boundary-aware neural model for nested named entity recognition. In: Proceedings of the 2019 Conference on Empirical Methods in Natural Language Processing and the 9th International Joint Conference on Natural Language Processing (EMNLP-IJCNLP), pp. 357–366 (2019)
25. Zhou, G., Zhang, J., Su, J., Shen, D., Tan, C.: Recognizing names in biomedical texts: a machine learning approach. Bioinformatics **20**(7), 1178–1190 (2004)

Incorporating Concept Information into Term Weighting Schemes for Topic Models

Huakui Zhang[1], Yi Cai[1(✉)], Bingshan Zhu[1], Changmeng Zheng[1], Kai Yang[2], Raymond Chi-Wing Wong[3], and Qing Li[4]

[1] School of Software Engineering, South China University of Technology,
Guangzhou, China
zhanghk1997@gmail.com, ycai@scut.edu.cn, zhubsscut@foxmail.com,
sethecharm@mail.scut.edu.cn
[2] Department of Information Systems, City University of Hong Kong,
Hong Kong, China
young_kind@foxmail.com
[3] Department of Computer Science and Engineering,
The Hong Kong University of Science and Technology, Hong Kong, China
raywong@cse.ust.hk
[4] Department of Computing, The Hong Kong Polytechnic University,
Hong Kong, China
csqli@comp.polyu.edu.hk

Abstract. Topic models demonstrate outstanding ability in discovering latent topics in text corpora. A coherent topic consists of words or entities related to similar concepts, $i.e.$, abstract ideas of categories of things. To generate more coherent topics, term weighting schemes have been proposed for topic models by assigning weights to terms in text, such as promoting the informative entities. However, in current term weighting schemes, entities are not discriminated by their concepts, which may cause incoherent topics containing entities from unrelated concepts. To solve the problem, in this paper we propose two term weighting schemes for topic models, CEP scheme and DCEP scheme, to improve the topic coherence by incorporating the concept information of the entities. More specifically, the CEP term weighting scheme gives more weights to entities from the concepts that reveals the topics of the document. The DCEP scheme further reduces the co-occurrence of the entities from unrelated concepts and separates them into different duplicates of a document. We develop CEP-LDA and DCEP-LDA term weighting topic models by applying the two proposed term weighting schemes to LDA. Experimental results on two public datasets show that CEP-LDA and DCEP-LDA topic models can produce more coherent topics.

Keywords: Topic model · Latent Dirichlet Allocation · Term weighting scheme

© Springer Nature Switzerland AG 2020
Y. Nah et al. (Eds.): DASFAA 2020, LNCS 12113, pp. 227–244, 2020.
https://doi.org/10.1007/978-3-030-59416-9_14

Table 1. An example about tennis and the recognized entities in it. Entities are in the left white rectangles and one of the concepts is shown in the right shaded ellipse for each entity.

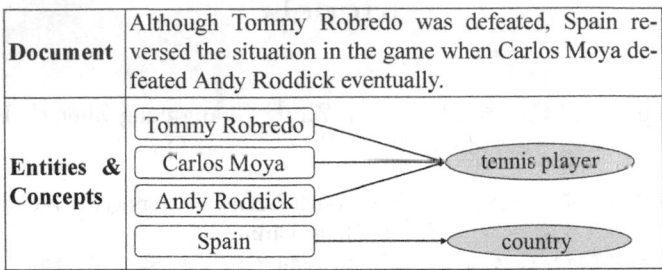

1   Introduction

With the rise of the Internet, massive amounts of data are generated every day. Topic models, as exemplified by Latent Dirichlet Allocation (LDA) [3], play a critical role in the field of text mining to analyze the data. Topic models assume that each document has a distribution over topics, and each topic has a distribution over words. They aim to discover implicit topics and offer people a quick understanding of a text corpus. Other than mining topics, topic models also make a significant contribution to many natural language processing (NLP) tasks [1,5,17,27].

The major criterion of a good topic model is that it produces useful and coherent topics. If words or entities in a topic are interpretable and associate with a single semantic concept, the topic is coherent [16]. However, general but highly frequent words, such as "good" and "think", tend to dominate and scatter across most topics produced by current topic models [8]. These general words lead to considerable incoherent topics without any specific meaning. Term weighting schemes are explored for topic models to alleviate the influences of these general terms (*i.e.*, words) by giving them lower weights and promoting the informative terms [8,9,13,25]. Notably, Krasnashchok *et al.* [9] regard entities in text as important terms which represent distinct objects in the world and play an essential role in describing events and facts, and they propose Document Independent Named Entity Promoting (NEP) term weighting scheme [9] for topic models to generate more coherent topics by promoting the entities.

A concept is an abstract idea of categories of entities or things [15]. In a document, there usually exist some concepts that cover more entities than other concepts. These concepts correlate more with the main topics of the document, and thus the entities under these concepts carry greater importance and should be given more weights. For example, in the document in Table 1, most entities (*e.g.*, "Carlos Moya") belong to the concept "tennis player", which reveals that the primary topic of the document is related to tennis. While the three tennis-related entities should have higher weights, entity "Spain" should have a lower weight because its concept "country" is not related to main tennis topic of document. However, current term weighting schemes such as the NEP scheme do not consider the relationship between the concepts of entities and the topics of the documents. Rather, it gives all the entities the same weights by increasing the same frequency to each entity. It should be noted that topic models tend to assign highly frequent and co-occurred words (or entities) to the same topic [6,23]. Therefore, for topic models with the NEP scheme, entities (*e.g.*, "Spain") are highly likely to be assigned to the topics (*e.g.*, tennis) that are unrelated to their concepts, hence the topics become incoherent.

To alleviate the problem of the current term weighting schemes which bring entities from unrelated concepts into the same topics and lead to incoherence, we propose two term weighting schemes for topic models, namely, Concept Based Entity Promoting (CEP) scheme and Duplicated Concept Based Entity Promoting (DCEP) scheme. In the CEP scheme, if an entity shares concepts with more entities, it is regarded to relate more to the main topics of the document and is given more weight by increasing more frequency. The entities that are irrelevant to the main topics have lower frequencies, so that the influence (*i.e.*, probability) of these entities on the unrelated topics is diminished in topic models and the topic coherence is improved. However, the CEP scheme still mix up entities from different unrelated concepts into the same topic in a document, leading to topic incoherence. Since topic models discover topics based on the co-occurrence of words or entities [6,23], the avoidance of the co-occurrence of the entities from unrelated concepts in a document can help to improve the topic coherence. We therefore propose DCEP term weighting scheme to separate entities from different concepts into different duplicates of a document, and to promote entities from one concept in each duplicate document. Consequently, topic models with the DCEP scheme can produce more coherent topics as the entities from unrelated concepts have higher probability to be assigned to different topics. We develop CEP-LDA and DCEP-LDA term weighting topic models by applying the CEP and DCEP term weighting schemes to LDA. The contributions of this paper can be summarized as follows:

- To address the problem that topic models with term weighting schemes produce incoherent topics, we propose the CEP term weighting scheme which gives more weights to entities whose concepts associate more with the topics of the document. To the best of our knowledge, this is the first study to integrate concept information into term weighting scheme for topic models.
- To alleviate the problem that CEP scheme mixes up entities from irrelevant concepts and leads to topic incoherence, we further extend the CEP scheme to DCEP term weighting scheme so as to reduce the co-occurrence of these unrelated entities and separate them into different duplicates of a document.
- We develop two term weighting topic models, CEP-LDA and DCEP-LDA, by applying the two proposed schemes to LDA. Experiments on two public datasets demonstrate that CEP-LDA and DCEP-LDA models are capable of discovering more coherent topics than NEP-LDA.

The remaining part of the paper is organized as follows. Section 2 briefly describes the related work. Section 3 presents the proposed CEP and DCEP term weighting schemes, and two topic models CEP-LDA and DCEP-LDA. The detailed experiments and analysis are shown in Sect. 4, followed by the conclusion in Sect. 5.

2 Related Work

Term weighting schemes assign weights to terms which represent their contribution in a specific task. Term weighting schemes are traditionally studied in information retrieval [20]. The most famous term weighting scheme is term frequency–inverted document frequency (TFIDF) [18] which explores term frequency and document frequency simultaneously. Thereafter, term weighting schemes are successfully applied to various NLP tasks, such as text categorization [10].

Topic models such as LDA are criticized for producing incoherent topics which are filled with general and highly frequent words. Wilson et al. [25] firstly prove that term weighting schemes can also benefit topic models to produce more coherent topics by assigning weights to words. They propose two term weighting topic models log-LDA and PMI-LDA which combines term weighting schemes and LDA. Log-WLDA utilizes log function and gives lower weights to highly frequent words and PMI-WLDA adopts pointwise mutual information (PMI) to calculate the relevance between words and documents as the weights.

Lee et al. [12] propose Weighted Topic Model (WTM) and Balance Weighted Topic Model (BWTM) that utilize IDF method to measure representativeness of words in a topic. Truica et al. [21] verify the effectiveness of different term weighting schemes on the LDA, including term frequency (TF), TFIDF, and the Okapi BM25. Bekoulis et al. [2] transform a document in a graph-of-words representation, attempting to capture the relationships between words in a context window and treat the number of co-occurrence words as the term weights of words.

It is ulteriorly observed that some topics generated by LDA contain irrelevant words scattering across these topics. These words are named as topic-indiscriminate words. TWLDA model [8] applies supervised Balanced Distributional Concentration (BDC) weighting scheme [22] to find these words, and assigns lower weights to them in a two-step training process. Extending from TWLDA model, an iterative term weighting framework ITWF [28] is further proposed which can be applied to the variants of LDA.

It is pointed out that the previous works [8,25] mainly focus on assigning lower weights to the general words, but words with higher weights are not necessarily informative. An entropy-based term weighting scheme is designed to measure the informativeness of words, and combined with log and BDC weighting schemes [13].

However, the previous term weighting topic models modify the generative process of LDA and increase the complexity of computation. NEP-LDA [9] offers new insights into the way to combining term weighting schemes and topic models. In NEP-LDA, entities are recognized as the informative words and directly promoted by increasing their frequencies in documents. Then standard training algorithms for LDA is reused on those modified documents. Inspired by NEP scheme, we further incorporate concept information into the term weighting schemes for topic models.

3   Model

In order to generate more coherent topics, we propose two term weighting schemes, CEP scheme and DCEP scheme, for topic models which utilize concept information of entities. The CEP term weighting scheme gives more weights to entities from the concepts that reflect the topics of the documents. The DCEP scheme further reduces the co-occurrence of the entities from unrelated concepts for more coherent topics. We develop two term weighting topic models, CEP-LDA and DCEP-LDA topic model, by applying the proposed schemes to LDA.

3.1   Latent Dirichlet Allocation

LDA is the most widely studied topic model. In LDA, documents are characterized as mixtures over topics, and topics are mixtures over all the words in the vocabulary of a corpus. LDA assumes the generative process of the entire corpus as follows:

1. For each topic $k = 1$ to K:
   (a) Draw word distribution $\phi_k \sim Dirichlet(\beta)$
2. For each document m in corpus D:
   (a) Draw topic distribution $\theta_m \sim Dirichlet(\alpha)$
   (b) For each word with index $i = 1$ to N_m in document m:
      i. Draw a topic $z_{m,i} \sim Multinomial(\theta_m)$
      ii. Draw a word $w_{m,i} \sim Multinomial(\phi_{z_{m,i}})$

where Dirichlet prior α and β and the topic number K are hyperparameters in LDA. N_m represents the number of words in document m. Figure 1 demonstrates the graphical representation of LDA model which expresses the conditional dependence between the random variables. The training goal of LDA is to reverse the generation process, outputting the topic distribution θ_m for each document m and the word distribution ϕ_k for each topic k.

3.2   CEP Term Weighting Scheme and CEP-LDA Model

If a concept covers more entities, it expresses more about the main topics of the document and is more substantial. Equivalently, if an entity shares semantic concepts with more entities in a document, this entity should be given more weights and thus be increased more frequency in the CEP scheme. Oppositely, if an entity shares concepts with fewer entities, it will be promoted less. In a document, if an entity diverges more in concepts from other entities, it may convey less important information and should have relatively lower frequency than

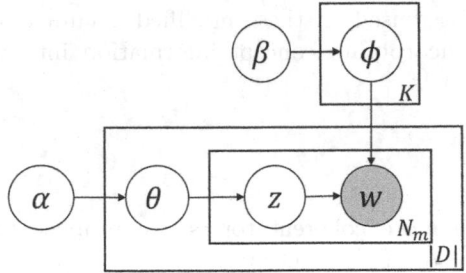

Fig. 1. Graphical representation of LDA model.

other entities. With lower frequency, an entity will have lower probability in a topic. Therefore, even if such an entity is incorrectly assigned to an irrelevant topic, the impact on the coherence is lessened due to its low probability. Moreover, it increases the chances that entities from the same concepts fall into the same topic because their frequencies are increased more. Consequently, the CEP scheme can facilitate topic models to find more coherent topics.

More specifically, in each document m in a corpus D, the CEP term weighting scheme is applied to the frequency of each type of word (*i.e.*, term) w as below:

$$N'_{m,w} = \begin{cases} N_{m,w} + C_{m,w} \cdot \max_{v} N_{m,v} & \text{if } w \in \tilde{T}_m \\ N_{m,w} & \text{if } w \in T_m \end{cases} \tag{1}$$

where $N'_{m,w}$ and $N_{m,w}$ represent the promoted and original frequency of word w in document m. A word is either an ordinary word or an entity. T_m denotes the set of ordinary words and $\tilde{T}_m$ denotes the set of entities occurring in document m. $C_{m,w}$ represents the number of different types of entities (including entity w) in document m which at least share one concept with entity w. Besides, $\max_{v} N_{m,v}$ is the maximum term frequency in document m. The CEP scheme does not change the frequencies of the ordinary words by reason of their comparatively secondary status when describing facts or events in texts as in [9].

Figure 2 demonstrates the original and promoted frequencies of some words in the document of Table 1 after applying different term weighting schemes. NEP scheme increases the frequencies of the entities by the maximum term frequency in the document which equals to two. The CEP scheme promotes the entities of the three tennis players by six because each shares the same concept with two more entities. The frequency of entity "Spain" is only increased by two. Because the frequency of "Spain" is less than the frequencies of the tennis players, it will have lower influence if it is assigned to the tennis-related or other unrelated topics. At the same time, there are higher opportunities that the same topic is chosen for the three tennis players.

CEP-LDA model is the combination of the CEP term weighting scheme and LDA. The CEP term weighting scheme does not change the generative process of topic models. In CEP-LDA model, after the CEP scheme is applied to the

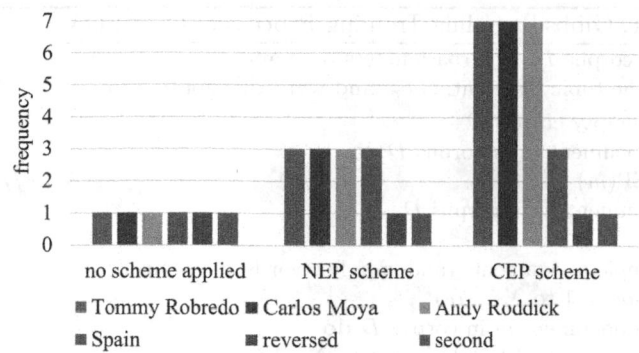

Fig. 2. Frequencies of words in the document in Table 1 under different term weighting schemes.

corpus, the training algorithm of LDA such as Gibbs sampling or variational inference can be directly reused on the modified corpus. We present the training process of CEP-LDA using collapsed Gibbs sampling algorithm in Algorithm 1. The CEP scheme is firstly applied to each document in the corpus (Line 1–5). The detailed process of the CEP scheme is presented in Algorithm 2. Then collapsed Gibbs sampling algorithm of LDA is adopted on the corpus. The topic of each word is iteratively sampled (Line 6–14) according to the following conditional distribution:

$$p(z_{m,i}|\mathbf{z}_{\neg(m,i)}, \mathbf{w}, \alpha, \beta) \propto (n^k_{m,\neg(m,i)} + \alpha) \cdot \frac{n^w_{k,\neg(m,i)} + \beta}{\sum_v^V (n^v_{k,\neg(m,i)} + \beta)} \qquad (2)$$

where α and β are hyperparameters, and $z_{m,i}$ is the topic assignment for the ith word $w_{m,i}$ in document m. Notations $\mathbf{z}$ and $\mathbf{w}$ represent all the topic assignments and words in the corpus, n^k_m is the number of words assigned to topic k in document m and n^w_k is the number of times that word w is assigned to topic k. Subscript $\neg(m,i)$ means the exclusion of the word $w_{m,i}$. V is the vocabulary of the corpus. Finally, the posterior probability of topic k in document m (Line 15) is computed as:

$$\theta_{m,k} = \frac{n^k_m + \alpha}{\sum_u^K (n^u_m + \alpha)} \qquad (3)$$

where K represents the pre-defined topic number. The posterior probability of word w in topic k (Line 16) is computed as:

$$\phi_{k,w} = \frac{n^w_k + \beta}{\sum_v^V (n^v_k + \beta)} \qquad (4)$$

Algorithm 1. Gibbs Sampling Training Process of CEP-LDA.

INPUT: The corpus D, hyperparameters α, β and K
OUTPUT: The topic distribution θ_m and word distribution ϕ_k

 1: Create an empty corpus $\tilde{D}$
 2: **for** each document m in corpus D **do**
 3:    $\tilde{m} = \text{CEP}(m)$ // See Alg. 2
 4:    Add document $\tilde{m}$ to corpus $\tilde{D}$
 5: **end for**
 6: Initialize topic assignments randomly for words in corpus $\tilde{D}$
 7: **for** *iterition* $= 1$ to N_{iter} **do**
 8:    **for** each document m in corpus $\tilde{D}$ **do**
 9:       **for** each word with index $i = 1$ to N_d **do**
10:          Draw a topic $z_{m,i} \sim p(z_{m,i}|\mathbf{z}_{\neg m,i}, \mathbf{w}, \alpha, \beta)$ // See Eq. 2
11:          Update n_m^k and n_k^w
12:       **end for**
13:    **end for**
14: **end for**
15: Compute topic distribution θ_m // See Eq. 3
16: Compute word distribution ϕ_k // See Eq. 4

3.3   DCEP Term Weighting Scheme and DCEP-LDA Model

Although the CEP scheme attempts to reduce the probability of an entity in an unrelated topic, it still mix up entities from unrelated concepts in a document to some extend and may produce incoherent topics. For example, in the document of Table 2, entities "China" and "United States" share the same concept "country". Entities "Xiaomi" and "Google" are the instances of concept "technology company" which is unrelated to concept "country". After applying the CEP scheme to the document, frequencies of the four entities are increased the same. Because of the high and equal frequencies, the four entities from the two unrelated concepts are still likely to be assigned to the same topic while all having high probability in the topic. Under such a circumstance, topic models fail to yield coherent topics by applying the CEP scheme.

We design the DCEP term weighting scheme to alleviate the problem by reducing the co-occurrence of the entities from different concepts. Based on the number of concepts of entities in a document, the DCEP scheme duplicates a document several times and create a list of new documents. Then it increases the frequencies of entities from different concepts in different duplicates of this document. The entities that differ about concepts are promoted separately in different duplicates. In each duplicate document, entities from one promoted concept have higher frequencies than other entities and higher probability to fall in the same topic. If there are two semantically similar concepts, the entities that belong to both concepts can act as bridges to gather other entities from either concept into the same topic. Oppositely, entities from different concepts that diverges much are less likely to end in the same topic.

Algorithm 2. CEP term weighting scheme

INPUT: Document m

OUTPUT: Document m after applying the CEP term weighting scheme

1: Compute max term frequency of document m: $M_m = \max\limits_{v} N_{m,v}$

2: Recognize entities in document m and form entity set $\widetilde{T}_m$

3: **for** each entity $t \in \widetilde{T}_m$ **do**

4:   Query concepts $concept(t)$ for entity t

5: **end for**

6: **for** each entity $t \in \widetilde{T}_m$ **do**

7:   **for** each entity $t' \in \widetilde{T}_m$ **do**

8:     **if** exists intersection between $concept(t)$ and $concept(t')$ **then**

9:       Add M_m entities of type t to document m

10:      **end if**

11:   **end for**

12: **end for**

13: **return** document m

Table 2. An example about companies and the recognized entities in it. Entities are in the left white rectangles and one of the concepts is shown in the right shaded ellipse for each entity.

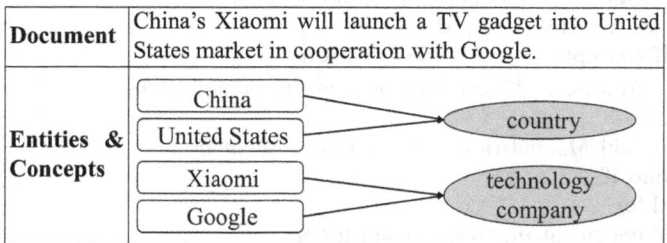

Document	China's Xiaomi will launch a TV gadget into United States market in cooperation with Google.
Entities & Concepts	China — United States — → country Xiaomi — Google — → technology company

More formally, the DCEP term weighting scheme is described as below. The DCEP scheme firstly counts the entities under each concept. In document m, if there exist $n_{m,i} \geq n_c$ entities that share the same concept $h_{m,i}$, the concept will be added to the concept set H_m and these entities will constitute the entity set $T'_{m,i}$. Hyperparameter n_c denotes the least number of entities belonging to a concept so that they can be promoted in a new duplicate document. The entities in document m that are not in the set $T'_{m,i}$ will end up in the set $T''_{m,i}$. The DCEP scheme duplicates document m for $|H_m|$ times, constructing a new list of documents $m' = \{m'_1, ..., m'_{|H_m|}\}$ to replace the original document m. Then, in each duplicate document $m'_i \in m'$, the frequency of each word is promoted as follows:

$$\widehat{N}_{m,i,w} = \begin{cases} N_{m,i,w} + n_{m,i} \cdot \max\limits_{v} N_{m,v} & \text{if } w \in T'_{m,i} \\ N_{m,i,w} + \max\limits_{v} N_{m,v} & \text{if } w \in T''_{m,i} \\ N_{m,i,w} & \text{if } w \in T_{m,i} \end{cases} \quad (5)$$

Algorithm 3. DCEP term weighting scheme

INPUT: Document m, hyperparameter n_c
OUTPUT: Document list m'
1: Compute max term frequency of document m: $M_m = \max_v N_{m,v}$
2: Recognize entities in document m and form entity set $\widetilde{T}_m$
3: **for** each entity $t \in \widetilde{T}_m$ **do**
4:    Query concepts $concept(t)$ for entity t
5:    Add concepts $concept(t)$ to concept set G_m
6: **end for**
7: **for** each concept $g_{m,i} \in G_m$ **do**
8:    **if** $n_{m,i} \geq n_c$ entities in $\widetilde{T}_m$ belong to concept $g_{m,i}$ **then**
9:        Add concept $g_{m,i}$ to concept set H_m
10:    **end if**
11: **end for**
12: Create empty document list m'
13: **if** $|H_m| \leq 1$ **then**
14:    $\tilde{m} = \text{CEP}(m)$ // See Alg. 2
15:    Add document $\tilde{m}$ to document list m'
16: **else**
17:    **for** each concept $h_{m,i} \in H_m$ **do**
18:        Make a duplicate document m'_i of document m
19:        **for** each entity $t \in \widetilde{T}_m$ **do**
20:            **if** concept $h_{m,i}$ in $concept(t)$ **then**
21:                Add $n_{m,i} \cdot M_m$ entities of type t to document m'_i
22:            **else**
23:                Add M_m entities of type t to document m'_i
24:            **end if**
25:        **end for**
26:        Add document m'_i to document list m'
27:    **end for**
28: **end if**
29: **return** Document list m'

---

where $\widehat{N}_{m,i,w}$ and $N_{m,i,w}$ denote the promoted and original frequency of word w in the duplicate document m'_i. $T_{m,i}$ is the set of ordinary words. If $|H_m| \leq 1$ in document m, it indicates that only one or no concept takes on a dominating role in the document. Under such a circumstance, the CEP scheme is still applied to document m.

Let us consider the document in Table 2 as an example. If $n_c \geq 3$, the document will simply apply the CEP scheme because there are not adequate entities under any concepts, and thus no duplicates of the document. If $n_c = 2$, there will be two concepts in H_m, "country" and "technology company", and therefore the document is duplicated twice. In the first duplicate document, entities "China" and "United States" are added more frequency because of the concept "country". Entities "Xiaomi" and "Google" from concept "technology company" are favored and promoted in the second duplicate. Compared to the CEP scheme which adds the same frequency to all the entities and tend to mix them together in the same topic with high probability, the DCEP scheme can deal with entities from different concepts in turn to form different coherent topics.

Algorithm 3 shows the detailed algorithm of applying the DCEP term weighting scheme to a document. DCEP-LDA model combines the DCEP term weighting scheme and LDA. The training algorithm of DCEP-LDA can be simply obtained by replacing the CEP scheme (Line 3–4) in Algorithm 1 with the DCEP scheme.

4 Experiment

We conduct experiments to evaluate the performance of our proposed CEP-LDA and DCEP-LDA models. NEP-LDA model [9] is the first term weighting topic model which treats entities as the informative terms and gives weights to entities by increasing frequencies without modifying the generative process of LDA. It is also a classical model that only seeks to generate coherent topics by giving more weights to the informative words without considering their concept information. Therefore, we choose NEP-LDA and standard LDA as baseline models.

4.1 Dataset and Concept Information

We perform experiments on two text datasets: 20 Newsgroups[1] with 18846 newsgroups documents and Reuters corpus[2] with 10788 news documents. They are widely employed in natural language processing and data mining tasks. To recognize the entities in documents, we adopt a named entity recognition tool, NeuroNER [4], on each document and utilize all types of the output entities. Further preprocessing procedures include tokenization, removal of stop words and terms with document frequency less than 3, removal of documents with less than 3 words, and lemmatization. Entity recognition is not performed on the datasets for standard LDA.

We employ the Microsoft Concept Graph [26] to query concept information of entities in the experiments. It is mined from billions of web pages and provides millions of concepts for considerable entities. Each entity recognized by NeuroNER is queried in Microsoft Concept Graph. For an entity, Microsoft Concept Graph returns a list of concepts sorted by the basic-level categorization (BLC) [24]. BLC simulates human preference when selecting appropriate concepts of an entity. The higher a BLC score of a concept is, the more people will have it in mind first. In the hope of discovering topics conforming to human cognition, we use the top 20 concepts of each entity sorted by BLC in the Microsoft Concept Graph. The concepts are not too specific that semantically similar entities for humans do not share the same concept, nor too abstract that the same concept exists between unrelated entities. We assume that two entities share the same concept if there is an intersection between their concept sets in Microsoft Concept Graph.

---

[1] http://qwone.com/~jason/20Newsgroups.
[2] http://www.nltk.org/book/ch02.html.

4.2 Experimental Setting

The performance of the topic models is usually measured by topic coherence. Prevailing coherence metrics include PMI [16], log conditional probability [14], normalized pointwise mutual information (NPMI) [11], C_v [19], etc. Empirically, C_v is verified to correlate the most with human judgment in interpretability and coherence of topics. Therefore, we use C_v as the coherence metric in the experiments. English Wikipedia from 2019/03/01 is served as the external corpus of C_v metric. Except when used to evaluate the results of the standard LDA, entity recognition is also performed on each article in Wikipedia.

For standard LDA, we use the implementation in Gensim[3] which is based on the online variational Bayes inference [7]. We implement term weighting topic model NEP-LDA by combining NEP scheme and LDA. Topic number K ranges from 20 to 100 with the interval of 20 in the experiments. Hyperparameters α and β are both set to $1/K$ as default in Gensim. For our proposed DCEP-LDA model, n_c varies from 2 to 6. The number of iterations through the corpus during training is 100. The topic coherence is evaluated on the top 10 words per topic, and the performance of a model is quantified by the average coherence of all the topics. For each model with different settings of topic number, we conduct experiments for 5 times under random initializations and then average the results.

4.3 Result

Quantitative Analysis. Table 3 and Table 4 depict the C_v coherence results of the baseline models and proposed CEP-LDA and DCEP-LDA models on 20 Newsgroups and Reuters corpus. From the results, we can observe that overall CEP-LDA and DCEP-LDA outperform LDA and NEP-LDA on topic coherence on both datasets. Averaging the results under all the topic numbers, the improvement of CEP-LDA over NEP-LDA is about 0.058 on 20 Newsgroups and 0.048 on Reuters corpus. In most settings, DCEP-LDA performs better than CEP-LDA. Considering the best performance of DCEP-LDA, DCEP-LDA achieves an average 0.038 and 0.081 higher score in C_v coherence than CEP-LDA on 20 Newsgroups and Reuters corpus. It confirms that by alleviating the influences of entities in unrelated topics, CEP-LDA can produce more coherent topics. Compared to CEP-LDA, DCEP-LDA further separates entities by their concepts to avoid entities from irrelevant concepts falling into the same topics, and improves the topic coherence.

On 20 Newsgroups dataset, NEP-LDA performs better than LDA when topic number is small but becomes worse when topic number is larger than 60, which is also demonstrated in the previous work [9]. It shows that attempting to increase the frequencies of entities without considering the concepts is not enough to improve the coherence. More scientifically, we design NEP-LDA* model in which each entity is promoted by twice the maximum term frequency of each document, and LDA** and NEP-LDA** in which each document is duplicated once

---

[3] https://radimrehurek.com/gensim/index.html.

Table 3. Mean and standard deviation of C_v coherence results on 20 Newsgroups with different topic number K. Except when topic number is 20, improvements of DCEP-LDA over LDA and NEP-LDA are statistically highly significant ($p < 0.01$) based on Student t-Test.

Model	$K = 20$	$K = 40$	$K = 60$	$K = 80$	$K = 100$
LDA	0.511 ± 0.011	0.495 ± 0.014	0.504 ± 0.007	0.491 ± 0.008	0.465 ± 0.011
LDA**	0.528 ± 0.014	0.521 ± 0.010	0.507 ± 0.008	0.498 ± 0.008	0.489 ± 0.007
NEP-LDA	0.574 ± 0.022	0.509 ± 0.019	0.467 ± 0.017	0.441 ± 0.007	0.459 ± 0.013
NEP-LDA*	0.558 ± 0.034	0.509 ± 0.010	0.488 ± 0.012	0.458 ± 0.010	0.443 ± 0.013
NEP-LDA**	0.588 ± 0.027	0.523 ± 0.013	0.497 ± 0.012	0.468 ± 0.008	0.461 ± 0.013
CEP-LDA	0.613 ± 0.015	0.559 ± 0.027	0.542 ± 0.016	0.509 ± 0.013	0.517 ± 0.013
DCEP-LDA ($n_c = 2$)	0.594 ± 0.019	0.594 ± 0.005	0.587 ± 0.019	0.548 ± 0.005	0.542 ± 0.003
DCEP-LDA ($n_c = 3$)	0.575 ± 0.027	0.603 ± 0.014	**0.589 ± 0.013**	**0.559 ± 0.010**	**0.546 ± 0.012**
DCEP-LDA ($n_c = 4$)	0.608 ± 0.022	0.607 ± 0.009	0.575 ± 0.006	0.555 ± 0.010	0.534 ± 0.006
DCEP-LDA ($n_c = 5$)	0.605 ± 0.029	**0.619 ± 0.016**	0.576 ± 0.018	0.544 ± 0.009	0.534 ± 0.005
DCEP-LDA ($n_c = 6$)	**0.619 ± 0.043**	0.606 ± 0.020	0.573 ± 0.011	0.542 ± 0.010	0.521 ± 0.012

based on the original document and the document after applying NEP scheme. According to Table 3 and Table 4, LDA**, NEP-LDA* and NEP-LDA** still behave worse than CEP-LDA and DCEP-LDA in most cases. It proves that our proposed models can effectively facilitate a topic to contain entities from similar concepts and gain more coherence.

Moreover, the results exhibit that with large topic numbers, DCEP-LDA reaches the optimal performance when $n_c = 3$ on 20 Newsgroups and when $n_c = 2$ on Reuters corpus. As the topic number becomes smaller, n_c needs to be larger to obtain higher coherence. The reason may be that when n_c varies, the different concepts used by DCEP-LDA influence the coherence of the output topics. More specifically, a topic model with a smaller topic number is supposed to produce broader topics like war, while a higher topic number corresponds to more specific topics such as World War I and World War II. Each entity also has broad and specific concepts. A broad concept embraces more entities and a specific concept includes less entities. n_c controls the least number of entities from the same concept to be promoted in a new duplicate document. When n_c is small, concepts involving a small number of entities, *i.e.*, specific concepts, may be widely used in DCEP-LDA model. Therefore, if topic number is high, entities belonging to those concepts tend to be assigned to the same specific topics, resulting in better coherence. Oppositely, when n_c is higher, the adopted broader concepts benefit generating broader topics if topic number is small.

However, a lower n_c implies more duplicate documents used to train the DCEP-LDA model and consumes more time. Table 5 shows the number of documents under different term weighting schemes on 20 Newsgroups dataset and the average training time of topic models. It shows that when n_c is small, the DCEP term weighting scheme does not significantly increase the number of documents and the training time but helps LDA to achieve outstanding performance. However, when $n_c = 2$, the number of documents is nearly doubled and the training

Table 4. Mean and standard deviation of C_v coherence results on Reuters corpus with different topic number K. Except when $n_c = 5$ and $n_c = 6$, improvements of DCEP-LDA over LDA and NEP-LDA are statistically highly significant ($p < 0.01$) based on Student t-Test.

Model	$K = 20$	$K = 40$	$K = 60$	$K = 80$	$K = 100$
LDA	0.423 ± 0.012	0.420 ± 0.005	0.417 ± 0.003	0.409 ± 0.008	0.409 ± 0.009
LDA**	0.436 ± 0.013	0.425 ± 0.008	0.427 ± 0.007	0.423 ± 0.003	0.412 ± 0.008
NEP-LDA	0.412 ± 0.024	0.420 ± 0.012	0.391 ± 0.003	0.373 ± 0.007	0.371 ± 0.010
NEP-LDA*	0.419 ± 0.030	0.411 ± 0.014	0.373 ± 0.010	0.362 ± 0.010	0.349 ± 0.013
NEP-LDA**	0.426 ± 0.013	0.419 ± 0.004	0.401 ± 0.008	0.381 ± 0.014	0.376 ± 0.010
CEP-LDA	0.482 ± 0.013	0.466 ± 0.009	0.428 ± 0.007	0.415 ± 0.014	0.414 ± 0.008
DCEP-LDA ($n_c = 2$)	0.536 ± 0.025	**0.531 ± 0.003**	**0.516 ± 0.005**	**0.510 ± 0.011**	**0.507 ± 0.008**
DCEP-LDA ($n_c = 3$)	**0.546 ± 0.012**	0.517 ± 0.014	0.492 ± 0.010	0.483 ± 0.015	0.462 ± 0.014
DCEP-LDA ($n_c = 4$)	0.510 ± 0.017	0.497 ± 0.014	0.450 ± 0.010	0.447 ± 0.009	0.427 ± 0.007
DCEP-LDA ($n_c = 5$)	0.504 ± 0.029	0.480 ± 0.014	0.437 ± 0.010	0.426 ± 0.018	0.413 ± 0.010
DCEP-LDA ($n_c = 6$)	0.499 ± 0.017	0.475 ± 0.018	0.439 ± 0.008	0.422 ± 0.014	0.425 ± 0.005

Table 5. Number of documents and the average run time under different models on 20 Newsgroups dataset with 60 topics.

Model	# Documents	Time
LDA	18182	294.0 s
NEP-LDA	18163	276.6 s
CEP-LDA	18163	274.8 s
DCEP-LDA ($n_c = 2$)	34045	1012.2 s
DCEP-LDA ($n_c = 3$)	20139	348.0 s
DCEP-LDA ($n_c = 4$)	18932	287.2 s
DCEP-LDA ($n_c = 5$)	18574	287.0 s
DCEP-LDA ($n_c = 6$)	18432	280.2 s

time is more than three times that of LDA. Hence there is a trade-off between time and topic coherence when choosing an appropriate hyperparameter n_c to train the DCEP-LDA model.

Qualitative Analysis. Table 6 demonstrates 10 words with the highest probabilities in five topics learned by DCEP-LDA, CEP-LDA and NEP-LDA model respectively on 20 Newsgroups with the topic number $K = 60$. Each column shows the most semantically related topics from the three topic models. The five topics can be summarized by baseball teams, baseball players, ice hockey players, comics and display format. In the first topic, what NEP-LDA finds at best is the mixture of teams such as "Dodgers", cities such as "Houston" and irrelevant word "Edu". DCEP-LDA discovers entities all about baseball teams, so the topic is more coherent. In the topic, half of the entities share the concept "Major League Baseball team" in Microsoft Concept Graph, and other shared

Table 6. Five topics learned from 20 Newsgroups by DCEP-LDA, CEP-LDA and NEP-LDA.

Model	DCEP-LDA ($n_c = 3$)				
Top words	Cincinnati Reds	Eddie Murray	Paul Coffey	Moon Knight	BMP
	Chicago White Sox	Ozzie Smith	Al Macinnis	Wolverine	GIF
	Seattle Mariners	Robin Yount	Adam Oates	New Mutants	TIFF
	Colorado Rockies	Dave Winfield	Dave Andreychuk	Silver Sable	GIFs
	St. Louis Cardinals	Dale Murphy	Pat Lafontaine	Sabretooth	PCX
	Milwaukee Brewers	Kirby Puckett	Cam Neely	Alpha Flight	JPEG
	Atlanta Braves	Yount	Brett Hull	New Warriors	VESA
	New York Mets	Jack Morris	Dale Hawerchuk	Jim Lee	image
	Toronto Blue Jays	Wade Boggs	Doug Gilmour	Rob Liefeld	TGA
	Detroit Tigers	Darrell Evans	Phil Housley	Deathlok	TARGA
C_v	0.958	0.829	0.846	0.805	0.763
Model	CEP-LDA				
Top words	New York Mets	Dave Winfield	Brett Hull	Moon Knight	BMP
	Los Angeles Dodgers	Ron Santo	Ron Francis	New Warriors	JPEG
	Atlanta Braves	Eddie Murray	Dave Andreychuk	Silver Sable	GIF
	Milwaukee Brewers	Seaver	Chris Chelios	Captain America	TIFF
	Toronto Blue Jays	Ryne Sandberg	Curtis Joseph	Sabretooth	GIFs
	California Angels	Darryl Strawberry	Brendan Shanahan	Erik Larsen	Atari ST
	Colorado Rockies	Roy Campanella	Doug Gilmour	Infinity Gauntlet	Amiga
	Detroit Tigers	Toronto	Paul Coffey	Wolverine	UUCP
	Kansas City Royals	Ozzie Smith	Al Macinnis	New Mutants	TGA
	Minnesota Twins	Dick Allen	Adam Oates	Alpha Flight	Windows
C_v	0.957	0.425	0.868	0.793	0.595
Model	NEP-LDA				
Top words	Edu	Era	Owen	Wolverine	JPEG
	Dodgers	Morris	Jun	Liefeld	GIF
	Houston	Roger	Chicago Tribune	New Mutants	TIFF
	St. Louis	Red Sox	Cal	Sabretooth	UUCP
	Bonds	Utah	True	Bagged	BMP
	Angels	Clemens	Doug Gilmour	Avengers	TARGA
	Cleveland	Alomar	Ron Francis	Star Trek	Simtel20
	hit	Jays	Bos	Miller	image
	Reds	Larson	Scott	Omega Men	JFIF
	Cincinnati	Prof	Joe Mullen	Alpha Flight	GIFs
C_v	0.569	0.303	0.149	0.408	0.554

concepts include "league team", "professional sport franchise", etc. CEP-LDA find the coherent topic of baseball teams as well. In the second topic, entities from DCEP-LDA are all about baseball players. However, in CEP-LDA, city "Toronto" invades the baseball-related topic. NEP-LDA still outputs the combination of entities about baseball and cities which form the most incoherent topic. In the third topic, DCEP-LDA and CEP-LDA present entities all about ice hockey players, but there are irrelevant entities such as the daily newspaper "Chicago Tribune" in the topic from NEP-LDA. DCEP-LDA shows entities all about Marvel comics and display formats in the fourth and last topics. However, noisy entities such as computer system "Atari ST" appear in last topic from CEP-LDA and irrelevant entities such as "Bagged" and "Simtel20" appear in the last two topics from NEP-LDA. On the whole, DCEP-LDA captures more coherent topics than CEP-LDA and NEP-LDA which performs the worst.

5 Conclusion

Term weighting schemes are important to topic models in discovering latent topics in text corpus. To help topic models to generate more coherent topics, in this paper we propose CEP as a term weighting scheme which gives more weights to entities from concepts that reveal the topics of a document. We further propose DCEP term weighting scheme to reduce the co-occurrence of entities from irrelevant concepts and separate them into different topics. We develop CEP-LDA and DCEP-LDA topic models, and experimental results on 20 Newsgroups and Reuters corpus show that they both can produce more coherent topics. For future work, we plan to apply our proposed term weighting schemes to more topic models to explore their flexibility.

Acknowlegement. This work was supported by the Fundamental Research Funds for the Central Universities, SCUT (No. 2017ZD048, D2182480), the Science and Technology Planning Project of Guangdong Province (No. 2017B050506004), the Science and Technology Programs of Guangzhou (No. 201704030076, 201802010027, 201902010046), the Hong Kong Research Grants Council (project no. PolyU 1121417), and an internal research grant from the Hong Kong Polytechnic University (project 1.9B0V).

References

1. Arun, K., Govindan, V.: A hybrid deep learning architecture for latent topic-based image retrieval. Data Sci. Eng. **3**(2), 166–195 (2018). https://doi.org/10.1007/s41019-018-0063-7
2. Bekoulis, G., Rousseau, F.: Graph-based term weighting scheme for topic modeling. In: 2016 IEEE 16th International Conference on Data Mining Workshops (ICDMW), pp. 1039–1044. IEEE (2016)
3. Blei, D.M., Ng, A.Y., Jordan, M.I.: Latent Dirichlet allocation. J. Mach. Learn. Res. **3**(Jan), 993–1022 (2003)
4. Dernoncourt, F., Lee, J.Y., Szolovits, P.: Neuroner: an easy-to-use program for named-entity recognition based on neural networks. In: Proceedings of the 2017 Conference on Empirical Methods in Natural Language Processing: System Demonstrations, pp. 97–102 (2017)
5. He, J., Liu, H., Zheng, Y., Tang, S., He, W., Du, X.: Bi-labeled LDA: inferring interest tags for non-famous users in social network. Data Sci. Eng. **5**, 1–21 (2019). https://doi.org/10.1007/s41019-019-00113-0
6. Heinrich, G.: Parameter estimation for text analysis. Technical report (2005)
7. Hoffman, M., Bach, F.R., Blei, D.M.: Online learning for latent Dirichlet allocation. In: Advances in Neural Information Processing Systems, pp. 856–864 (2010)
8. Kai, Y., Yi, C., Zhenhong, C., Ho-fung, L., Raymond, L.: Exploring topic discriminating power of words in latent Dirichlet allocation. In: Proceedings of COLING 2016, the 26th International Conference on Computational Linguistics: Technical Papers, pp. 2238–2247 (2016)
9. Krasnashchok, K., Jouili, S.: Improving topic quality by promoting named entities in topic modeling. In: Proceedings of the 56th Annual Meeting of the Association for Computational Linguistics (Volume 2: Short Papers), pp. 247–253 (2018)

10. Lan, M., Tan, C.L., Su, J., Lu, Y.: Supervised and traditional term weighting methods for automatic text categorization. IEEE Trans. Pattern Anal. Mach. Intell. **31**(4), 721–735 (2008)
11. Lau, J.H., Newman, D., Baldwin, T.: Machine reading tea leaves: automatically evaluating topic coherence and topic model quality. In: Proceedings of the 14th Conference of the European Chapter of the Association for Computational Linguistics, pp. 530–539 (2014)
12. Lee, S., Kim, J., Myaeng, S.H.: An extension of topic models for text classification: a term weighting approach. In: 2015 International Conference on Big Data and Smart Computing (BIGCOMP), pp. 217–224. IEEE (2015)
13. Li, X., Zhang, A., Li, C., Ouyang, J., Cai, Y.: Exploring coherent topics by topic modeling with term weighting. Inf. Process. Manag. **54**(6), 1345–1358 (2018)
14. Mimno, D., Wallach, H.M., Talley, E., Leenders, M., McCallum, A.: Optimizing semantic coherence in topic models. In: Proceedings of the Conference on Empirical Methods in Natural Language Processing, pp. 262–272. Association for Computational Linguistics (2011)
15. Murphy, G.L.: The Big Book of Concepts. MIT Press, Boston (2002)
16. Newman, D., Lau, J.H., Grieser, K., Baldwin, T.: Automatic evaluation of topic coherence. In: Human Language Technologies: The 2010 Annual Conference of the North American Chapter of the Association for Computational Linguistics, pp. 100–108. Association for Computational Linguistics (2010)
17. Ren, D., Cai, Y., Lei, X., Xu, J., Li, Q., Leung, H.: A multi-encoder neural conversation model. Neurocomputing **358**, 344–354 (2019)
18. Robertson, S.: Understanding inverse document frequency: on theoretical arguments for IDF. J. Doc. **60**(5), 503–520 (2004)
19. Röder, M., Both, A., Hinneburg, A.: Exploring the space of topic coherence measures. In: Proceedings of the eighth ACM International Conference on Web Search and Data Mining, pp. 399–408. ACM (2015)
20. Salton, G., Buckley, C.: Term-weighting approaches in automatic text retrieval. Inf. Process. Manag. **24**(5), 513–523 (1988)
21. Truica, C.O., Radulescu, F., Boicea, A.: Comparing different term weighting schemas for topic modeling. In: 2016 18th International Symposium on Symbolic and Numeric Algorithms for Scientific Computing (SYNASC), pp. 307–310. IEEE (2016)
22. Wang, T., Cai, Y., Leung, H., Cai, Z., Min, H.: Entropy-based term weighting schemes for text categorization in VSM. In: 2015 IEEE 27th International Conference on Tools with Artificial Intelligence (ICTAI), pp. 325–332. IEEE (2015)
23. Wang, X., McCallum, A.: Topics over time: a non-Markov continuous-time model of topical trends. In: Proceedings of the 12th ACM SIGKDD International Conference on Knowledge Discovery and Data Mining, pp. 424–433. ACM (2006)
24. Wang, Z., Wang, H., Wen, J.R., Xiao, Y.: An inference approach to basic level of categorization. In: Proceedings of the 24th ACM International on Conference on Information and Knowledge Management, pp. 653–662. ACM (2015)
25. Wilson, A.T., Chew, P.A.: Term weighting schemes for latent Dirichlet allocation. In: Human Language Technologies: The 2010 Annual Conference of the North American Chapter of the Association for Computational Linguistics, pp. 465–473. Association for Computational Linguistics (2010)
26. Wu, W., Li, H., Wang, H., Zhu, K.Q.: Probase: a probabilistic taxonomy for text understanding. In: Proceedings of the 2012 ACM SIGMOD International Conference on Management of Data, pp. 481–492. ACM (2012)

27. Yang, K., Cai, Y., Huang, D., Li, J., Zhou, Z., Lei, X.: An effective hybrid model for opinion mining and sentiment analysis. In: 2017 IEEE International Conference on Big Data and Smart Computing (BigComp), pp. 465–466. IEEE (2017)
28. Yang, K., Cai, Y., Leung, H., Lau, R.Y., Li, Q.: ITWF: a framework to apply term weighting schemes in topic model. Neurocomputing **350**, 248–260 (2019)

How to Generate Reasonable Texts with Controlled Attributes

Yanan Zheng[1], Yan Wang[2], Lijie Wen[1(✉)], and Jianmin Wang[1]

[1] School of Software, Tsinghua University, Beijing, China
zyanan93@gmail.com, {wenlj,jimwang}@tsinghua.edu.cn
[2] School of Information, Central University of Finance and Economics, Beijing, China
dayanking@gmail.com

Abstract. The controllable text generation (CTG) task is crucial for text-related applications, such as goal-oriented dialogue systems and text style-transfer applications, etc. However, existing CTG methods commonly ignore the co-occurrence dependencies between multiple controlled attributes, which are implicit in domain knowledge. As a result, rarely co-occurring controlled values are highly likely to be given by users, which finally leads to non-committal generated texts that are out of control. To address this problem, we initially propose the Dependency-aware Controllable Text Generation (DCTG) model that reduces trivial generations by automatically learning the co-occurrence dependencies and adjusting rarely co-occurring controlled values. Our DCTG highlights in (1) modeling the co-occurrence dependencies between controlled attributes with neural networks, (2) integrating dependency losses to guide each component of our model to collaboratively work for generating reasonable texts based on the learned dependencies, and (3) proposing a novel *Reasonableness* metric measuring to which degree generations comply with real co-occurrence dependencies. Experiments prove that DCTG outperforms state-of-the-art baselines on three datasets in multiple aspects.

Keywords: Controllable text generation · Co-occurrence dependency · Reasonableness

1 Introduction

The task of controllable text generation (CTG) [6] enables machines to automatically generate texts under the condition that specific attributes can be manually controlled. It builds the foundation of multiple advanced applications, including goal-oriented dialogue systems [13] and text style transfer [3], etc. Currently, the CTG has attracted much attention from both academia and industry.

There already have been pioneering works [6,12] for CTG, which are mainly contributed by generative neural models. They are generally based on the sequence-to-sequence framework, where they first encode required contextual

---

Y. Zheng and Y. Wang—Both are first authors with equal contributions.

© Springer Nature Switzerland AG 2020
Y. Nah et al. (Eds.): DASFAA 2020, LNCS 12113, pp. 245–262, 2020.
https://doi.org/10.1007/978-3-030-59416-9_15

information into real-valued vectors (denoted as hidden representations) and then decode them into texts. Particularly, for purposes of control, the hidden representations are made **disentangled**. It means certain attributes would be explicitly associated with specific dimensions (sets of dimensions) of hidden representations. In this way, manually modifying the values of corresponding dimensions would perturb generated texts in terms of related attributes in an interpretable way.

Despite significant advances, they're still far from being practically applicable. Existing works usually take discrete value forms for controlled attributes, which contradicts the fact that text-related attributes are more of continue values and change with varying degree. Besides, multiple controlled attributes are assumed to be independent. Namely, the attribute representations are supposed to independently learn respective attribute values, without considering the **co-occurrence dependencies** between them. For instance, intuitively attribute value *sentiment = positive* appears more frequently together with *location = park*, but rarely co-occurs with *location = cemetery*. Unfortunately, ignoring such co-occurrence dependencies is problematic. When giving such rarely co-occurred attribute values, the CTG process is highly likely to fail, generating non-committal texts that are out of control, as Fig. 1 shows.

Cases	Controlled Attribute Values	Generated Texts
Out-of-control case	sentiment="positive"	I have no idea
	location = "cemetery"	That's alright
Under-control case	sentiment="positive"	I really like to play in the part
	location = "park"	It is great to have a picnic here

Fig. 1. Exemplar samples to demonstrate how co-occurrence dependencies effect generated texts. Commonly/rarely co-occurred attribute combination values are highly likely to generate under-control/out-of-control cases that hold specific controlled information/trivial information.

To further understand it, potential explanations of the problem indicated in Fig. 1 are as follows. Since controlled attribute values are independently considered, there could be generating representations of both commonly co-occurred (reasonable) values (e.g., *sentiment = positive* and *location = park*) and rarely co-occurred (unreasonable) value combinations (e.g., *sentiment = positive* and *location = cemetery*). When decoding with reasonable representations, it will naturally generate the text *I really enjoy playing with friends in the park*, which is of high positiveness and high relevance with *park* at the same time. However, it is hard to find plausible sentences that carry two unmatched attribute values at the same time. Thus, when decoding with unreasonable representations, it will struggle to balance between them, as is argued in [4], and finally generate a sentence that is ambiguous on both attributes, leading to trivial generation *I have no idea.*

Based on the above analysis, we address the challenges above. We are inspired to particularly consider co-occurrence dependencies when constructing disentangled representations, such that models have the ability to adjust unreasonable representations and will further reduce generating trivial/out-of-control texts. Note that adjustment by co-occurrence dependencies is supposed to be slight without causing drastic changes and damaging controllability. Thus discrete representations used in previous methods [6,10] are not suitable any more. Motivated by the work [1] that operates in a continuous real-valued space, unlike previous works that give controlled attribute signals using designated discrete one-hot vectors, here we use sentences that holds controlled attribute signals to replace the discrete ones. Then our model is able to extract the continuous real-valued disentangled representations carrying given controlled signals from the sentences, with co-occurrence dependencies considered as the same time. Figure 2 illustrates how we extract two controlled signals in a continuous manner from given sentences while considering the co-occurrence dependencies between them. Note that $v_{sentiment}$ and $v_{location}$ would be eventually adjusted based on the co-occurrence dependency between the two attributes.

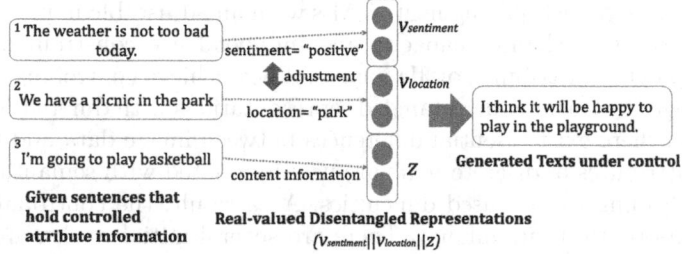

Fig. 2. Illustrative cases for how the proposed method works. Input sentences 1 and 2 specify controlled attribute values (i.e., $v_{sentiment}$ and $v_{location}$ represent *sentiment = positive* and *location = park*). Sentence 3 is encoded as z for content preservation. The concatenated vector $v_{sentiment}||v_{location}||z$ forms disentangled representations and are for generating controlled texts.

The co-occurrence dependencies between the attributes of a real-life dataset are usually more complicated than the above examples for illustration. On the one hand, the number of combinations of attribute values could be quite large; on the other hand, many dependencies are implicit in domain knowledge. It is difficult for ordinary users to identify co-occurrence dependencies for text generation and thus our work is necessary.

In this paper, we initially propose the Dependency-aware Controllable Text Generation model (DCTG). To the best of our knowledge, this is the first work to identify the problem of ignoring co-occurrence dependencies between attribute values in CTG. It is based on the generative variational auto-encoder framework and combines discriminative networks. DCTG highlights in following aspects. **First**, DCTG considers co-occurrence dependencies between controlled attributes by introducing a dependency-aware attribute network. **Second**, to collaboratively consider attribute values and reasonably extract/adjust their representations, a mutual dependency loss is integrated to guide the training of attribute network. **Third**, to quantitatively evaluate the compliance with real co-occurrence dependencies, we further propose the metric, *reasonableness*. **Fourth**, for effective optimization of DCTG, we present a staged algorithm extended from wake-sleep by augmenting it from two phrases into multiple ones. Experiments prove that our method significantly outperforms state-of-the-arts in multiple aspects under various practical scenarios.

2   Related Work

The controllable generation task has achieved promising progress in computer vision. For instance, the DC-IGN [8] generates new images of the same object with variations in pose and lighting. The InfoGAN [2] extends the generative adversarial net(GAN) by maximizing mutual information between latent variables and observations, where it achieves controlling styles/shapes when generating digit images and controlling hairstyles/sunglasses when generating human face images. The β-VAE [5] augments VAEs with an adjustable hyper-parameter that balances latent channel capacity and independence constraints, and succeeds manipulating attributes of 3D images. They achieve controlling the generation of images by learning disentangled representations with different strategies.

However, there exist essential differences between image data and text data, where the attributes of discrete texts are usually related with semantics and are subjective, leading to increased difficulties. As a result, the controllable generation of texts is still in its infancy. There are several initial works, and most of them are based on the Seq2Seq framework and simply incorporate controlling information to generate specific texts. For instance, [14] generates preferred product reviews by adding metadata, such as user, product and rating. [12] directly joins topic information into Seq2Seq to generate informative and interesting responses. However, the deterministic nature of Seq2Seq-based methods limits their performance. To overcome it, several probabilistic models are also proposed. The SentiGAN [11] extends GAN to have multiple generators, each focusing on generating texts with specific sentiment. Unluckily, GAN-based methods learn probabilistic features in an implicit way, and appear to be unstable. The majority are based on VAEs that explicitly learn probabilistic features, e.g., [6] achieve controlling the sentiment of generated texts by combining the VAE and discriminative networks that effectively impose sentiment semantics.

While these works are impressive, they are still far from being practically applicable. First, they only consider single controlled attribute. Second, they make strong assumptions that all controlled attributes are independent, which ignores natural co-occurrence dependencies between attributes of texts. It would ultimately leads to non-committal generated texts that are out of control. Our work exactly focuses on this problem, and keeps controllability of multiple attributes by emphasizing co-occurrence dependencies between them.

3 Dependency-Aware Controllable Text Generation

3.1 Problem Formalization

We first introduce notations and formally define our problem. This work mainly focus on cases with two controlled attributes. Given some dataset $\mathcal{D} = \{(x_i, l_{a,i}, l_{b,i})\}_{i=1}^{N}$, consisting of N i.i.d instances where each contains one sentence x_i and two attribute labels $l_{a,i}$ and $l_{b,i}$, the **goal of CTG** is to build a probabilistic model to describe the generative process of texts, such that one could use it to generate new texts with the same attributes as are given/controlled.

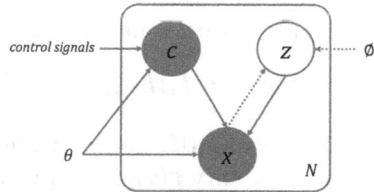

Fig. 3. Our PGM. Solid lines are generative models parameterized by θ. Dashed lines are inference models parameterized by ϕ. Blue circles are observed variables and white are unobserved ones. (Color figure online)

Our CTG problem can be represented with three variables: controlled attribute-set variable c carrying control signals, a latent variable z that captures other latent information than attributes, and observed sentence variable x. Note that the controlled attribute-set variable could represent more than one attributes, e.g., in this case there are two attributes (denoted as a and b), c is of pair value $c = (a, b)$. The whole process can be represented by the probabilistic graphical model (PGM) in Fig. 3. Specifically, the process is as follows.

1. Manually provide the pair value c_i, where it carries two attribute values that we expect x_i to carry.
2. Sample a latent representation z_i from prior $p(z)$.
3. Generate a sentence x_i through $p(x|z = z_i, c = c_i)$.

It defines the joint generative model $p(z, x, c) = p(z)p(c)p(x|z, c)$. We would like to use deep neural networks to model the probability distribution items. We refer to $p(x|z, c)$ as the *decoder network*, where it generates texts conditioned on inputs. We denote $p(c)$ as the *dependency-aware attribute network*, where it extracts attribute representations from given sentences that carry controlled signals. To model the distribution of z, we introduce an *stochastic encoder network with adversary* representing the approximated posterior distribution $q(z|x)$. Details will be introduced next. Note that for brevity, we omit subscript i that indicate number of instances.

3.2 Overview Architecture

Preliminary: Variational Encoder-Decoder. We propose Dependency-aware Controllable Text Generation (DCTG) model. DCTG is based on the variational encoder-decoder (VED) [1,9]. It consists of a stochastic encoder and a decoder.

Stochastic Encoder. It uses a recurrent network (e.g., GRU). Given an input sentence $x = \{w_1...w_T\}$, it encodes it into a list of hidden states h_i, as follows.

$$h_t = f_{\text{GRU}_1}(h_{t-1}, e(w_t)) \tag{1}$$

where $e(w_t)$ is word embedding of w_t, and h_t is the tth hidden states. The last encoder hidden states h_T is usually considered the summary of the whole sentence. It is used to infer the parameters of latent distribution (e.g., mean μ and variance σ^2 of a Gaussian). Thus, latent variable z can be sampled from it. f_μ and f_σ are two-layer perceptrons with relu activations.

$$\mu = f_\mu(h_T), \quad \log \sigma^2 = f_\sigma(h_T), \quad z \sim N(\mu, \sigma^2) \tag{2}$$

Decoder. The decoder uses another GRU. During training, it generates words by sampling from generative probability $p(\hat{x}_t|x_{<t}, z)$ which is as follows.

$$s_t = f_{\text{GRU}_2}(s_{t-1}, e(w_t), z), \hat{x}_t \sim p(\hat{x}_t|x_{<t}, z) = softmax(f_t(s_t)) \tag{3}$$

where f_{GRU_2} is recurrent unit for decoder, s_t is decoder hidden states at the t step, f_t is a fully connected layer and *softmax* is soft-max operation. During inferring, the new sequence is generated by sampling from $p(\hat{x}_t|\hat{x}_{<t}, z)$, as follows.

$$s_t = f_{\text{GRU}_2}(s_{t-1}, z), \hat{x}_t \sim p(\hat{x}_t|\hat{x}_{<t}, z) = softmax(f_t(s_t))$$

Loss. The network is optimized by minimizing a lower bound on log-likelihood.

$$\mathcal{L}_{elbo} = \mathbb{E}_{q(z|x)}[\log p(\hat{x}|z)] + KL(q(z|x)||p(z)) \leq \log p(x) \tag{4}$$

Overview Architecture of DCTG. Figure 4 shows its architecture. DCTG is based on the VED and particularly adopts a stochastic encoder with adversary and a dependency-aware attribute network. It highlights in several aspects.

1. For controllability, DCTG follows the idea of individually learning attribute representations and concatenate them all, to form disentangled latent representations (In Fig. 4, the convolutional modules learns attribute representations respectively. $z||v_a||v_b$ is the final disentangled representations).
2. For disentanglement, the encoder adopts the adversarial strategy [3] to exclude controlled attribute information from z (The facilitated adversarial module removes attribute-related information from z).
3. To consider co-occurrence dependencies between attributes and make it agree with real situations, DCTG adds the dependency modules along with convolutional modules to add constraints.

4. To ensure controlled attribute signals being flexibly represented and adjusted, we propose to provide sentences carrying related attribute values instead of discrete one-hot vectors. Controlled attribute signals are extracted from sentences (v_a and v_b).

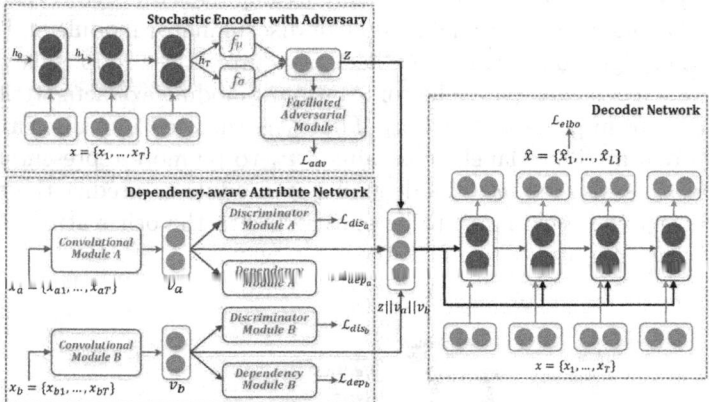

Fig. 4. DCTG overall architecture. It has an stochastic encoder with adversary, a decoder and a dependency-aware attribute network. The attribute network particularly introduces dependency modules to capture the co-occurrence dependencies between two attributes.

3.3 Stochastic Encoder with Adversary

Comparing with classic stochastic encoder in general VED, this stochastic encoder with adversary holds different goals. The former aims to encode all information from inputs, while the latter aims to selectively encode information, with designated attribute information removed.

While most parts are the same as is illustrated in Subsect. 3.2, this component additionally introduce a adversarial module. After obtaining the latent representation z according to Eq. 1 and Eq. 2, it further feeds z into adversarial modules (a two-layer perceptron) to predict controlled attribute labels. And it aims to minimize the predict loss, namely to make it hard to predict attribute labels. In this way, z is not able to predict attribute labels, and thus is forced to rarely learned attribute-related information.

3.4 Dependency-Aware Attribute Network

The dependency-aware attribute network aims to extract attribute signals in the form of real-valued continuous vectors from given sentences that carry controlling information. In the case of two controlled attributes, there are two input sentences, each related to one controlled attribute, respectively $x_{a_i} = \{w_{a_{i,1}}...w_{a_{i,T}}\}$ for attribute a and $x_{b_i} = \{w_{b_{i,1}}...x_{w_{i,T}}\}$ for b. It then outputs the extracted attribute representations, which is (v_{a_i}, v_{b_i}). Unlike previous work where both representations are independent, v_{a_i} and v_{b_i} from dependency-aware attribute network match each other.

As Fig. 4 shows, each attribute basically associates with a group of modules, each group having a convolutional module, a discriminator module and a dependency module. Figure 5 illustrates detailed structure of one group (take the group for attribute a as an example). The convolutional module extracts attribute representation v_a from given sentence x_a. The v_a is then fed into discriminator to predicts its real attribute label, constraining v_a to be more representative with attribute a. v_a is also fed into the dependency module to predict the real label of another attribute, guiding v_a to be matched with the other attribute values. The other group for attribute b is in the same way.

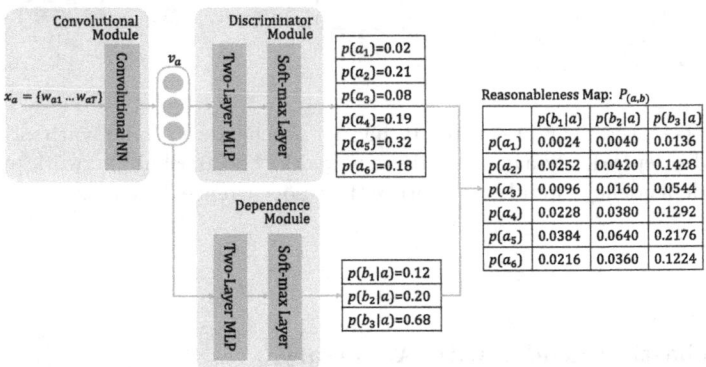

Fig. 5. Dependency-aware attribute network. For each attribute, it requires a convolutional, a discriminator and a dependency module. The convolutional module extracts real-valued attribute representation v_a from the given sentence x_a that carry controlled attribute signals. The v_a is then fed into discriminator to predicts its real attribute label. v_a is also fed into the dependency module to predict the real label of another attribute.

Convolutional Modules. They are fed with controlling sentences (x_a and x_b) and extract corresponding attribute representations (v_a and v_b). The process is as follows, where f_{cnn_1} and f_{cnn_2} are convolutional units.

$$v_a = f_{cnn_1}(x_a), \quad v_b = f_{cnn_2}(x_b)$$

Discriminator Modules. They use attribute representations (v_a and v_b) to discriminate respective attribute as given labels (l_a and l_b). They are as follows, where f_{s_1} and f_{s_2} are soft-max operations, f_{t_1} is fully connected layers with relu activations and f_{t_2} is fully connected layer with soft-max function.

$$p(a) = f_{s_1}(f_{t_1}(v_a)), p(b) = f_{s_2}(f_{t_2}(v_b))$$

Dependency Modules. Considering that co-occurrence dependencies are implicit and subtle, and cannot be expressed with descriptive rules, the most intuitive approach is to modeling them from a probabilistic perspective, i.e., modeling conditional probabilities between controlled attributes. Take attribute a as an example, the module is input with representations v_a and predicts the distribution over the co-occurred attribute b, where it learns $p(b|v_a)$. The dependency module for attribute b is formulated in similar way, $p(a|v_b)$.

$$p(b|v_a) = f_{s_3}(f_{t_3}(v_a)), \quad p(a|v_b) = f_{s_4}(f_{t_4}(v_b))$$

where f_{s_3} and f_{s_4} are fully connections with soft-max operations, f_{t_3} and f_{t_4} are full layer connections with relu activations. Special cases are that when attributes are independent, dependency modules will learn nothing from data, thus the model degenerates into those with independence assumptions [5,6].

Reasonableness. To measure to which degree the controlled attribute-values of sentence agree with the co-occurrence dependencies behind dataset, we propose a new metric *reasonableness* (R for short), where it is $R(x) = p_{(a,b)}(x)$ defined in a continuous space. It is specifically the joint probability over extracted attribute values and can be directly learned by our dependency-aware attribute networks by multiplying both values $p(a,b) = p(a)p(b|a)$, as is indicated by Fig. 5.

3.5   Staged Optimization Procedure

DCTG requires special optimization strategy since it consists of modules that collaboratively work with different goals. Inspired by the wake-sleep algorithm [7] which trains multi-layer networks with stochastic neurons in an unsupervised way, we propose a staged optimization algorithm extended from it.

Encoder. The encoder network has two parameter sets θ_{enc} for recurrent encoding module and θ_{adv} for adversarial modules. The recurrent encoding module maximizes $\mathcal{L}_{enc}(\theta_{enc})$ in Eq. 5, where it has two terms respectively the $\mathcal{L}_{elbo}$ same as Eq. 4 and $\mathcal{L}_{adv}$. λ is a balancing hyper-parameter ranging from 0 to 1, and α is a KL weight variable to prevent KL vanishing [1]. The facilitated adversarial module minimizes $\mathcal{L}_{adv}(\theta_{adv})$.

$$
\begin{aligned}
\mathcal{L}_{enc} &= \mathcal{L}_{elbo} + \lambda * \mathcal{L}_{adv} \\
\mathcal{L}_{adv} &= -(\mathbb{E}[\log p(l_a|z)] + \mathbb{E}[\log p(l_b|z)]) \\
\mathcal{L}_{elbo} &= \mathbb{E}_{q_\phi(z|x)}[\log p_\theta(x|c, z)] - \alpha \mathrm{KL}[q_\phi(z|x)||p_\theta(z)]
\end{aligned}
\tag{5}
$$

Dependency-aware Attribute Network. Three parameter sets are θ_{con} for convolutional modules, θ_{dis} for discriminator modules and θ_{dep} for dependency modules. The dependency modules maximize $\mathcal{L}_{dep}(\theta_{dep})$ as Eq. 6. The discriminators maximize $\mathcal{L}_{dis}(\theta_{dis})$ in Eq. 7. The convolutional module maximizes $\mathcal{L}_{con}(\theta_{con})$ in Eq. 8, where β is a balancing hyper-parameter in $[0, 1]$.

$$\mathcal{L}_{dep_a}(\theta_{dep_a}) = \mathbb{E}[\log p(l_b|a)], \mathcal{L}_{dep_b}(\theta_{dep_b}) = \mathbb{E}[\log p(l_a|b)] \tag{6}$$

$$\mathcal{L}_{dis_a}(\theta_{dis_a}) = \mathbb{E}[\log p(l_a|a)], \mathcal{L}_{dis_b}(\theta_{dis_b}) = \mathbb{E}[\log p(l_b|b)] \tag{7}$$

$$\mathcal{L}_{con_a}(\theta_{con_a}) = \mathcal{L}_{dis_a} + \beta * \mathcal{L}_{dep_a}, \mathcal{L}_{con_b}(\theta_{con_b}) = \mathcal{L}_{dis_b} + \beta * \mathcal{L}_{dep_b} \tag{8}$$

Decoder. The decoder is optimized by maximizing $\mathcal{L}_{elbo}(\theta_{dec})$.

For training, it follows a similar strategy as the wake-sleep algorithm, but is extended from previous two stages into multiple stages, where each stage optimizes one module using corresponding loss mentioned above. Empirically, modules require different training time to reach optima, where generative parts (encoder and decoder) trains slower while attribute networks train faster. However, we expect all modules to be fully trained approximately at the same time. Motivated by work [6], we pre-train generative parts until near convergence and then start collaboratively train all components until they converge.

4   Experiments

4.1   Experimental Setup

Datasets. This work deals with a more complicated scenario (two controlled attributes), thus datasets in previous works that handle single attribute are no longer suitable. We collect three datasets using widely-accepted datasets in text classification. All the datasets consists of real-life texts with more than one human-annotated attributes. Their statistics are shown in Table 1.

MOV. It is collected from Large Movie Review Dataset[1]. Each review has a sentiment label (positive or negative, 2 classes) and movie score label (0–7, 8 classes). The two attributes conform to the fact that positive reviews are more likely to be related to higher rating scores and vice versa.

YELP. We collect a dataset from YELP website[2] by randomly selecting restaurant reviews with rating scores (0–4, 5 classes) and quality levels (high/medium/low,3 classes). Empirical co-occurrence dependencies are that reviews indicating better quality usually associate with higher restaurant rating scores.

SYN. A synthetic dataset is built by partially combining YELP and IMDB[3]. All classes are ensured to be balanced. Thus, each data has a textual review and

---

[1] http://ai.stanford.edu/~amaas/data/sentiment/.
[2] https://www.yelp.com/dataset.
[3] https://www.imdb.com/interfaces/.

two distinct attributes, the subject of review (movie or restaurant, 2 classes) and the rating score (5 classes). The dependencies are that, according to results in psychology, people tend to be more harsh rating movies than rating restaurants.

Table 1. Statistics of experimental datasets.

dataset	# train	# valid	# test	# vocab
MOV	25.0K	10.0K	15.0K	42.0K
YELP	8.1K	1.0K	3.5K	24.0K
SYN	36.0K	5.0K	5.0K	36.0K

Baselines. We collect the following state-of-the-arts as baselines for comparison. They are based on VAE framework and allow controlling multiple attributes, thus are comparable with our DCTG. (1) Controlled text generation (HuCTG for short) [6]: It combines VED and discriminative networks. But, it independently considers controlled attributes. (2) Conditional VAE (CVAE) [10]: It is based on variational neural models and incorporate attributes as conditions.

Implementation Details. For fair comparison, we implement DCTG and baselines using Tensorflow 1.4.0 in a Linux server with three GTX 1080Ti GPUs. We use a valid set to tune parameters and finally measure the performance on the test set. To avoid randomness, each experiment is performed 6 times and the average results are reported. For pre-processing, we follow [6] to transform all letters to lowercase and map all out-of-vocabulary words to a special token <unk>. Models are optimized using Adam with a learning rate of 0.001. We employ single-layer unidirectional GRUs for both encoder and decoder, respectively with 128 and 256 units. The embedding dimension is 128. The dimension of latent variable z and attribute variables are all set 16. The CNN has 128 filters with filter size to be 3,4,5. For DCTG, it has attribute networks with 128/64 dimensions for two-layer MLPs. The batch size is fixed to be 128. The maximum lengths are set to be 15/30/24 for MOV/YELP/SYN, which are average lengths of datasets. All texts are padded or truncated to maximum lengths. To cope with KL vanishing, the KL annealing technique [1] is used by increasing the weight of KL term from 0 to 1 from 6000th step. During training, gradients clipping is used with maximum gradient norm 5. During inferring, beam search decoding is used with beam size to be 5.

4.2   Metric-Based Evaluation

Automatic Metrics. We first perform automatic evaluation from two aspects, respectively **generative performance** and **control performance**.

Generative performance means evaluating the quality of generated texts, in other words, whether generated contents are relevant and grammatical. We adopt widely-accepted metrics: per-word perplexity (PPL) and word error rate (WER).

1. PPL measures how well generative probabilistic models predict target texts. Given a predicted text $\{w_1...w_N\}$ and a well-trained model p, it is defined as the exponentiation of word entropy, which is $\text{PPL} = 2^{H[p(w)]} = 2^{-\frac{1}{N}\sum_{n=1}^{N}\log p(w_n|w_{<n})}$. Smaller PPL means better generative performance.
2. WER is also widely-accepted for generative performance. Given predicted text and target text, by comparing them word-by-word, there are three types of errors, including substitutions (S), deletions (D) and insertions (I). The WER calculates the total ratio of the three types of defined errors, which is $\text{WER} = \frac{S+D+I}{N}$. Lower values are better.

Control performance evaluates whether the given attribute signals are precisely reflected in generated texts. We follow [6] to use attribute accuracy (ACC). It measures agreements between given attribute labels and predicted attribute values of generations. We additionally train ideal attribute classifiers (which adopts the same network architecture as the discriminator modules) using the same data together with labels. Given a predicted text, we obtain its attribute value using classifiers, then compare it with ground-truth attribute label and compute accuracies. Larger ACC indicates more effective control.

Table 2. Automatic evaluation results on the three datasets in generative performance (PPL&WER) and control effect (ACC).

(a) Generative performance results. Lower values are better.

Model	YELP		MOV		SYN	
	PPL	WER	PPL	WER	PPL	WER
CVAE	49.9	0.83	58.1	0.86	43.2	0.91
HuCTG	52.7	0.86	59.2	0.87	40.1	0.88
DCTG	**45.1**	**0.72**	**40.4**	**0.69**	**29.3**	**0.83**

(b) Results of control effects. Larger ACC is better. Each dataset has two attributes. YELP: *quality(3)* and *rating score(5)*. MOV: *sentiment (2)* and *movie score(8)*. SYN: *subject (2)* and *rating score(5)*.

Model	YELP		MOV		SYN	
#Attr.	*quality(3)*	*rating(5)*	*sentiment(2)*	*movie(8)*	*subject (2)*	*rating(5)*
CVAE	0.40	0.25	0.54	0.14	0.64	0.20
HuCTG	0.42	0.28	0.56	0.18	0.69	0.26
DCTG	**0.45**	**0.35**	**0.62**	**0.21**	**0.72**	**0.31**

Results and Analysis. Table 2 shows results of metric-based evaluation. We have several observations. DCTG outperforms both baselines in all aspects significantly. DCTG outperforms baselines by more than 7 nats and 5% respectively in PPL and WER, implying better generation quality. DCTG shows better control effects by at least 3% improvements in ACC, which implies better effects in controlling attributes. The results are analyzed as follows.

1. Since co-occurrence dependencies are considered, DCTG is capable of reducing possibilities of incorrectly extracting latent representations that hold unreasonable controlled attribute values. Therefore, provided with matched/reasonable attribute representations, the decoder are less likely to generate non-committal texts, showing better quality and better inheriting controlled signals.
2. Another possible reason lies in the difference that DCTG adopts facilitated adversarial network to remove controlled information from unrelated parts of disentangled representations, to ensure the uniqueness of controlled signal sources, while baselines do not. Thus texts can be generated as requested and are more in line with given standards.

4.3 Human Evaluation

Metrics and Settings. In addition to objective metric-based evaluation, we also carried out subjective human evaluation. In particular, we randomly select 5 cases from each dataset respectively. For each case, we use DCTG as well as baselines to generate texts. Thus, we obtained 45 generated samples in total (5 cases × 3 models × 3 datasets = 45). We compare our DCTG with each baseline, forming 30 tuples (5 case × 3 datasets × 2 comparisons = 30). Each tuple contains (text$_1$, text$_2$, label$_1$, label$_2$), where text$_1$ and text$_2$ respectively come from DCTG and one of the baselines, label$_1$ and label$_2$ respectively are their ground-truth attribute values. We let 30 volunteers who are not related to this work to annotate these samples by the following rules. (1) Volunteers are prevent from knowing from which models the texts generate. (2) Each volunteer is asked to independently score all comparison tuples, among win and loss (win: text$_1$ is better; loss: text$_2$ is better) (3) Before scoring, each volunteer is trained with a few cases to make sure they have comprehensively understand the key factors to be considered, including being grammatical, being appropriate and being under-control. (4) For all the evaluation results, we adopt the strategy of majority voting to judge which one is better within each comparison.

Results. Table 3 is human evaluation results. From the results, we can see that, DCTG outperforms baselines in human evaluation. The performance advantages of DCTG over baselines are stable, however, are not dominant. Comparing with automatic evaluation results, human evaluation shows smaller advantages. The reasons are as follows. When performing automatic evaluation, we use the whole test sets which cover a certain percentage reasonable/unreasonable inputs. The robustness to different inputs is the main advantage of DCTG, which just demonstrates the improved gap between DCTG and baselines. When performing human evaluation, we just use several randomly-chosen samples, which are less representative. However, even with random examples, DCTG also shows certain improvements. This indirectly prove its effectiveness.

Table 3. Results of human evaluation

Comparison	Win	Loss
DCTG vs CVAE	51.8%	48.2%
DCTG vs HuCTG	53.3%	46.7%

4.4 Investigation on Reasonableness

Evaluating Reasonableness. We evaluate compliance with co-occurrence dependencies using our proposed *reasonableness* (R). As is discussed, the dependency module of DCTG learns co-occurrence dependencies from large training corpus. We respectively input generated texts from models into DCTG and output R values, to measure them under the same measurement. The reasonableness of generated texts could reflect the reasonableness of latent representations. Table 4 shows the results. We can see generated texts from DCTG have significantly larger R values than those from baselines, proving the effectiveness of the introduction of co-occurrence dependencies.

Table 4. Reasonableness results. The larger, the better.

Model	YELP	MOV	SYN
CVAE	0.023	0.011	0.012
HuCTG	0.004	0.013	0.019
DCTG	**0.062**	**0.026**	**0.036**

Visualizing Controlled Attribute-Pair Representations. To show effectiveness of adjustments by co-occurrence dependencies, we visualize the controlled attribute-pair representations respectively from DCTG and DCTG(w/o), whose dependency modules and dependency loss are removed. The controlled attribute-pair representation is defined as $v_a\|v_b$, the concatenation of each attribute representation. We feed the same conflicted data into both well-trained models to obtain their respective $v_a\|v_b$, and generate new sentences. The $v_a\|v_b$ are reduced into 2-dimensional vectors using T-SNE and are visualized. And they are labeled by whether attribute values are *reasonable/match* or not, where labels are determined by classifying generated new sentences with ideal classifiers (mentioned in Sect. 4.2). Here MOV dataset is taken for illustration. MOV has two attributes: sentiment (2 classes) and rating score (8 classes), where natural dependencies are that positive reviews should correspond to higher rating scores while negative reviews associate with lower ones. Attribute-pair representations from MOV are recognized as reasonable if two attribute values match (e.g. positive-4/5/6/7 or negative-0/1/2/3) and vice versa. Figure 6 shows the results.

From Fig. 6, we can see: comparing DCTG and DCTG (w/o), the ratio of dark blue points, representing matched/reasonable generated texts that conform to underlying dependencies, are obviously increased. This proves adjustment effects brought by dependency modules and dependency losses. By considering co-occurrence dependencies, unmatched/unreasonable attribute pairs are reduced.

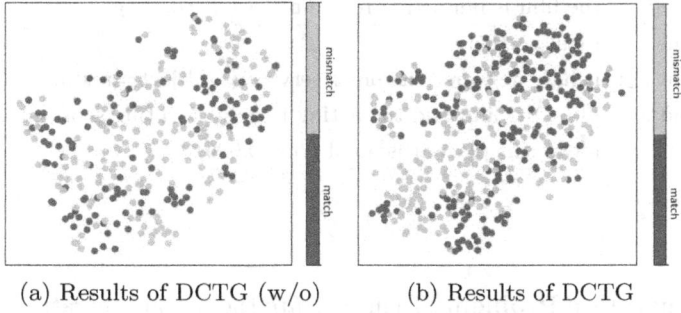

(a) Results of DCTG (w/o)   (b) Results of DCTG

Fig. 6. Visualization of attribute-pair representations using t-sne for DCTG(w/o) and DCTG on MOV. Dark/light blue points are matched/mismatched cases. (Color figure online)

4.5   Further Analysis with Case Study

Text-to-Text Synthesis. Text-to-text synthesis is one of the applicable scenarios for CTG. Its goal is to synthesize new texts conditioned on the given inputs. Take SYN dataset as an example, we input different sentences into encoder (e.g., x_1) and attribute network (e.g., x_2 and x_3). DCTG can synthesize new sentences that display the same review subject as x_2 and rating score as x_3 while keep other information similar to x_1. Table 5 displays several samples.

We have the following observations. (1) DCTG can synthesize well-formulated sentences with attributes respectively controlled by different source inputs. (2) R values truly reflect the compliance with real dependencies within dataset. Factual experiences are that people tend to be harsher when rating movies than restaurants and statistics of the dataset also verify it. Therefore, when $subject = \text{``}rest\text{''}$ and $score = 5$, R has a higher value, since

$p(subject = \text{``rest''}, score = 5)$ is empirical of high probability, as the third example shows. When $subject = \text{``mov''}$ and $score = 5$, R value is relatively lower, since $p(subject = \text{``mov''}, score = 5)$ is empirical of lower probability, as the second example shows.

Table 5. Text-to-text synthesis examples.

Input x_1:	it is closed already
Input x_2:	the food is terrible ("subject = restaurant")
Input x_3:	the film is good ("rating score" = 4)
Output:	this place is good one for eating ($R = 0.024$)
Input x_1:	how do you like it
Input x_2:	the film is awful ("subject = movie")
Input x_3:	i love this place ("rating score" = 5)
Output:	the film is fantastic i recommend ($R = 0.015$)
Input x_1:	i will go there
Input x_2:	it has the worst customer service ("subject = restaurant")
Input x_3:	i like the film and the acting is great ("rating score" = 5)
Output:	i love this place it is good ($R = 0.026$)

Trivial Generation Problem. To investigate the trivial generation issue, with MOV, we intentionally input two sentences (x_2 and x_3) with conflicted attribute values (e.g., negative-4/5/6/7 or positive-0/1/2/3) into the dependency-aware attribute network and another sentence (x_1) with neutral sentiment into encoder, and decode the generated sentences. Cases are generated respectively from DCTG and HuCTG, and we manually count the proportion of trivial generations in each model. Statistical results are that trivial generations account for **79%** in HuCTG while **53%** in DCTG. Table 6 shows some examples.

First, we can conclude the ratio of trivial generations for DCTG is significantly reduced. DCTG generates more specific texts when assigning unreasonable attribute values, while larger proportion of cases from HuCTG are noncommittal. This indicates that, considering co-occurrence dependencies makes model more robust towards rare/uncommon cases that are not in line with mainstream dependencies. Second, when the two attribute values are highly conflicted, generated texts from DCTG are generally controlled by one of the attributes. We speculate that, after being slightly adjusted, influence of both attributes are different and there would be a dominant one leading the generation, e.g., "sentiment" leads in the first and "rating score" leads in the second.

Table 6. Cases with unmatched values to investigate trivial generation problem.

Input x_1:	i will go to see the movie
Input x_2:	the acting is terrible ("sentiment = negative")
Input x_3:	the film is good ("movie rating" = 4)
HuCTG Out:	ok, that is alright
DCTG Out:	i really do not like the story
Input x_1:	it is a book
Input x_2:	i like the movie very much("sentiment = positive")
Input x_3:	the film is so terrible ("movie rating" = 0)
HuCTG Out:	i have no idea
DCTG Out:	it is terrible and i do not like it

5 Conclusion and Discussion

This is the first work to emphasize the problem of ignoring co-occurrence dependencies between controlled attributes in CTG. We propose DCTG that addresses it by collaboratively processing two controlled attributes under the guidance of co-occurrence dependencies. Thus, when extracting attribute representations from input controlled signals, signals can be accurately identified with less possibilities of being mistaken; meanwhile, the model is capable of automatically performing slight adjustment when unreasonable signals are given. Experiments prove that, comparing with state-of-the-arts, DCTG can generate texts that are grammatical and content-relevant, better inherit controlled signals and better comply with real co-occurrence dependencies.

Acknowledgements. The work was supported by the National Key Research and Development Program of China (No. 2019YFB1704003, No. 2016YFB1001101), the National Nature Science Foundation of China (No. 71690231, No. 61472207, No. 61773415), and Tsinghua BNRist.

References

1. Bowman, S.R., Vilnis, L., Vinyals, O., Dai, A.M., Jozefowicz, R., Bengio, S.: Generating sentences from a continuous space. In: CoNLL, pp. 10–21. ACL (2016)
2. Chen, X., Duan, Y., Houthooft, R., Schulman, J., Sutskever, I., Abbeel, P.: Infogan: interpretable representation learning by information maximizing generative adversarial nets. In: NIPS, pp. 2172–2180 (2016)
3. Fu, Z., Tan, X., Peng, N., Zhao, D., Yan, R.: Style transfer in text: exploration and evaluation. In: AAAI, pp. 663–670. AAAI Press (2018)
4. Ghosh, S., Chollet, M., Laksana, E., Morency, L.P., Scherer, S.: Affect-LM: a neural language model for customizable affective text generation. In: ACL (1), pp. 634–642. Association for Computational Linguistics (2017)
5. Higgins, I., et al.: beta-vae: learning basic visual concepts with a constrained variational framework. In: ICLR (Poster) (2017). https://openreview.net/

6. Hu, Z., Yang, Z., Liang, X., Salakhutdinov, R., Xing, E.P.: Toward controlled generation of text. In: ICML, Proceedings of Machine Learning Research, vol. 70, pp. 1587–1596. PMLR (2017)
7. Ikeda, S., Amari, S., Nakahara, H.: Convergence of the wake-sleep algorithm. In: NIPS, pp. 239–245. The MIT Press (1998)
8. Kulkarni, T.D., Whitney, W.F., Kohli, P., Tenenbaum, J.B.: Deep convolutional inverse graphics network, In: NIPS. pp. 2539–2547 (2015)
9. Shen, X., Su, H., Niu, S., Demberg, V.: Improving variational encoder-decoders in dialogue generation. In: AAAI, pp. 5456–5463. AAAI Press (2018)
10. Sohn, K., Lee, H., Yan, X.: Learning structured output representation using deep conditional generative models. In: NIPS, pp. 3483–3491 (2015)
11. Wang, K., Wan, X.: Sentigan: generating sentimental texts via mixture adversarial networks. In: IJCAI, pp. 4446–4452 (2018). https://www.ijcai.org/
12. Xing, C., et al.: Topic aware neural response generation. In: AAAI, pp. 3351–3357. AAAI Press (2017)
13. Zhao, T., Zhao, R., Eskenazi, M.: Learning discourse-level diversity for neural dialog models using conditional variational autoencoders. In: ACL (1), pp. 654–664. Association for Computational Linguistics (2017)
14. Zhou, M., Lapata, M., Wei, F., Dong, L., Huang, S., Xu, K.: Learning to generate product reviews from attributes. In: EACL (1), pp. 623–632. Association for Computational Linguistics (2017)

Keep You from Leaving: Churn Prediction in Online Games

Angyu Zheng[1,2], Liang Chen[1,2]($\boxtimes$), Fenfang Xie[1,2], Jianrong Tao[3],
Changjie Fan[3], and Zibin Zheng[1,2]

[1] School of Data and Computer Science, Sun Yat-sen University, Guangzhou, China
{zhengangy,xieff5}@mail2.sysu.edu.cn,
{chenliang6,zhzibin}@mail.sysu.edu.cn
[2] National Engineering Research Center of Digital Life, Sun Yat-sen University,
Guangzhou, China
[3] NetEase Fuxi AI Lab, Hangzhou, China
{hztaojianrong,fanchangjie}@corp.netease.com

Abstract. Customer retention is a crucial problem for game companies since the revenue is heavily influenced by the size of their user bases. Previous studies have reached a consensus that the cost of attracting a new player can be six times than retaining the players, which indicates an accurate churn prediction model is essential and critical for the strategy making of customer retention. Existing works more focus on studying login information (e.g. login activity traits of users) ignoring the rich in-game behaviors (e.g. upgrading, trading supplies) which could implicitly reflect user's preference from their inter-dependencies. In this paper, we propose a novel end-to-end neural network, named *ChurnPred*, for churn prediction problem. In particular, we not only consider the login behaviors but also in-game behaviors to model user behavior patterns more comprehensively. For time series of login activities, we leverage a LSTM-based structure to learn intrinsic temporal dependencies so as to capture the evolution of activity sequences. For in-game behaviors, we develop a time-aware filtering component to better distinguish the behavior patterns occurring in a specific period and a multi-view mechanism to automatically extract the multiple combinations of these behaviors from various perspectives. Comprehensive experiments conducted on real-world data demonstrate the effectiveness of the proposed model compared with state-of-the-art methods.

Keywords: Churn prediction · Online games · Neural network · In-game behaviors · Login activities

1 Introduction

The huge revenue generated by online games including massively multiplayer online role-playing games (MMORPGs) has attracted many game companies, which results in increasingly intense competition in the game market. Customer

Y. Nah et al. (Eds.): DASFAA 2020, LNCS 12113, pp. 263–279, 2020.
https://doi.org/10.1007/978-3-030-59416-9_16

retention is becoming a major concern, since: 1) *the cost of attracting a new player can be six times than retaining the players* [23]; 2) long-term players usually generate higher profits than the new ones. As an important part of the user retention, it is crucial to know early on whether players will choose to stay or leave the game in the early stage, which is also called as churn prediction problem.

An accurate churn prediction model is essential and critical for the strategy making of the customer retention. Once the churners are identified by the prediction model, game managers can take some measures to prevent those from leaving the game such as providing some reward tasks to stimulate the user's interest or pushing notifications with fresh play strategies that the user interests. Moreover, the prediction results of the churn prediction model can provide the game platform with a reference to understand the overall preferences of the game players and accordingly make appropriate strategies. An increasing number of churners may become a strong signal for game operators to adjust game strategy in advance.

Previous research for the churn prediction problem in online games (e.g. MMORPGs) focuse on mining salient features to indicate whether a user is about to leave the game. They prefer to exploit handcraft features after a comprehensive analysis on multiple characteristics and complete the churn prediction task by using traditional machine-learning-based methods [3,4,7,8,10]. The limitations of previous investigations are mainly two-fold: 1) Heavily depending on domain-specific knowledge and artificial features, which is not widespread to different application scenarios. For example, some features are not universal or difficult to collect for online games such as "click count" and "rests used" in [10], "sum of inter-session length per week" in [3], "social activity" and "item upgrade" in [8], "rate of group interactions" in [2]. 2) Mainly utilizing features derived from the statistics of login information, while ignoring users' behavior information in the game. These information is important for the churn prediction since it could further indicate the users' preference for the game. Players put many efforts into perfecting their roles, such as constantly performing tasks to upgrade or trading supplies to enhance their equipment, which demonstrates a kind of preference for their characters of the game. Tao et al. have proven the importance of users' in-game behavioral information in bot detection [16].

There exist several challenges of churn prediction in online games. As mentioned above, users' behaviors in online games are mainly classified in two aspects: login information (e.g. session statistic, login frequency) and in-game behavioral information (e.g. a series of in-game behaviors such as upgrading, trading supplies). First, these data are in different types since the former is often expressed as real-value vectors, while each element of the latter data is a discrete value representing a specific action. It is challenging to model these data together to capture user-game interactions and inherent behavior patterns. Second, since each player has her/his own lifetime, short- and long-term modeling is required for capturing the evolution of users' preferences and temporal patterns better. Third, users' behaviors are closely related to their daily life (details will be given in Sect. 3). For example, the length of users' engagement with the games on weekdays is different from that on weekends, or some events such as trading specific items or fighting battles can only take place on some special days (e.g., festivals). Therefore, it is essential to additionally consider the influence of these information when modeling.

To alleviate the above mentioned challenges, in this paper, we propose a novel end-to-end neural network approach, named *ChurnPred*, for churn prediction in online games. We consider login information and in-game information together to model user behaviors more comprehensively, from which potential behavior patterns are automatically learned without manually extracting features. Considering the impact of lifetime of users on login behaviors, we leverage LSTM models to learn the short- and long-term users' preferences. As we find in Sect. 3 that some behaviors are closely related to the day of occurrence, we propose a time-aware filtering component to better distinguish these characteristic behaviors based on the period of events. Besides, we propose a multi-view mechanism to automatically extract the multiple combinations of in-game behaviors from various perspectives which would lead to the departure of users.

To summarize, main contributions of this paper are listed as follows:

- We develop a novel end-to-end neural network approach, named *ChurnPred*, via considering login behaviors and in-game behaviors for churn prediction in online games. Additionally, we propose time-aware filtering mechanism to better distinguish the behavior patterns occurring in that period and a multi-view mechanism to extract the multiple combinations of in-game behaviors from various perspectives which would imply the departure of users.
- We conduct comprehensive experiments on a real-world dataset of three different periods to verify the effectiveness of the proposed model. Experimental results shows the superiority of our model for churn prediction in online games.

2   Related Work

Customer churn behaviors have been consistently analyzed across a wide range of industries, since most companies are convinced the number and stickiness of users play an importance role on their competitiveness and vitality in the market. Most of these works [10,14,23] focus more on extracting outstanding features and exploring the classification performance among the traditional classifiers such as logistic regression [11], random forests [21]. They model churn prediction as a binary classification problem and tend to summarize the difference of the samples by using statistical techniques for better identification. These studies depend much on domain-specific knowledge and artificial features, which is not universal to different application scenarios. Recently, some studies have suggested more advanced models on the churn prediction. Some works [13,18] propose survival analysis model by modeling the playtime of players. Since deep learning has achieve great success in various domain such as detection [19] and recommender [5,20], some researches [1,9,17] focus on leveraging the deep neural network for churn prediction problems, which motivates us to employ deep neural network models.

Only a few papers are directly related to the online games including MMO-PRGs. Borbora et al. design a lifecycle-based approach for modeling churn behavior and propose three dimensions to construct derived features for a distance-based schema *wClusterDist* for better classification [3]. However, the lifecycle-based approach ignores the time of users' registration and time consumption on the game. Those loyal customers who have been playing for a long time tend to be less active in observation and thus may be easily mistaken as churners. Runge et al. focus on predicting churn for high-value players of casual social games since they find that the top 7% of paying players contribute around 50% of the total revenue and acquire a series of features for classification [14]. Castro et al. propose a frequency analysis approach for feature representation from login records. The approach converts the login records into a fixed-length arrays as the inputs and use probabilistic classifiers with the k-nearest neighbors algorithm for classification [4]. The above investigations mainly focus on login information (i.e. login frequency), but do not consider users' in-game behavioral information of online games (e.g.MMORPGs). In-game behaviors are crucial for user behavioral modeling, since it contains rich information about the user including the players' specific events in the game and the chronological order of these events. These data will contribute a lot to fully reflect or accurately capture the tendency of players to leave the game.

3   Dataset Description

In this section, we give some detailed information of the real-world dataset from a MMOPRG released by the NetEase Games[1]. This dataset is collected from a server including user logs from 22 June, 2018 to 20 September, 2018 and over 880,000 users with hundreds of millions of behavioral sequences. In this dataset, 485 regular events are defined based on the game content and user logs has been automatically established for each player to record the events as well as the times when the player trigger them.

In this dataset, we define two classes of users: churners and non-churners. Usually, churners represent the users who leave the game permanently. To be less ambiguous, we define churners as those who are consistently inactive for over 7 days [12,23]. Let *leave_day* denote the day that user leave the game. To compare two types of users at the same stage, we mainly focus on the users who have left the game during a specific period and those who haven't. We define the period as a churn window which is denoted as [*observed_day*$_1$, *observed_day*$_2$]. The users whose *leave_day* fall in this window will be considered as "churners",

---

[1] NetEase Games is the one of China's largest MMORPG developer companies, which has published dozens of popular games including Ghost II, Tianxia 3 and Fantasy Westward Journey Online.

and those whose *leave_day* are after the *observed_day₂* are defined as "non-churners". In the following section, we adopt this setting for both "churners" and "non-churners".

In order to find out how long the user has been playing the game before they leave, we examine the distribution of the lifetime of all users in this dataset shown in Fig. 1. We observe that the number of churners fluctuates periodically. This indicates that users will leave the game with relatively high probability after they have played for a certain number of days (15/16/32/33). The predictive model needs to capture this characteristic by considering users' lifetime when predicting the probability of the user departure.

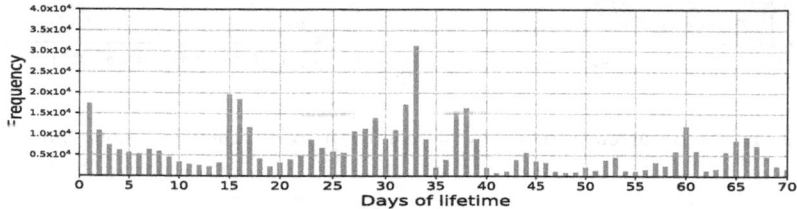

Fig. 1. The distribution of the lifetime of users in a real-world dataset.

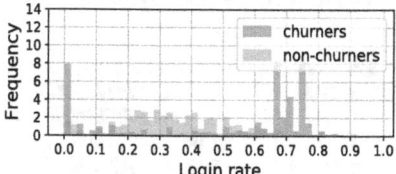

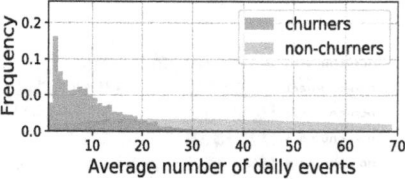

Fig. 2. The login rate of churners and non-churners

Fig. 3. The average number of daily events of churners and non-churners

To better understand what motivates users continue to play the game, we examine the difference of login information and in-game behavioral information between churners and non-churners. We observe several striking features.

Figure 2 shows the percentage of login days to the whole lifetime between churners and non-churners. We can see that the non-churners are concentrated in the range of 0.2 to 0.5 while churners have high distribution at both ends. Some churners have a low login rate due to various reasons such as lack of interest in the game. But interestingly, the figure also reveals that users with high login rates have a higher probability of leaving. This phenomenon that users log into the game frequently before they leave is helpful for game operators to take some churn preventive measures, such as pushing notification. In Fig. 3, the average daily events of churners is relatively small and the distribution of non-churners performs stable. Intuitively, the number of events reflects the duration of playing. Churners always have a fewer events per days because they have fewer times to stay engaging with the game due to low motivation while non-churners are more willing to spend their time to play the game and thus have more events.

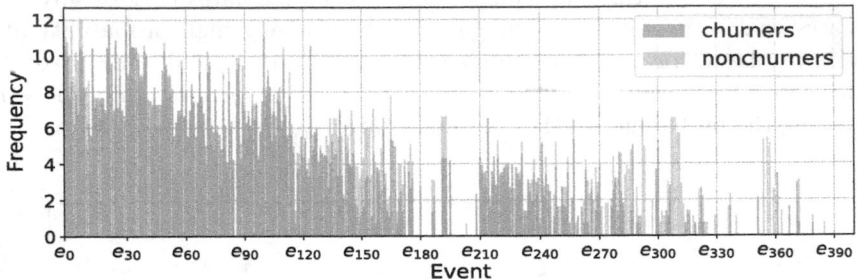

Fig. 4. The occurrence frequency of each event of churners and non-churners

Fig. 5. The behavioral sequences of churners and non-churners. Each color block represents the user's behavior in the game. (Color figure online)

We then investigate the in-game behaviors of users. The frequency of each events for churners and non-churners is plotted in the Fig. 4. We can see that there are some differences on the event frequency between these two types of users. Some events occur more often in certain types of users or with a relatively high frequency. For example, e_{150} has a higher frequency for non-churners and e_{310} occurs commonly in non-churners but rarely in churners. For the sequence of events, we randomly sample 5 churners and 5 non-churners in churn windows, and extract the sequences of their last 200 events prior to the *leave_day* and the *oberseved_day*$_1$, respectively. The result is shown in Fig. 5. During this period, the behaviors of non-churners are usually diverse and each is of short duration while the behavior of churners is monotonous and each last for a long time. It can be clearly seen that there are significant differences in the behaviors between churners and non-churners, which further indicates that short-term behaviors reflect whether the user stays in the game or not. Some studies focus on long-term behavior modeling, which not only faces lengthy behavior information, but also increases the complexity of the model and training time.

4   Model Architecture

In this section, we present the details of the proposed model. The architecture is illustrated in Fig. 6. The model can be divided into three main components: 1) an in-game behavior encoder that models the in-game behavioral information of each user as a context embedding vector. 2) a login behavior encoder that models the login information of each user in online game as a context embedding vector. 3) the fusion and prediction layer that aggregates above two kinds of embedding vectors and outputs the final possibility of whether the user leaves the game.

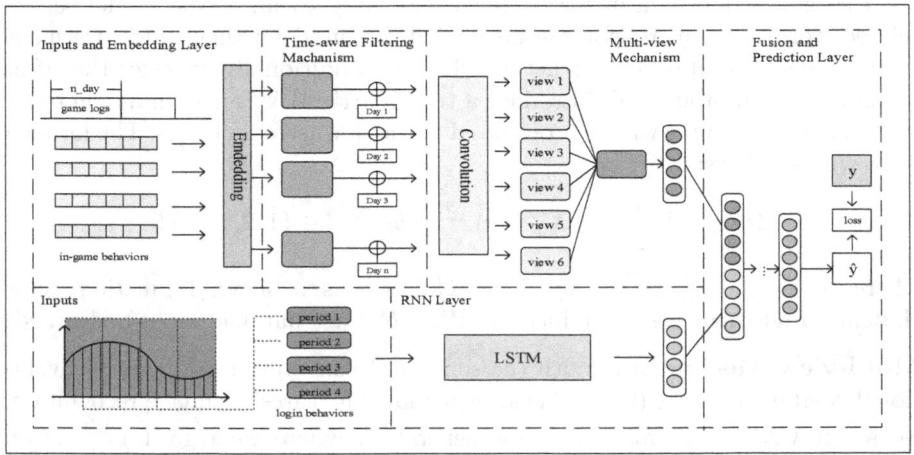

Fig. 6. The architecture of ChurnPred.

4.1   In-Game Behavior Encoder

Inputs. In terms of in-game information, we collect the daily events $e_{ut}^{(d)} \in E$ for user u and arrange them in chronological order which denoted as in-game behavioral sequences $S_u^{(d)} = \{e_{u1}^{(d)}, ..., e_{ut}^{(d)}, ..., e_{uB}^{(d)}\}$ where E is the set of events, d represents the day of events, B denotes the length of $S_u^{(d)}$. As we discussed above, users' total historical behaviors are lengthy and massive which may greatly increase the complexity of the model and training time. In this paper, we use the data of T_1 days before the day *observed_day*$_1$ as our input which is denoted as $S_u = \{S_u^{(1)}, S_u^{(2)}, .., S_u^{(T_1)}\}$.

Embedding Layer. Given $S_u^{(d)} = \{e_{u1}^{(d)}, ..., e_{ut}^{(d)}, ..., e_{uB}^{(d)}\}$, events are embedded into content vectors in a latent space through an embedding layer. In the discretization process, each event identity $e_{ut}^{(d)} \in E$ are encoded into an one-hot vector $o_{ut}^{(d)}$ with $|E|$-dimension. As the inputs are high-dimensional binary vectors, we use the embedding layer to transform them into dense representations. The event embedding vector $x_{ut}^{(d)}$ can be obtained as follows:

$$x_{ul}^{(d)} = W_e^T o_{ut}^{(d)}, \quad t \in \{1, 2, ..., B\} \tag{1}$$

where $W_e \in \mathbb{R}^{|E| \times L}$ denotes the latent factor matrix (embedding matrix) and L is the predefined value used to set the dimension of latent vectors.

Time-Aware Filtering Mechanism. In the analysis above, we find that user's behavior is closely related to the day it occurs. Hence, we propose a time-aware gating mechanism to capture these characteristic behaviors based on the time period. Dauphin et al. in [6] propose the gated linear unit (GLU) where they use this gating mechanism for language modeling to allow the model selects related words or features for the next word. Inspired by their work, we make some changes based on this structure where we additionally consider the effect of period on the inputs. We introduce a time matrix $W^{(d)}$ for each day in order to select what features will be propagated to the downstream layers. The formula is shown as follows:

$$D_u^{(d)} = X_u^{(d)} \odot \sigma(X_u^{(d)} * W^{(d)} + b^{(d)}), d \in \{1, 2, ..., T_1\} \tag{2}$$

where $X_u^{(d)} = \{x_{ut}^{(1)}, x_{ut}^{(2)}, .., x_{ut}^{(B)}\} \in \mathbb{R}^{B \times L}$, σ is a sigmoid function, $\odot$ is Hadamard (element-wise) product and $W^{(d)}, b^{(d)}$ are parameters to be learned.

Multi-view Mechanism. With the success of convolution filters of Convolutional Neural Networks (CNN) in capturing local features for image recognition, we adopt CNN units for multi-view generation where we regard $V_u^{(d)}$ as an "image" of behavioral information and the sequential patterns as local features of this "image". Convolutional filters represented as $kh \times kw$ matrices, which they slide over the "images" and then summary the multiple combinations of behaviors in various views. We use B filters to encode the in-game behaviors of each day respectively. Each filters $F^{(d)} \in \mathbb{R}^{kh \times kw}$ slide over $D_u^{(d)}$ as follows:

$$v_u^{lk(d)} = D_{u,\{l:l+kh-1,k:k+kw-1\}}^{(d)} \oplus F^{(d)} \tag{3}$$

$$V_u^{(d)} = \{v_u^{lk(d)} | 1 \leq l \leq B - kh + 1, 1 \leq k \leq L - kw + 1\} \tag{4}$$

where $\oplus$ is the sum of element-wise product, $D_{u,\{l:l+kh-1,k:k+kw-1\}}$ denotes the convolutional area of $D_u^{(d)}$ with rows from l to $(l+th-1)$ and the columns from k to $(k+tw-1)$.

Note that the obtained views from the above formulas do not contribute equally to the final results. We introduce an attention mechanism [24] to address this problem. Traditional attention mechanism is used to learn the attentive weights for multiple vectors. In this paper, we modify the formulas in order to learn the weights from multiple matrices (i.e. views). The representation of final view V_u is formed by a weighted sum of these generated views which is calculated as follows:

$$H_u^{(d)} = tanh(V_u^{(d)}) \tag{5}$$

$$\alpha_u^{(d)} = \frac{exp(H_u^{(d)} \oplus W_a)}{\sum_{i=1}^{T_1} exp(H_u^{(i)} \oplus W_a)} \tag{6}$$

$$V_u = \sum_{i=1}^{T_1} \alpha^{(d)} V_u^{(d)}, \tag{7}$$

where $V_u^{(d)}, H_u^{(d)}, W_a, V_u \in \mathbb{R}^{(B-kh+1) \times (L-kw+1)}$, $\alpha_u^{(d)}$ is the attentive weight of the view $V_u^{(d)}$ and W_a, b_a are training parameters. To make the final view into a latent vector, We use max-pooling to summarize the characteristics of the final view. The formula is as follows:

$$c_u^{in} = max - pooling(V_u) \tag{8}$$

where $c_u^1 \in \mathbb{R}^{B-kh+1}$ is the context representation for in-game behavioral information.

4.2 Login Behavior Encoder

Inputs. login behaviors in online games can be expressed as login frequency, play time etc. In this paper, we use daily play time for each user to describe the login information. We define a time window with the size of T_1 days and consider T_2 consecutive time windows before the *observed_day*$_1$. The input can be expressed as a sequence $M_u = \{m_1, m_2, .., m_{T_2}\}$ where m_t is a $|T_1|$-dimensional vector representing the duration of each day in the t-th windows.

Recurrent Neural Network (RNN) Layer. We apply a multi-layer LSTM (Long Short-Term Memory) for long- and short-term modeling since it takes various periods of daily data as time series and has strong ability in learning intrinsic temporal dependencies so as to capture the variation of activity sequences. Each layer of LSTM computes as follows:

$$i_t = \sigma(W_i * h_{t-1} + W_i * m_t + b_i) \tag{9}$$

$$f_t = \sigma(W_f * h_{t-1} + W_i * m_t + b_f) \tag{10}$$

$$\tilde{c}_t = tanh(W_c * h_{t-1} W_i * m_t + b_c) \tag{11}$$

$$c_t = f_t \odot c_{t-1} + i_t \odot \tilde{c}_t \tag{12}$$

$$g_t = \sigma(W_g * h_{t-1} + W_g * m_t + b_g) \tag{13}$$

$$h_t = g_t \odot tanh(c_t) \tag{14}$$

where i_t, f_t, g_t and c_t are an input gate, a forget gate, an output gate and memory state at time t, respectively. h_t represents the hidden state vector and we set

$h_0 = \mathbf{0}$ by default. $W_i, W_f, W_c, W_g, b_i, b_f, b_c, b_g$ are training parameters. The output of the last LSTM will be considered as the context representation of login information $c_u^2 = h_{T_2}$.

4.3 Fusion and Prediction Layer

After obtaining two kinds of context embedding vectors, i.e. c_u^{in} and c_u^{out}, we concatenate these vectors into a unified vector c_u which will be considered as high-level representation of behavioral features. We feed it into a fully connected feed forward neural network and output the final probability for churn prediction. The unified embedding via fusion can be denoted as:

$$c_u = [c_u^1, c_u^2] \tag{15}$$

$$y_u = \sigma(Wp * c_u + b_p)) \tag{16}$$

where $[.]$ is a concatenate operation, W_p, b_p are parameters in this layer (Fig. 7).

4.4 Loss Function and Optimization

At last, we adopt cross-entropy as our loss function for model optimization. To prevent over-fitting, we adopt l_2 regularization on the parameters in our loss function. The objective function is defined as follows:

$$\mathcal{L} = -\sum [y_i \log \hat{y}_i + (1 - y_i) \log(1 - \hat{y}_i)] + \lambda \|\Theta\|^2 \tag{17}$$

where $\hat{y}_i$ is the probability of becoming churners for user u_i and y_i is the corresponding truth score. If user u is a churner, then we have $y_i = 1$; otherwise, $y_i = 0$. Θ represents all of model parameters that will be learned in the training phase and λ is the regularization weight. We use Adam optimizer to learn the model.

5   Experiment

In this section, we aim to answer the following research questions:

- **RQ1:** How does *ChurnPred* perform as compared with widely used methods and the state-of-the-art ones in churn prediction?
- **RQ2:** What are the effects of the in-game behavior encoder and login behavior encoder in our proposed method?
- **RQ3:** How do different hyper-parameter settings (e.g. dimension of embedding vectors) affect the performance of *ChurnPred*?

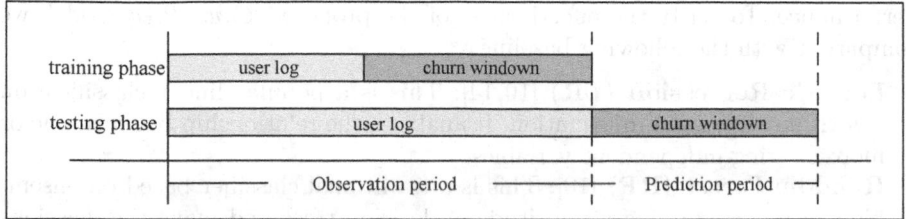

Fig. 7. Label generation process. We use different churn windows in the training and testing phase where the churn window of the testing set is behind the training set.

5.1 Dataset and Experimental Setup

We conduct the experiments on a real-world dataset described in Sect. 3. In particular, we extract the daily events of the users in the game and arrange them in chronological order serve as the features of in-game behavioral information (i.e. behavior sequences). The length of each daily behavior sequence will be considered as the features of login information (i.e. the daily play time) preprocessed by normalization. When constructing the training and testing samples, inspired by the paper [9], we adopt a similar splitting process to eliminate the problem of data leakage. Besides, a down-sampling approach is applied to avoid a skewed distribution [3,10], i.e. the ratio of churners to non-churners is 1:2. In order to better evaluate the performance of our model, we divide the dataset into three subsets where the churn windows in the testing phase are three consecutive weeks. The description of these datasets are illustrated in Table 1.

Table 1. Detailed statistics of the three periodic dataset. We use three subset of the raw dataset with different churn windows for testing.

Dataset	Phase	Churn window	Churners	Non-churners	Total users
MMORPG_1	Train	2018-07-20–2018-07-26	40907	81814	122721
	Test	2018-07-27–2018-08-02	103395	206790	310185
MMORPG_2	Train	2018-07-27–2018-08-02	103395	206790	310185
	Test	2018-08-03–2018-08-09	28157	56314	84471
MMORPG_3	Train	2018-08-03–2018-08-09	28157	56314	84471
	Test	2018-08-10–2018-08-16	50550	101100	151650

5.2 Evaluation Metrics and Baselines

Three widely used evaluation metrics, i.e. Precision, F1-Score and Accuracy, are adopted as metrics and performance is recorded when achieves the best F1-Score. Each experiment is run 5 times to take the best F1-Score as the final performance. To verify the effectiveness of the proposed *ChurnPred* model, we compare it with the following baselines:

- **Logistic Regression (LR)** [10,14]: This is a popular linear classification algorithm with login information. It analyzes the relationship between one or more existing independent variables.
- **Random Forest (RF)** [10]: This is a traditional classifier based on ensemble learning containing a multitude of decision trees and make the decisions together for classification. The inputs are as same as LR.
- **Multi-layer Perceptron (MLP)** [14]: Multi-layer perceptron is an artificial neural network which maps a set of input vectors into a low-dimensional space. We implement MLP with 2 fully-connected layers with the inputs of login information.
- **wClusterDist** [3]: wClusterDist is a distance-based classification schema conducted on login information as well as the derived features in three semantic dimensions of engagement, enthusiasm and persistence.
- **LSTM+Attention (ATT-LSTM)** [15]: This is an attention-based LSTM model for classifying early churn users whose input is the user behavior event sequence binned at constant intervals. The inputs are sequences of user in-game behaviors after registration.
- **PLSTM+** [22]: This is a two-step framework involving interpretable clustering and churn prediction. The prediction model is based on LSTM by leveraging the correlations among users' multidimensional activities and the underlying user type is derived from the interpretable clustering. Similar to its original inputs, we take the daily occurrences of the 10 most frequent in-game behaviors as inputs for prediction.

5.3   Parameter Settings

Neural network-based models are all implemented in Pytorch[2] including Churn-Pred, ATT-LSTM, PLSTM+ and MLP. These models are optimized with the Adam optimizer, and the batch size is set as 512 by default. In terms of hyper-parameters, we apply a grid search for hyperparameters on neural networks: the learning rate is tuned among {0.0001, 0.001, 0.01}, the size of hidden layer and the embedding matrix is in {8, 16, 32, 64} and the threshold is in {0.1, 0.2, 0.3, 0.4, 0.5, 0.6, 0.7, 0.8, 0.9}. For ChurnPred, the convolution is done by convolution kernels with the width of 3 and the height equals to the size of embedding matrix. For PLSTM+, we set the λ in the loss function as 1 and use 2 hidden layers in each LSTM. For wClusterDist, we set the number of clusters as 5. For ATT-LSTM, we use 2-layer LSTMs and set the dropout as 0.5.

5.4   Performance Comparison (RQ1)

Table 2 shows the performance comparison of the proposed model and the state-of-the-art ones. Key observations from the experimental results are listed as follows:

---

[2] https://pytorch.org/.

Table 2. The overall performance on MMOPRG_1, MMORPG_2 and MMOPRG_3.

Method	MMORPG_1			MMORPG_2			MMORPG_3		
	Precision	F1-Score	Accuracy	Precision	F1-Score	Accuracy	Precision	F1-Score	Accuracy
wClusterDist	0.3395	0.5068	0.3515	0.3458	0.5139	0.3696	0.3424	0.5101	0.3599
ATT-LSTM	0.3334	0.4999	0.3340	0.3333	0.4997	0.3338	0.3334	0.5000	0.3339
PLSTM+	0.3959	0.3503	0.6116	0.4275	0.4651	0.6090	0.3225	0.1450	0.6324
RF	0.6024	0.2456	0.6841	0.4306	0.5098	0.5995	0.4270	0.3515	0.6326
LR	0.5027	0.5589	0.6690	0.4072	0.5426	0.5432	0.4109	0.3803	0.6155
MLP	0.5923	0.6140	0.7329	0.3826	0.5142	0.5062	0.4032	0.5363	0.5386
ChurnPred	**0.6043**	**0.7022**	**0.7631**	**0.4577**	**0.5459**	**0.6250**	**0.4807**	**0.5720**	**0.6478**

- Among the conventional methods LR, RF and MLP, RF has the best average Precision while MLP has the best average F1-score on three datasets, which shows that RF is relatively correct on predicted churners but fails to find out more true samples since RF mistakes the churners as non-churners in most cases. MLP have a higher F1-score among these methods. The possible reason is that the model predicts non-churners as churners as much as possible, which recalls more and more true samples and thus increases the F1-score with the decline in precision.
- In the comparison models, both of PLSTM+ and ATT-LSTM use the in-game behavioral information of users as inputs but show different performance. PLSTM+ performs poorly, showing that the frequency of users' behavioral events is unable to fully describe the recent behavioral information of users. Instead, ATT-LSTM uses behavioral sequences as inputs and achieves better performance which implies the potential behavior patterns in the user's behavior sequences have ability of indicating whether users leave the game.
- RF, LR, MLP and wClusterDist all use login information as inputs. In these models, MLP performs the best on average F1-score metrics followed by wClusterDist. The result shows that MLP can capture these dynamic changes in login sequences while RF and LR lack the ability to encode this information. wClusterDist benefits from the derived features in three semantic dimensions of engagement, enthusiasm and persistence which describes changes in the users' login status, resulting in better performance.
- ChurnPred generally outperforms all baselines. This is largely due to considerations on login information and in-game behavioral information in online games. For in-game behaviors, it leverages the multi-view mechanism to learn the potential behavioral patterns. For login information, it is sensitive to the changes on daily play time which indicates the model capture the dynamic characteristics in login information. By integrating the two kinds of information, the model has been greatly improved.

5.5 Component Analysis (RQ2)

In order to evaluate the performance between login behavior encoder and in-game behavior encoder in our proposed method, we design three different models:

ChurnPred-α retains login behavior encoder, ChurnPred-β uses only in-game behavior encoder and ChurnPred adopts the above two kinds of components. These three models are conducted on $MMORPG\_1$ dataset and keep the same model parameters when training. The results are shown in Fig. 8. We can see that ChurnPred achieves the best performance, ChurnPred-β is the second and ChurnPred-α is the third. It shows that in-game behavioral sequences implies the potential behavior pattern, which contains more information about the user's intention of leaving when compared with login information in online games. Further, the results demonstrate the effectiveness of our proposed ChurnPred in encoding the intrinsic sequential patterns and login patterns, both of which contributes a lot in the decision-making process.

5.6 Parameter Sensitivity (RQ3)

To investigate the robustness of the $ChurnPred$ model, we study how the different choices of parameters affect the performance. Except for the parameter being tested, we set other parameters to default values. The experiments are conducted on $MMORPG\_1$ dataset.

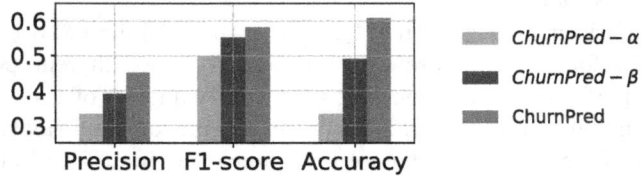

Fig. 8. Effect of in-game behavior and login information encoders.

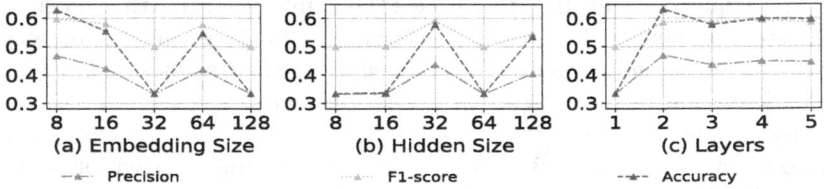

Fig. 9. Effect of the hyper-parameters.

Effect of Embedding Size. Figure 9(a) shows the performance in different dimension size of embedding matrix. We can observe that model performance generally declines with the increase of dimensions, which shows that the proposed model is sensitive to the dimension of the embedding matrix. choosing a reasonable dimension length gives the model superior performance and vice versa.

Effect of Hidden State Dimension. We keep the same hyper-parameters and vary the dimension of hidden state $hidden\_dim$ in LSTM component in the range of $\{8, 16, 32, 64, 128\}$ to investigate whether ChurnPred can benefit from the dimension size. The experimental results are illustrated in Fig. 9(b). As we can see, the model have the best performance when $hidden\_dim = 2$ and perform poorly in most cases, which means that the dimension size of the hidden state needs to be selected appropriately and otherwise it will get worse.

Effect of Layer Numbers. Figure 9(c) shows the performance in various number of hidden layers n_layer in LSTM component. The best performance is obtained when $n\_layer = 2$. After that, as the number of layers increases, the performance begin to descend slowly and become stable. This suggests that two layers are enough for the model to achieve significant performance and more layers will not contribute to better performance.

6 Conclusion and Future Work

In this paper, we investigate the problem of churn prediction in online games. We first explore and analyze user behaviors of a real-world MMORPG including engagement, days of lifetimes, in-game behaviors etc. According to the analysis insights, we develop a churn prediction model named *ChurnPred* by leveraging in-game behaviors and login behaviors of online games. We propose a time-aware filtering mechanism and a multi-view mechanism for behavior modeling. Comprehensive experiments conducted on a real-world dataset demonstrate the effectiveness of the proposed model by comparing with state-of-the-art methods. As future work, we will consider the social influence on the in-game behaviors. We argue that richer information could help the model make better decisions on the churn prediction. Further, the scalability problem of the proposed model will be considered in the future.

Acknowledgments. The paper was supported by the National Natural Science Foundation of China (61702568, U1711267), the Program for Guangdong Introducing Innovative and Entrepreneurial Teams (2017ZT07X355) and the Fundamental Research Funds for the Central Universities under Grant (17lgpy117). Liang Chen is the corresponding author.

References

1. Bertens, P., Guitart, A., Periáñez, Á.: Games and big data: a scalable multi-dimensional churn prediction model. In: 2017 IEEE Conference on Computational Intelligence and Games (CIG), pp. 33–36. IEEE (2017)
2. Borbora, Z., Srivastava, J., Hsu, K.W., Williams, D.: Churn prediction in MMORPGs using player motivation theories and an ensemble approach. In: 2011 IEEE Third International Conference on Privacy, Security, Risk and Trust and 2011 IEEE Third International Conference on Social Computing, pp. 157–164. IEEE (2011)

3. Borbora, Z.H., Srivastava, J.: User behavior modelling approach for churn prediction in online games. In: 2012 International Conference on Privacy, Security, Risk and Trust and 2012 International Conference on Social Computing, pp. 51–60. IEEE (2012)
4. Castro, E.G., Tsuzuki, M.S.: Churn prediction in online games using players' login records: a frequency analysis approach. IEEE Trans. Comput. Intell. AI Games 7(3), 255–265 (2015)
5. Chen, L., Liu, Y., He, X., Gao, L., Zheng, Z.: Matching user with item set: collaborative bundle recommendation with deep attention network. In: Proceedings of the 28th International Joint Conference on Artificial Intelligence, pp. 2095–2101. AAAI Press (2019)
6. Dauphin, Y.N., Fan, A., Auli, M., Grangier, D.: Language modeling with gated convolutional networks. In: Proceedings of the 34th International Conference on Machine Learning, vol. 70, pp. 933–941. JMLR.org (2017)
7. Kawale, J., Pal, A., Srivastava, J.: Churn prediction in MMORPGs: a social influence based approach. In: 2009 International Conference on Computational Science and Engineering, vol. 4, pp. 423–428. IEEE (2009)
8. Kwon, H., Jeong, W., Kim, D.W., Yang, S.I.: Clustering player behavioral data and improving performance of churn prediction from mobile game. In: 2018 International Conference on Information and Communication Technology Convergence (ICTC), pp. 1252–1254. IEEE (2018)
9. Liu, X., et al.: A semi-supervised and inductive embedding model for churn prediction of large-scale mobile games. In: 2018 IEEE International Conference on Data Mining (ICDM), pp. 277–286. IEEE (2018)
10. Milošević, M., Živić, N., Andjelković, I.: Early churn prediction with personalized targeting in mobile social games. Expert Syst. Appl. 83, 326–332 (2017)
11. Nie, G., Wang, G., Zhang, P., Tian, Y., Shi, Y.: Finding the hidden pattern of credit card holder's churn: a case of China. In: Allen, G., Nabrzyski, J., Seidel, E., van Albada, G.D., Dongarra, J., Sloot, P.M.A. (eds.) ICCS 2009. LNCS, vol. 5545, pp. 561–569. Springer, Heidelberg (2009). https://doi.org/10.1007/978-3-642-01973-9_63
12. Pudipeddi, J.S., Akoglu, L., Tong, H.: User churn in focused question answering sites: characterizations and prediction. In: Proceedings of the 23rd International Conference on World Wide Web, pp. 469–474. ACM (2014)
13. Ren, K., et al.: Deep recurrent survival analysis. arXiv e-prints arXiv:1809.02403, September 2018
14. Runge, J., Gao, P., Garcin, F., Faltings, B.: Churn prediction for high-value players in casual social games. In: 2014 IEEE Conference on Computational Intelligence and Games, pp. 1–8. IEEE (2014)
15. Sato, K., Oka, M., Kato, K.: Early churn user classification in social networking service using attention-based long short-term memory. In: U., L.H., Lauw, H.W. (eds.) PAKDD 2019. LNCS (LNAI), vol. 11607, pp. 45–56. Springer, Cham (2019). https://doi.org/10.1007/978-3-030-26142-9_5
16. Tao, J., Xu, J., Gong, L., Li, Y., Fan, C., Zhao, Z.: NGUARD: a game bot detection framework for NetEase MMORPGs. In: Proceedings of the 24th ACM SIGKDD International Conference on Knowledge Discovery & Data Mining, pp. 811–820. ACM (2018)
17. Umayaparvathi, V., Iyakutti, K.: Automated feature selection and churn prediction using deep learning models. Int. Res. J. Eng. Technol. (IRJET) 4(3), 1846–1854 (2017)

18. Viljanen, M., Airola, A., Heikkonen, J., Pahikkala, T.: Playtime measurement with survival analysis. IEEE Trans. Games 10(2), 128–138 (2017)
19. Wu, J., et al.: Who are the phishers? Phishing scam detection on ethereum via network embedding. arXiv preprint arXiv:1911.09259 (2019)
20. Xie, F., Chen, L., Ye, Y., Zheng, Z., Lin, X.: Factorization machine based service recommendation on heterogeneous information networks. In: 2018 IEEE International Conference on Web Services (ICWS), pp. 115–122. IEEE (2018)
21. Xie, Y., Li, X., Ngai, E., Ying, W.: Customer churn prediction using improved balanced random forests. Expert Syst. Appl. 36(3), 5445–5449 (2009)
22. Yang, C., Shi, X., Jie, L., Han, J.: I know you'll be back: interpretable new user clustering and churn prediction on a mobile social application. In: Proceedings of the 24th ACM SIGKDD International Conference on Knowledge Discovery & Data Mining, pp. 914–922. ACM (2018)
23. Yuan, S., Bai, S., Song, M., Zhou, Z.: Customer churn prediction in the online new media platform: a case study on juzi entertainment. In: 2017 International Conference on Platform Technology and Service (PlatCon), pp. 1–5. IEEE (2017)
24. Zhou, P., et al.: Attention based bidirectional long short-term memory networks for relation classification. In: Proceedings of the 54th Annual Meeting of the Association for Computational Linguistics (Volume 2: Short Papers), pp. 207–212 (2016)

Point-of-Interest Demand Discovery Using Semantic Trajectories

Ying Jin[1], Guojie Ma[1(✉)], Shiyu Yang[1], and Long Yuan[2]

[1] East China Normal University, Shanghai, China
yjin@stu.ecnu.odu.cn, {xmlin,gjma,syyang}@sei.ecnu.edu.cn
[2] Nanjing University of Science and Technology, Nanjing, China
longyuan@njust.edu.cn

Abstract. Semantic trajectories have become unprecedentedly available because of the rapidly growing popularities of location-sharing services. People's lifestyles and Point-of-Interest demands are hidden in such data. Extracting people's POI needs for different regions from semantic trajectories plays an important role in site selection, which can be widely used in city planning, facility location and other applications. However, most of existing works either use traditional trajectories which need to infer semantic with external information and lead to inaccuracy, or just focus on specific category. Semantic trajectory mining provides us a new way to address the challenges. Based on above motivation, we study the *regional POI demand discovery* problem using semantic trajectories. In this paper, we carefully analyze the features of semantic trajectory data and people' mobility patterns. Then, we propose an effective POI demand modeling method. Furthermore, we propose two efficient algorithms to identify the regional POI demands. The proposed algorithms extract regional patterns and compute the regional POIs demand according to POI demand model. Finally, the ranked POIs demands for regions are obtained. We evaluate the proposed modeling method and algorithms in terms of efficiency and effectiveness on two real data sets. The results show that our proposed methods outperform the competitor for both efficiency and effectiveness.

Keywords: POI discovery · Semantic trajectory · Mobility pattern mining

1 Introduction

With the rapid urbanization process, modern cities have developed urban regions with diverse functionality which naturally have a variety of demands for different Point-of-Interests (POIs) [28,29]. Discovery of regional POI demand, which can help governments allocate resources efficiently and provide suggestions for business investors, is becoming more and more important. Considering a cafe franchise want to open a new store in an urban region, with the help of regional

---

Y. Jin and G. Ma—The joint first authors.

© Springer Nature Switzerland AG 2020
Y. Nah et al. (Eds.): DASFAA 2020, LNCS 12113, pp. 280–296, 2020.
https://doi.org/10.1007/978-3-030-59416-9_17

POI demand, the investor can identify the potential demand for cafe in this region which is important for his investment decision.

Nowadays, POI demand analysis is still largely dependent on manual survey which is time-consuming. Besides, the markets and land resources are easy to change, if the analysis is conducted on the outdated data, the result inevitably leads to failure. Recently, with the advance of location positioning technique and high prevalence of location-sharing applications such as Foursquare, an increasing volume of semantic trajectories is extracted by combining traditional trajectory with semantic data [1], where each point in a semantic trajectory not only contains a particular address and a corresponding timestamp when person visited this site but also is enriched with a semantic category, such as cafe, gym or office. The appearance of semantic trajectories provides a new way for efficient and effective POI demand analysis which reflects the detailed underlying dynamics of residents in the city.

There are several approaches to recommend proper site location using human mobility data such as traditional or semantic trajectories using angle, velocity and other attributes. Unfortunately, most of existing works are proposed for specific demand [11,14,15,19,32], for instants, cultural planning or gas station. Specific focus leads to the ignorance of other significant categories and loss of generality of common demand discovery. Meanwhile another part of existing works focuses on traditional trajectory data [15], which means that they do not consider the semantic information and are not able to completely infer the POI category information.

In order to address these challenges, we study general POI demand discovery problem with an important economic logic *Foot Voting* [25]. Charles Tiebout points out that people have the ability to choose what they want by traveling. In other words, if people from one region frequently travel to other regions for specific category such as coffee shop, it is much likely that people need fresh or better coffee shop in their origin region. Therefore we can conclude that coffee shop is one of the POI demands of people's origin region. Based on the above observation and the help of people's frequent mobility patterns, the regional POI demands can be identified. Furthermore, governments and companies can understand POI demand better for future planning.

In this paper, we first propose a regional POI demand modeling which takes several relevant features into consideration and come up with a well designed regional POI demand modeling method. Then we develop efficient algorithms for regional POI demand discovery which consist of pre-processing of the raw semantic trajectories, cross-regional pattern mining and POI demand mining. Furthermore, we introduce optimization techniques which are based on some interesting observations to enrich the mining results. Finally, we evaluate our proposed method on two real datasets and show two illustrating cases in London and New York respectively. The experimental results show the effectiveness and efficiency of our proposed methods.

We conclude the main contributions of this paper as follows:

- We propose a POI demand modeling method based on the observation of *Foot Voting*.

- We design two efficient algorithms to compute the regional POI demand using semantic trajectories.
- We evaluate our proposed model and algorithms using real data sets and provide detailed analysis.
- Two case studies are introduced to show the effectiveness of the proposed methods.

The rest of this paper is organized as follows. We briefly review the related work in Sect. 2. In Scct. 3, we first define a few terms, then introduce our POI demand modeling and the formal problem definition. Our proposed mining algorithms are presented in Sect. 4 with some interesting observations. The experimental evaluation and illustrating case study are provided in Sect. 5. Finally, we conclude this paper in Sect. 6.

2   Related Work

2.1   Human Mobility Analysis

Understanding human mobility is crucial to location-based services and many related researches with mobility data, such as mobile phone data and transportation data [2,16,23]. [24] explores the urban Region-of-Interest to study agglomeration economies using online map search queries. [26] recommends a region with reliable POIs to a user with deep metric learning.

As we all know, each region has different specific needs. A good location has an effective impact on business and city planning. So correct POI demand analysis is key to site selection. With the help of mobility data, people can improve the accuracy and efficiency of site selection with comparison to traditional manual surveys or analysis models based on census [21,22]. Researchers mainly study specific POI category demand [11,13,14,19], for example, [32] designs a method to properly allocate cultural resources in urban area. However, [15] develops a systematic framework integrating POI and demographic data to identify various demands for developed and underdeveloped regions using traditional trajectories.

Human lifestyle [8] is another research field improved by the popularity of mobility data [20]. Some studies try to find the relation between multiple types of human lifestyles [31] and [10] uses shopping records to extract shopping patterns for divergent urban regions incorporating mobility patterns.

Existing POI demand identification works mainly focus on traditional human mobility pattern which may lead to mis-inference. And researches on assisting decision making with semantic data is few. Different from the above works, we design a more general framework for revealing people's lifestyles in cross-regional behaviors extracted from semantic trajectories to identify their life demands of each region. And recommend POI category from both region and semantic category perspectives in the framework.

2.2 Trajectory Pattern Mining

Trajectory pattern mining is a hot topic in spatial-temporal data mining. [18] explores propagation patterns and influential patterns in traffic and weather data with LSTM. According to the *Foot Voting* principle [25], people's movement can reflect POI demands to some extent. Therefore, frequent pattern mining using semantic trajectories [3,6] can be adopted to discover the POI demand. [9] proposes spatio-temporal containment pattern which requires similar transition time on visiting same sequences of places. [30] utilizes collaborative group of similar POIs rather than independent POIs to mine fine-grained frequent patterns. [12] proposes a probabilistic model to capture movement between semantic regions with coherent topic. They all focus on extracting globally frequent patterns in the entire data space. [7] proposes a new density scheme to quantify frequency of locally significant sequential patterns based on clustering. [4,5] study co-movement patterns problem which is closely related to frequent pattern mining.

However, there still exist challenges on mining POI demands due to the sparsity of trajectory data, especially for the regional POI demands discovery problem. People's different destinations usually distribute in various regions and they often start from diverse origins. This problem becomes even more challenging if we consider the semantic information for each visits in people's trajectories.

3 Preliminaries

In this section, we first define some important terms. Then we introduce the POI demand modeling using semantic trajectories. Finally we formally define the POI demand discovery problem.

3.1 Semantic Trajectories

Let $\mathcal{C} = \{c_1, c_2, \cdots, c_n\}$ is a set of semantic categories. Let $\mathcal{P} = \{p_1, p_2, \cdots, p_m\}$ be a set of places where each $p \in \mathcal{P}$ is defined as a tuple $(p.lon, p.lat, p.cat)$ where $p.lon$ and $p.lat$ denote p's latitude and longitude respectively and $p.cat \in \mathcal{C}$ is p's category. Following the existing definitions [7,30], we define *semantic trajectory* as follows:

Definition 1 *(Semantic Trajectory). A semantic trajectory T is defined as a sequence of pairs of place and a corresponding timestamp $\langle (p_1, t_1), (p_2, t_2), \cdots, (p_l, t_l) \rangle$, where $t_i < t_j$ if $i < j$ and l is the length of the trajectory.*

3.2 Region Partition

There are several methods to partition the urban area into regions, such as grid-based [17], road network-based and neighborhood-based [15] method. For the ease of presentation, we adopt grid-based method for region partition. Please note our proposed method can be used for other partition methods directly, as mapping POIs to regions does not rely on the partition methods.

Given a urban map, we divide the urban area into a set of $g \times g$ grid cells. Then we get a set of regions $\mathcal{R} = \{r_1, r_2, \cdots, r_{|\mathcal{R}|}\}$, where $|\mathcal{R}|$ equals to $g \times g$. According to POIs' location in semantic trajectory T, we can assign each of them into a region grid, as shown in Fig. 1.

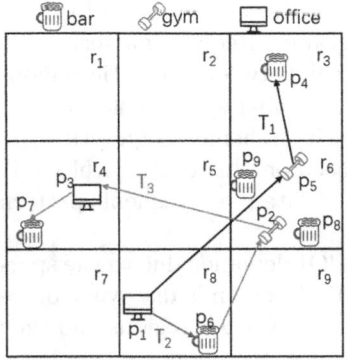

Trajectory	Sequence of POIS	Cross-Regional Patterns
T_1	$<p_1, p_5, p_4>$	$<(o, r_8), (g, r_6)>$ $<(g, r_6), (b, r_3)>$
T_2	$<p_1, p_6>$	
T_3	$<p_6, p_2, p_3, p_7>$	$<(b, r_8), (g, r_6)>$ $<(g, r_6), (o, r_4)>$

Fig. 1. An example of semantic trajectories (in different colors), T_1, T_2, T_3 and Regional Pattern, where $p_1, p_2, \cdots, p_9$ are places of interest (POIs), $r_1, r_2, \cdots, r_9$ are spatial regions and o, g, b are categories of POIs denoting office, gym and bar respectively.

After mapping the POIs into grid regions, we can generate regional patterns from a semantic trajectories according to the following definition.

Definition 2 *(Regional Pattern). Given a semantic trajectory T, a regional Pattern O of T is a sequence of tuples $O = \langle (c_1, r_i), (c_2, r_j), \cdots, (c_m, r_m) \rangle$, where each $c_i \in C$ and r_i, r_j and $r_m \in R$.*

A regional pattern O may contain several intra-region movements, e.g. movement from p_3 to p_7 in trajectory T_3 in Fig. 1. Such movement does not provide the POI demand information as the user's POI needs can be satisfied in the given region, say r_4 in the example. Therefore we cannot infer any POI demand for this region by considering the intra-region movements. In order to mine the region POI demand, we define the cross-region pattern as follows:

Definition 3 *(Cross-Regional Pattern). For any adjacent category-region pairs $\langle c_n, r_i \rangle$ and $\langle c_m, r_j \rangle$ in a given regional pattern, if $i \neq j$, we call such category-region pair as cross-regional pattern.*

A toy example to clarify the above definitions is as following.

Example 1. As shown in Fig. 1, given 3 semantic categories T_1, T_2 and T_3, there are 4 cross-regional pattern $\langle (o, r_8), (g, r_6) \rangle$, $\langle (g, r_6), (b, r_3) \rangle$, $\langle (b, r_8), (g, r_6) \rangle$ and $\langle (g, r_6), (o, r_4) \rangle$.

Next we define the regional category number to reflect the POIs appearance in a given region as follows.

Definition 4 *(Regional Category Number). Given a region r_i, we use regional category number $n_{i,j}$ to denote the count of POI with category c_j in region r_i.*

We maintain a list $F_{r_i} = \langle (c_1, n_{i,1}), (c_2, n_{i,2}), \cdots, (c_m, n_{i,m}) \rangle$ to count how many POIs of each kind of category c_i in this region r_i, where m is the number of categories in this region. Besides gathering regional category number for each kind of category in each region, we also count the global sum of category c_m and the total number of POIs in region r_j.

Due to the unbalanced development of urban regions, only counting the POI numbers may not reflect the real POI demand accurately. For example, the number of POIs in rural area is usually much smaller than that in city centers. Besides, if there already exists a lot of POIs of same category, we shouldn't suggest the same type of POI for this region because it will lead unbalanced region development and intensify competition which may lead vendor's failure. So it is important to formulate the regional category density.

Next, we define two types of semantic category density, namely, *global category density* and *local category density* which are calculated in the following two equations respectively.

$$d - global_{j,m} = \frac{n_{j,m}}{|c_m|}, \tag{1}$$

where $n_{j,m}$ is the number of category m in region j and $|c_m|$ is total number of category m in the dataset.

$$d - local_{j,m} = \frac{n_{j,m}}{|POI_j|}, \tag{2}$$

where $|POI_j|$ is total number of POI in region j.

Based on the density defined above, we propose regional category density to reveal the category distribution information for a given region as follows.

Definition 5 *(Regional Category Density). A density list of given region r_j, $D_{r_j} = \langle (c_1, d_{j,1}), (c_2, d_{j,2}), \cdots, (c_m, d_{j,m}) \rangle$, where m is the total number of semantic categories in this region r_j. A regional category density $d_{j,m} = d - global_{j,m} \times d - local_{j,m}$.*

The key idea of calculating regional category density is that only using local-level density cannot reflect the actual development of region. Assuming this region has very few vendors, any categories in this region can have a high local-level density value, however people need more various vendors. We will omit their demands if we only focus regions with lower local-level density. And high global-level density doesn't mean that they can fulfill each person's need because it may be a very flourishing area which need more shops than other regions.

3.3   Regional POI Demand Modeling

Before introducing the regional POI demand modeling, we first introduce need number which quantifies people's demand for a specific category in the region.

Given a cross-regional pattern E, any length-2 sub-pattern $\langle$(origin.category, origin.region), (destination.category, destination.region)$\rangle$ in E, we update origin region need number of destination's category $\langle origin.region, destination.category \rangle$ by adding $\frac{1}{d}$, where d is regional category density of destination's category in origin's region. The formal definition of need number is given as follow.

Definition 6. *(Need Number)* $need_{j,i}$ *is the need number representing demand of* c_i *in* r_j. *Every time the demand of* c_i *in* r_j *emerges in cross-regional pattern* E, $need_{j,i}$ *adds* $\frac{1}{d_{j,i}}$.

The need number reflects the demand of category in the given region. We use $\frac{1}{d}$ as the need number increase step. According to our analysis in Sect. 3.2, the regional category density d reflects the influence of local density and global density of the category in a given region which is important when considering the unbalance development in urban area. A toy example to show how to compute the need number is provided as follow.

Example 2. As shown in Fig. 1, T_1 is a cross-regional pattern, and there exists 2 length-2 sub-pattern $\langle(o, r_8), (g, r_6)\rangle$ and $\langle(g, r_6), (b, r_3)\rangle$. And T_3 contains a length-3 cross-regional pattern, which includes 2 length-2 sub-pattern $\langle(b, r_8), (g, r_6)\rangle$ and $\langle(g, r_6), (o, r_4)\rangle$. We take bar in region r_6 as example. Bar in region r_6's local density is $\frac{2}{4}$ and its global density is $\frac{2}{5}$, so final regional category density of Bar in r_6 is 0.2, and r_6's need number of bar is $\frac{1}{0.2} = 5$.

The need number $need_{i,j}$ quantifies the demand of category c_j in the region r_i. And larger $need_{i,j}$ means a stronger demand for the category. Now we are ready to formalize the problem studied in this paper.

Problem Statement: Given places set $\mathcal{P}$, categories set $\mathcal{C}$ and grid parameter g which partition the space into $g \times g$ regions, the aim of our problem is that, for each region, to compute the need number of categories which are demanded in this region and return the rank of categories according to their need numbers.

4   Regional POI Demand Discovery

In this section, we first introduce the framework of our proposed method for regional demand mining. Then we present our algorithms that efficiently compute the need numbers and return ranked regional demands in detail.

4.1   Framework Overview

Figure 2 shows the framework of proposed regional POI demand discovery method. We take check-ins data, map data and POIs data as the input and each of these data goes through an offline preprocessing step. Specifically, the check-ins data are used to construct semantic trajectories. Then the semantic trajectories are separated into sub-trajectories according to the max time gap.

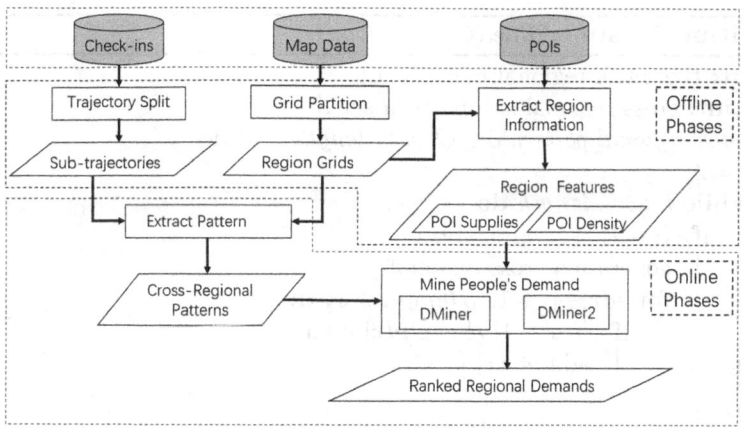

Fig. 2. An overview of framework

The map data are partitioned into regions by the grid size parameter g. And the POIs data together with the region information are used to extract regional POIs information as the region features.

The time difference between two adjacent check-ins is called time gap. In our daily life, the reason for people's movement is the demand for a variety of purposes or just semantic categories, if they need a kind of POI category strongly, they will go to this site as soon as possible. According to actual experience, a strong demand driven movement often happens in a short time period, for example period is from several hours up to a few days. So we introduce a max time gap threshold Δt, and split semantic trajectories into sub-trajectories to make sure that each time gap in one sub-trajectories is smaller than Δt. Another task in offline phase is to convert the semantic trajectories to regional patterns as we defined in Definition 2.

In the online phase, we conduct our proposed mining algorithm to extract cross-regional pattern, compute the need numbers and return ranked regional demands accordingly. Next, we will introduce our proposed algorithms in details.

4.2   Cross-Regional Pattern Extraction

In order to compute the need numbers, we first extract cross-regional patterns from regional patterns set $\mathcal{O}$ which are generated in the offline phase. We filter out pattern which length is less than 2 because it will not produce cross-regional pattern. As shown in Algorithm *patternMine()*, we first scan remaining patterns to check two adjacent category-regional pairs of a pattern whether located in the same region or not without considering category, in order to find a cross-region pattern. We add such category-region pair into the result set and try to extend this length-2 cross-regional pattern by repeatedly checking location information demonstrated as line 7. we finish the extension of this pattern until the next check-in is in the same region and start to find another cross-regional pattern from the remaining patterns.

Algorithm 1: patternMine ($\mathcal{O}$)

---

1 **Input:** the set of regional patterns $\mathcal{O}$
2 **Output:** cross-regional sub-pattern set $\mathcal{E}$
3 **for** *each regional pattern $o \in \mathcal{O}$ with length ≥ 2* **do**
4     $i = 2$;
5   **while** $i <= o.length$ **do**
6   **if** $o[i-1].r! = o[i].r$ **then**
7   generate a cross-regional pattern e ;
8   **for** $idx \in [i+1,\ o.length+1)$ **do**
9   **if** $o[idx-1].r! = o[idx].r$ **then**
10   add $o[idx]$ to e ;
11   **else**
12   i = idx+1;
13                 $\mathcal{E} = \mathcal{E} \cup e$;
14   break;
15   **end**
16   **end**
17   **else**
18   i = i+1;
19   **end**
20   **end**
21 **end**
22 return $\mathcal{E}$;

Example 3. T_3 as demonstrated in Fig. 1 can be translated into regional pattern $\langle(b,\ r_8),\ (g,\ r_6),\ (o,\ r_4),\ (b,\ r_4)\rangle$. We scan first two adjacent (category, region) pairs $(b,\ r_8)$ and $(g,\ r_6)$, and find these check-ins distributed in two regions r_8 and r_6 so we get a length-2 cross-regional pattern. Move to next pair $(o,\ r_4)$ which is placed at r_4 so the cross-regional pattern is extended to length-3. However, $(b,\ r_4)$ is also in region r_4, hence T_3 only includes a length-3 cross-regional pattern.

4.3 Computing Need Numbers for Regional Demand Mining

Next step is mining people's need from cross-regional pattern set $\mathcal{E}$ obtained by *patternmine()*. Algorithm **DMiner** shows how to compute the need numbers. According to daily experience, person can travel from one region to another region for a specific demand no matter the category of his(her) current starting point and the destination region of trip. Same category need starting from same region may ended in different regions. So in our algorithm, the idea to simplify the POIs scatter problem is that we only put focus on origin's starting region and destination's semantic category.

DMiner scans cross-regional pattern e in $\mathcal{E}$ from the first beginning and captures any two adjacent items in e to generate new category-region pairs.

Algorithm 2: DMiner ($\mathcal{E}$)

1 **Input:**cross-regional pattern set $\mathcal{E}$
2 **Output:**set of regional demand candidates $\mathcal{M}$
3 **for** *each e in $\mathcal{E}$* **do**
4   **for** *i = 1 to e.length-1* **do**
5   origin = $e[i]$ //$e[i]$ is the i-th check-in in e;
6   destination = $e[i+1]$;
7   generate a new need pair
        $m := ((destination.category, origin.region), 1/d_{x,y})$ //x is
        origin.region, y is destination.category
8         $\mathcal{M} = \mathcal{M} \cup m$;
9         $need_{x,y} + = 1/d_{x,y}$
10   **end**
11 **end**
12 **return** $\mathcal{M}$;

And the need number is continually updated according to the definitions (Line 9). After proceeding all the cross-regional patterns in $\mathcal{E}$, the regional demand candidates set $\mathcal{M}$ is obtained.

4.4 Optimization

By far, we only split cross-regional pattern e into a set of length-2 sub-patterns in *DMiner*. For example, if there exists a cross-regional pattern $\langle a, b, c \rangle$ (a, b, c all include category and region information), in *DMiner* we only pay attention to the pattern $\langle a, b \rangle$, $\langle b, c \rangle$. However, in real applications, people may not move from one region to another region for a specific category directly, they may stop-by somewhere first and then move to the destination. Trajectories split by max time gap ensure that stationary point in pattern doesn't cost too much time for visiting. So we can take $\langle a, c \rangle$ into consideration as well. In the optimized algorithm, we add another moving arrow for potential cross-regional category-region pair which may be farther in cross-regional pattern. And we define a new weighting factor σ to reflect the importance of such kind of extended cross-regional patterns.

$$\sigma = \frac{1}{j-i} \qquad (3)$$

where i and j stands for origin's and destination's place index in cross-regional pattern e, where $1 \leq i < j \leq e.length$. So σ of need acquired from two adjacent cross-regional pair is 1 as same as the weight in *DMiner*. In the optimized algorithm, the need number is updated by multiplying weight factor σ for the categories which have extended cross-regional pattern.

We call the optimized algorithm **DMiner2** which connects two category-region pairs if they are in different regions. Because cross-regional pattern may contain some behaviors happened in same region, for example cross-regional pattern $\langle$(bar, r_8), (gym, r_2), (office, r_8)$\rangle$, bar and office both locate in r_8. **DMiner2** should examine category distribution again.

4.5   Complexity Analysis

Our proposed framework consists of two online phases, namely cross-regional pattern extraction and need number computation. In the cross-regional pattern extraction phase, **patternMine** scans each regional pattern in regional pattern set $\mathcal{O}$ and records the adjacent movement pairs which are in different regions. Therefore the complexity of **patternMine** is $O(N)$ where N is the total length of the trajectory data set. In the need number computation phase, **DMiner** and **DMiner2** checks the cross-regional patterns generated in **patternMine** and generates regional demand candidates. Regional category density can be easily calculated by pre-stored regional category density list. The time complexity of **DMiner** and **DMiner2** is also $O(N)$, as in the worst case, **DMiner** and **DMiner2** have to check all movement pairs in the trajectory data set. Therefore, the overall time complexity of our framework is $O(N)$ which is linear to the size of data set. The experimental result also confirms the efficiency of our method.

Having the need numbers of the needed categories in a given region, we can return the ranked categories according their need numbers as regional POI demand.

5   Experiment

In this section, we evaluate performance of our proposed algorithms in real data sets. All algorithms are implemented in JAVA conducted on a computer running Linux (CentOS 7.3.1611) with 40 Intel Xeon CPU E5-2630 v4 2.2 GHz and 128 GB memory.

5.1   Dataset

In the experiments, we use two real-world data sets which are selected from the world-wide Foursquare check-ins data sets issued by Yang *et al.* [27]. Specifically, BR, US is the part of these numerous data sets where POIs and check-ins located at United Kingdom and United States respectively. The details of these datasets are listed in Table 1.

5.2   Competitors

We compare our proposed methods with state-of-the-art semantic trajectory mining algorithm **RegMiner** [7].

Since **RegMiner** is not designed for regional demand mining, we made the following modifications: First, we adopt the idea of **GridMiner** in [7] to fit **RegMiner** for our grid partition. Second, for the frequent threshold, we set

Table 1. The statistics of data sets

Dataset	BR	US
Number of POIs	54,278	168,625
Number of trajectories	4,893	13,489
Number of categories	414	427

1.5 as default which is much smaller than the value used in [7]. In our grid based partition, large frequent threshold will reduce number of the frequent patterns significantly and results in insufficient need demand, therefore we set the frequent threshold a reasonable small number which can archive balance between efficiency and effectiveness. We call the modified **RegMiner** as **RegMiner-Grid** in the rest of this paper.

5.3 Parameter Setting

We examine the impact of parameter for algorithms on BR dataset. Default parameters are set as follows: max time gap is 24 h and grid number is 100.

a. Varying grid number
The whole region is split into g × g size of small grids. Figure 3(a) shows grid number has a large impact on regional demand number. Different region distributions create various cross-regional patterns and result in diverse regional demands and large need number difference. On the other hand, smaller g such as 30 forms larger region area which lets trajectories hard to pass through. In the rest of the experiments, we set g as 100 and the length of each cell is round 6km and 8 km for BR and US which is reasonable for a neighborhood area in real cities.

b. Varying max time gap
We split raw trajectories into small trajectories which time between each two adjacent check-ins is no more than max time gap to filter out not very strong demand meeting. We conduct the experiments with max time gap varying from 12 h to 48 h. In Fig. 3(b), Δt represents max time gap. It shows that larger max time gap can produce large number of demands which confirms our analysis. In the rest of the experiments, we set Δt as 24 h.

5.4 Efficiency Study

In this section, we study the efficiency of the algorithms on BR with regard to two parameters, grid number and max time gap.

As shown in Fig. 4(a), the running time of all algorithms increases as the grid number increases. This is because the large grid numbers will produce more cross-regional patterns as the region is small. Therefore, it takes more time to compute the numbers for our algorithms and compute the frequent patterns for *RegMiner-Grid*. And our algorithms are always better than *RegMiner-Grid*,

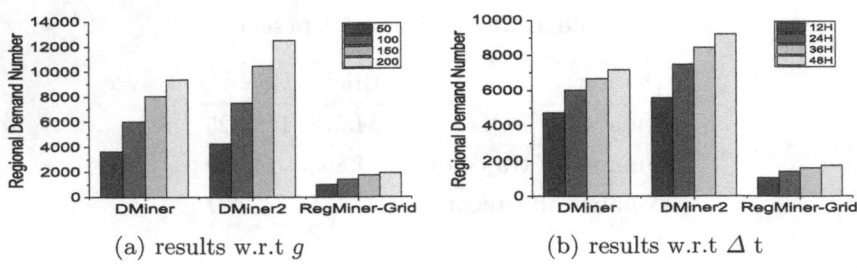

(a) results w.r.t g (b) results w.r.t Δt

Fig. 3. Regional demand number

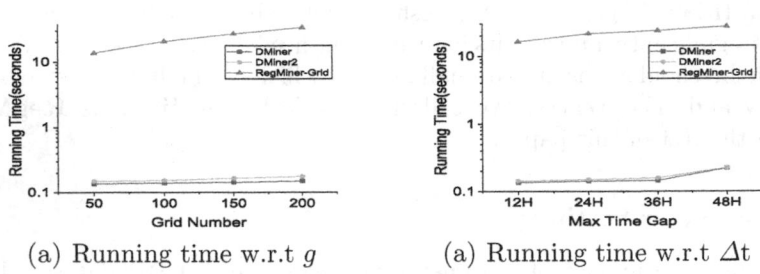

(a) Running time w.r.t g (a) Running time w.r.t Δt

Fig. 4. Running time on BR

as *RegMiner-Grid* takes more time when mining the frequent patterns with complicated computation of the support.

Similar trend can be observed in Fig. 4(b). The reason is that setting large max time gap will produce longer regional patterns and increase the computation for all the algorithms.

5.5 Effectiveness Study

In order to evaluate the effectiveness of the algorithms, we select New York city from US and Greater London from BR as represented. We divide the data sets into training and testing set as follows. We choose the first 80% check-ins to construct the regional patterns for training, and the remaining 20% check-ins are used for testing. First, Given a region, we rank the demands for POI categories and give a top-k ranking list. We use Hit@k as metric. For a region, if top-k predicted demands meet any actual open POI, hit number pluses 1. And hit@k is hit number divided by total number of regions. Figure 5 shows final result. Our algorithms outperforms the competitor in almost all cases.

5.6 Illustrating Cases

In order to better illustrate the ranking results for regions, we pick up several example regions with the top 5 identified demands in New York as shown in Table 2. As shown in the table, our method can effectively discovery the most needed categories and newly opened POIs in the ground-truth confirms that the proposed method is effective.

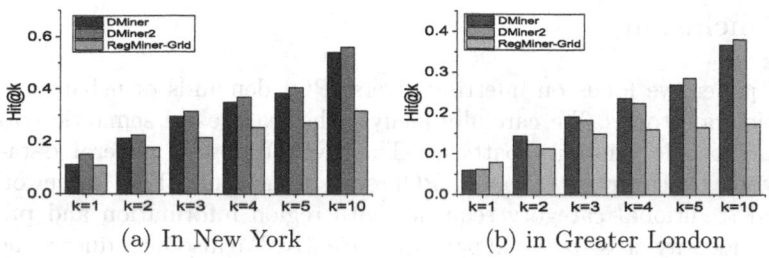

(a) In New York   (b) in Greater London

Fig. 5. Hit@k

Table 2. Identified POI demands for regions in New York

Region	Identified demands p@5	Groundtruth
84266	**House**; **Gas Station**; Drugstore; **Fast Food Restaurant**; American Restaurant	Residential Building; House; Gas Station Fast Food Restaurant; Convenience Store
84669	Community; **Department Store**; **Furniture Store**; **Road**; Drugstore	Department Store; Furniture Store; Road; Hotel; Bank
85461	Miscellaneous Shop; Bank; **Doctor'sOffice**; **Bakery**; **Automotive Shop**	Doctor's Office; Chinese Restaurant; Italian Restaurant; Bakery; Automotive Shop

Besides, We choose two hot tourism destinations, e.g. region 5116 in London and region 5367 in New York and list 10 representative regional demand in these regions. In reality, region 5116 is in London, which includes Kensington Palace, Battersea park and other famous spots. And Region 5367 is a part of Manhattan. There exists a lot check-ins scattered in theses regions, so our approaches are more easier to mine their regional category needs as shown in Fig. 6. Need Number is too large so these number are divided by 10^5 and 10^7 respectively in London and New York to show clearly.

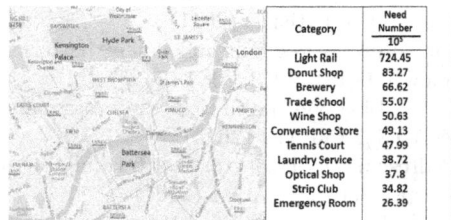

Category	Need Number 10^5
Light Rail	724.45
Donut Shop	83.27
Brewery	66.62
Trade School	55.07
Wine Shop	50.63
Convenience Store	49.13
Tennis Court	47.99
Laundry Service	38.72
Optical Shop	37.8
Strip Club	34.82
Emergency Room	26.39

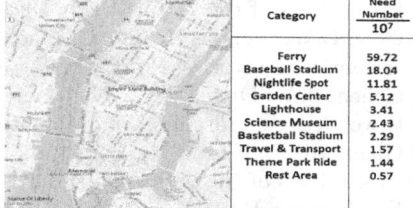

Category	Need Number 10^7
Ferry	59.72
Baseball Stadium	18.04
Nightlife Spot	11.81
Garden Center	5.12
Lighthouse	3.41
Science Museum	2.43
Basketball Stadium	2.29
Travel & Transport	1.57
Theme Park Ride	1.44
Rest Area	0.57

(a) Region 5116 in London   (b) Region 5367 in New York

Fig. 6. Regional demand in real area

6 Conclusion

In this paper, we focus on inferring diverse POI demands of urban area using semantic trajectories. We carefully analyze the features of semantic trajectory data and people' mobility patterns. Then we propose a general data-driven framework **DMiner** for regional POI demand mining. The framework uses enriched traditional category sequence with region information and **pattern-Mine** to identify cross-regional pattern efficiently. We also introduce some interesting observations to enrich the results and further propose a improved method **DMiner2**. We apply our framework on real data sets to show the effectiveness and efficiency with comparison to state-of-the-art locally frequent pattern mining method. Furthermore, we also present several example mining results for readers' better understanding.

Acknowledgements. We sincerely thank the anonymous reviewers for their feedback which helped improve our work. The research of Shiyu Yang is supported by NSFC61802127 and Shanghai Sailing Program 18YF1406700. The research of Long Yuan is supported by NSFC61902184 and NSF of Jiangsu Province BK20190453

References

1. Alvares, L.O., Bogorny, V., Kuijpers, B., de Macedo, J.A.F., Moelans, B., et al.: A model for enriching trajectories with semantic geographical information. In: Proceedings of the 15th Annual ACM International Symposium on Advances in Geographic Information Systems, p. 22. ACM (2007)
2. Batran, M., Mejia, M., Kanasugi, H., Sekimoto, Y., Shibasaki, R.: Inferencing human spatiotemporal mobility in greater Maputo via mobile phone big data mining. ISPRS Int. J. Geo-Inf. **7**(7), 259 (2018)
3. Cao, H., Mamoulis, N., Cheung, D.W.: Mining frequent spatio-temporal sequential patterns. In: Proceedings of the 5th IEEE ICDM, pp. 82–89. IEEE (2005)
4. Chan, H.K.H., Long, C., Yan, D., Wong, R.C.W.: Fraction-score: a new support measure for co-location pattern mining. In: Proceedings of the 35th IEEE ICDE, pp. 1514–1525. IEEE (2019)
5. Chen, L., Gao, Y., Fang, Z., Miao, X., Jensen, C.S., et al.: Real-time distributed co-movement pattern detection on streaming trajectories. Proc. VLDB Endow. **12**(10), 1208–1220 (2019)
6. Chen, Z., Shen, H.T., Zhou, X.: Discovering popular routes from trajectories. In: Proceedings of the 27th IEEE ICDE, pp. 900–911. IEEE (2011)
7. Choi, D.W., Pei, J., Heinis, T.: Efficient mining of regional movement patterns in semantic trajectories. Proc. VLDB Endow. **10**(13), 2073–2084 (2017)
8. Cohen, S.A., Duncan, T., Thulemark, M.: Lifestyle mobilities: the crossroads of travel, leisure and migration. Mobilities **10**(1), 155–172 (2015)
9. Giannotti, F., Nanni, M., Pinelli, F., Pedreschi, D.: Trajectory pattern mining. In: Proceedings of the 13th ACM SIGKDD, pp. 330–339. ACM (2007)
10. Hu, T., Song, R., Wang, Y., Xie, X., Luo, J.: Mining shopping patterns for divergent urban regions by incorporating mobility data. In: Proceedings of the 25th ACM International on Conference on Information and Knowledge Management, pp. 569–578. ACM (2016)

11. Karamshuk, D., Noulas, A., Scellato, S., Nicosia, V., Mascolo, C.: Geo-spotting: mining online location-based services for optimal retail store placement. In: Proceedings of the 19th ACM SIGKDD, pp. 793–801. ACM (2013)
12. Kim, Y., Han, J., Yuan, C.: TOPTRAC: topical trajectory pattern mining. In: Proceedings of the 21th ACM SIGKDD, pp. 587–596. ACM (2015)
13. Li, Q., Yu, Z., Guo, B., Lu, X.: Inferring housing demand based on express delivery data. In: Proceedings of the 6th IEEE International Conference on Big Data, pp. 1445–1454. IEEE (2018)
14. Li, Y., Zheng, Y., Ji, S., Wang, W., Gong, Z., et al.: Location selection for ambulance stations: a data-driven approach. In: Proceedings of the 23rd SIGSPATIAL, p. 85. ACM (2015)
15. Liu, Y., Liu, C., Lu, X., Teng, M., Zhu, H., et al.: Point-of-interest demand modeling with human mobility patterns. In: Proceedings of the 23rd ACM SIGKDD, pp. 947–955. ACM (2017)
16. Liu, Y., Liu, C., Yuan, N.J., Duan, L., Fu, Y., et al.: Exploiting heterogeneous human mobility patterns for intelligent bus routing. In: Proceedings of the 14th IEEE ICDM, pp. 360–369. IEEE (2014)
17. Ma, S., Zheng, Y., Wolfson, O.: T-share: a large-scale dynamic taxi ridesharing service. In: Proceedings of the 29th IEEE ICDE, pp. 410–421. IEEE (2013)
18. Moosavi, S., Samavatian, M.H., Nandi, A., Parthasarathy, S., Ramnath, R.: Short and long-term pattern discovery over large-scale geo-spatiotemporal data. In: Proceedings of the 25th ACM SIGKDD, pp. 2905–2913. ACM (2019)
19. Niu, H., Liu, J., Fu, Y., Liu, Y., Lang, B.: Exploiting human mobility patterns for gas station site selection. In: Navathe, S.B., Wu, W., Shekhar, S., Du, X., Wang, X.S., Xiong, H. (eds.) DASFAA 2016. LNCS, vol. 9642, pp. 242–257. Springer, Cham (2016). https://doi.org/10.1007/978-3-319-32025-0_16
20. Noulas, A., Scellato, S., Mascolo, C., Pontil, M.: An empirical study of geographic user activity patterns in foursquare. In: Proceedings of the 5th International AAAI Conference on Weblogs and Social Media. AAAI (2011)
21. Pilinkienė, V.: Market demand forecasting models and their elements in the context of competitive market. Eng. Econ. **60**(5) (2008)
22. Pilinkienė, V.: Selection of market demand forecast methods: criteria and application. Inžinerinė ekonomika (3) 19–25 (2008)
23. Shi, H., Li, Y., Cao, H., Zhou, X., Zhang, C., et al.: Semantics-aware hidden Markov model for human mobility. IEEE Trans. Knowl. Data Eng. (2019)
24. Sun, Y., Zhu, H., Zhuang, F., Gu, J., He, Q.: Exploring the urban region-of-interest through the analysis of online map search queries. In: Proceedings of the 24th ACM SIGKDD, pp. 2269–2278. ACM (2018)
25. Tiebout, C.M.: A pure theory of local expenditures. J. Polit. Econ. **64**(5), 416–424 (1956)
26. Xu, H., Zhang, Y., Wei, J., Yang, Z., Wang, J.: Spatiotemporal-aware region recommendation with deep metric learning. In: Li, G., Yang, J., Gama, J., Natwichai, J., Tong, Y. (eds.) DASFAA 2019. LNCS, vol. 11448, pp. 491–494. Springer, Cham (2019). https://doi.org/10.1007/978-3-030-18590-9_73
27. Yang, D., Zhang, D., Qu, B.: Participatory cultural mapping based on collective behavior data in location-based social networks. ACM Trans. Intell. Syst. Technol. (TIST) **7**(3) (2016). Article no. 30
28. Yao, Z., Fu, Y., Liu, B., Hu, W., Xiong, H.: Representing urban functions through zone embedding with human mobility patterns. In: IJCAI, pp. 3919–3925. Morgan (2018)

29. Yuan, J., Zheng, Y., Xie, X.: Discovering regions of different functions in a city using human mobility and POIs. In: Proceedings of the 18th ACM SIGKDD, pp. 186–194. ACM (2012)
30. Zhang, C., Han, J., Shou, L., Lu, J., La Porta, T.: Splitter: mining fine-grained sequential patterns in semantic trajectories. Proc. VLDB Endow. **7**(9), 769–780 (2014)
31. Zhong, Y., Yuan, N.J., Zhong, W., Zhang, F., Xie, X.: You are where you go: inferring demographic attributes from location check-ins. In: Proceedings of the 8th ACM International Conference on Web Search and Data Mining, pp. 295–304. ACM (2015)
32. Zhou, X., Noulas, A., Mascolo, C., Zhao, Z.: Discovering latent patterns of urban cultural interactions in WeChat for modern city planning. In: Proceedings of the 24th ACM SIGKDD, pp. 1069–1078. ACM (2018)

Learning from Heterogeneous Student Behaviors for Multiple Prediction Tasks

Haobing Liu, Yanmin Zhu[✉], and Yanan Xu

Department of Computer Science and Engineering, Shanghai Jiao Tong University,
Shanghai, China
{liuhaobing,yzhu,xuyanan2015}@sjtu.edu.cn

Abstract. Prediction tasks about students have practical real-world significance at both student level and university level. For example, predicting if a student will fail to graduate can alert the university student affairs office to take predictive measures to help the student improve academic performance. In this paper, we focus on making multiple predictions together, since leaning the model for a specific task may have the data-sparsity problem. With the rapid development of smart campus, the university is accumulating a large amount of heterogeneous data of student behaviors, such as entering libraries behavior, entering dormitory behavior. In this paper, we propose to learn from heterogeneous student behaviors for making multiple predictions about students. However, leveraging heterogeneous behaviors have two main challenges. First, *student profiles have a large impact on their behaviors and have not been well modeled in previous studies.* Second, *behaviors of different days will have different degrees of impact and should be treated unequally.* To address these challenges, we propose a novel variant of LSTM and a novel attention mechanism. The proposed LSTM is able to learn student profile-aware representation from the heterogeneous behavior sequences. The proposed attention mechanism can dynamically learn the different importance degrees of different days for every student. With multi-task learning, we can deal with multiple perdition tasks at the same time to alleviate the data-sparsity problem. Qualitative and quantitative experiments on a real-world dataset collected at Shanghai Jiao Tong University (SJTU) have demonstrated the effectiveness of our model.

Keywords: LSTM · Attention mechanism · Heterogeneous student behaviors · Multi-task learning

1 Introduction

Recently, more and more people are concerned about educational field. By utilizing data mining techniques in this field, there arise various significant prediction tasks for better understanding students and the settings which students learn in, such as academic performance prediction [30,31], library circulation predication [26,28], graduation failure prediction [23]. With the help of these tasks, educators could know future grades of students, future library circulation or whether

© Springer Nature Switzerland AG 2020
Y. Nah et al. (Eds.): DASFAA 2020, LNCS 12113, pp. 297–313, 2020.
https://doi.org/10.1007/978-3-030-59416-9_18

students pass/fail for a specific given course. Then educators could facilitate personalized education, do library strategic plan or design in-time intervention.

Previous works about these prediction tasks mostly focus on the factors including values of historical situations (such as historical grades [8,30], historical library circulation [26,28]) and student demographic information (i.e., student profiles) [17,21]. These factors are relatively stable over the long run and are difficult to change via educational management. Besides, in online learning environments (e.g., massive open online courses), students' digital records collected by online learning platforms such as logs about video-watching behavior, time spent on specific questions, test/quiz grades have been leveraged [2,3,14,16,19]. The digital records can directly reflect students' efforts and are key predictors. But these records are rarely digitized in traditional education.

Thanks to the development of information technology in college, there is a clear trend to augment physical facilities with sensing, computing and communication capabilities [33]. These facilities unobtrusively record students' digital footprints such as logs of entering libraries and logs of entering dormitory. The digital footprints of students encode heterogeneous behaviors which are helpful for many prediction tasks. For example, academic efforts can be learned from entering libraries records and entering dormitory records. Academic efforts are key predictors for predicting academic performance, the number of borrowed books or the number of failed courses. In other words, students' hard study (i.e., entering libraries frequently, early; going back to dormitory late) can be paid back and may result in borrowing many books from libraries. Once the digital footprints are available, they can be used to improve prediction performances. In this paper, we collect digital footprints of $10k$ students spanning one academic year from campus smart card usage for entering libraries and dormitory. One footprint record mainly contains *student identity number* and *the timestamp of the record*.

Based on the above thoughts, we want to leverage heterogeneous student behaviors to deal with multiple prediction tasks. Here we take Predicting Academic Performance (PAP), Predicting the Number of Borrowed Books (PNBB), and Predicting the Number of Failed Courses (PNFC) as three motivating examples of prediction tasks which can be implemented using our proposed model. However, leveraging heterogeneous behaviors confronts two main challenges. The first challenge is that *student profiles have a large impact on their behaviors and have not been well modeled in previous studies*. Similar behaviors of different kinds of students may mean differently. For example, there are two students: student 1 and student 2. Their records of entering libraries are similar. But student 1 is a freshman; student 2 is a senior. Student 2 would have less homework to do than student 1. In return, it means student 2 works harder than student 1. Thus academic performance of student 2 should be better than student 1. The second challenge is that *behaviors of different days to the task will have different degrees of impact and should be treated unequally*. For example, behaviors of different days have different degrees of impact for indicating students' efforts. The academic efforts of students on different days will change due to many reasons such as holidays, moods, study habits.

To address the above challenges, we propose an Attentional Profile-Aware Multi-Task model (APAMT). More specifically, for heterogeneous behaviors, each kind of daily behavior sequence is modeled by a variant of LSTM named Profile-Aware LSTM. By adding student profiles in the gates of LSTM, LSTM can consider student profiles when modeling daily behavior sequence, so as to improve the performances of prediction tasks. Besides, a novel attention mechanism is designed over Profile-Aware LSTM to dynamically learn the different importance degrees of different days for every student for improving the prediction results. Moreover, existing methods to deal with prediction tasks in educational field focus on each individual task, which is sub-optimal as valuable student information is not shared across different tasks and there exists a data-sparsity problem. In our dataset, only about 10% of students failed courses in one semester. As a consequence, it is necessary to leverage multi-task learning.

In summary, the main contributions of this paper are as follows:

- We propose an Attentional Profile-Aware Multi-Task model (i.e., APAMT). APAMT can learn personalized and general student representations from student profiles and student heterogeneous behaviors to deal with multiple prediction tasks in educational field.
- We design a variant of LSTM called Profile-Aware LSTM to capture student profiles when modeling heterogeneous daily behaviors. We design a novel attention mechanism for dynamically finding out informative days. We adopt multi-task learning for enabling the deep neural network to learn general and reliable student representations and alleviating the data-sparsity problem.
- We evaluate our proposed model on a large-scale real-world dataset. The experimental results demonstrate that our method outperforms the competing baselines and every component of our model is well-designed, benefiting the prediction.

The rest of this paper is organized as follows. We first introduce the related work of our research in Sect. 2. Next, we introduce related notations followed by the problem statement in Sect. 3. Following that, we propose our model in Sect. 4. Then, Sect. 5 presents qualitative and quantitative results of different methods. Finally, we conclude the paper in Sect. 6.

2   Related Work

Predicting Academic Performance. PAP task is the most frequently studied among prediction tasks in educational field. In this paper, we choose Weighted Average Grade (WAG) which is on a 100-point scale to quantitatively describe the academic performance of a student in one semester. WAG can be seen as the Cumulative Grade Point Average (CGPA). Most methods used for academic performance prediction are based on traditional classification/regression techniques such as linear regression [9]. Besides traditional methods, some researchers seek novel solutions. For example, matrix factorization techniques are utilized in some researches [24]. Feed forward neural networks are adopted in some works [29]. LSTMs are also leveraged [8]. Ensemble approaches are also studied [30]. As for employing students' behaviors to predict student performance, Wang et al. [27] found correlations between students' GPAs and automatic sensing behavioral data obtained from smartphones and chose a linear regression model. However, the passive sensing behavioral data they used is only collected from a small number of student and the collecting way is not universal enough. Yao et al. [31] studied the effect of social influence on predicting academic performance based on students' multiple behaviors. The effect of students' behaviors is very indirect. These studies ignore the influence of student profiles on modeling student daily behaviors and treat all days equally.

Predicting the Number of Borrowed Books. Most studies about library circulation prediction focus on modeling historical time series. Methods used include support vector regression [26], feed forward neural networks [28] and so on. Students' information hasn't been used in library circulation prediction.

Predicting the Number of Failed Courses. Existing studies about failure prediction mainly focus on classifying students into two categories: either pass or fail for a specific given course. Some studies do not distinguish this task with academic performance prediction task [32]. But we distinguish these two tasks and we aim to predict the number of failed courses. Methods used in failure prediction include k-nearest neighbour method [25], ensemble method [32], feed forward neural networks [23] and so on.

Multi-task Learning. Multi-task learning (MTL) was first analyzed by Caruana detaily [4]. Multi-task learning could improve learning efficiency and prediction accuracy for each task when compared to training a separate model for each task. One important reason is that multi-task learning allows sharing of statistical strength and transferring of knowledge between related tasks. Thus the shared representations can capture more underlying factors and become more general. Multi-task learning has been used successfully in many fields, such as computer vision [7,18], natural language processing [6].

To the best of our knowledge, our work is the first study that uses deep multi-task learning to deal with multiple prediction tasks in educational field.

3   Preliminaries

In this section, we first fix some notations and introduce the problem statement.

Entering Libraries Records. When students enter libraries, they need to swipe their campus cards. Thus records are generated. One entering libraries record can be represented as $r_{Lib} = (s, t_{Lib})$, where s denotes student s and t_{Lib} denotes the timestamp of the record.

Entering Dormitory Records. Similar to entering libraries records, one entering dormitory record is represented as $r_{Dorm} = (s, t_{Dorm})$, where s denotes student s and t_{Dorm} denotes the timestamp.

Student Profile Records. One record of this sub-dataset can be represented as (s, d^s), where d^s is an attribute set about demographic information of student s. In this paper, according to the dataset, the attributes include province, nationality, gender, grade, school, and department. If other demographic information like age was available, it could also be added.

Student Final Course Grade Records. Given course c_θ, one record can be represented as $r_{Grade} = (s, t, c_\theta, credit(c_\theta), grade^s(c_\theta))$, where t is the index of the whole semesters that student s involves in; $credit(c_\theta)$ is the credit of course c_θ and $grade^s(c_\theta)$ is the final grade student s achieves in course c_θ.

Problem Statement. In this paper, we have three tasks to deal with.

PAP task: Given digital footprints (i e , $\{r_{Lib}\}$ and $[r_{Dorm}])$ generated in the first half (to give the prediction results ahead of time) of the semester T, profiles d^s and final course grade records r_{Grade} generated in all previous $T - 1$ semesters of student s, our goal is to predict academic performance (i.e., WGA) of student s at the end of semester T.

PNBB task: Given digital footprints (i.e., $\{r_{Lib}\}$ and $\{r_{Dorm}\}$) generated in the first half (to give the prediction results ahead of time) of the semester T, profiles d^s and the number of borrowed books in each previous semester (the number of all previous semesters is $T - 1$) of student s, our goal is to predict the number of borrowed books of student s at the end of semester T.

PNFC task: Given digital footprints (i.e., $\{r_{Lib}\}$ and $\{r_{Dorm}\}$) generated in the first half (to give the prediction results ahead of time) of the semester T, profiles d^s and final course grade records r_{Grade} generated in all previous $T - 1$ semesters of student s, our goal is to predict the number of failed courses of student s at the end of this semester T.

4   Proposed APAMT Model

The main structure of our proposed Attentional Profile-Aware Multi-Task model (APAMT) is illustrated in Fig. 1. Detailed structures of task-specific modules are shown in Fig. 2. The rest of this section is organized as follows. First, we will introduce how to model heterogeneous student behaviors with Profile-Aware LSTM and attention-based pooling. After generating personalized student representation, we will leverage task-specific information and design task-specific feed forward neural networks to deal with multiple prediction tasks together.

4.1   Inputs and Dense Embedding

Student profiles d^s are represented in the form of one high-dimensional vector including many one-hot encoded vectors. To reduce the dimension and get a

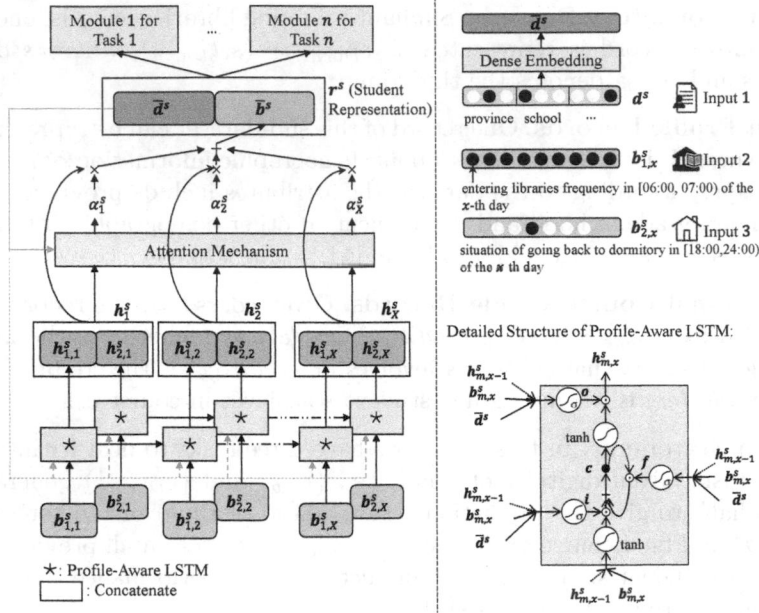

Fig. 1. The main structure of APAMT.

better representation, we use a dense embedding layer. The transformation is formalized as:

$$\bar{d}^s = W_d d^s, \tag{1}$$

where W_d is mapping matrix.

Thinking that the combination of entering libraries behavior and going back to dormitory behavior can reveal students' academic efforts, we extract behavior sequence of entering libraries and behavior sequence of going back to dormitory from $\{r_{Lib}\}$ and $\{r_{Dorm}\}$.

More specifically, we divide one day into 24 time slots by hour (i.e., $[00 : 00, 01 : 00), [01 : 00, 02 : 00), ..., [23 : 00, 24 : 00)$). According to $\{r_{Lib}\}$, almost 100% of entering libraries records are generated in 07:00–23:00. So we use 16 elements to record entering libraries frequency in 07:00–23:00 for each day as the upper-right of Fig. 1 shows. In this way, we get behavior sequence of entering libraries: $b_{1,1}, b_{1,2}, ..., b_{1,x}, ..., b_{1,X}$ (x is the index. $X = 63$ because the number of days in half semester is 63).

One going back to dormitory record is defined as the last record of entering dormitory of the day. Based on $\{r_{Dorm}\}$, around 84% of going back to dormitory records are generated in 18:00–24:00. So we use a vector with a length of 6 to record the situation of going back to dormitory in 18:00–24:00 for each day as the upper-right of Fig. 1 shows. In this way, we get behavior sequence of going back to dormitory: $b_{2,1}, b_{2,2}, ..., b_{2,x}, ..., b_{2,X}$.

4.2   Profile-Aware LSTM

RNN is widely used to deal with sequence data and has achieved good performance in various domains. There are many well-known variants of RNN models, such as LSTM [12], GRU [5], bidirectional RNNs [20]. But student profiles can not be considered when modeling student behavior sequence with these variants of RNN models. Similar behaviors of different kinds of students may mean differently. So we propose a new variant of LSTM called Profile-Aware LSTM. We treat student profiles as a strong signal in the gates of Profile-Aware LSTM (as Eq. (2), (3) and (5) show). That is to say, what to extract, what to remember and what to forward are extensively affected by student profiles. Behavior sequence is the only input of Profile-Aware LSTM (as Eq. (4) shows).

Profile-Aware LSTM model is formulated as follows:

$$i_x = \sigma(W_{ib}b_{m,x}^s + W_{ih}h_{m,x-1}^s + W_{id}\bar{d}^s + b_i), \tag{2}$$

$$f_m = \sigma(W_{fb}h_{m,x}^s + W_{fh}h_{m,x-1}^s + W_{fd}\bar{u}^s + b_f), \tag{3}$$

$$c_x = f_x \odot c_{x-1} + i_x \odot \tanh(W_{cb}b_{m,x}^s + W_{ch}h_{m,x-1}^s + b_c), \tag{4}$$

$$o_x = \sigma(W_{ob}b_{m,x}^s + W_{oh}h_{m,x-1}^s + W_{od}\bar{d}^s + b_o), \tag{5}$$

$$h_{m,x}^s = o_x \odot \tanh(c_x), \tag{6}$$

where $b_{m,x}^s$ and $h_{m,x}^s$ are one input element and the corresponding output of Profile-Aware LSTM unit, i.e., hidden state at time x, respectively. $m = 1, 2$. W terms denote weight matrices and b terms are bias vectors. σ is the element-wise sigmoid function and $\odot$ is the element-wise product.

We use two Profile-Aware LSTMs to model two kinds of behaviors respectively.

4.3   Attention-Based Pooling

The hidden representation of all heterogeneous behaviors of the x-th day can be formalized as:

$$h_x^s = h_{1,x}^s \oplus h_{2,x}^s, \tag{7}$$

where $\oplus$ is concatenation operation.

Behaviors of different days to the task will have different degrees of impact. For example, the academic efforts of students on different days may change due to many reasons. Inspired by the success of attention mechanism in machine translation [1], we apply a novel attention mechanism over Profile-Aware LSTM to draw information from the sequence by different weights. In the model, we consider each vector h_x^s as heterogeneous behaviors representation of the x-th day, and represent the sequence by a weighted sum of the vector representation of all the days. The attention weight makes it possible to perform proper credit assignment to days according to their importance to the student. Mathematically, We compute attention weight α_x^s for each day with the following equations:

$$a_x^s = W_{a0} \tanh(W_{a1} h_x^s + W_{a2} \bar{d}^s + b_a), \tag{8}$$

$$\alpha_x^s = \frac{\exp(a_x^s)}{\sum_{x=1}^{X} \exp(a_x^s)}, \tag{9}$$

where W terms denote weight matrices; b_a is bias vector. Similar to Profile-Aware LSTM, student profiles also contribute to the attention weights.

The advanced student behavior representation is generated using the following equation:

$$\bar{b}^s = \sum_{x=1}^{X} \alpha_x^s h_x^s, \tag{10}$$

The student representation r^s is the concatenation of $\bar{d}^s$ and $\bar{b}^s$:

$$r^s = \bar{d}^s \oplus \bar{b}^s. \tag{11}$$

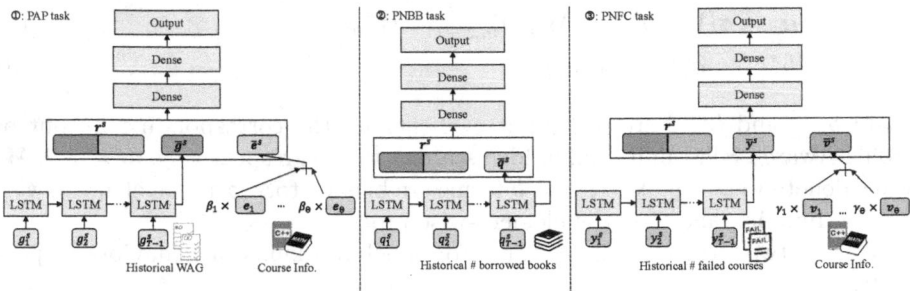

Fig. 2. The detailed structures of different modules w.r.t. different tasks.

4.4 Multiple Prediction Tasks

After obtaining the personalized student representation, we define several related tasks to learn simultaneously as Fig. 2 shows. For each task, the other tasks are viewed as regularization. Information about historical WAG, information about historical number of borrowed books, information about historical number of failed courses and information about courses are task-specific. We hope learned student representation does not contain these task-specific features. So we do not merge all information together as common multi-task learning.

PAP Task: As mentioned in Sect. 2, we use WAG to quantitatively describe the academic performance. Given $\{r_{Grade}\}$, WAG is calculated with the following equation:

$$g_t^s = \sum_{\theta=1}^{\Theta} \frac{credit(c_\theta) grade^s(c_\theta)}{\sum_{\theta=1}^{\Theta} credit(c_\theta)}, \tag{12}$$

where Θ is the number of courses chosen by student s in semester t. In this way, we get historical WAG sequence of student s: $g_1^s, g_2^s, ..., g_t^s, ..., g_T^s$. Historical WAG sequence reveals students' trends of academic performance. Note that the length of historical WAG sequence may vary from person to person, so we adopt a dynamic LSTM to model the sequence and get the higher representation $\bar{g}^s$.

We find that students get higher grades easily in some courses such as CS362 as Fig. 3 shows. This means different courses have different levels of difficulty. So for each course, we extract descriptive statistics (i.e., minimum, maximum, median, first quartile, third quartile, mean, standard deviation) as features. These features can describe the properties of distribution from multiple aspects. The feature vector of course c_θ is represented as e_θ. Next, we aggregate feature vectors of all courses by leveraging course credit information:

$$\bar{e}^s = \sum_{\theta=1}^{\Theta} \frac{credit(c_\theta)e_\theta}{\sum_{0-1}^{\Theta} credit(c_0)}. \tag{13}$$

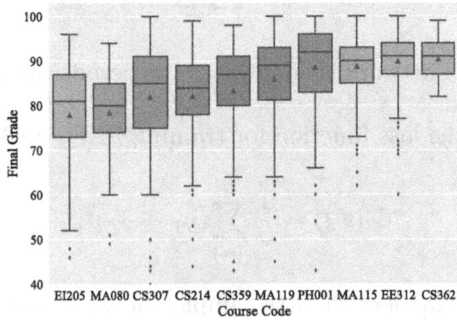

Fig. 3. Grade distributions of some different courses set in Department of Computer Science and Engineering.

Then we feed r^s, $\bar{g}^s$ and $\bar{e}^s$ into a feed forward neural network and get the prediction result $\hat{g}_T^s$ as the left of Fig. 2 illustrated.

We use the mean squared error (MSE) as the loss function for training PAP task:

$$\mathcal{L}_1(\Phi_1) = \frac{1}{U} \sum_{i=1}^{U} (g_T^i - \hat{g}_T^i)^2, \tag{14}$$

where u donates one training sample; U is the number of training samples; g_T^i denotes the label of the i-th sample and Φ_1 is all trainable parameters for PAP task.

PNBB Task: Similarly, historical number of borrowed books sequence reveals students' trends of the number of borrowed books. We utilize another dynamic

LSTM to model historical number of borrowed books sequence and get the high-level features $\bar{q}^s$. Then r^s and $\bar{q}^s$ are fed to another feed forward neural network which could model the complex interactions between the high-level features and give the final prediction result $\hat{q}_T^s$ as the middle of Fig. 2 shows.

We use MSE as the loss function for training PNBB task:

$$\mathcal{L}_2(\Phi_2) = \frac{1}{U} \sum_{i=1}^{U} (q_T^i - \hat{q}_T^i)^2, \tag{15}$$

where q_T^i denotes the label of the i-th sample and Φ_2 is all trainable parameters for PNBB task.

PNFC Task: LSTM is leveraged to model historical number of failed courses sequence. We also extract some features such as course failure rate and descriptive statistics. The feature vector of course c_θ is represented as v_θ as the right of Fig. 2 illustrated. We merger information of every course by:

$$\bar{v}^s = \sum_{\theta=1}^{\Theta} \frac{v_\theta}{\Theta}. \tag{16}$$

Then a shallow neural network is adopted as the decoder and the final prediction result $\hat{y}_T^s$ is generated.

We use MSE as the loss function for training PNFC task:

$$\mathcal{L}_3(\Phi_3) = \frac{1}{U} \sum_{i=1}^{U} (y_T^i - \hat{y}_T^i)^2, \tag{17}$$

where y_T^i denotes the label of the i-th sample and Φ_3 is all trainable parameters for PNFC task.

4.5   Optimization

The total loss is computed as the sum of the three individual losses:

$$\mathcal{L}_{Total} = \lambda_1 \mathcal{L}_1 + \lambda_2 \mathcal{L}_2 + \lambda_3 \mathcal{L}_3, \tag{18}$$

where λ is weight parameter which is decided based on the importance of the task in the overall loss. In this paper, we choose ($\lambda_1 = \lambda_2 = \lambda_3 = 1$) for our experiments assuming that theses tasks are equally important.

We adopt the adaptive moment estimation (Adam) [13] as the optimizer. Adam is an optimization method that can compute adaptive learning rates for each parameter and converges faster.

In order to improve the generalization capability of our models, we adopt dropout [22] to prevent the potential overfitting problem.

5 Experiments

In this section, we will describe the detailed experimental settings and discuss the results.

5.1 Dataset

The data were collected at SJTU with an enrollment of $10k$ undergraduate students. For protecting privacy, the data are collected and analyzed anonymously. This study has been approved by the Institutional Review Board (IRB). Dataset statistics are shown in Table 1.

Table 1. Dataset statistics.

Item	Value
# Students	10,000
Student behaviors time span	09/12/2016–01/15/2017 (i.e., Fall 2016 semester)
	02/20/2017–06/25/2017 (i.e., Spring 2017 semester)
# Library entrance records	867,571
# Dormitory entrance records	1,783,595
# Demographic records	10,000
# Courses	2,482

5.2 Baselines and Metric

We compare our proposed method with the following models and MSE is adopted as the evaluation metric:

- **HA:** We give the prediction result by the average value of historical situations.
- **LSTM** [8]: LSTM is widely used to model sequence data.
- **BRR** [9]: Bayesian Ridge Regression (BRR) is a generalized linear model which has L_2 regularization.
- **SVR** [26]: Support Vector Regression (SVR) is a variant of support vector machine (SVM) for supporting regression tasks. SVR is a minimum-margin regression which could model the non-linear relation between features.
- **RF:** Random Forest (RF) is an ensemble method with decision trees as base learners. It is based on "bagging" idea and its performance is much better than decision tree.
- **GBDT:** Gradient Boosting Decision Tree (GBDT) is another kind of ensemble method using decision trees as base learners. GBDT is a generalization of boosting to arbitrary differentiable loss functions.
- **FNN** [23,29]: Feedforward Neural Network (FNN) consists of multiple layers of nodes. Each layer is fully connected to the next layer in the network.

5.3 Implementation Details

For baselines, we extract features from heterogeneous student behaviors as Guan et al. suggested [10]. As for the data preprocessing, we represent the categorical features with one-hot encoding. We process numerical inputs with the Min-Max normalization to ensure they are within a suitable range. For WAG, the number of borrowed books and the number of failed courses, because we use tanh as the activation function in the output layer, we scale them into $[-1, 1]$. In the evaluation, we re-scale the predicted value back to the normal value, compared with the groundtruth. For the other numerical inputs, we scale them into $[0, 1]$. Around half of the data (Fall 2016) are used as the training set and the other half (Spring 2017) are used for testing.

The hyperparameters of all models are tuned with a ten-fold cross-validation method on the training dataset. We only present the optimal settings are as follows. The dense embedding layer has 30 neurons. The dimensions of the hidden states in the Profile-Aware LSTMs which handle entering libraries and going back to dormitory behaviors are set as 12 and 4 respectively. The dimension of the hidden state in the dynamic LSTM which handles historical WAG/number of borrowed books/number of failed courses sequence is set as 5. The shallow feed forward neural networks for giving the final prediction results have the same structure: $100 \rightarrow 100 \rightarrow 1$. We adopt PReLU [11] as activation functions in the first 2 dense layers. We apply dropout to each dense layer with a dropout rate equal to 0.4.

Table 2. Comparison of different methods. The results with the best performance are marked in bold.

Compared methods	PAP	PNBB	PNFC
	MSE	MSE	MSE
HA	31.85	63.50	0.344
LSTM	28.46	57.21	0.319
BRR	27.68	50.06	0.306
SVR	26.81	49.83	0.275
RF	18.24	30.17	0.197
GBDT	18.87	29.73	0.220
FNN	17.72	28.64	0.183
APAMT trained w. single task	15.10	26.43	0.177
APAMT w. standard LSTM	15.08	25.92	0.174
APAMT w/o attention mechanism	15.13	27.04	0.177
APAMT	**14.52**	**24.77**	**0.167**

5.4   Results and Discussion

Comparison with Baselines. We compare our model with baselines. All baselines are trained with single task. Quantitative comparison between different models is shown in Table 2. From the table, we can see that APAMT achieves the best performances with the lowest MSE 14.52 on PAP task, the lowest MSE 24.77 on PNBB task and the lowest MSE 0.167 on PNFC task.

We can see that LSTM performs not well, as it only utilizes historical WAG/number of borrowed books/number of failed courses values. Other baselines further consider student demographic information and student behaviors and therefore achieve better performances. FNN will perform better among baselines. It can model complex relations among features with deep learning. Ensemble models (i.e., RF and GBDT) also perform well. Usually, ensemble methods will utilize multiple learning algorithms to obtain better prediction performance than could be obtained from any of the constituent learning algorithms alone.

It is worth mentioning that APAMT achieves 18.1%, 13.5%, 8.7% relative improvements on PAP, PNBB, PNFC tasks, compared with the best baseline, i.e., FNN. One important reason is that extracting features manually from heterogeneous behaviors may lead to loss of lots of undiscovered useful information.

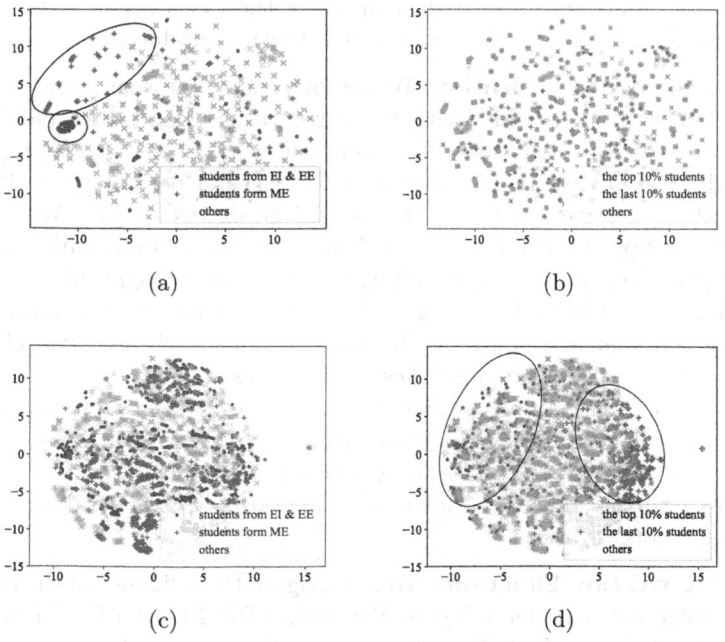

Fig. 4. (a) and (b) show visualizations of learned student representations r. (c) and (d) show visualizations of learned representations after one task-specific layer.

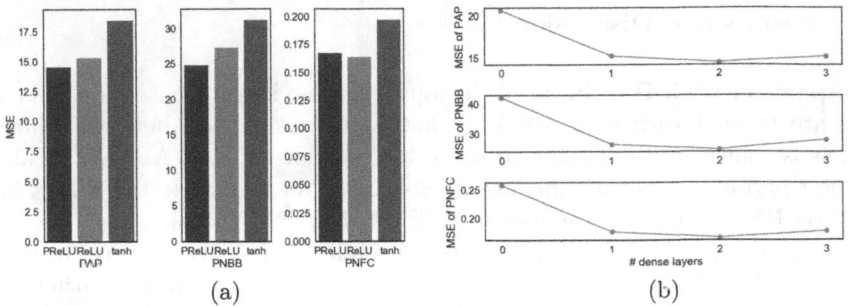

(a)   (b)

Fig. 5. MSE with activation functions (a) and number of dense layers (b).

Ablation Studies. Table 2 also provides the comparison results of variants of our proposed method. First, we study the effectiveness of multi-task learning. We train APAMT with single task. From the table we can see that multi-task learning achieves 3.8%, 6.3%, 5.6% relative improvements on PAP, PNBB, PNFC tasks compared with single-task learning. Second, we prove the benefit of Profile-Aware LSTM. We replace Profile-Aware LSTM with standard LSTM. The result is that APAMT achieves lower MSE values (a reduction of 3.7%, 4.4% and 4.0%, respectively) with the help of Profile-Aware LSTM. Third, we remove the attention mechanism and the performances of the tasks become much poorer. This demonstrates the effectiveness of our attention mechanism.

Representations Visualization. We remove course information $\bar{e}$ and $\bar{v}$ from APAMT and retrain APAMT with the three tasks. Figure 4(a) and (b) show visualizations of learned student representations r. Figure 4(c) and (d) show visualizations of learned representations after the first dense layer in PAP task based module. The technique we use is t-SNE algorithm [15]. We randomly choose two groups of students (EI & EE (i.e., Electronic Information and Electrical Engineering) students and ME (i.e., Mechanical Engineering) students) and mark these students. From Fig. 4(a), we can clearly find two clusters of EI & EE students and ME students. But we can not clearly find two clusters in Fig. 4(c). We can only distinguish these two groups.

Next, we mark the top 10% students and the last 10% students according to the mean of all WAGs. From Fig. 4(b), we can not distinguish these two groups of students. But there are clearly two clusters in Fig. 4(d).

This experiment indicates student representation r is general and could be transferred to other tasks.

Effect of Activation Functions. We investigate the influence of the activation function which exists in dense layers. We choose PReLU, ReLU and tanh to do the experiment. Figure 5(a) shows the results. We observe that on our dataset, PReLU is more suitable while tanh performs the worst.

Effect of the Number of Dense Layers. As we utilize feed forward neural networks as decoders, a problem worth studying is that how many dense layers are appropriate. Experimental results are shown in Fig. 5(b). As the number of layers grows, the performance grows. When the number of dense layers is 3, the performance drops. We think overfitting problem occurs.

6 Conclusion

In this paper, we propose an Attentional Profile-Aware Multi-Task model (i.e., APAMT) to deal with multiple prediction tasks about students. With APAMT, we can learn personalized and general student representations from student profiles and student heterogeneous behaviors. Once there arise new prediction tasks, we only need to retrain simple and shallow feed forward neural networks with the representations. Of course, APAMT can also be retrained for new tasks with all the existing tasks. Besides, the learned model of APAMT can also be used as initialization, and the whole network is fine-tuned for new tasks. All in all, APAMT has flexibility and extension. Qualitative and quantitative experiments on a real world dataset have demonstrated the effectiveness of APAMT. We believe APAMT can even be utilized to model heterogeneous behaviors of one person rather than one student.

Acknowledgments. This research is supported in part by the 2030 National Key AI Program of China 2018AAA0100503 (2018AAA0100500), National Science Foundation of China (No. 61772341, No. 61472254), Shanghai Municipal Science and Technology Commission (No. 18511103002, No. 19510760500, and No. 19511101500), the Program for Changjiang Young Scholars in University of China, the Program for China Top Young Talents, the Program for Shanghai Top Young Talents, Shanghai Engineering Research Center of Digital Education Equipment, and SJTU Global Strategic Partnership Fund (2019 SJTU-HKUST).

References

1. Bahdanau, D., Cho, K., Bengio, Y.: Neural machine translation by jointly learning to align and translate. In: ICLR (2015)
2. Brinton, C.G., Chiang, M.: MOOC performance prediction via clickstream data and social learning networks. In: INFOCOM, pp. 2299–2307 (2015)
3. Calvo-Flores, M.D., Galindo, E.G., Jiménez, M.P., Pineiro, O.P.: Predicting students' marks from Moodle logs using neural network models. Curr. Dev. Technol.-Assist. Educ. 1(2), 586–590 (2006)
4. Caruana, R.: Multitask learning. Mach. Learn. 28(1), 41–75 (1997). https://doi.org/10.1023/A:1007379606734
5. Chung, J., Gulcehre, C., Cho, K., Bengio, Y.: Empirical evaluation of gated recurrent neural networks on sequence modeling. arXiv preprint arXiv:1412.3555 (2014)
6. Collobert, R., Weston, J.: A unified architecture for natural language processing: deep neural networks with multitask learning. In: ICML, pp. 160–167 (2008)
7. Dai, J., He, K., Sun, J.: Instance-aware semantic segmentation via multi-task network cascades. In: CVPR, pp. 3150–3158 (2016)
8. Fei, M., Yeung, D.Y.: Temporal models for predicting student dropout in massive open online courses. In: International Conference on Data Mining Workshop (ICDMW), pp. 256–263 (2015)

9. Feng, M., Heffernan, N., Koedinger, K.: Addressing the assessment challenge with an online system that tutors as it assesses. UMUAI **19**(3), 243–266 (2009). https://doi.org/10.1007/s11257-009-9063-7

10. Guan, C., Lu, X., Li, X., Chen, E., Zhou, W., Xiong, H.: Discovery of college students in financial hardship. In: ICDM, pp. 141–150 (2015)

11. He, K., Zhang, X., Ren, S., Sun, J.: Delving deep into rectifiers: surpassing human-level performance on imagenet classification. In: ICCV, pp. 1026–1034 (2015)

12. Hochreiter, S., Schmidhuber, J.: Long short-term memory. Neural Comput. **9**(8), 1735–1780 (1997)

13. Kingma, D.P., Ba, J.: Adam: a method for stochastic optimization. In: ICLR (2015)

14. Lopez, M.I., Luna, J., Romero, C., Ventura, S.: Classification via clustering for predicting final marks based on student participation in forums. International Educational Data Mining Society (2012)

15. van der Maaten, L., Hinton, G.: Visualizing data using t-SNE. JMLR **9**, 2579–2605 (2008)

16. Minaei-Bidgoli, B., Kashy, D.A., Kortemeyer, G., Punch, W.F.: Predicting student performance: an application of data mining methods with an educational web-based system. In: FIE 2003 33rd Annual Frontiers in Education, vol. 1, p. T2A-13 (2003)

17. Nghe, N.T., Janecek, P., Haddawy, P.: A comparative analysis of techniques for predicting academic performance. In: 2007 37th Annual Frontiers in Education Conference-Global Engineering: Knowledge Without Borders, Opportunities Without Passports, FIE 2007, p. T2G-7 (2007)

18. Ranjan, R., Patel, V.M., Chellappa, R.: HyperFace: a deep multi-task learning framework for face detection, landmark localization, pose estimation, and gender recognition. PAMI **41**(1), 121–135 (2017)

19. Romero, C., López, M.I., Luna, J.M., Ventura, S.: Predicting students' final performance from participation in on-line discussion forums. Comput. Educ. **68**, 458–472 (2013)

20. Schuster, M., Paliwal, K.K.: Bidirectional recurrent neural networks. IEEE Trans. Sig. Process. **45**(11), 2673–2681 (1997)

21. Shahiri, A.M., Husain, W., et al.: A review on predicting student's performance using data mining techniques. Procedia Comput. Sci. **72**, 414–422 (2015)

22. Srivastava, N., Hinton, G., Krizhevsky, A., Sutskever, I., Salakhutdinov, R.: Dropout: a simple way to prevent neural networks from overfitting. JMLR **15**(1), 1929–1958 (2014)

23. Sukhbaatar, O., Usagawa, T., Choimaa, L.: An artificial neural network based early prediction of failure-prone students in blended learning course. Int. J. Emerg. Technol. Learn. **14**(19), 77–92 (2019)

24. Sweeney, M., Lester, J., Rangwala, H.: Next-term student grade prediction. In: International Conference on Big Data (Big Data), pp. 970–975 (2015)

25. Tanner, T., Toivonen, H., et al.: Predicting and preventing student failure-using the k-nearest neighbour method to predict student performance in an online course environment. Int. J. Learn. Technol. **5**(4), 356–377 (2010)

26. Tian, M.: Application of chaotic time series prediction in forecasting of library borrowing flow. In: International Conference on Internet Computing and Information Services, pp. 557–559 (2011)

27. Wang, R., Harari, G., Hao, P., Zhou, X., Campbell, A.T.: SmartGPA: how smartphones can assess and predict academic performance of college students. In: UbiComp, pp. 295–306 (2015)

28. Wang, R., Tang, Y., Li, L.: Application of BP neural network to prediction of library circulation. In: International Conference on Cognitive Informatics and Cognitive Computing, pp. 420–423 (2012)
29. Wang, Y., Liao, H.C.: Data mining for adaptive learning in a TESL-based e-learning system. Expert Syst. Appl. **38**(6), 6480–6485 (2011)
30. Xu, J., Han, Y., Marcu, D., Van Der Schaar, M.: Progressive prediction of student performance in college programs. In: AAAI, pp. 1604–1610 (2017)
31. Yao, H., Nie, M., Su, H., Xia, H., Lian, D.: Predicting academic performance via semi-supervised learning with constructed campus social network. In: Candan, S., Chen, L., Pedersen, T.B., Chang, L., Hua, W. (eds.) DASFAA 2017. LNCS, vol. 10178, pp. 597–609. Springer, Cham (2017). https://doi.org/10.1007/978-3-319-55699-4_37
32. Yu, H.F., et al.: Feature engineering and classifier ensemble for KDD cup 2010. In: KDD Cup (2010)
33. Zhang, D., Guo, B., Li, B., Yu, Z.: Extracting social and community intelligence from digital footprints: an emerging research area. In: Yu, Z., Liscano, R., Chen, G., Zhang, D., Zhou, X. (eds.) UIC 2010. LNCS, vol. 6406, pp. 4–18. Springer, Heidelberg (2010). https://doi.org/10.1007/978-3-642-16355-5_4

A General Early-Stopping Module
for Crowdsourced Ranking

Caihua Shan[1], Leong Hou U[2], Nikos Mamoulis[3], Reynold Cheng[1],
and Xiang Li[1(✉)]

[1] Department of Computer Science, University of Hong Kong,
Pok Fu Lam, Hong Kong
{chshan,ckcheng,xli2}@cs.hku.hk
[2] State Key Laboratory of Internet of Things for Smart City,
Department of Computer and Information Science, University of Macau,
Macau, China
ryanlhu@um.edu.mo
[3] Department of Computer Science, University of Ioannina, Ioannina, Epirus, Greece
nikos@cs.uoi.gr

Abstract. Crowdsourcing can be used to determine a total order for
an object set (e.g., the top-10 NBA players) based on crowd opinions.
This ranking problem is often decomposed into a set of microtasks (e.g.,
pairwise comparisons). These microtasks are passed to a large number
of workers and their answers are aggregated to infer the ranking. The
number of microtasks depends on the budget allocated for the problem.
Intuitively, the higher the number of microtask answers, the more accurate the ranking becomes. However, it is often hard to decide the budget
required for an accurate ranking. We study how a ranking process can
be terminated early, and yet achieve a high-quality ranking and great
savings in the budget. We use statistical tools to estimate the quality of
the ranking result at any stage of the crowdsourcing process, and terminate the process as soon as the desired quality is achieved. Our proposed
early-stopping module can be seamlessly integrated with most existing
inference algorithms and task assignment methods. We conduct extensive experiments and show that our early-stopping module is better than
other existing general stopping criteria.

1 Introduction

Crowdsourcing has been used to address a variety of problems, such as entity
matching [28], image labeling [14], and object ranking [12,16]. These problems,
which are typically hard for computers to solve, can be easier for humans. In
this paper, we study the use of crowdsourcing on *ranking* objects. This approach,
which has received a lot of attention from different research communities [6,16,
21], is particularly helpful when ranking cannot be done objectively. For example,
to determine the greatest athletes of all times or the best pictures of a landmark,
we could solicit opinions from the crowd and aggregate them to a ranking that

© Springer Nature Switzerland AG 2020
Y. Nah et al. (Eds.): DASFAA 2020, LNCS 12113, pp. 314–330, 2020.
https://doi.org/10.1007/978-3-030-59416-9_19

maximizes the consensus. In addition, crowdsourced ranking can be used to filter data for subsequent machine learning tasks. For instance, ranking answers to a question posted in a forum and selecting only the top ones can ease the burden of natural language processing.

To conduct crowdsourced ranking, existing solutions typically decompose the ranking process into a set of small and easy-to-answer microtasks, such as pairwise comparisons [31]. The microtasks are then distributed via crowdsourcing platforms, such as Amazon Mechanical Turk (AMT) [1] and FigureEight [2], to crowd workers by offering incentives, e.g., money, reputation, etc. The final ranking is computed by an inference algorithm based on the answers collected from the crowd. Naturally, the ranking accuracy is proportional to the number of collected answers to microtasks, i.e., the *total budget* paid by the requester.

Recent studies [6,8,12] attempt to improve the *inference algorithm* $\mathcal{I}$ and fine-tune the *task assignment* $\mathcal{T}$ (i.e., by dispatching tasks to suitable workers), in order to spend the budget more effectively. Typically, the microtask answers are collected in batches. Let A_i be the ith batch of answers; Inference algorithm module $\mathcal{I}$ infers the *interim ranking* from $A_1 \cup \ldots \cup A_i$; Task assignment module $\mathcal{T}$ is used to determine the next batch of microtasks and assign them to crowdsourcing platforms.

According to a recent experimental survey on crowdsourced ranking [31], there is no single winner method that outperforms all others in all performance factors (accuracy, convergence rate, efficiency, scalability). In addition, most approaches require the budget to be set in advance, but they offer no guideline on how to set this value. Hence, it is expected that the requester sets a large enough budget, hoping that the ranking process will converge to a stable ranking. This raises an interesting question: *can we spend less and achieve approximately the same ranking, as if we had spent all the budget?*

To answer this question, we first investigate how much budget could be saved when some representative inference algorithms are applied, i.e., Copeland [22], CrowdBT [8], Iterative [12], and Local [12]. Details about these methods are given in Sect. 4.1. We carry out the top-10 query tasks on two public datasets, namely peopleAge [31] and peopleNum [15]. Figure 1 shows how the *accuracy* of these algorithms varies as the budget increases. As an accuracy measure, we utilize Kendall's tau distance between the rankings progressively inferred and the ground truth ranking. All methods converge to a *stable state*[1], where the change of the distance induced by the inferred ranking is very small. In Fig. 1(a) and (b), CrowdBT reaches a stable state after using just 40% of the budget, whereas all other methods converge when 60% of the budget is used. Obviously, we can *stop early* the crowdsourcing process when we reach a stable state. We now face the following challenge: *how do we know if the ranking process has reached a stable state?*

To tackle this challenge, we develop a novel Early-Stopping (ES) module that attempts to predict the next batch of answers by probabilistic analysis. We then use Monte Carlo simulation [19], based on the prediction model, to construct

---

[1] A formal definition of the stable state is provided in the Sect. 2.2.

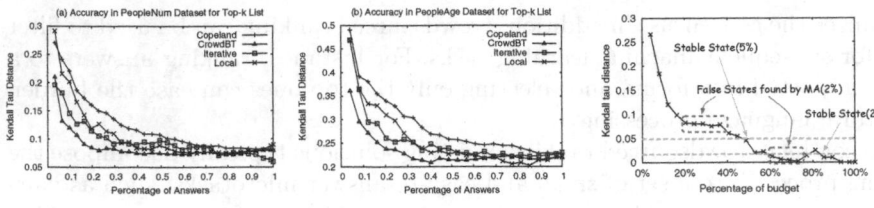

Fig. 1. Accuracy vs. budget   **Fig. 2.** Examples of stable state

the distribution of the final answer and, in turn, derive the *expected accuracy* of the final state. This helps us to assess when the ranking process reaches its stable state, subject to a budget B. To early-stop the process, our ES module requires an *accuracy tolerance* θ parameter, i.e., the acceptable accuracy that we can afford to lose when compared to the ranking that will be obtained if all the budget is used up.

Our ES module can seamlessly be used by most ranking processes with minimal effort. The only requirement is that the process provides interfaces for the inference and task assignment modules, and accepts a programming call to terminate the crowdsourcing process, when our module determines that the expected accuracy already satisfies tolerance θ.

The main contributions of this paper are summarized as follows:

- To the best of our knowledge, we are the first to propose a general Early-Stopping (ES) module for crowdsourced ranking.
- Our ES module is orthogonal to any inference algorithm or task assignment method, and does not interfere with the flow of the crowdsourced ranking process.
- We thoroughly evaluate our ES module with subjective and objective tasks, different inference algorithms and task assignment methods, varying budgets and accuracy tolerances. Our module can save even half of the budget given to the ranking processes.

The rest of the paper is organized as follows. We formulate the problem and provide definitions and notations in Sect. 2. Our ES module is described in detail in Sect. 3. The experimental evaluations are shown in Sect. 4. We discuss related work in Sect. 5 and conclude in Sect. 6.

2   Preliminaries

We first define crowdsourced ranking and top-k queries as follows.

Definition 1 (Crowdsourced Ranking). *Given a set of n objects $\mathcal{O} = \{o_1, ..., o_n\}$, use human workers to decide a total order $\sigma = \{o_i \prec o_j \prec ...\}$.*

Definition 2 (Crowdsourced Top-k Query). *Given a set of n objects $\mathcal{O} = \{o_1, ..., o_n\}$, use human workers to find a ranked list $\sigma^k = \{o_i \prec o_j \prec ...\}$ of size k, such that for any $o_i \in \sigma^k \wedge o_l \notin \sigma^k$, $o_i \prec o_l$.*

Note that the operator $\prec$ is a conclusion drawn from the crowd's answers. For instance, given some replies to a question posted in a forum, we can ask the crowd to conduct pairwise comparisons between the replies, and then use existing inference algorithms to process the crowd's input and find the top-5 replies. Note that comparing two replies is not machine friendly since it not only requires strong natural language processing techniques but also a good understanding of the question, i.e., domain expertise.

2.1 Distance Between Rankings

In our solution, we need to measure the distance (i.e., difference) between the ranking inferred at an intermediate state and the ranked list at the final state. To measure the distance between two rankings, a common practice is to use *Kendall's tau distance*, i.e., the number of inverse pairs of objects.

We use the normalized Kendall's tau distance for complete rankings and top-k ranked lists as defined in Eq. 1 and Eq. 2, respectively:

$$\mathbb{D}(\sigma_1, \sigma_2) = \frac{\sum_{(o_i,o_j) \in O \times O, i < j} \mathbb{1}(o_i \prec o_j, \sigma_1) \times \mathbb{1}(o_i \succ o_j, \sigma_2)}{n(n-1)/2} \tag{1}$$

$$\mathbb{D}(\sigma_1^k, \sigma_2^k) = \frac{\sum_{(o_i,o_j) \in O \times O, i < j} \mathbb{1}(o_i \prec o_j, \sigma_1^k) \times \mathbb{1}(o_i \succ o_j, \sigma_2^k)}{k^2} \tag{2}$$

where $\mathbb{1}$ is the indicator function that equals to 1 when its predicate is true, or 0 otherwise. When σ_1 and σ_2 are reversed, the numerator of Eq. 1 takes its maximum possible value $n(n-1)/2$, and Eq. 1 reaches the highest value of 1. As for Eq. 2, the numerator takes its maximum value k^2 when objects in σ_1^k and σ_2^k have no intersection.

2.2 Stable State and Optimal Stopping Point

Publishing a batch of microtasks into the crowdsourced platform is a common strategy to accelerate the speed of collections. Let p_i be the state after collecting the ith batch of answers A_i and $\sigma_i = \mathcal{I}(A_1 \cup ... \cup A_i)$ is the ranked list at p_i. The stopping module should check whether to stop at each p_i. Without loss of generality, we assume that the budget B is the total number of microtasks we plan to publish and the number of microtasks, n_{batch}, is the same in each batch. B/n_{batch} is the total number of batches needed to collect all answers. We then give a formal definition of the stable state that we mentioned in the Introduction:

Definition 3 (Stable State). *Given the whole collection process $\{A_1, A_2, \cdots, A_{B/n_{batch}}\}$ and an accuracy tolerance $\theta \in [0, 1]$ from the requester, p_l is called as a* stable state *of the process if:*

1. $\forall p_i, p_j \in [p_l, p_{final}]$, $\mathbb{D}(\sigma_i, \sigma_j) \leq \theta$ 2. $\nexists p_i < p_l$, p_i is a stable state
where $l \in [1, B/n_{batch}]$ and $p_{final} = B/n_{batch}$.

The first condition secures that the distances between the rankings at any two states (from p_l to the final) do not exceed θ. The second condition secures the maximality that no earlier (better) stable state can be found in the entire process. It is obvious only one stable state exists in each collection process.

The stopping point p_{sc} is the moment decided by a stopping criterion (SC) to early stop the ranking process. Based on the stable state definition, we can say that

Corollary 1 (The Optimal Stopping Point). *The optimal point $p_{optimal}$ to early stop a ranking process is when the process turns into the stable state, i.e., $p_{optimal} = p_l$.*

The optimal stopping point guarantees the optimality because it saves up as much as possible the budget and ensures the distances from the ranked list at the stopping point to the final are always smaller than the accuracy tolerance θ.

For example, Fig. 2 shows the distance between the current and the final ranking at all states of the process. We show two optimal stopping points with $\theta = 5\%$ or $\theta = 2\%$. Basically we may save more budget with larger θ. Here we save 50% budget for $\theta = 5\%$, and 10% budget for $\theta = 2\%$.

One may wonder whether some simple method, e.g., Moving Average and Weighted Moving Average [3], can find $p_{optimal}$. We also show two kinds of intervals in Fig. 2. The first purple rectangle is an interval that tends to be stable during a certain time but descends gradually as more budget consumes. The second one also tends to be stable but the change of rankings is larger than θ as more budget consumes. Given a current point p_i, moving average uses the previous rank lists in a certain window size to represent the inferred rankings in the future. It is easy to drop out into these intervals and cause the process to stop earlier than it should. Besides, it is hard for users to set the best parameter values for them, such as the window size. Bad parameters lead to the worst stopping position. To avoid stopping at these intervals, we propose a novel ES module that attempts to discover the optimal stopping point.

3   Early-Stopping Module

3.1   Predicting the Next Answer Set

Consider a crowdsourcing rank process $\mathcal{R}$, based on an inference module $\mathcal{I}$ and a task assignment module $\mathcal{T}$, that has already collected the ith batch answer set $(A^c = A_1 \cup ... \cup A_i)$. We predict the next batch of answers by a three-stage process, including (1) determining new tasks t_{new}, (2) predicting the answers a_{new} of t_{new}, and (3) estimating the influence of worker reliability.

Determining New Tasks, t_{new}. Recall that the microtasks of crowdsourced ranking are pairwise comparisons (o_i, o_j). Given the collected answer set A^c, the task assignment module $\mathcal{T}$ decides the importance of tasks. The most important n_{batch} tasks are distributed to crowdsourcing platforms as the next batch. We predict answers for these tasks in our subsequent prediction model.

Predicting the Answer, a_{new}. Given the collected answer set A^c and a chosen task $t_{new} = (o_i, o_j)$, we want to predict the answer to t_{new}. We assume that the workers are reliable since they have to obey the crowdsourcing platform policy, e.g., gain reputation via user feedback. Thereby, we can regard the answer a_{new} of the task $t_{new} = (o_i, o_j)$ as a Bernoulli distribution of the probability of $o_i \prec o_j$, denoted as P_{ij}. Formally, it can be written as $a_{new} \sim \text{Bernoulli}(P_{ij})$ where P_{ij} is the probability of $o_i \prec o_j$. Several models for P_{ij} has been suggested in previous crowdsourcing studies [5,18,26]. For instance, the Bradley-Terry (BT) model [5] defines $P_{ij} = \frac{e^{s_i}}{e^{s_i} + e^{s_j}}$, where s_i is the latent score of object o_i. The Thurstonian model [26] defines $P_{ij} = \Phi(s_i - s_j)$, where Φ is the normal cumulative distribution function. However, some inference modules [10,11] do not build on the latent scores of objects.

We attempt to design a new estimation model that is suitable for most inference modules. We estimate the probability P_{ij} independently, i.e., P_{ij} only based on the previous answer set of the task (o_i, o_j). Suppose that the current answer set is A^c; we build an observed matrix M, where M_{ij} is the number of answers reporting $o_i \prec o_j$ in A^c. P_{ij} depends on M_{ij} and M_{ji}.

We use maximum a posteriori probability (MAP) to calculate $\hat{P}_{ij}$:

$$\hat{P}_{\text{MAP}}(M) = \arg\max_{P} Pr(P \mid M) = \arg\max_{P} \prod_{i,j \mid i<j} Pr(P_{ij} \mid M_{ij}, M_{ji})$$

$$= \arg\max_{P} \prod_{i,j \mid i<j} \frac{Pr(M_{ij}, M_{ji} \mid P_{ij}) \, Pr(P_{ij})}{\int_0^1 Pr(M_{ij}, M_{ji} \mid p_{ij}) \, Pr(p_{ij}) \, dp_{ij}} \propto \arg\max_{P} \prod_{i,j \mid i<j} Pr(M_{ij}, M_{ji} \mid P_{ij}) \, Pr(P_{ij})$$

$$(3)$$

If we assume the prior distribution of P_{ij} as $Beta(1,1)$ which is the conjugate prior for the Bernoulli distribution, the posterior distribution of P_{ij} is $Pr(P_{ij} \mid M_{ij}, M_{ji}) \sim Beta(M_{ij} + 1, M_{ji} + 1)$. The reason behind using $Beta(1,1)$ is that we believe that we have equal probability to get either $o_i \prec o_j$ or $o_i \succ o_j$. It could also be interpreted as Laplace smoothing to avoid some undefined calculation, e.g., $Beta(0,0)$. The MAP of $\hat{P}_{ij}$ equals the mode of the posterior distribution, which is

$$\hat{P}_{ij} = \frac{M_{ij} + 1}{M_{ij} + M_{ji} + 2}. \tag{4}$$

Alternatively, we could also use maximum likelihood estimate (MLE) to calculate $\hat{P}_{ij}$:

$$\hat{P}_{\text{MLE}}(M) = \arg\max_{P} Pr(M \mid P) = \arg\max_{P} \prod_{i,j \mid i<j} Pr(M_{ij}, M_{ji} \mid P_{ij})$$

$$= \prod_{i,j \mid i<j} \binom{M_{ij} + M_{ji}}{M_{ij}} P_{ij}^{M_{ij}} (1 - P_{ij})^{M_{ji}} = \arg\max_{P} \prod_{i,j \mid i<j} P_{ij}^{M_{ij}} (1 - P_{ij})^{M_{ji}} \tag{5}$$

The MLE of $\hat{P}_{ij}$ equals to $\frac{M_{ij}}{M_{ij} + M_{ji}}$. Similarly, if we replace M_{ij} and M_{ji} by $M_{ij} + 1$ and $M_{ji} + 1$, respectively, by the Laplace smoothing, then the MLE equation will be identical to Eq. 4 (from MAP).

In summary, we estimate P_{ij} from M based on A^c and then sample an answer a_{new} by Bernoulli(P_{ij}) for the task (o_i, o_j).

Estimating the Influence of Worker Reliability. In this section, we discuss how worker reliability influences the predicting process of answer a_{new}. As mentioned in Sect. 3.1, the posterior distribution P_{ij} can be estimated based on the collected answers A^c. The estimation framework is built on our underlying assumption that *every worker is reliable*.

We attempt to add the effect of workers' reliability (i.e., the probability of answering correctly). Assume that we already know the average worker reliability rel in A^c, the probability of a new answer a_{new} should be revised as $P'_{ij} = P_{ij} \times rel + (1 - P_{ij}) \times (1 - rel)$. It means that workers give reliable answers with the probability rel while giving untrustworthy and opposite answers with the probability $1 - rel$. The worker reliability can be provided by the platforms and calculated based on workers' answer history in other projects. If the platforms do not provide this function, we could also set a lower bound of the required quality of workers or do the qualification test to filter bad workers before the actual assignments. This lower bound or qualified reliability is regarded as rel.

Generating Answers in the Next Batch A_{i+1}. So far, we have discussed how to predict the next task answer a_{new} based on the collected answers A^c and worker reliability. To predict the answers A_{i+1} obtained in the next batch, we apply an iterative process that generates answers one after another. Algorithm 1 shows the pseudo code of the iterative process. We first estimate P_{ij} in line 2–6. Then we utilize the assignment module $\mathcal{T}$ to get the importance of tasks. We select the first n_{batch} important tasks, predict the answers respectively and add into A_{i+1} in line 7–12.

We can also predict a "complete" answer set A (obtained when we use up the budget B). Based on Algorithm 1, we predict A_{i+1} based on $A^c = A_1 \cup ... \cup A_i$. Similarly, A_{i+2} is predicted based on $A_1 \cup ... \cup A_{i+1}$, A_{i+3} is predicted based on $A_1 \cup ... \cup A_{i+2}$ and so on. Finally, we can predict $A = A^c \cup A_{i+1} \cup A_{i+2} \cup A_{i+3}...$ until the size of A is equal to the given budget B.

3.2 Calculating Deviation

In the last section, we showed how to predict a "complete" answer set A. In this section, we discuss how to judge whether the current point satisfies the definition of the optimal stopping point.

Expected Distance Between Rankings. Given a "complete" and deterministic answer set A, the inference module $\mathcal{I}$ can be used to compute each interim ranking $\sigma_i = \mathcal{I}(A_1 \cup ... \cup A_i)$ and the distance $\mathbb{D}(\sigma_i, \sigma_j)$ between each two interim rankings (cf. Eq. 1 and 2). However, the probabilistic process may create many possible worlds, i.e., many possible answer sets $\mathbb{A} = \{A^1, A^2...\}$. If we know the occurrence probability of each possible world $Pr(A')$ where

---

Algorithm 1. *Predicting the Next Answer Set*

Input: Current answer set A^c, Inference module $\mathcal{I}$, Task assignment module $\mathcal{T}$, the number of tasks in a batch n_{batch}

1 Initialize $A_{i+1} = \varnothing$

2 // *Step 1: Build the matrix M and P*
3 Built matrix M based on the answer in A^c
4 **for** *all possible (i, j)* **do**
5   Estimate $P_{ij} = \frac{M_{ij}+1}{M_{ij}+M_{ji}+2}$ by Eq. 4
6   Calculate P'_{ij} by P_{ij} with worker reliability rel

7 // *Step 2: Getting the next n_{batch} important tasks from $\mathcal{T}$*
8 $T = \mathcal{T}(A^c)$
9 **for** *each t_{new} in T* **do**
10   // *Step 3: Predict the answer of $t_{new} = (o_i, o_j)$*
11   Sample $a \sim \text{Bernoulli}(P'_{ij})$
12     $A_{i+1} = A_{i+1} \cup \{a\}$

13 **return** A_{i+1};

$A' \in \mathbb{A}$, the expected distance between the ith and jth batches can be defined as $\mathrm{E}[\mathbb{D}_{ij}] = \sum_{A' \in \mathbb{A}} Pr(A') \times \mathbb{D}(\mathcal{I}(A'_1 \cup ... \cup A'_i), \mathcal{I}(A'_1 \cup ... \cup A'_j))$.

However, it is difficult to calculate the occurrence probability because it is impossible to conduct a brute-force search for all possible worlds. To tackle this problem, we apply the Monte Carlo method, that allows an estimation of the sampling distribution of almost any statistic using random sampling method. The Monte Carlo method helps to generate a list of possible worlds, i.e., "complete" answer sets $\{A^1, A^2, ..., A^s, ...|s \in [1, n_{\text{sample}}]\}$. Given a pair (i, j), we are able to compute a list of pairs of rankings (σ_i^s, σ_j^s) and the corresponding distances $\mathbb{D}_{ij}^s$. By the law of large numbers, the expected distance $\mathrm{E}[\mathbb{D}_{ij}]$ can be approximated by taking the sample mean $\overline{\mathbb{D}}_{ij} = \frac{1}{n_{\text{sample}}} \sum_{s=1}^{n_{\text{sample}}} \mathbb{D}(\mathcal{I}(A_1^s \cup ... \cup A_i^s), \mathcal{I}(A_1^s \cup ... \cup A_j^s))$. If p_{current} is the earliest point satisfying $\forall p_i, p_j \in [p_{\text{current}}, p_{\text{final}}]$, $\overline{\mathbb{D}}_{ij} \leq \theta$, p_{current} is the stopping point decided by our ES module.

The Number of Required Samples. In the Monte Carlo method, it is important to decide the number of required samples such that the quality is secured. Following common practice, we use Hoeffding's inequality [13] to decide it.

Hoeffding's Inequality. Let $X_1, ..., X_n$ be independent random variables bounded by the interval $[0, 1] : 0 \leq X_i \leq 1$. Define the mean of these variables as $\overline{X} = \frac{1}{n}(X_1 + ... + X_n)$. Then we have $Pr(\mathrm{E}[\overline{X}] - \overline{X} \geq t) \leq e^{-2nt^2}$ where $t \geq 0$.

We regard a possible world answer set A^s as a sample. The distance $\mathbb{D}_{ij}^s$ can be regarded as an independent random variable given (i, j). Based on Hoeffding's Inequality, we have $Pr(\mathrm{E}[\mathbb{D}_{ij}] - \overline{\mathbb{D}}_{ij} \geq t) \leq e^{-2nt^2}$. This inequality could be transformed into a confidence interval of $\mathrm{E}[\mathbb{D}_{ij}]$:

$$Pr(\mathrm{E}[\mathbb{D}_{ij}] \leq \overline{\mathbb{D}}_{ij} + t) > 1 - e^{-2nt^2}, \tag{6}$$

where $\overline{\mathbb{D}}_{ij}$ is computed using Sect. 3.2. We require at least $\frac{\ln(1/\alpha)}{2t^2}$ samples to acquire $(1 - \alpha)$-confidence interval for $\mathrm{E}[\mathbb{D}_{ij}] \leq \overline{\mathbb{D}}_{ij} + t$.

Given the targeted accuracy tolerance θ, if we find that $\overline{\mathbb{D}}_{ij} \leq \theta - t$, we can also derive $Pr(\mathrm{E}[\mathbb{D}_{ij}] \leq \overline{\mathbb{D}}_{ij} + t \leq \theta) > 1 - e^{-2nt^2}$. We summarize it as the following theorem.

Theorem 1. *Given two points p_i and p_j, we secure that $\mathrm{E}[\mathbb{D}_{ij}] \leq \theta$ with confidence $(1 - \alpha)$ after we random sample $\frac{\ln(1/\alpha)}{2t^2}$ "complete" answer sets and find $\overline{\mathbb{D}}_{ij} \leq \theta - t$, for some $0 < t < \theta$.*

Here we set the confidence level $\alpha = 5\%$ and the estimation error t as an order of magnitude smaller than θ which secures enough samples to give a good estimation. We need to sample $n_{\text{sample}} \approx 10^4$ for $\theta = 0.1$, and $n_{\text{sample}} \approx 10^6$ when we set $\theta = 0.01$. The workload of sampling can be accelerated by multithreading or distributed computation.

We then analyze the number of samples to secure all $\mathrm{E}[\mathbb{D}_{ij}] \leq \theta$ with high probability from the current to the final state, i.e., judge whether the following formula holds: $\forall p_i, p_j \in [p_{\text{current}}, p_{\text{final}}], \ \mathrm{E}[\mathbb{D}_{ij}] \leq \theta$.

Assume that number of batches for remaining budget is $m = \frac{B - |A^c|}{n_{\text{batch}}}$, there are $(m+1)m/2$ different expected distances needed to compute and check. If we acquire confidence $(1 - \alpha')$ for all the expected distances, the confidence $(1 - \alpha)$ and the number of samples for each expected distance can be set as

$$\alpha = \frac{\alpha'}{(m+1)m/2} \quad \text{and} \quad n_{\text{sample}} = \frac{\ln((m+1)m/2) + \ln(1/\alpha')}{2t^2}. \tag{7}$$

We utilize the union bound to prove them. Let $\mathrm{E}[\mathbb{D}_{ij}] \leq \overline{\mathbb{D}}_{ij} + t$ for a pair (p_i, p_j) be an event. The confidence $(1 - \alpha)$ means the probability that one event fails is α. Then based on the union bound, we derive that the probability that at least one of the events fails is no greater than the sum of the probabilities of the individual events, which is $\sum_{i=1}^{(m+1)m/2} \alpha = \alpha'$. In other words, the probability that no event fails is at least α', which satisfies our requirement.

Putting It All Together. We put all of these techniques together to finalize the ES module, as shown in Algorithm 2.

4   Experimental Evaluation

In this section, we thoroughly evaluate our ES module on two real public datasets. Based on the different inference algorithms and task assignment approaches, we compare our ES module with some standard quality estimation methods.

4.1   Experimental Settings

Datasets. We use two real public datasets collected in AMT.

Algorithm 2. *Early-Stopping module*

Input: Current answer set A^c, Inference module $\mathcal{I}$, Distance function $\mathbb{D}$, Budget B,
accuracy tolerance θ, confidence interval α'

1 Calculate number of batches for remaining budget $m = \frac{B-|A^c|}{n_{\text{batch}}}$

2 Estimate the number of samples n_{sample} by Eq. 7

3 Initialize distance array d and $\overline{\mathbb{D}}$

4 **for** $1 \leq s \leq n_{sample}$ **do**

5 $\quad$ Set a temporary answer set $A = A^c$

6 $\quad$ Create a temporary array of ranked lists σ and set $\sigma[0] = \mathcal{I}(A^c)$

7 $\quad$ **for** $1 \leq j \leq m$ **do**

8 $\quad\quad$ Predict a batch of answers A_j based on A by Alg. 1

9 $\quad\quad$ $A = A \cup A_j$

10 $\quad\quad$ $\sigma[j] = \mathcal{I}(A)$

11 $\quad$ **for** $0 \leq i \leq m-1$ **do**

12 $\quad\quad$ **for** $i+1 \leq j \leq m$ **do**

13 $\quad\quad\quad$ $d[s][i][j] = \mathbb{D}(\sigma[i], \sigma[j])$

14 **for** $0 \leq i \leq m-1$ **do**

15 $\quad$ **for** $i+1 \leq j \leq m$ **do**

16 $\quad\quad$ $\overline{\mathbb{D}}[i][j] = \frac{1}{n_{\text{sample}}} \sum_{1 \leq s \leq n_{\text{sample}}} d[s][i][j]$

17 **if** $\overline{\mathbb{D}}[i][j] \leq \theta - t, \forall i, j$ **then**

18 $\quad$ Invoke a programming call to terminate the rank process $\mathcal{R}$

19 **else**

20 $\quad$ Continue collecting the next batch of answers

- *PeopleNum* [15] concerns 39 images taken in a mall, each of which includes multiple persons. The goal is to find the images with the most people in them. 6066 answers were collected from 197 workers. Each pair of images is answered by at least 5 workers.
- *PeopleAge* [31] has 50 human photos with ages from 50 to 100. The goal is to find the photos that include the youngest person. There are 4930 answers from 150 workers. Each pair of photos is answered 3 times at least.

PeopleAge is hard because it is relatively subjective and different workers may have different opinions on age. The difficulty of *PeopleNum* is medium because it costs some time to count the persons.

Inference Modules $\mathcal{I}$. According to [31], we select some recommended inference algorithms and task assignment strategies to work with our ES module. For rank inference algorithms, we choose 4 methods:

- *Copeland* is a basic election approach where the objects are sorted by the times they win/lose in the comparisons.
- *Local* is a heuristic-based method based on a comparison graph, where nodes are objects and edges are built based on the pairwise comparisons. The score of an object is defined by the number of winning objects minus the number of losing objects in its 1-hop and 2-hop neighborhood.
- *Iterative* is an extended version of *local* supporting top-k queries. It keeps discarding the bottom half of the objects in the inference process and then re-computes the scores of the surviving objects. It repeats these two processes until k objects are left.

- *CrowdBT* is a representative method that uses the Bradley-Terry (BT) model to estimate the latent score s_i of the object o_i. It models the probability $o_i \prec o_j$ as $\frac{e^{s_i}}{e^{s_i}+e^{s_j}}$. Based on the crowdsourced comparisons A, it computes scores for the objects by maximizing $\sum_{o_i \prec o_j \in A} \log(\frac{e^{s_i}}{e^{s_i}+e^{s_j}})$.

Task Assignment Modules $\mathcal{T}$. We implemented 4 task assignment strategies based on commercial systems and existing work.

- *Random* is the strategy used by Amazon Mturk; tasks are assigned to coming workers at random and all tasks are answered the same number of times.
- *Greedy* chooses the pair of objects with the highest product of scores as the next task.
- *Complete* finds the top-x objects with the highest scores, where x is the largest integer satisfying $\frac{x(x-1)}{2} \leq n_{\text{batch}}$, and sets their pairwise comparisons as the next tasks.
- *CrowdBT* is an active learning method which selects the pair of objects which maximizes the information gain based on the estimated scores.

Based on the characteristics of the inference algorithms and the task assignment strategies, we form and test 7 rank processes $\mathcal{R}$: *Copeland-Random, Iterative-Random, Local-Random, CrowdBT-Random, Local-Greedy, Local-Complete*, and *CrowdBT-CrowdBT*.

Competitors. In order to evaluate our ES module, we also investigate two alternative stopping criteria based on statistical analysis.

- *Moving Average (MA)* stops when the following equation is smaller than θ at the first time. We calculate the distances between all pairs of consecutive rankings or top-k lists, generated at the last w points before the current stage and average them. Suppose we already collected i batches of answers:

$$\text{MA}(i, w) = \frac{\sum_{j=1}^{w} \mathbb{D}(\mathcal{I}(A_1 \cup ... \cup A_{i-j}), \mathcal{I}(A_1 \cup ... \cup A_{i-j+1}))}{w} \quad (8)$$

- *Weighted Moving Average (WMA)* is similar to MA, except that we assign different weights to the distances based on how far away they are from the current stage. The distance between the latest two rankings has the largest weight w, the second latest $w - 1$, etc., and so on.

$$\text{WMA}(i, w) = \frac{\sum_{j=1}^{w}(w - j + 1)\mathbb{D}(\mathcal{I}(A_1...A_{i-j}), \mathcal{I}(A_1...A_{i-j+1}))}{w(w + 1)/2} \quad (9)$$

Evaluation Metrics. We define the optimal stopping point p_{optimal} in the Sect. 2.2. To evaluate the effectiveness of different stopping criteria, we analyze the difference between p_{optimal} and the stopping point p_{sc} predicted by a stopping criterion. Mathematically, it can be written as $\Delta_{\text{sc}} = \frac{|p_{\text{optimal}} - p_{\text{sc}}|}{B/n_{\text{batch}}}$.

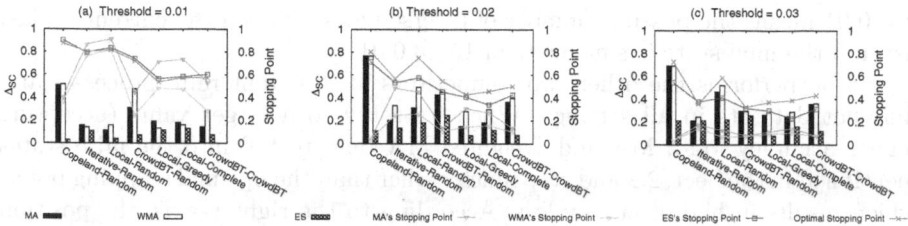

Fig. 3. Δ_{sc} & stopping points in PeopleNum dataset for top-10 lists

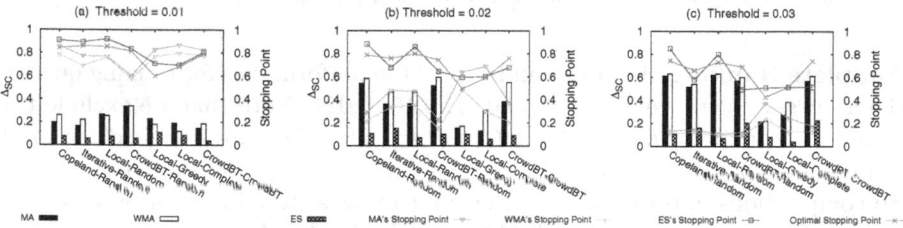

Fig. 4. Δ_{sc} & stopping points in PeopleAge dataset for top-10 lists

4.2 Experimental Results

Implementation Details. We compare our ES module with two competitors, MA and Weighted MA, on two datasets for ranking or top-k queries. The objective is to show the superiority and robustness of ES on top of different rank processes $\mathcal{R}$.

The total budget is set to the number of answers in each original dataset. The number of microtasks in a batch is set to 200. To get an answer of a pairwise comparison (o_i, o_j), we randomly sample an answer from the answer set of (o_i, o_j) without replacement. If some pairs are running out of answers, we will simulate the next answer by a worker that has average reliability. To solve the cold-start problem of some task assignment strategies, we pre-generate an answer to every comparison. We also choose the best window size for MA and Weighted MA, which is 20 for PeopleNum dataset and 10 for PeopleAge dataset, respectively. Besides, a little change of initial answers for the cold-start problem will change the next sequence of microtasks. Thus, we run the collection process 10 times, and report the average performance.

We use two y-axes in Fig. 3, 4, 5 and 6. The left y-axis is Δ_{sc}, which is defined in Sect. 4.1. The right y-axis is the relative stopping point of MA, Weighted MA, ES and the optimal stopping point, which divided by the maximum possible stopping point, B/n_{batch}.

Top-k Ranking. Figures 3 and 4 show Δ_{sc} and the stopping point of our ES module and the two alternative stopping criteria for top-k queries. Each stopping criterion is evaluated with seven rank processes (cf. Sect. 4.1). We set $k = 10$ by default. The accuracy tolerance θ is set to $\{0.01, 0.02, 0.03\}$. For instance,

$\theta = 0.01$ means the possible number of inverse pairs between the current ranked list and the final state is smaller than $10^2 \times 0.01 = 1$.

ES outperforms the other two competitors for different rank processes and different datasets in all settings. When we set θ to a larger value (accepting higher accuracy loss), MA and Weighted MA tend to fall into the false states mentioned in the Sect. 2.2 and stop much earlier than the optimal stopping point, which results in high accuracy loss. According to the right y-axis, the position of $p_{optimal}$ varies from 0.5 to 0.9. The stopping point of our ES module is very close to $p_{optimal}$ when compared with the stopping points of MA and Weighted MA. This reveals that ES is effective in finding $p_{optimal}$.

Complete Ranking. Figures 5 and 6 show the performance for ranking queries. The accuracy tolerance θ is set to $\{0.01, 0.15, 0.02\}$. Note that we exclude two inference algorithms, *Iterative* and *Complete*, since they are designed for top-k queries. Similar to top-k queries, our ES module is much better than the other two competitions in terms of Δ_{sc}. The curve of ES's stopping point is very close to that of $p_{optimal}$ compared with MA and Weighted MA.

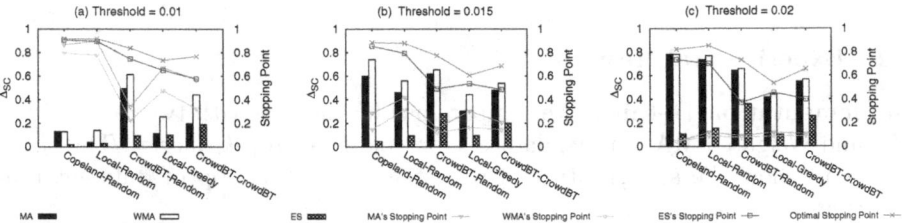

Fig. 5. Δ_{sc} & stopping points in PeopleNum dataset for rankings

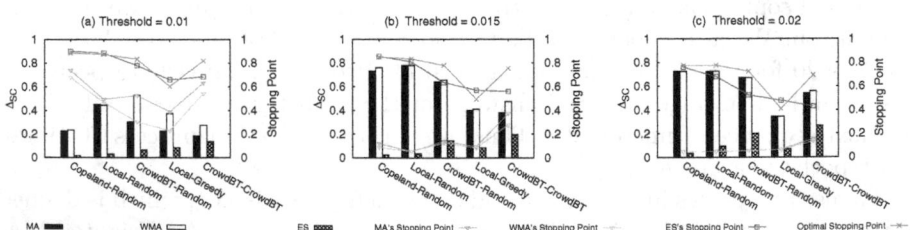

Fig. 6. Δ_{sc} & stopping points in PeopleAge dataset for rankings

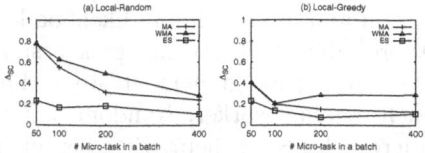

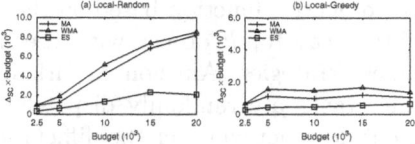

Fig. 7. Δ_{sc} in varied n_{batch} **Fig. 8.** Δ_{SC} in varied B

4.3 Parameter Analysis

In this section, we test the effect of the total budget B and the number of microtasks in one batch n_{bach}. We evaluate these parameters with two rank processes, *Local-Random* and *Local-Greedy* on PeopleNum dataset.

Figure 7 shows the effect of n_{batch}. In these experiments, we set the budget B equal to the total number of answers in the original dataset and set $\theta = 0.02$. ES is the clear winner since its Δ_{sc} is always less than or equal to 0.2 and outperforms MA and Weighted MA. In addition, MA and Weighted MA perform worse when n_{batch} becomes small (i.e., fewer microtasks in a batch), which means that the distance between two consecutive batches does not represent the distance between the current state and the final state.

Figure 8 evaluates the effect of the budget B. Note that we use the absolute number of answers instead of a percentage in the y-axis. We set $\theta = 0.02$ and $n_{batch} = 200$ as default. We try $\{2.5, 5.0, 10.0, 20.0\} * 10^3$. Δ_{sc} of ES is always smaller than the corresponding Δ_{sc} of MA and Weighted MA. Particularly, errors of MA and Weighted MA increase dramatically when B increases in *Local-Random*. This is because increasing budget B improves the quality of the final result and the position of the optimal stopping point moves backwards. But the stopping points predicted by MA and Weighted MA do not change.

5 Related Work

Crowdsourced Ranking. The ranking problem has a long history and has been studied in the past several decades. Simple traditional ranking algorithms, e.g., BordaCount [4] and Copeland [22], rank objects by the times they win/lose in the comparisons. But these algorithms do not consider that the crowd may give incorrect answers. How to deal with noisy answers and control worker qualities is the key component in almost all crowdsourcing problems [17,24,25]. Several *inference algorithms* and *task assignment strategies* are proposed to solve it.

Inference algorithms in raking problems can be divided into two categories: heuristic-based solutions from the DB community approach the problem as a top-k operation in databases, and machine-learning algorithms formalize it as a leaning problem and maximize the likelihood of top-k objects. Heuristic score-based algorithms [12,20,27,29] rank objects by estimating the underlying score of objects. CrowdBT [8] and CrowdGauss [21] are ML algorithms, which set the objective function based on the assumption and use maximum likelihood to obtain the top-k object with the highest probability. Regarding task assignment strategies, Amazon MTurk follows a random assignment strategy; i.e., microtasks are randomly dispatched to each coming worker. Random assignment does not consider the difficulties of microtasks. Some heuristic assignment methods [12] aim at maximizing the probability of obtaining the top-k result, e.g., by selecting most promising object pairs (e.g., with the largest latent scores) to compare. [6] avoids some unnecessary comparisons by setting a bound for the object latent score. Active learning methods are also used in CrowdBT [8] and CrowdGauss [21] to compare objects with the largest expected information gain.

According to a recent experimental study [31], different inference and assignment methods have their own advantages and there does not exist a single best one. Machine-learning methods typically have high quality. Still, global inference heuristics that utilize global comparison results achieve comparable and even higher quality than ML methods. Local inference heuristics have poor quality, but have higher efficiency and scalability. For task assignment, active-learning methods achieve higher quality than heuristics, but they have low efficiency.

Stopping Criteria. Stopping criteria have been defined for various crowdsourcing problems. [23] designs an early-stopping strategy for multiple-choice-question problems (e.g., choosing the opinion positive, neutral, or negative in a sentence). [30] uses Sequential Probability Ratio Test to decide when to stop for multi-labeling tasks (e.g., labeling pictures as a portrait or a landscape). Besides, [7] uses Chao92 estimator to evaluate the level of completion for entity collection (e.g., collecting a set of active NBA players). The settings of all these problems are quite different from crowdsourced ranking because microtasks are independent in these problems while correlated in the ranking problem.

Some previous studies on crowdsourced ranking define their special stopping conditions. For instance, [9] assumes that each object has a latent score and answers to pairwise comparisons follow the Bradley-Terry model [5]. [16] asks the crowd to give a numerical answer in $[0, 1]$ for a pairwise comparison and calculates the confidence interval of the result. However, these approaches are based on special assumptions that cannot generalize to most situations.

6   Conclusion

In this paper, we proposed a general stopping criterion for crowdsourced ranking. We demonstrated the robustness of our method in different situations, including subjective or objective tasks, diverse inference modules or task assignment modules and different budget and tolerance parameter values.

Acknowledgement. Leong Hou U was funded by the National Key R&D Plan of China (2019YFB2102100), the FDCT Macau (SKL-IOTSC-2018-2020), and UM RC (MYRG2019-00119-FST). Caihua Shan and Reynold Cheng were supported by HK RGC (RGC Projects HKU 17229116, 106150091, and 17205115), HKU (Projects 104004572, 102009508, and 104004129), and HK ITF (ITF project MRP/029/18).

Nikos Mamoulis has been co-financed by the European Regional Development Fund, Research–Create–Innovate project "Proximiot" (T1EDK-04810).

References

1. Amazon mechanical turk. https://www.mturk.com
2. Figure eight. https://www.figure-eight.com
3. Moving average. https://en.wikipedia.org/wiki/Moving_average
4. Adelsman, R.M., Whinston, A.B.: Sophisticated voting with information for two voting functions. J. Econ. Theory **15**(1), 145–159 (1977)
5. Bradley, R.A., Terry, M.E.: Rank analysis of incomplete block designs: I. The method of paired comparisons. Biometrika **39**(3/4), 324–345 (1952)
6. Busa-Fekete, R., Szorenyi, B., Cheng, W., Weng, P., Hüllermeier, E.: Top-k selection based on adaptive sampling of noisy preferences. In: ICML (2013)
7. Chai, C., Fan, J., Li, G.: Incentive-based entity collection using crowdsourcing. In: ICDE, pp. 341–352. IEEE (2018)
8. Chen, X., Bennett, P.N., Collins-Thompson, K., Horvitz, E.: Pairwise ranking aggregation in a crowdsourced setting. In: WSDM, pp. 193–202. ACM (2013)
9. Chen, X., Chen, Y., Li, X.: Asymptotically optimal sequential design for rank aggregation. arXiv preprint arXiv:1710.06056 (2017)
10. Davidson, S.B., Khanna, S., Milo, T., Roy, S.: Using the crowd for top-k and group-by queries. In: ICDT, pp. 225–236. ACM (2013)
11. Eriksson, B.: Learning to top-k search using pairwise comparisons. In: Artificial Intelligence and Statistics, pp. 265–273 (2013)
12. Guo, S., Parameswaran, A., Garcia-Molina, H.: So who won? Dynamic max discovery with the crowd. In: SIGMOD, pp. 385–396. ACM (2012)
13. Hoeffding, W.: Probability inequalities for sums of bounded random variables. J. Am. Stat. Assoc. **58**(301), 13–30 (1963)
14. Karger, D.R., Oh, S., Shah, D.: Efficient crowdsourcing for multi-class labeling. In: SIGMETRICS, vol. 41, no. 1, pp. 81–92 (2013)
15. Khan, A.R., Garcia-Molina, H.: Hybrid strategies for finding the max with the crowd. Technical report, Stanford InfoLab (2014)
16. Kou, N.M., Li, Y., Wang, H., Hou U, L., Gong, Z.: Crowdsourced top-k queries by confidence-aware pairwise judgments. In: SIGMOD, pp. 1415–1430. ACM (2017)
17. Li, G., Wang, J., Zheng, Y., Franklin, M.J.: Crowdsourced data management: a survey. TKDE **28**(9), 2296–2319 (2016)
18. Lu, T., Boutilier, C.: Learning mallows models with pairwise preferences. In: ICML, pp. 145–152 (2011)
19. Metropolis, N., Ulam, S.: The Monte Carlo method. J. Am. Stat. Assoc. **44**(247), 335–341 (1949)
20. Negahban, S., Oh, S., Shah, D.: Iterative ranking from pair-wise comparisons. In: Advances in Neural Information Processing Systems, pp. 2474–2482 (2012)
21. Pfeiffer, T., Gao, X.A., Chen, Y., Mao, A., Rand, D.G.: Adaptive polling for information aggregation. In: AAAI (2012)
22. Pomerol, J.C., Barba-Romero, S.: Multicriterion Decision in Management: Principles and Practice, vol. 25. Springer, Boston (2012)
23. Raykar, V., Agrawal, P.: Sequential crowdsourced labeling as an epsilon-greedy exploration in a Markov Decision Process. In: Artificial Intelligence and Statistics, pp. 832–840 (2014)

24. Shan, C., Mamoulis, N., Li, G., Cheng, R., Huang, Z., Zheng, Y.: T-Crowd: effective crowdsourcing for tabular data. In: ICDE, pp. 1316–1319 (2018)
25. Shan, C., Mamoulis, N., Li, G., Cheng, R., Huang, Z., Zheng, Y.: A crowdsourcing framework for collecting tabular data. TKDE (2019)
26. Thurstone, L.L.: A law of comparative judgment. Psychol. Rev. **34**(4), 273 (1927)
27. Venetis, P., Garcia-Molina, H., Huang, K., Polyzotis, N.: Max algorithms in crowdsourcing environments. In: WWW, pp. 989–998. ACM (2012)
28. Wang, J., Kraska, T., Franklin, M.J., Feng, J.: CrowdER: crowdsourcing entity resolution. PVLDB **5**(11), 1483–1494 (2012)
29. Wauthier, F., Jordan, M., Jojic, N.: Efficient ranking from pairwise comparisons. In: ICML, pp. 109–117 (2013)
30. Welinder, P., Perona, P.: Online crowdsourcing: rating annotators and obtaining cost-effective labels. In: CVPRW, pp. 25–32. IEEE (2010)
31. Zhang, X., Li, G., Feng, J.: Crowdsourced top-k algorithms: an experimental evaluation. PVLDB **9**(8), 612–623 (2016)

Guaranteed Delivery of Advertisements to Targeted Audiences Under Deduplication and Frequency Capping Constraints

Abhay Gupta, Ayush Bhatnagar, Aditya Ramana Rachakonda[✉],
and Ravindra Chittapur

Flipkart Internet Pvt. Ltd., Bangalore, India
{abhay.g,ayush.bhatnagar,aditya.rachakonda,
ravindra.chittapur}@flipkart.com

Abstract. In this work, we specify a guaranteed delivery booking system which helps the publishers provide view-guarantees to advertisers. We provide these guarantees while ensuring that content is not repeated to users in a visit (deduplication) and users are not overwhelmed by the same content across visits (frequency capping). We discuss the application of the guaranteed delivery system to two different use-cases: one in e-commerce and another in video streaming systems. We pose the booking problem as an optimisation of revenue under several constraints. We show that, the optimisation can be solved efficiently and such a system could provide near-real-time responses and act as a self-serve platform for advertisers. We also address the various practical considerations in providing such guarantees.

1 Introduction

In a typical e-commerce store-front, content on products is delivered to the customers either through a search interface or via banners or widgets that contain promotional information. Content shown in response to a search query has a specific intent associated with it whereas promotional content displayed through banners or widgets need not necessarily have an intent.

Content could be promoted for one of two major reasons. First is to show content which the user might be interested in and this would improve customer engagement and in turn improve the value to both the customer and the company. The second reason—the one driving this work—is to show content which lets the customer explore merchandise from various categories of the e-commerce store. Here the goal is to give visibility to the content of advertisers. This is akin to a store front in a brick and mortar shop which serves the purpose of piquing the customer's interest and thus drive engagement.

This problem is generally solved by affixing banners to the page displayed, or by allowing the content to be pinned to pages of users who satisfy certain

Y. Nah et al. (Eds.): DASFAA 2020, LNCS 12113, pp. 331–346, 2020.
https://doi.org/10.1007/978-3-030-59416-9_20

targeting criteria. We propose a system where the merchandisers request views of a target audience and the system provides a maximum bookable quantity and provides guarantees on the delivery once the booking is confirmed.

This work closely follows literature on guaranteed delivery of advertisements and builds on it to enable e-commerce store fronts. In the existing literature one of the core assumptions is that there is only one advertisement per page. But in a store-front—and for that matter even for advertisements on web pages— there can be more than one promotional content on a page. This constrains the guarantees further by a couple of expcricntial requirements like, (i) Deduplication: Not allowing duplicate content on a page and (ii) Frequency capping: Not showing a content more than a finite number of times to a customer during their multiple visits.

The contributions of this work are as follows: (i) A booking system which maximises content views, (ii) Unique content in any given visit, (iii) Frequency of content per user across visits finitely capped. This paper is organised as follows: Sect. 2 explores the relevant literature in this field, Sect. 3 gives an overview of the components in a basic guaranteed delivery system. Section 4 delves deeper into the current problem by formulating the guarantees and constraints required to solve this problem. Section 5 provides a brief interlude into a different domain where our solution becomes pertinent. We then present our practical observations in Sect. 6 and experiments in Sect. 7 before concluding.

2   Related Literature

Guaranteed delivery for advertisements by publishers has been an active area of research in past few years. Theoretically a very generic solution has been proposed by Vee et al. [12] which can be used for online bipartite matching, allocation and budgeted bidders. Their solution gives a near optimal allocation for users coming in online fashion. They propose a compact allocation plan of requests by advertisers on publishers website for multiple users as convex optimization problem with linear constraints. Here we can see the robustness of solution under sampling of original problem. Extending this work Bharadwaj et al. [2] proposed SHALE for display advertising, where early stop feature in dual space gives near optimal primal solve and linear time allocation in large systems. Both of these work assume one advertisement for each user visit while in practice we may want to show more than one ad when a user visits. Hence they do not focus on de-duplication property or on frequency capping constarint.

In allocation plans we can see representativeness as key objective to maximize along with reducing penalties for under deliveries. Bharadwaj et al. and Yang et al. [14] model allocation by maximizing it. They employ different methods to generate allocation plans. Yang et al. also model maximizing revenue from non-guaranteed advertisers and with clicks or conversions obtained from guaranteed ads. Chakrabarti et al. [5] address the joint problem of maximizing the CTR (click through rate) of ads considering the user engagement aspect along with minimizing under-delivery with the help of traffic shaping probabilities. To the best of our knowledge, there is little prior work concerning the booking problem. Booking of users' slots for different advertisers becomes problem when we start considering practical issues like,

1. More than one ad is shown on the page at the same time.
2. Every ad on a page is unique when a user visits the page.
3. Advertiser defined caps on the number of views per user.
4. Advertisers can target different cohorts of users or supplies.

Frequency capping has been addressed in the past but in the context of one advertisement per page. Treating it as online stochastic bipartite matching problem Feldman et al. [7] provided an approximate algorithm. Shanahan et al. [9] proposed frequency capping policies for each user segment via Markov Decision Process. Farahat [6] presents the idea of having frequency capping constraints in a linear optimization program for allocation. Buchbinder et al. [4] analyze greedy algorithms for special cases with frequency cap and also gives a primal-dual algorithm that holds even when various user segments are targeted by different advertisers and may help in improving the competitive ratio. Hojjat et al. [8] and Shi et al. [10] consider other aspects as well like fair allocation of ads to users(representativeness), user-level pacing and diversification along with frequency caps to solve the allocation problem. They propose a two phase framework to solve this problem in which first is to get the optimal allocation plan like we see in [2] but with frequency capping constraints and second is to get the pattern pools for each supply node. Zinkevich [15] present a weighted method for guaranteed delivery with focus on the frequency capping constraint. Our formulation is partially influenced by this constraint.

To the best of our knowledge, there is very little work on booking as an optimisation in guaranteed delivery. This merits a separate discussion around formulation because unlike allocation booking if implemented correctly is a time critical step where responses are expected in the matter of seconds.

3 Guaranteed Delivery

A guaranteed delivery (GD) system provides view-guarantees to advertisers on targeted audience segments at an agreed upon price. On failing to deliver the views the publisher pays a penalty for every view which was guaranteed but could not be delivered. The various components of a GD system are shown in Fig. 1 and described below.

Audience Manager is the system which divides the total number of content views generated by all users into *disjoint* segments of views. Typically this is done by dividing views using user attributes and then by context attributes. The final disjoint segments are termed as the **supply** nodes. In our GD system, each supply node is uniquely identified by a combination of the following: (**Gender × Location × Affinity × PageID × SlotID**). But in practice, we allow advertisers to target only on user attributes and not on context attributes. Hence targeting is restricted to user groups (**Gender** × **Location** × **Affinity**) and not all supply nodes.

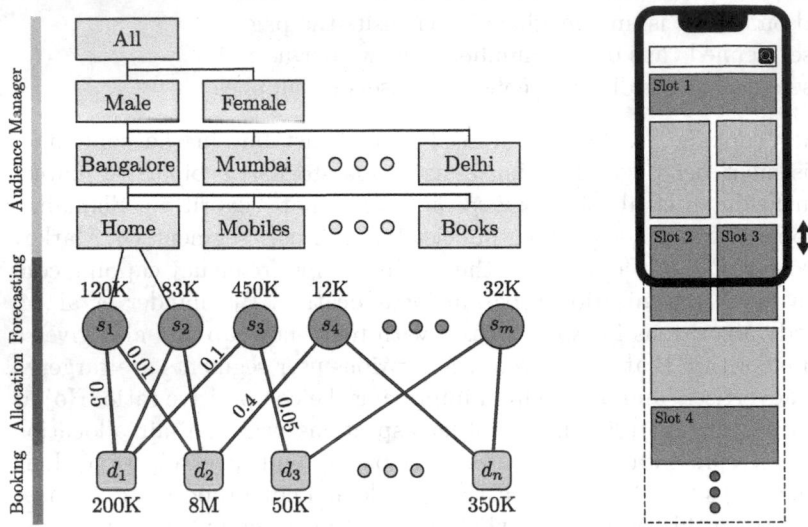

Fig. 1. GD system   Fig. 2. Mobile e-commerce layout

Forecasting system predicts the number of page views for each supply node for several days into the future. We use s_i to indicate the forecast of the views of the ith supply node. In practice, we use ARIMAX [3] with sale and calendar events as exogenous variables and Holt-Winters [13] to choose the best forecast based on validation data. We also found that bottom-up forecasting—independent forecasts for each supply node—worked best. For each supply node we can forecast two months into the future.

Booking is the process of adding/booking a new promotional content or advertisement to the GD system. It creates a contract between the publisher and the advertiser through the following steps:

1. Advertiser specifies a targeting criterion which reduces to a set of supply nodes to which they want to show an advertisement at an agreed upon price and penalty.
2. The GD booking system responds with a maximum number of views that the system can provide to that advertiser. This is a time-critical step and it is expected to be completed in the time taken for a transaction.
3. The advertiser books a number of views which is less than or equal to the maximum number of views provided by the system.

Each new booking, termed as **demand**, represents the number of views agreed upon by the booking system and the advertiser. The views of the jth demand node are represented as d_j. The corresponding price (value) and penalty are represented as ν_j and p_j respectively. The booking system also defines the mapping $\Gamma(j)$ which maps every booking to a set of supply nodes. The supply and demand nodes can be thought of as a bipartite graph and booking defines the edges of this graph. During booking the edge weights x_{ij} represent the hypothetical allocation of a supply node i to a demand node j. The under-delivery of a campaign is represented as u_j. Under-delivery can be either due to booking more valuable advertisements or it could be due to change in forecasts between bookings. The problem formulated as a linear programming problem as below:

$$\underset{x,u}{\text{maximise}} \left(\nu_{\mathbf{k}} \sum_{i=1}^{m} s_i x_{i\mathbf{k}} - \sum_{j=1}^{\mathbf{k}-1} p_j u_j \right) \tag{1}$$

$$\text{subject to} \sum_{i \in \Gamma(j)} s_i x_{ij} + u_j \geq d_j, \ \forall j \tag{2}$$

$$\sum_{j \in \Gamma(i)} x_{ij} \leq 1, \ \forall i \tag{3}$$

$$x_{ij}, u_j \geq 0, \ \forall i, \forall j \tag{4}$$

where $\mathbf{k}$ is the advertisement being booked. This optimisation will yield the largest hole that can be created to accommodate $\mathbf{k}$ while minimising the under-delivery of previously booked advertisements. Equations 2, 3, 4 are the demand, supply and non-negativity constraints respectively.

Allocation is the process by which we display a targeted advertisement to a user. It allocates a set of views from each supply node to a targeted demand node. It is represented as x_{ij} which indicates the fraction of views of supply node i which will be shown to the content provided by the demand node j. The formulation for allocation is very similar in constraints but the objective is to reduce under delivery.

$$\underset{x,u}{\text{minimise}} \sum_{j=1}^{n} p_j u_j \tag{5}$$

$$\text{subject to} \sum_{i \in \Gamma(j)} s_i x_{ij} + u_j \geq d_j, \ \forall j \tag{6}$$

$$\sum_{j \in \Gamma(i)} x_{ij} \leq 1, \ \forall i \tag{7}$$

$$x_{ij}, u_j \geq 0, \ \forall i, \forall j \tag{8}$$

Some approaches [2] add a fairness criterion called representativeness represented as θ_{ij} which would be considered a fair allocation and re-write Eq. 5 as:

$$\underset{x,u}{\text{minimise}} \left(\sum_{j=1}^{n} \sum_{i=1}^{m} s_i (x_{ij} - \theta_{ij})^2 + \sum_{j=1}^{n} p_j u_j \right) \tag{9}$$

The allocation and booking formulation given here would suffice if we were to have only one advertisement per page and if we do not limit the number of views of the same advertisement to a user. In practice, these assumptions do not hold as there can be more than one advertisement per page—at least in our use cases—and advertisers do not like getting a large number of views for one advertisement from the same user. In the next section we reformulate the optimisation problems to honour deduplication and frequency capping.

4   Booking Reformulation

Before reformulating the optimisation problem let us take a brief foray into the business problem of running an e-commerce store-front and the practical issues.

4.1   E-Commerce Store-Front

A typical e-commerce store-front as depicted in Fig. 2 consists of a search bar followed by several rectangle pieces of content. The content can be either promotional (like advertisements) or recommendations based on the user's past activity or any other non-commerce content (like shipping status).

There are several advertisement slots per page and it can be seen that all slots do not garner the same number of views. The view is an event that happens when a content is in the view-port. The view counts are dependent on the vertical scroll behaviour of the user[1].

User Affinity. In an e-commerce store different users would tend to have different interests. Some might be book-lovers, others might be interested in DIY goods and some others might shop for home appliances. Based on a user's past activity if we find that a user is likely to shop for a certain category of goods then we term it as that user's affinity towards that category. Advertisers like targeting affinities as it gets them a very relevant user base.

In our GD system, we take the set of top 3 affinities of a user. Given that we have around 20 high-level affinities we can define around $\binom{20}{3}$ disjoint affinities. If an advertiser chooses book-lovers as their target audience then we choose all sets which have book-lovers as one of the affinities for that advertisers.

---

[1] Visits from a mobile device make up more than 90% of our traffic and hence without loss of generality we assume the device to be a mobile phone.

4.2 Deduplication

Deduplication can be solved at serving time by removing duplicates and serving alternate content in their place. Doing so will not violate the constraint but will end up causing significant under-delivery. In a page with several slots the booking system might assume all of them are available for an advertisement causing under-delivery. To resolve this issue we transform a set of supply nodes in a page taken in the descending order of views $\{s_1, s_2, \ldots, s_k\}$ into an equivalent number of σ-supply nodes $\{\sigma_1, \sigma_2, \ldots, \sigma_k\}$ as in Fig. 3(a) to 3(b).

First, let us define $\{\omega_1, \omega_2, \ldots, \omega_k\}$ as follows:

$$\omega_i = \begin{cases} s_k, & \text{if } i = 1 \\ s_{k-i+1} - s_{k-i+2} & \text{otherwise} \end{cases} \qquad (10)$$

Now let us define k σ-supply nodes $\{\sigma_1, \sigma_2, \ldots, \sigma_k\}$ as in Eq. 11,

$$\sigma_i = \omega_i \times (k - i + 1) \qquad (11)$$

Each ω_i represents the number of unique times a user would scroll till a depth $k - i + 1$ and the corresponding σ_i represents the total number of views. This transformation enables us to constrain each user to be allotted not more than ω_i views from σ_i, for anything larger than ω_i would lead to duplicates.

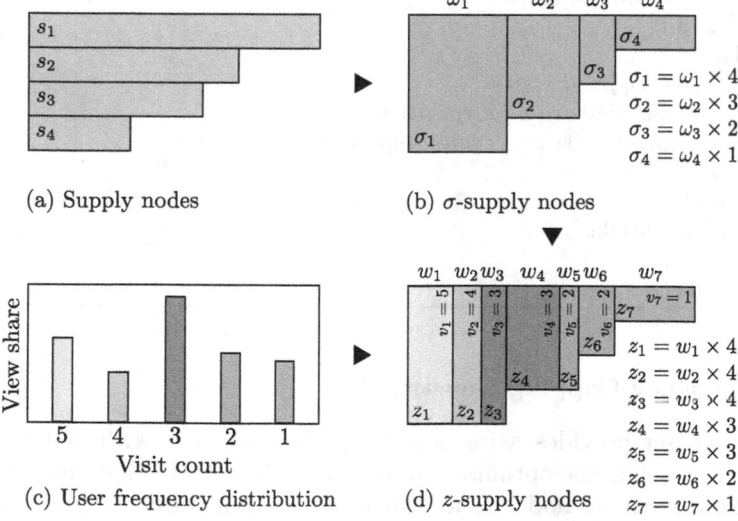

Fig. 3. Visualising supply nodes

Algorithm 1. Transformation of supplies in a user group for fcap constraint

---

1: **Inputs:**

$\sigma = [\sigma_1, \sigma_2, \ldots, \sigma_k]$, $\omega = [\omega_1, \omega_2, \ldots, \omega_k]$,

$f = [f_1, f_2, \ldots, f_n]$ s.t. $\sum_{i=1}^{V} f_i = 1$

2: **Outputs:**

$z = [z_1, z_2, \ldots, z_b]$, $w = [w_1, w_2, \ldots, w_b]$, $v = [v_1, v_2, \ldots, v_b]$

3: **Initialize:**

$z = [], w = [], v = []$

$i \leftarrow j \leftarrow l \leftarrow 1$

$\text{total\_visits} \leftarrow \sum_k \omega$

$\text{allotted\_visits} \leftarrow 0$

$\text{remaining\_visits} \leftarrow \omega_j$

4: **while** $\text{allotted\_visits} \leq \text{total\_visits}$ **do**

5:     $\text{required\_visits} \leftarrow f_i \times \text{total\_visits}$

6:     $\text{height} \leftarrow \sigma_j / \omega_j$

7:     $v_l \leftarrow V - i + 1$

8:     **if** $\text{required\_visits} \geq \text{remaining\_visits}$ **then**

9:         $w_l \leftarrow \text{remaining\_visits}$

10:        $j \leftarrow j + 1$

11:        **if** $\text{required\_visits} = \text{remaining\_visits}$ **then**

12:            $i \leftarrow i + 1$

13:        **else**

14:            $f_i \leftarrow f_i - (\text{remaining\_visits} / \text{total\_visits})$

15:            $\text{allotted\_visits} \leftarrow \text{allotted\_visits} + w_l$

16:            $\text{remaining\_visits} \leftarrow \omega_j$

17:        **end if**

18:    **else**

19:        $w_l \leftarrow \text{required\_visits}$

20:        $\text{allotted\_visits} \leftarrow \text{allotted\_visits} + w_l$

21:        $\text{remaining\_visits} \leftarrow \text{remaining\_visits} - w_l$

22:        $i \leftarrow i + 1$

23:    **end if**

24:    $z_l = w_l \times \text{height}$

25:    $l \leftarrow l + 1$

26: **end while**

4.3 Frequency Capping Constraint

Every advertiser provides a frequency cap ψ_j associated with demand d_j. In order to reformulate the optimisation to honour these frequency caps we need to re-transform σ-supply nodes to a form where we can define frequency capping constraints. Before doing that, let us introduce the notion of user frequency distribution.

A user group is the set of user attributes to which an advertisement is targeted. We term every unique combination of (**Gender** × **Location** × **Affinity**) as a user group. Every user falls in exactly one user group. For every user group we compute a distribution of number of users visiting v number of times in the given forecasting period. This means that for every user group we have the information about the fraction of users that visit once, twice, thrice in a forecasting period as shown in Fig. 3(c). This histogram is provided by our forecasting system. Note that we do not allow targeting at a page level as that would not enable us to honour the frequency capping constraint.

Now we impose the user frequency distribution on the σ-supply nodes to transform them into z-supply nodes which enable us to define frequency capping constraints over deduplication constraints.

As a thought exercise, let us assume that the users who visit only once scroll the deepest and the users who visit most frequently do not go beyond the first slot in the page. This makes the optimisation simpler as the deep scrolls (σ_1, σ_2) will not have frequency cap constraints, as they are from users who do not revisit and hence will not have frequency caps. And in the shallow scrolls ($\sigma_{k-1}, \sigma k$) the frequency cap constraints can be modelled in a straight-forward way (as shown by Shi et al. [10]), due to the lack of deduplication problems. In reality, this assumption will be obviously wrong and the true nature might be closer to the fact that the number of visits and the depth of scrolling would be independent. But to ensure we provide the right guarantees, we assume the contrary, that the users who visit most will also scroll the most and the users who visit the least also scroll the least. This is the worst case scenario with respect to guarantees on frequency capping.

We do this by selecting the traffic in the descending order of visit count from the histogram and assigning it to the σ-supply nodes as given in Fig. 3(d). Whenever we switch from one visit count bucket to another we break the σ-supply node and the corresponding ω value. These new supply nodes are termed z-supply nodes and the equivalents of ω values are called w values. The exact transformation is detailed in Algorithm 1. Note that unlike the earlier transformation Fig. 3(b), this transformation increases the number of supply nodes in a page at most by V where V is the number of visit count buckets. As a part of this transformation we also assign a v_i with every pair of z_i and w_i making them a triplet.

So the final formulation of our booking problem is:

$$\text{maximise}_{x,u} \left(\nu_{\mathbf{k}} \sum_{i=1}^{m} z_i x_{i\mathbf{k}} - \sum_{j=1}^{k-1} p_j u_j \right) \tag{12}$$

$$\text{subject to} \sum_{i \in \Gamma(j)} z_i x_{ij} + u_j \geq d_j, \ \forall j \tag{13}$$

$$\sum_{j \in \Gamma(i)} x_{ij} \leq 1, \ \forall i \tag{14}$$

$$z_i x_{ij} \leq w_i, \ \forall i, \tag{15}$$

$$z_i x_{ij} \leq \min(\psi_j, v_i) \times (w_i/v_i), \ \forall i, \forall j \tag{16}$$

$$u_j \leq \kappa d_j, \ \forall j \text{ where } 0 \leq \kappa \leq 1 \tag{17}$$

$$x_{ij}, u_j \geq 0, \ \forall i, \forall j \tag{18}$$

In the optimisation above, we can observe that the objective (Eq. 12) mirrors that of the booking objective provided in Sect. 3 (Eq. 1) in all forms except that the supply nodes are replaced by z-supply nodes. The demand, supply and non-negativity constraints (Eqs. 2, 3, 4) are similarly formulated (Eqs. 13, 14, 18). The deduplication constraint (Eq. 15) states that any z-supply node is never assigned more than w views. In the frequency capping constraint (Eq. 16) the ratio w_i/v_i gives the unique number of users. Every user is given no more than the frequency cap ψ_j number of views of an advertisement. Equation 17 is a fairness constraint which states that a higher priced campaign can never fully eliminate a lower priced campaign. In practice we use a κ of 0.5.

4.4 Allocation

As we saw earlier the allocation optimisation (Eqs. 5, 9) and the booking optimisation (Eq. 1) share the same set of constraints while differing in the objectives. This remains to be the case in our formulation as well. The computational time constraints to solve the allocation problem are relaxed to a few hours instead of a few seconds in which we need to book a new advertisement. So, we use a quadratic objective—variant of the allocation provided in SHALE (Eq. 9)—as given below:

$$\underset{x,u}{\text{minimise}} \left(\sum_{j=1}^{n} \sum_{i=1}^{m} z_i (x_{ij} - \theta_{ij})^2 + \sum_{j=1}^{n} p_j u_j \right) \tag{19}$$

5   Guaranteed Video Ads

Online video ads is an application where guaranteed delivery through affinity based targeting seems to be the best way to optimise content. Traditional performance advertising through CTR modelling requires a response from the user to work. The response can be a click or a conversion. But video ads typically are not linked to a response, as it is very hard to build such systems for television which is the primary medium for video consumption. The only means to reach a relevant set of users is through targeting based on user affinities. There has been prior work on using guaranteed delivery in videos by Sumita et al. [11].

The optimisation formulation presented in the paper is perfectly extensible for video advertisements. The supply node can be mapped to (Gender × Location × Affinity × **VideoID** × SlotID)   instead   of   (Gender × Location × Affinity × **PageID** × SlotID) and the rest of the paper naturally falls into its place. A web page is scrollable and hence slots higher up have more views than slots lower below. Similarly a video can be played and ad slots earlier on will garner more views than ad slots towards the end. Deduplication and frequency caps are pertinent for online videos as well.

6   Practical Considerations

Booking over Multiple Days. Most of the time advertisers would want to book an advertisement over several days sometimes even weeks. For booking, compute the maximum bookable views for each day in parallel and report the sum along with the distribution of views to ensure transparency of pacing. For allocation we take the booked amount and the demand overhang from the previous day and compute the allocation plan. This splitting by days ensures us to horizontally scale as per the requirements.

Booking Cache. Another optimisation we employ for better turnaround times is to precompute the maximum allocatable booking for a set of frequently targeted user bases. This computation needs to be performed once for each cached audience targets after the successful completion of a booking transaction. And the computation for a targeting is independent of others (for caching purposes) and hence can be horizontally scaled.

Fallbacks. Not all slots will be booked by guaranteed delivery and hence as a fallback we use performance advertising where the user response is modelled as $Pr(click|view)$ and $Pr(conversion|view)$.

Simplifying Frequency Capping Constraint. The final transformation of supplies for modelling frequency capping constraint yields a triplet (z_i, w_i, v_i) for every z-supply node in any user group, say $\mathcal{G}$. Here v_i of a z-supply denotes that the visits in that supply of user segment are solely made up of users who visit exactly v_i number of times. Let's define a set of user groups that are targeted by an advertiser j as $\mathcal{S}(j)$. Note that a user group is the one which contains multiple supply nodes s_i which we transform into z_i.

Instead of the constraint in Eq. 16, where there is one constraint for every atomic supply, we can instead write the constraint for every advertiser and user groups targeted by that advertiser, thus reducing the number of individual constraints in the solver. Note that the users visiting less than or equal to ψ_j will not see the advertisement more than ψ_j times. We show this in Eq. 21 which turns out to be the deduplication constraint i.e. Eq. 15. Therefore we exclude the frequency capping constraint for transformed supplies having v_i value less than or equal to ψ_j. For users visiting more than ψ_j times we reformulate Eq. 20 to Eq. 22. We create a single constraint for each demand (d_j) and for each user group $(\mathcal{G} \in \mathcal{S}(j))$ it targets. The LHS of the inequality is the supply allotted from the z-supply nodes with v_i greater than ψ_j while in the RHS we have ψ_j times the unique users with the number of visits greater than ψ_j in those transformed supplies.

$$z_i x_{ij} \leq \min(\psi_j, v_i) \times (w_i/v_i), \ \forall i, \forall j \qquad (20)$$

$$\text{if } v_i \leq \psi_j \implies z_i x_{ij} \leq v_i \times \frac{w_i}{v_i} \implies z_i x_{ij} \leq w_i, \ \forall i, \forall j \qquad (21)$$

$$\sum_{i \in \{i | z_i \in \mathcal{G} \wedge v_i > \psi_j\}} z_i x_{ij} \leq \psi_j \times \sum_{i \in \{i | z_i \in \mathcal{G} \wedge v_i > \psi_j\}} (w_i/v_i), \ \forall j, \forall \mathcal{G} \in \mathcal{S}(j) \qquad (22)$$

7 Experimental Setup and Results

In the set of experiments we want to show how quick and robust we are in our formulations.

Data. We test our approaches on simulated graphs that have a scale of real world data we face on usual business days. The number of supply nodes or user segments is 234150, the number of demands nodes is 100 and the number of edges they make are 587485. We also distributed the edges in a manner representative of the targeting that we observe in practice. The cost to advertiser of a guaranteed delivery advertisement is higher than that of a performance based advertisement. Hence in practice we typically see around 30–70 such advertisements at any given time. In our experiments we assumed that we would take up to 100 such advertisements. We used Mosek 9.0.89 [1] solver to solve our linear program (LP) on Intel(R) Xeon(R) CPU E5-2690 v4 @ 2.60 GHz machine.

7.1 Analysis of Time as Demands Arrive Progressively

When an advertiser has a demand with well-defined targets we would want to inform her about the maximum amount of views we can allocate as soon as possible. Hence the time taken to complete the optimisation has to be in the duration of a transaction—less than a few minutes. With every new demand coming in, the number of variables and constraints keeps on increasing. So in order to speed up the procedure, for every new demand we use the optimal solution of the previous LP as a warm start.

In this experiment we want to show with new demand coming in we would be able to solve our optimisation problem within few seconds irrespective of how many supplies they target. Figure 4 shows the variation of time taken to solve the formulation and obtain the maximum visits that we can promise for different demands coming in. The arrival order of demands is shuffled a hundred times and hence for each shuffled order of arrival the whole booking process has to be carried out. The X-axis shows the index of the arrival of demand and Y-axis shows the spread of time taken to solve the optimisation for different demand indices across the hundred booking procedures. Thus at each demand index we would have 100 corresponding time values as we have repeated booking procedure 100 times for all 100 demands in random order coming in.

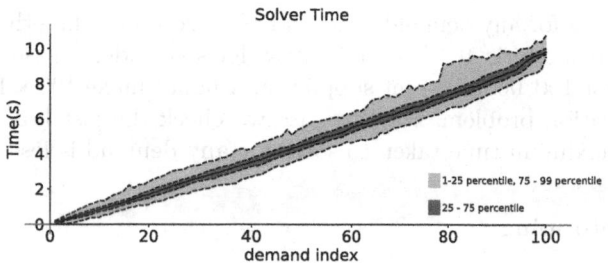

Fig. 4. Time vs demand

From Fig. 4 we can see that the time varies almost linearly as the number of demands grow. Here shuffling makes sure that in whatever order demands come with whatever targets they want and corresponding edges they make, we still solve our formulation within 10 s. Each new demand increases the variables and constraints in the booking system and as a result the time for solving the optimisation also increases but in a linear fashion. Thus when a new demand will come we will be able to reply with how much we can allocate him within few seconds.

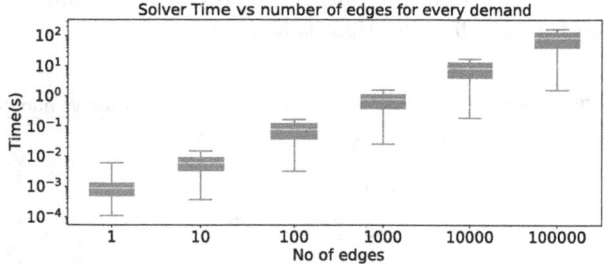

Fig. 5. Time vs number of edges

7.2 Variation in Time as Number of Targets Increase

We wanted to check the time taken supposing every demand targets the same number of supply nodes but targets nodes between demands are different. Figure 5 shows this experiment where each demand targets exactly 1 supply, then 10 supplies, then 100 and so on till 100,000 different supplies each. The X-axis represents the number of targeted supplies by each demand. The Y-axis represents the time taken to solve the LP problem. The box plot shows the distribution of time taken on the arrival of each demand. Say for the first case where each demand is just targeting 1 supply node, the box plot shows the time taken to solve for all 100 demands coming in. We can see that the least time taken for booking for any demand is around 10^{-4} seconds while the highest time taken for any demand is 10^{-2} seconds. Now let's consider a case where all 100 demands ask for 100,000 different supplies and hence make $100 \times 100,000$ edges in our optimisation problem. For this case we check the last box plot. And we see that the maximum time taken to solve for any demand is less than 2 min.

7.3 Early Stopping

One of the biggest sources of error in the GD system comes from the errors in traffic forecasting and hence a slightly sub-optimal solution to the optimisation problem would not be of much concern. Early stopping can on the other hand speed up the transaction time significantly. In this experiment, we check the trade-off between saving time and error introduced due to early stopping. We enable early stopping by setting the maximum iterations parameter in our solver.

Figure 6 shows the trade-off between error and time as the iterations for early-stopping is varied. The X-axis shows the maximum allowed iterations for each demand, the left Y-axis shows the error or revenue loss and the right Y-axis shows the maximum time for any single demand in that batch. We can see that if stop early at just few iterations like 10 the revenue loss is huge even though the time taken is minimal. While as we increase the maximum iterations, we see a sudden jump to optimality but this jump, comes at a significant cost in terms of time. After this jump the optimisation converges and hence maximum iterations has no further effect on time taken.

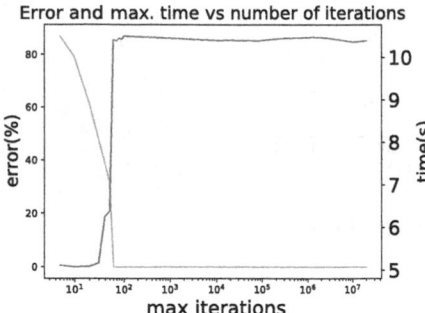
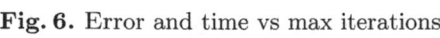
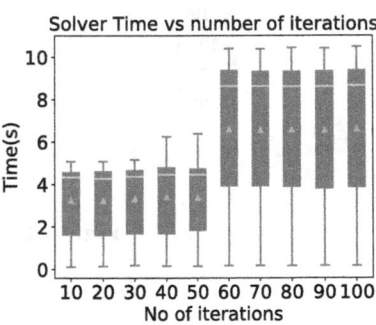

Fig. 6. Error and time vs max iterations

Fig. 7. Solver time vs number max iterations.

We compute the sub-optimality in terms of the difference of the total revenue generated at the end of the complete booking procedure with the revenue generated when we stop early. In Fig. 7 we present a finer view of this jump and across several runs—in each run we randomise the order of bookings. And we see this abrupt jump from sub-optimality to optimality once again. Hence it seems almost impossible to tune maximum iterations to give any benefit in the time taken for a booking.

7.4   Effect of Variation in the Forecasts on Optimality

We obtain our views in a supply nodes from a forecasting system which uses historic data to predict future. There is always a difference between what we predict and what actually occurs. It might be possible that we may forecast more than the actual visits thus leading to under-delivery for us. The opposite leaves us with under-booking and money left on the table. In this experiment, we analyse this effect of the instability in forecasts on under-delivery and under-booking.

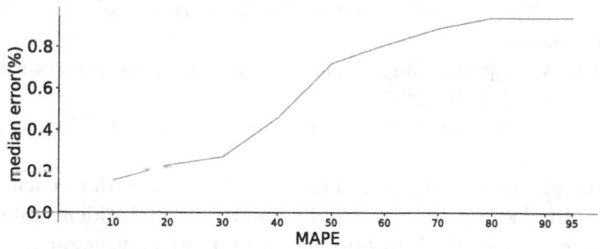

Fig. 8. Error vs the variance in the forecasts

We measure the error we make by observing the revenue we loose if the actual users visiting the platform varies highly from the forecasts. It is expected that as the variance increases the error will also increase. In order to simulate real visits by actual users visits we added variance into the forecast and then do the booking for these perturbed supplies. In Fig. 8 the X-axis is the variance in forecast of supply numbers inside each user segment. We have revenue from the forecast supplies and then we also calculate revenue from the perturbed supplies, these two giving us the error in percentage for revenue which is the Y-axis. From this figure it is clear that even with the highest variance in forecast we receive an error of 0.94%. This shows that our formulation is robust to forecasting errors with respect to actual visits.

8   Conclusions

In this paper, we proposed a formulation to enable booking and allocation of guaranteed delivery campaigns on pages with more than one advertisement. We also formulated the deduplication and frequency capping constraints and through experiments we have seen that we can book such advertisements in the duration of a transaction—in a few seconds. We discuss the practical considerations of implementing such a system. We observed through experiments that the formulation scales linearly in computation times with the number of demands and is also robust to forecasting errors.

References

1. ApS, M.: MOSEK Optimizer API for Python 9.0.89 (2019). https://docs.mosek. com/9.1/pythonapi/index.html
2. Bharadwaj, V., et al.: SHALE: an efficient algorithm for allocation of guaranteed display advertising. In: KDD, pp. 1195–1203 (2012)
3. Box, G.E., et al.: Time Series Analysis: Forecasting and Control. Wiley, Hoboken (2015)
4. Buchbinder, N., Feldman, M., Ghosh, A., Naor, J.: Frequency capping in online advertising. J. Sched. **17**(4), 385–398 (2014). https://doi.org/10.1007/s10951-014-0367-z
5. Chakrabarti, D., Vee, E.: Traffic shaping to optimize ad delivery. TEAC **3**(2), 1–20 (2015). Article no. 11
6. Farahat, A.: Privacy preserving frequency capping in internet banner advertising. In: WWW, pp. 1147–1148 (2009)
7. Feldman, J., et al.: Online stochastic matching: beating 1–1/e. In: Foundations of Computer Science, pp. 117–126 (2009)
8. Hojjat, A., et al.: Delivering guaranteed display ads under reach and frequency requirements. In: Twenty-Eighth AAAI Conference on Artificial Intelligence (2014)
9. Shanahan, J., den Poel, D.: Determining optimal advertisement frequency capping policy via Markov decision processes to maximize click through rates. In: NIPS Workshop: Machine Learning in Online Advertising, pp. 39–45 (2010)
10. Shi, W., et al.: Online guaranteed-delivery advertising under frequency capping. In: BIGCOM, pp. 225–230 (2018)
11. Sumita, H., et al.: Online optimization of video-ad allocation. In: IJCAI, pp. 423–429 (2017)
12. Vee, E., et al.: Optimal online assignment with forecasts. In: EC, pp. 109–118 (2010)
13. Winters, P.R.: Forecasting sales by exponentially weighted moving averages. Manag. Sci. **6**(3), 324–342 (1960)
14. Yang, J., et al.: Inventory allocation for online graphical display advertising using multi-objective optimization. In: ICORES 2012, pp. 293–304 (2012)
15. Zinkevich, M.: Optimal online frequency capping allocation using the weight approach (2010). http://martin.zinkevich.org/publications/weights.pdf

Graph Data

Efficient Parallel Cycle Search in Large Graphs

Zhu Qing[1], Long Yuan[2(✉)], Zi Chen[1], Jingjing Lin[1], and Guojie Ma[1]

[1] East China Normal University, Shanghai, China
Skullpirate.qing@gmail.com, zchen@stu.ecnu.edu.cn, jingle_1984@foxmail.com,
gjma@sei.ecnu.edu.cn
[2] Nanjing University of Science and Technology, Nanjing, China
longyuan@njust.edu.cn

Abstract. Cycle is a fundamental structure in graphs. Motivated by the wide applications of cycle search, namely computing the cycles related to a vertex in the graph, we investigate efficient parallel algorithm to address the cycle search problem in large graphs. We first propose a two-phase paradigm tailored for the parallel cycle search problem. Based on the paradigm, we further devise a workload estimation method to improve the efficiency and scalability of the algorithm by balancing the work assigned to different threads. We experimentally evaluate our algorithms on real datasets and the results demonstrate the effectiveness of our approach.

Keywords: Cycle search · Parallel algorithm · Graph

1 Introduction

Graphs have been widely adopted to represent the relationships of entities in real applications such as social networks [29], web search [8], road networks [16,17], collaboration networks [15], and biology [25]. With the proliferation of graph applications, research efforts have been devoted to many problems in managing and analyzing graph data [18,24,26–28]. Among them, the cycle is fundamental structure of a graph and has been studied in. Formally, given a graph $G = (V, E)$, a path from u to v, denoted by $p(u, v)$, is a sequence of vertices $u = v_0, v_1, \ldots, v_n = v$ such that $(v_{i-1}, v_i) \in E$ and there is not repeated vertices in $v_0, v_1, \ldots, v_n$. A cycle is a path $p = v_0, v_1, \ldots, v_n$ where $v_0 = v_n$.

Applications. Computing cycles in a graph can be used in many application scenarios. For example:

(1) *Automobile Insurance Fraud Detection.* In automobile insurance fraud detection, a collision network is a graph in which each car represents a vertex and there is an edge between two vertices if the corresponding cars involved in the same collision. A cycle in a collision network is a strong indicator of the insurance fraud behaviour and computing the cycles in the collision network can be beneficial for detecting suspect fraud behaviours [3].

© Springer Nature Switzerland AG 2020
Y. Nah et al. (Eds.): DASFAA 2020, LNCS 12113, pp. 349–367, 2020.
https://doi.org/10.1007/978-3-030-59416-9_21

(2) *Investment Risk Detection*. In investment risk detection, cycle search is an effective way to deal with wash trades. To conduct a wash trade, traders usually set up an agreement to construct a network. Every trader may connect to exactly two other trading neighbours forming a single continuous pathway for transactions. These transactions form a clockwise cycle. Fraudsters expand their balance sheet by wash trade. So where there is a cycle in trade networks, there may exist investment risk [5].

(3) *Stock Manipulation Criminal Detection*. In stock manipulation criminal detection, a criminal transaction network is formed by nominee accounts given by penny stock companies. These nominee accounts are controlled by criminal gangs. The criminal gangs use some abnormal manipulative trading with others to give the market a false impression that there were real demands for these stocks. A cycle in the transaction network usually indicates a potential crime [10,14].

Motivations. Due to its wide application scenarios, computing the cycle structure in a graph has been extensively studied in the literature [4]. However, all the existing works focus on the cycle detection problem, namely, computing all the cycles in the entire graph, which is generally time-consuming especially on large graphs. Moreover, from the application scenario perspective, users are more interested in the cycles related to a specific vertex instead of all the cycles in the graph. For example, in the application of automobile insurance fraud detection [3]. The insurance companies generally know some suspicious users and they are more interested in the cycles containing cars of these suspicious users. Therefore, we study the *cycle search* problem in this paper, namely, given a vertex $q \in V(G)$, computes all the cycles containing q in G.

Driven by current commodity, single multi-core servers can easily fit graphs with over a hundred billion edges in memory and these multi-core servers have sufficient memory bandwidth to get quite good speedups over sequential codes [22], we adopt the single shared-memory multi-core platform and aim to devise efficient parallel algorithms to address the cycle search problem.

Our Approach. To address the cycle search problem in parallel, we propose a new paradigm for parallel cycle search in the paper. Our paradigm contains two phases, namely, prefix expansion and parallel search. In prefix expansion, we extend query vertex to a batch of path prefix into a task queue. In parallel search phase, every thread steals task from the task queue and continue searching for cycles. Following these two phases, our algorithm can answer the cycle search efficiently.

Contributions. In the paper, we make the following contributions:

(1) *A new parallel paradigm for cycle search problem.* We are the first to propose a paradigm for parallel cycle search. And we can improve the paradigm by the distribution of the graph.

(2) *A novel algorithm to search the cycles.* Following the expansion-parallel-search paradigm, we devise a new parallel cycle search algorithm. Our new

parallel cycle search algorithm is highly effective and scalable. Besides, we also prove that our algorithm is work efficient in theory.

(3) *Extensive performance studies on large real datasets.* We conduct extensive experimental studies to evaluate the proposed algorithms on eight real graphs, one of which contains 65 million vertices and 1.8 billion edges. The experimental results demonstrate the good parallelism and scalability of our algorithm.

2   Preliminaries

We model a graph as $G(V, E)$, where (1) $V(G)$ represents the set of vertices; (2) $E(G)$ represents the set of edges in G. We denote the number of vertices as n and the number of edges as m, i.e., $n = |V(G)|$ and $m = |E(G)|$. For a vertex $u \in V(G)$, we use $nbr(u, G)$ to denote the neighbour set of u in G, i.e., $nbr(u, G) = \{v \in V(G)|(u, v) \in E(G)\}$. The degree of a vertex $u \in V$, denoted by $deg(u, G)$, is the number of neighbours of u, i.e., $deg(u, G) - |nbr(u, G)|$. In this paper, we omit G when it is explicit in context. A *path* p from vertex u to v is a sequence of vertices $u = v_0, v_1, \ldots, v_n = v$ which every adjacent vertices are joined by $(v_{i-1}, v_i) \in E(G)$. We can use $p(u, v)$ to represent a path from vertex u to v. The length of path p, denoted by $len(p)$, is the number of edges in the path. A *cycle* is a *path* p with $v_0 = v_n$ and $len(p) \geq 3$. A simple cycle is a cycle with no repetitions of vertices and edges, except the starting and the ending vertex.

Definition 1 (Length Constraint). *We say a path or cycle p satisfy the length constraint if $len(p) \leq k$, where k is a given integer.*

Definition 2 (Length Constraint Cycle Search). *Given a graph G, a query vertex q and a length constraint k, cycle search computes all simple cycles $\{p|$ $v_0 = q \bigwedge len(p) \leq k\}$ in G.*

Problem Statement. In this paper, we study the problem of parallel cycle search. Given a graph G, a vertex q, and a length constraint k, we need to search all cycles p which contain vertex q and $len(p) \leq k$. We use the standard PRAM model machine proposed in [23]. It assumes that a set of similar types of processors, all the processors share a common memory unit and a memory access unit connects the processors with the single shared memory. And the cost of parallel algorithms is analyzed in two measures: work and span. The work of an algorithm corresponds to the total number of primitive operations performed by the algorithm. The span of an algorithm basically corresponds to the longest sequence of dependences in the computation. In this paper, we discuss the problem on the undirected graph, and the algorithm in this paper is easy to extend to the directed graph.

Cycle search problem is NP-Hard. We can prove it by reducing the Hamiltonian cycle problem to cycle search problem. Because the length of the Hamiltonian path is n, if the cycle search with length n can be solved in the polynomial time, we just need to check if there is a cycle with length n, then the Hamiltonian cycle will be solved. Therefore the problem is NP-Complete.

3   Baseline Algorithm

3.1   Single Thread Algorithm

In this section, we first introduce the DFSEnum algorithm, which is a single thread algorithm. For q, we have neighbours $nbr(q)$ and for every edge in $\{(q,t)|t \in nbr(q)\}$ where there is a $path(q,t)$, there is a cycle including q. Thus the key is to find all simple paths $\{p \mid p \in path(q,t) \cap len(p) < k\}$. We can easily come up with a simple algorithm based on depth-first search (DFS) to find all simple paths between q and t.

The inputs of the Algorithm 1 are the graph G, the query vertex q and the length constraint k. When we enter the procedure Search-Path, two conditions need to be satisfied: (1) whether the vertex n is the target vertex t, (2) whether the current path is under the length constraint. If the vertex n is the target vertex and the length of the current path is under the constraint, we report the path. If the length of the current path exceeds the limit, we discard the path and pop back the vertex. Then we move on to the next vertex in $nbr(n)$. The algorithm stops until all paths under the length k have been explored.

Algorithm 1. DFS-Enum(Graph G, Vertex q, Length k)

1: $p \leftarrow$ empty path
2: p.push(q)
3: $visited[] \leftarrow false$
4: **for** each t in $nbr(q)$ **do**
5:     remove (q,t) from G
6:     Search-Path(G, p, q, t, $k-1$, $visited$)
7:     add (q,t) back to G

8: **Procedure** Search-Path(Graph G, Path p, Vertex n, Vertex t, Length l, Bool $visited[]$)
9: **if** $n = t$ **then**
10:     report p;
11: **if** $l = 0$ **then**
12:     return ;
13: **for** m in $nbr(n)$ **do**
14:     **if** not $visited(m)$ **then**
15:         $visited(m) \leftarrow$ true
16:         p.push(m);
17:         Search-Path(G, p, m, t, $l-1$, $visited$)
18:         p.pop();
19:         $visited(m) \leftarrow$ false

Example 1. Consider the graph G in Fig. 1, assuming that the vertex 18 is the target vertex t and path length constraint k is 5. In the DFSEnum algorithm, after entering the vertex 12, the current path is $(1, 4, 8, 12)$ and the $nbrs(12)$ is $\{17, 18, 19\}$. When get to the vertex 17, we find the lenght exceeded limit and the vertex 17 is not the target. We discard the path and follow the arrow back to the vertex 12. Following the $nbrs(12)$, we enter the vertex 18 and find our target vertex. The path $(1, 4, 8, 13, 18)$ will be reported.

Drawbacks of Existing Solution. The complexity of the search algorithm is $O(m^k)$, in which m is the maximum degree of the graph. Thus the single thread algorithm is too slow for applications in the real world. As shown in Algorithm 1, DFSEnum does not make full use of today's computation architecture with a large amount of memory and multi-cores in one processor. The procedure Search-Path can be parallelized to solve these problems.

4   A New Approach

4.1   Expansion-Parallel-Search Paradigm

As discussed in Sect. 3, DFSEnum cannot fully utilize the available architecture. Motivated by this, we propose a new paradigm that parallelizes the problem. To solve the problem, we take the DFSEnum into two parts: the serial part and the parallel part. Therefore our paradigm has two phases, namely, prefix expansion phase and parallel search phase.

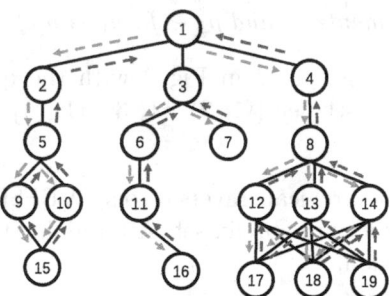

Fig. 1. Depth-first search

In the prefix expansion phase, we generate a set of prefix $\{p_1, p_2, \ldots, p_k\}$, which is a prefix set of all paths. When the number of prefixes exceeds the number of threads, the expansion phase stops. In the parallel search phase, we send every prefix into threads, and each thread will rebuild the program state to continue searching.

Using this paradigm, we can fully use the multi-cores in today's servers. However, to make our paradigm practically applicable, the following issues should be addressed when designing our algorithm:

- Correctness: We should be able to create a correct prefix set which can promise no paths are missed or duplicated in the parallel search phase.
- Efficiency: We should be able to get a more balanced prefix set. Because some graphs obey power-law, there is the imbalanced data distribution in these graphs.

In the following, we will introduce how to address these issues one by one.

4.2 Naive Expansion

We give two concepts to help us judge whether the prefix set is correct. It is trivial to just consider the expansion alone. For example, we can arbitrarily select a batch of prefixes that walks randomly from the query vertex. However, this approach doesn't satisfy the correctness of expansion. We must generate a set of prefixes to make sure there are no paths duplicated or leaked in the parallel search.

Definition 3 (Prefix Relation). *Given two paths p_1 and p_2, $p_1 = (v_0, v_1, \ldots, v_n)$, $p_2 = (v_0, v_1, \ldots, v_k)$. When $0 \leq k \leq n$, $p_2 = prefix(p_1)$.*

Definition 4 (Legal Expansion). *Given a graph G, a query vertex q, a length constraint k. The answer set S includes all paths that less than k from q. A legal expansion is a path set L that for every $p \in S$, there are $prefix(p) \in L$. And there is no such two elements p_1 and $p_2 \in L$, p_1 is $prefix(p_2)$.*

Example 2. Consider the graph G in Fig. 2 with the query vertex 1 and the length constraint 5, the path set $\{(1, 2), (1, 3), (1, 4)\}$ is a legal expansion of vertex 1.

We use the idea of hierarchical traversal to split DFSEnum and integrate the shallow traversal results into the prefix set. After giving the algorithm, we prove it using the legel expansion.

Algorithm Design. The algorithm is shown in Algorithm 2, which gives a set of prefixes starting from q. The inputs of the algorithm are the graph G, the query vertex q, the target vertex t, the length constraint k and the number of threads *threads*.

In each recursion, we get a sequence $p(v_1, v_2, v_3, \ldots, v_k)$. There are three possible situations: (1) If v_k is equal to target, we report it as an answer; (2) If the $u = nbr(v_k)$ is present in $\{v_i | i \in 2..k\}$, the path is ignored; (3) For other cases, we attach the vertex to the back of the path until the length reaches the limit. Once the length of the *path* reaches the limit, we collect it as a seed for the multi-thread processing.

Example 3. For the given graph in Fig. 2 with the length constraint 5, the number of threads 4, the expansion sets generated by the algorithm is $\{(1,2,5),(1,3,6),(1,3,7),\ (1,4,8)\}$.

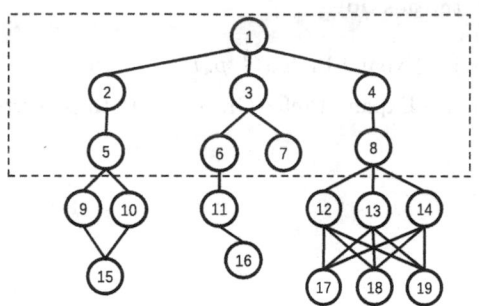

Fig. 2. Naive expansion

Lemma 1. *The prefix generated by naive expansion is a legal expansion.*

Proof. We can prove it by mathematical induction. First, the initial prefix set $\{(s)\}$ is a legal expansion. Next, we expand the sequences $(v_1, v_2, v_3, \ldots, v_k)$ from the previous set by attaching all the $nbr(v_k)$ to the back of sequence in each iteration. And the sequence will be extended to $\{(v_1, v_2, v_3, \ldots, v_k, t)|t \in nbr(v_k)\}$. We do the same jobs for every sequence in the previous set, therefore, we do not omit any prefix. Duplicate vertices are not permitted in $nbr(v_k)$. Thus the prefixes are different from each other in simple graph. In conclusion, the prefix generated by naive expansion is a legal expansion.

4.3 Parallel Search

In this section, we give the details of the parallel search algorithm. The algorithm will send prefixes to each thread and make each thread to continue searching. We use the work stealing model as a dynamic scheduler.

Algorithm Design. As shown in Algorithm 3, the function Parallel-Search accepts the graph G, the target vertex t, the length limit k, and a prefix set $prefixes$. We search paths for every prefix in each thread. In Search-Path-From-Prefix, the function accepts the graph G, a prefix of path p, the target vertex t, the total length limit k, and a bool set *visited*. We rebuild the visited set by marking the vertices in p as visited in each thread. In each recursion, the algorithm takes the last vertex of the path and expand legal vertex as rules in Sect. 3.

Algorithm 2. Naive-Expansion(Graph G, Vertex q, Vertex t, Length k, Int *threads*)

1: $ans \leftarrow \{(q)\}$
2: $visited[] \leftarrow$ false
3: $visited[q]$ = true
4: **while** $len(ans) <$ threads **do**
5:    **for** p in ans **do**
6:       ans $\leftarrow$ Recursive-Expand-Prefix(G, p, t, k, $visited$)

7: **Procedure** Recursive-Expand-Prefix(Graph G, Path p, Vertex t, Length k, Bool $visited[]$)
8: $u \leftarrow$ last vertex of p
9: **if** $u = t$ **then**
10:    report p;
11: $ans \leftarrow \emptyset$
12: **if** $k = 0$ **then**
13:    collect p into ans
14:    return ans
15: **for** n in $nbr(u)$ **do**
16:    **if** not $visited(n)$ **then**
17:       $visited(n) \leftarrow$ true
18:       p.push(n)
19:       collect ans from Recursive-Expand-Prefix(G, p, t, $k-1$, $visited$);
20:       p.pop()
21:       $visited(n) \leftarrow$ false
22: return ans

Lemma 2. *Algorithm 2 and 3 compute paths start from u under the length k correctly.*

Proof. When we follow a $path(u,v)$ to enter v, the *visited* only contains the vertices along the $path(u,v)$ in 1. If there are two paths, $path_1(u,v)$ and $path_2(u,v)$, the *visited* of $path_1(u,v)$ and the *visited* of $path_2(u,v)$ are independent from each other. We build the *visited* of each paths correct in Algorithm 3. So each thread can do search procedure correctly. And by Lemma 1, the naive expansion is legal. In conclusion, we get the answer correctly.

Drawbacks of Naive Solution. In the naive expansion algorithm, the imbalance of the workloads always happens. So we use a work stealing [2] scheduler for the parallel search. But the effectiveness of the work stealing scheduler is limited. In the social graph, there are always some small dense groups connected with outside. In this application, we should detect these groups and divide them into different threads. We need to estimate how many paths appear under each prefix and assign these prefixes to threads based on workload.

Algorithm 3. Parallel-Search(Graph G, Vertex t, Length k, Paths $prefixes[]$)

1: openmp parallel for
2: **for** $p \in prefixes$ **do**
3:    $visited[] \leftarrow$ false
4:    mark vertices in p as visited
5:    Search-Path-From-Prefix(G, p, t, $k - len(p)$, $visited$)

6: **Procedure** Search-Path-From-Prefix(Graph G, Path p, Vertex t, Length k, Bool $visited[]$)
7: $u \leftarrow$ last vertex of p
8: **if** $u = t$ **then**
9:    report p;
10: **if** $k = 0$ **then**
11:    return ;
12: **for** n in $nbr(u)$ **do**
13:    **if** not $visited(n)$ **then**
14:       $visited(n) \leftarrow$ true
15:       p.push(n)
16:       Search-Path-From-Prefix(G, p, v, $k - 1$, $visited$);
17:       p.pop()
18:       $visited(n) \leftarrow$ false;

5   Smart Expansion

In this section, we propose the smart expansion algorithm and the DAG-Tail-Index. First, we will see how to expand prefixes from the query vertex after we getting the workloads. Then we will show that it is impossible to get a completely accurate workload. Finally, we will put forward a fuzzy estimation index of workload and a method to calculate it.

5.1   Prefix Container and Smart Expansion

Prefix container is a completely accurate workload for parallel search. It tells us how many paths under the length constraint follow the prefix. In the distribution phase, we need to extend those prefixes with many paths forward so that they can be evenly distributed among each thread. The formal definition is below.

Definition 5 (Prefix Container). *There is a graph G, a path prefix p, a length limit k. The prefix container is the number of paths that start with path prefix.*

Example 4. If we have a prefix sequence $(1, 2, 3)$ and the length constraint is 5. Assuming there are two paths $(1, 2, 3, 4, 5)$ and $(1, 2, 3, 4, 6)$ under the length constraint, the $\Omega((1, 2, 3))$ is 2.

As we can see, $\Omega(prefix)$ indicates the time complexity of the thread receiving the prefix. An intuitive idea about the algorithm is that after we get the set of prefixes, we divide the prefix with the highest $\Omega(prefix)$ by extending one frontier of the path.

Algorithm Design. The algorithm is shown as Algorithm 4. The inputs of the algorithm are the graph G, the query vertex q, the target vertex t, the path length constraint k, the number of threads $threads$, and the $\Omega(prefix)$. And the algorithm return sets of the path prefix.

We first push the path that only contains the query vertex into the queue. In each iteration, we pop the path with the largest $\Omega(prefix)$ from the priority queue. Then we divide the path into two situations: (1) If the path is already long enough, we discard the prefix; (2) If the target vertex appears, the result will be reported. Therefore, we propose a new index to replace $\Omega(prefix)$, which is easier to calculate.

Lemma 3. *The result of smart expansion is a legal expansion.*

Proof. We also use mathematical induction. First, the initial prefix set $\{(q)\}$ is a legal expansion. Next, when a prefix from the priority queue is chosen to be expanded, all the neighbours of this prefix's the last vertex are tested. This operation promises no missing paths. Duplicate vertices are not permitted in $nbr(v_k)$, therefore, the prefixes are different from each other. In conclusion, prefixes in priority queue is a new legal expansion.

Algorithm 4. Smart-Expansion(Graph G, Vertex q, Vertex t, Length k, Int $threads$, Int $\Omega[]$)

```
 1: q ← priority queue
 2: init-path ← (cur)
 3: q.push(Ω(init-path), init-path)
 4: while q.size() < threads do
 5:     (Ω(path), path) = q.pop()
 6:     if len(path) ≥ k then
 7:         discard the path
 8:     n ← the last vertex of p
 9:     for m ∈ nbr(n) do
10:         if m = t then
11:             report p
12:             continue
13:         if m not in p then
14:             cur-path ← path expand m
15:             push (Ω(cur-path), cur-path) into q
16: return q
```

5.2   DAG-Tail-Index

It is easy to see that if each $\Omega(prefix)$ is known, all paths are searched. For the difficulty of computation of the prefix container, we propose a new index to help us process expansion. The index has two requirements: (1) The index must be easy to calculate; (2) The index can give us the approximate number of the paths with given prefixes.

Lemma 4. *Calculating $\Omega(prefix)$ is as difficult as cycle search.*

Proof. The $\Omega(prefix) = \Sigma\{\Omega(prefix\text{-}expansion)\}$. Then we get the expansion recursively until the length of prefix is equal to the length limit. After getting $\Omega(prefix)$, we have already done the cycle search.

The DAG-Tail-Index intuitively simplifies the problem into computing the number of paths from an arbitrary vertex to the farthest vertices.

Definition 6 (Farthest Vertices Set). *Given a graph G, a query vertex q, a length constraint k. Farthest vertices set is $\{y|\forall y \in nbr(x)dist(y,q) \geq dist(x,q) \wedge dist(y,q) \leq k\}$, and $dist(a,b)$ means the shortest distance between a and b.*

The simplification is based on the shortest path. The farthest vertex is always the last vertex of the path which is used as the end of the work. In this way, we put the graph as a view of the divergent network where the vertices near the query vertex point to those farther. We use the shortest distance from the query vertex to build the DAG.

Definition 7 (Shortest Path Based DAG). *Given a graph G, query vertex q. Shortest path based DAG is a graph that the vertex of this DAG is equal to the G, and the edge set is $\{(x,y)|dist(x,q) < dist(y,q)\}$. The $dist(x,q)$ means the shortest distance between x and q in the G.*

If there are edges (x,y) and (y,x), we only keep one direction (x,y) in which x is closer to the query vertex q than y. Then we turn the Graph G into a *DAG*. The definition of the DAG Tail index is below.

Definition 8 (DAG-Tail-Index). *Given a DAG D, a length constraint k. For a vertex v, the number of paths from the vertex to the farthest vertex is called the DAG-Tail-Index of the vertex v.*

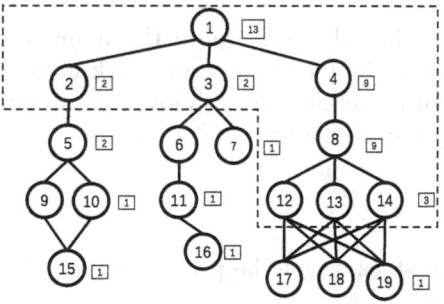

Fig. 3. Smart expansion

Example 5. For the given graph in Fig. 3 with the query vertex 1 and the length constraint 5, the farthest vertex set is $\{15, 16, 17, 18, 19\}$. The blocks near the vertices show their indexes and the result of smart expansion is $\{(1,2), (1,3), (1,4,8,12), (1,4,8,13), (1,4,8,14)\}$.

5.3   Calculation of DAG-Tail-Index

Based on the definition of the DAG-Tail-Index, a simple algorithm is introduced in this section. After building shortest path based DAG, we can calculate the DAG-Tail-Index using depth-first search.

Algorithm Design. The Algorithm 5 shows the procedure. The inputs of the algorithm are the Graph DAG, the query vertex q, the target vertex t, the length constraint k, an integer array that gives shortest-distance $shortest$, a bool array to record $visited$, and an integer array to record $priority$.

The vertices that we encounter are divided into three conditions: (1) If the vertex is v or the length reaches k, we set the priority of the vertex as 1. For another vertex, we traversal its neighbours; (2) If the neighbour has been visited, we just add the priority of son vertices to the parent vertex; (3) If the neighbour has not been visited, we enter the son vertices and calculate the priority recursively.

Algorithm 5. Smart-Priority(Graph DAG, Vertex q, Vertex t, Length k, Int $shortest[]$, Bool $visited[]$,Int $priority[]$)

1: **if** $shortest\text{-}len(q) \geq k$ **or** $q = t$ **then**
2:     $priority(q) \leftarrow 1$
3:     **return**
4: $visited[q] \leftarrow$ true;
5: **for** n in $nbr(q)$ **do**
6:     **if** not $visited(n)$ **then**
7:         Smart-Priority(DAG, n, v, k, $shortest$, $visited$, $priority$)
8:     $priority(q) \leftarrow priority(q) + priority(n)$;

However, it is still difficult to compute the number of prefixes per path. Because we use the breadth-first search framework in the expansion phase, we usually get a prefix that is the shortest path for u. As a result, we use the priority of the last vertex in prefix as the $\Omega(prefix)$.

5.4   Analysis

There are three major steps to get the priority index. We prove that it can be done fast and effective.

Theorem 1. *The Algorithm 4 and 3 are work efficient parallel algorithm.*

Proof. The breadth-first search for the graph and searching the farther set is $O(n + m)$. The proof is omitted. And it is easy to see that Smart-Priority just visit every vertex and edge once. The complexity of smart expand is $O(T)$ in which T is the number of threads.

For there are infinite processors, we use parallel-search in multi-round. The result of prefix obtained in the previous round will be treated as input of next round. work and span are caculated as below.

$$\text{Span}(m, k) = \begin{cases} m, & \text{if k} = 1 \\ \frac{m^k}{p^k} + \text{Span}(m, k-1), & \text{other condition} \end{cases} \quad (1)$$

$$\text{Work}(m, k) = \begin{cases} m, & \text{if k} = 1 \\ O(m^k + \text{Work}(m, k-1)), & \text{other condition} \end{cases} \quad (2)$$

As $p \geq m$, $\text{Span}(m, k) = O(k * m)$ and $\text{Work}(m, k) = (m^k)$ where m is the maximum degree of the graph.

Therefore our parallel algorithm that can be done in $O(k * m)$ with m^{k-1}/k processors is efficient since the work $O(m^k)$ is as good as any sequential algorithm. And the experiment shows it brings a nice improvement to our performance. The analysis of data distribution can help us to improve the efficiency of the parallel algorithm.

6   Evaluation

In this section, we conduct experimental studies by comparing speedup, scalability, and variance between NExp, SExp, and DFSEnum. Datasets are shown in Table 1. The first four are small datasets, and the last four are large datasets.

Table 1. Datasets used in experiments

Datasets	Type	Number of vertices	Number of edges	Average degree
Amazon	Communities	334, 863	925, 872	2.76
DBLP	Network	317,080	1,049,866	3.31
Web-Google	Web	875,713	5,105,039	5.82
Youtube	Communities	1,134,890	2,987,624	2.63
wiki-topcats	Communities	1,791,489	28,511,807	15.91
LiveJournal	Social	3,997,962	34,681,189	17.35
Twitter7	Social	17,069,982	476,553,560	27.92
Friendster	Social	65, 608, 366	1, 806, 067, 135	27.52

Algorithms. We implement and compare following the three algorithms:

DFSEnum: Single thread depth-first search.
NExp: Naive Expansion and dynamic scheduler.
SExp: Smart Expansion and dynamic scheduler.

Table 2. Speed Up and Baseline time Experiments

Path Length	5			6			7			8		
Algorithm	SExp	NExp	Time	SExp	NExp	Time	SExp	NExp	Time	SExp	NExp	Time
Amazon	13.57	2.48	0.26	15.07	2.98	4.83	18.83	3.12	45.08	19.59	3.88	317.76
DBLP	14.16	3.03	2.96	16.25	3.75	12.04	18.57	3.23	51.32	21.36	3.86	463.12
web-Google	15.19	3.15	2.83	15.86	3.31	15.92	20.18	3.72	78.37	22.60	3.87	646.42
Youtube	15.66	3.38	1.72	17.46	3.43	13.26	21.80	3.69	107.76	21.98	4.03	973.16
wiki-topcats	15.57	3.31	4.43	16.87	3.38	23.74	20.37	3.92	328.12	21.32	4.48	1367.59
LiveJournal	14.32	3.42	5.41	17.83	3.75	63.24	21.32	3.06	356 ?	22.52	4.83	1421.11
Twitter7	15.52	3.18	5.81	16.52	3.78	43.13	21.91	4.05	415.44	22.42	4.64	1634.96
Friendster	15.57	3.22	4.28	17.87	3.72	52.78	22.62	4.23	430.88	22.92	5.25	2192.87

The NExp and SExp are developed using C++ with openmp [6]. We evaluate the program on an Intel(R) Core(R) E5 CPU with 44 cores(at 2.2 GHz) and 128GB of memory. We choose some random vertices and compute the average time of results.

Exp-1: Speedup. In this experiment, we compare speedup when we vary the length of the path from 5 to 8. The results are shown in Table 2. We present T_1/T_{32} in the first two columns and the processing time(s) of DFSEnum in the last column. T_1 means the running time of single thread and T_{32} means the running time of 32 threads.

From Table 2, (1) we can see that in all datasets, the speedup of SExp is better than NExp. NExp performance bad because of the imbalance of the data. The thread delays the total time of the performance when one prefix has a heavy amount of paths to search. SExp outperforms NExp. Because of the proper estimation of running time of tasks, SExp divides the tasks evenly. The speedup of SExp is better than NExp; (2) The speedup will increase as the length of paths increases. As we know $T_x = T_{exp} + T_{search}$, the expansion step is serial while the search steps are parallel. As the length of paths increases, search steps take up most of the time.

Exp-2: Scalability. In this experiment, we compare the scalability of the algorithms. We process the scalability experiment in all datasets under the length constraint 8 when we vary the number of threads from 1 to 32.

The result is shown in Fig. 4, 5, respectively. The running time of both algorithms decreases as the number of threads increases. This is because all algorithms can split tasks into parts and reduce the total running time. But the performance gap increases as the number of threads increases. Due to the similar reason as previous analysis, the imbalance of data causes the gap increases as the number of threads increases.

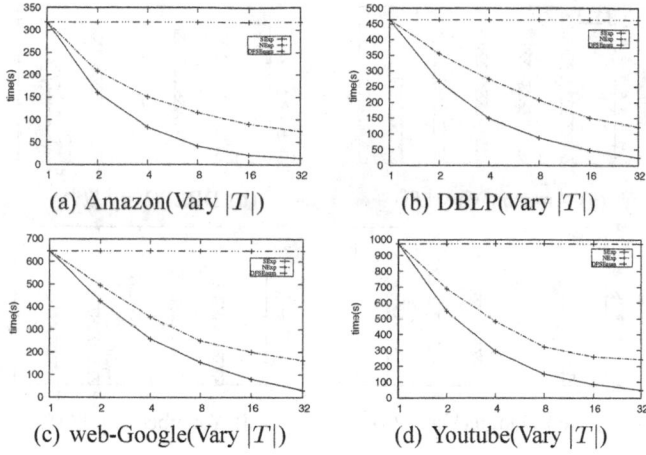

(a) Amazon(Vary $|T|$)   (b) DBLP(Vary $|T|$)

(c) web-Google(Vary $|T|$)   (d) Youtube(Vary $|T|$)

Fig. 4. Scalability (small)

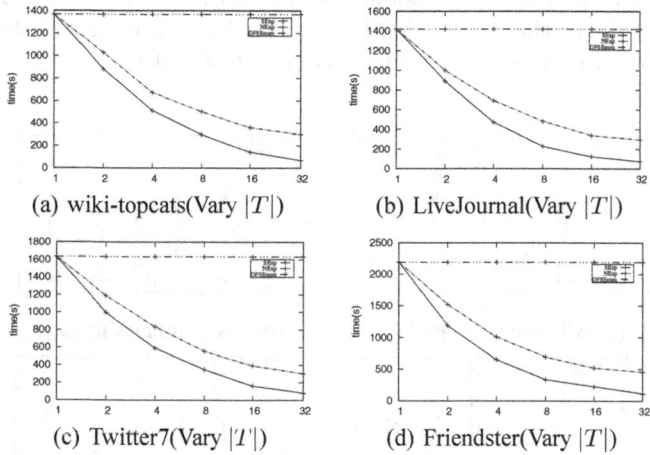

(a) wiki-topcats(Vary $|T|$)   (b) LiveJournal(Vary $|T|$)

(c) Twitter7(Vary $|T|$)   (d) Friendster(Vary $|T|$)

Fig. 5. Scalability (large)

Exp-3: Time Difference between Threads. In this experiment, we compare the time difference between threads when we vary the number of threads from 2 to 32 and the length constraint is 8. We compare the maximum time of threads minus the minimum time of threads in all datasets.

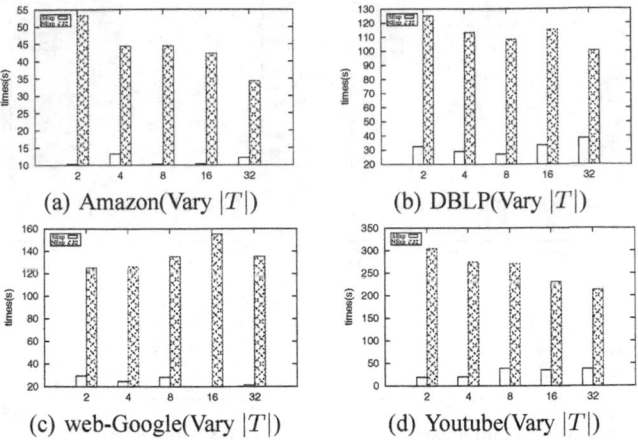

(a) Amazon(Vary $|T|$) (b) DBLP(Vary $|T|$)

(c) web-Google(Vary $|T|$) (d) Youtube(Vary $|T|$)

Fig. 6. Time difference between threads (small)

Figure 6, 7 show the time difference of threads. And the difference between NExp is much larger than SExp. As discussed before, threads with heavy search tasks are avoided due to the average assignment of tasks.

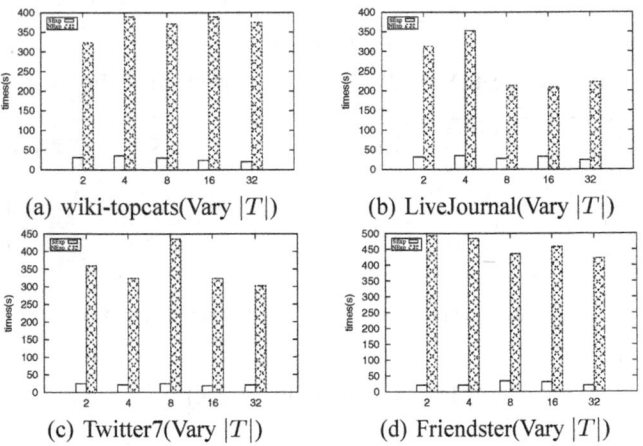

(a) wiki-topcats(Vary $|T|$) (b) LiveJournal(Vary $|T|$)

(c) Twitter7(Vary $|T|$) (d) Friendster(Vary $|T|$)

Fig. 7. Time difference between threads (large)

7   Related Work

Cycle detection is a fundamental problem in graph analysis and has been extensively studied in the literature. For the single thread cycle detection algorithm,

[4] describes an algorithm by depth-first search based algorithm. A solution based on an index is proposed in [19]. For distributed cycle detection algorithm, [20] gives us a solution based on the vertex-centric programming model and [9] proves that, for every $k \geq 3$, there exists a 1-sided error distributed property testing algorithm for C_k-*freeness*, performing in $O(1/\epsilon)$ rounds in the CON-GEST model. The incremental cycle detection has been studied in literature(e.g., [1,12,21]).

There are also many works in applications of cycle search. [3] gives an application of cycle detection in organized groups of fraudsters, which brings more leakage revenue to the insurance industry, especially the automobile industry. [5] tells us the cycle is an important network topology in the wash trade of the financial market. [14] tells that where is a stock manipulation ring, there is a risk of fraud. The detection of rings will give users information about stock manipulation.

The general pattern match is also important in graphs. And many studies are conducted in pattern mining. [13] gives a general-purpose distributed pattern matching system.Graphflow [11] applies a worst-case optimal join algorithm to incrementally evaluate subgraph matching for each update. IncIsoMat [7] is proposed to continuously identify subgraph matching upon the update of the graph where a candidate subgraph region is computed to reduce the search space.

8 Conclusion

In this paper, we study the parallel cycle search algorithm in large graphs. After investigating the drawbacks of existing solutions, we propose a new expansion-parallel-search paradigm for the cycle search problem. Based on the expansion-parallel-search paradigm, we devise a smart expansion that can divide tasks based on the distribution of the data for the cycle search problem. Besides, we also prove that our algorithm is work efficient in theory. We conduct extensive experiments on real graphs and the results demonstrate the efficiency and scalability of our proposed algorithm.

Acknowledge. Long Yuan is supported by NSFC61902184 and NSF of Jiangsu Province BK20190453.

References

1. Bernstein, A., Chechi, S.: Incremental topological sort and cycle detection in expected total time, pp. 21–34, January 2018
2. Blumofe, R.D., Leiserson, C.E.: Scheduling multithreaded computations by work stealing. J. ACM **46**(5), 720–748 (1999)
3. Bodaghi, A., Teimourpour, B.: Automobile insurance fraud detection using social network analysis. In: Moshirpour, M., Far, B.H., Alhajj, R. (eds.) Applications of Data Management and Analysis. LNSN, pp. 11–16. Springer, Cham (2018). https://doi.org/10.1007/978-3-319-95810-1_2

4. Bondy, J.A., Murty, U.S.R.: Graph theory with applications (1976)
5. Cao, Y., Li, Y., Coleman, S., Belatreche, A., McGinnity, T.M.: Detecting wash trade in the financial market. In: 2014 IEEE Conference on Computational Intelligence for Financial Engineering and Economics (CIFEr), pp. 85–91. IEEE (2014)
6. Dagum, L., Menon, R.: OpenMP: an industry-standard API for shared-memory programming. IEEE Comput. Sci. Eng. **5**(1), 46–55 (1998)
7. Fan, W., Wang, X., Wu, Y.: Incremental graph pattern matching. ACM Trans. Database Syst. **38**(3), 18:1–18:47 (2013)
8. Feng, X., Chang, L., Lin, X., Qin, L., Zhang, W., Yuan, L.: Distributed computing connected components with linear communication cost. Distrib Parallel Databases **36**(3), 555–592 (2018). https://doi.org/10.1007/s10619-018-7232-6
9. Fraigniaud, P., Olivetti, D.: Distributed detection of cycles. ACM Trans. Parallel Comput. **6**(3), 12:1–12:20 (2019)
10. Jiang, Z.-Q., et al.: Trading networks, abnormal motifs and stock manipulation. Quant. Financ. Lett. **1**(1), 1–8 (2013)
11. Kankanamge, C., Sahu, S., Mhedbhi, A., Chen, J., Salihoglu, S.: Graphflow: An active graph database. In Proceedings of the 2017 ACM International Conference on Management of Data, SIGMOD 2017, pp. 1695–1698, New York. ACM (2017)
12. Kosaraju, S., Sullivan, G.: Detecting cycles in dynamic graphs in polynomial time. In: Proceedings 20th Annual ACM Symposium on Theory Computing, pp. 398–406, January 1988
13. Lai, L., et al.: Distributed subgraph matching on timely dataflow. Proc. VLDB Endow. **12**(10), 1099–1112 (2019)
14. Lee, P.S., Owda, M., Crockett, K.: the detection of fraud activities on the stock market through forward analysis methodology of financial discussion boards. In: Arai, K., Kapoor, S., Bhatia, R. (eds.) FICC 2018. AISC, vol. 887, pp. 212–220. Springer, Cham (2019). https://doi.org/10.1007/978-3-030-03405-4_14
15. Liu, B., Yuan, L., Lin, X., Qin, L., Zhang, W., Zhou, J.: Efficient (α, β)-core computation: an index-based approach. In: Proceedings of WWW, pp. 1130–1141 (2019)
16. Ouyang, D., Long Yuan, L., Qin, L.C., Zhang, Y.: Efficient shortest path index maintenance on dynamic road networks with theoretical guarantees. PVLDB **13**(5), 602–615 (2020)
17. Ouyang, D., Yuan, L., Zhang, F., Qin, L., Lin, X.: Towards efficient path skyline computation in bicriteria networks. In: Pei, J., Manolopoulos, Y., Sadiq, S., Li, J. (eds.) DASFAA 2018. LNCS, vol. 10827, pp. 239–254. Springer, Cham (2018). https://doi.org/10.1007/978-3-319-91452-7_16
18. Qing, Z., Yuan, L., Zhang, F., Qin, L., Lin, X., Zhang, W.: External topological sorting in large graphs. In: Pei, J., Manolopoulos, Y., Sadiq, S., Li, J. (eds.) DASFAA 2018. LNCS, vol. 10827, pp. 203–220. Springer, Cham (2018). https://doi.org/10.1007/978-3-319-91452-7_14
19. Qiu, X., Cen, W., Qian, Z., Peng, Y., Zhang, Y., Lin, X., Zhou, J.: Real-time constrained cycle detection in large dynamic graphs. PVLDB **11**(12), 1876–1888 (2018)
20. Rocha, R., Thatte, B: Distributed cycle detection in large-scale sparse graphs, August 2015
21. Shmueli, O.: Dynamic cycle detection. Inf. Process. Lett. **17**(4), 185–188 (1983)
22. Shun, J., Blelloch, G.E.: Ligra: a lightweight graph processing framework for shared memory. In: ACM SIGPLAN Symposium on Principles and Practice of Parallel Programming, PPoPP 2013, Shenzhen, China, 23–27 February 2013, pp. 135–146 (2013)

23. Vishkin, U.: Using simple abstraction to reinvent computing for parallelism. Commun. ACM **54**(1), 75–85 (2011)
24. Wu, X., Yuan, L., Lin, X., Yang, S., Zhang, W.: Towards efficient k-TriPeak decomposition on large graphs. In: Proceedings of International Conference on Database Systems for Advanced Applications, pp. 604–621 (2019)
25. Long Yuan, L., Qin, X.L., Chang, L., Zhang, W.: Diversified top-k clique search. VLDB J. **25**(2), 171–196 (2016)
26. Yuan, L., Qin, L., Lin, X., Chang, L., Zhang, W.: I/O efficient ECC graph decomposition via graph reduction. VLDB J. **26**(2), 275–300 (2016). https://doi.org/10.1007/s00778-016-0451-4
27. Long Yuan, L., Qin, X.L., Chang, L., Zhang, W.: Effective and efficient dynamic graph coloring. PVLDB **11**(3), 338–351 (2017)
28. Yuan, L., Qin, L., Lin, X., Chang, L., Zhang, W.: I/O efficient ECC graph decomposition via graph reduction. VLDB J. **26**(2), 275–300 (2016). https://doi.org/10.1007/s00778-016-0451-4
29. Yuan, L., Qin, W.Z., Chang, L., Yang, J.: Index-based densest clique percolation community search in networks. IEEE TKDE **30**(5), 922–935 (2018)

Cross-Graph Representation Learning for Unsupervised Graph Alignment

Weifan Wang[1,2], Minnan Luo[1,2(✉)], Caixia Yan[2], Meng Wang[3], Xiang Zhao[4], and Qinghua Zheng[1,2,5]

[1] Center for Intelligent Understanding of Communication Content, State Key Laboratory of Communication Content Cognition, Beijing 100733, China
[2] MOEKLINNS Lab, College of Computer Science and Technology, Xi'an Jiaotong University, Xi'an, China
{weifanw_stu,yancaixia}@stu.xjtu.edu.cn, {minnluo,qhzheng}@xjtu.edu.cn
[3] School of Computer Science and Engineering, Southeast University, Nanjing, China
meng.wang@seu.edu.cn
[4] Key Laboratory of Science and Technology on Information System Engineering, National University of Defense Technology, Changsha, China
xiangzhao@nudt.edu.cn
[5] National Engineering Lab for Big Data Analytics, Xi'an Jiaotong University, Xi'an, China

Abstract. As a crucial prerequisite for graph mining, graph alignment aims to find node correspondences across multiple correlated graphs. The main difficulty of graph alignment lies in how to seamlessly bridge multiple graphs with distinct topology structures and attribute distributions. A vast majority of earlier efforts tackle this problem based on alignment consistency, which directly measures the attribute and structure similarity of nodes. However, alignment consistency is prone to be violated due to the radically different patterns owned by different graphs. Another group of methods tackle the problem in a supervised manner by learning a mapping function that maps the node representations of both the source and target graphs into the same feature space. However, these methods heavily rely on observed anchor links between different graphs while these anchor links are usually limited or even absent in many real-world applications. To address these issues, we propose an unsupervised cross-graph representation learning framework to jointly learn the node representations of different graphs in a unified deep model. Specifically, we employ an auto-encoder model to learn the cross-graph node representations based on both attribute and structure reconstruction, where source and target graphs share the same encoder but are decoded by their respective decoders. To step further, we also introduce a discriminator to better align the learned representations for different graphs via adversarial training. Extensive experiments on both synthetic and real-world datasets demonstrate the effectiveness of the proposed approach.

The original version of this chapter was revised: an institution affiliation was missing in the authors' section for the following authors: Weifan Wang, Minnan Lu, and Qinghua Zheng. The missing institution has been now added. The correction to this chapter is available at https://doi.org/10.1007/978-3-030-59416-9_49

Y. Nah et al. (Eds.): DASFAA 2020, LNCS 12113, pp. 368–384, 2020.
https://doi.org/10.1007/978-3-030-59416-9_22

Keywords: Graph alignment · Cross-graph representation learning · Adversarial training

1 Introduction

Recent years have witnessed an increasing attention on graph analysis in the data mining community. In previous literature, a surge of algorithms for a *single* graph have been proposed for various graph mining tasks, such as link prediction [23], node classification [7], and anomaly detection [26]. Despite their efficacy, these methods heavily rely on the assumption that all the nodes appear in the same graph, while fail to consider the fact that the same object may be involved in *multiple* graphs simultaneously. Unfortunately, we usually do not have access to the shared nodes to build connections between different graphs. Thus, finding node correspondence across different graphs (a.k.a. graph alignment), has become a fundamental problem and crucial step for many graph mining tasks. In this field, the shared nodes among different graphs are denoted as *anchor nodes* and the relationships among them are defined as *anchor links*.

The key point of graph alignment lies in how to seamlessly integrate both graph structure and attribute information. Due to the distinct topology structures and attribute distributions among different graphs, these information cannot be directly utilized to calculate the similarity between nodes for alignment. To tackle this issue, extensive research efforts have been devoted in the past decade. Earlier efforts mainly deal with this problem based on the consistency principle for both topology and attribute. For example, several methods [10,21,30] infer anchor links based on the topology consistency assumption that correspondent nodes should have consistent connectivity structure patterns across different networks. Nonetheless, these methods fail to take the rich attribute information of nodes into consideration, which may also be beneficial for the alignment task. For this issue, Kong *et al.* [9] and Zhang *et al.* [28] extract discriminative social features for a pair of user accounts in two disjoint social networks to facilitate the alignment task. Zhang *et al.* [29] formulates the attribute and structure matrices from different graphs into a quadratic function w.r.t S based on the alignment consistency. The final alignment results could be derived by solving this function. Heimann *et al.* [6] proposes to use node representations generated based on degree distribution, and, if available, attribute information to calculate the similarity between nodes. Despite the empirical success of above methods, it could be easily violated because of the distinct patterns owned by different graphs, which would lead to sub-optimal alignment results.

Recently, there is an emerging trend that utilizes representation learning to tackle the above problem with a two-stage pipeline [13,15,32]. First, graph embedding techniques [5,18,22] are employed to learn the raw node representations for both graphs. Second, a mapping function from one graph embedding space to the other graph embedding space is learned based on the observed anchor links. Based on the learned mapping function, the node representations of both graphs can be mapped into the same space, and thus a similarity matrix can be calculated by measuring the similarity between each pair of node representations. These approaches bridge the gap between different graphs by using the mapping function learned from the observed anchor links. At the same time, they also make better use of the structural regularities of networks through representation learning. However, most of them fall into a supervised paradigm and rely on a large amount of training data, *i.e.*, observed anchor links, thus the performance cannot be guaranteed if the training data is small. To this end, how to align different graphs based on representation learning in an unsupervised manner still remains a daunting task.

Taking all the above mentioned challenges into consideration, we propose a cross-graph representation learning framework for unsupervised graph alignment. Specifically, we learn the node representations of source and target graphs simultaneously using two auto-encoders that share the same encoder function. For each auto-encoder, both the structure decoder and the attribute decoder are incorporated to guarantee that enough information could be retained into the learned representations. To further reduce the discrepancy existing in attribute and structure distribution of different graphs, we employ a discriminator to differentiate the learned node representations from different graphs, and thus the encoder would play another role as generator to compose a adversarial training procedure with the added discriminator.

The main contributions are summarized as follows:

1) We first analyze the limitations of existing alignment algorithms and elaborate the prominent property of the proposed Cross-graph Representation Learning for Unsupervised Graph Alignment.
2) We propose a cross-graph representation learning method accompanying with adversarial training to directly generate comparable node representations.
3) We conduct extensive experiments on both synthetic and real-world datasets to show the superiority of the proposed method against existing graph alignment methods.

The rest of this paper is organized as follows. In Sect. 2, we briefly introduce the notations and problem definitions utilized in this paper. Section 3 elaborates the formulations of the proposed cross-graph representation learning framework for unsupervised graph alignment. In Sect. 4, extensive experiments over both synthetic and real-world datasets are conducted to verify the effectiveness and superiority of the proposed method. Section 5 gives a brief review of the related works. Conclusions are given in Sect. 6.

2   Preliminary and Problem Definition

In this paper, attributed network (graph) is represented as a triplet $\mathcal{G} = \{\mathcal{V}, \mathcal{E}, \boldsymbol{X}\}$, where the set $\mathcal{V} = \{v_1, v_2, v_3, \cdots, v_n\}$ collects all the n nodes of graph $\mathcal{G}$; $\mathcal{E}$ refers to the set of edges between nodes in graph $\mathcal{G}$; $\boldsymbol{X}$ is the node attribute matrix, written as $\boldsymbol{X} = [\boldsymbol{x}_1, \boldsymbol{x}_2, \cdots, \boldsymbol{x}_n]^\top \in \mathbb{R}^{n \times d}$ with $\boldsymbol{x}_i \in \mathbb{R}^d$ being the attribute vector of node $v_i \in \mathcal{V}$. Without loss of generality, we assume that the edges in graph $\mathcal{G}$ are undirected and unweighted. In this sense, the topological structure information of the attributed network is characterized by an adjacency matrix $A \in \mathbb{R}^{n \times n}$, where $A(v_i, v_j) = 1$ if the unordered pair of two nodes v_i and v_j are connected in graph $\mathcal{G}$, and $A(v_i, v_j) = 0$ otherwise. Following the well established graph convolutional network (GCN) [7], layer-wise latent representations of the nodes are induced based on the properties of their neighborhoods, $i.e.$,

$$H^{(l+1)} = \sigma \left(R^{-\frac{1}{2}} \tilde{A} R^{-\frac{1}{2}} H^{(l)} W^{(l)} \right), \tag{1}$$

where $H^{(l)} \in \mathbb{R}^{n \times d^{(l)}}$ and $H^{(l+1)} \in \mathbb{R}^{n \times d^{(l+1)}}$ refer to the input and output of the convolution layer l; $\sigma(\cdot)$ is a non-linear operation (such as ReLU); $R \in \mathbb{R}^{n \times n}$ is a diagonal matrix with diagonal element $R(k, k) = \sum_i \tilde{A}_{k,i}$ for $k = 1, 2, \cdots, n$ and $\tilde{A} = A + I \in \mathbb{R}^{n \times n}$; $W^{(l)}$ is the trainable weight matrix of the l-th layer. For the first layer, we take attribute matrix $X \in \mathbb{R}^{n \times d}$ as its input $H^{(0)}$. By stacking L convolution layers to the graph encoder, node representations of graph $\mathcal{G}$ could be generated as output of the last convolutional layer, $i.e.$,

$$Z = f(\mathcal{W}; \mathcal{G}) = \sigma \left(R^{-\frac{1}{2}} \tilde{A} R^{-\frac{1}{2}} \cdots \sigma \left(R^{-\frac{1}{2}} \tilde{A} R^{-\frac{1}{2}} X W^{(1)} \right) \cdots W^{(L)} \right), \tag{2}$$

where $\mathcal{W} = \{ W^{(1)}, W^{(2)}, \cdots, W^{(L)} \}$ collects all of the parameters in L convolutional layers.

With the above notations and preliminaries, we formally define the studied problem as follows.

Problem 1. **Unsupervised Graph Alignment with Representation Learning:** Given a source graph $\mathcal{G}_s = \{ \mathcal{V}_s, \mathcal{E}_s, X_s \}$ and a target graph $\mathcal{G}_t = \{ \mathcal{V}_t, \mathcal{E}_t, X_t \}$ without any observed anchor links, the problem aims to identify all the hidden anchor links across graph $\mathcal{G}_s$ and $\mathcal{G}_t$ based on the learned nodes representation Z_s and Z_t correspondingly.

It is noteworthy that the proposed problem is different from most existing supervised models that rely on predefined anchor links to bridge the distinct distributions of node representations for graph alignment. Specifically, this paper mainly focuses on identifying hidden anchor links based on the generated representations without any need of observed anchor links or prior information.

3   Methodology

In this section, we elaborate the formulation of the proposed framework, which mainly consists of two essential components, $i.e.$, (1) cross-graph reconstruction, and (2) adversarial learning. The architecture is illustrated in Fig. 1 for a better understanding.

3.1 Cross-Graph Reconstruction

Given the source graph $\mathcal{G}_s = \{\mathcal{V}_s, \mathcal{E}_s, \boldsymbol{X}_s\}$ and the target graph $\mathcal{G}_t = \{\mathcal{V}_t, \mathcal{E}_t, \boldsymbol{X}_t\}$ with their adjacency matrices $\boldsymbol{A}_s \in \mathbb{R}^{m \times m}$ and $\boldsymbol{A}_t \in \mathbb{R}^{n \times n}$ respectively, we learn the node representations $\boldsymbol{Z}_s \in \mathbb{R}^{m \times p}$ and $\boldsymbol{Z}_t \in \mathbb{R}^{n \times p}$ by sharing the same parameters of convolution layers $\mathcal{W}$, i.e.,

$$\boldsymbol{Z}_s = f\left(\mathcal{W}; \mathcal{G}_s\right) = \sigma\left(\boldsymbol{R}_s^{-\frac{1}{2}} \tilde{\boldsymbol{A}}_s \boldsymbol{R}_s^{-\frac{1}{2}} \cdots \sigma\left(\boldsymbol{R}_s^{-\frac{1}{2}} \tilde{\boldsymbol{A}}_s \boldsymbol{R}_s^{-\frac{1}{2}} \boldsymbol{X}_s \boldsymbol{W}^{(1)}\right) \cdots \boldsymbol{W}^{(L)}\right),$$

$$\boldsymbol{Z}_t = f\left(\mathcal{W}; \mathcal{G}_t\right) = \sigma\left(\boldsymbol{R}_t^{-\frac{1}{2}} \tilde{\boldsymbol{A}}_t \boldsymbol{R}_t^{-\frac{1}{2}} \cdots \sigma\left(\boldsymbol{R}_t^{-\frac{1}{2}} \tilde{\boldsymbol{A}}_t \boldsymbol{R}_t^{-\frac{1}{2}} \boldsymbol{X}_t \boldsymbol{W}^{(1)}\right) \cdots \boldsymbol{W}^{(L)}\right).$$

This strategy aims to bridge the gap between different graphs $\mathcal{G}_s$ and $\mathcal{G}_t$, and thus makes the node representations of both graphs comparable.

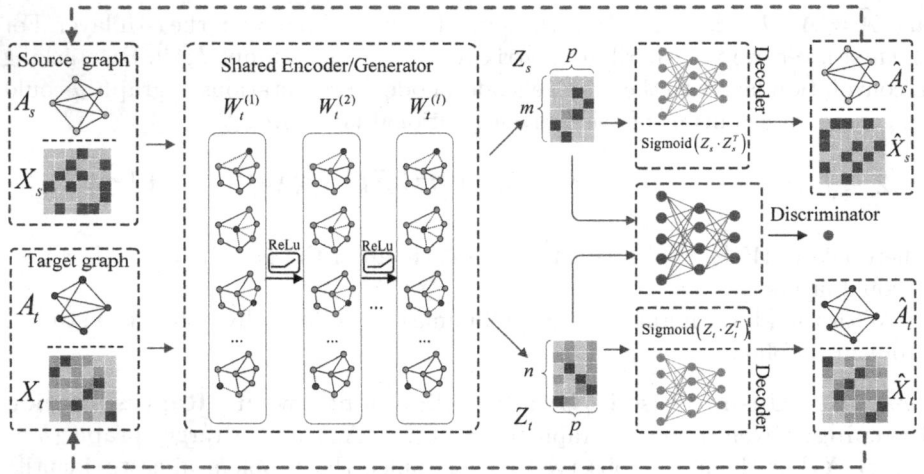

Fig. 1. The proposed framework CrossUGA for unsupervised graph alignment.

In the decoder part, both attribute and structure reconstruction are taken into consideration to ensure the generated representations could retain as much information from the original graph as possible. Inspired by [8], the structure reconstruction decoder takes latent node representations as input and then predicts whether there exists a link between a pair of nodes. In such a way, the reconstructed adjacency matrices are calculated by

$$\hat{\boldsymbol{A}}_s = Sigmoid\left(\boldsymbol{Z}_s \boldsymbol{Z}_s^\top\right) \text{ and } \hat{\boldsymbol{A}}_t = Sigmoid\left(\boldsymbol{Z}_t \boldsymbol{Z}_t^\top\right), \tag{3}$$

where $Sigmoid(\cdot)$ refers to the sigmoid activation. In this sense, the decoder loss for the structure reconstruction of graphs $\mathcal{G}_s$ and $\mathcal{G}_t$ are formulated as

$$\mathcal{L}_s^{stru}\left(\mathcal{W}; \boldsymbol{A}_s, \hat{\boldsymbol{A}}_s\right) = \sum_{u=1}^{m}\sum_{v=1}^{m} \boldsymbol{A}_s\left(u, v\right)\log \hat{\boldsymbol{A}}_s\left(u, v\right) + \left(1 - \boldsymbol{A}_s\left(u, v\right)\right)\log\left(1 - \hat{\boldsymbol{A}}_s\left(u, v\right)\right),$$

$$\mathcal{L}_t^{stru}\left(\mathcal{W}; \boldsymbol{A}_t, \hat{\boldsymbol{A}}_t\right) = \sum_{u=1}^{n}\sum_{v=1}^{n} \boldsymbol{A}_t\left(u, v\right)\log \hat{\boldsymbol{A}}_t\left(u, v\right) + \left(1 - \boldsymbol{A}_t\left(u, v\right)\right)\log\left(1 - \hat{\boldsymbol{A}}_t\left(u, v\right)\right).$$

Regarding to the decoding of attribute information, we leverage a simple dense layer to reconstruct the attributes in the source and target graph, respectively

$$\hat{\boldsymbol{X}}_s = f_{relu}\left(\boldsymbol{W}_s \boldsymbol{Z}_s + \boldsymbol{b}_s\right) \text{ and } \hat{\boldsymbol{X}}_t = f_{relu}\left(\boldsymbol{W}_t \boldsymbol{Z}_t + \boldsymbol{b}_t\right), \tag{4}$$

where f_{relu} refers to the Relu activation. The reconstruction errors on attributes of graphs $\mathcal{G}_s$ and $\mathcal{G}_t$ are calculated using the Frobenius norm, *i.e.*,

$$\begin{aligned}
\mathcal{L}_s^{attr}\left(\mathcal{W}, \boldsymbol{W}_s, \boldsymbol{b}_s; \boldsymbol{X}_s\right) &= \left\|\boldsymbol{X}_s - \hat{\boldsymbol{X}}_s\right\|_F, \\
\mathcal{L}_t^{attr}\left(\mathcal{W}, \boldsymbol{W}_t, \boldsymbol{b}_t; \boldsymbol{X}_t\right) &= \left\|\boldsymbol{X}_t - \hat{\boldsymbol{X}}_t\right\|_F.
\end{aligned} \tag{5}$$

Taking both the structure and attribute information into consideration, the total reconstruction errors for graphs $\mathcal{G}_s$ and $\mathcal{G}_t$ are formulated as

$$\begin{aligned}
\mathcal{L}_s^{rec}\left(\mathcal{W}, \boldsymbol{W}_s, \boldsymbol{b}_s; \mathcal{G}_s\right) &= \alpha \mathcal{L}_s^{stru}\left(\mathcal{W}, \boldsymbol{A}_s\right) + (1 - \alpha) \mathcal{L}_s^{attr}\left(\mathcal{W}, \boldsymbol{W}_s, \boldsymbol{b}_s; \boldsymbol{X}_s\right), \\
\mathcal{L}_t^{rec}\left(\mathcal{W}, \boldsymbol{W}_t, \boldsymbol{b}_t; \mathcal{G}_t\right) &= \alpha \mathcal{L}_t^{stru}\left(\mathcal{W}, \boldsymbol{A}_t\right) + (1 - \alpha) \mathcal{L}_t^{attr}\left(\mathcal{W}, \boldsymbol{W}_t, \boldsymbol{b}_t; \boldsymbol{X}_t\right),
\end{aligned} \tag{6}$$

where hyper-parameter $\alpha \in [0, 1]$ controls the balance of structure and attribute reconstruction. Moreover, we formulate the loss on cross-graph reconstruction of both source graph $\mathcal{G}_s$ and target graph $\mathcal{G}_t$ by

$$\mathcal{L}^{rec}\left(\mathcal{W}, \mathcal{M}; \mathcal{G}_s, \mathcal{G}_t\right) = \mathcal{L}_s^{rec}\left(\mathcal{W}, \boldsymbol{W}_s, \boldsymbol{b}_s; \mathcal{G}_s\right) + \beta \mathcal{L}_t^{rec}\left(\mathcal{W}, \boldsymbol{W}_t, \boldsymbol{b}_t; \mathcal{G}_t\right), \tag{7}$$

where $\mathcal{M} = \{\boldsymbol{W}_s, \boldsymbol{b}_s, \boldsymbol{W}_t, \boldsymbol{b}_t\}$ collects all parameters of the decoder involved in the reconstruction procedure. Hyper-parameter β controls the impact of reconstruction for the target graph during the cross-graph representation learning.

3.2 Adversarial Training

The adversarial training plays an important role in reducing discrepancy existing in attribute and structure distribution among different graphs. Let the representation of source graph $\mathcal{G}_s$ be the *real data*, and the representation of target graph $\mathcal{G}_t$ be the *fake data* generated by the cross-graph encoder. We impose a discriminator $D : \mathbb{R}^p \rightarrow \mathbb{R}$ to distinguish the fake representations $\boldsymbol{Z}_t$ from $\boldsymbol{Z}_s$. Without loss of generality, the discriminator D is comprised of two fully connected neural network layers, *i.e.*, $\forall \boldsymbol{Z}_s(i) \in \mathbb{R}^p$,

$$D\left(\boldsymbol{\Theta}; \boldsymbol{Z}_s(i)\right) = \boldsymbol{W}_D^{(2)} f_{relu}\left(\boldsymbol{W}_D^{(1)} \boldsymbol{Z}_s(i) + \boldsymbol{b}_D^{(1)}\right) + \boldsymbol{b}_D^{(2)}, \tag{8}$$

where $\boldsymbol{\Theta} = \left\{\boldsymbol{W}_D^{(1)}, \boldsymbol{b}_D^{(1)}, \boldsymbol{W}_D^{(2)}, \boldsymbol{b}_D^{(2)}\right\}$ is the set of parameters in the neural network layers. The responsibility of discriminator is to distinguish the fake representations $\boldsymbol{Z}_t$ from $\boldsymbol{Z}_s$, while the cross-graph encoder aims to confuse the discriminator by generating representations for graphs $\mathcal{G}_s$ and $\mathcal{G}_t$ with similar patterns. As a result, the adversarial loss function is derived as

$$\mathcal{L}_D^{adv}\left(\boldsymbol{\Theta}; \boldsymbol{Z}_s, \boldsymbol{Z}_t\right) = \mathbb{E}_{\boldsymbol{Z}_t \sim f(\mathcal{W}; \mathcal{G}_t)}\left[D\left(\boldsymbol{\Theta}; \boldsymbol{Z}_t\right)\right] - \mathbb{E}_{\boldsymbol{Z}_s \sim f(\mathcal{W}; \mathcal{G}_t)(\mathcal{G}_s)}\left[D\left(\boldsymbol{\Theta}; \boldsymbol{Z}_s\right)\right], \tag{9}$$

$$\mathcal{L}_G^{adv}\left(\mathcal{W}; \boldsymbol{Z}_t\right) = -\mathbb{E}_{\boldsymbol{Z}_t \sim f(\mathcal{G}_s)}\left[D\left(\boldsymbol{\Theta}; \boldsymbol{Z}_t\right)\right]. \tag{10}$$

Algorithm 1. The proposed CrossUGA algorithm.

Input: Source graph $\mathcal{G}_s = \{\mathcal{V}_s, \mathcal{E}_s, \boldsymbol{X}_s\}$ and target graph $\mathcal{G}_t = \{\mathcal{V}_t, \mathcal{E}_t, \boldsymbol{X}_t\}$, learning rate η_1, η_2 and η_3, the number of steps to apply to the encoder and discriminator, k_G and k_D.

1: Initialize $\mathcal{W}$, $\mathcal{M}$ and Θ
2: **repeat**
3:     **for** k_G steps **do**
4:         compute $\mathcal{L}^{rec}$ and $\mathcal{L}_G^{adv}$ according to Eq. 7 and 10, respectively;
5:         $\mathcal{W} \leftarrow Adam(\nabla \mathcal{W}, \mathcal{L}^{rec}, \mathcal{L}_G^{adv}, \eta_1)$;
6:         $\mathcal{M} \leftarrow Adam(\nabla \mathcal{W}, \mathcal{L}^{rec}, \eta_2)$;
7:     **end for**
8:     **for** k_D steps **do**
9:         compute $\mathcal{L}_D^{adv}$ according to Eq. 9;
10:         $\Theta \leftarrow Adam(\nabla \Theta, \mathcal{L}_D^{adv}, \eta_3)$;
11:     **end for**
12: **until** convergence;
13: **Output** $\boldsymbol{Z}_s, \boldsymbol{Z}_t$.

In summary, the overall loss function of the proposed cross-graph representation learning for unsupervised graph alignment is formulated as

$$\min_{\Theta} \max_{\mathcal{W}, \mathcal{M}} -\mathcal{L}^{rec}(\mathcal{W}, \mathcal{M}; \mathcal{G}_s, \mathcal{G}_t) + \lambda \left(\mathcal{L}_D^{adv}(\Theta; \boldsymbol{Z}_s, \boldsymbol{Z}_t) - \mathcal{L}_G^{adv}(\mathcal{W}; \boldsymbol{Z}_t) \right), \quad (11)$$

where trade-off parameter λ is utilized to balance the reconstruction loss and adversarial loss. By simultaneously playing the min-max game, we can eventually enforce the node representations of two graphs in the same distribution.

3.3   Model Inference

Note that there are three sets of parameters to estimate in the proposed optimization problem (11), including $\mathcal{W}$, $\mathcal{M}$, and Θ. We optimize this objective function by alternately updating each set of parameters. Algorithm 1 summarizes the procedure for learning the model. It first calls the encoders to generate node representations $\boldsymbol{Z}_s$ and $\boldsymbol{Z}_t$ simultaneously. Then it updates parameters in the $\mathcal{M}$ for reconstruction based on Eq. (6). As the encoder also plays the role of generator in the min-max game, $\mathcal{W}$ should also be updated based on Eq. (10). After a certain number of epochs k_G, the model turns to update the Θ in discriminators for another k_D epochs based on Eq. (9).

4   Experiments

In this section, we present the experimental results on both synthetic and real-world datasets to demonstrate the effectiveness of the proposed CrossUGA. We also include sensitive analysis to assess the impact of the controlling hyperparameters β and λ. Specifically, we conduct experiments to answer the following research questions:

Table 1. Details of datasets.

	Douban Offline/Online	Lastfm/Myspace	Flickr	Wiki
Number of nodes	3,906/1,118	4,115/1,104	7,575	2,405
Number of attributes	538	1,010	12,047	4,973
Number of edges	17,981/4,732	3,989/1,135	479,476	24,357
Number of anchor links	1,118	1,104	7,575	2,405

- **Q1** How effective is the proposed framework in tackling graphs with distinct topology structures and attribute distributions?
- **Q2** Whether the proposed framework can work well for graphs of different scales?
- **Q3** Whether the node representations trained by the proposed framework are well distributed in the same space?

4.1   Experimental Setup

Datasets. In this paper, to verify the proposed model can deal with the alignment task in most cases, we employ two synthetic datasets and two real-world datasets to evaluate the alignment performance. The detailed statistics for used datasets are summarized in Table 1.

- **Synthetic datasets:** We follow the method proposed by Derr *et al.* [3] to generate synthetic dataset from a single graph. Specifically, we randomly discard $\alpha_e\%$ edges from the original graph $\mathcal{G}$ and get the source graph $\mathcal{G}_s$. The target graph $\mathcal{G}_t$ can be generated in the same manner. We choose **Flickr** [11] and **Wiki**[1] to generate synthetic datasets using the above method. Both of them possess rich accompanying attributes on the nodes.
- **Real-world datasets: Douban** dataset provided by [29] consists of two networks with different scales. Besides the size information illustrated in Table 1, a prior alignment preference H based on the degree similarity is also provided. Another dataset, *i.e.*, **Lastfm-Myspace**, contains two subgraphs extracted from the original graphs [31]: Lastfm and Myspace. Following [29], we use the username similarity to construct a prior alignment preference based on Jaro-Winkler [4] distance.

Implementation Details. For the Douban dataset, we employ a two-layer GCN to encode both graphs simultaneously, where the number of hidden units is set to 512. For the attribute decoder, the hidden units of the fully connected layer is set to 512. In terms of the discriminator, we use a two-layer fully connected network with 256 hidden units and Leaky ReLU activation function. Besides, we set the hyper-parameters $\beta = 0.4$ and $\lambda = 0.3$. For the Lastfm-Myspace dataset, we use a single-layer GCN with 2,048 hidden units for the encoder. The number

---

[1] https://github.com/thunlp/OpenNE/tree/master/data/wiki.

of hidden units in the attribute decoder is set to 2,048. Meanwhile, the discriminator is built with two fully connected layers (512 neurons and 512 neurons). For this dataset, we set the hyper-parameters $\beta = 0.6$ and $\lambda = 0.2$. As for the synthetic datasets, we use a single-layer GCN with 512 hidden units. The number of hidden units in the attribute decoder is set to $1,024$. The discriminators for the synthetic datasets are designed to be the same as that of Lastfm-Myspace. Besides, we set the hyper-parameters $\beta = 0.2$ and $\lambda = 0$.

Evaluation Metrics. In this paper, we employ Precision@k [6] as the evaluation metric for graph alignment. Precision@k measures whether the positive matching occurs in the top-k candidates, *i.e.*, the top k nodes possessing the highest similarity with the source node. It is computed by

$$\text{Precision@}k = \frac{|\text{Correct alignments in top-}k \text{ candidate pairs}|}{|\text{Ground truth node pairs}|}$$

where |Ground truth node pairs| refers to the number of anchor links.

Comparison Methods. In this paper, we compare CrossUGA with three centrality-based algorithms and three state-of-the-art alignment methods. Here, the compared methods are listed as follows:

- **Centrality-based algorithms** are simple baselines that use degree, betweenness, and closeness centrality for the alignment task [3]. Once we compute the centrality for each node in both graphs, we can measure the distance between each pair of nodes and obtain the similarity matrix.
- **Isorank** [21] measures the node similarity based on network topology and then propagates the similarity in the product graph until convergence. The key idea of Isorank is that two nodes from different graphs are more possible to be aligned if their neighborhoods are similar as well.
- **FINAL** [29] is the first method that takes both node attribute and topology information into consideration when tackling the alignment task. Notably, both FINAL and Isorank can include a prior alignment preference matrix H to assist the alignment task.
- **REGAL** [6] is another approach that takes advantage of both structure and attribute information. It first generates node representations conditioned on degree distribution, and then measures the distance between each pair of nodes based on node attributes and the generated node representations.

4.2   Experimental Results

Performance on synthetic datasets. For the synthetic datasets constructed from Flickr and Wiki with the sub-graph generation approach [3], we regard the difference level between two generated graphs as structure noise. In this sense, higher difference level in structure means the alignment task would be more difficult. We evaluate the performance of the competitors by increasing the difference level λ_e of two graphs from 0 to 0.5. Experimental results on Precision@1 and

Precision@5 are shown in Fig. 3 and Fig. 2, respectively. Due to the absence of prior information, Isorank performs poorly over the synthetic datasets. That is why we do not show its experimental results. It is reasonable that the alignment performances decline with the increase of structure noise. However, the precision of some baselines such as Isorank and REGAL decreases sharply when the noise level increases, which shows their poor performance toward handling graphs with distinct topology structures. Our proposed CrossUGA outperforms different baselines with respect to different levels of noise. It might because CrossUGA learns the node representation with the GCN based cross-graph encoding, which mitigates the adverse effects caused by the structure noise.

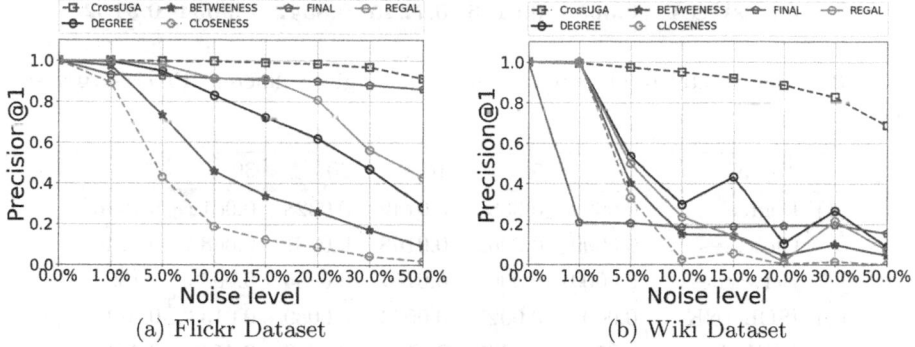

(a) Flickr Dataset   (b) Wiki Dataset

Fig. 2. Effect of structure noise on Precision@1

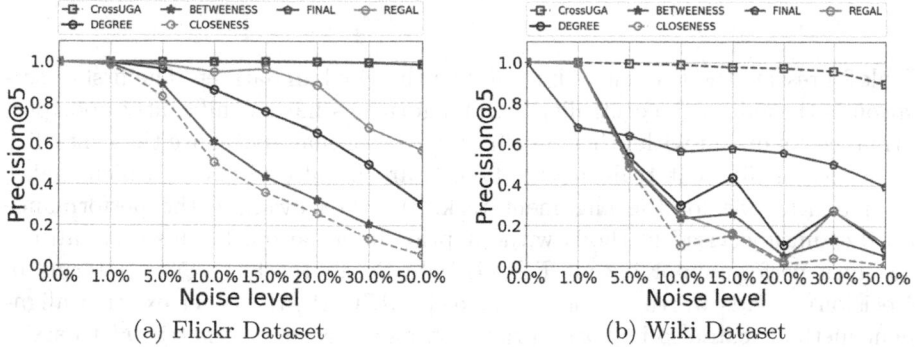

(a) Flickr Dataset   (b) Wiki Dataset

Fig. 3. Effect of structure noise on Precision@5.

Performance on Real-World Datasets. In addition to synthetic datasets, we also compare CrossUGA against other baselines on real-world datasets.

Table 2. Experimental results on Douban given different Precision@K settings.

	Top-K	1	5	10	20	30	50
(1)	Degree	0.0036	0.0072	0.0098	0.0188	0.0223	0.0403
	Closeness	0.0054	0.0116	0.0233	0.0492	0.0707	0.1208
	Betweeness	0.0018	0.0072	0.0143	0.0304	0.0438	0.0742
(2)	ISORANK	0.0018	0.0036	0.0089	0.0143	0.0224	0.0358
	REGAL	0.0152	0.0626	0.0841	0.1512	0.1843	0.2496
	FINAL	0.1145	0.3023	0.4499	0.5671	0.6503	0.7549
(3)	$ISORANK^+$	0.0662	0.0859	0.1047	0.1324	0.1565	0.2013
	$FINAL^+$	0.2496	0.5411	0.6467	0.7728	0.8318	0.9114
	CrossUGA	**0.3658**	**0.6163**	**0.7245**	**0.8542**	**0.9034**	**0.9132**

Table 3. Experimental results on Lastfm-Myspace given different Precision@K settings.

	Top-K	1	5	10	20	30	50
(1)	Degree	0.0009	0.0053	0.0142	0.0328	0.0612	0.1046
	Closeness	0.0009	0.0062	0.0168	0.0381	0.0683	0.1144
	Betweeness	0.0009	0.0062	0.0151	0.0355	0.0638	0.1090
(2)	ISORANK	0.0009	0.0027	0.0044	0.0089	0.0133	0.0142
	REGAL	0.2754	0.3307	0.3732	0.4212	0.4547	0.4918
	FINAL	0.3546	0.4929	0.5346	0.5789	0.6011	0.6215
(3)	$ISORANK^+$	0.1339	0.2766	0.3590	0.4007	0.4016	0.4043
	$FINAL^+$	0.4814	0.5878	0.6073	0.6259	0.6339	0.6463
	CrossUGA	**0.5762**	**0.6020**	**0.6179**	**0.6286**	**0.6401**	**0.6524**

Table 2 presents the Precision@k results on the Douban dataset. The first observation is that all of the centrality-based algorithms have significantly poor performance compared with other baselines. It is reasonable because the centrality properties of different real-world networks are usually different, which makes them undesirable for the alignment task. We then evaluate the performance of other unsupervised methods without prior information. In this case, all the baselines perform poor except FINAL, which can reach 11.45% in terms of Precision@1. It is worth noting that, except REGAL, the other existing alignment methods can also impose a prior alignment preference matrix H to assist the alignment task. With the help of prior information, a significant improvement on Precision@K can be achieved. Once we added the prior information [29] to the FINAL model (indicated as FINAL+), its Precision@1 value improves from 11.45% to 24.96%. This phenomenon indicates that the prior information has a significant influence on these algorithms. Notably, we can also observe that our model performs better than all the baselines even without any prior information.

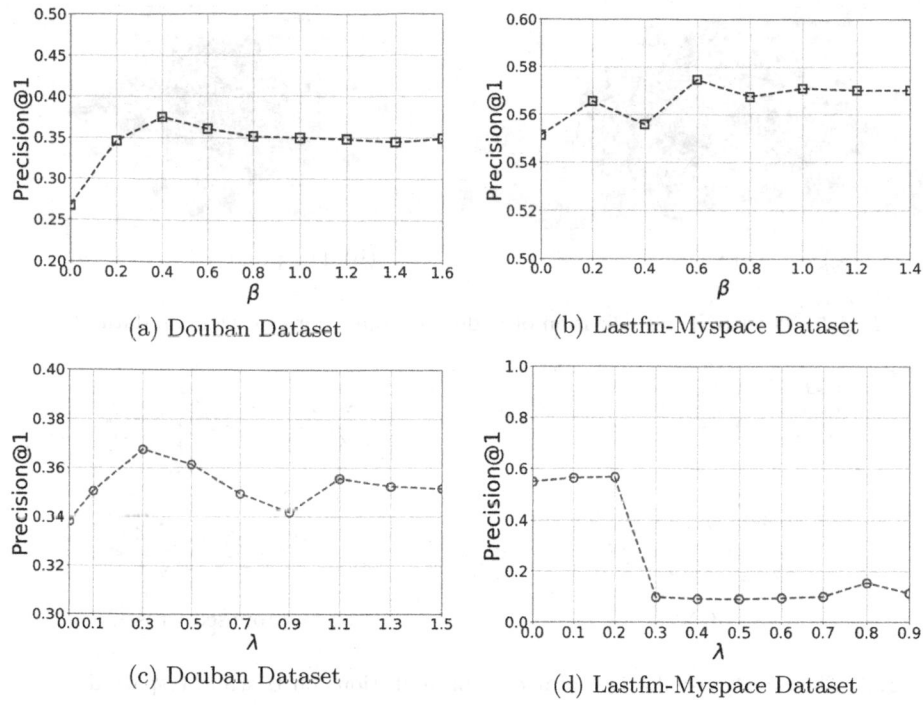

Fig. 4. Sensitive analysis for β and λ on real-world datasets.

CrossUGA can achieve 46.55% improvement in precision@1 compared with the best performed baseline FINAL and is also the highest when we take different Precision@k settings. Additionally, as mentioned in Sect. 1, the prior information is usually difficult to obtain. Thus our model shows stronger capabilities in graph alignment and is more practical compared with the above baselines.

We also report the experimental results over Lastfm-Myspace in Table 3. From the table we can derive the same conclusion that no matter the baselines use prior information or not, the proposed CrossUGA always achieves the best performance, achieving 19.69% performance improvement compared with FINAL+. These results prove that the proposed CrossUGA is able to work well for graphs of different scales and also outperform all of these baselines on both synthetic and real-world datasets.

4.3 Sensitivity Analysis

To investigate the effect of hyper-parameters, we present the performance on precision@1 over the real-world datasets by varying the controlling parameters β and λ.

Sensitive Analysis for β**.** We first discuss the impact of parameter β on the performance of proposed CrossUGA. As shown in Fig. 4a and Fig. 4b, when the

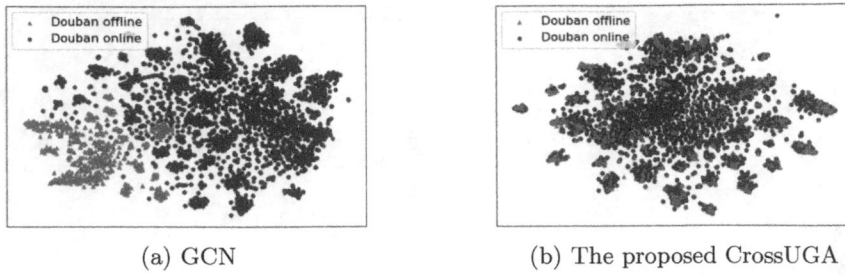

(a) GCN   (b) The proposed CrossUGA

Fig. 5. The t-SNE visualization of node representations on Douban dataset.

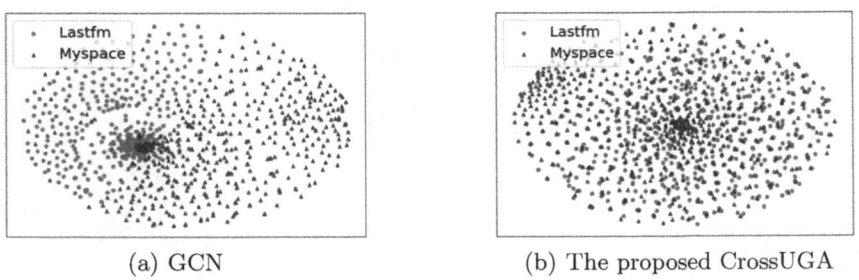

(a) GCN   (b) The proposed CrossUGA

Fig. 6. The t-SNE visualization of node representations on Lastfm-Myspace dataset.

model reconstructs both graphs simultaneously through the process of cross-graph representation learning *i.e.*, $\beta \geq 0$, the performance of our model gains a notable improvement and becomes flattening up to a point if we keep increases the value of β. This proves that the cross-graph embedding learning procedure indeed makes the learned representations possess similar distributions.

Sensitive Analysis for λ. Then we discuss the impact of controlling parameter λ. As shown in Fig. 4c and Fig. 4d, choosing λ around 0.3 tends to yield the best performance for Douban dataset. As for the Lastfm-Myspace dataset, the best choice of λ is 0.2. Larger controlling parameter λ tends to degrade the alignment performance. It proves that employing the discriminator with proper λ can indeed better align the node representations from different graphs, and thus make it more comparable.

4.4   Qualitative Analysis

To verify if the proposed CrossUGA can indeed map the node representations into the same space, we visualize the node representations before and after the learning procedure on real-world datasets. In Fig. 5 and 6, it can be observed that the node representations generated by GCN independently cannot be aligned because of the difference of the graph topology. After using our proposed CrossUGA, the node representation of both graphs are successfully projected into the same space and the node representations become closer after the cross-graph representation learning procedure.

5   Related Work

Graph Alignment. Graph alignment has been employed in various fields like link prediction, information diffusion, and recommendation. Many research efforts have been devoted to solving this challenging problem. The early methods tried to align different graphs based on the alignment consistency principle – including both topology and attribute consistency. For example, Bayati et al. [1] formulates graph alignment as an integer quadratic programming problem based on the total number of shared edges across graphs and develops an effective solution based on message passing. Singh et al. [21] only utilizes topology information to calculate similarity among nodes and propagates the similarity scores in the product graph until convergence. Zhang et al. [27] promotes alignment transitivity penalty for multiple anonymized graphs. Koutra et al. [10] formulates the bipartite network alignment problem and uses the alternating projected gradient descent to solve the problem. Zhang et al. [30] proposes a method that jointly deals with graph alignment and graph completion at the same time to alleviate the adverse effects of incomplete networks. Kong et al. [9] extracts heterogeneous features from multiple heterogeneous graphs to predict the anchor links, including user's social, spatial, temporal, and text information. Zhang et al. [29] first investigates the alignment problem for attributed graphs. Heimann et al. [6] devises a method to calculate the similarity between nodes using the degree-based node representations and attribute information to align the nodes.

Recently, with the development of graph embedding [12,25] and deep learning, representation learning has been used to improve the effectiveness of alignment algorithms. These methods first embed nodes into low-dimensional feature space, then learn a mapping function using the observed anchor links to map the representations into the same space. For example, Man et al. [15] leverages the observed anchor links between two graphs to complete the edges that are available in one graph but absent in the other one. Then by imposing specific embedding methods [18] on the extended graphs, they construct the node representations for both graphs. After learning the mapping function, it successfully maps the node representations into the same space and calculates the similarity matrix for the alignment task. Zhou et al. [32] further improves the quality of mapping functions by leveraging the anchor nodes in a dual learning process. Liu [13] uses the same mapping function as PALE. It also takes the neighborhood of a node into consideration during representation learning.

Graph Representation Learning. Nowadays, graph analysis aims to extract useful information hidden in graphs which could promote a wide range of applications, such as link prediction [14,16], node classification [17], and network clustering [19,20]. Graph representation learning targets at converting nodes in the graph into a low dimensional feature space, which significantly improves the performance and computation efficiency of various graph mining algorithms. Perozzi *et al.* [18] successfully generalizes the neural language models to learn social representations of a graph's vertices, by modeling a stream of random walks. Then the LINE algorithm proposed by Tang *et al.* [22] deals with the embedding problem for large graphs by optimizing an objective that takes both the local and global structure into consideration. node2vec [5] learns node embeddings by biased random walks on top of the Deepwalk algorithm. With the development of deep learning, deep neural networks based methods have been applied to graph representation learning. Wang *et al.* [24] proposes to use auto-encoders to preserve the first and second order node proximity for representation learning. Cao *et al.* [2] adopts a random walking model to capture graph structural information directly. The model consists of random surfing, positive point wise mutual information calculation, and stacked denoising auto-encoders. Graph Convolutional Network (GCN) [7] successfully learns hidden layer representations that encode both local graph structure and features of nodes by stacking several nonlinear convolutional layers.

6   Conclusion

In this paper, we propose CrossUGA, an unsupervised alignment framework that is able to directly generate comparable node embeddings by using cross-graph representation learning. The proposed method does not require any anchor links or prior information. At the same time, it also makes better use of the structural regularities of graphs through representation learning. By training these representations in an adversarial process, we further mitigate the distribution differences between different graphs, thus the refined representations could be directly aligned. Extensive experiments show the superiority of the proposed CrossUGA against existing alignment methods.

Acknowledgement. This work was supported by National Nature Science Foundation of China (No. 61872287, No. 61532015, and No. 61872446), Innovative Research Group of the National Natural Science Foundation of China (No. 61721002), Innovation Research Team of Ministry of Education (IRT_17R86), and Project of China Knowledge Center for Engineering Science and Technology. Besides, this research was funded by National Science and Technology Major Project of the Ministry of Science and Technology of China (No. 2018AAA0102900).

References

1. Bayati, M., Gerritsen, M., Gleich, D.F., Saberi, A., Wang, Y.: Algorithms for large, sparse network alignment problems. In: ICDM (2009)
2. Cao, S., Lu, W., Xu, Q.: Deep neural networks for learning graph representations. In: AAAI (2016)
3. Chen, C., et al.: Unsupervised adversarial graph alignment with graph embedding. arXiv preprint arXiv:1907.00544 (2019)

4. Cohen, W., Ravikumar, P., Fienberg, S.: A comparison of string metrics for matching names and records. In: ACM KDD Workshop on Data Cleaning and Object Consolidation (2003)
5. Grover, A., Leskovec, J.: node2vec: Scalable feature learning for networks. In: ACM SIGKDD (2016)
6. Heimann, M., Shen, H., Safavi, T., Koutra, D.: Regal: representation learning-based graph alignment. In: ACM CIKM (2018)
7. Kipf, T.N., Welling, M.: Semi-supervised classification with graph convolutional networks. arXiv preprint arXiv:1609.02907 (2016)
8. Kipf, T.N., Welling, M.: Variational graph auto-encoders. arXiv preprint arXiv:1611.07308 (2016)
9. Kong, X., Zhang, J., Yu, P.S.: Inferring anchor links across multiple heterogeneous social networks. In: ACM CIKM (2013)
10. Koutra, D., Tong, H., Lubensky, D.: Big-align: fast bipartite graph alignment. In: ICDM (2013)
11. Li, J., Hu, X., Tang, J., Liu, H.: Unsupervised streaming feature selection in social media. In: ACM CIKM (2015)
12. Li, Q., Zhong, J., Li, Q., Cao, Z., Wang, C.: Enhancing network embedding with implicit clustering. In: Li, G., Yang, J., Gama, J., Natwichai, J., Tong, Y. (eds.) DASFAA 2019. LNCS, vol. 11446, pp. 452–467. Springer, Cham (2019). https://doi.org/10.1007/978-3-030-18576-3_27
13. Liu, L., Cheung, W.K., Li, X., Liao, L.: Aligning users across social networks using network embedding. In: IJCAI (2016)
14. Lü, L., Zhou, T.: Link prediction in weighted networks: the role of weak ties. EPL (Europhys. Lett.) **89**, 18001 (2010)
15. Man, T., Shen, H., Liu, S., Jin, X., Cheng, X.: Predict anchor links across social networks via an embedding approach. In: IJCAI (2016)
16. Menon, A.K., Elkan, C.: Link prediction via matrix factorization. In: Gunopulos, D., Hofmann, T., Malerba, D., Vazirgiannis, M. (eds.) ECML PKDD 2011. LNCS (LNAI), vol. 6912, pp. 437–452. Springer, Heidelberg (2011). https://doi.org/10.1007/978-3-642-23783-6_28
17. Moore, C., Yan, X., Zhu, Y., Rouquier, J.B., Lane, T.: Active learning for node classification in assortative and disassortative networks. In: ACM SIGKDD (2011)
18. Perozzi, B., Al-Rfou, R., Skiena, S.: DeepWalk: online learning of social representations. In: ACM SIGKDD (2014)
19. Ramaswamy, L., Gedik, B., Liu, L.: A distributed approach to node clustering in decentralized peer-to-peer networks. IEEE Trans. Parallel Distrib. Syst. **16**(9), 814–829 (2005)
20. Sasikumar, P., Khara, S.: K-means clustering in wireless sensor networks. In: CICN (2012)
21. Singh, R., Xu, J., Berger, B.: Pairwise global alignment of protein interaction networks by matching neighborhood topology. In: Speed, T., Huang, H. (eds.) RECOMB 2007. LNCS, vol. 4453, pp. 16–31. Springer, Heidelberg (2007). https://doi.org/10.1007/978-3-540-71681-5_2
22. Tang, J., Qu, M., Wang, M., Zhang, M., Yan, J., Mei, Q.: Line: large-scale information network embedding. In: WWW (2015)
23. Trouillon, T., Welbl, J., Riedel, S., Gaussier, É., Bouchard, G.: Complex embeddings for simple link prediction. In: ICML (2016)
24. Wang, D., Cui, P., Zhu, W.: Structural deep network embedding. In: ACM SIGKDD (2016)

25. Xiong, Y., Zhang, Y., Fu, H., Wang, W., Zhu, Y., Yu, P.S.: DynGraphGAN: dynamic graph embedding via generative adversarial networks. In: Li, G., Yang, J., Gama, J., Natwichai, J., Tong, Y. (eds.) DASFAA 2019. LNCS, vol. 11446, pp. 536–552. Springer, Cham (2019). https://doi.org/10.1007/978-3-030-18576-3_32
26. Xue, L., Luo, M., Peng, Z., Li, J., Chen, Y., Liu, J.: Anomaly detection in time-evolving attributed networks. In: Li, G., Yang, J., Gama, J., Natwichai, J., Tong, Y. (eds.) DASFAA 2019. LNCS, vol. 11448, pp. 235–239. Springer, Cham (2019). https://doi.org/10.1007/978-3-030-18590-9_19
27. Zhang, J., Philip, S.Y.: Multiple anonymized social networks alignment. In: ICDM (2015)
28. Zhang, J., Yu, P.S.: PCT: partial co-alignment of social networks. In: WWW (2016)
29. Zhang, S., Tong, H.: Final: fast attributed network alignment. In: ACM SIGKDD (2017)
30. Zhang, S., Tong, H., Tang, J., Xu, J., Fan, W.: iNEAT: incomplete network alignment. In: ICDM (2017)
31. Zhang, Y., Tang, J., Yang, Z., Pei, J., Yu, P.S.: COSNET: connecting heterogeneous social networks with local and global consistency. In: ACM SIGKDD (2015)
32. Zhou, F., Liu, L., Zhang, K., Trajcevski, G., Wu, J., Zhong, T.: DeepLink: a deep learning approach for user identity linkage. In: INFOCOM (2018)

Predicting Hospital Readmission Using Graph Representation Learning Based on Patient and Disease Bipartite Graph

Zhiqi Liu[1], Lizhen Cui[1,2(✉)], Wei Guo[1,2], Wei He[1,2], Hui Li[1,2], and Jun Gao[3]

[1] School of Software, Shandong University, Jinan, China
sdu_sde_lzq@163.com,
{clz,guowei,hewei,lih}@sdu.edu.cn
[2] Joint SDU-NTU Centre for Artificial Intelligence Research (C-FAIR),
Shandong University, Jinan, China
[3] Department of Computer Science, Peking University, Beijing, China
gaojun@pku.edu.cn

Abstract. Accurate hospital readmission prediction is conducive to reducing medical waste, improving the quality and efficiency of public health services, and providing better medical services for more people. The readmission of each patient is closely related to their disease history. Therefore, it is of great help to accurately predict the readmission by using the patient's diagnosis history information. However, the diagnosis history of some patients may be very short, and it is difficult to use the features of individual patients to predict their readmission. In this paper, a hospital readmission prediction model based on patient and disease bipartite graph, PDGraph, is proposed. In this method, heterogeneous graph is used to establish the correlations between patients and diseases, which can express the historical disease information of patients and the latent relationships between patients with the same disease. By constructing the bipartite graph of patients and diseases, one patient establishes an indirect relationship with patients with the same diseases through disease nodes. Thus, the features of other related patients can be used to assist the hospital readmission prediction and improve the prediction effect. Then, PDGraph embedding generation algorithm is designed to aggregate the information of disease and related patients to each patient to improve the predictive performance. Our proposed model was tested on a real dataset, and the results show that the proposed method is more accurate in the prediction task than baselines.

Keywords: Heterogeneous graph · Hospital readmission prediction · Graph representation learning

1 Introduction

The hospital readmission is defined as a patient who is admitted shortly after discharge. Hospital rehospitalization events are frequent and costly, which brings

Y. Nah et al. (Eds.): DASFAA 2020, LNCS 12113, pp. 385–397, 2020.
https://doi.org/10.1007/978-3-030-59416-9_23

huge burden to patients and medical system [1,2]. As an important indicator to measure the quality of medical services [3], the high readmission rate has become a growing focus for the government, medical institutions, insurance companies and patients. Policy makers in the United States [4] medical insurance and Medicaid Service Center (CMS) and the United Kingdom [5] even reduce the payment for patients who are readmitted within 30 days after discharge, so as to impose economic penalties on hospitals with high readmission rate. Therefore, solving the problem of hospital readmission prediction from the perspective of data analysis has attracted more and more attention in the research field [6]. Accurate hospital readmission predictions can help clinicians develop better treatment plans, help medical institutions identify patients at risk for intervention, make researchers better understand medical results of complex patient groups, and help medical insurance institutions actively prevent and reduce the cost of medical insurance, so as to provide better medical services for more people.

Reviewing previous studies on hospital readmission prediction, most early studies used various regression techniques to establish prediction models. In recent studies, machine learning algorithms, such as decision tree and support vector machine, have been applied more and more [6]. Recently, many people have also applied deep learning to the prediction of hospital readmission, which has achieved good results [9,10]. In recent years, some people predict hospital readmission based on graphs [11]. In order to solve the problem of vertical and heterogeneous electronic health records (EHR), they propose to use temporal graph to represent the sequence of medical events.

The hospital readmission of each patient is closely related to their diagnosis history and personal health information. Therefore, with the help of the patient's medical history and personal health information, it is very helpful to accurately predict the hospital readmission. However, some patients have a short history of diagnosis and it is difficult to predict their readmission time based on their own features. To solve this problem, the features of other patients with the same disease can be used to assist the hospital readmission prediction and improve the prediction effect. Moreover, even for patients with a long history of diagnosis, the prediction effect can be improved by learning from the features of other related patients. Therefore, this paper uses patient and disease bipartite graph to establish the correlation between patients and diseases, which can express the historical disease information of patients and the indirect relationship between patients with the same disease. and make full use of the health information of patients.

In this paper, we propose a hospital readmission prediction framework based on heterogeneous graph representation learning. First of all, according to the patient's medical records, the patient and disease bipartite graph is constructed to establish the correlation between patients and diseases and to establish the indirect relationship between patients with the same diseases. Then, PDGraph embedding generation algorithm is designed to aggregate information from the diseases and related patients for each patient. Finally, aggregate information is used to predict hospital readmission.

We summarize our main contributions as follows:

- We construct Patient and Disease Bipartite Graph to establish the correlation between patients and diseases, which can express the historical disease information of patients and the indirect relationship between the patients with the same disease, and can make good use of the health information of patients. Thus, the information of other patients with the same disease can be used to assist the hospital readmission prediction and improve the prediction effect.
- A hospital readmission prediction method based on Patient and Disease Bipartite Graph is proposed. The PDGraph embedding generation algorithm is designed to aggregate information from the diseases and related patients for each patient. Finally, we use the aggregation information of patient nodes to predict hospital readmission.
- The proposed method is validated on a real-word healthcare datasets. Experimental results show that the proposed method is promising and effective in prediction, and our model outperformes the baselines in the hospital readmission prediction experiment.

The rest of this paper is organized as follows. Section 2 reviews related work, and the details of the methodology is discussed in Sect. 3. Experiments and results analysis are given in Sect. 4, and Sect. 5 concludes this paper.

2 Related Work

Reviewing previous studies on hospital readmission prediction, most early studies used various regression techniques to build prediction models. In recent studies, machine learning algorithms, such as decision tree and support vector machine, have been increasingly applied [6]. In paper [7], support vector machine, decision tree and naive bayesian model were used to predict the rehospitalization risk of icu patients. In paper [8], multilayer perceptron, decision tree, k-nearest neighbor algorithm and bayesian classifier are used to predict patients' rehospitalization, and neural network is recommended as a classification training method.

In the last few years, the prediction methods of hospital readmission can be roughly divided into two categories. One is to apply deep learning to hospital readmission prediction, and the other is to predict hospital readmission based on temporal graph.

As we all know, deep learning has been widely applied in various fields and achieved good results, such as speech recognition, machine translation, image recognition and so on. Recently, many people have also applied deep learning to the prediction of hospital readmission, with good improvement. Chopra et al. [9] designed a regression neural network model to predict whether the patients would be hospitalized again, and compared with the accuracy of the basic classifier (e.g., SVM, random forest, simple neural network). The results showed that RNN showed the highest predictive ability among all the models used. Using LSTM, Reddy et al. [10] predicted hospital readmission within 30 days by extracting temporal relationships in longitudinal EHR clinical data. The results show that compared with traditional classification methods (such as ANN and penalty logistic regression), deep learning method has significant performance improvement.

As an important source of big data, graphs have been widely used in social media marketing, knowledge discovery, transportation network and other fields [15]. In recent years, some people predict hospital readmission based on graphs [11]. They proposed using temporal graph to the sequences of medical events to address the longitudinal and heterogeneous properties of electronic health records (EHR). Temporal graph can capture the temporal relation of medical events in each event sequences, and has strong robustness, anti-noise and anti-irregular observation ability. Based on the representation of temporal graphs, a method of identifying temporal phenotypes was further developed to identify the most important and interpretable graph basis as phenotypes, which could help us better understand the evolution patterns of diseases. Finally, by expressing the temporal graph with phenotypes, the expression coefficient was used to predict hospital readmission. In this method, some features are acquired based on graphs. In the end, the traditional machine learning method is used to predict readmission.

In summary, the current methods for solving the problem of hospital readmission prediction are generally using traditional machine learning classifiers, or using RNN and its variants in deep learning. However, the existing methods do not take into account the latent correlations between the patients who have had the same disease. Therefore, our method uses heterogeneous graph to establish the correlations between patients and diseases, which can express the historical disease information of patients and the latent relationships between patients who have had the same disease. Then through the representation learning of heterogeneous graph, personalized vector representation of each patient can be learned for hospital readmission prediction, which can achieve better prediction effect.

3   Methodology

In this section, we will introduce the details of the hospital readmission prediction method using heterogeneous graph representation learning. First, we introduce how to build the Patient and Disease Bipartite Graph based on the medical record histories of patients. Then, we describe the details of our prediction method based on the constructed bipartite graph.

3.1   Patient and Disease Bipartite Graph

Hospital readmission is influenced by many factors, especially the patient's personal health information and the disease information. Moreover, the predictive effect of hospital readmission for each patient can be improved by using the features of other relevant patients to assist the hospital readmission prediction.

Therefore, this paper constructs a "patient-disease" bipartite graph to combine patient information and disease information, and by constructing a bipartite graph, the patient can have a deep connection with relevant patients through the disease. The left in Fig. 1 shows a simple example of Patient-Disease Bipartite Graph construction with three patients and five diseases. After constructing the bipartite graph, we can find the related patients for each patient. For example, through the two paths shown on the right side of Fig. 1, $P2 \rightarrow D \rightarrow P1$ and $P2 \rightarrow D \rightarrow P1 \rightarrow C \rightarrow P3$, we can find that patient P1 and patient P3 are related patients of patient P2.

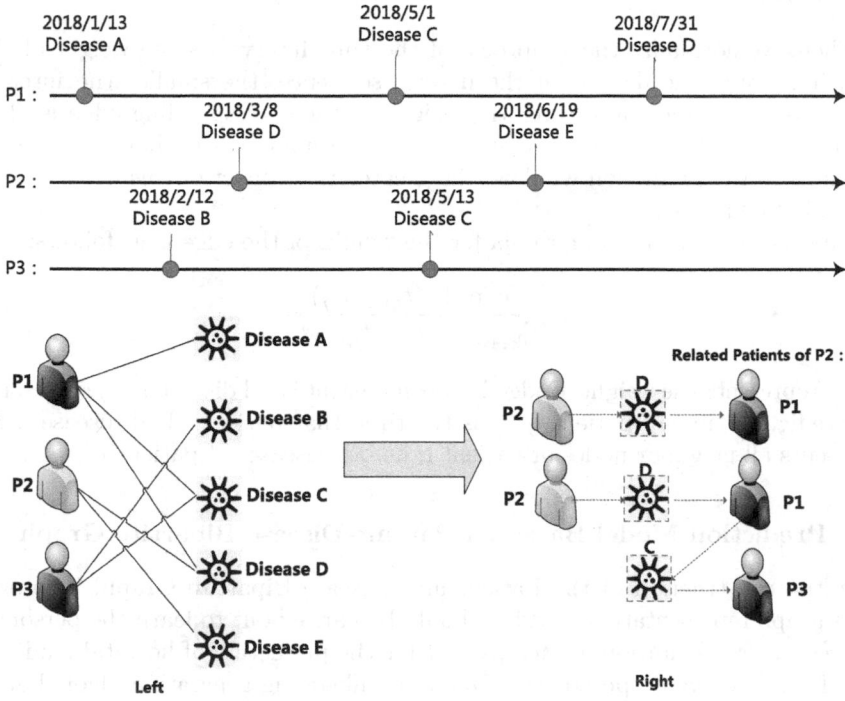

Fig. 1. Left: A simple example of Patient-Disease Bipartite Graph construction with three patients and five diseases. Right: A simple example shows how to find related patients of P2 through the bipartite graph.

First, the diseases are extracted from the patients' medical record history, and the diseases of each patient are serialized according to the timestamp of the disease.

Definition 1 *(Disease Sequence Set). Suppose we have a set of disease sequences $\{s_n | n = 1, 2, 3, ...N\}$, where N is the number of disease sequences. Each disease sequence s_n is represented as $< (d_{n1}, t_{n1}), (d_{n2}, t_{n2}), ...(d_{nL_n}, t_{nL_n}) >$, where L_n is the length of s_n, a disease d_{ni} takes place at timestamp t_{ni}, and $t_{np} \leq t_{nq}$, for all $p < q$.*

A simplified example of a medical event sequence is shown in Fig. 1. Then, based on the patients' disease sequence set, we construct a patient-disease bipartite graph. All patients are taken as patient node set of the bipartite graph, and the unique disease of the disease set $\langle d_{n1}, d_{n2}, ..., d_{nL_n} \rangle$ is taken as disease node set of the bipartite graph. The edge between the patient and the disease indicates that the patient suffered from the disease.

Definition 2 *(Patient-Disease Bipartite Graph). Suppose we have a patient-disease bipartite graph $\mathcal{G}(V_p + V_d, \mathcal{E})$, where V_p is the set of pateient nodes and V_d is the set of disease nodes. $\mathcal{E}$ is the set of edges, which indicate the correlation between patients and diseases, and each edge has a weight.*

Then, we normalize the reciprocal of the time interval as the weight of the edge. The later one disease in the disease sequence, the smaller the interval of the disease is and the greater the weight of the corresponding edge is. The underlying idea behind this weight computation approach is that the closer a disease is to the prediction window, the greater the impact of this disease is on hospital readmission.

The specific calculation formula for the weight of the edge is as follows:

$$e_{ij} = \frac{\exp\left(1/\left(t_{ip} - t_{ij}\right)\right)}{\sum_{k \in N_i} \exp\left(1/\left(t_{ip} - t_{ij}\right)\right)} \tag{1}$$

e_{ij} represents the weight of edge between patient i and disease j, t_{ip} represents the prediction time of patient i, t_{ij} is the time that patient i had disease j, N_i represents all neighbor nodes of patient i, i.e. all diseases of patient i.

3.2 Prediction Model Based on Patient-Disease Bipartite Graph

After the construction of the Patient and Disease Bipartite Graph, heterogeneous graph representation learning should be carried out to learn the personalized vector representation of each patient for the prediction of hospital readmission. Therefore, we proposed the PDGraph embedding generation algorithm to learn the medical heterogeneous graph we constructed, which aggregated node neighborhood information layer by layer, and finally we used the aggregation information of patient nodes to predict hospital readmission.

PDGraph Embedding Generation Algorithm. In this section, we introduce the details of PDGraph embedding generation algorithm. The intuition of our algorithm is that patient nodes aggregate information from the linked disease nodes at each iteration, meanwhile disease nodes aggregate information from the linked patient nodes at each iteration. As the iteration continues, patient nodes and disease nodes incrementally gain more and more information from further reaches of the Patient-Disease Bipartite Graph.

Step 1 in Fig. 2 illustrates the idea of PDGraph embedding generation algorithm. Algorithm 1 describes the process of embedding generation in the case

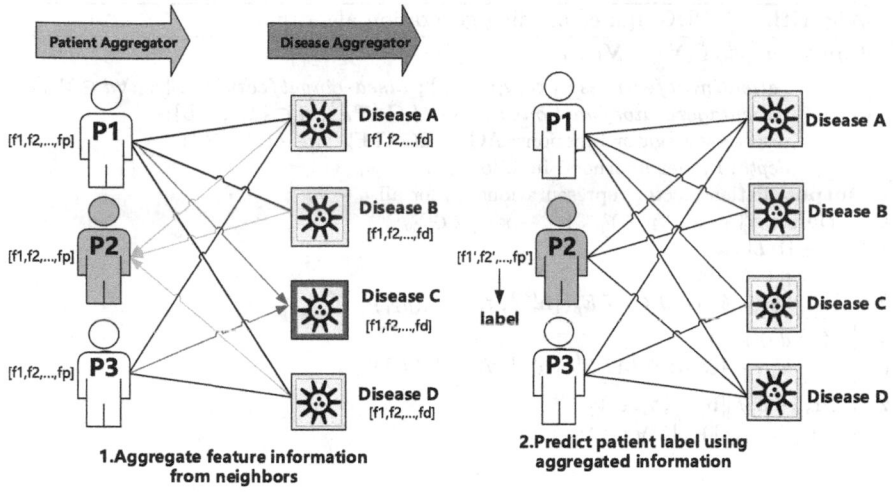

Fig. 2. An example of the idea of our method.

where the patient-disease bipartite graph, $G(V_p + V_d, \mathcal{E})$, and features of patient nodes and disease nodes are provided as input. Each iteration in the outer loop of Algorithm 1 proceeds as follows, where l represents the current iteration in the outer loop and $\mathbf{h}^l$ represents a node's representation at this step: First, each patient node $p \in V_p$ aggregates the representations of the linked disease nodes, $\mathbf{h}_u^{l-1}, \forall u \in \mathcal{N}(p)$, to obtain the next layer representation of the patient node h_p^l. It should be noted that this aggregation step depends on the representations generated at the previous iteration (i.e., $l-1$), and the $l=0$ representations are defined as the input features of patient nodes. For each disease node, do similar operations, but the aggregator method is different.

Aggregator. As shown in Algorithm 1, for each iteration, we need to aggregate the neighborhood information of patient node and disease node. In this paper, different aggregators are used to aggregate neighborhood information for patient node and disease node, which are named patient aggregator and disease aggregator respectively. And our aggregator method inspired by Hamilton et al. [12] and Velickovic et al. [13].

The inputs for two kinds of aggregators are both two sets of node features. $h_p = \{h_{p1}, h_{p2}, \ldots, h_{pm}\}, h_{pi} \in \mathcal{R}^{F_p}$ is the set of patient node features, where m is the number of patient nodes, and F_p is the number of features in each patient node. $h_d = \{h_{d1}, h_{d2}, \ldots, h_{dn}\}, h_{di} \in \mathcal{R}^{F_d}$ is the set of disease node features, where n is the number of disease nodes, and F_d is the number of features in each disease node. The aggregator produces two new sets of node features, $\{h'_{p1}, h'_{p2}, \ldots, h'_{pm}\}, h'_{pi} \in \mathcal{R}^{F'_p}$ and $h'_d = \{h'_{d1}, h'_{d2}, \ldots, h'_{dm}\}, h'_{di} \in \mathcal{R}^{F'_d}$, as its output.

Algorithm 1 PDGraph embedding generation algorithm

Input: $Graph : \mathcal{G}(\mathbf{V}_\vee + \mathbf{V}_\Gamma, \mathcal{E})$;

$\quad\quad\quad patient\ input\ features : \{\mathbf{x}_p, \forall p \in \mathcal{V}_p\}$; $disease\ input\ features : \{\mathbf{x}_d, \forall d \in \mathcal{V}_d\}$;

$\quad\quad\quad patient\ aggregator\ functions : AGGREGATE_p^l, \forall l \in \{1, \ldots, L\}$;

$\quad\quad\quad$ disease aggregator functions: $AGGREGATE_d^l, \forall l \in \{1, \ldots, L\}$;

$\quad\quad\quad depth$: L; neighborhood function: $\mathcal{N}$.

Output: Patient vector representations $\mathbf{z}_p$ for all $p \in \mathcal{V}_p$

1 **Initialize** $\mathbf{h}_p^0 \leftarrow \mathbf{x}_p, \forall p \in \mathcal{V}_p$, $\mathbf{h}_d^0 \leftarrow \mathbf{x}_d, \forall d \in \mathcal{V}_d$;

2 **for** $l \in [1, L]$ **do**

3 $\quad$ **for** $p \in \mathcal{V}_p$ **do**

4 $\quad\quad$ $h_p^l \leftarrow AGGREGATE_p^l(\{\mathbf{h}_u^{l-1}, \forall u \in \mathcal{N}(p)\})$

5 $\quad$ **for** $d \in \mathcal{V}_d$ **do**

6 $\quad\quad$ $h_d^l \leftarrow AGGREGATE_d^l(\{\mathbf{h}_u^{l-1}, \forall u \in \mathcal{N}(d)\})$

7 $\quad$ $\mathbf{h}_p^l \leftarrow \mathbf{h}_p^l / \left\| \mathbf{h}_p^l \right\|_2, \forall p \in \mathcal{V}_p$

$\quad\quad$ $\mathbf{h}_d^l \leftarrow \mathbf{h}_d^l / \left\| \mathbf{h}_d^l \right\|_2, \forall d \in \mathcal{V}_d$

8 $\mathbf{z}_p \leftarrow \mathbf{h}_p^L, \forall p \in \mathcal{V}_p$

Patients should have different concerns about different diseases, because the later the disease is, the greater the impact on patient hospital readmission is. Therefore, we need to determine the weight of the edge between the disease and the patient. The weights, i.e. attention coefficients, is calculated as follows:

$$\alpha\left(h_{\text{pi}}, h_{\text{dj}}, e_{ij}\right) = \frac{\exp\left(\sigma\left(\mathbf{a}^\text{T}\left[W_p h_{\text{pi}} || e_{ij} W_d h_{\text{dj}}\right]\right)\right)}{\sum_{k \in N_{\text{pi}}} \exp\left(\sigma\left(\mathbf{a}^\text{T}\left[W_p h_{\text{pi}} || e_{ij} W_d h_{\text{dj}}\right]\right)\right)} \quad (2)$$

Where T represents transposition; $||$ represents the connection operation; σ represents a nonlinearity; N_{pi} represents the neighbors of patient node i; h_{pi} is the features of patient node i; h_{dj} is the features of disease node j; e_{ij} is the current attention coefficient that indicates the importance of node j to node i. It is the attention coefficient of the previous layer, and it is the initial weight of the edge at the first layer.

Patient Aggregator. The attention coefficients are used to compute a linear combination of the features corresponding to them, to obtain the final output features for each patient node,

$$h_{pi}^l = \sigma\left(\sum_{j \in N_{pi}} \alpha\left(h_{pi}^{l-1}, h_{dj}^{l-1}, e_{ij}^{l-1}\right) W^{l-1} h_{dj}^{l-1}\right) \quad (3)$$

Disease aggregator. Similar to patient aggregator, disease aggregator uses the attention coefficients to compute a linear combination of the features corresponding to them as the final output features for each disease node,

$$h_{dj}^l = \sigma\left(\sum_{i \in N_{dj}} \alpha\left(h_{pi}^{l-1}, h_{dj}^{l-1}, e_{ij}^{l-1}\right) W^{l-1} h_{pi}^{l-1}\right) \quad (4)$$

Where h_{pi}^{l-1} represents the features of patient node i at layer $l-1$; h_{dj}^{l-1} represents the features of disease node j at layer $l - 1$; e_{ij}^{l-1} is the weight of the edge which links node j to node i at layer $l - 1$; W^{l-1} is the corresponding weight matrix at layer $l-1$, which is used to propagate information between different layers of the model; α is the weight calculation function mentiond before; σ is a nonlinearity.

Predict Hospital Readmission. By PDGraph embedding generation algorithm, we aggregate information from the diseases and related patients for each patient. Thus, the good patient representations z_p for all $p \in V_p$ are obtained. Then, as shown in step 2 in Fig. 2, we use aggregated information (i.e., z_p) to predict hospital readmission for each patient. Since we obtain good representation of each patient by the method mentioned before, we simply use a softmax layer to predict hospital readmission,

$$\hat{y} = \text{softmax}(z_p) \tag{5}$$

where $\hat{y}$ indicates whether the patient will be readmitted.

4 Experiment

4.1 Datasets

We use a real-world healthcare dataset of patients with coronary heart disease to evaluate the effectiveness of our method, including the diagnosis information and the health examination information. Our datasets include the records of 710 patients for 6 years, from 2011 to 2016.

The statistics of the dataset is summarized in Table 1. The Coronary Heart Disease dataset includes 710 patients and 435 distinct diseases. Among these patients 381 are hospitalized within one year after CHD confirmation, and the rest 329 patients are not. The average number of diseases per patient is 4.269, and the maximum number of diseases per patient is 14. Each patient has at least one diagnosis, up to 14, and most patients have no more than 10 diagnoses.

4.2 Experimental Settings

Here we give some details of the our model, and the baseline approaches to compare with. Our task is to predict whether the patient with coronary heart disease will be hospitalized or not within 180 days after discharge from hospital. All of methods use a 5-fold cross validation method to evaluate method performance, in order to more accurately evaluate the performance of each method. And the classification performance is measured by Precision, Recall, F1-score and Accuracy.

Baseline Approaches. For comparison purpose, we also implemented the following baselines:

- LR: Reviewing previous studies on hospital readmission prediction, a variety of regression techniques are mostly used to construct the prediction model in the early stage, and logistic regression is one of the most commonly used algorithms [6]. Logistic regression is a statistical model that in its basic form uses a logistic function to model a binary dependent variable.
- SVM: Support vector machine is a common supervised learning model to analyze data used for classification. In the most recent studies, machine learning algorithms have been increasingly used, among which SVM is one of the most commonly used algorithms [6].
- DT: Decision tree algorithm is a basic classification and regression algorithm, and in our task, we use it to perform a binary classification task. Classification decision tree model is a tree structure that describes the classification of instances.
- RF: Random forests or random decision forests are an ensemble learning method for classification task that operates by constructing a multitude of decision trees at training time and outputting the class that is the mode of the classes of the individual trees.

Table 1. Statistics of dataset.

Cohorts	Coronary heart disease dataset
# Patients	710
Total # distinct diseases	435
Avg. # of diseases per patient	4.269
Max # of diseases per patient	14

Our Model. Our task is to predict the risk of hospital readmission for each patient with coronary heart disease. We set the prediction window as 180 days, and all the rest records before prediction window belong to observation window. First, we use the records in observation window to construct the patient and disease bipartite graph, and embed the basic health information of patients as the features of patient nodes, and use the medical concept embedding method [14] to learn appropriate disease vector representation as the features of disease nodes. The basic health information of patients includes the average hospital days, the average hospital costs, the hospital frequency, gender, age, BMI, whether smoking or not, etc. Then, we train our model described in Sect. 3.2 to obtain the optimized parameters. After that, we predict hospital readmission for each testing patient.

Table 2. Results of predicting hospital readmission. Pre, Rec, F1 and Acc represent Precision, Recall, F1-score and Accuracy, respectively. The prediction performance over 5-fold cross validation on real-world data sets.

	LR	SVM	DT	RF	PDGraph
Pre	0.5070	0.5139	0.5397	**0.5932**	0.5857
Rec	0.7347	0.7551	0.6939	0.7143	**0.7884**
F1	0.6000	0.6116	0.6071	0.6481	**0.6721**
Acc	0.5200	0.5300	0.5600	0.6200	**0.6364**

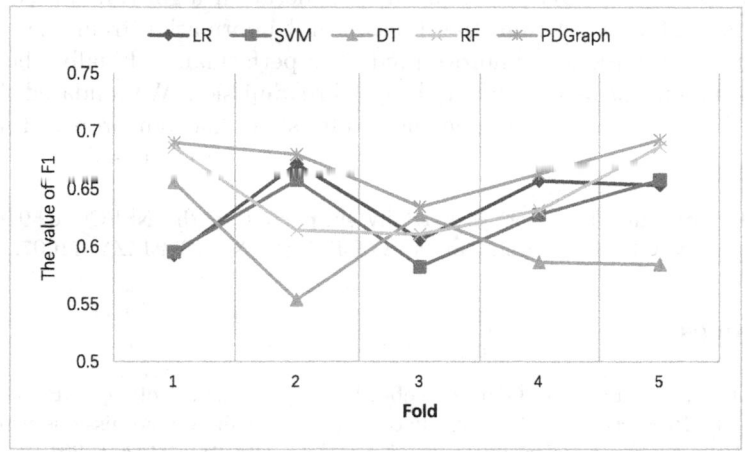

Fig. 3. The F1-score of each fold for all five methods

4.3   Prediction Performance

The experimental results are shown in Table 2. It contains the comparison among four classification performance measures (Pre, Rec, F1, Acc), and five prediction methods (LR, SVM, DT, RF, PDGraph). Among them, LR, SVM, DT and RF are machine learning methods commonly used to predict hospital readmission, and PDGraph is our method based on patient and disease bipartite graph. Pre, Rec, F1 and Acc represent Precision, Recall, F1-score and Accuracy, respectively.

From Table 2, We can see that PDGraph has the dominating overall prediction accuracy on coronary heart disease data sets and its performance is promising. PDGraph outperforms the other methods by reaching the F1-score 0.6721 and the accuracy 0.6364. And the value of recall of PDGraph is much higher than other methods, indicating that our method can better find hospital readmission patients.

Figure 3 shows the F1-score measure across all the folds for all five methods. We can see that our method has a great advantage compared with the other four methods. Although the predictive performance of our method fluctuates in different folds and even has a big decline in fold-3, we can still see that our method is more competitive than the other four methods.

5   Conclusion

In this paper, we propose a hospital readmission prediction model based on heterogeneous graph representation learning. Specifically, a "patient-disease" bipartite graph is constructed according to the patients' medical records, through which each patient can have a deep correlation with other patients with the same disease. Then, PDGraph embedding generation algorithm was designed to aggregate information from the diseases and information from the relevant patients for each patient to improve predictive performance. Finally, the aggregate information was used to predict hospital readmission. We validated the proposed model on a real dataset, and the results show that our proposed method is more accurate in the prediction tasks compared with the baselines.

Acknowledgement. This work is partially supported by the NSFC No. 91846205, the Shandong Key R&D Program No. 2018YFJH0506, No. 2019JZZY011007.

References

1. Wallmann, R., Llorca, J., Gómez-Acebo, I., Ortega, Á.C., Roldan, F.R., Dierssen-Sotos, T.: Prediction of 30-day cardiac-related-emergency-readmissions using simple administrative hospital data. Int. J. Cardiol. **164**(2), 193–200 (2013)
2. Dharmarajan, K., et al.: Diagnoses and timing of 30-day readmissions after hospitalization for heart failure, acute myocardial infarction, or pneumonia. J. Hosp. Med. **8**(12), 689–695 (2013)
3. Baillie, C.A., et al.: The readmission risk flag: using the electronic health record to automatically identify patients at risk for 30-day readmission. In: Rado, G.T., Suhl, H., (eds.) Magnetism, vol. III, pp. 271–350. Academic, New York (1963)
4. Centers for Medicare and Medicaid Services (CMS), HHS. Medicare program; hospital inpatient prospective payment systems for acute care hospitals and the long-term care hospital prospective payment system and Fiscal Year 2014 rates; quality reporting requirements for specific providers; hospital conditions of participation; payment policies related to patient status, final rules. Fed. Regist. **78**(160) 50495 (2013)
5. Kmietowicz, Z.: Hospitals will be fined for emergency readmissions, says Lansley. BMJ: Br. Med. J. **340**, 340 (2010)
6. Artetxe, A., Beristain, A., Grana, M.: Predictive models for hospital readmission risk: a systematic review of methods. Comput. Methods Programs Biomed. **164**, 49–64 (2018)
7. Braga, P., Portela, F., Santos, M.F., Rua, F.: Data mining models to predict patient's readmission in intensive care units. In: ICAART 2014-Proceedings of the 6th International Conference on Agents and Artificial Intelligence, vol. 1, pp. 604–610 (2014)
8. Garmendia, A., Graña, M., Lopez-Guede, J.M., Rios, S.: Predicting patient hospitalization after emergency readmission. Cybern. Syst. **48**(3), 182–192 (2017)

9. Chopra, C., Sinha, S., Jaroli, S., Shukla, A., Maheshwari, S.: Recurrent neural networks with non-sequential data to predict hospital readmission of diabetic patients. In: Proceedings of the 2017 International Conference on Computational Biology and Bioinformatics, pp. 18–23 (2017)
10. Reddy, B.K., Delen, D.: Predicting hospital readmission for lupus patients: an RNN-LSTM-based deep-learning methodology. Comput. Biol. Med. **101**, 199–209 (2018)
11. Liu, C., Wang, F., Hu, J., Xiong, H.: Temporal phenotyping from longitudinal electronic health records: a graph based framework. In: Proceedings of the 21th ACM SIGKDD International Conference on Knowledge Discovery and Data Mining, pp. 705–714 (2015)
12. Hamilton, W., Ying, Z., Leskovec, J.: Inductive representation learning on large graphs. In: Advances in Neural Information Processing Systems, pp. 1024–1034 (2017)
13. Velickovic, P., Cucurull, G., Casanova, A., Romero, A., Lio, P., Bengio, Y.: Graph attention networks. In: Proceedings of the International Conference on Learning Representations (2017)
14. Choi, E., Schuetz, A., Stewart, W.F., Sun, J.: Medical concept representation learning from electronic health records and its application on heart failure prediction. arXiv:1602.03686 (2016)
15. Fan, W., Hu, C.: Big graph analyses: from queries to dependencies and association rules. Data Sci. Eng. **2**(1), 36–55 (2017)

Aspect-Level Attributed Network Embedding via Variational Graph Neural Networks

Hengliang Wang[✉] and Kedian Mu

School of Mathematical Sciences, Peking University, Beijing, China
wanghl@pku.edu.cn

Abstract. Attributed information network embedding (AINE) has been widely used in network analysis. Existing AINE methods mainly focus on preserving network proximities and minimizing the reconstruction loss of node attribute information from a single aspect. However, complex network data may stem from different aspects. For example, a social network may consist of working relationship networks, alumni associations and so on. In this paper, we propose a novel model, called Aspect-level Attributed Network Embedding (AANE), to embed nodes by learning different aspect-level information. Specifically, we use a transform matrix to model aspect-level network topological structure and node attributes. Then, we leverage graph neural networks to learn aspect-level embedding. To learn a robust representation, we aggregate different aspect-level embeddings via the attention mechanism in a variational manner. Experimental results on four real-world network datasets demonstrate that AANE outperforms the state-of-the-art network embedding methods.

Keywords: Attributed information network embedding · Graph neural networks · Variational auto-encoder

1 Introduction

In the era of information explosion, attributed information networks (AINs) [6] have been widely used in social media and e-commerce. AIN is a powerful tool to store and access relational data. Data mining tasks on AINs, such as community detection [4], node classification [25], and link prediction [11], have attracted continuous attention. Network embedding [5,17], which maps nodes into a low-dimension space, plays an important role in data mining tasks on AINs. Particularly, unsupervised network embedding is more flexible and more general because it is hard and expensive to obtain the labels of nodes in most cases.

Unsupervised attributed information network embedding methods can be categorized into two classes [9]. The first class, such as DANE [4] and ANRL

Y. Nah et al. (Eds.): DASFAA 2020, LNCS 12113, pp. 398–414, 2020.
https://doi.org/10.1007/978-3-030-59416-9_24

[25], usually uses random walk based model [17] to capture the linkage information and an auto-encoder to capture the content information of nodes. The second class, like DGI [21], embeds nodes into a low-dimensional space through mutual information maximization. However, existing methods usually learn node representations from a single aspect, ignoring that network data may stem from different aspects. For instance, a social network, as illustrated in Fig. 1, consists of working relationship networks, alumni associations, hobby networks and so on. Citation networks are made up of citations of different topics. More specifically, a person may have different character traits and social relationships in different circumstances, and a paper may draw knowledge and cite references from two or more fields. So, from different aspects, nodes may have different features and the network topological structure may be different. The observed network information is a blend of different aspect-level data. Actually, aspect-level analysis has shown its positive effect in handling complex information in many fields, such as heterogeneous information network based recommendation [6] and sentiment classification [24]. Thus, it will be better to apply aspect-level analysis to attributed information networks, rather than from a single aspect.

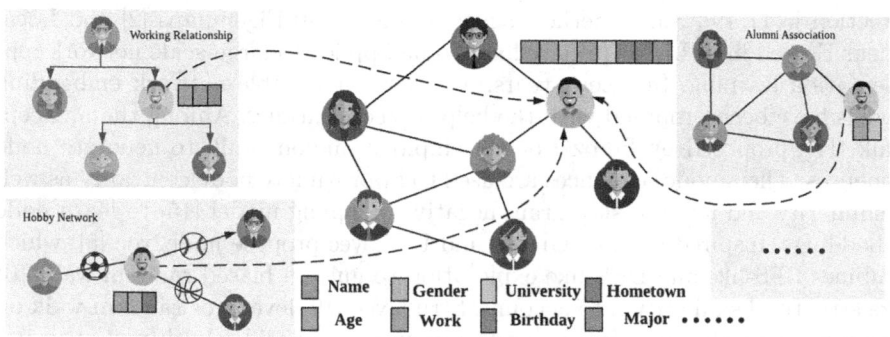

Fig. 1. Illustration of a social network with different aspect-level data.

In this paper, we propose a method called Aspect-level Attributed Network Embedding (AANE), which learns a robust representation in a variational manner. We first design a transform matrix to capture aspect-level attributes and topology information. Then, nodes are embedded into a low-dimensional representation space according to the attribute information and topology information of each aspect. By combining the node embeddings of different aspects via attention mechanism [1] in a variational manner, our model obtains the final embedding of each node. Our model focuses on unsupervised AIN embedding and it can be easily applied to plain networks, heterogeneous information networks, signed information networks and so on. Besides, our model can be fine-tuned in a supervised way if the labels are available. Our contributions are as follows:

- We present a unified method AANE, which analyses attributed information networks in an aspect-level way, and then integrates the topology information as well as content information of different aspects in a low dimensional space.
- We design an aspect-level encoder, which uses a transform matrix to capture different aspect-level network topology information and node attributes.
- We conduct experiments on four datasets: Cora, Citeseer, Pubmed and Wiki. The experiment results demonstrate the effectiveness of AANE.

2   Related Work

In this section, we first give a brief introduction to unsupervised network embedding. Next, we focus on attributed information network embedding.

2.1   Unsupervised Network Embedding

Network embedding attempts to map nodes into a low-dimensional space that preserves the topology information of the network. Network embedding has been widely used in a variety of tasks, such as social recommendation and community detection [5,17,19]. Early methods, such as Laplacian Eigenmaps [2] and Local Linear Embedding (LLE) [18], are hard to be applied to large-scale network representation learning. In recent years, a variety of scalable network embedding models have been proposed with the help of deep learning. Among them, Deep-Walk [17], proposed by Perozzi et al., employs random walk to generate node sequences. Then, node sequences are used to approximate node centrality as well as similarity and fed into skip-gram negative sampling model [15] to learn node embeddings. Inspired by this, Grover and Leskovec propose node2vec [5], which combines BFS-like and DFS-like exploration to guide a biased random walk. To take structural similarity into account, Struc2vec [19] leverages random walk on a context graph that enables the node sequences to consider both node proximity and structural similarity. Instead of using a random walk-based model, LINE [20] employs a factorization based model to preserve both the first-order and the second-order proximity. GraRep [3] is proposed to capture high-order proximity. However, these models fail to consider the node attribute information.

2.2   Attributed Information Network Embedding

Attributed information network embedding (AINE) aims to integrate node attribute information and topology information to learn node representations. With the help of node attributes, AINE is promising to be more representative than plain network embedding [25]. TADW [23] employs matrix factorization to combine topological structure and text features of nodes. DANE [4] uses an auto-encoder to capture node attribute information and proposes a strategy to capture the consistency information between topological structure and node attributes. ANRL [25] mainly focuses on the aggregation information of the first-order proximity and node attributes under the help of the neighbor enhancement autoencoder. Recently, graph neural networks (GNNs) [22] are proved to be an effective framework for network representation learning. VGAE [11], proposed by Kipf and Welling, uses a graph convolutional network [12] and an inner product decoder to learn node embeddings in an unsupervised manner. To capture the mutual information between node representations (local information) and graph-level summaries (global information), Velickovic et al. [21] propose a GNN-based model to learn node embedding by applying Deep InfoMax [8] to network data. However, these works fail to analyze the aspect-level information of a network.

3 Aspect-Level Attributed Network Embedding

3.1 Problem Definition

An attributed information network is an undirected graph $\mathcal{G} = (\mathcal{V}, \mathcal{A}, \mathcal{E}^{\mathcal{V}}, \mathcal{E}^{\mathcal{A}})$ with adjacency matrix $\mathbf{A} \in \mathbb{R}^{N \times N}$ and the attribute matrix $\mathbf{X} = \mathbb{R}^{N \times D}$, where $\mathcal{V}$ is node set and $\mathcal{A}$ is attribute set. $N = |\mathcal{V}|$ is number of nodes and $D = |\mathcal{A}|$ is number of attributes. $\mathcal{E}^{\mathcal{V}} \subset \mathcal{V} \times \mathcal{V}$ is the edge set and $\mathcal{E}^{\mathcal{A}} \subset \mathcal{V} \times \mathcal{A}$ is the set of node attributes.

Given an AIN $\mathcal{G} = (\mathcal{V}, \mathcal{A}, \mathcal{E}^{\mathcal{V}}, \mathcal{E}^{\mathcal{A}})$, the goal of attributed network embedding is to learn a mapping function f that maps each node $v_j \in \mathcal{V}$ to a low dimension vector $\mathbf{z}_j \in \mathbb{R}^d$, where d is the embedding size. Moreover, the mapping function f preserves not only network topological structure but also node attribute information. We denote the latent representation matrix for all nodes as $\mathbf{Z} \in \mathbb{R}^{N \times d}$.

3.2 The Architecture of AANE

AANE is a variational model that employs the aspect-level encoder (inference model) to capture the content information and topological structure of complex attributed information networks. We demonstrate the framework of our model in Fig. 2. The details of AANE are described as follows.

Given an AIN, $\mathcal{G} = (\mathcal{V}, \mathcal{A}, \mathcal{E}^{\mathcal{V}}, \mathcal{E}^{\mathcal{A}})$ with adjacency matrix $\mathbf{A}$ and the attribute matrix $\mathbf{X}$, the log-probability of the observed adjacency matrix $\mathbf{A}$ and the attributed matrix $\mathbf{X}$ is defined as follows.

$$\begin{aligned}
\log p(\mathbf{A}, \mathbf{X}) &= \log \int_{\mathbf{Z}} p(\mathbf{A}, \mathbf{X}, \mathbf{Z}) d\mathbf{Z} \\
&= \log \int_{\mathbf{Z}} p(\mathbf{A}, \mathbf{X}, \mathbf{Z}) \frac{q_\phi(\mathbf{Z}|\mathbf{A}, \mathbf{X})}{q_\phi(\mathbf{Z}|\mathbf{A}, \mathbf{X})} d\mathbf{Z} \\
&\geq \mathbb{E}_{q_\phi}[\log(\frac{p_\theta(\mathbf{A}, \mathbf{X}|\mathbf{Z}) p(\mathbf{Z})}{q_\phi(\mathbf{Z}|\mathbf{A}, \mathbf{X})})],
\end{aligned} \tag{1}$$

where $p(\mathbf{Z})$ is the prior distribution of $\mathbf{Z}$ and inference model (encoder) q_ϕ is parameterized by aspect-level encoder, which will be introduced in the following subsection. By assuming $q_\phi(\cdot)$ to be mean-field distribution, we have

402   H. Wang and K. Mu

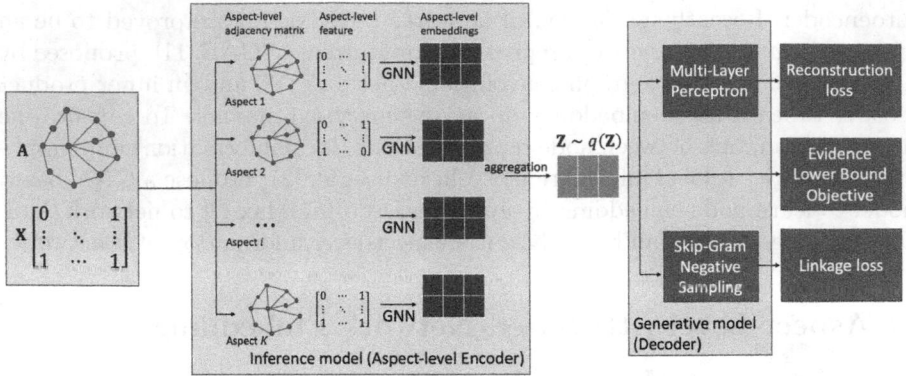

Fig. 2. The framework of AANE. The overall architecture of AANE consists of two components: inference model (aspect-level encoder) and generative model (decoder). The inference model is to capture aspect-level network topological structure and node attributes. The generative model is to preserve network structure and node attributes.

$$q_\phi(\mathbf{Z}|\mathbf{A},\mathbf{X}) = \prod_{j=1}^{N} q_\phi(\mathbf{z}_j|\mathbf{A},\mathbf{X}). \tag{2}$$

As for the generative model (decoder) p_θ, we assume that the linkage information and the content information are independent of each other when conditioned on Z.

$$\log p_\theta(\mathbf{A},\mathbf{X}|\mathbf{Z}) = \log p_\theta(\mathbf{A}|\mathbf{Z}) + \log p_\theta(\mathbf{X}|\mathbf{Z}), \tag{3}$$

where the first term is a reconstruction error for the topological structure of $\mathcal{G}$, while the second term is for the content information of nodes. By substituting the Eq. 2, Eq. 3 into Eq. 1, we have the corresponding evidence lower bound objective (ELBO) as follows.

$$\log p(\mathbf{A},\mathbf{X}) \geq \mathbb{E}_{q_\phi}[\log(p_\theta(\mathbf{A}|\mathbf{Z}))] + \mathbb{E}_{q_\phi}[\log(p_\theta(\mathbf{X}|\mathbf{Z}))] - D_{KL}(q_\phi(\mathbf{Z}|\mathbf{A},\mathbf{X})||p(\mathbf{Z})) \tag{4}$$

where $D_{KL}(\cdot||\cdot)$ denotes the Kullback–Leibler divergence [13]. Following the setting of [10], we let the prior distribution $p(\mathbf{Z})$ to be the centered isotropic multivariate Gaussian, the approximate posterior q_ϕ to be a mutli-variate Gaussian with diagonal co-variance. Then, the last term $D_{KL}(q_\phi(\mathbf{Z}|\mathbf{A},\mathbf{X})||p(\mathbf{Z}))$ in Eq. 4 can have an analytical form.

$$p(\mathbf{Z}) = \mathcal{N}(0,\mathbf{I}) \tag{5}$$

$$q_\phi(\mathbf{z}_j|\mathbf{A},\mathbf{X}) = \mathcal{N}(\boldsymbol{\mu}_{\mathbf{z}_j},\sigma_{\mathbf{z}_j}^2\mathbf{I}) \tag{6}$$

$$D_{KL}(q_\phi(\mathbf{Z}|\mathbf{A},\mathbf{X})||p(\mathbf{Z})) = \frac{1}{2}\sum_{j=1}^{N}((\sigma_{\mathbf{z}_j}^2 + \boldsymbol{\mu}_{\mathbf{z}_j}^2) - \log(\sigma_{\mathbf{z}_j}^2) - 1) \tag{7}$$

Similar to variational auto-encoder, our model is optimized with the reparameterization trick and Stochastic Gradient Variational Bayes (SGVB) algorithm [10].

3.3 Aspect-Level Encoder

In this subsection, we introduce the aspect-level encoder $q_\phi(\mathbf{Z}|\mathbf{A}, \mathbf{X})$ in detail. As discussed earlier, a complex AIN is made up of multi-aspect information. Moreover, both the topological structure and the content information may differ in different aspects. To address this issue, we first get the latent representation of each aspect, then we fuse all the aspect-level representation into the final representation $\mathbf{Z}$.

We design a transform matrix to extract the node feature and topological structure under different aspects. For the i-th aspect, we denote the transform matrix as $\mathbf{M}^{(i)} \in \mathbb{R}^{D_a \times D}$. Here, $\mathbf{M}^{(i)}$ is a learnable matrix and D_a is the dimension of aspect-level node attribute. On the i-th aspect, $\mathbf{M}^{(i)}$ serves as a feature extractor for each node. The i-th aspect-level attributes of node v_j is defined as follows.

$$\mathbf{x}_j^{(i)} = \mathbf{M}^{(i)} \cdot \mathbf{x}_j, i = 1, 2, \cdots, K \tag{8}$$

where $\mathbf{x}_j$ is the original feature of v_j and K is the aspect number. Based on the aspect-level attributes, the aspect-level connection strength between v_j and its neighbor v_k is modeled by an attention mechanism.

$$a_{jk}^{(i)} = \frac{\exp(a(\mathbf{x}_j^{(i)}, \mathbf{x}_k^{(i)}))}{\sum\limits_{k' \in Nei(j)} \exp(a(\mathbf{x}_j^{(i)}, \mathbf{x}_{k'}^{(i)}))} = \frac{\exp(a(\mathbf{M}^{(i)} \cdot \mathbf{x}_j, \mathbf{M}^{(i)} \cdot \mathbf{x}_k))}{\sum\limits_{k' \in Nei(j)} \exp(a(\mathbf{M}^{(i)} \cdot \mathbf{x}_j, \mathbf{M}^{(i)} \cdot \mathbf{x}_{k'}))}, \tag{9}$$

where $Nei(j)$ denotes the set of neighbor nodes of v_j. For $(v_j, v'_k) \notin \mathcal{E}^{\mathcal{V}}$, we set $a_{jk'}^{(i)} = 0$. We use $\mathbf{A}^{(i)} = (a_{jk}^{(i)})_{N \times N}$ to denote the aspect-level adjacency matrix.

To get the aspect-level latent representations, it is important to take both topological structure and content information into account. GNN [22] is a powerful tool to integrate the node feature as well as the topological structure and it has been proved to be effective in network representation learning. Thus, we employ a two-layer graph convolutional network (GCN) to get aspect-level representations. For the i-th aspect with aspect-level feature $\mathbf{X}^{(i)} = \mathbf{M}^{(i)} \cdot \mathbf{X}$ and adjacency matrix $\mathbf{A}^{(i)}$, the two-layer GCN of aspect i is defined as follows.

$$\mathbf{H}_1^{(i)} = \sigma(\tilde{\mathbf{A}}^{(i)} \mathbf{X}^{(i)} \mathbf{W}_0^{(i)}), \tag{10}$$

$$[\boldsymbol{\mu}_{\mathbf{Z}^{(i)}}, \boldsymbol{\sigma}_{\mathbf{Z}^{(i)}}^2] = \sigma(\tilde{\mathbf{A}}^{(i)} \mathbf{H}_1^{(i)} \mathbf{W}_1^{(i)}), \tag{11}$$

where $\boldsymbol{\mu}_{\mathbf{Z}^{(i)}}, \boldsymbol{\sigma}_{\mathbf{Z}^{(i)}}^2$ denote the mean and variance of $\mathbf{Z}^{(i)}$. $\tilde{\mathbf{A}}^{(i)} = (\mathbf{D}^{(i)})^{-\frac{1}{2}} \mathbf{A}^{(i)} (\mathbf{D}^{(i)})^{-\frac{1}{2}}$ is normalized adjacency matrix of $\mathbf{A}^{(i)}$. $\mathbf{D}^{(i)}$ is the diagonal degree matrix of $\mathbf{A}^{(i)}$ and $\mathbf{D}_{ll}^{(i)} = \sum_p \mathbf{A}_{lp}^{(i)}$. $\mathbf{W}_0^{(i)}$ and $\mathbf{W}_1^{(i)}$ are learnable parameters and $\mathbf{H}_1^{(i)}$ is hidden representations of nodes. $\sigma(\cdot)$ is a non-linear activation function, such as $ReLU(\cdot)$ [16] and $tanh(\cdot)$ function. In our experiment, we use $tanh(\cdot)$ function.

Here we assume that $\mathbf{Z}^{(i)}$ are independent of each other and $\mathbf{Z}^{(i)} \sim \mathcal{N}(\boldsymbol{\mu}_{\mathbf{Z}^{(i)}}, \boldsymbol{\sigma}^2_{\mathbf{Z}^{(i)}})$. After obtaining the mean and variance of aspect-level representation $\mathbf{Z}^{(i)}$, we propose two ways to fuse them to get the final representation. The first one is to average all aspects.

$$\mathbf{Z}_{avg} = \frac{1}{K}\sum_{i=1}^{K}\mathbf{Z}^{(i)} \sim \mathcal{N}(\frac{1}{K}\sum_{i=1}^{K}\boldsymbol{\mu}_{\mathbf{Z}^{(i)}}, \frac{1}{K^2}\sum_{i=1}^{K}\boldsymbol{\sigma}^2_{\mathbf{Z}^{(i)}}\mathbf{I}) \tag{12}$$

This method does not distinguish the different importance of each aspect. However, different aspects may have different contributions to the final representation. Attention mechanism [1], which can learn the weight of each aspect, has been proved to be an effective tool in information fusing. We use the attention mechanism to fuse all aspects in a weighted manner. We denote e_i as the attention weight of the i-th aspect. Then, we have

$$\mathbf{Z}_{att} = \sum_{i=1}^{K}e_i\mathbf{Z}^{(i)} \sim \mathcal{N}(\sum_{i=1}^{K}e_i\boldsymbol{\mu}_{\mathbf{Z}^{(i)}}, \sum_{i=1}^{K}e_i^2\boldsymbol{\sigma}^2_{\mathbf{Z}^{(i)}}\mathbf{I}) \tag{13}$$

$$e_i = \frac{\exp(a(\mathbf{Z}^{(i)}))}{\sum_{j=1}^{K}\exp(a(\mathbf{Z}^{(j)}))}, \tag{14}$$

where $a(\cdot)$ is the scoring function, which is a two-layer perceptron in our experiment.

3.4 Decoder

The decoder aims to reconstruct the topological structure and attribute information from the latent representation $\mathbf{Z}$. Here, we assume that the linkage information and the content information are independent of each other when conditioned on Z. Then, we have

$$\log p_\theta(\mathbf{A}, \mathbf{X}|\mathbf{Z}) = \log p_\theta(\mathbf{A}|\mathbf{Z}) + \log p_\theta(\mathbf{X}|\mathbf{Z}). \tag{15}$$

To reconstruct the content information, we use a two-layer perceptron $g(\mathbf{Z})$ to preserve the node attributes.

$$\mathbf{X} \sim \mathcal{N}(g(\mathbf{Z}), \mathbf{I}), \quad g(\mathbf{Z}) = \sigma(\mathbf{W}_{\theta,2}(\sigma(\mathbf{W}_{\theta,1}\mathbf{Z} + b_{\theta,1})) + b_{\theta,2}).$$

To model the topology information, we employ the Skip-Gram Negative Sampling (SGNS) model to capture the linkage information. SGNS model has been widely used in network embedding [5,17,25]. SGNS model assumes that nodes with similar content should have similar latent representations. Given a random walks set RW, we have

$$\log p_\theta(\mathbf{A}|\mathbf{Z}) = \sum_{j=1}^{N}\sum_{r \in RW}\sum_{-j \leq b \leq j, b \neq 0}\log p(v_{j+b}|v_j), \tag{16}$$

where v_{j+b} is the context node of node v_j in the random walk r and b is the window size. The conditional probability $p(v_{j+b}|v_j)$ represents the likelihood of observing the context nodes given the node v_j.

$$p(v_{j+b}|v_j) = \frac{\exp((\mathbf{z}_{j+b})^T \mathbf{z}_j)}{\sum\limits_{v_w \in \mathcal{V}} \exp((\mathbf{z}_w)^T \mathbf{z}_j)}. \tag{17}$$

Similar to DeepWalk [17], $p_\theta(\mathbf{A}|\mathbf{Z})$ is optimized by negative sampling [15]. Thus, the overall objective function of our model is as follows:

$$\begin{aligned}
\mathcal{O} =& \mathbb{E}_{q_\phi}[p_\theta(\mathbf{A}|\mathbf{Z})] + \mathbb{E}_{q_\phi}[p_\theta(\mathbf{X}|\mathbf{Z})] - D_{KL}(q_\phi(\mathbf{Z}|\mathbf{A},\mathbf{X})||p(\mathbf{Z})) \\
=& -\frac{1}{N^2}||\mathbf{X} - g(\mathbf{Z})||_F^2 + \sum_{j=1}^{n} \sum_{r \in RW} \sum_{-j \le b \le j, b \ne 0} \frac{\exp((\mathbf{z}_{j+b})^T \mathbf{z}_j)}{\sum\limits_{v_w \in \mathcal{V}} \exp((\mathbf{z}_w)^T \mathbf{z}_j)} \\
& + \frac{1}{2N} \sum_{j=1}^{N} (1 + \log(\sigma_{\mathbf{z}_j}^2) - (\sigma_{\mathbf{z}_j}^2 + \mu_{\mathbf{z}_j}^2)).
\end{aligned} \tag{18}$$

Furthermore, if the labels of nodes are available, our model can be trained in a supervised manner with a classifier.

$$\mathcal{O}_{sup} = \mathbb{E}_{q_\phi}[p_\theta(\mathbf{A}|\mathbf{Z})] + \mathbb{E}_{q_\phi}[p_\theta(\mathbf{X}|\mathbf{Z})] - D_{KL}(q_\phi(\mathbf{Z}|\mathbf{A},\mathbf{X})||p(\mathbf{Z})) + \sum_{j \in \mathbf{L}} p(\mathbf{z}_j|y_j; \theta_{cls}), \tag{19}$$

where $\mathbf{L}$ is the set of labelled nodes and θ_{cls} is the parameter set of the classifier.

3.5 Applications to Different Types of Networks

Our model can be easily applied to different types of networks. For plain networks without node attributes, we can use the one-hot representation of node ID as node attributes. As for heterogeneous information networks, we can use the node type as node attributes. Moreover, the connection matrix of meta-paths can be employed as the aspect-level adjacency matrix in our model. Signed information networks are an aggregation of positive (friendly) and negative (antagonistic) interactions. Thus, the connection matrix of positive signs and negative signs can be used as aspect-level adjacency matrices in our model. Then, the transform matrices are used to capture aspect-level node attributes. After obtaining the aspect-level adjacency matrix and node attributes, the decoder described in Sect. 3.4 is employed to capture linkage information and content information.

4 Experiments

In this section, we evaluate the performance of AANE on four AIN datasets: Citeseer, Pubmed, Cora, and Wiki[1], and compare it with the state-of-the-art network embedding methods.

4.1 Experiment Settings

Datasets. The statistics of the datasets are summarized in Table 1. Cora, Citeseer and Pubmed are citation networks. Each node in the network represents a scientific publication and edges between nodes represent citation links between publications. The attribute of nodes is the bag-of-words representations or TF-IDF word vectors [14] of the corresponding publication. The publications in datasets are classified into several classes, which are the label information of each node. For instance, publications in the Citeseer dataset are classified into one of the following six groups: Agents, AI, DB, IR, ML, and HCI. Nodes in the Wiki dataset are webpages from 17 categories and edges are hyperlinks between webpages. Node attribute is a TF-IDF vector of web content.

Table 1. Statistics of the datasets and corresponding parameter settings

Datasets	#nodes	#edges	#attributes	#labels	#neurons of decoder	#aspect-level dim
Citeseer	3312	4660	3703	6	200-1000-3703	1000
Cora	2708	5278	1433	7	200-1000-1433	1000
Pubmed	19717	44338	500	3	200-200-500	200
Wiki	2405	12761	4973	17	200-1000-4973	1000

Baselines. To evaluate the performance of AANE, we compare it with several network embedding methods:

Attribute-only

- AE [7] is the auto-encoder model that only takes node attributes as input. The number of hidden neurons is the same as the decoder of AANE.

Structure-only

- DeepWalk (DW) [17] employs random walk to generate node sequences and learns node embeddings by feeding node sequences into Skip-Gram Negative Sampling model. The length of node sequences is set to 80, and the window size is 10.

---

[1] https://linqs.soe.ucsc.edu/data.

- Node2Vec [5] is a variant model of DeepWalk. Different from DeepWalk, Node2Vec combines BFS-like and DFS-like exploration to guide a biased random walk.
- LINE [20] uses a factorization-based model to preserve both the first-order and the second-order proximity.
- GraRep [3] is a factorization-based model that can capture global structural information of the network.

Attribute + Structure

- TADW [23] employs matrix factorization to combine the topological structure and text features of nodes.
- GAE/VGAE [11] learns node embeddings by a graph convolution network encoder and an inner product decoder. VGAE is a variational version of GAE.
- DANE [4] uses two auto-encoders to capture node attribute information and topology information respectively and proposes a strategy to focus on the consistency information between the topological structure and node attributes.
- ANRL [25] leverages the neighbor enhancement auto-encoder to capture the aggregate information of the first-order proximity and node attributes.

AANE-variants

- AANE-AVG averages all aspect-level representations to get the final representation.
- AANE-ATT uses attention mechanism to fuse the aspect-level representations as defined in Eq. 13.

Table 2. Node classification result of Citeseer

Method	10%		30%		50%	
	Micro-F1	Macro-F1	Micro-F1	Macro-F1	Micro-F1	Macro-F1
AE	0.5438	0.5131	0.6373	0.5996	0.6691	0.6156
DW	0.5052	0.4645	0.5783	0.5329	0.5900	0.5486
Node2Vec	0.5233	0.4832	0.6110	0.5651	0.6335	0.5972
GraRep	0.4817	0.4589	0.5511	0.5118	0.5707	0.5048
LINE	0.5139	0.4726	0.5761	0.5384	0.6075	0.5700
TADW	0.6048	0.5344	0.6481	0.5769	0.6578	0.5897
GAE	0.6058	0.5532	0.6550	0.5814	0.6540	0.5808
VGAE	0.6115	0.5662	0.6386	0.5824	0.6443	0.5837
DANE	0.6443	0.6043	0.7137	0.6718	0.7393	0.6965
ANRL	0.6849	0.6322	0.7275	0.6721	0.7279	0.6805
AANE-AVG	0.7098	0.6355	0.7305	0.6754	0.7415	0.6768
AANE-ATT	**0.7132**	**0.6562**	**0.7370**	**0.6844**	**0.7548**	**0.6982**

Parameter Settings. In experiments, the aspect-level feature dimension is set to be 1000. The aspect number is set to be 4. The number of decoder layers is set to be 2. The architecture of decoder is summarized in Table 1. Learning rate and batch size are set to as 10^{-4} and 512. For the skip-gram model, we set the window size as 10, the walk length as 80, the number of walks as 10. At last, the embedding size is set to be 200 for all baselines and AANE. The parameter sensitivity is analysed in Sect. 4.4.

4.2   Node Classification

We conduct experiments on node classification to validate the effectiveness of AANE. After obtaining the node embedding, we use a standard SVM classifier in sklearn with default parameter setting to classify nodes into different classes. To conduct a comprehensive evaluation, we random select {10%, 30%, 50%} nodes as the training set and the rest as the testing set. Similar to previous studies [4, 25], we use Micro-F1 (Mi-F1) and Macro-F1 (Ma-F1) score as evaluation metrics. We repeat this process 10 times and report the average results. The performance of DW, Node2Vec, LINE, GraRep, TADW, GAE/VGAE, and DANE are cited from [4]. The classification results are demonstrated in Table 2, 3, 4, 5, respectively. The best result is boldfaced and the next best is underlined. From these results, we have the following observations:

- "Attribute-only" methods outperform "Structure-only" methods a lot in Wiki as well as Citeseer, and get comparable results in Pubmed. "Structure-only" methods outperform "Attribute-only" methods a lot in Cora. This is because different dataset has different characteristics. For Wiki and Citeseer, node attribute contributes more than topology information, while topology information contributes more to Cora. However, "Attribute+Structure" methods outperform these two methods in most situations. Thus, it is meaningful to take both node attributes and topological structure into account.
- Our model achieves the best performance in most cases. Furthermore, the gain is statistically significant in Citeseer and Cora. The results verify the effectiveness of our proposed model.
- AANE-ATT outperforms AANE-AVG in most situations. This is because attention mechanism has more flexibility to aggregate all aspect-level representations than average them directly.

4.3   Ablation Study

To evaluate the contributions of each component of AANE, we compare it with its four variants to verify the effectiveness of variational auto-encoder, aspect-level encoder, linkage information $p_\theta(\mathbf{A}|\mathbf{Z})$ and content information $p_\theta(\mathbf{X}|\mathbf{Z})$.

   To validate the effectiveness of variational auto-encoder, we remove the variational part of our model and denote this variant as "AANE-var". We replace the aspect-level encoder with a two-layer graph convolutional network to verify

Table 3. Node classification result of Pubmed

Method	10%		30%		50%	
	Micro-F1	Macro-F1	Micro-F1	Macro-F1	Micro-F1	Macro-F1
AE	0.8245	0.8232	0.8395	0.8387	0.8430	0.8419
DW	0.8047	0.7873	0.8168	0.8034	0.8156	0.8034
Node2Vec	0.8027	0.7849	0.8110	0.7965	0.8103	0.7981
GraRep	0.7951	0.7785	0.8031	0.7901	0.8051	0.7937
LINE	0.8037	0.7892	0.8129	0.8007	0.8110	0.7994
TADW	0.8358	0.8343	0.8586	0.8584	0.8643	0.8633
GAE	0.8285	0.8238	0.8263	0.8191	0.8284	0.8203
VGAE	0.8299	0.8240	0.8350	0.8291	0.8361	0.8299
DANE	0.8608	0.8579	0.8731	0.8706	0.8775	0.8749
ANRL	0.8424	0.8422	0.8586	0.8559	0.8424	0.8422
AANE-AVG	<u>0.8696</u>	<u>0.8661</u>	<u>0.8795</u>	<u>0.8764</u>	<u>0.8804</u>	<u>0.8757</u>
AANE-ATT	**0.8716**	**0.8688**	**0.8797**	**0.8765**	**0.8813**	**0.8797**

Table 4. Node classification result of Cora

Method	10%		30%		50%	
	Micro-F1	Macro-F1	Micro-F1	Macro-F1	Micro-F1	Macro-F1
AE	0.6587	0.6146	0.7315	0.7074	0.7563	0.7310
DW	0.7568	0.7498	0.8064	0.7943	0.8287	0.8177
Node2Vec	0.7477	0.7256	0.8201	0.8121	0.8235	0.8162
GraRep	0.7568	0.7441	0.7927	0.7893	0.7999	0.7921
LINE	0.7338	0.7191	0.8122	0.8105	0.8353	0.8254
TADW	0.7510	0.7234	0.8006	0.7801	0.8354	0.8187
GAE	0.7691	0.7573	0.8059	0.7921	0.8095	0.7989
VGAE	0.7888	0.7736	0.8054	0.7909	0.8117	0.7994
DANE	0.7867	0.7748	0.8281	0.8127	0.8502	0.8377
ANRL	0.7806	0.7635	0.8270	0.8148	0.8368	0.8223
AANE-AVG	<u>0.8121</u>	<u>0.8060</u>	**0.8592**	**0.8489**	<u>0.8597</u>	<u>0.8496</u>
AANE-ATT	**0.8228**	**0.8153**	<u>0.8576</u>	<u>0.8457</u>	**0.8604**	**0.8501**

the effectiveness of aspect-level encoder. We mark this model as "AANE-ale". Besides, we remove the reconstruction loss to evaluate the contributions of linkage information and remove the Skip-gram model to evaluate the contributions of content information. We name these two models as "AANE-attr" and "AANE-topo". The result in Citeseer is demonstrated in Table 7. We have the following analyses by observing the results.

Table 5. Node classification result of Wiki

Method	10%		30%		50%	
	Micro-F1	Macro-F1	Micro-F1	Macro-F1	Micro-F1	Macro-F1
AE	0.6656	0.5070	0.6948	0.5535	0.7049	0.5736
DW	0.5621	0.4536	0.6479	0.5267	0.6675	0.5942
Node2Vec	0.5603	0.4131	0.6099	0.4760	0.6376	0.5203
GraRep	0.5801	0.4393	0.6223	0.5143	0.6642	0.5341
LINE	0.5806	0.4634	0.6538	0.5425	0.6766	0.5656
TADW	0.7266	0.6300	0.7565	0.6434	0.7764	0.6519
GAE	0.6245	0.4842	0.6526	0.5038	0.6567	0.5076
VGAE	0.6591	0.5215	0.6817	0.5621	0.7041	0.5790
DANE	<u>0.7293</u>	<u>0.6180</u>	0.7702	**0.6597**	<u>0.7839</u>	<u>0.6838</u>
ANRL	0.6679	0.5362	0.7257	0.6392	0.7340	0.6436
AANE-AVG	0.7207	0.6017	<u>0.7781</u>	0.6478	0.7822	0.6623
AANE-ATT	**0.7370**	**0.6193**	**0.7805**	<u>0.6585</u>	**0.7897**	**0.6973**

- AANE performs better than AANE-var among all settings, validating that AANE learns a more robust embedding with the help of variational auto-encoder. It is worth mentioning that AANE-var still outperforms above baselines among all settings, which demonstrates the effectiveness of our model.
- Aspect-level encoder can improve the performance a lot by comparing AANE with AANE-ale. AANE outperforms AANE-ale 9.54% with 10% labeled nodes in terms of Micro-F1. This is because that the aspect-level encoder can capture the information of different aspects, which makes the embedding more representative (Tables 3, 4 and 5).
- Similar to the previous observation, attribute information contributes more than topology information in Citeseer by comparing the result of AANE-topo with AANE-attr. Moreover, the results demonstrate that our model provides an effective way to take both topology information and attribute information into consideration (Table 6).

Table 6. Description of AANE and its variants

Methods	Variational	Aspect-level encoder	Topological loss	Reconstruction loss
AANE	✓	✓	✓	✓
AANE-var	×	✓	✓	✓
AANE-ale	✓	×	✓	✓
AANE-topo	✓	✓	×	✓
AANE-attr	✓	✓	✓	×

Table 7. Results of AANE and its variants

Method	10%		30%		50%	
	Micro-F1	Marco-F1	Micro-F1	Macro-F1	Micro-F1	Macro-F1
AANE	0.7132	0.6562	0.7370	0.6844	0.7548	0.6982
AANE-var	0.7037	0.6530	0.7119	0.6708	0.7409	0.6889
	−1.33%	−0.49%	−3.41%	−1.99%	−1.84%	−1.33%
AANE-ale	0.6511	0.6154	0.7020	0.6623	0.7289	0.6833
	−8.71%	−6.22%	−4.75%	−3.23%	−3.43%	−2.13%
AANE-topo	0.6733	0.6226	0.7130	0.6644	0.7236	0.6751
	−5.59%	−5.12%	−3.26%	−2.92%	−4.13%	−3.31%
AANE-attr	0.5888	0.5543	0.6596	0.6187	0.6896	0.6488
	−17.44%	−15.53%	−10.50%	−9.60%	−8.64%	−7.08%

4.4 Parameter Sensitivity

In this subsection, we study the parameter sensitivity in AANE for node classification. We evaluate how different sizes of the embedding dimensions, different sizes of the aspect-level dimensions and different values of the aspect number affect the performance, respectively. The results in Citeseer are illustrated in Fig. 3.

Embedding dimensions As illustrated in Fig. 3(a) and 3(d), we vary the embedding size from [25, 50, 100, 200, 400], other hyper-parameters keep the same. From the results, we can see that the trend under different settings is similar. The Macro-F1 score and Micro-F1 score increase at first and decrease when the embedding size increases. Besides, we can find that the performance of our model is comparatively stable when the embedding size range from 100 to 200.

Aspect-level dimensions We vary the aspect-level dimensions from [200, 400, 600, 800, 1000]. The results are demonstrated in Fig. 3(b) and 3(e). It is can be seen that the Macro-F1 score and Micro-F1 score increase as the aspect-level dimensions increase. It will cost more space if we use a larger aspect-level dimension. Thus, there exists a trade-off between the performance and the cost of model training.

Aspect number We vary the aspect number from 2 to 16 and the results are reported in Fig. 3(c) and Fig. 3(f). From the results, we can see that the Macro-F1 score and Micro-F1 score increase as first and decrease when the aspect number increases. The aspect number is suggested to set a range from 2 to 8. Besides, we find that the curves are "unimodal", thus it is easy to find a suitable setting for aspect number by grid searching.

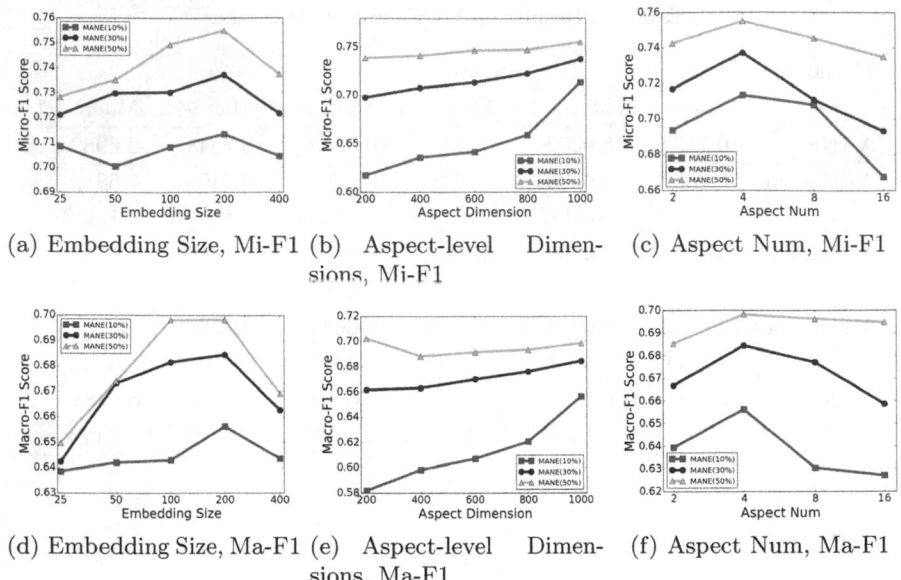

(a) Embedding Size, Mi-F1 (b) Aspect-level Dimensions, Mi-F1 (c) Aspect Num, Mi-F1

(d) Embedding Size, Ma-F1 (e) Aspect-level Dimensions, Ma-F1 (f) Aspect Num, Ma-F1

Fig. 3. Parameter Sensitivity

5 Conclusion

In this paper, we proposed a novel model, called AANE, to learn different aspect-level information of attributed information networks in a variational manner. We designed an aspect-level encoder to capture aspect-level topology information and node attribute information, which achieved sssignificant improvement for unsupervised attributed information network embedding. We employed the skip-gram negative sampling model and multi-layer perceptron to preserve network topology information and node content information. To learn a more robust representation, our model was optimized in a variational manner. Furthermore, our model can be easily applied to different types of networks and can be fine-tuned in a supervised way if the labels are available. Experimental results on four real-world network datasets verified the effectiveness of our model.

Acknowledgements. This work was partly supported by the National Natural Science Foundation of China under Grant No. 61572002, No. 61170300, No. 61690201, and No. 61732001.

References

1. Bahdanau, D., Cho, K., Bengio, Y.: Neural machine translation by jointly learning to align and translate. In: 3rd International Conference on Learning Representations, ICLR 2015 Conference Track Proceedings, San Diego, CA, USA, 7–9 May 2015 (2015)

2. Belkin, M., Niyogi, P.: Laplacian eigenmaps and spectral techniques for embedding and clustering. In: Neural Information Processing Systems: Natural and Synthetic, NIPS 2001, Vancouver, British Columbia, Canada, 3–8 December 2001, pp. 585–591 (2001)

3. Cao, S., Lu, W., Xu, Q.: GraRep: learning graph representations with global structural information. In: Proceedings of the 24th ACM International Conference on Information and Knowledge Management, CIKM 2015, Melbourne, VIC, Australia, 19–23 October 2015, pp. 891–900 (2015)

4. Gao, H., Huang, H.: Deep attributed network embedding. In: Proceedings of the Twenty-Seventh International Joint Conference on Artificial Intelligence, IJCAI 2018, Stockholm, Sweden, 13–19 July 2018, pp. 3364–3370 (2018)

5. Grover, A., Leskovec, J.: node2vec: scalable feature learning for networks. In: Proceedings of the 22nd ACM SIGKDD International Conference on Knowledge Discovery and Data Mining, San Francisco, CA, USA, 13–17 August 2016, pp. 855–864 (2016)

6. Han, X., Shi, C., Wang, S., Yu, P.S., Song, L.: Aspect-level deep collaborative filtering via heterogeneous information networks. In: Proceedings of the Twenty-Seventh International Joint Conference on Artificial Intelligence, IJCAI 2018, Stockholm, Sweden, 13–19 July 2018, pp. 3393–3399 (2018)

7. Hinton, G.E., Salakhutdinov, R.R.: Reducing the dimensionality of data with neural networks. Science 313(5786), 504–507 (2006)

8. Hjelm, R.D., et al.: Learning deep representations by mutual information estimation and maximization. In: 7th International Conference on Learning Representations, ICLR 2019, New Orleans, LA, USA, 6–9 May 2019 (2019)

9. Hu, W., et al.: Pre-training graph neural networks. CoRR abs/1905.12265 (2019)

10. Kingma, D.P., Welling, M.: Auto-encoding variational Bayes. In: 2nd International Conference on Learning Representations, ICLR 2014 Conference Track Proceedings, Banff, AB, Canada, 14–16 April 2014 (2014)

11. Kipf, T.N., Welling, M.: Variational graph auto-encoders. CoRR abs/1611.07308 (2016)

12. Kipf, T.N., Welling, M.: Semi-supervised classification with graph convolutional networks. In: 5th International Conference on Learning Representations, ICLR 2017 Conference Track Proceedings, Toulon, France, 24–26 April 2017 (2017)

13. Kullback, S., Leibler, R.A.: On information and sufficiency. Ann. Math. Stat. 22(1), 79–86 (1951)

14. Leskovec, J., Rajaraman, A., Ullman, J.D.: Mining of Massive Datasets, 2nd edn. Cambridge University Press, Cambridge (2014)

15. Mikolov, T., Sutskever, I., Chen, K., Corrado, G.S., Dean, J.: Distributed representations of words and phrases and their compositionality. In: Advances in Neural Information Processing Systems 26: Proceedings of 27th Annual Conference on Neural Information Processing Systems 2013, Lake Tahoe, Nevada, United States, 5–8 December 2013, pp. 3111–3119 (2013)

16. Nair, V., Hinton, G.E.: Rectified linear units improve restricted Boltzmann machines. In: Proceedings of the 27th International Conference on International Conference on Machine Learning. ICML 2010 (2010)

17. Perozzi, B., Al-Rfou, R., Skiena, S.: DeepWalk: online learning of social representations. In: The 20th ACM SIGKDD International Conference on Knowledge Discovery and Data Mining, KDD 2014, New York, NY, USA, 24–27 August 2014, pp. 701–710 (2014)

18. Polito, M., Perona, P.: Grouping and dimensionality reduction by locally linear embedding. In: Neural Information Processing Systems: Natural and Synthetic, NIPS 2001, Vancouver, British Columbia, Canada, 3–8 December 2001, pp. 1255–1262 (2001)
19. Ribeiro, L.F.R., Saverese, P.H.P., Figueiredo, D.R.: struc2vec: learning node representations from structural identity. In: Proceedings of the 23rd ACM SIGKDD International Conference on Knowledge Discovery and Data Mining, Halifax, NS, Canada, 13–17 August 2017, pp. 385–394 (2017)
20. Tang, J., Qu, M., Wang, M., Zhang, M., Yan, J., Mei, Q.: LINE: large-scale information network embedding. In: Proceedings of the 24th International Conference on World Wide Web, WWW 2015, Florence, Italy, 18–22 May 2015, pp. 1067–1077 (2015)
21. Velickovic, P., Fedus, W., Hamilton, W.L., Liò, P., Bengio, Y., Hjelm, R.D.: Deep graph infomax. In: 7th International Conference on Learning Representations, ICLR 2019, New Orleans, LA, USA, 6–9 May 2019 (2019)
22. Xu, K., Hu, W., Leskovec, J., Jegelka, S.: How powerful are graph neural networks? In: 7th International Conference on Learning Representations, ICLR 2019, New Orleans, LA, USA, 6–9 May 2019 (2019)
23. Yang, C., Liu, Z., Zhao, D., Sun, M., Chang, E.Y.: Network representation learning with rich text information. In: Proceedings of the Twenty-Fourth International Joint Conference on Artificial Intelligence, IJCAI 2015, Buenos Aires, Argentina, 25–31 July 2015. pp. 2111–2117 (2015)
24. Zhang, C., Li, Q., Song, D.: Aspect-based sentiment classification with aspect-specific graph convolutional networks. In: Proceedings of the 2019 Conference on Empirical Methods in Natural Language Processing and the 9th International Joint Conference on Natural Language Processing, EMNLP-IJCNLP 2019, Hong Kong, China, 3–7 November 2019, pp. 4567–4577 (2019)
25. Zhang, Z., et al.: ANRL: attributed network representation learning via deep neural networks. In: Proceedings of the Twenty-Seventh International Joint Conference on Artificial Intelligence, IJCAI 2018, Stockholm, Sweden, 13–19 July 2018, pp. 3155–3161 (2018)

Semantic Region Retrieval from Spatial RDF Data

Dingming Wu[1]($\boxtimes$), Can Hou[1], Erjia Xiao[1], and Christian S. Jensen[2]

[1] College of Computer Science and Software Engineering, Shenzhen University, Shenzhen, China
dingming@szu.edu.cn,
{houcan2017,xiaoerjia}@email.szu.edu.cn
[2] Department of Computer Science, Aalborg University, Aalborg, Denmark
csj@cs.aau.dk

Abstract. The top-k most relevant Semantic Place retrieval (kSP) query on spatial RDF data combines keyword-based and location-based retrieval. The query returns semantic places that are subgraphs rooted at a place entity with an associated location. The relevance to the query keywords of a semantic place is measured by a looseness score that aggregates the graph distances between the place (root) and the occurrences of the keywords in the nodes of the tree. We observe that kSP queries may retrieve semantic places that are spatially close to the query location, but with very low keyword relevance. When any single nearby place has low relevance, returning instead multiple relevant places maybe helpful. Hence, we propose a generalization of semantic place retrieval, namely semantic region (SR) retrieval. An SR query aims to return multiple places that are spatially close to the query location such that each place is relevant to one or more query keywords. An algorithm and optimization techniques are proposed for the efficient processing of SR queries. Extensive empirical studies with two real datasets offer insight into the performance of the proposals.

Keywords: Semantic region · Spatial RDF data · Query processing

1 Introduction

Large knowledge bases like DBpedia [1] and YAGO [2] typically adopt the Resource Description Framework (RDF) data model, which represents data as collections of (*subject, predicate, object*) triples. Currently, YAGO includes knowledge of more than 10 million entities (persons, organizations, cities, etc.) and contains more than 120 million facts about these entities. The English version of DBpedia describes 4.58 million entities, including 1,445,000 persons,

This work is supported in part by grant No. 2019A1515011721 from Natural Science Foundation of Guangdong, China and the DiCyPS project, funded by Innovation Fund Denmark.

Y. Nah et al. (Eds.): DASFAA 2020, LNCS 12113, pp. 415–431, 2020.
https://doi.org/10.1007/978-3-030-59416-9_25

735,000 places, 411,000 creative works, 241,000 organizations, 251,000 species, and 6,000 diseases.

RDF data is traditionally accessed using a structured query language, like SPARQL [20,25,30]. However, it is not friendly to common users, since query issuers need to understand the language itself and to be aware of the data domain. Hence, SPARQL limits data access mostly to domain experts. This leaves room for a *keyword search* model on RDF data [8,18,27]. This model allows common users to access RDF knowledge bases using ad-hoc keyword queries. RDF data can be modeled as a directed graph with subjects and objects as vertices and predicates as edges. In the keyword search model [18], outgoing edges from subjects that connect to types or literals are removed, and all the keywords in the URIs, types, and literals of such entities are collected to form a document of each vertex. A keyword query retrieves a set of (small) subgraphs, where the vertices in each subgraph collectively cover all the given keywords.

The recent *top-k relevant Semantic Place retrieval* (kSP) query [29] on spatial RDF data takes a query location and a set of query keywords as parameters and combines keyword-based and location-based retrieval. The query returns k *semantic places* that are subgraphs rooted at place entities that have associated locations. Specifically, a kSP query returns the top-k *Tightest Qualified Semantic Places* (TQSP) according to a scoring function that considers both the spatial distance of a semantic place to the query location and the graph proximity of the occurrences of the query keywords in the RDF graph of a place. A *qualified semantic place* satisfies two conditions: (i) it is a tree rooted at a *place entity* (i.e., a vertex in the RDF graph associated with a spatial location), (ii) the documents associated with the vertices in the tree collectively cover all query keywords. A *looseness* score of a qualified semantic place is an aggregate of the graph distances between the place (root) and the occurrences of the query keywords covered by the nodes of the tree rooted at the place [8,18,27]. The kSP query returns the k places with the smallest *combined looseness and spatial distance* with respect to the query parameters. However, we observe that kSP queries may retrieve places that are spatially close to the query, but with poor looseness score, or places that have good looseness score, but far from the query. Consider the example kSP query q in Fig. 1 with keywords "childhood" and "scientific." The top-1 semantic place, shown in Fig. 3, is rooted at p_1. Although p_1 is spatially close to the query location in Fig. 1, the looseness of the semantic place rooted at p_1 is large, i.e., "scientific" is six edges away and "childhood" is eight edges away from p_1, which means that p_1 may not satisfy the user's intent. When a single place cannot satisfy a user's intent, returning instead several relevant places that are close to each other may be helpful. In practice, they can be considered as one place, since users can easily visit them. Take again query q in Fig. 1 with keywords "childhood" and "scientific" as an example. Returning two spatially close places p_2 and p_3 is more helpful than returning p_1. Places p_2 and p_3 collectively satisfy the user's intent, since "childhood" is close to p_2 and "scientific" is close to p_3 on the RDF graph, shown in Fig. 2.

Motivated by the above observation, we propose a generalization of semantic place retrieval called semantic region (SR) retrieval. Specifically, an SR query takes a spatial range and a set of query keywords as arguments and returns the qualified semantic region that minimizes a scoring function. The semantic region is composed of a subgraph $T(r, P)$ connecting a set of places that are in the query spatial range and the so-called keyword-relevant paths of the query keywords. The scoring function considers both the graph proximity of the occurrences of query keywords in the RDF graph to the places and the graph proximity among the places. An SR query aims to retrieve multiple places that are spatially close to the query location such that each place is relevant to one or more the query keywords.

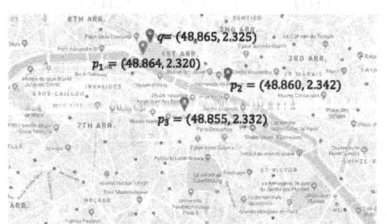

Fig. 1. Map of places in Figs. 2 and 3 and query location.

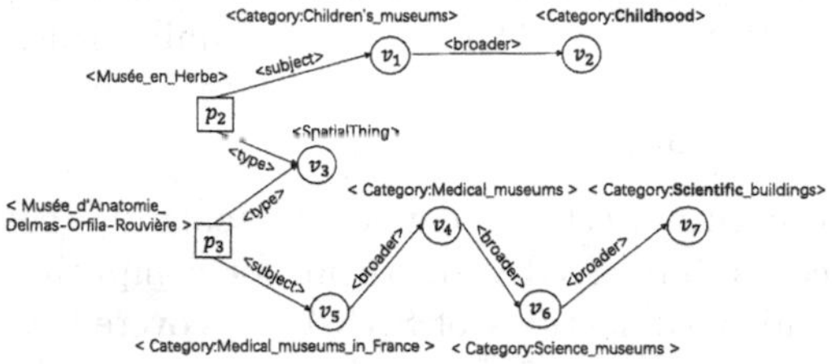

Fig. 2. Semantic region.

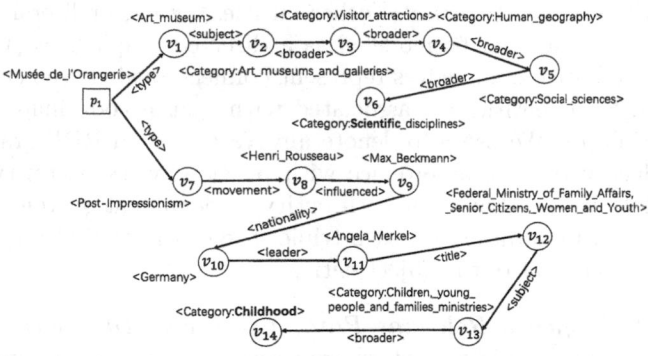

Fig. 3. Semantic place.

A straightforward method to process the SR query is to first find the place set P_0 in the query spatial range and then to enumerate all the subsets of P_0. The next step is to construct the semantic region for each subset of places and to compute its score. The semantic region with the smallest score is returned. However, this method is inefficient, since considering all subsets of P_0 is time consuming and unnecessary. In addition, constructing the semantic region for a subset of places is expensive. It involves finding the graph proximity of the query keywords to each place and computing the graph proximity among the places. We propose the SRRA algorithm for efficiently computing SR queries. A lemma guarantees that the number of places in the semantic region of an SR query cannot exceed the number of query keywords, thus reducing the number of subsets of places to be computed. Also, it first finds a candidate semantic region of the query and derives a lower bound on the scores of un-computed subsets. Then, the subsets with bound no less than the candidate can be pruned. In addition, a lower bound is derived on the graph proximity among the places. During the process of constructing $T(r, P)$, this bound is used to prune unpromising semantic regions. To further improve the performance of the SRRA algorithm, two additional pruning rules are proposed. The SRRA algorithm first considers subsets of places of size 2 and then expands small subsets to larger subsets by adding places. The proposed pruning rules use the places already in the processed subsets to prune the places to be added, so that more subsets of places can be pruned.

Outline. Section 2 defines the semantic region retrieval query and relevant concepts. The SRRA algorithm for computing SR queries is presented in Sect. 3, and optimizations of SRRA are covered in Sect. 4. Our empirical study is the subject of Sect. 5. Related work is reviewed in Sect. 6, and we conclude in Sect. 7.

2 Problem Definition

An RDF data set is a collection of (*subject, predicate, object*) triples, where *subjects* are entities linked to *objects* (other entities, types, or literals) via *predicates*. Such a data set can be modeled as a directed graph $G = (V, E)$, where vertices refer to entities, and edges represent connections between entities based on *predicates*. Some entities are associated with spatial coordinates λ. We call such entities places. We use v to denote any vertex in an RDF graph, while p denotes a place vertex. In accordance with previous work on querying spatial RDF data [29], we construct, for each entity, a document ψ from the entity's URI and literals. In addition, for each triple, the description of the predicate is added to the document of the object entity.

Definition 1 *Keyword-Relevant Path.* *Given an RDF graph $G = (V, E)$, a keyword w, and a place p, a w-relevant path of p is a path with the fewest edges from p to a vertex whose document contains w. Formally, let $\gamma(p, v)$ be the shortest path from place p to vertex v, and let $d(p, v)$ be the length (number of edges) of $\gamma(p, v)$. Let $V(w)$ be the set of vertices whose documents contain keyword w. A w-relevant path of p is defined as $\Gamma_w(p) = \gamma(p, v^*)$, where $v^* = \arg\min_{v \in V(w)} d(p, v)$.*

Definition 2 *Keyword-Distance of a Place.* *In an RDF graph $G = (V, E)$, the distance between a place p and a keyword w, denoted by $d_g(p, w)$, is the number of edges in $\Gamma_w(p)$ (a w-relevant path of p).*

According to Definitions 1 and 2, a place p is relevant to a keyword w (denoted as $p \sim w$) if it is connected to a vertex whose document contains the keyword. A small keyword-distance of a place indicates that this place is relevant to the keyword. If no documents of any of the vertices connected to a place p (including the document of p itself) contain keyword w, the keyword-distance $d_g(p, w)$ is undefined. In this case, place p is irrelevant to keyword w.

Definition 3 *Keyword-Distance of a set of Places*. *In an RDF graph $G = (V, E)$, the distance between a keyword w and a set of places P is defined as $d_g(P, w) = \min_{p \in P} d_g(p, w)$.*

Example 1. Figure 4 shows an example RDF graph. Figure 5 shows (part of) the documents attached to the vertices in Fig. 4. Considering keyword w_3, there are two paths from p_2 to the vertices (i.e., v_1 and v_6) whose documents contain w_3. The w_3-relevant path of p_2 is the shorter path, i.e., $\Gamma_{w_3}(p_2) = p_2 \rightarrow v_5 \rightarrow v_6$. The distance between p_2 and w_3 is $d_g(p_2, w_3) = 2$. Similarly, the w_3-relevant path of p_1 is $\Gamma_{w_3}(p_1) = p_1 \rightarrow v_3 \rightarrow v_2 \rightarrow v_1$. The distance between p_1 and w_3 is $d_g(p_1, w_3) = 3$. Consider the set of places $P = \{p_1, p_2\}$. The distance between w_3 and P is $d_g(P, w_3) = 2$.

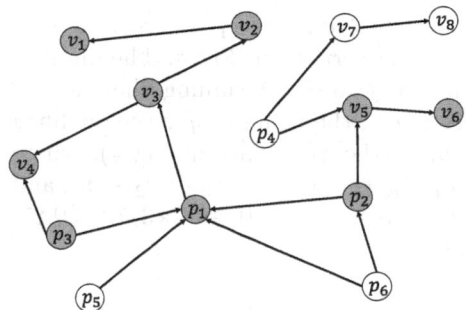

Vertices	Document
v_1	w_2, w_3, w_5
v_4	w_1, w_4, w_5
v_6	w_3, w_6
v_8	w_1, w_5, w_6

Fig. 4. RDF graph.   **Fig. 5.** Documents.

A *semantic region* $R(P) = (T(r, P), \{\Gamma_w(p) \mid p \in P\})$ is a connected subgraph of the RDF graph. It consists of a tree $T(r, P)$ with root r and the places in P as leaves, and the keyword-relevant paths of the places in P. A special case is a semantic region with only one place, i.e., $|P| = 1$, which is called a semantic place [29]. This paper studies the case where a semantic region contains at least two places, i.e., $|P| > 1$.

A **Semantic Region (SR) retrieval query** q takes two parameters: a spatial range $q.r$ and a keyword set $q.\psi$. Given an SR query q, a qualified semantic region $R(P)$ of q satisfies two properties: (i) all the places in $R(P)$ are in the query spatial range $q.r$, and (ii) for each keyword w in $q.\psi$, there exists a relevant place p in $R(P)$. The qualified semantic region w.r.t. an SR query is formally defined in Definition 4.

Definition 4 Qualified Semantic Region (QSR). *Given an SR query q, a qualified semantic region $R_q(P) = (T(r, P), \{\Gamma_w(p) \mid p \in P, w \in q.\psi\})$ satisfies $\forall p \in P \ (p.\lambda \in q.r) \wedge \forall w \in q.\psi \ \exists p \in P \ (\Gamma_w(p) \neq \emptyset)$.*

Definition 5 Semantic Region Retrieval. *Given an SR query q on an RDF graph G, the result of q is the qualified semantic region $R_q(P) = (T(r, P), \{\Gamma_w(p) \mid p \in P, w \in q.\psi\})$ that minimizes the following scoring function.*

$$f(R_q(P)) = \alpha \cdot \frac{\min(cscore(T(r, P)), L)}{L} + (1 - \alpha) \cdot \frac{\min(kscore(P), L)}{L}$$

$$cscore(T(r, P)) = \sum_{p \in P} d(r, p) \qquad kscore(P) = \max_{w \in q.\psi} d_g(P, w)$$

where L is the maximum allowed number of edges (e.g., $L{=}10$), $cscore(T(r, P))$ is the graph proximity of the places in P, $kscore(P)$ indicates the relevance of the set of places P w.r.t. the query keywords, and parameter α is used to balance the importance of $cscore(T(r, P))$ versus $kscore(P)$.

Given an SR query, if there exist multiple QSRs that minimize the scoring function, the firstly found such QSR is returned as the answer for simplicity.

Example 2. Consider an SR query q with keywords $q.\psi = \{w_1, w_2, w_3\}$. Figure 5 shows (part of) the documents attached to the vertices in Fig. 4. The omitted content does not contain any of the query keywords. Assuming that all the places in Fig. 4 are in the query spatial range $q.r$, the result of q is the qualified semantic region $R_q(P) = (T(r, P), \{\Gamma_w(p)\})$ (the gray part in Fig. 4), where $P = \{p_1, p_2, p_3\}$, $r = p_1$, $\Gamma_{w_1}(p_3) = p_3 \rightarrow v_4$, $\Gamma_{w_2}(p_1) = p_1 \rightarrow v_3 \rightarrow v_2 \rightarrow v_1$, and $\Gamma_{w_3}(p_2) = p_2 \rightarrow v_5 \rightarrow v_6$. Given $\alpha = 0.5$, its score is $0.5 \times 2/10 + 0.5 \times 3/10 = 0.25$, where $cscore(T(r, P)) = 2$ and $kscore(P) = 3$.

3   Semantic Region Retrieval Algorithm

3.1   Data Structures

The semantic region retrieval algorithm (SRRA) uses three main data structures. An R*-tree indexes the locations of all places in the RDF graph. A disk-resident inverted index I indexes the documents of all vertices in the RDF graph. This index consists of two main components: (1) a vocabulary of all distinct terms in the collection of documents and (2) a posting list for each term t in the vocabulary. The posting list for term t is a list of the *ids* of all vertices v whose document ψ contains term t. An additional disk-resident inverted index I^α indexes the α-radius word neighborhoods of all places in the RDF graph [29]. The α-radius word neighborhood $WN(p)$ of a place p contains the set of word-distance pairs $\{(w_i, d_g(p, w_i))\}$, where the shortest graph distance from p to w_i is no larger than α, i.e., $d_g(p, w_i) \leq \alpha$.

Algorithm 1. SRRA(q, *Rtree*, G, I, I^α)

1: **for each** keyword w_i in $q.\psi$ **do**
2:     Load posting list pl_i of w_i from I
3:     Load posting list pl_i^α of w_i from I^α
4: $P_0 \leftarrow$ *Rtree.RangeQuery*($q.r$)
5: **for each** keyword w in $q.\psi$ **do**
6:     $v \leftarrow \arg_p \min d_g(p, w)$
7:     Add v to P_c
8: Compute $f(R_q(P_c))$
9: $R^c \leftarrow R_q(P_c)$
10: $j \leftarrow 2$
11: **while** $j \leq |q.\psi|$ **do**   ▷ Lemma 1
12:     **if** $\mathcal{P} \leftarrow$ *GenerateCover*(R^c, j) $\neq$ *NULL* **then**
13:         **for each** P_i in $\mathcal{P}$ **do**
14:             Compute $\{\Gamma_w(p) \mid p \in P_i, w \in q.\psi\}$
15:             Compute $T(r, P_i)$ ▷ Lemma 4 is applied for pruning.
16:             Compute $f(R_q(P_i))$
17:             **if** $f(R^c) > f(R_q(P_i))$ **then**
18:                 $R^c \leftarrow R_q(P_i)$
19:     $j{+}{+}$
20: **return** R^c

3.2 Algorithm SRRA

The semantic region retrieved by the *SR* query q is formed by the subset of places in the query spatial range that minimizes the scoring function $f(R_q(P))$. A straightforward way of finding the result is to compute the scores of the qualified semantic regions formed by each subset of the places in the query spatial range. This method is inefficient. First, the number of the subsets of places in the query spatial range may be large; second, constructing the semantic region formed by a set of places P is expensive as it involves computing the keyword-relevant path of each place $\Gamma_w(p)$ for each query keyword and the subgraph $T(r, P)$ that connects all the places in P. Algorithm SRRA tries to reduce the search space in three ways. (i) We show that the number of places in the result region cannot exceed $|q.\psi|$, so SRRA prunes subsets of places larger than $|q.\psi|$. (ii) SRRA first computes a candidate QSR with the best *kscore*(P) using index structure I^α. It also derives bounds on the scores of other subsets of places. Then, subsets with bounds larger than the score of the candidate QSR are pruned. (iii) SRRA derives a lower bound on the *cscore*($T(r, P)$) of the QSRs. During the process of constructing $T(r, P)$, this bound is used for early termination of the computation of unpromising QSRs.

Algorithm 1 shows the pseudo code of SRRA. Given an *SR* query q, it first loads the posting lists $\{pl_i\}$ and $\{pl_i^\alpha\}$ of each query keyword w_i from both I and I^α. Then the places P_0 in the query range $q.r$ are retrieved from the R*-tree via a range query. Next, a candidate QSR R^c is constructed by using the nearest places of each query keyword, i.e., $v \leftarrow \arg_p \min d_g(p, w)$. Ties are broken arbitrarily. Having the candidate QSR R^c, the algorithm tries to find a better QSR in terms of $f(R_q(P))$ from the places in P_0. If one is found, R^c is replaced. In the end, R^c is returned as the answer to query q.

To find a better QSR, algorithm SRRA generates place sets of size j, $j \in [2, |q.\psi|]$, from P_0, since an SR query aims to retrieve a result containing at least two places and at most $|q.\psi|$ places (according to Lemma 1). However, considering all place sets of size j is time consuming. Algorithm SRRA instead calls Algorithm 2 to obtain promising place sets. Algorithm 2 derives a lower bound $kd^B(P^j)$ (Lemma 2) on the keyword distance of each place set and a lower bound $f^B(R_q(P^j))$ (Lemma 3) on the score of the QSR formed by each place set. The place sets $\mathcal{P}$ whose lower bounds on their scores are smaller than the score of the candidate QSR are returned to Algorithm 1 to compute the corresponding QSRs $R_q(P_i)$. To compute the QSR for a set of places P_i, the keyword-relevant path of each place in P_i for each query keyword is calculated using a variant of Dijkstra's Algorithm [29]. Next, $T(r, P)$ is computed using an existing Algorithm [18]. Since $T(r, P)$ is constructed incrementally, Lemma 4 is applied to terminate the computation early if the current QSR cannot obtain a better score than the candidate.

Lemma 1. *The result of an SR query q contains at most $|q.\psi|$ places.*

Proof. Suppose the result $R_q(P)$ of an SR query q contains $|q.\psi| + n$ places, i.e., $|P| = |q.\psi| + n$. Create a subset P' of P in the following way: for each query keyword $w_i \in q.\psi$, let p_i be the place in P having the shortest keyword distance, i.e., $p_i = \arg\min_{p_i \in P} d_g(p, w)$; add p_i to P'. Then, we have $cscore(T(r, P)) > cscore(T(r, P'))$, since $P' \subset P$. Also, by construction, $kscore(P) \geq kscore(P')$. Hence, we obtain $f(R(P)) > f(R(P'))$, which leads to a contradiction. In addition, $|P'| \leq |q.\psi|$. The equality holds when each place added to P' is distinct. This proves the lemma.

Algorithm 2. GENERATECOVER(R^c, j)

1: **for each** P^j **do**
2:     Compute $kd^B(P^j)$
3:     Compute $f^B(R_q(P^j))$ ▷ Pruning Rule 1
4:     **if** $f^B(R_q(P^j)) < f(R^c)$ **then**
5:         Add P^j to $\mathcal{P}$
6: **return** $\mathcal{P}$

Lemma 2. *Given a place set P^j, for each place $p \in P^j$ and for each keyword $w \in q.\psi$, if p does not have the word-distance pair $\{(w, d_g(p, w))\}$ in α-radius word neighborhood $WN(p)$, we set $d_g(p, w) = \alpha + 1$. Otherwise, $d_g(p, w)$ is the value in $WN(p)$. A lower bound on $kscore(P^j)$ is as follows:*

$$kd^B(P^j) = \max_{w \in q.\psi} d_g(P, w) = \max_{w \in q.\psi} \min_{p \in P} d_g(p, w)$$

Proof. For each place $p \in P^j$ and for each keyword $w \in q.\psi$, if p does not have the word-distance pair $\{(w, d_g(p, w))\}$ in α-radius word neighborhood $WN(p)$, it must hold that $d_g(p, w) \geq \alpha + 1$. When computing $kd^B(P^j)$ for such places, $\alpha + 1$ is used instead of their real keyword distances. And $kd^B(P^j)$ is computed based on all real keyword distances. Obviously, $kd^B(P^j) \leq kscore(P^j)$.

Lemma 3. *Given a place set P^j, a lower bound on the score of semantic region $R_q(P^j)$ is as follows:*

$$f^B(R_q(P^j)) = \alpha \cdot \frac{\min(|P^j| - 1, L)}{L} + (1 - \alpha) \cdot \frac{\min(kd^B(P^j), L)}{L}$$

Proof. Given a place set P^j, $cscore(T(r, P))$ takes its minimum value $|P^j| - 1$ when one of the places is the root and all the other places connect to the root via one edge. According to Lemma 2, $kd^B(P^j) \leq kscore(P^j)$. Hence, we obtain $f^B(R_q(P^j)) \leq f(R_q(P^j))$.

Pruning Rule 1. *Given an SR query q, let P be the subset of the places in the query spatial range generated by Algorithm 2. According to Lemma 3, if $f^B(R_q(P)) \geq f(R^c)$, P cannot be the result and is pruned.*

Lemma 4. *Let R^c be the candidate QSR. A lower bound on $cscore(T(r, P))$ is defined as follows (normalization parameter L is ignored for convenience):*

$$cscore^B(P) = \frac{f(R^c) - (1 - \alpha) \cdot kscore(P)}{\alpha}$$

Proof. First, $f(R^c)$ is the score of the candidate QSR. Second, $kscore(P)$ is the keyword distances of the places in P. Then $cscore^B(P)$ is derived according the scoring function using $f(R^c)$ and $kscore(P)$, which is the worst allowed value for $R(P)$ to become the result.

Example 3. Consider the SR query q with keywords $q.\psi = \{w_1, w_2, w_3\}$ in the running example in Fig. 4 and 5, assuming that all the places are in the query range $q.r$, i.e., $P_0 = \{p_1, p_2, \cdots, p_6\}$. Inverted index I^α contains the α-radius word neighborhood of all the places. The candidate QSR R^c is formed by place set $P_c = \{p_1, p_2, p_3\}$, and $f(R_q(P_c)) = 0.5 \times 2/10 + 0.5 \times 3/10 = 0.25$, where $\alpha = 0.5$, $cscore(T(r, P_c)) = 2$ and $kscore(P_c) = 3$. Consider place set $P = \{p_2, p_3, p_4\}$. Here, $kd^B(P) = \max\{1, 4, 2\} = 4$, and $f^B(R_q(P)) = 0.5 \times 2/10 + 0.5 \times 4/10 = 0.3 > f(R_q(P_c))$. According to Pruning Rule 1, set P cannot be the result and is pruned.

4   Optimization

In order to find the subset of places in the query spatial range of an SR query q that minimizes the scoring function, algorithm SRRA generates place sets of size j, $j \in [2, |q.\psi|]$. For each generated place set, it is expensive to compute the corresponding semantic region. Although algorithm SRRA uses a candidate QSR to prune some subsets of places, many subsets still have to be computed when the number of query keywords is large. Next, we propose two pruning techniques to further prune subsets of places that cannot be the result. The correctness of the pruning rules are guaranteed by Lemmas 5 and 6.

Definition 6. *Place p_i is dominated by place p_j with respect to keyword set ψ, denoted by $p_j \preceq_\psi p_i$, if $\forall w \in \psi \, (d_g(p_j, w) \le d_g(p_i, w))$.*

Lemma 5. *Given an SR query q, let P_1 and P_2 be subsets of places in the query spatial range, and let $P_1 \subset P_2$. If $\forall p \in P_2 \setminus P_1 \, \exists p_0 \in P_1 \, (p_0 \preceq_\psi p)$ then $f(R_q(P_1)) \le f(R_q(P_2))$.*

Proof. Since $P_1 \subset P_2$ and $\forall p \in P_2 \setminus P_1 \, \exists p_0 \in P_1 \, (p_0 \preceq_\psi p)$, we have $kscore(P_1) \le kscore(P_2)$. Because $P_1 \subset P_2$, we have $cscore(T(r, P_1)) \le cscore(T(r, P_2))$. This proves that $f(R_q(P_1)) \le f(R_q(P_2))$.

Pruning Rule 2. *Given an SR query q, let P be the subset of the places in the query spatial range generated by Algorithm 2. Let $\mathcal{P}$ contain all the sets of places in the query spatial range and $\forall P_i \in \mathcal{P} \, (P \subseteq P_i)$. If $\forall p \in P_i \setminus P \, \exists p_0 \in P \, (p_0 \preceq_\psi p)$, according to Lemma 5, $R_q(P_i)$ cannot have a better score than $R_q(P)$ and can be pruned.*

Example 4. Consider the RDF graph in Fig. 4. Given $\psi = \{w_1, w_2, w_3\}$, let $P_1 = \{p_1, p_2\}$ and $P_2 = \{p_1, p_2, p_5\}$. According to Definition 6, $p_1 \preceq_\psi p_5$, since $\forall w \in \psi \, d_g(p_1, w) \le d_g(p_5, w)$. According to Pruning Rule 2, P_2 can be pruned.

Definition 7. *Place p_i is dominated by a set of places P with respect to a keyword set ψ, denoted by $P \preceq_\psi p_i$, if $\forall w \in \psi \, \exists p_j \in P \, (d_g(p_j, w) \le d_g(p_i, w))$.*

Lemma 6. *Given an SR query q, let P_1 and P_2 be subsets of places in the query range, and let $P_1 \subset P_2$. If $\forall p \in P_2 \setminus P_1 \, \exists P' \subseteq P_1 \, (P' \preceq_\psi p)$, $f(R_q(P_1)) \le f(R_q(P_2))$.*

Proof. Since $P_1 \subset P_2$ and $\forall p \in P_2 \setminus P_1 \, \exists P' \subseteq P_1 \, (P' \preceq_\psi p)$, we have $kscore(P_1) \le kscore(P_2)$. Because $P_1 \subset P_2$, we have $cscore(T(r, P_1)) \le cscore(T(r, P_2))$. This proves that $f(R_q(P_1)) \le f(R_q(P_2))$.

Pruning Rule 3. *Given an SR query q, let P be the subset of the places in the query spatial range generated by Algorithm 2. Let $\mathcal{P}$ contain all the sets of places in the query spatial range, and let $\forall P_i \in \mathcal{P} \, (P \subseteq P_i)$. If $\forall p \in P_i \setminus P \, \exists P' \subseteq P \, (P' \preceq_\psi p)$, according to Lemma 6, $R_q(P_i)$ cannot have a better score than $R_q(P)$ and can be pruned.*

Example 5. Consider the RDF graph in Fig. 4. Given $\psi = \{w_1, w_2, w_3\}$, let $P_1 = \{p_1, p_2\}$ and $P_2 = \{p_1, p_2, p_6\}$. According to Definition 7, $P_1 \preceq_\psi p_6$, since $d_g(p_1, w_1) < d_g(p_6, w_1)$, $d_g(p_1, w_2) < d_g(p_6, w_2)$, and $d_g(p_2, w_3) < d_g(p_6, w_3)$. According to Pruning Rule 3, P_2 can be pruned.

5   Empirical Study

This section evaluates the performance of the SRRA algorithm (proposed in Sect. 3) and of SRRA*, which is the SRRA algorithm combined with the optimization techniques presented in Sect. 4.

5.1   Data and Queries

The data used in our experiments are from DBpedia and Yago (version 2.5). DBpedia's directed RDF graph contains 8,099,955 vertices and 72,193,833 edges, and the dictionary contains 2,927,026 unique words. The documents of all vertices are organized by an inverted index. The average posting list length is 56.46, which means that a word appears on average in the documents of 56.46 vertices in the graph. Among all vertices, 883,665 are places with coordinates. Yago's directed RDF graph has 8,091,179 vertices and 50,415,307 edges, and its dictionary contains 3,778,457 distinct words. The documents of all vertices are organized by an inverted index with average posting list 7.83. A total of 4,774,796 vertices are places with coordinates.

Generating SR queries at random reduces the probability of obtaining any results. To generate more meaningful SR queries, we follow the spatial and keyword distribution of the datasets. For each generated query, its spatial range is a rectangle centered at a point location selected at random from the data. Since the SR query aims to retrieve a semantic region rather than a semantic place, we avoid using keywords that are close to a single place. Specifically, query keywords are generated in the following way. We randomly select a vertex p with low degree[1] from the RDF graph, and we randomly select a keyword from its document. We randomly choose up to $|q.\psi|$ vertices and randomly extract $|q.\psi|$ keywords from the distinct words in the documents of these vertices.

5.2   Setup

The query processing time is evaluated when varying the number of query keywords $|q.\psi|$, α in the scoring function, and the size of the query spatial range $q.r$. We vary one parameter while keeping the others fixed. Table 1 lists the values of the parameters. The values in bold are the (fixed) default values. For each setting, we run 100 queries and measure the average runtime. To evaluate the effectiveness of the proposed techniques, the computations on graph are also reported, including the times of constructing subgraphs connecting places and the times of computing the keyword-relevant paths. All methods were implemented in Java and evaluated on 3.4 GHz quad-core machine running Ubuntu 12.04 with 16 GBytes memory. For both datasets, the RDF graph is assumed to be memory-resident. Although the inverted indexes used can also fit in main memory, we choose to follow the setting of commercial search engines, where the inverted index is disk-resident. This is reasonable because for each query,

---

[1] Vertices with degree less than 12 on Yago and less than 20 on DBpedia.

Table 1. Parameter settings.

Parameter	Values
$|q.\psi|$	2, **3**, 4, 5
α	0.1, 0.3, **0.5**, 0.7, 0.9
$|q.r|$	$625\,\mathrm{km}^2$, $\mathbf{784}\,\mathbf{km^2}$, $900\,\mathrm{km}^2$, $1600\,\mathrm{km}^2$

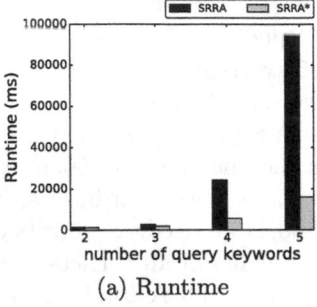

(a) Runtime

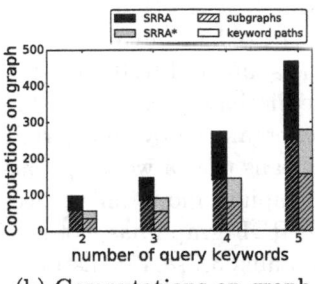

(b) Computations on graph

Fig. 6. Varying the number of query keywords (Yago).

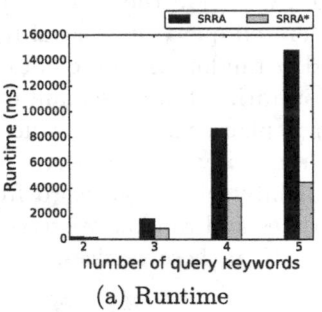

(a) Runtime

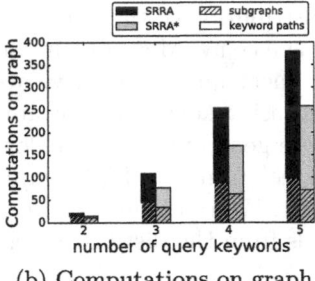

(b) Computations on graph

Fig. 7. Varying the number of query keywords (DBpedia).

only a small portion of the inverted index is relevant and needs be kept in main memory. In addition, such a design is scalable when more textual data is added to an RDF knowledge base.

5.3 Performance Evaluation

Varying the Number of Query Keywords. Figures 6 and 7 show the cost of both SRRA and SRRA* on datasets Yago and DBpedia, respectively. As expected, the runtime and the computations on graph increase as the number of keywords increases, since more RDF graph vertices need to be explored to discover QSRs covering all the query keywords. SRRA* is significantly faster than SRRA, and the performance gap widens with the number of keywords. For both algorithms, the cost of constructing QSRs dominates the runtime. SRRA* is more efficient than SRRA, confirming the effectiveness of the pruning techniques proposed in Sect. 4.

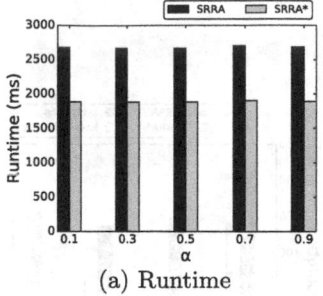
(a) Runtime

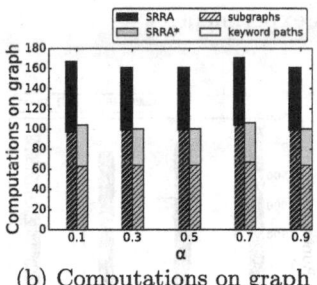
(b) Computations on graph

Fig. 8. Varying α (Yago).

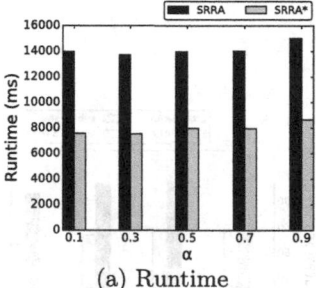
(a) Runtime

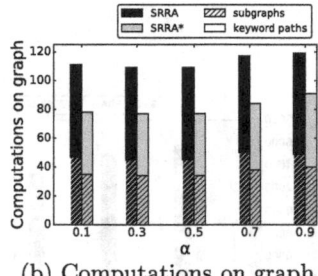
(b) Computations on graph

Fig. 9. Varying α (DBpedia).

Varying α. Figures 8 and 9 shows the performance of SRRA and SRRA* on Yago and DBpedia when varying α in the scoring function. Large α favor semantic regions where places are closely connected, while small α favor semantic regions where places are close to the query keywords. On both datasets, the performance of the two algorithms are not sensitive to α. The runtime is strongly correlated with the computations on graph. SRRA* outperforms SRRA consistently for all values of α.

Varying the Size of the Query Spatial Range. Figures 10 and 11 show the computational costs of SRRA and SRRA* on the two datasets. As the size of query spatial range increases, the costs of the algorithms slightly decreases. Intuitively, if the query spatial range is large, a lot of places are involved in the computation, so that the computational cost is expected to be high. However, we observe from the datasets that a large query spatial range tends to find the semantic region with more places and each place has short keyword relevant path, so that the derived bound on the score is small which is able to prune more sets of places. The amount of computations on graph in Figs. 10b and 11b is the evidence of this observation. Again, SRRA* is more efficient than SRRA in this experiment.

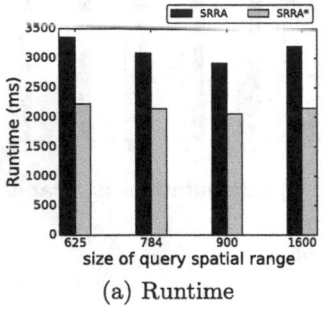

(a) Runtime

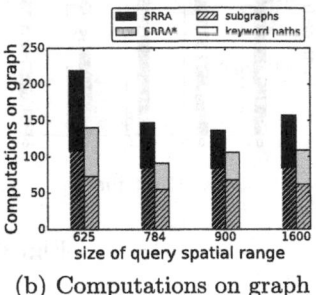

(b) Computations on graph

Fig. 10. Varying the size of the query spatial range (Yago).

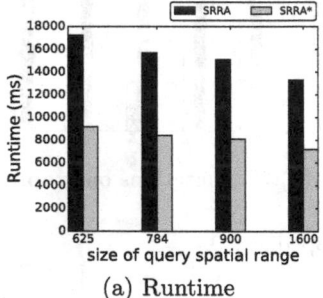

(a) Runtime

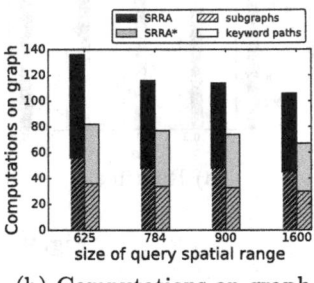

(b) Computations on graph

Fig. 11. Varying the size of the query spatial range (DBpedia).

6   Related Work

Keyword Search on Graph Data. Traditional graph search algorithms convert queries into searches in feature spaces, such as paths [26], frequent-patterns [31], and sequences [16], which focus predominantly on the structure of the graph rather than on the semantic content of the graph. However, keyword search over graph data [3,6,7,12,14,15,17] takes both the content and the graph structure into account. These two sources of information improve the overall quality of the results. Moreover, interesting answers that are often difficult to obtain via rigidly-formatted structured queries may be discovered by keyword search. A recent survey covers keyword search on schema graphs (e.g., relational data and XML documents) and schema-free graphs [28]. Keyword-based search is also studied on temporal graphs [22]. Zhong et al. [32] investigate diverse set of most relevant results for a given keyword query on graphs.

Keyword Search on RDF Data. RDF data is traditionally queried using structured query languages, like SPARQL. Due to the advantages of keyword queries over RDF data, SPARQL queries thus have been augmented with keywords for ranked retrieval of RDF data [9]. Elbassuoni et al. study a keyword-based retrieval model over RDF graphs [8] that identifies a set of maximal subgraphs whose vertices contain the query keywords. These subgraphs are ranked based on statistical language models (LMs) [24]. Different from directly searching for keywords on RDF data, Tran et al. [27] first construct a set of k query subgraphs based on the query keywords and then let users choose the appropriate query graph. There are studies focus on the scalable and efficient processing of keyword queries on large RDF graphs [18,27]. These two studies follow the definition of BLINKS [14] for the result subgraphs. Next, k-nearest keyword (k-NK) search on RDF graphs [19] finds the k closest pairs of vertices, (v_i, u_i) that contain two given keywords q and w, respectively. Keyword query interpretation [10] uses a sequence of structured queries to personalize the interpretation of a new query on RDF databases. Personalized keyword search on RDF [11] returns ranked results using the Ranking SVM approach that trains ranking functions based on historical user feedback. Diversified keyword search on RDF graphs [4] finds diversifies results in terms of both the content and the structure of the results. A path-oriented RDF index for keyword search query [5] improves the query processing performance based on associations across RDF paths. A query graph assembly approach [13] converts keyword queries into graph queries. SPARQL and keyword search has been integrated to find SPARQL matches that are closest to all keywords in RDF graphs [23]. Lin et al. [21] translate keyword queries to SPARQL queries using a type-based summary which summarizes all the inter-entity relationships from RDF data.

All these studies concern the querying of general graph and RDF data using keyword-based constraints. Semantic place retrieval [29] from RDF data is the most relevant work, which combines keyword-based and location-based retrieval. The semantic region retrieval studied in this paper is a generalization of semantic place retrieval. It makes up for the shortcomings of semantic place retrieval, addressing the cases where a single place cannot satisfy a users' intent.

7   Conclusion

We propose a novel semantic region retrieval (SR) query that takes as parameters a query spatial range $q.r$ and a set of query keywords $q.\psi$, and returns the qualified semantic region in an RDF graph that minimizes a scoring function. The scoring function takes the graph proximity of the places in the region and the graph proximity of the places w.r.t. the query keywords into account. Compared to existing semantic place retrieval, the SR query targets for the situation when a single place cannot satisfy the users' requirements. It retrieves multiple nearby relevant places. In order to support efficiently processing of SR queries, we propose algorithm SRRA that follows the branch-and bound paradigm. The most expensive part of the algorithm is computing keyword-relevant paths and connected subgraphs that cover sets of places. To improve the performance of SRRA, we propose two pruning rules that are able to reduce the number of computed semantic regions. The proposed techniques are evaluated on DBpedia and Yago, two large real RDF data sets. The results show that applying all techniques enables processing SR queries efficiently.

References

1. Dbpedia. http://wiki.dbpedia.org
2. Yago.   http://www.mpi-inf.mpg.de/departments/databases-and-information-systems/research/yago-naga/yago/
3. Agrawal, S., Chaudhuri, S., Das, G.: DBXplorer: a system for keyword-based search over relational databases. In: ICDE, pp. 5–16 (2002)
4. Bikakis, N., Giannopoulos, G., Liagouris, J., Skoutas, D., Dalamagas, T., Sellis, T.: RDivF: diversifying keyword search on RDF graphs. In: Aalberg, T., Papatheodorou, C., Dobreva, M., Tsakonas, G., Farrugia, C.J. (eds.) TPDL 2013. LNCS, vol. 8092, pp. 413–416. Springer, Heidelberg (2013). https://doi.org/10.1007/978-3-642-40501-3_49
5. Cappellari, P., De Virgilio, R., Maccioni, A., Roantree, M.: A path-oriented RDF index for keyword search query processing. In: Hameurlain, A., Liddle, S.W., Schewe, K.-D., Zhou, X. (eds.) DEXA 2011. LNCS, vol. 6861, pp. 366–380. Springer, Heidelberg (2011). https://doi.org/10.1007/978-3-642-23091-2_31
6. Cohen, S., Mamou, J., Kanza, Y., Sagiv, Y.: XSEarch: a semantic search engine for XML. In: VLDB, pp. 45–56 (2003)
7. Dalvi, B.B., Kshirsagar, M., Sudarshan, S.: Keyword search on external memory data graphs. PVLDB 1(1), 1189–1204 (2008)
8. Elbassuoni, S., Blanco, R.: Keyword search over RDF graphs. In: CIKM, pp. 237–242 (2011)
9. Elbassuoni, S., Ramanath, M., Schenkel, R., Weikum, G.: Searching RDF graphs with SPARQL and keywords. IEEE Data Eng. Bull. 33(1), 16–24 (2010)
10. Fu, H., Anyanwu, K.: Effectively interpreting keyword queries on RDF databases with a rear view. In: Aroyo, L., et al. (eds.) ISWC 2011. LNCS, vol. 7031, pp. 193–208. Springer, Heidelberg (2011). https://doi.org/10.1007/978-3-642-25073-6_13
11. Giannopoulos, G., Biliri, E., Sellis, T.: Personalizing keyword search on RDF data. In: Aalberg, T., Papatheodorou, C., Dobreva, M., Tsakonas, G., Farrugia, C.J. (eds.) TPDL 2013. LNCS, vol. 8092, pp. 272–278. Springer, Heidelberg (2013). https://doi.org/10.1007/978-3-642-40501-3_27
12. Guo, L., Shao, F., Botev, C., Shanmugasundaram, J.: XRANK: ranked keyword search over XML documents. In: SIGMOD, pp. 16–27 (2003)
13. Han, S., Zou, L., Yu, J.X., Zhao, D.: Keyword search on RDF graphs - a query graph assembly approach. In: CIKM, pp. 227–236 (2017)

14. He, H., Wang, H., Yang, J., Yu, P.S.: BLINKS: ranked keyword searches on graphs. In: SIGMOD, pp. 305–316 (2007)
15. Hristidis, V., Papakonstantinou, Y.: DISCOVER: keyword search in relational databases. In: VLDB, pp. 670–681 (2002)
16. Jiang, H., Wang, H., Yu, P.S., Zhou, S.: GString: a novel approach for efficient search in graph databases. In: ICDE, pp. 566–575 (2007)
17. Kacholia, V., Pandit, S., Chakrabarti, S., Sudarshan, S., Desai, R., Karambelkar, H.: Bidirectional expansion for keyword search on graph databases. In: VLDB, pp. 505–516 (2005)
18. Le, W., Li, F., Kementsietsidis, A., Duan, S.: Scalable keyword search on large RDF data. TKDE **26**(11), 2774–2788 (2014)
19. Lian, X., Hoyos, E.D., Chebotko, A., Fu, B., Reilly, C.: k-nearest keyword search in RDF graphs. J. Web Semant. **22**, 40–56 (2013)
20. Libkin, L., Reutter, J.L., Soto, A., Vrgoc, D.: TriAL: a navigational algebra for RDF triplestores. ACM Trans. Database Syst. **43**(1), 5:1–5:46 (2018)
21. Lin, X., Ma, Z., Yan, L.: RDF keyword search using a type-based summary. J. Inf. Sci. Eng. **34**(2), 489–504 (2018)
22. Llu, Z., Wang, C., Chen, Y.: Keyword search on temporal graphs, pp. 1807–1808, ICDE (2018)
23. Peng, P., Zou, L., Qin, Z.: Answering top-k query combined keywords and structural queries on RDF graphs. Inf. Syst. **67**, 19–35 (2017)
24. Ponte, J.M., Croft, W.B.: A language modeling approach to information retrieval. In: SIGIR, pp. 275–281 (1998)
25. Prud'Hommeaux, E., Seaborne, A., et al.: SPARQL query language for RDF. W3C recommendation 15 (2008)
26. Shasha, D., Wang, J.T.L., Giugno, R.: Algorithmics and applications of tree and graph searching. In: PODS, pp. 39–52 (2002)
27. Tran, T., Wang, H., Rudolph, S., Cimiano, P.: Top-k exploration of query candidates for efficient keyword search on graph-shaped (RDF) data. In: ICDE, pp. 405–416 (2009)
28. Wang, H., Aggarwal, C.C.: A survey of algorithms for keyword search on graph data. In: Aggarwal, C., Wang, H. (eds.) Managing and Mining Graph Data. Advances in Database Systems, vol. 40, pp. 249–273. Springer, Boston (2010). https://doi.org/10.1007/978-1-4419-6045-0_8
29. Wu, D., Zhou, H., Shi, J., Mamoulis, N.: Top-k relevant semantic place retrieval on spatiotemporal RDF data. VLDB J. **29**(4), 893–917 (2020)
30. Wylot, M., Hauswirth, M., Cudré-Mauroux, P., Sakr, S.: RDF data storage and query processing schemes: a survey. ACM Comput. Surv. **51**(4), 84:1–84:36 (2018)
31. Yan, X., Yu, P.S., Han, J.: Substructure similarity search in graph databases. In: SIGMOD, pp. 766–777 (2005)
32. Zhong, M., Wang, Y., Zhu, Y.: Coverage-oriented diversification of keyword search results on graphs. In: DASFAA, pp. 166–183 (2018)

RE-GCN: Relation Enhanced Graph Convolutional Network for Entity Alignment in Heterogeneous Knowledge Graphs

Jinzhu Yang[1,2], Wei Zhou[1,2(✉)], Lingwei Wei[1,2], Junyu Lin[1], Jizhong Han[1], and Songlin Hu[1,2(✉)]

[1] Institute of Information Engineering, Chinese Academy of Sciences, Beijing 100093, China
{yangjinzhu,zhouwei,weilingwei,linjunyu,hanjizhong,husonglin}@iie.ac.cn
[2] School of Cyber Security, University of Chinese Academy of Sciences, Beijing 100049, China

Abstract. Entity alignment is a fundamental task of matching synonymous entities from different knowledge graphs (KGs). Most of the existing methods perform this task by evaluating the similarity among entity embeddings learned from heterogeneous KGs, where Graph Convolutional Network (GCN) based embedding is widely adopted for capturing complex network structure. However, the semantics and directional information of relations are ignored in previous GCN based efforts, which affect the integrality of embedding definitely and decrease the efficiency consequently. To overcome this shortcoming, this paper proposes a Relation-Enhanced Graph Convolutional Network (RE-GCN) method for entity alignment including two stages. First, to take advantage of the semantics of the relations, a novel triadic graph is designed to integrate relation nodes into the primal graph by using triadic closure. In a triadic graph, both relations and entities nodes could be organized in a unified network. The corresponding triadic graph convolution is utilized together with the primal one to learn the relation and entity embeddings, simultaneously. Second, in order to make use of direction information of the relations, a bidirectional context aggregation mechanism is proposed to aggregate the embeddings from the first stage. The final aggregation embeddings are utilized for entity alignment. On three real-world multilingual datasets, experimental results demonstrate that RE-GCN produces a more excellent performance compared with some state-of-the-art entity alignment methods.

Keywords: Entity alignment · Relation enhanced · Graph Convolutional Network · Heterogeneous knowledge graphs

© Springer Nature Switzerland AG 2020
Y. Nah et al. (Eds.): DASFAA 2020, LNCS 12113, pp. 432–447, 2020.
https://doi.org/10.1007/978-3-030-59416-9_26

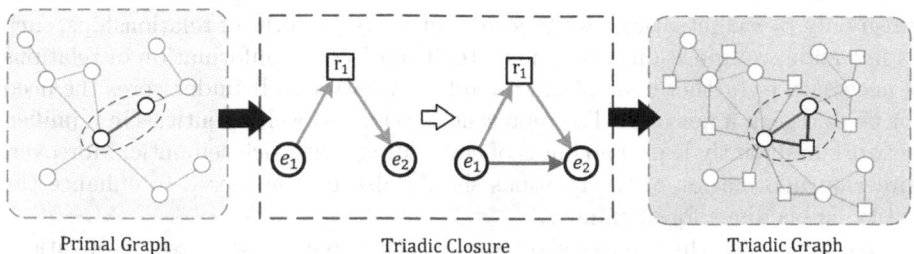

Primal Graph   Triadic Closure   Triadic Graph

Fig. 1. The primal graph is an unweighted and undirected network and preserves the equivalent relations between entities. The triadic graph is derived from a primal graph to preserve structure information between entities and relations. The relations in KGs are added in the triadic graph as vertices, and the interaction is constructed between entities and relations from triadic closure. Over the course of triadic closure, the formation of closure edge makes the open triad become a closed triad.

1 Introduction

Knowledge graphs (KGs), with a massive set of machine-readable entity-relation triples, have become an important resource for many knowledge-driven applications in areas like question answering, semantic search and recommender systems, etc. In reality, most of the existing KGs are constructed separately (e.g., YAGO [16] and DBpedia [1]), or even in different languages. These KGs inevitably contain heterogeneous but semantically consistent knowledge. That is the main reason why heterogeneous KGs integration draws extensive attention in recent years.

Many efforts have been devoted to integrating KGs by aligning entities, which work on knowledge representation learning to bridge the language gap among multilingual KGs. Traditional researches [3,7,28] mainly adopt machine translation techniques to learn entity representations. However, the translation based models are constrained by the strong assumption *head entity + relation ≈ tail entity*, resulting in a low efficiency for capturing the complex structure information [22]. Most recently, several approaches [10,21] are proposed to utilize Graph Convolutional Network (GCN) to embed KG entities from a graph perspective, which broadly follows a recursive neighborhood aggregation scheme to capture the structural information within the neighborhood. Nevertheless, since the vanilla GCN operates on the unweighted and undirected graphs, the useful relation semantic and direction information of multi-relational KGs would be ignored. Although several variants of GCN [13,14,22] tend to consider relation information between entities. They only choose to enable relation-aware weights for different neighbors of an entity.

However, in fact, it is not enough to distinguish between relations only with weights. For instance, the relations in the triples (*Sun Yat_sen, spouse, Soong Ching_ling*) and (*Soong Mei_ling, sister, Soong Ching_ling*) are *'spouse'* and *'sister'*, respectively. As relation *'spouse'* and *'sister'* are both intimate relationship, the semantic differences between the above two relations are arduous to distinguish only by weights. Besides, KGs contain many patterns of relationships, such as inversion, composition, transition, etc. The direction information of relations is necessary to further understand the relation patterns. It underscores the need for us to design a new model to represent relations as well as entities in a unified network and jointly learn two kinds of embeddings with rich semantic. Moreover, direction information of the relations should also be considered to enhance the entity embeddings for alignment.

To overcome the above shortcoming, this paper proposes a Relation-Enhanced Graph Convolutional Network (RE-GCN) method for entity alignment, including two stages. On the one hand, in order to enable relation embedding as well as entity one, the triadic closure is utilized to extend the primal graph to a novel triadic graph. Both the primal graph convolution and the corresponding triadic convolution are formulated to learn entity and relation embeddings, simultaneously. As shown in Fig. 1, the primal graph [13] only preserves connection structure among entities, where vertices denote entities and relations are only treated as equivalent connecting edges. The triadic graph preserves interaction structure among entities and relations, which is constructed from the course of triadic closure to add relations as extended vertices to the primal graph. In the triadic graph, the triple facts in KGs are organized as a triadic closure, which increases the strength and the stability of the tie between triples [15]. On the other hand, in order to further capture the directional interactions among entities, both input and output contextual information of a focal entity are considered for embedding. Specifically, the head entities and relations of a focal entity are regarded as its input context. At the same time, the tail entities and relations of a focal entity are regarded as its output context. Accordingly, a bidirectional context aggregation(BCA) mechanism is proposed to aggregate the directional interactions from two individual neighborhood sub-graphs information for entity alignment.

The main contributions are summarized as follows:

- A novel knowledge embedding model RE-GCN is presented to represent relations as well as entities, simultaneously, where a multiple structural graph convolution driven by a triadic graph and primal graph is integrated.
- A bidirectional context aggregation mechanism is designed to learn entity embeddings for alignment with the awareness of both relation semantic and direction.
- On three real-world multilingual datasets, experimental results demonstrate that RE-GCN produces a more excellent performance compared with some state-of-the-art entity alignment methods.

The rest of this paper is organized as follows. We review related works briefly in Sect. 2. In Sect. 3, we formally define the problem of entity alignment in multilingual KGs and some essential notions. The proposed RE-GCN will be described in Sect. 4. In Sect. 5, extensive results are presented on three real-world multilingual datasets to evaluate the effectiveness and efficiency of RE-GCN. Finally, we conclude the paper in Sect. 6.

2 Related Work

2.1 Knowledge Alignment

Conventional knowledge alignment methods usually require well-designed hand-crafted features [12] in different knowledge graphs. Due to the complexity of the alignment problem, the embedding of the above single view feature is insufficient to align two KGs. [26,27] learned representations of entities in KGs from multi-view features and brought a big boost to the hit precision of alignment. However, such methods rely on knowledge graphs providing sufficient multi-granularity features, which is usually expensive to obtain. Inspired by the study of knowledge represent learning [2,20], many embedding-based methods have proposed to model known aligned triple facts for multilingual knowledge graphs alignment [3,7,8]. Based on these methods, [28] used the newly-labeled alignment in an incremental manner and leveraged it to guide the subsequent training iteratively. In order to tackle the problem of error propagation in [28], [18] proposed improvements mechanism by checking the newly-labeled alignment roll back to the unlabeled state. Apart from this, the method represented by [17] combined embedding-based models with entity features to align the knowledge graphs. [29] regarded that the neighborhood sub-graph knowledge of entities that implies more richer alignment information for aligning entities. They considered neighborhood information of focal entities with translation based embeddings and have achieved promising results. In this paper, we explicitly aggregate neighborhood contextual information through a BCA mechanism with the awareness of both relation semantic and direction.

2.2 Graph Convolutional Networks

Recently, there has been a surge of interest in Graph Conventional Network (GCN). GCN and its variants belong to a family of graph message passing architectures where each node aggregates feature vectors of its neighbors to compute its new feature vector recursively [23]. Since the vanilla GCN operates on the unweighted and undirected graphs, many researches [13,14,22] tend to consider relation information to enhance the integrality of embeddings in multi-relational networks. Recently, Graph Attention Networks have aggregated neighborhood information according to trainable attention weights [19], which achieve state-of-the-art performance on many fundamental tasks. GCN has recently been practiced with a variety of successful applications [4,25]. Since the graph representation learning models GCN can naturally be embedded with node features, [21] brought the GCN to the knowledge graphs alignment for the first time, they indicated the neighbor-aware contextual information of an entity in the KG is crucial to the KG alignment task. GMNN [24] formulated the entity alignment problem as a graph matching problem. They roughly matched the sub-graphs of focal entities and failed to capture relation information in the neighborhood sub-graph structure. RDGCN [22] has recently proposed to model relation information for entity alignment in multi-relational KGs. They pre-incorporated entity features with relation information to fed into the GCN with high way gates mechanism. Their method only enabled specific weights to aggregate neighbor entities and did not explicitly formulate the semantic representations for the relations. Therefore, this paper proposes a novel RE-GCN to study the entity and relation embeddings simultaneously.

3 Preliminaries

Knowledge in a typical KG is usually organized into triples of (*head entity, relation, tail entity*), also abridged as (*h, r, t*). Let $G = (E, R, T)$ denote the knowledge graph, where E, R, T are the sets of entities, relations and triples respectively. Given two knowledge graphs from different sources or languages as $G_1 = (E_1, R_1, T_1)$ and $G_2 = (E_2, R_2, T_2)$. The task of heterogeneous knowledge alignment is to align synonymous entities cross the two KGs. As a starting point, a small set of synonymous entities among KGs, which have already prior aligned and can be used as training data. We define these synonymous entities as *alignment seeds* $\mathbb{L} = \{(e_{i_1}, e_{i_2})|e_{i_1} \in E_1 \wedge e_{i_2} \in E_2\}$. We study the knowledge alignment problem as automatically identity synonymous entities based on initial *alignment seeds*. With reference to the setting of [28], we assume that all of the alignments between relations are known. For notations, we use the bold lowercase letters to represent vector and bold uppercase letters to matrice. We construct two graph definitions to learn the representations of entities and relations in the KGs organized as follows:

3.1 Primal Graph

A primal graph is defined as $\mathcal{G}_p = \langle \mathcal{V}_p, \mathcal{E}_p \rangle$, which is an unweighted and undirected network among entities, where $\mathcal{V}_p = \{e \,|e \in E\}$ represents the set of vertices and $\mathcal{E}_p = \{r \,|r \in R\}$ represents the set of edges. The primal graph preserves the equivalent connection structure between entities.

3.2 Triadic Graph

In order to model relation information properly, we regard both relations and entities as vertices in a triadic graph. We introduce the triadic graph as $\mathcal{G}_t = (\mathcal{V}_t, \mathcal{E}_t)$, which is derived from the primal graph $\mathcal{G}_p$ through the course of triadic closure, where $\mathcal{V}_t = \mathcal{V}_p \cup \mathcal{E}_p$ and the path edges $\mathcal{P}$ between the relation node and the entity node are added to construct the $\mathcal{E}_t = \mathcal{E}_p \cup \mathcal{P}$. Take the triple (e_0, r_1, e_1) as an example, we add the path edges $\langle e_1 \rightarrow r_1 \rangle$ and $\langle r_1 \rightarrow e_0 \rangle$ to the triadic graph which preserve the relation fact from e_0 through r_1 to e_1. Then we construct the triadic edge $\langle e_1 \rightarrow e_0 \rangle$ to make the open triad become a closed triad. The triadic graph organizes triple structures in KGs as a triadic closure, which preserves interaction structure among entities and relations.

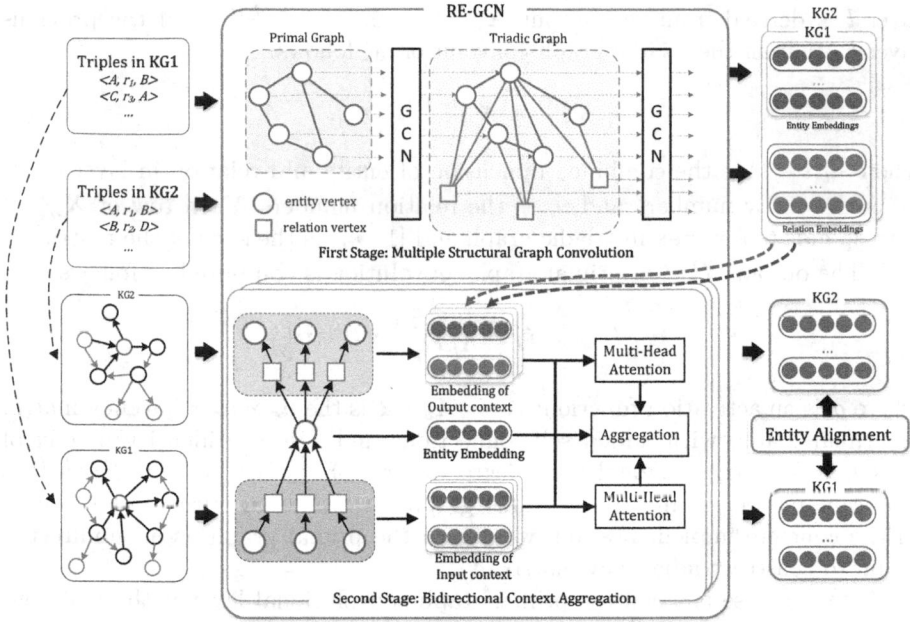

Fig. 2. The overview of RE-GCN model.

4   Methodology

In this section, we describe the proposed RE-GCN method in detail. The overview of RE-GCN model is illustrated in Fig. 2, including two stages. First, RE-GCN jointly studies the embeddings of entities and relations via unifies multiple graph convolution driven by a primal graph and triadic graph. Second, we propose a BCA mechanism to enhance the entity embeddings for alignment via aggregating the contextual information with the awareness of both relation semantic and direction. In this way, we evaluate the similarity of entity aggregation embeddings to align entities cross heterogeneous KGs.

4.1   Multiple Structural Graph Convolution

In order to represent relation as well as the entities, RE-GCN unifies multiple graph convolution driven by a primal graph and triadic graph. Consequently, RE-GCN consists of multiple stacked graph convolutional layers. The node messages are passing in the primal graph and triadic graph alternately to study the entity and relation embeddings, simultaneously.

Primal Graph Convolution. The messages passing of primal graph convolution is in the primal graph iteratively. The input of primal graph convolutional layer l is derived from the output $\boldsymbol{X}_o^{t(l-1)} \in \mathbb{R}^{(n_e+n_r) \times d_t(l-1)}$ of the previous layer $l-1$ from the triadic graph convolution as follows:

$$\boldsymbol{X}_i^{p(l)} = \boldsymbol{X}_o^{t(l-1)}[1:n_e], \tag{1}$$

where $d_t(l-1)$ is the combined dimension of entity and relation in layer $l-1$, n_e is the entity numbers and n_r is the relation numbers. Each row of $\boldsymbol{X}_o^{t(l-1)}$ corresponds to a vertex in triadic graph and $[1:n_e]$ is the slice of the matrix by row. The output $\boldsymbol{X}_o^{p(l)}$ of primal graph convolution is computed as follows:

$$\boldsymbol{X}_o^{p(l)} = \sigma(\hat{\boldsymbol{D}}_p^{-\frac{1}{2}} \hat{\boldsymbol{A}}_p \hat{\boldsymbol{D}}_p^{-\frac{1}{2}} \boldsymbol{X}_i^{p(l)} \boldsymbol{W}_p^l), \tag{2}$$

where σ is an activation function; $\hat{\boldsymbol{A}}_p = \boldsymbol{A}_p + \boldsymbol{I}$ is the $n_e \times n_e$ adjacency matrix of primal graph, with added self-connections and $\boldsymbol{I}$ is the identity matrix of $n_e \times n_e$; $\hat{\boldsymbol{D}}_p$ is the diagonal node degree matrix of $\hat{\boldsymbol{A}}_p$; $\boldsymbol{W}_p^l \in \mathbb{R}^{d_t(l-1) \times d_p(l)}$ is the trainable weight matrix of primal graph convolutional layer at the l layer. In the concrete implementation, we regard the primal graph as an undirected graph to construct adjacency matrix $\boldsymbol{A}_p$.

A special case is when the primal graph convolutional layer is the first convolution layer. Let $\boldsymbol{X}_i^{e(0)} \in \mathbb{R}^{n_e \times d_e(0)}$ denote the initial entity representation matrix. In our model, the initial representations of entities are initialized with word embeddings of entity names, which have great potentials for capturing the entity similarity [26].

Triadic Graph Convolution. The messages passing of triadic graph convolution is in the triadic graph. Graph convolution in RE-GCN is alternated between the primal graph convolution layer and triadic graph convolution layer. The input of triadic graph convolutional layer l is derived from the output $\boldsymbol{X}_o^{e(l)} \in \mathbb{R}^{n_e \times d_e(l)}$ of the previous layer l from the primal convolution. $\boldsymbol{X}_i^{t(l)}$ is computed as follows:

$$\boldsymbol{X}_i^{t(l)} = Concat(\boldsymbol{X}_o^{e(l)}; \boldsymbol{X}_o^{t(l-1)}[n_e : n_e + n_r]), \tag{3}$$

where $[n_e : n_e + n_r]$ is the slice of the matrix from row n_e to n_r, $Concat(\cdot ; \cdot)$ is the concatenation of two matrix. The output representations of $\boldsymbol{X}_o^{t(l+1)}$ in triadic graph convolutional layer is defined as follows:

$$\boldsymbol{X}_o^{t(l+1)} = \sigma(\hat{\boldsymbol{D}}_t^{-\frac{1}{2}} \hat{\boldsymbol{A}}_t \hat{\boldsymbol{D}}_t^{-\frac{1}{2}} \boldsymbol{X}_i^{e(l)} \boldsymbol{W}_t^l), \tag{4}$$

where $\hat{\boldsymbol{A}}_t = \boldsymbol{A}_t + \boldsymbol{I}_t$ is the $n_e \times n_e$ adjacency matrix of triadic graph, with added self-connections and $\boldsymbol{I}_t$ is the identity matrix of $(n_e + n_r) \times (n_e + n_r)$; $\hat{\boldsymbol{D}}_t$ is the diagonal node degree matrix of $\hat{\boldsymbol{A}}_t$; $\boldsymbol{W}_t^l \in \mathbb{R}^{d_e(l) \times d_e(l+1)}$ is the trainable weight matrix of triadic graph convolutional layer at the l layer. We also regard the triadic graph as an undirected graph to construct adjacency matrix $\boldsymbol{A}_t$.

Note that when the model loads the triadic graph convolutional layer for the first time, we need to define the feature information of relations to construct a mixed feature matrix of entities and relations. Since the names of the relation in the knowledge graph are often not regular. We approximate the relation representation in triadic graph refer to [22] as follows:

$$x_k^{r(0)} = Concat(\frac{\sum_{e_h \in H_k} x_h^{e(0)}}{|H_k|}; \frac{\sum_{e_t \in T_k} x_t^{e(0)}}{|T_k|}), \tag{5}$$

where $x_k^{r(0)}$ denote the initial representation of relation r_k which is concatenated by its averaged head and tail entity representations of triples in knowledge graph; H_k is the head entities set of r_k and T_k is the tail entities set of r_k; $x_h^{e(0)}$ and $x_t^{e(0)}$ are initial representation of entity e_h and e_t. Through the multiple graph convolution from different network structures, we can study the representations of entities and relations simultaneously. Then the final embeddings of entity and relation are computed as $\bar{X}^e = X_o^t[1 : n_e]$ and $\bar{X}^r = X_o^t[n_e : n_e + n_r]$, where X_o^t is the output of final triadic graph conventional layer.

4.2 Bidirectional Context Aggregation

In the KGs, the neighborhood sub-graph knowledge of entities that implies more richer alignment information for aligning entities [29]. In this section, we design a directional context aggregation method to incorporate neighborhood information with the awareness of both relation semantic and direction.

We regard the neighborhood context of a focal entity as a sub-graph contains relations and entities within input and output two directions. The head entities and relations of a focal entity are regarded as its input context. At the same time, the tail entities and relations of a focal entity are regarded as its output context. For instance, as elaborated in Fig. 3 (a), the sub-graph of focal entity e_0 consists of head entities and tail entities associated with relations. Head entity e_1, e_2 and e_3 connect to e_0 through r_1, r_2 and r_3, which forms the input context. e_1 and r_1 can denote as the input context pair $\langle r_1, e_1 \rangle$ of focal entity e_0. And output context can be obtained by a similar procedure.

The aggregation model is illustrated in Fig. 3 (b). As we have represented entities and relations at the above stage, for a neighbor pair $\langle r, e \rangle$, the context embedding can represented as $\bar{x}^c = \bar{x}^r \odot \bar{x}^e$, where $\bar{x}^e \in \bar{X}^e$ and $\bar{x}^r \in \bar{X}^r$ are the entity and relation embeddings, $\odot$ is the elementwise multiplication operation. We utilize multi-head attention to encode input context and output context, respectively. An attention mechanism can be described as mapping a query and a set of key-value pairs to output as follows:

$$Attention(q, K, V) = \xi(\frac{qK^T}{\sqrt{d}}V). \tag{6}$$

Take input context aggregation as example, for an entity e_k, q(query) is the embedding of e_k represented as $\bar{x}_k^e$. K(key) and V(value) are input context matrix $\bar{X}_t^{c(i)}$ which consist of e_t's input context embeddings; $\xi(\cdot)$ is the activation

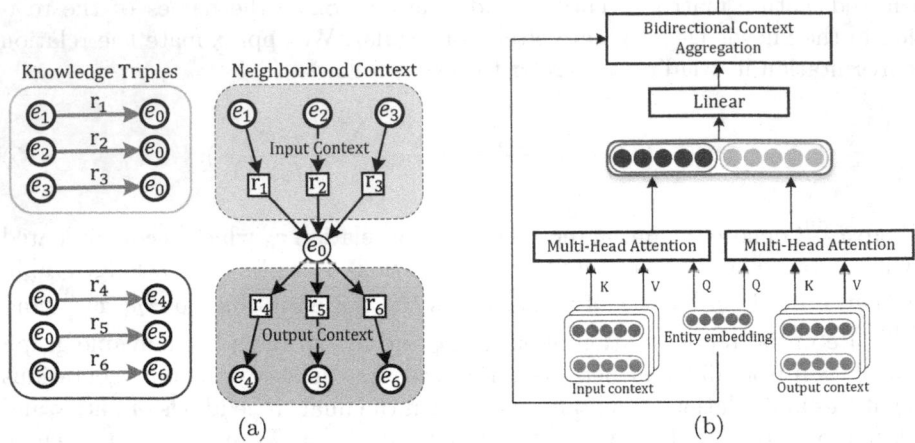

Fig. 3. (a) shows the sub-graph extracts from neighborhood context of a focal entity and (b) shows the framework of the bidirectional context aggregation model.

function. d is the key vector's dimension. $\sqrt{d}$ is denoted as the scaling factor. So the multi-head attention based input encoder module as follows:

$$
\begin{aligned}
MultiHead(\bar{\boldsymbol{x}}_k^e, \bar{\boldsymbol{X}}_k^{c(i)}) &= Concat(head_1;...;head_h)\boldsymbol{W}_a^{c(i)}, \\
where\ head_j &= Attention(\bar{\boldsymbol{x}}_k^e \cdot \boldsymbol{W}_{q_j}^{c(i)}, \bar{\boldsymbol{X}}_t^{c(i)}\boldsymbol{W}_{K_j}^{c(i)}, \bar{\boldsymbol{X}}_t^{c(i)}\boldsymbol{W}_{V_j}^{c(i)}),
\end{aligned}
\tag{7}
$$

and the projections are parameter matrices $\boldsymbol{W}_{q_j}^{c(i)}$, $\boldsymbol{W}_{K_j}^{c(i)}$, $\boldsymbol{W}_{V_j}^{c(i)}$. $\boldsymbol{W}_a^{c(i)}$ is the transform matrix of the context aggregation. The output context is aggregated similarly. Therefore the input and output context aggregation of e_k is computed as follows:

$$
\begin{aligned}
\boldsymbol{c}_k^i &= MultiHead(\bar{\boldsymbol{x}}_k^e, \bar{\boldsymbol{X}}_k^{c(i)}), \\
\boldsymbol{c}_k^o &= MultiHead(\bar{\boldsymbol{x}}_k^e, \bar{\boldsymbol{X}}_k^{c(o)}),
\end{aligned}
\tag{8}
$$

then we use the following module to concatenate entity embeddings with the above context aggregation.

$$
\boldsymbol{a}_k = Concat(MLP(\boldsymbol{c}_k^i;\ \boldsymbol{c}_k^o); \bar{\boldsymbol{x}}_k^e),
\tag{9}
$$

where MLP is a single linear layer for the context transformation.

4.3 Entity Alignment

For both KGs G_1 and G_2, RE-GCN can get the entity representations separately. We utilize a margin-based score function as the training objective, which defined as:

$$
\mathcal{L} = \sum_{(e_{i_1},e_{i_2})\in\mathbb{L}^+} [E(e_{i_1},e_{i_2}) - \gamma_1]_+ + \mu \sum_{(e_{j_1},e_{j_2})\in\mathbb{L}^-} [\gamma_2 - E(e_{j_1},e_{j_2})]_+,
\tag{10}
$$

Table 1. Summary of the DBP15K datasets.

Datasets		# Entities	# Relations	# Relation triples	# Aligned entity
ZH-EN	ZH	66,469	2,830	153,929	1,5000
	EN	98,125	2,317	237,674	1,5000
JA-EN	JA	65,744	2,043	164,373	1,5000
	EN	95,680	2,096	233,319	1,5000
FR-EN	FR	66,858	1,379	192,191	1,5000
	EN	105,889	2,209	278,590	1,5000

where $[a]_+ = max\{0, a\}$ denotes the maximum between 0 and a. We denote alignment seeds as $\mathbb{L}^+$ and non-aligned entities as $\mathbb{L}^-$. As for hyper-parameters, γ_1 and γ_2 control the loss boundary. And $\mu \to [0, 1]$ is the preference parameter to trade off the two objectives. $E(\cdot)$ is the function to evaluate entities similarity cross different KGs which is also assigned as the probability of entity alignment. The proposed objective function has two desirable properties. First, aligned entities are expected to have high similarity. And another property is that non-aligned entities are expected to have a low similarity.

5   Experiments

In this section, we compare RE-GCN with some existing baseline methods for entity alignment in heterogeneous KGs and conduct some analysis.

5.1   Experiment Settings

Datasets. We evaluate the RE-GCN on three real-world datasets from DBP15K [17]. These datasets are extracted from the multilingual versions of DBpedia. Each dataset contains aligned entity pairs from two KGs in different languages. The details are summarized in Table 1. Followed by [18], we split 30% for training and 70% for testing.

Implementation Details. We implement our experiment by Pytorch 1.0. Our experiments are conducted on a personal workstation with an Intel Xeon E3 3.3 GHz CPU, a NVIDIA GeForce GTX 2080 Ti GPU.

In our approach, we adopt the Ada-Grad [6] method for learning the parameters. The optimal parameter settings for each method are either determined by experiments or taken from the suggestions by previous works [22]. All dimensions of entity embeddings and relation embeddings ware set to 300. In this work, we employ $h = 8$ parallel attention heads in Eq. (7). We set margin $\gamma_1 = 0.9$ and $\gamma_2 = 0.2$ in Eq. (10) and for the trade-off term of the two learning objectives, we set $\mu = 0.5$. The learning rate is set to 0.001, and batch size of the experiment is

Table 2. The performance for all models on the DBP15K datasets.

Models	ZH-EN			JA-EN			FR-EN		
	Hits@1	Hits@10	MRR	Hits@1	Hits@10	MRR	Hits@1	Hits@10	MRR
JE	21.27	42.77	–	18.92	39.97	–	15.38	38.84	–
MTransE	30.83	61.41	0.364	27.86	57.45	0.349	24.41	55.55	0.335
IPTransE	40.59	73.47	0.516	36.69	69.26	0.474	33.30	68.54	0.451
JAPE	41.18	74.46	0.490	36.25	68.50	0.476	32.39	66.68	0.430
BootEA	62.94	84.75	0.703	62.23	85.39	0.701	65.30	87.44	0.731
NAEA	65.01	86.73	0.720	64.14	87.27	0.718	67.32	89.43	0.752
GCN	41.25	74.38	0.549	39.91	74.46	0.546	37.29	74.49	0.532
KECG	47.77	83.50	0.598	48.97	84.40	0.610	48.64	95.06	0.610
GMNN	62.90	77.89	0.645	63.48	76.86	0.667	79.72	91.21	0.829
RDGCN	69.69	84.23	0.750	76.27	89.59	0.811	87.82	95.59	0.901
RE-GCN(w/ T)	70.11	87.77	0.763	77.18	90.45	0.817	91.90	97.22	0.938
RE-GCN(w/o R)	69.38	**90.93**	0.769	77.02	93.17	0.826	92.12	98.02	0.943
RE-GCN(w/o D)	67.82	90.40	0.757	76.14	93.05	0.821	91.85	98.07	0.942
RE-GCN(w/o RD)	65.27	89.55	0.702	73.54	93.02	0.804	90.72	97.96	0.933
RE-GCN	**73.49**	90.29	**0.798**	**79.90**	**93.27**	**0.845**	**93.28**	**98.13**	**0.951**

set to 500. The initial embeddings of the entity in the present paper is referred to [22].

Two standard measures: Mean Reciprocal Rank(MRR) and Hit-Precision (Hits@1 and Hits@10) are considered as evaluation metrics. A Hits@k score is computed by measuring the proportion of correct alignment ranked in top-k. And MRR is the average of the reciprocal ranks of results. We prefer higher Hits@k and MRR that indicate better alignment. Note that Hits@1 should be more preferred, and it is equivalent to precision widely-used in conventional entity alignment [26].

Comparison Methods. We compare RE-GCN with two kinds of baseline methods: 6 recent translation based models, such as JE [7], MTransE [3], IPTransE [28], JAPE [17], BootEA [18], NAEA [29]. And 4 GCN based models, such as GCN [21], KECE [10], GMNN [24], RDGCN [22].

Model Variants. We use four variants of the RE-GCN model to assess the robustness of different components of our model: 1) RE-GCN(w/ T): a two layers **T**riadic Graph Convolution Network with BCA mechanism. 2) RE-GCN(w/o **R**): the variant of RE-GCN model which aggregate neighborhood context without consider relation information. 3) RE-GCN(w/o **D**): the variant of RE-GCN model which aggregate neighborhood context without consider direction information. 4) RE-GCN(w/o RD): the variant of RE-GCN model which aggregates neighborhood context without consider relation and direction information.

5.2   Knowledge Alignment Results

The results of all models are shown in Table 2. In this experiment, some results of baseline models are directly copied from their papers since the same datasets are used. The other experiment results are implemented with the source code provided by the authors. From Table 2, we can observe that our model RE-GCN consistently outperforms all baselines on the three datasets. Looking into the results, RE-GCN gets 4.76% to 6.22% on Hits@1, 2.66% to 7.19% on Hits@10, and 4.19% to 6.40% on MRR improvements over the strongest baseline RDGCN model in three datasets.

Comparison with Translation-Based Baselines. Comparing with translation-based baselines, RE-GCN has achieved statistically significant improvements increase. JE [7], MTransE [3] are the plain translation-based KG embedding models and they obtain the worst alignment performance. JAPE [17] combines the attribute information of entities to KG triples with a joint objective in an unsophisticated way. NAEA [29] considered neighborhood information of a focal entity and lacks clear modeling of rich relation information. IPTransE [28], BootEA [18] conducted entity alignment in a bootstrapping process and labels likely alignment as training data, which gives the perspectives to take advantage of limited prior-aligned users data. We believe that a bootstrapping process can further improve the performance of RE-GCN, and we leave this for future work. The above translation-based are constrained by the strong assumption *head entity + relation ≈ tail entity*, which makes it inefficient for the model to capture the complex structure information [22]. Therefore, most of these methods inevitably have limited performance.

Comparison with GCN-Based Baselines. GCN-based model [21, 22, 24] can naturally utilize node attribute to aggregate neighborhood information iteratively over the entire graph [10], which clearly outperforms most translation based models. GCN [21] is the vanilla GCN model driven by primal entity graph, which studies entity embeddings without considering the relation information. KECG [10] combines a translation based model and GCNs together to learn the embeddings of the entities. They take advantage of the two kinds of methods, but also inherit the disadvantages of them. GMNN [24] formulates the entity alignment as a graph matching problem and roughly aggregates neighborhood entity embeddings with similarity. This naive method cannot exploit the rich information in the neighborhood context of a focal entity. RDGCN [22] incorporates entity features with relation information and enable specify different weights to aggregate neighborhood information. Their model does not explicitly formulate the semantic representations for the relations and has no considering the direction of the relations. With the enhance of relation semantic and direction, our model achieved the best performance comparison with GCN-based baselines.

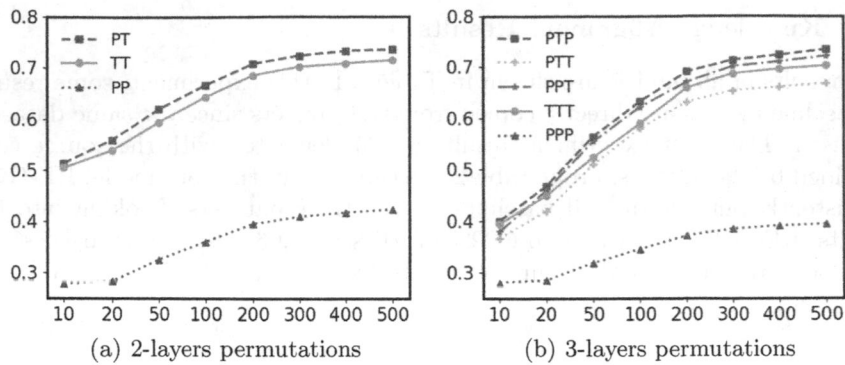

(a) 2-layers permutations   (b) 3-layers permutations

Fig. 4. Performance of different convolution layers arrangement. The abbreviated letters 'P' and 'T' represent the graph convolution layers driven by the primal graph and the triadic graph. The arrangement of the convolution layers is the same as the alphabetical order. The x-axes are the epochs of training processes, and the y-axes are Hits@1 scores.

Ablation Studies. In Table 2, we also compare our model with the ablation of some model components on overall performance. We find that a model with all of these components can achieve the best performance. The result of RE-GCN (w/o RD) is worse than other variants, which verified aggregation of neighborhood context with relation semantic and direction is not surprising very important. The performance of RE-GCN (w/o R) is better than RE-GCN (w/o D), which shows that directional information is more critical than relation information in the aggregation scheme.

5.3   Model Analysis

Impact of Convolution Layers Arrangement. In this paper, RE-GCN stacks of multiple graph convolutional layers with different structures. To analyze the robustness of this architecture, we show the performance of different graph convolution layer arrangements during training progresses. Figure 4 (a) illustrates the arrangement of two-layers graph convolution. RE-GCN(PT) is architecture proposed in the present paper, also abridged as PT. RE-GCN(TT) and RE-GCN(PP) are the two-layers graph convolution of triadic graph convolutional layers and primal graph convolutional layers. As shown in Fig. 4 (a), RE-GCN(PT) outperforms the other models, because of this arrangement using multiple graph convolution, which leverages complex structure information. Figure 4 (b) illustrates the arrangement of three-layers graph convolution. Similar to the two-layers graph convolution, RE-GCN(PTP) performs better than other variant models. The performance of RE-GCN(PPT) is very close to RE-GCN(PTP). RE-GCN(PTT) performs the worst in graph convolutions across different graph structures. This result due to the high degree connectivity of multiple triadic graphs leading to excessive smoothing of entity features.

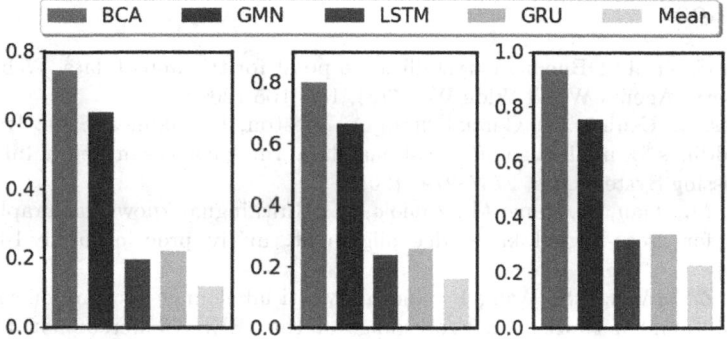

Fig. 5. Performance evaluation of five aggregators on three datasets. The x-axes are shown in the legend, and the y-axes are Hits@1 scores.

Comparison of Context Aggregation Models. In order to verify the validity of the aggregation method for the neighborhood knowledge of a focal entity in our model, we compare the performance impact of some aggregators on neighborhood context. The *Mean* aggregator simply average each dimension of entity embeddings in the neighborhood. Recurrent neural networks (RNNs) have excellent sequence modeling capacity, especially the two improved variants of the long-short term memory (LSTM) networks [9] and the gated recurrent unit (GRU) networks [5]. Therefore, we consider the two alternative methods for comparison. GMN is the graph embedding model from [11]. As detailed in Fig. 5, five neighborhood context aggregators show similar patterns on three datasets. BCA model outperforms other four aggregators which illustrates the BCA model can incorporate neighborhood subgraph-level information of entities effectively.

6 Conclusion

In this paper, we propose a novel RE-GCN to study the entity and relation embeddings, simultaneously, where a multiple structural graph convolution driven by a triadic graph and primal graph is integrated. Then, the neighborhood context information of entities with the awareness of relation semantic and directions are explicitly aggregated to align entities cross heterogeneous KGs. On three real-world multilingual datasets, experimental results demonstrate that RE-GCN produces a more excellent performance compared with some state-of-the-art entity alignment methods.

References

1. Bizer, C., et al.: DBpedia-a crystallization point for the web of data. Web Semant. Sci. Serv. Agents World Wide Web **7**(3), 154–165 (2009)
2. Bordes, A., Usunier, N., Garcia-Duran, A., Weston, J., Yakhnenko, O.: Translating embeddings for modeling multi-relational data. In: Advances in Neural Information Processing Systems, pp. 2787–2795 (2013)
3. Chen, M., Tian, Y., Yang, M., Zaniolo, C.: Multilingual knowledge graph embeddings for cross-lingual knowledge alignment. arXiv preprint arXiv:1611.03954 (2016)
4. Chen, Z.M., Wei, X.S., Wang, P., Guo, Y.: Multi-label image recognition with graph convolutional networks. In: Proceedings of the IEEE Conference on Computer Vision and Pattern Recognition, pp. 5177–5186 (2019)
5. Cho, K., Van Merriënboer, B., Bahdanau, D., Bengio, Y.: On the properties of neural machine translation: encoder-decoder approaches. arXiv preprint arXiv:1409.1259 (2014)
6. Duchi, J., Hazan, E., Singer, Y.: Adaptive subgradient methods for online learning and stochastic optimization. J. Mach. Learn. Res. **12**(Jul), 2121–2159 (2011)
7. Hao, Y., Zhang, Y., He, S., Liu, K., Zhao, J.: A joint embedding method for entity alignment of knowledge bases. In: Chen, H., Ji, H., Sun, L., Wang, H., Qian, T., Ruan, T. (eds.) CCKS 2016. CCIS, vol. 650, pp. 3–14. Springer, Singapore (2016). https://doi.org/10.1007/978-981-10-3168-7_1
8. He, F., et al.: Unsupervised entity alignment using attribute triples and relation triples. In: Li, G., Yang, J., Gama, J., Natwichai, J., Tong, Y. (eds.) DASFAA 2019. LNCS, vol. 11446, pp. 367–382. Springer, Cham (2019). https://doi.org/10.1007/978-3-030-18576-3_22
9. Hochreiter, S., Schmidhuber, J.: Long short-term memory. Neural Comput. **9**(8), 1735–1780 (1997)
10. Li, C., Cao, Y., Hou, L., Shi, J., Li, J., Chua, T.S.: Semi-supervised entity alignment via joint knowledge embedding model and cross-graph model. In: Proceedings of the 2019 Conference on Empirical Methods in Natural Language Processing and the 9th International Joint Conference on Natural Language Processing (EMNLP-IJCNLP), pp. 2723–2732 (2019)
11. Li, Y., Gu, C., Dullien, T., Vinyals, O., Kohli, P.: Graph matching networks for learning the similarity of graph structured objects. arXiv preprint arXiv:1904.12787 (2019)
12. Mahdisoltani, F., Biega, J., Suchanek, F.M.: Yago3: a knowledge base from multilingual wikipedias (2013)
13. Monti, F., Shchur, O., Bojchevski, A., Litany, O., Günnemann, S., Bronstein, M.M.: Dual-primal graph convolutional networks. arXiv preprint arXiv:1806.00770 (2018)
14. Schlichtkrull, M., Kipf, T.N., Bloem, P., van den Berg, R., Titov, I., Welling, M.: Modeling relational data with graph convolutional networks. In: Gangemi, A., et al. (eds.) ESWC 2018. LNCS, vol. 10843, pp. 593–607. Springer, Cham (2018). https://doi.org/10.1007/978-3-319-93417-4_38
15. Simmel, G.: The Sociology of Georg Simmel, vol. 92892. Simon and Schuster (1950)
16. Suchanek, F.M., Kasneci, G., Weikum, G.: YAGO: a large ontology from Wikipedia and wordnet. Web Semant. Sci. Serv. Agents World Wide Web **6**(3), 203–217 (2008)
17. Sun, Z., Hu, W., Li, C.: Cross-lingual entity alignment via joint attribute-preserving embedding. In: d'Amato, C., et al. (eds.) ISWC 2017. LNCS, vol. 10587, pp. 628–644. Springer, Cham (2017). https://doi.org/10.1007/978-3-319-68288-4_37

18. Sun, Z., Hu, W., Zhang, Q., Qu, Y.: Bootstrapping entity alignment with knowledge graph embedding. In: IJCAI, pp. 4396–4402 (2018)
19. Veličković, P., Cucurull, G., Casanova, A., Romero, A., Lio, P., Bengio, Y.: Graph attention networks. arXiv preprint arXiv:1710.10903 (2017)
20. Wang, Z., Zhang, J., Feng, J., Chen, Z.: Knowledge graph embedding by translating on hyperplanes. In: Twenty-Eighth AAAI Conference on Artificial Intelligence (2014)
21. Wang, Z., Lv, Q., Lan, X., Zhang, Y.: Cross-lingual knowledge graph alignment via graph convolutional networks. In: Proceedings of the 2018 Conference on Empirical Methods in Natural Language Processing, pp. 349–357 (2018)
22. Wu, Y., Liu, X., Feng, Y., Wang, Z., Yan, R., Zhao, D.: Relation-aware entity alignment for heterogeneous knowledge graphs. arXiv preprint arXiv:1908.08210 (2019)
23. Xu, K., Hu, W., Leskovec, J., Jegelka, S.: How powerful are graph neural networks? arXiv preprint arXiv:1810.00826 (2018)
24. Xu, K., et al.: Cross-lingual knowledge graph alignment via graph matching neural network. arXiv preprint arXiv:1905.11605 (2019)
25. Yao, L., Mao, C., Luo, Y.: Graph convolutional networks for text classification. In: Proceedings of the AAAI Conference on Artificial Intelligence, vol. 33, pp. 7370–7377 (2019)
26. Zhang, Q., Sun, Z., Hu, W., Chen, M., Guo, L., Qu, Y.: Multi-view knowledge graph embedding for entity alignment. arXiv preprint arXiv:1906.02390 (2019)
27. Zhang, S., Tong, H., Maciejewski, R., Eliassi-Rad, T.: Multilevel network alignment. In: The World Wide Web Conference, pp. 2344–2354. ACM (2019)
28. Zhu, H., Xie, R., Liu, Z., Sun, M.: Iterative entity alignment via joint knowledge embeddings. In: IJCAI, pp. 4258–4264 (2017)
29. Zhu, Q., Zhou, X., Wu, J., Tan, J., Guo, L.: Neighborhood-aware attentional representation for multilingual knowledge graphs. In: Proceedings of the 28th International Joint Conference on Artificial Intelligence, pp. 1943–1949. AAAI Press (2019)

Efficient Graph Hierarchical Decomposition with User Engagement and Tie Strength

Maryam Ghafouri[1], Kai Wang[1(✉)], Fan Zhang[2], Ying Zhang[3], and Xuemin Lin[1]

[1] The University of New South Wales, Sydney, Australia
{m.ghafouri,kai.wang}@unsw.edu.au, lxue@cse.unsw.edu.au
[2] Guangzhou University, Guangzhou, China
zhangf@gzhu.edu.cn
[3] The University of Technology Sydney, Ultimo, Australia
ying.zhang@uts.edu.au

Abstract. Graph decomposition methods using k-core and k-truss hierarchically group vertices and edges from external to internal by degrees of vertices or tie strength of edges. As both the user engagement of nodes and the strength of relationships are important, the (k,s)-core model is proposed in the literature to discover strong communities. Nevertheless, the decomposition algorithm regarding (k,s)-core is not yet investigated. In this paper, we propose (k,s)-core algorithms to decompose a graph into its hierarchical structures considering both user engagement and tie strength. We first present the basic (k,s)-core decomposition methods. Then, we propose the advanced algorithms DES and DEK which index the support of edges to enable higher-level cost-sharing in the peeling process. In addition, effective pruning strategies are applied to DES/DEK to further enhance performance. Moreover, we build a novel index based on the decomposition result and investigate an efficient (k,s)-core query algorithm based on our index. Extensive experimental evaluations on 12 real-world datasets verify the efficiency of our proposed decomposition algorithms and show that our index-based query algorithm can speed up the state-of-the-art query algorithms by up to three orders of magnitude.

Keywords: Graph decomposition · Cohesive subgraph · Index · Query

1 Introduction

Graph hierarchical decomposition has been widely studied in the literature [27] and proved useful in many real-world applications such as community detection [22,24,26], network analysis [2,5,23,28,29], and protein function prediction [1]. Recent works on graph decomposition are based on cohesive subgraph models. Decomposition generates a nested chain of cohesive subgraphs to discover the

© Springer Nature Switzerland AG 2020
Y. Nah et al. (Eds.): DASFAA 2020, LNCS 12113, pp. 448–465, 2020.
https://doi.org/10.1007/978-3-030-59416-9_27

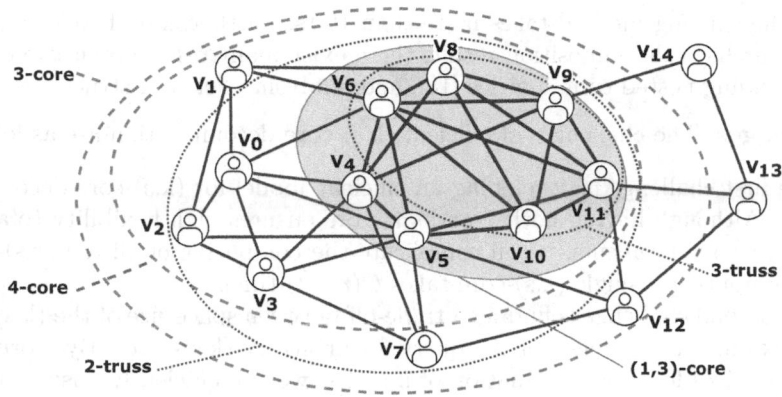

Fig. 1. Running example

hierarchical structure of those subgraphs. Among those cohesive subgraph models, k-core [13,19] and k-truss [4,15] are two of the most well-known models where k-core is vertex oriented and each vertex in it has a degree of at least k while k-truss is edge oriented and each edge in it is a strong tie (i.e., contained in at least k triangles). However, none of k-core or k-truss decomposition methods considers the vertex engagement and tie strength at the same time while they are both important. In some cases, although people have a strong connection with only a few friends or family members, they also have some weaker relationships with some more other people and even weaker ties with a larger group of casual acquaintances [12]. Figure 1 depicts an example of a graph G, consisting of 15 nodes. Here, some levels of k-core decomposition are shown by dashed lines and some levels of k-truss decomposition are depicted by dotted lines. Despite the fact that the induced subgraph of $\{v_4, v_5, v_6, v_8, v_9, v_{10}, v_{11}\}$ is tightly connected and every user has at least one strong relation (with three common friends) with the other users, it can not be found by k-truss or k-core. Motivated by this, Zhang et. al [25] propose the (k,s)-core model to fulfil various requirements to be either user engaged or with a good tie strength. Under the (k,s)-core model, this subgraph can be found as (1,3)-core. In real-world applications, the request of arbitrary (k,s)-core computation may happen not only once in a graph. The proposed online (k,s)-core computation method in [25] needs $O(m^{1.5})$ time to compute the (k,s)-core for given k and s where m denotes the number of edges. Thus, it is impractical when we request several queries with various range of k and s in a large graph. In this paper, we study the *(k,s)-core decomposition problem* which is never addressed in the literature. Specifically, given a graph G, we aim to find all the (k,s)-cores in G. Utilizing the result of (k,s)-core decomposition, an offline space efficient index can be built and we can return an arbitrary (k,s)-core efficiently within $O(m)$ time based on the index. For instance, to answer 100 random (k,s)-core queries on WikiTalk dataset with 4 million edges, our index-based query algorithm takes about 1 s while the existing method takes more than 160 s. Furthermore, benefiting from the hierarchical decomposition result, there exist many other applications such as identifying nested communities [18], and analysing network structures [2,5].

Challenges. The challenges of efficient (k,s)-core decomposition are as follows:

- The first challenge is developing an efficient model for (k,s)-core decomposition. Although having both k and s factors ensures high flexibility to adjust different requirements, it can complicate the computing of all the (k,s)-cores as computing a single (k,s)-core takes $O(m^{1.5})$ time.
- The second challenge is finding a trade-off between space size of the (k,s)-core index and the efficiency of the query for arbitrary (k,s)-cores. By storing all the vertices for any combination of k and s, we can efficiently answer all the queries, however, the storage cost could be very huge. So we need to wisely select and store results of any vertex in a (k,s)-core number set which can help identify tightly interlinked groups with similar thresholds.

Our Solution. Firstly, we propose **BasicDES** and **BasicDEK** algorithms which start with a pre-computed k-core and then iteratively computing (k,s)-core number of nodes regarding a dedicated k from 1 to k_{max} or a defined s from 1 to its maximum value. To reduce redundant computation in our basic algorithms, we introduce *Strong Neighbour Number* to understand the effect of removing an edge to the core number of its incident nodes. However, in the basic algorithms, there are a lot of support and engagement calculations among all the iterations. Motivate by this issue, We improve the basic models in **DEK** and **DES** by introducing *Core Support* which indexes support of edges for different core values in a pre-computed *Core Support List* for possible cost-sharing. In addition, in DES we avoid redundant computation by updating the engagements of affected nodes in outer loop computations. Finally, to speed up the (k,s)-core queries, we build the **Basic Index** and the **Advanced Index** utilizing the decomposition result.

Contributions: To summarize, we make the following contributions:

- We define *(k,s)-core decomposition model* to capture the hierarchy of subgraphs regarding both user engagement and tie strength.
- We propose efficient algorithms for (k,s)-core decomposition by exploring possible cost-sharing and avoiding redundant work. In addition, we analyse the time and space complexity of the proposed algorithms (Sect. 3).
- We investigate non-trivial indexing techniques to support efficient (k,s)-core queries. In addition, we compact the index and optimize the query process to achieve higher performance (Sect. 4.1).
- We conduct *extensive experiments* on 12 real-world datasets and show that our (k,s)-core decomposition algorithms can efficiently find cohesive substructures over real-world datasets (Sect. 5). Also, our index-based query algorithm significantly outperforms the state-of-the-art method to query (k,s)-cores by up to three orders of magnitude.

Table 1. The summary of notations

Notation	Definition
$G(V,E)$	An unweighted and undirected graph
u,v,w	Vertexes in G
$e(u,v)$	An edge with u and v as endpoints in G
$N(u,G)$	Set of adjacent vertices of u in G
$E(u,G)$	Set of edges where each edge is incident to u in G
$deg(u,G)$	The number of adjacent vertices of u in G
$sup(e,G)$	The number of triangles each containing e in G
$eng(u,G)$	The number of edges where each edge e has $sup(e,G) \geq s$ and e is incident to u in G
$C_k(G)/C_{k,s}(G)$	k-core/(k,s)-core of G
$c(v)$	Core number of a vertex v
$\triangle_{uvw}$	The triangle formed by vertices u, v and w
$sup_k(e,C_k)$	Support of an edge $e(u,v)$ in C_k which is the number of $\triangle_{uvw}$ contain $e(u,v)$ and w has a core number of at least k

2 Preliminary

2.1 Basic Definitions

Table 1 summarizes the notations frequently used throughout the paper.

Consider an undirected, unweighted graph $G = (V, E)$, where V is the set of vertices and $E \subseteq V \times V$ is the set of edges in G. We denote $n = |V|$, $m = |E|$ and assume $m > n$. The degree of vertex $u \in G$, is noted by $deg(u,G)$.

Definition 1 (k-core). *Given a graph G and an integer k, the subgraph C_k of G is the k-core of G if it is the maximal subgraph in which all vertices have degree at least k.*

Definition 2 (Support). *A cycle of length 3 in a graph G is called a triangle. We note the support of an edge $e(u,v)$ in G by $sup(e,G)$, to represent the number of triangles that contain e.*

$$sup(e,G) = |\triangle_{uvw} : \triangle_{uvw} \in \triangle_G| \tag{1}$$

Definition 3 (k-truss). *Given a graph G, an integer k, the k-truss of G is defined as the maximal subgraph where each edge has a support of at least k.*

2.2 (k,s)-Core

Definition 4 (Strong tie). *Given an integer s, an edge e is called a strong tie in G if $sup(e,G) \geq s$; otherwise, it is assumed as weak.*

Definition 5 (Engagement). *The engagement of u in G, denoted by $eng(u, G)$, represents the number of strong ties incident to u with $sup(e, G) \geq s$.*

Definition 6 (Strong engagement). *For an integer k, a vertex u is strongly engaged in G if u is incident to at least k strong ties in G, i.e., $eng(u, G) \geq k$, otherwise, it is weakly engaged.*

Definition 7 ((k,s)-core). *Given a graph G, two integers k and s, the (k,s)-core $C_{k,s}(G)$ of G is the maximal subgraph where each vertex engages at least k strong ties.*

Definition 8 ((k,s)-core number). *The (k,s)-core numbers of v is set of (k,s) pairs denoted as $\phi(v)$. For each (k,s) pair in $\phi(v)$, there is a (k,s)-core containing v, and there is no (k+1,s)-core or (k,s+1)-core containing v.*

Although the lack of considering both user engagement and tie strength is answered in the (k,s)-core model [25], there is no any (k,s)-core decomposition model or any efficient indexing technique for answering queries yet.

2.3 Problem Statement

In this paper, we study the problem of **(k,s)-core decomposition**, that is, to compute the (k,s)-cores for all possible k and s values in a given graph. This problem can be transferred to compute the (k,s)-core numbers of all the vertices since finding the induced subgraph of vertices takes only linear time.

3   Solutions for (k,s)-Core Decomposition

In this section, we focus on efficient algorithms for (k,s)-core decomposition.

3.1 Basic (k,s)-Core Decomposition Methods

We first explain our basic decomposition methods. Following the fact from [25], when $k > 0$, (k,s)-core of G is a subgraph of k'-core of G (i.e., $C_{k,s}(G) \subseteq C_{k'}(G)$) where $k' = max(k, s + 1)$). So, we compute the k-core as a base for (k,s)-core computation and use proper $C_{k'}(G)$ in different levels of decomposition. We start by core decomposition and assign core number to each node as a primitive engagement when $s = 0$. Also, by considering the minimum support for calculating engagement, we may need to update the engagements of those endpoint nodes.

Example 1. By considering engagements of at least 3, we can discard v_{13} and v_{14} and consequently related edges of $e(v_{13}, v_{14})$, $e(v_9, v_{14})$, $e(v_{11}, v_{13})$ and $e(v_{12}, v_{13})$ in Fig. 1. In (k,s)-core decomposition with two parameter of k and s, for example we also consider $s > 1$, then we should check the engagements of their neighbours (v_9, v_{11} and v_{12}). In fact, removing edge $e(v_{11}, v_{13})$ or $e(v_{12}, v_{13})$ decreases the support of edge $e(v_{11}, v_{12})$ from 2 to 1 as there is no more $\triangle v_{11}v_{12}v_{13}$. This may decreases $eng(v_{11})$ and $eng(v_{12})$.

For solving this problem, we need to find a way to understand if this edge is counted towards the current engagement of endpoint node. A node in (k,s)-core with $eng(v) = l$ have l or more incident edges with sufficient support and removing one of its incident edges may or may not make $eng(v) = l - 1$. So, we introduce *Strong Neighbours Number* $strsum_{k,s}(v, G)$ as below:

Definition 9 (Strong Neighbours Number). *We define the Strong Neighbours Number of a vertices v in edge $e(v, u)$ in the graph G by $strsum_{k,s,e(v,u)}$ (v, G), to represent the number of edges in G which $sup(e(v, w)) \geq s$ and $eng(w) \geq k$ and $w \neq u$.*

$$strsum_{k,s,e(v,u)}(v, G) = |\bigcup(N(v)|(e(v,u) \geq s, eng(u) \geq k)|, w \neq u; \quad (2)$$

Lemma 1. *When the support of an edge e becomes less than the support threshold (i.e., $sup(e(v, u)) < s$), the engagement of v is decreased by 1 only if $strsum_{k,s,e(v,u)}(v, G) < eng(v)$, that is:*

$$eng(v) = eng(v) - 1, if \ strsum_{k,s,e(v,u)}(v, G) < eng(v); \quad (3)$$

Proof: If $strsum_{k,s,e(v,u)}(v, G) \geq eng(v)$, we have more than eng(v) edges with $sup(e(v, w)) \geq s$ which is enough for the definition of engagement in (k,s)-core. Thus, the core number of v remains unchanged. Otherwise, $eng(v)$ should be decreased by 1 since one of its strong tie becomes weak tie. Thus, this lemma holds.

BasicDES: Basic (k,s)-Core Decomposition, Iterating First on s Then k. In this method, we define the maximum k value for every node regarding a fixed s. We nested two main loops, the outer loop is iterating on s until all the nodes are removed and takes control of complete repetitions of the inner loop which works on k. This is represented in Algorithm 1.

The algorithm starts by initiating an empty result set $(\phi(v))$ for each vertex v in line 1 and then with k-core computation in line 2. Then, starting from $s = 1$ in each iteration on s, it uses the (s+1)-core (line 4) as G' and initializes the engagements of nodes by their core number (line 5) and sorts them in line 7 by the engagements. Next, the algorithm calculates support of each edge in G' and sorts them in line 8. Then, in line 9 to 10 the engagements of nodes who have weak ties are updated.

Iterating in the inner loop from $k = 1$ to k_{max} and while the graph is not empty, we update the graph G' by removing every vertex with the engagement of less than current k and update their neighbours (line 12 to 20). Obviously, the deletion of an edge will respectively decrease the engagement of its neighbour if this edge had support of at least s. Also, the deletion of an edge may cause a reduction in the support of other edges of its triangles and consequently the engagements of the other nodes on the triangles (line 16 to 19). The algorithm returns all (k,s)-core numbers for each vertex $v \in G$ in line 22.

Algorithm 1: *BasicDES*(G)

Input : G: a social network
Output: ϕ_v : (k,s)-core numbers for each vertex v $\in$ G
1 $\phi_v \leftarrow \emptyset$ for each $v \in G$; $s \leftarrow 1$;
2 Run core decomposition(G);
3 **while** *the graph is not empty* **do**
4       $k \leftarrow s + 1$; $G' \leftarrow C_k(G)$;
5       $eng(u) \leftarrow c(u)$ for each $u \in G'$;
6   compute $sup(e, G')$ for each $e \in G'$
7   order the vertices in G' with increasing order of $eng(u)$ for each u;
8   order the edges in G' with increasing order of $sup(e, G')$ for each e;
9   **for** $(sup(e(v, u), G') < s)$ **do**
10        $eng(\{v, u\}) \leftarrow$ UpdateEngagement($\{v, u\}$) ;   // by equation 3
11   **for** $k = 1, ..., k_{max}$ **do**
12   **while** *exists* $u \in G'$ *and* $eng(u) < k$ **do**
13   **foreach** *vertex* $v \in N(u, G')$ *and* $eng(v) > k$ **do**
14   **if** $sup(e(u, v)) \geq s$ **then**
15   eng(v) $\leftarrow$ UpdateEngagement(v)
16   **foreach** $w \in N(u) \cap N(v)$ *and* $eng(w) > k$ *and* $sup(e(v, w)) \geq s$ **do**
17   sup(e(v, w)) $\leftarrow$ sup(e(v, w)) - 1 and reorder;
18   **if** $sup(e(v, w)) < s$ **then**
19                $eng(\{v, w\}) \leftarrow$ UpdateEngagement($\{v, w\}$)
20          $G' \leftarrow (G' \setminus (u \cup E(u, G')))$; $\phi_u \leftarrow \phi_u \cup (k - 1, s)$; $k \leftarrow k + 1$;
21      $s \leftarrow s + 1$
22 **return** ϕ_v for each vertex $v \in G$;

BasicDEK: Basic (k,s)-Core Decomposition, Iterating First on k Then s. The only difference between this method and BasicDES is that here the outer loop iterates on k and inner loop on s, so the line (line 9 and 10) move to inner iteration on s.

Example 2. We start by decomposed graph G in Fig. 1 which consists of 15 vertices in 3 levels from 2 to 4. Then starting from $k = 1$, we copy the k-core with core numbers more than 1 which is here the whole graph. Then, we calculate and sort the support of every edge in this level of decomposition. In the next step, we calculate and sort engagements of nodes with respect to current k in G'. Then step by step, we increase s and update the graph G'.

While $k = 1$ and $s > 0$, we select elements of support list with the support of less than one to update their engagements. The support of edges $e(v_9, v_{14})$ and $e(v_{13}, v_{14})$ are zero, so we need to update the core number of v_9, v_{14} and v_{13} if required. However, as explained before, updating engagements by the support of these two edges do not have any effect on core numbers of v_9 and v_{13} while the engagement of v_{14} should reduce from 2 to 0 and consequently we need to remove this node for $k = 1$ and $s > 0$.

Time Complexity Analysis. Note that the order can be updated in $O(1)$ time in Line 9, 5, and whenever we have UpdateEngagement, by using bin sort following [7]. The computation of support of all the edges takes $O(m^{1.5})$ time [21]. The removal of all vertices and edges takes $O(m)$ time in each inner loop and updating supports for the edges takes $O(m^{1.5})$ time. So the time complexity of BasicDES is $O(s_{max} \times \sum_{s=1}^{s_{max}} 2 \times |E(C_{1,s}(G))|^{1.5})$. Similarly, the time complexity of the algorithm BasicDEK is $O(k_{max} \times \sum_{k=1}^{k_{max}} 2 \times |E(C_{k,1}(G))|^{1.5})$.

Space Complexity Analysis. For the space complexity, the algorithm DES requires O(m+n) memory space to keep the input graph and also for the inner loop it requires $O(m)$ space for supports. Thus the space complexity of Algorithm 2 is $O(m)$.

Drawbacks of the Basic Solutions. In the baseline algorithms, we need to calculate supports and engagements in each outer iteration. Since the support of every edge is derived by the number of common neighbours of its endpoint vertices, and these common neighbours have different core numbers, the support of an edge may vary in different levels of decomposition and we need to continuously update them. Consequently, the engagements of related nodes that are derived from supports need updating. Considering this problem, we should avoid a noticeable amount of redundant computation in the baseline algorithm.

3.2 Efficient (k,s)-Core Decomposition Methods

Since the support of every edge is derived by the number of the common neighbours of its endpoint vertices and these common neighbours have different core numbers, the support of an edge may vary in different levels of decomposition. While we beneficiary from using the pre-calculated k-core, we can not use a fixed support list. Therefore, we need to compute the support of every edge in every outer iteration of (k,s)-core decomposition. However, counting the number of $\triangle_{uvw}$ which contain $e(u, v)$ and w has a core number of at least k is expensive. To relax this issue, here we define the support of an edge in the $C_k(G)$ by the number of common neighbours who have the core number of at least k as below:

Definition 10 (Core Support). *We define the Core Support of an edge $e(u, v)$ in the graph by $coreSup(e, C_k(G))$, to represent the number of $\triangle_{uvw}$ which contain $e(u, v)$ and w has a core number of k.*

$$coreSup(e, C_k(G)) = |\bigcup(\triangle_{uvw}|(\triangle_{uvw} \in \triangle_G, c(w) = k))|; \qquad (4)$$

Example 3. In the represented graph in Fig. 1, edge $e(v_5, v_{12})$ is contained in two triangles $\triangle v_5 v_{12} v_7$ and $\triangle v_5 v_{12} v_{11}$ and consequently has two common neighbours of v_7 with $c(v_7) = 3$ and v_{11} with $c(v_{11}) = 4$. So $coreSup(e(v_5, v_{12}), C_4(G)) = 1$ and $coreSup(e(v_5, v_{12}), C_3(G)) = 1$.

Definition 11 (Support in $C_k(G)$). *We define the Support of an edge $e(u, v)$ in C_k as sup_k, to represent the number of $\triangle_{uvw}$ which contain $e(u, v)$ and w has a core number of k as below:*

$$sup(e(u, v), C_k(G)) = |\bigcup(\triangle_{uvw}|(\triangle_{uvw} \in \triangle_G, c(w) \geq k))|; \tag{5}$$

Calculate by below formula:

$$sup(e(u, v), C_k(G)) = \sum_{i=k}^{k_{max}} coreSup(e, C_i(G)) \tag{6}$$

Lemma 2. *When $k > 0$, we can use Core Support to have the support of an edge for different k values from Eq. 4.*

Proof: While the support of edge $e(u, v)$ is derived by the number of common neighbours of its endpoint vertices (Eq. 1), these common neighbours have different core numbers and are removed in various levels of decomposition. Since Core number $c(w)$ of a vertex w is equal to the highest-order core that w belongs to it but not to any higher core, to have the support of an edge in the current order of core, we can count the number of $\triangle_{uvw}$ which contains $e(u, v)$ if w has a core number of at least k.

Example 4. In Example 3, we calculate $coreSup(e(v_5, v_{12}), C_4(G)) = 1$ and $coreSup(e(v_5, v_{12}), C_3(G)) = 1$. Following the Eq. 6, we have: $sup(e, C_4(G)) = 1$, $sup(e, C_3(G)) = 2$, $sup(e, C_2(G)) = 2$, $sup(e, C_1(G)) = 2$, $sup(e, C_0(G)) = 2$.

However, the edge e(u,v) will not exist after the minimum value of $c(u)$ and $c(v)$ and we do not need to calculate and support values after that.

Definition 12 (Support List). *We define the Support List of an edge $e(u, v)$ in G as $supList$, to represent its support value in different level of decomposition as below:*

$$supList(e(u, v)) = \bigcup_{k=0}^{min\{c(u), c(v)\}} sup(e(u, v), C_k(G)) \tag{7}$$

Example 5. Following the Example 4 and Eq. 7 we have: $supList(e(v_5, v_{12})) = \{2, 2, 2, 2\}$. Because the minimum value for the core number of v_5 and v_{12} is 3, we stop calculation when $k > 3$.

DES: Efficient (k,s)-Core Decomposition, Iterating First on s Then k.
The purpose of this decomposition is defining the maximum k value for every node regarding a fixed s while we step by step iterate s from 1 to minimum of s_{max} and $k_{max} - 1$. The Algorithm 2 represents this idea.

The algorithm starts by initiating an empty result set ($\phi(v)$) for each vertex v in line 1 and computing k-core in line 2. Then it computes *supList* of all the edges in line 3 by using Eq. 4, 6 and 7. In line 4 and 5 the engagements of nodes are initialized by their core number and nodes are sorted by their engagements.

Then, starting from $s = 1$ in each iteration of s, the (s+1)-core is used while the support of each edge in C_k is derived from *supList*. The edges are sorted in the next line with increasing order of their supports. Then, in the following lines from 10 to 13 the engagements of nodes who have weak ties are updated.

Algorithm 2: *DES*(G)

Input : G: a social network
Output: ϕ_v : (k,s)-core numbers for each vertex $v \in G$
1   $\phi_v \leftarrow \emptyset$ for each vertex $v \in G$;
2   Run core decomposition(G);
3   Compute $supList(e)$ for each $e \in G$;   // calculate by equation 6
4   $eng(u) \leftarrow c(u)$ for each $u \in G$;
5   order the vertices in G with increasing order of $eng(u)$ for each u;
6   **for** $s = 1, ..., min\{s_{max}, k_{max} - 1\}$ **do**
7      $k \leftarrow s + 1$
8   get $sup(e, C_k(G))$ from $supList(e)$ for each $e \in C_k(G)$
9   order the edges in $C_k(G)$ with increasing order of $sup(e, C_k(G))$;
10   **for** $(sup(e(v, u)) < s) \in C_k(G)$ **do**
11        $eng(\{v, u\}) \leftarrow$ UpdateEngagement($\{v, u\}$) ;   // by equation 3
12   **foreach** $e(w, y) \in \{\triangle_{vwy} \cup \triangle_{uwy}\}$ **and** $eng(w) > k$ **and** $eng(y) > k$ **and** $sup(e(w, y)) \geq s$ **do**
13   update $supList(e(w, y))$;
14   **while** *exists* $u \in G$ *with* $eng(u) = 0$ **do**
15   **foreach** *vertex* $v \in N(u, G)$ **and** $eng(v) > 0$ **do**
16   sup(e(v, w)) $\leftarrow$ sup(e(v, w)) - 1;
17   **if** $sup(e(v, w)) < s$ **then**
18              $eng(\{v, w\}) \leftarrow$ UpdateEngagement($\{v, w\}$)
19           $\phi_v \leftarrow \phi_v \cup (0, s); G \leftarrow (G\backslash v)$;
20     $G' \leftarrow C_k(G)$;
21   get $sup'(e)$ from $supList(e)$ for each $e \in G'$
22   run Algorithm 1 line 11 to 20, replace $sup(e)$ with $sup'(e)$;
23 **return** ϕ_v for each vertex $v \in G$;

As explained before, updating core numbers of nodes is not as simple as a k-core and we need to check their *Strong Neighbours Number* as defined in

Eq. 2 and Theorem 1. Obviously, decreasing the engagements of node v affects $supList(e(u,w))$ when $e(u,w) \in \Delta vuw$ (line 12 and 13).

In line 14 to 19, nodes who have no engagements are removed, the support of related edges and the result sets are updated. In the cases that updating the support of an edge make it weak, we need to update the engagements of its incidents nodes (line 17 and 18). For inner iteration on k the algorithm uses a copy of updated C_k (line 20) and supports of edges (line 21). The inner iteration is similar to line 12 to 20 in Algorithm 1. Finally, the algorithm returns the (k,s)-core numbers for any vertex in line 23.

DEK: Efficient (k,s)-Core Decomposition, Iterating First on k Then s. We skip the explanation of this model as it is similar to the DES model Sect. 3.2. The obvious difference is that here the outer loop iterates on k and inner loop on s. Therefore we can not update engagement by using the current s threshold in (line 10 to 19 in Algorithm 2) and consequently we need more time in inner computations.

Avoiding Redundant Work. To overcome the drawbacks of the baseline solution in Sect. 3.1, DES and DEK avoid plenty of support calculation by using the core support as explained before.

Time Complexity Analysis. Note that the order can be updated in $O(1)$ time in Line 9, 5, and whenever we have UpdateEngagement, by using bin sort following [7]. Computing the support list for all the edges takes $O(m^{1.5})$ time in total. The removal of all vertices and edges takes $O(m)$ time in each inner loop. So the time complexity of the algorithm DES is $O(m^{1.5} + min(s_{max}, k_{max} - 1) \times \sum_{s=1}^{min(s_{max},k_{max}-1)} |E(C_{1,s}(G))|^{1.5})$. Similarly, the time complexity of the algorithm DEK is $O(m^{1.5} + k_{max} \times \sum_{k=1}^{k_{max}} |E(C_{k,1}(G))|^{1.5})$.

Space Complexity Analysis. For the space complexity, the algorithm DES requires $O(m+n)$ memory space to keep the graph and $O(\sum_{(u,v)\in E(G)} c(u), c(v))$ space to keep the support list and also for inner loop it requires $O(m)$ space for supports. Thus space complexity of Algorithm 2 is $O(\sum_{(u,v)\in E(G)} c(u), c(v))$.

4   Space Efficient Index and Optimized Query Processing

4.1   Index

In this section, we propose the index and the method for answering (k,s)-core queries. Given a (k,s) value in a graph G, the problem is to find a sub-graph of G when all of its nodes have the engagement of at least k, when the support threshold is at least s. For ease of presentation, we refer a request of computing (k,s)-core for the given k, s as $Q_{k,s}$. We investigate this problem with the following three methods:

The Naive Method, Using (k,s)-Core Model. In this method, we traverse the whole graph to calculate (k,s)-core by using the Algorithm in [25]. However, it is not efficient when we need to answer a large number of queries. A lot of re-calculation for each query is the main reason that we need to decompose and index the graph.

Basic Index. Here we make the basic index while decomposing a graph by Algorithm 2. We store all the vertices of each $C_{k,s}(G)$ and record their locations by two-level pointer table. By visiting the location referred by the (k,s) value we can return the vertices of $C_{k,s}(G)$ in optimal time. The storage size takes $O(m * s_{max})$ space. This is because, for each vertex $v \in G$, it can have $O(deg(v))$ values for k and each of them links to $O(s_{max})$ buckets in the second level where v can exist.

Advanced Index. For answering storage size problem in Basic Index, we develop a compact index by reducing the number of times that a node is stored. Given a graph G, $C_{k,s'}$ is contained $C_{k,s}$ in if $s \geq s'$. we develop a compact index by avoiding redundant storage by considering to only save $C_{k,s'}$ - $C_{k,s}$ for each s. Also, in the advanced index, the edges are returns by using a neighbours list which is sorted by the core number of nodes. Thus we can avoid searching all the neighbours by stopping at nodes with the core number of less than requested k. The advanced index takes only $O(m)$ space since for each vertex $v \in G$, it has at most $deg(v)$ values for k and we store only the maximal s number for a k value.

4.2 Query Processing

The first method to process queries is following Algorithm 2 in [25]. This naive method does not require any index and calculates $C_{k,s}$ by using a pre-computed k-core. The second method uses the basic index and can return nodes of $C_{k,s}$ in optimal time by traversing bucket for k and then visiting bucket s. Then it calculates edges of $C_{k,s}$ using neighbour list. The last method uses a compact

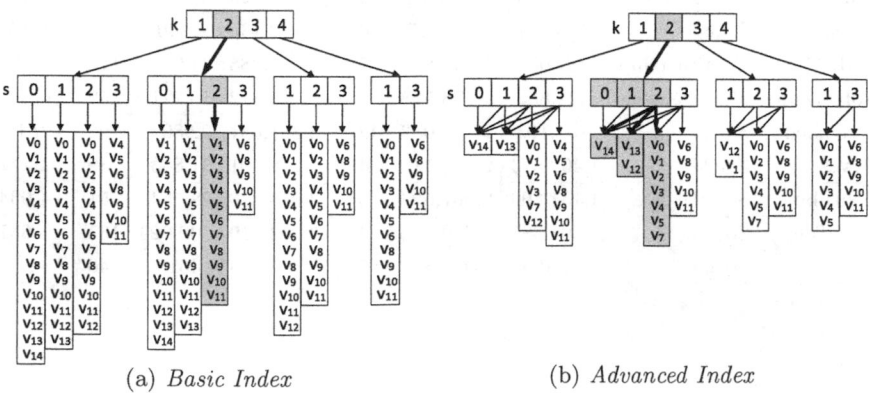

(a) *Basic Index*   (b) *Advanced Index*

Fig. 2. Index on running example graph

index for returning nodes of $C_{k,s}$ by first traversing to the related bucket for requested k and then retrieving all the nodes in the bucket with the value between zero to s.

Example 6. Following the running example, we show the basic index in Fig. 2(a). For instance, node v_{11} is stored 13 times in the Basic Index. The result of $Q_{2,2}$ ($C_{2,2}$) is stored in grey bucket following pointer $k = 2$ and then $s = 2$. We also show the compact index in Fig. 2(b). Here for finding $C_{2,2}$, we follow all the arrows which pointing to $s \geq 2$, showed in grey colour.

5   Experiment

5.1   Experimental Setting

In this section, to evaluate the efficiency of our proposed techniques. All programs were implemented in standard C++ and compiled with G++ 8.2.0 at -O3 level in Linux. All experiments were performed on a machine with Intel Xeon 3.00 GHz CPU with 64 GB memory.

Datasets. 12 real-life networks were deployed in our experiments and we assume all vertices in each network are initially engaged. All datasets are from http://snap.stanford.edu/ and http://socialcomputing.asu.edu/. Table 2 shows the statistics of the 12 datasets.

Table 2. Statistic of datasets

Dataset	Type	$|V|$	$|E|$	d_{avg}	$|\triangle|$	d_{max}	k_{max}	s_{max}
ArXiv	Coauthorship	18,771	198,050	21	1,351,441	504	56	350
Brightkite	Social	58,228	214,078	7	494,728	1134	52	272
Facebook	Social	63,731	817,035	25	3,500,542	1098	52	265
Amazon	Misc	334,863	925,872	6	667,129	549	6	161
Gowalla	Social	196,591	950,327	10	2,273,138	14730	51	1297
DBLP	Coauthorship	317,080	1,049,866	7	2,224,385	343	113	213
NotreDame	Miscellaneous	449,885	1,496,528	9	5,812	10,721	152	682
Livemocha	Social	104,103	2,193,083	42	3,361,651	2,980	92	881
Hyves	Social	1,402,673	2,777,419	4	752,401	31,883	39	1,141
Youtube	Social	1,134,890	2,987,624	5	3,056,386	28,754	51	4,034
WikiTalk	Social	2,394,385	4,659,565	4	9,203,519	100,029	131	1,631
Flixster	Social	2,611,083	7,918,801	2	1,949	1431	40	41

Algorithms and Methods. We compare the performance of following decomposition methods:

- **BasicDEK:** Naive (k,s)-core decomposition, iterating first on k.
- **BasicDES (Algorithm 1):** Naive (k,s)-core decomposition, iterating first on s.
- **DEK:** Efficient (k,s)-core decomposition, iterating first on k.
- **DES (Algorithm 2):** Efficient (k,s)-core decomposition, iterating first on s.

We compare the space usage of:

- **Basic index:** Stores all the vertices for each k and s ($C_{k,s}$);
- **Advanced index:** Wisely selects and store the vertices for each k and s and uses the sorted neighbour list by the core number of nodes.

In addition, we evaluate the performance of our indexes in handling queries:

- **Naive method:** Uses the state-of-the-art (k,s)-core computation algorithm in [25] to compute $C_{k,s}$ for each $Q_{k,s}$.
- **Basic query processing:** Uses the basic (k,s)-core index.
- **Advanced query processing:** Uses our advanced (k,s)-core index.

5.2 Performance on Decomposition

Total Decomposition Time. Figure 3 summarizes the performances of our decomposition algorithms by showing the running time for various datasets. The figure shows that DES and DEC are always faster than BasicDEK and BasicDES, thanks to using the *Core Support* and our *pruning strategies*. DES outperforms the other three algorithms on all the datasets because of less calculation in inner loops. DES updates the engagements of nodes by the support of edges in outer iteration which saves a lot of computations which is not possible in DEK.

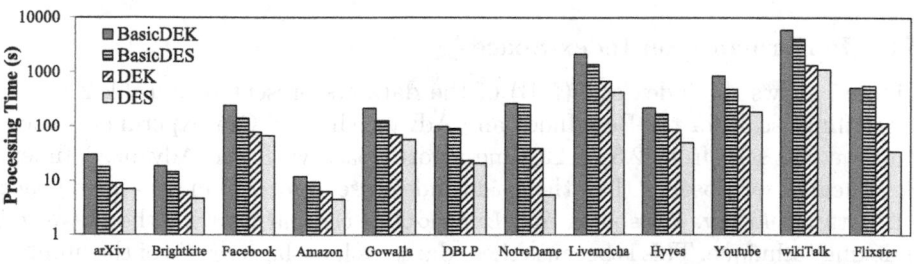

Fig. 3. Algorithms performances

Decomposition Time in Different Iterations. Although the numbers of iterations are the same in some of the datasets, the spent time in various iterations which has a great impact on total time is different. Figure 4(a) to 4(l) show the amount of spent times in different iterations of our algorithms. The spent time in all of the datasets are less in DES. With less number of triangles, the performance of DES is clearly better, because DES updates the engagements of nodes by the support of edges in the outer iteration, so having less number of triangles means weaker ties and consequently, the engagements of a lot of nodes are decreasing in early iterations on s towards zero. As an example, DES is 48 times faster than BasicDEK in `NoterDome` datasets with 1.5 million edges and the graph is empty after 12 iterations on s.

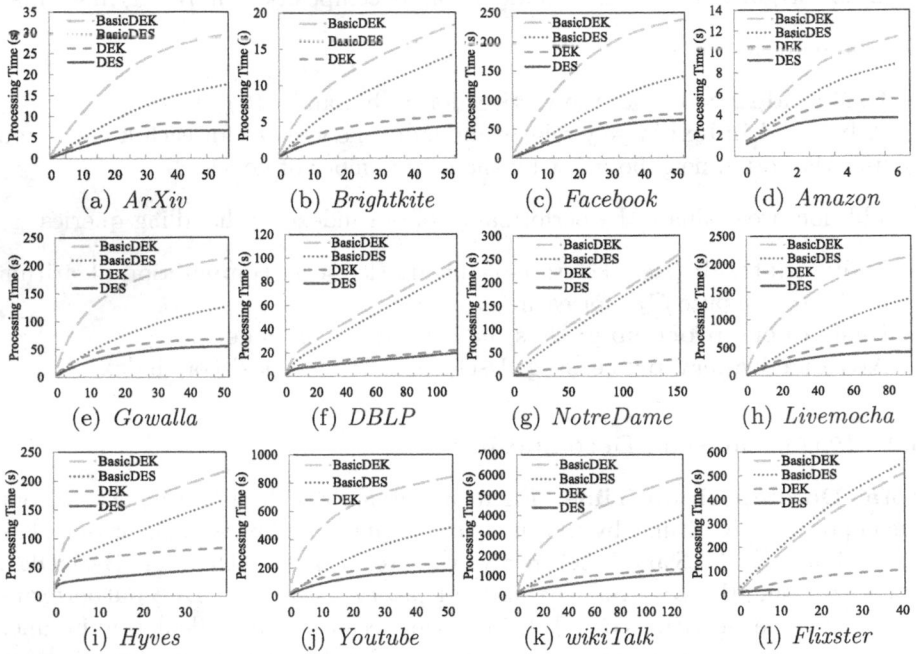

Fig. 4. Running time in iterations

5.3   Performance on Index Space

Figure 5 shows the index size (MB) of the datasets presented in Table 2 in the logarithmic scale for the BasicIndex and AdvancedIndex. Our experiments show that we can save from 2.5 to 20 times more space with the Advanced Index. Specifically, we observe that the basic index uses more than 10 times space (in datasets `ArXiv`, `Facebook`, and `Livemocha`) comparing with the advanced indexing technique. This is because these datasets have larger ratio of the number of triangles to the number of nodes which means that for each k-bucket in Basic Index, more nodes are stored in more s-buckets.

5.4   Performance on Query Processing

We evaluate and compare the performance of answering 100 random queries in our different datasets with the three query methods in Fig. 6. Although computing k'-core in advance in the naive method reduces the candidate set for further

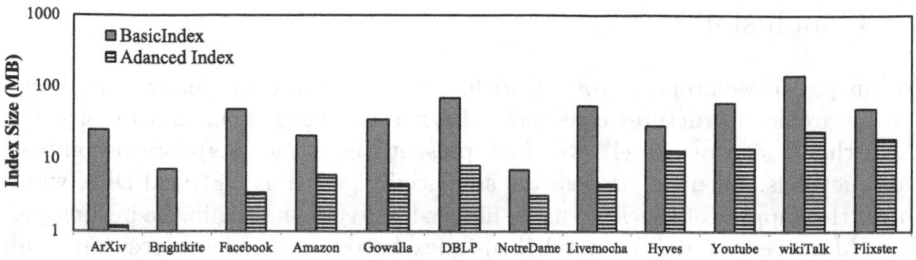

Fig. 5. Index size

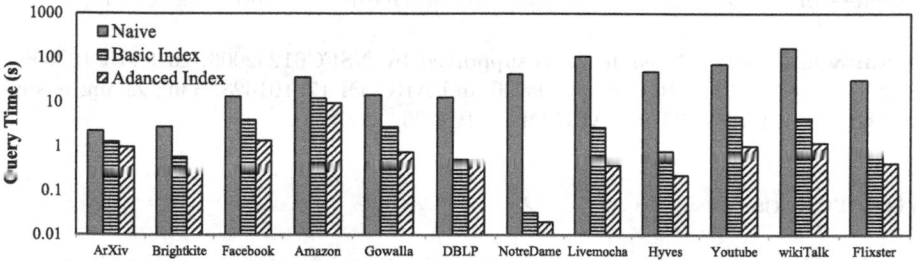

Fig. 6. Processing time for 100 queries in different datasets

computation and consequently saves time, its performance is worse and shows the need for having a proper index. For instance, on WikiTalk dataset with 4 million edges, our advanced index-based method takes about 1 s while the existing method takes more than 160 s to finish. Also, on NotreDame dataset, our advanced index-based query algorithm significantly outperforms the state-of-the-art method by more than three orders of magnitude. This is because the number of triangles is small in this dataset which leads to a limited number of nodes in the resulting (k,s)-cores.

6   Related Work

Various popular models for hierarchical decomposition of graph are proposed in recent literature including; **degree based decomposition** such as k-core [11,19], **tie-strength based decomposition** such as k-truss [4,9], **density based decomposition** which following the concept of locally-dense subgraph with different density value [14,20], **connectivity based decomposition** such as (k-ECC) [3] and the other variants like (k,s)-core [25], S-core on weighted network [6], CoreCube in multilayer graphs [10], k-(r,s)-nucleus [16,17], (k,d)-core [8]. Zhang et al. [25] developed (k,s)-core model but no decomposition method is introduced. In addition, we propose index-based (k,s)-core computation methods which significantly outperform their algorithm.

7 Conclusion

In this paper, we propose novel algorithms to decompose and index a graph into its hierarchical structures considering both user engagement and tie strength (i.e., the (k,s)-core model). We first present the basic (k,s)-core decomposition methods. Then, we propose the advanced algorithms DES and DEK which index the support of edges to enable higher-level cost-sharing in the peeling process. Moreover, we build a novel (k,s)-index based on the decomposition result and investigate efficient on line search algorithms based on our index. Extensive experimental evaluations on real-world datasets verify the efficiency and effectiveness of our proposed decomposition algorithms and indexing techniques.

Acknowledgment. Xuemin Lin is supported by NSFC61232006, 2018YFB1003504, ARC DP200101338, ARC DP180103096 and ARC DP170101628. Ying Zhang is supported by FT170100128 and ARC DP180103096.

References

1. Altaf-Ul-Amine, M., et al.: Prediction of protein functions based on k-cores of protein-protein interaction networks and amino acid sequences. Genome Inform. **14**, 498–499 (2003)
2. Alvarez-Hamelin, J.I., Dall'Asta, L., Barrat, A., Vespignani, A.: Large scale networks fingerprinting and visualization using the k-core decomposition. In: Advances in Neural Information Processing Systems, pp. 41–50 (2006)
3. Chang, L., Yu, J.X., Qin, L., Lin, X., Liu, C., Liang, W.: Efficiently computing k-edge connected components via graph decomposition. In: SIGMOD, pp. 205–216. ACM (2013)
4. Cohen, J.: Trusses: cohesive subgraphs for social network analysis, June 2019
5. Dorogovtsev, S.N., Goltsev, A.V., Mendes, J.F.F.: K-core organization of complex networks. Phys. Rev. Lett. **96**(4), 040601 (2006)
6. Eidsaa, M., Almaas, E.: S-core network decomposition: a generalization of k-core analysis to weighted networks. Phys. Rev. E **88**(6), 062819 (2013)
7. Khaouid, W., Barsky, M., Srinivasan, V., Thomo, A.: K-core decomposition of large networks on a single pc. PVLDB **9**(1), 13–23 (2015)
8. Lee, P., Lakshmanan, L.V., Milios, E.: Cast: a context-aware story-teller for streaming social content. In: CIKM, pp. 789–798. ACM (2014)
9. Li, Z., et al.: Discovering hierarchical subgraphs of k-core-truss. Data Sci. Eng. **3**(2), 136–149 (2018)
10. Liu, B., Zhang, F., Zhang, C., Zhang, W., Lin, X.: CoreCube: core decomposition in multilayer graphs. In: Cheng, R., Mamoulis, N., Sun, Y., Huang, X. (eds.) WISE 2020. LNCS, vol. 11881, pp. 694–710. Springer, Cham (2019). https://doi.org/10.1007/978-3-030-34223-4_44
11. Malliaros, F.D., Papadopoulos, A.N., Vazirgiannis, M.: Core decomposition in graphs: concepts, algorithms and applications. In: EDBT, pp. 720–721 (2016)
12. Mattie, H., Engø-Monsen, K., Ling, R., Onnela, J.P.: Understanding tie strength in social networks using a local "bow tie" framework. Sci. Rep. **8** (2018). https://doi.org/10.1038/s41598-018-27290-8

13. Matula, D.W., Beck, L.L.: Smallest-last ordering and clustering and graph coloring algorithms. JACM **30**(3), 417–427 (1983)
14. Qin, L., Li, R.H., Chang, L., Zhang, C.: Locally densest subgraph discovery. In: Proceedings of the 21th ACM SIGKDD International Conference on Knowledge Discovery and Data Mining, pp. 965–974. ACM (2015)
15. Saito, K., Yamada, T., Kazama, K.: Extracting communities from complex networks by the k-dense method. IEICE Trans. Fundam. Electron. Commun. Comput. Sci. **91**(11), 3304–3311 (2008)
16. Sariyüce, A.E., Pinar, A.: Fast hierarchy construction for dense subgraphs. PVLDB **10**(3), 97–108 (2016)
17. Sariyuce, A.E., Seshadhri, C., Pinar, A., Catalyurek, U.V.: Finding the hierarchy of dense subgraphs using nucleus decompositions. In: WWW, pp. 927–937. International World Wide Web Conferences Steering Committee (2015)
18. Sariyüce, A.E., Seshadhri, C., Pinar, A., Çatalyürek, Ü.V.: Nucleus decompositions for identifying hierarchy of dense subgraphs. TWEB **11**(3), 16 (2017)
19. Seidman, S.B.: Network structure and minimum degree. Soc. Netw. **5**(3), 269–287 (1983)
20. Tattı, N.: Density-friendly graph decomposition. TKDD **13**(5), 54 (2019)
21. Wang, J., Cheng, J.: Truss decomposition in massive networks. PVLDB **5**(9), 812–823 (2012)
22. Wang, K., Cao, X., Lin, X., Zhang, W., Qin, L.: Efficient computing of radius-bounded k-cores. In: ICDE, pp. 233–244. IEEE (2018)
23. Wang, K., Lin, X., Qin, L., Zhang, W., Zhang, Y.: Vertex priority based butterfly counting for large-scale bipartite networks. PVLDB **12**(10), 1139–1152 (2019)
24. Wang, K., Lin, X., Qin, L., Zhang, W., Zhang, Y.: Efficient bitruss decomposition for large-scale bipartite graphs. In: ICDE. IEEE (2020)
25. Zhang, F., Yuan, L., Zhang, Y., Qin, L., Lin, X., Zhou, A.: Discovering strong communities with user engagement and tie strength. In: Pei, J., Manolopoulos, Y., Sadiq, S., Li, J. (eds.) DASFAA 2018. LNCS, vol. 10827, pp. 425–441. Springer, Cham (2018). https://doi.org/10.1007/978-3-319-91452-7_28
26. Zhang, F., Zhang, Y., Qin, L., Zhang, W., Lin, X.: When engagement meets similarity: efficient (k,r)-core computation on social networks. PVLDB **10**(10), 998–1009 (2017)
27. Zhang, Y., Qin, L., Zhang, F., Zhang, W.: Hierarchical decomposition of big graphs. In: ICDE, pp. 2064–2067, April 2019
28. Zhang, Y., Parthasarathy, S.: Extracting analyzing and visualizing triangle k-core motifs within networks. In: ICDE, pp. 1049–1060. IEEE (2012)
29. Zhao, F., Tung, A.K.: Large scale cohesive subgraphs discovery for social network visual analysis. PVLDB **6**(2), 85–96 (2012)

Role-Oriented Graph Auto-encoder Guided by Structural Information

Xuan Guo[1], Wang Zhang[1], Wenjun Wang[1], Yang Yu[1], Yinghui Wang[1], and Pengfei Jiao[1,2(✉)] (iD)

[1] College of Intelligence and Computing, Tianjin University, Tianjin 300350, China
{guoxuan,wangzhang,wjwang,yuyangyy,wangyinghui}@tju.edu.cn
[2] Center of Biosafety Research and Strategy, Tianjin University, Tianjin 300092, China
pjiao@tju.edu.cn

Abstract. Roles in a complex network usually represent the local connectivity patterns of nodes, which reflect the functions or behaviors of corresponding entities. Role discovery has great meaning for understanding the formation and evolution of networks. While the importance of role discovery in networks has been realized gradually, a variety of approaches of role-oriented network representation learning are proposed. Almost all the existing approaches are dependent on manual high-order structural properties which are always fragmentary. They suffer from unstable performances and poor generalization ability, because their handcraft structural features sometimes miss the characteristics of different networks. In addition, graph neural networks (GNNs) have great potential to automatically capture structural properties, but it is hard to be given the rein to for the difficulty of designing role-oriented unsupervised loss. To overcome these challenges, we provide an idea that leverage low-dimensional extracted structural features as guidance to train graph neural networks. Based on the idea, we proposed GAS, a novel graph auto-encoder guided by structural information, to learn role-oriented representations for nodes. Results of extensive experiments show that GAS has better performance than other state-of-the-art approaches.

Keywords: Role discovery · Network embedding · Graph convolution networks · Graph auto-encoder

1 Introduction

Graph or Network is the natural representation structure of irregular data in numerous application domains, including social networks [28], proteomics [31], etc. Specifically, nodes and edges in a network are used to represent real-world entities and their relationships. In this way, different problems in many domains can be transformed into corresponding research problems on networks. While

---

X. Guo and W. Zhang—These authors contributed equally to this work.

© Springer Nature Switzerland AG 2020
Y. Nah et al. (Eds.): DASFAA 2020, LNCS 12113, pp. 466–481, 2020.
https://doi.org/10.1007/978-3-030-59416-9_28

modeling complex systems in reality, networks contain a lot of useful hidden information which is worth mining out and analyzing considerately. **Community Detection** [11] and **Role Discovery** [21,24] are such two research fields of mining network information at the mesoscopic level.

Community detection and role discovery are two kinds of graph clustering problems based on different criteria. As shown in Fig. 1, the nodes play different roles as reflected in their local connectivity patterns while forming communities having more connections inside than outside. Correspondingly, real-world entities always perform various functions and behaviors in groups, such as employers and employees at different positions forming companies. Naturally, studying communities can help to learn the shared interests and objectives of entities while studying roles are conductive to capturing the distinctions between relationships. Therefore, communities and roles are of great significance for understanding the formation and evolution of networks. However, community detection has been profoundly studied for a long time while role discovery has attracted little but increasing attention in recent years.

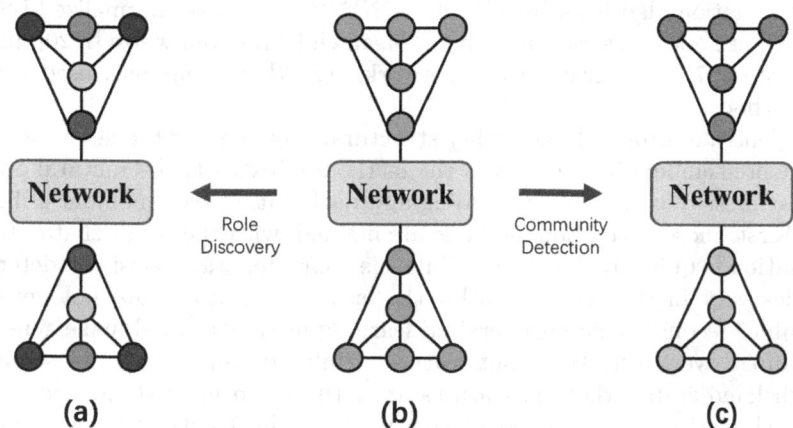

Fig. 1. Comparison between role discovery and community detection. (a) The result of role discovery. (b) The original network. (c) The result of community detection.

Essentially, role discovery is the process of capturing structural properties of nodes. Thus, classic metrics computed based on node-centric structure, such as PageRank [18] and other node centralities, could be considered as role measures. But these metrics can only represent roles from a particular viewpoint and usually have high computational complexity, which limit their applications for complex and massive analysis and machine learning tasks on large-scale networks.

Fortunately, **Network Embedding** (also known as **Network Representation Learning**), which uses low-dimensional vectors to preserve original node information in networks, has shown great power on representing large-scale networks. Compared with the above metrics, the learned embeddings are more versatile representations. While losing complex graph structure and preserving much information in vectors, the embeddings can be easily and effectively utilized for large amounts of tasks of network analysis and machine learning. However, most of existing network embedding algorithms [5,19,25] are based on proximity of nodes, which means the closer nodes in the network have more similar embeddings. In other words, these algorithms are oriented to communities. As the importance of roles has been realized gradually, some role-oriented network embedding approaches have been proposed recently.

The aim of role-oriented network embedding is to encode node-centric structural information and transform the structural similarities between nodes into the geometric relationships in embedding space. Guided by the purpose, almost all of role-oriented network embedding approaches are in two steps: (S1) Capture the structural properties of nodes. (S2) Mapping structural properties and similarities into embeddings. Most role-oriented embedding approaches leverage high-order structural features to capture sturctural information. For example, role2vec [1] and HONE [23] leverage small induced subgraphs called motifs while RolX [8], GLRD [3] and DMER [12] take advantages of a recursive feature aggregation algorithm ReFeX [9]. DRNE [27] uses layer normalized LSTMs to represent nodes on sorted neighbors. Meanwhile, random walks [1,20], matrix factorization [7,8] and graph neural networks [12,27] are commonly used as mapping methods.

Evidently, obtaining high-quality structural properties is the key to learning role-oriented embeddings. However, the methods of extracting structural properties that most role-oriented embedding approaches use have a number of limitations. First, those extraction methods are manual, with the result that obtained information is quite fragmentary. While the characteristics decisively determining roles vary in different networks, the extracted features are not generally applicable. Second, some unsupervised learning methods would make generated embeddings overfitting the input features while ignoring the graph structure. Though hand-craft structural features are intuitive to understand and easy to handle, they suffer from massive information loss. Third, extraction of high-order structural features such as motifs could be quite time-consuming.

What's more, **graph neural networks (GNNs)** have the natural ability to learn structural properties due to its propagation mechanism on the edges. However, it is pretty difficult to design the role-oriented unsupervised loss. Though some works tried in different ways including reconstructing input features and approximating embeddings by recursively aggregation on neighborhood, they still face limitations mentioned above for over-dependency on manual extraction process. What role-oriented GNN models need is only little guidance with which they can extract high-quality structural information automatically.

To address aforementioned problems, we propose **GAS**, a novel graph autoencoder guided by structural information. In GAS, we use graph convolutional layers [14] to capture structural properties. We replace the symmetric normalized adjacency matrix in each graph convolutional layer with the unnormalized adjacency matrix to distinguishing local structures more powerfully. We leverage structural features as guidance information instead of inputs so that our method can greatly alleviate the problems caused by over-dependence on hand-craft features. Additionally, the features we use are obtained by aggregating neighbor's primary features only once and their dimensions are very low. Without lots of unnecessary computations, our model is highly efficient.

In summary, the contributions of our paper are as follows:

1. We are the first to provide the idea of using structural features as guidance information to train role-oriented graph neural networks.
2. We propose GAS, a novel graph auto-encoder guided by structural information for role-oriented tasks. We leverage features in very low dimensions to GAS for high efficiency and effectiveness.
3. While performing better than other state-of-the-art embedding methods in a variety of experiments on several real-world datasets, the correctness of our guidance idea and the effectiveness of our approach are verified.

2 Related Work

Graph is irregular structure and real-world networks are always in large-scale and sparse. Therefore, it is too difficult to utilize graph structure data directly as inputs of complex and massive network tasks. Inspired by word embedding methods, which generate dense representations in low dimensions for sparse distributed words, **Network Embedding** methods are proposed to encode nodes into low-dimensional embedding space.

DeepWalk [19] is the first to introduce the classic language model Skip-Gram [17] to network representation learning. It leverages random walks to generate sequences composed of nodes as the inputs of Skip-Gram. Then Skip-Gram produces representations of nodes. On the basis of DeepWalk, Node2vec [5] makes random walks biased by adding two hyper-parameters in order to capture both homogeneity and structural properties of nodes. However, embeddings of the nodes that are close in the network are still similar due to the similar node contexts. To be appliable for large-scale networks, LINE [25] uses an objective function that preserves direct links (first-order proximity) and shared neighbors (second-order proximity) of nodes and an edge-sampling algorithm for optimizing the objective. Therefore, these methods are all designed for capturing proximity of nodes and not feasible for role-orient tasks.

Some role-oriented network embedding approaches have been proposed recently. ReFeX [9] extracts local and egonet features and aggregates the features of neighbors recursively. As an efficient method of high-order structural feature extraction, ReFeX is applied extensively in many other role-oriented embedding approaches. For example, RolX [8] leverages ReFeX to extract structural features and generates embeddings via Non-negative Matrix Factorization. Soon afterwards, GLRD [3] extends RolX by adding sparsity and diversity constraints to the NMF formulation. Similarly, xNetMF in REGAL [7] firstly obtains structural features by counting of node degrees of k-hop neighbors of each node. Then it uses Singular Value Decomposition to encode the similarity calculated based on both structure and attributes to representations.

There are several approaches based on random walks. Role2vec [1] designs a feature based random walk for learning role-oriented embeddings. It replaces the sequences of nodes in DeepWalk with sequences of motif-based feature values so that structural information could be kept in the representations. In contrast to Role2vec which leveraging features to random walks in a direct way, Struc2vec [20] constructs a hierarchy of complete graphs by transforming degree-based structural similarities to weights of edges. After construction, Skip-Gram are trained on the multi-layer network.

Graph neural networks have great potential to capture local connectivity patterns due to their propagation mechanisms on edges. Nevertheless, to our best known, only two role-oriented embedding methods leverage graph neural networks. DRNE [27] uses layer normalized LSTMs [10] to handle graph data entered. In essence, it is an semi-manual method of capturing structural properties. DRNE also defines a recursive aggregation process to learn regular equivalence of nodes. DMER [12], a deep mutual encode model combining graph convolutional networks [14] and feature-based auto-encoder, is an attempt to reduce dependency on manual processes. It should be noted that the propagation mechanisms could be a double-edged sword. A large number of aggregation processes might smooth embeddings of connected nodes to much, which is really harmful to role-oriented embeddings.

Additionally, HONE [23] and GraphWave [2] use different diffusion methods to learn the local connectivity patterns of nodes.

It's apparent almost all of above role-oriented embedding approaches can be summed up in two steps: structural properties extraction and mapping. While the quality of extracted properties determines the effectiveness of learned representations, these approaches face lots of problems caused by their mutual extraction methods.

3   Method

In this section, we introduce the notations and the details of our proposed role-oriented network embedding framework named GAS. As the overview is shown in Fig. 2, our framework are roughly divided in three parts: (a) Extract structural features as the guidance information; (b) Use a graph auto-encoder for encoding nodes to role-oriented embeddings which are reconstructed to features by the decoder; (c) Compute the loss based on guidance features and reconstructed features for training the graph auto-encoder.

3.1   Notations

Given a undirected unweighted network $G = (V, E)$, where $V = \{v_1, ..., v_n\}$ is the set of n nodes and $E \subseteq V \times V$ is the set of edges among the nodes. For each node $v \in V$, the set of its neighborhood is denoted as $\mathcal{N}(v) = \{u|(v, u) \in E\}$.

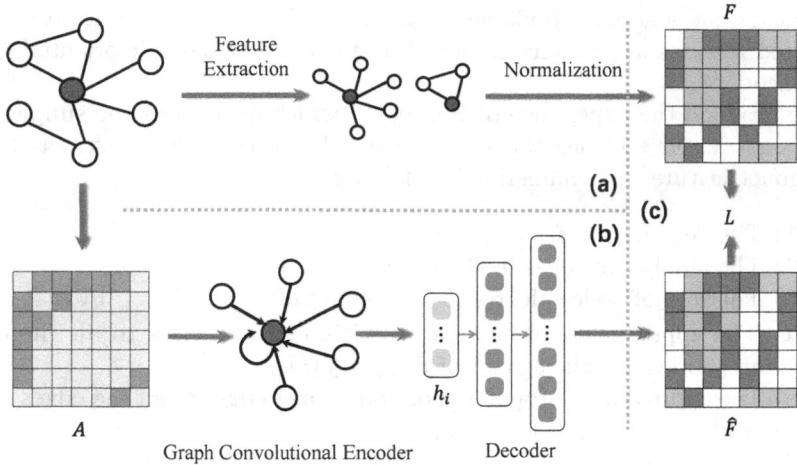

Fig. 2. Overview of our proposed GAS framework. (a): Structural feature extraction. (b): Encoder-decoder architecture. (c): Loss computation based on artificially extracted features and features reconstructed by decoder.

Table 1. Main notations and their definitions.

Notation	Definition
$G = (V, E)$	The graph G with node set V and edge set E
$A \in \mathbb{R}^{n \times n}$	The adjacency matrix of G
$D \in \mathbb{R}^{n \times n}$	The degree matrix of G
$F \in \mathbb{R}^{n \times d}$	The extracted structural matrix of G
$\mathcal{N}(v) = \{u | (v, u) \in E\}$	The set of node v's neighbors G
$\mathcal{E}(v) = (V_{\mathcal{E}(v)}, E_{\mathcal{E}(v)})$	The egonet of node v
$T(v)$	The set of triangles node v participates in

$A \in \mathbb{R}^{n \times n}$ is the adjacency matrix of G. $A_{ij} = 1$ if v_i and v_j are linked in G, otherwise $A_{ij} = 0$. $\mathcal{E}(v) = (V_{\mathcal{E}(v)}, E_{\mathcal{E}(v)})$ denotes the egonet of node v, where $V_{\mathcal{E}(v)} = \mathcal{N}(v) \cup \{v\}$ and $E_{\mathcal{E}(v)} = \{(u, u') | (u, u') \in E \wedge u, u' \in V_{\mathcal{E}(v)}\}$ are the sets of nodes and edges in $\mathcal{E}(v)$ respectively. $T(v) = \{\{v, u, u'\} | (v, u), (v, u'), (u, u') \in E\}$ means the set of triangles node v participates in. The symbol of degree matrix is $D_{ii} = \sum_j A_{ij}$. $F \in \mathbb{R}^{n \times m}$ represents the extracted structural feature matrix, where each row F_i is the m-dimensional feature vector of node v_i. The notations mainly used in this paper are sumarized in Table 1.

3.2 Feature Extraction

Role-oriented network representation learning is unsupervised. While treating hand-craft structural features as inputs, the generated embeddings would fit features. This kind of dependence on features is too strong and makes embedding approaches not generally appliable. To alleviate the problems, we choose to use extracted features as guidance information for training our role-oriented graph auto-encoder.

We draw on the experience of ReFeX [9] which aggregates the simple local and egonet features of neighbors recursively. For each node v, extracted local and egonet features are enumerated as follows:

- **(F1)** The degree of v: $f_1 = |\mathcal{N}(v)|$.
- **(F2)** The number of edges in the egonet of v: $f_2 = |E_{\mathcal{E}(v)}|$.
- **(F3)** The sum of node's degree in the egonet of v: $f_3 = \sum_{\mathcal{E}(v)} |\mathcal{N}(u)|$.
- **(F4)** The approximate proportion of within-egonet edges to all the edges entering and leaving the egonet of v: $f_4 = f_2/f_3$.
- **(F5)** The approximate proportion of non-egonet edges to all the edges entering and leaving the egonet of v: $f_5 = 1 - f_2/f_3$.
- **(F6)** The number of triangles v participates in: $f_6 = |T(v)|$.
- **(F7)** The clustering coefficient of v: $f_7 = 2f_6/(f_1(f_1 - 1))$.

Then each kind of above features are normalized to range $(0, 1)$. We construct the primary structural feature matrix $\widetilde{F}$ in which each row is a 7-dimensional vector composed of normalized features. We calculate Finally, the features are aggregated by computing the mean and sum of node features in each egonet as follows:

$$F = \widetilde{F} \circ \hat{D}^{-1}\hat{A}\widetilde{F} \circ \hat{A}\widetilde{F}, \tag{1}$$

where $\circ$ is the concatenation operator. $\hat{A} = A + I$ is the adjacency matrix of graph G with added self-loops where $I \in \mathbb{R}^{n \times n}$ is the identity matrix, and $\hat{D}_{ii} = \sum_j \hat{A}_{ij}$. Because a small F is enough as guidance information, we only aggregates the features only once. The dimension of every node's ultimate feature vectors is only $m = 21$. Intuitively, the full process of feature extraction is simple and efficient while high-order structrual information are captured.

3.3   Graph Auto-encoder

Our encoder consists of multi layers of graph convolutional networks (GCN) [14]. The original GCN use the propagation rule as follows:

$$H^{(l)} = \sigma(\hat{D}^{-\frac{1}{2}}\hat{A}D^{-\frac{1}{2}}H^{(l-1)}\Theta^{(l)}), \tag{2}$$

where $l = 1, 2, \cdots, L$. $H^{(l-1)} \in \mathbb{R}^{n \times d}$ and $\Theta^{(l)} \in \mathbb{R}^{d \times c}$ represent the activation matrix and the trainable weight matrix of the lth layer respectively. $H^{(0)}$ is $\hat{A}$ or a randomly initialized matrix. $\sigma(\cdot)$ denotes a nonlinear activation function.

As discussed in [30], the propagation rule of original GCN is essentially a variety of mean-pooling. Sometimes mean-pooling does not perform well for distinguishing local structures, which is lethal to role-oriented tasks. For greater discrimination, we apply following sum-pooling propagation rule in our graph convolutional encoder:

$$H^{(l)} = \sigma(\hat{A}H^{(l-1)}\Theta^{(l)}). \tag{3}$$

The output of the Lth layer of graph convolutional network, i.e. $H^{(L)}$, is the representation matrix whose ith row $H_i^{(L)}$ is the representation of node v_i.

Then we use multi-layer perceptrons to decode the representations as follows:

$$\hat{H}^{(s)} = \sigma(\hat{H}^{(s-1)} W^{(s)} + b^{(s)}), \tag{4}$$

where $s = 1, 2, \cdots, S$. $\hat{H}^{(s-1)} \in \mathbb{R}^{n \times d'}$ is the activation matrix in the sth layer, $W^{(l)} \in \mathbb{R}^{d' \times c'}$ and $b^{(s)}$ are the trainable weight matrix and the biases of the sth-layer perceptron respectively. $\hat{H}^{(0)} = H^{(L)}$. The reconstructed structural features are generated by the last layer of perceptron:

$$\hat{F} = \hat{H}^{(S)} = \sigma(\hat{H}^{(S-1)} W^{(S)} + b^{(S)}), \tag{5}$$

which is used to construct loss function.

3.4 Training

In contrast to most existing methods which treat hand-craft structural features as inputs, we use extracted features as guidance of training for our algorithm. Thus, we let the reconstructed feature matrix $\hat{F}$ approach the extracted feature matrix F by minimizing the guidance loss which is defined as follows:

$$\mathcal{L}_g = \left\| \hat{F} - F \right\|_{fro}^2, \tag{6}$$

where $\|\cdot\|_{fro}$ denotes the Frobenius norm. In order to increase the robustness of our model, we introduce the following L2 regularization to the parameters of our graph convolutional auto-encoder:

$$\mathcal{L}_{reg} = \sum_{l=1}^{L} \left\| \Theta^{(l)} \right\|_{fro}^2 + \sum_{s=1}^{S} (\left\| W^{(s)} + b^{(s)} \right\|_2^2). \tag{7}$$

The final loss function is as follows:

$$\mathcal{L} = \mathcal{L}_g + \lambda \mathcal{L}_{reg}, \tag{8}$$

where λ is the weight of $\mathcal{L}_{reg}$. As we discussed above, the embeddings obtained via most existing methods fit the mutually extracted features. In contrast, our approach GAS can provide embeddings containing richer structural information which can reconstruct the extracted features while minimizing the guidance loss.

3.5 Computational Complexity

Let $|V|$ denotes the number of nodes, $|E|$ denotes the number of edges, f be the number of extracted primary local and egonet features. $f = 7$ in our method. For a input real-world network, computing primary local and egonet features takes $O(|V|)$ [9]. Though we express the aggregation process as matrix multiplications,

Table 2. Detailed statistic of the datasets.

Dataset	# Nodes	# Edges	# Classes	Density(%)
Brazil	131	1,003	4	11.7792
Europe	399	5,995	4	7.5503
USA	1,190	13,599	4	1.9222
Reality-call	6,809	7,680	3	0.0331
Actor	7,779	26,752	4	0.0884

each aggregation actually take $O(|E|f)$ due to the sparsity of the network. While aggregating only once, the total time complexity of feature extraction is $O(|E|f + |V|f)$. Thus, the process of feature extraction in our framework is highly efficient.

Each layer of graph convolutional networks has complexity $O(|E|dc)$ [14], where d is the dimension of input representations and c is the dimension of output representations. Compared with other graph neural networks propagating on all the edges, i.e. without sampling in each node's neighborhood, our encoder composed of GCNs is one of the most efficient models.

4   Experiments

4.1   Datasets

To verify the effectiveness of our proposed approach GAS, we conduct experiments on following real-world networks:

- **Air-traffic networks** [20]: There are three air-traffic networks, including American, Brazilian and European air-traffic networks (shortly denoted as USA, Brazil, and Europe). In these networks, nodes represent airports and edges represent commercial flights existing between airports. Airports are grouped based on the volume of airplanes or people.
- **Actor co-occurance network** [15]: It is an actor only network extracted from a film-director-actor-writer network [26]. In this network, nodes mean actors and edges between them mean that they have appeared on the same Wiki pages. Actors are labeled based on the number of words of their Wiki pages. For convenience, we use Actor to denote this network.
- **Phone call Network** [22]: This real phone call data records a total of 52050 calls from 6809 users during the period from September 2004 to January 2005. We express it as a static network in which nodes denote users and edges denote communication between them. The users are divided into different classes based on their frequencies of calls. For convenience, we use Reality to denote this network.

The details of these datasets are provided in Table 2.

Table 3. The micro-averaged F1 score on different datasets (The mean results of 10 runs; OM means out of memory).

Dataset	Brazil	Europe	USA	Reality	Actor
DeepWalk	0.4050 (8)	0.4064 (8)	0.4936 (8)	0.5098 (7)	0.3560 (7)
Node2vec	0.4145 (7)	0.4441 (7)	0.4988 (7)	0.4917 (8)	0.3609 (6)
RolX	0.7107 (6)	0.5495 (4)	0.6424 (2)	0.6538 (5)	0.4723 (3)
GraphWave	0.7300 (4)	0.5331 6)	0.5180 (6)	0.8255 (3)	OM
Struc2vec	0.7262 (5)	0.5788 (2)	0.6113 (5)	0.6074 (6)	0.4679 (4)
DRNE	0.7555 (2)	0.5574 (3)	0.6159 (4)	0.8389 (2)	0.4751 (2)
Features	0.7365 (3)	0.5373 (5)	0.6227 (3)	0.7740 (4)	0.4653 (5)
GAS	**0.7995 (1)**	**0.5825 (1)**	**0.6737 (1)**	**0.8458 (1)**	**0.4822 (1)**

Table 4. The macro-averaged F1 score on different datasets (The mean results of 10 runs; OM means out of memory).

Dataset	Brazil	Europe	USA	Reality	Actor
DeepWalk	0.4009 (8)	0.4009 (8)	0.4763 (7)	0.3332 (7)	0.3456 (7)
Node2vec	0.3994 (7)	0.4218 (7)	0.4818 (6)	0.3240 (8)	0.3473 (6)
RolX	0.7053 (6)	0.5364 (5)	0.6352 (2)	0.4290 (5)	0.4586 (4)
GraphWave	0.7144 (5)	0.4953 (6)	0.4730 (8)	0.5180 (3)	OM
Struc2vec	0.7205 (4)	0.5752 (2)	0.6036 (4)	0.3874 (6)	0.4611 (3)
DRNE	0.7446 (2)	0.5475 (3)	0.6013 (5)	0.5244 (2)	0.4682 (2)
Features	0.7206 (3)	0.5422 (4)	0.6141 (3)	0.4986 (4)	0.4542 (5)
GAS	**0.7940 (1)**	**0.5799 (1)**	**0.6658 (1)**	**0.5327 (1)**	**0.4815 (1)**

4.2 Model Configuration

We adopt two layers of graph convolutional networks as the encoder and two layers of multi-layer perceptrons. For the nonlinear activation function $\sigma(\cdot)$, sigmoid function is selected. We set the dimension of embeddings to 128 and the weight of L2 regularization to 0.8. The models is initialized using Glorot initialization [4] and trained using the Adam SGD optimizer [13] with a learning rate of 0.001 for at most 200 epochs. We also use an early stopping strategy on the loss $\mathcal{L}$ with a patience of 15 epochs.

4.3 Baselines

We compared our model with several state-of-the-art network representation learning approaches including both classic models and role-oriented models. The dimension of embeddings is set to 128 to all the baselines except Features and DRNE [27]. The baselines and their parameter settings are listed as follows:

- **Features**: Features denotes the handcraft structural features referenced ReFeX [9] which we use as guidance information.
- **DeepWalk** [19]: DeepWalk learns node representations by leveraging Skip-Gram [17] to node sequences generated by random walks. We set window size to 10, walk length to 80 and each node's number of walks to 20.
- **Node2vec** [5]: Node2vec uses a biased random walk method to capture more neighborhood information than DeepWalk. To capture more structural information, we set hyper-parameter $p = 1$ and $q = 3$. The parameters of random walks are the same as those of DeepWalk.
- **RolX** [8]: RolX decompose the feature matrix generated by ReFeX [9] using non-negative matrix factorization. For different networks, we tune the number of aggregation recursions to get the best results.
- **GraphWave** [17]: GraphWave treats spectral graph wavelets as probability distributions and generate embeddings by characterizing the distributions. We use its default settings.
- **Struc2vec** [20]: Struc2vec applies random walk method on a reconstructed multi-layer networks. We tune the layer number of the reconstructed hierarchy for different networks and the parameters of random walks are the same as those of DeepWalk.
- **DRNE** [27]: DRNE uses layer normalized LSTMs to represent nodes and captures the regular equivalence by recursively aggregating the representations. The dimension of embeddings is set as 32, with which DRNE gets the best results. The other parameters are set as default.

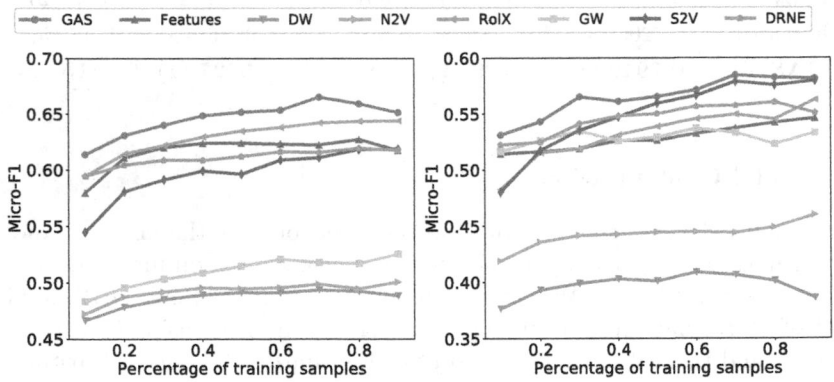

Fig. 3. The micro-averaged F1 score for role-oriented node classification on different dataset splits. Left: USA. Right: European. The shorthands DW, N2V, GW and S2V denote methods DeepWalk, Node2vec, GraphWave and Struc2vec respectively.

4.4   Role-Oriented Node Classification

We conduct role-oriented node classification tasks to evaluate the proposed graph auto-encoder guided by structural information. For each dataset, a linear logistic

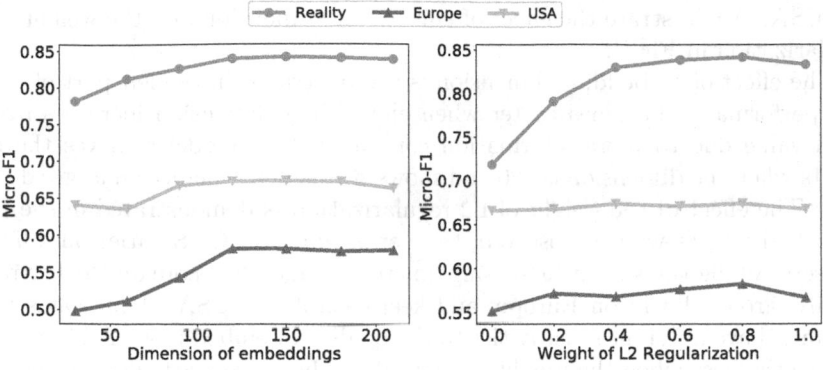

Fig. 4. Parameter Sensitivity w.r.t. the dimension of embeddings (left), the weight of L2 regularization (right).

regression classifier trained and tested using embeddings generated by each baseline and our model. We randomly sample 70% node embeddings as the training set and the other embeddings are used as the test set. The micro-averaged F1 score and macro-averaged F1 score are reported in Table 3 and Table 4 respectively, where the ranks of results are in brackets.

We have following observations:

- Role-oriented embedding methods including RolX, GraphWave and DRNE performs much better than classic embedding methods including DeepWalk and Node2vec, which verifies the no-free-lunch theorem [29] and the necessity of role-oriented network representation learning.
- Role-oriented baseline methods get fluctuating results because node roles in different networks are determined by different features. That is one of our motivation to use manually extracted features as guidance information.
- The results of our extracted features are not bad though their dimension is only 21. That indicates the extracted features contain a certain amount of structural information, which is their foundation to be used as guidance.
- Compared with Features, our approach GAS has improved performance greatly, which verifies the correctness of the idea using extracted structural features as guidance information.
- Our GAS overperforms all of the baselines on all the datasets. GAS is a state-of-the-art method for role-oriented network representation learning.

We also report the results of role-oriented node classification tasks using different train/test splits of the networks in Fig. 3. It can be observed that our model GAS still performs better than baselines on different splits.

4.5   Parameter Sensitivity

To evaluate how parameters influence the performance of our proposed GAS, role-oriented node classification tasks are conducted to datasets Reality, Europe and USA. We illustrate the effect of embedding dimension and the weight of L2 regularization in Fig. 4.

The effect of embedding dimension is demonstrated in the left part of Fig. 4. The performance becomes better when embedding dimension increases from a small value due to more information contained. Our model achieves the best results when the dimension is 120 and shows stable performance on larger dimensions. The effect of the weight of L2 regularization is demonstrated in the right part of Fig. 4. As we can observed, the performance of GAS varies on different datasets. While the weight increasing, micro-averaged F1 score on Reality raises rapidly, grows slowly on Europe, and keeps stable on USA. It indicates these networks have different sensitivities to the quality of embeddings. All the results achieve the best when the weight is about 0.8. The score starts decreasing when the weight exceeds 0.8.

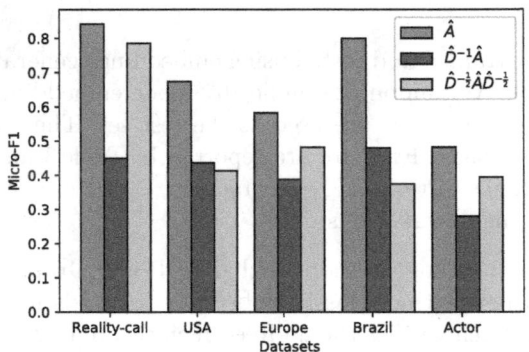

Fig. 5. Effectiveness w.r.t the propagation rules of graph convolutional encoder.

4.6 Propagation Rule Analysis

Graph neural networks could capture structural information due to its propagation mechanisms on edges. For GAS, we leverage graph convolutional networks as the encoder. And we use sum-pooling propagation rule defined as Eq. 3 for its great power of distinguishing local structures. To verify the point, we change the propagation rule of GAS to that of original GCN and mean-pooling propagation rule [6] defined as Eq. 2 and Eq. 9 respectively.

$$H^{(l)} = \sigma(\hat{D}^{-1}\hat{A}H^{(l-1)}\Theta^{(l)}). \tag{9}$$

The results are reported in Fig. 5 where we denotes the three propagation rules shortly as $\hat{A}$, $\hat{D}^{-1}\hat{A}$ and $\hat{D}^{-\frac{1}{2}}\hat{A}\hat{D}^{-\frac{1}{2}}$. The sum-pooling does perform much better than the other two methods. Original GCN and mean-pooling propagation rule perform differently due to the distinctions of datasets.

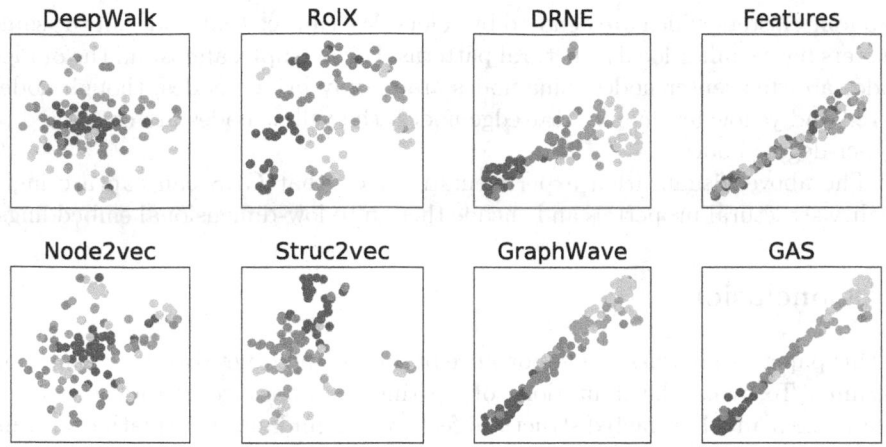

Fig. 6. Visualization of node representations on Brazil network.

4.7 Visualization

We illustrate the embeddings which are generated by our approach GAS and baselines in Fig. 6. Here, the embeddings are projected to two dimensions using t-SNE [16] and the colors of nodes represents their labels. The closer the ebeddings of nodes with the same label are, the better effectiveness are demonstrated. Thus, the same observations described in Sect. 4.4 can be obtained again from Fig. 6.

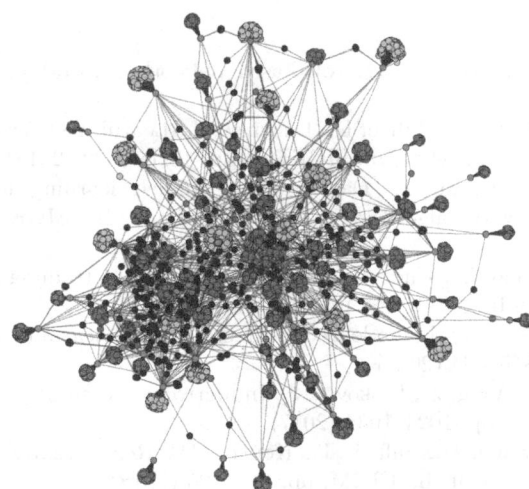

Fig. 7. The result of clustering nodes by using K-means based on embeddings.

We also adopt K-means algorithm on embeddings generated by GAS to cluster the nodes. As shown in the Fig. 7, we divide the nodes of Reality network into four clusters which are denoted by colors. We can see that nodes in the same clusters have similar local structural patterns. For example, almost all the orange nodes are star-center nodes; blue nodes are mainly bridge nodes; though nodes in red and yellow are mainly star-edge nodes, the yellow nodes are connected to higher-degree nodes.

The above visualization experiments indicate that GAS can capture high-quality structural properties and encode them into low-dimensional embeddings.

5   Conclusion

In this paper, we discuss the importance of role-oriented network representation learning. To avoid the limitations of existing methods, we introduce a novel idea using manual extracted structural features as guidance information to train a role-oriented graph neural network model. And we implement the idea via our proposed approach GAS which leverages sum-pooling propagating graph convolutional layers as encoder and handcraft structural features as the guidance of training. The extensive experiments verify the correctness of our idea and the effectiveness of GAS.

Acknowledgments. This work was supported by the National Natural Science Foundation of China (61902278, 91746205, 91746107, 51438009), the National Key R&D Program of China (2018YFC0831000, 2018YFC0809800, 2016QY15Z2502-02) and the Science and Technology Key R&D Program of Tianjin (18YFZCSF01370).

References

1. Ahmed, N.K., et al.: role2vec: role-based network embeddings. In: DLG KDD (2019)
2. Donnat, C., Zitnik, M., Hallac, D., Leskovec, J.: Learning structural node embeddings via diffusion wavelets. In: SIGKDD, pp. 1320–1329 (2018)
3. Gilpin, S., Eliassi-Rad, T., Davidson, I.: Guided learning for role discovery (GLRD): framework, algorithms, and applications. In: SIGKDD, pp. 113–121 (2013)
4. Glorot, X., Bengio, Y.: Understanding the difficulty of training deep feedforward neural networks. In: AISTATS, pp. 249–256 (2010)
5. Grover, A., Leskovec, J.: node2vec: scalable feature learning for networks. In: SIGKDD, pp. 855–864 (2016)
6. Hamilton, W.L., Ying, Z., Leskovec, J.: Inductive representation learning on large graphs. In: NIPS, pp. 1024–1034 (2017)
7. Heimann, M., Shen, H., Safavi, T., Koutra, D.: Regal: representation learning-based graph alignment. In: CIKM, pp. 117–126 (2018)
8. Henderson, K., et al.: RoLX: structural role extraction & mining in large graphs. In: SIGKDD, pp. 1231–1239 (2012)
9. Henderson, K., et al.: It's who you know: graph mining using recursive structural features. In: SIGKDD, pp. 663–671 (2011)
10. Hochreiter, S., Schmidhuber, J.: Long short-term memory. Neural Comput. 9(8), 1735–1780 (1997)

11. Holland, P.W., Leinhardt, S.: Local structure in social networks. Sociol. Methodol. **7**, 1–45 (1976)
12. Ke, H., et al.: Deep mutual encode model for network embedding from structural identity. IEEE Access **7**, 177484–177496 (2019)
13. Kingma, D.P., Ba, J.: Adam: a method for stochastic optimization. In: ICLR (2014)
14. Kipf, T., Welling, M.: Semi-supervised classification with graph convolutional networks. In: ICLR (2017)
15. Ma, X., Qin, G., Qiu, Z., Zheng, M., Wang, Z.: RiWalk: fast structural node embedding via role identification. arXiv preprint arXiv:1910.06541 (2019)
16. van der Maaten, L., Hinton, G.: Visualizing data using t-SNE. J. Mach. Learn. Res. **9**(Nov), 2579–2605 (2008)
17. Mikolov, T., Sutskever, I., Chen, K., Corrado, G.S., Dean, J.: Distributed representations of words and phrases and their compositionality. In: NIPS, pp. 3111–3119 (2013)
18. Page, L., Brin, S., Motwani, R., Winograd, T.: The pagerank citation ranking: bringing order to the web. Technical report, Stanford InfoLab (1999)
19. Perozzi, B., Al-Rfou, R., Skiena, S.: DeepWalk: online learning of social representations. In: SIGKDD, pp. 701–710 (2014)
20. Ribeiro, L.F., Saverese, P.H., Figueiredo, D.R.: struc2vec: learning node representations from structural identity. In: SIGKDD, pp. 385–394 (2017)
21. Rossi, R.A., Ahmed, N.K.: Role discovery in networks. IEEE Trans. Knowl. Data Eng. **27**(4), 1112–1131 (2014)
22. Rossi, R.A., Ahmed, N.K.: The network data repository with interactive graph analytics and visualization. In: AAAI, pp. 4292–4293 (2015)
23. Rossi, R.A., Ahmed, N.K., Koh, E.: Higher-order network representation learning. In: WWW (2018)
24. Rossi, R.A., Jin, D., Kim, S., Ahmed, N.K., Koutra, D., Lee, J.B.: From community to role-based graph embeddings. arXiv preprint arXiv:1908.08572 (2019)
25. Tang, J., Qu, M., Wang, M., Zhang, M., Yan, J., Mei, Q.: Line: large-scale information network embedding. In: WWW, pp. 1067–1077 (2015)
26. Tang, J., Sun, J., Wang, C., Yang, Z.: Social influence analysis in large-scale networks. In: SIGKDD, pp. 807–816 (2009)
27. Tu, K., Cui, P., Wang, X., Yu, P.S., Zhu, W.: Deep recursive network embedding with regular equivalence. In: SIGKDD, pp. 2357–2366 (2018)
28. Wasserman, S., Faust, K.: Social Network Analysis: Methods and Applications, vol. 8. Cambridge University Press, Cambridge (1994)
29. Wolpert, D.H., Macready, W.G.: No free lunch theorems for optimization. IEEE Trans. Evol. Comput. **1**(1), 67–82 (1997)
30. Xu, K., Hu, W., Leskovec, J., Jegelka, S.: How powerful are graph neural networks? In: ICLR (2019)
31. Zitnik, M., Leskovec, J.: Predicting multicellular function through multi-layer tissue networks. Bioinformatics **33**(14), i190–i198 (2017)

Dynamic Graph Repartitioning: From Single Vertex to Vertex Group

He Li[1]([⊠]), Hang Yuan[1], Jianbin Huang[1]([⊠]), Jiangtao Cui[1], and Jaesoo Yoo[2]([⊠])

[1] School of Computer Science and Technology, Xidian University, Xi'an, Shaanxi, China
{heli, jbhuang, cuijt}@xidian.edu.cn,
h_yuan@stu.xidian.edu.cn
[2] Department of Information and Communication Engineering, Chungbuk National University, Cheongju, Chungbuk, South Korea
yjs@cbnu.ac.kr

Abstract. With the increase of large graph data arising in applications like Web, social network, knowledge graph, and so on, there is a growing need for partitioning and repartitioning large graph data in graph data systems. However, the existing graph repartitioning methods are known for poor efficiency in the dynamic environment. In this paper, we devise an efficient lightweight method to identify and move the candidate vertices to achieve graph repartitioning in the dynamic environment. Different from previous approaches that just focus on the case of moving a single vertex as a basic unit, we show that the movement of some closely connected vertices as a group can further improve the quality of graph repartitioning result. We conduct experiments on a large set of real and synthetic graph data sets, and the results showed that the proposed method is more efficient comparing with existing method in several aspects.

Keywords: Graph repartitioning · Large graph data · Graph algorithm · Lightweight method

1 Introduction

Nowadays, applications with very large graph structured data are becoming more and more common. Google has reported that manages more than a trillion links of knowledge graph. DBpedia has extracted 1.89 billion graph links from Wikipedia. The WWW contains more than 50 billion web pages and more than one trillion unique URLs [1]. The friendship network of Facebook recently reported more than 1 billion of users and 140 billion of friend links [2]. The linked open data [3] had collected over 20 billion RDF triples from 295 interlinked datasets on the Web. Such graphs are too massive to be managed on a single machine system. A typical approach is to partition it across a graph data system. The problem of optimal graph partitioning expects to divide the vertices of a given graph into equal sized components and the number of edges connecting vertices among different components is minimum. This has been extensively studied in the past and proved NP-Hard [4].

© Springer Nature Switzerland AG 2020
Y. Nah et al. (Eds.): DASFAA 2020, LNCS 12113, pp. 482–497, 2020.
https://doi.org/10.1007/978-3-030-59416-9_29

Most previous methods focus on static graph partitioning, such as the classical graph partitioning method Metis [5] and its variants. However, most of the graphs encountered in the real-world are inherently dynamic, the graph structures evolved over time. For example, the accounts and relationships receive thousands of update per second in the online services such as Facebook and Twitter, new vertices and edges being added at high rates and in some cases, vertices and edges may be removed. It is critical to keep up with graph update, monitoring and adapting partitions over time.

In this paper, we focus on graph repartitioning in the dynamic environment. A straightforward method for graph repartitioning is that periodically running the existing static graph partitioning methods [5–7] to obtain the graph repartitioning results continuously. However, the high complexity of computation makes them no longer suitable for large dynamic graph data. Recently, some methods have been proposed for dynamic graph partitioning problems [8–10]. However, they perform vertex movement in an asynchronous mode, which would cause migration interference. Additionally, we found that taking a single vertex as a basic unit for movement will limit the quality of graph repartitioning results.

Inspired by the existing lightweight methods, this paper introduces a new method to identify and move the appropriate vertex to achieve graph repartitioning in the dynamic environment. Instead of taking a single vertex as a basic unit for vertex movement, we propose a vertex-group based vertex movement method. By doing this, the graph repartitioning result could be improved by facilitating load balance as well as decreasing total edge cut among the distributed partitions. More specifically, we propose a label propagation algorithm (LPA) [11] based method to detect the vertex-group within a given partition locally. Different from the existing methods, the proposed method does not require to process the entire graph data and the label assignment and updating is only started from the selected boundary vertices of a given partition in this paper. The experimental results indicate that the proposed method is more efficient comparing with existing method in several aspects.

The remainder of this paper is organized as follows. Section 2 provides a brief review of related works on graph partitioning and repartitioning. Section 3 gives the description of preliminaries. In Sect. 4, we first give a basic method for graph repartitioning and then detail the proposed vertex-group based method. Section 5 discusses the experimental results. Finally, we conclude the paper in Sect. 6.

2 Related Work

There are a lot of distributed graph database systems have been developed to support large graph data management, such as Trinity [12], Pregel [13], HyperGraphDB [14], Neo4j [15], and Tao [16]. Most of them apply a simple hash function to allocate each vertex of the graph into different data partitions. The hash based approach is easy to be implemented in dynamic environments, but the main disadvantage is the lack of control of the graph structure to be destroyed.

Traditional Graph Partitioning: The classical graph partitioning method Metis [5] and its parallel version ParMetis [17] were proposed to produce high quality result by adopting graph theory. However, they require to access to the global structure of the entire graph before performing graph partitioning, which make them inapplicable for large dynamic graphs in distributed environments. After that, Sheep [18] proposed to support graph partitioning in a distributed system. It first transforms the given graph into an elimination tree, and then performs the graph partitioning on the elimination tree. [19] designed a multi-level algorithm on top of Trinity [12]. However, they also required the knowledge of global graph structure. Ja-Be-Ja [20] is a distributed algorithm for graph partitioning without global knowledge. However, it has to process the entire graph to ensure obtaining the graph partitioning result, which is not the case for graph repartitioning in a dynamic environment. Recently, streaming graph partitioning [6, 7] have been proposed for very large graph data. After that, several improved methods [22–24] were proposed to improve the quality of streaming graph partitioning result. In [25], an overview of streaming graph partitioning techniques based on their assumptions was introduced. However, the streaming techniques cannot be straightly adopted to handle graph repartitioning in the dynamic environment.

Dynamic Graph Repartitioning: In order to process the dynamic graph partitioning problem, some lightweight methods [8–10, 26] have been proposed. [8] and [9] assumed a heterogeneous system which can be considered as the special case of the environment in [10]. Leopard [26] introduced a dynamic graph partitioning algorithm build on the existing streaming approaches [7]. It focused on integrating replication policy [27] with the graph repartitioning. Lightweight means that they only rely on a small amount of information about the graph structure to perform graph repartitioning over the dynamic graph data. However, adopting the existing lightweight method in the dynamic environment have problems in several aspects: 1) adopting asynchronous ways to migrate vertices would incur migration interference; 2) the processing of a single vertex as a basic unit limits the quality of the graph partitioning result to some extent; 3) lacking balanced mechanisms between load balances and crossing edges for graph repartitioning. In this paper, we focus on resolving the above mentioned problems for graph repartitioning in the dynamic environment.

3 Preliminaries

3.1 Basic Concepts

We assume a graph $G = (V, E)$, where V denotes the vertices set, and E denotes the edges set. Note that, the graph can be either directed or undirected, unweighted or weighted on both vertices and edges. In what for ease of presentation, we assume the case of an undirected graph with unweighted vertices and edges. Initially, the given graph G can be divided into different partitions and distributed across a set of k storage nodes by adopting existing static graph partitioning methods such as Metis [5] and streaming based method [6]. An initial k partitioning set of graph G can be defined as $P = \{P_i: \cup_{i=1}^{k} P_i = G,$ and $P_s \cap P_t = \emptyset$ for any $s \neq t, 1 \leq s, t \leq k\}$, where P denotes a partitioning set of graph G decomposed with size k, and each partition P_i is called a partition element.

Definition 1 (Boundary vertex). *If a vertex v_i of P_i having neighboring vertices in the other partitions, we define that vertex v_i is a boundary vertex of partition P_i.*

Definition 2 (Edge cut [21]). *Given a graph partition pair P_s and P_t, the edge cut is the set of crossing edges that can divide the given partition pair into two disjoint partitions by removing them, where the remove of the subset of it cannot divide the partition pair into two disjoint partitions.*

If a given graph G is decomposed of k partitions, the edge cut is the set of crossing edges that can divide graph G into k disjoint sub-graph by removing them, where the remove of the subset of it cannot divide the given graph G into k disjoint partitions. For a subset of vertices $S \subseteq V$, let $e(S, S)$ be the set of edges with both vertices in S, and let $e(S, V \backslash S)$ be the set of edges with vertices across the edge cut. The edge cut valu $ec(S, V \backslash S)$ is measured by the number of crossing edges in an edge cut set, i.e., $ec(S, V \backslash S) = |e(S, V \backslash S)|$. If the given graph G is decomposed of k partitions, the total edge cut value (Tec) of the k partitioning set P is defined as

$$Tec(P) = \frac{1}{2} \sum\nolimits_{i=1}^{k} ec(P_i, V \backslash P_i), P_i \in P. \tag{1}$$

Let $W(P_i)$ be the weight of partition P_i, here we adopt the number of vertices in P_i to measure the weight of partition P_i, and it can also be replaced by the number of edges if necessary. $\frac{1}{k} \sum_{j=1}^{k} W(P_j)$ denotes the average weight of all the partitions. When $|V| = n, \frac{1}{k} \sum_{j=1}^{k} W(P_j) = \frac{n}{k}$. A partition P_i is said to be overloaded when $W(P_i) > \frac{(1+\varepsilon)n}{k}$, and a partition P_i is said to be underloaded when $W(P_i) < \frac{(1-\varepsilon)n}{k}$, where ε $(0 \leq \varepsilon \leq 1)$ is a user allowed imbalance ratio of the distributed partitions, i.e., how imbalance the partitions are allowed to be. Then, the summation of the total load imbalance (Tib) of the given partitioning set P can be defined as

$$Tib(P) = \sum\nolimits_{i=1}^{k} \left| W(P_i) - \frac{n}{k} \right|. \tag{2}$$

3.2   Problem Statement

Dynamic Graph Repartitioning: It is obvious that moving a vertex from the overloaded partition to the underloaded partition could decrease the load imbalance ratio of the graph partitioning set, and moving the vertex to the partition which has more connectivity than that of the current one could reduce edge cut. Then, the problem of graph repartitioning in the dynamic environment can be transformed to exchange the appropriate vertices among the distributed partitions continuously to maintain the optimization of the graph repartitioning result. The objective of graph repartitioning is to find a possible repartitioning set $P' = \{P'_i : \cup_{i=1}^{k} P'_i = G\}$, s.t. $Tib(P')$ and $Tec(P')$ are minimized with the given partitioning set $P = \{P_i : \cup_{i=1}^{k} P_i = G\}$. We define an objective function f,

$$f(P') = \gamma * \frac{Tec(P) - Tec(P')}{|E|} + (1 - \gamma) * \frac{Tib(P) - Tib(P')}{|V|}, \tag{3}$$

where $Tec(P)$ and $Tib(P)$ denote the total edge cut value and load imbalance of the given initial partitioning set P. γ $(0 \leq \gamma \leq 1)$ is a weight value which is used to control the balance between the edge cut value and load imbalance of different partitions. The divisor $|E|$ and $|V|$ are used to provide us a proper scaling between the edge cut value and load imbalance of the different partitions.

4   The Proposed Method

4.1   A Basic Method

Since the complex connectivity of the graph data, the neighboring vertices will be distributed in different partitions inherently. If the neighboring vertices in different partitions moved independently, whether their neighbors in the other partitions have been moved is unpredictable.

Example 1: Consider the given graph $G = \{P_1, P_2, P_3\}$ in Fig. 1(a), P_1, P_2, and P_3 are partitions distributed in different storage nodes. It is clear that moving vertex b from partition P_1 to P_2 can decrease edge cut value since it has more neighboring vertices in partition P_2. Similarly, it is preferable to move vertex d from partition P_2 to P_1 and move vertex h from partition P_3 to P_2. However, as shown in Fig. 1(b), when moving vertex d from partition P_2 to P_1, vertex h in P_3 has to be moved to P_1 and vertex b in P_1 is not necessary to be moved to P_3.

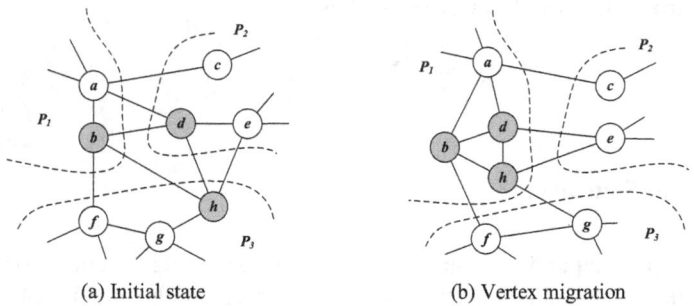

(a) Initial state   (b) Vertex migration

Fig. 1. Illustration of migration interference in graph repartitioning among different partitions.

In order to mitigate this migration interference, we design a sequential method to move vertices among the partitions. Before vertex movement, we first determine which vertex should be moved out from their local partitions. It is obvious that moving the vertex to the partition which has more connectivity can reduce total edge cut and moving the vertex from the overloaded partition to the underloaded partition can improve load balance. Therefore, if two connected vertices located on different partitions, they may become candidates for reassignment when the movement of which could decrease edge cut value or improve the load balance of the partitions.

Definition 3 (Edge-cut gain). *The edge cut gain of moving vertex v from partition P_s to partition P_t is defined by the difference between the number of its neighboring vertices in P_s and in P_t.*

Consider a partition pair (P_s, P_t) and let v be a boundary vertex in partition P_s, the edge cut gain $ec: gain^{s \to t}(v)$ is used to denote the decrease of edge cut value between P_s and P_t when moving v from P_s to P_t.

$$ec:\ gain^{s \to t}(v) = N_t(v) - N_s(v), \tag{4}$$

where $N_t(v)$ and $N_s(v)$ denote the number of neighbors of vertex v *in* P_t *and in* P_s, respectively.

Algorithm 1 (*Basic Graph Repartitioning*)

if the partitioning has not converged **then**

load information exchange

foreach partition $P_i \in P$ **do**

find P_i with maximum overload ratio;

Identify boundary vertices of P_i;

foreach boundary vertex $v \in P_i$ **do**

compute $ec:gain^{s \to t}(v)$ of vertex v;

find v with maximum $ec:gain^{s \to t}(v)$;

if $ec:gain^{s \to t}(v) > 0 \&\& W(P_s) > \frac{(1-\varepsilon)n}{k} \&\& W(P_t) < \frac{(1+\varepsilon)n}{k}$ **then**

$migration(v, P_t)$;

$continue$;

end if

$CheckPartitionConvergence()$;

end if

As the boundary vertex has relationships with the other partitions directly, the movement of the boundary vertex may affect edge cut value among the distributed partitions. When the partition with maximum overload ratio is selected, the vertex movement is started from the boundary vertex of it. The boundary vertices are proposed to move to their target partitions when $W(P_s) > \frac{(1-\varepsilon)n}{k}$, $W(P_t) < \frac{(1+\varepsilon)n}{k}$ and $ec: gain^{s \to t}(v) > 0$, where n denotes the size of vertex set V, $W(P_s)$ and $W(P_t)$ denote the weights of their current partitions and target partitions. When the candidate vertex has to be migrated to more than one partition, the partition with maximum gain value is selected as its target partition. Note that once a boundary vertex is identified as a candidate vertex and moved to its target partition, its neighboring vertices in the current partition will become new boundary vertices. In each time, the partition with maximum overload ratio is selected to perform vertex movement. Like this, the vertex movement is processed until we cannot find any vertex with positive edge cut gain or the load balance criterion ε is violated. The pseudo-code of this process is shown in Algorithm 1.

4.2 Vertex-Group Based Method

Most of the graph partitioning and repartitioning methods take a single vertex as a basic unit for processing. Intuitively, it is clear that the movement of a single vertex with negative gain value will degrade the edge cut among the partitions for graph repartitioning. However, we found that in some cases the migration of some vertices with negative gain values as a whole could further reduce the total edge cut value among the distributed partitions. For instance, as shown in Fig. 2, there are two partitions P_1 and P_2, ec: $gain^{1\rightarrow2}(e) = -1$, ec: $gain^{1\rightarrow2}(f) = -1$, and ec: $gain^{2\rightarrow1}(d) = -3$. As is well known, moving any single vertex d, e, and f from P_1 to P_2 cannot decrease the edge cut value between partition P_1 and P_2. However, moving them as a whole from P_1 to P_2 can further result in a decrease of the total edge cut.

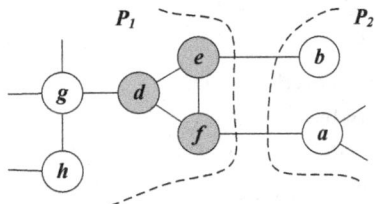

Fig. 2. Illustrating the effect of moving vertices as a group.

Since the movement of vertices as a group can further reduce the total edge cut value among the distributed partitions, the vertex movement is processed only based on the single vertex that will limit the quality of the graph repartitioning result. Especially, the advantage of the vertex group based movement is obvious for high overloaded partitions. We define a vertex-group to represent the vertices group in vertex migration processing.

Definition 4 (Vertex-group).   *Given a partition $P_i = \{V_i, E_i\}$, $C(v) = \{V_i', E_i'\}$ is a vertex-group of P_i represented by a vertex v, if $V_i' \subseteq V_i$, $E_i' \subseteq E_i$, and migrating $C(v)$ as a whole from its local partition to another partition could decrease the total edge cut value.*

Theorem 1.   *Given a partitioning set $P = \{P_i: \cup_{i=1}^{k} P_i = G\}$ and a partition $P_i \in P$, C is a vertex-group of P_i iff $C \subseteq P_i$ and $|N_c^i| < |N_c^j|$, for $i \neq j$ and $1 \leq j \leq k$, where N_c^i and N_c^j denote the neighboring set of C within partition P_i and P_j, respectively.*

According to the property of the vertex-group, the vertex and edge of the original graph can be reduced into a smaller graph with shrinking the vertex within the same vertex-group into a super-vertex. The weight of the connectivity of the vertex-group is integrated based on the original vertex. Then, we can get the edge cut gain of moving a vertex-group among different partitions. The edge cut gain of moving a given vertex-group from partition P_s to partition P_t is defined as $ec: gain^{s \rightarrow t}(C) = N_t(C) - N_s(C)$, where $N_t(C)$ and $N_s(C)$ denote the number of neighboring vertices of the vertex-group C in partition P_t and P_s, respectively.

Here, we propose a label propagation algorithm (LPA) based method to detect the vertex-group within a given partition locally. Different from the original LPA method, the label assignment and update is started from the boundary vertices of a given partition. Each source vertex updates its label by using the majority voting rule (5) in parallel, i.e.

$$c(v) = argmax \sum_{u \in N_v^i} w(u), \tag{5}$$

where $c(v)$ is the new label of vertex v and N_v^i is the set of neighbors of vertex v within partition P_i where $v \notin P_i$. Initially, the label of the boundary vertex is the partition ID that the maximum number of its external neighbors in. Afterwards, the vertex propagates the label to its neighboring vertices within it in the same partition.

The new vertex which receives the message of label propagation updates its label by using the same majority voting rule (5). Note that, when the vertex which receives the message of label propagation has already been assigned a label, it updates its new label by using the majority voting rule (6), i.e.

$$c(x) = argmax(c(x_1), \ldots, c(x_i), \ldots, c(x_j)), \tag{6}$$

where $x_1, \ldots, x_i, \ldots,$ and x_j are the neighbors of the vertex x including itself that have already updated their labels. $c(x)$ returns the label that the maximum number of its neighbors carry. Since we adopt the partition ID as the label for propagation, the maximum number of different labels within a given partition will be less than that of the number of partitions.

The vertices are expanded by absorbing new vertices that connected with them and have the common label. By doing this, the vertex has the same label as the maximum number of its neighbors are formed within a same group in a given partition. The vertex-group is formed when this process found that the edge cut gain of the vertices group with $ec: gain^{s \rightarrow t}(C) > 0$. There are two auxiliary information associated with each vertex-group, such as the edge cut gain and the aggregated vertex weight within it. The processing of vertex-group detection is performed in parallel in a given partition of different boundary vertices. The termination condition of vertex-group detection is different with the original LPA method. The vertex-group detection is terminated when moving which violate the size constraint of the partitions, such as $W(P_s) - \sum_{C \in Ps} W(C) < \frac{(1-\varepsilon)n}{k}$. At this time, the algorithm rollback to find the vertex-groups which have the maximum edge cut gain. By doing this, the proposed method does not require to process the entire graph data which is different from the existing communication methods. The pseudo-code of this vertex-group detection algorithm is given in Algorithm 2. Afterwards, the vertex-group detection and movement are performed in the next partition which has maximum overload ratio. Like Algorithm 1, it is processed sequentially in each partition until we cannot find any vertex-group with positive edge cut gain or the load balance criterion ε is violated.

Algorithm 2 (*Vertex-group Detection*)

Begin from the boundary vertices of the partition P_s:

foreach boundary vertex $v \in P_s$ **do**

// The process of the boundary vertices is performed in parallel;

assign a new label to v according to the rule (5);

//run LPA under the size constraint of P_s;

while $W(P_s) > \frac{(1-\varepsilon)n}{k}$ **do**

the vertex which has a label performs LPA;

the vertex updates the label according to the rule (6);

if $W(P_t) + W(C)) < \frac{(1+\varepsilon)n}{k}$ **then**

$W(P_s) -= W(C)$;

continue;

else

break;

end if

end while

rollback to find the vertex-groups with minimum edge cut;

4.3 Complexity Analysis

In this section, we provide the complexity analysis of the proposed method. The proposed method is designed for graph repartitioning by performing vertex movement among the distributed partitions. During the processing in each partition, the vertex only needs to know the locations of its neighbors and the load information of the target partition.

Theorem 2. *In each partition, the cost of processing graph repartitioning takes at most $O(|CS_i| + |CS_i|*log(|CS_i|))$ with CS_i denotes the set of candidate vertices that have to be checked for movement in partition P_i.*

Proof. For Algorithm 1, we will move up to $O(|CS_i|)$ candidate vertices in partition P_i and perform extracting at most $O(|CS_i|*log(|CS_i|))$ neighbors from the moving of the candidate vertices. Then we can get that the time complexity of Algorithm 1 in partition P_i is $O(|CS_i| + |CS_i|*log(|CS_i|))$. Algorithm 2 requires an additional memory, which including at most k arrays of size $O(|CS_i|/k)$ to record the information about the vertex-groups in partition P_i. The label propagation takes at most $O(|S_i|)$ vertices. Actually, the movement of the vertex is far less than $|S_i|$ under the constraint of load balance. The update of the label takes at most $O(r*|S_i|)$ with r denotes the number of iterations. Since the time complexity of building the group is bounded by the update of the label, the cost of Algorithm 2 is $O(r*|S_i|)$.

Theorem 3. *After a bounded number of iterations, the sequential migration algorithm converges to a stable partitioning state.*

Proof. In the proposed method, the vertex and vertex-group are selected for moving only when migrating them could improve edge cut value or load balance. We have to consider three cases:

1) $W(P_i) > \frac{n}{k}$, let $Tec(P)$ denote the total edge cut value and $Tib(P)$ denote the total load imbalance. In general, the values of $Tec(P)$ and $Tib(P)$ are expected to be decreased with the migration of the selected vertices. This implies that the migration process will be terminated when a stable value is achieved;

2) $W(P_i) \approx \frac{n}{k}$, that is to say the partition is considered as load balance under before vertex movement. In this case, the migration of vertex v will increase the value of $Tib(P)$. However, the migration of candidate vertices with high gain values can be used to amortize the increase of $Tib(P)$ and this will be terminated at a certain point, such as $\delta(v, P_s, P_t) = 0$;

3) $W(P_i) < \frac{n}{k}$, note that the proposed method selects high overloaded partition $(argmax_{1 \le i,j \le k}\{P_i|W(P_i) - n/k, P_i \in P\})$ to perform migration process. Then, the vertex migration process will not be occurred in the partition with $W(P_i) < \frac{n}{k}$. Instead, the specified partition will receive vertices from the other partitions during the processing of the first two cases. With the reception of the candidate vertices the specified partition will tend to balance.

5 Experiments

In this section, we present the evaluation result of the proposed dynamic graph repartitioning (DGR) method comparing with Streaming [6] and Hermes [10]. Hermes is considered as the closest to the proposed method. Planar [9] is a special case of Hermes which assume a heterogeneous network architecture. We implement three of the proposed methods, which including DGR-V(single vertex based movement), DGR-G(vertex-group based movement), and DGR-B(adjusting the parameter γ).

5.1 Experimental Setting

Datasets: Five real-world data sets [28] provided by the work of Stanford University named DBLP, Youtube, RoadNet-PA, LiveJournal, Orkut, and two synthetic graph data sets generated following the Lancichinetti Fortunato Radicchi (LFR) benchmark [29] were used to evaluate the performance. The two synthetic graph data sets represent different size and sparsity. The detail descriptions of the seven datasets are shown in Table 1. Initially, we select 70% of the seven graph datasets randomly and partition them by using the streaming based graph partitioning method [6]. In order to simulate the dynamic environment, we select the remaining 30% of the seven graph datasets proportionally to insert into the initial partitions. To keep up with Hermes, the load balance criterion ε is set to 0.1 in the experiments.

Table 1. Summary description of different graph datasets.

Data name	Number of vertices	Number of edges	Average degree
DBLP	317,080	1,049,866	6.62
Youtube	1,134890	2,987,624	5.27
RoadNet	1,088,092	1,541,898	2.83
LiveJournal	3,997,962	34,681,189	17.35
Orkut	3,072,441	117,185,083	76.28
LFR1	10,000,000	9,672,167	1.93
LFR2	30,000,000	174,470,043	11.63

Setting: All experiments were conducted on a Hadoop File System with 16 storage nodes. Each storage node runs on Ubuntu OS with i7-3.6 GHz CPU and 32 GB RAM. All the algorithms were coded in Java 1.7.

Metrics: We consider the following three metrics, such as edge cut, load balance, and migration efficiency.
Edge cut (EC), the edge cut is the basic metric to evaluate the quality of the graph partitioning results. Given a partition set P, the edge cut (EC) ratio is defined as

$$EC\ ratio = \frac{Tec(P)}{|E|}. \tag{7}$$

And the edge cut improvement of graph repartitioning result P' is defined as

$$EC\ improvement = \frac{Tec(P) - Tec(P')}{Tec(P)}. \tag{8}$$

Load balance (LB), given a partition set P, the load balance (LB) ratio is defined as

$$LB\ ratio = \frac{Tib(P)}{|V|}. \tag{9}$$

And the load balance improvement of graph repartitioning result P' is defined as

$$LB\ improvement = \frac{Tib(P) - Tib(P')}{Tib(P)}. \tag{10}$$

Migration efficiency, migration efficiency is an important factor for graph repartitioning in dynamic environment. We use migration interference (MI) to count up the number of vertices that cause migration interference during vertex migration and total migrations (TM) to count the number of total vertices that have to be moved to achieve graph repartitioning.

5.2   Experimental Results

We first compare the parameter γ of the proposed method DGR-B that affects the balance of edge cut value and load imbalance ratio. As discussed in previous, the two goals (minimum edge cut value and minimum load imbalance ratio) of graph repartitioning are always in conflict. Figure 3 shows the results on Youtube dataset, and the results of the other datasets are shown on Table 2. When $\gamma = 0$, it means that the proposed method DGR-B only focuses on reducing the load imbalance ratio and the edge cut value of the partition is ignored completely. All the results showed that the load balance improvement is maximum when $\gamma = 0$. However, the corresponding value of edge cut improvement is minimum. With the increase of γ, the vertex whose gain is greater than 0 has a chance to be migrated during the graph repartitioning. The *EC* improvement will gradually increase. However, the weight of load balance will decrease, which will result in the reduction of *LB* improvement. Then, we select the optimal parameter γ with the intersection position for DGR-B in the following experiments.

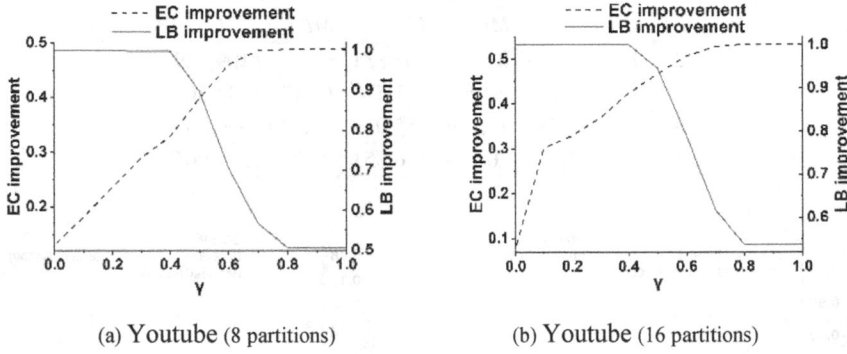

(a) Youtube (8 partitions)   (b) Youtube (16 partitions)

Fig. 3. The result of edge cut improvement and load balance improvement according to the value of parameter γ.

Convergence Speed Comparison: Both Hermes and the proposed method perform vertex migration in an iterative mode. For each movement of the iteration, the edge cut ratio and load balance ratio will be decreased. For DGR-B, the objective function that balancing the edge cut and load balance can make the vertex movement of the graph repartitioning converge rapidly. Hermes adopts a parameter N in the algorithm which will affect convergence speed. A large value of N will result in faster convergence of iterations but it will cause more migration interference and load imbalance, as shown in Table 3 and Fig. 5, respectively. In order to be fair, Hermes is performed with two different values of N, where $N = 500$ and $N = 2000$. Figure 4 shows the result of iteration times over the Youtube dataset. The edge cut ratio and load balance ratio of Hermes, DGR-V, DGR-G, and DGR-B tending to be stable after several iterations. The edge cut ratio and load balance ratio of the proposed method are decreased sharply with the movement of the selected vertices and tend to be stable more rapidly than Hermes.

Table 2. The selection of optimal parameter γ on different datasets

Dataset name	γ of different number of partitions			
	2	4	8	16
DBLP	0.7	0.8	0.8	0.7
RoadNet-PA	0.6	0.6	0.7	0.7
Youtube	0.5	0.4	0.5	0.5
LiveJournal	0.6	0.6	0.6	0.6
Orkut	0.3	0.2	0.2	0.3
LFR1	0.7	0.7	0.8	0.8
LFR2	0.5	0.6	0.6	0.5

Table 3. The result of migration interference and total migration.

$|P|$	DGR-V		Hermes ($N = 500$)		Hermes ($N = 2000$)	
	MI	TM	MI	TM	MI	TM
2	0	100,549	0	107,831	0	109,129
4	0	297,360	6,106	341,570	6,912	344,369
8	0	324,783	15,896	355,023	16,599	360,059
16	0	317,837	20,196	336,851	21,246	372,065

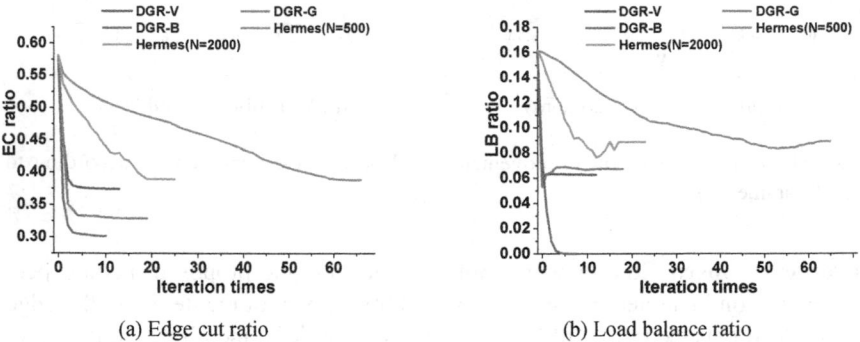

(a) Edge cut ratio   (b) Load balance ratio

Fig. 4. The result of convergence speed under the edge cut ratio and load balance ratio.

Migration Efficiency Comparison: Table 3 shows the result of migration interference (MI) and total migration (TM) over Youtube dataset. DGR-V performs vertex migration among the different partitions in a sequential method, the result of migration interference is 0. Hermes performs vertex migration in parallel, the migration interference will occur inherently. Therefore, a lot of vertex migration will cause migration interference. However, the result of migration interference of both Hermes and DGR-V are 0 when the number of partition is 2. This is because the vertex migration of Hermes is also performed in a sequential model when the number of partition is only 2. In this case, the migration interference is not occurred. When the number of partition is larger than 2, the advantage of the proposed method is obvious. For Hermes, there are more vertices to be migrated at a time when $N = 2000$, and the higher the probability of migration interference is occurred.

Dynamic Graph Repartitioning Result: Figure 5 shows the result of graph repartitioning methods on both edge cut ratio and load balance ratio over all the datasets comparing with the initial state. Since the streaming based graph partitioning algorithm joining the punishment mechanism to guarantee the load balance of the graph partitioning result, a vertex with high edge cut gain will be ignored and assigned to a partition with large storage space. Therefore, the edge cut ratio of streaming based graph partitioning method is a little high comparing with the other graph repartitioning methods. However, its load balance ratio is relatively low comparing with the other methods. Both the proposed method DGR-V and Hermes take the single vertex as a basic unit for vertex migration to achieve graph repartitioning, the results of edge cut ratio of them are similar. However, DGR-V can avoid migration interference and the number of iterations of DGR-V will be less than that of Hermes. The proposed method DGR-G takes the vertex-group as a basic unit for vertex migration to achieve graph repartitioning, the edge cut ratio of the graph repartitioning is significantly reduced comparing with DGR-V and Hermes in most cases. This is because the migration of the group of vertices which have negative edge cut gains can further reduce the total edge cut. As for DGR-B, it has a slightly higher edge cut ratio comparing with DGR-G. This is because it focuses on balancing the edge cut and load balance of the graph repartitioning result. However, the advantage of the load balance ratio of DGR-B is obvious.

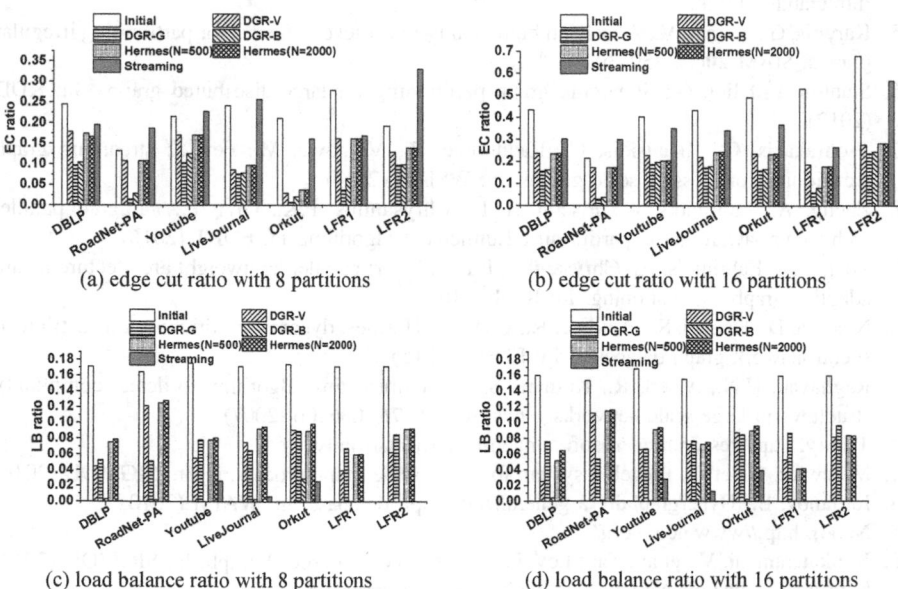

(a) edge cut ratio with 8 partitions   (b) edge cut ratio with 16 partitions

(c) load balance ratio with 8 partitions   (d) load balance ratio with 16 partitions

Fig. 5. The quality of graph repartitioning result in both edge cut ratio and load balance ratio.

6 Conclusions

This paper addresses the problem of graph repartitioning in the dynamic environment. We devise an efficient lightweight method to identify and move the candidate vertices to achieve graph repartitioning in the dynamic environment. In order to get a competitive graph repartitioning result, instead of migrating a single vertex as a basic unit the candidate vertex is processed based on vertex-group. Extensive experiments are conducted to evaluate the efficiency of the proposed methods on different types of real-word and synthetic graph datasets. The results show that the considering of vertex-group is more efficient than the other methods. Additionally, the results also show that the load balance ratio of DGR-B can be improved by nearly 90% comparing with Hermes.

Acknowledgements. This work was supported by the Natural Science Foundation of China (No. 61602354), Natural Science Foundation of Shaanxi Province (No. 2019JM-227), and the National Research Foundation of Korea (NRF) grant funded by the Korea government (MSIT) (No. 2019R1A2C2084257).

References

1. http://www.wordwidewebsize.com/
2. http://www.facebook.com/press/info.php?statistics/
3. http://www.w3.org/
4. Garey, M.R., Johnson, D.S.: A guide to the Theory of NP-Completeness. Computers and Intractability (1990)
5. Karypis, G., Kumar, V.: A fast and high quality multi-level schemes for partitioning irregular graphs. SIAM **20**(1), 359–392 (1998)
6. Stanton, I., Kliot, G.: Streaming graph partitioning for large distributed graphs. In: KDD (2012)
7. Tsourakakis, C., Gkantsidis, C., Radunovic, B., Vojnovic, M.: Fennel: streaming graph partitioning for massive scale graphs. In: WSDM (2014)
8. Zheng, A., Labrinidis, A., Pisciuneri, P., Chrysanthis, P.K., Givi, P.: Paragon: parallel architecture-aware graph partitioning Refinement algorithm. In: EDBT (2016)
9. Zheng, A., Labrinidis, A., Chrysanthis, P.K.: Planar: parallel lightweight architecture-aware adaptive graph re-partitioning. In: ICDE (2016)
10. Nicoara, D., Kamali, S., Daudjee, K., Chen L.: Hermes: dynamic partitioning for distributed social network graph databases. In: EDBT (2015)
11. Raghavan, U.N., Albert, R., Kumara, S.: Near linear time algorithm to detect community structures in large-scale networks. Phys. Rev. E **76**, 036106 (2007)
12. Trinity. http://research.microsoft.com/en-us/projects/trinity/
13. Malewicz, G., et al.: Pregel: a system for large-scale graph processing. In: SIGMOD (2010)
14. Iordanov, B.: Hypergraphdb: a generalized graph database. In: WAIM (2010)
15. Neo4j. http://www.neo4j.org/
16. Venkataramani, V., et al.: Tao: how Facebook serves the social graph. In: SIGMOD (2012)
17. http://glaros.dtc.umn.edu/gkhome/metis/parmetis/overview/
18. Margo, D., Seltzer, M.: A scalable distributed graph partitioner. In: VLDB (2015)

19. Wang, L., Xiao, Y., Shao, B., Wang, H.: How to partition a billion-node graph. In: ICDE (2014)
20. Rahimian, F., Payberah, A.H., Girdzijauskas, S., Jelasity, M., Haridi, S.: JA-BE-JA: a distributed algorithm for balanced graph partitioning. In: SASO (2013)
21. Rosen, K.H.: Discrete Mathematics and its Applications. China Machine Press (2012)
22. Ioanna, F., Kotidis, Y.: Online and on-demand partitioning of streaming graphs. In: the IEEE International Conference on Big Data (2015)
23. Mayer, C., et al.: ADWISE: adaptive window-based streaming edge partitioning for high-speed graph processing. In: ICDCS (2018)
24. Xu, N., Cui, B., Chen, L., Huang, Z., Shao, Y.: Heterogeneous environment aware streaming graph partitioning. TKDE 27(6), 1560–1572 (2015)
25. Abbas, Z., Kalavri, V., Carbone, P., Vlassov, V.: Streaming graph partitioning: an experimental study. VLDB 11(11) (2018)
26. Huang, J., Abadi, J.: Leopard: Lightweight edge-oriented partitioning and replication for dynamic graphs. VLDB 9(7), 540–551 (2016)
27. Jayanta, M., Deshpande, A.: Managing large dynamic graphs efficiently. In: SIGMOD (2012)
28. http://snap.stanford.edu/data
29. https://en.wikipedia.org/wiki/Lancichinetti%E2%80%93Fortunato%E2%80%93Radicchi_benchmark/

Modeling Heterogeneous Edges to Represent Networks with Graph Auto-Encoder

Lu Wang[1,2,3], Yu Song[1,2,3], Hong Huang[1,2,3(✉)], Fanghua Ye[4],
Xuanhua Shi[1,2,3], and Hai Jin[1,2,3]

[1] National Engineering Research Center for Big Data Technology and System,
Huazhong University of Science and Technology, Wuhan, China
`wluluo@gmail.com`, {`yusonghust,honghuang,xhshi,hjin`}`@hust.edu.cn`
[2] Service Computing Technology and Systems Laboratory,
Huazhong University of Science and Technology, Wuhan, China
[3] School of Computer Science and Technology,
Huazhong University of Science and Technology, Wuhan, China
[4] Department of Computer Science, University College London, London, UK
`smartyfh@outlook.com`

Abstract. In the real world, networks often contain multiple relationships among nodes, manifested as the heterogeneity of the edges in the networks. We convert the heterogeneous networks into multiple views by using each view to describe a specific type of relationship between nodes, so that we can leverage the collaboration of multiple views to learn the representation of networks with heterogeneous edges. Given this, we propose a *regularized graph auto-encoders* (RGAE) model, committed to utilizing abundant information in multiple views to learn robust network representations. More specifically, RGAE designs shared and private graph auto-encoders as main components to capture high-order nonlinear structure information of the networks. Besides, two loss functions serve as regularization to extract consistent and unique information, respectively. Concrete experimental results on realistic datasets indicate that our model outperforms state-of-the-art baselines in practical applications.

Keywords: Network embedding · Network analysis · Deep learning

1 Introduction

The research of network analysis has made rapid progress in recent years. In fact, network data are usually complex and therefore hard to process. To mine network data, one fundamental task is to learn a low-dimensional representation for each node, such that network properties are preserved in the vector space. As a result, various downstream applications, such as link prediction [22], classification [36],

---

L. Wang and Y. Song—Equal contribution.

© Springer Nature Switzerland AG 2020
Y. Nah et al. (Eds.): DASFAA 2020, LNCS 12113, pp. 498–515, 2020.
https://doi.org/10.1007/978-3-030-59416-9_30

and community detection[10], can be directly conducted in such vector space. As for learning representations for networks, there are two main challenges that have not yet been fully resolved:

(1) Preservation of heterogeneous relationships between nodes. There usually exist diverse and different types of relationships between nodes, leading to the heterogeneity of edges. For example, in the twitter network, four types of relationships may be observed in the interactions between two users, that is one user may retweet, reply, like, and mention another user's tweet. Thus it is reasonable to build four types of edges between the two users with each type of edge corresponding to one type of relationship. Although these edges reflect the similarity between the two users, we can not ignore the slight difference at the "semantic" level. Therefore, taking heterogeneity of edges into consideration for representing such networks is quite significant. In literature, several heterogeneous network embedding approaches (e.g. PTE [29], Metapath2vec [4], and HIN2Vec[7]) have been proposed to represent heterogeneous nodes or edges into the same semantic vector space. However, these methods only learn a final representation for all relationships jointly but ignore the different semantic meanings of edges. Therefore, in order to explore the heterogeneity of edges, it is necessary to learn a relation-specific representation for each type of relationship.

(2) Preservation of high-order node proximities. As described in LINE [30], it defines two loss functions to preserve both 1-st and 2-nd order proximities together. However, it is also meaningful to further integrate the information of k-th-order neighbors for enhancing the representation of nodes with small degrees. Moreover, most existing network embedding methods are equivalent to implicit matrix factorization [23], which is a shallow model that fails to capture high-order nonlinear proximities between nodes. GraRep [2] aims to capture the k-th-order proximity by factorizing the k-step ($k = 1, 2, \cdots, K$) transition matrices. However, the matrix factorization technique is usually time inefficient and hard to learn nonlinear relationships between nodes. SDNE [34] designs a deep auto-encoder framework to extract the nonlinear structural information of networks, but it still only considers 1-st and 2-nd order proximities without preserving even higher order proximities between nodes. Consequently, to preserve the complex network information, a better solution should leverage high-order nonlinear structural information to yield more robust network representations.

Recently, it has witnessed that multi-view learning is applied successfully in a wide variety of applications, especially for mining heterogeneous data, such as clustering [13], computer vision [16], and information retrieval [21]. In this regard, we convert heterogeneous edges into multiple views for a network, and solving a multi-view learning problem to learn representations for such networks. To be more specific, we abstract each relationship as a view of the network, reflecting a type of proximity between nodes, thus the original network can be further interpreted as a multi-view network. Finally, we formalize the task as a multi-view network embedding problem. Existing multi-view network embedding methods, such as MVE [24] and MINEs [19], first learn a single-view network representa-

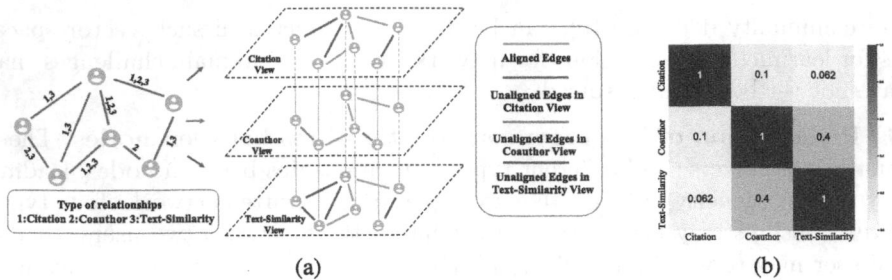

Fig. 1. (a) Illustration of converting heterogeneous relationships to multiple views of the network. (b) Consistent and unique information carried by each pair of AMiner network views.

tion using skip-gram model then fuse them directly. Since their fusion strategies, i.e. averaging and adding, are both linear functions, they fail to capture the complex nonlinear information, leading to a sub-optimal result. Besides, there are some works [27,37,40] learning a unified representation and a view-specific representation for each view simultaneously, but they are shallow models without considering the high-order proximities between nodes.

Targeting at modeling the heterogeneity of edges and preservation of high-order node proximities for learning network representations, we propose a novel **R**egularized **G**raph **A**uto-**E**ncoders framework, namely RGAE. To better illustrate our motivation, we first introduce a case study on a multi-view AMiner network (see details in Sect. 4.1). As shown in Fig. 1 (a), it contains two types of information, consistent information and unique information, as its edges are partial aligned as well as partial distinct between different views. Different views may share some consistent information. At the same time, each of them also carries some unique information that others do not have. We further follow a similar method [27] to perform a statistical analysis. Given a pair of views, the edge sets are $\mathcal{E}_1$ and $\mathcal{E}_2$. We treat the Jaccard coefficient between the two sets as the proportion of consistent information. As we can see in Fig. 1 (b), there exists noticeable consistent information between coauthor and text similarity views while other pairs of views are quite negligible. Thus we conclude that it is unreasonable to preserve only consistent or unique information for multi-view network embedding. As a result, RGAE model aims to preserve consistent and unique information simultaneously, as well as capturing high-order nonlinear proximities between nodes. The contributions of our model are threefold:

(1). In consideration of preserving heterogeneous information of edges as much as possible, we design two kinds of graph auto-encoders to deal with consistent and unique information respectively: one is the shared across view and the other is private to each view. Through these deep and nonlinear graph auto-encoders, our RGAE model is able to represent complex high-order structural information.
(2). We further introduce two regularized loss functions, i.e. the similarity loss and the difference loss, to explicitly avoid the information redundancy of the

Table 1. Summary of symbols

Symbol	Definition	Symbol	Definition
$\mathcal{U}$	Node set	$\mathcal{E}_i$	Edge set of view i
$\|V\|$	Number of views	D	Dimension of Y
N	Number of nodes	d	$= \lfloor D/(\|V\|+1) \rfloor$
$\mathbf{A}_i \in \mathbb{R}^{N \times N}$	Adjacency matrix of view i	α, β, γ	Hyper-parameters
$\mathbf{Y}_{i,p} \in \mathbb{R}^d$	Private embedding of view i	$\mathbf{I}_N \in \mathbb{R}^{N \times N}$	An identity matrix
$\mathbf{Y}_{i,s} \in \mathbb{R}^d$	Shared embedding of view i	$\tilde{\mathbf{A}}_i$	$= \mathbf{A}_i + I_N$
$\mathbf{Y}_{con} \in \mathbb{R}^d$	Consistent embedding	$\tilde{\mathbf{D}}_i(m,m)$	$= \sum_n \tilde{\mathbf{A}}_i(m,n)$
$\mathbf{Y} \in \mathbb{R}^D$	Final network embedding	$\mathbf{X}_1 \oplus \mathbf{X}_2$	Concatenation in the last dimension

two types of graph auto-encoders. The similarity loss is used to extract consistent information from shared graph auto-encoders. The difference loss aims to encourage the independence between shared and private graph auto-encoders, so the unique information can also be well preserved at the same time.

(3). To evaluate the performance of the RGAE model, we conduct abundant experiments on four real-world datasets. The experimental results demonstrate that the proposed model is superior to existing state-of-the-art baseline approaches as well as examining the novelty of our model.

2 Problem Formulation and Notations

We first briefly define a multi-view network, multi-view network embedding and list the main notations used throughout this paper in Table 1:

Definition 1. Multi-View Network. *A multi-view network is a network defined as $G = \{\mathcal{U}, \mathcal{E}_1, \mathcal{E}_2, \cdots, \mathcal{E}_{\|V\|}\}$, where $\mathcal{U}$ is a node set shared by all views, and $\mathcal{E}_i$ $(1 \le i \le \|V\|)$ is the edge set of the i-th view, which reflects a specific type of relationship between nodes.*

Problem 1. Multi-View Network Embedding. Given a multi-view network $G = \{\mathcal{U}, \mathcal{E}_1, \mathcal{E}_2, \cdots, \mathcal{E}_{\|V\|}\}$, the multi-view network embedding problem aims to learn a low-dimensional embedding representation $\mathbf{Y} \in \mathbb{R}^D$ $(D \ll N)$. More specifically, an intermediate view-specific embedding representation $\mathbf{Y}_{i,p} \in \mathbb{R}^d$ is learned to preserve the unique information of view i and a shared embedding representation $\mathbf{Y}_{con} \in \mathbb{R}^d$ is learned to preserve the consistent information among all views. The final embedding representation $\mathbf{Y}$ is obtained from all view-specific embedding representations and the shared embedding representation by an aggregation function.

3 Method

In this section, we introduce our proposed **R**egularized **G**raph **A**uto-**E**ncoders framework, namely RGAE, for tackling the multi-view network embedding problem in detail. An illustrative example of the RGAE model is shown in Fig. 2.

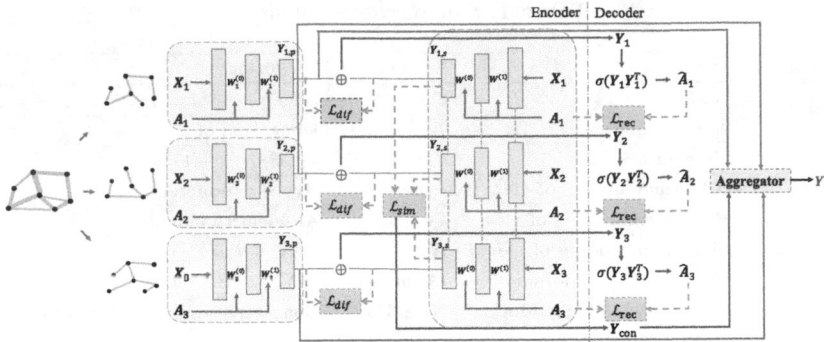

Fig. 2. The framework of RGAE. The illustration takes a network with three views as an example.

3.1   The Shared and Private Graph Auto-Encoders

Graph convolutional network (GCN) [11] is built on the idea of message passing, and convolves the representation of the central node with the representations of its neighbors to derive an updated representation of the central node. Our shared and private graph auto-encoders are both motivated as an extension of existing GCN that is able to learn valuable information for graphs. By stacking multiple GCN layers as an encoder and a simple inner production operation as a decoder, the graph auto-encoders in the RGAE model is capable of extracting consistent and unique information in a multi-view network. Specifically, given a multi-view network denoted as $G = \{\mathcal{U}, \mathcal{E}_1, \mathcal{E}_2, \cdots, \mathcal{E}_{|V|}\}$, for a specific view i, the propagation rule of l-th layer in the private encoder is formulated as:

$$\mathbf{Y}_{i,p}^{(l+1)} = \sigma(\tilde{\mathbf{D}}_i^{-\frac{1}{2}}\tilde{\mathbf{A}}_i\tilde{\mathbf{D}}_i^{-\frac{1}{2}}\mathbf{Y}_{i,p}^{(l)}\mathbf{W}_i^{(l)}) \tag{1}$$

where the $\sigma(\cdot)$ is the non-linear activation function. In this paper, we choose *relu* as activation function in all cases. $\mathbf{W}_i^{(l)}$ is the weight matrix, and $\mathbf{Y}_{i,p}^{(0)} = \mathbf{X}_i$ is the feature matrix for view i. Specially, if the node features are not available the $\mathbf{X}_i$ will be an identity matrix, as described in [11].

The key point of the shared encoder is that the weight matrices in all layers are shared across different views[1], which is clearly different from the private graph auto-encoder. In detail, the propagation rule of the l-th layer in the shared graph encoder is formulated as:

$$\mathbf{Y}_{i,s}^{(l+1)} = \sigma(\tilde{\mathbf{D}}_i^{-\frac{1}{2}}\tilde{\mathbf{A}}_i\tilde{\mathbf{D}}_i^{-\frac{1}{2}}\mathbf{Y}_{i,s}^{(l)}\mathbf{W}^{(l)}) \tag{2}$$

Note that the weight matrix $\mathbf{W}^{(l)}$ is only shared in view-wise rather than layer-wise. Through this shared architecture we can project all views into the same semantic space so that the process of extracting the consistent information is

---

[1] Note the node set is shared across all views.

more interpretable. We can also allow different views to influence mutually and collaborate implicitly.

The GCN layer is motivated by a first-order approximation of the localized spectral filters on graph-structured data [3]. In this regard, it is possible to stack multiple GCN layers in both shared encoders and private encoders to capture the high-order proximity between nodes. The final outputs of these stacked shared encoders and private encoders are denoted as $\mathbf{Y}_{i,s}$ and $\mathbf{Y}_{i,p}$ for each view respectively. During the forward pass, the graph decoder in view i aims to calculate the reconstructed adjacency matrix $\hat{\mathbf{A}}_i$. In order to utilize the complete information to make a better reconstruction, we first concatenate the outputs of the shared encoder and private encoder for view i, then we utilize the inner production operation to yield the reconstructed adjacency matrix, as described in [12], which is computed as follow:

$$\mathbf{Y}_i = \mathbf{Y}_{i,s} \oplus \mathbf{Y}_{i,p}, \quad \hat{\mathbf{A}}_i = sigmoid(\mathbf{Y}_i \mathbf{Y}_i^{\mathrm{T}}) \tag{3}$$

Since the adjacency matrix preserves the topology information of the graph, it is momentous to minimize the reconstruction loss. It has been demonstrated that minimizing the reconstruction loss is helpful to preserve the similarity between nodes [26]. Due to the sparsity of networks, there exist a great deal of zero elements and the number of zero elements and non-zero elements is extremely unbalanced in the adjacency matrix. As a result, we minimize the reconstruction error by optimizing the Balanced Cross-Entropy loss, which allows the model to pay more attention to the non-zero elements thus ignores the redundant noises from zero elements. For the view i, we compute the reconstruction loss as follows:

$$\mathcal{L}_i^{rec} = \sum_{a_i^{(m,n)} \in \mathbf{A}_i, \hat{a}_i^{(m,n)} \in \hat{\mathbf{A}}_i} [-a_i^{(m,n)} log(\hat{a}_i^{(m,n)})\varsigma - (1 - a_i^{(m,n)}) log(1 - \hat{a}_i^{(m,n)})] \tag{4}$$

where the ς is a weighting factor to balance the importance of the non-zero elements, defined as $\frac{\#zero \quad elements}{\#non-zero \quad elements}$ in $\mathbf{A}_i$.

3.2 Regularization

Similarity Loss. Intuitively, the consistent information can be extracted from the outputs of the shared encoders. Since we have projected all these outputs into the same semantic space, it is meaningful to make them collaborate to vote for the consistent representation. In this process, we encourage the consistent representation $\mathbf{Y}_{con}$ to be similar to the shared representation $\mathbf{Y}_{i,s}$ of each view as much as possible. As the importance of views may be different, we further allow the model to assign different weights to them. Taking all these into consideration, we introduce the following similarity loss to regularize the extraction process:

$$\mathcal{L}^{sim} = \sum_{i=1}^{|V|} \lambda_i^\gamma \|\mathbf{Y}_{con} - \mathbf{Y}_{i,s}\|_F^2, \quad \sum_{i=1}^{|V|} \lambda_i = 1, \lambda_i \geq 0 \tag{5}$$

where λ_i is the weight for view i, and γ moderates the weight distribution. By learning proper weights, the extraction process can let the consistent representation focus on the most informative views. Naturally, the consistent representation is calculated as the weighted combinations of the outputs of the shared encoders, which illustrates the collaboration between different views.

Difference Loss. In order to preserve the unique information, the difference loss is also introduced to encourage the isolation between consistent embeddings and unique embeddings. As the consistent information and unique information have essential differences, they should be distinguished clearly to avoid the information redundancy. In other words, the shared embeddings and private embeddings should describe the information of multiple views in different perspectives, thus we define the difference loss via an orthogonality constraint between the private embedding and shared embedding in each view:

$$\mathcal{L}_i^{dif} = \|\mathbf{Y}_{i,s} \odot \mathbf{Y}_{i,p}\|_F^2, \quad i = 1, 2, \cdots, |V| \tag{6}$$

where the $\odot$ is the row-wise inner production. Obviously, the difference loss will drive the shared embeddings to be orthogonal with the private embeddings, thus they will be as dissimilar as possible. In this way, the shared and private encoders are able to encode different aspects of the multi-view network. In this paper, we treat the output of the private graph encoder for each view as its private representation.

3.3   The Aggregation Process

As introduced above, our RGAE model includes the three types of losses, i.e. the reconstruction loss, the similarity loss, and the difference loss. In order to train these losses jointly, the overall loss of our proposed model is summarized as follow:

$$\mathcal{L} = \sum_{i=1}^{|V|} \mathcal{L}_i^{rec} + \alpha * \mathcal{L}^{sim} + \beta * \sum_{i=1}^{|V|} \mathcal{L}_i^{dif} \tag{7}$$

where α and β are hyper-parameters to control the importance of similarity loss and difference loss respectively. Up to now, we have obtained the representations of consistent and unique information. Finally, we design an aggregation process to yield the final network representation, which can be illustrated as:

$$\mathbf{Y} = Aggregator(\mathbf{Y}_{con}, \mathbf{Y}_{1,p}, \cdots, \mathbf{Y}_{|V|,p}) \tag{8}$$

The aggregator should be able to integrate both the consistent and unique information effectively, and it can be add, average, pooling and some other designed functions. In this paper, we choose concatenation as the aggregation function since it has been proven to be useful and efficient in many existing network embedding methods [15,27,30]. As shown in Table 1, the total dimension D has been assigned to each graph auto-encoder equally, thus after the concatenation process the final network embedding will still satisfy $\mathbf{Y} \in \mathbb{R}^D$.

3.4   Implementation

In practice, we utilize Tensorflow for an efficient GPU-based implementation of the RGAE model. Then the parameters of RGAE model except λ_i can be efficiently optimized automatically with back propagation algorithm. To save space, we omit details here. Since the sparsity of network data, we use sparse-dense matrix multiplication for Eqs. (1) and (2), as described in [11]. Specially, for the view weight λ_i in Eq. (5), we follow the same method [1] to update it. Let's denote $\|\mathbf{Y}_{con} - \mathbf{Y}_{i,s}\|_F^2$ as $\mathbf{B}_i$, then Eq. (5) is equivalent to $\sum_{i=1}^{|V|} \lambda_i^\gamma \mathbf{B_i} - \xi(\sum_{i=1}^{|V|} \lambda_i - 1)$, where ξ is Lagrange multiplier. By taking the derivative of this formula with respect to λ_i as zero, we can obtain the update rule of λ_i: $\lambda_i \leftarrow \dfrac{(\gamma \mathbf{B_i})^{\frac{1}{1-\gamma}}}{\sum_{i=1}^{|V|}(\gamma \mathbf{B_i})^{\frac{1}{1-\gamma}}}$. It is efficient to use one parameter γ for controlling the distribution of view weights during the optimization process dynamically. According to the update rule, we would assign equal weights to all views when γ closes to ∞. When γ closes to 1, the weight for the view whose $\mathbf{B}_i$ value is smallest will be assigned as 1, while others are almost ignored since their weights are close to 0.

4   Experiments

4.1   Experimental Setup

We select four multi-view network datasets in different fields. The statistic analysis is shown in Table 2.

Table 2. Overview of datasets

Task	Dataset	Views	Nodes	Edges	Labels	Type
Multi-class Node Classification	AMiner	3	8,438	2,433,356	8	Academic
	PPI	6	4,328	1,661,756	50	Biological
Multi-label Node Classification	Flickr	2	34,881	3,290,030	171	Social
Link Prediction	YouTube	4	5,108	3,263,045	–	Social

- AMiner [31]: AMiner network is an academic network representing the relationships between authors. It consists of three views: author-citation, co-authorship, and text similarity. Text similarity between two authors is calculated by TF-IDF from titles and abstracts in their papers. An author establishes connections with his top ten similar authors and we only preserve authors in eight research fields as [4]. The research fields are treated as node labels.
- PPI [5]: The PPI network is a human protein-protein interaction network. Six views are constructed based on the co-expression, co-occurrence, database, experiment, fusion, and neighborhood information. Gene groups are treated as node labels.

- Flickr [32]: It is a social network of online users on Flickr with two views. One view is the friendship network among bloggers. The other is a tag-proximity network in which a node connects with its top 10 similar nodes according to their tags. We treat community memberships as node labels.
- YouTube [38]: It is a social network consists of four views: the friendship, the number of common friends, the number of common subscribers, and the number of common favorite videos between two users.

In order to evaluate the effectiveness of RGAE, we compare our model with three types of baselines. The **single-view** based baselines include:

- Deepwalk [22]: It is a well-known baseline for network embedding. We set the number and the length for each node as 80 and 40 respectively following the recommendations of the original paper. The window-size is set as 10.
- GraRep [2]: It aims to capture the k-order proximities by factorizing the k-step transition matrices. We set k as 5.
- SDNE [34]: It utilizes the auto-encoders to preserve the neighbor structure of nodes. The first-order and second-order proximity are proposed to preserve the global and the local network structure. We set the number of layers as 3, and the hidden size as [800,400,128].
- GAE [12]: It stacks GCN layers as an encoder and the inner production operation as a decoder. The reconstruction loss helps it to capture structural information in an unsupervised manner. We set the number of layers and hidden sizes same as SDNE.

The **heterogeneous** network embedding methods include:

- PTE [29]: It is a heterogeneous network embedding method which can also be used to jointly train the embedding, because multi-view network is a special type of heterogeneous network. We set the number of negative samples as 5.
- Metapath2vec [4]: It utilizes meta-paths guided random walk to generate the node sequences then uses skip-gram model to learn the node representations. We set the number, the length of walks and window size same as deepwalk. We perform experiment using one of all possible meta-paths at a time, and report the best result.

The **multi-view** based baselines include:

- Deepwalk-con: It applies Deepwalk to get a d dimensional representation for each view then concatenates these representations from all K views to generate a unified representation with $K * d$ dimensions.
- MultiNMF [17]: It is a multi-view matrix factorization algorithm, which extracts consistent information by a joint matrix factorization process.
- MVE [24]: It combines single view embeddings by weights learned from attention mechanism to construct a multi-view network embedding. We set the parameters of random walk and skip-gram model same as Deepwalk, and other parameters are same as the original paper.

- MNE [40]: It combines the information of multiple view by preserving a high dimensional common embedding and a lower dimensional embedding for each view. The dimensions of the additional vectors are set as 10.
- MTNE-C [37]: It combines the common embedding and node-specific embedding of each node to be a complete embedding for the closeness measurement. We follow the default parameter setting in the original paper.

For RGAE and all baselines except Deepwalk-con, the embedding dimension is set as 128. The number of graph auto-encoder layers is set as 3, and two hidden layers' dimensions are set as 800 and 400 respectively. Both α and β are selected from [0.1, 0.3, 0.5, 0.7, 1.0, 1.5, 2.0], and γ is selected from [0.05, 0.5, 5, 10, 50, 100, 500]. The learning rate is selected from [0.001, 0.01, 0.1]. As node features are not available for our datasets the feature matrix will be an identity matrix. We treat the node embedding learned by various methods as feature to train linear classifiers for multiclass classification, and train one-vs-rest classifiers for multilabel classification. For link prediction, we use the cosine similarity between node pairs as features to train a logistic classifier to predict the link existence. Follow the setting in [24], we use other three views to train embeddings and predict the link existence in friend view. To generate negative edges, we randomly sample an equal number of node pairs which have no edge connecting them. We report the best results among multiple views for single-view based baselines. To guarantee a fair comparison, we repeat each method ten times and the average metrics are reported.

4.2 Experimental Results

Node Classification. We evaluate the performance of our method and three categories of baselines using the Micro-F1 and Macro-F1 scores. Table 3 shows the comparison on three datasets. As can be seen, our RGAE model outperforms all baselines except for Macro-F1 on Flickr dataset. For example, on AMiner dataset, it achieves a sustainable performance gain of 1%, 2%, and 3% with the percentage of training data increasing. It is noted that RGAE always outperforms GAE consistently, which shows that with making good use of information from multiple views, we are indeed able to learn a robust representation for a multi-view network. The superiority of RGAE over SDNE further verifies that it is reasonable to model the heterogeneity of edges. Although GraRep captures high order proximities between nodes, the matrix factorization process makes it hard to preserve non-linear network information, which is not compared with our model. One may see that the existing multi-view network embedding approaches are also not comparable to our RGAE model. The reason is that either they are not possible to consider the uniqueness of each view, like Metapath2Vec and MVE, or they are not possible to capture high-order proximities between nodes, such as MTNE-C and MNE. All these observed results show that the RGAE model can indeed capture more complete non-linear information from multiple views.

508   L. Wang et al.

Table 3. Node classification results w.r.t. Micro-F1(%) and Macro-F1(%) with different training ratio. '-' means out of memory error.

Datesets	Category	Methods	0.1		0.3		0.5	
			Micro	Macro	Micro	Macro	Micro	Macro
AMiner	Single-View	Deepwalk	69.9	68.4	74.3	73.3	75.1	74.3
		GraRep	23.3	20.5	44.8	41.8	61.9	60.6
		SDNE	64.8	62.5	70.3	68.0	70.8	69.4
		GAE	60.4	54.8	62.5	57.7	63.6	59.3
	Heterogeneous	PTE	52.9	46.9	56.6	52.7	58.1	55.2
		Metapath2Vec	70.6	70.1	75.3	73.5	76.2	74.9
	Multi-View	Deepwalk-con	61.4	59.0	74.2	72.6	76.1	74.9
		MultiNMF	57.4	52.6	66.4	64.1	66.8	62.8
		MVE	73.6	72.7	78.8	77.5	78.9	77.6
		MNE	73.6	72.2	79.2	77.8	79.6	78.1
		MTNE-C	54.5	48.8	57.2	53.9	58.6	55.2
		RGAE	**74.9**	**73.3**	**80.6**	**79.7**	**82.0**	**80.9**
PPI	Single-View	Deepwalk	8.9	4.2	10.9	6.1	12.1	7.3
		GraRep	4.0	2.0	5.1	3.1	13.1	10.0
		SDNE	11.8	10.7	14.7	13.4	17.6	15.0
		GAE	9.5	4.3	12.3	8.0	13.7	9.1
	Heterogeneous	PTE	12.8	9.5	19.7	11.7	22.0	14.0
		Metapath2Vec	13.4	10.0	20.2	12.8	22.3	15.7
	Multi-View	Deepwalk-con	9.9	6.2	11.9	8.5	13.6	9.9
		MultiNMF	15.3	11.9	17.8	15.2	20.3	17.5
		MVE	11.7	9.9	12.1	10.6	13.3	10.8
		MNE	13.3	11.8	14.1	12.2	15.6	12.1
		MTNE-C	3.4	1.6	4.0	2.0	6.2	3.5
		RGAE	**19.0**	**15.1**	**24.4**	**21.0**	**25.0**	**21.3**
Flickr	Single-View	Deepwalk	51.7	32.1	51.9	27.6	53.2	27.8
		GraRep	52.4	32.2	53.8	**35.0**	55.9	35.8
		SDNE	47.6	32.1	48.2	32.6	49.6	30.5
		GAE	34.5	9.1	37.0	10.4	38.4	11.1
	Heterogeneous	PTE	55.7	30.4	56.4	34.3	56.2	31.0
		Metapath2Vec	55.7	30.8	56.6	33.9	56.7	32.2
	Multi-View	Deepwalk-con	51.9	32.6	52.5	28.2	53.7	28.3
		MultiNMF	-	-	-	-	-	-
		MVE	52.0	32.5	53.0	28.9	54.3	28.8
		MNE	52.4	**33.1**	53.5	29.9	54.8	29.8
		MTNE-C	23.9	5.2	23.3	4.8	22.9	4.6
		RGAE	**56.7**	32.9	**57.6**	33.7	**58.4**	**36.2**

Link Prediction. We select the YouTube dataset to verify the performance of link prediction. Table 4 shows that the RGAE model significantly outper-

Table 4. Link Prediction results on YouTube dataset w.r.t. ROC_AUC Score(%) and Average Precision Score (AP)(%) with different training ratio

Category	Methods	0.1		0.3		0.5	
		ROC_AUC	AP	ROC_AUC	AP	ROC_AUC	AP
Single-View	Deepwalk	74.4	73.6	74.7	74.0	78.4	77.2
	GraRep	80.2	79.6	80.3	79.8	80.7	80.0
	SDNE	81.8	82.7	82.3	83.0	85.0	85.3
	GAE	77.0	77.7	77.3	78.2	80.3	79.6
Heterogeneous	PTE	69.5	63.8	70.1	64.8	69.1	64.7
	Metapath2Vcc	78.5	73.8	80.6	75.8	81.9	79.7
Multi-View	Deepwalk-con	78.9	78.0	79.8	78.9	84.7	83.1
	MultiNMF	80.3	80.2	81.9	82.3	82.2	82.8
	MVE	82.0	82.4	83.0	82.8	83.4	83.1
	MNE	82.3	82.7	83.3	83.5	84.1	84.6
	MTNE-C	52.4	53.0	62.3	60.0	00.1	65.8
	RGAE	**82.7**	**83.2**	**85.5**	**85.2**	**86.3**	**85.9**

forms all baseline methods. The results verify again that RGAE indeed can preserve the abundant information in multi-view networks. It is noticeable that the SDNE even outperforms all multi-view and heterogeneous network embedding approaches. By designing two kinds of graph auto-encoders, RGAE utilizes both consistent and unique information from multiple views to describe the node proximity in a detailed way, which achieves better performance than SDNE. As a result, we conclude that RGAE is able to explore the structural properties of multi-view networks.

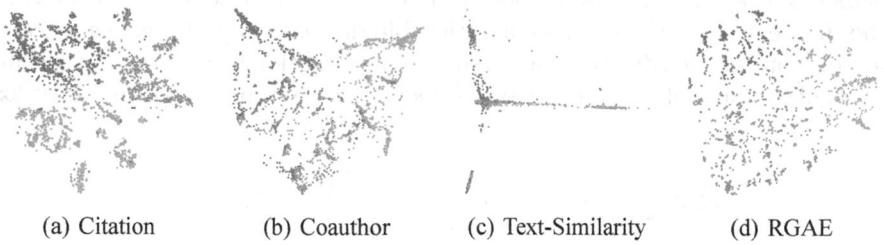

| (a) Citation | (b) Coauthor | (c) Text-Similarity | (d) RGAE |

Fig. 3. 2d t-SNE Visualization for AMiner Dataset. Each point represents a node and colors represent labels. red: computational linguistics; blue: computer graphics; green: theoretical computer science (Color figure online)

Network Visualization. We project the embeddings of AMiner dataset onto 2d vectors with t-SNE [20]. Figure 3 shows the network visualizations of the RGAE model as well as each view's visualization obtained by its shared and private encoders. The difference between RGAE model and the single-view model is that single-view model lacks not only the constraints of the loss function to divide the consistent information and unique information in a view, but also the cooperation and supplementary between different views. In order to make the visualization results more clear and legible, we select three from the eight categories of nodes for visualization, and each color represents a research field. We can see that our multi-view based approach works better than learning each view individually. Citation view may achieve relatively good representation effect, but there are still a few nodes that have not been assigned to the correct cluster. Therefore, it still needs more useful information from other views to complement and properly correct it to get a robust representation. The visualization of RGAE, by contrast, separates the three research fields clearly, which illustrates the necessity of modeling heterogeneous edges with consideration of all types of relationships.

4.3 Influence of Loss Functions

The visualization results have proven the importance of both consistent and unique information. In this part, we research the effect of the loss functions. In our RGAE model, there exist two loss functions, i.e. the similarity loss and the difference loss, that regularize the processes of extracting the consistent and unique information respectively. To evaluate the influences of the two loss functions, we remove similarity loss, difference loss, and both of them respectively, and show the performance in Fig. 4. The histogram clearly shows the importance of the two loss functions for our RGAE model. When we remove the similarity loss function, there is slight decline in performance. Because without similarity loss function, the quality of consistent information will be affected. Whereas there is relatively little consistent information among the views, and the proportion of the dimensions of the common representation in the final representation is small, so that the performance declination will not be quite severe. When there is no difference loss, there will be a noticeable decrease in performance, because the isolation between different view's specific information becomes worse without the regularization of difference loss. Moreover, if we remove the similarity loss

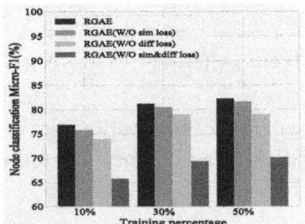
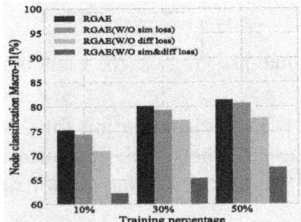

(a) Node classification on AMiner dataset w.r.t Micro-F1(%)

(b) Node classification on AMiner dataset w.r.t Macro-F1(%)

Fig. 4. The effectiveness of the similarity loss and difference loss in our RGAE model

and difference loss simultaneously, the performance of the RGAE model declines further dramatically. All these observations can demonstrate the necessity of the similarity loss and difference loss, but the degree of influence varies between the two losses.

4.4   Parameter Sensitivity

With results presented in Fig. 5, we focus on the parameter sensitivity of RGAE model, including the number of embedding dimensions, α, β, and γ. We perform node classification on AMiner dataset and link prediction on YouTube dataset to evaluate the parameter sensitivity. To explore the contributions of these parameters, we fix others to evaluate the effect of one parameter at a time on the experimental results.

Overall, different datasets and tasks have different sensitivities to embedding dimensions. On AMiner dataset, the performance increases with the dimension increasing then stabilizes when the dimension reaches 64. While on the YouTube dataset, the model performs well when the dimension is 32 and the performance decreases slightly when the dimension continues to increase. Compared with the AMiner dataset, the Youtube dataset achieves good results in lower dimensions. When the proportion of the training data set is small, a large number of dimensions tend to cause overfitting.

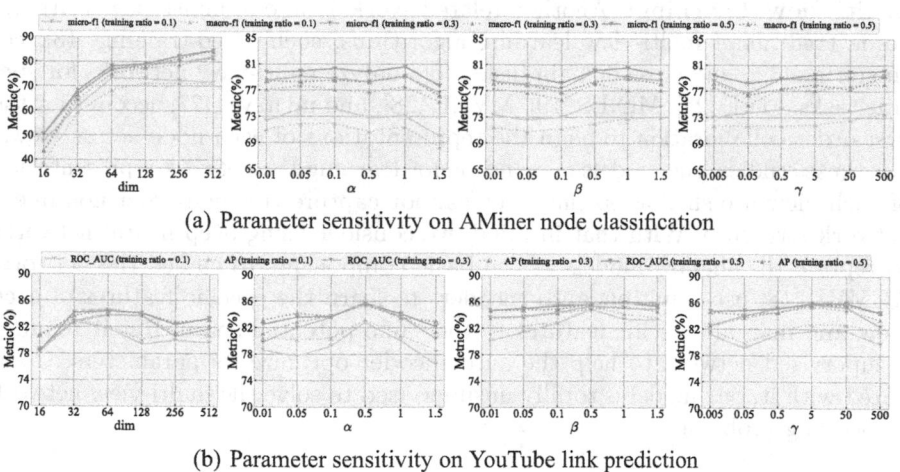

(a) Parameter sensitivity on AMiner node classification

(b) Parameter sensitivity on YouTube link prediction

Fig. 5. Performance of the RGAE models under varying hyper-parameters

The curves of the experimental metrics with the parameters α or β are not monotonic. Their overall trends are both first rising and then falling. Because when the proportion of similarity loss function and difference loss function are too large, the proportion of reconstruction loss will be weakened, which will affect the representation abilities of graph auto-encoders. As for γ, we find that it actually influences the results for both tasks. As we can see, it is more suitable to set the value of γ larger than 5.

5   Related Work

Network Embedding: Network embedding is dedicated to mapping nodes in a network into a low-dimensional vector space for preserving structural information. Earlier studies such as Deepwalk [22], node2vec [8], and Struc2vec [25] use skip-gram model to preserve network structures through neighborhood sampling. Traditional deep neural networks also get widespread attention because of its nonlinear underlying structure. SDNE [34], SiNE [35], and Deepcas [14] have a strong advantage in retaining the highly nonlinear structure of the network. More recent methods adopt graph neural network to perform convolutional operations on graphs. GCN [11], GATs [33], and GraphSAGE [9] are all representative works as end-to-end approaches for network representation learning. These studies are directed at homogeneous networks. Heterogeneous network embedding has also attracted attention because of its practical significance. PTE [29] is an extension method of LINE on heterogeneous networks. Besides, Metapath2vec [4], HIN2vec [7], and RHINE [18] use meta path to capture the structure and semantic information in heterogeneous networks.

Multi-view Learning: Another related work is about multi-view learning. Some traditional multi-view learning algorithms, such as co-training [13], co-clustering [39], and cross-domain fusion [6] analyze multi-view networks for specific tasks. MVE [24], MINES [19], MVNE [28], and mvn2vec [27] account for the first-order collaboration to align the representations of each node across views. For these studies, the models responsible for learning the network representation of each view are shallow so that they cannot capture the high-order non-linear network structure. With that in mind, we consider using deep neural networks to replace the shallow models as the basic components to embed the network. ACMVL [18] uses multiple auto-encoders to learn the specific features of each view and map all specific features to the same potential space. But it requires a supervised network to help the auto-encoder optimize its parameters. Compared with it, our model is totally unsupervised to solve the multi-view network embedding problem.

6   Conclusion

In this paper, we explore how to model the heterogeneity of edges by solving a multi-view network embedding problem and propose a novel RGAE model. More specifically, our model makes use of two types of graph auto-encoders to extract consistent and unique information of views respectively, and innovatively proposes two loss functions to distinguish these two types of information. Experimental results not only indicate the superiority of the proposed model but also investigate the contributions of two loss functions. In the future, we plan to apply the framework to more applications. A meaningful direction is to use multi-view learning to represent general heterogeneous networks, that is, the nodes and edges of the network have multiple types at the same time.

Acknowledgement. The research was supported by National Natural Science Foundation of China (No. 61802140) and Hubei Provincial Natural Science Foundation (No. 2018CFB200).

References

1. Cai, X., Nie, F., Huang, H.: Multi-view k-means clustering on big data. In: Proceedings of the Twenty-Third International Joint Conference on Artificial Intelligence (2013)
2. Cao, S., Lu, W., Xu, Q.: GraRep: learning graph representations with global structural information. In: Proceedings of the 24th ACM International on Conference on Information and Knowledge Management, pp. 891–900. ACM (2015)
3. Defferrard, M., Bresson, X., Vandergheynst, P.: Convolutional neural networks on graphs with fast localized spectral filtering. In: Proceedings of the 30th Advances in Neural Information Processing Systems, pp. 3844–3852 (2016)
4. Dong, Y., Chawla, N.V., Swami, A.: metapath2vec: scalable representation learning for heterogeneous networks. In: Proceedings of the 23rd ACM SIGKDD International Conference on Knowledge Discovery and Data Mining, pp. 135–144. ACM (2017)
5. Franceschini, A., et al.: String v9.1: protein-protein interaction networks, with increased coverage and integration. Nucleic Acids Res. **41**(D1), D808–D815 (2012)
6. Franco, J.S., Boyer, E.: Fusion of multiview silhouette cues using a space occupancy grid. In: Proceedings of the Tenth IEEE International Conference on Computer Vision (ICCV 2005), vols. 1, 2, pp. 1747–1753. IEEE (2005)
7. Fu, T., Lee, W.C., Lei, Z.: Hin2vec: explore meta-paths in heterogeneous information networks for representation learning. In: Proceedings of the 2017 ACM on Conference on Information and Knowledge Management, pp. 1797–1806. ACM (2017)
8. Grover, A., Leskovec, J.: node2vec: scalable feature learning for networks. In: Proceedings of the 22nd ACM SIGKDD International Conference on Knowledge Discovery and Data Mining, pp. 855–864. ACM (2016)
9. Hamilton, W., Ying, Z., Leskovec, J.: Inductive representation learning on large graphs. In: Advances in Neural Information Processing Systems, pp. 1024–1034 (2017)
10. He, K., Sun, Y., Bindel, D., Hopcroft, J., Li, Y.: Detecting overlapping communities from local spectral subspaces. In: Proceedings of the 2015 IEEE International Conference on Data Mining, pp. 769–774. IEEE (2015)
11. Kipf, T.N., Welling, M.: Semi-supervised classification with graph convolutional networks. arXiv preprint arXiv:1609.02907 (2016)
12. Kipf, T.N., Welling, M.: Variational graph auto-encoders. arXiv preprint arXiv:1611.07308 (2016)
13. Kumar, A., Daumé, H.: A co-training approach for multi-view spectral clustering. In: Proceedings of the 28th International Conference on Machine Learning (ICML 2011), pp. 393–400 (2011)

14. Li, C., Ma, J., Guo, X., Mei, Q.: DeepCas: an end-to-end predictor of information cascades. In: Proceedings of the 26th International Conference on World Wide Web, pp. 577–586 (2017)
15. Li, J., Wu, L., Liu, H.: Multi-level network embedding with boosted low-rank matrix approximation. arXiv preprint arXiv:1808.08627 (2018)
16. Li, S.Z., Zhu, L., Zhang, Z.Q., Blake, A., Zhang, H.J., Shum, H.: Statistical learning of multi-view face detection. In: Heyden, A., Sparr, G., Nielsen, M., Johansen, P. (eds.) ECCV 2002. LNCS, vol. 2353, pp. 67–81. Springer, Heidelberg (2002). https://doi.org/10.1007/3-540-47979-1_5
17. Liu, J., Wang, C., Gao, J., Han, J.: Multi-view clustering via joint nonnegative matrix factorization. In: Proceedings of the 2013 SIAM International Conference on Data Mining, pp. 252–260. SIAM (2013)
18. Lu, R., Liu, J., Wang, Y., Xie, H., Zuo, X.: Auto-encoder based co-training multi-view representation learning. In: Yang, Q., Zhou, Z.-H., Gong, Z., Zhang, M.-L., Huang, S.-J. (eds.) PAKDD 2019. LNCS (LNAI), vol. 11441, pp. 119–130. Springer, Cham (2019). https://doi.org/10.1007/978-3-030-16142-2_10
19. Ma, Y., Ren, Z., Jiang, Z., Tang, J., Yin, D.: Multi-dimensional network embedding with hierarchical structure. In: Proceedings of the Eleventh ACM International Conference on Web Search and Data Mining, pp. 387–395. ACM (2018)
20. van der Maaten, L., Hinton, G.: Visualizing data using t-SNE. J. Mach. Learn. Res. **9**(Nov), 2579–2605 (2008)
21. Pan, Y., Yao, T., Mei, T., Li, H., Ngo, C.W., Rui, Y.: Click-through-based cross-view learning for image search. In: Proceedings of the 37th International ACM SIGIR Conference on Research & Development in Information Retrieval, pp. 717–726. ACM (2014)
22. Perozzi, B., Al-Rfou, R., Skiena, S.: DeepWalk: online learning of social representations. In: Proceedings of the 20th ACM SIGKDD International Conference on Knowledge Discovery and Data Mining, pp. 701–710. ACM (2014)
23. Qiu, J., Dong, Y., Ma, H., Li, J., Wang, K., Tang, J.: Network embedding as matrix factorization: unifying DeepWalk, LINE, PTE, and node2vec. In: Proceedings of the Eleventh ACM International Conference on Web Search and Data Mining, pp. 459–467 (2018)
24. Qu, M., Tang, J., Shang, J., Ren, X., Zhang, M., Han, J.: An attention-based collaboration framework for multi-view network representation learning. In: Proceedings of the 2017 ACM on Conference on Information and Knowledge Management, pp. 1767–1776. ACM (2017)
25. Ribeiro, L.F., Saverese, P.H., Figueiredo, D.R.: struc2vec: learning node representations from structural identity. In: Proceedings of the 23rd ACM SIGKDD International Conference on Knowledge Discovery and Data Mining, pp. 385–394. ACM (2017)
26. Salakhutdinov, R., Hinton, G.: Semantic hashing. Int. J. Approx. Reason. **50**(7), 969–978 (2009)
27. Shi, Y., et al.: mvn2vec: preservation and collaboration in multi-view network embedding. arXiv preprint arXiv:1801.06597 (2018)
28. Sun, Y., Bui, N., Hsieh, T.Y., Honavar, V.: Multi-view network embedding via graph factorization clustering and co-regularized multi-view agreement. In: Proceedings of the 2018 IEEE International Conference on Data Mining Workshops (ICDMW), pp. 1006–1013. IEEE (2018)

29. Tang, J., Qu, M., Mei, Q.: PTE: predictive text embedding through large-scale heterogeneous text networks. In: Proceedings of the 21th ACM SIGKDD International Conference on Knowledge Discovery and Data Mining, pp. 1165–1174. ACM (2015)
30. Tang, J., Qu, M., Wang, M., Zhang, M., Yan, J., Mei, Q.: Line: large-scale information network embedding. In: Proceedings of the 24th International Conference on World Wide Web (2015)
31. Tang, J., Zhang, J., Yao, L., Li, J., Zhang, L., Su, Z.: ArnetMiner: extraction and mining of academic social networks. In: Proceedings of the 14th ACM SIGKDD International Conference on Knowledge Discovery and Data Mining, pp. 990–998. ACM (2008)
32. Tang, L., Liu, H.: Relational learning via latent social dimensions. In: Proceedings of the 15th ACM SIGKDD International Conference on Knowledge Discovery and Data Mining, pp. 817–826. ACM (2009)
33. Veličković, P., Cucurull, G., Casanova, A., Romero, A., Lio, P., Bengio, Y.: Graph attention networks. arXiv preprint arXiv:1710.10903 (2017)
34. Wang, D., Cui, P., Zhu, W.: Structural deep network embedding In: Proceedings of the 22nd ACM SIGKDD International Conference on Knowledge Discovery and Data Mining, pp. 1225–1234. ACM (2016)
35. Wang, S., Tang, J., Aggarwal, C., Chang, Y., Liu, H.: Signed network embedding in social media. In: Proceedings of the 2017 SIAM International Conference on Data Mining, pp. 327–335. SIAM (2017)
36. Wang, S., Tang, J., Aggarwal, C., Liu, H.: Linked document embedding for classification. In: Proceedings of the 25th ACM International on Conference on Information and Knowledge Management, pp. 115–124. ACM (2016)
37. Xu, L., Wei, X., Cao, J., Yu, P.S.: Multi-task network embedding. Int. J. Data Sci. Anal. 8(2), 183–198 (2018). https://doi.org/10.1007/s41060-018-0166-2
38. Yang, J., Leskovec, J.: Defining and evaluating network communities based on ground-truth. Knowl. Inf. Syst. 42(1), 181–213 (2013). https://doi.org/10.1007/s10115-013-0693-z
39. Yao, X., Han, J., Zhang, D., Nie, F.: Revisiting co-saliency detection: a novel approach based on two-stage multi-view spectral rotation co-clustering. IEEE Trans. Image Process. 26(7), 3196–3209 (2017)
40. Zhang, H., Qiu, L., Yi, L., Song, Y.: Scalable multiplex network embedding. In: Proceedings of the 27th International Joint Conference on Artificial Intelligence, vol. 18, pp. 3082–3088 (2018)

AOT: Pushing the Efficiency Boundary of Main-Memory Triangle Listing

Michael Yu[1]([✉]), Lu Qin[2], Ying Zhang[2], Wenjie Zhang[1], and Xuemin Lin[1]

[1] University of New South Wales, Kensington, Australia
{mryu,wenjie.zhang,lxue}@cse.unsw.edu.au
[2] University of Technology Sydney, Ultimo, Australia
{lu.qin,ying.zhang}@uts.edu.au

Abstract. Triangle listing is an important topic significant in many practical applications. Efficient algorithms exist for the task of triangle listing. Recent algorithms leverage an orientation framework, which can be thought of as mapping an undirected graph to a directed acylic graph, namely *oriented graph*, with respect to any global vertex order. In this paper, we propose an adaptive orientation technique that satisfies the orientation technique but refines it by traversing carefully based on the out-degree of the vertices in the oriented graph during the computation of triangles. Based on this adaptive orientation technique, we design a new algorithm, namely AOT, to enhance the edge-iterator listing paradigm. We also make improvements to the performance of AOT by exploiting the local order within the adjacent list of the vertices.

We show that AOT is the first work which can achieve best performance in terms of both practical performance and theoretical time complexity. Our comprehensive experiments over 16 real-life large graphs show a superior performance of our AOT algorithm when compared against the state-of-the-art, especially for massive graphs with billions of edges. Theoretically, we show that our proposed algorithm has a time complexity of $\Theta(\sum_{\langle u,v \rangle \in E} \min\{deg^+(u), deg^+(v)\}))$, where E and $deg^+(x)$ denote the set of directed edges in an oriented graph and the out-degree of vertex x respectively. As to our best knowledge, this is the best time complexity among in-memory triangle listing algorithms.

Keywords: Triangle · Enumeration · Graph algorithm

1 Introduction

Triangle-listing is one of the most fundamental problems in graphs, with numerous applications including structural clustering [25], web spamming discovery [4], community search [5,18], higher-order graph clustering [26], and role discovery [6]. A large number of algorithms have been proposed to efficiently enumerate all triangles in a given graph. These include in-memory algorithms [15,19,20,27], I/O efficient algorithms [7,8,11,12], and parallel/distributed algorithms [10,16,21], etc. In this paper, we focus on in-memory triangle-listing

© Springer Nature Switzerland AG 2020
Y. Nah et al. (Eds.): DASFAA 2020, LNCS 12113, pp. 516–533, 2020.
https://doi.org/10.1007/978-3-030-59416-9_31

algorithms and aim to achieve the best performance from both theoretical and practical aspects.

State-of-the-Art. The existing state-of-the-art in-memory triangle-listing algorithms are based on vertex ordering and orientation techniques [9,15]. Given an undirected simple graph, these algorithms first compute a total-order η for all its graph vertices; one example of such ordering is the non-increasing degree order. With the total-order η, a direction can then be specified for each undirected edge (u, v) such that $\eta(u) < \eta(v)$. Once complete, the graph orientation technique converts the initial undirected graph G into a directed acyclic graph $\boldsymbol{G}$. With an oriented graph, the original problem of triangle-listing on an undirected simple graph G is recast to a problem of finding three vertices u, v, w so that directed edges $\langle u, v \rangle$, $\langle v, w \rangle$, $\langle u, w \rangle$ exist in $\boldsymbol{G}$. For directed triangle instances, we refer to the role of vertex u with 2 out-going edges that form a triangle as a pivot.

Motivation. We give an example for finding triangles in an oriented-graph [9]. For each pivot vertex u, the method first initializes an index to the out-neighbors of u; after that, for each out-neighbor v of u, it traverses the out-neighbor w of v and checks to see whether w is also an out-neighbor of v in the index. The advantage of this technique is twofold: First, by simply processing all pivot vertices using the above procedure, it already guarantees that each triangle is generated only once without performing the normal pruning for duplicate triangle solutions. Secondly, parallelization of the algorithm is easy if we process sets of pivot vertices independently. This algorithm has the time complexity of $\Theta(\Sigma_{v \in V} deg^+(v) \cdot deg^-(v))$ and is bounded by $O(m^{1.5})$ [9], where V is the set of vertices in $\boldsymbol{G}$; $deg^+(v)$ and $deg^-(v)$ are the numbers of out-neighbors and in-neighbors of v in $\boldsymbol{G}$ respectively; and m is the number of edges in $\boldsymbol{G}$.

A dominant cost of the above algorithm is that of look-up operations, where the algorithm searches the out-neighbors of each pivot. A natural question is raised: Is it possible to significantly reduce the number of look-up operations needed by the algorithm? To answer this question, we first find the time complexity of the former algorithm is equivalent to that of $\Theta(\Sigma_{\langle u,v \rangle \in E} deg^+(v))$, where E is the set of directed edges in $\boldsymbol{G}$. In other words, for each directed edge $\langle u, v \rangle \in E$, the algorithm will always spend $deg^+(v)$ amount of look-up operations irrespective of whether $deg^+(v) \leq deg^+(u)$ holds. We find that if we are able to spend $deg^+(u)$ operations in the case that $deg^+(v) > deg^+(u)$ for the edge $\langle u, v \rangle \in E$, the cost of the algorithm can be further lessened, therefore it motivates us to explore new ways to further leverage the properties from graph orientation at a finer level, to improve the algorithm both theoretically and practically.

Challenges. Faced with the above problem, we ask intuitively: Can we tackle the asymmetry by manually reversing the direction of each edge $\langle u, v \rangle \in E$ if $deg^+(v) > deg^+(u)$ and then reuse the same algorithm on the now modified oriented graph? Unfortunately, this solution is infeasible. To explain, reversing the direction of the selected edges can result in cycles ($\langle u, v \rangle$, $\langle v, w \rangle$, and $\langle w, u \rangle$) in

Table 1. The Summary of notations

Notation	Definition
$G = (V, E)$	An undirected graph with vertices V and edges E
$\boldsymbol{G}$	A directed graph with vertices V and directed edge $\boldsymbol{E}$
u, v, w, x, y	Vertices in the graph
(u, v)	An undirected edge between vertices u and v
$\langle u, v \rangle$	A directed edge from vertex u to v
(u, v, w)	A triangle with vertices u, v and w
$deg(u)$	The degree of the vertex u
$deg^+(u)$	The out-degree of u in oriented graph

the oriented graph $\boldsymbol{G}$, such cyclic triangles will be missed by the aforementioned algorithm. To ensure algorithmic correctness, for each undirected edge (u, v), up to two orientations need to be kept simultaneously: the original orientation in $\boldsymbol{G}$ and the orientation specified by the comparison of $deg^+(u)$ and $deg^+(v)$ because the two orientations can be inconsistent. Therefore, to make our idea practically applicable, the following issues will be addressed in this paper: (1) How can we integrate the two orientations to improve the algorithm complexity and also ensure that each triangle is enumerated once and only once? and (2) Can we further improve the efficiency of the algorithm practically by exploring some local vertex orders?

Contributions. In this paper, we answer the above questions and make the following contributions.

(1) We have designed a new triangle listing algorithm named *Adaptive Oriented Triangle-Listing* (AOT) by developing novel adaptive orientation and local ordering techniques, which can achieve the best time complexity among the existing algorithms in the literature.
(2) We conduct an extensive performance study using 16 real-world large graphs at billion scale, to demonstrate the high efficiency of our proposed solutions. The experimental results show that our AOT algorithm is faster than the state-of-the-art solutions by up to an order of magnitude. It is also shown that AOT can be easily extended to parallel setting, significantly outperforming the state-of-the-art parallel solutions.

Organization. The rest of the paper is organized as follows. Section 2 provides a problem definition and states the notations used and introduce two state-of-the-art methods. Section 3 explains some motivation and explains our proposed algorithm. Section 4 describes the experimental studies conducted and reports on findings from the results. Section 5 presents the related work. Section 6 concludes the paper.

2   Background

In this section, we formally introduce the problem and the state-of-the-art techniques. Table 1 is a summary of the mathematical notations used in this paper.

2.1   Notations and Problem Definition

Let $G = (V, E)$ be an undirected simple graph, where V and E are a set of vertices and a set of edges, respectively. Below, we also use V(G) and E(G) to denote V and E of a graph G. The number of vertices and the number of edges is denoted as n and m for $n = |V|$ and $m = |E|$, respectively. For undirected graph G, we denote the set of neighbors of vertex u in G as $N(u)$ and denote the degree of u in G as $deg(u)$ which is equal to $|N(u)|$. For a directed graph $\boldsymbol{G} = (V, \boldsymbol{E})$, we use $\boldsymbol{E}$ to denote the set of directed edges $\{\langle u, v\rangle\}$ where u and v are the starting and ending vertex respectively. We denote the set of outgoing-neighbors of vertex u in G as $N^+(u)$, and the out-degree as $deg^+(u) = |N^+(u)|$. Likewise, we denote the in-neighborhood of vertex u in $\boldsymbol{G}$ as $N^-(u)$, and the in-degree as $deg^-(u) = |N^-(u)|$. By (u, v), we denote an undirected edge between two vertices u and v. A **triangle** is a set of three vertices fully connected to each other. We denote by (u, v, w) a triangle consisting of three vertices u, v and w.

Problem Statement. Given an undirected simple graph $G = (V, E)$, we aim to develop an efficient main-memory algorithm to list all triangles in the graph G one by one, with both good time complexity and practical performance.

2.2   Compact Forward (CF) Algorithm

We consider the method *Compact-forward* (CF) [15] as a state-of-the-art for triangle listing; although it was designed in 2008, its efficiency for triangle listing is still referred to frequently [9]. There are two key components in the CF algorithm: the *"edge-iterator"* computing paradigm and the *orientation* technique.

Edge-Iterator. The "edge-iterator" is a recurring computing paradigm for triangle listing, its strategy for triangle listing is to find triangles with reference to pairs of adjacent vertices. Given an edge (u, v), any triangle that includes the edge must contain a third vertex w that has connections to both of u and v. Thus, we can obtain any triangles containing edge (u, v) based on the intersection of $N(u)$ and $N(v)$. For each edge, the edge-iterator returns the set of triangles associated with that edge, and when repeated on all edges, the set of all triangle solutions is made available.

Orientation Technique. An orientation technique is recently leveraged in triangle listing algorithms, this involves the generation of a directed (i.e., oriented) graph $\boldsymbol{G}$ from an initially undirected input graph G [15]. Each undirected edge is mapped to a directed edge where the direction (i.e., orientation) is decided by the rank of its endpoints in a vertex-ordering (e.g., out-degree [15]). We refer to vertex u as a *pivot vertex* if u has two out-going edges. We can association a triangle in the undirected graph with only one pivot vertex to ensure one and only one instance of this triangle in the output, which significantly improves the performance.

Algorithm 1: CF(G)

Input   : G : an undirected graph
Output : All triangles in G
1 $G \leftarrow$ Orientation graph of G based on degree-order;
2 **for** each vertex $u \in G$ **do**
3   **for** each out-going neighbor v do
4          $T \leftarrow N^+(u) \cap N^+(v)$;
5   **for** each vertex $w \in T$ **do**
6   Output the triangle (u, v, w);

Compact Forward (CF) Algorithm. The CF algorithm is designed based on the edge-iterator and the orientation technique. We show its pseudocode in Algorithm 1. In line 1, undirected graph G is transformed into a directed graph G via the *orientation* technique. (Line 2 onward follows the edge-iterator framework.) In Line 3, triangles are enumerated by iterating through the outgoing-neighborhoods rather than the full neighborhood. In Line 4, a *merge-based intersection* identifies the common out-going neighbors of u and v, denoted by T. A set of triangles (u, v, w) is then output for every vertex $w \in T$.

Algorithm 2: kClist(G)

Input   : G : an undirected graph
Output : All triangles in G
1 $G \leftarrow$ Orientation graph of G based on degeneracy order η ;
2 **for** each vertex $u \in G$ **do**
3   **for** any two out-going neighbors $\{v, w\}$ of u with $\eta(v) < \eta(w)$ **do**
4   **if** there is a directed edge $\langle v, w \rangle \in E$ **then**
5   Output triangle (u, v, w);

Analysis. Since all triangles identified are unique, a naive traversal of the oriented graphs edges (the outgoing-neighborhoods for each vertex) yields the complete set of unique solutions without explicit duplicate pruning. In terms of time complexity, the merge-based intersection operation at Line 4 takes $\Theta(deg^+(u) + deg^+(v))$, assuming that the directed adjacency lists of u and v are sorted. In total, the CF algorithm has a complexity of $\Theta(\sum_{\langle u,v \rangle \in E} deg^+(u) + deg^+(v))$.

Remark 1. There is also an alternative implementation of the CF algorithm that adopts hash tables for the intersection operation, namely CF-Hash. Suppose a hash table has been built for each vertex based on the out-going neighbors in the oriented graph. At Line 4 of Algorithm 1, we may choose the vertex with larger number of neighbors as the hash table for intersection operation with $\Theta(\min\{deg^+(u), deg^+(v)\})$ look-up cost. This can come up with a better time complexity of $\Theta(\sum_{\langle u,v \rangle \in E} \min\{deg^+(u), deg^+(v)\}))$. However, as reported in [15, 21] and our experiments, the practical performance of hash-based CF algorithm is not competitive compared to the above merge-based CF algorithm. Thus, the merge-based CF algorithm is used as the representative of CF algorithm in the literature.

2.3   K-Clique Listing Algorithm (kClist)

We introduce the second state-of-the-art algorithm for in-memory triangle listing. The kClist algorithm [9] lists cliques for a queried size k, we restrict our discussion to the relevant use-case when $k = 3$ for listing triangles. kClist follows the node-iterator triangle listing paradigm which is described below.

Node-Iterator. The "node-iterator" triangle listing paradigm lists triangles by inspecting for adjacency between vertex pairs within one vertex neighborhood. For example, consider the neighboring vertices of node u, if there is an edge between two neighbors v_2 and v_3, then the triangle solution (u, v_2, v_3) is output.

k-Clique Listing (kClist) Algorithm. The kClist algorithm begins by generating an oriented graph G based on the degeneracy ordering [2]. We use η to denote the degeneracy ordering here. In lines 3–5 of Algorithm 2, for every two out-going neighbor v and w where $\eta(v) < \eta(w)$, the existence of a directed edge $\langle v, w \rangle$ is assessed; for each edge found, a triangle solution is output.

Analysis. The running time of kClist is $\Theta(m + \sum_{u \in V} deg^+(u) \times deg^-(u))$, this can also be expressed as $\Theta(\sum_{\langle u,v \rangle \in E} deg^+(v))$. It is apparent that the time complexity of kClist is an improvement compared to the CF algorithm which takes $\Theta(\sum_{\langle u,v \rangle \in E} (deg^+(u) + deg^+(v)))$ time, its practical performance is also shown to be efficient.

3   Our Approach

We introduce our adaptive orientation technique and implement it in our algorithm, AOT, to push the efficiency boundary for main-memory triangle listing algorithms.

3.1   Motivation and Problem Analysis

Since the proposal of the orientation technique, its nice properties and good practical performance have allowed it to gradually become a valuable technique utilized in subsequent studies of triangle listing.

Shortcoming of Orientation Technique. We recognize the prevalent usage of this orientation technique, however, we respond by showing that although current methods leverage the salient benefits of orientation, there are still finer benefits that are overlooked. We argue that there are still ways to further leverage

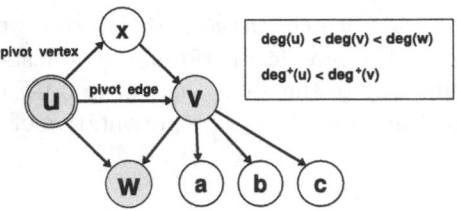

Fig. 1. Limit of orientation technique

properties that can improve the existing performances of triangle-listing. Our goal is therefore to maximize the benefits of the orientation technique.

In the following discussion of oriented edges, relative to a vertex u, we refer to edges $\langle u, v \rangle$ as *positive edges* if the out-degree relation of its adjacent vertex v has an out-degree value that is greater or equal to that of the pivot vertex $(deg^+(u) \leq deg^+(v))$; we also refer to edges $\langle u, v \rangle$ as *negative edges* if the pivot vertex has the greater out-degree value $(deg^+(u) > deg^+(v))$.

We refer to the time complexity of the kClist algorithm and see that it is $\Theta(\sum_{\langle u,v \rangle \in E} deg^+(v))$ when listing triangles. However, this is not optimal for triangle listing. In Fig. 1, consider the point in the triangle listing computation where triangles of edge $\langle u, v \rangle$ are processed. With respect to pivot vertex u, $deg^+(v)$ is larger than that of $deg^+(u)$ since $4 > 3$. The aforementioned complexity is not favorable for processing this ordinary edge. Its issue is because its cost is strictly that of $deg^+(v)$ (i.e., 4). Our observation is that, if we can reverse the direction of the edge $\langle u, v \rangle$ to follow the out-degree vertex-order, we can process $\langle u, v \rangle$ more favorably with $deg^+(u)$ (i.e., 3) and come up with a better time complexity.

Solutions are Non-trivial. Obviously, the optimal instance for a running time of $\Theta(\sum_{\langle u,v \rangle \in E} deg^+(v))$ is an oriented graph G where all edges are positive. However, most graphs do not exhibit that property: in most cases, not all graphs edges $\{\langle u, v \rangle\}$ are necessarily positive at the same. Recall Fig. 1: while edges such as $\langle u, x \rangle$ and $\langle u, w \rangle$ are positive, negative edges such as $\langle u, v \rangle$ are also possible.

We remedy the existence of negative edges by making a series of modifications to the computed orientation of negative edges after it is oriented. One naive way of achieving this is to manually change the direction of the oriented edge. For example, there is a negative edge $\langle u, v \rangle$ in Fig. 1, we see that it can become a positive edge if its direction is simply changed to $\langle v, u \rangle$. This methodology is limited because it ultimately undermines the total order used in the orientation, moreover, changing $\langle u, v \rangle$ creates a cycle subgraph (u, x, v, u); this is a critical complication since triangle (u, x, v) would surely be omitted and missing from the result set of existing methods.

Ultimately, the out-degree of a vertex is a result of the orientation of its incident edges, and therefore depends directly on the total ordering used for the orientation techniques, it is difficult to significantly reduce the number of negative edges by manually changing its orientation.

The Main Idea. As an alternative, we instead suggest modifying the computing order of u and v on the fly when encountering negative edges instances $\{\langle u, v\rangle\}$. We notice that the CF algorithm cannot take advantage of this because its complexity of $\Theta(deg^+(u) + deg^+(v))$ for every edge $\langle u, v\rangle$ suggests that the design of CF is insensitive to the direction of the edge. We also notice that the kClist algorithm cannot do this either, because the accessing order of the vertices has to strictly follow the degeneracy order on the oriented graph to ensure the correctness of the algorithm. We have showed that two state-of-the-art techniques cannot trivially take advantage of this observation. In contrast, our algorithm does not depend on any total order, any total order will be acceptable.

Following the above analysis, we are motivated to develop a technique that tightens the boundary for efficient triangle listing, by taking advantage of the resulting out-going degree order of each incoming edge, and adaptively listing triangle based on its property. Our key idea involves selecting the optimal pivot vertices for each triangle accordingly, such that each triangle is found only from the vertex with a smaller out-going degree. This way we achieve the time complexity $\Theta(\min\{deg^+(u), deg^+(v)\})$ for every edge $\langle u, v\rangle \in E$, which is now *optimal* for a given oriented graph following the edge-iterator paradigm.

When finding the intersection between the out-going neighbors of adjacent vertices u and v (i.e. $N^+(u) \cap N^+(v)$ for an oriented edge $\langle u, v\rangle$), there is a larger and a smaller out-degree vertex, we use the hash-join approach as the appropriate method to perform the set-intersection. Note that one hash-table here contain the out-going neighbors for one single vertex. Following the hash-join approach, we choose to look-up the out-going neighbors of the vertex with the lesser out-degree in the hash structure of the vertex with the greater out-degree. However, with one endpoint fixed, within its adjacent neighborhood, the endpoint with the lesser out-degree vertex varies, to accomplish the former statement efficiently is hard because it is not known in advance which endpoint has the smaller out-degree vertex. The known solution requires both hash tables for either endpoints be available when the edge is visited. There are two methods for constructing the two indexes in advance: (1) Building hash tables of all graph vertices prior to listing. Where this is a naive solution, it is computationally infeasible due to its high storage demand and a high look-up cost. (2) For each vertex u, building a hash table for all for its out-going neighbors on the fly. This is also infeasible because one vertex is likely to need to rebuild its hash table multiple times throughout the listing stage.

Categorizing Triangles. To facilitate understanding of technique, we discuss two categorizes for each triangle in an oriented graph G: *positive triangle* or *negative triangle*. The category of each triangle depends on its pivot edge: given an oriented triangle, were refer to it as positive if its pivot edge $\langle x, y\rangle$ is positive i.e. $\eta(x) < \eta(y)$ and $deg^+(x) \geq deg^+(y)$; otherwise, it is negative if $\eta(x) < \eta(y)$ and $deg^+(x) < deg^+(y)$, where η is the vertex ordering used in the orientation.

An example instance of positive and negative triangles is shown in Figs. 2(a)-(b). We consider the two triangles from a sample graph with a common vertex u, we note that without additional structural information from the graph, the

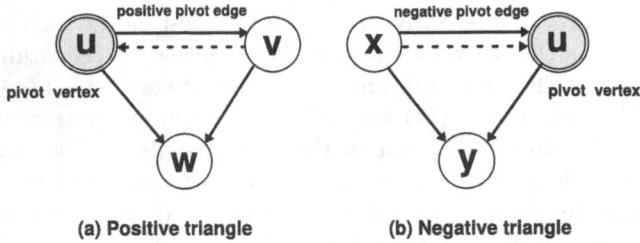

(a) Positive triangle   (b) Negative triangle

Fig. 2. Motivation for adaptive orientation

induced subgraphs u, v, w and x, u, y are isomorphic. However, with attention to pivot edges $\langle u, v \rangle$ and $\langle x, u \rangle$, we observe that the two triangles are different in terms of the out-going degree order (the dotted line points to the vertex with the higher out-degree), and there for their orientation is different.

We propose seperate computations for the two types of triangles due to their subtle differences, by selecting different respective piviot veritices. The selection of the pivot vertex affects the amount of computation to list the triangle. If it is a positive triangle, we remain consistent with the orientation technique and use the vertex with two out-going edges as the *pivot vertex* (e.g. the vertex u in Fig. 2(a)). However, if it is a negative triangle, we select a different vertex as the pivot vertex (e.g. u in Fig. 2(b)).

A direct benefit from the above selection is that, every vertex $u \in G$ is now the pivot vertex for both *positive* and *negative* triangles solutions, where the previous technique rigidly processes all triangles as positive triangles. In the traditional orientation technique, both triangles would be processed equally and listed by vertices u and x respectively, this was because the pivot vertex of each triangle is strictly the vertex with two out-going edges and does not account for our positive or negative triangle definitions. A desirable property of our *adaptive orientation technique* is that this way each vertex u only needs to build a hash table once for its out-going neighbors.

To conclude: For positive triangles with pivot vertex u, for each out-going neighbor v of u (e.g. v in Fig. 2(a)), we will look-up if each out-going neighbors w of v (e.g. w in Fig. 2(a)) is also in the hash table, to see if w is also an out-going neighbor of u. For the negative triangles with pivot vertex u, for each in-coming neighbor x of u (e.g. x in Fig. 2(b)), we will look-up if each out-going neighbor y of x (e.g. y in Fig. 2(b)) is also in the hash table, to see if y is also an out-going neighbor of u.

As we later show in the theoretical analysis in Sect. 3.2, our proposed *adaptive orientation* technique achieves the time complexity of $\Theta(\sum_{\langle u,v \rangle \in E} \min\{deg^+(u), deg^+(v)\}))$ because, in terms of the hash-based intersection, the look-up operations will always be performed on the vertex with larger out-degree values for each oriented edge.

3.2   The Algorithm

We introduce the algorithm with our proposed adaptive orientation technique. With reference to the pseudo-code in Algorithm 3, In line 1, the orientated graph G is generated following the degree vertex order. In lines 2–13, a vertex u acts as pivot vertex and lists its associated positive and negative triangles. For each pivot vertex u, Line 3 generates a bitmap hash table H based on its adjacency neighborhood.

For pivot vertex u, all *positive triangles* are enumerated in Lines 4–8. That is, for each out-going neighbor v of u with $deg^+(v) < deg^+(u)$ (i.e. positive pivot edge), we find its out-going neighbors which are also out-going neighbors of u by looking up the hash table H as illustrated in Fig. 2(a).

Similarly, all *negative triangles* for pivot vertex u are enumerated in Lines 9–13. For each in-coming neighbor x of u with $deg^+(x) < deg^+(u)$ (i.e. negative pivot edge), we find its out-going neighbors which are also out-going neighbors of u by looking up the hash table H as illustrated in Fig. 2(b).

Algorithm 3: Our Algorithm – AOT (G)

    Input   : G : an undirected graph
    Output : All triangles in G
1 $G \leftarrow$ orientation graph of G based on degree-order;
2 **for** $u \in V(G)$ **do**
3   Set-up the hash table H with IDs of the out-going neighbors of u $(N^+(u))$;
4   **for** every out-going neighbor v of u **do**
5   **if** $deg^+(v) < deg^+(u)$ **then**
6   **for** every out-going neighbor w of v **do**
7   **if** Find w in H **then**
8   output triangle (u, v, w);

9   **for** every in-coming neighbor x of u **do**
10   **if** $deg^+(x) < deg^+(u)$ **then**
11   **for** every out-going neighbor y of x **do**
12   **if** Find y in H **then**
13   output triangle (u, x, y);

Correctness. To explain the correctness of our algorithm, we recall that each oriented triangle in G belongs to either a positive type triangle or a negative type triangle, we note that this is true for any vertex total-order.

Given an oriented triangle (u, v, w): such that u is the pivot vertex, and $\langle u, v \rangle$ is its pivot edge as illustrated in Fig. 1. If $deg^+(v) < deg^+(u)$, then (u, v, w) is a positive triangle with pivot vertex u; given w is the common out-going neighbor of u and v, a triangle will be output at Line 8 of Algorithm 3. Otherwise, if the triangle is not positive i.e., if $deg^+(u) < deg^+(v)$[1], (u, v, w) is a negative triangle with pivot vertex v, this oriented triangle will be output at Line 13 of Algorithm 3 when v is the pivot vertex, because w is the common out-going neighbor of u

---

[1] Recall that ties are broken by vertex ID.

and v. Evidently, this oriented triangle (u, v, w) will not be output under any other scenario when following the oriented triangle technique. Consequently, this showed that (u, v, w) will be output once and only once, the correctness of the Algorithm 3 follows.

Time Complexity. We use a bitmap with size $|V|$ to implement the hash table H, where $H[v.ID] = 1$ if the vertex v is the out-going neighbor of the pivot vertex. For each pivot vertex u visited, we can use $\Theta(deg^+(u))$ time to initiate or clean the hash table H. Thus, the maintenance of H takes $\Theta(2m)$ time.

Recall that for a pivot edge $\langle u, v \rangle$, the set of triangles it outputs can be a mix of either positive or negative triangles. For every pivot edge $\langle u, v \rangle$, the time complexity for its positive triangles is $\Theta(deg^+(v))$ with $deg^+(v) < deg^+(u)$ since the time complexity of Line 8 is $\Theta(1)$. Similarly, the time complexity for its negative triangles is $\Theta(deg^+(u))$ with $deg^+(u) < deg^+(v)$ since the time complexity of Line 13 is $\Theta(1)$. It follows that the total time complexity of our Algorithm 3 is $\Theta(\sum_{\langle u,v \rangle \in E} \min\{deg^+(u), deg^+(v)\}))$.

Example 1. In Fig. 3, the oriented graph has 14 vertices and 21 edges. Out of the 21 edges, 9 for which have a $deg^+(v)$ value of greater than 0. For $\sum_{\langle u,v \rangle \in E} deg^+(v))$: Edges $\langle v_1, v_3 \rangle$, $\langle v_5, v_7 \rangle$ and $\langle v_9, v_{11} \rangle$ each incur a cost of 3. Edges $\langle v_2, v_4 \rangle$, $\langle v_6, v_8 \rangle$, $\langle v_{10}, v_{12} \rangle$ each incur a cost of 2. Edges $\langle v_3, v_4 \rangle$, $\langle v_7, v_8 \rangle$ and $\langle v_{11}, v_{12} \rangle$ each also incur a cost of 2. The remaining edges incur no cost. In total, $\sum_{\langle u,v \rangle \in E} deg^+(v)) = 3 + 3 + 3 + 2 + 2 + 2 + 2 + 2 + 2 = 21$. For $\sum_{\langle u,v \rangle \in E} \min\{deg^+(u), deg^+(v)\}$: Edges $\langle v_1, v_3 \rangle$, $\langle v_5, v_7 \rangle$ and $\langle v_9, v_11 \rangle$ each incur a cost of 1. Edges $\langle v_2, v_4 \rangle$, $\langle v_6, v_8 \rangle$, $\langle v_{10}, v_{12} \rangle$ each also incur a cost of 1. Edges $\langle v_3, v_4 \rangle$, $\langle v_7, v_8 \rangle$ and $\langle v_{11}, v_{12} \rangle$ each incur a cost of 2. The remaining edges incur no cost. In total, $\sum_{\langle u,v \rangle \in E} \min\{deg^+(u), deg^+(v)\}) = 1 + 1 + 1 + 1 + 1 + 1 + 2 + 2 + 2 = 12$.

The former is a calculation of the computation required by the state-of-the-art, the latter is the computations required by our algorithm. In comparison, Example 1 illustrates that our algorithm incurs significantly fewer computation to list triangles. Where the costs for some edges is the same between two algorithms, our algorithm uses less computation for edges $\langle v_1, v_3 \rangle$, $\langle v_5, v_7 \rangle$, $\langle v_9, v_{11} \rangle$, $\langle v_2, v_4 \rangle$, $\langle v_6, v_8 \rangle$ and $\langle v_{10}, v_{12} \rangle$.

Remark 2. Note that the bitmap hash table cannot be deployed by CF-Hash technique. Clearly, on large graphs we cannot afford to construct $|V|$ bitmap hash tables each of which has size $|V|$. On the other hand, it is time consuming to build H on the fly because, unlike we build the hash table H only once[2] for each vertex in AOT algorithm, H might be built multiple times for a vertex because it's hash table will be chosen (i.e., build on the fly) by CF-Hash algorithm once its hash table size is smaller than that of pivot vertex.

---

[2] When it is chosen as the pivot vertex.

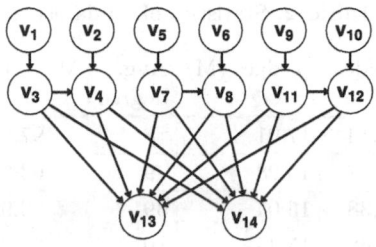

Fig. 3. Example graph

Space Complexity
We only need to keep the graph G, the oriented graph $\boldsymbol{G}$ and the global hash table H, as a result, Algorithm 3 is space efficient, with space complexity $O(m + n)$ where m is the number of edges and n is the number of vertices in G.

Exploiting Local Order. In addition to the global vertex order, we also consider a local vertex ordering used to store vertices within the scope for each vertex neighborhood list (i.e. *local order*). In Algorithm 3, the dominant cost is the hash table look-ups happen at Lines 7 and 12. There is a good chance that a vertex w will be repeatedly checked because of the overlap of the neighborhood. Ideally, the ID of w should be kept in the CPU cache such that the following look-up of w can be processed efficiently. We may design sophisticate local ordering strategy with some assumptions on the workload such that the neighbors of a (pivot) vertex is well organized by their neighborhood similarity. However, we cannot afford such cost for the preprocessing. In this paper, we order the vertices in the adjacent list of a vertex by the decreasing order of their degree; that is, we visit the vertices at Lines 4 and 9 in Algorithm 3 following the degree order. This is because we believe the vertex with a high degree is more likely to have common neighbors with other vertices. For each vertex, we can keep its neighbors with this local order in the adjacent list. Our empirical study confirms the efficiency of this local order strategy.

4   Experimental Study

Algorithms. To show the efficiency of our proposed technique, we compare our proposed algorithm with the following state-of-the-art methods. In total, we make comparisons between the four algorithms listed below.

- **CF** [15,21]. The CF algorithm, presented in Sect. 2.2.
- **CF-Hash** [15,21]. A variant of CF, where the intersection of two adjacency lists are implemented by hashing.
- **kClist** [9]. The kClist algorithm for triangle listing, presented in Sect. 2.3.
- **AOT**. Our proposed algorithm with adaptive orientation and local ordering, presented in Sect. 3.2.

Table 2. Statistics of 16 datasets.

Graph	#nodes (M)	#edges (M)	Avg. degree	Max. degree	#Triangles (M)
web-baidu-baike	2.14	17.01	8	97,848	25.21
uk-2014-tpd	1.77	15.28	9	63,731	259.04
actor	0.38	15.04	39	3,956	346.81
flicker	1.62	15.48	10	27,236	548.65
uk-2014-host	4.77	40.21	8	726,244	2,509.74
sx-stackoverflow	6.02	28.18	5	44,065	114.21
ljournal-2008	5.36	49.51	9	19,432	411.16
soc-orkut	3.00	106.35	35	27,466	524.64
hollywood-2011	2.18	114.49	53	13,107	7,073.95
indochina-2004	7.41	150.98	20	256,425	60,115.56
soc-sinaweibo	58.66	261.32	4	278,489	212.98
wikipedia_link_en	12.15	288.26	24	962,969	11,686.21
arabic-2005	22.74	553.90	24	3,247	36,895.36
uk-2005	39.46	783.03	20	5,213	21,779.37
it-2004	41.29	1,027.47	25	9,964	48,374.55
twitter-2010	41.65	1,202.51	29	2,997,487	34,824.92

The source-code for the assessment of *CF*, *kClist*, and *CF-Hash* are acquired from their respective authors. We note that for *CF* and *CF-Hash*, we use the implementation from [21] named *TC-Merge* and *TC-Hash* respectively, due to their more efficient implementations.

Datasets. The datasets used in the experiments are listed in Table 2. We used 16 large real-world graphs with up to a billion edges. Networks are treated as undirected simple graphs, and are processed appropriately.

Settings. The tests are run on a 64 bit Linux machine with a Intel(R) Xeon(R) CPU E5-2650 v3 @ 2.30 GHz processor, the L1, L2 and L3 cache of 32K, 256K, and 25600K respectively, with 591 GB of available RAM.

4.1   Results Against the State-of-the-Art

Figure 4 reports the relative running times of the algorithms tested. The measured time captures the elapsed time between the point when the graph is loaded until the point of successful program termination. For the state-of-the-art methods, the kClist algorithm requires fewer running time than the CF algorithm. For datasets containing up to 100 million edges, kClist is observed to significantly outperform CF; this gap in running time is less significant for graphs where the edge count is greater than 100 million. There are also instances where CF is more efficient than kClist, as observed in the social-network *soc-sinaweibo*.

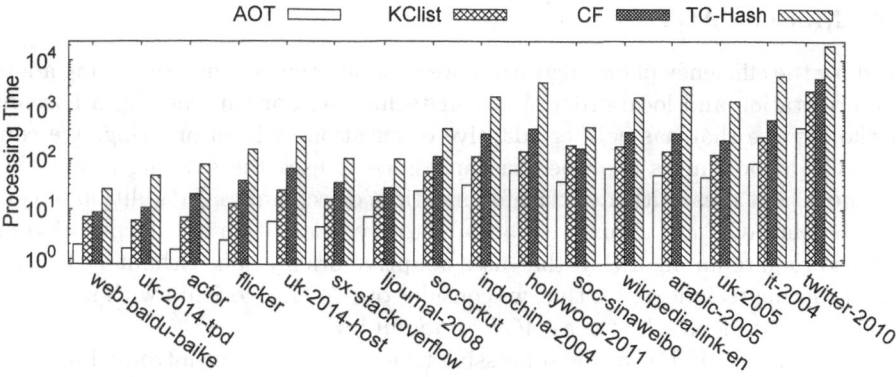

Fig. 4. Performance analysis

In comparison, our algorithm AOT consistently outperforms the two state-of-the-art, which supports the tightened running bound of $\sum_{\{u,w\} \in E} min(deg^+(u), deg^+(v))$ from its theoretical analysis. We notice that on a large graph *twitter-2010* that has 41.65 million vertices, 1.2 billion edges and contains 35 billion triangles, the observed running times of kClist and CF are 2,381 s and 4,230 s respectively. In contrast, our algorithm listed all triangles in *twitter-2010* in 433 s and achieved a speedup of 10-times. It is noticed that hash-based CF (CF-Hash) is consistently outperformed by AOT with big margins, though two algorithms have the same asymptotic behavior. This is because the high efficiency of look-up operation of the bitmap hash table as well as the local ordering technique in AOT algorithm. Recall that, without the adaptive orientation technique proposed in this paper, hash-based CF cannot take this advantage. This reflects the non-trivial nature of our adaptive orientation technique.

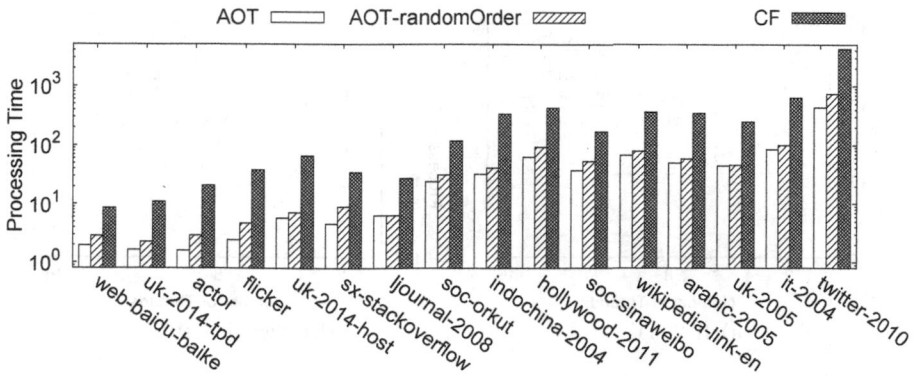

Fig. 5. Incremental improvements

4.2 More on AOT

To show the efficiency of our algorithm, we evaluate the benefits for having adaptive orientation and local ordering in our technique. For this setting, a baseline method is one that has neither adaptive orientation or local ordering. We consider CF algorithm as a proper baseline since it uses the existing orientation technique, but uses neither of the aforementioned techniques. In addition to considering the AOT algorithm with both adaptive orientation and local ordering. We also require an algorithm that uses adaptive orientation without utilizing a local ordering technique, for this, we consider our AOT algorithm with a random local ordering, denoted later as *AOT-randomOrder*.

As we can see in Fig. 5, the processing time decreases after introducing adaptive orientation and the local ordering strategy. In comparison to the baseline processing time, the adaptive orientation contributes a greater drop in processing time compared to that from the later adoption of the local-order strategy Where the difference between *AOT-randomOrder* and CF is greater than that between *AOT* and *AOT-randomOrder*. This highlights that our adaptive orientation technique performs better than the orientation technique in its current state. Furthermore, the results also show that using a local order reduces the running time needed on most graphs; this can be explained by an improvement in the algorithms cache performance.

4.3 Parallel Experiments

Our algorithm *AOT* can be easily made parallel. This is achieved by processing vertices in parallel. As a result, we analyze the parallelism of our algorithm and compare it against the state-of-the-art methods. *TC-Merge* (i.e., parallel implementation of *CF* proposed in [15]), *TC-Hash* and *kClist* all provided parallel implementations of their algorithms. For this parallel experiment, we consider the two largest datasets *It*-2004 and *Twitter*-2010.

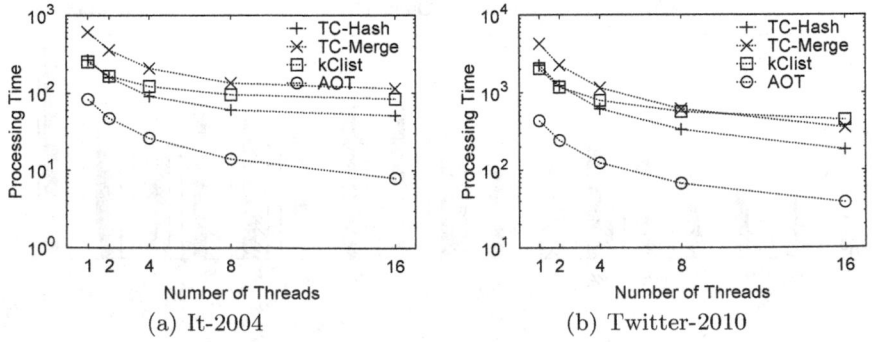

(a) It-2004   (b) Twitter-2010

Fig. 6. Evaluating parallel performance

As seen in Fig. 6, increasing the number of threads decreases the amount of processing time needed to list all triangles, this is expected and true for all four algorithms tested. In the case of *kClist*, the drop is less pronounced for both networks after 4 threads. In the case of *TC-Merge* and *TC-Hash*, the drop in processing time is not visible when handling *It*-2004 past 8 threads. In contrast, this decrease is visible for our method *AOT* across both datasets. All in all, *AOT* is consistently the fastest method in this parallel experiments.

5 Related Work

Triangle Listing. In-memory algorithms for listing triangles have been extensively studied in the literature. The edge-iterator [1] and node-iterator [13] are two popular triangle listing computing paradigms, which share the same asymptotic behavior [20]. A lot of subsequent algorithms are mostly improvements based on the original two paradigms. While Ortmann was the first to formalize a generalized framework based on undirected graph orientation, past literature Forward and Compact Forward(CF) had previously considered triangle-listing on induced directed graphs with respect to a vertex ordering [20]. In literature, the orientation technique is observed beyond triangle-listing; it is also applied for higher-order structure enumeration [9]. In more recent years, the topics of interest have shifted to parallel/distributed processing (e.g., [16,21]), efficient I/O external memory methods (e.g., [7,12], and the asymptotic cost analysis of triangle listing in random graphs [24].

Triangle Counting. The triangle counting is a related problem to the triangle listing problem, solving the listing problem solves the counting problem. The triangle counting problem is the task to find the total number of triangles in a graph G. Compared to listing algorithms, counting algorithms find ways to compute the number without relying on the exploration of triangle instances. Many algorithms have been designed to count triangles (e.g., [3,14,17]). Approximate methods are useful for settings that handle large-scale graphs, or settings where a given approximation is as useful as knowing the exact triangle count (e.g., [22,23]).

6 Conclusion

The triangle listing is a fundamental problem in graph analysis with a wide range of applications. This problem has been extensively studied in the literature. Although many efficient main memory algorithms based on the efficient orientation technique have been proposed, in this paper, we pushed the efficiency boundary of the triangle listing and developed a new algorithm with best theoretical time complexity and practical performance. On the theoretical side, we showed that our proposed algorithm has the time complexity $\Theta(\sum_{\langle u,v \rangle \in E} \min\{deg^+(u), deg^+(v)\}))$ where E is the directed edges in the oriented graph, which is the best known theoretical time complexity for the problem of in-memory triangle listing so far. On the practical side, our comprehensive experiments over 16 real-life large graphs show the superior performance of our AOT algorithm compared with two state-of-the-art techniques, especially on large-scale graphs with billions of edges.

Acknowledgement. Lu Qin is is supported by ARC DP160101513. Ying Zhang is supported by FT170100128 and ARC DP180103096, Wenjie Zhang is supported by ARC DP180103096 and ARC DP200101116. Xuemin Lin is supported by 2018YFB1003504, ARC DP200101338, NSFC61232006, ARC DP180103096 and DP170101628.

References

1. Batagelj, V., Mrvar, A.: A subquadratic triad census algorithm for large sparse networks with small maximum degree. Soc. Netw. **23**(3), 237–243 (2001)
2. Batagelj, V., Zaveršnik, M.: Generalized cores. arXiv preprint cs/0202039 (2002)
3. Becchetti, L., Boldi, P., Castillo, C., Gionis, A.: Efficient semi-streaming algorithms for local triangle counting in massive graphs. In: Proceedings of SIGKDD 2008 (2008)
4. Becchetti, L., Boldi, P., Castillo, C., Gionis, A.: Efficient algorithms for large-scale local triangle counting. TKDD **4**(3), 1–28 (2010)
5. Berry, J.W., Hendrickson, B., LaViolette, R.A., Phillips, C.A.: Tolerating the community detection resolution limit with edge weighting. Phys. Rev. E **83**(5), 056119 (2011)
6. Chou, B.-H., Suzuki, E.: Discovering community-oriented roles of nodes in a social network. In: Bach Pedersen, T., Mohania, M.K., Tjoa, A.M. (eds.) DaWaK 2010. LNCS, vol. 6263, pp. 52–64. Springer, Heidelberg (2010). https://doi.org/10.1007/978-3-642-15105-7_5
7. Chu, S., Cheng, J.: Triangle listing in massive networks and its applications. In: Proceedings of KDD 2011 (2011)
8. Chu, S., Cheng, J.: Triangle listing in massive networks. TKDD **6**(4), 1–32 (2012)
9. Danisch, M., Balalau, O., Sozio, M.: Listing k-cliques in sparse real-world graphs. In: Proceedings of WWW 2018 (2018)
10. Giechaskiel, I., Panagopoulos, G., Yoneki, E.: PDTL: parallel and distributed triangle listing for massive graphs. In: Proceedings of ICPP 2015 (2015)
11. Hu, X., Tao, Y., Chung, C.W.: Massive graph triangulation. In: Proceedings of SIGMOD 2013 (2013)
12. Hu, X., Tao, Y., Chung, C.: I/O-efficient algorithms on triangle listing and counting. ACM Trans. Database Syst. **39**(4), 1–30 (2014)
13. Itai, A., Rodeh, M.: Finding a minimum circuit in a graph. SIAM J. Comput. **7**(4), 413–423 (1978)
14. Kolda, T.G., Pinar, A., Plantenga, T.D., Seshadhri, C., Task, C.: Counting triangles in massive graphs with MapReduce. SIAM J. Sci. Comput. **36**(5), S48–S77 (2014)
15. Latapy, M.: Main-memory triangle computations for very large (sparse (power-law)) graphs. Theor. Comput. Sci. **407**(1–3), 458–473 (2008)
16. Park, H.M., Myaeng, S.H., Kang, U.: PTE: enumerating trillion triangles on distributed systems. In: Proceedings of SIGKDD 2016 (2016)
17. Pavan, A., Tangwongsan, K., Tirthapura, S., Wu, K.: Counting and sampling triangles from a graph stream. PVLDB **6**(14), 1870–1881 (2013)

18. Radicchi, F., Castellano, C., Cecconi, F., Loreto, V., Parisi, D.: Defining and identifying communities in networks. PNAS **101**(9), 2658–2663 (2004)
19. Schank, T.: Algorithmic aspects of triangle-based network analysis. Ph.D. thesis, Universitat Karlsruhe (TH) (2007)
20. Schank, T., Wagner, D.: Finding, counting and listing all triangles in large graphs, an experimental study. In: Nikoletseas, S.E. (ed.) WEA 2005. LNCS, vol. 3503, pp. 606–609. Springer, Heidelberg (2005). https://doi.org/10.1007/11427186_54
21. Shun, J., Tangwongsan, K.: Multicore triangle computations without tuning. In: Proceedings of ICDE 2015 (2015)
22. Tsourakakis, C.E., Kang, U., Miller, G.L., Faloutsos, C.: DOULION: counting triangles in massive graphs with a coin. In: Proceedings of SIGKDD 2009 (2009)
23. Türkoglu, D., Turk, A.: Edge-based wedge sampling to estimate triangle counts in very large graphs. In: Proceedings of ICDM 2017 (2017)
24. Xiao, D., Cui, Y., Cline, D.B., Loguinov, D.: On asymptotic cost of triangle listing in random graphs. In: PODS, pp. 261–272. ACM (2017)
25. Xu, X., Yuruk, N., Feng, Z., Schweiger, T.A.: Scan: a structural clustering algorithm for networks. In: Proceedings of SIGKDD 2007 (2007)
26. Yin, H., Benson, A.R., Leskovec, J., Gleich, D.F.: Local higher-order graph clustering. In: Proceedings of SIGKDD 2017 (2017)
27. Zhang, Y., Parthasarathy, S.: Extracting, analyzing and visualizing triangle k-core motifs within networks. In: Proceedings of ICDE 2012 (2012)

Efficient Closeness Centrality Computation for Dynamic Graphs

Zhenzhen Shao[1], Na Guo[1,2], Yu Gu[1]($\boxtimes$), Zhigang Wang[3], Fangfang Li[1], and Ge Yu[1]

[1] Northeastern University, Shenyang 110169, Liaoning, China
guyu@mail.neu.edu.cn
[2] Shenyang Aerospace University, Shenyang 110136, Liaoning, China
[3] Ocean University of China, Qingdao 266100, Shandong, China

Abstract. As a classic metric, closeness centrality can measure the importance of a node in a graph by its proximity to the other nodes. However, exactly calculating closeness centrality of all nodes is significantly time-consuming. Besides, graphs usually evolve with inserted and/or deleted edges, which exacerbates the performance issue if we recompute results from scratch. The paper proposes a preliminary algorithm for calculating exact closeness centrality by using biconnected components and articulation points. Firstly, a large graph is divided into a series of biconnected components which are connected by articulation points. Then distance between arbitrary nodes on the whole graph can be converted into multiple distances between different biconnected components. We further propose an incremental update technique to dynamically maintain the computation results when graphs are changing, like inserting and/or deleting edges, by efficiently detecting all the affected shortest paths to update the closeness centrality based on articulation points. We finally conduct extensive experiments over real graphs to validate the efficiency and effectiveness of our techniques.

Keywords: Dynamic graph · Exact closeness centrality · Articulation point

1 Introduction

Centrality is used to measure the importance of nodes in a graph, which plays a very important role in real applications, especially for social networks. There are many centrality metrics [1], such as degree centrality [2], betweenness centrality [3,4], closeness centrality [5,6], and eigenvector centrality [7,8]. Among them, closeness centrality as the focus of this paper, is widely used [9–12].

Supported by the National Key R&D Program of China (2018YFB1003400), the National Natural Science Foundation of China (61872070, U1811261, 61902366) and Liao Ning Revitalization Talents Program (XLYC1807158).

Y. Nah et al. (Eds.): DASFAA 2020, LNCS 12113, pp. 534–550, 2020.
https://doi.org/10.1007/978-3-030-59416-9_32

On the other hand, real-world graphs change dynamically. For example, in social networks, if two unrelated people establish relationship, a new edge will be created. In contrast, an edge will be deleted. Such insertion and deletion can be performed very frequently. Clearly, if every update triggers a re-computation of closeness centrality from scratch, the expensive cost is not acceptable. Thus, the efficient processing for dynamic graphs consists of two stages: executing a preliminary algorithm for the initial static graph in the off-line manner and running an incremental algorithm on line when an update occurs. Some pioneering works have explored efficient solutions to closeness evaluation over dynamic graphs and the representative exact algorithms are CC [13] and CENDY [14]. However, two key issues have not been sufficiently considered.

Leveraging the Static Algorithm to Facilitate the Incremental Maintenance. Both CC and CENDY ignore the optimization of this step. They just employ the BFS (Breath First Search)-based algorithm for the entire graph to obtain initial results in the off line stage, from which the later incremental maintenance cannot benefit. In contrast, we make an improvement to propose a static algorithm which can better support the incremental maintenance. Specifically, we introduce the biconnected component in the static algorithm and reserve some necessary intermediate results to avoid redundant computation of the online stage.

Constraining the Incremental Calculation in the Local Regions. CC uses the divide and conquer strategy based on biconnected components only for the on-line stage. CC finds the affected nodes within the affected biconnected component, but the closeness centrality of the affected nodes is still calculated in the whole graph. For the remaining nodes, the algorithm finds the articulation point corresponding to each node in the remaining ones and update them. Therefore, the number of affected node sets is also very large. On the other hand, CENDY finds the affected shortest path in the entire graph, and puts the pair of vertices corresponding to the affected shortest path in two sets. The algorithm uses each node in the set with fewer nodes as the source node but the evaluation needs to be performed on the entire graph to calculate the amount of change. In this paper, we devise an incremental method which can limit the incremental calculation to the affected biconnected component and avoid the deficiency of CC and CENDY.

Based on the above analysis, our main contributions can be concluded as follows:

1. *Preliminary method for the initial graph.* Firstly we propose a preliminary algorithm. We divide a large graph into small biconnected components by articulation points. The distance between nodes in the large graph can be converted to the distance between biconnected components. Then we connect the distance by articulation points. The algorithm can reserve some useful intermediate results for the incremental maintenance and thus avoid redundant computation.

2. *Incremental method for the dynamic graph.* Based on the preliminary algorithm, we propose an incremental algorithm in the dynamic graph which includes the insertion and deletion of edges. The incremental algorithm is efficient due to limiting the computation in the local regions and leveraging the results of the preliminary algorithm.
3. *Experiment.* Compared with the existing algorithms, ours can yield up to one order-of-magnitude performance gains on public datasets.

The reminder of this paper is organized as follows. Section 2 investigates the related works. Section 3 introduces the basic concepts and definitions. Section 4 proposes preliminary off-line algorithm for the initial graphs, and Sect. 5 explores a novel on-line incremental method to handle high-speed updates. Section 6 reports our experiment results. Our work is finally concluded in Sect. 7.

2   Related Work

Closeness Centrality over Static Graphs. Calculating the exact closeness centrality of the static graph usually employs BFS. The time consumption of BFS is very large in a large graph. Therefore, many attempts in different perspectives are made to improve performance, like approximate variants [15–17], distributed computations [18,19], and top-k query [20,21].

Closeness Centrality on Dynamic Graphs. Normally, graphs in applications evolve over time. Specifically, dynamic top-k closeness centrality is explored in [22]. [13,14,23] aim to evaluate exact closeness centrality of all the nodes in dynamic graphs. [23] focuses on directed graphs, which is not suitable for the efficient processing of undirected graphs. The other two approaches namely CC [13] and CENDY [14] stand out for updating closeness centrality in generic evolving graphs. These two algorithms calculate the change based on the entire graph, while our algorithm can limit the calculation within subgraphs.

Other Centrality Algorithms. There are some other centrality algorithms. For example, [2] focuses on betweenness centrality. And [24] aims to deal with pagerank, which is a variant of eigenvector centrality. Due to different definitions and application scenarios, the above methods can not be directly used to solve closeness centrality.

3   Preliminaries

For simplicity, we use the undirected and unweighted graph as an example to introduce our technique. Our algorithms can be easily extended to the directed and weighted graphs.

3.1 Problem Definition

Given a connected graph $G(V, E)$, the closeness centrality value $C(v)$ of node v in G is the derivative of the sum of the distance d_{uv} from any other node u to it in G as shown in Formula (1). Formally:

$$C(v) = \frac{1}{\sum\limits_{u \in V, u \neq v} d_{uv}} \tag{1}$$

3.2 Related Concepts

In the following, we introduce the related concepts including articulation point, bridge edge and biconnected component. The algorithm that we use to find the biconnected components is Tarjan [25].

Definition 1 (articulation point). *In the connected graph $G(V, E)$, if we delete a vertex and its adjacent edges, G is divided into two or more non-connected subgraphs, then the node is called articulation point.*

Definition 2 (bridge edge). *In the connected graph $G(V, E)$, if we delete an edge $e(u, v)$, G is divided into two non-connected subgraphs, then the edge is called bridge edge.*

Definition 3 (biconnected component). *If a connected graph has no articulation points, we call the connected graph as a biconnected component.*

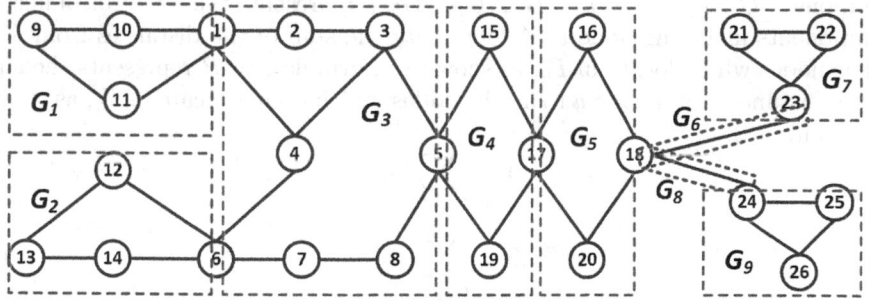

Fig. 1. Articulation points and biconnected components

Figure 1 shows an example. If we remove node 1, the original graph becomes two disconnected subgraphs, so node 1 is an articulation point. In the same way, nodes 6, 5, 17, 18, 23, 24 are also articulation points. There are no articulation points in the subgraph formed by nodes 1, 9, 10, and 11, so this subgraph is a biconnected component. Note that, the subgraph formed by the remainder nodes and connected to 1 is not a biconnected component, because it contains articulation points 5, 6, etc. In Fig. 1, different biconnected components are circled by colored dotted lines, and nodes connecting different biconnected components are articulation points. We can see that several adjacent biconnected components may share a common articulation point. The Tarjan algorithm can enumerate biconnected components of a given undirected graph by performing DFS only once. Further, edge e(18, 23) is thereby removed, and the entire graph becomes two disconnected subgraphs. $e(18, 23)$ is called a bridge edge.

4   Preliminary Algorithm for the Initial Graph

In this section we introduce the preliminary algorithm for the initial graphs. Firstly, we calculate the closeness centrality of articulation points. We then calculate the closeness centrality of the nodes which are located in the biconnected components where the articulation points reside. Finally, we design the whole process of the algorithm and calculate the closeness centrality of all nodes.

4.1   The Closeness Centrality of Articulation Point

After we find the biconnected components and articulation points, we will get a adjacent relations graph which is similar to Fig. 2 (The edges represent the articulation points and rectangles represent biconnected components). Biconnected components are connected to each other by articulation points. Firstly we introduce a few symbols. $G_{bc} = \{G_1, G_2, G_3, \cdots, G_t\}$ represents the biconnected component set of graph G. If u is a node of graph G, s_{uG_i} represents the sum of the distance from node u to other nodes which locate in biconnected component G_i. $\Gamma_u = \{G_i | u \text{ in } G_i \wedge G_i \in G_{bc}\}$ represents the set of biconnected components including node u. A represents the sum of the distances from u to other nodes which locate in Γ_u, as shown in Formula (2). B represents the sum of the distances from node u to all the nodes which do not locate in Γ_u, as shown in formula (3).

$$A = \sum_{G_i \in \Gamma_u} s_{uG_i} \tag{2}$$

$$B = \sum_{G_i \notin \Gamma_u} s_{uG_i} \tag{3}$$

In Formula (2), we can get the result by one BFS from node u in G_i. The calculation of Formula (3) is a little bit complicated. Under the hypotheses of Lemma 1, s_{uG_i} in Formula (3) can be computed by Formula (4). In Formula (4), $|G_i|$ represents the number of nodes in G_i, a_u is the nearest articulation point from node u in G_i, and d_{ua_u} represents the length of the shortest path from u to a_u. In particular, when u is an articulation point, d_{ua_u} can be computed by accumulating the distance between articulation points visited on the path. The distance between any two articulation points can be calculated directly by performing BFS in their common biconnected component, which can be calculated in advance, and shared in process of calculating the $C(u)$ of every articulation

---

Algorithm 1. the closeness centrality of articulation point

Input: an articulation point u of G, G_{bc}
Output: $C(u)$
1: $\Gamma_u = \{G_i | u \text{ in } G_i \wedge G_i \in G_{bc}\}$, $\Gamma_{past} = \emptyset$
2: $A = 0$, $B = 0$
3: sort G_{bc} according to the order of BFS traversal from u
4: **for each** $g \in G_{bc}$ **do**
5:   **if** $g \in \Gamma_u$ **then**
6:     $A = A + s_{ug}$
7:   **else**
8:     $a = \Gamma_{past} \cap g$ // $\cap$ is the operate of finding the common articulation point
9:     $B = B + d_{ua} * (|g| - 1) + s_{ag}$
10:   **end if**
11:   $\Gamma_{past} = \Gamma_{past} \cup g$
12: **end for each**
13: $C(u) = \frac{1}{A+B}$

---

point u. Next, we give Lemma 1 to prove the important property of articulation points.

$$s_{uG_i} = d_{ua_u} * (|G_i| - 1) + s_{a_u G_i} \tag{4}$$

Lemma 1. *If nodes u and v are not in the same biconnected component, the path from u to v must pass articulation points.*

Proof: We use contradiction to prove. Assume there is a shortest path p_{uv} from u to v, which does not cross any articulation points. Then the deletion of arbitrary articulation point must not affect the p_{uv}. But if the articulation points of biconnected components which p_{uv} crosses are removed, the biconnected components which u and v are located in will be disconnected. That means p_{uv} doesn't exist, which contradicts our assumption.

According to Lemma 1, if u and a_u are not in the same biconnected component, the shortest path from u to a_u must pass some articulation points. Assuming that they are $a_{u1}, a_{u2}, a_{u3}, \cdots, a_{uk}$, d_{ua_u} can be computed by Formula (5).

$$d_{ua_u} = d_{ua_{u1}} + \sum_{j=1}^{k-1} d_{a_{uj}a_{u(j+1)}} + d_{a_{uk}a_u} \tag{5}$$

Based on this analysis, we design our algorithm as shown in Algorithm 1. Figure 2 shows an example. If we calculate the closeness centrality of articulation point u, A is calculated by traversing the biconnected components which include articulation point u, so $A = s_{uG_1} + s_{uG_5}$. The calculation of B is the sum of s_{uG_2}, s_{uG_3}, s_{uG_4}, s_{uG_6}. Then $B = s_{uG_2} + s_{uG_3} + s_{uG_4} + s_{uG_6}$, where $s_{uG_2} = d_{ua_1} * (|G_2| - 1) + s_{a_1 G_2}$, $s_{uG_3} = d_{ua_2} * (|G_3| - 1) + s_{a_2 G_3}$, $s_{uG_4} = (d_{ua_1} + d_{a_1 a_3}) * (|G_4| - 1) + s_{a_3 G_4}$, and $s_{uG_6} = d_{ua_4} * (|G_6| - 1) + s_{a_4 G_6}$. $s_{a_1 G_2}$, $s_{a_2 G_3}$, $s_{a_3 G_4}$, $s_{a_4 G_6}$ can be calculated by traversing G_2, G_3, G_4, G_6 respectively. The closeness centrality of u is thereby $\frac{1}{A+B}$.

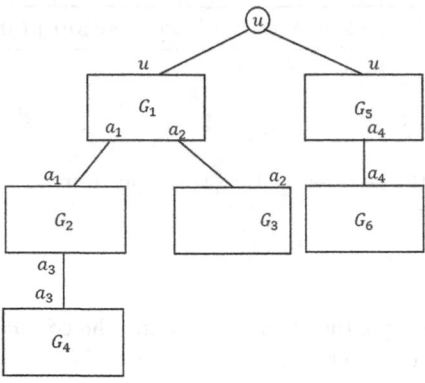

Fig. 2. Calculating articulation points

4.2 The Closeness Centrality of Nodes in Γ_u

The closeness centrality of nodes in Γ_u can be computed using the results of articulation point u, which can avoid some repetitive calculations. After we calculate $C(u)$, we can also get the number of nodes in each subgraph if node u is removed from G. For each node v which belongs to Γ_u is not u, the cost of calculation can be reduced by using the partial results. We use $G_{u\bigcup v}$ to represent the biconnected component where nodes u and v are located. Then $G_{u\bigcup v} \in \Gamma_u$ is true. Similar to calculating the closeness centrality of articulation point u, here we divide the calculation of $C(u)$ into two parts which are ΔA and ΔB. ΔA represents the difference between $s_{vG_{u\bigcup v}}$ and $s_{uG_{u\bigcup v}}$, and ΔB represents the difference between $s_{v(G\backslash G_{u\bigcup v})}$ and $s_{u(G\backslash G_{u\bigcup v})}$. The calculation of ΔA and ΔB is shown as formula (6) and formula (7) respectively. $A_{G_{u\bigcup v}} = \{a_i | a_i \in G_{u\bigcup v} \wedge iscut[a_i] = 1\}$ represents the set of articulation points in $G_{u\bigcup v}$, where $iscut[a_i] = 1$ represents that node a_i is an articulation point. If we remove $G_{u\bigcup v}$, graph G is divided into several subgraphs which are $G'_{a_1}, G'_{a_2}, G'_{a_3}, \cdots$. G'_{a_i} represents the subgraph which includes articulation point a_i. $|G'_{a_i}|$ represents the number of nodes in G'_{a_i}. When we get ΔA and ΔB, we can calculate $C(v)$ by formula (8). We design our algorithm as shown in Algorithm 2.

$$\Delta A = s_{vG_{u\bigcup v}} - s_{uG_{u\bigcup v}} \tag{6}$$

$$\Delta B = \sum_{a_i \in A_a} (d_{va_i} - d_{ua_i}) * |G'_{a_i}| \tag{7}$$

$$C(v) = \frac{1}{\frac{1}{C(u)} + \Delta A + \Delta B} \tag{8}$$

Algorithm 2. the closeness centrality of node in Γ_u

Input: an articulation point u, Γ_u, G_{bc},
Output: $C(v)$ of each node v in Γ_u
1: **for each** $g \in \Gamma_u$ **do**
2:　　find $A_g = \{a_i | a_i \text{ in } g \wedge iscut[a_i] = 1\}$
3:　　**for each** $a_i \in A_g$ **do**
4:　　　find G'_{a_i}
5:　　　get $|G'_{a_i}|$
6:　　**end for each**
7:　　**for each** v in g **do**
8:　　　$\Delta A = 0$, $\Delta B = 0$
9:　　　BFS traverse g from v, get s_{vg}, and also d_{va_i} of $a_i \in A_g$
10:　　　$\Delta A = s_{vg} - s_{ug}$
11:　　　**for each** $a_i \in A_g$ **do**
12:　　　　$\Delta B = (d_{va_i} - d_{ua_i}) * |G'_{a_i}|$
13:　　　**end for each**
14:　　　$C(v) = \dfrac{1}{\frac{1}{C(u)} + \Delta A + \Delta B}$
15:　　**end for each**
16: **end for each**

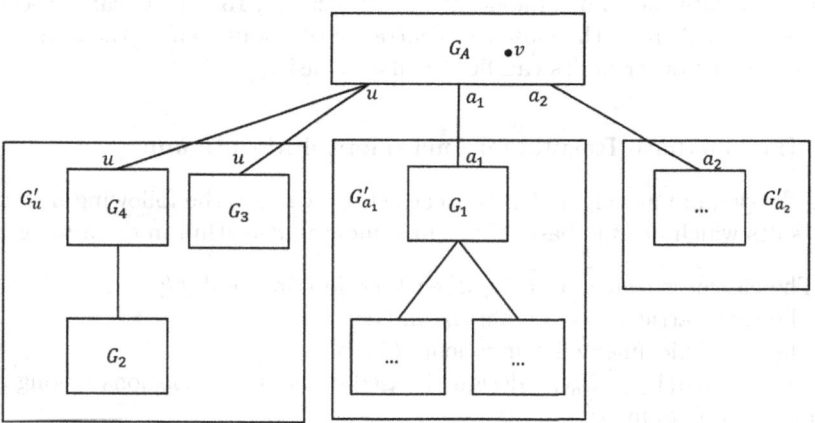

Fig. 3. The example of calculating nodes in Γ_u

Figure 3 shows an example. Assuming we have calculated the closeness centrality of node u, and now we want to calculate the closeness centrality of node v. Node u and v are both in G_A, and the set of articulation points in G_A includes u, a_1 and a_2. If G_A is removed, we can get the same number of subgraphs as articulation points which are G'_u, G'_{a_1}, and G'_{a_2}. After we calculate the closeness centrality of node u, we get $c(v)$, $|G_4|$, $|G'_{a_1}|$, and $|G'_{a_2}|$. We can get s_{vG_A} by traversing G_A from node v, so ΔA is calculated by $\Delta A = s_{vG_A} - s_{uG_A}$. ΔB can be calculated by $\Delta B = d_{vu} * |G_4 \cup G_2 \cup G_3| + (d_{va_1} - d_{ua_1}) * |G'_{a_1}| + (d_{va_2} - d_{ua_2} * |G'_{a_2}|)$. The closeness centrality of node v can be obtained by formula (8).

4.3   Putting Together

Firstly we get the articulation points and the biconnected components. Secondly, we calculate the shortest distance of between articulation points which are locate in the same biconnected component, the sum of the shortest distance from artic- ulation points to other nodes which are in the same biconnected component, and the number of nodes in each biconnected component. The calculation can be fin- ished only in each biconnected component, and each articulation point saves the related information. Then we calculate the closeness centrality of a articulation point by Algorithm 1, and the closeness centrality of other nodes belonging to the same biconnected component by Algorithm 2. Algorithm 1 and Algorithm 2 are performed alternately until the closeness centrality of all the nodes in the graph have been calculated. A concrete example is given in the following.

In Fig. 1, after we calculate the closeness centrality of articulation point 1, according to the intermediate results we can easily calculate the closeness cen- trality of nodes 9, 10, 11, 2, 3, 4, 5, 6, 7, 8. Then we calculate the closeness centrality of articulation point 17. According to the intermediate results we can easily calculate the closeness centrality of nodes 15, 19, 16, 18, 20. In addition we calculate the closeness centrality of articulation points 23, 24, and 6 in turn, and further calculate the value of nodes 21, 22, 25, 26, 12, 13, 14. As can be seen, we only need to calculate the closeness centrality of about half of the articulation points, and the other nodes can be calculated easily.

4.4   Intermediate Results for Incremental Maintenance

After the preliminary algorithm is executed, we will get the following intermedi- ate results which are the basis of the incremental algorithm in dynamic graphs.

(1) The closeness centrality $C(v)$ of each node v in graph G;
(2) The set of articulation points A_G in G;
(3) The set of biconnected components G_{bc} of G;
(4) Graph $G_{arti}(V_{arti}, E_{arti})$ designed based on adjacent relations among artic- ulation points in G;
(5) Graph $G_{bcg}(V_{bcg}, E_{bcg})$ designed based on adjacent relations among bicon- nected components of G.

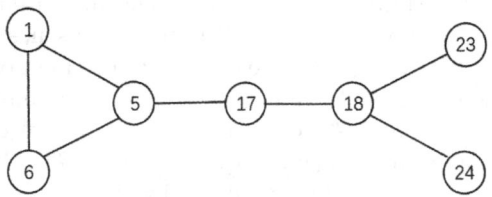

Fig. 4. G_{arti} of Fig. 1.

Nodes of graph G_{arti} represent articulation points in G. There are edges between articulation points belonging to the same biconnected component. Nodes of graph G_{bcg} represent biconnected components of G. In G_{bcg}, nodes represent biconnected components, and each edge represents the adjacency of a biconnected component pair, which is actually their common articulation point. G_{arti} and G_{bcg} of Fig. 1 are shown in Fig. 4 and Fig. 5 respectively.

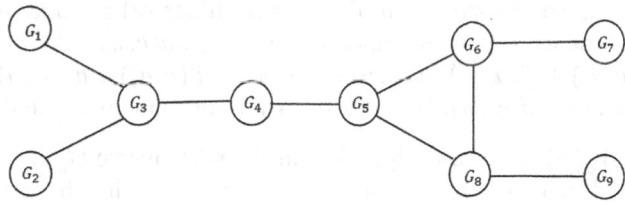

Fig. 5. G_{bcg} of Fig. 1.

5 Incremental Maintenance for Dynamic Graphs

5.1 The Change of Graph

We get graph G' after we insert/delete an edge $e(a,b)$ into/from graph G. Firstly, we traverse G and G' respectively from node a, and we get the distance from a to other nodes in G. If $d'(a,u) \neq d(a,u)$, this indicates that node u is affected by edge $e(a,b)$. We then add u to V'_a for further incremental update. If $d'(b,u) \neq d(b,u)$, this indicates that node u is affected by edge $e(a,b)$. We add u to V'_b. We employ the definition of unstable vertex pair in [14]. If $d'(u,v) \neq d(u,v)$, (u,v) is called an unstable vertex pair, otherwise (u,v) is called a stable vertex pair. If $d'(u,v) \neq d(u,v)$, there must be $u \in V'_a$ and $v \in V'_b$.

After edge $e(a,b)$ is inserted in the graph G, if nodes a and b are in the same biconnected component, affected biconnected component G'_{affect} is the biconnected component that they are located in. If not, G_{bc} and G_{bcg} are changed. We need to merge some biconnected components as G'_{affect}. We traverse G'_{affect} and G_{affect} from node a (b) to get V'_a (V'_b). If V'_a or V'_b have articulation points, the nodes belonging to the subgraph connected to G'_{affect} through the articulation points are also affected nodes, and we save this type of affected nodes in the V'_{ab}. We find all node pairs in G'_{affect}, and calculate the change of closeness centrality δ. In addition, we define an array which is represented by $fnode$. For each node t in G'_{affect}, we set $fnode[t] = t$. Assuming the articulation points are $a_1, a_2, a_3, \cdots, a_k$ in G'_{affect}, the subgraphs connected to G'_{affect} by the articulation points are $G'_{a_1}, G'_{a_2}, G'_{a_3}, \cdots, G'_{a_k}$ respectively.

5.2 Incremental Algorithm

Next, we propose Theorem 1 to instruct how to calculate the nodes outside the affected biconnected components through the articulation points instead of performing BFS in the entire updated graph, and then prove it. We set

$fnode[t] = a_i$, $t \in G'_{a_i}, i = 1, 2, 3, \ldots, k$, and the amount of change for each node in G'_{a_i} is equal to the amount of change node a_i according to Theorem 1, so we only need calculate δ^{a_i}.

Theorem 1. *The change of the sum of distance for each node in G'_{a_i} is equal to the change of articulation point a_i.*

Proof: For each node v in G'_{a_i}, because G'_{a_i} does not change with the graph update, the change of the sum of the distance from v to other nodes in G'_{a_i} is zero, and a_i is the same as v. For each node u in $G' \backslash G'_{a_i}$, $d(v, u) - d(v, a_i) \mid d(a_i, u)$, $d'(v, u) = d'(v, a_i) + d'(a_i, u)$, $d'(v, u) - d(v, u) = d'(v, a_i) + d'(a_i, u) - d(v, a_i) - d(a_i, u) = d'(a_i, u) - d(a_i, u)$. It is obvious that the change is equal too.

Assuming $|V'_a| \leq |V'_b|$, for each node v in V'_a, we traverse G'_{affect} and G_{affect} from v. For each u in V'_b, if u is an articulation point, the change of v is $\delta^v = \delta^v + ((d'(v, u) - d(v, u)) * |G'_u|)$, otherwise the change of v is $\delta^v = \delta^v + (d'(v, u) - d(v, u))$. If v is an articulation point, the change of u is $\delta^u = \delta^u + ((d'(v, u) - d(v, u)) * |G'_v|)$, otherwise the change of u is $\delta^u = \delta^u + (d'(v, u) - d(v, u))$. Finally we update the closeness centrality of nodes by Formula (9). In Formula (9), $\frac{1}{C(v)}$ is the sum of the distance from v to other nodes in G. $\delta^{fnode[v]}$ is the change of the sum of the distance from v to other nodes. The pseudo code is shown in Algorithm 3.

$$C'(v) = \frac{1}{\frac{1}{C(v)} + \delta^{fnode[v]}} \tag{9}$$

Algorithm 3. the proposed incrementally updating algorithm(IUA)

Input: $G(V, E)$, G_{bc}, A_G, $C(v)$ of each $v \in V$, the changed edge $e(u, v)$
Output: the closeness centrality $C'(v)$ of node v in G'
1: update G_{bc}, A_G and $fnode$, and find G'_{affect}, get V'_a, V'_b, V'_{ab}
2: **for each** $v \in V'_a$ (Suppose $|V'_a| \leq |V'_b|$) **do**
3:     perform BFS starting from v in G'_{affect} and G_{affect} respectively
4:     **for each** $u \in V'_b$ **do**
5:         **if** $iscut[v] = 1$ **then**
6:             $\delta^u = \delta^u + ((d'(v, u) - d(v, u)) * |G'_v|)$
7:         **else**
8:             $\delta^u = \delta^u + (d'(v, u) - d(v, u))$
9:         **end if**
10:         **if** $iscut[u] = 1$ **then**
11:             $\delta^v = \delta^v + ((d'(v, u) - d(v, u)) * |G'_u|)$
12:         **else**
13:             $\delta^v = \delta^v + (d'(v, u) - d(v, u))$
14:         **end if**
15:     **end for each**
16: **end for each**
17: $updatenode = V'_a \cup V'_b \cup V'_{ab}$
18: **for each** v in $updatenode$ **do**
19:     $C'(v) = \frac{1}{\frac{1}{C(v)} + \delta^{fnode[v]}}$
20: **end for each**

5.3 Analysis of Complexity

When edge (a, b) is inserted/deleted into/from graph G, the worse case is that a and b are not in the same biconnected components. Firstly, we find (and update) G_{affect} and get V'_a and V'_b by traversing it, which requires $O(|V_{affect}| + |E_{affect}|) + O(|V_{bcg}| + |E_{bcg}|)$ time. We then need to update intermediate results, such as G_{arti}, A_{G_i}, and $fnode$, which takes $O(|V_{arti}| + |E_{arti}|) + O(|V|)$ time. To summarize, the overall maintenance time complexity is $O(|V| + |E|)$. For each node in V'_a, BFS in G_{affect} and G'_{affect} is performed respectively. So the computation time cost is $O(|V'_a|(|(|V_{affect}| + |E_{affect}|)|))$.

Table 1 shows the time complexity of different algorithm. In CENDY, $|V|+|E|$ is large. In CC, V_{cid} is large. In IUA (the incrementally update algorithm), $|V'_a|$ and $|V_{affect}| + |E_{affect}|$ are both small. $|V_{bcg}| + |E_{bcg}|$ and $|V_{bcg}| + |E_{bcg}|$ is so small that they can be ignored. IUA has more advantages in efficiency.

Table 1. The compare of time complexity

Algorithm	The time complexity
IUA	$O(|V_{affect}| + |E_{affect}|) + O(|V|) + O(|V'_a|(|V_{affect}| + |E_{affect}|))$
CENDY	$O(|V| + |E|) + O(|V'_a|(|V| + |E|))$
CC	$O(|V| + |E|) + O(|V_{cid}|(|V_{affect}| + |E_{affect}|))$

6 Experiments

6.1 Settings

All algorithms are run on the win10 system. The computer memory is 8G, and CPU is 3.2 Hz. The employed graph datasets are obtained from [2], which are shown in Table 2. The datasets Cagr, Erdos02, Erdos972 and com-dblp are collaboration graphs. Epa is a web graph. Eva is a media network. Wiki-Vote is a voting network. Contact and email-EuAll are communication networks.

Table 2. The datasets

Dataset	$|V|$	$|E|$	BCn_rate	$|MBC|\_rate$
Cagr	4158	13428	0.6376	0.7519
Epa	4253	8897	0.5086	0.9864
Eva	4475	4654	0.0523	0.9940
Erdos972	5440	8940	0.3184	0.9992
Erdos02	6927	11850	0.3097	0.9996
Wiki-Vote	7066	100736	0.6773	0.9996
Contact	13373	79823	0.6224	0.9877
email-EuAll	224832	340795	0.1601	0.9999
com-dblp	317080	1049866	0.3241	0.9991

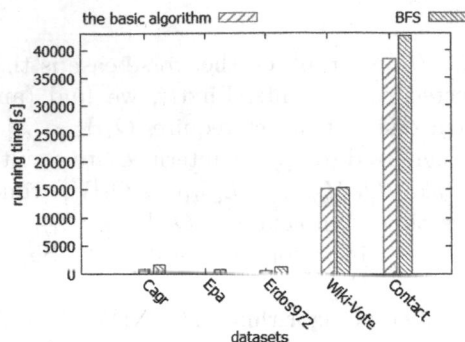

Fig. 6. Runtime comparison of algorithms for static graph.

Table 3. The ratio of V_a' and V_b' respectively

Dataset	$|V_a'|/|V|$	$|V_b'|/|V|$
Cagr	0.08	0.67
Epa	0.01	0.13
Eva	0.002	0.03
Erdos972	0.005	0.1
Erdos02	0,001	0.02
Wiki-Vote	0.001	0.04
Contact	0.001	0.04
email-EuAll	0.001	0.03
com-dblp	0.0005	0.1

The number of nodes $|V|$ and edges $|E|$, the number rate of small biconnected components BCn_rate, and the number rate of nodes in the biggest biconnected components $|MBC|\_rate$ are listed in Table 2. $BCn\_rate = \frac{BC_{2\_n}}{BC\_n}$ is computed by the number BC_{2_n} of biconnected components formed by two nodes and the total number of biconnected components. $|MBC|\_rate = \frac{|V\_maxBC|}{|V|}$ is computed by the number $|V\_maxBC|$ of nodes in the biggest biconnected component and the total number of nodes. From the value of parameters, BCn_rate and $|MBC|\_rate$ of the Wiki-Vote and Contact are relatively large, thus with many extreme biconnected components. Eva has a large $|MBC|\_rate$ but small BCn_rate value, meaning that most of the biconnected components occupies few of nodes, and the dataset is very sparse.

6.2   The Experiment Results

(1) The experiment result of the preliminary algorithm

As far as we know, calculating the exact closeness centrality of all nodes in a static graph usually employs BFS currently, so the preliminary algorithm in this paper is compared with the BFS. The experimental results using seconds (s) as the time unit are shown in Fig. 6.

The static algorithm is more than twice as fast as BFS in Cagr, Epa and Erdos972. However, the performance benefit is marginal for Wiki-Vote and Contact. This is because the biconnected components are heavily skewed in Wiki-Vote and Contact. That is, the largest biconnected component occupies most of the graph, while the remaining 99% are formed by two nodes mostly. In this scenario, it takes a lot of time to calculate the distance between the articulation points in the largest biconnected component, which shows that most of the remaining nodes are articulation points, whose closeness centralities need to be calculated. The static algorithm is more efficient than BFS, and can help conveniently design and speedup the incremental algorithm for the on-line update.

Table 4. The experimental results of insertion edges

Dataset	IUA(s)	CENDY(s)	CC(s)
Cagr	33.39	99.83	158.67
Epa	9.81	41.43	71.37
Eva	0.69	60.79	0.42
Erdos972	4.21	9.22	38.63
Erdos02	2.14	14.66	12.67
Wiki-Vote	39.18	41.33	451.3
Contact	84.66	135.38	1932.76
email-EuAll	496.21	2031.29	4961.02
com-dblp	612.65	3192.12	6002.13

(2) The experiment result of incremental algorithm Insertion of Edges: In order to evaluate the efficiency of IUA, the average execution time(s) is used as the metric. We insert 100 edges randomly, and update the results every time for each insertion. The various corresponding average percentages of $|V_a'|$ and $|V_b'|$ are shown in Table 3, and the efficiency is evaluated in Table 4.

In Table 3, we can observe that $|V_a'|$ is remarkably smaller than $|V_b'|$ on each dataset. With such a small $|V_a'|$, only a few of BFS are required. Therefore IUA yield better update efficiency. Although Table 4 indicates that IUA has different efficiencies in different graphs, in most cases, it can greatly improve the performance. As an exception, we can see that IUA is not as efficient as CC on Eva dataset, because Eva is sparse and IUA requires maintaining biconnected components which is a little time consuming.

The scalable results performed over two small graphs Cagr and Wiki-Vote, and two large graphs email-EiAll and com-dblp, are shown in Fig. 7. We can observe that IUA is not only efficient, but also relatively stable in execution, indicating that IUA can scale very well with the dynamic update. Note that the fluctuations of curves in Fig. 7, are caused by randomly inserting edges.

Deletion of Edges: For deletions, we delete 100 edges, and update the results every time once a deletion operation is finished. We use the average runtime as the evaluation. Table 5 lists all the runtime results.

We can generally draw the similar conclusion for deletion and insertion of edges. The only exception is Eva. The results are similar in the term of scalability on the datasets with various ratios of V_a' and V_b'. Details are omitted due to space limitation.

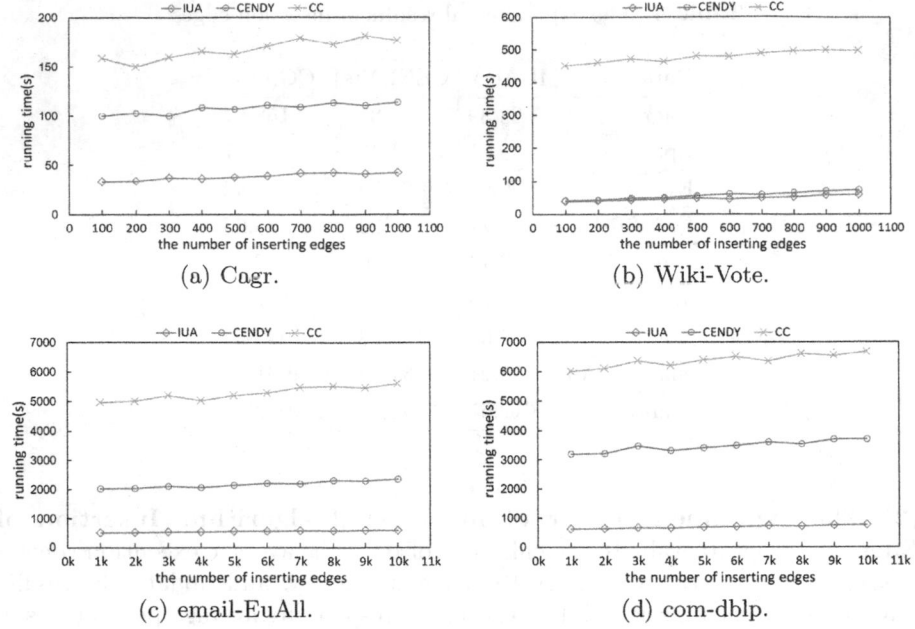

Fig. 7. The experiment results of inserting edges.

Table 5. The experimental results of deletion edges

Dataset	IUA(s)	CENDY(s)	CC(s)
Cagr	33.23	100.03	164.14
Epa	9.86	41.43	71.28
Eva	0.1	60.75	0.4
Erdos972	4.2	49.12	38.79
Erdos02	2.13	14.63	12.71
Wiki-Vote	39.2	41.32	449.92
Contact	84.46	135.55	1915.79
email-EuAll	489.52	2011.79	4897.85
com-dblp	598.07	3001.34	5988.13

7   Conclusions

In this paper, we focus on the efficiency problem of computing the exact closeness centrality for the evolving graphs. First, we propose a preliminary algorithm instead of performing BFS in the off-line stage, which leverages the biconnected component and reserves key intermediate results to boost the later incremental maintenance. Further, based on the preliminary algorithm, we explore an incremental algorithm to handle on-line updates by constraining the evaluation into affected biconnected components. The experimental results show that our proposed algorithms are superior to the previous ones.

References

1. Paolo, B., Vigna, S.: Axioms for centrality. Internet Math. **10**(3–4), 222–262 (2014)
2. Saxena, A., Malik, V., Iyengar, S.R.S.: Estimating the degree centrality ranking. In: 12th International Conference on COMmunication Systems and NETworkS (COMSNETS), pp. 1–2 (2016)
3. Jamour, F., Skiadopoulos, S., Kalnis, P.: Parallel algorithm for incremental betweenness centrality on large graphs. IEEE Trans. Parallel Distrib. Syst. **29**(3), 659–672 (2018)
4. Wang, C., Lin, Z.: An efficient approximation of betweenness centrality for uncertain graphs. IEEE Access **7**, 61259–61272 (2019)
5. Bergamini, E., Borassi, M., Crescenzi, P., Marino, A., Meyerhenke, H.: Computing top-k closeness centrality faster in unweighted graphs. ACM Trans. Knowl. Disc. Data (TKDD) **13**(5), 1–40 (2019)
6. Ayta, V., Turac, T.: Closeness centrality in some splitting networks. Comput. Sci. J. Moldova **26**(3), 251–269 (2018)
7. Lv, L., Zhang, K., Zhang, T., Li, X., Zhang, J., Xue, W.: Eigenvector centrality measure based on node similarity for multilayer and temporal networks. IEEE Access **7**, 115725–115733 (2019)
8. Pedroche, F., Tortosa, L., Vicent, J.-F.: An eigenvector centrality for multiplex networks with data. Symmetry **11**, 1–23 (2019)
9. Newman, M.E.J.: Scientific collaboration networks. II. Shortest paths, weighted networks, and centrality. Phys. Rev. E **64**, 016132 (2001)
10. Sporns, O., Honey, C.J., Kotter, R.: Identification and classification of hubs in brain networks. PLoS ONE **2**(10), e1049 (2007)
11. Carbaugh, J., Fletcher, M., Gera, R., Lee, W.C., Nelson, R., Debnath, J.: Extracting information based on partial or complete network data. J. Fundam. Appl. Sci. **10**(4), 76–83 (2018)
12. Iyengar, S.R.S., Madhavan, C.E.V., Zweig, K.A., Natarajan, A.: Understanding human navigation using network analysis. Topics Cognitive Sci. **4**(1), 121–134 (2012)
13. Sariyce, A.E., Kaya, K., Saule, E., et al.: Incremental algorithms for closeness centrality. In: International Conference on Big Data, pp. 487–492. IEEE (2013)
14. Yen, C.-C., Yeh, M.-Y., Chen, M.-S.: An efficient approach to updating closeness centrality and average path length in dynamic networks. In: IEEE International Conference on Data Mining (ICDM), pp. 867–876. IEEE (2013)
15. Cohen, E., Delling, D., Pajor, T., Werneck, R.F.: Computing classic closeness centrality, at scale. In: 2nd ACM Conference on Online Social Networks (COSN), pp. 37–50. ACM (2014)
16. Kim, J., Ahn, H., Park, M., Kim, S., Kim, K.P.: An estimated closeness centrality ranking algorithm and its performance analysis in large-scale workflow-supported social networks. Trans. Internet Inf. Syst. (TIIS) **10**(3), 1454–1466 (2016)
17. Guo, t., Cao, X., Cong, G., Lu, J., Lin, X.: Random-radius ball method for estimating closeness centrality. In: 31th AAAI Conference on Artificial Intelligence (AAAI), pp. 125–131. AAAI (2017)

18. Sariyce, A.E., Saule, E., Kaya, K., et al.: Incremental closeness centrality in distributed memory. Parallel Comput. **47**, 3–18 (2015)
19. Santos, E.E., Korah, J., Murugappan, V., Subramanian, S.: Efficient anytime anywhere algorithms for closeness centrality in large and dynamic graphs. In: International Parallel and Distributed Processing Symposium Workshops (IPDPSW), pp. 1821–1830. IEEE (2016)
20. Olsen, P.W., Labouseur, A.G., Hwang, J.-H.: Efficient top-k closeness centrality search. In: 30th International Conference on Data Engineering (ICDE), pp. 196–207. IEEE (2014)
21. Bergamini, E., Borassi, M., Crescenzi, P., Marino, A., Meyerhenke, H.: Computing top-k closeness centrality faster in unweighted graphs. ACM Trans. Knowl. Disc. from Data **13**(5), 1–40 (2017)
22. Bisenius, P., Bergamini, E., Angriman, E., Meyerhenke, H.: Computing Top-k closeness centrality in fully-dynamic graphs. In: 20th SIAM Workshop on Algorithm Engineering and Experiments (ALENEX), pp. 21–35 (2018)
23. Kas, M., Carley, K.M., Carley, L.R.: Incremental closeness centrality for dynamically changing social networks. In: International Conference on Advances in Social Networks Analysis and Mining (ASONAM), pp. 1250–1258. IEEE/ACM (2013)
24. Inariba, W., Akiba, T., Yoshida, Y.: Distributed algorithms on exact personalized PageRank. In: 17th Proceedings of the 2017 ACM International Conference on Management of Data (SIGMOD), pp. 479–494. ACM (2017)
25. Hopcroft, J.E., Tarjan, R.E.: Efficient algorithms for graph manipulation (Algorithm 447). Commun. ACM **16**(6), 372–378 (1973)

GQA_RDF: A Graph-Based Approach Towards Efficient SPARQL Query Answering

Xi Wang[1], Qianzhen Zhang[1], Deke Guo[1(✉)], Xiang Zhao[1(✉)],
and Jianye Yang[2]

[1] Science and Technology on Information Systems Engineering Laboratory,
National University of Defense Technology, Changsha, China
{dekeguo,xiangzhao}@nudt.edu.cn
[2] Hunan University, Changsha, China

Abstract. Due to the increasing use of RDF data, efficient processing of SPARQL queries over RDF datasets has become an important issue. In graph-based RDF data management solution, SPARQL queries are translated into subgraph patterns and evaluated over RDF graphs via graph matching. However, answering SPARQL queries requires handing *RDF reasoning* to model *implicit* triples in RDF data, which is largely overlooked by existing graph-based solutions. In this paper, we investigate to equip graph-based solution with the important RDF reasoning feature for supporting SPARQL query answering. (1) We propose an on-demand saturation strategy, which only selects an RDF fragment that may be potentially affected by the query. (2) We provide a filtering-and-verification framework to efficiently compute the answers of a given query. The framework groups the equivalent entity vertices in the RDF graph to form semantic abstracted graph as index, and further computes the matches according to the multi-grade pruning supported by the index. (3) In addition, we show that the semantic abstracted graph and the graph saturation can be efficiently updated upon the changes to the data graph, enabling the framework to cope with dynamic RDF graphs. (4) Extensive experiments over real-life and synthetic datasets verify the effectiveness and efficiency of our approach.

1 Introduction

The Resource Description Framework (RDF)[1] is a graph-based data model promoted by the W3C for modeling Web Objects as part of the prospective semantic web. An RDF dataset is in essence a set of *triples*, each of the form $\langle s, p, o \rangle$ for $\langle \text{subject}, property, \text{object} \rangle$. A triple indicates a relationship between s and o captured by p. Consequently, a collection of triples can be modelled as a *directed labeled* graph where the graph vertices denote subjects and objects while graph

---

X. Wang and Q. Zhang—Both authors contributed equally to this work.
[1] https://www.w3.org/RDF/.

© Springer Nature Switzerland AG 2020
Y. Nah et al. (Eds.): DASFAA 2020, LNCS 12113, pp. 551–568, 2020.
https://doi.org/10.1007/978-3-030-59416-9_33

edges are used to denote predicates, as shown in Fig. 1. In order to query RDF data, the W3C recommends a formal language, namely, SPARQL[2]. For example, to retrieve the actor in a science fiction film who won an America award, one may formulate the query using SPARQL:

Q_1:*Select ?m Where { ?m ⟨won⟩ ?p. ?n ⟨hasActor⟩ ?m. ?m ⟨rdf : type⟩ Actor. ?p ⟨rdf : type⟩ America_Award. ?n ⟨type⟩ Science_Fiction_ Film. }*

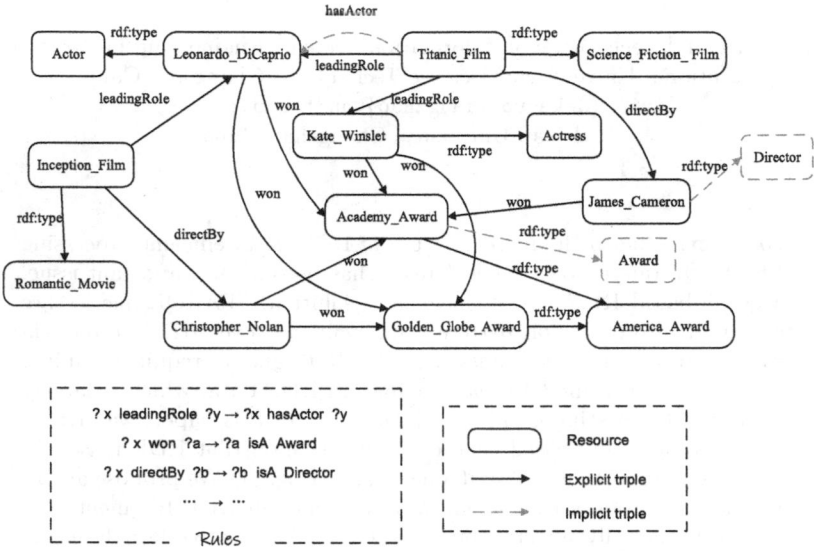

Fig. 1. Sample RDF graph

From the perspective of data management, there exist two types of solutions—relational and graph-based—to RDF data [1]. Using relational databases does not always offer an elegant solution towards efficiently RDF query evaluation, and still lacks best practices currently [2]. Recently, graph-based solution emerges, attributed to the fact that RDF is a universal graph model of data. In graph-based solution, a SPARQL query is translated into a graph pattern P, which is then evaluated over the RDF graph G. The query evaluation process is performed via matching the variables in P with the elements of G such that the returned graph is contained in G (pattern matching). The main focus of this article is on a well-known subset of SPARQL consisting of (unions of) basic graph pattern (BGP) queries, which is identified in the SPARQL recommendation, are more expressive than relational conjunctive queries [3].

The major advantage of graph-based solution lies in that RDF query[3] becomes easier to formulate without losing its modeling capability, and more

---

[2] https://www.w3.org/TR/sparql11-query/.

[3] In this paper, we may use SPARQL BGP query" and RDF query" interchangeably.

importantly, graph pattern matching, without optimization strategies, is able to perform, if not better, as good as relational RDF query engines [4]. In succession, a few novel graph-based systems were put forward [4–6]. In particular, gStore [5] uses a carefully designed index VS*-tree to process RDF queries. TurboHom++ [4] transforms RDF graphs into labeled graphs and applies subgraph homomorphism methods to RDF query processing. AMbER [6] is a graph-based RDF engine that represents the RDF data and SPARQL queries into multigraphs and the query evaluation task is transformed to the problem of subgraph homomorphism.

All the aforementioned work can be summarized as graph-based efforts for RDF query evaluation (not answering) since they ignore the essential RDF feature called *entailment*, which allows model *implicit information* within RDF graph. Taking entailment into account is crucial, without which leads to incomplete answers. For instance, assume the claim that "Titanic has an actor Leonardo DiCaprio" is not in the RDF data; nonetheless, we can derive ⟨Titanic_Film, *hasActor*, Leonardo_DiCaprio⟩, on the basis of the explicit triple ⟨Titanic_Film, *leadingRole*, Leonardo_DiCaprio⟩ and the description "leadingRole belongs to the subproperty of hasActor" in terms of RDFS. RDFS represents an ontology language that can be used to enhance the description of RDF graphs. As a result, RDF query answering can be split into a reasoning step and a query evaluation step.

There are two disparate reasoning steps, i.e., *saturation* and *reformulation* [7,8], in relational-based approaches. Saturation-based query answering exhaustively makes explicit all of the implicit information. Reformulation-based query answering performs rewriting a query into an equivalent large union of conjunctive queries and posing them against the original RDF data [9,10]. While saturation leads to efficient query evaluation, it requires large amount of time to compute, space to store, and must be recomputed upon updates; query reformulation adversely affects query response times due to syntactically great complexity and subtle interplay between RDF and SPARQL dialects.

In this paper, we investigate to close the gap by supplementing reasoning mechanism to existing graph-based systems. Conceptually, we strike a balance between *saturation* and *reformulation*, and propose to deal with entailment by using an *on-demand saturation* strategy. That is, we need not make explicit all of the implicit data in the RDF graph, since most implicit information is irrelevant to the query; instead, we carefully choose only the RDF fragment that is revelent to the query, and then, saturate it accordingly. Based on the reasoning mechanism, we propose a filtering-and-verification framework, namely, GQA$_{RDF}$, for computing the answers of a given query.

Contributions. In short, the major contributions under the framework we have made are summarized below:

- We group the equivalent entity vertices in the RDF graph to form multi-grade abstracted graph as index.
- Using the index, we develop a filtering strategy, which extracts a small subgraph of G as a compact representation of the query results.

- We propose a new encoding method for further refining the candidates of each query vertex and conduct subgraph matching calculations.
- We provide techniques to incrementally maintain the index and the graph saturation upon the changes to the RDF graph, enabling the framework to cope with dynamic data graphs.

Experiment results demonstrate that our techniques significantly outperform the state-of-the-art RDF data management system.

2   Preliminaries

RDF data is a set of triples of the form $\langle s, p, o \rangle$, where s is an entity or a class, and p denotes one attribute associated to one entity or a class, and o is an entity, a class, or a literal value. We consider only well-formed triples, as per the W3C RDF standard, both entity and class can be represented by IRIs (Internationalized Resource Identifiers). In this work, we will not distinguish between an "entity" and a "literal" since we have the same operations. As an alternative, RDF data is expressed as an RDF graph, formally defined as follows.

Definition 1 (RDF graph). *An RDF graph is a directed labeled graph $G = (U_G, E_G, \Sigma_G, L_G)$, where U_G is a set of vertices that correspond to all subjects and objects in RDF data, $E_G \subseteq U_G \times U_G$ is the set of directed edges that connect the subjects and objects, Σ_G is a finite set of labels for vertices and edges, and the labeling function L_G maps each vertex or edge to a label in Σ_G. More precisely, a vertex of a subject has a label corresponding to its IRI, while a vertex of an object can possess a label of either IRI or literal. The label of an edge is its corresponding property.*

Definition 2 (RDF schema). *RDF Schema (RDFS) is a valuable feature of RDF that allows enhancing the descriptions in RDF graphs. RDFS triples declare semantic constraints between the classes and the properties used in those graphs.*

Definition 3 (RDF entailment). *The W3C named RDF entailment the mechanism, through which, implicit RDF triples can be derived, based on a set of explicit triples and some entailment rules.*

Table 1. Instance-level entailment

Constraints	Description	Entailment rules	Entailed triples
$\prec_{sc}$	subclass	$s' \prec_{sc} s''$; s rdf:type s'	s rdf:type s''
$\prec_{sp}$	subproperty	$p \prec_{sp} p'$; $s\ p\ s'$	$s\ p'\ s'$
$\leftharpoondown_d$	domain	$p \leftharpoondown_d s$; $s_1\ p\ o$	s_1 rdf:type s
$\rightharpoonup_r$	range	$p \rightharpoonup_r s$; $s_1\ p\ o$	o rdf:type s

In this research, we concentrate ourselves on the core entailment of RDFS regime. Using RDFS, we can recover a large amount of implicit information, part of which may be answers to queries. Specifically, Table 1 enumerates the possible RDFS constraints and the corresponding entailment rules. The first two columns show the allowed semantic constraints, and the notations to express them, where *domain* and *range* denote the first and second attribute of every property (edge label), respectively. The last two columns show the entailment rules to get the *entailed triples*. Since the overwhelming practical impact of querying only the instance-level (implicit and explicit) data, we focus on query answering only for instance-level queries (cf. Table 1).

We consider the most fundamental building block of SPARQL, which consists of (unions of) basic graph pattern (BGP) queries[4].

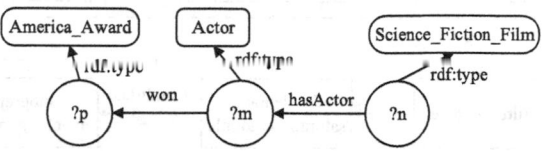

Fig. 2. An illustrate of query pattern graph

Definition 4 (BGP query). *A BGP can be modelled as a directed labeled query pattern graph $Q = (V_Q, E_Q)$, where V_Q is a collection of subject and object vertices, which can be IRIs, literals or variables, $E_Q \subseteq V_Q \times V_Q$ is a set of directed edges that connect the corresponding subjects and objects, each of which has an edge label of literal or variable. Figure 2 shows a BGP query, and the circles in it represent variable vertices.*

Definition 5 (Query evaluation). *Given a query pattern $Q = (V_Q, E_Q)$ that has n vertices $\{v_1, \ldots, v_n\}$. A set of n vertices $\{u_1, \ldots, u_n\}$ in G is said to be a match, or embedding, of Q, if and only if the following conditions hold:*

- *if v_i is a literal vertex, v_i and u_i have the same literal value;*
- *if v_i is an entity vertex, v_i and u_i have the same IRI;*
- *if v_i is a variable vertex, there is no constraint on u_i; and*
- *if there is an edge $\langle v_i, v_j \rangle \in E_Q$ with property p, there is an edge $\langle u_i, u_j \rangle \in E_G$ with the same property p.*

Definition 6 (Query answering). *Query answering is the evaluation of Q against G that takes the entailment into account. The answers of Q are constituted of returned bindings to query variables.*

---

[4] https://www.w3.org/TR/rdf-sparql-query/#BasicGraphPatterns.

3 Framework

Recall that the SPARQL BGP query answering problem is a major challenge that is largely overlooked by existing graph-based efforts towards RDF data management. To this end, we provide a novel filtering-and-verification framework named GQA_{RDF}. Generally speaking, our approach consists of two stages: *offline index construction* and *online RDF query answering* (see Fig. 3). We briefly review the two stages before we discuss them in details in upcoming sections.

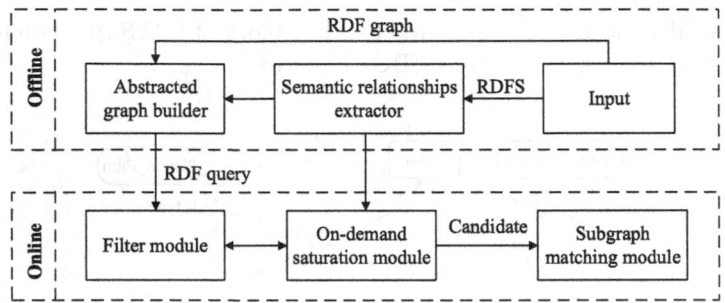

Fig. 3. Solution framework of GQA_{RDF}

Offline Index Construction. The offline process is used to build the semantic abstracted graph as index. We describe the main components. Firstly, we construct an auxiliary data structure, namely, STP, which is a series of sets that represent the semantic inclusion relation in RDFS. Then, based on STP, we merge the entity vertices in the RDF graph that is adjacent to equivalent class vertices (have equivalent type) to construct an abstracted graph as index. The index is precomputed once, and is dynamically maintained upon changes to G.

Online Query Processing. The online process is used to calculate the answers of a given query. Upon receiving an RDF query Q, the framework extracts a small subgraph as a compact representation of all the matches that are similar to Q, by visiting the abstracted graphs. If such a subgraph is empty, the framework determines that Q has no answers. Otherwise, we use the proposed on-demand saturation strategy to obtain the candidates of each variable vertex and conduct subgraph matching to calculate the answer. Specially, we propose a new encode module to encode the neighborhood structure around a vertex into a bitstring, and prune the candidates via "Bloom filter".

4 Semantic Abstracted Graph

In this section, we propose an effective index to reduce the space cost and facilitate the query processing.

4.1 Semantic Relationships Extraction

In order to construct the *abstracted graph*, we need to group and merge the equivalent entity vertices in G, where two entity vertices are equivalent if they are adjacent to equivalent class vertex (have the equivalent type). To this end, we construct an auxiliary data structure named STP by using the semantic relation in RDFS, such that given a class vertex t and an entity vertex u, one can check whether u has type t. STP is comprised of the following four sets.

- SubPro($\cdot$): given an edge property p in RDFS, SubPro(p) is a set of edge properties that are the *subproperty* of p;
- SubClass($\cdot$): given a class vertex t in RDFS, SubClass(t) is a set of class vertices that are the *subclass* of t;
- Domain($\cdot$): given a class vertex t in RDFS, Domain(t) is a set of edge properties that belong to the *domain* of t; and
- Range($\cdot$): given a class vertex t in RDFS, Range(t) is a set of edge properties that belong to the *range* of t.

To obtain SubPro($\cdot$), we extract all triples in RDFS with edge property "*rdfs:subPropertyOf*", i.e., $\langle p_1, rdfs:subPropertyOf, p_2 \rangle$. Then, the vertex p_1 is extracted to form the set SubPro (p_2). The other three sets can be constructed in a similar flavor as the set SubPro($\cdot$). Note that, in the STP construction process, we need to obtain corresponding superclass vertices for constructing the index.

Definition 7 (Superclass vertex). *We say a class vertex t_s is a **superclass vertex** if there exists no other class vertex t such that $t_s \in$ SubClass(t).*

To achieve the superclass vertices, we use a counter num(t) (initialize to 0) for every class vertex t in RDFS to count the times of t that is extracted to construct SubClass($\cdot$). For example, in processing a trip in RDFS with edge property "*rdfs:subClassOf*", i.e., $\langle t_1, rdfs:subClassOf, t_2 \rangle$, t_1 is extracted to form the set SubClass (t_2). Then, we set num(t_1) $\leftarrow$ num(t_1) $+ 1$. Intuitively, we say a class vertex t_s is a superclass vertex if t_s has a 0 count (i.e., num(t_s) $= 0$). The class vertices $\{t\}$ within SubClass($\cdot$) are sorted in descending order of vertex weights $w(t)$ where $w(t) = \frac{1}{\text{num}(t)}$.

4.2 Semantic Abstracted Graph

Relying on the semantic class constraint set in STP, we construct a semantic abstracted graph as index to reduce the space cost further.

Given an RDF graph $G = (U, E, L)$, a *concept graph* $G_c = (U_c, E_c, L_c)$ is a directed graph by ignoring edge labels. In detail, (1) U_c is a partition of U, where each $\mathcal{U}_c \in U_c$ is a set of entity vertices; (2) each $\mathcal{U}_c$ has a label $L_c(\mathcal{U}_c)$ from the superclass vertices obtained in STP, such that for any entity vertex $u \in \mathcal{U}_c$ of type t_u, $t_u \in$ SubClass($L_c(\mathcal{U}_c)$); (3) $\langle \mathcal{U}_c^1, \mathcal{U}_c^2 \rangle$ is an edge in E_c if and only if for each entity vertex u_1 in $\mathcal{U}_c^1$ (resp. u_2 in $\mathcal{U}_c^2$), there is an entity vertex u_2 in $\mathcal{U}_c^2$

(resp. u_1 in $\mathcal{U}_c^1$), such that $\langle u_1, u_2 \rangle$ (resp. $\langle u_2, u_1 \rangle$) is an edge in G. Specially, if u has no type, we can use STP to derive corresponding type of u. To differentiate the vertices of the concept graph from the vertices of Q and G, we call vertices of the abstracted graph as **nodes**. Here, a entity vertex u of type t_u means there is a class vertex t_u that is adjacent to u.

Figure 4 shows the concept graph G_c of the RDF graph in Fig. 1. Each node $\mathcal{U}_c$ in G_c represents a set of entity vertices whose types belong to $\mathsf{SubClass}(L_c(\mathcal{U}_c))$. In the node $Film$, the types of $Inception\_Film$ (i.e., $Science\_Fiction\_Film$) and $Titanic\_Film$ (i.e., $Romantic\_Movie$) both belong to $\mathsf{SubClass}(Film)$.

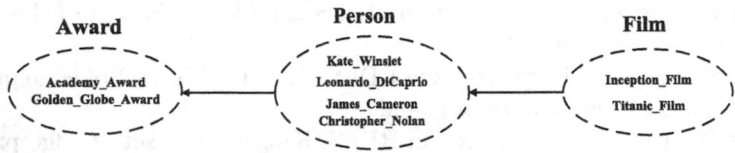

Fig. 4. Concept graph

Definition 8 (Semantic abstracted graph). *A semantic abstracted graph is multi-grade concept graph, where*

- *the first grade, $G_{c_1} = (U_{c_1}, E_{c_1}, L_{c_1})$, represents the initial concept graph constructed by using the superclass vertices;*
- *the i-th ($i \geq 2$) grade, $G_{c_i} = (U_{c_i}, E_{c_i}, L_{c_i})$, is a more detailed concept graph constructed from $G_{c_{i-1}}$ in the $(i-1)$-th grade by dividing each node $\mathcal{U}_{c_{i-1}}$ ($\mathcal{U}_{c_{i-1}} \in U_{c_{i-1}}$) into smaller partitions. In this case, (1) each $\mathcal{U}_{c_i}$ ($\mathcal{U}_{c_i}$ is in $\mathcal{U}_{c_{i-1}}$) has a label $L_{c_i}(\mathcal{U}_{c_i})$, which is the child-class of $L_{c_{i-1}}(\mathcal{U}_{c_{i-1}})$; (2) $\langle \mathcal{U}_{c_i}^1, \mathcal{U}_{c_i}^2 \rangle$ ($\mathcal{U}_{c_i}^1 \in \mathcal{U}_{c_{i-1}}^1$, $\mathcal{U}_{c_i}^2 \in \mathcal{U}_{c_{i-1}}^2$) is an edge in E_{c_i} if and only if for each entity vertex u_1 in $\mathcal{U}_{c_i}^1$ (resp. u_2 in $\mathcal{U}_{c_i}^2$), there is a entity vertex u_2 in $\mathcal{U}_{c_i}^2$ (resp. u_1 in $\mathcal{U}_{c_i}^1$), such that $\langle u_1, u_2 \rangle$ (resp. $\langle u_2, u_1 \rangle$) is an edge in G.*

An important issue is to get the child-class vertices of a given class vertex t_u. Recall that we can obtain the subclass vertices $\{t_u^n\}$ of t_u based on $\mathsf{SubClass}(t_u)$ in STP, each of which has a weight $w(t_u^n)$. Note that, the closer t_u^n is to t_u, the greater the value of $w(t_u^n)$ is. As a result, we say $\{t_u^1, \ldots, t_u^i\}$ ($1 < i \leq n$) is the set of child-class vertices of t_u if they have the same and greatest value of weights in $\mathsf{SubClass}(t_u)$. In specific, if $\mathsf{SubClass}(t_u) = \emptyset$, we say the child-class vertex of t_u is itself. Figure 5(b) depicts a semantic abstracted graph of the RDF graph in Fig. 1, which is also a two-grade concept graph.

Our empirical study showed that three-grade concept graph are enough for optimization. Thus, we set the grade as 3 in our experiments.

Semantic Abstracted Graph Construction. In G_{c_1}, we first construct the node set U_{c_1} as a vertex partition of G, where each node $\mathcal{U}_{c_1}$ of U_{c_1} consists of the entity vertices of type $L_{c_1}(\mathcal{U}_{c_1}) \in \mathsf{SubClass}(t_s)$. The edge set E_{c_1} is also constructed accordingly. We then check the condition whether for each edge $\langle \mathcal{U}_{c_1}^1, \mathcal{U}_{c_1}^2 \rangle$, each vertex u_1 (resp. u_2)in $\mathcal{U}_{c_1}^1$ (resp. $\mathcal{U}_{c_1}^2$) has a child in $\mathcal{U}_{c_1}^2$ (resp. parent in $\mathcal{U}_{c_1}^1$). If not, we refine U_{c_1} by splitting and merging the node $\mathcal{U}_{c_1}^1$ (resp. $\mathcal{U}_{c_1}^2$) to make the condition satisfied. G_{c_i} is updated accordingly with the new node and edge set. The refinement process repeats until a fixpoint is reached. In G_{c_i} ($i \geq 2$), we replace the class vertices used in $G_{c_{i-1}}$ with corresponding child-class vertices and adopt the same procedure to construct G_{c_i}.

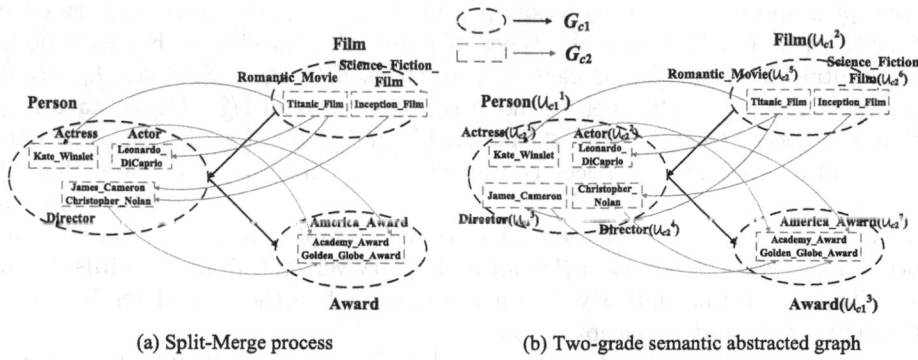

(a) Split-Merge process   (b) Two-grade semantic abstracted graph

Fig. 5. Construction of abstracted graph

For example in Fig. 5(a), nodes *Person* and *Film* are divided into a set of nodes {*Actress, Actor, Director*} and {*Romantic_Movie, Seience_Fiction_Film*} in G_{c_2}, respectively. Since the entity vertex *Christopher_Nolan* in *Director* has no neighbor in node *Romantic_Movie*, we split the node *Director* into two nodes to produce G_{c_2} (Fig. 5(b)) as the 2-*nd* grade concept graph.

5 Query Pruning and Answering

In this section, we illustrate the filtering phase of the query answering framework based on the abstracted graph index, and then obtain the answers of the query by adding the on-demand saturation strategy.

5.1 Multi-grade Filtering

In order to retrieve the final answers, we need to obtain candidates for each variable vertex in the query. Instead of performing the subgraph matching directly over the RDF graph, we extract a (typically small) subgraph of G that contains all the matches of the query based on the abstracted graph.

We first search the query graph over G_{c_1}. For each variable v in Q, we can obtain the corresponding superclass t_s of v based on STP. Let cand(v) denote the candidates of v, which is initialized as the set of nodes labeled t_s in G_{c_1}.

We conduct a fixpoint computation for each query edge $\langle v, v' \rangle$ (v' is not a class vertex) using $\mathsf{cand}(v)$ and $\mathsf{cand}(v')$. Regarding each node $\mathcal{U}_{c_1} \in \mathsf{cand}(v)$, we check if there is a node $\mathcal{U}'_{c_1}$ in $\mathsf{cand}(v')$ such that edge $\langle \mathcal{U}_{c_1}, \mathcal{U}'_{c_1} \rangle$ in G_{c_1} has the same direction as $\langle v, v' \rangle$. If not, $\mathcal{U}_{c_1}$ (and all the data vertices contained in it) is no longer a candidate for v, and will be removed from $\mathsf{cand}(v)$. Specially, if $\mathsf{cand}(v)$ is empty, then we can say the query Q has no answers over the RDF graph.

Multi-grade Pruning. Since the semantic abstracted graph is a multi-grade concept graph, we can refine candidates by going through i-th ($i \geq 2$) grade concept graph one-by-one. For example, in the 2-nd grade, given a query edge $\langle v, v' \rangle$, let t_v and t'_v denote the types of v and v', respectively. For each node $\mathcal{U}_{c_2}$ contained in $\mathcal{U}_{c_1}$ ($\mathcal{U}_{c_1} \in \mathsf{cand}(v)$), we check if (1) $t_v \in \mathsf{SubClass}(L_{c_2}(\mathcal{U}_{c_2}))$ (or $t_v = L_{c_2}(\mathcal{U}_{c_2})$); (2) there is node $\mathcal{U}'_{c_2}$ contained in $\mathcal{U}'_{c_1}$ ($\mathcal{U}'_{c_1} \in \mathsf{cand}(v')$) that is adjacent to $\mathcal{U}_{c_2}$ and $t'_v \in \mathsf{SubClass}(L_{c_2}(\mathcal{U}'_{c_2}))$ (or $t'_v = L_{c_2}(\mathcal{U}'_{c_2})$). If not, $\mathcal{U}_{c_2}$ (and all the entity vertices contained in it) can be pruned. Note that, if the type t_v of v is equal to $L_{c_2}(\mathcal{U}_{c_2})$, then we will not check the query edges adjacent to v any more in larger grades concept graphs. To differentiate v from other query vertices, we use a *flag* for each query vertex (initialize to **false**) and set $flag[v] = $ **true**. Similarly, one may further refine the candidates by going through larger grades concept graphs.

Consider the semantic abstracted graph in Fig. 5(b), and the SPARQL query graph in Fig. 2. In G_{c_1}, we initialize $\mathsf{cand}(?p) = \{\mathcal{U}^3_{c_1}\}$, $\mathsf{cand}(?m) = \{\mathcal{U}^1_{c_1}\}$, $\mathsf{cand}(?n) = \{\mathcal{U}^2_{c_1}\}$. After checking, we find all the candidate nodes satisfy the edge constraint and will not be pruned. Then, in G_{c_2}, we refine the candidates set of each variable vertex based on the child-class of each superclass used in G_{c_1}. After the refinement, $\mathsf{cand}(?p) = \{\mathcal{U}^7_{c_2}\}$, $\mathsf{cand}(?m) = \{\mathcal{U}^2_{c_2}\}$, $\mathsf{cand}(?n) = \{\mathcal{U}^6_{c_2}\}$.

5.2   On-Demand Saturation

To obtain complete answers of the query, in this section, we present an on-demand saturation strategy, which consists of two stages: edge property saturation and entity type saturation.

Edge Property Saturation. Edge property saturation is used to check whether a data edge can match a query edge with respect to property, either directly or via entailment. That is, if a data edge has a different property from a query edge, we examine the subproperties entailed by the data edge, to see if any of them matches the query edge.

To this end, let $\langle v, v' \rangle$ be an outing going edge labeled p_v adjacent to v. For each candidate entity vertex u in $\mathsf{cand}(v)$, we check whether there exists an outgoing edge $\langle u, u' \rangle$ labeled p_u adjacent to u such that $p_u = p_v$ or $p_u \in \mathsf{SubPro}(p_v)$. If not, u will be pruned from $\mathsf{cand}(v)$. Otherwise, if $p_u \in \mathsf{SubPro}(p_v)$ and there is no other outing edge adjacent to u with the property p_v, we add the outgoing edge $\langle u, u' \rangle$ labeled p_v into u.

Entity Type Saturation. Entity type saturation is used to check if a entity vertex matches a query vertex with respect to type in the query graph.

Given a variable vertex v of type t_v s.t. $flag[v] = $ **false**, for each entity vertex u in cand(v), we check if one of the following three conditions hold: (1) $t_u \in$ SubClass(t_v) where t_u is the type of u; (2) there exists an outgoing edge $\langle u, u' \rangle$ labeled p_u adjacent to u such that $p_u \in$ Domain(t_v); (3) there exists an incoming edge $\langle u', u \rangle$ labeled p_u adjacent to u such that $p_u \in$ Range(t_v). If not, u will be pruned from cand(v).

5.3 RDF Query Answering

Note that, in the filtering process, we ignore the edge property information for each query edge. In this section, we use the *neighborhood encoding* technology to further prune invalid candidates.

Neighborhood Encoding. Neighborhood encoding has been widely adopted to assist various operations in managing RDF data [11], which describes each vertex as a bit string, namely, *vertex signature*. In a similar flavor, we choose to encode, for each vertex in RDF graph, its adjacent edge properties and the corresponding neighbor vertex properties into bit strings via *Bloom filter* [12].

Let $\langle u, u' \rangle$ labeled p_u be an adjacent edge of an entity vertex u in G, m the length of p_u's bit string, n the length of u''s bit string. Bloom filter uses a set of hash functions H to set $\overline{m}$ out of m bits to be "1", and set $\overline{n}$ out of n bits to be "1", where $\overline{m}$ and $\overline{n}$ represent the number of independent hash functions, respectively. The bit string of u, denoted by $Bit(u)$, is formed by performing *bitwise OR* operations over all it's adjacent edge bit strings. Note that given a variable vertex v, if the adjacent neighbor of v is also a variable vertex, we set the bit string of the vertex with all "0" (same as variable edge). u is a candidate of v only if $Bit(v)$ & $Bit(u) = Bit(v)$, where '&' is the *bitwise AND* operator.

Out-edge	Out-vertex	Out-edge+vertex	In-edge	In-vertex	In-edge+vertex

Fig. 6. Bit string of a vertex

The encoding method in [5] divides the bit string of the vertex into two parts: the first part represents the outgoing edge properties information, while the second represents the properties information of linked neighbors. Such method can be insufficient in fully harness the neighborhood information for candidate pruning. In this connection, we propose to encode the neighborhood of a vertex using six parts, as depicted in Fig. 6. The first two parts describe the information of outgoing edges information and linked vertices. In the third part, we bind each edge with the neighbor corresponding to it. The last three parts are the information about incoming edges, which are processed in a similar manner as for outgoing edges. In order to avoid the "false drop" problem that may exist in the encoding method, we follow the method in [5] to set the length of each part as 100 and use 3 different hash functions.

Then, upon receiving the final concise candidates set of each query vertex, we conduct subgraph homomorphism calculations to obtain the answers of the query. Here, we adopt the cost model proposed in the state-of-the-art algorithm, i.e., CPI [13], for computing an efficient matching order and conduct subgraph homomorphism matching accordingly.

6   Rationale of Maintenance

In this section, we investigate the incremental maintenance of the semantic abstracted graph index and the graph saturation, which further enables the RDF query answering to cope with dynamic data graphs.

6.1   Index Maintenance upon Updates

Instead of recomputing the semantic abstracted graph and the saturation from the scratch each time the RDF graph is updated, we relay on an incremental maintain strategy.

Handling Edge Insertions. Consider an edge $\langle u, u' \rangle$ inserted into G, we take a *split-merge-propagation* strategy for each grade in the abstracted graph as follows. In the 1-st grade, we first identify $\mathcal{U}_{c_1}$ and $\mathcal{U}'_{c_1}$ in G_{c_1} that contains u and u', respectively. We then separate u' from $\mathcal{U}'_{c_1}$, and *split* $\mathcal{U}_{c_1}$ similarly if $\mathcal{U}_{c_1}$ and $\mathcal{U}'_{c_1}$ violate the structural constraints of a concept graph due to the edge insertion. Next, we check whether the separated data vertices can be *merged* into other nodes in G_{c_1}, due to satisfying the edge constraints. Since the updates of nodes $\mathcal{U}_{c_1}$ (resp. $\mathcal{U}'_{c_1}$) may *propagate* to its adjacent nodes, we should further check the neighbor nodes of $\mathcal{U}_{c_1}$ (resp. $\mathcal{U}'_{c_1}$) in the same way until there is no update in G_{c_1}. Similarly, after updating G_{c_1}, we update G_{c_i} ($i \geq 2$) following the same *split-merge-propagation* strategy.

Handling Edge Deletions. Consider an edge $\langle u, u' \rangle$ deleted from G, we take a similar operations as the updating procedure of edge insertions. Omitted in the interest of space, we do not describe here.

6.2   Saturation Maintenance upon Updates

To maintain the saturation efficiently, an important issue is to keep track of the multiple ways in which an edge was entailed. This is significant when considering both implicit data and updates: for a given update, we must decide whether this adds/removes one reason why a triple belongs to the saturation. A naïve implementation would record the inference paths of each implied triple, that is, all sequences of reasoning rules that have lead to that triple being present in the saturation. However, the volume of such justification grows very fast and thus the approach does not scale. Instead, we chose to keep track of the *number of reasons* why an edge has been inferred. In subproperty saturation, the number of reason is 1 since an implied edge only entailed by one explicit edge. In entity type saturation, for each data vertex u in cand(v), we use the notation $Type(u)$ to record the number of reasons that can entail u has the same type as v. Then, for a given edge insertion (resp. edge deletion), we will decide whether this adds (resp. deletes) one reason why an type edge belongs to the saturation. When this count reaches 0, the implied type edge should be deleted.

7   Experiments

In this section, we report experiment results and analyses.

7.1   Experiment Setup

The proposed algorithms were implemented using C++, running on a Linux machine with two Core Intel Xeon CPU 2.2 Ghz and 32 GB main memory. Particularly, three algorithms were implemented: (1) GQA$_{RDF}$, our algorithm; (2) Turbolum++, which extends existing subgraph homomorphism method to handle SPARQL queries [4]; (3) gStore, which tags each vertex with a signature and match signatures of data vertices and pattern vertices one by one [5].

Experiments were carried out on real-life RDF and synthetic datasets (as shown in Table 2). For query evaluation, we choose to use the SPARQL BGP queries in [14] over Yago and use the SPARQL BGP queries in [15] over LUBM, each of which has six queries ($Q_1 \sim Q_6$).

Table 2. Graph datasets

Dataset	Edge	Predicate	Entity
Yago	20,263,756	21,843	2,218,624
LUBM10M	12,237,135	18	1,684,231
LUBM20M	25,124,227	18	3,243,658
LUBM30M	32,457,671	18	4,752,538

7.2   Evaluating the Effectiveness of On-Demand Saturation

In this subsection, we evaluate the effectiveness of our on-demand saturation technology, which is scaled by the number of match results. For the sake of simplicity, we use Q_i^y to represent the query Q_i in Yago, and use Q_i^l to represent the query Q_i in LUBM. We ran experiments with both datasets and report the results obtained for all queries. The conclusions are reported below.

Table 3 shows the total number of match results. It is not surprising to notice that GQA$_{RDF}$ can get more complete match results for almost all the queries than gStore. Especially, in Q_2^y, Q_4^y and Q_3^l, the number of match results is 0 if we use gStore. This is because in Q_2^y, the edge label *"placedIn"* does not exist in original

Table 3. Match results

Queries	Yago		LUBM 10M	
	gStore	GQA$_{RDF}$	gStore	GQA$_{RDF}$
Q_1	1,638	3,271	211	495
Q_2	0	1,063	2,201	6,731
Q_3	397	1,817	0	4,062
Q_4	0	18,849	1,336	1,849
Q_5	125	428	20	231
Q_6	863	1,093	784	784

RDF graph, however, GQA$_{RDF}$ can use the constraint $isLocatedIn \prec_{sp} placedIn$ to get the entailed triples which satisfy the query. Similarly, in Q_4^y and Q_3^l, some edges in pattern graph but not in RDF graph will be entailed, and added to the RDF graph to get more match results. In general, the comparisons verify the effectiveness of our proposed on-demand saturation strategy.

7.3   Evaluating the Efficiency and Scalability of GQA$_{RDF}$

We evaluated the performance of GQA$_{RDF}$, gStore and TurboHom++ using both Yago and LUBM, and their scalability using LUBM. In these experiments, the indexes were precomputed, and thus their construction time were not counted. Note that, gStore and TurboHom++ cannot handle SPARQL query answering since they ignore the essential RDF feature called entailment. As a result, we adopt the *reformulation* reasoning strategy, and **rewrite** the queries that are used in gStore and TurboHom++ to directly compute all the answers.

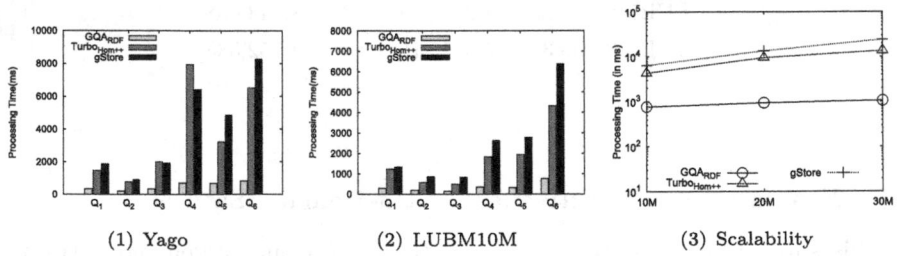

(1) Yago   (2) LUBM10M   (3) Scalability

Fig. 7. Performance evaluation-I

Query Answering Time. Figure 7(1) and Fig. 7(2) show the query answering time for each RDF query graph over Yago and LUBM, respectively. Since TurboHom++ needs offline process for transforming the RDF graph into labeled graph and gStore needs offline process for building the VS*-tree index, we only consider the online performance for each competitors. GQA_{RDF} consistently out-performs its competitors. This is due to our on-demand saturation strategy that can avoid large amounts of subgraph matching calculations for rewritten queries. Specially, in Yago, GQA_{RDF} outperforms TurboHom++ by up to 11.28 times (see query Q_4^y), gStore by up to 10.19 times (see query Q_6^y); in LUBM, GQA_{RDF} out-performs TurboHom++ by up to 5.89 times (see query Q_5^l), gStore by up to 8.47 times (see query Q_5^l). Note that, in most cases, gStore has the worst performance, since it traverses the RDF graph in a BFS order, which will produce redundant Cartesian products.

Evaluating the Scalability. Figure 7(3) shows the performance results of GQA_{RDF} against existing algorithms regarding the scalability by using LUBM for varying the dataset size. Here, we vary the size of the RDF graph from 12,237,135 (LUBM10M) to 32,457,671 (LUBM30M). We use Q_{6b} since the performance gap is largest at this case. It reveals that GQA_{RDF} consistently outperforms its com-petitors regardless of the dataset size. In generally, the scalability suggests that GQA_{RDF} can handle reasonably large real-life graphs as those existing algorithms for deterministic graphs. Specially, GQA_{RDF} outperforms TurboHom++ by up to 12.75 times and gStore by up to 22.57 times.

7.4   Evaluating the Effectiveness of Semantic Abstracted Graph

Using synthetic and real-life datasets, we next investigate (1) the index building cost of GQA_{RDF} and its competitors, including time cost and physical memory; (2) the memory reduction mr $= \frac{|M_I|}{|M|}$, where $|M_I|$ and $|M|$ are the physical memory cost of the index and the data graph, respectively; (3) the filtering rate fr $= \frac{|G_{sub}|}{|G|}$, where $|G_{sub}|$ is the average size of the induced subgraphs in the filtering phase, and G is the size of G. The result is shown below.

Table 4. Effectiveness of index

Dataset	GQA_{RDF}		gStore	
	mr	fr	mr	fr
Yago	0.43	0.13	0.64	0.27

Figure 8(1) and Fig. 8(2) show the space cost and time cost of index con-struction using LUBM, respectively. Since TurboHom++ does not construct any index, we only compare GQA_{RDF} with gStore. We see that GQA_{RDF} has consis-tently better performance than its competitors regardless of memory and time. What's more, the figure reads a non-exponential increase as the data size grows. In specific, GQA_{RDF} outperforms gStore by up to 11.24 times and 40.31 times, in terms of the memory cost and time cost, respectively.

Table 4 gives the effectiveness of the index using Yago. It reveals: (1) GQA_{RDF} beats gStore regardless of mr and fr; (2) the semantic abstracted graph contains

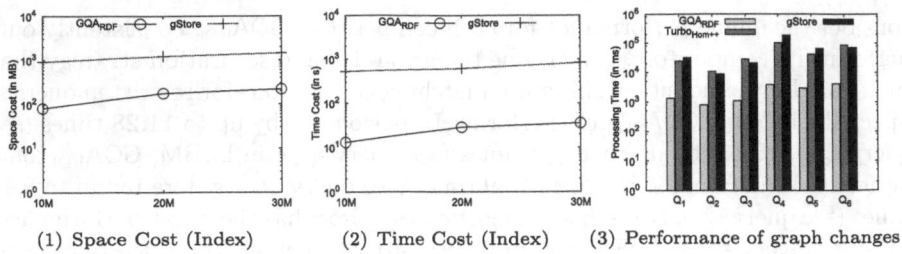

(1) Space Cost (Index)   (2) Time Cost (Index)   (3) Performance of graph changes

Fig. 8. Performance evaluation-II

much less nodes and edges over the RDF graph, and takes less than half of its physical memory cost; (3) using semantic abstracted graph can effectively filter the search space, that is, the size of G_{sub} for verification is only 17% over Yago.

We finally compare the performance of GQA$_{RDF}$ and its competitors upon RDF graph changes. We use Yago dataset and fix edge insertions $|E_I|$ = 1,376,286. Since updating one edge at a time is too slow for TurboHom++ and will reach the timeout (1-h) for all queries. As a result, we insert edges in batches of 100K (= 100×10^3) for it. Figure 8(3) tells us that GQA$_{RDF}$ greatly outperforms its competitors. Specially, GQA$_{RDF}$ performs TurboHom++ by up to 26.43 even the edge updates are inserted in bathes for TurboHom++.

8 Related Work

We categorize the related work as follows.

Relational-Based RDF Query Evaluation. Relational-based RDF stores use relational models to store RDF data and translate SPARQL queries into relational algebraic expressions. SW-Store [16] uses a column-oriented store as its underlying store, triples are stored as sorted by the subject column. RDF-3X [1, 17] and Hexastore [18] model RDF triples as big three-attribute tabular structures and build six clustered clustered B+-trees as indexes for each permutation of subject, predicate and object. H-RDF-3X [19] is a distributed RDF processing engine where RDF-3X is installed in each cluster node.

Graph-Based Query Evaluation. Graph-based stores use graph traversal approaches, i.e., subgraph homomorphism, and graph indexing. TurboHom++ [4] eliminates corresponding query vertices/edges from a query graph by embedding the types of an entity into a vertex label set to boost query performance. GRIN [20] uses graph partitioning and distance information to construct the index for graph queries. gStore [5] tags each vertex with a signature and matches signatures of data vertices and query vertices by using the VS*-tree index. Grass [21] performs the graph pattern matching by the concept of fingerprint for star subgraph to prune search space.

Query Answering. RDF query answering needs to take the *entailment* into account, as ignoring which leads to incomplete answers. 3store [7], Jena [22],

OWLIM [8], Sesame [23] support saturation-based query answering, based on (a subset of) RDF entailment rules. The work by Goasdoue et al. [24] extends above studied by the support of blank nodes. Algorithms in [25] consider some novel rules to reformulate relational conjunctive queries. However, above query answering approaches are relational-based, and there is no graph-based methods towards efficient query answering.

9   Conclusion

In this paper, we have studied *graph-based approach for efficient query answering*. We devise GQA_{RDF} to provide effective support. On top of it, we propose an on-demand saturation strategy, which only selects an RDF fragment that may be potentially affected by the query. In addition, we devise a semantic abstracted graph index for discovering candidate vertices, which brings a constant-time reduction of candidate search space. The semantic abstracted graph and the graph saturation can be efficiently updated upon the changes to the data graph. Finally, comprehensive experiments performed on real and benchmark datasets demonstrate that GQA_{RDF} outperforms its alternatives.

Acknowledgement. This work is partially supported by National Natural Science Foundation of China under Grant No. 61872446, Natural Science Foundation of Hunan Province under Grant No. 2019JJ20024, National key research and development program under Grant Nos. 2018YFB1800203 and 2018YFE0207600.

References

1. Neumann, T., Weikum, G.: The RDF-3X engine for scalable management of RDF data. VLDB J. **19**(1), 91–113 (2010)
2. Sakr, S., Wylot, M., Mutharaju, R., Phuoc, D.L., Fundulaki, I.: Linked Data: Storing, Querying, and Reasoning. Springer, Cham (2018). https://doi.org/10.1007/978-3-319-73515-3
3. Wylot, M., Hauswirth, M., Cudré-Mauroux, P., Sakr, S.: RDF data storage and query processing schemes: a survey. ACM Comput. Surv. **51**, 84:1–84:36 (2018)
4. Kim, J., Shin, H., Han, W., Hong, S., Chafi, H.: Taming subgraph isomorphism for RDF query processing. PVLDB **8**(11), 1238–1249 (2015)
5. Zou, L., Mo, J., Chen, L., Özsu, M.T., Zhao, D.: gStore: answering SPARQL queries via subgraph matching. PVLDB **4**(8), 482–493 (2011)
6. Ingalalli, V., Ienco, D., Poncelet, P., Villata, S.: Querying RDF data using a multigraph-based approach. In: EDBT 2016, Bordeaux, France, 15–16 March 2016, pp. 245–256 (2016)
7. Harris, S., Gibbins, N.: 3store: efficient bulk RDF storage. In: PSSS1, Sanibel Island, Florida, USA, 20 October 2003
8. Bishop, B., Kiryakov, A., Ognyanoff, D., Peikov, I., Tashev, Z., Velkov, R.: OWLIM: a family of scalable semantic repositories. Semant. Web **2**(1), 33–42 (2011)
9. Calvanese, D., De Giacomo, G., Lembo, D., Lenzerini, M., Rosati, R.: Tractable reasoning and efficient query answering in description logics: the DL-Lite family. J. Autom. Reasoning **39**(3), 385–429 (2007)

10. Gottlob, G., Orsi, G., Pieris, A.: Ontological queries: rewriting and optimization. In: ICDE 2011, 11–16 April 2011, Hannover, Germany, pp. 2–13 (2011)
11. Zou, L., Özsu, M.T.: Graph-based RDF data management. Data Sci. Eng. **2**(1), 56–70 (2017)
12. Bloom, B.H.: Space/time trade-offs in hash coding with allowable errors. Commun. ACM **13**(7), 422–426 (1970)
13. Bi, F., Chang, L., Lin, X., Qin, L., Zhang, W.: Efficient subgraph matching by postponing cartesian products. In: SIGMOD Conference 2016, San Francisco, CA, USA, 26 June–01 July 2016, pp. 1199–1214 (2016)
14. Zou, L., Özsu, M.T., Chen, L., Shen, X., Huang, R., Zhao, D.: gstore: a graph-based SPARQL query engine. VLDB J. **23**(4), 565–590 (2014)
15. Zeng, L., Zou, L.: Redesign of the gstore system. Front. Comput. Sci. **12**(4), 623–641 (2018)
16. Abadi, D.J., Marcus, A., Madden, S., Hollenbach, K.: Sw-store: a vertically partitioned DBMS for semantic web data management. VLDB J. **18**(2), 385–406 (2009)
17. Neumann, T., Weikum, G.: x-RDF-3X: Fast querying, high update rates, and consistency for RDF databases. PVLDB **3**(1), 256–263 (2010)
18. Weiss, C., Karras, P., Bernstein, A.: Hexastore: sextuple indexing for semantic web data management. PVLDB **1**(1), 1008–1019 (2008)
19. Huang, J., Abadi, D.J., Ren, K.: Scalable SPARQL querying of large RDF graphs. PVLDB **4**(11), 1123–1134 (2011)
20. Udrea, O., Pugliese, A., Subrahmanian, V.S.: GRIN: a graph based RDF index. In: AAAI, 22–26 July 2007, Vancouver, British Columbia, Canada, pp. 1465–1470 (2007)
21. Lyu, X., Wang, X., Li, Y.-F., Feng, Z., Wang, J.: GraSS: an efficient method for RDF subgraph matching. In: Wang, J., et al. (eds.) WISE 2015. LNCS, vol. 9418, pp. 108–122. Springer, Cham (2015). https://doi.org/10.1007/978-3-319-26190-4_8
22. Carroll, J.J., Dickinson, I., Dollin, C., Reynolds, D., Seaborne, A., Wilkinson, K.: Jena: implementing the semantic web recommendations. In: WWW 2004, New York, USA, 17–20 May, pp. 74–83 (2004)
23. Broekstra, J., Kampman, A., van Harmelen, F.: Sesame: a generic architecture for storing and querying RDF and RDF schema. In: Horrocks, I., Hendler, J. (eds.) ISWC 2002. LNCS, vol. 2342, pp. 54–68. Springer, Heidelberg (2002). https://doi.org/10.1007/3-540-48005-6_7
24. Goasdoué, F., Manolescu, I., Roatis, A.: Efficient query answering against dynamic RDF databases. In: EDBT Genoa, Italy, 18–22 March, pp. 299–310 (2013)
25. Bursztyn, D., Goasdoué, F., Manolescu, I.: Optimizing reformulation-based query answering in RDF. In: EDBT 2015, Brussels, Belgium, 23–27 March, pp. 265–276 (2015)

Efficient Closest Community Search over Large Graphs

Mingshen Cai[1] and Lijun Chang[2(✉)]

[1] Canva, Sydney, Australia
sam.cai@canva.com
[2] The University of Sydney, Sydney, Australia
lijun.chang@sydney.edu.au

Abstract. This paper studies the closest community search problem. Given a graph G and a set of query vertices Q, the closest community of Q in G is the connected subgraph of G that contains Q, is most cohesive (*i.e.*, with the largest possible minimum vertex degree), is *closest* to Q, and is maximal. We show that this can be computed via a two-stage approach: (1) compute the maximal connected subgraph g_0 of G that contains Q and is most cohesive, and (2) iteratively remove from g_0 the vertex that is furthest to Q and subsequently also other vertices that violate the cohesiveness requirement. The last non-empty subgraph is the closest community of Q in G. We first propose baseline approaches for the two stages that run in $\mathcal{O}(n+m)$ and $\mathcal{O}(n_0 \times m_0)$ time, respectively, where n (resp. n_0) and m (resp. m_0) are the number of vertices and edges in G (resp. g_0). Then, we develop techniques to improve the time complexities of the two stages into $\mathcal{O}(n_0 + m_0)$ and $\mathcal{O}(m_0 + n_0 \log n_0)$, respectively. Moreover, we further design an algorithm CCS with the same time complexity as $\mathcal{O}(m_0 + n_0 \log n_0)$, but performs much better in practice. Extensive empirical studies demonstrate that CCS can efficiently compute the closest community over large graphs.

1 Introduction

The graph model has been widely used to capture the information of entities and their relationships, where entities are represented by vertices and relationships are represented by edges [13]. With the proliferation of graph data, research efforts have been devoted to managing, mining and querying large graphs. In this paper, we study the problem of community search for a given set of query vertices, where a community is a group of vertices that are densely connected to each other [7,9].

Traditionally, the problem of community detection has been extensively studied (*e.g.*, see the survey [7] and references therein), which aims to mine the community structures in a graph. Essentially, it partitions vertices of a graph into disjoint or overlapping groups such that each group represents one community. Community detection is a one-time task, and the result is the same set

---

The work was done while Mingshen Cai was with The University of Sydney.

© Springer Nature Switzerland AG 2020
Y. Nah et al. (Eds.): DASFAA 2020, LNCS 12113, pp. 569–587, 2020.
https://doi.org/10.1007/978-3-030-59416-9_34

of communities for different users and thus does not reflect users' personalized information. To remedy the non-personalization issue of community detection, there is a growing interest to search communities for user-given query vertices which facilitates a user-centric personalized search (*e.g.*, see the tutorial [9] and references therein). This querying problem is known as the *community search* problem. In principle the total number of distinct communities that are discoverable by community search can be much larger than n—the number of vertices in the data graph—and even may be exponential, while most of the community detection methods can only identify at most n distinct communities. As a result, community search has many applications [6,8,11], such as advertisements targeting, recommendation in online social networks, and metabolic network analysis.

Given a data graph $G = (V, E)$ and a set of one or more query vertices $Q \subset V$, the problem of community search aims to find a connected subgraph of G that contains all query vertices, and is (most) cohesive. In the literature, the cohesiveness of a subgraph is usually measured by its minimum vertex degree (aka *k-core*) [2,6,12,14], minimum number of triangles each edge participates in (aka *k-truss*) [10], or edge connectivity [3]. Among them, the minimum vertex degree-based cohesiveness measure is popularly used due to its simplicity and easy computability. However, there could be an exponential number of subgraphs of G that contain Q and have the same cohesiveness (*i.e.*, minimum vertex degree). In light of this, Cui et al. [6] reports an arbitrary one satisfying the requirements as the result, while Sozio and Gionis [14] introduces a distance threshold τ such that all vertices in the reported subgraph should be within distance τ from the query vertices. For the former, it is obviously not a good idea to report an arbitrary one since vertices in the result could be far away from the query vertices, while for the latter it may not be an easy task to specify an appropriate distance threshold τ.

In this paper, we formulate the *closest community search* problem. Specifically, the closest community of Q in G is the *connected* subgraph of G that *contains all query vertices*, *is most cohesive* (*i.e.*, with the largest possible minimum vertex degree), *is closest to Q*, and *is maximal*. Here, the closeness of a subgraph is measured by the largest value among the shortest distances between query vertices and other vertices in the subgraph. Compared to [6], closest community only includes vertices that are close and thus relevant to the query vertices Q. Compared to [14], closest community search does not require end-users to input a distance threshold τ, but automatically finds the subgraph that satisfies the smallest τ.

We show that the closest community of Q in G can be computed via a two-stage approach: (1) stage-I computes the maximal connected subgraph g_0 of G that contains Q and is most cohesive, and (2) stage-II iteratively removes from g_0 the vertex that is furthest to Q and subsequently also other vertices that violate the cohesiveness requirement due to the removal of their neighbors. Then, the last non-empty subgraph will be the closest community of Q in G. We first propose baseline approaches for the two stages that run in $\mathcal{O}(n + m)$ and $\mathcal{O}(n_0 \times m_0)$ time, respectively, where n (resp. n_0) and m (resp. m_0) are the number of vertices and edges in G (resp. g_0). Then, we develop techniques to improve the time complexities of the two stages into $\mathcal{O}(n_0 + m_0)$ and $\mathcal{O}(m_0 + n_0 \log n_0)$, respectively. As a result, we have the IndexedLO algorithm whose time complexity is $\mathcal{O}(m_0 + n_0 \log n_0)$; this is near-optimal in the worst case, since the closest community of Q could be g_0 itself whose size is $\mathcal{O}(n_0 + m_0)$. Nevertheless, in practice the closest community of Q could be much smaller than g_0, as it is expected that the closest community of Q usually contains only a few vertices that are close to Q. Thus, we further develop an algorithm CCS that has the same time complexity as IndexedLO but performs much better in practice. Our contributions are as follows.

- We formulate the closest community search problem (Sect. 2), and develop a Baseline approach (Sect. 4.1).
- We develop techniques to improve the time complexity and obtain the IndexedLO algorithm that runs in $\mathcal{O}(m_0 + n_0 \log n_0)$ time, which is near-optimal (Sect. 4.2).
- We design a CCS algorithm that has the same time complexity as IndexedLO but runs faster in practice (Sect. 4.3).
- We conduct extensive empirical studies to demonstrate the efficiency and effectiveness of our techniques (Sect. 5).

Proofs of all lemmas and theorems are omitted due to limit of space.

2   Preliminaries

For presentation simplicity, we focus our discussions on an undirected and unweighted graph $G = (V, E)$,[1] where V and E are the vertex set and edge set of G, respectively. We use n and m to denote the number of vertices and the number of edges of G, respectively. We denote the undirected edge between vertices u and v by (u, v). The set of neighbors of a vertex u is denoted by $N(u) = \{v \in V \mid (u, v) \in E\}$, and the degree of u is denoted by $deg(u) = |N(u)|$. A path between u and v is $(v_0, v_1, \ldots, v_l)$ such that $v_0 = u$, $v_l = v$ and $(v_{i-1}, v_i) \in E$ for $1 \leq i \leq l$; the length of the path is l. The distance between u and v, denoted $\delta(u, v)$, is defined as the shortest length among all paths between u and v.

Given a set $Q \subset V$ of query vertices, the **query distance** of a vertex $v \in V$ is the maximum value among the distances between v and vertices of Q, i.e., $\delta(Q, v) = \max_{u \in Q} \delta(u, v)$. For example, for the graph in Fig. 1 and $Q = \{q_1, q_2\}$, $\delta(Q, v_1) = 1$, $\delta(Q, v_3) = 2$, and $\delta(Q, v_7) = 3$. Then, the query distance of a subgraph containing Q is the maximum query distance of its vertices. For example, the query distance of the subgraph induced by vertices $\{q_1, q_2, v_1, v_2, \ldots, v_9\}$ is 3, the query distance of the subgraph induced by vertices $\{q_1, q_2, v_1, v_2, \ldots, v_6\}$ is 2, and the query distance of the subgraph induced by vertices $\{q_1, q_2, v_1, v_2\}$ is 1.

---

[1] The techniques we propose in this paper can be straightforwardly extended to directed graphs and weighted graphs.

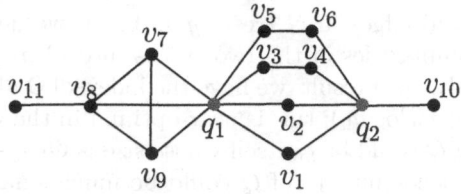

Fig. 1. An example graph

Given a set Q of query vertices, we aim to find the closest community of Q in G. Intuitively, (1) the community should be connected and contain all query vertices, (2) the community should be cohesive such that the vertices are tightly connected, and (3) the community should be close to the query vertices such that it is relevant to the query. In this paper, for presentation simplicity we adopt the minimum vertex degree to measure the cohesiveness of a subgraph, while our techniques can be easily extended to other cohesiveness measures such as trussness [10] or edge connectivity [3]. We formally define the closest community as follows.

Definition 1. *Given a graph $G = (V, E)$ and a set of query vertices $Q \subset V$, the* ***closest community*** *of Q in G is the* ***connected*** *subgraph g of G that contains Q and satisfies the following three conditions.*

1. ***Most Cohesive:*** *the minimum vertex degree of g is the largest among all connected subgraphs of G containing Q.*
2. ***Closest:*** *g has the smallest query distance among all subgraphs satisfying the above conditions.*
3. ***Maximal:*** *g is maximal.*

The closest community of $Q = \{q_1, q_2\}$ in Fig. 1 is the subgraph induced by $\{q_1, q_2, v_1, v_2\}$, where the minimum vertex degree is 2 and the query distance is 1.

Problem Statement. Given a graph $G = (V, E)$ and a set of query vertices $Q \subset V$, we study the problem of efficiently computing the closest community of Q in G.

We assume that the input graph G is connected, and a tie-breaker (*e.g.*, vertex ID, or personalized PageRank values [2]) is introduced such that all vertices have different query distances. In the running examples, we use vertex ID for tie breaking.

3   General Idea

The general idea of our approaches is based on the concept of (k, d)-community.

Definition 2. *Given a graph $G = (V, E)$, a set of query vertices $Q \subset V$, and integers k and d, the (k, d)-**community** of Q in G is the **connected** subgraph g of G that contains Q and satisfies the following three conditions:*

1. **Cohesive:** *the minimum vertex degree of g is at least k.*
2. **Close:** *the query distance of g is at most d.*
3. **Maximal:** *g is maximal.*

It is easy to see that the closest community of Q in G is the (k, d)-community of Q in G that exists and has the largest k and the smallest d. Note that, the (k, d)-community of Q (if exists) is unique. Moreover, the (k, d)-communities of Q for different k values and different d values form hierarchical structures. That is, for a fixed d, the (k_1, d)-community of Q is a subgraph of the (k_2, d)-community of Q if $k_1 > k_2$; for a fixed k, the (k, d_1)-community of Q is a subgraph of the (k, d_2)-community of Q if $d_1 < d_2$. Thus, we can compute the closest community of Q by a two-stage framework.

Algorithm 1: TwoStageFramework

---
1 $(k_Q, g_0) \leftarrow$ Stage-I(G, Q);
2 **return** Stage-II(g_0, Q, k_Q);

Stage-I. In the first stage, we compute the (k, ∞)-community of Q in G that has the largest k value. Denote this value of k as k_Q, and denote the (k_Q, ∞)-community of Q by g_0. Then, k_Q is the largest k value such that Q is in a connected component of the k-core of G, and g_0 is the connected component of the k_Q-core of G that contains Q. This is because, for any k, the (k, ∞)-community of Q is the connected component of the k-core that contains Q, where the k-*core* of a graph is the maximal subgraph g such that every vertex in g has at least k neighbors in g. Note that, the k-core is unique. For the graph in Fig. 1, the entire graph is a 1-core, the subgraph induced by vertices $\{q_1, q_2, v_1, v_2, \ldots, v_9\}$ is a 2-core, the subgraph induced by vertices $\{q_1, v_7, v_8, v_9\}$ is a 3-core, and there is no 4-core. Thus, for $Q = \{q_1, q_2\}$ in Fig. 1, $k_Q = 2$ and the (k_Q, ∞)-community of Q is the subgraph induced by vertices $\{q_1, q_2, v_1, v_2, \ldots, v_9\}$.

Stage-II. In the second stage, we compute the (k_Q, d)-community of Q that exists and has the smallest d value. As all vertices not in g_0 are guaranteed to be not in the (k_Q, d)-community of Q for any d, we can focus our computations on g_0. Thus, we iteratively reduce the graph g_0 to obtain the (k_Q, d)-community of Q with the next largest d value, and the final non-empty subgraph is the result. For example, the (k_Q, ∞)-community of $Q = \{q_1, q_2\}$ is the subgraph induced by vertices $\{q_1, q_2, v_1, v_2, \ldots, v_9\}$. The next (k_Q, d)-communities that will be discovered are the subgraphs induced by vertices $\{q_1, q_2, v_1, v_2, \ldots, v_8\}$, $\{q_1, q_2, v_1, v_2, \ldots, v_6\}$, $\{q_1, q_2, v_1, v_2, v_3, v_4\}$, and $\{q_1, q_2, v_1, v_2\}$, respectively, where the last one is the closest community of Q.

4 Our Approaches

We first propose a Baseline approach in Sect. 4.1, then improve its time complexity in Sect. 4.2, and finally improve its practical performance in Sect. 4.3.

4.1 A Baseline Approach

Baseline Stage-I: Baseline-S1. A naive approach for stage-I in Algorithm 1 would be iteratively computing the k-core of G for k values decreasing from n to 1, and stopping immediately if Q is contained in a connected component of the computed k-core. However, the worst-case time complexity will be quadratic to the input graph size, which is prohibitive for large graphs. To aim for a better time complexity, we propose to first compute the core number for all vertices, where the **core number** of a vertex u, denoted $\text{core}(u)$, is the largest k such that the k-core contains u. For the graph in Fig. 1, $\text{core}(q_1) = \text{core}(v_7) = \text{core}(v_8) = \text{core}(v_9) = 3$, $\text{core}(v_{10}) = \text{core}(v_{11}) = 1$, and the core numbers of all other vertices are 2. Note that, the core number for all vertices in G can be computed by the *peeling algorithm* in linear time [1]. Then, the k-core of G is the subgraph induced by vertices whose core numbers are at least k [4]. Thus, we can compute k_Q, the largest k value such that Q is in a connected component of the k-core of G, by conducting a prioritized search from an arbitrary vertex of Q. That is, we grow the connected component from an arbitrary vertex of Q, and each time we include, into the connected component, the vertex that has the largest core number among all vertices that are connected to (a vertex of) the connected component. Once the connected component contains all vertices of Q, the minimum core number among all vertices of the connected component then is k_Q. The pseudocode of our baseline approach for stage-I is shown in Algorithm 2, denoted Baseline-S1.

Example 1. Consider $Q = \{q_1, q_2\}$ and the graph in Fig. 1, and assume we conduct the prioritized search from q_1. The algorithm will first visit the vertices $\{q_1, v_7, v_8, v_9\}$ that have core numbers 3 and are connected to q_1. Then, the algorithm will visit a subset of the vertices $\{v_1, v_2, q_2, v_3, v_4, v_5, v_6\}$ that have core numbers 2. Thus, $k_Q = 2$, and the (k_Q, ∞)-community of Q is the subgraph induced by vertices $\{q_1, q_2, v_1, v_2, \ldots, v_9\}$.

The correctness of Baseline-S1 (Algorithm 2) can be verified from the definitions of k_Q and (k_Q, ∞)-community, and the property that the k-core of G is the subgraph induced by vertices whose core numbers are at least k. The time complexity of Baseline-S1 is proved by the theorem below.

Theorem 1. *The time complexity of* Baseline-S1 *is* $\mathcal{O}(n + m)$ *where n and m are the number of vertices and the number of edges of G, respectively.*

Baseline Stage-II: Baseline-S2. In the second stage, we aim to iteratively reduce the graph g_0, obtained from the first stage, to compute the (k_Q, d)-community of Q with the next largest d value. Intuitively, the vertex that is

---

Algorithm 2: Baseline-S1

Input: Graph $G = (V, E)$ and a set of query vertices $Q \subset V$
Output: k_Q and the (k_Q, ∞)-community of Q

1 Run the peeling algorithm of [1] to compute the core number for all vertices of G;
2 Initialize a priority queue $\mathcal{Q}$ to contain an arbitrary vertex of Q;
3 $k_Q \leftarrow n$;
4 **while** *not all vertices of Q have been visited* **do**
5      $u \leftarrow$ pop the vertex with the maximum core number from $\mathcal{Q}$;
6   Mark u as visited;
7   **if** $\text{core}(u) < k_Q$ **then** $k_Q \leftarrow \text{core}(u)$;
8   **for each** *neighbor $v \in N(u)$* **do**
9   **if** *v is not in $\mathcal{Q}$ and has not been visited* **then** Push v into $\mathcal{Q}$;

10 $g_0 \leftarrow$ the connected component of the k_Q-core of G that contains Q;
11 **return** (k_Q, g_0);

Algorithm 3: Baseline-S2

Input: A set of query vertices $Q \subset V$, an integer k_Q, and a graph g_0 that contains Q and has minimum vertex degree k_Q
Output: Closest community of Q

1 Compute the query distance for all vertices of g_0;
2 $i \leftarrow 0$;
3 **while true do**
4      $u \leftarrow$ the vertex in g_i with the largest query distance;
5      $g_{i+1} \leftarrow$ the connected component of the k_Q-core of $g_i \backslash \{u\}$ that contains Q;
6   **if** $g_{i+1} = \emptyset$ **then break** ;
7   **else** $i \leftarrow i + 1$;

8 **return** g_i;

---

furthest from the query vertices in g_0 will not be in the next (k_Q, d)-community; thus, we can remove this vertex from g_0 and then reduce the resulting graph to the connected component of the k_Q-core that contains Q. The final non-empty subgraph will be the closest community of Q.

The pseudocode of our baseline approach for stage-II is shown in Algorithm 3, denoted **Baseline-S2**. Line 1 computes the query distance for all vertices of g_0. Then, at Lines 4–5, we iteratively remove from g_i the vertex that is furtherest from the query vertices (*i.e.*, has the largest query distance), and compute the connected component g_{i+1} of the k_Q-core of the graph $g_i \backslash \{u\}$ that contains Q. If there is no such g_{i+1} (*i.e.*, $g_{i+1} = \emptyset$), then g_i is the closest community of Q and the algorithm terminates (Line 6). Otherwise, we increase i and continue the next iteration (Line 7).

Example 2. Continue Example 1. $k_Q = 2$ and g_0 is the subgraph induced by vertices $\{q_1, q_2, v_1, v_2, \ldots, v_9\}$. v_9 is the vertex that has the largest query distance in g_0. Then, g_1 is computed as the connected component of the k_Q-core of $g_0\backslash\{v_9\}$ that contains Q, which is the subgraph induced by vertices $\{q_1, q_2, v_1, v_2, \ldots, v_8\}$. v_8 is the vertex that has the largest query distance in g_1, and g_2 is computed as the subgraph induced by vertices $\{q_1, q_2, v_1, v_2, \ldots, v_6\}$. Similarly, g_3 is the subgraph induced by vertices $\{q_1, q_2, v_1, v_2, v_3, v_4\}$, and g_4 is the subgraph induced by vertices $\{q_1, q_2, v_1, v_2\}$. Now, v_2 is the vertex that has the largest query distance in g_4. After removing v_2 from g_4, the k_Q-core of $g_4\backslash\{v_2\}$ does not contain all vertices of Q. Thus, the algorithm terminates, and g_4 is the closest community of Q.

The correctness of Baseline-S2 (Algorithm 3) is straightforward. The time complexity of Baseline-S2 is proved by the theorem below.

Theorem 2. *The time complexity of* Baseline-S2 *is* $\mathcal{O}(n_0 \times m_0)$ *where* n_0 *and* m_0 *are the number of vertices and the number of edges of* g_0, *respectively.*

As a result, the total time complexity of Baseline that first runs Baseline-S1 and then runs Baseline-S2 is $\mathcal{O}(n + m + n_0 \times m_0)$. Note that, n_0 and m_0 in the worst case can be as large as n and m, respectively. Thus, the time complexity of Baseline is quadratic to the input graph size in the worst case.

4.2   Improving the Baseline Approach

The Baseline approach proposed in Sect. 4.1 is too slow to process large graphs due to its quadratic time complexity $\mathcal{O}(n + m + n_0 \times m_0)$. In this subsection, we propose techniques to improve the time complexity for the two stages of Baseline.

LinearOrder-S2: **Improving** Baseline-S2. As shown by our empirical studies in Sect. 5, Baseline-S2 takes more time than Baseline-S1 in Baseline. Thus, we first aim to reduce the time complexity of stage-II of Baseline, *i.e.*, Baseline-S2. The main cost of Baseline-S2 comes from Line 5 of Algorithm 3 that in each iteration computes the connected component of the k_Q-core of $g_i\backslash\{u\}$ that contains Q. To avoid this quadratic cost, we do not immediately search for the connected component of the k_Q-core that contains Q in each iteration. Instead, we separate the computation into two steps: step-1 builds the entire hierarchical structure for the (k_Q, d)-communities of Q for all different d values by ignoring the connectedness requirement, and step-2 searches for the connected (k_Q, d)-community of Q that has the smallest d value. This is based on the fact that the (k_Q, d_1)-community of Q is a subgraph of the (k_Q, d_2)-community of Q if $d_1 < d_2$.

To build the hierarchical structure for the (k_Q, d)-communities of Q for all different d values, we propose to compute a linear ordering for vertices of g_0; recall that g_0 is the (k_Q, ∞)-community of Q. Specifically, we encode the hierarchical structure by a linear ordering seq of vertices of g_0 and a subsequence targets of seq, such that *there is one-to-one correspondence between each (k_Q, d)-community for a different d value and each suffix of* seq *that starts* *from a vertex of* targets. Figure 2 shows such an example. Note that, to be more precise, we here refer to a variant of (k_Q, d)-community that does not necessarily to be connected, *i.e.*, we remove the connected requirement from Definition 2. To compute the linear ordering, we iteratively remove from g_0 the vertex that has the largest query distance (and add it to the end of seq and targets), and then subsequently remove from g_0 all vertices that violate the k_Q-core requirement (and add them to the end of seq).

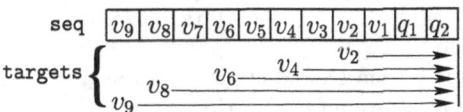

Fig. 2. Hierarchical structure of (k_Q, d)-communities for all different d values

Given seq and a vertex $u \in$ seq, let seq_u denote the suffix of seq that starts from u. Then, the closest community of Q will be the connected component, of the subgraph induced by seq_u, containing Q, where u is the right-most vertex of targets such that Q is connected in the subgraph induced by seq_u. For example, in Fig. 2, the closest community of $Q = \{q_1, q_2\}$ simply is the subgraph induced by $\text{seq}_{v_2} = \{v_2, v_1, q_1, q_2\}$. It is worth mentioning that, in general Q may be *disconnected* in the subgraph seq_v where v is the last vertex of targets. This is because we do not check the connectedness of Q during the computation of seq and targets for the sake of time complexity. To get the closest community of Q from seq and targets, we can use a disjoint-set data structure [5] to incrementally maintain the connected components of the subgraphs of g_0 induced by vertices of suffices of seq.

The pseudocode of our improved algorithm for stage-II is shown in Algorithm 4, denoted LinearOrder-S2. Lines 1–14 compute the hierarchical structure for the (k_Q, d)-communities of Q for all different d values, and Lines 15–21 find the closest community of Q from the hierarchical structure. Note that, in order to efficient check whether Q is entirely contained in a single set of the disjoint-set data structure $\mathcal{S}$ at Line 21, we maintain a counter for each set recording the number of Q's vertices that are in this set. The counter can be maintained in constant time after each union operation of Line 20, and Line 21 can be tested in constant time; we omit the details.

Example 3. Reconsider Example 2. $k_Q = 2$ and g_0 is the subgraph induced by vertices $\{q_1, q_2, v_1, v_2, \ldots, v_9\}$. Firstly, v_9 is the vertex with the largest query distance, so v_9 is removed from the graph and is appended to both seq and targets; no other vertices are removed as a result of the k_Q-core requirement. Secondly, v_8 is the vertex with the largest query distance, and it is removed from the graph and is appended to both seq and targets; subsequently, v_7 is also removed from the graph and is appended to seq due to the violation of the k_Q-core requirement. So on so forth. The final results are $\text{seq} = (v_9, v_8, v_7, v_6, v_5, v_4, v_3, v_2, v_1, q_1, q_2)$

Algorithm 4: LinearOrder-S2

/* Compute the hierarchical structure for the (k_Q, d)-communities */
1 Compute the query distance for all vertices of g_0;
2 Sort vertices of g_0 in decreasing order with respect to their query distances;
3 seq $\leftarrow \emptyset$; targets $\leftarrow \emptyset$;
4 $g' \leftarrow g_0$; $deg(u) \leftarrow$ the degree of u in g' for all vertices $u \in g'$;
5 **while** g' *is not empty* **do**
6    $u \leftarrow$ the vertex in g' with the largest query distance;
7   **if** $Q \cap$ seq $= \emptyset$ **then** Append u to targets;
8    $Q \leftarrow \{u\}$;   /* Q is a queue */;
9   **while** $Q \neq \emptyset$ **do**
10   Pop a vertex v from Q, and append v to seq;
11   **for each** *neighbor w of v in g'* **do**
12        $deg(w) \leftarrow deg(w) - 1$;
13   **if** $deg(w) = k_Q - 1$ **then** Push w into Q ;
14   Remove v from g';

/* Search for the closest community of Q */
15 Initialize an empty disjoint-set data structure $\mathcal{S}$;
16 **for each** *vertex $u \in$ targets in the reverse order* **do**
17   **for each** *vertex $v \in$ seq between u (inclusive) and the next target vertex (exclusive)* **do**
18   Add a singleton set for v into $\mathcal{S}$;
19   **for each** *neighbor w of v in g_0* **do**
20   **if** $w \in \mathcal{S}$ **then** Union v and w in $\mathcal{S}$;
21   **if** Q *is entirely contained in a single set of* $\mathcal{S}$ **then break** ;
22 **return** all vertices in the set of $\mathcal{S}$ that contains Q;

---

and targets $= (v_9, v_8, v_6, v_4, v_2)$ as shown in Fig. 2. As the subgraph induced by $\text{seq}_{v_2} = \{v_2, v_1, q_1, q_2\}$ is connected and contains both q_1 and q_2, the closest community of $Q = \{q_1, q_2\}$ is the subgraph induced by vertices seq_{v_2}.

Theorem 3. *The time complexity of* LinearOrder-S2 *is* $\mathcal{O}(m_0 + n_0 \log n_0)$.

Indexed-S1: Improving Baseline-S1. By improving Baseline-S2 to LinearOrder-S2 which has a time complexity of $\mathcal{O}(m_0 + n_0 \log n_0)$, stage-I (*i.e.*, Baseline-S1), which processes the entire input graph and takes $\mathcal{O}(n + m)$ time, now becomes the bottleneck. Thus, in the following we propose to utilize an index structure to improve Baseline-S1.

    Baseline-S1 computes two things: k_Q and g_0 where g_0 is the connected component of the k_Q-core of G that contains Q. We first discuss how to efficiently get g_0 from G based on an index structure if k_Q is known. Recall that, for any k, the k-core of G is the subgraph induced by vertices whose core number are at least k. Thus, *in the index structure, we precompute and store the core number for all vertices of G, and moreover we sort the neighbors of each vertex in* *the graph representation in decreasing order with respect to their core numbers.* Thus, to search for g_0, we can conduct a pruned breath-first search which starts from an arbitrary vertex of Q and visits only vertices whose core numbers are at least k_Q. It can be verified that, the vertices and edges visited during the pruned breath-first search form the g_0.

Secondly, to efficiently compute k_Q, we further maintain a maximum spanning tree of the edge-weighted graph of G where the weight of edge (u, v) equals $\max\{\mathtt{core}(u), \mathtt{core}(v)\}$. For example, the weighted graph and the maximum spanning tree for the graph in Fig. 1 are shown in Fig. 3(a) and Fig. 3(b), respectively. It can be verified by a similar argument as in [3] that k_Q equals the minimum weight among all edges in the paths between q_1 and q_i for $2 \leq i \leq |Q|$ in the maximum spanning tree, where $Q = \{q_1, q_2, \ldots, q_{|Q|}\}$. For example, the path between q_1 and q_2 in Fig. 3(b) is (q_1, v_3, v_4, q_2) and $k_{\{q_1,q_2\}} = 2$. Note that, by further processing the maximum spanning tree using the techniques in [3], k_Q can be computed in $\mathcal{O}(|Q|)$ time; we omit the details.

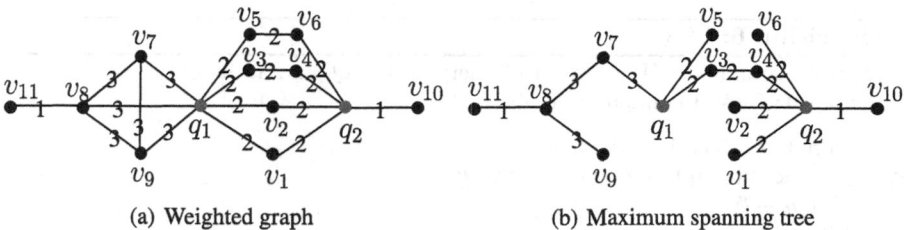

(a) Weighted graph   (b) Maximum spanning tree

Fig. 3. Weighted graph and maximum spanning tree

Algorithm 5: Indexed-S1

---
1 Compute k_Q based on the index $\mathcal{I}$;
2 Conduct a pruned breadth-first search on G by starting from an arbitrary
   vertex of Q and visiting only vertices whose core numbers are at least k_Q;
3 $g_0 \leftarrow$ the subgraph of G induced by vertices visited at Line 2;
4 **return** (k_Q, g_0);

The pseudocode of our index-based algorithm for stage-I is shown in Algorithm 5, which is self-explanatory.

Theorem 4. *The time complexity of* Indexed-S1 *is* $\mathcal{O}(n_0 + m_0)$.

By invoking Indexed-S1 for stage-I and LinearOrder-S2 for stage-II, we get an algorithm that computes the closest community of Q in $\mathcal{O}(m_0 + n_0 \log n_0)$ time; denote this algorithm as IndexedLO.

4.3   The CCS Approach

The time complexity of IndexedLO is near-optimal in the worst case, because the closest community of Q could be g_0 itself whose size is $\mathcal{O}(n_0 + m_0)$. Nevertheless, the closest community of Q could be much smaller than g_0 in practice, as it is expected that the closest community of Q usually contains only a few vertices that are close to Q. Motivated by this, in this section we propose a CCS approach to improve the performance of IndexedLO in practice. The general idea of CCS follows the framework of [2]. That is, instead of first computing g_0—the connected component of the k_Q-core of G that contains Q—and then shrinking g_0 to obtain the closest community of Q as shown in Algorithm 1, we start from working on a small subgraph containing Q and then progressively expand it by including next few further away vertices. As the vertices are added to the working subgraph in increasing order according their query distances, once the working subgraph has a connected k_Q-core that contain all vertices of Q, the closest community of Q can be computed from the working subgraph by invoking LinearOrder-S2.

Algorithm 6: CCS

Input: Graph $G = (V, E)$, a set of query vertex Q, and an index $\mathcal{I}$
Output: Closest community of Q

1 Compute k_Q based on the index $\mathcal{I}$;
2 $h_0 \leftarrow$ the subgraph of G induced by Q;
3 $i \leftarrow 0$; $g \leftarrow \emptyset$;
4 **while true do**
5 $\quad$ $g' \leftarrow$ the connected component of the k_Q-core of h_i that contains Q;
6 $\quad$ $g \leftarrow$ LinearOrder-S2(Q, k_Q, g');
7 $\quad$ **if** $g = \emptyset$ **then**
8 $\quad\quad$ $i \leftarrow i + 1$; $h_i \leftarrow h_{i-1}$;
9 $\quad\quad$ **while** $h_i \neq G$ **and** *the size of h_i is less than twice of h_{i-1}* **do**
10 $\quad\quad\quad$ Get the next vertex u that has the smallest query distance;
11 $\quad\quad\quad$ Add to h_i the vertex u and its adjacent edges to existing vertices of h_i;
12 $\quad$ **else break**;
13 **return** g;

The pseudocode of CCS is shown in Algorithm 6. We first compute k_Q based on the index $\mathcal{I}$ (Line 1), and initialize the working subgraph h_0 to be the subgraph of G induced by Q (Line 2). Then, we go to iterations (Lines 5–12). In each iteration, we try to compute the closest community of Q in h_i by invoking LinearOrder-S2 on the connected component of the k_Q-core of h_i that contains Q (Lines 5–6). Let g be the result. If g is not empty, then it is guaranteed to be the closest community of Q in G (Line 12). Otherwise, the current working subgraph h_i does not include all vertices of the closest community of Q, and we need to grow the working subgraph (Lines 8–11). To grow the working subgraph, we (1) include vertices in increasing order according to their query distances, and (2) grow the working subgraph exponentially at a rate of two. Here, the size of a graph is measured by the summation of its number of vertices and its number of edges. We will prove shortly that the time complexity of this strategy will be $\mathcal{O}(m_0 + n_0 \log n_0)$ in the worst case. Note that, if we grow the working subgraph at the rate of adding one vertex, then it is easy to see that the time complexity would be quadratic (*i.e.*, $\mathcal{O}(n_0 \times m_0)$).

Example 4. Reconsider $Q = \{q_1, q_2\}$ and the graph in Fig. 1, and recall that the vertices in increasing query distance order are $q_1, q_2, v_1, v_2, \ldots, v_{11}$. $k_Q = 2$. The initial working subgraph h_0 consists of vertices q_1 and q_2 and is of size 2, as shown in Fig. 4. The second working subgraph h_1 is of size 5, as shown in Fig. 4. h_1 does not have a 2-core, and we continue growing the working subgraph. The third working subgraph h_2 is the subgraph induced by vertices $\{q_1, q_2, v_1, v_2, v_3\}$, and g is computed as the subgraph induced vertices $\{q_1, q_2, v_1, v_2\}$ which is the closest community of Q. Thus, the algorithm terminates and reports g as the closest community of Q.

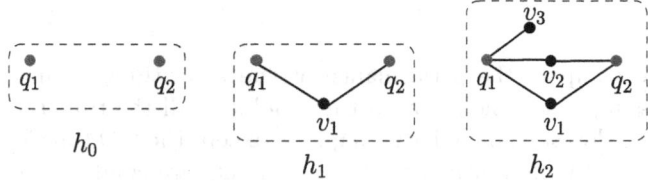

Fig. 4. Running example of CCS

Although CCS may need to process many subgraphs of g_0, we prove in the theorem below that its worst-case time complexity is $\mathcal{O}(m_0 + n_0 \log n_0)$.

Theorem 5. *The worst-case time complexity of* CCS *is* $\mathcal{O}(m_0 + n_0 \log n_0)$.

5 Experiments

In this section, we conduct extensive empirical studies to evaluate the performance of our algorithms on real-world graphs. We evaluate the following four algorithms.

- Baseline, which invokes Baseline-S1 (Algorithm 2) for stage-I and Baseline-S2 (Algorithm 3) for stage-II.
- LinearOrder, which invokes Baseline-S1 (Algorithm 2) for stage-I and LinearOrder-S2 (Algorithm 4) for stage-II.

- IndexedLO, which invokes Indexed-S1 (Algorithm 5) for stage-I and LinearOrder-S2 (Algorithm 4) for stage-II.
- CCS (Algorithm 6).

All the algorithms are implemented in C++.

Datasets. We use six real graphs that are downloaded from the Stanford Network Analysis Platform[2] in our evaluation. Statics of these graphs are shown in Table 1, where $core_{max}$ denotes the maximum core number among vertices in a graph.

Table 1. Statistics of real graphs

Graphs	n	m	$core_{max}$
Email	36,692	183,831	43
Amazon	334,863	925,872	6
DBLP	317,080	1,049,866	113
Youtube	1,134,890	2,987,624	51
LiveJournal	3,997,962	34,681,189	360
Orkut	3,072,441	117,185,083	253

Setting. We compare the performance of the algorithms by measuring their query processing time. The reported time includes all the time that is spent in computing the closest community for a query, except the I/O time for reading the graph from disk to main memory. All experiments are conducted on a machine with 2.9 GHz Intel Core i7 CPU and 16 GB main memory.

5.1   Experimental Results

In this testing, the query vertices for a graph are randomly selected from its 5-core. The total running time of the four algorithms on the six graphs is shown in Fig. 5. We can see that the algorithms in sorted order from slowest to fastest are Baseline, LinearOrder, IndexedLO, and CCS. This results align with our theoretical analysis. That is, the time complexities of these four algorithms are $\mathcal{O}(n + m + n_0 \times m_0)$, $\mathcal{O}(n + m + m_0 + n_0 \log n_0)$, $\mathcal{O}(m_0 + n_0 \log n_0)$, and $\mathcal{O}(m_0 + n_0 \log n_0)$, respectively, where n_0 usually is much smaller than n, and m_0 usually is much smaller than m. Baseline cannot finish with 10 min, except for the two small graphs Email and Amazon. The improvement of CCS over LinearOrder is up-to 607 times. The improvement of CCS over IndexedLO is up-to 148 times, despite having the same worst-case time complexity.

   To get a more detailed analysis of the algorithms, we separate the total running time into the running time of stage-I and the running time of stage-II, for each algorithm. The results are shown in Table 2. Recall that the algorithm for

---

[2] http://snap.stanford.edu/.

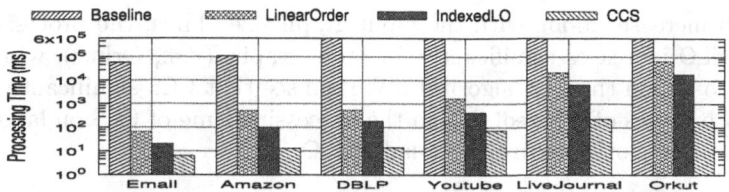

Fig. 5. Total running time of the algorithms (ms)

stage-I of LinearOrder is the same as that of Baseline, and the algorithm for stage-II of IndexedLO is the same as that of LinearOrder. We can see that Indexed-S1 (used in stage-I of IndexedLO) significantly improves upon Baseline-S1 (used in stage-I of Baseline and LinearOrder) as a result of the index-based approach, and the improvement is more than one order of magnitude. Regarding stage-II, we can see that LinearOrder-S2 (used in LinearOrder and IndexedLO) significantly improves upon Baseline-S2 (used in Baseline) due to the improved time complexity from quadratic (specifically, $\mathcal{O}(n_0 \times m_0)$) to near-linear (specifically, $\mathcal{O}(m_0 + n_0 \log n_0)$).

Table 2. Stage-I and stage-II time of the algorithms (ms)

Graphs	Baseline		LinearOrder		IndexedLO		CCS
	Stage-I	Stage-II	Stage-I	Stage-II	Stage-I	Stage-II	Total
Email	56.01	56,322	56.10	12.66	7.48	12.22	6.31
Amazon	445.14	104,581	445.03	68.52	35.89	68.24	12.85
DBLP	493.02	>10 min	493.95	120.84	59.5	120.77	14.00
Youtube	1,385	>10 min	1,385	291	128.49	291	74.07
LiveJournal	19,343	>10 min	19,343	4,178	2374.39	4,178	226.74
Orkut	58,815	>10 min	58,815	13,620	4295.06	13,620	176.63

Now, let's compare the two stages within each algorithm. We can see that for Baseline, stage-II (Baseline-S2 with time complexity $\mathcal{O}(n_0 \times m_0)$) dominates stage-I (Baseline-S1 with time complexity $\mathcal{O}(n + m)$) due to the quadratic time complexity of stage-II, and stage-II takes more than 10 min for graphs DBLP, Youtube, LiveJournal, and Orkut. This motivates us to improve Baseline-S2 to LinearOrder-S2 that runs in $\mathcal{O}(m_0 + n_0 \log n_0)$ time, which leads to our second algorithm LinearOrder. Due to the improved time complexity of LinearOrder-S2, we can see that stage-I of LinearOrder (*i.e.*, Baseline-S1) now dominates due to processing the entire input graph. This motivates us to utilize an index structure that is built offline to improve the online query processing time, which results in our third algorithm IndexedLO that has a time complexity of $\mathcal{O}(m_0 + n_0 \log n_0)$. The time complexity of IndexedLO is near-linear to the size of the initial graph

g_0, which increases along with the input graph size. Thus, the processing time of IndexedLO increases significantly for large graphs (*e.g.*, Orkut), which motivates us to design the CCS algorithm. We can see that CCS significantly outperforms both stages of IndexedLO, and the processing time of CCS on large graphs increases much slower than that of IndexedLO.

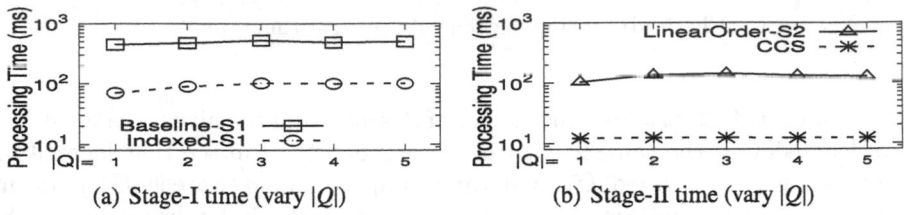

(a) Stage-I time (vary $|Q|$)   (b) Stage-II time (vary $|Q|$)

Fig. 6. DBLP with distance 1 among query vertices

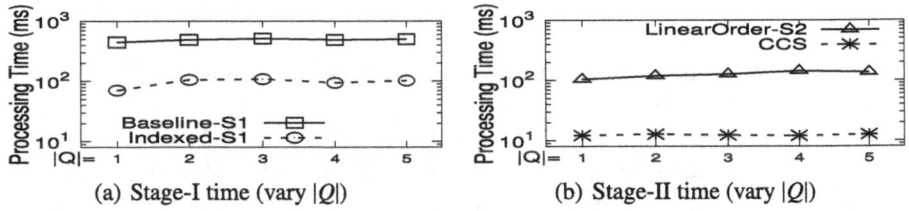

(a) Stage-I time (vary $|Q|$)   (b) Stage-II time (vary $|Q|$)

Fig. 7. DBLP with distance 2 among query vertices

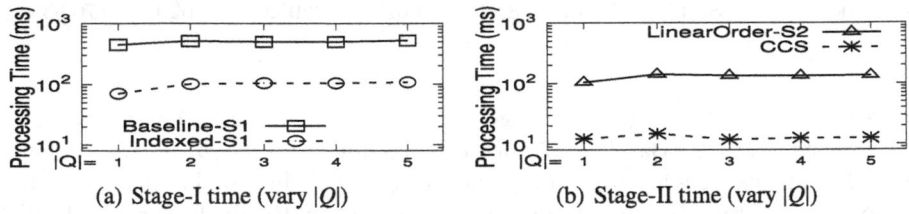

(a) Stage-I time (vary $|Q|$)   (b) Stage-II time (vary $|Q|$)

Fig. 8. DBLP with distance 3 among query vertices

Vary Query Size. In this testing, we evaluate the impact of the number of query vertices on the performance of the algorithms. In particular, we separately consider the algorithms for stage-I and for stage-II. For stage-I, we compare Indexed-S1 with Baseline-S1, and for stage-II, we compare CCS with

LinearOrder-S2. Note that, (1) we do not include Baseline-S2 because it is too slow as shown in Table 2, and (2) we compare CCS with LinearOrder-S2 although the reported time of CCS is its total processing time. We vary the number of query vertices $|Q|$ from 1 to 5. For each query size, we generate three sets of queries such that the distances among the query vertices are 1, 2, and 3, respectively. The results on DBLP are shown in Fig. 6, Fig. 7 and Fig. 8. We can see that the processing time for both stages increases slightly when the number of query vertices increases. Nevertheless, this is not significant, and CCS still significantly outperforms the other algorithms.

Case Study. We conduct a case study for the closest community search on the DBLP coauthor graph, which is built based on the dataset *BigDND: Big Dynamic Network Data*[3] extracted from DBLP. The dataset includes all author publication information stored in DBLP up-to October 2014. In our coauthor graph, each vertex represents one author, and there is an edge between u and v if they have published at least 3 papers together. The final coauthor graph has $367,202$ vertices and $821,205$ edges.

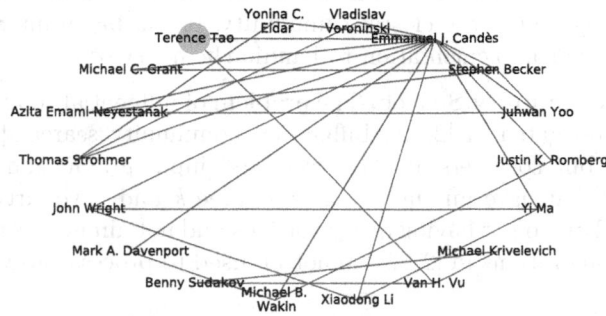

Fig. 9. Closest community search for "Terence Tao"

In the case study, we search for the closest community of "Terence Tao", an Australian-American mathematician who is one of the Fields Medal recipient in 2006. The result is shown in Fig. 9, which has 18 authors. Terence Tao has published more than 3 papers together with Van H. Vu and Emmanuel J. Candes. The most cited paper of Tao's is *Robust uncertainty principles: exact signal reconstruction from highly incomplete frequency information*, which is a collaborated work with Emmanuel J. Candes and Justin Romberg. Emmanuel J. Candes also has over 80 papers recorded in our dataset, so there are a lot of scholars that coauthor with him as well, as shown in Fig. 9, there are 13 nodes that represent his coauthors.

---

[3] http://projects.csail.mit.edu/dnd/.

6   Related Works

Community Search. Given a set of one or more query vertices Q, community search aims to find cohesive subgraphs that contain Q. In the literature, the cohesiveness of a subgraph is usually measured by minimum degree (aka k-core) [6,14], minimum number of triangles each edge participates in (aka k-truss) [10], or edge connectivity [3]. In this paper, we use the minimum degree-based cohesiveness measure in our closest community search problem. The technique of [6] cannot be used for closest community search as it inherently ignores the distance between vertices. Although the technique of [14] can be extended to compute the closest community which corresponds to our Baseline approach, it is infeasible for large graphs as shown by our experiments. On the other hand, the closest community search problem is recently studied in [10] which uses the trussness-based cohesiveness measure, the general idea of the algorithm in [10] is similar to our combination of Indexed-S1 and Baseline-S2. We have shown that Baseline-S2 cannot process large graphs due to its quadratic time complexity. In order to process large graphs, heuristic techniques (such as bulk deletion and local exploration) are used in [10] which destroys the *exactness*; that is, the computed result may be not the closest community. It will be an interesting future work to extend our implementation to handle the query of [10].

Influential Community Search. The problem of influential community search is recently investigated in [2,12]. Influential community search does not have query vertices but considers a vertex-weighted input graph, and aims to find top subgraphs that have minimum vertex degree k and have largest minimum vertex weight. Due to not having query vertices and not aiming for most cohesive subgraph, the algorithms in [2,12] cannot be used to process closest community search queries.

7   Conclusion

In this paper, we formulated the closest community search problem based on the minimum degree-based cohesiveness measure. We firstly developed a Baseline algorithm, and then progressively improved it to IndexedLO, and CCS. We theoretically analyzed their time complexities, and conducted extensive empirical studies to evaluate the efficiency and effectiveness of the algorithms.

References

1. Batagelj, V., Zaversnik, M.: An o(m) algorithm for cores decomposition of networks. CoRR cs.DS/0310049 (2003)
2. Bi, F., Chang, L., Lin, X., Zhang, W.: An optimal and progressive approach to online search of top-k influential communities. PVLDB **11**(9), 1056–1068 (2018)
3. Chang, L., Lin, X., Qin, L., Yu, J.X., Zhang, W.: Index-based optimal algorithms for computing steiner components with maximum connectivity. In: Proceedings of SIGMOD 2015 (2015)

4. Chang, L., Qin, L.: Cohesive Subgraph Computation over Large Sparse Graphs. SSDS. Springer, Cham (2018). https://doi.org/10.1007/978-3-030-03599-0
5. Cormen, T.H., Leiserson, C.E., Rivest, R.L., Stein, C.: Introduction to Algorithms, 3rd edn. The MIT Press, Cambridge (2009)
6. Cui, W., Xiao, Y., Wang, H., Wang, W.: Local search of communities in large graphs. In: Proceedings of SIGMOD 2014, pp. 991–1002 (2014)
7. Fortunato, S.: Community detection in graphs. Phys. Rep. **486**(3–5), 75–174 (2010)
8. Guimerà, R., Nunes Amaral, L.A.: Functional cartography of complex metabolic networks. Nature **433**(7028), 895–900 (2005)
9. Huang, X., Lakshmanan, L.V.S., Xu, J.: Community search over big graphs: models, algorithms, and opportunities. In: Proceedings of ICDE 2017, pp. 1451–1454 (2017)
10. Huang, X., Lakshmanan, L.V.S., Yu, J.X., Cheng, H.: Approximate closest community search in networks. Proc. VLDB Endow. **9**(4), 276–287 (2015)
11. Li, J., Wang, X., Deng, K., Yang, X., Sellis, T., Yu, J.X.: Most influential community search over large social networks. In: Proceedings of ICDE 2017, pp. 871–882 (2017)
12. Li, R.H., Qin, L., Yu, J.X., Mao, R.: Influential community search in large networks. Proc. VLDB Endow. **8**(5), 509–520 (2015)
13. Robinson, I., Webber, J., Eifrem, E.: Graph Databases. O'Reilly Media Inc., Sebastopol (2013)
14. Sozio, M., Gionis, A.: The community-search problem and how to plan a successful cocktail party. In: Proceedings of KDD 2010, p. 939 (2010)

PDKE: An Efficient Distributed Embedding Framework for Large Knowledge Graphs

Sicong Dong[1], Xin Wang[1,2]([✉]), Lele Chai[1], Jianxin Li[3], and Yajun Yang[1,2]

[1] College of Intelligence and Computing, Tianjin University, Tianjin, China
[2] Tianjin Key Laboratory of Cognitive Computing and Application, Tianjin, China
{sicongdong,wangx,lelechai,yjyang}@tju.edu.cn
[3] School of Information Technology, Deakin University, Melbourne, Australia
jianxin.li@deakin.edu.au

Abstract. Knowledge Representation Learning (KRL) methods produce unsupervised node features from knowledge graphs that can be used for a variety of machine learning tasks. However, two main issues in KRL embedding techniques have not been addressed yet. One is that real-world knowledge graphs contain millions of nodes and billions of edges, which exceeds the capability of existing KRL embedding systems; the other issue is the lack of a unified framework to integrate the current KRL models to facilitate the realization of embeddings for various applications. To address the issues, we propose PDKE, which is a distributed KRL training framework that can incorporate different translation-based KRL models using a unified algorithm template. In PDKE, a set of functions is implemented by various knowledge embedding models to form a unified algorithm template for distributed KRL. PDKE implements training arbitrarily large embeddings in a distributed environment. The effeciency and scalability of our framework have been verified by extensive experiments on both synthetic and real-world knowledge graphs, which shows that our approach outperforms the existing ones by a large margin.

Keywords: Knowledge Representation Learning · Knowledge Graphs · Distributed framework · Knowledge embedding

1 Introduction

With the proliferation of Knowledge Graphs (KG), the applications of knowledge graphs have a rapid growth in recent years. In fact, a KG is a type of large-scale Semantic Web [1], which is constructed to represent millions of objects and billions of relations in the real world, such as Freebase [2], DBpedia [9], and YAGO [19]. In the Semantic Web community, the *Resource Description Framework* (RDF) has been widely recognized as a flexible graph-like data model to represent large-scale KGs. An RDF triple is represented as (h, r, t), where h

© Springer Nature Switzerland AG 2020
Y. Nah et al. (Eds.): DASFAA 2020, LNCS 12113, pp. 588–603, 2020.
https://doi.org/10.1007/978-3-030-59416-9_35

is the head entity, t the tail entity, and r the relation connecting the head and tail. A triple indicates an existing fact that two entities are connected by the relation. Take $(Cameron, directs, Titanic)$ as an example, the statement claims a fact that the director $Cameron$ directs the movie $Titanic$. Although a set of triples is effective in representing graph-structured data, KGs' inherent graph nature may incur high complexity when they are involved in most learning tasks.

To tackle this issue, a new research direction called Knowledge Representation Learning (KRL) is proposed. The key idea is to embed the components of a KG containing entities and relations into a continuous vector space in order to simplify operations while retaining the inherent structure of the KG. The relations of triples are represented as various types of operators between vectors of head and tail entities, which can be further used for various machine learning tasks, such as knowledge graph completion [3], relation extraction [18], entity visualization [5], and entity classification [17].

Among the existing KRL models, translation-based models, such as TransE [3], TransH [21], and TransR [13], have exhibited high accuracy on benchmark datasets (e.g., FB15K and WN18). However, the following issues are largely ignored in previous works: (1) the scalability is not yet considered in the existing models, which mainly focus on the synthetic benchmark datasets instead of real-world large-scale KGs; (2) there is a lack of a unified algorithm framework that can incorporate at least a set of models in the same category (e.g., translation-based) to facilitate applications of these models.

To this end, we propose a novel PyTorch-based Distributed Knowledge Embedding (PDKE) framework[1] to uniformly train the translation-based models. PDKE uses a partitioning scheme, which is proposed in [11], to support models that are too large to fit in memory on a single machine. Therefore, the PDKE framework supports distributed training, in which all computing sites participate the training process in parallel without performing synchronization. In PDKE, an efficient negative sampling technique is adopted, which can uniformly sample entities from data and reuse negative examples in batch processing to reduce memory consumption. PDKE realizes a unified algorithm framework, which can incorporate translation-based KRL models. We have conducted extensive experiments for the PDKE framework on both synthetic and real-world KGs. The experimental results show that our framework is comparable to the baselines in accuracy. Meanwhile, the PDKE framework can smoothly perform training on real-world KGs, which shows that our framework is scalable when dealing with large KGs. Our contributions in this paper can be summarized as follows:

(1) We propose a PyTorch-based Distributed Knowledge Embedding framework, which uses entity and relation partitioning to support distributed training in order to achieve the scalability for large KGs.
(2) PDKE realizes a unified algorithm framework that can incorporate translation-based models to facilitate applications of these models. KRL models can be implemented through the API interface provided by PDKE.

---

[1] https://github.com/RweBs/PDKE.

(3) Extensive experiments have been conducted to verify the efficiency and scalability of the proposed framework on both synthetic and real-world KGs. The results show that the PDKE framework can significantly improve training efficiency and reduce memory consumption without reducing accuracy.

The rest of this paper is organized as follows. Section 2 reviews related works. In Sect. 3, we introduce preliminaries for the distributed embedding framework. In Sect. 4, we describe in detail the proposed algorithms for learning embeddings of entities and relations in knowledge graphs. Section 5 shows the experimental results, and we conclude in Sect. 6.

2   Related Work

Recent years have witnessed great advances in Knowledge Graph Embedding (KGE) techniques, which can be classified into the following categories: (1) traditional KRL models [3,8,13,21]; (2) the unified training framework [7,10,11,13]. Currently, the capability of existing unified framework is limited, which is only able to incorporate a few KRL models (i.e., TransE [3], TransH [21], TransR [13], and TransD [8]) and perform training on small benchmark datasets.

2.1   Traditional KRL Models

Existing facts stored in knowledge graphs are exploited for training by most currently available KRL models, which can be classified into two categories: translation-based models and semantic matching models.

(1) Translation-based models. TransE [3] is the initial work in this category, which is extended by a series of following works, e.g., TransH [21], TransR [13], and TransD [8]. TransE represents entities and relations as vectors in the same space. TransH embeds entities and relations into different hyperplanes, and thus solves the problem of different types of entity vectors with similar distances during the multi-relation embedding process, which cannot be solved in TransE. In TransR, an entity usually has more than one property at the same time, and different relations focus on various properties of the entity. However, the high complexity of TransR has become its main drawback. TransD uses projection vectors to replace the projection matrix in TransR, which significantly reduces time complexity while achieving the same effect as TransR.

(2) Semantic matching models. Related works on the semantic matching model includes RESCAL [16], DistMult [22], HolE [15], ComplEx [20], etc. RESCAL associates each entity with a vector to capture its latent semantics, and represents each relation as a matrix that models the pairwise interactions between factors. DistMult restricts the matrices mentioned in RESCAL to diagonal matrices to simplify the model, which causes DistMult to handle only symmetric relations. HolE represents all entities and relations

as vectors in a vector space, which allows it to have both the expressive power of RESCAL and the simplicity of DistMult. ComplEx extends DistMult by introducing complex-valued embeddings, which allows it to better model asymmetric relations.

2.2 The Unified Training Framework

The existing unified training frameworks generally perform single-process training on one machine, which requires a relatively long training time. To address the low efficiency of the single-process training, the Parameter Server (PS) [12] distributed architecture is proposed to implement parallel training, which uses parameter server to store model parameters and clients for processing training data. Multiple clients perform training in parallel and communicate asynchronously with the server, which improves training efficiency. With reasonable scheduling, the PS architecture can avoid conflicts during parallel training. Based on the PS architecture, a series of unified training frameworks are constructed, which can be classified as follows:

(1) Standalone KRL framework. KB2E [13] is a graph embedding toolkit that integrates the unified implementation of various KRL models. However, KB2E cannot perform distributed training, which makes it difficult to satisfy the requirements of large-scale KGs. In the OpenKE [7] framework, GPU acceleration and parallelization mechanisms are applied to the whole training procedure, which can speed up the training process. Nevertheless, the parallelization mechanism is actually executed on a single machine, not on a distributed cluster, thus OpenKE still does not support embedding for large-scale KGs.

(2) Distributed KRL framework. SANSA [10] is an open-source distributed stack for computation over large-scale KGs. SANSA provides efficient scalability, fault tolerance, and wide interfaces to execute various applications for users. In SANSA, the distributed machine learning layer is built on top of the architecture and implements TransE, which is the most basic translation-based KRL model. Nevertheless, the accuracy of the TransE in SANSA is quite low since the embedding module of SANSA is still in the alpha development phase and has bugs in the distributed updating process of the training model. PBG is a large-scale graph embedding system, which consists of distributed execution models based on block decomposition and a negative sampling strategy for distributed workers. Unlike previous works, our PDKE framework is a unified algorithm framework that can incorporate all translation-based KRL models.

More recently, DKRL proposed in [4] is a distributed representation learning algorithm based on Spark [23]. DKRL incorporates different translation-based KRL models and are able to train them in parallel, which is most similar work to ours. However, our PDKE framework is based on the Parameter-Server architecture and implemented on the PyTorch distributed learning library, which enables

PDKE to handle larger KGs than DKRL. Furthermore, PDKE leverages entity and edge partitioning to avoid conflicts in the update process to solve the problem in SANSA. We also devise an efficient negative sampling technique in PDKE, which can sample negative triples uniformly from the data and reuse the negative examples in batch processing to reduce memory consumption.

3   Preliminaries

In this section, we introduce the definitions of relevant background knowledge.

Definition 1 (Knowledge Graph). *Knowledge graph is denoted as $G = (V, R, T)$, where V and R are the entity set and relation set, respectively, $T = \{(h, r, t)\} \subseteq V \times R \times V$ is the set of triples.*

Inspired by the graph partitioning method in [11], we introduce an entity and edge partitioning strategy on knowledge graphs.

Definition 2 (Entity Partition). *Entity Partition $P = \{p_1, p_2, ..., p_n\} (1 \leq n \leq |V|)$ is a subset of $\mathscr{P}(V)$, where V is entity set and $\mathscr{P}(V)$ is the power set of V. P satisfies the following conditions: (1) $\forall p_i \in P, p_i \neq \emptyset$; (2) $\forall p_i, p_j \in P$; $i \neq j \rightarrow p_i \cap p_j = \emptyset$; (3) $\bigcup_{i=1}^{n} p_i = P$.*

After entities are divided into n partitions (n is defined by the user), edges can be divided into n^2 partitions.

Definition 3 (Edge Partition). *Edge Partition $Q = \{q_{ij} \mid q_{ij} = \{(p_i, p_j)\} \wedge 1 \leq i, j \leq n\}$ is a multi-set combined by ordered pairs of entities, which satisfies the following conditions: (1) $\forall q_{ij} \in Q, q_{ij} \neq \emptyset$; (2) $\forall q_{ij}, q_{rs} \in Q; i \neq r \wedge j \neq s \rightarrow q_{ij} \cap q_{rs} = \emptyset$; (3) $\bigcup_{i=1}^{n}(\bigcup_{j=1}^{n} q_{ij}) = Q$.*

PDKE is a distributed parallel embedding framework that we proposed for large-scale KGs. The computation tasks of PDKE are implemented on top of a distributed cluster of multiple machines. The PDKE framework are formally defined as follows:

Definition 4 (PDKE framework). *Given a KG S as the input data, let C be a set of machines in a distributed cluster, each computing site $s \in C$ has two states, i.e., active or inactive. The function getState(): $C \rightarrow \{active, inactive\}$ gets current state of a computing site. The master site $s_m \in C$. In the initial stage, only master site is active, the other slave sites are inactive. An inactive site would be invoked while receiving the signal from the master site. During the computation process, the function* trainExecution(α, γ, Trans(X)) *may be executed in parallel on each computing site, where α is the learning rate, γ the margin,* Trans(X) *the KRL model. When each computing site s_i starts working, it (1) first calls the function* acquireToken() *to request a token from the lock server in order to access the corresponding resources, (2) generates sample triples in the edge partition Q, (3) executes the loss functions and gradient for the update procedure, (4) returns tokens to lock server, and (5) starts the next iteration or stops training. The parallel training continues until all sites are inactive.*

In the entire PDKE framework, the master site is the most critical one which is responsible for resource allocation and management, work scheduling, as well as training.

4   Algorithm Framework

In this section, we propose a distributed algorithm framework for parallel knowledge embedding, which employs the entity and relation partitioning introduced in Sect. 3. First, we illustrate the architecture of our framework, then we describe the implementation of distributed algorithms. Finally, we analyze the complexity results of the proposed method.

4.1   Architecture

The popularity of large-scale real-world KGs, with millions of nodes and billions of edges, demands the efficiency and scalability of the knowledge embedding approach. The architecture of PDKE for KRL is depicted in Fig. 1. The numbered arrows in Fig. 1 respectively indicate: ① given a knowledge graph, the framework loads the KG and performs the partitioning algorithm; ② the initializer initializes parameters of a KRL model in preparation for distributed training; ③ the executors process training in parallel and get embedding vectors and trained models; ④ the embedding vectors are used for downstream machine learning tasks.

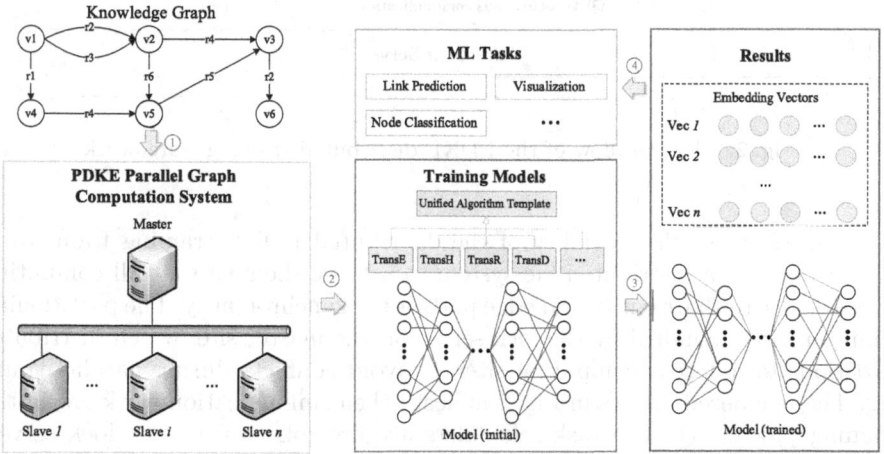

Fig. 1. The PDKE architecture

The design rationale of the PDKE framework is in line with the Template Method design pattern [6]. It is worth noting that the PDKE algorithm framework can accommodate all translation-based KRL models, not limited to the

four exemplary models mentioned above. New models can be easily added by
providing concrete classes that implement the Template Method interface in
PDKE.

Existing works have shown that the PS architecture is effective for training
with large sparse models. PDKE uses the PS architecture to support representation learning for large-scale knowledge graphs. In the PDKE architecture, the
parameter server stores all embeddings in the form of key-value pairs. Each time
the SGD function is called, the clients request the required embedding parameters from the parameter server and asynchronously send the gradients to the
server to update the parameters.

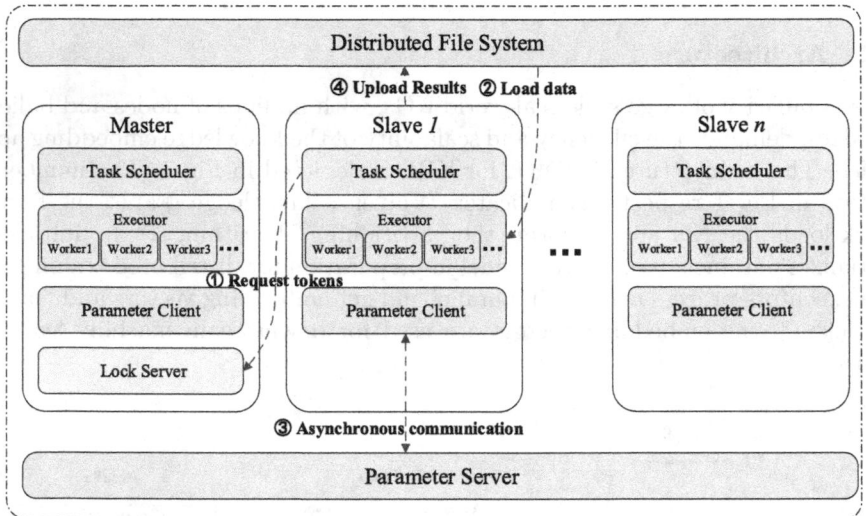

Fig. 2. The workflow of the PDKE distributed training framework

Figure 2 shows the workflow of the distributed PDKE training framework.
PDKE employs a distributed file system to achieve the goal that all computing
sites are able to share entity and edge partitions asynchronously. The partitioning
management is handled by the lock server on the master site, which distributes
partitions to different computing sites to avoid conflicts during parallel training. The numbered arrows in Fig. 2 indicate the communication workflow in the
training process. ① The task schedulers acquire tokens from the lock server;
② the executors load data from the distributed file system and perform training in parallel; ③ during the training process, the clients communicate with the
parameter server asynchronouslys; ④ the computing sites upload the embedding
results to the distributed file system.

4.2   Distributed Training Model

We propose a distributed training model to address the parallel training issue. Algorithm 1 presents an overview of the distributed training process. In the initial phase, input data is stored in the distributed file system, and all computing sites are in the inactive state. After the data is preprocessed, the master site independently completes the tasks of entity and edge patitioning. Entities are divided into n partitions, where n is chosen such that each partition can fit into memory or to meet the conditions required by the parallel execution (line 4). Edges are divided into n^2 partitions that is detemined by the types of head and tail entities (line 5). After entity and edge partitioning is complete, the master site starts the lock server to manage the access tokens, which are needed by the computing sites during training execution (line 6). Once the access tokens have been obtained from the lock server, different computing sites can load partitions, implement training, and update parameters in parallel without conflicts. Trans(X) represents a translation-based KRL model (e.g., TransE), which is usually stored on the parameter server in the form of a set of parameters generated by $\mathtt{dataInit}(T_p, \mathtt{Trans}(X))$. The computing sites start the training procedures in parallel by communicating with the distributed file system and the parameter server synchronously (lines 8–10). The training procedure will be terminated when reaching the maximum number of iterations, which is equal to the parameter *epoch*.

Algorithm 1: PDKE-Training

Input: A set of RDF triples $S = \{(h, r, t) \mid h, t \in V, r \in E\}$
Parameter: max training iterations *epoch*, embedding dimension d, learning rate α, margin γ
Output: Embedding results of S: $Vec(S) = \{(\boldsymbol{h}, \boldsymbol{r}, \boldsymbol{t}) \mid h, t \in V, r \in E\}$

1 $Vec(S) \leftarrow \emptyset$;
2 $V, R, T \leftarrow$ dataPreprocess(S) ;   /* Load RDF triple set S */
3 if s_i is *master* then
4       $V_p \leftarrow$ split V into patitions ;
5       $T_p \leftarrow$ split T into patitions ;
6   startLockServer();

7 dataInit(T_p, Trans(X)) ;   /* $X \in \{E, H, R, D\}$ */
8 for *each computing site s_i is inactive* do
9   while *not end of epoch* do
10          $\{(\boldsymbol{h}, \boldsymbol{r}, \boldsymbol{t})\} \leftarrow$ trainExecution(α, γ, Trans(X));
                                  /* train on each site in parallel */

11 $Vec(S) \leftarrow Vec(S) \cup \{(\boldsymbol{h}, \boldsymbol{r}, \boldsymbol{t})\}$;
12 return $Vec(S)$;

On each site, the training procedure is performed as shown in Algorithm 2. Access tokens are acquired in order that the computing sites are able to use resources on the distributed file system. In each iteration, the executor calls getSample($pid, rand\_seed[s_i]$) to sample a set of positive triples (line 3), and uses getNegative($pid, rand\_seed[s_i]$) to generate corresponding negative triples (line 4). Then, the executor uniformly divides the positive samples into nc chunks and calculates the *loss* parameter for each chunk. If the *loss* > 0, which indicates that the positive sample score is higher than the negative one, the Gradient Descent (GD) function is invoked to update the embedding results (line 9). After the training process is completed, computing sites update embeddings stored on the distributed file system, free up occupied resources, and return the access tokens.

Algorithm 2: trainExecution($\alpha, \gamma, \text{Trans}(X)$)

Input: number of chunks nc, learning rate α, margin γ, and algorithm
        $Trans(X)$
Output: Embedding results: $\{(h, r, t)\}$
1 $pid \leftarrow$ acquireToken();
                            /* pid is the index number of the partition */
2 $T_{pid} \leftarrow$ getEmbeddings(pid) ;   /* T_{pid} is the embedding vectors */
3 $T_{pos} \leftarrow$ getSample($pid, rand\_seed[s_i]$) ;
4 $T_{neg} \leftarrow$ getNegative($pid, rand\_seed[s_i]$) ;   /* $T_{pos}, T_{neg} \subseteq T_{pid}$ */
5 $\{(h, r, t)\} \leftarrow$ split T_{pos} into nc chunks ;
6 **while** *not end of nc* **do**
7 $\quad$ $loss \leftarrow \gamma + f_r(\{(h, r, t)\}) - f_r(T_{neg})$;
8 $\quad$ **if** $loss > 0$ **then**
9 $\quad\quad$ $\lfloor$ $\{(h, r, t)\} \leftarrow$ update$\{(h, r, t)\}$ *w.r.t.* GD;
10 $\quad$ **else**
11 $\quad\quad$ $\lfloor$ $\{(h, r, t)\}$;

12 returnToken(pid) ;
13 **return** $\{(h, r, t)\}$;

As shown in Table 1, the PDKE framework leverages the Template Method design patterns to accommodate multiple translation-based embedding models by exposing initialization and score functions of concrete models as an abstract interface. For the concrete models that we have implemented, (1) TransE [3] represents the relation as a translation vector r so that the entity embeddings h and t can be connected by r; (2) TransH [21] introduces relation-specific hyperplanes and models a relation r as a vector r on a hyperplane with w_r as the norm vector, where h_p and t_p represent the projection vectors of the entity embeddings h and t on the hyperplane of the relation r, respectively; (3) in TransR [13], entities h and t are represented as vectors h and t in an entity space $\mathbb{R}^n$, each relation is represented as a vector r in a specific space $\mathbb{R}^m$, where the projection matrix $M_r \in \mathbb{R}^{m \times n}$ projects the vectors h and t to the relation space $\mathbb{R}^m$ to obtain the vectors h_p and t_p; (4) TransD [8] simplifies TransR by decomposing the projection matrix M_r into a product of two vectors $h_p^\top$ and r_p.

Table 1. KRL models implemented in the PDKE framework

Trans(X)	dataInit()	Score function $f_r(T)$	Time complexity
TransE [3]	h: head vector	$-\|h + r - t\|_{1/2}$	$O(N_t)$
	t: tail vector		
	r: relation vector		
TransH [21]	h: head vector	$h_p = w_r^\top \cdot h \cdot w_r$	$O(2mN_t)$
	t: tail vector	$t_p = w_r^\top \cdot t \cdot w_r$	
	r: relation vector	$-\|h_p + r - t_p\|_{1/2}$	
	w_r: norm vector		
TransR [13]	h: head vector	$-\|M_r \cdot h + r - M_r \cdot t\|_{1/2}$	$O(2mnN_t)$
	t: tail vector		
	r: relation vector		
	M_r: projection matrix		
TransD [8]	h: head vector	$h_\perp = h_p^\top \cdot h \cdot r_p + [h^\top, 0^\top]^\top$	$O(2nN_t)$
	t: tail vector	$t_\perp = t_p^\top \cdot t \cdot r_p + [t^\top, 0^\top]^\top$	
	r: relation vector	$-\|h_\perp + r - t_\perp\|_{1/2}$	
	h_p: projection vector		
	t_p: projection vector		
	r_p: projection vector		

The correctness and time complexity of the PDKE algorithms are guaranteed by the following theorems.

Theorem 1. *Given a knowledge graph G, Algorithm 1 and 2 give the correct embedding vector sets Vec(S) in the $O(|epoch|)$ number of iterations, where epoch is the total number of iterations.*

Proof. (Sketch) The correctness of the algorithms can be proved as follows: (1) In each training iteration, each computing site may choose an edge partition T_{pid} and sample from edge partitions, where pid is the index number of the partition. A set of positive triples T_{pos} of size $|batchsize|$ is obtained from T_{pid}, meanwhile, the function getNegative(pid, $rand\_seed[s_i]$) is called to generate the corresponding negative samples T_{neg}, where $rand\_seed[s_i]$ is a random seed. (2) The loss function is $loss = \gamma + f_r(T_{pos}) - f_r(T_{neg})$. If $loss > 0$, which means that the positive sample score is higher than the negative one, the GD function is invoked to update the embedding results. Each time GD is called, the distance between $h + r$ and t would be closer, which means that the score of the triple is increasing, and the results become better. The *loss* value of the embedding results in each partition is gradually decreasing. (3) After the iteration of $|epoch|$ rounds are completed, we can get the optimal embedding vectors $Vec(S)$.   □

Theorem 2. *The time complexity of the PDKE algorithm is bounded by $O(|epoch| \cdot |batchsize| \cdot |n|^2/|k|)$, where $|epoch|$ is the total number of iterations, $|batchsize|$ is the maximum number of the sampled triples, $|n|$ and $|k|$ represent the number of entity partitions and the number of computing sites, respectively.*

Proof. (Sketch) The time complexity consists of three parts: (1) The algorithm has $|epoch|$ iterations; (2) in each iteration, all computing sites need to process $|n^2|$ edge partitions; (3) when dealing with an edge partition, $|batchsize|$ positive and negative samples are generated. The above time complexity is $O(|epoch| \cdot |batchsize| \cdot |n|^2)$. Since the algorithm is executed in parallel on $|k|$ sites, the time complexity of PDKE is $O(|epoch| \cdot |batchsize| \cdot |n|^2/|k|)$.   □

5   Experiments

In this section, we evaluate the performance of our framework. We conducted extensive experiments to verify the efficiency and scalability of the proposed algorithms on both synthetic and real-world KGs.

5.1   Experimental Settings

The proposed algorithms are implemented in Python using PyTorch, which were deployed on a 4-site cluster in the *Tencent Cloud*[2]. Each site in this cluster installs a 64-bit CentOS 7.6 Linux operating system, with a 6 Intel(R) Xeon(R) cores (two sockets) and two hyperthreads per core, for a total of 12 virtual cores, and 96 GB of RAM. Our algorithm was executed on Python 3.7 and PyTorch 1.2. In the comparison experiments, the parameters used in PDKE are similar to the previous research work [11], and we adjust the best results of grid search with learning rate between 0.001–0.2, margin between 0.05–0.2, and negative batch size between 100–500.

Table 2. Datasets used in the experiments

#Dataset	#Relation	#Entity	#Train	#Valid	#Test
FB15K	1,345	14,951	483,142	50,000	59,071
WN18	18	40,943	141,142	5,000	5,000
DBpedia	663	5,526,333	17,197,311	500,000	597,701

The evaluation task of link prediction [20] is usually implemented on two popular benchmark datasets, i.e., Freebase [2] and WordNet [14]. (1) Freebase is a famous knowledge base, which is consisted by a large volume of general facts. (2) WordNet is a semantic lexical knowledge graph and has been widely used in the field of natural language processing. In this paper, we use two subsets of the benchmark knowledge bases, i.e., FB15K and WN18. In order to verify the efficiency and scalability of PDKE, we conducted experiments on a real-world knowledge graph DBpedia[3], which is a dataset extracted from Wikipedia. As listed in Table 2, we summarize the statistics of these datasets.

---

[2] https://cloud.tencent.com/.
[3] http://wiki.dbpedia.org/.

5.2   Experimental Results

The link prediction task is widely employed to predict missing entities or the entities that are able to be incorporated into knowledge graphs. After learning the representation of entities and relations, we used link prediction to evaluate the quality of entity and relation embeddings. Mean Rank, Mean Reciprocal Rank (MRR), and Hits@N are used to evaluate the results. Mean Rank is the average rank of correct triples, and MRR represents the average reciprocal rank of the correct triples. Hits@N is the percentage of rankings that are less than N, which are the metrics commonly used to evaluate the validity of experimental results.

Table 3. Experimental results on link prediction

Dataset	WN18				FB15K			
Metrics	Mean		Hits@10		Mean		Hits@10	
	Raw	Filt	Raw	Filt	Raw	Filt	Raw	Filt
TransE (Baseline)	263	251	0.754	**0.892**	243	125	**0.349**	0.471
TransH (Baseline)	318	303	**0.754**	0.867	**211**	84	**0.425**	0.585
TransR (Baseline)	**232**	219	**0.783**	**0.917**	226	**78**	0.438	0.655
TransD (Baseline)	242	229	**0.792**	0.925	211	**67**	**0.494**	**0.742**
TransE (PDKE)	**254**	226	**0.761**	0.858	234	119	0.335	**0.485**
TransH (PDKE)	**295**	276	0.745	**0.874**	261	114	0.386	**0.607**
TransR (PDKE)	237	**215**	0.773	0.912	**214**	107	**0.475**	**0.692**
TransD (PDKE)	**232**	**203**	0.781	**0.937**	**208**	81	0.462	0.738

Exp 1. Effectiveness of the Algorithms in Accuracy. To verify the validity of our methods, we conducted extensive experiments on the two benchmark datasets mentioned above, i.e., WN18 and FB15K. We conducted a comparison experiment on a stand-alone machine to compare the accuracy of our method with that of the baselines, with that of the baselines [8]. During 40 epochs training, 300-dimensional embeddings are trained with a ranking loss over negatives using cosine similarity. Table 3 shows that our approach are highly competitive compared to the existing works [3,8,13,21], which verifies the correctness of our algorithms.

As shown in Fig. 3, PDKE has comparable accuracy to OpenKE and KB2E in most evaluations. Since KB2E does not implement the TransD model, the experimental results of TransD on KB2E in the two figures are blank. It is worth noting that the TransE model implemented by OpenKE performs exceptionally well on the FB15K dataset, mainly because OpenKE has made some improvements on the original TransE model. The results show that PDKE can achieve comparable accuracy to previous works on a stand-alone machine, and also supports distributed training that is not available in existing works.

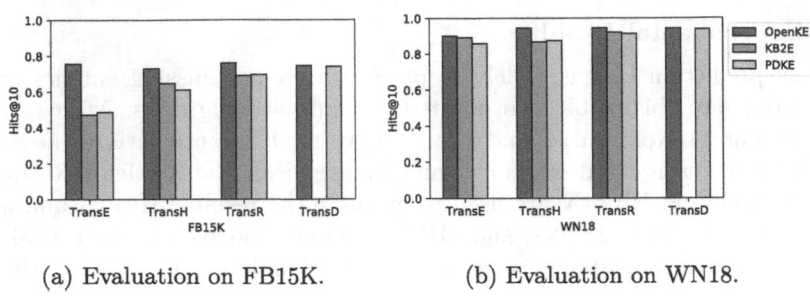

(a) Evaluation on FB15K.   (b) Evaluation on WN18.

Fig. 3. Accuracy comparison with OpenKE and KB2E.

Exp 2. Time Efficiency of the Algorithms. In order to verify the time efficiency of our method, we conducted experiments on a cluster of four machines. OpenKE and KB2E are only available on a single machine, so we chose the distributed system SANSA [10] as a baseline. Since SANSA cannot deal with the DBpedia dataset due to its large scale, we conducted the comparisons only on the FB15K dataset.

Table 4. Evaluation on FB15K

Models	Mean rank	Hits@10	Time(s)
TransE(PDKE)	**268**	**0.317**	**5,157**
TransH(PDKE)	295	0.355	6,995
TransR(PDKE)	247	0.467	9,537
TransD(PDKE)	242	0.524	8,392
TransE(SANSA)	7,340	0.008	8,094

Among the typical translation-based models, SANSA only implemented the TransE model in its beta version. As shown in Table 4, the training time on PDKE decreased by 36.29% compared to SANSA, however, the accuracy of SANSA is much lower than PDKE In order to find the reasons for the low accuracy of SANSA, we checked the source code and found that there were errors in the update procedure of SANSA. All entities in datasets are updated in each iteration, which caused conflicts in the distributed environment.

Due to the partitioning of entities and edges, all computing sites can independently perform the training process and asynchronously exchange resources on the distributed file system, which saves a significant amount of consumed by the synchronization process and speeds up the model training process. Meanwhile, experimental results show that distributed training techniques based on entity and relation partitioning could not affect the accuracy. In summary, the experimental results validates the time efficiency of the PDKE framework, which is consistent with our previous analysis.

Exp 3. Scalability of the Algorithms. In order to verify the scalability of our method, we performed experiments on a cluster of four machines using the DBpedia dataset to study the impact of the number of partitions and the cluster size on the training accuracy and efficiency.

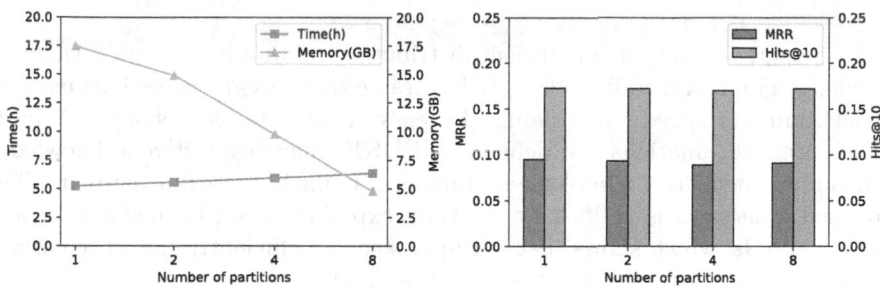

Fig. 4. The impact of partition numbers

The results in Fig. 4 show that when training on single machine, as the number of partitions increases, the peak memory usage decreases, and the training time almost linearly increases. The main reason is that the increase in the number of partitions makes the size of each partition smaller, thereby reducing the memory consumption for a certain period of time, but it brings additional I/O overhead. The results in Fig. 4 show that different numbers of partitions would not affect the accuracy of the results, which verifies the scalability of our method on a single machine.

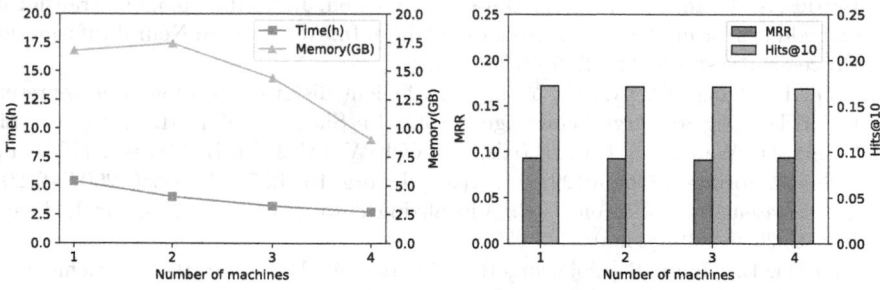

Fig. 5. The impact of cluster size

For the experiments on multiple machines, we set the number of partitions to twice the number of machines. Figure 5 shows the effect of cluster size on the training results. As the number of machines increases, the training time gradually decreases, and the peak memory usage first increases and then decreases. The reason is that, in a distributed setting, the training model as a whole can be shared across all machines rather than partitioned among different machines. The accuracy of the algorithms are the same in different cluster sizes, which verifies that our method is scalable in a distributed environment.

6   Conclusion

In this paper, we propose an efficient distributed training framework PDKE for knowledge graph embedding. The PDKE framework integrates various existing models and can speed up training efficiency in distributed settings. A basic set of interface functions are defined in PDKE, allowing different knowledge embedding models to be implemented under a unified algorithm template. The proposed framework is verified by extensive experiments on both synthetic and real-world KGs, which shows that our approach can efficiently train the current translation-based KRL models with great scalability.

Acknowledgments. This work is supported by the National Natural Science Foundation of China (61972275), the Natural Science Foundation of Tianjin (17JCY-BJC15400), and the Australian Research Council Linkage Project (LP180100750).

References

1. Berners-Lee, T., Hendler, J., Lassila, O.: The semantic web. Sci. Am. **284**(5), 34–43 (2001)
2. Bollacker, K., Evans, C., Paritosh, P., Sturge, T., Taylor, J.: Freebase: a collaboratively created graph database for structuring human knowledge. In: Proceedings of the 2008 ACM SIGMOD International Conference on Management of Data, pp. 1247–1250. AcM (2008)
3. Bordes, A., Usunier, N., Garcia-Duran, A., Weston, J., Yakhnenko, O.: Translating embeddings for modeling multi-relational data. In: Advances in Neural Information Processing Systems, pp. 2787–2795 (2013)
4. Chai, L., Wang, X., Liu, B., Yang, Y.: Efficient distributed knowledge representation learning for large knowledge graphs. In: Shao, J., Yiu, M.L., Toyoda, M., Zhang, D., Wang, W., Cui, B. (eds.) APWeb-WAIM 2019. LNCS, vol. 11641, pp. 398–413. Springer, Cham (2019). https://doi.org/10.1007/978-3-030-26072-9_29
5. Der Maaten, L.V., Hinton, G.E.: Visualizing data using t-SNE. J. Mach. Learn. Res. **9**, 2579–2605 (2008)
6. Gamma, E., Helm, R., Johnson, R., Vlissides, J.: Design Patterns. Elements of Reusable Object-oriented Software. Pearson Education, London (1995)
7. Han, X., et al.: Openke: an open toolkit for knowledge embedding. In: Proceedings of the 2018 Conference on Empirical Methods in Natural Language Processing: System Demonstrations, pp. 139–144 (2018)
8. Ji, G., He, S., Xu, L., Liu, K., Zhao, J.: Knowledge graph embedding via dynamic mapping matrix. In: Proceedings of the 53rd Annual Meeting of the Association for Computational Linguistics and the 7th International Joint Conference on Natural Language Processing of the Asian Federation of Natural Language Processing, ACL 2015, 26–31 July 2015, Beijing, China, Volume 1: Long Papers, pp. 687–696 (2015). https://www.aclweb.org/anthology/P15-1067/

9. Lehmann, J., et al.: Dbpedia-a large-scale, multilingual knowledge base extracted from Wikipedia. Semant. Web **6**(2), 167–195 (2015)
10. Lehmann, J., et al.: Distributed semantic analytics using the SANSA stack. In: d'Amato, C., et al. (eds.) ISWC 2017. LNCS, vol. 10588, pp. 147–155. Springer, Cham (2017). https://doi.org/10.1007/978-3-319-68204-4_15
11. Lerer, A., et al.: Pytorch-biggraph: a large-scale graph embedding system. arXiv preprint arXiv:1903.12287 (2019)
12. Li, M.: Scaling distributed machine learning with the parameter server. In: Proceedings of the 2014 International Conference on Big Data Science and Computing BigDataScience 2014, ACM, New York, pp. 3:1–3:1. (2014). http://doi.acm.org/10.1145/2640087.2644155
13. Lin, Y., Liu, Z., Sun, M., Liu, Y., Zhu, X.: Learning entity and relation embeddings for knowledge graph completion. In: Twenty-Ninth AAAI Conference on Artificial Intelligence (2015)
14. Miller, G.A.: Wordnet: a lexical database for English. Commun. ACM **38**(11), 39–41 (1995)
15. Nickel, M., Rosasco, L., Poggio, T.: Holographic embeddings of knowledge graphs arXiv Artificial Intelligence (2015)
16. Nickel, M., Tresp, V.: Tensor factorization for multi-relational learning. In: Blockeel, H., Kersting, K., Nijssen, S., Železný, F. (eds.) ECML PKDD 2013. LNCS (LNAI), vol. 8190, pp. 617–621. Springer, Heidelberg (2013). https://doi.org/10.1007/978-3-642-40994-3_40
17. Nickel, M., Tresp, V., Kriegel, H.P.: A three-way model for collective learning on multi-relational data. ICML. **11**, 809–816 (2011)
18. Riedel, S., Yao, L., McCallum, A., Marlin, B.M.: Relation extraction with matrix factorization and universal schemas. In: Proceedings of the 2013 Conference of the North American Chapter of the Association for Computational Linguistics: Human Language Technologies, pp. 74–84 (2013)
19. Suchanek, F.M., Kasneci, G., Weikum, G.: Yago: a core of semantic knowledge. In: Proceedings of the 16th international conference on World Wide Web, pp. 697–706. ACM (2007)
20. Trouillon, T., Welbl, J., Riedel, S., Gaussier, E., Bouchard, G.: Complex embeddings for simple link prediction, pp. 2071–2080 (2016)
21. Wang, Z., Zhang, J., Feng, J., Chen, Z.: Knowledge graph embedding by translating on hyperplanes. In: Proceedings of the Twenty-Eighth AAAI Conference on Artificial Intelligence AAAI 2014, pp. 1112–1119. AAAI Press (2014). http://dl.acm.org/citation.cfm?id=2893873.2894046
22. Yang, B., Yih, W., He, X., Gao, J., Deng, L.: Embedding entities and relations for learning and inference in knowledge bases. arXiv Computation and Language (2014)
23. Zaharia, M., Chowdhury, M., Franklin, M.J., Shenker, S., Stoica, I.: Spark: cluster computing with working sets. HotCloud **10**(10–10), 95 (2010)

Type Preserving Representation of Heterogeneous Information Networks

Chunyao Song[1,3]([✉]), Jiawen Guo[1], Tingjian Ge[2], and Xiaojie Yuan[1]

[1] Tianjin Key Laboratory of Network and Data Science Technology,
College of Computer Science, Nankai University, Tianjin, China
{chunyao.song,guojiawen,yuanxj}@nankai.edu.cn
[2] University of Massachusetts, Lowell, USA
ge@cs.uml.edu
[3] Jiangsu Key Laboratory of Big Data Security and Intelligent Processing,
Nanjing University of Posts and Telecommunications, Nanjing, China

Abstract. In the current information explosion era, many complex systems can be modeled using networks/graphs. The development of artificial intelligence and machine learning has also provided more means for graph analysis tasks. However, the high-dimensional large-scale graphs cannot be used as input to machine learning algorithms directly. One typically needs to apply representation learning to transform the high-dimensional graphs to low-dimensional vector representations. As for network embedding/representation learning, the study on homogeneous graphs is already highly adequate. However, heterogeneous information networks are more common in real-world applications. Applying homogeneous-graph embedding methods to heterogeneous graphs will incur significant information loss. In this paper, we propose a numerical signature based method, which is highly pluggable—given a target heterogeneous graph G, our method can complement any existing network embedding method on either homogeneous or heterogeneous graphs and universally improve the embedding quality of G, while only introducing minimum overhead. We use real datasets from four different domains, and compare with a representative homogeneous network embedding method, a representative heterogeneous network embedding method, and a state-of-the-art heterogeneous network embedding method, to illustrate the improvement effect of the proposed framework on the quality of network embedding, in terms of node classification, node clustering, and edge classification tasks.

Keywords: Heterogeneous network · Network embedding · Representation learning

1 Introduction

In this big data era, information is being generated at a rapid rate. The development of artificial intelligence and machine learning provides a good platform for

© Springer Nature Switzerland AG 2020
Y. Nah et al. (Eds.): DASFAA 2020, LNCS 12113, pp. 604–612, 2020.
https://doi.org/10.1007/978-3-030-59416-9_36

using these data. Among all the generated data, lots of them can be modeled as graphs, such as co-authorship networks, computer networks, infrastructure networks, interaction networks, online social networks, and protein-protein interactions. However, the high dimensionality and structural information of complex networks make it difficult to apply machine learning algorithms directly. Therefore, network embedding/representation learning, which assigns nodes in a network to low-dimensional representations and effectively preserves the network structure [2], provides a way for machine learning methods to be used on complex networks.

There have been extensive studies on homogeneous graphs, which only consider network topologies. However, in real world applications, lots of nodes and edges of complex networks are in different types, which also carry a lot of useful information. Ignoring such type/label information would result in significant information loss.

When we try to perform representation learning on a heterogeneous information network (HIN), where both nodes and edges are associated with distinct types, if we apply homogeneous network embedding methods on such graphs, we will not be able to encode type information in the learned vectors. Many researchers realized this. Therefore, several embedding methods specifically for HINs have been proposed. Most of them are random walk based methods, where node types are used to guide random walks. However, some of them depend heavily on expert knowledge. The edge types correlate significantly with the adjacent node types too. Moreover, for those methods, it is difficult to ensure that the type information of a node's neighborhood has been completely represented.

As a result, an intuition is whether we can completely represent the type information of a node's neighborhood in HINs and use the existing fully developed homogeneous network embedding methods to represent the topology of HINs, and combine the two parts to produce high quality HIN representation results. We propose a numerical signature based method, which leverages the properties of prime numbers to encode the type information of a node's neighborhood, and concatenates the result to existing embedding vectors to get the final representation of the given HIN, improving the embedding quality accordingly.

Our Contributions: We formally state the problem of heterogeneous information network embedding, and formally define a HIN node's neighborhood for the first-order proximity (Sect. 3). We propose a numerical signature based framework for HIN representation learning, which can be applied to any existing network embedding method, and improve the embedding quality on HINs with minimum overhead (Sect. 4). We perform a comprehensive evaluation on real datasets from four different domains, and compare with three different embedding methods, using node classification, node clustering, and edge classification tasks as examples, to illustrate the accuracy improvement and low overhead of the proposed method on HIN embedding over existing methods (Sect. 5).

2   Related Work

Cui et al. give an excellent survey [2] on network embedding. Shi et al. give a survey on heterogeneous network analysis [13]. Dave et al. give a study [1] on the problem that which topological structure of graph can be captured by embedding. HOPE [12], Node2Vec [8] and SDNE [15] are all network embedding methods on homogeneous networks. There are also studies on attributed network embedding, where nodes are accompanied with attributes, or text, or image contents. To name a few, Neural-Brane [3] and DANE [7] all belong to this category. However, this problem is different from ours, as it only considers node contents, and does not differentiate edges/links of different types.

Considering the characteristics of heterogeneous network, Huang et al. develop a dynamic programming approach [9] which preserves meta path similarity for HIN embedding. Recently, Dong et al. propose metapath2vec [4]. Hussein et al. propose a JUMP & STAY method [10] to guide the random walk, and set the probability that a walker jump to another type of nodes to preserve the neighborhood node type information.

However, all the existing HIN embedding methods have strict restrictions on edge types. In other words, they either assume that, when the two endpoint node types are known, the edge type is determined as well, or simply ignore the edge types. However, in practical applications, we often observe that the node types and edge types are more or less independent, or there are many-to-many mappings (a single type of edge may connect nodes of multiple types at either end). Can we also preserve the information from both node types and independent edge types for representation learning? This paper aims to solve this problem.

3   Preliminaries

Definition 1. *An Undirected Heterogeneous Information Network (HIN) is defined as a graph $G = (V, E)$ where V is a set of vertices $\{v_1, v_2, \ldots, v_n\}$ and E is a set of edges $\{e_1, e_2, \ldots, e_m\}$. There is a vertex type function $T_v : V \rightarrow \Sigma_N$, and there is an edge type function $T_e : E \rightarrow \Sigma_E$, with $|\Sigma_N| \geq 1$ and $|\Sigma_E| \geq 1$.*

Most previous HIN embedding work focuses on embedding with $|\Sigma_N| \geq 1$, and the edge types are determined once the two endpoints' types of an edge are known. In this work, we allow $|\Sigma_N| > 1$ and $|\Sigma_E| > 1$, and the edge types and node types can be independent and the mapping can be many-to-many. In order to encode the node and edge type features, we need to define the neighborhood of a node. In this work, we consider two kinds of neighborhood.

Definition 2. *A Direct Neighborhood of a node v is denoted as N_{dv}, where N_{dv} consists of v and a set of nodes V_v such that $\forall v_i \in V_v$, $(v_i, v) \in E$, and a set of edges E_v such that $\forall e_i \in E_v$, an endpoint of e_i is v.*

Definition 3. *An Ego-Network* *of a node v is denoted as N_{en}, where N_{en} consists of v and a set of nodes V_v such that $\forall v_i \in V_v$, $(v_i, v) \in E$, and a set of edges E_v such that $\forall e_i \in E_v$, the two endpoints of $e_i \in N_{dv}$.*

4 Numerical Signature Based Heterogeneous Information Network Representation

In this section, we present the framework of **N**umerical **S**ignature based **HIN R**epresentation (NSHR), which is compatible with and complement any existing homogeneous or HIN embedding methods.

We adopt the same objective function as in [4] and extend it to fit in HINs. As for a HIN $G = (V, E, \Sigma)$, where Σ defines the type set of nodes and edges in G, the local structure of a node v also considers the node and edge types in v's neighborhood. So now the objective function is:

$$arg\ max_\theta \prod_{v \in V} [\prod_{c \in N_{t(v)}} p(c|v; \theta) \oplus \prod_{c \in N_{\Sigma(v)}} p(c|v; \theta)] \tag{1}$$

where $N_{t(v)}$ represents the topological neighborhood of v, $N_{\Sigma(v)}$ represents the neighborhood type set of v, and $\oplus$ stands for a representation concatenation. And $p(c|v; \theta)$ in (1) is the conditional probability of having a context node c given a node v.

Thus in this way, the task of HIN representation learning has been divided into two parts, where the first part is to learn the topological neighborhood features of a node v, and the second part is to learn the neighborhood type set information features of a node v. For the first part, any existing network embedding methods can be applied, as they all reflect topological information. For the second part, we will present a numerical signature based method as follows, and combine the two parts to get the final representation.

In order to maximize the network probability in terms of local type set information, we need to differentiate different nodes' neighborhood type set information. That is, nodes with similar neighborhood type set should have similar type set representations, and vice versa. To achieve this, we use prime numbers to represent different node and edge types; so each distinct type is associated with a particular prime number. Then we build a numerical signature representation for a node v to represent v's neighborhood type set information as:

$$NT(v) = \prod_{m \in N_{HIN}(v)} prime(m) \tag{2}$$

where $N_{HIN}(v)$ represents the neighborhood of v in HINs. In this work, we consider two kinds of neighborhood as shown in Definitions 2 and 3.

It is possible that a numerical signature is too large and cannot be held within one integer. In that case, we start a new dimension if the integer for the current dimension times the next prime number would exceed the maximum integer. Hence the whole signature could be broken down into multiple integers,

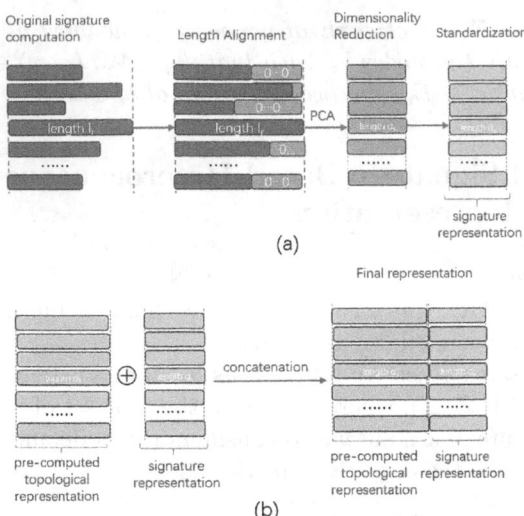

Fig. 1. (a) The procedure of numerical signature representation to present type information. (b) Concatenating the topological information representation to get the final representation.

whose product is the whole signature. Suppose that for a network G, adopting either of the two kinds of neighborhood, after the signature computation, each node v_i of G will have a signature vector of length sv_i. The length of the longest signature vector will be used as the length of signature representation l_r. All other signature vectors shorter than l_r will be padded 0s on the right up to the length l_r. Therefore, all nodes with similar local type set information will result in similar signature representations of the same length. After getting the signature vectors of length l_r, we use PCA [11] for dimensionality reduction to fit our particular dimensionality requirements. We then do standardization to get the signature ready for our framework. The whole process of signature preparation is illustrated in Fig. 1 (a).

After getting the topological representation meeting the dimensionality requirement and the neighborhood type set representation, we concatenates the two parts to return the final representation of the given HIN as in Fig. 1 (b).

5   Experiments

5.1   Datasets and Setup:

We use the following four real-world datsets: **Phone** [5], **Enron Email** [6] (preprocessed into 20 edge types), **Foursquare** [16] (8 node types including time, check-in, user, and 5 categories of points of interest) and **DBIS** [14].

We compare our method with (1) a representative homoegeneous network embedding method **node2vec** [8], and use the parameters $p = 1$ and $q = 1$ as in

[4]; (2) a representative HIN embedding method **metapath2vec** [4], and apply the most meaningful metapaths; (3) a state-of-the-art HIN embedding method **JUST** [10], and use $\alpha = 0.5$ and $m = 1$. For all these methods, we use walk length $l = 80$, the number of walks per node $r = 10$, and the representation learning dimensions $d = 100$. For our methods, we adjust the signature dimensions d_s for evaluation. The maximum integer used for computing the signature representation is set according to the computation resource limitation and the number of types of the dataset. In our experiments, we choose 1,000,000 as the maximum integer for Enron, and 1,000 for the other three datasets. We repeat each experiment 5 times, and report the average scores for evaluation. All algorithms are implemented in Python and run on a machine with an Intel Core i7 3.40 GHz processor and a 64 GB memory[1].

5.2 Evaluation Results

Node Classification: The node representations are learned from the full dataset using the three competing methods, as well as our framework using two kinds of neighborhood. We use a simple logistic regression classifier for the classification task and report Macro-F1 score. Micro-F1 score is omitted due to space limitation. The size of the training set is set to 80% and the remaining 20% is used as the test set.

Figure 2 shows the results, where we report the best results by adjusting the parameter d_s from 1 to 30. The NSHR framework using direct neighborhood is reported as *sig*, and the framework using ego-network is reported as *sig-ego*. We can see that our framework can improve the quality of learning results of baseline methods by as much as from 20% to more than four times in general on all datasets. In general, our methods improve the quality of existing methods up to more than four times, and give superior results for rare-type classification.

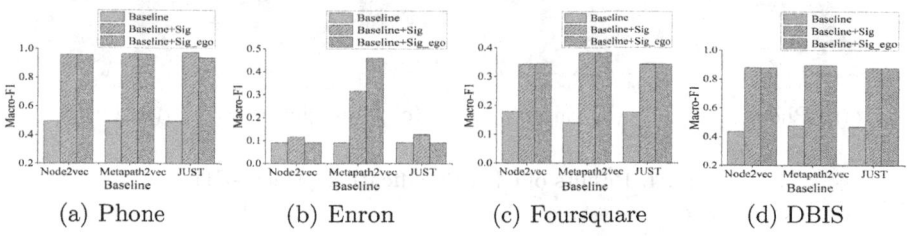

(a) Phone   (b) Enron   (c) Foursquare   (d) DBIS

Fig. 2. Results of edge classification (Macro-F1)

---

[1] All datasets and code are publicly available at https://github.com/guaw/sig_py.

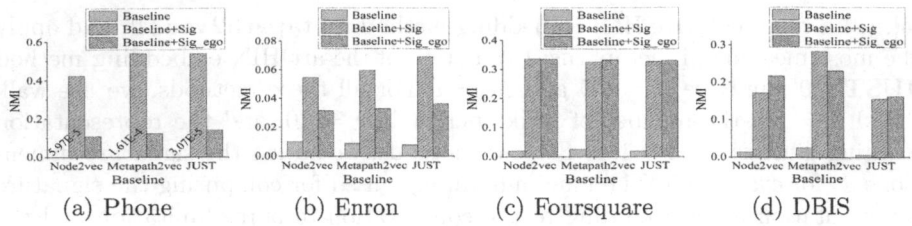

Fig. 3. Results of node clustering

Node Clustering: We use k-means for node clustering and report NMI in Fig. 3. We can see that our framework improves the performance of its corresponding baseline significantly. In most cases, direct-neighborhood performs better than ego-network. This is because for node clustering, node types themselves contribute to the final result the most. In general, our framework improves the performance of the corresponding baseline by up to five orders of magnitude.

Edge Classification: The representation vector of an edge is the concatenation of those of its two endpoints. We use logistic regression to do edge classification. We only show the results of Macro-F1 in Fig. 4 due to space limitation. The results of Micro-F1 are similar to those of Macro-F1. We can see that before applying our framework, node2vec performs the best among the three in most cases. This is because, traditional HIN embedding methods ignore the possible independence between edge and node types. After incorporating our framework, the predictive quality of all baselines increases by 10% to 70%.

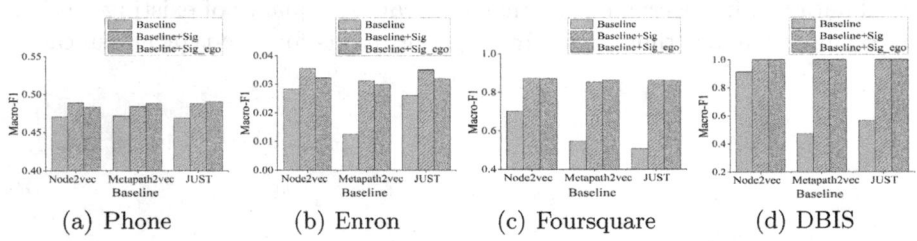

Fig. 4. Results of edge classification (Macro-F1)

Runtime Performance: Fig. 5 shows the learning time of applying our framework, where the final representation learning time consists of applying the baseline method as well as computing the signatures. We can see from Fig. 5 that the time needed for computing the signatures are negligible, compared to the cost of baseline methods.

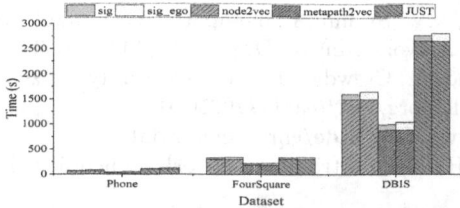

Fig. 5. A breakdown of execution times of various components

Summary: Our evaluations provide strong evidence that the proposed framework can improve the representation learning quality of the baseline methods on HINs significantly, with negligible extra running time. We have also done experiments that consider either topological features or neighborhood type features alone. However, as both parts are important to HINs, ignoring either of them would result in inferior evaluation results. Thus we did not report them in the paper. The experiments also demonstrate that our framework provides strong support for edge types that are more or less independent of node types.

6 Conclusions

In this work, we present a numerical signature based heterogeneous information network representation learning framework, which is compatible with and complements any existing homogeneous or HIN embedding methods. Under the same original dimensionality, with only about one-tenth extra time of existing embedding methods, the framework can improve the representation learning quality for downstream predictive analysis by two to three times, in terms of node classification, node clustering, and edge classification tasks.

Acknowledgements. Chunyao Song is supported in part by the NSFC under the grants 61702285, 61772289, U1836109, U1936206, and U1936105, the NSF of Tianjin under the grant 17JCQNJC00200, and Jiangsu Key Laboratory of Big Data Security & Intelligent Processing, NJUPT under the grant BDSIP1902. Tingjian Ge is supported in part by NSF grant IIS-1633271.

References

1. Bonner, S., Kureshi, I., Brennan, J., Theodoropoulos, G., McGough, A.S., Obara, B.: Exploring the semantic content of unsupervised graph embeddings: an empirical study. Data Sci. Eng. **4**(3), 269–289 (2019). https://doi.org/10.1007/s41019-019-0097-5
2. Cui, P., Wang, X., Pei, J., Zhu, W.: A survey on network embedding. IEEE Trans. Knowl. Data Eng. **31**(5), 833–852 (2019)
3. Dave, V.S., Zhang, B., Chen, P.Y., Hasan, M.A.: Neural-brane: neural Bayesian personalized ranking for attributed network embedding. Data Sci. Eng. **4**(2), 119–131 (2019). https://doi.org/10.1007/s41019-019-0092-x

4. Dong, Y., Chawla, N.V., Swami, A.: metapath2vec: scalable representation learning for heterogeneous networks. In: KDD, pp. 135–144 (2017)
5. Eagle, N., Pentland, A.: Crawdad dataset mit/reality (v. 2005–07-01). downloaded from http://crawdad.org/mit/reality/20050701
6. Enron: http://www.ahschulz.de/enron-email-data/
7. Gao, H., Huang, H.: Deep attributed network embedding. In: IJCAI, vol. 18, pp. 3364–3370 (2018)
8. Grover, A., Leskovec, J.: node2vec: scalable feature learning for networks. In: SIGKDD, pp. 855–864 (2016)
9. Huang, Z., Mamoulis, N.: Heterogeneous information network embedding for meta path based proximity (2017). arXiv:1701.05291v1
10. Hussein, R., Yang, D., Cudre-Mauroux, P.: Are meta-paths necessary? Revisiting heterogeneous graph embeddings. In: CIKM, pp. 437–446 (2018)
11. Lever, J., Krzywinski, M., Altman, N.: Principal component analysis. Nat. Methods 14, 641–642 (2017)
12. Ou, M., Cui, P., Pei, J., Zhang, Z., Zhu, W.: Asymmetric transitivity preserving graph embedding. In: SIGKDD, pp. 1105–1114 (2016)
13. Shi, C., Li, Y., Zhang, J., Sun, Y., Yu, P.S.: A survey of heterogeneous information network analysis. TKDE 29, 17–37 (2017)
14. Sun, Y., Han, J., Yan, X., Yu, P.S., Wu, T.: Pathsim: meta path-based top-k similarity search in heterogeneous information networks. VLDB 4(11), 992–1003 (2011)
15. Wang, D., Cui, P., Zhu, W.: Structural deep network embedding. In: SIGKDD, pp. 1225–1234 (2016)
16. Yang, D., Zhang, D., Qu, B.: Participatory cultural mapping based on collective behavior data in location based social networks. TIST 7(3), 1–23 (2015)

Keyword Search over Federated RDF Systems

Qing Wang, Peng Peng[(✉)], Tianyao Tong, Zhen Tian, and Zheng Qin

Hunan University, Changsha, China
{wangqing160,hnu16pp,cat0109,ztian,zqin}@hnu.edu.cn

Abstract. In this paper, we study the problem of keyword search over federated RDF systems. We utilize the full-text search interfaces provided by SPARQL endpoints and the authoritative documents of URIs to map keywords to the classes, and generates SPARQL queries by exploring the schema graph. Then, we send the generated queries to the SPARQL endpoints and evaluate these queries. Experiments show that our approaches are effective and efficient.

1 Introduction

Recently, *Resource Description Framework* (RDF) has been widely used in various applications to mark *resources* in the Web. An RDF dataset is a collection of triples, denoted as ⟨subject, property, object⟩. We can also represent an RDF dataset as a graph, where subjects and objects are vertices and triples are edges with labels between vertices.

As many data providers represent data in RDF model and provide the SPARQL interfaces in their own sites, the federated RDF systems [6,9] are put forward. In federated RDF systems, different RDF datasets are stored on different "autonomous" sites, and the data providers only provide the query interface to access their RDF datasets. In this paper, an autonomous site with a SPARQL query interface is called a *SPARQL endpoint*. The federated RDF system provides an interface to receive and handle the user requests over multiple SPARQL endpoints.

The federated RDF systems usually only support the SPARQL query to complete the data acquisition. However, in many applications, keyword search is more frequently used and easy to understand. Many studies [2,3] have been carried out on keyword search over other types of RDF systems. However, few solutions to federated RDF systems have been proposed.

For example, Fig. 1 shows an example RDF graph in a federated RDF system, which consists of four SPARQL endpoints. Assume an user wants to find out the anti-inflammatory that John Robert Vane is related to. John Robert Vane is a scientist that discovered how aspirin, an anti-inflammatory drug, produces pain-relief effects. Hence, the user may input two keywords, "anti-inflammatory" and "John Robert Vane", to specify his needs. We should utilize the two keywords to find out the relevant substructures returned to the user.

© Springer Nature Switzerland AG 2020
Y. Nah et al. (Eds.): DASFAA 2020, LNCS 12113, pp. 613–622, 2020.
https://doi.org/10.1007/978-3-030-59416-9_37

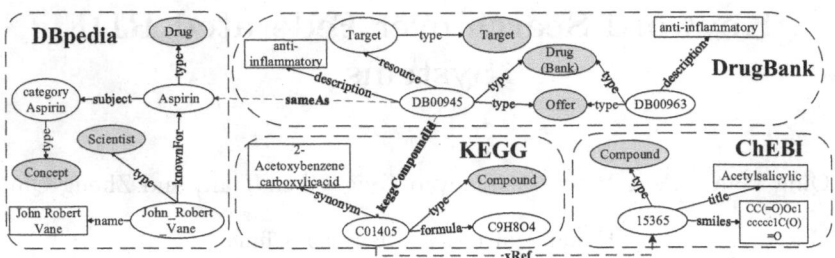

Fig. 1. Example federated RDF graph

In this paper, we propose a keyword search technique over federated RDF systems. In the offline phase, we combine the schemas of different SPARQL endpoints to construct a schema graph. In the online phase, we first utilize the SPARQL query interfaces and authoritative documents to map keywords to the candidate classes in the schema graph. Then, we traverse the schema graph to construct some queries to model users' query intentions. We evaluate the queries over federated RDF systems to find results returned to users.

In summary, our main contributions are summarized as follows:

- We put forward a SPARQL query interface-based approach for mapping keywords to the RDF graph over federated RDF systems.
- We propose an algorithm over the schema graph to construct SPARQL queries connecting the vertices corresponding to the keywords. We can evaluate these queries to find results returned.
- Finally, we evaluate our approach in real federated RDF datasets and confirm the superiority of our approach.

2   Preliminaries

In this section, we introduce some definitions used in this paper.

First, an *RDF graph* G can be defined as $\langle V, E, L, f \rangle$, where $V = V_L \cup V_E \cup V_C$ is a set of vertices that correspond to all subjects and objects in RDF data and V_L, V_E and V_C denote all literal vertices, resource vertices and class vertices; $E \subseteq V \times V$ is a multiset of directed edges that correspond to all triples in RDF data. $L = L_A \cup L_R \cup \{type\}$ is a set of edge labels, i.e. properties. L_A is the set of named attributes, L_R is the set of named relationships between resources, and $type$ connects resources to their classes. $f : E \rightarrow L$ is a function, and for each edge $e \in E$, $f(e)$ is its corresponding property.

On the other hand, a *federated RDF system* is a combination of many SPARQL endpoints at different sites [6]. Moreover, according to the principles for the web of Linked Data [4], resources, classes and properties are identified by their URI. For each URI, there exists a document describing it, which is considered as an *authoritative document*. We model the relationship between URIs and their authoritative documents by using the mapping *adoc*, and we can retrieve the authoritative document of a resource by looking up its URI.

A *SPARQL query Q* is a collection of triple patterns with variables and constraint filters, which can be represented as a query graph with variables and constraint filters. Then, given a SPARQL query Q over RDF graph G, a match μ is a subgraph of G homomorphic to Q and satisfying all constraint filters [12].

Given a set of keywords $KW = \{w_1, w_2, w_3, \ldots, w_n\}$ and a federated RDF system W, a result is a substructure over W that connects the vertices matching the keywords. In this paper, we convert KW to a set of SPARQL queries $\mathbb{Q}$ over W of top-k smallest sizes and get their results as the final results.

3 Overview

In this section, we give an overview of three main steps involved in our specific execution process as shown in Fig. 2. The first step is *keyword mapping*. We build up a schema graph for the federated RDF graph in the offline phase, which can intuitively capture the relationships between different classes. We also look up the authoritative documents of classes and properties in the schema graph and build up the invert indices for them. All the above indices are maintained in the control site. In the online phase, we first compute out a set of candidate classes in the schema graph for each keyword through the SPARQL query interfaces or the authoritative documents of classes and properties. The class vertices in the schema graph mapping to keywords are called *keyword elements* in this paper. After keyword mapping, the second step is *SPARQL query construction*. We explore the schema graph to find a substructure that is connected to all keyword elements. For each substructure, some SPARQL queries are constructed through the mapping of graph elements to query elements. We construct a set of SPARQL queries, $\mathbb{Q}$, to generate results for the keywords. The last step is *query execution*. We send $\mathbb{Q}$ to their relevant SPARQL endpoints and evaluate them there.

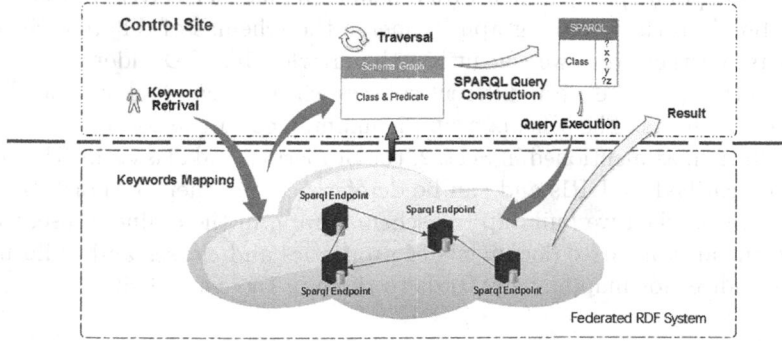

Fig. 2. System architecture

4 Keyword Mapping

In this section, we describe the detailed process of mapping keyword to the schema graph by using the full-text search interfaces in SPARQL endpoints.

4.1 Schema Graph

In this paper, to guide the keyword mapping and query construction process, we introduce the schema graph, which intuitively captures only relations between classes of resources. A schema graph S is defined as a triple $S = \{V^S, E^S, L^S\}$, where $V^S = V_C \cup \{Resource\}$ is a set of vertices corresponding to class vertices in G. Here, we use $Resource$ to represent the class of the resources with no given class. $E^S = V^S \times V^S$ is a set of directed edges, and $\overrightarrow{t_i t_j} \in E^S$ if and only if there is an edge $\overrightarrow{v_i v_j} \in E$ where v_i has a class t_i and v_j has a class t_j. $L^S = L_R$ is the set of edge labels, and $\overrightarrow{t_i t_j} \in E^S$ has a property p if and only if there is an edge $\overrightarrow{v_i v_j} \in E$ of property p where v_i has a class t_i and v_j has a class t_j. For example, Fig. 3 shows the schema graph for our example federated RDF graph.

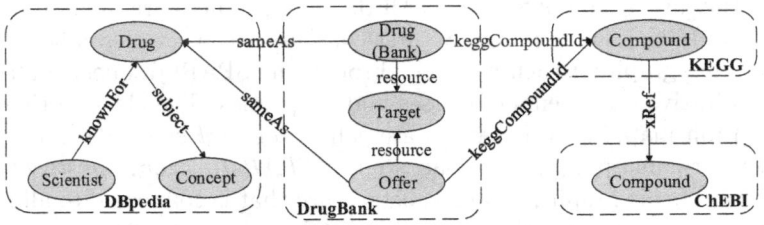

Fig. 3. Example schema graph

How to build up the schema graph is also a challenge. Fortunately, many SPARQL endpoints provide their own schemas to link themselves to users. Thus, we can build up the schema graph by merge the schemas of different SPARQL endpoints. Furthermore, we can utilize the crawler, like LDspider [7], to figure out edges that cross between different sources, since we can look up the URIs to retrieve their hosts. The schema graph is maintained in the control site.

In addition, as mentioned in Sect. 2, the properties and classes in RDF model are also identified by URIs and can be dereferenced by their authoritative documents. Thus, when we build up the schema graph in the offline phase, we also look up the authoritative documents of properties and classes and build up the inverted indices for mapping keywords to them in the control site.

4.2 Mapping Process

In real applications, keywords entered by users might refer to resources, classes or properties. In our approach, the full-text search interfaces are used to map keywords to resources, while the descriptions of classes and properties in the control site are used to map keywords to classes and properties. Note that, these two mapping processes are executed concurrently, because resource mapping only concerns the full-text search interfaces in the SPARQL endpoints and class and property mapping only concerns the descriptions of classes and properties in the control site. Many existing RDF repositories used for building up the SPARQL endpoints, like Sesame[1] and Virtuoso[2], provide the full-text search interfaces for users to access to the internal structure of string literals rather than treating such literals as opaque items.

Based on the results, we can annotate the corresponding class vertices in the schema graph with the keywords, and get an augmented schema graph annotated with keywords. For example, we can find out that the class mapping to "John Robert Vane" is "Scientist" in DBpedia, and the classes corresponding to keyword "anti-inflammatory" are "Drug (Bank)" and "Offer" in DrugBank. Then, we get the schema graph annotated with keywords as shown in Fig. 4.

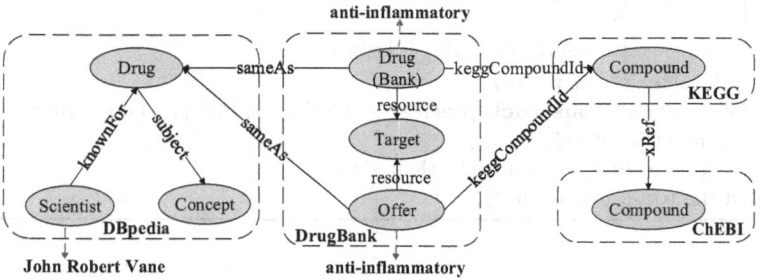

Fig. 4. Example schema graph annotated with keywords

5   SPARQL Query Construction

In this section, we introduce our method for SPARQL construction based on the results of keyword mapping. After keyword mapping, some class vertices in the schema graph are annotated with keywords, which are called *keyword elements*. Then, we explore the schema graph from the keyword elements to generate the substructures connecting them for constructing SPARQL queries. Our algorithm for query construction is displayed in Algorithm 1.

Generally, we maintain a result set RS_i and a priority queue PQ_i for each keyword w_i. The exploration starts with keyword elements that are placed into the queues (Lines 1–3 in Algorithm 1). At each step, we pick a queue PQ_i $(i = 1, \ldots, n)$ and pop its head to expand in a round-robin manner. When a vertex v is popped from queue PQ_i, we have computed its distance to keyword w_i, so we insert it into result set RS_i and try to add its neighbors into

---

[1] http://rdf4j.org/.

[2] https://virtuoso.openlinksw.com/rdf-quad-store/.

Algorithm 1: SPARQL Query Construction Algorithm

Input: The schema graph $S = \{V^S, E^S, L^S\}$, a set of keywords
$KW = \{w_1, w_2, w_3, \ldots, w_n\}$ mapping to keyword elements
$\{C_1, C_2, C_3, \ldots, C_n\}$, the priority queues $PQ_1, \ldots, PQ_n$.

Output: Constructed queries $\mathbb{Q}$.

1 **for** *each set C_i of keyword elements for keyword w_i* **do**
2   **for** *each keyword element v_C in C_i* **do**
3   Insert $(v_C, \emptyset, 0)$ into PQ_i;
4 **while** *not all queues are empty* **do**
5   **for** $i = 1, \ldots, n$ **do**
6   Pop the head of PQ_i (denoted as $(v, p, |p_i|)$);
7   **for** *each adjacent edge $\overrightarrow{vv'}$ (or $\overrightarrow{v'v}$) from v in E^S* **do**
8   Set $p'' = p \cup \overrightarrow{vv'}$ (or $p'' = p \cup \overrightarrow{v'v}$);
9   **if** *p'' is a simple path* **then**
10   **if** *there exists another element $(v', p', |p'|)$ in PQ_i* **then**
11   **if** $|p'| > |p| + 1$ **then**
12   Delete $(v', p', |p'|)$, and insert $(v', p'', |p_i| + 1)$ in PQ_i;
13   **else**
14   Insert $(v', p'', |p| + 1)$ in PQ_i;
15 **for** *each vertex v_C in V^S* **do**
16   Call function **ConstructQueries**$(v_C, \{RS_1, \ldots, RS_n\})$ to construct a query and insert it into $\mathbb{Q}$;
17 Sort all queries in $\mathbb{Q}$ according to their sizes.
18 Return the top-k queries in $\mathbb{Q}$.

---

the queue PQ_i (Lines 4–14 in Algorithm 1). We run the exploration algorithm until all vertices (in schema graph S) have been explored by all keywords. Then, each class vertex can correspond to a substructure connecting all keywords. We call a function *ConstructQueries* to construct SPARQL queries for these substructures (Lines 15–16 in Algorithm 1). In *ConstructQueries*, a vertex v is associated with a distinct variable $var(v)$, and $var(v)$ is also associated with a triple pattern that has the type of v in the schema graph (Line 5 in Function ConstructQueries). If v is a keyword element through resource mapping, it is associated with some triple patterns that map it to its corresponding keyword through the full-text search interface (Line 7 in Function ConstructQueries). If v is a keyword element through property mapping, the triple pattern with the mapping property is inserted into the constructed query (Line 9 in Function ConstructQueries). In addition, for each edge $\overrightarrow{vv'}$, its is mapped to a triple pattern $\langle var(v), L^S(\overrightarrow{vv'}), var(v') \rangle$ (Line 10–11 in Function ConstructQueries). Last, we sort the constructed queries according to their sizes and return the queries of the top-k smallest sizes (Lines 17–18 in Algorithm 1).

Function ConstructQueries(v_C, $\{RS_1, ..., RS_n\}$)

---

1 Initialize a query Q;
2 **for** $i \leftarrow 1$ *to* n **do**
3   Get p_i in RS_i that connects v_C to keyword elements in C_i;
4   **for** *each vertex v in p_i* **do**
5   Insert $var(v)$ and a triple pattern $\langle var(v), type, v \rangle$ into Q;
6   **if** *v is a keyword element from resource mapping* **then**
7   Insert some triple patterns mapping v to its keyword through the full-text search interface into Q;
8   **if** *v is a keyword element mapping to property $L^S(\overrightarrow{vv'})$* **then**
9   Insert a triple pattern $\langle var(v), L^S(\overrightarrow{vv'}), var(v') \rangle$;
10   **for** *each edge $e = \overrightarrow{vv'}$ in p_i* **do**
11   Insert a triple pattern $\langle var(v), L^S(\overrightarrow{vv'}), var(v') \rangle$ into Q;
12 Return Q;

---

6 Query Execution

After we construct a set of SPARQL queries, we should execute them to get their results. First, we decompose each query in $\mathbb{Q}$ to a set of subqueries expressed over relevant SPARQL endpoints. Then, we send the subqueries to their relevant SPARQL endpoints and evaluate them. Results of subqueries are returned to the control site and joined together to form final results presented to users. Moreover, when we join the results of subqueries, we can utilize the optimizations for joins [6,9], which group a set of join variables' matches in some subqueries and rewritten other subqueries using FILTER or UNION operators.

7 Experiments

In this section, we evaluate our method over a well-known real federated RDF benchmark. We compare our system with a federated keyword search engine, FuhSen [1], which has released their codes in GitHub[3].

7.1 Setting

FedBench [8] is a benchmark suite to test both the efficiency and effectiveness of federated RDF systems. It includes 4 life science domain datasets and 6 cross domain datasets. To assess the effectiveness of our approach, we have asked colleagues to provide 8 keyword queries for each datasets ($L_1 - L_8$ for life science and $C_1 - C_8$ for cross domain) along with the descriptions in natural language of the underlying information need.

We conduct all experiments on a cluster of machines running Linux on Alibaba Cloud, each of which has one CPU with two core of 2.5 GHz and 32 GB

---

[3] https://github.com/LiDaKrA/FuhSen-reactive.

memory. The prototype is implemented in Java. At each site, we install Sesame 2.8.10 to build up a SPARQL endpoint for a dataset in FedBench. Each SPARQL endpoint can only communicate with the control site through HTTP requests.

7.2 Effectiveness Study

In this section, we do experiments to show the effectiveness of our methods. We use the mean average precision (MAP) [11] to assess the effectiveness of the results. Table 1 reports the MAP values of the sixteen queries. Generally, we observe that our method gets rather better results than FuhSen. This is because FuhSen directly merges all keywords into one search constraint of a SPARQL query and cannot find answers for multiple keywords mapping to different resources across different endpoints. However, our method can find out the relevant substructures across multiple sites.

Furthermore, we find that the experimental result in life science is better than that in cross domain. The reason is that the datasets of cross domain have more complex schemas than that of life science. Thus, keywords may result in more ambiguity in cross domain than in life science.

Table 1. MAP values

	Our method	FuhSen
FedBench (Life Science)	0.87	0.30
FedBench (Cross Domain)	0.65	0.28

7.3 Efficiency Study

In this experiment, we compare the performance of our method with FuhSen [1]. Figure 5 shows the performance of different approaches. Generally speaking, our method can outperform FuhSen in most cases. FuhSen translate the input keywords into a simple query that need retrieve the whole RDF datasets in the sites, which take much more time than our method.

8 Related Work

For keyword search over federated RDF systems, one paper [5] utilizes the centralized technique in [2] to generate local queries for different SPARQL endpoints, and then synthesizes the local queries to form a federated query. Thus, it requires that the SPARQL endpoints should support to translate keywords to SPARQL queries, Hermes [10] build up a global keyword index for mapping keywords and generating query graphs across multiple sources. Then, Hermes evaluates these query graphs and return the evaluation results. Both of them are not practical in real federated RDF systems. FuhSen [1] develops an instance of

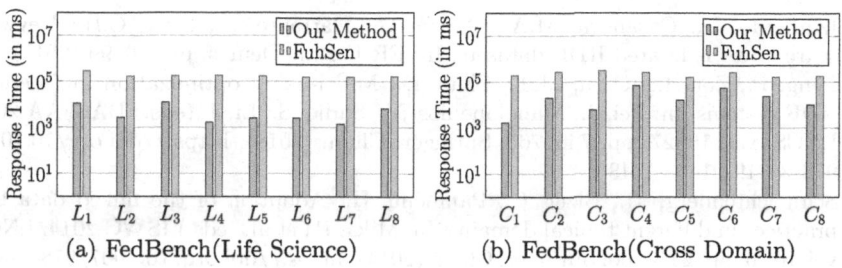

(a) FedBench(Life Science)   (b) FedBench(Cross Domain)

Fig. 5. Performance comparison

the RDF Wrapper component, which translates the keywords into a SPARQL query against the SPARQL endpoints. The union of matches are ranked returned to users. FuhSen fails to handle the cases that users input multiple keywords and results crossing multiple SPARQL endpoints need to be returned

9 Conclusions

In this paper, we propose a keyword search approach over federated RDF systems. By mapping the keywords to the schema graph derived from the federated RDF system, we construct SPARQL queries of the smallest sizes from the keywords, and evaluate them over the underlying federated RDF systems. Experiments show that our method is efficient and effective.

Acknowledgement. The corresponding author is Peng Peng, and this work was supported by NSFC under grant 61702171 and 61772191, National Key R&D Projects (2018YFB0704000, 2017YFB0902904), Hunan Provincial Natural Science Foundation of China under grant 2018JJ3065, Science and Technology Key Projects of Hunan Province (2015TP1004, 2018TP1009, 2018TP2023, 2018TP3001), Transportation Science and Technology Project of Hunan Province (201819), Science and Technology ChangSha City (kq1804008) and the Fundamental Research Funds for the Central Universities.

References

1. Collarana, D., Lange, C., Auer, S.: FuhSen: a platform for federated, RDF-based hybrid search. In: WWW, pp. 171–174 (2016)
2. García, G., Izquierdo, Y., Menendez, E., Dartayre, F., Casanova, M.A.: RDF keyword-based query technology meets a real-world dataset. In: EDBT, pp. 656–667 (2017)
3. Han, S., Zou, L., Yu, J.X., Zhao, D.: Keyword search on RDF graphs - a query graph assembly approach. In: CIKM, pp. 227–236 (2017)
4. Hartig, O.: SPARQL for a web of linked data: semantics and computability. In: Simperl, E., Cimiano, P., Polleres, A., Corcho, O., Presutti, V. (eds.) ESWC 2012. LNCS, vol. 7295, pp. 8–23. Springer, Heidelberg (2012). https://doi.org/10.1007/978-3-642-30284-8_8

5. Izquierdo, Y., Casanova, M.A., García, G., Dartayre, F., Levy, C.H.: Keyword search over federated RDF datasets. In: ER Forum/Demos, pp. 86–99 (2017)
6. Peng, P., Zou, L., Özsu, M.T., Zhao, D.: Multi-query optimization in federated RDF systems. In: Pei, J., Manolopoulos, Y., Sadiq, S., Li, J. (eds.) DASFAA 2018. LNCS, vol. 10827, pp. 745–765. Springer, Cham (2018). https://doi.org/10.1007/978-3-319-91452-7_48
7. Schmachtenberg, M., Bizer, C., Paulheim, H.: Adoption of the linked data best practices in different topical domains. In: Mika, P., et al. (eds.) ISWC 2014. LNCS, vol. 8796, pp. 245–260. Springer, Cham (2014). https://doi.org/10.1007/978-3-319-11964-9_16
8. Schmidt, M., Görlitz, O., Haase, P., Ladwig, G., Schwarte, A., Tran, T.: FedBench: a benchmark suite for federated semantic data query processing. In: Aroyo, L., et al. (eds.) ISWC 2011. LNCS, vol. 7031, pp. 585–600. Springer, Heidelberg (2011). https://doi.org/10.1007/978-3-642-25073-6_37
9. Schwarte, A., Haase, P., Hose, K., Schenkel, R., Schmidt, M.: FedX: optimization techniques for federated query processing on linked data. In: Aroyo, L., et al. (eds.) ISWC 2011. LNCS, vol. 7031, pp. 601–616. Springer, Heidelberg (2011). https://doi.org/10.1007/978-3-642-25073-6_38
10. Tran, T., Wang, H., Haase, P.: Hermes: data Web search on a pay-as-you-go integration infrastructure. J. Web Semant. 7(3), 189–203 (2009)
11. Turpin, A., Scholer, F.: User performance versus precision measures for simple search tasks. In: SIGIR, pp. 11–18 (2006)
12. Zou, L., Özsu, M.T., Chen, L., Shen, X., Huang, R., Zhao, D.: gStore: a graph-based SPARQL query engine. VLDB J. 23(4), 565–590 (2014)

Mutual Relation Detection for Complex Question Answering over Knowledge Graph

Qifan Zhang[1], Peihao Tong[3], Junjie Yao[1,2(✉)], and Xiaoling Wang[1]

[1] School of Computer Science and Technology,
East China Normal University, Shanghai, China
qifanwz@gmail.com, xherot@gmail.com
[2] Key Laboratory of Advanced Theory and Application in Statistics and Data
Science, Ministry of Education, East China Normal University, Shanghai, China
{junjie.yao,xlwang}@cs.ecnu.edu.cn
[3] Pinduoduo Inc., Shanghai, China

Abstract. Question Answering over Knowledge Graph (KG-QA) becomes a convenient way to interact with the prevailing information. The user's information needs, i.e., input questions become more complex. We find that the comparison, relation, and opinion questions are witnessed a significant growth, especially in some domains. However, most of the current KG-QA methods cannot appropriately handle the inherent complex relation and coverage characteristics within the questions.

In this work, we propose to utilize the relation information with the questions and knowledge graph in a mutual way, improving the final question answering performance. Wse design local and global attention models for relation detection. We combine the features for relation detection in an attention matching model. Experiments on our new dataset and common dataset reveal its advantages both in accuracy and efficiency.

1 Introduction

Question answering over knowledge graph(KG-QA) has attracted many attentions and acheived remarkable progress in recent years [2,3,14,15]. With the great benefits of KG-QA, we have witnessed an information access paradigm shift, from a proactive search to voice/question oriented automatic assistant in recent years. Under the hood of these services, structured knowledge graphs play an essential role, which are constructed from a wide range of related data sources. Common ways of KG-QA include semantic parsing, retrieval and recent neural matching based. Though impressive performance, KG-QA is still a challenging problem. The difficulty issues lie at not only the vague question description but

J. Yao—This work was supported by National Key R&D Program of China (No. 2017YFC0803700), NSFC grant (61972151, 61972155).

Y. Nah et al. (Eds.): DASFAA 2020, LNCS 12113, pp. 623–631, 2020.
https://doi.org/10.1007/978-3-030-59416-9_38

also a growing variety of complex relation types within the diverse knowledge graphs [12, 20].

Take an insurance product KG as our motivation scenario, we have constructed a knowledge graph for insurance products (InsKG, abbrv. later in this paper). Currently, it has more than 200k nodes, consisting of insurance categories, types, attributes, diseases, detailed terms, etc. We have set up a KG-QA service on top of it. With intuitive answers, we collected almost 100k questions from ordinary users, in less than one year. A part of this knowledge graph and its question examples are shown in Fig. 1. These new questions cover a wide range of question types and usually need several hops to identify the answers in the target knowledge graph. The required answers also connect different kinds of relation connection. These new input questions are difficult to well process under current KG-QA methods, requiring more complex relation detection and composition.

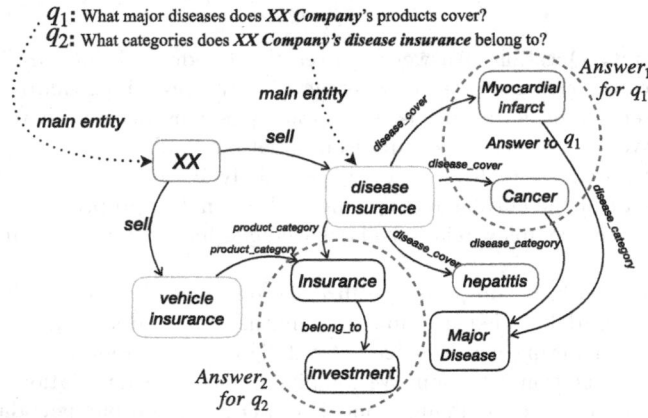

Fig. 1. Complex Questions and Multi-Hop Answers in KG-QA

Relation detection is not new for knowledge graph communities. Especially, some recent work [7, 19] made impressive progress for relation inference in knowledge graph or type detection for improving question answering. However, they either focus on relation matching or type extension, and are difficult to support complex and long questions. It is still challenging to effectively process the user's growing complex questions for the knowledge graph.

In this paper, we propose a Mutual Relation Detection (MRD) framework with attention mechanism [6, 17]. We combine the relation detection and question answering together in a natural way. We utilize the features extracted from question logs and knowledge graph for the relation detection. Also, we utilize the question logs and knowledge graph as global features to enrich the relation detection. Experiments on two real datasets demonstrate its improved performance on relation detection.

The contributions of this paper can be briefly summarized as follows. We exploit the rich features embedded in questions and knowledge graphs to improve relation detection, and finally the KG-QA. We then utilize the attention model to match the relation detection features in the complex KG-QA task, in a natural way. The experimental results demonstrate the effectiveness of our proposed approach, especially in domain knowledge graphs.

2   Related Work

Question Answering over knowledge Graph: Semantic parsing-based methods compile the input natural language questions into logical forms, with the help of a combinatory grammar [4] or dependency-based compositional semantics [9]. Recent deep learning methods usually transform questions and answers into the form of semantic vectors [3], and then conduct the matching, ranking operations. These methods are impressive and useful, but encounter difficulties in handling the complex user questions.

Relation Detection: With the benefits for relation inference, knowledge graph completion and even collective classification, relation detection in knowledge graph are becoming more and more important. [5,7] discussed the reasoning framework and translation based methods for relation detection in knowledge graph. [10,20] presented type selection approach. [19] discussed relation detection for precise question match with edge descriptions. This paper differs from these recent work, and we focus on answer relation detection and composition in a mutual way.

Attention Models: [18] designed an attentive max-pooling layer for CNN to answer factual questions. [6] discussed attention based end-to-end model with the global knowledge graph features for question answering. [8] introduced the interactive model for question answering. We proceed to design a mutual attention model, combining both question and knowledge graph features, from the local and global perspectives.

3   Mutual Relation Detection

3.1   Relation Detection Framework

Figure 2 shows the general design of the proposed approach. Given an input question, we first extract the local features within the input question and embed the candidate relations. As well as the local question analysis and knowledge graph extraction, we also enrich global features, leveraging the existing question corpus and the global knowledge graph context to improve the relation detection performance in a mutually way. The extraction covers the local and global aspects, and generate the question and graph features.

We extract relation features from the question corpus with the help of LSTM model. Graph global type and context features are served into the relation detection task. We then utilize the attention based matching models to process the

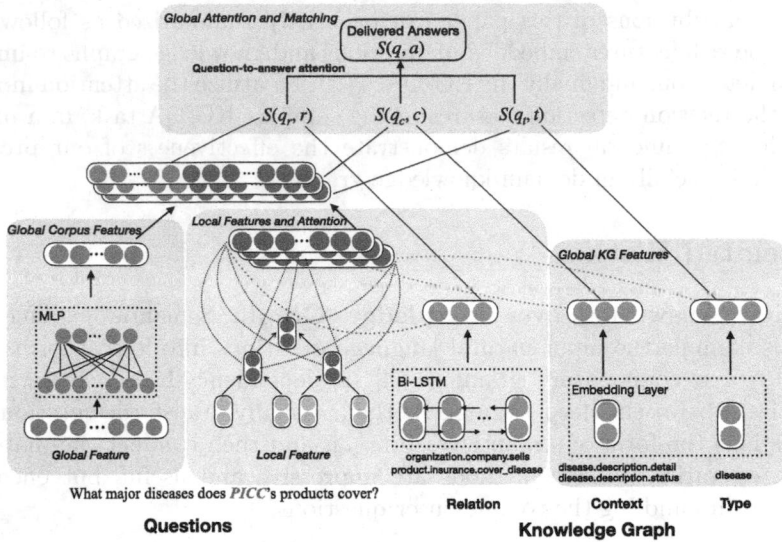

Fig. 2. Framework of Mutual Relation Detection in KG-QA

local question parts and the global features. In the training procedure, we employ the pairwise training strategy. The loss function is defined as follows, where a denotes the correct answer, a' denotes the wrong answer and γ is the margin which is always a small positive real number within 1.

$$\mathcal{L}_{q,a,a'} = \sum_{a \in P_q} \sum_{a' \in N_q} [\gamma + S(q,a') - S(q,a)]_+ \tag{1}$$

3.2 Local and Global Feature Extraction

Relation Features in Questions. We utilize the tree-structured LSTM model, a variant of recursive neural networks [13] for question feature extraction. The architecture of the network will be constructed according to the tree structure of the extracted concept layers from the input question. We set up constituency trees for each question, and use Tree-LSTM to handle the constituency tree. The constituency tree is intuitive to cover different semantic modules within it, beneficial for the question representation since the left subtree contains noun information, while the right contains the verb relation.

Global Question Features: Though Tree-LSTM model can leverage local word patterns with the help of tree patterns, it is difficult to capture global information, especially from many existing questions. To extract a global view of topics from the questions, we propose to utilize global term features to represent question as a supplement to the Tree-LSTM model. Given a vocabulary of words $V = (w_1, w_2, \cdots, w_{|V|})$, the question will be represented as

$q_{tf} = \{n_1, n_2, \cdots, n_{|V|}\}$ where n_i represents the frequency or other weights of the word w_i appearing in the question. Then a linear layer and tanh function are chosen to handle the global question representation. In this way, we generate a dense global representation for each question.

Relation Features in Knowledge Graph. In the formulation of the relation detection as a mutual matching problem, we take not only relation name descriptions but also more rich tail entity type and context information into consideration.

Relation Modeling: Here we choose word-level features to represent relations. Formally, the relation will be denoted as $r = \{w_{r_1}, w_{r_2}, \cdots, w_{r_n}\}$. Take the relation "product.insurance.cover._disease" as example, we will split the relation name into words sequence as "product", "insurance", "cover" and "disease". The relation can be regarded as a word sequence. The pre-trained word embedding vectors such as GloVe [11] are used to initialize the embedding for words in the relation sequence. Finally, one max-pooling is be used to generate the final representation $h^a(r)$ from the outcome of the Bi-LSTM model.

Global Graph Feature Modeling: We continue to exploit the relation's corresponding tail entity types as a feature source. The difficult issue is that the tail entity types are confusing. We propose a method to collect tail entity type for each relation with the global information of the KG. For each relation, we collect all the tail entity of this relation and then rank the numbers of entity types. Shown in Fig. 3, the type "cardiopathy", "neoplasm" and "inflammation" will be filtered since they are not the global type for relation "disease_cover".

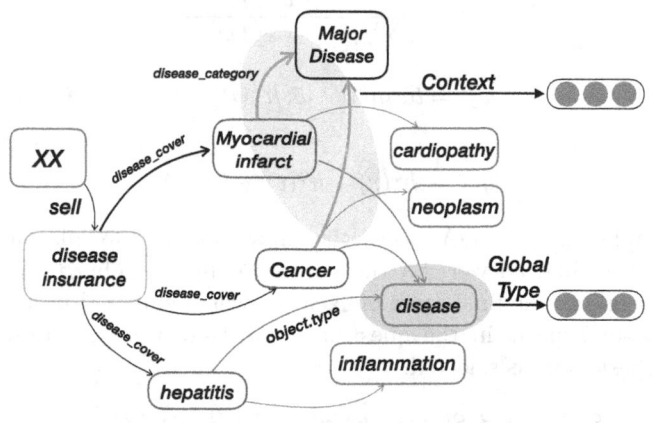

Answer Relation： *sell -> disease_cover*

Fig. 3. Global type and question context

Local Graph Feature Modeling: The context information is also taken into consideration in order to provide a local structure view for corresponding relations.

For each candidate relation, we collect all the relations connected to the tail entity as the context of the candidate relation.

3.3   Mutual Attention Matching Models

Local Attention. We combine the h_{root}, h_{left} and h_{right} from question features. The weight of attention is evaluated by the relevance between each feature node on question representation and answer aspect representation.

$$\alpha_j^i = \frac{\exp(w_{ij})}{\sum_{k=1}^{3} \exp(w_{ik})} \qquad (2)$$

$$w_{ij} = tanh(W^T[h_j; a_i] + b) \qquad (3)$$

Here α_j^i denotes the attention weight between an answer aspect a_i and tree node representation h_j where $h_j \in \{h_{left}, h_{root}, h_{right}\}$ and $a_i \in \{h^a(r), h^a(t), h^a(c)\}$.

Global Attention. Questions should also take varying attention to different answer aspects. Different questions will concentrate on different answer aspects, which leads to question-towards-answer attention, shown in Fig. 2. We generate the question-towards-answer attention distribution β, which are β_r, β_t, β_c respectively, denoting the attention weight for each answer aspect. This weight distribution reflects the importance of different answers aspects w.r.t. the input question.

$$\beta_{a_i} = \frac{\exp(w_{a_i})}{\sum_{a_j \in r,t,c} \exp(w_{a_j})} \qquad (4)$$

$$w_{a_i} = tanh(W^T[\bar{q}; h^a(i)] + b) \qquad (5)$$

$$\bar{q} = \frac{1}{3}(h^q(r) + h^q(t) + h^q(c)) \qquad (6)$$

For example, in some QA cases, the answer type may play a key role in determining the final answer. So the corresponding weight β_{e_t} will be larger than other weights. The final score of each answer is summed up by scores from different answer aspects in the question-towards-answer attention. Candidate with the highest score is selected.

$$S(q,a) = \beta_r S(h^q(r), h^a(r)) + \beta_t S(h^q(t), h^a(t)) \\ + \beta_c S(h^q(c), h^a(c)) \qquad (7)$$

4 Experiments

4.1 Experimental Setup

We conduct extensive experiments on two datasets. One is the insKG dataset we have created and released, as the specific domain knowledge graph. A subset with 200k nodes is used in this experiment. Another one is the commonly used WebQuestions [1] dataset, as the open domain knowledge graph dataset.

In the WebQuestions dataset, there are about 4.8k q-a pairs, containing 3,116 training pairs training and 1,649 testing pairs. In the insKG dataset, we carefully select 1,527 q-a pairs for training and 794 q-a pairs for testing.

4.2 Improved QA Accuracy

Table 1 shows the QA tests on WebQuestions and InsKG datasets. The proposed model outperforms the baslines and achieve significant improvomonto. In WebQuestions, global feature is not significant. In contrast, the global feature contributes a lot in the improvement.

Table 1. QA performance

Methods	WebQuestions	InsKG
Bi-CNN [16]	77.74	84.08
Bi-LSTM [6]	79.32	86.07
Residual network [19]	82.53	89.67
Proposed approach	**84.11**	**95.34**
w/o global feature	83.38	92.30
w/o context and type feature	83.02	93.82

4.3 Training Process

To test the efficiency of the model structure, we diagnose the model training process in InsKG dataset in Fig. 4. Our model can always have a swift convergence, compared with other baselines.

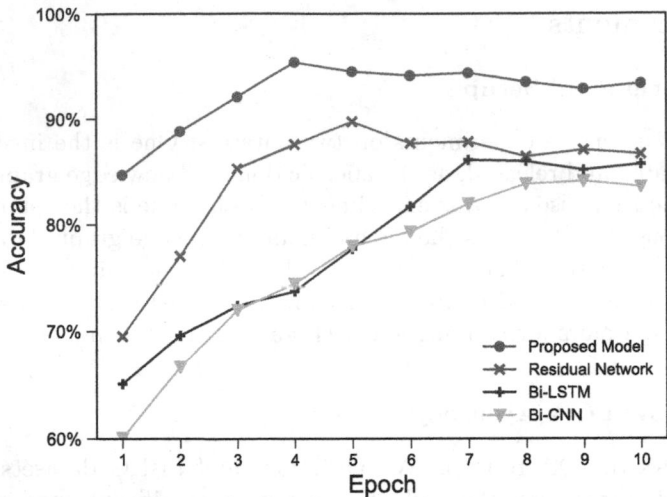

Fig. 4. Training Process on InsKG

5 Conclusion

In this paper, we propose a mutual relation detection approach for question answering over knowledge graph. We design an attention based matching framework, which includes comprehensive feature selection and composition. Experiments demonstrate its advantage not only in increasing complex specific domain knowledge graphs but also improves the open domain ones. In the ongoing work, we are exploiting its potential for users' ad hoc relation inference and suggestion problems.

References

1. Berant, J., Chou, A., Frostig, R., Liang, P.: Semantic parsing on freebase from question-answer pairs. In: Proceedings of EMNLP, pp. 1533–1544 (2013)
2. Bollacker, K.D., Evans, C., Paritosh, P., Sturge, T., Taylor, J.: Freebase: a collaboratively created graph database for structuring human knowledge. In: Proceedings of SIGMOD, pp. 1247–1250 (2008)
3. Bordes, A., Weston, J., Usunier, N.: Open question answering with weakly supervised embedding models. In: Calders, T., Esposito, F., Hüllermeier, E., Meo, R. (eds.) ECML PKDD 2014. LNCS (LNAI), vol. 8724, pp. 165–180. Springer, Heidelberg (2014). https://doi.org/10.1007/978-3-662-44848-9_11
4. Cai, Q., Yates, A.: Large-scale semantic parsing via schema matching and lexicon extension. In: Proceedings of ACL, pp. 423–433 (2013)
5. Fan, Z., Wei, Z., Li, P., Lan, Y., Huang, X.: A question type driven framework to diversify visual question generation. In: Proceedings of IJCAI, pp. 4048–4054 (2018)

6. Hao, Y., et al.: An end-to-end model for question answering over knowledge base with cross-attention combining global knowledge. In: Proceedings of ACL, pp. 221–231 (2017)
7. He, X., Qian, W., Fu, C., Zhu, Y., Cai, D.: Translating embeddings for knowledge graph completion with relation attention mechanism. In: Proceedings of IJCAI, pp. 4286–4292 (2018)
8. Li, H., Min, M.R., Ge, Y., Kadav, A.: A context-aware attention network for interactive question answering. In: Proceedings of KDD, pp. 927–935 (2017)
9. Liang, P., Jordan, M.I., Klein, D.: Learning dependency-based compositional semantics. Comput. Linguist. **39**(2), 389–446 (2013)
10. Miyanishi, T., Hirayama, J.i., Kanemura, A., Kawanabe, M.: Answering mixed type questions about daily living episodes. In: Proceedings of IJCAI, pp. 4265–4271 (2018)
11. Pennington, J., Socher, R., Manning, C.D.: Glove: global vectors for word representation. In: Proceedings of EMNLP, pp. 1532–1543 (2014)
12. Saha, A., Pahuja, V., Khapra, M.M., Sankaranarayanan, K., Chandar, S.: Complex sequential question answering: towards learning to converse over linked question answer pairs with a knowledge graph. In: Proceedings of AAAI, pp. 705–713 (2018)
13. Tai, K.S., Socher, R., Manning, C.D.: Improved semantic representations from tree-structured long short-term memory networks. In: Proceedings of ACL, pp. 1556–1566 (2015)
14. Yang, M., Duan, N., Zhou, M., Rim, H.: Joint relational embeddings for knowledge-based question answering. In: Proceedings of EMNLP, pp. 645–650 (2014)
15. Yao, X., Durme, B.V.: Information extraction over structured data: question answering with freebase. In: Proceedings of ACL, pp. 956–966 (2014)
16. Yih, W., Chang, M., He, X., Gao, J.: Semantic parsing via staged query graph generation: question answering with knowledge base. In: Proceedings of ACL, pp. 1321–1331 (2015)
17. Yin, J., Zhao, W.X., Li, X.M.: Type-aware question answering over knowledge base with attention-based tree-structured neural networks. J. Comput. Sci. Technol. **32**(4), 805–813 (2017)
18. Yin, W., Yu, M., Xiang, B., Zhou, B., Schütze, H.: Simple question answering by attentive convolutional neural network. In: Proceedings of COLING, pp. 1746–1756 (2016)
19. Yu, M., Yin, W., Hasan, K.S., dos Santos, C.N., Xiang, B., Zhou, B.: Improved neural relation detection for knowledge base question answering. In: Proceedings of ACL, pp. 571–581 (2017)
20. Zhang, Y., Dai, H., Kozareva, Z., Smola, A., Song, L.: Variational reasoning for question answering with knowledge graph. In: Proceedings of AAAI, pp. 6069–6076 (2018)

DDSL: Efficient Subgraph Listing
on Distributed and Dynamic Graphs

Xun Jian[1]($\boxtimes$), Yue Wang[2], Xiayu Lei[1], Yanyan Shen[3], and Lei Chen[1]

[1] The Hong Kong University of Science and Technology, Hong Kong, China
{xjian,xylei,leichen}@cse.ust.hk
[2] Shenzhen Institute of Computing Sciences, Shenzhen University,
Shenzhen, China
ywangby@connect.ust.hk
[3] Shanghai Jiao Tong University, Shanghai, China
shenyy@sjtu.edu.cn

Abstract. Subgraph listing is a fundamental problem in graph theory and has wide applications in many areas. Modern graphs can usually be large-scale and highly dynamic, which challenges the efficiency of existing subgraph listing algorithms. In this paper, we propose an efficient join-based approach, called *Distributed and Dynamic Subgraph Listing* (DDSL), which can incrementally update the results instead of running from scratch. Extensive experiments are conducted on real-world datasets. The results show that DDSL outperforms existing methods in dealing with both static and dynamic graphs in terms of the responding time.

Keywords: Distributed graph · Dynamic graph · Subgraph listing

1 Introduction

In this paper, we study subgraph listing, one of the fundamental problems in graph theory. Given two undirected and unlabeled graphs d and p, it requires to list all subgraphs of the *data graph* d, which are isomorphic to the *pattern graph* p. Such a subgraph is also called a match. Despite its NP-hardness [2], subgraph listing has wide applications in areas like sociology, chemistry, telecommunication and bioinformatics [8,10].

The large size and high dynamic of real-world graphs challenge the efficiency of subgraph listing algorithms. Although existing distributed solutions like [1,7, 9] achieve good performance on static graphs, they fall short in exact subgraph listing on distributed and dynamic graphs.

In this paper, we propose *Dynamic and Distributed Subgraph Listing* (DDSL), which is able to solve the exact subgraph listing problem on distributed and dynamic graphs. Considering that disks are preferred to store massive matching results, which might be updated subsequently to graph changes, we develop our method in MapReduce [3]. The whole approach can be divided into two

Y. Nah et al. (Eds.): DASFAA 2020, LNCS 12113, pp. 632–640, 2020.
https://doi.org/10.1007/978-3-030-59416-9_39

stages. The initial stage follows a general distributed join framework [7], where matches of *join units* (subgraphs of the pattern graph p in pre-defined forms) are listed from a distributed storage of the data graph d, and those matches are joined to recover the matches of p. In the incremental updating stage, we design an algorithm which can update the distributed storage according to the graph changes with a low cost. To update the matches, we design a novel *Navigated Join* (Nav-join) approach to extract a *patch set* that contains only the newly-appeared matches. Then we can simply merge the old matches with the patch set, and filter out the matches that no longer exist. By expectation, our approach has a lower cost compared to running from scratch under mild assumptions.

2 Preliminaries

Given an undirected and unlabeled graph g, we use $V(g)$ and $E(g)$ to denote the vertex set and edge set in g, respectively. An edge connecting v_i and v_j is denoted by (v_i, v_j) (or equivalently (v_j, v_i)). Edge (v_i, v_j) is *incident* to both v_i and v_j. For any vertex $v \in V(g)$, denote $\mathcal{N}_g(v)$ as the *neighbors* of v, which is defined as $\mathcal{N}_g(v) = \{u | (v, u) \in E(g)\}$, and $deg(v) = |\mathcal{N}_g(v)|$ as the degree of v.

Given two graphs d and p, subgraph listing requires outputing all subgraphs of d, which are isomorphic [11] to p. Here d is called the *data graph*, and p is called the *pattern graph*. Each isomorphism f from p to a valid subgraph of d is called a *match*, and we denote $M(p, d)$ as the set of all matches of p in d.

The *automorphism* of a graph g is the isomorphism $f : V(g) \mapsto V(g)$. In this work, we use *Symmetric Breaking* (SimB) [4] to avoid duplicate results caused by the automorphisms of p. In this case, for each valid subgraph of d, we can find only one *match*.

A dynamic graph is defined as an initial graph d, followed by several updates U_1, U_2, ..., where each update U_i contains a set $E_d(U_i)$ of edges to delete and a set $E_a(U_i)$ of edges to insert. Assuming that after applying each of those updates, we get the updated graphs d', d'', ..., our goal is to output the match set $M(p, d)$, $M(p, d')$, $M(p, d'')$, ... efficiently. For simplicity, we only consider one update, because if we can compute $M(p, d')$ efficiently, we can handle the next one by treating d' as the new initial graph.

Problem Statement. Given a distributed file system, which can store and load data as key-value pairs, a pattern graph p, a data graph d, and a graph update U, we consider two problems:

1. To compute $M(p, d)$ efficiently.
2. To compute $M(p, d')$ efficiently given $M(p, d)$, where d' is the updated graph.

3 DDSL: Initial Subgraph Listing

We use all graphs with *radius = 1* as join units, which are called R1 units. Given an R1 unit q, we can find at least one vertex, who is the common neighbor of all other vertices. We randomly pick such a vertex as the *anchor vertex* of q.

To support directly listing the matches of any R1 unit without join, we use the Neighbor-Preserved (NP) storage mechanism. Specifically, for each vertex v_i, we store its *local graph* $loc(v_i) = d[\{v_i\} \cup \mathcal{N}_d(v_i)]$ in partition $d_{h(i)}$, where h is an arbitrary partition function.

Perceptually, u_i lies on the "center" of $loc(u_i)$, so we call u_i a *center vertex* of d_j if $h(i) = j$. For non-center vertices of d_j, we call them *border vertices*. To list matches of a join unit q, we use an alternative version $M_{ac}(q, d_i)$ which requires that q's anchor vertex must be matched to one of d_i's center vertices. In this way, the union of all $M_{ac}(q, d_i)$ will be $M(q, d)$[1].

3.1   Pattern Decomposition and Join

With the two building blocks decided, we can perform the subgraph listing within the join framework. Given a pattern graph p, we decompose p into a set of join units $Q = \{q_1, q_2, \ldots, q_k\}$, such that (1) Each q_i is an R1 unit, and (2) $\bigcup_{q_i \in Q} q_i = p$.

We then list the matches of all the join units in Q directly from the NP storage, and join the matches together. Assuming that we have two matches $f_1 \in M(p_1, d)$ and $f_2 \in M(p_2, d)$, then f_1 can be joined with f_2 if $\forall v \in V(p_1) \cap V(p_2) : f_1(v) = f_2(v)$. This guarantees that there exists no conflict when merging the mappings in f_1 and f_2, and the vertex set $\{f_i(v) | \forall v \in V(p_1) \cap V(p_2)\}$ is called the join keys. After the join, we need to check each result, and drop every match that maps two or more vertices in p to the same vertex in d.

To find a good decomposition as well as a join order to reduce the I/O cost, we apply techniques like match size estimation and computation cost model as in [7]. We refer the reader to [5] for details.

4   DDSL: Incremental Updating

In this section we address the problem of handling dynamic graphs. Assuming that a batch U of edge updates is applied on the original data graph d, resulting in a new data graph d', we update $\Phi(d)$ and $M(p, d)$ in three steps:

1. Update $\Phi(d)$ to $\Phi(d')$ according to U;
2. Compute a patch set $M_{new}(p, d')$ containing all newly-appeared matches, i.e., $M_{new}(p, d') = M(p, d') \backslash M(p, d)$;
3. Compute $M(p, d')$ by first filtering matches in $M(p, d)$ that should be removed, and then merging the result with $M_{new}(p, d')$.

4.1   Updating the NP Storage

To update the NP storage $\Phi(d)$, essentially we need to update each local graph $loc(u_i)$ correctly.

---

[1] All the proofs can be found in [5].

Algorithm 1: Update NP storage

Input : $\Phi(d)$, h, U.
Output: $\Phi(d')$.

1 **Function** *NBRSet(d_k, i, U)*   // compute $\mathcal{N}_{d'}(u_i)$
2 | return $\mathcal{N}_{d_k}(u_i) \setminus \{u_l | \forall (u_i, u_l) \in E_d(U)\} \cup \{u_l | \forall (u_i, u_l) \in E_a(U)\}$;
3 **Function** *map(d_k, h, U)*
4 | **foreach** $(u_i, u_j) \in E_a(U)$ **do**
5 | | **if** $h(i) = k$ && $h(i) \neq h(j)$ **then** Output$(h(j), \text{NBRSet}(d_k, i, U))$;
6 | | **if** $h(j) = k$ && $h(i) \neq h(j)$ **then** Output$(h(i), \text{NBRSet}(d_k, j, U))$;
7 **Function** *reduce(d_k, h, U, $\mathcal{N}_{d'_k}$)*
8 | **foreach** $(u_i, u_j) \in E_d(U)$ **do** delete edge (u_i, u_j) from d_k ;
9 | **foreach** $(u_i, u_j) \in E_a(U)$ **do** insert edge (u_i, u_j) into d_k using $\mathcal{N}_{d'_k}$;
10 | Output$(updated\ d_k)$;

Edge Insertion. There are two possible situations that inserting an edge can lead to the change of $loc(u_i)$.

1. Inserting edge (u_i, u_j), which means u_j becomes a new neighbor of u_i. In this case, we need to check all edges adjacent to u_j, and add edge (u_j, u_k) into $loc(u_i)$ if u_k is u_i's neighbor.
2. Inserting edge (u_j, u_k), where u_j and u_k are both u_i's neighbors. In this case, we only need to add (u_j, u_k) into $loc(u_i)$.

Edge Deletion. Edge deletion is the reverse of edge insertion, so it can be handled by the above two situations with all edge insertions replaced with edge deletions. The only difference is that, in situation (1), we can just delete all edges in $loc(u_i)$ which are adjacent to u_j.

In DDSL we deal with all cases in a single MapReduce round, which is summarized in Algorithm 1. Each mapper takes d_k and U as the input, which causes $S(\Phi(d)) + m \cdot |E(U)|$ I/O cost. All mappers output the neighbor sets of vertices in U, which are shuffled to the reducer. This incurs at most $3 \cdot \sum_{u_i \in U} |\mathcal{N}_{d'}(u_i)|$ communication cost. The reducers read d_k, U and $\mathcal{N}_{d'_k}$, and then output $\Phi(d')$, so the I/O cost of reduce is $S(\Phi(d)) + m \cdot |E(U)| + \sum_{u_i \in U} |\mathcal{N}_{d'}(u_i)| + S(\Phi(d'))$. In summary, the total cost of updating $\Phi(d)$ is

$$2 \cdot S(\Phi(d)) + 2 \cdot m \cdot |E(U)| + 4 \cdot \sum_{u_i \in U} |\mathcal{N}_{d'}(u_i)| + S(\Phi(d'))$$

4.2 Updating the Match Set

The update of the match set can be divided into two categories: the removed matches and the newly-appeared matches. The removed matches exist in $M(p, d)$, but are no longer valid because some edges are deleted. They can be removed by checking each match in $M(p, d)$, and removing those who contain edges in $E_d(U)$. The extra I/O cost comes from reading the deleted edge set $E_d(U)$ by each mapper, which is in total $m \cdot |E(U)|$.

The newly-appeared matches do not exist in $M(p, d)$, but appear in $M(p, d')$. According to Lemma 1, we can use $E_a(U)$ to identify these matches, which consist the patch set $M_{new}(p, d')$.

Lemma 1. *A match in $M(p, d')$ is not in $M(p, d)$ if and only if it maps any edge in $E(p)$ to an inserted edge in $E_a(U)$.*

In DDSL, we design a *navigated join (Nav-join)* to compute $M_{new}(p, d')$ with a lower cost based on two assumptions:

- The inserted edge number is small compared to $|E(d)|$, so $|M_{new}(p_i, d', q_i)|$ for any p_i and q_i should be small.
- The size of $M(p_i, d)$ for a small p_i is usually much larger than $|E(d)|$.

Instead of joining two match sets, we may use a partition-and-expand strategy to reduce the join cost. Basically, for a join $p_i = p_j \cup q_k$, where q_k is a join unit, we can send each $f \in M_{new}(p_j, d')$ to several partitions. Then inside each partition d'_x, we expand f to get the matches of p_i. If we choose the partitions carefully, we can guarantee the correctness of the result. Suppose that $M_{new}(p_j, d')$ takes $S_{new}(p_j)$ storage, the total cost is now at most $S(\Phi(d')) + (4m + 1) \cdot S_{new}(p_j) + S_{new}(p_i)$. According to our assumptions, this cost should be lower than the original bushy-join cost. Based on this, we design the Nav-join to compute $M_{new}(p, d', q_i)$ as follows:

1. Find a left-deep tree w.r.t. the join unit set Q, where q_i is the lowest leaf.
2. Extract $M_{new}(q_i, d', q_i)$ from each partition separately with the constraint that every match must map at least one edge in q_i to an inserted edge.
3. For a join in the tree, we compute the result using Nav-join by partitioning the matches on the left side, and expanding them in each part of the NP storage.
4. Repeat step (3) from the bottom of the tree to the root, and the final result is $M_{new}(p, d', q_i)$.

The Optimal Left-Deep Tree. In a join $p_i = p_i^l \cup p_i^r$, the mappers take $M_{new}(p_i^l, d', q_i)$ as input, and output the matches sent to each d'_k, which are shuffled to the reducers. The reducers take $\Phi(d')$ and received matches as input, and output $M_{new}(p_i, d', q_i)$. According to assumption (1), the main cost would be reading $\Phi(d')$, i.e., $S(\Phi(d'))$. Assuming a left-deep tree involves j join units, then the total cost is $j \cdot S(\Phi(d'))$, which comes from 1 unit match listing and $j-1$ Nav-joins. Thus, the optimal left-deep tree is the one involving the minimum number of join units.

Match Navigation. In step (3), supposing the join is $p_i = p_i^l \cup p_i^r$, we decide whether f should be sent to d'_k as follows:

1. If p_i^r's anchor vertex v is used to generate the join-key, and $f(v) = u_j$, then f can only be joined with matches in $M(p_i^r, loc'(u_j))$, where $loc'(u_j)$ is the local graph of u_j in d'. In this case, we only send f to $d'_{h(j)}$.

2. Otherwise, we generate the join-key of f. If a match f' can be joined with f, f' must have the same join-key, and thus $f'(v)$ must be the common neighbors of all vertices in the join-key. For each vertex u_j in the join-key, we send f to $d'_{h(j)}$.

Parallelize All Trees. For each $q_i \in Q$ we need to compute $M_{new}(p, d', q_i)$ according to its left-deep tree. If we compute all sets in serialization, the total cost is $S(\Phi(d')) \cdot |Q|^2$. We noticed that in each join and unit match listing, the input $\Phi(d')$ can be shared, so we compute all match sets in parallelism. In each MapReduce round, we process the same level of all left-deep trees simultaneously. Since all left-deep tress has the same height $|Q| - 1$, the calculation can be done in exact $|Q|$ rounds, and the total cost is thus $S(\Phi(d')) \cdot |Q|$.

Match Deduplication. For $M_{new}(p, d', q_i)$, there might be a match f, which maps an edge in q_i to an inserted edge, and another edge in q_j to an inserted edge. This f will also appear in $M_{new}(p, d', q_j)$ according to our algorithm. To avoid such duplications, we assign a total order $\{q_i < q_j \ if \ i < j\}$ on Q, then $\forall f \in M_{new}(p, d', q_i)$, we keep it only if for any $q_j < q_i$, f does not map an edge in q_j to an inserted edge. In other words, f can map an edge in q_j to an inserted edge if and only if $q_j > q_i$.

Theorem 1. *By assigning the total order in the Nav-join, there will be no duplicate matches or lost matches.*

5 Experiments

5.1 Experiment Setup

Datasets and Queries. In our experiments, we use 4 commonly-used real-word graphs WebGoogle (WG), WikiTalk (WT), LiveJournal (LJ), and UK-2002 (UK) as the data graph. Datasets WG, WT and LJ can be downloaded from SNAP[2], and dataset UK can be downloaded from WEB[3]. The size of each dataset is listed in Table 1. For the pattern graphs, we pick 5 commonly used ones from recent works [6,7,9], which are shown in Fig. 1.

Table 1. Sizes of datasets.

	WG	WT	LJ	UK
$|V|$	0.87M	2.39M	4.84M	18.5M
$|E|$	5.1M	5.0M	34M	227.5M

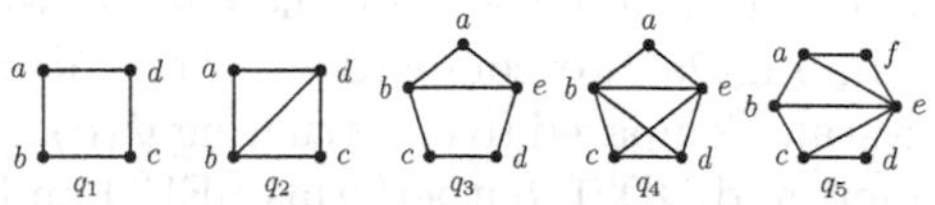

Fig. 1. Pattern graphs.

[2] http://snap.stanford.edu/data/index.html.
[3] http://law.di.unimi.it.

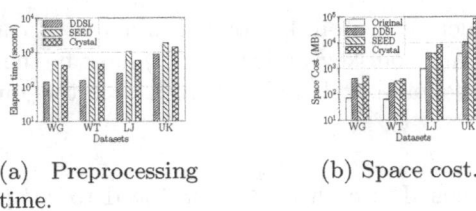

(a) Preprocessing time.

(b) Space cost.

Fig. 2. Preprocessing cost.

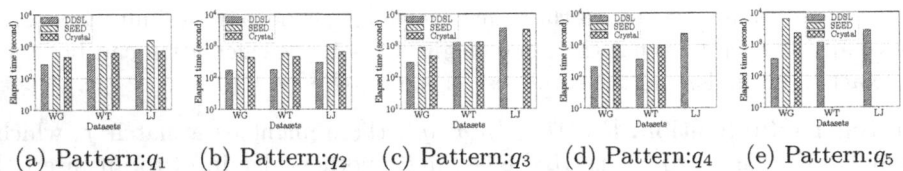

(a) Pattern:q_1 (b) Pattern:q_2 (c) Pattern:q_3 (d) Pattern:q_4 (e) Pattern:q_5

Fig. 3. Performance on static graphs: vary pattern.

Compared Methods. In the experiments on static graphs, we compare DDSL with two state-of-the-art distributed approaches SEED [7] and Crystal [9]. In the experiments on dynamic graphs, we compare to Delta-BigJoin [1]. Since edges in Delta-BigJoin have directions, we replace each undirected edge (u, v) with two directed edges (u, v) and (v, u).

Running Environment. All methods in our experiments are running on a cluster of 11 machines. The master has 47 GB RAM, two Intel Xeon X5650 CPUs, and one 900 GB HDD. Each slave has 125 GB RAM, two Intel Xeon E5-2630 CPUs, and one 900 GB HDD. By default we set the number of mappers and reducers to be 200, each with 4 GB memory space. For Delta-BigJoin, we set the number of processes to be 200.

5.2 Experiments on Static Graphs

We first evaluate the computation and space cost of preprocessing the data graph. Then we investigate the cost of listing all matches of a given pattern.

In Fig. 2a, we compare the preprocessing time of DDSL with SEED and Crystal. Compared to constructing $\Phi(d)$, the cost for listing all 3-cliques is much larger, and DDSL outperforms SEED and Crystal by up to 5 times.

Besides the construction time, we also compare the space cost of each method's underlying storage. For each method, the total file size across the cloud is shown in Fig. 2b. Compared to the original graph, the NP storage takes at most 4.6 times of extra space, while SEED and Crystal can take more than 7 and 10 times of extra space, respectively.

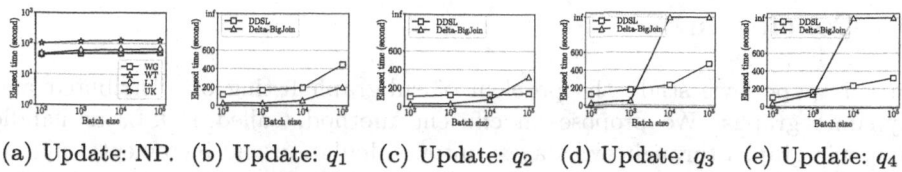

(a) Update: NP.   (b) Update: q_1 (c) Update: q_2 (d) Update: q_3 (e) Update: q_4

Fig. 4. Performance of incremental updating.

In Fig. 3 we show the overall running time of each method on all pattern graphs. The missing bars mean that the running time is larger than 10^4 s. In general, DDSL outperforms other two methods in most of the situations. It is slightly slower than Crystal only for processing q_1 and q_3 on LJ. For these two patterns, all three methods performs similar joins while listing the matches, and thus DDSL does not have notable advantages over other two methods. For other three patterns, DDSL has the best performance on all datasets.

5.3 Experiments on Dynamic Graphs

Experiments in this part also contain two parts. The first part is to evaluate the cost of updating the NP storage, and the second part is to evaluate the cost of updating the matches of a pattern. For both two parts, we vary the batch size in $\{10^2, 10^3, 10^4, 10^5\}$, and generate the update batch by randomly picking $b/2$ edges in d to delete, and generating $b/2$ edges that do not exist in d to insert.

To evaluate the cost of updating the NP storage, we count the time of updating the NP storage on each dataset. As Fig. 4a shows, DDSL can update the NP storage very efficiently. In comparison to Fig. 2, the updating time is less than the construction time even for the largest batch size. We also noticed that for each dataset, the updating time remains nearly unchanged as the batch size grows, which means the message size during the updating also grows slowly.

To evaluate the performance of updating the match set, we count the overall elapsed time of DDSL and Delta-BigJoin. For DDSL, we also include the time for updating of the NP storage, to illustrate its overall performance. For Delta-BigJoin, we randomly assign a direction to each edge in the query, and average the running time in 5 runs. The inf indicates that either the running time is too long, or the memory usage exceeds our capacity.

As Fig. 4b to Fig. 4e show that, except for q_2, the increasing of running time of Delta-BigJoin is much faster than that of DDSL. On the other hand, DDSL performs stabler. The updating time of all 4 patterns remains to be low. Comparing the updating time with the running time on LJ in Fig. 3, the updating time for every pattern is much smaller than that on static graphs even for the 10^5 batch size.

6 Conclusion

In this paper, we study the problem of subgraph listing on distributed and dynamic graphs. We propose an efficient method, called DDSL, to handle dynamic graphs through two stages: initial calculation and incremental updating. Extensive experiments show that DDSL can handle static subgraph listing with a competitive performance compared with the state-of-the-art distributed methods. Moreover, DDSL can efficiently handle dynamic subgraph listing without computing from scratch.

Acknowledgment. The work is partially supported by the Hong Kong RGC GRF Project 16214716, AOE project AoE/E-603/18, the National Science Foundation of China (NSFC) under Grant No. 61729201, Science and Technology Planning Project of Guangdong Province, China, No. 2015B010110006, Hong Kong ITC grants ITS/044/18FX and ITS/470/18FX, Didi-HKUST joint research lab Grant, Microsoft Research Asia Collaborative Research Grant, Wechat Research Grant and Webank Research Grant.

References

1. Ammar, K., McSherry, F., Salihoglu, S., Joglekar, M.: Distributed evaluation of subgraph queries using worst-case optimal low-memory dataflows. VLDB Endow. (2018)
2. Cook, S.A.: The complexity of theorem-proving procedures. In: ACM STOC (1971)
3. Dean, J., Ghemawat, S.: MapReduce: simplified data processing on large clusters. Commun. ACM **51**, 107–113 (2008)
4. Grochow, J.A., Kellis, M.: Network motif discovery using subgraph enumeration and symmetry-breaking. In: Speed, T., Huang, H. (eds.) RECOMB 2007. LNCS, vol. 4453, pp. 92–106. Springer, Heidelberg (2007). https://doi.org/10.1007/978-3-540-71681-5_7
5. Jian, X., Wang, Y., Lei, X., Chen, L.: DDSL: efficient subgraph listing on distributed and dynamic graphs. ArXiv e-prints, October 2018
6. Kim, H., et al.: Dualsim: parallel subgraph enumeration in a massive graph on a single machine. In: ACM SIGMOD (2016)
7. Lai, L., Qin, L., Lin, X., Zhang, Y., Chang, L., Yang, S.: Scalable distributed subgraph enumeration. VLDB Endow. **8**, 974–985 (2016)
8. Pržulj, N.: Biological network comparison using graphlet degree distribution. Bioinformatics **23**, e177–e183 (2007)
9. Qiao, M., Zhang, H., Cheng, H.: Subgraph matching: on compression and computation. VLDB Endow. **11**, 176–188 (2017)
10. Shervashidze, N., Vishwanathan, S., Petri, T., Mehlhorn, K., Borgwardt, K.: Efficient graphlet kernels for large graph comparison. In: Artificial Intelligence and Statistics (2009)
11. West, D.B., et al.: Introduction to Graph Theory. Prentice Hall, Upper Saddle River (2001)

DSP: Deep Sign Prediction in Signed Social Networks

Wei Yang, Yitong Wang[✉], and Xinshu Li

School of Computer Science, Fudan University, Shanghai, China
{17210240021,yitongw,xsli18}@fudan.edu.cn

Abstract. In a signed social network, users can express emotional tendencies such as: like/dislike, friend/foe, support/oppose, trust/distrust to others. Sign prediction, which aims to predict the sign of an edge, is an important task of signed social networks. In this paper, we attempt to tackle the problem of sign prediction by proposing a Deep Sign Prediction (DSP) method, which uses deep learning technology to capture the structure information of the signed social networks. DSP considers the "triangle" structures each edge involves comprehensively, and takes both the "balance" theory and the "status" theory into account. We conduct experiments and evaluations on five real signed social networks and compare the proposed DSP method with multiple state-of-the-art methods. The experimental results show that the proposed DSP method is very effective and outperforms other methods in terms of four metrics (AUC, binary-F1, micro-F1, macro-F1).

Keywords: Sign prediction · Balance theory · Status theory · Triangle structure

1 Introduction

With the emergence of online social networks, individuals show more interests in participating in social intercourse on the Internet. Numerous studies focus on unsigned social networks while only a few of them have studied the signed ones. Due to the existence of negative edges, many effective unsigned social network analysis methods cannot be applied to signed social networks directly [4–6]. Signed social networks are usually based on balance theory [1, 2] and status theory [3], both of which are proposed by observing social phenomena. At the same time, with the rapid development of deep learning technology, many scholars have begun to adopt the idea of network embedding to solve the problem of sign prediction. Although these methods have achieved good sign prediction performance, they have some drawbacks. Firstly, most methods basing on balance theory [9, 11] obtain the node embedding by optimizing single balance triangle each edge involves during each round of training process. These methods can have some limitations: 1. The interactions between multiple triangles each edge involves are ignored. 2. Most methods only consider triangles that satisfy the balance theory, and ignore those violating the theory, which will lead to the key information loss. 3. There is no common neighbor between the two endpoints of an edge, which is called a "bridge" edge in the paper [9]. Thus, how to properly model this

© Springer Nature Switzerland AG 2020
Y. Nah et al. (Eds.): DASFAA 2020, LNCS 12113, pp. 641–649, 2020.
https://doi.org/10.1007/978-3-030-59416-9_40

type of edges is also an essential aspect. Secondly, for some methods based on skip-gram models [12, 13], they use shallow models to train node embedding and cannot capture the non-linear structure information of the network well. Thirdly, a sign prediction method should fuse balance theory and status theory reasonably to obtain optimal sign prediction performance [9], but there are few methods considering both theories together. Last but not least, as stated in the paper [7], it is necessary to specifically design a solution framework for sign prediction problem.

The main contributions of this paper are:

- This paper proposes an end-to-end framework: Deep Sign Prediction (DSP) method, which uses the deep learning technology and optimizes a loss function specifically designed for sign prediction.
- This paper extends the balance theory by considering all possible "triangle" structures each edge involves and solves the drawbacks of former methods which only model single balanced triangle each edge involves.
- In this paper, a two-layer neural network architecture is designed to combine the balance theory with status theory reasonably.
- We conduct experiments and evaluations on five real signed social networks and compare the proposed DSP method with multiple state-of-the-art methods. Experimental results show that our method outperforms other methods in terms of four metrics (AUC, binary-F1, micro-F1, macro-F1).

2   Related Work

Signed Network Embedding: Signed network embedding methods can be roughly divided into following four categories. The first category does not consider any sociological theory. In [10], Yuan et al. propose a SNE method, which uses a log-bilinear model to train the target embedding of nodes along a given path. The second category makes use of balance theory. For example, SiNE [11] method is based on the extended structural balance theory. In SIGNet [12], the authors propose a scalable signed network embedding method. In [13], Kim et al. propose the SIDE method, which fully encodes the direction and sign of the edges in the learned embedding space. The third category is based on status theory. In SSNE [14], the authors design an energy-based ranking loss function based on status theory. The last type considers both two theories. For example, the BESIDE method in [9].

Sign Prediction: There are many methods solving sign prediction from different perspectives, apart from signed network embedding methods mentioned above. For example, in [8], Leskovec et al. manually extract degree features of the nodes and triad features of edges to train a logistic regression classifier for sign prediction. In [15], Javari et al. design a probability prediction model based on the local and global structure of networks in order to deal with the sparsity problem of signed social networks.

3 Preliminary

Signed Social Network: A signed social network can be modeled as a directed signed graph $G = (V, E, E^+, E^-, S)$, where V, E, E^+, E^- represent the sets of all nodes, signed edges, positive edges, and negative edges in the network; S is a signed adjacency matrix, and each entry S_{ij} of S represents the relationship from node i to j (Specifically, $S_{ij} = 1, -1, 0$ indicates positive, negative, no relationship in the current network).

Sign Prediction: Given a signed social network G, sign prediction aims to predict the sign of edges that are not observed in current network.

4 The Proposed Method

4.1 Model "Triangle" Structures Each Edge Involves

In a signed social network, there are multiple situations for the interaction between any directed edge e_{ij} and any node k. Nodes i, j, and k can form a triangle, which may not necessarily conform to balance theory, or they cannot even form a triangle. And, e_{ij} may be involved in multiple "triangles" at the same time. As shown in Fig. 1, without considering the edge sign, edge e_{ij} and node k can form four possible "triangle" structures (dashed line indicates that edge may not exist). Each "triangle" type corresponds to interactions between the neighbor structure of node i and that of the node j in directed edge e_{ij}. For example, the first type of "triangle" corresponds to the interaction between the out-neighbor structure of node i and the in-neighbor structure of node j.

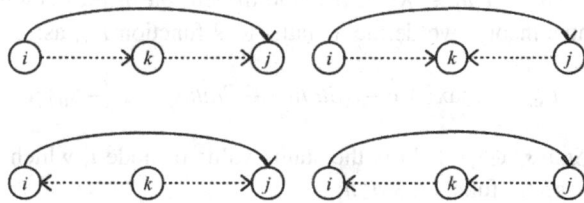

Fig. 1. Four possible "triangle" structures each edge involves.

According to Fig. 1, we generate a "balance" neighbor structure vector for two endpoints of the directed edge e_{ij}:

$$b\_st_i = \left[S_i^{out}; S_i^{out}; S_i^{in}; S_i^{in}\right], \quad b\_en_j = \left[S_j^{in}; S_j^{out}; S_j^{in}; S_j^{out}\right] \tag{1}$$

in formula (1): $b\_st_i, b\_en_j \in R^{1 \times 4|V|}$; $S_i^{out} \in R^{1 \times |V|}$ is the i th row of the matrix S, and $S_i^{in} \in R^{1 \times |V|}$ is the i th column of the matrix S.

By constructing b_st_i and b_en_j for each edge e_{ij}, and training b_st_i and b_en_j simultaneously, our method can consider the four "triangle" types in Fig. 1. This solution extends the balance theory and considers all possible "triangle" structures each edge involves comprehensively. Next we want to find a function f, which takes b_st_i or b_en_j as input, and output the "balance" embedding b_em_i or b_em_j. Namely,

$$b\_em_i = f(b\_st_i), \ b\_em_j = f(b\_en_j) \tag{2}$$

in formula (2): $b\_em_i \in R^{1 \times d}$ and d is the dimension of "balance" embedding.

4.2 Modeling Directed Edges by Status Theory

For a user in signed social networks, her status is determined by two parts: her "subjective" status/self-evaluation, and her "objective" status, which is evaluated by others. The "subjective"/"objective" status can be reflected by the user's out-neighbor/in-neighbor structure. Then for a node i, we want to find a function $g(\cdot, \cdot)$ which inputs the S_i^{out} and S_i^{in} and outputs a "status" neighbor structure vector: s_ne_i.

$$s\_ne_i = g(S_i^{out}, S_i^{in}) \tag{3}$$

we use the vector addition to define the function g. In formula (3): $s\_ne_i \in R^{1 \times |V|}$.

After obtaining the "status" neighbor vectors of node i, j, we will learn two functions: st_h and en_h to obtain the "status" embedding: s_em_i, s_em_j respectively.

$$s\_em_i = st\_h(s\_ne_i), \ s\_em_j = en\_h(s\_ne_j) \tag{4}$$

in formula (4): $s\_em_i, s\_em_j \in R^{1 \times d}$, d is the dimension of the "status" embedding.

Based on status theory, we define a status loss function L_{st}, as:

$$L_{st_{ij}} = \max(0, \delta - (Status_i - Status_j) \times (-S_{ij})) \tag{5}$$

in formula (5): $Status_i \in (-1, 1)$ is the status value of node i, which is generated by the non-linear mapping function sta_h;

$$Status_i = sta\_h(s\_em_i) \tag{6}$$

S_{ij} is the sign of e_{ij}; δ is the threshold of the difference between the two status values, and we set it to 0.5 according to the previous experimental research.

4.3 Deep Sign Prediction Model

Our network architecture is divided into two parts: the first part is used to extend balance theory, and the second part is used to consider the status theory. The input of DSP is an edge. The detailed network architecture of the DSP method is shown in Fig. 2.

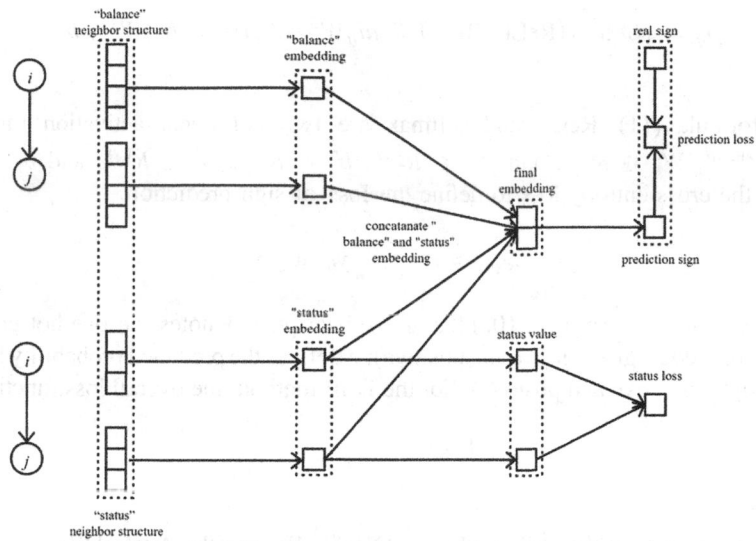

Fig. 2. Network architecture of the DSP method

First, we use a two-layer fully connected neural network to define function f.

$$b\_em_i = \tanh\left(\tanh\left(b\_st_i W^0 + b^0\right)W^1 + b^1\right) \tag{7}$$

in formula (7): tanh is a non-linear activation function; $W^0 \in R^{4|V| \times 2d}$ and $W^1 \in R^{2d \times d}$ are the weight parameters; $b^0 \in R^{1 \times 2d}$ and $b^1 \in R^{1 \times d}$ are the bias parameters.

For the functions st_h and en_h, they are defined by using a layer of fully connected neural network, respectively.

$$s\_em_i = \tanh\left(s\_ne_i W^2 + b^2\right), \ s\_em_j = \tanh\left(s\_ne_j W^3 + b^3\right) \tag{8}$$

in formula (8): $W^2, W^3 \in R^{|V| \times d}$; $b^2, b^3 \in R^{1 \times d}$.

We also use a layer of fully connected neural network to define the function sta_h.

$$Status_i = \tanh\left(s\_em_i W^4 + b^4\right) \tag{9}$$

in formula (9): $W^4 \in R^{d \times 1}$; $b^4 \in R^{1 \times 1}$.

Then, we concatenate "balance" embedding and "status" embedding of two endpoints of each edge as the final feature representation.

$$final_{ij} = \left[b\_em_i; b\_em_j; s\_em_i; s\_em_j\right] \tag{10}$$

in formula (10): $final_{ij} \in R^{1 \times 4d}$ is the final embedding vector.

For the prediction layer, we use a three-layer fully connected neural network to generate the edge's prediction value.

$$p_{ij} = \text{softmax}\left(\text{ReLU}\left(\text{ReLU}\left(\textit{final}_{ij}W^5 + b^5\right)W^6 + b^6\right)W^7 + b^7\right) \tag{11}$$

in the formula (11): ReLU and softmax are two non-linear activation functions; $W^5 \in R^{4d \times d}$, $W^6 \in R^{d \times \frac{d}{2}}$, and $W^7 \in R^{\frac{d}{2} \times 2}$; $b^5 \in R^{1 \times d}$, $b^6 \in R^{1 \times \frac{d}{2}}$, and $b^7 \in R^{1 \times 2}$. We use the cross-entropy loss to define the loss of sign prediction.

$$L_{sign_{ij}} = -\sum_m y_{ij_m} \log p_{ij_m} \tag{12}$$

in the formula (12): $m \in \{0, 1\}$ is the subscript. y denotes the one-hot encoding vector of the edge sign (negative and positive); p defines the predicted probability for each type of sign (negative and positive). For the DSP method, the overall loss function is:

$$L = \frac{1}{|E|} \sum_{e_{ij} \in E} \left(L_{sign_{ij}} + L_{st_{ij}}\right) \tag{13}$$

The input scale of the DSP method is $O(|E|)$. We use the Adam [17] algorithm to optimize the DSP model. The learning rate is 0.0001, and the batch size is 128.

5 Experiments

5.1 Datasets

We conduct experiments and evaluations on five real online signed social networks. The specific statistical information of five datasets is shown in Table 1.

Table 1. The statistical information of five datasets

Dataset	Node	Edge	Positive (%)	Negative (%)
Alpha	3783	24186	93.65%	6.35%
OTC	5881	35592	89.99%	10.01%
RfA	7118	107080	78.41%	21.59%
Slashdot	82140	549202	77.40%	22.60%
Epinions	131828	641372	85.30%	14.70%

5.2 Baseline Methods

We compare the proposed DSP method with several state-of-the-art sign prediction methods: two feature engineering methods (All23 [8] and FxG [16]), two unsigned network embedding methods (DW [4] and N2V [6]), three signed network embedding methods (SIGNet [12], SIDE [13], and BESIDE [9]), and the part of extends balance theory in DSP model (DSP_B). For the above methods, we use the same parameters setting recommended by the original papers. For the unsigned network embedding methods, we ignore edge sign during training process. For the node embedding methods, we concatenate the node embedding to obtain the edge embedding, and then train a logistic regression model for sign prediction. Our method uses the DSP framework for sign prediction and sets the dimension of the embedding vector $d = 40$.

5.3 Sign Prediction

As in previous studies [9], we use AUC, binary-F1, micro-F1, and macro-F1 to evaluate the performance of sign prediction. We randomly divide the datasets into a test set and a training set with a ratio of 2–8. The experimental results are shown in Table 2.

From Table 2, we can see that the DSP method has obtained the best experimental results in most cases. It is better than All23 and FxG, which shows the powerful learning ability of deep model. The performance of two unsigned network embedding methods is relatively poor, which means the unsigned network embedding methods cannot adapt to sign prediction. By comparing DSP with SIGNet and SIDE, we find that using deep models and considering both balance theory and status theory together can achieve better sign prediction performance. DSP is superior to BESIDE, indicating that comprehensive consideration of all possible "triangle" structures each edge involves can capture the latent features related to sign prediction well. The results also indicate that solution framework specifically designed for sign prediction problem is crucial to achieve better sign prediction performance by comparing DSP with other methods of signed network embedding. In most cases, the DSP method is better than DSP_B, which shows that combining balance theory with status theory reasonably can achieve the best sign prediction performance.

Table 2. The result of sign prediction

Dataset	Metric	All23	FxG	DW	N2V	SIGNet	SIDE	BESIDE	DSP_B	DSP
Alpha	AUC	0.8878	0.8793	0.8460	0.8451	0.8678	0.8787	0.8833	0.9143	**0.9200**
	binary-F1	0.9718	0.9452	0.9681	0.9689	0.9651	0.9682	0.9695	0.9741	**0.9742**
	micro-F1	0.9464	0.8988	0.9388	0.9403	0.9342	0.9397	0.9422	0.9511	**0.9513**
	macro-F1	0.7151	0.6411	0.6051	0.6256	0.6963	0.6945	0.7186	0.7808	**0.7837**
OTC	AUC	0.9109	0.8919	0.8649	0.8664	0.8793	0.8854	0.9069	0.9320	**0.9350**
	binary-F1	0.9644	0.9308	0.9591	0.9588	0.9550	0.9569	0.9628	**0.9714**	**0.9714**
	micro-F1	0.9344	0.8769	0.9240	0.9235	0.9180	0.9210	0.9322	**0.9481**	**0.9481**
	macro-F1	0.7734	0.6877	0.7117	0.7112	0.7461	0.7444	0.7912	0.8447	**0.8450**
RfA	AUC	0.8718	0.8925	0.8080	0.8091	0.9038	0.8369	0.9072	0.9198	**0.9210**
	binary-F1	0.9047	0.9082	0.8935	0.8894	0.9162	0.8955	0.9193	0.9238	**0.9242**
	micro-F1	0.8442	0.8495	0.8205	0.8133	0.8657	0.8257	0.8701	0.8778	**0.8787**
	macro-F1	0.7388	0.7450	0.6614	0.6452	0.7889	0.6851	0.7940	0.8111	**0.8125**
Slashdot	AUC	0.8873	0.8141	0.8049	0.8045	0.8852	0.8466	0.8903	0.9258	**0.9271**
	binary-F1	0.9063	0.8617	0.8780	0.8776	0.9030	0.8919	0.9131	**0.9266**	0.9262
	micro-F1	0.8462	0.7803	0.7965	0.7959	0.8472	0.8265	0.8617	**0.8847**	0.8843
	macro-F1	0.7394	0.6641	0.6325	0.6320	0.7718	0.7264	0.7878	**0.8289**	**0.8289**
Epinion	AUC	0.9433	0.9240	0.8673	0.8682	0.9214	0.9197	0.9391	0.9643	**0.9664**
	binary-F1	0.9555	0.9441	0.9400	0.9399	0.9556	0.9579	0.9660	**0.9712**	**0.9712**
	micro-F1	0.9213	0.9032	0.8927	0.8926	0.9231	0.9262	0.9411	**0.9501**	**0.9501**
	macro-F1	0.8060	0.7906	0.7177	0.7183	0.8337	0.8300	0.8734	**0.8925**	0.8924

We compare the prediction performance of each algorithm on a test set that contains only "bridge" edges. The experimental results on "bridge" edges are shown in Table 3. From Table 3, we can see that BESIDE achieves the best performance on all baseline methods, which means that BESIDE method with status theory is quite useful for modeling "bridge" edges. The proposed DSP and DSP_B methods are both superior to BESIDE, showing that considering the neighbor structures of two endpoints of each edge comprehensively, the "bridge" edges can be trained and predicted well.

Table 3. The performance of sign prediction on the "bridge" edges.

Dataset	Metric	All23	FxG	DW	N2V	SIGNet	SIDE	BESIDE	DSP_B	DSP
Alpha	AUC	0.8321	0.8093	0.7769	0.7840	0.8021	0.8313	0.8208	0.8696	**0.8742**
	binary-F1	0.9804	0.9014	0.9796	0.9809	0.9642	0.9716	0.9798	**0.9817**	0.9810
	micro-F1	0.9618	0.8237	0.9602	0.9628	0.9323	0.9454	0.9608	**0.9648**	0.9634
	macro-F1	0.6313	0.5356	0.5915	0.5942	0.6583	0.6370	0.7160	**0.7535**	0.7435
OTC	AUC	0.8442	0.8065	0.7948	0.8003	0.8121	0.8120	0.8584	0.8755	**0.8814**
	binary-F1	0.9645	0.8820	0.9667	0.9681	0.9540	0.9580	0.9683	**0.9708**	**0.9708**
	micro-F1	0.9324	0.7956	0.9363	0.9390	0.9147	0.9213	0.9407	**0.9457**	0.9455
	macro-F1	0.6283	0.5585	0.6208	0.6299	0.6802	0.6635	0.7651	**0.7977**	0.7958
RfA	AUC	0.8064	**0.8867**	0.7899	0.7696	0.8527	0.8027	0.8590	0.8853	0.8860
	binary-F1	0.8184	0.8536	0.8174	0.8035	0.8426	0.8136	0.8595	0.8749	**0.8750**
	micro-F1	0.7238	0.8057	0.7390	0.7129	0.7885	0.7401	0.8057	0.8277	**0.8279**
	macro-F1	0.6210	0.7823	0.6801	0.6355	0.7600	0.6920	0.7722	0.7994	**0.8001**
Slashdot	AUC	0.8615	0.7951	0.7844	0.7846	0.8674	0.8277	0.8724	0.9085	**0.9094**
	binary-F1	0.8930	0.8492	0.8783	0.8734	0.8939	0.8837	0.9086	**0.9178**	0.9172
	micro-F1	0.8218	0.7654	0.7890	0.7881	0.8337	0.8146	0.8547	**0.8709**	0.8705
	macro-F1	0.6805	0.6610	0.6153	0.6122	0.7550	0.7138	0.7778	0.8098	**0.8100**
Epinion	AUC	0.8575	0.8573	0.7918	0.7948	0.8409	0.8709	0.8609	0.9039	**0.9066**
	binary-F1	0.8962	0.8694	0.8832	0.8837	0.9036	0.9142	0.9306	**0.9395**	0.9389
	micro-F1	0.8211	0.8064	0.8090	0.8090	0.8463	0.8639	0.8873	**0.9025**	0.9017
	macro-F1	0.6244	0.7476	0.6800	0.6752	0.7622	0.7931	0.8159	**0.8443**	0.8440

6 Conclusion and Future Work

This paper presents a DSP method specifically for solving sign prediction task. DSP makes use of the powerful learning ability of deep learning to capture the complex structure of signed social networks. At the same time, the DSP method extends the balance theory, comprehensively considers all possible "triangle" structures each edge involves. Finally, the DSP method reasonably combines balance theory with status theory. We perform two types of comparative experiments on the five real signed social network datasets. The experimental results on four commonly used evaluation metrics show the superiority of our proposed methods.

Although DSP achieves excellent sign prediction performance, there are still some directions that can be further explored. For example, in the future, we will explore more ways of combining balance theory with status theory. Moreover, we will explore the attribute information of nodes in the next research work.

References

1. Heider, F.: Attitudes and cognitive organization. J. Psychol. **21**(1), 107–112 (1946)
2. Cartwright, D., Harary, F.: Structural balance: a generalization of Heider's theory. Psychol. Rev. **63**(5), 277–293 (1956)
3. Leskovec, J., Huttenlocher, D., Kleinberg, J.: Signed networks in social media. In: Proceedings of SIGCHI, pp. 1361–1370. ACM (2010)
4. Perozzi, B., Al-Rfou, R., Skiena, S.: Deepwalk: online learning of social representations. In: Proceedings of SIGKDD, pp. 701–710 (2014)
5. Tang, J., Qu, M., Wang, M., Zhang, M., Yan, J., Mei, Q.: Line: large-scale information network embedding. In: Proceedings of WWW, pp. 1067–1077 (2015)
6. Grover, A., Leskovec J.: node2vec: scalable feature learning for networks. In: Proceedings of the 22nd ACM SIGKDD International Conference on Knowledge Discovery and Data Mining, pp. 855–864 (2016)
7. Cui, P., Wang, X., Pei, J.: A survey on network embedding. In: Proceedings of IEEE Transactions on Knowledge and Data Engineering (2018)
8. Leskovec, J., Huttenlocher, D., Kleinberg, J.: Predicting positive and negative links in online social networks. In: Proceedings of WWW, pp. 641–650. ACM (2010)
9. Chen, Y., Qian, T., Liu, H., Sun, K.: "Bridge" enhanced signed directed network embedding. In: The 27th ACM International Conference on Information and Knowledge Management, pp. 773–782. ACM (2018)
10. Yuan, S., Wu, X., Xiang, Y.: SNE: signed network embedding. In: Kim, J., Shim, K., Cao, L., Lee, J.-G., Lin, X., Moon, Y.-S. (eds.) PAKDD 2017. LNCS (LNAI), vol. 10235, pp. 183–195. Springer, Cham (2017). https://doi.org/10.1007/978-3-319-57529-2_15
11. Wang, S., Tang, J., Aggarwal, C., Chang, Y., Liu, H.: Signed network embedding in social media. In: Proceedings of SDM, pp. 327–335. SIAM (2017)
12. Islam, M.R., Aditya Prakash, B., Ramakrishnan, N.: SIGNet: scalable embeddings for signed networks. In: Phung, D., et al. (eds.) PAKDD 2018. LNCS (LNAI), vol. 10938, pp. 157–169. Springer, Cham (2018). https://doi.org/10.1007/978-3-319-93037-4_13
13. Kim, J., Park, H., Lee, J., Kang U.: SIDE: Representation learning in signed directed networks. In: Proceedings of WWW, pp. 509–518 (2018)
14. Lu, C., Jiao, P., Liu, H., Wang, Y., Xu, H., Wang, W.: SSNE: status signed network embedding. In: Yang, Q., Zhou, Z.-H., Gong, Z., Zhang, M.-L., Huang, S.-J. (eds.) PAKDD 2019. LNCS (LNAI), vol. 11441, pp. 81–93. Springer, Cham (2019). https://doi.org/10.1007/978-3-030-16142-2_7
15. Javari, A., Qiu, H., Barzegaran, E., Jalili, M., Chang, K.: Statistical link label modeling for sign prediction: smoothing sparsity by joining local and global information. In: Proceedings of ICDM, pp. 1039–1044 (2017)
16. Kumar, S., Spezzano, F., Subrahmanian, V., Faloutsos, C.: Edge weight prediction in weighted signed networks. In: Proceedings of ICDM, pp. 221–230 (2016)
17. Kingma, D., Ba, J.: Adam: a method for stochastic optimization. In: Proceedings of ICLR (2014)

MinSR: Multi-level Interests Network for Session-Based Recommendation

Tao Lei[1], Yun Xiong[1,2(✉)], Peng Tian[1], and Yangyong Zhu[1,2]

[1] Shanghai Key Laboratory of Data Science, School of Computer Science,
Fudan University, Shanghai, China
{tlei18,yunx,tianpeng,yyzhu}@fudan.edu.cn
[2] Shanghai Institute for Advanced Communication and Data Science,
Fudan University, Shanghai, China

Abstract. Session-based recommendation, which is the task of predicting user behavior based on anonymous sessions in the recommendation domain, has drawn increasing interests in recent years. Most existing studies focus on modeling a session as a sequence and only capturing the item-level dependency. Although newly impressive progress has been made to session-based recommendation utilizing graph neural networks, those methods are deficient in incorporating multi-level coupling relations and capturing the session-level information. In this paper, we propose a multi-level interests network (MinSR) based on Graph Neural Networks (GNN) and Attention mechanism, which can simultaneously integrate multi-level interests in the recommendation process and provide a framework for exploiting both current and global session relationships. On the aspect of the current session, we extract *Current Preference* (CP) and *Interest Point* (IP) for each session using graph neural network and attention network. On the aspect of the global session, we generate *Global Tendency* (GT) via self-attention graph pooling for the session graph. Finally, by inherently combining them in a unified framework, our method can take into account both current and global session dependencies. Extensive experimental results based on two real-world datasets demonstrate that the proposed MinSR achieves competitive results compared with the state-of-the-art approaches.

Keywords: Session-based recommendation · Graph neural network · Attention mechanism · Graph pooling

1 Introduction

Recently, session-based recommendation (SR) has attracted wide attention, which aim to predict user next action from an ongoing session or recent historical sessions, as shown in Fig. 1a.

Many works have been proposed for SR, which model each session as a sequence of items. Previously, Markov Chain based approaches, such as FMC [11], predict the next action based on the previous ones. It is obvious that an

© Springer Nature Switzerland AG 2020
Y. Nah et al. (Eds.): DASFAA 2020, LNCS 12113, pp. 650–657, 2020.
https://doi.org/10.1007/978-3-030-59416-9_41

independent combination of past actions may limit the accuracy of recommendation under the circumstances. The past few years have witnessed the enormous success of deep learning in recommender systems. A multitude of relevant works [2,7,8] using the recurrent neural network (RNN) for SR obtain promising results, by reason of RNN's intrinsic advantages for modeling sequential dependency. Except for RNN, STAMP [6] exploits Multilayer Perceptron (MLP) networks and an attention net to capture the hybrid features of current and general interests. More recently, some methods [9,10] take advantage of Graph Neural

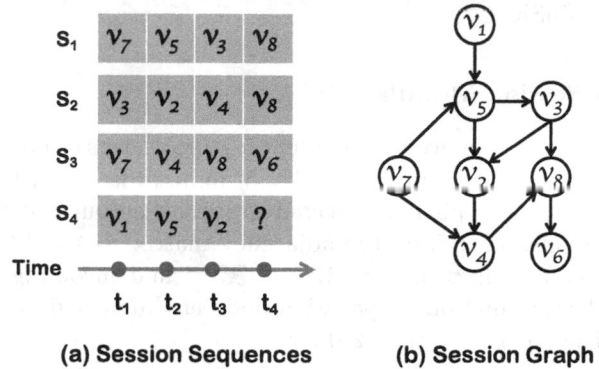

(a) Session Sequences   (b) Session Graph

Fig. 1. Session sequences and session graph.

Networks to make recommendation, where session sequences are modeled as graph-structured data (see Fig. 1b). Compared with previous conventional sequential methods, GNN can capture complex transitions of items. Based on the session graph, Wu et al. [9] propose the session-based recommendation with graph neural networks (SR-GNN) to explore rich transitions among items. Similar to STAMP [6], SR-GNN also constructs each session representations via the global preference and the current interest. More recently, GC-SAN [10] leverages self-attention mechanism and graph neural network for learning long-range dependency. Although GNN based models have been proven useful in learning users' interests from a session graph, existing literature only consider modeling each session as a combination of the global preference and the current interest and neglect the entire session graph information.

To address the above issues, we propose a novel **multi-level interests network** for session-based recommendation, named as MinSR, which can provide a framework for exploiting both current and global session relationships and model users' interests from multi-level. On the aspect of the current session, we extract *Current Preference* (CP) and *Interest Point* (IP) for each session using graph neural network and attention network. On the aspect of the global session, we generate *Global Tendency* (GT) via self-attention graph pooling [4] for the session graph. Finally, by inherently combining them in an attention network, our method can take into account both current and global session dependencies simultaneously.

It is worth noting that different from previous GNN-based models [9, 10], MinSR provides flexibility to represent users' interests via the attentive combination of CP, IP, and GT.

2   Proposed Method

In this section, we introduce the proposed MinSR, a novel multi-level interests network for SR. Our model contains three modules: (1) current session module, (2) global session module, and (3) prediction module. Figure 2 presents the whole architecture of MinSR.

2.1   Current Session Module

Based on the session graph, we obtain latent feature vectors of nodes (i.e., items) via gated graph sequence neural networks [5] in accordance with SR-GNN [9]. Note that the session graph is a directed graph on account of the sequential order between items. Therefore, the adjacency matrix $A_t \in \mathbb{R}^{n \times 2n}$ consists of two blocks, outgoing edges matrix $A_t^{out} \in \mathbb{R}^{n \times n}$ and incoming edges matrix $A_t^{in} \in \mathbb{R}^{n \times n}$. The information propagation between different nodes via outgoing and incoming edges can be formalized as:

$$x_t = A_t([v_1, v_2, \ldots, v_n]W_z + b_z) \tag{1}$$

where $W_z \in \mathbb{R}^{d \times 2d}$ is the learnable parameter matrix and $b_z \in \mathbb{R}^d$ is the bias vector. Thus x_t can obtain the information from edges in both directions. The same as Gated Recurrent Unit [1], the remaining update operations incorporate information from the previous time-step and from other nodes to update each node's hidden state x_{ti}.

Current Preference (CP). After feeding all session graphs into the gated graph neural network, we can obtain the latent feature vectors of all nodes. Then a session sequence $s_t = \{v_{t1}, v_{t2}, v_{t3}, \ldots, v_{tn}\}$ can be represented as $x_t = \{x_{t1}, x_{t2}, x_{t3}, \ldots, x_{tn}\}$ where x_{ti} denotes node embedding. Consistent with previous session-based recommendation methods, we consider the global embedding of a session sequence s_t by aggregating all node vectors x_t as current preference. To draw global dependency in the current session, we use the attention mechanism to learn the importance of different items for CP.

$$h_i = \frac{1}{n} \sum_{i \in n} q^T tanh(W_1 x_{tn} + W_2 x_{ti} + b)$$

$$\beta_i = \frac{exp(h_i)}{\sum_{i=1}^{p} exp(h_i)} \tag{2}$$

$$S_{cp} = \sum_{i=1}^{t} \beta_i x_{ti}$$

Interest Point (IP). For a session sequence s_t, the last clicked-item plays an important role in predicting the next action. Therefore, we model the crucial role as the interest point defined as the last clicked-item vector, i.e., x_{tn}.

$$S_{ip} = x_{tn} \tag{3}$$

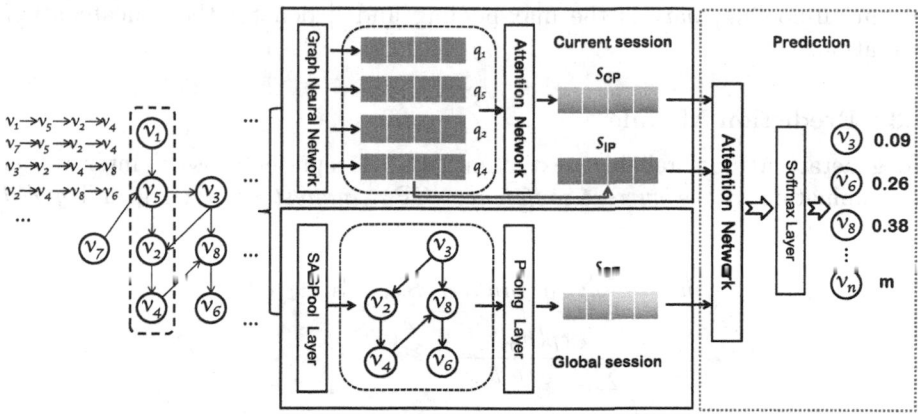

Fig. 2. The overall framework of the proposed MinSR.

2.2 Global Session Module

Considering the information in the global session graph can have an effect on user behavior, we adopt self-attention graph pooling (SAGPool) [4] to generate a graph embedding as Global Tendency (GT). In the session graph, we utilize the widely used graph convolution network [3] to learn node embedding.

$$h_{conv}^{(l)} = \sigma(\widetilde{D}^{-\frac{1}{2}}\widetilde{A}\widetilde{D}^{-\frac{1}{2}}h^{(l-1)}\Theta) \tag{4}$$

where $h^{(l-1)}$ is the node representation of $(l-1)$-th layer, $\widetilde{A}$ is the adjacency matrix of session graph $\mathcal{G}$, $\widetilde{D} = \sum_j \widetilde{A}_{ij}$, and Θ is the convolution weight. The critical point of SAGPool is the graph pooling layer that uses the same graph convolution network to provide the self-attention score $P \in \mathbb{R}^{N \times 1}$ in the back of a graph convolution layer:

$$P_{pool} = \sigma(\widetilde{D}^{-\frac{1}{2}}\widetilde{A}\widetilde{D}^{-\frac{1}{2}}h_{conv}^{(l)}W) \tag{5}$$

Here, W is a layer-specific trainable weight matrix, $h_{conv}^{(l)}$ is the input feature matrix of the graph and σ denotes an action function, such as $tanh$. Then we set a hyperparameter, the pooling ratio $k \in (0,1]$ that determines the number of nodes to stay. The top $\lfloor kN \rfloor$ nodes are selected based on the value of P.

$$idx = f_{top}(P, \lfloor kN \rfloor) \tag{6}$$

where f_{top} is the function that returns the indices of remaining nodes.

Global Tendency (GT). Like other pooling approaches, a readout layer is used to aggregate node features. The stack of graph convolution layers, graph pooling layers and readout layers are concatenated to form the hierarchical pooling architecture. The final output that can serve as global tendency S_{gt} is as follows:

$$S_{gt} = [\widehat{P}_{mean}||\widehat{P}_{max}] \tag{7}$$

where $\widehat{P}$ is the output of the self-attention graph pooling network, $mean$ is the mean-pooling, max is the max-pooling and $||$ denotes the concatenation operation.

2.3 Prediction Module

To generate a more reliable next item, MinSR represents users' interests as a combination of the *current preference* (CP), *interest point* (IP), and *global tendency* (GT).

$$h_m = \frac{1}{n} \sum q^T tanh(W_1 S_{cp} + W_2 S_i + b)$$

$$\alpha_i = \frac{exp(h_m)}{\sum_{i=1}^{p} exp(h_m)} \tag{8}$$

$$S = \sum_{i=1}^{t} \alpha_i S_i$$

Finally, we predict the next action for a session sequence s_t by applying a softmax function, where the score of each candidate item is computed via multiplying its embedding by users' interests representation S as follows:

$$\hat{y}_i = \frac{exp(S^T x_i)}{\sum_{i=1}^{n} exp(S^T x_i)} \tag{9}$$

During model training, we can minimize the Cross-Entropy of the ground-truth and the prediction over training data with the L2-norm. The objective function is defined as follows:

$$L = -\sum_{i=1}^{m} y_i log(\hat{y}_i) + (1 - y_i)log(1 - \hat{y}_i) + \eta ||\theta||^2 \tag{10}$$

where y_i denotes the ground truth item, η is regularization factor and θ is model parameters.

3 Experiments

In this section, we compare our proposed algorithm with state-of-the-art traditional and deep learning based recommendation methods as well as recently developed graph-based approaches on two benchmark datasets. The Diginetica dataset is obtained from CIKM Cup 2016, and the Yoochoose dataset comes from the RecSys Challenge 2015. We report the performance of all models on frequently used metrics P@K and MRR@K.

Comparison Against Baselines. Table 1 shows the results of comparing MinSR with the traditional methods (i.e., POP, S-POP, Item-KNN and BPR-MF) and the deep learning based approaches (i.e., GRU4Rec, NARM and STAMP) on the two benchmark datasets in terms of P@20 and MRR@20. We can see that MinSR performs the best and significantly outperforms the traditional methods and the deep learning based models on two datasets, which shows the effectiveness of our proposed method on SR.

Table 1. The performance of comparing MinSR with the traditional and deep learning based methods on the two benchmark datasets in terms of P@k and MRR@k (k = 20).

Datasets	Yoochoose1/64		Yoochoose1/4		Diginetica	
	P@20	MRR@20	P@20	MRR@20	P@20	MRR@20
POP	6.71	1.65	1.33	0.30	0.89	0.20
S-POP	30.44	18.35	27.08	17.75	21.06	13.68
Item-KNN	51.60	21.81	52.31	21.70	35.75	11.57
BPR-MF	31.31	12.08	3.40	1.57	5.24	1.98
GRU4Rec	60.64	22.89	59.53	22.60	29.45	8.33
NARM	68.32	28.63	69.73	29.23	49.70	16.17
STAMP	68.74	29.67	70.44	30.00	45.64	14.32
MinSR	**70.53**	**30.06**	**70.80**	**31.35**	**51.85**	**17.81**

Table 2 presents the data of comparing MinSR with the graph neural networks based approach on the Diginetica dataset in terms of P@k and MRR@k ($k \in [5, 10, 15, 20]$). For graph-based methods, we can see that the recent method SR-GNN and our MinSR perform quite well. This suggests that building session graphs using session sequences can preserve complex relations among items, which can provide additional information in predicting process. The main reasons why MinSR works well are three fold: 1) the session graph can represent complex transitions of items; 2) the model further exploits both current and global session relationships; 3) most importantly, MinSR captures user interests via the attentive combination of CP, IP, and GT.

Table 2. The performance of comparing MinSR with the graph neural networks based method on the Diginetica dataset in terms of P@k and MRR@k ($k \in [5, 10, 15, 20]$).

Datasets	Diginetica							
	P@5	MRR@5	P@10	MRR@10	P@15	MRR@15	P@20	MRR@20
SR-GNN	26.82	15.13	38.41	16.65	45.68	17.20	50.73	17.59
MinSR	**27.44**	**15.40**	**38.81**	**16.92**	**46.07**	**17.37**	**51.85**	**17.81**

Model Analysis. As shown in Table 3, we examine the contributions of two main components, namely, graph neural network and user interest, using the best-performing MinSR model on the Diginetica dataset.

Table 3. The performance of comparing MinSR with eight variants on the Diginetica datasets in terms of P@k and MRR@k ($k \in [5, 10, 15, 20]$).

Datasets	Diginetica							
	P@5	MRR@5	P@10	MRR@10	P@15	MRR@15	P@20	MRR@20
MinSR-IP	25.41	14.27	36.25	15.70	43.61	16.24	48.91	16.51
MinSR-CP	27.00	15.12	38.55	16.65	46.06	17.19	51.54	17.50
MinSR-GT	0.35	0.18	0.54	0.21	0.70	0.22	0.81	0.22
MinSR-IP+CP	26.82	15.13	38.41	16.65	45.68	17.20	50.73	17.59
MinSR-IP+GT	25.41	14.31	36.36	15.78	43.50	16.33	48.61	16.60
MinSR-GT+CP	26.96	15.08	38.40	16.61	45.95	17.19	51.40	17.46
MinSR-GAT	26.58	15.08	37.91	16.57	45.14	17.11	50.57	17.47
MinSR-SAGE	26.80	15.21	37.94	16.47	45.36	17.27	51.85	17.48
MinSR	**27.44**	**15.40**	**38.81**	**16.92**	**46.07**	**17.37**	**51.85**	**17.81**

4   Conclusion

In this paper, we propose MinSR, a novel multi-level interests network for session-based recommendation, which is able to provide a framework for exploiting both current and global session relationships. Especially, our MinSR can capture users' interests from multi-level. On the aspect of the current session, we extract *Current Preference* (CP) and *Interest Point* (IP) for each session using graph neural network and attention mechanism. On the aspect of the global session, we generate *Global Tendency* (GT) via self-attention graph pooling for the session graph. Finally, by inherently combining them in an attention network, our method can take into account both current and global session dependencies simultaneously. Different from previous GNN-based models, MinSR provides flexibility to represent users' interests via the attentive combination of CP, IP and GT. Extensive experimental results on two real-world datasets demonstrate that the proposed MinSR achieves competitive results compared with the state-of-the-art approaches.

Acknowledgements. This work is supported in part by the National Natural Science Foundation of China Projects No. U1636207, No. U1936213, the Shanghai Science and Technology Development Fund No. 19DZ1200802, No. 19511121204.

References

1. Cho, K., et al.: Learning phrase representations using RNN encoder-decoder for statistical machine translation. In: Proceedings of the 2014 Conference on Empirical Methods in Natural Language Processing (EMNLP), pp. 1724–1734 (2014)

2. Hidasi, B., Karatzoglou, A., Baltrunas, L., Tikk, D.: Session-based recommendations with recurrent neural networks. In: 4th International Conference on Learning Representations, Conference Track Proceedings, ICLR 2016, San Juan, Puerto Rico, 2–4 May 2016 (2016)

3. Kipf, T.N., Welling, M.: Semi-supervised classification with graph convolutional networks. In: 5th International Conference on Learning Representations, Conference Track Proceedings, ICLR 2017, Toulon, France, 24–26 April 2017 (2017)

4. Lee, J., Lee, I., Kang, J.: Self-attention graph pooling. In: International Conference on Machine Learning, pp. 3734–3743 (2019)

5. Li, Y., Tarlow, D., Brockschmidt, M., Zemel, R.S.: Gated graph sequence neural networks. In: 4th International Conference on Learning Representations, Conference Track Proceedings, ICLR 2016, San Juan, Puerto Rico, 2–4 May 2016 (2016)

6. Liu, Q., Zeng, Y., Mokhosi, R., Zhang, H.: Stamp: short-term attention/memory priority model for session-based recommendation. In: Proceedings of the 24th ACM SIGKDD International Conference on Knowledge Discovery & Data Mining, pp. 1831–1839. ACM (2018)

7. Quadrana, M., Karatzoglou, A., Hidasi, B., Cremonesi, P.: Personalizing session-based recommendations with hierarchical recurrent neural networks. In: Proceedings of the Eleventh ACM Conference on Recommender Systems, pp. 130–137. ACM (2017)

8. Tan, Y.K., Xu, X., Liu, Y.: Improved recurrent neural networks for session-based recommendations. In: Proceedings of the 1st Workshop on Deep Learning for Recommender Systems, pp. 17–22. ACM (2016)

9. Wu, S., Tang, Y., Zhu, Y., Wang, L., Xie, X., Tan, T.: Session-based recommendation with graph neural networks. In: Proceedings of the AAAI Conference on Artificial Intelligence, vol. 33, pp. 346–353 (2019)

10. Xu, C., et al.: Graph contextualized self-attention network for session-based recommendation. In: Proceedings of the 28th International Joint Conference on Artificial Intelligence, pp. 3940–3946. AAAI Press (2019)

11. Yengibarian, N.B.: Factorization of markov chains. J. Theor. Probab. 17(2), 459–481 (2004)

Efficient Core Maintenance of Dynamic Graphs

Wen Bai[1], Yuxiao Zhang[1], Xuezheng Liu[1], Min Chen[3], and Di Wu[1,2(✉)]

[1] School of Data and Computer Science, Sun Yat-Sen University, Guangzou, China
{baiw6,zhangyx27}@mail2.sysu.edu.cn, {liuxzh36,wudi27}@mail.sysu.edu.cn
[2] Guangdong Key Laboratory of Big Data Analysis and Processing,
Guangzhou, China
[3] School of Computer Science and Technology, Huazhong University
of Science and Technology, Wuhan, China
minchen@ieee.org

Abstract. $k-$core is one type of cohesive subgraphs such that every vertex has at least k degree within the graph. It is widely used in many graph mining tasks, including but not limited to community detection, graph visualization and clique finding. Frequently decomposing a dynamic graph to get its $k-$cores brings expensive cost since $k-$cores evolve as the dynamic graph changes. To address this problem, previous studies proposed several maintenance solutions to update $k-$cores based on a single inserted (removed) edge. Unlike previous studies, we maintain affected $k-$cores from the sparsest to the densest, so the cost of our method is determined by the largest core number of a graph. Experimental results show that our approach can significantly outperform the previous algorithms up to 3 order of magnitude for real graphs tested.

Keywords: $k-$core · Core maintenance · Dynamic graph

1 Introduction

$k-$core [10] is defined as the maximal subgraph of a simple graph G such that every vertex in the subgraph has at least k degree. The problem of finding the core number of all vertices in G is called core decomposition [4], which is widely used in many real-world applications, including large graph visualization [1], community detection [5], and network analysis [2].

Most graphs in our life are highly dynamic, whose edges are inserted into or removed from the graph over time. The core number of vertices should be updated to reveal the up-to-date structure of the graph. Clearly, it is uneconomical to recalculate the core number of all vertices while a few edges change. Instead, core maintenance [6,9] is proposed, whose goal is to update the core number of influenced vertices rather than decompose the entire graph. Unfortunately, existing solutions can only deal with a single edge each time, which leads to high cost when a graph with numerous inserted (removed) edges.

© Springer Nature Switzerland AG 2020
Y. Nah et al. (Eds.): DASFAA 2020, LNCS 12113, pp. 658–665, 2020.
https://doi.org/10.1007/978-3-030-59416-9_42

To overcome above drawbacks, we provide a novel solution to maintain core number of vertices with multiple inserted (removed) edges simultaneously. Compared with previous studies, our solution is relevant to the maximum core number of a graph. We conduct extensive experiments to evaluate the performance of our method and the existing solution. Experimental results show that our method can significantly outperform the previous algorithm up to 3 orders of magnitude for large real graphs tested.

The main contributions of our paper can be summarized as follows:

- With the aid of quasi$-k-$core, a similar but more loose concept to $k-$core, we can estimate the vertices affected by a set of inserted (removed) edges.
- Unlike existing approaches, our maintenance solution can update the core number of vertices in affected $k-$cores from the sparsest to the densest.
- Through executing extensive experiments on real graphs, our solution performs better than the existing approach.

The rest of this paper is organized as follows: Sect. 2 provides some preliminaries. The details of our solution are introduced in Sect. 3. Section 4 reports experimental results and Sect. 5 describes the related work about our paper. Finally, Sect. 6 concludes the paper.

2   Preliminaries

Usually, G represents a simple graph, which consists of a vertex set $V(G)$ and an edge set $E(G)$ such that $E(G) \subseteq V(G) \times V(G)$. For convenience, $|G| = |V(G)| + |E(G)|$ is used to represent the size of $|G|$, where $|V(G)|$ and $|E(G)|$ are the size of vertices and edges respectively. Additionally, K_0 indicates an empty graph without vertices or edges.

Given an arbitrary vertex $v \in V(G)$, we define $N(G, v) = \{u : (u, v) \in E(G)\}$ as the set of neighbors of v. Clearly, $|N(G, v)|$ is the degree of v in G, denoted by $d(G, v)$. For convenience, we also use $v \in G$ $((u, v) \in G)$ to replace $v \in V(G)$ $((u, v) \in E(G))$, where u and v are two adjacent vertices of an edge in G.

To clearly illustrate the relation between two graphs G_1 and G_2, we generalize four set notations on graphs: $G_1 \subseteq G_2$ represents G_1 is a subgraph of G_2; $G_1 \cap G_2$ refers to the intersection graph of G_1 and G_2; $G_1 \cup G_2$ is the union graph of G_1 and G_2; $G_1 \setminus G_2$ depicts the difference graph of G_1 and G_2 such that $E(G_1 \setminus G_2) = E(G_1) \setminus E(G_2)$.

$k-$core [10] is a well-established metric to evaluate the importance of vertices as well as their connections in the graph. Besides, $k-$core has two important properties: uniqueness and nestedness [4,8].

Definition 1. *A $k-$core is the largest subgraph of a graph G, denoted by $C(G, k)$, such that $d(C(G, k), v) \geq k$ for an arbitrary vertex $v \in C(G, k)$.*

Generally, we require $k \geq 1$. When $k = 0$, $0-$core is the graph itself. If not specified, we assume isolated vertices have been removed from G. Besides, we use $C(G, k) = K_0$ to represent an empty $k-$core.

Similar to existing studies [4], we define the core number of vertices in G. If a vertex v is located in $k-$core but not contained in $(k+1)-$core, then its core number is k, denoted by $\phi(G, v) = k$. Additionally, the maximum core number of vertices in G is denoted as $\phi(G)$.

3   Solution

Existing methods obey the core update theorem [6,9], while an edge is inserted into (removed from) a graph, the vertices affected by this edge will change their core number at most 1. When numerous edges change, existing methods repeatedly identify influenced vertices for each edge and some of them may change their core number many times. If the number of edges is very large, the maintenance cost will become expensive.

To address the above issues, we propose a novel solution, which updates core number of influenced vertices from the sparsest $k-$core to the densest. To this end, we first propose the quasi$-k-$core to estimate the candidate vertices for each influenced $k-$core. Secondly, we identify the partial$-k-$core of each affected $k-$core and update their core number. Lastly, we increase k until all affected $k-$cores are updated.

For convenience, we use G_c to represent the current graph and G_p to indicate the previous graph before changing. Correspondingly, we define $S_i = G_c \setminus G_p$ $(S_r = G_p \setminus G_c)$ as the insertion (removal) graph.

3.1   Quasi$-k-$core

Consider that most graphs are sparse, not all $k-$cores will be affected by inserted (removed) edges. To find influenced $k-$cores, an intuitive idea is to decompose S_i (S_r). Since some vertices of S_i (S_r) lack adjacent edge information in G_c (G_p), we decompose S_i (S_r) to a set of quasi$-k-$cores with the aid of G_c (G_p).

Consider that the steps of quasi core decomposition on S_i and S_r are similar, we use S (e.g. S_i or S_r) and G (e.g. G_c or G_p) to represent two arbitrary graphs for ease of presentation. To supplement extra edge information of vertices in S, we define the neighborhood graph S on G, which consists of vertices in S and their adjacent neighbors within one step in G. Similar to $k-$core, quasi$-k-$core is also unique and nested. Otherwise, it contradicts to the maximal property of quasi$-k-$core.

Definition 2. $S(G) = (V(S(G)), E(S(G)))$ *is the neighborhood graph of S on G such that* $V(S(G)) = V(S) \cup \{v : v \in N(G, u) \wedge u \in V(S)\}$ *and* $E(S(G)) = E(S) \cup \{(u, v) : u \in S \wedge v \in N(G, u)\}$. *Specially, if $S \cap G = K_0$, then $S(G) = S$.*

Definition 3. *The quasi$-k-$core $\hat{C}(S, G, k)$ is the largest subgraph of S on G such that $d(\hat{C}(G), v) \geq k$ for an arbitrary $v \in \hat{C}(S, G, k)$, where $\hat{C}(G)$ is the neighborhood graph of $\hat{C}(S, G, k)$ on G.*

To get a set of quasi$-k-$cores, we can revise the decomposition method of $k-$cores. Through recursively removing unsatisfied vertices from S for each k, we can get a set of quasi$-k-$cores. Besides, we can also define quasi core number for each vertex, which is similar to core number.

3.2   Insertion Case

Our insertion algorithm has four steps: firstly, we decompose S_i to a set of quasi$-k-$cores with the aid of G_c; secondly, we expand each quasi$-k-$core to a candidate graph; thirdly, we get the partial$-k-$core from the candidate graph; lastly, we update the core number of vertices in the partial$-k-$core and continue the next loop until all affected $k-$cores are updated.

Note that inserted edges may increase the core number of adjacent vertices of the quasi$-k-$core, but they are not contained in the quasi$-k-$core. To find all affected vertices, we expand the quasi$-k-$core to a candidate graph, which contains all possible affected vertices. Additionally, we terminate the search path when edges are contained in the previous $k-$core since they must belong to the current $k-$core.

Definition 4. $F(k)$ *is a candidate graph whose vertex* $v \in C(G_c, k-1)$ *satisfying* $d(C(G_c, k-1), v) \geq k$ *is reachable from* $u \in \hat{C}(S_i, G_c, k)$ *via a path and satisfies* $(u', v') \notin C(G_p, k)$ *for an arbitrary edge* $(u', v') \in F(k)$.

We can observe that $F(k)$ contains all vertices that may be contained in $C(G_c, k) \setminus C(G_p, k)$. So, $C(G_c, k) \subseteq F(k) \cup C(G_p, k)$ holds. Since $F(k)$ contains some redundant vertices, we identify the partial$-k-$core from $F(k)$, denoted by $P(k) = C(G_c, k) \setminus C(G_p, k)$, which is the difference graph of $C(G_c, k)$ and $C(G_p, k)$. Since $\hat{C}(P(k), C(G_p, k), k)$ is a subgraph of $P(k)$ and for any $v \in P(k)$, $d(P(C(G_p, k)), v) \geq k$ holds, we have $\hat{C}(P(k), C(G_p, k), k) = P(k)$.

To get $P(k)$ from $F(k)$, we observe that $P(k) = \hat{C}(P(k), C(G_p, k), k)$. Since $P(k) \subseteq F(k)$, we have $P(k) \subseteq \hat{C}(F(k), C(G_p, k), k)$. On the contrary, if a vertex $v \in \hat{C}(F(k), C(G_p, k), k) \setminus P(k)$, there must be a vertex $u \in C(G_p, k)$ which can be reachable from v such that $d(F(C(G_p, k)), u) < k$ via a path. Again, this is a contradiction. Consider another case $(u, v) \in \hat{C}(F(k), C(G_p, k), k) \setminus P(k)$, since $u, v \in P(k)$, $P(k) \subseteq P(k) \cup (u, v)$. When $C(G_p, k) = K_0$, we can directly get $C(G_c, k)$ from $F(k)$ since $C(G_c, k) \subseteq F(k)$.

Based on above discussions, we implement Algorithm 1 to maintain $k-$cores for the insertion case. In detail, it first decomposes S_i to a map of quasi core numbers and corresponding vertex sets. Then the algorithm updates the core number of influenced vertices from $k = 2$ to $\hat{\phi}(S_i, G_c)$ (the maximal quasi core number of S_i on G_c) according to two cases mentioned above.

Clearly, the time complexity of Algorithm 1 is $O(|S_i| + \sum_{k=1}^{\hat{\phi}(S_i, G_c)} 2|F(k)|)$, where $O(2|F(k)|)$ is the cost to get $F(k)$ and the partial$-k-$core. Note that $\hat{\phi}(S_i, G_c)$ is much less than $|V(G_c)|$, where $|V(G_c)|$ is the number of vertices in G_c. As for the space complexity, it only costs $O(|G_c|)$ to store the entire graph.

Algorithm 1: Insertion Case (IC)

Input: S_i: the insertion graph, G_c: the current graph, ϕ: a map of vertices and their core number.

Output: ϕ: a map of vertices and their core number.

1 decompose S_i to a set of quasi$-k-$cores;
2 $\phi(v) \leftarrow 1$ for $v \in S_i$;
3 $k \leftarrow 2$;
4 **while** $k \leq \hat{\phi}(S_i, G_c)$ **do**
5   expand the quasi$-k-$core to a candiadte graph;
6   **if** $k \leq \phi(G_p)$ **then**
7   get $\hat{C}(F(k), C(G_p, k), k)$ from $F(k)$;
8          $\phi(v) \leftarrow k$ for $v \in \hat{C}(F(k), C(G_p, k), k)$;
9          $k \leftarrow k + 1$;
10   **else**
11   execute core decomposition on $F(k)$;
12   **for** $v \in F(k)$ **do**
13             $\phi(v) \leftarrow \phi(F(k), v)$ if $\phi(F(k), v) \geq k$;
14   **break**;
15 **return** ϕ;

3.3 Removal Case

Our removal algorithm contains three steps: firstly, we decompose S_r to a set of quasi$-k-$cores with the aid of G_p; secondly, we delete the common edges in $\hat{C}(S_r, G_p, k) \cap C(G_p, k)$ and recursively remove influenced vertices that cannot be located in $C(G_p, k)$; thirdly, we continue the loop until all affected $k-$cores are updated.

The implementation of Algorithm 2 is relatively simple. Firstly, it decomposes S_r to a map of vertices and their quasi core number (line 1). Secondly, for each influenced $k-$core, it deletes common edges in $\hat{C}(S_r, G_p, k) \cap C(G_p, k)$, recursively removes influenced vertices and updates the core number of affected vertices. The time complexity of Algorithm 2 is $O(|S_r| + \sum_{k=1}^{\hat{\phi}(S_r, G_p)} |C(G_p, k)|)$. Since it at most traverses the entire affected $k-$core for each k, and the space complexity is $O(|G_p|)$.

4   Experiments

Our real graphs are downloaded from Koblenz Network Collection[1], including 10 real graphs (seen Table 1), where *Stanford* is a direct graph and *Youtube* is a temporal graph. For the directed graph, we ignore the edge direction and regard it as a simple graph. Then for the temporal graph, we sort their edges by the timestamp. While for the remainder graphs, we keep the initial order of edges as the corresponding graph files.

---

[1] http://konect.uni-koblenz.de/.

Algorithm 2: Removal Case (RC)

Input: S_r: the removal graph, G_p: the previous graph, ϕ: a map of vertices and their core number.

Output: ϕ: a map of vertices and their core number.

1   decompose S_r to a set of quasi$-k-$cores;
2   $\hat{\phi}(S_r, G_p) \leftarrow \phi(G_p)$ if $\hat{\phi}(S_r, G_p) > \phi(G_p)$;
3   $k \leftarrow 1$;
4   **while** $k \leq \hat{\phi}(S_r, G_p)$ **do**
5   let $\mathcal{Q}$ be an empty queue;
6   **for** $(u, v) \in \hat{C}(S_r, G_p, k) \cap C(G_p, k)$ **do**
7   remove (u, v) from $C(G_p, k)$;
8   push u (v) into $\mathcal{Q}$ if $d(C(G_p, k), u) < k$ $(d(C(G_p, k), v) < k)$;
9   adjust $C(G_p, k)$ by removing vertices in $\mathcal{Q}$;
10   update core number of affected vertices in ϕ;
11     $k \leftarrow k + 1$;
12 **return** ϕ;

All algorithms are implemented in C++ and compiled with GCC 7.4.0 at -O2 optimization level. All experiments are executed sequentially on the Linux operating system Ubuntu 18.04, which is running on a machine with two Xeon E5-2683v4@2.1 GHz CPUs and 128 GB RAM.

Table 1. The detail of graphs

G	Amazon	Douban	Flixster	Gowalla	Hyves	Livemocha	Skitter	Stanford	Wordnet	Youtube
$|V(G)|$	334, 863	154, 908	2, 523, 386	196, 591	1, 402, 673	104, 103	1, 696, 415	281, 903	146, 005	3, 223, 585
$|E(G)|$	925, 872	327, 162	7, 918, 801	950, 327	2, 777, 419	2, 193, 083	11, 095, 298	1, 992, 636	656, 999	9, 375, 374
$|\phi(G)|$	6	15	68	51	39	92	111	71	31	88

Similar to the most of existing studies, we adopt the execution time is as the metric of our experiments. In our experiments, we select the traversal approach [9] as the baseline, which contains **Trav-I** for the insertion case and **Trav-R** for the removal case. To support numerous edges, we recursively execute the traversal approach multiple times. Before experiments, we set some necessary parameters. We set the 2-hops for **Trav-I** and 1-hop for **Trav-R** in experiments, the details of these algorithms can be seen in [9].

For the insertion case, the last m edges are used to construct the insertion graph S_i and the remainder are used to construct G_p. As for the removal case, the first m edges are used to construct removal graph S_r and all edges are used to construct G_p. Generally, we vary m from $100, 000$ to $200, 000$ for tracing the evolution of the performance of two approaches.

Table 2 shows the execution time on all graphs for the insertion case. Compared with **Trav-I**, **IC** achieves the best performance on all graphs. Table 3 shows the execution time on all graphs for the removal case. Since both two

Table 2. The execution time for the insertion case (unit: second)

m	100, 000		120, 000		150, 000		180, 000		200, 000	
Methods	IC	Trav-I	IC	Trav-I	IC	Trav-I	IC	Trav-I	IC	Trav-I
Amazon	**6.02**	254.66	**6.79**	296.50	**7.52**	344.93	**8.34**	377.53	**8.92**	392.49
Douban	**3.36**	30.22	**3.75**	33.77	**4.79**	49.18	**5.41**	67.17	**5.89**	90.68
Gowalla	**4.72**	11.21	**5.87**	13.00	**7.23**	14.65	**8.75**	16.65	**10.39**	18.22
Stanford	**59.79**	154.22	**62.36**	177.53	**66.70**	220.50	**70.94**	257.38	**72.09**	275.71
Wordnet	**6.76**	14.96	**7.68**	18.45	**8.95**	24.78	**10.24**	29.22	**10.97**	33.29
Flixster	**48.62**	1222.00	**56.03**	1474.87	**64.67**	1674.03	**73.05**	2365.18	**78.25**	2657.49
Hyves	**7.43**	1715.22	**8.42**	2070.69	**9.32**	2616.87	**10.41**	3164.22	**10.93**	3419.63
Livemocha	**66.84**	73.95	**73.09**	88.01	**81.30**	104.80	**89.32**	144.65	**94.50**	176.27
Skitter	**4.27**	10.88	**5.02**	11.53	**6.70**	12.81	**8.69**	14.48	**10.36**	15.57
Youtube	**284.04**	336.86	**297.46**	394.72	**312.28**	488.06	**326.43**	596.92	**334.13**	731.56

Table 3. The execution time for the removal case (unit: second)

m	100, 000		120, 000		150, 000		180, 000		200, 000	
Methods	RC	Trav-R	RC	Trav-R	RC	Trav-R	RC	Trav-R	RC	Trav-R
Amazon	**2.51**	2.96	**3.02**	3.54	**3.75**	4.39	**4.58**	5.25	**5.13**	5.79
Douban	**3.25**	6.08	**3.93**	7.54	**4.55**	8.93	**5.32**	10.29	**5.84**	10.80
Gowalla	**7.88**	10.33	**9.67**	12.38	**12.14**	16.38	**15.05**	19.92	**16.53**	22.79
Stanford	**8.37**	10.33	**10.21**	12.34	**12.54**	14.64	**14.93**	16.81	**16.65**	18.87
Wordnet	**4.26**	5.56	**5.18**	6.64	**6.41**	7.90	**7.50**	8.79	**8.30**	9.80
Flixster	**12.93**	27.29	**15.71**	33.67	**19.14**	41.27	**22.14**	49.07	**24.35**	52.11
Hyves	**5.85**	12.80	**6.59**	14.11	**7.72**	16.12	**9.41**	19.13	**10.35**	20.68
Livemocha	**20.32**	30.18	**24.71**	38.63	**31.25**	48.22	**37.37**	58.04	**40.66**	63.12
Skitter	**8.77**	9.94	**10.15**	11.91	**12.74**	15.51	**15.30**	19.21	**16.95**	21.50
Youtube	**9.82**	14.18	**12.09**	17.84	**14.24**	20.34	**16.74**	22.53	**17.84**	24.44

algorithms do not search candidate vertices in the removal case, the execution time is obviously less than that of the insertion case. Even so, the performance of **RC** is still better than **Trav-R** on all graphs.

5   Related Work

$k-$core decomposition, which assigns each vertex v with a core number to reveal the connected state of v and its neighbors, is strongly related to graph degeneracy [10]. Numerous $k-$core decomposition algorithms are proposed to handle different cases. To handle $(k, h)-$core of a temporal graph, which is an extension of $k-$core, Wu et al. [11] proposed two distributed algorithms to deal with massive temporal graphs. Besides, the probabilistic core decomposition was also studied recently in [3], where $(k, \eta)-$cores were proposed.

$k-$core and its extensions have been extensively used in numerous applications. To solve the maximal clique problem, Lu et al. [7] devised a randomized algorithm by utilizing $k-$core and $k-$truss. With the aid of $k-$core, variants of community detection problems are addressed such as local communities detection [5]. Alvarezhamelin *et al.* [2] used $k-$core as a tool to analyze large scale graphs such as social network and Internet graph.

6 Conclusions

In this paper, we propose a novel solution to tackle $k-$core maintenance of dynamic graphs, which provides an effective solution to maintain the core number of vertices affected by multiple inserted (removed) edges simultaneously. We confirm our approaches by conducting extensive experiments on 10 real graphs. The results show that our solution can outperform the existing algorithm up to 3 order of magnitude for real graphs tested.

Acknowledgment. This work was supported by the National Natural Science Foundation of China under Grant U1911201, Guangdong Special Support Program under Grant 2017T X04X148, the Fundamental Research Funds for the Central Universities under Grant 19LGZD37, 19LGYJS57.

References

1. Alvarez-Hamelin, J.I., Dall'Asta, L., Barrat, A., Vespignani, A.: Large scale networks fingerprinting and visualization using the k-core decomposition. In: Advances in Neural Information Processing Systems, pp. 41–50 (2006)
2. Alvarezhamelin, J.I., Dall'Asta, L., Barrat, A., Vespignani, A.: K-core decomposition of internet graphs: hierarchies, self-similarity and measurement biases. Netw. Heterogen. Media **3**(2), 371–393 (2017)
3. Bonchi, F., Gullo, F., Kaltenbrunner, A., Volkovich, Y.: Core decomposition of uncertain graphs. In: Proceedings of the 20th ACM SIGKDD International Conference on Knowledge Discovery and Data Mining, pp. 1316–1325. ACM (2014)
4. Cheng, J., Ke, Y., Chu, S., Özsu, M.T.: Efficient core decomposition in massive networks. In: 2011 IEEE 27th International Conference on Data Engineering (ICDE), pp. 51–62. IEEE (2011)
5. Cui, W., Xiao, Y., Wang, H., Wei, W.: Local search of communities in large graphs. In: ACM SIGMOD International Conference on Management of Data, pp. 991–1002. ACM (2014)
6. Li, R.H., Yu, J.X., Mao, R.: Efficient core maintenance in large dynamic graphs. IEEE Trans. Knowl. Data Eng. **26**(10), 2453–2465 (2014)
7. Lu, C., Yu, J.X., Wei, H., Zhang, Y.: Finding the maximum clique in massive graphs. Proc. VLDB Endowment **10**(11), 1538–1549 (2017)
8. Montresor, A., De Pellegrini, F., Miorandi, D.: Distributed k-core decomposition. IEEE Trans. Parallel Distrib. Syst. **24**(2), 288–300 (2013)
9. Sarıyüce, A.E., Gedik, B., Jacques-Silva, G., Wu, K.L., Çatalürek, Ü.V.: Incremental k-core decomposition: algorithms and evaluation. VLDB J. **25**(3), 425–447 (2016)
10. Seidman, S.B.: Network structure and minimum degree. Soc. Netw. **5**(3), 269–287 (1983)
11. Wu, H., Cheng, J., Lu, Y., Ke, Y., Huang, Y., Yan, D., Wu, H.: Core decomposition in large temporal graphs. In: 2015 IEEE International Conference on Big Data (Big Data), pp. 649–658. IEEE (2015)

Discovering Cliques in Signed Networks Based on Balance Theory

Renjie Sun, Qiuyu Zhu, Chen Chen, Xiaoyang Wang[✉], Ying Zhang, and Xun Wang

Zhejiang Gongshang University, Zhejiang, China
renjiesun.zjgsu@gmail.com, qiuyuz.zjgsu@gmail.com,
yingz.au@gmail.com, {chenc,xiaoyangw,wx}@zjgsu.edu.cn

Abstract. Enumerating cohesive subgraphs is a fundamental problem for signed network analysis. In this paper, we propose a novel model, called maximal signed k-clique, which aims to find cohesive subgraphs in signed networks based on clique property and balance theory. Given a signed graph G, a set of nodes C is a maximal signed k-clique if (1) $|C| \geq k$ and C is a clique without any unbalanced triangle; and (2) C is maximal. We show the problem of enumerating all maximal signed k-cliques is NP-hard. Novel pruning techniques are proposed to significantly filter the searching space. An efficient algorithm, SKC, is developed to handle large networks. Comprehensive experiments on four real-world datasets are conducted to demonstrate the efficiency and effectiveness of the proposed algorithms.

Keywords: Signed network · Balanced triangle · Signed clique

1 Introduction

Mining cohesive subgraphs is a fundamental task in network analysis and many cohesive subgraph models are proposed in the literature, such as k-core [10], k-truss [13] and clique [3]. Most existing research about cohesive subgraph mining focuses on unsigned graphs, i.e., treating all connections between users as positive relationships. However, social interactions involve both positive relationship (e.g., friend) and negative relationship (e.g., enemy). Ignoring the signed edge information may fail to characterize the cohesiveness of subgraphs.

For signed network analysis, the balance theory is widely adopted, which is formulated by Heider in the 1940s [6]. In the balance theory, many observations are based on the concept of balanced triangle, which serves as a fundamental role for signed network analysis. In a signed network, a triangle is balanced, if there are odd number of positive edges in the triangle [2]. As shown in Fig. 1, T_1 and T_2 are balanced triangles, while T_3 and T_4 are unbalanced triangles. A balanced triangle with three positive edges (T_1) means that "the friend of my friend is my friend", while the one with one positive edge and two negative edges

Y. Nah et al. (Eds.): DASFAA 2020, LNCS 12113, pp. 666–674, 2020.
https://doi.org/10.1007/978-3-030-59416-9_43

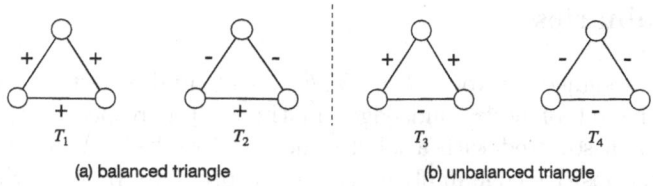

(a) balanced triangle   (b) unbalanced triangle

Fig. 1. Example of balanced and unbalanced triangles

(T_2) indicates "the enemy of my enemy is my friend". In a real social network, a community with more balanced triangles tends to be more stable [6].

Intuitively, in a signed graph, a stable cohesive subgraph should be densely-balanced, i.e., nodes should be densely connected and the subgraph should be free from unbalanced triangles. Based on this intuition, in this paper, we propose a novel cohesive subgraph model for signed networks, called the maximal signed k-clique, which meets three criteria: (1) it is a clique with size no less than k; (2) it does not contain any unbalanced triangle; and (3) it is maximal, i.e., any super graph of it cannot meet the first two criteria. The found cliques can be very important for many applications, such as discovering balanced communities or cooperative groups in signed social networks.

Recently, there are some works that try to identify cohesive subgraphs from signed networks. For instance, Giatsidis et al. [5] propose an s-core model, which requires each node in the subgraph to have sufficient number of positive and negative neighbors. Our work is closely related to [9]. In [9], Li et al. propose a signed clique model, called (α, k)-clique, to find cliques with more positive edges and fewer negative edges. Specifically, each node in the found cliques should have no more than k negative neighbors and at least αk positive neighbors. Unfortunately, even though this model sets hard constraints on the number of positive/negative neighbors, it may still involve a lot of unbalanced triangles such as T_3 and T_4 in Fig. 1, which may lead to unstable communities.

The main challenges of the proposed problem lie in the following aspects. Firstly, our problem is NP-hard, implying it is non-trivial to identify the maximal signed k-cliques. Secondly, it is challenging to support both clique and balance constraints simultaneously, since existing methods usually focus on one type of the constraints. To the best of our knowledge, we are the first to investigate the maximal signed k-clique problem. Our principal contributions are summarized as follows.

- We formally define the maximal signed k-clique model and show its hardness.
- Novel pruning methods are developed by leveraging the properties of balanced triangle to safely skip unpromising nodes and edges.
- Efficient algorithms are developed for the maximal signed k-clique enumeration based on the classic Bron-Kerbosch framework [1].
- To evaluate the proposed techniques, we conduct comprehensive experiments on 4 real-world datasets.

2   Preliminaries

We consider a signed network $G = (V, E)$ as an undirected graph, where V and E are the set of nodes and edges in the graph, respectively. Each edge $e \in E$ in G is associated with a label either "+" or "−". An edge with label "+" denotes a positive edge implying these two users are friends, while an edge with label "−" denotes a negative edge denoting the hostile relationship. Let $NB(u) = \{v | (u, v) \in E\}$ be the set of neighbor nodes of u. We denote the degree of u in G as $d_u(G) = |NB(u)|$. A triangle Δ is a cycle of length 3. In signed networks, balanced triangle is very important to keep the stability of a community, which is defined as follows.

Definition 1 (Balanced triangle). *Given a signed graph G, we say a triangle is balanced, denoted by Δ^+, if it has odd number of positive edges.*

As shown in Fig. 1, given a signed graph, there exist 4 types of triangles. T_1 and T_2 are balanced triangles, while T_3 and T_4 are unbalanced triangles. To model the cohesiveness of a subgraph, we employ the clique model.

Definition 2 (Clique). *Given a signed graph G, an induced subgraph C is a clique, if all pairs of nodes in C are mutually connected.*

Intuitively, an interesting community or cohesive subgraph in signed networks should be 1) densely connected, i.e., clique; and 2) free from unbalanced structures, i.e., unbalanced triangles. In addition, for network analysis, an important community should have sufficient number of people. Thus, we propose the signed k-clique model to describe the cohesive subgraphs in signed networks.

Definition 3 (Signed k-clique). *Given a signed graph G and a parameter k, a signed k-clique is an induced subgraph C that satisfies: (i) k-clique constraint: C is a clique and the number of nodes in C is no less than k, i.e., $|C| \geq k$; and (ii) balance theory constraint: C does not contain any unbalanced triangle.*

Definition 4 (Maximal signed k-clique). *An induced subgraph C is a maximal signed k-clique in G if C is a signed k-clique and there is no super graph of C that is a signed k-clique.*

Problem Statement. Given a signed graph G and a positive integer k, we aim to develop efficient algorithms to enumerate all the maximal signed k-cliques.

Problem Hardness. When there are only positive edges in the graph, the maximal signed k-clique problem is reduced to the maximal k-clique problem in unsigned graphs, which is NP-hard [7]. Therefore, the problem studied in this paper is also NP-hard.

3 Enumerating All Maximal Signed k-Cliques

Naively, we can extend the existing methods, such as Bron and Kerbosch framework [1], to enumerate cliques and verify them based on size and balance theory constraints. However, it will explore a lot of unnecessary searching space. In this section, novel pruning strategies are firstly proposed to filter the unpromising nodes and edges that are certainly not contained in any maximal signed k-clique. Then, the SKC algorithm is developed by integrating all the pruning strategies.

3.1 Pruning Strategies

As we know, k-core is a widely used model, where each node has at least k neighbors. In the following, we firstly use k-core model to prune the space.

Lemma 1. *k-core based pruning rule Given a signed graph G, a subgraph $S \subseteq G$ cannot be a signed k-clique, if S does not belong to $(k-1)$ core.*

Proof. Based on the definition of k-clique, any node in a k-clique should have at least $k-1$ neighbors, which meets the definition of $(k-1)$-core. Thus, the lemma holds.

Given a node u (resp. an edge (u,v)), we use Δ_u^+ (resp. $\Delta_{(u,v)}^+$) and $|\Delta_u^+|$ (rep. $|\Delta_{(u,v)}^+|$) to denote balanced triangles that contain u (resp. (u,v)) and the cardinality of Δ_u^+ (resp. $\Delta_{(u,v)}^+$), respectively. Then, based on the properties of triangle and clique, we can safely prune unpromising nodes based on Lemma 2 and filter unsatisfied edges based on Lemma 3 to reduce the searching space.

Lemma 2. *Node-based pruning rule. For any node u in a signed k-clique, the number of the balanced triangles containing u must be no less than $\frac{(k-1)(k-2)}{2}$.*

Proof. Given a signed k-clique C with size $|C| \geq k$, for any node $u \in C$, the number of neighbors of u (i.e., $|C|-1$) is no less than $k-1$ according to the properties of clique. All pairs of nodes in clique are connected, it implies that there are at least $\frac{(k-1)(k-2)}{2}$ balanced triangles containing u. Thus, if node u involves in less than $\frac{(k-1)(k-2)}{2}$ balanced triangles, it cannot be in any signed k-clique. Therefore, the lemma holds.

Lemma 3. *Edge-based pruning rule. For any edge e in a signed k-clique, the number of the balanced triangles containing e is no less than $k-2$.*

Proof. Clearly, there will be $|\Delta_{(u,v)}^+|$ common neighbors for both u and v in a signed k-clique. Suppose an edge $e(u,v)$ is contained in less than $k-2$ balanced triangles (i.e., $|\Delta_{(u,v)}^+| < k-2$). It implies edge $e(u,v)$ cannot exist in a signed k-clique, since the subgraph induced has less than k nodes, contradicting the definition of the signed k-clique. Thus, the lemma holds.

Algorithm 1: SKC Algorithm

Input : G: signed graph, k: clique constraint
Output : Maximal signed k-cliques
1 $G \leftarrow$ compute $(k-1)$-core in G;   /* Lemma 1 */
2 $\Delta_u^+, \Delta_{(u,v)}^+ \leftarrow$ Compute balanced triangles for each node u and edge (u,v) in G;
3 **while** $\exists u \in G$ with $|\Delta_u^+| < \frac{(k-1)(k-2)}{2}$ or $(u,v) \in G$ with $|\Delta_{(u,v)}^+| < k-2$ **do**
4   delete u or (u,v) from G;
5   **for each** $\Delta_{uvw} \in \Delta_u^+$ or $\Delta_{(u,v)}^+$ **do**
6   update the Δ information for the left nodes and edges in Δ_{uvw};

7 ENUMSKC$(\varnothing, U, \varnothing)$;   /* Lines 8-23 */

8 **Procedure** ENUMSKC(C, U, X);
9 **if** $U = \varnothing$ **then**
10   **if** $X = \varnothing \wedge |C| \geq k$ **then** report C as a maximal signed k-clique;
11   **return**

12 $u \leftarrow \arg\max_{v \in \{X \cup U\}} |U \cap NB(v)|$; $L \leftarrow U \backslash NB(u)$;
13 **for each** *node* $v \in L$ **do**
14     $U' \leftarrow \{U \cap NB(v)\}$;
15   **for each** $u \in U'$ **do**
16   **if** $\exists w \in C$ with Δ_{uvw} is unbalanced **then** $U' = U' \backslash \{u\}$;

17     $X' \leftarrow$ process X similar as U;
18   ENUMSKC$(C \cup \{v\}, U', X')$;
19     $U \leftarrow U \backslash \{v\}$; $X \leftarrow X \cup \{v\}$;

3.2 SKC Algorithm

In this section, we present the maximal signed k-clique enumeration (SKC) algorithm. Algorithm 1 shows the details of SKC. It first derives the $(k-1)$-core to prune some unpromising nodes based on Lemma 1 (Line 1). In Line 2, we compute the balanced triangles for each node u and edge (u,v) in G. According to Lemma 2 and 3, we further filter unsatisfied nodes and edges until none of them violates these two lemmas (Lines 3–6).

After filtering the searching space, we try to enumerate all the maximal signed k-cliques by extending the Bron and Kerbosch framework [1] in Line 7. The details of ENUMSKC procedure are shown in Lines 8–19. Note that it admits three input parameters $\{C, U, X\}$, where C is the temporary result, U is the set of possible candidates and X is the excluded set. To improve the performance, in Line 12, we first choose the best pivot node u from $X \cup U$ to minimize the size of L based on the pivoting technique, and remove the neighbors of u from L. In the loop, we first pick a node v from L and add it to C. In Line 14, we derive the set U' by removing the non-neighbors of v from U. In Lines 15–16, we use balance theory constraint to remove nodes from U'. Next we process X following the similar procedure as that of U in Line 17. Then, we repeat the ENUMSKC procedure for new C, U and X (Line 18) until U is empty (Line 9). If U and X

are both empty and the size of nodes in C is no less than k, it reports C as a newly found maximal signed k-clique (Lines 9–11). Otherwise, we backtrack to the last node picked and move it from U to X in Line 19.

4 Experiments

4.1 Experiment Setup

Algorithms. To the best of our knowledge, there is no existing work on the problem studied in this paper. Therefore, we add pruning rules one by one to evaluate the performance of SKC. In the experiments, we implement and evaluate the following algorithms.

- **SKC-C:** SKC framework with only the k-core based pruning rule.
- **SKC-CN:** SKC framework with the k-core and node-based pruning rules.
  SKC. SKC framework with all the pruning techniques, i.e., Algorithm 1.

Datasets. Four real datasets are utilized in our experiments. Table 1 shows the details of 4 real datasets that are utilized in our experiments. Bitcoin[1], Slashdot[1] and Wiki[2] are all real signed networks. Bitcoin is who-trusts-whom networks, where each edge represents the reputation, i.e., positive edge represents the trust while negative edge represents the distrust. The Slashdot dataset, collected from Slashdot, contains friend and foe links between the users. Wiki contains interpreted interactions between the users of the English Wikipedia that have edited pages about politics, where each interaction is given a positive or negative value. Youtube[1] is a large unsigned social network to evaluate the scalability of algorithms. Following the procedure in [9], we generate the signed labels by randomly picking 70% of the edges as the positive edges and the remaining edges as negative edges.

Table 1. Statistics of datasets

Dataset	$n = |V|$	$m = |E|$	$|E^+|$	$|E^-|$	$|\triangle^+|$	$|\triangle^-|$
Bitcoin	7,605	14,125	12,973	1,152	19,629	2,524
Slashdot	82,144	500,481	382,915	117,566	499,187	80,378
Wiki	138,593	717,573	631,547	86,026	2,737,424	264,899
Youtube	1,157,828	2,987,625	2,091,338	896,287	1,625,861	1,430,525

Parameters and Workload. To evaluate the performance of the proposed techniques, we conduct experiments by varying k. The response time and the

---

[1] http://snap.stanford.edu.
[2] http://konect.uni-koblenz.de.

number of maximal signed k-cliques are reported to demonstrate the efficiency and effectiveness of the methods, respectively. For each setting, we run the algorithm 10 times and report the average value. All the programs are implemented in standard C++. All the experiments are performed on a PC with an Intel i5-9600KF 3.7 GHz CPU and 64 GB RAM.

4.2   Efficiency and Effectiveness Evaluation of SKC

Efficiency Evaluation. To evaluate the efficiency, we compare the response time of SKC-C, SKC-CN and SKC on all the datasets by varying k. The results are shown in Fig. 2. As can be seen, by adding more pruning techniques, the algorithm becomes faster. SKC constantly outperforms the others on all datasets. As shown, when k increases, the response time deceases for all the algorithms. This is because the number of maximal k-cliques becomes smaller for larger k. In addition, algorithm becomes faster when more pruning rules are involved, which verifies the pruning power of the proposed techniques.

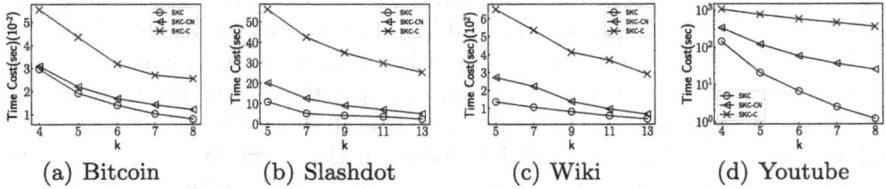

(a) Bitcoin   (b) Slashdot   (c) Wiki   (d) Youtube

Fig. 2. Efficiency evaluation of SKC by varying k

Effectiveness Evaluation. To evaluate the effectiveness of the proposed model, we report the number of cliques found based on the normal k-clique model and the proposed signed k-clique model. For the normal k-clique model, we ignore the labels on the edges and enumerate the k-cliques. Figure 3 shows the results conducted on all datasets by varying k. As observed, the number of normal k-cliques is larger than that of our model, which indicates that there are many unbalanced k-cliques in the signed networks. The results greatly demonstrate the effectiveness of the proposed model.

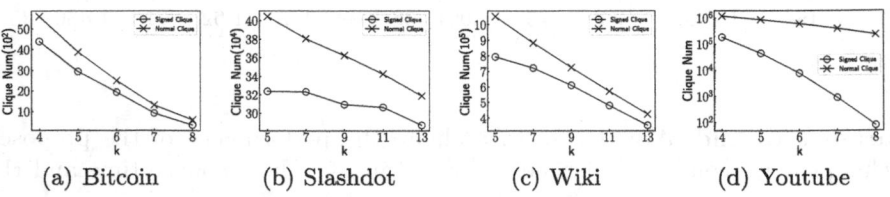

(a) Bitcoin   (b) Slashdot   (c) Wiki   (d) Youtube

Fig. 3. Effectiveness evaluation of SKC by varying k

5   Related Work

In graph analysis, clique enumeration serves as an important role in various applications [3,4,12]. To enumerate all the maximal cliques, Bron and Kerbosch [1] propose the classic backtracking method, called Bron-Kerbosch algorithm, which requires only polynomial storage space and escapes recomputing the same clique. Furthermore, Cheng et al. [4] develop an I/O-efficient maximal clique enumeration algorithm. Balance theory is proposed by Heider [6] and generalized by Cartwright [2].Balance theory has been widely used to investigate the properties of networks. In [8], Leskovec et al. use balance theory for link prediction. In recent years, mining signed networks has attracted a lot of attention. Yang et al. [11] propose a framework based on agent-based random walk model to extract communities in signed networks. Giatsidis et al. [5] extend the k-core model for the signed graphs. Li et al. [9] propose the (α, k)-clique model, which is very close to our problem. It tries to find cliques with more positive edges and fewer negative edges. As discussed, this model may still involve a lot of unbalanced structures. In addition, the proposed techniques cannot be extended to support the problem studied in this paper.

6   Conclusion

In this paper, we conduct the first research to investigate the maximal signed k-clique problem based on balance theory in signed graphs. We formalize the problem and show it is NP-hard. Novel pruning techniques are proposed to filter the unpromising nodes and edges. Advanced algorithms are developed to accelerate the enumeration of cliques. We conduct extensive experiments on four real-world signed networks to evaluate the effectiveness and efficiency of the proposed techniques.

Acknowledgments. Xiaoyang Wang is supported by NSFC61802345. Chen is supported by ZJNSF LQ20F020007.

References

1. Bron, C., Kerbosch, J.: Algorithm 457: finding all cliques of an undirected graph. Commun. ACM **16**(9), 575–577 (1973)
2. Cartwright, D., Harary, F.: Structural balance: a generalization of Heider's theory. Psychol. Rev. **63**(5), 277 (1956)
3. Cheng, J., Ke, Y., Fu, A.W.C., Yu, J.X., Zhu, L.: Finding maximal cliques in massive networks. ACM Trans. Database Syst. (TODS) **36**(4), 1–34 (2011)
4. Cheng, J., Zhu, L., Ke, Y., Chu, S.: Fast algorithms for maximal clique enumeration with limited memory. In: KDD (2012)
5. Giatsidis, C., Cautis, B., Maniu, S., Thilikos, D.M., Vazirgiannis, M.: Quantifying trust dynamics in signed graphs, the s-cores approach. In: ICDM (2014)
6. Heider, F.: Attitudes and cognitive organization. J. Psychol. **21**(1), 107–112 (1946)

7. Johnson, D.S., Garey, M.R.: Computers and Intractability: A Guide to the Theory of NP-Completeness. WH Freeman, New York (1979)
8. Leskovec, J., Huttenlocher, D., Kleinberg, J.: Predicting positive and negative links in online social networks. In: WWW, pp. 641–650 (2010)
9. Li, R.H., et al.: Efficient signed clique search in signed networks. In: ICDE, pp. 245–256. IEEE (2018)
10. Seidman, S.B.: Network structure and minimum degree. Soc. Netw. 5(3), 269–287 (1983)
11. Yang, B., Cheung, W., Liu, J.: Community mining from signed social networks. IEEE Trans. Knowl. Data Eng. 19(10), 1333–1348 (2007)
12. Yuan, L., Qin, L., Lin, X., Chang, L., Zhang, W.: Diversified top-k clique search. VLDBJ 25(2), 171–196 (2016)
13. Zhu, W., Zhang, M., Chen, C., Wang, X., Zhang, F., Lin, X.: Pivotal relationship identification: the k-truss minimization problem. In: IJCAI (2019)

Spatial Data

Group Task Assignment with Social Impact-Based Preference in Spatial Crowdsourcing

Xiang Li[1], Yan Zhao[1(✉)], Jiannan Guo[2], and Kai Zheng[3]

[1] School of Computer Science and Technology, Soochow University, Suzhou, China
`xli96@stu.suda.edu.cn, zhaoyan@suda.edu.cn`
[2] China Mobile Cloud Centre, Suzhou, China
`guojiannan@cmss.chinamobile.com`
[3] University of Electronic Science and Technology of China, Chengdu, China
`zhengkai@uestc.edu.cn`

Abstract. With the pervasiveness of GPS-enabled smart devices and increased wireless communication technologies, Spatial Crowdsourcing (SC) has drawn increasing attention in assigning location-sensitive tasks to moving workers. In real-world scenarios, for the complex tasks, SC is more likely to assign each task to more than one worker, called Group Task Assignment (GTA), for the reason that an individual worker cannot complete the task well by herself. It is a challenging issue to assign worker groups the tasks that they are interested in and willing to perform. In this paper, we propose a novel framework for group task assignment based on worker groups' preferences, which includes two components: Social Impact-based Preference Modeling (SIPM) and Preference-aware Group Task Assignment (PGTA). SIPM employs a Bipartite Graph Embedding Model (BGEM) and the attention mechanism to learn the social impact-based preferences of different worker groups on different task categories. PGTA utilizes an optimal task assignment algorithm based on the tree-decomposition technology to maximize the overall task assignments, in which we give higher priorities to the worker groups showing more interests in the tasks. Our empirical studies based on a real-world dataset verify the practicability of our proposed framework.

Keywords: Spatial crowdsourcing · Group task assignment · Social impact-based preference

1 Introduction

With the ubiquitous deployment of wireless networks and mobile devices (e.g., smart phones), Spatial Crowdsourcing (SC), an emerging paradigm utilizing the distributed mobile devices to monitor diverse phenomena about human activities, has attracted much attention from both academic and industry communities. The main idea of spatial crowdsourcing is recruiting a set of available

© Springer Nature Switzerland AG 2020
Y. Nah et al. (Eds.): DASFAA 2020, LNCS 12113, pp. 677–693, 2020.
https://doi.org/10.1007/978-3-030-59416-9_44

workers to perform the location-specific tasks by physically traveling to these locations, called *task assignment*.

Most existing SC researches focus on single task assignment, which assumes that tasks are simple and each task can only be assigned to a single worker. For example, Tong et al. [12] design several efficient greedy algorithms to solve the proposed Global Online Micro-task Allocation (GOMA) problem in spatial crowdsourcing. [7] considers task assignment and scheduling at the same time, in which an approximate approach is developed that iteratively improves the assignment and scheduling to achieve more completed tasks. However, in real-world scenarios, an individual worker may not be able to perform a complex task (e.g., monitoring the traffic flow in an area or moving heavy stuff) independently since completing the task alone exceeds the capability of this worker. In such scenarios, each task should be assigned to a group of workers, which is named *Group Task Assignment*.

Group task assignment requires a group of workers to perform each task by physically traveling to the location of this task at a particular time. Some previous studies have explored the group task assignment problem in spatial crowdsourcing. For instance, [8] proposes a Team-Oriented Task Planning (TOTP) problem, which makes feasible plans for workers and satisfies the skill requirements of different tasks on workers. Gao et al. [9] develop a Top-k team recommendation framework in spatial crowdsourcing, in which a team leader is appointed among each recommended team of workers in order to coordinate different workers conveniently. Cheng et al. [3] consider the collaboration in task assignment, in which workers are required to cooperate and accomplish the tasks jointly for achieving high total cooperation quality scores. Nevertheless, they fail to effectively incorporate the group preference, which is an essential factor for improving the quality of group task assignment in spatial crowdsourcing as the group members may not be willing to perform the task assigned to them when they are not interested in this task. We next illustrate the group task assignment problem through a motivation example.

Figure 1 shows an example of the group task assignment problem, in which each task is required to be assigned to two workers. There exist five workers $(w_1, ..., w_5)$ and two tasks (s_1, s_2). Each worker is associated with her current location and her reachable distance range. Each task is labeled with its location where it will be performed. In addition, Fig. 1 also depicts the preferences of different available worker groups for each task. The problem is to assign tasks to suitable worker groups so as to maximize the total task assignments. In SC, it is an intuitive move to assign the nearby tasks to workers without violating the spatio-temporal constraint (i.e., the assigned tasks should be located in the reachable ranges of the corresponding workers and workers can arrive in the locations of assigned tasks before the deadlines of tasks). Therefore, we can obtain a task assignment, $\{<s_1, \{w_1, w_2\}>, <s_2, \{w_4, w_5\}>\}$, with the overall group preference of 0.33. Nevertheless, when we assign the worker group, $\{w_4, w_5\}$, to task s_2, the group is likely to quit performing s_2 as they show little interest in s_2 (i.e., the group preference on s_2 is only 0.04), which may leave s_2

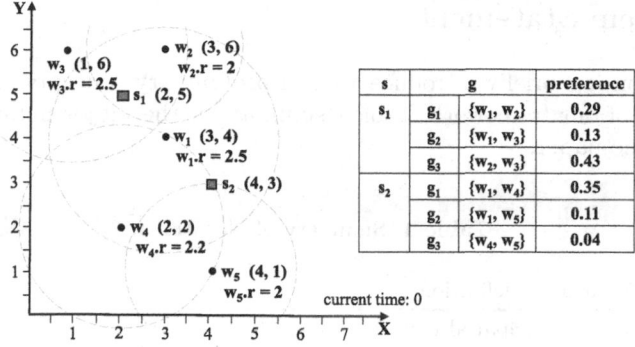

Fig. 1. Running example

uncompleted. If we assign tasks by giving higher priorities to the worker groups who are more interested in the tasks, we can get the task assignment result, $\{<s_1, \{w_2, w_3\}>, <s_2, \{w_1, w_4\}>\}$, the total group preference of which is 0.78.

In this paper, we develop a group task assignment framework based on worker groups' preferences. The framework is comprised of two primary components. First, we utilize the powerful Bipartite Graph Embedding Model (BGEM) [15] and the attention mechanism to learn the embedding of task categories and worker groups in a low-dimensional space from group-task interaction data. In order to overcome the limitations of data-sparsity problem, we integrate the worker-task interaction data and social network structure information (which is used for extracting the social impact of workers) during the process of preference modeling. Secondly, we apply the tree-decomposition-based algorithm [19] to assign tasks to worker groups to maximize the task assignments by giving higher priorities to the worker groups that show more interest in the tasks.

The contributions made by this paper can be summarized as follows:

- We identify a novel task assignment problem in SC, namely Group Task Assignment (GTA), in which each task needs to be completed by a group of workers.
- We adopt the Bipartite Graph Embedding Model (BGEM) and the attention mechanism to learn the social impact-based preferences of different worker groups on different task categories, in which the worker-task interaction, group-task interaction and social network structure information are taken into account in order to address the data sparsity problem.
- A task assignment algorithm based on tree decomposition is introduced, following the optimization strategy by maximizing the overall task assignments and giving higher priorities to worker groups with higher preferences on tasks.
- As demonstrated by the experiments, our proposed algorithms can efficiently and effectively form available worker groups for tasks that can achieve an optimal task assignment.

2 Problem Statement

In this section, we briefly introduce a set of preliminary concepts, and then give an overview of our framework. Table 1 summarizes the major notations used in the rest of the paper.

Table 1. Summary of Notations

Notation	Definition
s	Spatial task
S	A set of tasks
$s.l$	Location of spatial task s
$s.p$	Published time of spatial task s
$s.e$	Expiration time of spatial task s
$s.c$	Category of spatial task s
$s.numW$	Number of workers that s requires to be assigned
w	Worker
W	A set of workers
$w.l$	Location of worker w
$w.r$	Reachable radius of worker w
$w.on$	Online time of worker w
$w.off$	Offline time of worker w
$AWS(s)$	Available worker set of task s
$AWG(s)$	Available worker group of task s
A	A spatial task assignment

2.1 Preliminary Concepts

Definition 1 (Spatial Task). *A spatial task, $s = <s.l, s.p, s.e, s.c, s.numW>$, is a task to be performed at location s.l, published at time s.p, and will expire at s.e, where $s.l : (x, y)$ is a point in the 2D space. Each task s is also labelled with a category s.c (e.g., moving heavy stuff) and s.numW is the number of workers allowed to be assigned to perform s at the same time instance.*

Definition 2 (Worker). *A worker, denoted by $w = <w.l, w.r, w.on, w.off>$, is a carrier of a mobile device who volunteers to perform spatial tasks. A worker can be in an either online or offline mode. A worker is online when she is ready to accept tasks. An online worker is associated with her current location w.l and her reachable circular range with w.l as the center and w.r as the radius, where w can accept assignment of spatial tasks. Besides, a worker with her online time,*

$w.on$, is also associated with her offline time, $w.off$, before which the worker can be assigned tasks.

In our model, a worker can handle only one task at a certain time instance, which is reasonable in practice. Once the server assigns a task to a worker, the worker is considered being offline until she completes the assigned task.

Definition 3 (Available Worker Set). Given a task s to be assigned and a set of workers in the vicinity of s, the available worker set for task s, denoted as $AWS(s)$, should satisfy the following three conditions: $\forall w \in AWS(s)$:
1) $t_{now} + t(w.l, s.l) \leq s.e$, and
2) $d(w.l, s.l) \leq w.r$, and
3) $t_{now} + t(w.l, s.l) \leq w.off$,
where t_{now} is the current time, $t(w.l, s.l)$ is the travel time from $w.l$ to $s.l$, and $d(w.l, s.l)$ is the travel distance (e.g., Euclidean distance) between $w.l$ and $s.l$.

For the sake of simplicity, we assume all the workers share the same velocity, such that the travel time between two locations can be estimated with their Euclidean distance, e.g., $t(w.l, s.l) = d(w.l, s.l)$.

Definition 4 (Available Worker Group). Given a task s to be assigned and its available worker set $AWS(s)$, the available worker group for task s, denoted as $AWG(s)$, should satisfy the following three conditions:
1) $AWG(s) \subset AWS(s)$, and
2) $|AWG(s)| = s.numW$, and
3) $\forall w_i, w_j \in AWG(s), t_{now} + t(w_i.l, s.l) \leq w_j.off$,
where $|AWG(s)|$ denotes the number of worker in $AWG(s)$.

In the rest of the paper, we will use worker group and group interchangeably when the context is clear.

Definition 5 (Spatial Task Assignment). Given a set of workers W_i and a set of tasks S_i at time instance t_i, a spatial task assignment, denoted by A_i, consists of a set of $<task, AWG>$ pairs in the form of $<s_1, AWG(s_1)>$, $<s_2, AWG(s_2)>, ...$ We use $|A_i|$ to denote the number of task assignments.

Problem Statement: Given a set of workers W_i and a set of tasks S_i at the current time instance t_i on a SC platform, the Group Task Assignment (GTA) problem aims to find the optimal assignment with the maximum number of task assignments (i.e., $max\{|A_i|\}$) by considering the preferences of worker groups.

2.2   Framework Overview

As shown in Fig. 2, our framework consists of two major components: 1) Social Impact-based Preference Modeling (SIPM) for worker groups; and 2) Preference-based Group Task Assignment (PGTA) based on worker groups' preferences.

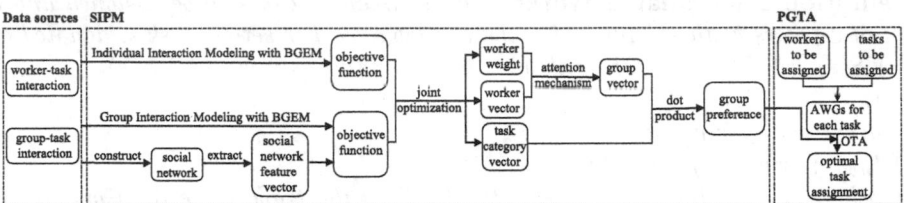

Fig. 2. Framework of our model

In the SIPM procedure, inspired by the success of [1,14] in learning (user) group preference based on both user-item and group-item interaction data, we utilize the Bipartite Graph Embedding Model (BGEM) and attention mechanism to obtain each worker group's preference on different categories of tasks by simultaneously leveraging both worker-task and group-task interaction data. Note that we say a worker interacts with a task if she has performed this task. More specifically, we utilize BGEM to model the individual interaction (i.e., worker-task interaction) and group interaction (i.e., group-task interaction) to learn the vector representation of workers and task categories in a low-dimensional space, respectively. Since the worker groups in spatial crowdsourcing are often formed in an ad hoc manner (called occasional groups) without any interaction with tasks, which means the group interaction data is sparse, we cannot effectively learn the vector representation of groups directly. To solve this problem, we introduce workers' social impact that represents workers' weights in a group when making decision about task selection. In particular, we integrate the worker-task interaction data with group-task interaction data to construct a social network, based on which we extract the social network information. In order to alleviate the sparsity of group-task interaction data, we employ a joint optimization approach to combine group-task interaction data with worker-task interaction data, in which we can obtain the embedding vectors of workers and task categories as well as workers' weights (i.e., workers' social impact). At the same time, the group vector can be calculated by the attention mechanism, which assigns different weights to different workers. Finally, we can obtain the group preference on task categories by taking dot product between group vector and task category vector.

In the PGTA phrase, given a set of workers and tasks to be assigned, we first obtain the Available Worker Groups (AWGs) for each task by considering trip constraints, i.e., workers' reachable range, workers' available time and tasks' expiration time. Then we employ the Optimal Task Assignment (OTA) algorithm based on tree decomposition to assign tasks to suitable worker groups in order to maximize the total task assignments and giving higher priorities to worker groups showing more preferences to tasks.

3   Social Impact-Based Preference Modeling

In this section, we first elaborate how the Bipartite Graph Embedding Model (BGEM) [15] learns each worker's embedding vector (representing her preference on different task categories) and each task category's embedding vector based on the historical worker-task interaction data (a.k.a. individual interaction data). Then in the group interaction modeling, we extract workers' social impact from the social network and employ the attention mechanism [1] to adapt the social impact to different worker groups. Finally, we design a joint optimization strategy, which can obtain the preference of each group on task categories by simultaneously leveraging both worker-task and group-task interaction data.

0.1   Individual Interaction Modeling

Given the interactions between workers and tasks, i.e., worker-task interaction data, we first construct a bipartite graph, $\mathcal{G}_{WC} = (W \cup C, E_{WC})$, where W denotes the worker set, C denotes all the categories of tasks, $W \cup C$ is the node set of $\mathcal{G}_{WC}$, E_{WC} is the set of edges between workers and task categories. An edge e_{ij} ($\in E_{WC}$) exists when worker w_i ($\in W$) has performed the tasks with category c_j ($\in C$). The weight h_{ij} of edge e_{ij} is set as $h_{ij} = \frac{N_{w_i}^{c_j}}{N_{w_i}}$, where $N_{w_i}^{c_j}$ denotes the number of tasks (with category c_j) worker w_i has performed and $N_{w_i} = \sum_{c \in C} N_{w_i}^c$ denotes the total number of tasks w_i has performed.

Due to the success of BGEM [15] in learning the embedding of heterogenous interaction entities, we employ it to model the individual worker-task interaction. For the given worker w_i, the probability of w_i interacting with the tasks with category c_j can be calculated in the following:

$$p(c_j|w_i) = \frac{\exp(\boldsymbol{w}_i \cdot \boldsymbol{c}_j)}{\sum_{c \in C} \exp(\boldsymbol{w}_i \cdot \boldsymbol{c})}, \tag{1}$$

where $\boldsymbol{w}_i$ is the embedding vector of worker w_i representing her preference, and $\boldsymbol{c}_j$ is the embedding vector of task category c_j.

In the sequel, we define the objective function of the BGEM. As we all know from [10], the target of BGEM is to minimize the KL-divergence between $\hat{p}(\cdot|w_i)$ and $p(\cdot|w_i)$, which represent the empirical distribution and the estimated neighbour probability distribution for each worker $w_i \in W$ respectively.

We employ d_i to represent the outdegree of worker node w_i, which can be calculated as $d_i = \sum_{c_j \in C} h_{ij}$ (where h_{ij} denotes the weight of the edge e_{ij}). We define the empirical distribution $\hat{p}(c_j|w_i) = h_{ij}/d_i$. Thus, the objective function can be obtained as follows:

$$O_{WC} = -\sum_{e_{ij} \in E_{WC}} h_{ij} \log p(c_j|w_i) = -\sum_{e_{ij} \in E_{WC}} \frac{N_{w_i}^{c_j}}{N_{w_i}} \log \frac{\exp(\boldsymbol{w}_i \cdot \boldsymbol{c}_j)}{\sum_{c \in C} \exp(\boldsymbol{w}_i \cdot \boldsymbol{c})}. \tag{2}$$

3.2   Group Interaction Modeling

In the similar way, we construct a bipartite graph, i.e., $\mathcal{G}_{GC} = (G \cup C, E_{GC})$, to represent the interactions between groups and task categories, where G is a set of groups, $G \cup C$ is the node set of $\mathcal{G}_{GC}$, E_{GC} represents a set of edges between groups and task categories. There exists an edge e_{ij} ($\in E_{GC}$) between group g_i ($\in G$) and task category c_j ($\in C$) if this group of workers has performed the tasks with category c_j ($\in C$). Moreover, the weight h_{ij} of the edge e_{ij} is simply set as $h_{ij} = \frac{N_{g_i}^{c_j}}{N_{g_i}}$, where $N_{g_i}^{c_j}$ denotes the number of tasks (with category c_j) worker group g_i has performed and N_{g_i} denotes the total number of tasks g_i has performed. Let g_i be the embedding vector for group g_i and c_j be the embedding vector for task category c_j. Our target is to obtain an embedding vector for each worker group to estimate the preference on all the task categories.

The objective function in group-task interaction data, which is similar to the worker-task interaction data, can be calculated in the following:

$$O_{GC} = - \sum_{e_{ij} \in E_{GC}} h_{ij} \log p(c_j | g_i) = - \sum_{e_{ij} \in E_{GC}} \frac{N_{g_i}^{c_j}}{N_{g_i}} \log \frac{\exp(g_i \cdot c_j)}{\sum_{c \in C} \exp(g_i \cdot c)}. \quad (3)$$

Nevertheless, in reality, there are few persistent groups while there are large amounts of occasional groups forming in an ad hoc manner to perform a task in spatial crowdsourcing. As a result, the group-task interaction data is over sparse with the cold-start nature (i.e., there have no or little group-task interaction) of occasional groups, which leads it difficult to directly learn the embedding vector of an occasional group. To tackle the sparsity and cold-start issue, we aggregate the embeddings of all the members in a group from the group-task interaction data. We observe that in decisions such as task selection, some group members may out-speak others in expressing their preference (due to prestige, authority, or other personality factors) and thus are more influential on the group's choice on tasks. In addition, the same worker in different groups may have different contributions on group's decision-making. Therefore, we introduce a coefficient $\alpha(k, i)$ to learn the weight of worker w_k in group g_i, which represents the group-aware personal social impact of w_k in deciding the choice of group g_i on tasks. Specifically, given an occasional group g_i, we define the embedding vector g_i as follows:

$$g_i = \sum_{w_k \in g_i} \alpha(k, i) w_k, \quad (4)$$

where $\alpha(k, i)$ is a learnable parameter (where a higher value indicates greater impact on a group's decision), and w_k denotes the embedding of worker w_k.

However, occasional groups temporarily gather together to perform a task in a time instance. It is difficult to learn the coefficient $\alpha(k, i)$ directly from the group-task interaction data because of the extreme data sparsity problem. Therefore, we introduce an additional positive numerical value λ_k for each worker w_k representing the global personal social impact, which does not depend on specific groups. We employ $\exp(\lambda_k)$ to represent the relative impact on deciding a group choice on tasks. Thus, $\alpha(k, i)$ can be calculated in Eq. 5, which is inspired by the attention mechanism [1].

$$\alpha(k, i) = \frac{\exp(\lambda_k)}{\sum_{w_k \in g_i} \exp(\lambda_k)}. \tag{5}$$

It is obvious that once we obtain the λ_k representing the global personal social impact for each worker w_k, we can easily obtain the $\alpha(k, i)$, which represents the group-aware personal social impact in a group. However, if a worker has only participated in very few group activities, it may suffer from over-fitting problems. Moreover, if a worker has never attended any group activities, we are not capable of learning the global personal social impact. As a result, we cannot learn the satisfying social impact only from the group-task interaction data.

In order to improve the accuracy of global personal social impact estimation, we construct a workers' social network based on both worker-task and group-task interaction data, based on which we extract the social network information, which benefits workers' global social impact estimation. In the social network, each worker maps to a node and an edge exists if two workers have cooperated with each other in the same group. The weight of the edge is set as the number of cooperations between the workers. Each worker (node) is associated with the number of tasks she has completed. Then we extract the social network structure information by various measures (e.g., degree centrality and betweenness centrality) and integrate the social network structure information into the learning process of worker's global social impact, which effectively alleviates the cold-start problem in group-task interaction data.

In particular, we can calculate a social network feature vector β_k for worker w_k and employ a feature selector vector h to assign different weights to different structure features [14]. We normalize all the feature values into the range [0,1]. Then, we take dot product between the social network feature vector β_k and the feature selector vector h as the Gaussian prior for the global personal social impact of worker, i.e., $\lambda_k \sim (\beta_k \cdot h + b, \rho_V^2)$ (b is a bias term). Due to the fact that global personal social impact may be affected by other unknown factors, we assume that λ_k follows the normal distribution with the mean $\beta_k \cdot h + b$ to learn the more robust personal global social impact.

In terms of the objective function, we should add a corresponding regularization term R_V, i.e., $\frac{1}{2\rho_V^2} \sum_{w_k \in W} (\lambda_k - (\beta_k \cdot h + b))^2$, into the objective function since we introduce a Gaussian prior for the personal social impact parameter λ_k. The hyper-parameter ρ_V^2 (i.e., variance) can control the weight of the regularization term. Therefore, the new objective function is as follows:

$$O_{VGC} = O_{GC} + R_V. \tag{6}$$

Considering the cold-start issue in group-task interaction data, we combine worker-task interaction data with group-task interaction data during the optimization process. More specifically, we design a joint optimization approach, which can simultaneously learn the embedding vectors of workers and task categories from the worker-task interaction data and group-task interaction data.

Besides, the global social impact of workers can be learned during the optimization process. Therefore, we combine O_{VGC} and O_{WC} to form a joint objective function, which is simply defined as follows:

$$O_{GWC} = O_{VGC} + O_{WC}. \tag{7}$$

Here, we adopt the standard Stochastic Gradient Descent (SGD) strategy [2] to minimize the objective function O_{GWC} in Eq. 7, as a result of which each worker's embedding vector w, each task category's embedding vector c and the model parameters (i.e., λ_h, h) can be learned. We can calculate the coefficient $\alpha(k, i)$ representing the group-aware personal social impact according to Eq. 5. Then each group's embedding vector g can be correspondingly obtained based on Eq. 4. Finally, we take dot product between each group's embedding vector and each task category's embedding vector to achieve the preference of each group on each task category.

4   Preference-Based Group Task Assignment

In this section, we first generate the available worker groups for each task based on the trip constraints (i.e., workers' reachable range, workers' available time and tasks' expiration time), and then a tree-decomposition-based algorithm [16,19] is employed to achieve the optimal task assignment.

4.1   Available Worker Group Set Generation

Finding the Reachable Workers for Each Task. Due to the constraint of workers' reachable distance, workers' available time and tasks' expiration time, each task can be completed by a small subset of workers in a time instance. Therefore, we firstly find the set of workers that can complete each task without violating the constraints. The reachable worker subset for a task s, denoted as RW_s, should satisfy the following conditions: $\forall w \in RW_s$:

1) $t_{now} + t(w.l, s.l) \leq s.e$, and
2) $d(w.l, s.l) \leq w.r$, and
3) $t_{now} + t(w.l, s.l) \leq w.off$,

where t_{now} denotes the current time, $t(w.l, s.l)$ is the travel time from $w.l$ to $s.l$ and $d(w.l, s.l)$ denotes the travel distance (e.g., Euclidean distance) between $w.l$ and $s.l$. The above three conditions guarantee that a worker w can travel from her location $w.l$ to a task s (which is located in her reachable range) directly before task s expires and during worker w's available time.

Finding the Available Worker Group Sets for Each Task. Given the reachable workers for each task s, we next find the set of available worker group, denoted as $\mathbb{AWG}(s)$, under the constraints of workers' available time in a group and the number of workers allowed to be assigned to perform a task s. Each available worker group in $\mathbb{AWG}(s)$, denoted as $AWG(s)$, should satisfy the following conditions:

1) $|AWG(s)| = s.numW$, and

2) $\forall w_j, w_k \in AWG(s), t_{now} + t(w_j.l, s.l) \leq w_k.off$,

where $|AWG(s)|$ is the number of worker in $AWG(s)$. The above two conditions guarantee that workers in a group can arrive at the location of task s without violating the available time of each other.

4.2 Optimal Algorithm

It is easy to know the global optimal result is the union of one possible Available Worker Group (AWG) of all tasks. We introduce an algorithm, i.e., tree-decomposition-based strategy [19], to achieve the optimal task assignment with the maximal preferences. More specifically, we first construct a task dependency graph according to the dependency relationship among tasks (two tasks are dependent with each other if they share the available workers; otherwise they are independent). Subsequently, we utilize a tree-decomposition strategy to separate all tasks into independent clusters (i.e., tasks in different clusters do not share the same available workers) and organize them into a balance tree structure, such that the tasks in sibling nodes of the tree do not share the same available workers. Facilitated by such a tree structure, we can solve the optimal assignment sub-problem on each sibling node independently. Then the optimal assignment can be found by a depth-first search through the tree.

Meanwhile, we assign tasks to the available worker groups with higher preference (i.e., social impact-based preferences) during the process of search to maximize the total task assignments by giving higher priorities to the worker groups with more interests in tasks.

5 Experiment

In this section, we conduct extensive experiments on a real-world dataset to evaluate the performance of our proposed algorithms. All the algorithms are implemented on an Intel(R) Xeon(R) CPU E5-2650 v4 @ 2.20 GHz with 256 GB RAM.

5.1 Experiment Setup

Dataset. We conduct our experiments on a check-in dataset from Twitter, which provides check-in data across USA except Hawaii and Alaska from September 2010 to January 2011 including locations of 62462 venues and 61412 users. The dataset is used widely in evaluation of SC platform [6]. Due to the lack of category information of venues in dataset, we generate the category information (i.e., task category information) associated with each venue from Foursquare with the aid of its API. When using the dataset in our experimental research, we assume the users in dataset are the workers of SC platform since users who check in to different spots may be good candidates to perform spatial tasks in the vicinity of those spots, and their locations are those of the most recent check-in points. We assume the spots are the tasks of SC platform, and employ its location and earliest check-in time of the day as the location and publish time of a task respectively. We extract 20 kinds of check-in categories to simulate the task categories, i.e., the categories of check-ins. Checking in a spot is equivalent to accepting a task.

As Twitter does not contain explicit group information, we extract implicit group task completion activities as follows: we assume if a set of users visit the same spot or different spots with the same category which are near to each other (e.g., the distance between any two spots is less 10 km in our experiments) in one hour, they are regarded as the members of a group.

Evaluation. We compare and evaluate the performance of following methods:

1) OGTA: Optimal Group Task Assignment based on tree-decomposition algorithm without considering worker group's preference.
2) AVG-OGTA: Optimal Group Task Assignment with average worker group's preference, where the average preference of a group g is set as $\frac{N_g^c}{N_g}$, where N_g^c denotes the number of tasks (with category c) worker group g has performed and N_g denotes the total number of tasks g has performed.
3) SIP-GGTA: Greedy Group Task Assignment with Social Impact-based Preference of worker groups. For the sake of efficiency, a basic Greedy Task Assignment algorithm is introduced to assign each task greedily to the worker groups with the maximal preferences until all the tasks are assigned or all the worker groups are exhausted.
4) SIP-OGTA: Optimal Group Task Assignment with Social Impact-based Preference of worker groups (i.e., our proposed algorithm).

Three metrics are compared among the above algorithms:

1) CPU cost: the CPU time cost for finding a task assignment in a time instance;
2) ASR: Assignment Success Rate is the ratio of successful assignments to the total assignments for all workers in a time instance. Note that once all the group members actually perform (check in) the tasks (spots) with the same category which are near to each other (e.g., the distance between the tasks is less 10 km in our experiments) in one hour, we regard this task assignment as a successful assignment.
3) Number of task assignments.

The default values of all parameters used in our experiments are summarized in Table 2.

Table 2. Experiment Parameters

Parameter	Default value
Valid time of tasks $e - p$	1.5 h
Number of each group $numW$	2
Workers' reachable radius r	2 km
Workers' available time $off - on$	3 h
Number of tasks $|S|$	3000

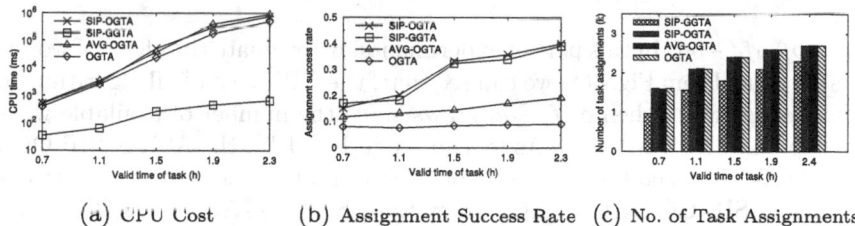

(a) CPU Cost   (b) Assignment Success Rate   (c) No. of Task Assignments

Fig. 3. Performance of Group Task Assignment: Effect of $e - p$

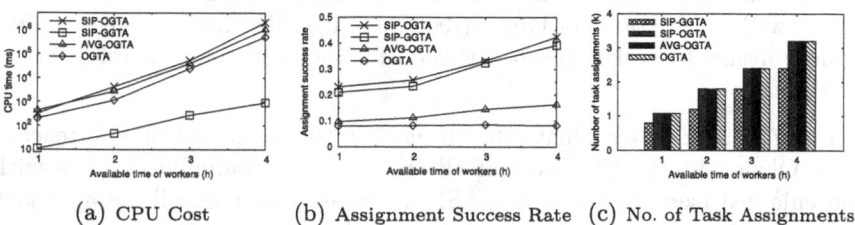

(a) CPU Cost   (b) Assignment Success Rate   (c) No. of Task Assignments

Fig. 4. Performance of Group Task Assignment: Effect of $off - on$

5.2   Experimental Results

Effect of $e - p$. We first study the effect of the valid time $e - p$ of tasks. As depicted in Fig. 3(a), longer expiration time will incur more CPU cost for all algorithms since more available worker groups need to be searched. As expected, the accuracy of all algorithms except OGTA increases as the valid time of task grows since a worker group has more chance to be assigned her interested tasks with the growing valid time of tasks (see Fig. 3(b)). SIP-OGTA and SIP-GGTA perform better than AVG-OGTA in terms of ASR, which demonstrates the benefit of considering social impact into worker groups' preference. OGTA keeps almost constant as it does not consider worker group' preference. Although SIP-GGTA is fastest among all the methods and has the similar ASR with SIP-OGTA, it assigns less tasks than other methods (i.e., OGTA, AVG-OGTA, SIP-OGTA), shown in Fig. 3(c).

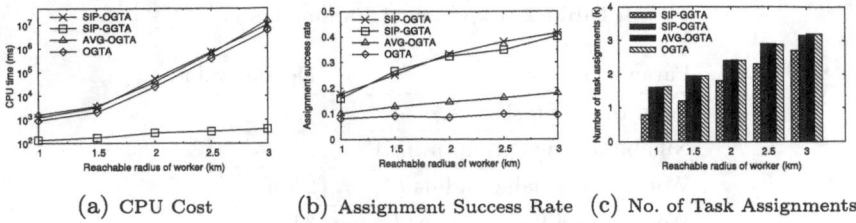

(a) CPU Cost   (b) Assignment Success Rate   (c) No. of Task Assignments

Fig. 5. Performance of Group Task Assignment: Effect of r

Effect of $off-on$**.** In this part of experiments, we evaluate the effect of workers' available time. From Fig. 4(a) we can see that, the CPU cost of all algorithms has an increasing trend when $off - on$ grows since the number of available worker groups for each task increases. As we can see in Fig. 4(b), the ASR of SIP-OGTA and SIP-GGTA methods consistently outperforms other methods by a noticeable margin and SIP-GGTA is slightly lower than SIP-OGTA. The ASR of all the methods has a similar tendency with $e - p$ when $off - on$ grows with the similar reason that worker groups have more chance to obtain their interested tasks with the increasing $off - on$. The number of task assignments grows quickly, almost linearly, with $off - on$ gets larger (see Fig. 4(c)). The intrinsic reason lies in the more available worker groups for each task as workers' available time gets longer.

Effect of r**.** Next, we evaluate the effect of r, the range of workers' reachable radius. Obviously, the CPU cost of all the methods gradually increase with r being enlarged (see Fig. 5(a)). The ASR increases with r for all the approaches that take worker groups' preferences into consideration since the larger the workers' reachable regions are, the more chance worker groups can be assigned their interested tasks. As illustrated in Fig. 5(c), we can see SIP-GGTA algorithm performs worse than others, which demonstrates the superiority of optimal task assignment strategy.

Effect of $numW$**.** Figure 6(a) illustrates the CPU cost decreases gradually when the number of workers for each group (i.e., $numW$) gets larger. The reason behind it is that the available worker groups for each task are less as $numW$ gets larger, which reduces the search space. When it comes to the assignment success rate, shown in Fig. 6(b), all algorithms show a decreasing trend. We cannot assign the tasks to the suitable groups because of the less available worker groups. However, SIP-OGTA method still shows a higher superiority than other algorithms. In addition, Fig. 6(c) demonstrates that the number of task assignments of SIP-GGTA has no advantage compared with other methods.

Effect of $|S|$**.** In the final set of experiments, we evaluate the scalability of all the proposed algorithms by changing the number $|S|$ of tasks from 1k to 5k. As expected, although the CPU cost increases as $|S|$ increases, SIP-OGTA performs

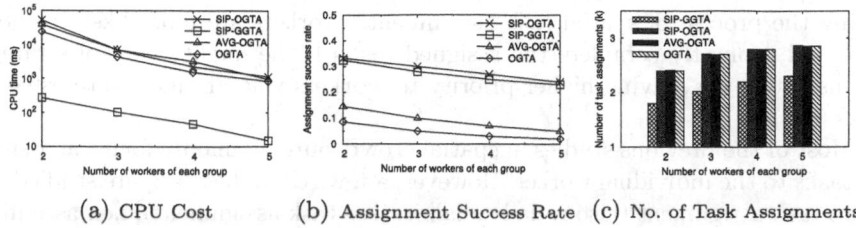

(a) CPU Cost   (b) Assignment Success Rate   (c) No. of Task Assignments

Fig. 6. Performance of Group Task Assignment: Effect of $numW$

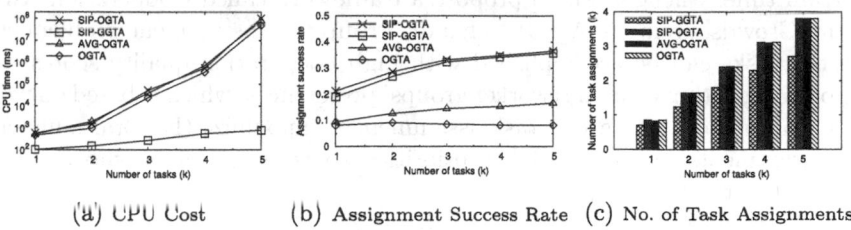

(a) CPU Cost   (b) Assignment Success Rate   (c) No. of Task Assignments

Fig. 7. Performance of Group Task Assignment: Effect of $|S|$

well in improving the assignment success rate and the number of task assignments, which is demonstrated in Fig. 7(b) and Fig. 7(c). Figure 7(a) indicates SIP-GGTA is the least time-consuming algorithm while other algorithms based on OGTA run much more slower, which is mainly due to the extra time cost for building the tree to be searched and searching the tree. In terms of assignment success rate, the accuracy of SIP-OGTA is a bit higher than SIP-GGTA and AVG-OGTA still increases slowly as $|S|$ grows, which is shown in Fig. 7(b). Similar to the previous results, The OGTA related algorithms outperform the SIP-GGTA method for all values of $|S|$ in the number of task assignments, which is depicted in Fig. 7(c).

6   Related Work

Spatial Crowdsourcing (SC) can be deemed as one of the main enablers to complete location-based tasks [5,13,17,18]. SC can be classified into two categories namely Server Assigned Tasks (SAT) and Worker Selected Tasks (WST) based on the task publishing modes. In particular, for the SAT mode which is popular in existing researches, SC server is responsible for directly assigning proper tasks to nearby workers, which aims to maximize the number of assigned tasks after collecting all the locations of workers/tasks on the server side [11] or maximize the reliability-and-diversity score of assignments [4]. For the WST mode, spatial tasks are published online and then broadcast to all workers, such that workers can choose any task according to their personal preferences by themselves [6]. Meanwhile, quality assurance is an intractable problem needing to be solved during the process of spatial task assignment. Workers are more likely to honestly and promptly complete the assigned tasks if the quality control strategy is considered, e.g., giving higher priority to workers who are more interested in tasks.

Most of the previous studies in spatial crowdsourcing mainly focus on assigning tasks to the individual worker. However, a few researches [3,8] are studied for group task assignment (also called collaborative task assignment), i.e., assigning tasks to a group of multiple workers. The groups are formed by workers in an ad-hoc way, also called occasional groups, who have a shared purpose only in a certain time. Cheng et al. [3] propose a framework called Cooperation-Aware Spatial Crowdsourcing (CA-SC) to handle group task assignment problem such that the tasks can be accomplished with high cooperation quality scores. Our proposed algorithm combines worker groups' preferences, which is based on workers' social impact, with group task assignment to maximize the total number of task assignments by giving higher priorities to worker groups who are more interested in the tasks.

7   Conclusion

In this paper, we propose a novel task assignment problem, called Group Task Assignment (GTA), in spatial crowdsourcing. In order to achieve effective task assignment, we addressed a few challenges by proposing different strategies to obtain the social impact-based preferences of different worker groups for each task category, and adopting an optimal algorithm to assign tasks. To the best of our knowledge, this is the first work in spatial crowdsourcing that considers the social impact-based preferences of worker groups and performs group task assignment based on these preferences. Extensive empirical study based on a real dataset confirms the practicability of our proposed framework.

Acknowledgement. This work is partially supported by Natural Science Foundation of China (No. 61972069, 61836007, 61832017, 61532018) and Alibaba Innovation Research (AIR).

References

1. Bahdanau, D., Cho, K., Bengio, Y.: Neural machine translation by jointly learning to align and translate. In: ICLR (2015)
2. Bottou, L.: Large-scale machine learning with stochastic gradient descent. In: Lechevallier, Y., Saporta, G. (eds.) Proceedings of COMPSTAT 2010, pp. 177–186. Springer, Heidelberg (2010). https://doi.org/10.1007/978-3-7908-2604-3_16
3. Cheng, P., Chen, L., Ye, J.: Cooperation-aware task assignment in spatial crowdsourcing. In: ICDE, pp. 1442–1453 (2019)
4. Cheng, P., et al.: Reliable diversity-based spatial crowdsourcing by moving workers. PVLDB 8(10), 1022–1033 (2015)
5. Cui, Y., Deng, L., Zhao, Y., Yao, B., Zheng, V.W., Zheng, K.: Hidden POI ranking with spatial crowdsourcing. In: SIGKDD, pp. 814–824 (2019)

6. Deng, D., Shahabi, C., Demiryurek, U.: Maximizing the number of worker's self-selected tasks in spatial crowdsourcing. In: SIGSPATIAL, pp. 314–323 (2013)
7. Deng, D., Shahabi, C., Zhu, L.: Task matching and scheduling for multiple workers in spatial crowdsourcing. In: SIGSPATIAL, p. 21 (2015)
8. Gao, D., Tong, Y., Ji, Y., Xu, K.: Team-oriented task planning in spatial crowdsourcing. In: Chen, L., Jensen, C.S., Shahabi, C., Yang, X., Lian, X. (eds.) APWeb-WAIM 2017. LNCS, vol. 10366, pp. 41–56. Springer, Cham (2017). https://doi.org/10.1007/978-3-319-63579-8_4
9. Gao, D., Tong, Y., She, J., Song, T., Chen, L., Xu, K.: Top-k team recommendation and its variants in spatial crowdsourcing. DSE **2**(2), 136–150 (2017)
10. Mikolov, T., Sutskever, I., Chen, K., Corrado, G.S., Dean, J.: Distributed representations of words and phrases and their compositionality. In: NIPS, pp. 3111–3119 (2013)
11. Tong, Y., Chen, L., Zhou, Z., Jagadish, H.V., Shou, L., Weifeng, L.: SLADE: a smart large-scale task decomposer in crowdsourcing. In: ICDE, pp. 2133–2134 (2019)
12. Tong, Y., She, J., Ding, B., Wang, L.: Online mobile micro-task allocation in spatial crowdsourcing. In: ICDE, pp. 49–60 (2016)
13. Xia, J., Zhao, Y., Liu, G., Xu, J., Zhang, M., Zheng, K.: Profit-driven task assignment in spatial crowdsourcing. In: IJCAI, pp. 1914–1920 (2019)
14. Yin, H., Wang, Q., Zheng, K., Li, Z., Yang, J., Zhou, X.: Social influence-based group representation learning for group recommendation. In: ICDE, pp. 566–577 (2019)
15. Yin, H., Zou, L., Nguyen, Q.V.H., Huang, z., Zhou, X.: Joint event-partner recommendation in event-based social networks. In: ICDE, pp. 929–940 (2018)
16. Zhao, Y., Li, Y., Wang, Y., Su, H., Zheng, K.: Destination-aware task assignment in spatial crowdsourcing. In: CIKM, pp. 297–306 (2017)
17. Zhao, Y., et al.: Preference-aware task assignment in spatial crowdsourcing. In: AAAI, pp. 2629–2636 (2019)
18. Zhao, Y., Zheng, K., Cui, Y., Su, H., Zhu, F., Zhou, X.: Predictive task assignment in spatial crowdsourcing: a data-driven approach (2020)
19. Zhao, Y., Zheng, K., Li, Y., Su, H., Liu, J., Zhou, X.: Destination-aware task assignment in spatial crowdsourcing: a worker decomposition approach. TKDE (2019)

Finish Them on the Fly: An Incentive Mechanism for Real-Time Spatial Crowdsourcing

Qiyu Liu[1], Libin Zheng[1(✉)], Yanyan Shen[2], and Lei Chen[1]

[1] The Hong Kong University of Science and Technology,
Clear Water Bay, Hong Kong
{qliuau,lzhengab,leichen}@cse.ust.hk
[2] Shanghai Jiao Tong University, Shanghai, China
yanyanshen14@gmail.com

Abstract. Proper incentive mechanism design for stimulating workers is a fundamental challenge in nowadays spatial crowdsourcing (SC) powered applications like Didi and Uber. Usually, extra monetary rewards are paid to workers as incentive to enhance their participation in the SC platform. However, deciding incentives in real-time is non-trivial as the spatial crowdsourcing market changes fast over time. Existing studies mostly assume an *offline* scenario where the incentives are computed considering a static market condition with the global knowledge of tasks and workers. Unfortunately, this setting does not fit the reality where the market itself would evolve gradually. In this paper, to enable online incentive determination, we formulate the problem of *Real-time Monetary Incentive for Tasks in Spatial Crowdsourcing (MIT)*, which computes proper reward for each task to maximize the task completion rate at real time. We propose a unified and efficient approach to the MIT problem with a theoretical effectiveness guarantee. The experimental results on real ride-sharing data show that, compared with the state-of-the-art offline algorithms, our approach decreases the total worker response time by two orders of magnitude with insignificant utility loss.

Keywords: Real-time spatial crowdsourcing · Competitive analysis · Incentive mechanism design

1 Introduction

With the popularization of mobile location based services, applications powered by Spatial Crowdsourcing (SC), e.g., ride-hailing services like Uber[1] and Didi[2], have been deeply influencing our daily lives. As the base of an SC business, making proper incentives for workers is of great importance to enhance

---

[1] https://www.uber.com/.
[2] http://www.didichuxing.com/.

© Springer Nature Switzerland AG 2020
Y. Nah et al. (Eds.): DASFAA 2020, LNCS 12113, pp. 694–710, 2020.
https://doi.org/10.1007/978-3-030-59416-9_45

the worker participation [12,14]. Due to its usefulness and importance, proper incentive mechanism design on SC platforms has attracted much attention from both industry and academia. As an intuitive and easy-to-implement approach, monetary rewards are adopted by many practical SC platforms. However, as indicated in [14], it is hard to devise an efficient and effective pricing scheme for SC platforms since the spatial-temporal factors and the relationship between supply and demand are changing in real time. Prior researches, based on either auction models [10,11,16] or constrained utility optimization models [5,13], typically assume a static (or semi-static) market where both the workers' arrival and the task distribution are homogeneous and time-invariant.

Specifically, Faradani et al. [3] and Gao et al. [5] modeled the market dynamics of traditional crowdsourcing platforms like AMT [1] in two modules: (1) the Non-Homogeneous Poisson Model that depicts workers' arrival pattern; and (2) the Discrete Choice Model that captures workers' task response behaviours. Such models are reasonable for traditional crowdsourcing platforms as the market is relatively stable. For example, both requesters and workers of AMT simply interact with a computer for issuing/answering the tasks (e.g., image labeling), which makes the process reliable and predictable. However, for spatial crowdsourcing, there are a non-negligible number of factors that can lead to a sudden change of the market, such as weather condition, traffic condition, cellular network signal condition, and etc. Note that, other important issues in spatial crowdsourcing like profit-aware task assignment [15,17] concentrate more on the matching between workers and tasks instead of SC market modeling.

To demonstrate the data heterogeneity in spatial crowdsourcing applications, regarding Didi's open dataset, we plot the drivers' arrival rate of a certain region in Chengdu in two time intervals: Nov. 1st 8:00–9:00 and 18:00–19:00, which is shown in Fig. 1. It is obvious that when both time intervals are in rush-hour, the worker arrivals differ a lot.

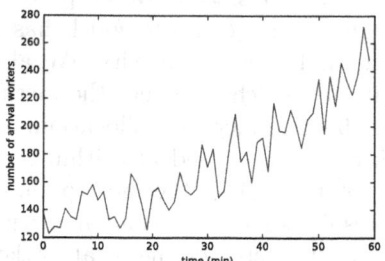

(a) The workers' arrival sequence between 8:00 to 9:00.

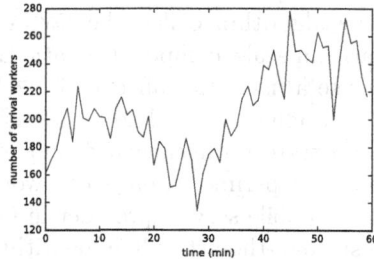

(b) The workers' arrival sequence between 18:00 to 19:00.

Fig. 1. Workers' arrival sequence of Chengdu on Nov. 1st, 2016.

To solve the dynamic SC market issue, in this paper, we consider the problem of Real-time <u>M</u>onetary <u>I</u>ncentive for <u>T</u>asks in Spatial Crowdsourcing (MIT). The core challenges can be summarized as two questions:

1. *How to effectively depict a dynamic SC market?* Different from traditional crowdsourcing platforms where the market is relatively static and could be well depicted via the statistics of historical data, SC market is dynamic and much harder to predict due to the spatial-temporal properties (e.g., it is difficult to predict when and where a traffic collision will occur).
2. *How to design a proper incentive mechanism for dynamic SC markets?* Intuitively, a proper price should be decided by leveraging the relation of *demand* against *supply*. For example, bad weather or poor transportation conditions will decrease the number of available workers who are willing to provide a service (i.e., *supply < demand*). Thus, extra money should be allocated as an incentive to attract workers to perform current tasks. In another scenario, where the available workers are more than the total issued tasks (i.e., *supply > demand*), less extra reward would be allocated to reduce the cost.

To tackle the aforementioned challenges, we propose a generalized worker arrival model to depict the dynamics of an SC market. Depending on how much we know about the future, the SC market model is categorized into three cases, oblivious case (no prior knowledge about the future workers' arrival), omniscient case (full knowledge about the future market), and predictable case where the worker's arrival can be modeled by some random process. Based on the market model, we formulate the generalized real-time monetary incentive allocation problem that finds an incentive allocation plan for a pool of SC tasks such that the expected utility is maximized and the expected cost is no larger than a total budget. Note that, the utility and cost functions can be customized and thus our formulation applies to a wide variety of spatial crowdsourcing applications, e.g., ride-hailing, food/parcel delivery, geographic data collection, and etc.

However, solving such a utility optimization problem is non-trivial, especially when we lack any prior knowledge towards the SC market. We first introduce an exact solution based on dynamic programming for the static case (i.e., omniscient case). For the fully dynamic market (i.e., oblivious case), we propose an online algorithm called the DYNAMIC THRESHOLD ALGORITHM which has a logarithm-scale competitive ratio and a polynomial time complexity. We also propose a heuristic called K-STEP WATCH AHEAD, which combines the merits of both offline and online solutions for a more effective incentive allocation. To demonstrate both efficiency and effectiveness of our proposed algorithms, we conduct experiments on a real-world SC dataset from Didi, the most popular shared mobile service provider in China. The results show that, compared with the state-of-the-art offline algorithms, our approach decreases the total worker response time by two orders of magnitude with insignificant utility loss.

The contributions and organization of this paper are as summarized below.

- We formally propose a dynamic SC market model and formulate the generalized incentive allocation problem (the MIT problem). (▷ See Sect. 2)
- We propose novel algorithms with rigorous competitive analysis to solve the MIT problem efficiently. (▷ See Sect. 3 and Sect. 4)
- We conduct experimental studies on a real dataset to demonstrate the performance of our proposed algorithms. (▷ See Sect. 5)

2   SC Market Modeling and Problem Definition

In this section, we formulate the *Real-time Monetary Incentive for Tasks in Spatial Crowdsourcing (MIT)* problem. We describe the nature of a spatial crowdsourcing platform, and then introduce our models for workers and tasks, respectively. Finally, we define the MIT problem and show that our MIT problem is highly extensible, which generalizes the existing studies on the incentive mechanism design.

2.1   SC Platform

The spatial crowdsourcing market is highly dynamic, where the demand and supply change dramatically in both spatial and temporal dimensions. To precisely depict an SC market, we partition the whole region (e.g., a city) into a set of grids $\{g_1, g_2, \cdots, g_G\}$. Generally, a spatial task, a.k.a. task, can be any type of request issued to the SC platform (e.g., a pick-up and delivery request in a ride-hailing service or food/parcel delivery services, a data collection request in geographical applications like Gigwalk, or a sensing task for network systems like [4]). We use st to represent a spatial task and denote ℓ_{st} and t_{st} as its location and issued time. Tasks with similar location and time compete with one another for the same pool of workers. Thus, we group the tasks falling into the same grid g and time interval (e.g., $8:00 \pm 10min$) as a batch, which is denoted by $T^{g,t}$.

2.2   SC Market Modeling

In our paper, we propose a generalized SC market model, which works with any degree of prior knowledge about the market. We follow the taxonomy shown in the previous literature [5] which profiles the SC market with two sub-models: *price response model* and *worker arrival model*. The *price response model* depicts workers' sensitivity toward monetary reward in a given region and at a given time, and the worker arrival model dynamically depicts the spatial-temporal distribution of available workers.

Price Response Model. We first define the *task acceptance ratio*.

Definition 1 (Task Acceptance Ratio). *For a spatial task st issued in grid g at time t with additional monetary incentive p, the task acceptance ratio w.r.t. p, denoted by $AR^{g,t}(p)$, is defined as the probability that a worker in g at time t accepts this task.*

We assume that workers make their decisions independently. Let $W^{g,t}$ denote the number of available workers and $N^{g,t}$ denote the number of accepted tasks in g at time t. Then $N^{g,t}$ follows a binomial distribution $\mathbf{B}(W^{g,t}, AR^{g,t}(p))$. In economic studies, the *Discrete Choice Model* is commonly used to model the probability that a customer will choose a specific product [9], which is also used by Gao et al. [5] to model the the task acceptance ratio in crowdsourcing. We follow these works to model the task acceptance ratio, i.e., $AR^{g,t}(p) = \frac{\exp(\frac{p}{\alpha}-\beta)}{\exp(\frac{p}{\alpha}-\beta)+\gamma}$

where the parameters α, β and γ can be estimated from the historical data by using maximal likelihood estimation.

Worker Arrival Model. The *Worker Arrival Model* captures the workers' arrival dynamics. Based on the prediction level, worker arrival models can be categorized into the three types: *Oblivious Case*, *Omniscient Case* and *Predictable Case*. We consider a sequence of time stamps, $t = 0, 1, \cdots, T$, and model the number of available workers $W^0, W^1, \cdots, W^T$ as follows.

1. *Oblivious Case (a.k.a. online case)*: W^t is known only at and after time t, which means we cannot make any assumption of W^t at time $t' < t$. This case is sometimes also called the *online scenario*.
2. *Omniscient Case (a.k.a. static/offline case)*: All $W^{t'}$'s are known since the first time stamp $t = 0$.
3. *Predictable Case*: In this case, we do not exactly know W^t at time $t' < t$, but we can model its distribution as $\Pr(W^t = k) = f(k, \boldsymbol{\theta}(t))$ where $\boldsymbol{\theta}(t)$ denotes some specific random process regarding t.

Intuitively, the oblivious/online case has the least knowledge of the future, whereas the omniscient/static case knows everything about the future, and the predictable case can be regarded as a compromise between the above two cases. Note that, the predictable case can also be regarded as *static* since the distribution that depicts the workers' arrival is also known in advance, which we will discuss in detail in Sect. 3.

2.3   Problem Statement

In this section, we formally define the dynamic incentive determination problem that applies to all the three cases discussed above. We first give the definitions of *state* and *state transition probability* of a local market, which refers to tasks/workers in the same grid g and time interval.

Definition 2 (Market State). *The state of a SC market in grid g at the time stamp t refers to the number of unfinished tasks at t, which is denoted by $N^{g,t}$ (N^t if g is given clearly). Then, a local market is described by a state sequence $N^0, \cdots, N^T$, where N^0 is the initial number of tasks issued to the SC platform.*

Definition 3 (State Transition Probability). *Given two states in successive time stamps N^t and N^{t+1}, the state transition process is denoted by $N^t \to N^{t+1}$, with the transition probability $\Pr(N^t \to N^{t+1})$.*

Intuitively, the value of state N^{t+1} is jointly determined by N^t and workers' engagement at time t. Workers' engagement is further influenced by the additional rewards, i.e., incentives. We give two examples below to describe the state transition under different worker arrival models.

Example 1 (State Transition for Oblivious and Omniscient Cases). For both the oblivious/online case and omniscient/static case, the number of workers at the time stamp t is known as W^t. The difference lies in that in the static case all W^t's are known in advance, whereas for the online case W^t is observed exactly at the time t. According to the *price response model*, with the reward value p^t, the state transition probability is calculated as follows:

$$\Pr(N^t \to N^{t+1}|p^t) = \begin{cases} 0, & \text{if } W^t < N^t - N^{t+1} \\ \Pr(\mathbf{B}(W^t, AR(p^t)) \geq N^t), & \text{if } N^{t+1} = 0 \\ \Pr(\mathbf{B}(W^t, AR(p^t)) = N^t - N^{t+1}), & \text{otherwise} \end{cases} \tag{1}$$

where $\mathbf{B}(W^t, AR(p^t))$ denotes the Binomial distributed random variable associated with W^t and $AR(p^t)$.

Example 2 (State Transition for the Predictable Case). As for the predictable case, we assume that the workers' arrival follows a Non-Homogeneous Poisson process, i.e., $W^t \sim \mathbf{Poisson}(\lambda(t))$, and $\lambda(t)$ is the arrival rate in time interval $[t, t+1]$. Thus, the task completion rate in this time interval is $\lambda(t) \cdot AR(p^t)$ and the state transition probability of the predictable case is:

$$\Pr(N^t \to N^{t+1}|p^t) = \begin{cases} \mathbf{Pois}(N^t - N^{t+1}|\lambda(t)AR(p^t)), & \text{if } N^{t+1} \neq 0 \\ \mathbf{Pois}(k \geq N^t|\lambda(t)AR(p^t)), & \text{otherwise} \end{cases} \tag{2}$$

where $\mathbf{Pois}(k|\lambda(t))$ represents the probability that a Poisson distributed random variable with the arrival rate $\lambda(t)$ taking the value k, i.e., $\mathbf{Pois}(k|\lambda(t)) = e^{-\lambda(t)} \frac{\lambda(t)^k}{k!}$.

The state transition probabilities depend on how much incentive we give to the workers. Intuitively, a high incentive increases the state transition probability, but introduces more monetary cost. To measure the benefit and cost of the state transitions, we define the utility and cost function as follows.

Definition 4 (State Transition Utility and Cost). *The state transition utility and cost are defined as function $U : (N^t \to N^{t+1}) \to \mathbb{R}^+$ and $C : (N^t \to N^{t+1}) \to \mathbb{R}^+$, respectively. Note that, both $U(\cdot)$ and $C(\cdot)$ can be any user-defined functions which is monotonically non-decreasing w.r.t. $N^t - N^{t+1}$.*

Definition 5 (Conditional Utility and Cost). *At the time stamp t, if the incentive value is p^t and the current state $N^t = n$, the conditional utility, denoted by $CU^t(p^t|N^t = n)$, is defined as the expected utility gain, i.e.,*

$$CU^t(p^t|N^t = n) = \mathbb{E}[U(N^t \to N^{t+1})|N^t = n] = \sum_{0 \leq k \leq n} U(n \to k) \cdot \Pr(n \to k|p^t), \tag{3}$$

where the state transition probability $\Pr(n \to k|p^t)$ is computed regarding Eq. (1) and Eq. (2). Similarly, the conditional cost $CC^t(p^t|N^t = n)$ is defined as,

$$CC^t(p^t|N^t = n) = \mathbb{E}[C(N^t \to N^{t+1})|N^t = n] = \sum_{0 \leq k \leq n} C(n \to k) \cdot \Pr(n \to k|p^t). \tag{4}$$

Definition 6 (Expected Utility and Cost). *At the time stamp* t, *the expected utility and expected cost, denoted by* $EU^t(p^t)$ *and* $EC^t(p^t)$ *respectively, are computed via examining all the possible states and their probabilities, i.e.,*

$$EU^t(p^t) = \sum_{0 \le n \le |\mathcal{T}|} CU^t(p^t|N^t = n) \cdot \Pr(N^t = n|p^t) \ and \tag{5}$$

$$EC^t(p^t) = \sum_{0 \le n \le |\mathcal{T}|} CC^t(p^t|N^t = n) \cdot \Pr(N^t = n|p^t). \tag{6}$$

The probability $\Pr(N^t - n|p^t)$ can be computed as follows,

$$\Pr(N^t = n|p^t) = \sum_{i=n}^{|\mathcal{T}|} \Pr(N^{t-1} = i) \cdot \Pr(i \to n|p^t), \tag{7}$$

where $|\mathcal{T}|$ is the initial (i.e., $t = 0$) number of tasks. We now formulate the *Real-time Monetary Incentive for Tasks in Spatial Crowdsourcing (MIT)* problem as follows.

Definition 7 (MIT Problem). *Considering a batch of issued tasks* $\mathcal{T}$, *the task acceptance ratio function* $AR^{g,t}(\cdot)$ *($AR(\cdot)$, in short), and the worker arrival model, the objective of the* MIT *problem is to find a reward/incentive sequence, denoted by* $p^0, \cdots, p^{T-1}$, *such that the expected total utility is maximized and the expected cost is not larger than a total cost budget* B, *i.e.,*

$$\max_{p^0, p^1, \cdots, p^{T-1}} \sum_{t=0}^{T-1} EU^t(p^t) \quad s.t. \quad \sum_{t=0}^{T-1} EC^t(p^t) \le B. \tag{8}$$

We further discuss several issues about the MIT problem.

Problem Input. For the input worker arrival model, if we focus on the oblivious case or omniscient case, the input should be the worker number sequence $W^0, W^1, \cdots, W^T$, otherwise (i.e., the predictable case), the input should be the distribution of W^t, i.e., $\Pr(W^t = k)$. In the subsequent sections, we would propose a unified algorithm that applies to all the aforementioned cases.

Generality. $U(\cdot)$ and $C(\cdot)$ are user-defined functions, which are usually related to the number of accomplished tasks. In this paper, *w.l.o.g.*, we choose the throughput for $U(\cdot)$, i,e., $U(N^t \to N^{t+1}) = N^{t+1} - N^t$, and the requester's expenditure for $C(\cdot)$, i.e., $C(N^t \to N^{t+1}) = c^t \cdot (N^{t+1} - N^t)$ where c^t equals the sum of *base price* and *monetary incentive* (i.e., p^t).

Hardness. The generalized *MIT* problem can be demonstrated as NP-hard by using a straightforward reduction from the *KNAPSACK* problem. However, the hardness still differ for different worker arrival models. Intuitively, for the *MIT* problem under the omniscient case or predictable case, the hardness is similar to that of the classical *KNAPSACK* problem where an $(1+\epsilon)$-approximation exists and there is a dynamic programming based pseudo polynomial time solution. On the other hand, for the *MIT* problem under the online case, the hardness inherits the hardness of *online KNAPSACK* [7,8,18] where no online algorithm yields a constant competitive ratio. We will further discuss the computation complexity in detail in Sect. 3 and Sect. 4, respectively.

3   DP-Based Optimal Solution

Before entering the first algorithm, we revisit and clarify some details of the SC market discussed in Sect. 2.2. We have already categorized the worker arrival model as three cases: oblivious case, omniscient case and predictable case. In contrast to the online case, the workers' arrival in the future under both the omniscient and predictable cases are *known* at $t = 0$. Specifically, for the predictable case, the future SC market information can be captured by a distribution that is also known in advance, e.g., the Non-Homogeneous Poisson Process. The only difference between the omniscient case and the predictable case is the way we calculate the state transition probability (see Example 1 and Example 2). Thus, we use *static case* to represent both *omniscient case* and *predictable case* hereafter.

We then introduce our first algorithm called OPT to solve the static case, which extends the dynamic programming algorithm of *Multi-Choice Knapsack* problem (MCKP) [6]. Note that the possible incentive value p^t belongs to a discrete space $\mathcal{P} = \{P_1, \cdots, P_M\}$ which contains M possible choices. Similarly, for a budget limit B, we construct another discrete price space $\mathcal{B} = \{bg_1, \cdots, bg_B\}$. Define $opt[m, b]$ as the optimal total expected utility value of the *MIT* problem with the first m incentive choices and budget constraint b where $b \in \mathcal{B}$. Then, for the static cases, since the market information are known in advance, we have the following recursion,

$$opt[m, b] = \begin{cases} \max_{0 \le t \le T-1} \left(opt[m - 1, b - EC^t(P_m)] + EU^t(P_m), 0 \right), & \text{if } EC^t(P_m) \le b \\ -\infty, & \text{otherwise.} \end{cases}$$

(9)

Note that the initial condition of the recursion is $opt[0, b] = 0$ for $\forall b \in \mathcal{B}$. The maximal total expected utility is stored in $opt[M, B]$ and $opt[M, B] = 0$ if there is no feasible incentive allocation plan that can satisfy the budget constraint.

With the recursion in Eq. (9) and the initial condition, we can enumerate and fill the DP array opt in a "bottom-up" fashion. After the enumeration of the DP table, the optimal incentive values allocation plan, which corresponds to the maximum total utility $opt[M][B]$, can be obtained by looking back to the DP table $opt[\cdot][\cdot]$. Note that, the way we calculate EC^t and EU^t differs from the input workers' arrival model, i.e., the omniscient case where $W^0, \cdots, W^{T-1}$ are given or the predictable case where the distribution $\Pr(W^t = k)$ is known.

Complexity Analysis. Apparently, the DP table $opt[\cdot][\cdot]$ takes space $O(MB)$ where M is the total number of possible choices of incentive values and B is the value of the total budget. For the time complexity, enumerating the DP table takes $O(MB)$ times calculation of Eq. (9), which involves $O(T)$ times calculation of EU^t and EC^t. The evaluation of EU^t and EC^t based on Eq. (3) and Eq. (5), takes time $O(|\mathcal{T}|^2)$ where $|\mathcal{T}|$ is the total number of the issued tasks at $t = 0$. Thus, the total time complexity of algorithm OPT is $O(MBT|\mathcal{T}|^2)$.

4 Approximate Online Algorithm

In Sect. 3, we propose algorithm OPT to handle the static cases including the omniscient case and the predictable case. OPT finds an optimal solution when the input workers' arrival model is static if there does exist a feasible solution (i.e., $opt[M, B] \neq 0$). The major drawbacks of this algorithm are twofold: (1) the *static* assumption on workers' arrival model is not practical enough; and (2) the high time complexity prevents the SC platform responding to task requests in real-time. To alleviate the first drawback, we introduce the *online case* in Sect. 2.2 where the workers' arrival sequence is totally unknown unless it is observed. However, solving the *MIT* problem under this case is nontrivial since very little information is provided as input, which might make the result obtained by an algorithm very far from the optimum value.

Algorithm 1: DYNAMIC-THRESHOLD ALGORITHM

Input: the number of available workers: $W^0, W^1, \cdots, W^{T-1}$, the task
acceptance ratio: $AR(p)$, the total budget: B, and maximum and
minimum ratio of value and cost: U, L.
Output: incentive values: $p^0, p^1, \cdots, p^{T-1}$.
1 define function $\Phi(x)$ as Eq. (10);
2 *spent* $\leftarrow 0$;
3 **for** $t = 0, 1, \cdots, T - 1$ **do**
4     $q \leftarrow$ empty priority queue;
5   **for** $i = 1, \cdots, M$ **do**
6        $gain[i] \leftarrow$ expected utility by taking price p_i;
7        $cost[i] \leftarrow$ expected cost by taking price p_i;
8        $q.enqueue(\text{Tuple}\,(i, gain[i]/cost[i]))$;
9     $(i, max\_util) \leftarrow q.dequeue()$;
10   **if** $max\_util < \Phi(spent/B)$ **then** $p^t \leftarrow 0$;
11   **else** $p^t \leftarrow p_i$; $spent \leftarrow spent + EC^t(p^t)$;
12   **yield** p^t;

4.1 Dynamic Threshold Algorithm

In this section, we propose an algorithm called DYNAMIC-THRESHOLD ALGORITHM for the fully online SC market. Compared with OPT, this algorithm obtains a true polynomial time complexity with a logarithm-scale competitive ratio.

The DYNAMIC-THRESHOLD ALGORITHM extends the online knapsack algorithm which has been investigated in [7,8,18]. The core idea of this algorithm borrows the idea of the greedy algorithm for the classic 0/1 *KNAPSACK* problem. At each timestamp t, we try to select the incentive value p^t maximizing the *utility density*, which is defined as the ratio of expected utility and expected cost, that is, $p^t = \arg\max_{p\in\mathcal{P}} \frac{EU^t(p)}{EC^t(p)}$ where $\mathcal{P}$ denotes the set that contains all possible selections of incentive/reward values. However, the simple greedy strategy is not a wise idea since we do not know the future SC market, i.e., the workers' arrival in the future, which will make the greedy-based strategy short-sighted. That is to say, we might use up the total budget too early and fail to allocate incentives at some more appropriate timestamp in the future. To handle this, the idea of "dynamic threshold" is adopted where a threshold function, denoted by $\Phi(x)$, is used to trace the remaining budget value, and we reject allocating any incentive if the maximum utility density is less than the dynamic threshold.

The details of the DYNAMIC THRESHOLD ALGORITHM are shown in Algorithm 1. In line 1, we first define the dynamic threshold function as

$$\Phi(x) = \begin{cases} L, & x \leq \frac{1}{1+\log(U/L)} \\ \left(\frac{U_e}{L}\right)^x \left(\frac{U}{L}\right), & \text{otherwise,} \end{cases} \tag{10}$$

where $x \in [0,1]$ which denotes the percentage of the total budget we have spent, and U, L are assumed as the upper-bound and lower bound of the utility density, which are regarded as input parameters. That is to say, $L \leq EU^t/EC^t \leq U$ for $\forall t = 0, \cdots, T-1$. Note that the reason we select $\Phi(x)$ as Eq. (10) and the properties of Eq. (10) are discussed in Sect. 4.2. In line 2, a variable *spent* is initialized to trace the value of spent budget up to the current time. Lines 3–12 apply the idea of a greedy strategy combined with the dynamic threshold. Line 4 initializes an empty priority queue at each timestamp t which is used to keep the maximum utility density. In lines 5–8, the algorithm calculates the utility densities for all possible incentive values, i.e., any $p \in \mathcal{P}$, and add them to the priority queue q (specifically, we insert a tuple containing both utility density value and its corresponding index i in $\mathcal{P}$ into the priority queue q). Line 9 takes out the maximum utility density, denoted by max_util, and its corresponding price index i from q. Lines 10–11 allocate the incentive/reward based on the dynamic threshold function. If the $max\_util \leq \Phi(spent/B)$, we set p^t to 0, otherwise, p^t is set to p_i and *spent* is updated to $spent + EC^t(p_i)$. Finally, line 12 outputs the current incentive value, p^t, in an online fashion.

Complexity Analysis. The space complexity of Algorithm 1 is determined by the size of the priority queue q, i.e., $O(M)$, where M is the number of possible incentive values. Then we move to the time complexity. Line 3 yields $O(T)$ loops. For the inner loop shown in lines 5–8, there are M times calculation of EU^t and EC^t and M times heap-based priority queue operations, which take time $O(M \cdot |\mathcal{T}|^2)$ and $O(M \log M)$, respectively. Thus, the total time complexity of Algorithm 1 is $O(M \cdot T \cdot (|\mathcal{T}|^2 + \log M))$. Note that, compared with algorithm OPT, the time complexity of Algorithm 1 is *true polynomial* since it does not depend on the input budget B.

4.2   Algorithm Analysis

To analyze the effectiveness of algorithms in an online fashion, we adopt the *competitive analysis framework* [2]. To conduct a competitive analysis, we first assume an omniscient adversary who knows the entire workers' arrival sequence $W^0, W^1, \cdots, W^T$. Regard the result from an optimal static solution as the optimal solution, and then compare it with the result outputted by an online algorithm. The worst ratio is known as the *competitive ratio*, which is used as the measurement for analyzing online algorithms. Note that, the *competitive ratio* can be regarded as the approximation ratio under an online input setting. The formal definition of the *competitive ratio* is shown as follows.

For an input sequence σ, denote $ALG(\sigma)$ as the objective value (for a maximization problem) obtained by an online algorithm $\mathcal{A}$ and $OPT(\sigma)$ as the objective value obtained by a optimal solution who knows the entire input sequence σ in advance. The competitive ratio of $\mathcal{A}$, denoted by $CR(\mathcal{A})$, is defined as[3]:

$$CR(\mathcal{A}) = \sup_{\sigma} \frac{OPT(\sigma)}{ALG(\sigma)}. \tag{11}$$

An online algorithm with competitive ratio $O(f(n))$ is called $O(f(n))$-competitive.

In the remaining part of this section, we conduct competitive analysis for our DYNAMIC THRESHOLD ALGORITHM, denoted by $\mathcal{DT}$, to show the effectiveness of this algorithm. The major theoretical results are shown as follows.

Theorem 1. *Denote the workers' arrival sequence* $W^0, \cdots, W^T$ *as* σ, $ALG(\sigma|\mathcal{DT})$ *as the total expected utility value of our algorithm* $\mathcal{DT}$, *and* $OPT(\sigma)$ *as the optimal utility value obtained by an omniscient adversary who knows the entire* σ. *Then, we have,*

$$CR(\mathcal{DT}) = \sup_{\sigma} \frac{OPT(\sigma)}{ALG(\sigma|\mathcal{DT})} = O\left(\log \frac{U}{L}\right), \tag{12}$$

where U *and* L *are the upper-bound and lower-bound of the utility density in Algorithm 1 respectively. That is to say, Algorithm 1 is* $O(\log U/L)$-*competitive.*

Proof. Before showing the proof, we first introduce some symbols: 1) P: the incentive value sequence obtained by Algorithm 1; 2) P^*: the optimal incentive value sequence; 3) $u(\cdot)$: the total utility of a subset of incentive value sequence; and 4) $c(\cdot)$: the total cost of a subset of incentive value sequence. We first have Lemma 1, which is trivial to prove, to show a decomposition of the total expected utility value outputted by Algorithm 1.

Lemma 1. *For any input sequence* σ, *it always holds for the output total utility value* $ALG(\sigma|\mathcal{DT})$,

$$ALG(\sigma|\mathcal{DT}) = u(P \cap P^*) + u(P - P^*). \tag{13}$$

Then, we bound the optimal total utility value OPT for any input sequence σ.

Lemma 2. *For any input sequence* σ, *assume that Algorithm 1 terminates with the remainder of budget* $X \cdot B$, *then an upper bound of the maximum total utility, i.e.,* $OPT(\sigma)$, *is given by,*

$$OPT(\sigma) \leq u(P \cap P^*) + \Phi(X) \cdot (B - c(P \cap P^*)). \tag{14}$$

---

[3] If the problem is a minimization problem, change "sup" to "inf".

Combining Lemma 1 and Lemma 2, we then have Lemma 3.

Lemma 3. *For any input sequence σ, it always holds that,*

$$\frac{OPT(\sigma)}{ALG(\sigma|\mathcal{DT})} \leq \frac{u(P \cap P^*) + \Phi(X) \cdot (B - c(P \cap P^*))}{u(P \cap P^*) + u(P - P^*)} \leq \frac{\Phi(X)}{\sum_{i \in P} \Phi(x_i) \cdot (x_{i+1} - x_i)},$$
(15)

where x_i denotes the fraction of total spent budget at the moment $i \in P$ is picked.

Then, in Lemma 4, we introduce a lower bound for the denominator term in Eq. (15), i.e., $\sum_{i \in P} \Phi(x_i) \cdot (x_{i+1} - x_i)$.

Lemma 4. $\sum_{i \in P} \Phi(x_i) \cdot (x_{i+1} - x_i) \geq \frac{\Phi(X)}{\log U/L + 1}$.

Combining Lemma 3 and Lemma 4, we can derive that, for any input sequence σ, it always holds that,

$$\frac{OPT(\sigma)}{ALG(\sigma|\mathcal{DT})} \leq \frac{\Phi(X)}{\sum_{i \in P} \Phi(x_i) \cdot (x_{i+1} - x_i)} \leq \frac{\Phi(X)}{\Phi(X)/(\log U/L + 1)} \leq O\left(\log \frac{U}{L}\right),$$
(16)

which proves Theorem 1.

4.3 k-Step Watch Ahead Heuristic

In Sect. 4.1 and Sect. 4.2, we introduce and analyze the DYNAMIC THRESHOLD ALGORITHM for the online spatial crowdsourcing market, which assumes no knowledge is available for workers' arrival in the future. Though much faster than the DP-BASED OPTIMAL ALGORITHM, since the input information is much more limited, the DYNAMIC THRESHOLD ALGORITHM may lose some total benefit. To balance efficiency (running time) and effectiveness (total utility value), in this subsection, we introduce an intuitive heuristic strategy, called K-STEP WATCH AHEAD HEURISTIC, which combines the merits of the DP-BASED OPTIMAL ALGORITHM, which focuses on the static cases, and the DYNAMIC THRESHOLD ALGORITHM, which focuses on the online scenario.

The intuition is straightforward. Instead of knowing or predicting the workers' whole arrival sequence, we predict only k steps ahead each time, which is the reason we name it "k-Step Watch Ahead". That is to say, at time t, we predict the future arrival sequence in $[t + 1, \cdots, t + k]$. Then, the DP-BASED OPTIMAL ALGORITHM is invoked on this k-size sequence. After that, we apply the dynamic threshold function to reject any incentive allocation p violating the constraint that p's utility density is less than the dynamic threshold. Such a heuristic strategy works well in practice since the short-term prediction of the SC market is usually better than the long-term prediction.

Algorithm 2: K-STEP WATCH AHEAD HEURISTIC

Input: the number of steps that we watch ahead: k, the task acceptance ratio: $AR(p)$, the total budget: B, and maximum and minimum ratio of value and cost: U, L.

Output: incentive values: $p^0, p^1, \cdots, p^{T-1}$.

1   define function $\Phi(x)$ as Eq. (10) ;

2   *spent* $\leftarrow$ 0 ;

3   **for** $t = 0, 1, \cdots, \lceil \frac{T}{k} \rceil - 1$ **do**

4   predict workers' arrival sequence $\sigma^t = W^t, W^{t+1}, \cdots, W^{t+k-1}$;

5   invoke DP-BASED OPTIMAL ALGORITHM on sequence σ^t to obtain the incentive sequence $p^t, p^{t+1}, \cdots, p^{t+k-1}$;

6   apply the dynamic threshold function $\Phi(x)$ on $p^t, p^{t+1}, \cdots, p^{t+k-1}$ and reject any p if $\frac{EU(p)}{EC(p)} < \Phi\left(\frac{spent}{B}\right)$;

7   update *spent*;

8   **return** $p^0, p^1, \cdots, p^{T-1}$;

The K-STEP WATCH AHEAD HEURISTIC is shown in Algorithm 2. In line 1 and line 2, we define the threshold function $\Phi(\cdot)$ and initialize the variable *spent*, which are the same as those in Algorithm 1. Then, in line 3, we divide the whole time interval into $\lceil \frac{T}{k} \rceil$ sub-intervals. In line 4, at timestamp $t = 0, 1, \cdots, \lceil \frac{T}{k} \rceil - 1$, we predict the SC market information for the next k timestamps, which returns a predicted workers' arrival sequence $\sigma^t = W^t, W^{t+1}, \cdots, W^{t+k-1}$. Line 5 invokes the DP-BASED OPTIMAL ALGORITHM on sequence σ^t and get the incentive value sequence $p^t, p^{t+1}, \cdots, p^{t+k-1}$. Note that, such result is optimal w.r.t. k-length workers' arrival sequence σ^t. In line 6, for any incentive allocation p^t in the incentive sequence obtained by dynamic programming, we test whether the utility density $\frac{EU^t(p^t)}{EC^t(p^t)}$ is less than the dynamic threshold $\Phi\left(\frac{spent}{B}\right)$. If yes, we reject the corresponding incentive allocation, i.e., set $p^t = 0$. Line 7 updates *spent* and line 8 returns the final incentive sequence $p^0, p^1, \cdots, p^{T-1}$.

It is easy to show that the space complexity and time complexity of the K-STEP WATCH AHEAD HEURISTIC are the same as those of the DP-BASED OPTIMAL ALGORITHM, which are $O(MB)$ and $O(MBT|\mathcal{T}|^2)$, respectively. However, the response time of Algorithm 2 is much better than that of algorithm OPT. The reason is that Algorithm 2 applies dynamic programming on a very short sequence and then makes progress, whereas, OPT invokes DP on the entire sequence.

5   Experimental Study

In this section, we conduct experiments on real datasets to demonstrate the effectiveness and efficiency of our proposed algorithms. All the experiments were run on a Linux server with Intel(R) Xeon(R) CPU X5675 @ 3.07 GHz and 16 GB memory, and all the algorithms were implemented in Java with JDK 10.

5.1 Experiment Setup

Data Preparation. We use Didi's open ride data[4] for our experimental study. For each ride, the data contains attributes like its issue time, arrival time, origin location, transaction states, and etc. The coordinate range of the tested region is [30.727, 104.043], [30.726, 104.129], [30.655, 104.129] and [30.653, 104.042], which specifies Chengdu city, one of the largest cities in China. The time frame of the data is from 1st to 30th, Nov. 2016. In our experiments, we focus on taxi transactions falling on November 1st, which contains 209,423 records. Nevertheless, it yields similar results to test the methods on other dates.

Parameter Setting. There are mainly three parameters for the experiments.

1. M: the number of incentive choices. The maximum incentive in our experiments is set to 50 RMB, which is divided by M to form a spectrum of incentives. For example, for $M = 50$ and $M = 100$, the gap between two adjacent incentives is $50/50 = 1$ and $50/100 = 0.5$ RMB, respectively. The range of M is set to $[5, 10, \underline{25}, 50, 100]$.
2. T: the time frame of a batch of orders, whose values are $\{5, 10, \underline{15}, 20, 25\}$ minutes.
3. B: the initial total budget. The unit of B is RMB. $B \in [2, 4, \underline{6}, 8, 10]$ ($\times$ 2k RMB).

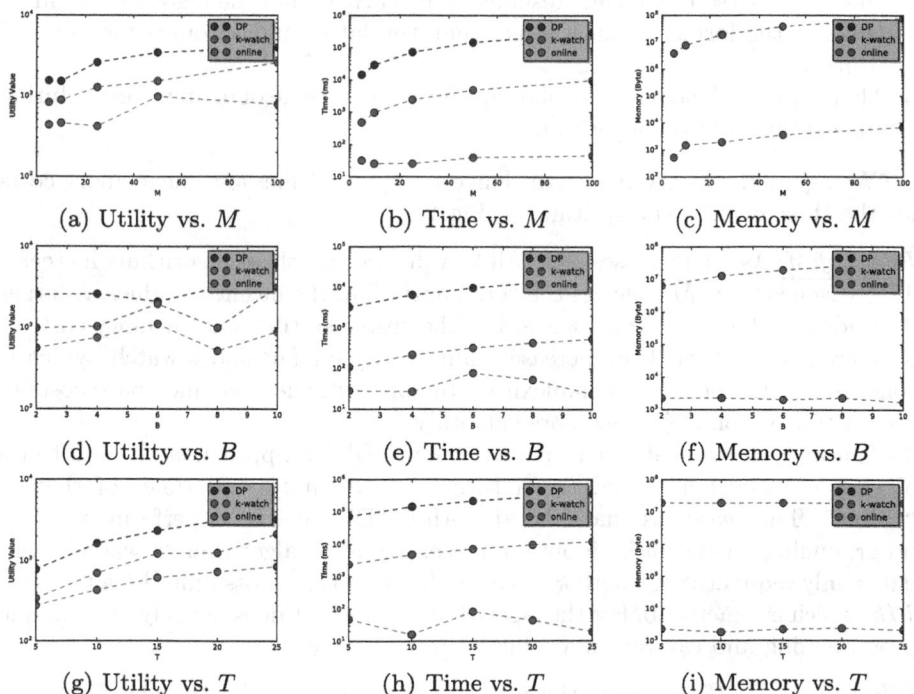

(a) Utility vs. M (b) Time vs. M (c) Memory vs. M

(d) Utility vs. B (e) Time vs. B (f) Memory vs. B

(g) Utility vs. T (h) Time vs. T (i) Memory vs. T

Fig. 2. Experimental results w.r.t. M, B and T.

---

[4] The data is available at https://outreach.didichuxing.com/research/opendata/.

In our experiments, we vary one parameter to test its effect, with other parameters fixed to their default values (marked with underlines).

Compared Algorithms. We compare our proposed three incentive allocation strategies: (1) offline optimal algorithm OPT ("DP" in short), (2) DYNAMIC THRESHOLD ALGORITHM in Algorithm 1 ("online" in short), and (3) K-STEP WATCH AHEAD HEURISTIC in Algorithm 2 ("k-watch" in short). In our experiment, we run DP on the omniscient case where the total input sequence is known in advance. Then, the optimal solution obtained by DP can be used to measure the effectiveness of the other two algorithms. Note that, for the K-STEP WATCH AHEAD ALGORITHM, the value of k is fixed to $T/5$, i.e., $k \in [1, 2, 3, 4, 5]$. For the predicting method in Line 4 of Algorithm 2, we use Auto Regressive Moving Average model (ARMA) to predict the k-length workers' arrival in the future.

5.2 Main Results

Measurements. We evaluate the algorithms in terms of the following aspects.

1. Expected utility value ("utility" in short), which is the objective function of the *MIT* problem;
2. Longest response time ("time" in short), which is equal to the maximum difference between the task issue time and the incentive allocated time. Note that, we choose the longest response time rather than the algorithm running time, as the former is much larger than the latter and accounts for workers' waiting.
3. Memory cost ("memory" for short), which is the usage of main memory during the execution of the algorithm.

We report the utility values, the longest response times and the memory costs for the three evaluated algorithms in Fig. 2.

Effect of M. As M increases, the utility values of all three algorithms increase. The reason is that, M specifies the "granularity" of the incentive values. A larger M leads to a larger solution space. For the response time and memory cost, as M increases, both of them increase dramatically for DP and k-watch, which is consistent with their time complexities. In contrast, the time and space costs of the algorithm "online" grow more smoothly.

It always shows that, the response time of "DP" is approximately $\sim$10 times of that of "k-watch", which is in turn approximately $\sim$10 times of that of "online". The reason is that, the algorithm "DP" needs to perform dynamic programming for the entire input sequence, while the algorithm "k-watch" evaluates only sequences of length k. As a result, their time costs differ by a factor of T/k, which is exactly 10. For the algorithm "online", it does not rely on dynamic programming and can return a solution immediately.

Effect of B. As B increases, the utility values obtained by the algorithms all increase since as budget means more incentives, which will engage more workers. Both the time and space cost of algorithms "DP" and "k-watch" increase as B

increases, since their time complexities are linear to B. In contrast, the time and space costs of the algorithm "online" remain stable over different values of B.

Effect of T. As T increases, the utility of the algorithms all increase as well. The reason is straightforward: a larger time frame indicates a larger number of tasks, and thus a higher utility. The response time of "DP" and "k-watch" become larger as T increases, while it almost keeps unchanged for the algorithm "online". For the memory cost, all three algorithms remain stable over different T since neither the DP array of algorithm "DP" and "k-watch" nor the priority queue of the algorithm "online" is dependent on T.

6   Conclusion

In this paper, we formulate a problem called *Real-time Monetary Incentive for Tasks in Spatial Crowdsourcing (MIT)*, which determines incentives for tasks in real time, aiming to maximize the number of completed tasks. We show that our *MIT* problem generalizes a spectrum of spatial crowdsourcing applications, To solve the problem, we propose three algorithms under different levels of future knowledge. We further show that they are efficient (true polynomial time solvable) and effective (logarithm-scale competitive) both theoretically and experimentally.

Acknowledgments. The work is partially supported by the Hong Kong RGC GRF Project 16207617, CRF project C6030-18G, AOE project AoE/E-603/18, the National Science Foundation of China (NSFC) under Grant No. 61729201, Science and Technology Planning Project of Guangdong Province, China, No. 2015B010110006, Hong Kong ITC Grants ITS/044/18FX and ITS/470/18FX, Didi-HKUST joint research lab Grant, Microsoft Research Asia Collaborative Research Grant, Wechat Research Grant and Webank Research Grant.

References

1. Amazon mechanical turk. https://www.mturk.com/. Accessed 11 Nov 2019
2. Borodin, A., El-Yaniv, R.: Online Computation and Competitive Analysis. Cambridge University Press, Cambridge (2005)
3. Faradani, S., Hartmann, B., Ipeirotis, P.G.: What's the right price? Pricing tasks for finishing on time. In: AAAI Workshops Human Computation, vol. WS-11-11. AAAI (2011)
4. Ganti, R.K., Ye, F., Lei, H.: Mobile crowdsensing: current state and future challenges. IEEE Commun. Mag. **49**(11), 32–39 (2011)
5. Gao, Y., Parameswaran, A.G.: Finish them!: pricing algorithms for human computation. PVLDB **7**(14), 1965–1976 (2014)
6. Kellerer, H., Pferschy, U., Pisinger, D.: The multiple-choice knapsack problem. In: Kellerer, H., Pferschy, U., Pisinger, D. (eds.) Knapsack Problems, pp. 317–347. Springer, Heidelberg (2004). https://doi.org/10.1007/978-3-540-24777-7_11
7. Kleinberg, R.D.: A multiple-choice secretary algorithm with applications to online auctions. In: SODA, pp. 630–631. SIAM (2005)

8. Marchetti-Spaccamela, A., Vercellis, C.: Stochastic on-line Knapsack problems. Math. Program. **68**, 73–104 (1995)
9. McFadden, D., et al.: Conditional logit analysis of qualitative choice behavior (1973)
10. Singer, Y., Mittal, M.: Pricing tasks in online labor markets. In: AAAI Workshops Human Computation, vol. WS-11-11. AAAI (2011)
11. Singla, A., Krause, A.: Truthful incentives in crowdsourcing tasks using regret minimization mechanisms. In: WWW, pp. 1167–1178. International World Wide Web Conferences Steering Committee/ACM (2013)
12. Tong, Y., Chen, L., Shahabi, C.: Spatial crowdsourcing: challenges, techniques, and applications. PVLDB **10**(12), 1988–1991 (2017)
13. Tong, Y., Wang, L., Zhou, Z., Chen, L., Du, B., Ye, J.: Dynamic pricing in spatial crowdsourcing: a matching-based approach. In: SIGMOD Conference, pp. 773–788. ACM (2018)
14. Tong, Y., Zhou, Z., Zeng, Y., Chen, L., Shahabi, C.: Spatial crowdsourcing: a survey. VLDB J. **29**(1), 217–250 (2019). https://doi.org/10.1007/s00778-019-00568-7
15. Xia, J., Zhao, Y., Liu, G., Xu, J., Zhang, M., Zheng, K.: Profit-driven task assignment in spatial crowdsourcing. In: IJCAI, pp. 1914–1920. ijcai.org (2019)
16. Yang, D., Xue, G., Fang, X., Tang, J.: Crowdsourcing to smartphones: incentive mechanism design for mobile phone sensing. In: MobiCom, pp. 173–184. ACM (2012)
17. Zhai, D., et al.: Towards secure and truthful task assignment in spatial crowdsourcing. World Wide Web **22**(5), 2017–2040 (2018). https://doi.org/10.1007/s11280-018-0638-2
18. Zhou, Y., Chakrabarty, D., Lukose, R.M.: Budget constrained bidding in keyword auctions and online knapsack problems. In: WWW, pp. 1243–1244. ACM (2008)

An Evaluation of Modern Spatial Libraries

Varun Pandey$^{(\boxtimes)}$, Alexander van Renen, Andreas Kipf, and Alfons Kemper

Technical University of Munich, Munich, Germany
{pandey,renen,kipf,kemper}@in.tum.de

Abstract. Applications such as Uber, Yelp, and Tinder rely on spatial data or locations from their users. These applications and services either build their own spatial data management systems or rely on existing solutions. The JTS Topology Suite (JTS), its C++ port GEOS, Google S2, ESRI Geometry API, and Java Spatial Index (JSI) are among the spatial processing libraries that those systems build upon. Applications and services depend on the indexing capabilities available in such libraries for high-performance spatial query processing. However, limited prior work has empirically compared these libraries. Herein, we compare these libraries qualitatively and quantitatively based on four popular spatial queries and using two real-world datasets. We also compare a lesser known library (jvptree) which utilizes Vantage Point Trees. In addition to performance evaluation, we also analyzed the construction time, and space overhead, and identified the strengths and weaknesses of each libraries and their underlying index structures. Our results demonstrate that there are vast differences in space consumption (up to 9.8 x), construction time (up to 5 x), and query runtime (up to 54 x) between the libraries evaluated.

1 Introduction

Recent years, have seen an exponential growth in location-enabled data fueled by services, such as: recommendations for nearby social events, businesses, or restaurants as well as navigation, location-based mobile advertising, and social media platforms. Google, Facebook, Uber, Foursquare, and Yelp are among the companies that provide such services. To handle location data from their users, these companies either build their own spatial data management systems from scratch or rely on existing solutions. The rise of location-based services has also encouraged the research community to develop systems that can efficiently handle, process, and analyze spatial data. HadoopGIS [1] and SpatialHadoop [2] were one of the first research efforts to focus on handling and processing spatial data at scale. Apache Spark and Impala saw a similar trend with a plethora of research introducing spatial support in the form of SpatialSpark [27], GeoSpark [28], Simba [25], STARK [6], LocationSpark [21], Sphinx [3], and SRX [23]. Popular database systems have also undergone a similar trend, e.g., Oracle Spatial [16], MemSQL [4], MongoDB [15], and HyPer [19]. Many of these systems or services

© Springer Nature Switzerland AG 2020
Y. Nah et al. (Eds.): DASFAA 2020, LNCS 12113, pp. 711–727, 2020.
https://doi.org/10.1007/978-3-030-59416-9_46

use open source libraries to implement the basic geometry types, indexes, and algorithms for spatial processing. Some of the most popular libraries for these purposes are JTS Topology Suite (JTS), its C++ port Geometry Engine Open Source (GEOS), Google S2 (S2), ESRI Geometry API, and Java Spatial Index (JSI). Today, these libraries are used in a variety of services and research projects. We highlight the major services and research projects using these libraries in Sect. 3. Given the prevalence and the relevance of these libraries in present day services and systems, we argue that it is necessary to evaluate them.

The paper is structured as follows: Sect. 2 formally defines the spatial queries evaluated and presents practical examples of these queries; Sect. 3 introduces modern spatial libraries; Sect. 4 presents the experimental setup used for evaluation, which is followed by the evaluation in Sect. 5; Sect. 6 discusses related work and Sect. 7 presents the conclusions.

2   Queries

2.1   Range Query

A range query takes a range r (i.e., the minimum and maximum for dimensions D) and a set of geometric objects S. It returns all objects in S that are contained within the range r. Formally,

$$Range(r, S) = \{s | s \in S \land \forall d \in D :$$
$$r\,[d]\,.\min \leq s\,[d] \leq r\,[d]\,.\max\}.$$

Practical Example: Retrieve all objects at the current zoom level in a map application (e.g., Google Maps) for a browser window.

2.2   Distance Query

A distance query takes a query point q, a distance d, and a set of geometric objects S. It returns all objects in S that lie within the distance d of query point q. Formally,

$$Distance(q, d, S) = \{s | s \in S \land \text{dist}(q, s) \leq d\}.$$

Practical Example: Retrieve all dating profiles within 5 km of a user's location.

2.3   k Nearest Neighbors (kNN) Query

A kNN query takes a set of points S, a query point q, and an integer $k \geq 1$ as input, and determines the k nearest points in S to q. Formally,

$$kNN(q, k, S) = \{s | s \in T \subseteq S \land |T| = k \land \forall t \in T,$$
$$\forall r \in S - T : d(q, t) \leq d(q, r)\}.$$

Practical Example: Find the five Greek restaurants closest to a user's location.

Table 1. Selected features of the libraries

Features	S2	GEOS	ESRI	JTS	JSI	jvptree
Language	C++	C++	Java	Java	Java	Java
Indexes	ShapeIndex, PointIndex, RegionTermIndexer	STRtree, Quadtree	Quadtree	STRtree, Quadtree, KD-tree	R-Tree	Vantage Point Tree
Geometry Type	Spherical	Planar	Planar	Planar	Planar	Metric space
Geometry Model	Point, Line, Area, Geometry Collections	Point, Line, Area, Geometry Collections	Point, Line, Area, Geometry Collections	Point, Line, Area, Geometry Collections	Point, Area	Point
License	Apache v2.0	LGPL	Apache v2.0	Dual license (EPL 1.0, BSD)	LGPL	MIT

2.4 Spatial Join

A spatial join takes two input sets of spatial records R and S and a join predicate θ (e.g., overlap, intersect, contains, within, or withindistance) and returns a set of all pairs (r, s) in which $r \in R$, $s \in S$, and the join predicate θ is fulfilled. Formally,

$$R \bowtie_\theta S = \{(r, s) \mid r \in R,\ s \in S,\ \theta(r, s) \text{ holds}\}.$$

Practical Example: Find the average cost of all taxi rides that originate from each neighborhood in New York City.

3   Libraries

In the following section, we describe the major features of the libraries evaluated. We also highlight major services, applications, and systems using these libraries. Table 1 summarizes the features of each library, and Table 2 summarizes the features of the indexes found in these libraries.

3.1   ESRI Geometry API

ESRI Geometry API[1] is a planar geometry library written in Java. It comes with a rich support for multiple geometry datatypes, such as point, multipoint, line, polyline, polygon, and envelope and OGC variants of these datatypes. It supports various topological operations, such as cut, difference, intersection, symmetric, union and various relational operations using a DE-9IM matrix such as contains, crosses, overlaps etc. ESRI Geometry API also supports a variety of I/O formats, WKT, WKB, GeoJSON, ESRI shape, and REST JSON. It also comes equipped with a Quadtree index which cannot be classified into a particular type in Quadtree family. The key property of any Quadtree is its decomposition

---

[1] https://github.com/Esri/geometry-api-java.

rule; in ESRI Quadtree a leaf node splits into four when the node element count reaches 5 elements, and these are pushed into the child quadrants if possible.

ESRI Geometry API is used in a variety of ESRI products such as ArcGIS, the ESRI GIS tools for Hadoop, and various ArcGIS APIs. It is also used by the Hive UDFs and by developers building geometry functions for third-party applications including Cassandra, HBase, Storm, and many other Java-based "big data" applications.

3.2 Java Spatial Index (JSI)

The Java Spatial Index (JSI)[2] is the main memory optimized implementation of the R-tree [5]. JSI relies heavily on trove4j[3] library to optimize its performance and reduce its memory footprint. The code is open source, and is released under the GNU Lesser General Public License, version 2.1 or later. The JSI spatial index is limited in features, and supports only a few operations. It is a lightweight R-tree implementation, specifically designed for the following features (in order of importance): fast intersection performance by using only main memory to store entries, low memory footprint, and fast updates. JSI's R-tree implementation avoids the creation of unnecessary objects through its use of primitive collections from the trove4j library. JSI supports rectangle and point datatypes, and has support for only two predicates for refinement, intersects, and contains. The R-tree index can be queried natively for ranges, and for kNN.

We found no reference of JSI being used in a major system or service, which we believe is primarily due to its limited capabilities. In spite of this, JSI is still regularly utilized in diverse research areas [9,10,13,14,22].

3.3 JTS Topology Suite and Geometry Engine Open Source

The JTS Topology Suite (JTS) is an open source Java library that provides an object model for planar geometry together with a set of fundamental geometric functions. JTS conforms to the Simple Features Specification for SQL published by the Open GIS Consortium[4]. GEOS (Geometry Engine Open Source)[5] is a C++ port of the JTS Topology Suite (JTS). Both JTS and GEOS provide support for basic spatial datatypes such as points, linestrings, and polygons as well as for indexes such as STR packed R-tree and MX-CIF Quadtree [11]. They also support a variety of geometric operations such as area, distance between geometries, length/perimeter, spatial predicates, overlay functions, and buffer computations. They also support a number of input/output formats including Well-Known Text (WKT), Well-Known Binary (WKB).

JTS is used in a large number of modern distributed spatial analytics systems including Hadoop-GIS [1], SpatialHadoop [2], GeoSpark [28], and SpatialSpark [27] and other research areas [20]. GEOS on the other hand is used in

[2] https://github.com/aled/jsi.
[3] http://trove4j.sourceforge.net/html/overview.html.
[4] https://www.opengeospatial.org/standards/sfa.
[5] https://trac.osgeo.org/geos/.

Table 2. Selected features of all indexes

Feature	S2	ESRI	JTS			JSI	jvptree
	PointIndex	Quadtree	k-d tree	Quadtree	STRtree	R-tree	jvptree
Implementation	Linear Quadtree	Quadtree	k-d tree	MX-CIF Quadtree	STR packed R-tree	R-tree	VPTree
Geometry	Point	Rectangle	Point	Rectangle	Rectangle	Rectangle	Point
Native queries	Range, Distance, kNN	Range	Range	Range	Range, kNN	Range, kNN	Distance, kNN
Updateable?	Yes	Yes	Insert: Yes Delete: No	Yes	No insertion after build	Yes	No
Fanout	32	4	2	4	10	20–50	2

a number of database systems and their spatial extensions such as MonetDB, PostGIS, SpatiaLite, Ingres, and it is also used by other frameworks, applications, and proprietary packages.

3.4   Google S2 Geometry

S2[6] library is primarily designed to work with spherical geometry, i.e., shapes drawn on a sphere rather than on a planar 2D map, making it especially suitable for working with geographic data. S2 supports a variety of spatial datatypes including points, polylines, and polygons. It has two index structures, namely (i) S2PointIndex, which indexes collections of points in memory and is a variant of Linear Quadtree [11], and (ii) S2ShapeIndex which is used to index arbitrary collections of shapes, i.e., points, polylines, and polygons in memory. S2 also defines a number of queries that can be issued against these indexes. Indexes also define iterators that allow more fine-grained access. S2 also accepts input in latitude-longitude (GPS) format.

In recent years, S2 has become a popular choice among various location-based services. It is used by Foursquare[7], on-demand ride hail services such as Uber[8], the location-based dating application Tinder[9], numerous database systems, such as MongoDB [15], HyPer [19], MemSQL [4], and in other research areas [7,8].

---

[6] https://github.com/google/s2geometry.
[7] https://www.fastcompany.com/3007394/how-foursquare-building-humane-map-framework-rival-googles/.
[8] https://www.infoq.com/presentations/uber-market-platform/.
[9] https://tech.gotinder.com/geosharded-recommendations-part-1-sharding-approach-2/.

3.5   Vantage Point Tree

We use the library jvptree[10] for an implementation of Vantage Point Tree. Vantage Point Trees [26] are based on metric space and have been extensively studied in image retrieval and nearest neighbor search algorithms for high dimensional data. Metric space is defined by a set, and a distance function to measure the distance between points in that set. Formally, metric space is defined as follows: Let X be a set and let $d \colon X \times X \to [0, \infty)$. The function d is a metric on X if for all $x, y, z \in X$:

1. $d(x,y) \geq 0$; and $d(x,y) = 0$ iff $x = y$;
2. $d(x,y) = d(y,x)$;
3. $d(x,z) \leq d(x,y) + d(y,z)$;

The ordered pair (X, d) is referred to as a metric space. Vantage Point Trees divide data by choosing a point in the input space, the vantage point p, before partitioning data points into two parts: those that are closer to the p than distance r, which go to the left child, and those further away than r, which become part of the right child. This process is done recursively at every level of the treeand the tree can then be traversed efficiently for distance and kNN queries. We refer readers to [26] for further detail on Vantage Point Trees.

4   Methodology

To benchmark libraries and measure memory costs we use language specific open-source tools. For Java-based libraries we use the Java Microbenchmark Harness (JMH)[11], which is a framework for building, running, and analyzing benchmarks. To measure the memory consumption in Java we use the JOL (Java Object Layout) tool[12] which is a toolbox to analyze object layout schemes in JVMs. To benchmark C++ based libraries we used Google Benchmark[13], and to measure the memory consumption of the indexes in C++ we used the Heap Profiler in TCMalloc[14].

For evaluation, we used two datasets, the New York City Taxi Rides dataset[15] (NYC Taxi Rides), and geo-tagged Tweets in the New York City area (NYC Tweets). Using the *shuf* command in Linux, we sampled a subset of 50 million rides (for the year 2015) and geo-tagged tweets from the two datasets. Figure 1 shows the distribution of the rides and tweets in the NYC region. It can be seen that the taxi rides are mostly centered around central New York while the tweets are distributed across the whole city. We further generated query datasets consisting of ranges (bounding boxes) for range query, query points and distances

---

[10] https://github.com/jchambers/jvptree.
[11] https://openjdk.java.net/projects/code-tools/jmh/.
[12] https://openjdk.java.net/projects/code-tools/jol/.
[13] https://github.com/google/benchmark.
[14] https://github.com/gperftools/gperftools.
[15] https://www1.nyc.gov/site/tlc/about/tlc-trip-record-data.page.

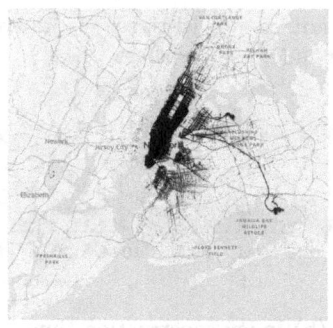
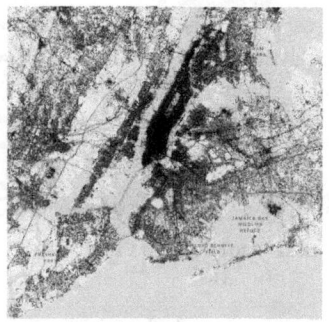

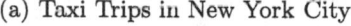

(a) Taxi Trips in New York City   (b) Tweets in New York City

Fig. 1. Datasets: NYC Taxi trips are clustered in central New York whereas Tweets are spread across the city

in case of the distance query, and query points in the case of the kNN query. For range queries and distance queries we created seven different query datasets for seven different selectivities, ranging from 0.0001% to 100%. For the kNN query dataset, we uniformly generated points within the NYC bounding box. Each of these query datasets consists of one million queries. For the point in polygon spatial join query, we used 289 polygons of neighborhood boundaries in NYC.

For the planar geometry libraries we projected the datasets to EPSG:32118 using *ogr2ogr* tool in GDAL. We used the *ogr2ogr* tool in GDAL to transform the latitude-longitude coordinates in the datasets. NYC Taxi datasets (both projected and non-projected), and its query datasets (both projected and non-projected) are available on our website[16], and the benchmark code used in the experiments is available on GitHub[17]. Twitter data was collected using Twitter's Developer API; the usage policy prohibits us from sharing the dataset.

5   Evaluation

All experiments were run single-threaded on a two-socket Ubuntu 18.04 machine equipped with an Intel Xeon E5-2660 v2 CPU (2.20 GHz, 3.00 GHz turbo)[18] and 256 GB DDR3 RAM. We use the *numactl* command to bind the thread and memory to one node to avoid NUMA effects. CPU scaling was also disabled during benchmarking using the *cpupower* command.

To evaluate queries we performed two experiments for each query. In the first experiment, we fixed the selectivity of the query to 0.1% (we fixed k to 10 in case of the kNN query) and varied the cardinality of the points dataset from 10 M to 50 M tuples. In the second experiment, we fixed the number of points to 50 M

---

[16] http://spatial-libs.db.in.tum.de.

[17] https://github.com/varpande/spatial-libs.

[18] CPU: https://ark.intel.com/content/www/us/en/ark/products/75272/intel-xeon-processor-e5-2660-v2-25m-cache-2-20-ghz.html.

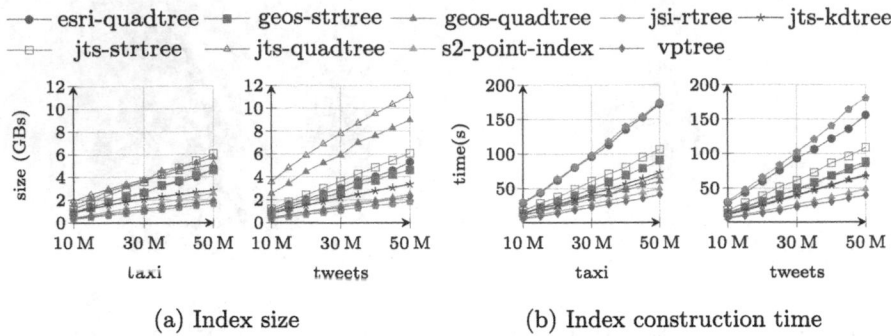

(a) Index size   (b) Index construction time

Fig. 2. Index sizes and construction times in various libraries for Taxi and Twitter Dataset

and varied the selectivity of the query from 0.0001% to 100%. (we varied k from 1 to 10,000 in case of the kNN query). For all these experiments we measure the throughput for each library in queries/s. In the case of point in polygon join query, we used 289 neighborhood polygons and varied number of points from 10 M to 50 M in the first experiment, whereas, in the second experiment we fixed the number of points to 50 M and varied the number of polygons. We report the join time (seconds) for the join query. The implementation of every query is covered under the respective section. If a particular index did not support a query natively, the query was implemented using the *filter and refine* [17] approach.

5.1 Indexing Costs

ESRI Quadtree and JSI R-tree accept the rectangular range to index, and an identifier for the rectangular range, whereas other index structures are more liberal and allow users to put any user data along with the rectangular range. To ensure experimental equality with respect to all index structures, we only stored the rectangular range to index and an identifier in each case and measured the size of these indexes in memory.

It is important at this point to categorize indexes in the libraries in order to better understand their behavior. Indexes in the libraries can be classified into two types: Point Access Methods (PAMs) and Spatial Access Methods (SAMs) [11]. PAMs are indexing methods that index point data, whereas SAMs index extended spatial objects such as rectangles, polygons etc. S2PointIndex, k-d tree, and vptree are PAMs and the rest are SAMs. Indexes can also be categorized as space-driven (following the embedding space hierarchy), or data-driven (following the data space hierarchy). Quadtrees are space-driven structures, whereas the other indexes are data-driven.

Figure 2 shows the sizes of indexes in various libraries and the time takes to construct them. S2PointIndex, k-d tree, and vptree are PAMs which store only points (at least two doubles) and hence their memory consumption is minimal.

S2PointIndex is a B-tree which stores 64-bit integers (cell ids), and the overhead in the inner nodes is minimal. The k-d tree in JTS stores only points, and moreover snaps duplicate points (points are considered duplicates if they satisfy a distance tolerance threshold[19]) instead of creating a new node. jvptree stores only a vantage point and radius at every node hence the intermediate nodes consume minimal memory. Other indexes are SAMs and store rectangles, thus consuming more memory than PAMs. This is expected since the trees store rectangles[20], each of which requires the storage of at least four doubles. It can also be seen from Fig. 2 that the R-tree in JSI consumes very little memory even though it stores rectangles. This is because JSI heavily relies on trove4j[21] collections which are generally faster to access, and consumes considerably less memory than Java's Util collections. There are two specific reasons for the low memory consumption: firstly (any) primitive collections store data directly in an array of primitives (int, long, double, char) and thus only a single reference to an array of primitives is needed instead of an array of refcrences to data objects. Secondly, each primitive data element consumes less memory than the Object (e.g. type int only requires 4 bytes instead of a 16 byte object Integer). The reason for better performance is that trove4j avoids the boxing and unboxing of elements every time a primitive value is queried to/from the collection. Furthermore, space-driven indexes, i.e. Quadtrees, consume more memory for the Twitter dataset. Since space-driven structures divide the space they index more internal nodes are formed if the space is larger. Since the Twitter dataset covers more space than the Taxi dataset, more internal nodes are generated (e.g. the JTS/GEOS Quadtree generates 4 million nodes for 50 million data points for Twitter dataset vs. 1.5 million for Taxi dataset), and the quadtrees are commensurately larger.

Index construction times have been measured using the benchmarking frameworks, and are averaged over several runs until the runtime is statistically stable. For both Taxi and Twitter datasets, jvptree is the fastest to construct, closely followed by S2PointIndex, whereas Quadtree in ESRI geometry API and R-tree in JSI are among the slowest to construct for all datasets.

5.2   Range Query

Implementation: All indexes, except for jvptree, provide a native interface for range queries. To implement range queries in jvptree we first compute the centroid q of the query rectangle. Following this, we determine the distance of the centroid q to one of the rectangle's corner vertices. The resulting circle (q, d) is always larger than the range query rectangle and can therefore be used as a *filter* to retrieve a list with qualifying points. This list is then *refined* to determine which points are actually contained within the range query rectangle. As

---

[19] We kept the tolerance value to 0.0 which means if the point coordinates are exactly the same only then they are snapped to the same node: https://locationtech.github.io/jts/javadoc/org/locationtech/jts/index/kdtree/KdTree.html.

[20] We store points from the datasets as degerate rectangles in SAMs.

[21] http://trove4j.sourceforge.net/html/benchmarks.shtml.

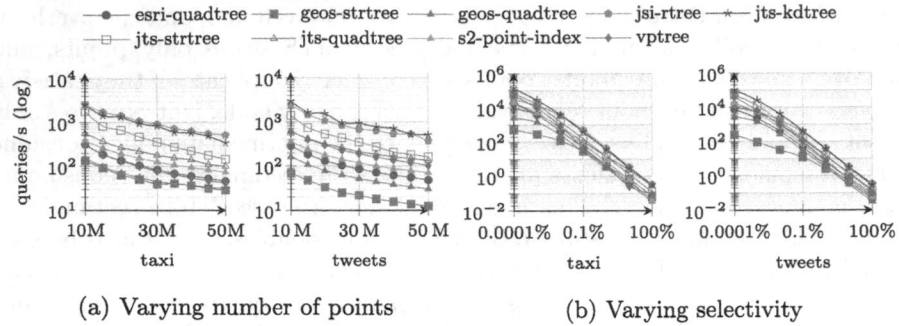

(a) Varying number of points   (b) Varying selectivity

Fig. 3. Range query performance varying the number of points and selectivity of the query rectangle for NYC Taxi and Twitter Datasets

mentioned earlier, the k-d tree in JTS keeps a count of points; in the case of duplicate points (up to a certain distance of tolerance), rather than creating a new node for each duplicate point. We ensure that we materialize all such points for the range query, but we do use them as an optimization in distance and join query to reduce the refinement costs (i.e. skip refinement for duplicate points if one point qualifies the refinement check). Another point to mention here is Quadtree implementation in ESRI geometry API requires tuning. The implementation expects a height parameter for the index. We extensively experimented with heights varying from 1 to 32 for both datasets. We found that the Quadtree performed best with heights 18 and 9 for the Taxi and Tweets datasets respectively.

Analysis: Figure 3 shows the range query performance of the various libraries on the Taxi and Twitter datasets. For both datasets, JTS k-d tree and JSI R-tree show the best throughput numbers (336 and 514 queries per second, respectively, in the Taxi dataset for 50 M points and 0.1% selectivity). The k-d tree are tailor made for range searches on points and thus exhibit among the

Table 3. CPU Counters - Range query datasize = 50M tweets, selectivity = 0.1 %, 1 thread, normalized by the number of range queries. All values are in **millions** except IPC.

	cycles	ipc	instr	L1 miss	LLC miss	branch miss
esri-quadtree	116	0.84	98	1.34	0.54	0.08
geos-quadtree	105	0.75	79	0.97	0.75	0.09
geos-strtree	236	0.37	88	4.04	**2.68**	0.51
geos-cfstrtree	91	0.87	80	1.21	**0.57**	0.46
jsi-rtree	8	1.25	10	0.13	0.06	0.03
jts-kdtree	8	1.12	9	0.14	0.02	0.04
jts-quadtree	68	1.17	80	0.82	0.27	0.19
jts-strtree	31	0.81	25	0.42	0.22	0.01
s2-pointindex	44	1.34	59	0.42	0.05	0.36
vptree	30	0.70	21	0.68	0.21	0.05

best performances for both datasets. The JSI R-tree is optimized for main memory usage and has the smallest height of all indexes (5 in both datasets). Many nodes of the tree are cached, and it thus suffers from the least number of cache

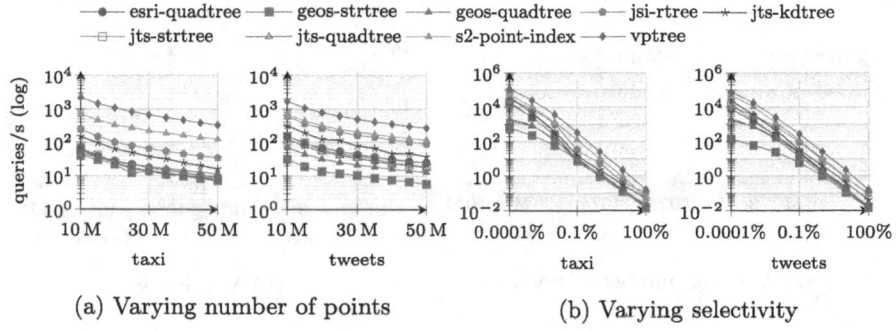

(a) Varying number of points

(b) Varying selectivity

Fig. 4. Distance query performance varying the number of points and selectivity of the query rectangle for NYC Taxi Dataset and Twitter Datasets

misses (see Table 3). An interesting case in the results is the low query throughput of the GEOS STRtree (28.5 queries per second in the Taxi dataset for 50 M points and 0.1% selectivity). The GEOS STRtree is much slower than the JTS STRtree. Upon investigation, we found that the reason for this is an implementation artifact. Table 3 shows that the GEOS STRtree suffers from a large number of LLC misses: 2.68 million in Twitter dataset and 1.28 million in Taxi dataset (data not shown in table). R-trees store multiple rectangles at every node. When the tree is queried, the decision to explore its branches from each node is based on whether the query range overlaps with any of these rectangles. In both JTS and GEOS, every node in the STRtree contains a maximum of 10 such rectangles by default. The GEOS STRtree stores a vector of **pointers** to these rectangles at every node. At each node, the algorithm in the range query iterates over these pointers, retrieves these rectangles from memory and checks if there is any overlap with the query range. Then, based on the overlap, it explores the various branches from the node. Retrieving these rectangles from memory causes many cache misses in the GEOS STRtree during the query execution. To validate this, we implemented a cache-friendly STRtree (designated as cfstrtree in Table 3) in GEOS on top of the existing tree. Essentially, another vector was introduced at every node in the tree, storing the objects of these rectangles in contiguous memory. We replaced the logic to check for overlap to use these rectangle objects rather than the pointers to them. This reduced the number of LLC misses in CFSTRtree, relative to STRtree, by a large number as shown in Table 3.

5.3 Distance Query

Implementation: S2PointIndex and jvptree provide native support for distance queries, so we directly issue the query point and the distance to these two indexes. The other indexes do not natively support distance queries. To implement distance queries in these indexes we again used the *filter and refine* paradigm. We first filtered using a rectangle, with each corner vertex at a distance of d from

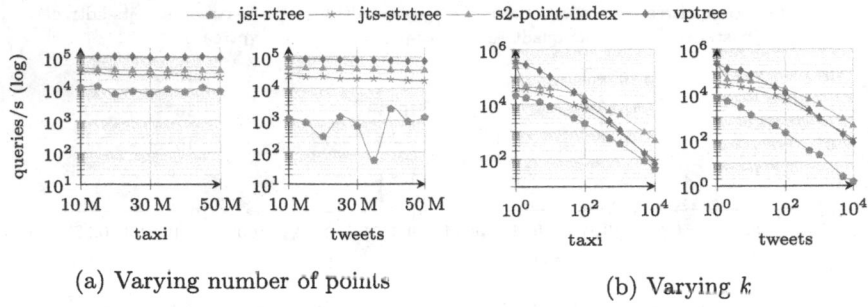

(a) Varying number of points   (b) Varying k

Fig. 5. kNN query performance varying the number of points and k for NYC Taxi and Twitter Datasets

the query point q. We issued a range query to the various range-based indexes using this rectangle. We then refined the resulting candidate set of points using a *withinDistance* predicate (available in ESRI Geometry API, JTS, and GEOS). For JSI, we implemented our own predicate which computes the Euclidean distance for all candidate points from the query point and checks if the candidate point is within distance $d * d$ rather than d from the query point. This allowed us to skip the square root operation when calculating the Euclidean distance.

Analysis: Figure 4 shows the distance query performance on Taxi and Twitter datasets. The performance for distance query is dominated by range query lookup for most indexes, apart from S2PointIndex and jvptree. These indexes support distance queries natively For the other indexes we deploy the filter and refine scheme. The performance of these indexes thus follow directly from the range query performance. JSI R-tree shows a slightly better performance than the JTS k-d tree, stemming from the fact that we optimized the Euclidean distance computation by skipping the square root operation. We also advice readers to use this approach for refinement in GEOS as well. The *isWithinDistance* function in GEOS returns whether two geometries are within a certain distance of each other. By profiling the function we noticed that this function makes six *malloc()* calls, for every candidate point, degrading the performance. Using our own predicate distance function we were able to speed up the distance query by up to 2x in GEOS. In many geometric operations, GEOS frequently allocates and frees memory, which is an overhead. This was similary observed by [27], where the authors used GEOS to introduce spatial processing in Impala.

5.4   kNN Query

Implementation: Of all the available indexes, only S2PointIndex, JTS STRtree, JSI R-tree, and jvptree support kNN queries natively. We directly issued the query point to these indexes and measured their performance. We did not implement any tree traversal algorithms for any other available tree

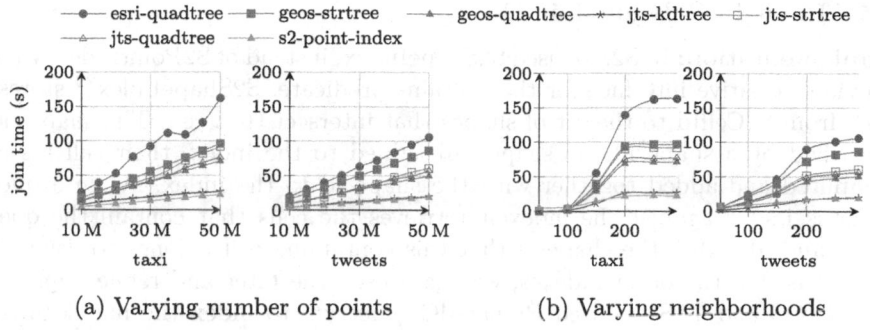

(a) Varying number of points (b) Varying neighborhoods

Fig. 6. Join query performance varying the number of points and neighborhoods for NYC Taxi and Twitter Datasets

because we wanted to measure the performance of the libraries without making any changes to their source codes.

Analysis: Figure 5 shows kNN query performance of various indexes on the Taxi and Twitter datasets. jvptree again took the crown as the best performing index for kNN queries, with S2PointIndex closely behind. It can be observed that for the Twitter dataset the performance of JSI R-tree fluctuates significantly. This can be explained by the manner in which the nearest neighbor algorithm works in JSI R-tree (and also in JTS STRtree) which is known as branch-and-bound traversal. The algorithm starts with the addition of the root node to a priority queue of size k. The algorithm then iterates over the tree continuously adding nodes until the priority queue is full. The algorithm then continues traversing the tree observing nodes and replacing the current farthest node in the queue with the node being observed, if it is closer. The JSI R-trees for different sized datasets are vastly different since the JSI R-tree is a *dynamic* R-tree, the nodes are split at various times during insertion based on multiple factors, and is also unbalanced, for different sized dataset. Thus during the tree traversal for kNN query, sometimes a large number of branches from a node can be dropped since they are not closer than the current farthest node in priority queue and sometimes they cannot be dropped. This can lead to multiple search paths to be evaluated and hence the fluctuation in performance. JTS STRtree packed R-tree does not suffer from this because it is a type of *static* and *bulk-loaded* R-tree and is at most times balanced. It is built once, and then more elements cannot be added to it. STRtree is built by first sorting the leaf node in the x dimension, dividing the nodes into splices after sorting, and then sorting each splice in y dimension. The tree is then built on top of these sorted nodes. The difference in tree node boundaries is still retained in JTS STRtree but is more profound in lower levels of the tree, rather than at various levels as in the case of the JSI R-tree. Thus, the JSI R-tree can sometimes quickly discard branches at the top of the tree and other times it cannot, and this is reflected in the query throughput.

5.5   Point-In-Polygon Join Query

Implementation: In S2, we used S2ShapeIndex, instead of S2PointIndex, which provides a native interface for the contains predicate. S2ShapeIndex[22] stores a map from S2CellId to the set of shapes that intersect that cell. The shapes are identified by a shape id. As shapes are added to the index, their cell ids are computed and added together with the shape id to the index. When a query point is issued against the index it retrieves the cells that contain the query point and identifies the shape(s) that this containing cell belongs to using the shape ids. For the other indexes, we again used the filter and refine approach. For GEOS and JTS we used PreparedGeometry[23] to index the line segments of all individual polygons, which helps in accelerating the refinement check. In JTS, we also used the k-d tree's points snapping technique to skip refinement for duplicate points in case one point qualifies or disqualifies the predicate check. In ESRI implementation, we used AcceleratedGeometry and set its *accelDegree* to *enumHot*[24] for the fastest containment performance.

Analysis: Figure 6 shows the join query performance on the Taxi and the Twitter datasets. Spatial join queries are notoriously expensive and this is reflected in the figure. The kd-tree and S2ShapeIndex exhibit the best performance. The kd-tree, as in the case for range query, can quickly identify the points that lie in the bounding box of a polygon. This candidate set of points is then refined using PreparedGeometry. As mentioned above, we skipped the refinement check for duplicate points if one such point qualified (or disqualified) the refinement check. The S2ShapeIndex natively supports the containment query and traverses the index appropriately and does not have to deal with refining many candidate sets of points. The performance of the other indexes followed directly from the range query performance. JTS/GEOS STRtree and Quadtree performed better than ESRI Quadtree because the refinement using PreparedGeometry is faster than AcceleratedGeometry in ESRI.

6   Related Work

To the best of our knowledge, no previous work has empirically evaluated the spatial libraries studied herein. [27] implemented spatial query processing in Apache Spark, and Apache Impala using JTS and GEOS, respectively. They did observe some of the differences in implementation between JTS and GEOS, but the work was largely a comparative study of spatial processing in Spark and Impala. [18] compared five Spark based spatial analytics systems, some of which used the JTS library for spatial query processing, while [12] compared two database systems which use Google S2 and GEOS for spatial processing. [24] evaluated various parallel in-memory spatial joins.

---

[22] http://s2geometry.io/devguide/s2shapeindex.html.

[23] https://locationtech.github.io/jts/javadoc/org/locationtech/jts/geom/prep/PreparedGeometry.html.

[24] https://esri.github.io/geometry-api-java/javadoc/com/esri/core/geometry/Geometry.GeometryAccelerationDegree.html.

Table 4. Strengths/Weaknesses of the Libraries

Library	Strengths	Weaknesses
ESRI	(1) Active development and support	(1) Quadtree requires tuning
	(2) Full geometric types, refinements, and operations	
JSI	(1) R-tree performance as a filter	(1) No active development
		(2) No geometric refinements
GEOS and JTS	(1) Active development and support	(1) Memory management in GEOS requires improvement
	(2) Full geometric types, refinements, and operations	
jvptree	(1) Best distance and kNN performance	(1) No geometric refinements
S2	(1) Best suited for geographic data	
	(2) Active development and support	
	(3) Many practical queries natively supported	

7 Conclusions

In this work we empirically compared popular spatial libraries using four different queries: range query, distance query, kNN query, and a point in polygon join query. We performed an experimental evaluation of these libraries using two real-world datasets. Table 4 summarizes the strengths and weaknesses of the spatial libraries. There is no clear winner for each of the considered queries, and this is mostly because all the indexes available in the libraries do not support all these queries natively (i.e. do not have specialized tree traversal algorithms for each query). ESRI geometry API and JTS/GEOS are complete planar geometry libraries, and are rich in features. They support multiple datatypes, and have a variety of topological and geometry operations. They are also under active development and has a community for support. They do, however, come with some drawbacks. ESRI Quadtree has to be tuned for the dataset that it indexes, and memory management in GEOS could be improved. The kd-tree in JTS is one of the best performing index in many queries, but does not support the kNN query. There are algorithms available to traverse the kd-tree efficiently in order to answer the kNN queries and implementing the algorithm in the index would be a welcome addition. The R-tree in JSI exhibited the best performance for range lookups, however, JSI is very limited in features, and is also not under active development. Google S2 is a spherical geometry library and is best suited to work with geographic data. It is active under development and is used in many multimillion-dollar industries. It also has many practically used queries that are implemented natively on various indexes. Finally, jvptree, is a library that implements the Vantage Point Tree, and exhibited the best performance for distance and kNN queries since it was specifically designed to answer these queries. The index can only be used as a filter for other queries, and users have to implement their own refinement operations for such queries.

References

1. Aji, A., et al.: Hadoop-GIS: a high performance spatial data warehousing system over mapreduce. PVLDB (2013). https://doi.org/10.14778/2536222.2536227
2. Eldawy, A., Mokbel, M.F.: SpatialHadoop: a MapReduce framework for spatial data. In: ICDE 2015. IEEE Computer Society (2015)
3. Eldawy, A., Sabek, I., Elganainy, M., Bakeer, A., Abdelmotaleb, A., Mokbel, M.F.: Sphinx: empowering impala for efficient execution of SQL queries on big spatial data. In: Gertz, M., et al. (eds.) SSTD 2017. LNCS, vol. 10411, pp. 65–83. Springer, Cham (2017). https://doi.org/10.1007/978-3-319-64367-0_4
4. Gomes, D.: MemSQL Live (2019). https://www.memsql.com/blog/memsql-live-nikita-shamgunov-on-the-data-engineering-podcast/
5. Guttman, A.: R-trees: a dynamic index structure for spatial searching. In: SIGMOD 1984 (1984)
6. Hagedorn, S., et al.: The STARK framework for spatio-temporal data analytics on spark. In: Datenbanksysteme für Business, Technologie und Web (BTW 2017) (2017)
7. Kipf, A., et al.: Approximate geospatial joins with precision guarantees. In: 34th IEEE ICDE 2018, Paris, France, April 16–19 2018 (2018)
8. Kipf, A., et al.: Adaptive main-memory indexing for high-performance point-polygon joins. In: Extending Database Technology, EDBT 2020 (2020)
9. Lee, K., Ganti, R.K., Srivatsa, M., Liu, L.: Efficient spatial query processing for big data. In: Proceedings of the 22nd ACM SIGSPATIAL (2014)
10. Lee, K., et al.: Lightweight indexing and querying services for big spatial data. IEEE Trans. Serv. Comput. (2019)
11. Liu, L., Özsu, M.T. (eds.): Encyclopedia of Database Systems. Springer, New York (2018). https://doi.org/10.1007/978-1-4614-8265-9
12. Makris, A., et al.: Performance evaluation of MongoDB and PostgreSQL for spatio-temporal data. In: EDBT Workshop. CEUR Workshop Proceedings (2019)
13. Malensek, M., et al.: Polygon-based query evaluation over geospatial data using distributed hash tables. In: Utility and Cloud Computing, UCC 2013 (2013)
14. Malensek, M., et al.: Evaluating geospatial geometry and proximity queries using distributed hash tables. Comput. Sci. Eng. **16**, 53–61 (2014)
15. MongoDB Releases - New Geo Features in MongoDB 2.4 (2013). https://www.mongodb.com/blog/post/new-geo-features-in-mongodb-24/
16. Oracle Spatial (2019). https://www.oracle.com/technetwork/database/options/spatialandgraph/overview/spatialfeatures-1902020.html/
17. Orenstein, J.A.: Redundancy in spatial databases. In: ACM SIGMOD 1989 (1989)
18. Pandey, V., Kipf, A., Neumann, T., Kemper, A.: How good are modern spatial analytics systems? PVLDB **11**(11), 1661–1673 (2018)
19. Pandey, V., et al.: High-performance geospatial analytics in hyperspace. In: Proceedings of the 2016 International Conference on Management of Data, SIGMOD Conference 2016, San Francisco, CA, USA, 26 June–01 July 2016 (2016)

20. Tahboub, R.Y., Rompf, T.: On supporting compilation in spatial query engines: (vision paper). In: ACM SIGSPATIAL (2016)
21. Tang, M., et al.: LocationSpark: a distributed in-memory data management system for big spatial data. PVLDB **9**(13), 1565–1568 (2016)
22. Tang, M., et al.: Similarity group-by operators for multi-dimensional relational data. IEEE Trans. Knowl. Data Eng. **28**, 510–523 (2016)
23. Theocharidis, K., Liagouris, J., Mamoulis, N., Bouros, P., Terrovitis, M.: SRX: efficient management of spatial RDF data. VLDB J. **28**(5), 703–733 (2019). https://doi.org/10.1007/s00778-019-00554-z
24. Tsitsigkos, D., et al.: Parallel in-memory evaluation of spatial joins. In: ACM SIGSPATIAL 2019 (2019). https://doi.org/10.1145/3347146.3359343
25. Xie, D., et al.: Simba: efficient in-memory spatial analytics. In: SIGMOD 2016 (2016)
26. Yianilos, P.N.: Data structures and algorithms for nearest neighbor search in general metric spaces. In: Proceedings of the Fourth Annual ACM/SIGACT-SIAM Symposium on Discrete Algorithms, Austin, Texas, USA, 25–27 January 1993 (1993)
27. You, S., Zhang, J., Gruenwald, L.: Large-scale spatial join query processing in cloud. In: 31st ICDE Workshops 2015 (2015)
28. Yu, J., et al.: GeoSpark: a cluster computing framework for processing large-scale spatial data. In: ACM SIGSPATIAL 2015 (2015)

Differentially Private Resource Auction in Distributed Spatial Crowdsourcing

Yin Xu[1], Mingjun Xiao[2(✉)], Xiang Zou[3], and An Liu[4]

[1] School of Cyberscience/Suzhou Institute for Advanced Study,
University of Science and Technology of China, Hefei, China
`xuyin218@mail.ustc.edu.cn`
[2] School of Computer Science and Technology/Suzhou Institute for Advanced Study,
University of Science and Technology of China, Hefei, China
`xiaomj@ustc.edu.cn`
[3] The Third Research Institute of the Ministry of Public Security, Shanghai, China
`xzou@eid.net.cn`
[4] School of Computer Science and Technology, Soochow University, Suzhou, China
`anliu@suda.edu.cn`

Abstract. In this paper, we study a new type of Spatial Crowdsourcing (SC), namely Distributed SC (DSC), which can support a variety of location-relative services demanded by different requesters with low latency and bandwidth costs. In DSC, requesters need to compete for limited resources so as to deploy their desired SC services, and the requested resources must be allocated together to meet the demand of the service. We model this competitive resource allocation problem as a combinatorial auction process. Since this problem is NP-hard, we design an approximation algorithm to solve it. Besides, the leakage of sensitive information such as bids may incur severe economic damage, and there is a lack of works that can provide efficient protection without a trustworthy third-party. Based on this, we propose a novel Differentially private Resource Auction (DRA) mechanism. A bid confusion strategy based on differential privacy is designed against the untrusted third-party. Moreover, we prove that DRA offers ϵ-differential privacy, γ-truthfulness, individual rationality and computational efficiency. Finally, extensive simulations on a real trace confirm the efficacy of DRA and indicate good performance in accordance with the design expectations.

Keywords: Distributed spatial crowdsourcing · Auction mechanism · Differentially private

1 Introduction

The dramatic proliferation of smart mobile devices enable a newly-emerged crowdsourcing paradigm, namely Spatial Crowdsourcing (SC). A typical SC system contains some task requesters, mobile users, and a server on the cloud. Through the SC server, requesters can crowdsource their tasks to mobile users

Y. Nah et al. (Eds.): DASFAA 2020, LNCS 12113, pp. 728–745, 2020.
https://doi.org/10.1007/978-3-030-59416-9_47

to be accomplished. So far, a lot of efforts have been devoted to designing diverse SC systems and the corresponding user recruitment, task assignment, incentive mechanisms, or privacy-preserving protocols, etc [5,17,21–23]. However, most of these existing SC systems only involve a single server platform, which can be categorized as centralized crowdsourcing paradigm. All user recruitment or task assignment would need to be conducted via the centralized SC server. As the number and types of SC services increase, these simple centralized systems are more and more unable to meet the experience demand of users. Distributed SC systems, which provide efficient and diverse services, are becoming popular.

In this paper, we investigate resource allocation in a Distributed Spatial Crowdsourcing (DSC) system with the help of edge computing. In general, a DSC system can support a variety of location-relative services demanded by different requesters. By the aid of edge computing, the DSC system can dynamically deploy these services to specified decentralized Edge Clouds (ECs) according to requesters' demand. The ECs can be formed of a number of small-scale computing and storage servers which are placed at network edges. Consequently, the services are more closer to mobile users which can reduce time latency and high bandwidth costs significantly. Figure 1 shows an example of a DSC system. Three requesters want to provide their SC services, each of which corresponds to one or more locations. On the basis of the demands, the DSC system can deploy these three services to nearby ECs which cover the related locations and recruit mobile users to perform their SC tasks.

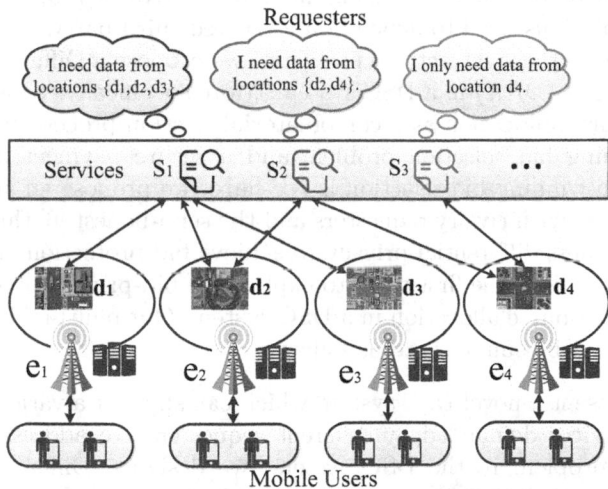

Fig. 1. The DSC system model

Different from traditional SC systems which mainly depend on a central cloud, the DSC system needs to deploy services on distributed ECs where the computing and communication resources are generally limited. Thus, requesters need to compete for the limited EC resources so as to deploy their desired SC services. As we know, auction is one of the most efficient and fair manners to deal with resource competition issues, and thus, it is also adopted in this paper. There are two challenges in the auction mechanism design. Firstly, the resources that each requester applies for might be distributed among multiple ECs and must be allocated together to support the corresponding SC service. For example, a requester in Fig. 1 needs to deploy service s_1 to collect the traffic congestion information among three locations $\{d_1, d_2, d_3\}$ within a certain period of time. Since it is meaningless to only collect partial data under the time constraint, s_1 is either successfully deployed on an EC bundle $\{e_1, e_2, e_3\}$ simultaneously or fails. Thus, it actually involves a distributed combinatorial resource allocation issue. Secondly, bids play an essential role in auctions, which generally imply the valuation of SC services, requesters' interests, and so on. Such information is sensitive to each requester. If it is revealed, potential adversaries might utilize the information to manipulate the auction, resulting in unfair resource competition. Hence, we need to protect requesters' bids from being revealed [10, 13].

Although many combinatorial auction-based resource allocation mechanisms have been proposed [12, 15, 16], most of them pay more attention to achieving critical economic properties without taking bid privacy into account. So far, only a handful of works take the privacy issues into consideration which usually can be divided into two classes. One class is to utilize cryptography techniques to encrypt bids [1, 2, 18–20]. This class of approaches can strongly protect bid privacy but will lead to huge computation and communication overheads. The other is to provide puzzle of bids using differential privacy [7–9, 13, 14]. However, most of the solutions need to depend on a trusted third-party.

In response to these intractable problems, we propose a Differentially private Resource Auction (DRA) in a DSC system. More specifically, we formalize each round of resource allocation as a combinatorial auction process, which includes a secure winning bid selection problem and a secure payment determination problem. Since winning bid selection is NP-hard, we propose an approximation algorithm. Faced with rivalry requesters and the semi-honest [6] third-party auctioneer, we harness differential privacy to achieve bid protection. To the best of our knowledge, this is the first work to exploit the bid-privacy preservation and combinatorial resource allocation in a DSC system. Our multi-fold contributions in this paper can be summarized as follows:

1. We first present a novel DSC system which can support a variety of location-relative services demanded by different requesters. To address the resource allocation problem in the DSC system, we design a Differentially private Resource Auction (DRA) mechanism in which requesters can compete for the resources of ECs so as to deploy their desired SC services.
2. We transform the competitive resource allocation problem with the indivisible requested resources into a secure combinatorial auction, including secure winning bid selection and secure payment determination. And we prove that the secure winning selection problem is NP-hard, so we propose a greedy algorithm which can achieve an acceptable approximation ratio.

3. To shield bid privacy from rivalry requesters and the untrusted third-party, we design a bid confusion strategy in a differentially privacy-preserving manner. The strategy allows each requester to upload confused bids without disclosing sensitive information.
4. We prove that the DRA mechanism not only satisfies differential privacy, but also guarantees γ-truthfulness, individual rationality and computational efficiency. And then we conduct extensive experiments on a real trace to verify the significant performances of the DRA mechanism.

The remainder of the paper is organized as follows. Section 2 introduces our model and problem. We present the design of the DRA mechanism in Sect. 3. The theoretical analysis is showcased in Sect. 4. In Sect. 5, we implement our mechanism and evaluate its performances. Section 6 reviews related works. Finally, we make a conclusion in Sect. 7.

2 Model and Problem Formulation

2.1 System Model

The model consists of three major entities: services, many ECs and the auctioneer. Services proposed by requesters need resources from the ECs, denoted by $S = \{s_1, s_2, ..., s_n\}$. The ECs possess certain resources which are used to deploy services, denoted as $E = \{e_1, e_2, ..., e_m\}$. Therefore, the services can be seemed as buyers, and the ECs play the role of sellers. The auction results contain the set of winning bids and the corresponding payments decided by the semi-honest auctioneer, which are denoted by W and P, respectively.

For each EC e_j, we use $<A_j, c_j>$ to denote the state information where A_j denotes resource capacity and c_j denotes the unit cost of resources. For each service s_i, the state information is denoted by a triple $<D_i, Q_i, b_i>$. Requesters bid on a bundle instead of an individual EC. We assume that a requester who

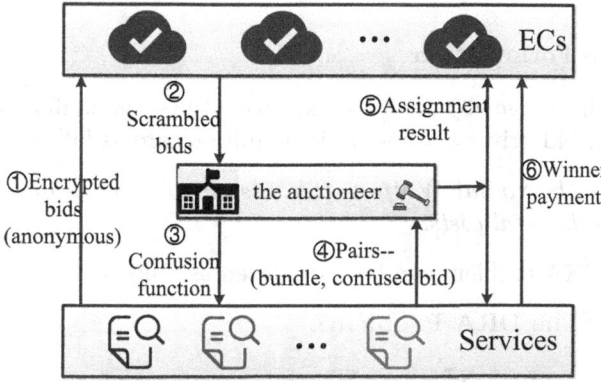

Fig. 2. The DRA system model

demands s_i is l_i-minded, which means that the requester can submit at most l_i bundles $D_i = \{D_{i,1}, D_{i,2}, ..., D_{i,l_i}\}$ along with a set of the unit bids $b_i = \{b_{i,1}, b_{i,2}, ..., b_{i,l_i}\}$ and a set of requested resources $Q_i = \{Q_{i,1}, Q_{i,2}, ..., Q_{i,l_i}\}$, where $D_{i,k} \subseteq E$ $(\forall k \in [1, l_i])$ is a bundle and $Q_{i,k}$ is the set of the corresponding requested resource quantities $\{q_{i,j} | \forall e_j \in D_{i,k}\}$. B denotes the set of all true bids.

Architecturally, the interactions among the various entities are depicted in Fig. 2. Now we would like to shed some light on how to fulfill the process.

Step 1: According to the preference for different bundles, the requester who demands s_i $(\forall i \in [1, n])$ determines the unit bid for each preferred bundle, forming a bundle-bid pair $(D_{i,k}, b_{i,k})$. For sake of preventing the bids from being revealed during the transmission process, requesters encrypt bids with a public key k_p which is broadcasted by the auctioneer. Then, all requesters upload encrypted bids to different ECs with anonymous communication technology [3]. It is noteworthy that each requester could upload different encrypted bids to different ECs but one encrypted bid can be uploaded to at most one EC.

Step 2: Each EC will transfer all encrypted and disordered bids to the auctioneer. Thanks to anonymous transmission, the auctioneer cannot know which bundle a bid belongs to.

Step 3: The auctioneer decrypts all encrypted bids by using its private key k_s. Then, it can know the distribution of true bids and generate a differential privacy confusion function based on exponential mechanism. Afterwards, the auctioneer publishes the designed confusion function to requesters.

Step 4: After knowing the bid confusion function, the requester who demands service s_i $(\forall i \in [1, n])$ replaces a true bid $b_{i,k}$ with a confused bid $\tilde{b}_{i,k}$ and reports the bundle-confused bid pairs to the auctioneer.

Step 5: Receiving the confused bids from each requester, the auctioneer executes the combinatorial auction algorithm to seek out the winning bids set and determine the corresponding payments, and then publishes the auction results.

Step 6: Finally, the DSC system deploys the winning services on requested ECs and recruits mobile users to perform their SC tasks, and then the related requesters pay the corresponding rewards to the DSC system.

2.2   Problem Formulation

In this paper, the design objective is maximizing the social welfare on the premise of guaranteeing bid privacy. Some basic definitions are as follows.

Definition 1. *The **Social Welfare** (SW) is the total valuations of the winning services minus the total costs.*

Then, the DRA problem can be formulated as follows.

Definition 2 (The DRA Problem).
Maximize:

$$SW = \sum_{b_{i,k} \in W} \sum_{q_{i,j} \in Q_{i,k}} (v_{i,k} - c_j) * q_{i,j} \tag{1}$$

Subject to:

$$\sum\nolimits_{i:(b_{i,k}\in W \cap q_{i,j}\in Q_{i,k})} q_{i,j} \leq A_j, \forall e_j \in E \tag{2}$$

$$\sum\nolimits_{k=1}^{l_i} 1_{\{b_{i,k}\in W\}} \leq 1, \forall s_i \in S \tag{3}$$

where $v_{i,k}$ denotes the true unit valuation that the requester evaluates if it run its demanded service s_i on bundle $D_{i,k}$.

Here, Eq. 2 claims that the total requested resources of services cannot exceed the capacity of each EC. Equation 3 indicates that a service can be only deployed on a bundle at most.

In addition to protecting bid privacy, we are not willing to sacrifice some critical economic properties, such as truthfulness, individual rationality and computational efficiency.

Definition 3 (Individual Rationality). *Each requester with the winning bid $b_{i,k}$ has a nonnegative utility, i.e., $u_i - v_{i,k} - p_{i,k} \geq 0$.*

Definition 4 (γ-truthfulness [11]). *An auction is γ-truthful in expectation iff $E[u_i(b_i', \boldsymbol{b}_{-i})] \geq E[u_i(b_i, \boldsymbol{b}_{-i})] - \gamma$ holds for any bid $b_i \neq b_i'$ and any bid profile of other services $\boldsymbol{b}_{-i}$, where γ is a small positive constant.*

Definition 5 (Computational Efficiency [20]). *If an auction mechanism can terminate in polynomial time, it has the property of computational efficiency.*

2.3 Preliminary

Differential privacy, which provides privacy for statistics publishing with strong theoretical guarantee, has emerged as the standard in data privacy. And the exponential mechanism is often used to design privacy-preserving mechanisms.

Definition 6 (Differential Privacy [4]). *A randomized mechanism M has ϵ-differential privacy if for any two input sets D_1 and D_2 differing on at most one element, and for any set of outcomes $O \subseteq Range(M)$, we have $Pr[M(D_1) \in O] \leq exp(\epsilon) \times Pr[M(D_2) \in O]$. $\epsilon > 0$ is the privacy budget—the smaller ϵ, the stricter protection and lower data availability.*

Definition 7 (Exponential Mechanism). *Given an outcome space O, an input set A, a score function f and a small constant ϵ, a random mechanism M satisfies ϵ-differential privacy, if $M(A, o) = \{o : |Pr[o \in O] \propto exp(\frac{\epsilon f(A,o)}{2\Delta f})\}$, where Δf is the sensitivity of the score function $f(A, o)$.*

For ease of reference, we list the main notations of this paper in Table 1.

Table 1. Description of major notations

Variable	Description
s_i, S	The i-th service, the set of all services
e_j, E	The j-th EC, the set of all ECs
$<A_j, c_j>$	Resource capacity, the unit cost of resources
$<D_i, Q_i, b_i>$	The set of preferred bundles, the set of requested resources, the set of the claimed unit bids
$D_{i,k}, Q_{i,k}$	A bundle and the set of corresponding requested resource quantities
$q_{i,j}$	Requested resource quantities for the EC e_j
$b_{i,k}, v_{i,k}$	The claimed bid and true valuation for bundle $D_{i,k}$
$\tilde{b}_{i,k}$	The confused bid from $b_{i,k}$
B, W, P	The set of all bids, all winning bids, all payments

3   Design of the DRA Mechanism

3.1   Problem Hardness Analysis

Firstly, we analyze the complexity of the DRA problem.

Theorem 1. *The DRA problem is NP-hard.*

Proof. We consider a special case of the DRA problem without privacy protection, where there is only one EC and each requester submits a bid for the EC at most. Then, the problem is reducible to determine a subset $B' \subseteq B$ so as to maximize $\sum_{b_{i,1} \in B'} (v_{i,1} - c_1) * q_{i,1}$, while meeting $\sum_{i:b_{i,1} \in B'} q_{i,1} \leq A_1$. This is equivalent to the 0–1 knapsack problem: maximize the total value $\sum_{i=1}^{n} v_i * x_i$ while ensuring $\sum_{i=1}^{n} w_i * x_i \leq C, x_i \in \{0, 1\}$. As we all know, the 0–1 knapsack problem is NP-hard, so the special DRA problem is NP-hard. Certainly, the general DRA problem with privacy protection is also NP-hard.

3.2   Basic Idea

We propose a full-fledged DRA mechanism in a DSC system which integrates the combinatorial auction with exponential mechanism. The goal of our mechanism design is to maximize the social welfare while achieving bid privacy, truthfulness, individual rationality and computational efficiency.

To address the issue of bid privacy, we design a global bid confusion function which confuses bids of requesters via exponential mechanism. Different from general designs for bid protection which need to depend on a trusted third-party, our design provides a stronger privacy assurance to requesters. Specifically, we make use of asymmetric encryption and anonymous communication technology to obtain encrypted bids, which can protect true bids from the ECs and generate the bid confusion function. Then, we use local differential privacy to shield bids from the untrusted third-party.

Given the bundle-confused bid pairs, we model the competitive resource allocation problem as a secure combinatorial auction, which includes secure winning bid selection and secure payment determination. Without true bids, we take the expectation of bids based on the bid confusion function as the input of the auction algorithm. Since the DRA problem is NP-hard, we propose a greedy algorithm to select winning bids to maximize the social welfare and design the corresponding payments without violating individual rationality.

3.3   Bid Confusion

In our paper, we take the advantage of exponential mechanism to design a bid confusion function, which maps a true bid b to a confused bid $\tilde{b}$. On the basis of the Definition 7, we can define the confusion function as follows.

$$Pr(\tilde{b}|b) \propto exp(\frac{\epsilon f(b, \tilde{b})}{2\Delta f}) \tag{4}$$

Here, $Pr(\tilde{b}|b)$ is the probability of mapping the true bid b to the confused bid $\tilde{b}$. $f(b, \tilde{b})$ is the score function measuring the closeness of the confused bid $\tilde{b}$ to the true bid b. The higher the score is, the closer the two are.

In order to satisfy the properties of the score function, we resort to a monotonically non-increasing function. In this end, the score function can be

$$f(b, \tilde{b}) = -\ln(|b - \tilde{b}| + 1) \tag{5}$$

It is desirable that the smaller the gap between a true bid b and a confused bid $\tilde{b}$, the higher the probability $Pr(\tilde{b}|b)$. At this time, the sensitivity of the score function is $\ln(|b_{max} - b_{min}| + 1) = \ln(\Delta b + 1)$, where b_{max} and b_{min} denote the maximum value and minimum value in B, and Δb equals $b_{max} - b_{min}$.

After designing the score function, the confusion function is

$$Pr(\tilde{b}|b) \propto exp(-\frac{\epsilon * \ln(|b - \tilde{b}| + 1)}{2\ln(\Delta b + 1)}) = \frac{exp(-\frac{\epsilon * \ln(|b - \tilde{b}| + 1)}{2\ln(\Delta b + 1)})}{\sum_{b' \in B} exp(-\frac{\epsilon * \ln(|b - b'| + 1)}{2\ln(\Delta b + 1)})} \tag{6}$$

Finally, the auctioneer publishes the designed confusion function to requesters. Each requester can utilize the confusion function and the true bid $b_{i,k}$ to calculate the probability $Pr(\tilde{b}_{i,k}|b_{i,k})$, and then select a confused bid $\tilde{b}_{i,k}$ judiciously based on different perception about privacy and the urgent need level.

3.4   Auction Mechanism Design

Secure Winning Bid Selection. The objective of our mechanism is maximizing the social welfare, but the paramount difficulty of selecting winners is that the auctioneer only holds the confused bids without the ability of inferring the true bids. Faced with the challenge, we employ the expected bids to approximate the true bids. Given the confusion function and the confused bid $\tilde{b}_{i,k}$, we can calculate the expected bid $E[b_{i,k}]$ as

---

Algorithm 1. Secure Winning Bid Selection

Require: S, E, B
Ensure: W
1: **Initialize** $G = \emptyset, W = \emptyset$;
2: //**Compute Grade:**
3: **for** $s_i \in S$ **do**
4:      **Initialize** $G_i = \emptyset$;
5:      **for** $D_{i,k} \in D_i$ **do**
6:          **Initialize** $g_{i,k} = 0, count = 0$;
7:          **for** $e_j \in D_{i,k}$ **do**
8:              $g_{i,k} = g_{i,k} + c_j, count = count + 1$;
9:          **end for**
10:          $g_{i,k} = E[b_{i,k}] - \frac{g_{i,k}}{count}; G_i = G_i + \{g_{i,k}\}$;
11:      **end for**
12:      $G = G + \{G_i\}$;
13: **end for**
14: //**Greedy Selection:**
15: **while** $S \neq \emptyset$ and $E \neq \emptyset$ and $B \neq \emptyset$ **do**
16:      **Record the index with the maximum grade** $g_{i,k}$ **as** (i^*, k^*);
17:      **Initialize** $flag = 1$;
18:      **for** $q_{i^*,j} \in Q_{i^*,k^*}$ **do**
19:          **if** $q_{i^*,j} > A_j$ **then**
20:              $flag = 0$ **and break**;
21:          **end if**
22:      **end for**
23:      **if** $flag = 1$ **then**
24:          **for** $q_{i^*,j} \in Q_{i^*,k^*}$ **do**
25:              $A_j = A_j - q_{i^*,j}$;
26:          **end for**
27:          $W = W + \{E[b_{i^*,k^*}]\}; S = S - \{s_{i^*}\}; G = G - \{G_{i^*}\}$;
28:      **else**
29:          $G_i = G_i - \{g_{i^*,k^*}\}$ **and Update** G;
30:          **if** $G_i = \emptyset$ **then**
31:              $S = S - \{s_{i^*}\}$;
32:          **end if**
33:      **end if**
34: **end while**

$$E[b_{i,k}] = \frac{\sum_{b_{i,k} \in B} Pr(\widetilde{b}_{i,k}|b_{i,k})Pr(b_{i,k})Pr_e(b_{i,k}) * b_{i,k}}{\sum_{b_{i,k} \in B} Pr(\widetilde{b}_{i,k}|b_{i,k})Pr(b_{i,k})Pr_e(b_{i,k})} \qquad (7)$$

where $Pr(b_{i,k}) = num(b_{i,k})/|B|$ means the probability of $b_{i,k}$ in the set B. The function $num(b_{i,k})$ is used for counting the frequency of $b_{i,k}$ in the set B and $|\cdot|$ means the cardinality of the set. Let $Pr_e(b_{i,k})$ denote the probability that a true bid $b_{i,k}$ exists in the bundle-bid pairs for bundle $D_{i,k}$, which can be calculated as

$$Pr_e(b_{i,k}) = \frac{\sum_{\widetilde{b}_{i,k} \in B_k} Pr(\widetilde{b}_{i,k}|b_{i,k})}{\sum_{b_{i,k} \in B} \sum_{\widetilde{b}_{i,k} \in B_k} Pr(\widetilde{b}_{i,k}|b_{i,k})} \qquad (8)$$

where B_k denotes the set of the confused bids of the requesters who desire to purchase resources from the bundle $D_{i,k}$.

Based on the above policy, the process of selecting the winning bids can be divided into the following steps.

Step 1: (Compute Grade) Firstly, We give a grade vector for each service. Grading rule is as the following formula. $g_{i,k}$ denotes the grade for the bundle $D_{i,k}$.

$$G_i = \{g_{i,k} = E[b_{i,k}] - \frac{\sum_{e_j \in D_{i,k}} c_j}{|D_{i,k}|} |\forall k \in [1, l_i]\}, \forall s_i \in S \qquad (9)$$

Step 2: (Greedy Algorithm) Due to the NP-hardness of the DRA problem, we design a greedy algorithm to determine the winning bids. More concretely, we greedily select an expected bid with the largest grade in each round. The detail is illustrated in Algorithm 1. In the first part, we compute a grade vector for each service in Lines 1–13. In the second part, we design a greedy winning bid selection strategy in Lines 14–34. In each round, we select the bundle with largest grade and record the index as (i^*, k^*) in Line 16. Next, we need to judge whether the selected bundle is eligible. If eligible, we hit a winning bid and update the related sets in Lines 23–27; otherwise, we delete the bundle grade in Lines 28–33.

Secure Payment Determination. Although the true bundle-bid pairs are privacy-preserving, the true bids must fall within the interval between b_{min} and b_{max}. For sake of individual rationality, we design the payment of each requester who demands the corresponding winning service as follows.

$$p_{i,k} = min\{|E[b_{i,k}] - (b_{max} - b_{min})|, b_{min}\} \qquad (10)$$

4   Theoretical Analysis

In this section, we prove how DRA achieves the desired design objectives: differential privacy, individual rationality, γ-truthfulness and computational efficiency.

Theorem 2. *The DRA mechanism satisfies ϵ-differential privacy.*

Proof. To facilitate the proof, we assume that there are two different true bids b_1 and b_2, and they are both obfuscated to $\tilde{b}$. The probability of mapping the bid b_1 (resp. b_2) to the confused bid $\tilde{b}$ is $Pr(\tilde{b}|b_1)$ (resp. $Pr(\tilde{b}|b_2)$). Then, we can derive an exponential upper-bound for $Pr(\tilde{b}|b_1)/Pr(\tilde{b}|b_2)$. The specific derivation process is as follows.

$$\frac{Pr(\tilde{b}|b_1)}{Pr(\tilde{b}|b_2)} = \frac{\dfrac{exp(-\frac{\epsilon*\ln(|b_1-\tilde{b}|+1)}{2\ln(\Delta b+1)})}{\sum_{b'\in B} exp(-\frac{\epsilon*\ln(|b_1-b'|+1)}{2\ln(\Delta b+1)})}}{\dfrac{exp(-\frac{\epsilon*\ln(|b_2-\tilde{b}|+1)}{2\ln(\Delta b+1)})}{\sum_{b'\in B} exp(-\frac{\epsilon*\ln(|b_2-b'|+1)}{2\ln(\Delta b+1)})}}$$

$$= \frac{exp(-\frac{\epsilon*\ln(|b_1-\tilde{b}|+1)}{2\ln(\Delta b+1)})}{exp(-\frac{\epsilon*\ln(|b_2-\tilde{b}|+1)}{2\ln(\Delta b+1)})} * \frac{\sum_{b'\in B} exp(-\frac{\epsilon*\ln(|b_2-b'|+1)}{2\ln(\Delta b+1)})}{\sum_{b'\in B} exp(-\frac{\epsilon*\ln(|b_1-b'|+1)}{2\ln(\Delta b+1)})} \quad (11)$$

As for the first half of the expression, denoted by *left*, we have

$$left = \frac{exp(-\frac{\epsilon*\ln(|b_1-\tilde{b}|+1)}{2\ln(\Delta b+1)})}{exp(-\frac{\epsilon*\ln(|b_2-\tilde{b}|+1)}{2\ln(\Delta b+1)})} = exp(\epsilon * \frac{\ln(|b_2-\tilde{b}|+1)-\ln(|b_1-\tilde{b}|+1)}{2\ln(\Delta b+1)})$$

$$= exp(\epsilon * \frac{\ln\frac{|b_2-\tilde{b}|+1}{|b_1-\tilde{b}|+1}}{2\ln(\Delta b+1)}) \le exp(\epsilon * \frac{\ln(\Delta b+1)}{2\ln(\Delta b+1)}) = exp(\frac{\epsilon}{2}) \quad (12)$$

Then, the last half of the expression is denoted by *right*. Since $\frac{1}{\Delta b+1} \le \frac{|b_2-\tilde{b}|+1}{|b_1-\tilde{b}|+1} \le \Delta b+1$, we have $\ln\frac{1}{\Delta b+1} \le \ln\frac{|b_2-\tilde{b}|+1}{|b_1-\tilde{b}|+1} \le \ln(\Delta b+1)$. Thus, we have

$$right = \frac{\sum_{b'\in B} exp(-\frac{\epsilon*\ln(|b_2-b'|+1)}{2\ln(\Delta b+1)})}{\sum_{b'\in B} exp(-\frac{\epsilon*\ln(|b_1-b'|+1)}{2\ln(\Delta b+1)})} \le \frac{\sum_{b'\in B} exp(-\frac{\epsilon*\ln(|b_2-b'|+1)}{2\ln(\Delta b+1)})}{\sum_{b'\in B} exp(\frac{\epsilon*[-\ln(|b_2-b'|+1)-\ln(\Delta b+1)]}{2\ln(\Delta b+1)})}$$

$$= \frac{\sum_{b'\in B} exp(-\frac{\epsilon*\ln(|b_2-b'|+1)}{2\ln(\Delta b+1)})}{\sum_{b'\in B} exp(-\frac{\epsilon*\ln(|b_2-b'|+1)}{2\ln(\Delta b+1)}) * exp(-\frac{\epsilon}{2})} = exp(\frac{\epsilon}{2}) \quad (13)$$

Finally, based on the above induction of *left* and *right*, we have

$$Pr(\tilde{b}|b_1)/Pr(\tilde{b}|b_2) = left * right \le exp(\frac{\epsilon}{2}) * exp(\frac{\epsilon}{2}) = exp(\epsilon) \quad (14)$$

According to Definition 6, the theorem holds.

Theorem 3. *The DRA mechanism meets the condition of individual rationality.*

Proof. We consider an arbitrary confused bid $\tilde{b}_{i,k}$ and calculate the corresponding expected bid $E[b_{i,k}]$ according to the Eq. 7. Then, the expected bid would encounter two conditions: $E[b_{i,k}] \in W$ and $E[b_{i,k}] \notin W$. If $E[b_{i,k}] \notin W$, the payment $p_{i,k} = 0$. Otherwise, the requester who demands s_i should pay $p_{i,k} = min\{|E[b_{i,k}] - (b_{max} - b_{min})|, b_{min}\}$. Obviously, there is $p_{i,k} \leq b_{min}$. Hence, given that $v_{i,k} \in [b_{min}, b_{max}]$, the utility of the requester is $v_{i,k} - p_{i,k} \geq 0$. According to Definition 3, the theorem holds.

Theorem 4. *The DRA mechanism satisfies $2\epsilon\Delta b$-truthful.*

Proof. Let b_1 and b_2 be two different true bids for the same bundle $D_{i,k}$ of service s_i. Using the Theorem 2, we have $Pr(\tilde{b}|b_1) \leq exp(\epsilon)Pr(\tilde{b}|b_2)$. Therefore, the utility expectation of the requester who demands s_i is

$$E[u_i(b_1)] = \sum_{\tilde{b} \in B}[u_i(\tilde{b})Pr(\tilde{b}|b_1)]$$
$$\leq \sum_{\tilde{b} \in B}[u_i(\tilde{b})exp(\epsilon)Pr(\tilde{b}|b_2)] = exp(\epsilon)E[u_i(b_2)] \qquad (15)$$

Due to $u_i = v_{i,k} - p_{i,k} \leq b_{max} - (E[b_{i,k}] - (b_{max} - b_{min})) = (b_{max} - b_{min}) + (b_{max} - E[b_{i,k}]) \leq 2\Delta b$, we have

$$E[u_i(b_2)] \geq exp(-\epsilon) * E[u_i(b_1)] \geq (1 - \epsilon) * E[u_i(b_1)]$$
$$\geq E[u_i(b_1)] - \epsilon E[u_i(b_1)] \geq E[u_i(b_1)] - 2\epsilon\Delta b \qquad (16)$$

According to Definition 4, we have completed the proof.

Theorem 5. *The DRA mechanism is computationally efficient.*

Proof. The DRA mechanism mainly is composed by the bid confusion and the secure winning bid selection. For the former, each requester can bid for at most $l_{max} = max\{l_i | i \in [1, n]\}$ bundles for each service, and there are at most n services in a certain period of time, so the computational overhead is $O(nl_{max})$. Next, the computational overhead of Algorithm 1 is $O(mn^2 l_{max}^2)$. Based on Definition 5, the DRA mechanism is computationally efficient.

5 Evaluations

5.1 Algorithms in Comparison

Since DRA is the first solution for the combinatorial auction and bid protection in a DSC system against the untrusted third-party, we compare it with the state-of-the-art bid protection algorithms with a trustworthy third-party [14] [8]. However, the model and problems in these works are different from ours so that we cannot compare them directly. Therefore, we tailor the basic idea in these algorithms for our model and carefully design three secure resource allocation algorithms for comparison: LIN-M [14], LOG-M [14] and DPS [8].

5.2 Simulation Setup

We artificially generate some ECs in the simulations, each of which has a limited resource capacity and a unit cost. The resource capacity and the unit cost are uniformly distributed over [10, 20] and [1, 5], respectively. For simplicity, we assume that bundles are determined, but the generation of bundles in each round of simulations is random. Then, we generate some services demanded by different requesters, and these requesters can bid for determined bundles. The bids and requested resource quantities are generated randomly from [10, 20] and [1, 5], respectively. The number of ECs is selected from 20 to 60 and the number of services ranges from 50 to 250. The differential privacy budget ranges from 0.1 to 1.1 and we set $\epsilon = 0.5$ as default. Moreover, all simulation parameters are listed in Table 2, where default values are in bold fonts. All experimental results are averaged on 100 random repetitions under the same setting.

We use three metrics to evaluate the performance of our mechanism:

- Social Welfare: as defined in Sect. 2.
- Total Payment: the payments paid by the requesters to the DSC system.
- Privacy Leakage: we use the Kullback-Leibler divergence [14] to evaluate the privacy leakage of DRA. Let b and $\tilde{b}$ be the true bid and the confused bid, respectively. $Pr(b = \tilde{b})$ means the probability when b equals $\tilde{b}$. In this paper, the privacy leakage is defined as $PL = \frac{1}{\sum_{b \in B} Pr_e(b) \ln(\frac{1}{Pr(b=\tilde{b})})}$.

Table 2. Evaluation setting

Parameter name	Values
Number of services	50, **100**, 150, 200, 250
Number of edge clouds	**20**, 30, 40, 50, 60
Privacy budget	0.1, 0.3, **0.5**, 0.7, 0.9, 1.1
Range of resource capacity and the unit cost	[10, 20], [1, 5]
Range of requested resource quantity and the unit bid	[1, 5], [10, 20]

5.3 Simulation Results

Evaluation of Social Welfare. We first compare the social welfare of DRA with that of LIN-M, LOG-M and DPS, and show the results in Fig. 3. Note that DPS can be considered optimal when selecting winners. The impact of the number of services on the social welfare when there are 20 ECs is shown in Fig. 3(a). We can see that the social welfare of all mechanisms increases slightly as the number of services grows. This is because with more services, the auctioneer may select more suitable services to allocate resources. We also observe that the social welfare of DPS is lower than those of DRA, LIN-M and LOG-M. This is because, DPS has a trusted third-party who knows all true bids so that it can select services with the highest grade. Moreover, our mechanism has higher social welfare compared to the LIN-M and LOG-M. This is because although our mechanism confuses true bids, we select winners by their expected bids rather than select them randomly with a certain probability in the LIN-M and LOG-M.

Figure 3(b) depicts the performance of four mechanisms on the social welfare against the number of ECs when there are 100 services. We find that the social welfare of four mechanisms increases when the number of ECs grows. The reason is that with more ECs, each requester will have more choices of the ECs for their desired services, and then the auctioneer can select more services as winners. Our mechanism has higher social welfare compared to the LIN-M and LOG-M with the same reason above.

Figure 3(c) reports the social welfare obtained by four mechanisms with different privacy budget when there are 20 ECs and 50 services. It is shown that there is a slight increase in the social welfare, because the larger the privacy budget is, the worse the differential privacy is achieved. But the influence is barely perceptible.

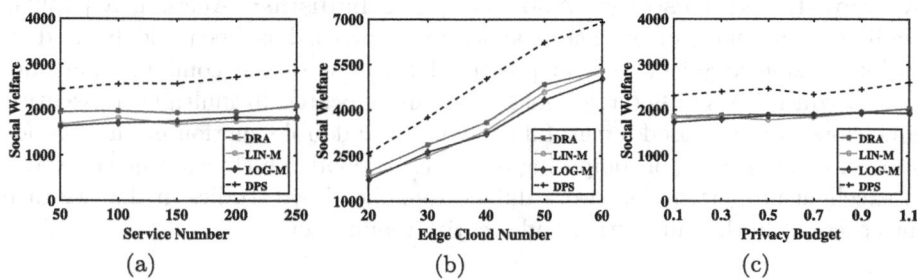

Fig. 3. Evaluation of Social Welfare. (a) Impact of the number of services. (b) Impact of the number of ECs. (c) Impact of privacy budget.

Evaluation of Total Payment. In Fig. 4(a), Fig. 4(b) and Fig. 4(c), we plot the impact of the number of services, the number of ECs and privacy budget on the total payment of four mechanisms, respectively. The results show that the total payment follows the same pattern as the social welfare. The reasons are similar to that discussed for Fig. 3. We also observe that the total payment of DRA is lower than that of LIN-M, LOG-M and DPS. This is because each payment of DRA is less than b_{min} to guarantee individual rationality. With less payment, requesters are more willing to deploy services on the DSC system, which will finally bring a lot of advantages to the DSC system.

Evaluation of Privacy Leakage. Figure 5 illustrates the impact of privacy budget on the privacy leakage. Along with the increase of privacy budget, the privacy leakage of DRA increases. This is because when the privacy budget is smaller, the probability of obfuscating any bid to other is higher, and then bid privacy is less likely to be compromised. Note that the privacy leakage values of LIN-M, LOG-M and DPS are positive infinity, because these mechanisms assume that there exists a trusted third-party and all bidders would submit true bids to it.

Evaluation of Computational Efficiency. Finally, we verify the computational efficiency of the DRA mechanism. We find that the running time of the DRA mechanism increases slowly when the number of services and ECs increase, as shown in Fig. 6. When the number of ECs is 60 and the number of services is 250, the execution time of DRA is less than 6s, which is much smaller than the auction cycle. This means that the DRA can work efficiently in real applications. These simulation results remain consistent with our theoretical analysis.

6 Related Work

Auction-Based Resource Allocation Mechanisms: Auction, a popular trading form that can efficiently allocate resources, has been widely used in various systems. Shi et al. [15] presented the first online combinatorial auction in which VMs of heterogeneous types are allocated in multiple consecutive time-slots. [12] proposed a truthful combinatorial double auction mechanism for allocation and pricing of computing resources in cloud, which can achieve a series of excellent properties. Our work differs from the above studies in that we take into account both competition and security requirements.

Privacy-Preserving Mechanisms: As for the security of bid information, some efforts have been made to protect the bid privacy with few methods such as cryptography techniques and differential privacy. Xiao et al. [20] proposed a secure reverse auction protocol for a novel spatial crowdsourcing, which protects the quotations of workers using homomorphic encryption. Although providing

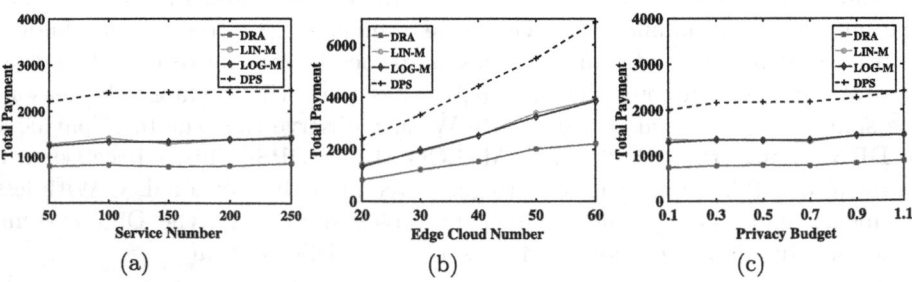

Fig. 4. Evaluation of Total Payment. (a) Impact of the number of services. (b) Impact of the number of ECs. (c) Impact of privacy budget.

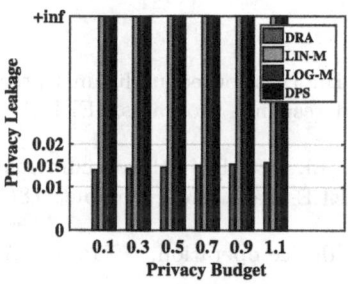

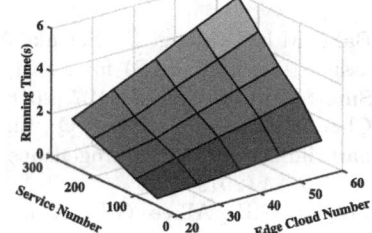

Fig. 5. Evaluation of Privacy Leakage

Fig. 6. Evaluation of Computational Efficiency

good performance in privacy preservation, the mechanisms like [1,2,18,19] are based on cryptography techniques and may bring about a large quantity of calculations. To bypass the drawback, the research [14] designed two frameworks for privacy-preserving auction-based incentive mechanisms based on differential privacy. However, it relies on a trusted platform so that only the bid information would not be revealed to other bidders. Hence, once the platform is semi-honest or vulnerable, the bid information would be leaked with a great probability.

7 Conclusion

In this paper, we study the resource allocation problem in a DSC system where requesters need to compete for the limited EC resources so as to deploy their desired SC services. We have formalized this competitive problem with the indivisible requested resources as a secure combinatorial auction, and we have proposed a mechanism named DRA to solve the problem. To shield bid privacy from rivalry requesters and the untrusted third-party, a bid confusion strategy based on differential privacy has been proposed to allow each requester to upload confused bids without disclosing sensitive information. We have proved that DRA ensures the properties of ϵ-differential bid privacy, γ-truthfulness, individual rationality and computational efficiency. Extensive simulations verify the performance of the DRA mechanism.

Acknowledgment. This research was supported by the National Key Research and Development Program of China (Grant No. 2017YFB0802302), the National Natural Science Foundation of China (NSFC) (Grant No. 61872330, 61572457, 61572336, 61379132, 61936015, U1709217), the NSF of Jiangsu Province in China (Grant No. BK20191194, BK20131174, BK2009150), Natural Science Research Project of Jiangsu Higher Education Institution (No. 18KJA520010), and Anhui Initiative in Quantum Information Technologies (Grant No. AHY150300).

References

1. Balli, M.F., Uludag, S., Selcuk, A.A., Tavli, B.: Distributed multi-unit privacy assured bidding (PAB) for smart grid demand response programs. IEEE Trans. Smart Grid **9**(5), 4119–4127 (2018)
2. Chen, Y., Tian, X., Wang, Q., Li, M., Du, M., Li, Q.: ARMOR: a secure combinatorial auction for heterogeneous spectrum. IEEE Trans. Mob. Comput. **18**(10), 2270–2284 (2019)
3. Cooper, G.H., AlLee, G.L., et al.: Anonymous device operation, US Patent App. 10/289,610, 14 May 2019
4. Dwork, C.: Differential Privacy. In: van Tilborg, H.C.A., Jajodia, S. (eds.) Encyclopedia of Cryptography and Security, pp. 338–340. Springer, Boston (2011). https://doi.org/10.1007/978-1-4419-5906-5_752
5. Gao, G., Wu, J., Xiao, M., Chen, G.: Combinatorial multi-armed bandit based unknown worker recruitment in heterogeneous crowdsensing. In: IEEE INFOCOM 2020 - IEEE Conference on Computer Communications (2020)
6. Goldreich, O.: Foundations of Cryptography: Basic Applications, vol. 2. Cambridge University Press, Cambridge (2009)
7. Han, K., Liu, H., Tang, S., Xiao, M., Luo, J.: Differentially private mechanisms for budget limited mobile crowdsourcing. IEEE Trans. Mob. Comput. **18**(4), 934–946 (2019)
8. Hu, Y., Zhang, R.: Differentially-private incentive mechanism for crowdsourced radio environment map construction. In: IEEE INFOCOM 2019 - IEEE Conference on Computer Communications, pp. 1594–1602, April 2019
9. Jin, W., Li, M., Guoy, L., Yang, L.: DPDA: a differentially private double auction scheme for mobile crowd sensing. In: 2018 IEEE Conference on Communications and Network Security (CNS), pp. 1–9, May 2018
10. Jin, X., Zhang, Y.: Privacy-preserving crowdsourced spectrum sensing. IEEE/ACM Trans. Network. **26**(3), 1236–1249 (2018)
11. Kothar, A., Parke, D.C., Sur, S.: Approximately-strategyproof and tractable multi-unit auctions. In: Proceedings of the 4th ACM Conference on Electronic Commerce, pp. 166–175. ACM (2003)
12. Kumar, D., Baranwal, G., Raza, Z., Vidyarthi, D.P.: A truthful combinatorial double auction-based marketplace mechanism for cloud computing. J. Syst. Softw. **140**, 91–108 (2018)
13. Li, D., Yang, Q., Yu, W., An, D., Zhang, Y., Zhao, W.: Towards differential privacy-based online double auction for smart grid. IEEE Trans. Inf. Forensics Secur. **15**, 971–986 (2020)
14. Lin, J., Yang, D., Li, M., Xu, J., Xue, G.: Frameworks for privacy-preserving mobile crowdsensing incentive mechanisms. IEEE Trans. Mob. Comput. **17**(8), 1851–1864 (2018)
15. Shi, W., Zhang, L., Wu, C., Li, Z., Lau, F.C.M.: An online auction framework for dynamic resource provisioning in cloud computing. IEEE/ACM Trans. Network. **24**(4), 2060–2073 (2016)
16. Singhal, R., Singhal, A.: A combinatorial economical double auction resource allocation model (CEDARA). In: 2019 International Conference on Machine Learning, Big Data, Cloud and Parallel Computing (COMITCon), pp. 497–502, February 2019
17. Tong, Y., Chen, L., Zhou, Z., Jagadish, H.V., Shou, L., Lv, W.: Slade: a smart large-scale task decomposer in crowdsourcing. In: 2019 IEEE 35th International Conference on Data Engineering (ICDE), pp. 2133–2134, April 2019

18. Wang, J., Karuppiah, M., Kumari, S., Kong, Z., Shi, W.: A privacy-preserving spectrum auction scheme using paillier cryptosystem with public verification. J. Intell. Fuzzy Syst. (Preprint) 1–12 (2019)
19. Wang, Q., Huang, J., Chen, Y., Wang, C., Xiao, F., Luo, X.: *prost*: privacy-preserving and truthful online double auction for spectrum allocation. IEEE Trans. Inf. Forensics Secur. **14**(2), 374–386 (2019)
20. Xiao, M., et al.: SRA: secure reverse auction for task assignment in spatial crowd-sourcing. IEEE Trans. Knowl. Data Eng. **32**, 782–796 (2019)
21. Xiao, M., Wu, J., Huang, L., Cheng, R., Wang, Y.: Online task assignment for crowdsensing in predictable mobile social networks. IEEE Trans. Mob. Comput. **16**(8), 2306–2320 (2017)
22. Yu, X., Li, G., Zheng, Y., Huang, Y., Zhang, S., Chen, F.: CrowdOTA: an online task assignment system in crowdsourcing. In: 2018 IEEE 34th International Conference on Data Engineering (ICDE), pp. 1629–1632, April 2018
23. Yuan, D., Li, Q., Li, G., Wang, Q., Ren, K.: PriRadar: a privacy-preserving framework for spatial crowdsourcing. IEEE Trans. Inf. Forensics Secur. **15**, 299–314 (2020)

Spatial Dynamic Searchable Encryption with Forward Security

Xiangyu Wang[1], Jianfeng Ma[1]($\boxtimes$), Ximeng Liu[2], Yinbin Miao[1], and Dan Zhu[1]

[1] School of Cyber Engineering, Xidian University, Xi'an, China
xy_wang@stu.xidian.edu.cn, jfma@mail.xidian.edu.cn, ybmiao@xidian.edu.cn
[2] College of Mathematics and Computer Science, Fuzhou University, Fuzhou, China
snbnix@gmail.com

Abstract. Nowadays, spatial search services bring unprecedented convenience in people's daily life (e.g., location-based services, social networking) and are becoming more and more popular. To protect the privacy of outsourcing data, several schemes have been proposed to achieve secure search over encrypted spatial databases. However, most existing schemes cannot support dynamic updates, which seriously hinders the practical application of spatial databases. To address this issue, in this paper, we propose two novel Spatial Dynamic Searchable Encryption (SDSE) constructions for outsourcing spatial databases, which achieve various security guarantees. First, we present a basic construction supporting dynamic update with sub-linear search complexity based on the order-revealing encryption and Quadtree. Then, to ensure that updates do not reveal any information underlying the prior modifications beyond some explicit leakage (i.e., forward security), we further give an improved construction according to constrained pseudo-random functions. Both the nearest neighbor search and geometric search are supported in our constructions, which meet almost all spatial search needs. The experiments using real-world dataset demonstrate that our constructions are efficient and feasible in practice.

Keywords: Searchable encryption · Spatial search · Dynamic updates · Forward security.

1 Introduction

With the increasing popularity of location-based services and social networking, spatial search has drawn great interest from both industrial and academic fields in recent years. Nearest Neighbor (NN) search and geometric search are two major spatial search queries in practice. For example, a user can find his/her closest friend by running NN search over a location check-in dataset in a social network. To find all the stores in a certain geometric area, a user can run a geometric search over a spatial database. For cost savings and great flexibility, more and more data owners are motivated to outsource their spatial search services to the cloud. However, directly outsourcing such services to an untrusted

Y. Nah et al. (Eds.): DASFAA 2020, LNCS 12113, pp. 746–762, 2020.
https://doi.org/10.1007/978-3-030-59416-9_48

cloud may raise serious privacy concerns [27]. Searchable Symmetric Encryption (SSE) [5,17,22,23], which allows clients to outsource databases to a server and directly search over encrypted data, is an ideal primitive to solve the above problem. With SSE, a client can obtain correct search results from a *honest-but-curious* server without revealing queries or data stored on it. In addition, the database has to be updated frequently to cope with practical application requirements. In the traditional SSE schemes, the client has to re-upload all the data to update the database, which incurs huge communication and computational overhead. To address this issue, Dynamic SSE (DSSE) [10] schemes were proposed to allow the client to update data without losing data confidentiality and searchability. However, the attacker can reveal the content of a past query by inserting a few new documents since the server can learn that the newly inserted document matches a previous search query [28]. To resist such attack, some forward security schemes [2,3] were proposed, which do not leak any information about previous search queries and new document when inserting a new document. Unfortunately, existing DSSE schemes are mainly focus on keyword database, most spatial search schemes, including NN search [6,19,25] and geometric search [18,20,21,26], cannot support dynamic updates, which greatly limits the application of spatial data. An ideal DSSE scheme for spatial data should meet the following requirements: (1) minimizing the number of communications, and it is best to achieve a single-roundtrip; (2) search complexity should be sub-linear to cope with large-scale data; (3) ensuring both efficiency and security. This means that heavy cryptographic primitives such as homomorphic encryption cannot be used. Finally, supporting dynamic updates should not incur privacy leakage, that is, to achieve forward security.

1.1 Our Contributions

In this paper, we propose two practical Spatial Dynamic Searchable Encryption (SDSE) constructions, which offer efficient spatial search and dynamic updates over encrypted databases. The main contributions of this paper are as follows.

1. After introducing formal definitions of SDSE, we propose Secure Quadtree (SQ-tree), a basic SDSE construction based on the Order-Revealing Encryption (ORE) [12] and Quadtree [7]. Using SQ-tree, a client can dynamically update an encrypted spatial database stored on a server and perform both NN search and geometric search over it with sub-linear search complexity.
2. We further improve the SQ-tree by leveraging the Constrained Pseudo-Random Functions (CPRF) [1,11] to construct a forward-secure SDSE, namely SQ-tree$_{fw}$. In SQ-tree$_{fw}$, when a new data object is inserted, the encrypted data object is salted with CPRF and directly inserted into a cache database instead of the SQ-tree. The salt of the newly inserted data will be taken off during the next search process, and the data is inserted into the SQ-tree after the search to maintain sub-liner search complexity.

3. We implement our proposed constructions in C/C++ and evaluate its performance over a real-world dataset. The experimental results show that our constructions are practical, which only requires less than 50 ms among 1 million data objects.

Table 1. Comparison with prior works. "FS" stands for forward security, "Geo" stands for geometric search. N is the dataset size, M is the maximum number of children in the deepest non-leaf node, n_{new} is the number of newly inserted data objects. $|v|$ is size of a search vector, $|x|$ is the query range of one-dimensional data in dataset, τ is the number of instances the server needs to evaluate, τ' is the size of the link list that the update applies to.

Schemes	Round-trip	Search cost	Query size	Update cost	FS	Search method
ASPE [25]	1	$\mathcal{O}(N)$	$\mathcal{O}(1)$	–	–	NN
[9]	$\mathcal{O}(\log_M N)$	$\mathcal{O}(M) + \mathcal{O}(M \log_M N)$	$\mathcal{O}(1)$	–	–	NN
[6]	$\mathcal{O}(N)$	$\mathcal{O}(N)$	$\mathcal{O}(1)$	–	–	NN
NNSE [19]	2	$\mathcal{O}(M) + \mathcal{O}(M \log_M N)$	$\mathcal{O}(1)$	–	–	NN
FastGeo [18]	1	$\mathcal{O}(|v| \cdot \tau)$	$\mathcal{O}(|x|)$	$\mathcal{O}(|v| \cdot \tau')$	✗	Geo
SQ-tree	2 or 1	$\mathcal{O}(M) + \mathcal{O}(4 \log_4 N)$	$\mathcal{O}(1)$	$\mathcal{O}(4 \log_4 N)$	✗	NN or Geo
SQ-tree$_{fw}$	2 or 1	$\mathcal{O}(M + n_{new}) + \mathcal{O}(4 \log_4 N)$	$\mathcal{O}(1)$	$\mathcal{O}(1)$	✓	NN or Geo

To the best of our knowledge, our constructions are the first to achieve both dynamic update and forward security on the encrypted spatial database. A comparison of our constructions with prior work is shown in Table 1.

1.2   Related Work

Dynamic Symmetric Searchable Encryption. At the first time, Song et al. [17] proposed the notion of Symmetric Searchable Encryption (SSE). Following this work, Curtmola et al. [5] introduced the idea of leakage to develop the security model of SSE and designed the first reversed-index-based SSE construction. However, these two schemes still cannot support dynamic deployments. Hence, Kamara et al. [10] presented a formal security definition for Dynamic SSE (DSSE) that supports data addition and deletion, and described a DSSE based on the inverted index. With trade-offs between security and practicality, almost all of the practical DSSE schemes leak information about documents. Recent researches on the real-world impact of this leakage, however, show that even small leakage can be used to break the privacy of search queries [15,28]. In particular, the file-injection attacks proposed by Zhang et al. [28] pointed that it is possible to reveal the contents of past search queries of DSSE schemes with a few injections of documents. This attack underlines the need for DSSE schemes with forward security. Therefore, to resist the above attack exploiting leakage in dynamic operations, some schemes [2,3] have been proposed to support forward-secure addition. Unfortunately, almost all of the above schemes only consider the textual keyword database rather than the spatial database.

Secure Spatial Data Search. Most existing works regarding spatial data focus on rich query capabilities, including NN search [6,9,19,25] and geometric search [18,20,26]. Specifically, Wong et al. [25] first proposed a secure k-NN scheme by introducing Asymmetric Scalar Product Preserving Encryption (ASPE), but their scheme is too weak to resist even Ciphertext-only Attack (CoA) [13]. Hu et al. [9] designed a new scheme using R-tree and private homomorphism, which has sub-linear search complexity. Unfortunately, using their scheme, the client needs to store a local index, and one-round communication has to be performed per layer of the tree. Elmehdwi et al. [6] presented a scheme for secure k-NN search based on the assumption of two non-colluding server model, while this scheme only achieves linear search complexity. Besides, the heavy cryptographic and blinding operations between the two servers in [6] significantly degrade the entire search process. To achieve practical secure NN search, Wang et al. [19] introduced Order-Preserving Encryption (OPE) [16] and R-tree. However, the ciphertexts of OPE leaks the order of the underlying plaintexts, which makes it weak against inference attack [14], and leakage-abuse attack [8]. Recently, Wang et al. [24] recovered most of OPE's ciphertext through file-injection attacks and pointed out that only forward security OPE schemes can resist such attacks. In addition, geometric search on encrypted spatial database [18,20,26] has also attracted widespread interest. To support arbitrary geometric range query, Wang et al. [20] presented a model actualizing range query for any geometric drawing over encrypted cloud data. Then, to improve the efficiency of [20] and support update, they designed another geometric range query method [18] using hash table and a set of link lists to construct two-level search structure. Recently, Xu et al. [26] achieve geometer range queries according to the polynomial fitting technique and the ASPE, and improve the search efficiency by introducing OPE-based R-tree. However, most of the above schemes cannot support dynamic updates, which greatly reduces the usability of the encrypted spatial database.

2 Perliminaries

2.1 Order-Revealing Encryption

In order to overcome the weakness of Order-Preserving Encryption (OPE) [16] which directly exposes the order from the ciphertext, Order-Revealing Encryption (ORE) [12] was proposed. ORE only allows ciphertext with corresponding tokens to compare their numerical order, which significantly reduces the disclosed knowledge. In this paper, we use a state-of-the-art ORE [12] scheme with left/right ciphertexts. Using this ORE, each plaintext m is encrypted to left ciphertext $\mathsf{ct_L}(m)$ and right ciphertxet $\mathsf{ct_R}(m)$. For two plaintexts m_1, m_2, only the $(\mathsf{ct_L}(m_1), \mathsf{ct_R}(m_2))$ or $(\mathsf{ct_R}(m_1), \mathsf{ct_L}(m_2))$ can be used to compare. If only the right ciphertexts of two messages are exposed to the server or an adversary, they are semantically secure [12]. The ORE scheme is a tuple of four algorithms ($\mathsf{ORE.Setup}$, $\mathsf{ORE.Enc_L}$, $\mathsf{ORE.Enc_R}$, $\mathsf{ORE.Compare}$) defined over a well-ordered domain $\mathcal{D}$ with the following properties:

- ORE.Setup$(1^\lambda) \rightarrow$ sk: Given a security parameter λ, this algorithm outputs a secret key sk.
- ORE.Enc$_L$(sk, m) $\rightarrow$ ct$_L(m)$: Given a secret key sk and a message $m \in \mathcal{D}$, this algorithm outputs a left ciphertext ct$_L(m)$.
- ORE.Enc$_R$(sk, m) $\rightarrow$ ct$_R(m)$: Given a secret key sk and a message $m \in \mathcal{D}$, this algorithm outputs a right ciphertext ct$_R(m)$.
- ORE.Compare(ct$_L(m_1)$, ct$_R(m_2)$) $\rightarrow b$: Given two ciphertext ct$_L(m_1)$, ct$_R(m_2)$, this algorithm outputs a bit $b \in \{-1, 0, 1\}$, where $b \leftarrow 1$ if $m_1 < m_2$; $b \leftarrow -1$ if $m_1 > m_2$; otherwise, $b \leftarrow 0$.

2.2   Trapdoor Permutations and Constrained Pseudorandom Functions

A TrapDoor Permutation (TDP) [2] π is a one-way permutation over a domain $\mathcal{X}$ such that, it is easy to compute π for any value of the domain with the public key TPK, but the inverse π^{-1} for any value of a co-domain $\mathcal{Y}$ only can be calculated with the secret key TSK (i.e., $\pi_{\mathsf{TSK}}^{-1}(\pi_{\mathsf{TPK}}(x)) \rightarrow x$, $\pi_{\mathsf{TPK}}(\pi_{\mathsf{TSK}}^{-1}(x)) \rightarrow x$). A Constrained PRF (CPRF) [1,11], which is associated with a family of boolean circuits $\mathcal{C}$, is a TDP. In CPRF, the master key holder who has secret key K is able to produce a constrained key K_C corresponding to a circuit $C \in \mathcal{C}$. The constrained key K_C allows evaluation of the PRF only on inputs x for which $C(x) = 1$. A CPRF $\tilde{F} : \{0,1\}^\lambda \times \mathcal{X} \rightarrow \mathcal{Y}$ consists two algorithms ($\tilde{F}.Constrain$, $\tilde{F}.Eval$) are defined as:

- $\tilde{F}.Constrain(K, C)$: Given a key $K \in \{0,1\}^\lambda$ and a circuit $C \in \mathcal{C}$, this algorithm outputs a constrained key K_C.
- $\tilde{F}.Eval(K_C, x)$: Given a constrained key K_C for circuit $\mathcal{C}$, and $x \in \mathcal{X}$, this algorithm outputs $y \in \mathcal{Y}$.

Let $\tilde{F}.Eval((\mathsf{TSK}, ST_0), c) = \pi_{\mathsf{TSK}}^{-c}(ST_0)$, where π^{-c} is the c-fold iteration of π^{-1}. We identify the circuit constraining to the range $\{0, ..., n\}$ with the integer n. The constrain algorithm will be $\tilde{F}.Constrain((\mathsf{TSK}, ST_0), n) = (\mathsf{TPK}, \pi_{\mathsf{TSK}}^{-n}(ST_0), n) = (\mathsf{TPK}, ST_n, n)$. The constrained evaluation function is $\tilde{F}.Eval((\mathsf{TPK}, ST_n, n), c) = \pi_{\mathsf{TPK}}^{n-c}(ST_c)$. In the rest of this paper, we write $\tilde{F}.Eval(K_C, x)$ as $\tilde{F}(K_C, x)$.

3   Spatial Dynamic Searchable Encryption (SDSE)

In SDSE, a client outsources a spatial database DB to a server and then performs search queries over it. Each data object p or search query q is a point of data space $\{0,1\}_T^d$, where d is the dimensions of data objects and T is the message space of each dimension. The database model in SDSE is a collection of (spatial data, document index) pairs denoted as $\mathsf{DB} = (\mathsf{p}_i, \mathsf{ind}_i)_{i=1}^N$, where $\mathsf{p}_i \in \{0,1\}_T^d$, $\mathsf{ind}_i \in \{0,1\}^\lambda$, and N is the size of database. A SDSE scheme Σ contains one algorithms and three protocols between a client and a server as follows:

- $(K_\Sigma, \sigma, \mathsf{EDB}) \leftarrow \mathsf{Setup}(1^\lambda, \mathsf{DB})$: Given a security parameter λ and a spatial database DB, this algorithms outputs the secret keys set K_Σ, the client's state σ, and the encrypted database EDB.
- $\mathcal{R} \leftarrow \mathsf{GeoSearch}(K_\Sigma, Q, \sigma; \mathsf{EDB})$: The client inputs (K_Σ, Q, σ), where Q is a geometric query, and the server inputs EDB to match results inside Q. After the protocol, the results $\mathcal{R}$ is returned to the client.
- $\mathcal{R} \leftarrow \mathsf{NNSearch}(K_\Sigma, q, \sigma; \mathsf{EDB})$: The client inputs (K_Σ, q, σ), where q is a location point, and the server inputs EDB to match the nearest neighbor of q. After the protocol, the results $\mathcal{R}$ is returned to the client.
- $\mathsf{Update}(K_\Sigma, \sigma, \mathsf{op}, \mathsf{in}; \mathsf{EDB})$: The client inputs $(K_\Sigma, \sigma, \mathsf{op}, \mathsf{in})$, where in is a set of spatial/document pairs and $\mathsf{op} \in \{\mathsf{add}, \mathsf{del}\}$ denotes a addition or deletion operations, and server inputs EDB. After the protocol, the input in is inserted into or deleted from the EDB.

Security. In SDSE scheme, an adversary should not learn any information about the content of the spatial database and the queries beyond some explicit leakage. Following the security definition of the DSSE [10], the notion of SDSE security is also captured using the real-world versus ideal-world game. A leakage function $\mathcal{L} = (\mathcal{L}^{\mathsf{Stp}}, \mathcal{L}^{\mathsf{Srch}}, \mathcal{L}^{\mathsf{Updt}})$ is used to capture the information learned by the adversary and its components express the information leaked by Setup, Search[1] and Update, respectively. The adversary's task is to distinguish between the experiments REAL and IDEAL.

Definition 1 (Adaptive Security of SDSE). *Let $\mathcal{L}$ be a leakage function, a SDSE scheme $\Sigma = (\mathsf{Setup}, \mathsf{Search}, \mathsf{Update})$ is said to be Σ-adaptively-secure, if for all PPT adversary $\mathcal{A}$ that make a polynomial $q(\lambda)$ of quires, there exists an efficient simulator $\mathcal{S}$ such that:*

$$|\Pr[\mathrm{REAL}_\mathcal{A}^\Sigma(\lambda) = 1] - \Pr[\mathrm{IDEAL}_{\mathcal{A}, \mathcal{S}, \mathcal{L}}^\Sigma(\lambda) = 1]| \leq negl(\lambda),$$

where $\mathrm{REAL}_\mathcal{A}^\Sigma$ and $\mathrm{IDEAL}_{\mathcal{A}, \mathcal{S}, \mathcal{L}}^\Sigma$ are defined as:

- $\mathrm{REAL}_\mathcal{A}^\Sigma$: *$\mathcal{A}$ chooses a database DB, $\mathsf{EDB} \leftarrow \mathsf{Setup}(1^\lambda, \mathsf{DB})$. After that, $\mathcal{A}$ adaptively performs Search or Update queries, and receives transcript generated from Search or Update. Finally, $\mathcal{A}$ observes real transcripts of all operations and outputs a bit b.*
- $\mathrm{IDEAL}_{\mathcal{A}, \mathcal{S}, \mathcal{L}}^\Sigma$: *$\mathcal{A}$ chooses a database DB, and receives EDB generated by the simulator $\mathcal{S}(\mathcal{L}^{\mathsf{Stp}}(\mathsf{DB}))$. Then $\mathcal{A}$ adaptively performs Search or Update queries, and gets a transcript generated from $\mathcal{S}(\mathcal{L}^{\mathsf{Srch}})$ or $\mathcal{S}(\mathcal{L}^{\mathsf{Updt}})$. Eventually, $\mathcal{A}$ observes all simulated transcripts and outputs a bit b.*

Forward security of DSSE was firstly defined in [4], and then formalized by Bost et al. [2]. Following their work, the forward security of SDSE can be defined as:

---

[1] Here, Search denotes both NNSearch and GeoSearch.

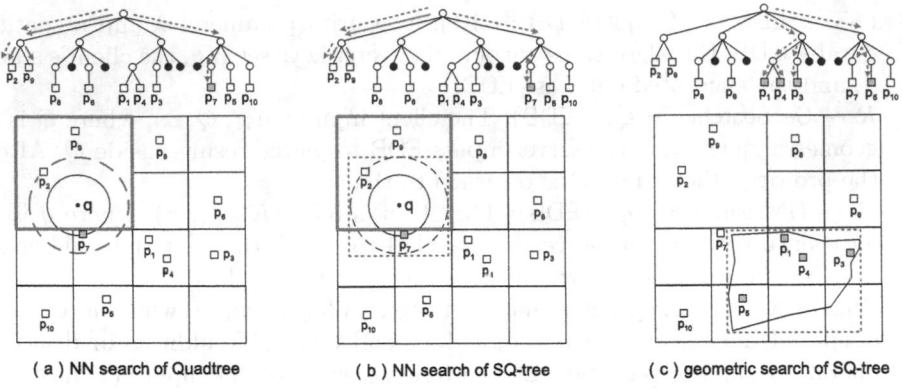

(a) NN search of Quadtree   (b) NN search of SQ-tree   (c) geometric search of SQ-tree

Fig. 1. Examples of search over Quadtree and SQ-tree

Definition 2 (Forward Security of SDSE). *Let* $\mathcal{L}^{Updt}$ *be a update leakage function defined as:*

$$\mathcal{L}^{Updt}(op, in) = \mathcal{L}'(op, (ind, c)),$$

where c *is the counter of updated document index* ind, $\mathcal{L}'$ *is a stateless function An* $\mathcal{L}$*-adaptively secure SDSE scheme is forward secure.*

4   Our Constructions

In this section, we first introduce a basic SDSE construction, Secure-Quadtree (SQ-tree), which is constructed on the basis of ORE and Quadtree. Then, we improve the SQ-tree to achieve forward security. For the convenience of description, in the rest of this paper we assume that the spatial data in DB is 2-dimensional. Note that our constructions can be extended to support any dimensions.

4.1   SQ-Tree: Basic SDSE Construction

Overview. Quadtree [7] is a dynamic tree construct which can improve the search efficiency of spatial queries. In a Quadtree, each deepest none-leaf node has a maximum capacity and the other none-leaf nodes have exactly four children. When the maximum capacity is reached and a new object should be inserted, the deepest none-leaf node splits. Figure 2(a) is an example Quadtree contains 10 data objects, where maximum capacity $M = 2$. To find the nearest neighbor of a query point q from the Quadtree, the server: (1) finds the deepest none-leaf node contains q; (2) takes the closest object (i.e., p_2) to q among all the data objects contained in the node; (3) generates a temporary circle, where the center is q and the radius is the distance between the q and the closest objects (i.e., p_2); (4) finds points inside the circle, and obtains the closest objects (i.e., p_7). The original nearest neighbor search in a Quadtree requires both *order compare* operation (e.g., whether a point is inside a rectangle) and *compute-then-compare* operations (e.g., whether a point is inside a circle and whether a circle intersects with a rectangle). However, there are currently no efficient encryption primitives that can satisfy both requirements at the same time. The ORE schemes can only support *order compare* operation and the homomorphic encryption based schemes are computation and communication expensive. Therefore, we follow the idea of [19] which replace the temporary circle with a circumscribed rectangle of the temporary circle, so that only the ORE is needed to search over the encrypted data. As shown in Fig. 2(b), after the first-round search, the server returns all data objects contained in the same node of q, and the client submits a new query that is a circumscribed rectangle of the temporary circle as described above. Then, the server returns all data objects contained in the circumscribed rectangle so that the client can find the nearest neighbor of q. In addition, we can achieve geometric search by translating the geometric to rectangles as shown in Fig. 2(c), the geometric is replaced by a rectangle so that the client can return all data objects inside the geometric.

Before describing the SQ-tree in detail, we first present two basic algorithms used in search process, namely InRec and Overlap. Given an encrypted query point $\mathsf{ct}_\mathsf{L}(q) = \{\mathsf{ct}_\mathsf{L}(x), \mathsf{ct}_\mathsf{L}(y)\}$ and an encrypted rectangle $\mathsf{ct}_\mathsf{R}(R^*) = \{\mathsf{ct}_\mathsf{R}(x_{min}), \mathsf{ct}_\mathsf{R}(x_{max}), \mathsf{ct}_\mathsf{R}(y_{min}), \mathsf{ct}_\mathsf{R}(y_{max})\}$, InRec is used to determine whether q is inside of R^*, where

$$\mathsf{InRec}(\mathsf{ct}_\mathsf{L}(q), \mathsf{ct}_\mathsf{R}(R^*)) = \begin{cases} 1 \leftarrow q \ inside \ of \ R^* \\ 0 \leftarrow q \ outside \ of \ R^* \end{cases}.$$

Given two encrypted rectangles $\mathsf{ct}_\mathsf{L}(R_1^*)$, $\mathsf{ct}_\mathsf{R}(R_2^*)$, Overlap is used to determine the overlap relationship of these two rectangles, where

$$\mathsf{Overlap}(\mathsf{ct}_\mathsf{L}(R_1^*), \mathsf{ct}_\mathsf{R}(R_2^*)) = \begin{cases} 0 \leftarrow R_1^* \ outside \ of \ R_2^* \\ 1 \leftarrow R_1^* \ inside \ of \ R_2^* \\ 2 \leftarrow R_1^* \ overlap \ with \ R_2^* \end{cases}.$$

Since the order of the messages can be revealed from their ORE ciphertexts, we can use the same method as used in plaintext to achieve InRec and Overlap. If $x_{max} \geq x \geq x_{min}$ and $y_{max} \geq y \geq y_{min}$, then q is inside of R^*; otherwise, q is outside of R^*. Similarly, if all points of R_1^* are inside of R_2^*, R_1^* is inside of R_2^*; if all points of R_1^* are outside of R_2^*, R_1^* is outside of R_2^*; otherwise, R_1^* is overlap with R_2^*. Note that in the above algorithms the left and right ciphertexts are interchangeable, as long as the query and data are encrypted in different ways.

Details of the SQ-Tree. Our SQ-Tree contains one algorithm Setup and three protocols NNSearch, GeoSearch, Update between a client and a server such that: Setup(1^λ, DB) → ($K_\Sigma, \sigma,$ EDB): Given a security parameter λ and a database DB, the client generates a secret key $\mathsf{sk}_i \leftarrow$ ORE.Setup(1^λ) for each dimen-

---

Algorithm 1: GeoSearch(K_Σ, σ, Q; EDB)$\rightarrow \mathcal{R}$:

@ **Client**: Send $\mathsf{ct_L}(Q) = \{\ \mathsf{ct_L}(x_{max}), \mathsf{ct_L}(x_{min}), \mathsf{ct_L}(y_{max}), \mathsf{ct_L}(y_{min})\}$ to server.

@ **Server**:
> From root node of the EDB, evaluate Flag $\leftarrow$ Overlap($\mathsf{ct_L}(Q), \mathsf{ct_R}(R_{node})$);
> **if** *Flag* $== 0$ **then** Stop search on this node;
> **else if** *Flag* $== 1$ **then**
>> Continue to search its children;
>> **if** *Reach the leaf-node* $\{ct_R(p), ind\}$ **then**
>>> Iflag $\leftarrow$ InRec($\mathsf{ct_R}(\mathsf{p}), \mathsf{ct_L}(Q)$);
>>> **if** *Iflag* $== 1$ **then** $\mathcal{R}$.Append(ind);
>
>> **else if** *Flag* $== 2$ **then** $\mathcal{R}$.Append(inds belong to the current node);
>
> **return** $\mathcal{R}$.

Algorithm 2: NNSearch(K_Σ, σ, q; EDB)$\rightarrow \mathcal{R}$:

@ **Client**: Send $\mathsf{ct_L}(q) = \{\mathsf{ct_L}(x), \mathsf{ct_L}(y)\}$ to the server.

@ **Server**:
> From root node of the EDB, evaluate Flag $\leftarrow$ InRec($\mathsf{ct_L}(q), \mathsf{ct_R}(R_{node})$);
> **if** *Flag* $== 0$ **then** Stop search on this node;
> **else if** *Flag* $== 1$ **then**
>> Continue to search its children;
>> **if** *Reach the deepest non-leaf node* **then**
>>> Return all data objects contained in current node;

@ **Client**: Obtain the nearest object of q from all returned objects, and generates a square query $sq = \{x_1, x_2, y_1, y_2\}$;

@ **Client & Server**: $\mathcal{R} \leftarrow$ GeoSearch(K_Σ, σ, sq; EDB).

---

sion of the data objects, the secret key set for a 2-dimensional database is $K_\Sigma = \{\mathsf{sk}_x, \mathsf{sk}_y\}$. Then, the client builds the Quadtree according to DB and encrypts every nodes and spatial data objects in the Quadtree. It is worth noting that the non-leaf nodes are encrypted by both ORE.Enc$_R$ and ORE.Enc$_L$, and the data objects are only encrypted by ORE.Enc$_R$. Each dimension of the data objects/nodes is encrypted by its corresponding key (i.e., a data object $\mathsf{p} = (x, y)$ is encrypted to $\mathsf{ct_R}(x) \leftarrow$ ORE.Enc$_R(\mathsf{sk}_x, x)$, $\mathsf{ct_R}(y) \leftarrow$ ORE.Enc$_R(\mathsf{sk}_y, y)$). Finally, the client outsources the EDB to the server.

GeoSearch(K_Σ, Q, σ; EDB): As described in Algorithm 1, given a geometric query, the client first translates the geometric into a rectangle $Q = \{x_{min}, x_{max}, y_{min}, y_{max}\}$, and generates the search query using K_Σ and ORE.Enc$_L$. Then, the client sends the search query to the server. The server responses all objects inside the query rectangle, and the client can find all objects inside the geometric.

NNSearch(K_Σ, q, σ; EDB): As shown in Algorithm 2, given a point $q = (x, y)$, the client generates a search query using K_Σ and ORE.Enc$_L$, and sends the search query to the server. After receiving the search query, the server finds the deepest non-leaf node contains q and returns all objects contained in the current node. In the second round query, the client generates a new circumscribed rectangle as described in overview, encrypts it using ORE.Enc$_L$, and sends the encrypted query rectangle to the server. The server responses all objects inside the query rectangle, and the client can find the nearest neighbor from the returned objects.

Update($K_\Sigma, \sigma, $op, in; EDB): Given a new object in, the client generates the ciphertexts according to ORE.Enc$_R$. The server finds the deepest non-leaf node contains in according to the ciphertexts. If the operator op $==$ add, and the current node contains less than M objects, the ciphertexts of in is inserted into this node; otherwise, the server and client split the current node through a new round of communication and insert the data objects into the corresponding node. If the operator op $==$ del, the in is encrypted by ORE.Enc$_L$, and the data object matching in is removed from the EDB.

4.2 SQ-Tree$_{fw}$: Forward Security SDSE Construction

In a forward security SDSE, an adversary $\mathcal{A}$ should not distinguish newly inserted data objects and the ciphertexts encrypted by a perfect encryption scheme, when they are just inserted into the database before performing any search operations. To achieve this goal, we add salt on the ciphertexts generated by the client, the salt is a hash value of an order counter **OC**. Since the salt causes the newly inserted data objects cannot be directly inserted into the index tree, the server uses a set EDB.Cash to temporarily store the newly inserted data. These data can be inserted into the index tree after the next search to ensure sub-linear search complexity. We use the CPRF $\tilde{F} : \{0,1\}^\lambda \times \{0, ..., n_{max}\} \to \{0,1\}^\lambda$ with respect to the class of range circuits $\mathcal{C}$ defined in Sect. 2.2 as the seed of salt. Since the principles of NN search and geometry search are similar, in the rest of this paper, the search query is a rectangular Q, and we will not repeat the specific search details, but focus on the forward security details.

As described in Algorithm 3, in Setup, besides the SQ-tree and ORE encryption keys SK as described above, two keys K, K' are generated by the client. To insert a new data object p into EDB (i.e., the $(c + 1)$-th addition, $c \geq 0$), client generates an order token OT_{c+1} based on $\tilde{F}$, its secret key K, and the new counter $c + 1$. The ind and ciphertexts of spatial data are salted by a hash function $H(K', OT_{c+1})$. As for search process, the client generates ciphertexts $ct_L(Q)$ of the search query Q and search token $ST \leftarrow \tilde{F}.Constrain(K, C_c)$, where C_c is the circuit evaluating to 1 on $\{0, ..., c\}$. Then, the client sends $\{K', c, ct_L(Q), ST\}$ to the server. The server can then calculate all the order tokens OT_c with K', and gets the original ciphertexts of data objects by desalting operations. At last, the client receives the correct comparison result which is calculated with the comparison algorithm of the ORE by the server. As shown in the black box, to maintain sub-linear search complexity, our SQ-tree$_{fw}$ uses *search-then-insert* mechanism. At the first time that the client submits a search query to the server, the server lookups both in SQ-tree and EDB.Cash. Thus, the newly added objects are desalted and can be inserted into the index tree as described

---

Algorithm 3: SQ-tree$_{fw}$: Forward-secure SDSE

Setup(1^λ):
  SK = $\{sk_x, sk_y\} \leftarrow$ ORE.Setup(1^λ), $K||K' \leftarrow \{0,1\}^{2\lambda}$, **OC** $\leftarrow$ 0;
  Generate EDB as described in SQ-tree;
  return ($K_\Sigma = \{SK, K, K'\}, \sigma;$ EDB).

Search(SK, $K_\Sigma, Q, \sigma;$ EDB):
  @ **Client:**
    $c \leftarrow$ **OC**, $ct_L(Q) \leftarrow$ ORE.Enc$_L$(SK, Q);
    $ST \leftarrow F.Constrain(K, C_c)$;
    Send $\{K', c, ct_L(Q), ST\}$ to the server.
  @ **Server:**
  for *each data object (i, e) in the current node and* **EDB**.*Cash* **do**
    $OT_i \leftarrow \tilde{F}(ST, i)$;
    $ct_R(p_i), ind_i \leftarrow e \oplus H(K', OT_i)$;
  @ **Client & Server:**
    Find the result $\mathcal{R}$ in the same way as described in SQ-tree;
    ┌───┐
    │ Insert the objects from the EDB.Cash into the index tree as described in │
    │ SQ-tree, the new node parameters are also salted;   │
    └───┘
  return ($\mathcal{R}, \sigma;$ EDB).

Update(K_Σ, op, in, $\sigma;$ EDB):
  @ **Client:**
    $c \leftarrow$ **OC**;
    $OT_{c+1} \leftarrow \tilde{F}(K, c+1)$, **OC** $\leftarrow c+1$, $ct_R(p) \leftarrow$ ORE.Enc$_R$(SK, p);
    $e \leftarrow (ct_R(p), ind) \oplus H(K', OT_{c+1})$;
    Send $(c+1, e)$ to the server.
  @ **Server:** EDB.Cash $\leftarrow (c+1, e)$.

---

in SQ-tree. When the client submits a query next time, the server can find all the search results through the index tree. In this way, although the search complexity of the first search after a new addition operation is slightly higher than that of SQ-tree, the second and subsequent search will maintain the ideal complexity.

5   Security Analysis

Security of the SQ-tree. In our SQ-tree, each non-leaf node is encrypted by both ORE.Enc$_L$ and ORE.Enc$_R$, each data object is encrypted only by ORE.Enc$_R$, and each query is encrypted only by ORE.Enc$_L$. Non-leaf nodes can compare with data objects, queries, and each others. The tree construct and the search path of queries are leaked. According to the properties of ORE used in SQ-tree, data objects are semantically secure with each other [12]. They only reveal their comparison with the search query during the search process.

Theorem 1 (Adaptive Security of SQ-tree). *Let* $Q = (x, y)$ *or* $Q = (x_{min}, x_{max}, y_{min}, y_{max})$ *be a search query, we define* $\mathcal{L}_Q^{SQ}$ *as*

$$\mathcal{L}_Q^{SQ} = \{CMP(x, x_i')_{i=1}^N, CMP(y, y_i')_{i=1}^N, CMP(x_{min}, x_i')_{i=1}^N,$$
$$CMP(x_{max}, x_N')_{i=1}^N, CMP(y_{min}, y_i')_{i=1}^N, CMP(y_{max}, y_i')_{i=1}^N, sp(Q), |EDB|\},$$

where (x_i', y_i') *is the spatial data stored in* DB, *CMP is the order pattern of two numbers,* $sp(Q)$ *is the search path of the* Q, $|EDB|$ *is the index tree structure. SQ-tree is secure with leakage function* $\mathcal{L}_Q^{SQ}$.

Proof. Since each dimension of the data objects is encrypted by ORE with a different key sk_i. Hence, for a database DB and any sequence of queries $q_1, ..., q_\ell$, we just need to invoke the simulator in the proof of ORE as described in [12] for each dimension of the data objects stored in EDB. This completes the proof. Due to space limitations, we skip further details.

Security of Our SQ-tree$_{fw}$. During the search process, the adversary can only see the CPRF keys for ranges corresponding to the inserted data objects, but cannot predict the evaluation of the PRF for inputs that outside of these ranges. Hence, before the first search for a newly inserted object, update leak no information. After first search for a newly inserted object p, p is inserted into EDB, which leaks the search path of p.

Theorem 2 (Forward Security of $SQ\text{-}tree_{fw}$**).** *Let* $\mathcal{L}_{forw}^{Updt^{1th}}$ *be the update leakage for a object just inserted into the database before performing any search operation,* $\mathcal{L}_{forw}^{Updt}$ *be the update leakage after search operation. Define* $\mathcal{L}_{FS} = (\mathcal{L}_{forw}^{Srch}, \mathcal{L}_{forw}^{Updt^{1th}}, \mathcal{L}_{forw}^{Updt})$ *as*

$$\mathcal{L}_{forw}^{Srch}(Q) = (\mathcal{L}_Q^{SQ}, UpHist), \mathcal{L}_{forw}^{Updt^{1th}}(add, p, ind) = \bot, \mathcal{L}_{forw}^{Updt}(add, p, ind) = sp(p),$$

where $sp(p)$ *is the search path of* p, *and* UpHist *contains all the data-updating histories. SQ-tree$_{fw}$ is* $\mathcal{L}_{FS}$*-adaptively-secure.*

Proof. The proof proceeds using a hybrid argument, we are going to derive several games from the real-world game $\text{REAL}_{\mathcal{A}}^{SDSE_{fs}}(\lambda)$.
Game G_0: is the real world SDSE security game $\text{REAL}_{\mathcal{A}}$

$$\Pr[\text{REAL}_{\mathcal{A}}^{SDSE_{fs}}(\lambda) = 1] = \Pr[G_0 = 1].$$

Game G_1: stores all the order tokens generated by CPRF $\tilde{F}(\cdot)$ in a map **OT**. Instead of calling the hash function H to generate the salts, the game picks random strings as salts and stores them in a map **H**. A function H' is used to ensure that two different salts for the inputs of the same tuple (K', OT_i) never be generated. If the map **H** does not include the tuple (K', OT_i), H' will randomly generate the result. But if the order token OT_i gets a collision with another order token, a flag *Error* will be set to be 1, and the function will return the corresponding salt of the equivalent token. Thus, according to the difference between G_0 and G_1 described above, we have: the advantage of distinguishing between G_0 and G_1 is smaller than the probability that the flag *Error* is set to be 1 in G_1: $|\Pr[G_0 = 1] - \Pr[G_1 = 1]| \leq \Pr[Error\ is\ set\ to\ 1\ in\ G_1]$.

Note that, the flag *Error* is set to be 1 in G_1, only if an efficient adversary $\mathcal{A}_1$ breaks the one-wayness of CPRF $\tilde{F}$. The error occurs only when the collision of at least two order tokens happens. In other words, the error occurs when the values generated by $\tilde{F}$ form a token without one-wayness. Thus, the advantage of distinguishing G_0 and G_1 can be reduced to that of breaking the one-wayness of CPRF. Also, if $\mathcal{A}_1$ makes m queries to the random oracle (apart from the ones already needed by the execution of the game), as OT_c is uniformly random, the probability H was called on (K', OT_i) is $m \cdot 2^{-\lambda}$. Hence,

$$\Pr[Error\ is\ set\ to\ 1\ in\ G_1] \leq \mathbf{Adv}_{\tilde{F},\mathcal{A}_1}^{\mathsf{cprf}}(\lambda) + \frac{m}{2^\lambda}.$$

Let N be the data number in EDB, we have

$$|\Pr[G_0 = 1] - \Pr[G_1 = 1]| \leq N \cdot \mathbf{Adv}_{\tilde{F},\mathcal{A}_1}^{\mathsf{cprf}}(\lambda) + \frac{Nm}{2^\lambda}.$$

Simulator. We use simulator $\mathcal{S}$ and the leakage function $\mathcal{L}_{FS}$ to describe the ideal forward security of SDSE scheme, where $\mathcal{L}_{FS}$ is defined in Theorem 2. The simulator uses the set $\mathbf{C}$ to store ciphertexts, the leakage of the order information is only revealed when the ciphertexts are going to execute the Search algorithm. We show that the simulator $\mathcal{S}$ and the game G_1 are indistinguishable. For data encryption, it is immediate as the scheme is outputting a fresh random bit string for each update in G_1. For data searching, using the adding history UpHist, the simulator constructs the oracle H'' which is subject to revealing the order correctly with the corresponding order token generated from OT_0. Hence,

$$|\Pr[G_1 = 1] - \Pr[\mathrm{IDEAL}_{\mathcal{A},\mathcal{S},\mathcal{L}_{FS}}^{\mathrm{SDSE}_{fs}}(\lambda)] = 1| = 0.$$

Conclusion. By combining all the contributions from all the games, there exists an adversary $\mathcal{A}_1$ such that

$$|\Pr[\mathrm{REAL}_{\mathcal{A}}^{\mathrm{SDSE}_{fs}}(\lambda) = 1] - \Pr[\mathrm{IDEAL}_{\mathcal{A},\mathcal{S},\mathcal{L}_{FS}}^{\mathrm{SDSE}_{fs}}(\lambda)] = 1| \leq N \cdot \mathbf{Adv}_{\tilde{F},\mathcal{A}_1}^{\mathsf{cprf}}(\lambda) + \frac{Nm}{2^\lambda}.$$

The right part of the reduction is negligible, our SQ-tree$_{\mathsf{fw}}$ are forward security.

6   Performance Evaluation

Setup. We implement and evaluate the proposed schemes in this paper. The code is written in C/C++. We use opensource code of ORE from [12] and the opensource code of CPRF $\tilde{F}$ from [3]. We use the AES-ECB as the keyed hash

Table 2. Performance of Setup in average (test 10 times for average)

Dataset Size	Setup time		Storage cost	
	32-bits	64-bits	32-bits	64-bits
2^{10}	0.119 s	1.123 s	0.425 MB	0.687 MB
2^{12}	0.478 s	4.945 s	1.789 MB	2.833 MB
2^{14}	1.911 s	18.582 s	7.162 MB	11.367 MB
2^{16}	7.596 s	81.853 s	28.655 MB	45.477 MB
2^{18}	30.583 s	289.496 s	114.623 MB	181.914 MB
2^{20}	122.336 s	1195.725 s	458.498 MB	727.644 MB

function, the security parameter λ is set as 128. For comparison, we also implement the NNSE [19] in C/C++. We ran our experiments on a computer running Ubuntu 14.04 with 16 Intel Xeon v2 CPU, 30 GB RAM. We use the Gowalla dataset[2], which has 6,442,890 location check-in collected from 196,591 users. We test our schemes over this dataset with different data size. For each size of the dataset, we set the plaintext length to 32-bits and 64-bits, respectively. The maximum capacity of deepest non-leaf nodes in SQ-tree is set as $M = 4$.

Experimental Results. The performance of Setup is presented in Table 2. As we can observe from Table 2, the setup time increases rapidly with the increase of the dataset size, because as the dataset size increases, the number of nodes needed to be encrypted is increasing. The running time of Setup in 32-bits setting is almost 10× faster than that in 64-bits setting, that is determined by the characteristics of the ORE. We can also see that the storage cost of the encrypted database grows slightly faster than the dataset size, because the database stores the Quadtree nodes in addition to storing the data objects. It is worth noting that the storage cost of a database in 32-bits setting is not half of that in 64-bits setting, this is because the ciphertext length of ORE is sub-linear increases with increasing bit-length of plaintext and the storage cost of ind is const.

In Fig. 2, we plot the performance of SQ-tree and SQ-tree$_{fw}$ in different settings. Since GeoSearch is also used in NNSearch, we only test the performance of NNSearch. We randomly select 100 data objects for NN search. The running time is the average of 100 queries. It is efficient to perform a spatial search among large-scale encrypted datasets with our SQ-tree. As we can see from Fig. 2(a), the running time of our SQ-tree and NNSE are sub-linear increase via increasing dataset size. The running time of our SQ-tree is faster than that of NNSE since the Quadtree will return more accurate neighbors than R-tree in the first round query, which makes the area of the second round query smaller, and the order compare of ORE is faster than that of the OPE used in NNSE.

---

[2] http://snap.stanford.edu/data/loc-gowalla.html.

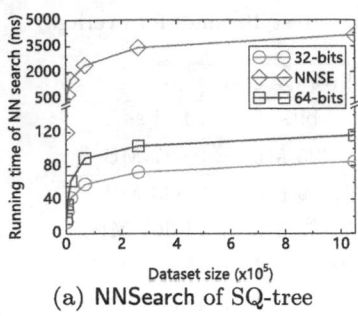
(a) NNSearch of SQ-tree

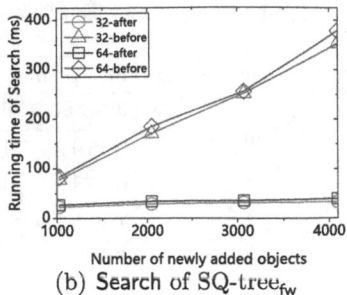
(b) Search of SQ-tree$_{fw}$

Fig. 2. Performance of Search.

In SQ-tree$_{fw}$, new data object is salted before insertion and is not inserted into the Quadtree. When the newly inserted data is searched, the salt is temporarily removed and the data can be inserted into the Quadtree. To fully test the performance of search, for a 2^{12} dataset, we insert $2^{10} \sim 2^{12}$ new data objects and then search them twice. In the first search, we show the performance of search the new data objects which haven't been searched before (i.e., the data objects added salt but without inserted into the Quadtree). And the second search test shows that the performance of search the new data objects which have been searched before (i.e., the data objects added salt and inserted into the Quadtree). The performance of SQ-tree$_{fw}$ in different settings is shown in Fig. 2(b). As shown in Fig. 2(b), the second search test runs significantly faster than the first search test. In the first search process, besides searching the data objects in the Quadtree, the server also needs to search all newly inserted data objects in the EDB.Cash that are not inserted into the Quadtree. In the second search process, the server can find out the data objects according to the Quadtree with sub-linear search complexity.

7 Conclusion

In this paper, we presented a formal definition of the Spatial Dynamic Searchable Encryption (SDSE) and proposed a secure SDSE scheme that supports dynamic update and sub-linear search complexity, called SQ-tree. When executing SQ-tree, it only leaks the order of numbers and the search path. To prevent file-injection attack [24], we also presented SQ-tree$_{fw}$, a forward-secure scheme that newly updated objects cannot be related to previous search results. Finally, we evaluated the practicality of our proposed schemes in a application environment.

Acknowledgments. This work was supported by the Key Program of NSFC Grant (U1405255), Shaanxi Science & Technology Coordination & Innovation Project (2016TZC-G-6-3), the Fundamental Research Funds for the Central Universities (SA-ZD161504, JB191506), the National Natural Science Foundation of China (61702404, U1804263, 61702105), and the National Natural Science Foundation of Shaanxi

Province (2019JQ-005). Xiangyu Wang was supported by the Doctoral Students' Short Term Study Abroad Scholarship, Xidian University.

References

1. Boneh, D., Waters, B.: Constrained pseudorandom functions and their applications. In: Proceedings of ASIACRYPT 2013, pp. 280–300 (2013)
2. Bost, R.: $\sum o \varphi o \varsigma$: forward secure searchable encryption. In: Proceedings of CCS 2016, pp. 1143–1154 (2016)
3. Bost, R., Minaud, B., Ohrimenko, O.: Forward and backward private searchable encryption from constrained cryptographic primitives. In: Proceedings of CCS 2017, pp. 1465–1482 (2017)
4. Cash, D., et al.: Dynamic searchable encryption in very-large databases: data structures and implementation. In: Proceedings of NDSS 2014 (2014)
5. Curtmola, R., Garay, J.A., Kamara, S., Ostrovsky, R.: Searchable symmetric encryption: improved definitions and efficient constructions. In: Proceedings of CCS 2006, pp. 79–88 (2006)
6. Elmehdwi, Y., Samanthula, B.K., Jiang, W.: Secure k-nearest neighbor query over encrypted data in outsourced environments. In: Proceedings of ICDE 2014, pp. 664–675 (2014)
7. Finkel, R.A., Bentley, J.L.: Quad trees a data structure for retrieval on composite keys. Acta Informatica 4(1), 1–9 (1974)
8. Grubbs, P., Sekniqi, K., Bindschaedler, V., Naveed, M., Ristenpart, T.: Leakage-abuse attacks against order-revealing encryption. In: Proceedings of IEEE S&P 2017, pp. 655–672 (2017)
9. Hu, H., Xu, J., Ren, C., Choi, B.: Processing private queries over untrusted data cloud through privacy homomorphism. In: Proceedings of ICDE 2011, pp. 601–612 (2011)
10. Kamara, S., Papamanthou, C., Roeder, T.: Dynamic searchable symmetric encryption. In: Proceedings of CCS 2012, pp. 965–976 (2012)
11. Kiayias, A., Papadopoulos, S., Triandopoulos, N., Zacharias, T.: Delegatable pseudorandom functions and applications. In: Proceedings of CCS 2013, pp. 669–684 (2013)
12. Lewi, K., Wu, D.J.: Order-revealing encryption: new constructions, applications, and lower bounds. In: Proceedings of CCS 2016, pp. 1167–1178 (2016)
13. Li, R., Liu, A., Liu, Y., Xu, H., Yuan, H.: Insecurity and hardness of nearest neighbor queries over encrypted data. In: Proceedings of ICDE 2019, pp. 1614–1617 (2019)
14. Naveed, M., Kamara, S., Wright, C.V.: Inference attacks on property-preserving encrypted databases. In: Proceedings of CCS 2015 (2015)
15. Ning, J., Xu, J., Liang, K., Zhang, F., Chang, E.: Passive attacks against searchable encryption. IEEE Trans. Inf. Forensics Secur. 14(3), 789–802 (2019)
16. Popa, R.A., Li, F.H., Zeldovich, N.: An ideal-security protocol for order-preserving encoding. In: Proceedings of IEEE S&P 2013, pp. 463–477 (2013)
17. Song, D.X., Wagner, D.A., Perrig, A.: Practical techniques for searches on encrypted data. In: Proceedings of IEEE S&P, pp. 44–55 (2000)
18. Wang, B., Li, M., Xiong, L.: Fastgeo: Efficient geometric range queries on encrypted spatial data. IEEE Trans. Dependable Secure Comput. 16(2), 245–258 (2019)
19. Wang, B., Hou, Y., Li, M.: Practical and secure nearest neighbor search on encrypted large-scale data. In: Proceedings of INFOCOM 2016, pp. 1–9 (2016)

20. Wang, B., Li, M., Wang, H.: Geometric range search on encrypted spatial data. IEEE Trans. Inf. Forensics Secur. **11**(4), 704–719 (2016)
21. Wang, X., et al.: Search me in the dark: Privacy-preserving boolean range query over encrypted spatial data. In: Proceedings of INFOCOM 2020, pp. 1–10 (2020)
22. Wang, X., Ma, J., Liu, X., Miao, Y.: Search in my way: practical outsourced image retrieval framework supporting unshared key. In: Proceedings INFOCOM 2019, pp. 2485–2493 (2019)
23. Wang, X., Ma, J., Miao, Y., Liu, X., Yang, R.: Privacy-preserving diverse keyword search and online pre-diagnosis in cloud computing. IEEE Trans. Serv. Comput. (2019)
24. Wang, X., Zhao, Y.: Order-revealing encryption: file-injection attack and forward security. In: Proceedings of ESORICS 2018, pp. 101–121 (2018)
25. Wong, W.K., Cheung, D.W., Kao, B., Mamoulis, N.: Secure KNN computation on encrypted databases. In: Proceedings of SIGMOD 2009, pp. 139–152 (2009)
26. Xu, G., Li, H., Dai, Y., Yang, K., Lin, X.: Enabling efficient and geometric range query with access control over encrypted spatial data. IEEE Trans. Inf. Forensics Secur. **14**(4), 870–885 (2019)
27. Yuan, H., Chen, X., Li, J., Jiang, T., Wang, J., Deng, R.: Secure cloud data deduplication with efficient re-encryption. IEEE Trans. Serv. Comput. (2019)
28. Zhang, Y., Katz, J., Papamanthou, C.: All your queries are belong to us: the power of file-injection attacks on searchable encryption. In: Proceedings of USENIX Security 2016, pp. 707–720 (2016)

Correction to: Cross-Graph Representation Learning for Unsupervised Graph Alignment

Weifan Wang, Minnan Luo, Caixia Yan, Meng Wang, Xiang Zhao, and Qinghua Zheng

Correction to:
Chapter "Cross-Graph Representation Learning
for Unsupervised Graph Alignment" in: Y. Nah et al. (Eds.):
Database Systems for Advanced Applications, LNCS 12113,
https://doi.org/10.1007/978-3-030-59416-9_22

In the original edition of this chapter, an institution affiliation was missing in the authors' section for the following authors: Weifan Wang, Minnan Lu, and Qinghua Zheng. The missing institution has been now added.

The updated version of this chapter can be found at
https://doi.org/10.1007/978-3-030-59416-9_22

Author Index